Windows Vista® Secrets®

Scott,
Thanks for
reading!
— Paul
Thurrott

Windows Vista® Secrets®
SP1 Edition

Paul Thurrott

Wiley Publishing, Inc.

Windows Vista® Secrets®: SP1 Edition

Published by
Wiley Publishing, Inc.
10475 Crosspoint Boulevard
Indianapolis, IN 46256
www.wiley.com

Copyright © 2008 by Wiley Publishing, Inc., Indianapolis, Indiana

Published simultaneously in Canada

ISBN: 978-0-470-24200-1

Manufactured in the United States of America

10 9 8 7 6 5 4 3 2 1

For general information on our other products and services or to obtain technical support, please contact our Customer Care Department within the U.S. at (800) 762-2974, outside the U.S. at (317) 572-3993 or fax (317) 572-4002.

Library of Congress Cataloging-in-Publication Data

Thurrott, Paul B.
  Windows Vista secrets / Paul Thurrott. — Sp1 ed.
    p. cm.
  Includes index.
  ISBN 978-0-470-24200-1 (cloth/website)
  1. Microsoft Windows (Computer file) 2. Operating systems (Computers) I. Title.
  QA76.76.O63T53 2008
  005.4'46—dc22
                    2008032157

To Stephanie, Mark, and Kelly

About the Author

The author of over 20 books, **Paul Thurrott** is the news editor of *Windows IT Pro Media* and editor of the SuperSite for Windows (**www.winsupersite.com**). He writes a weekly editorial for Windows IT Pro UPDATE (**www.windowsitpro.com/email**); a daily Windows news and information newsletter called *WinInfo Daily UPDATE* (**www.wininformant.com**); and a monthly column called "Need To Know" in *Windows IT Pro Magazine*. He blogs daily via the SuperSite Blog and appears weekly in the highly rated *Windows Weekly* podcast with Leo Laporte. You can follow Paul's exploits on Twitter (**www.twitter.com/thurrott**) and FriendFeed (**www.friendfeed.com/thurrott**).

About the Technical Editor

Joli Ballew is a technology trainer and writer in the Dallas area. She holds several certifications, including MCSE, MCTS, and MCDST, and is a 2008 Microsoft MVP. Joli writes books for several publishers, teaches computer classes at a local junior college, and works as a network administrator and Web designer for North Texas Graphics. She has written more than two dozen books, including two Microsoft certification titles, and has been published in over 15 languages. Joli maintains a Web site at **www.joliballew.com**.

Credits

Acquisitions Editor
Katie Mohr

Senior Development Editor
Kevin Kent

Technical Editor
Joli Ballew

Production Editor
Dassi Zeidel

Copy Editor
Luann Rouff

Editorial Manager
Mary Beth Wakefield

Production Manager
Tim Tate

**Vice President and
Executive Group Publisher**
Richard Swadley

**Vice President and Executive
Publisher**
Joseph B. Wikert

Project Coordinator, Cover
Lynsey Stanford

Compositor
Maureen Forys, Happenstance
Type-O-Rama

Proofreader
Candace English;
Jen Larsen, Word One

Indexer
Robert Swanson

Cover Designer
Ryan Sneed

Acknowledgments

Writing a book is always a time-consuming process, and while I had hoped that a revision like this would be easier than writing the original—well...it wasn't. With that in mind...

Thanks especially to Stephanie for putting up with the several months of downtime this update required. You are the glue that makes our family work. I love you.

Apologies to Mark and Kelly for any missed baseball and softball games. And yes, I heard "Shh...Daddy's working" more than once, so thanks for trying. You are both amazing.

Thanks, too, to everyone at Wiley, especially Katie and Kevin, who put up with constant delays and tardiness, not to mention the months-long drama that was the build-up to this version of the book. At least we have stories to tell.

Finally, thank you for buying this book or at least considering it.

Contents at a Glance

Contents

Preface

Welcome to the SP1 edition of *Windows Vista Secrets*, which I hope you'll agree is a vastly expanded and improved version of the original. I also hope you enjoy combing through this book as much as I enjoyed digging deep into Windows Vista to find the most valuable information for you.

—Paul Thurrott
thurrott@windowsitpro.com
July 2008

Web Site Supporting the Book

For updates, errata, new information, and an ongoing blog with interactive discussions, please visit **www.winsupersite.com**. This book is only the beginning: More secrets can be found online.

Icons Used in This Book

The following icons are used in this book to help draw your attention to some of the most important or most useful information in the book.

Secret

The Secret icon marks little-known facts that are not obvious to most Windows users. This information is rarely documented by Microsoft, and when it is, it's done so in a way that's not easy for users to find.

tip
The Tip icon indicates a helpful trick.

note
The Note icon points out items of importance.

cross ref
The Cross-Reference icon points to chapters where additional information can be found.

caution
The Caution icon warns you about possible negative side-effects or precautions you should take before making a change.

Read This First

Ⅰn this preliminary chapter, I provide a crash course in some of the major new features of Windows Vista. Give me just 15 minutes of your time and I'll show you the biggest changes in the operating system—before you may have to grapple with them yourself.

Don't Believe the Hype

In the time since Windows Vista first shipped to the public, the outcry from tech pundits, bloggers, and self-proclaimed experts has been loud and clear: Windows Vista is a piece of junk, they say. It's slower and less compatible than its predecessor, Windows XP, and doesn't offer enough additional functionality to justify the upgrade. Most egregiously, these guys are trying to paint Windows Vista as a failure, pointing to dubious statistics to prove that Microsoft's latest operating system isn't selling as well or as fast as XP.

Too bad it's all a bunch of baloney.

Of course, some of the claims are certainly true, but then they've been true of every single Windows version that ever came down the pike. Sometimes I wonder if these guys are so busy listening to the sounds of their voices that they've forgotten the past.

Yes, Windows Vista, like Windows XP before it, is slower on the same hardware and less compatible with existing hardware and software than its predecessor. That's what happens when you release a major new Windows version with huge architectural changes. But the advantages of Vista—in this case, its ability to work more efficiently with modern and upcoming hardware designs, for example—more than offset these statistical issues. More important, in real-world use, you'll never notice a day-to-day performance difference between Windows Vista and Windows XP on modern hardware. My advice has never changed: You're going to get the best experience with any new Windows version— including Vista—on a new PC.

Microsoft did indeed back-port a slew of Vista technologies to Windows XP for a variety of reasons. But as I'll discuss in this chapter, Windows Vista still includes an incredible number of new and unique features and functionality when compared to its predecessor. Most important, it passes the upgrade test. Once you've used Windows Vista, you'll have a hard time going back to XP because you'll miss so much of what makes Windows Vista special. It's certainly true in my case.

And let me put the "Vista is a failure" baloney into perspective. While many like to point to Vista's first-year sales—110 million units sold, by the way—as a problem because PC makers sold 250 million PCs during that same period, you might look at these figures in a different light. For example, at the time of Vista's first anniversary, there were almost 1 billion PCs in use around the world. That means Vista was able to secure over 10 percent usage share in its first year on the market. Guess what XP's usage share was after 1 year on the market? That's right; it was about the same: 10 percent. Yet today, these pundits are claiming that Vista is somehow lagging behind Windows XP. It's not true. By the time Vista hits its second anniversary, over 200 million people will be using this operating system every single day.

Some failure, eh?

But I don't have to defend Windows Vista. I'll just let it speak for itself. This chapter describes some of the many ways in which Windows Vista is superior to previous Windows versions. Windows Vista is a major Windows update and one that offers significant value over Windows XP. I'd never dream of going back. Neither, I suspect, will you.

The Value of Vista

We all waited more than five years for Windows Vista. As you may recall, Windows XP was released with much fanfare in October 2001. But instead of the next Windows version shipping in just a couple of years, as originally expected, Microsoft lost its way in the development process. Vista didn't make it to consumers until early 2007.

Was it worth the wait?

Absolutely. I believe Vista is a major advance over Microsoft's previous operating systems. If you're buying a new PC today, I don't hesitate to recommend that you get Vista rather than requesting XP or another, older operating system. (If you're upgrading an older PC to Vista, by contrast, be sure to first read Chapter 2.)

In 2001, Microsoft executives widely claimed that XP was "the most secure operating system we have ever delivered." In fact, XP and its new Web browser, Internet Explorer 6.0, were full of maddening security holes that previous operating systems didn't suffer from. ActiveX exploits, drive-by downloads, and many other kinds of weaknesses were quickly exploited by black-hat hackers. Microsoft has been issuing patches for XP and IE 6.0 ever since.

Windows Vista and the new Internet Explorer 7 browser are welcome steps toward changing that. Microsoft has added "hardening" features to Vista that should make remote exploits more difficult for hackers to carry out. The first-year vulnerability statistics bear out Microsoft's efforts in this area. Whereas Windows XP suffered from 65 vulnerabilities and 30 security updates, Windows Vista succumbed to just 36 vulnerabilities and 17 security updates in the same time period. This suggests that Vista is both more secure and more easily managed than its predecessor. (Media darling Mac OS X fared even worse: Mac OS X 10.4 "Tiger" suffered from 116 vulnerabilities and 17 security updates in its first year on the market. So much for those libelous "Switcher" ads that Apple once ran.)

Besides improved security, XP users who switch to Vista will also find enhancements in desktop searching, Windows Sidebar access to applets called *gadgets*, PC-to-PC content transfers, and even new games—mahjong and (finally!) chess. There are brand-spanking-new digital media and productivity applications and broader access to Windows capabilities, such as Tablet PC and Media Center PC support, that were previously available only in very specific Windows XP versions.

In these pages, I aim to give you a crash course on Windows Vista. In other words, read on and you can learn the most important new features of Vista in the time it takes to sip a perfectly made latte.

Windows Vista in 15 Minutes

It's impossible to cover all the new features of Windows Vista in a single chapter. Many features warrant their own chapters because there's a lot to say about them or I discovered secret information that isn't in Windows Vista's Help and Support system.

Other new Windows Vista features, although important, may be so straightforward that they don't have any particular secrets. When this is the case, I don't waste time or space on them in this book.

But even features that don't have hidden aspects may be important for you to know about when you turn Vista on for the first time. Exposing those hidden aspects to you is the purpose of the following overview.

The New Start Menu

In Windows Vista, the Start button is no longer called Start, and the Start Menu looks completely different from the menu you may be used to in Windows XP. However, it's still there at the bottom of the screen, and you may find it a bit better organized.

The old Start button has been replaced by a lighted sphere, called the Start Orb, that displays the Windows flag logo. (I'm going to keep calling it the Start button, as does Microsoft most of the time.) Instead of submenus that fly out to the right of the main menu, Windows Vista displays your most recently used programs in a primary window (see Figure 1).

Figure 1: The new Start Menu is a primary window containing your most recently used programs and a column of buttons that open windows for common tasks.

---

tip   If you don't like the new look, you can get the old Start Menu back by reverting to the familiar Windows 2000 submenu system. To do so, right-click the Start button, click Properties, select Classic Start Menu, and then click OK. This blast from the past is shown in Figure 2.

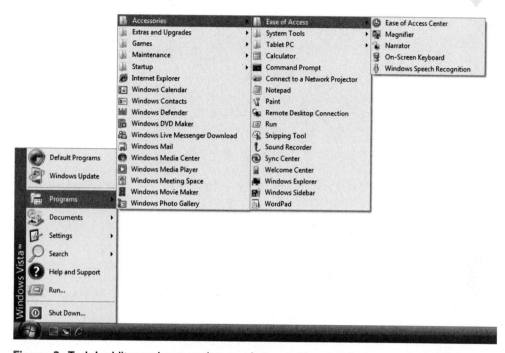

Figure 2: Tech Luddites and corporations not interested in retraining users may enjoy the classic Start Menu, but this is the last time you're going to see it in this book.

When you click All Programs in the new Start Menu, the menu switches to a display of collapsing folders. You can expand each folder to see all available programs, but the Start Menu keeps the list within the primary window.

Secret

What Happened to the Run Menu?

One thing you won't find on the default Start Menu is the Run option, which generations of Windows users have employed to start programs that may not appear on any menu. The omission isn't a problem—if you know the secret. Simply type the name of the program you want to run (such as **notepad**) into the Start Search bar just above the Start button and then press Enter. If you really, really want to reenable the Run command, you can do so: Right-click the Start button and choose Properties. Then click Customize next to the Start Menu option. In the Customize Start Menu window that appears, scroll down the list and check the option titled *Run command.* Click OK, and then click OK again.

Windows Aero

You'll see a slick new look to objects and applications in Vista if you have a version of the operating system that supports it and hardware that's modern enough to render it (and, you will, most likely).

This new interface, called Windows Aero, or just Aero, gives translucency to the so-called "window chrome" that surrounds most application windows. This enables you to see what lies beneath a window, whether the foreground app is stationary or you're dragging it to a new location.

> **tip** If the translucency of window chrome irritates you, you can switch it off. From the Start Menu, type **personalize** in Start Menu Search and then click Windows Color and Appearance. Uncheck the item titled *Enable transparency* and then click OK.

Perhaps more important than translucency is the new *live thumbnail* effect that Aero adds to the taskbar at the bottom of the screen. Hover your mouse over a button that represents a minimized application, and you'll see a live representation of what's in the app at that moment, as shown in Figure 3. This can be helpful in deciding which of several minimized applications to switch to.

Figure 3: Live taskbar thumbnails take the guesswork out of finding the right window.

To utilize the Aero interface (formerly code-named Aero Glass), you must be running Windows Vista Home Premium, Business, Enterprise, or Ultimate Edition. Vista Home Basic and Starter Editions need not apply.

Secret

Can Translucency Help Productivity?

Translucency may seem like an unimportant feature, but a source within Microsoft's Usability Labs told me that the bold colors of the window frames in Windows XP were found to distract the eye from whatever material was in the main application window. Lightening up the window colors—by making them partially translucent—was found to improve how quickly users could work with the content within applications.

> **cross ref** For more on the Aero interface, see Chapter 4.

Flip 3D

Many Windows users know about the Alt+Tab keyboard shortcut, whereby you hold down the Alt key and tap Tab repeatedly to switch to any application or window that's currently open, in sequence. Alt+Tab task switching is still available in Windows Vista, but it's been enhanced with thumbnail previews and renamed *Windows Flip*.

The Aero user interface adds a powerful enhancement to this form of task switching. Dubbed *Windows Flip 3D*, this new type of task switching shows you a revolving set of windows at an angle so you can see exactly what you're switching to, as shown in Figure 4. Instead of using Alt+Tab, you use the Windows key+Tab to activate Windows Flip 3D.

One of the windows that's always shown in the Flip 3D view is your Windows Desktop. That makes it easy to minimize all of your applications. Simply hold down the Windows key (either the left one or the right one), and then press Tab until the miniature window that looks like your Desktop is uppermost.

tip   You can reverse the order in which Flip 3D cycles through your open windows by holding down the Shift key in addition to the Windows key+Tab. In my tests, the Desktop window has always been displayed as the bottom-most application when I pressed the Windows key+Tab. To minimize all applications and display your Desktop, therefore, hold down the Windows key, then press Tab, Shift+Tab, and let go of the Windows key.

cross ref   Windows Flip 3D is also discussed in Chapter 4.

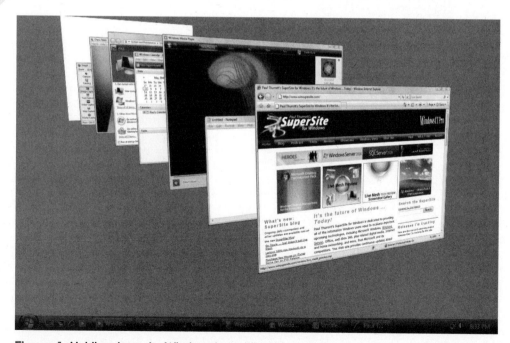

Figure 4: Holding down the Windows key while repeatedly pressing Tab cycles through miniature windows that show you what's in each of your open applications and your Desktop. It's a new Vista feature called Windows Flip 3D.

Programs Explorer Replaces Add/Remove Programs

Legions of Windows users have become accustomed to using the Add or Remove Programs dialog box in the Control Panel to uninstall and change applications. Unfortunately, Microsoft has renamed this feature in such a way that it is even harder to find than it was before.

To reconfigure or completely remove an application, you now use the Programs Explorer, shown in Figure 5. This applet also enables you to turn on or off many of the built-in features that come with Windows Vista, such as the Indexing Service.

Fortunately, the Programs Explorer is still available through the Control Panel. You just need to know to look for it in the Ps instead of the As.

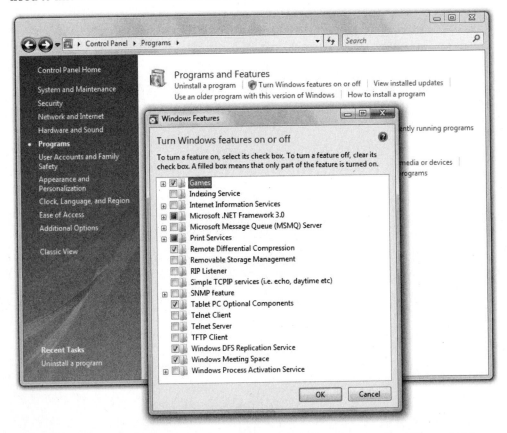

Figure 5: Programs Explorer helps you uninstall unwanted programs and enable or disable various Windows Vista features.

Putting Some Gadgets in Your Windows Sidebar

Apple users have long been able to take advantage of the Mac OS X Dashboard, and Windows users have been able to download Yahoo! Widgets (formerly Konfabulator

Widgets) in order to take advantage of small utilities, sometimes called widgets or gadgets. Now Windows Vista has its own special small utilities, which Microsoft calls *gadgets*.

Windows Vista gadgets live in the new Windows Sidebar—which you can move to the left or right side of the screen by right-clicking it and selecting Properties. Alternately, you can put gadgets on your Desktop by dragging them over from the Sidebar. The Windows Sidebar is shown in Figure 6.

Figure 6: In this view, the Windows Sidebar holds five gadgets: Calendar, CPU Meter, Currency Converter, Notes, and the Picture Puzzle.

cross ref   The Windows Sidebar is discussed in detail in Chapter 6.

Instant Search and the Search Pane

An interactive Instant Search bar is now a feature of every Explorer window in Vista, as well as Vista's Start Menu, Help and Support, and other applications. This may not slow the progress of third-party desktop search applications that are increasingly being promoted as Windows downloads from the major search engines, but Microsoft is, in fact, trying to build advanced search functions into Windows Vista to render such downloads unnecessary.

Figure 7 shows what you'll see if you type *.jpg* in the Start Search window and then click Search Everywhere. Pressing Enter after the search opens a more capable Search window in which you can refine your search or organize the results by file size and other attributes.

Figure 7: Entering a string into Start Menu Search and pressing Enter opens the Search window, where you can refine your search.

---

tip
Vista's search function becomes context-specific in many such applications. Figure 8 shows the Windows Vista Control Panel in Classic View, which is somewhat cluttered with applets. Figure 9, by contrast, shows the result after you enter a search string into the Control Panel's integrated search bar, which displays just applets with that word in their titles.

---

cross ref
You can read more about Windows Vista's extensive search features in Chapter 5.

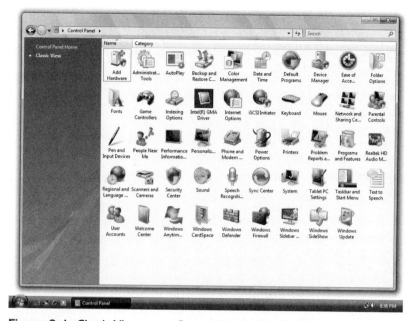

Figure 8: In Classic View, every Control Panel applet is shown, which can be hard to navigate.

Figure 9: By entering the word *options* into the Control Panel's search bar, only applets with that word in their titles are displayed, making your choice easier.

Internet Explorer 7.0 Catches Up

The improved security functionality in Internet Explorer 7 combined with the addition of long-requested features such as tabbed browsing make Microsoft's integrated Web browser a solid component of the OS, rather than the backward stepchild that was its predecessor, IE 6. (Users of Windows XP can and should download and install Internet Explorer 7 if an upgrade to Vista isn't immediately possible.)

Besides tabbed browsing, Internet Explorer 7 has (thankfully) copied several other features from Firefox, Opera, and other non-Microsoft browsers. These include the capability to add Internet search engines of your choice to IE's search bar and a default Shrink to Fit setting so Web pages will fit your printer's paper size.

However, Internet Explorer 7 has also gained a few new features that other browsers may need to copy:

- ◆ A new Quick Tabs feature graphically tiles all of your open tabs into a convenient thumbnail view, as shown in Figure 10. When you have a lot of tabs open, Quick Tabs can save you a substantial amount of time that you might otherwise spend clicking at random to get back to a particular site.

- ◆ Page Zoom is another handy feature. When you're viewing a Web page that's too small or too large, hold down the Ctrl key and press + or - to scale the page larger or smaller, respectively. Unlike competing browsers, Internet Explorer 7 scales both the text and the graphics, which makes for easier reading.

- ◆ There's also a small Page Zoom button on the extreme right of Internet Explorer 7's status bar. You can click it repeatedly to move through three preset zoom sizes.

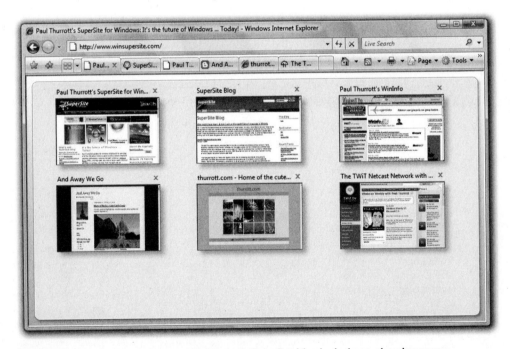

Figure 10: Quick Tabs in Internet Explorer 7 tiles all tabbed windows, showing you a thumbnail to help you switch to a desired Web page.

IE Protected Mode, Phishing Filter, and Other Security Features

Internet Explorer 7.0, when running under Windows Vista (not XP or earlier operating systems), operates by default in a special new *Protected Mode*. This means that dishonest Web sites that a user happens to visit cannot trick Internet Explorer 7 into changing Windows system files or other crucial configuration details.

A separate feature, but one that can work in concert with Protected Mode to keep users out of trouble, is Microsoft's new *Phishing Filter*. Internet Explorer 7 regularly downloads a list of Web addresses that appear to be fraudulent. These sites may get on the list because they're collecting passwords or credit card numbers from gullible consumers, they're uploading spyware to people's computers, or for other reasons. In any case, Internet Explorer 7 doesn't display known phishing sites, instead warning the user about the identified problems with the site.

The features just described are only two of the several Microsoft has added to Internet Explorer. Others include protection against cross-site scripting attacks (in which one site takes over a window used by another site), ActiveX suspension (which disables the most dangerous ActiveX controls), and Windows Defender (which guards against spyware).

cross ref See Chapter 19 to discover many more Internet Explorer 7 features.

cross ref For more about Windows Vista security features, turn to Chapter 8.

Support for RSS News Feeds

Internet Explorer 7.0 includes an easy way to subscribe to news feeds, regularly updated information that Web sites publish in the format known as Really Simple Syndication (RSS).

When a surfer visits a site that publishes one or more news feeds, an orange broadcast button on Internet Explorer 7's toolbar lights up. Clicking the button icon takes you to a page that explains the content of a feed and provides a link for subscribing to that feed, as shown in Figure 11.

After you've subscribed to a news feed, you can read it using Internet Explorer 7's Favorites Center pane. This pane is accessed by clicking the yellow star in IE's new toolbar and selecting Feeds. The latest news items can be sorted by date or title or filtered by categories provided by the author of the feed, as shown in Figure 12.

IE's native feed handling isn't as capable as a dedicated reader's, such as NewsGator (**www.newsgator.com**), or an online news aggregator's, such as Bloglines (**www.bloglines .com**). But the addition of RSS support in IE is certain to make this form of communications popular with a much larger chunk of Internet users than had discovered news feeds prior to Vista.

Figure 11: If a Web site publishes a news feed, IE's RSS icon lights up. Clicking the icon leads to a page with a link enabling you to subscribe to the feed.

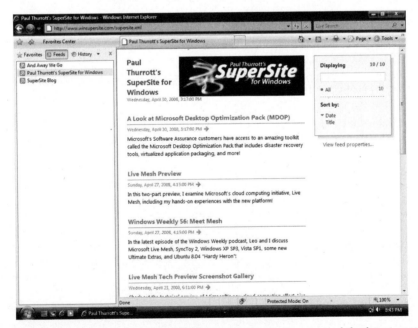

Figure 12: After you've subscribed to a news feed, you can read the latest posts in IE's Favorites Center.

Encrypt Entire Drives with BitLocker

News headlines in recent years have made the public aware of stolen laptops and desktop computers that contained the personal records of thousands, even millions, of individuals. These thefts might not have exposed anyone's personal data if the hard drives in the stolen computers had been encrypted and protected by strong passwords.

Various third-party solutions have long been available to encrypt sensitive data folders and entire hard drives. With Windows Vista, Microsoft now enters this market with a new feature called *BitLocker Drive Encryption*, or simply *BitLocker*.

BitLocker has some advantages over competing encryption products because, integrated as it is into Windows, it can check the integrity of a computer system before the Windows user interface is ever loaded. BitLocker can tell when a hard drive has been moved to a different computer—as would be the case if a drive had been stolen—and can defend against brute-force attacks.

BitLocker also integrates with Microsoft's Active Directory domain service scheme. The remote storage of digital keys that can unlock or restore data if a user forgets a password is a difficult and labor-intensive chore for IT administrators. BitLocker handles this by using Active Directory to escrow the keys securely, while still being able to help an authorized (but forgetful) user access crucial data that's stored in a password-protected drive.

Note that BitLocker is available only in Vista Ultimate and Enterprise Editions.

cross ref   You can read more about BitLocker in Chapter 8.

Use Easy Transfer to Move Data to a New PC

Moving all of your old documents and other data files and settings from one PC to another has been a royal pain for years. Microsoft provides a better solution to this problem with its Easy Transfer utility in Windows Vista. This program accepts files and preferences from Windows 2000 and Windows XP machines, as well as machines running Vista, so it's perfect for anyone upgrading.

You can select just data files to transfer to the new PC or transfer entire clumps of e-mail messages and contacts, Internet settings, or even complete user accounts, as shown in Figure 13. No information is deleted from the old PC, so you have plenty of time to confirm that the data has been transferred correctly before erasing anything on your obsolete system.

The transfer requires that you install an Easy Transfer program from Vista to the older computer. In addition, both the new system and the old one must be capable of exchanging data through one of the following methods:

- ◆ A local area network
- ◆ A USB Flash drive or external hard drive
- ◆ Recordable CDs or DVDs

Microsoft's hardware partners also sell a special USB-based Windows Easy Transfer cable. This works like the software-based Easy Transfer application but automates the process somewhat. You plug the provided cable into both machines and start the transfer from the new machine, as shown in Figure 14.

Figure 13: Files, settings, and user accounts may be transferred from Windows 2000, Windows XP, or Windows Vista machines to a new machine using Windows Easy Transfer.

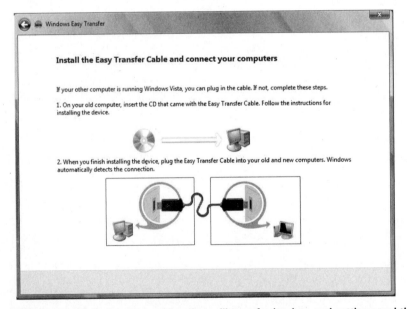

Figure 14: Both the old machine that will transfer its data and settings and the new machine that will receive them must be capable of exchanging information through a network, a recordable CD/DVD, a Flash drive, an external hard drive, or a special Easy Transfer cable.

Parental Controls

Vista's new Parental Controls capability helps you protect your children against inappropriate content online and in games and otherwise helps configure how and when they can use the PC. It is shown in Figure 15.

Secret

Don't Assume Too Much

If you think Parental Controls on your home PC are going to effectively bar your kids from seeing whatever they want on the Internet, you're fooling yourself. Most teenagers have access to dozens of PCs that you don't control—even cell phones can download Web content today. You're better off training your kids what not to install from the Web, such as free offers that actually contain spyware. That's a much bigger threat to your household's security than uncensored Internet access itself poses.

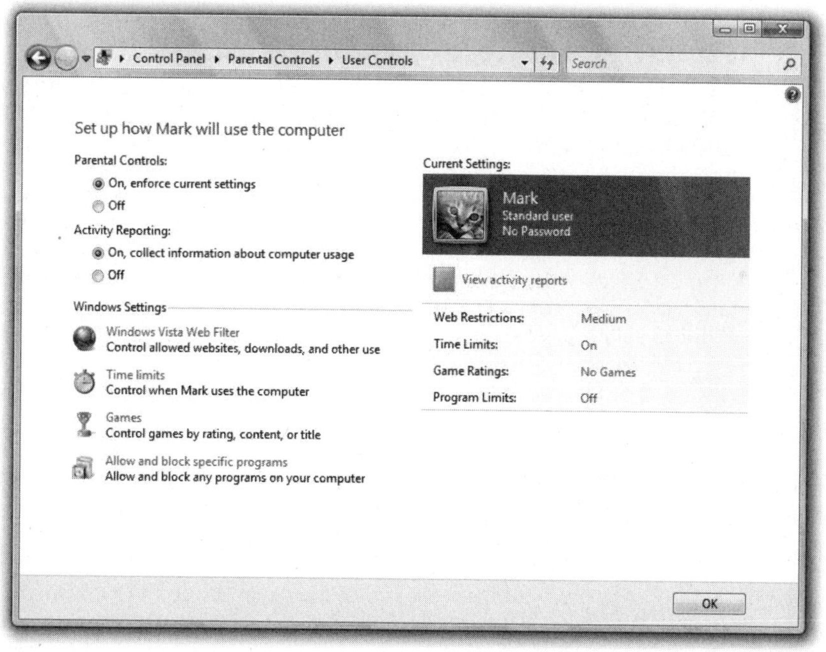

Figure 15: The Parental Controls feature in Windows Vista enables you to subscribe to the evaluation systems of several different organizations to restrict computer access to age-appropriate material.

New Games: Mahjong and Chess

No major version of Windows is complete without the inclusion of a new game or two, but Windows Vista takes this important principle to a whole new level. Not only are there several entirely new games—including Mahjong Titans and Chess Titans (the latter of which is shown in Figure 16), which represent respectable challenges for serious players of either game—but all of the old Windows games have been substantially updated with photorealistic and 3D imagery.

That old standby, Solitaire, for example, is much improved. Not only are the cards more crisp and vivid than ever before, but when you move a card from one pile to another, the exposed card turns itself over in a smooth animated effect. Right-clicking an eligible card moves it to the home position. And, if you have many eligible cards (such as when you've succeeded in placing all the cards in columns), right-clicking the green felt background of the game moves *all* the cards home.

All of the new Vista games benefit from enlarging their windows to full-screen. Watch closely when you do this, and you can actually see the objects in a game become richer and more realistic when they have more pixels to render themselves.

Secret

Thinking of Cheating at Solitaire?

Unfortunately, Vista's new Solitaire code seems to have broken one way that ne'er-do-wells have cheated at the game for years. You used to be able to click Game ➪ Undo when playing a Draw Three game, and the last three cards you turned over from the deck would go back on the pile. If you then *held down the Shift key* while clicking the deck, only one card at a time would turn over, allowing you to pick up a crucial card that wasn't originally on top of the stack. Whether by omission or design, that trick no longer works, and you'll just have to win at Solitaire the good old-fashioned way. (You can still, however, undo the turnover of your last three cards if you suddenly see a move on the board that might benefit.)

tip

Want to get better 3D rendering? If you think the special effects in Vista's new games are spectacular, you ain't seen nothin' yet. If your hardware supports it, you can get even better 3D effects by manipulating a little-used control. In Chess Titans, for example, pull down the Game menu and select the Options dialog box. If the pointer called Graphics Slider isn't all the way to the right end of the range, push it there with your mouse. When you click OK, you'll immediately see the playing pieces become sharper and smoother. I can't guarantee that this extra rendering effort will make your computer opponent a little stupider, but it's worth a shot.

Figure 16: The new Chess Titans game is an example of the photorealistic, 3D effects that Vista is capable of with Aero-compatible hardware.

cross ref Chapter 16 contains more discussion about games and Windows Vista.

Windows Media Player 11

Windows Media Player 11, a key part of Microsoft's campaign to make Windows the centerpiece of users' digital entertainment collections, is notably changed in Vista from earlier Media Player versions.

The Windows Media Player Media Library, for example, now provides more graphical views of your music library, as shown in Figure 17.

Ripping CDs to digital files has also been enhanced in WMP 11. Two new audio formats appear for the first time: Windows Media Audio Pro and lossless WAV (see Figure 18).

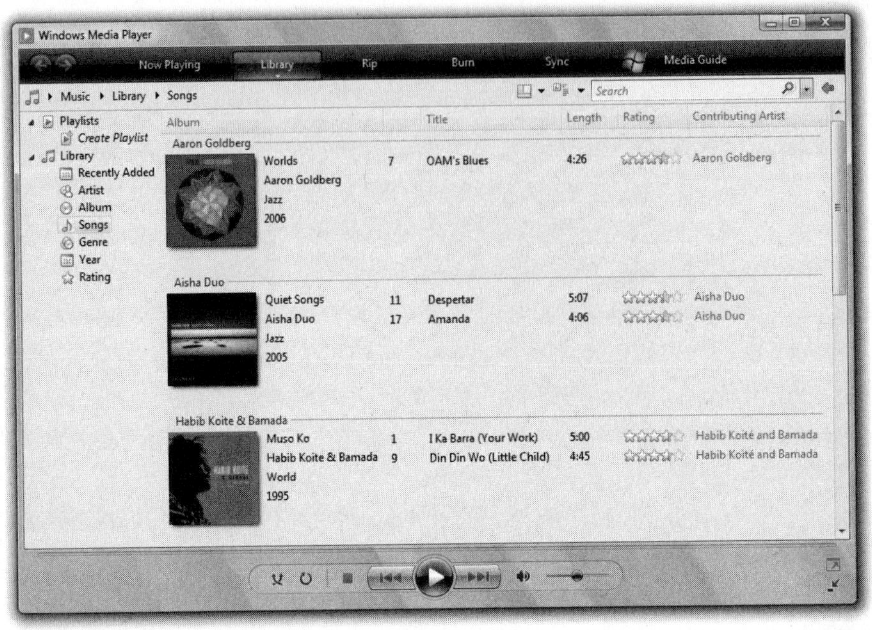

Figure 17: Windows Media Player 11 provides a variety of ways to organize, play, and view your music and video collection.

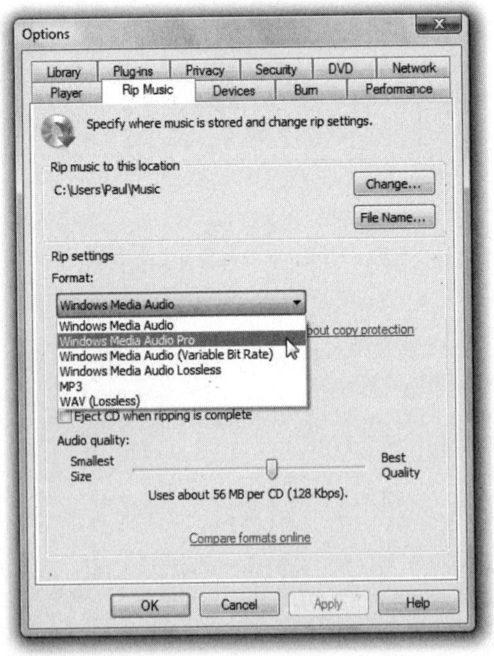

Figure 18: Microsoft's new Windows Media Player 11 supports even more formats to store CDs you've digitized.

The Pro format, strangely enough, digitizes sound at only 64 kilobits per second (64 Kbps), about half the bit rate of the older Windows Media Audio format. Lossless WAV, by contrast, is so high-quality—with a bit rate in the high hundreds of Kbps—that ripping a single CD to disk produces files that total approximately 600 MB.

Hard drives are cheap these days, so whether you really want or need the extra tonal range that comes from lossless ripping may depend on whether you've already filled up most of your disk space.

If you happen to have more than one CD drive installed on your PC, WMP 11 will rip files from all of them at once. That won't make feeding your disks into the CD trays any more fun, but it will get it over with faster.

In case you decide to reverse the process, and burn your digital files to CDs, WMP 11 has added new forms of support here, too. A disk-spanning feature calculates the number of CDs needed—if your collection exceeds the capacity of a single CD—and automatically burns your playlist over multiple disks.

cross ref Chapter 11 is all about Windows Media Player 11, while Chapter 12 describes Microsoft's related Zune initiative.

New Music and Video Services

Windows Media Player 11 boasts partnerships with several online audio and video services, including the selections of Audible.com, Napster, XM Satellite Radio, and many others, as shown in Figure 19.

Figure 19: Pick your online music store. Windows Media Player 11 integrates with a fistful of downloadable audio sources.

Windows Movie Maker and DVD Maker

Music doesn't get all the digital media action in Vista. For digital-video fans, Windows Movie Maker makes anyone with a camcorder or a video-capable camera or cell phone downright dangerous.

In case you like to subject your friends and family to your video masterpieces, Windows Movie Maker enables you to edit your raw video into a more bearable length. If you insist on your film noir running longer, however, you'll find a variety of special effects and transitions that can make almost any of your original content truly special, as shown in Figure 20.

Although they're two separate applications, Vista's Windows DVD Maker complements Movie Maker by presenting a way to burn your video creations and photo slide shows to a DVD movie for posterity. Windows DVD Maker is shown in Figure 21.

cross ref   Chapter 14 discusses Windows Movie Maker and Windows DVD Maker in much more detail.

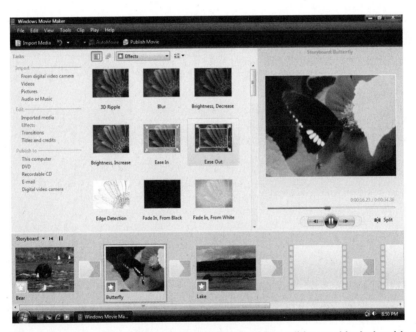

Figure 20: Microsoft's Windows Movie Maker video-editing tool includes titles and other special effects you can add to raw video.

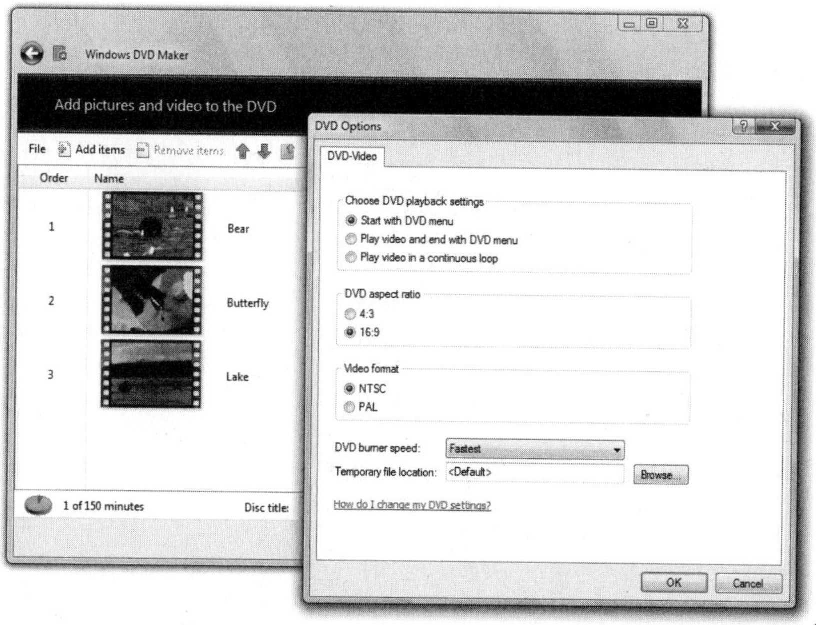

Figure 21: You may not win an Oscar, but you can try by burning as many DVDs as you want with Windows DVD Maker.

Windows Photo Gallery

Shown in Figure 22, Windows Photo Gallery is a built-in Windows Vista tool that you can use to organize, tag, enhance, and print photos from cameras, cell phones, and other digital devices.

A new thumbnail slider—a user-interface widget that's revealed by clicking the magnifying glass near the bottom of the window—enables you to quickly zoom your photo collection up and down to fit as few or as many images onto the screen as you may desire.

Windows Photo Gallery includes several tools that enable you to fix (or ruin) your original photos in your own particular way. For example, you can manually adjust the brightness, contrast, and color of a photo. A control for fixing red-eye is included for those pics that suffer from a wee bit too much flash. These tools are shown in Figure 23.

When you've got your photos the way you want them, Windows Photo Gallery can turn your selected images into slideshows, screen savers, e-mail attachments (with five levels of compression), and prints, or burn them onto CDs or DVDs. For those of you who like to edit your videos in Movie Maker (discussed previously), you can import videos into Photo Gallery. It displays each video as a thumbnail so you can mix and match video material with your stills.

Figure 22: Windows Photo Gallery helps you organize and tag your photo collections in numerous ways.

Figure 23: Windows Photo Gallery enables you to enhance your photos with simple editing tools.

tip

You can undo your fixes, no matter how many steps you took. In case your heavy-handed tweaks don't look so good, Photo Gallery retains the state your image started in. Simply click the Revert to Original icon to switch back to the picture the way it was before your "improvements."

cross ref

Chapter 13 includes more details on Windows Photo Gallery and its new successor, Windows Live Photo Gallery.

Windows Media Center

In Windows Vista Home Premium and Ultimate Editions, Windows Media Center turns your PC into a DVD player and digital video recorder all in one. Windows Media Center is shown in Figure 24.

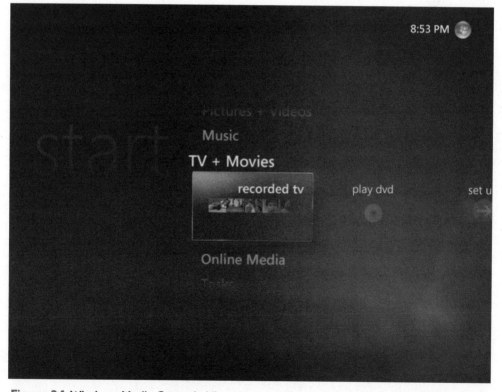

Figure 24: Windows Media Center in Vista supports wide-screen and high-definition programming with the appropriate hardware.

The Windows Vista version of Media Center has been developed to support wide-screen and high-definition monitors. It works fine on older 4:3 displays but takes full advantage of greater capabilities when present in the hardware found on a system (refer to Figure 24).

PCs that include a TV tuner enable users to watch, record, and pause live programming. With multiple tuners, it's possible to watch a program on one channel while recording another program on a different channel.

Besides TV and digital videos, Media Center also supports music and other audio files and digital photos. You can direct slide shows and music playlists as well as watch live or recorded video programming.

cross ref   See Chapter 15 for the latest on Windows Media Center.

But Wait; It Gets Better

You want more? No problem; I've got more: Thanks to Microsoft's ongoing efforts to improve Windows Vista, the software giant's latest operating system is just getting better and better over time. Since it first shipped Windows Vista, Microsoft has improved Windows Vista with a variety of fixes, culminating in the first major update to the system, dubbed Service Pack 1 (SP1). Additionally, Microsoft has shipped a number of online services via its Live services that make Vista even better, and has shipped companion products such as Windows Home Server.

Windows Vista Service Pack 1

There's an old saying when it comes to Windows: business users won't even think about upgrading to the new version until Microsoft ships the first service pack. For the uninitiated, service packs are a way for Microsoft to collect security fixes and other bug fixes into a single installable package. Corporations like service packs because they make it easier for them to keep up-to-date with the latest fixes; and if they happen to roll out a Windows version one, two, or several years after Microsoft first issued the OS, they can get the latest fixes in one whack. This can save a lot of time and effort.

Windows Vista Service Pack 1 is the first major update to Windows Vista, a collection of bug fixes, minor functional changes, and other additions to Microsoft's latest operating system.

Secret   As is the case with Vista itself, the feature set for SP1 has changed dramatically over time. Originally Microsoft hoped to ship a Media Center update code-named "Fiji" with SP1, but they had to delay that release.

From an end-user perspective, there are no major changes in Windows Vista, but that doesn't mean SP1 isn't interesting. Indeed, Microsoft has improved Vista in many ways with SP1, including the following:

♦ **Bug fixes:** Windows Vista SP1 includes a collection of previously released and new security fixes, bug fixes, and other minor updates.

♦ **A new kernel version:** SP1 includes an update to the Windows kernel to bring the Vista kernel (version 6.0) up-to-date with the version in Windows Server 2008 (version 6.1).

♦ **Kernel Patch Protection changes:** The Kernel Patch Protection ("PatchGuard") feature is designed to protect the Windows Vista kernel in 64-bit versions of the OS. However, security companies such as McAfee and Symantec complained that this feature kept them from integrating as tightly with the OS as they could in previous Windows versions, so Microsoft changed Kernel Patch Protection and released a set of APIs aimed at helping developers write code that interacts with this security feature.

♦ **Instant Search changes:** Microsoft changed Vista's Instant Search feature to allow third-party desktop search product makers to more closely integrate their products with Windows Vista. In the initially shipped version of Vista, the Instant Search indexer ran at full speed even if a third-party product was installed, reducing overall system performance. In SP1, this has been fixed.

♦ **Windows Genuine Advantage (WGA) changes:** Microsoft removed the annoying Reduced Functionality Mode (RFM) and Non-Genuine State (NGS) mode for Vista installs in expired non-activated and non-genuine states. Now with SP1, even expired non-activated Vista installs will work normally, though users are notified every hour that they need to activate.

♦ **Device compatibility:** This is up dramatically, from a bit over 40,000 compatible devices at launch to just under 80,000 devices with SP1. The number of logoed devices—devices that are certified by Microsoft to work properly with Vista—is also up dramatically, from about 2,000 at launch to over 17,000 with SP1. Improvements to Vista's drivers aren't limited to sheer numbers, either; changes to video, audio, and other drivers in SP1 have actually improved the battery life on laptops from several major PC makers by an average of 7 percent.

♦ **Application compatibility:** This has also improved significantly with SP1. While this area includes consumer-oriented applications, incompatible enterprise applications were the big deployment blockers during Vista's first year. Microsoft and its partners remediated over 150 enterprise application blockers during the development of SP1: These are applications that previously prevented one or more corporations from upgrading to Vista.

♦ **Reliability:** This is better in Vista SP1, too, Microsoft says. The company's telemetry data enables Microsoft to analyze various system disruptions in Vista, including such behaviors as nonresponding applications, application hangs and crashes, and system crashes. Compared to the release version of Vista, SP1 more than doubled the mean number of hours between disruptions, from about 17 hours to about 34 hours.

♦ **File copy improvements:** One of the biggest complaints users have had with Windows Vista concerns file copy operations, both locally on a single PC and over networks. Microsoft isolated the causes of these and provides the fixes in SP1. A number of areas are affected, including the performance of file copy operations and system responsiveness during these operations. According to the latest data, file copy operations are 44 to 71 percent faster with SP1 than they were under the original version of Vista. Microsoft has also improved the speed at which Vista resumes from Sleep or Hibernation in SP1.

◆ **Security:** This is another oft-discussed aspect of Vista, and Microsoft points to data showing that Vista is less vulnerable to electronic attacks than are rival operating systems and its own predecessor, Windows XP. SP1 includes a small change to the highly criticized User Account Control (UAC) feature in Vista and a change to BitLocker, enabling it to encrypt nonsystem disks.

◆ **End-user changes:** While Windows Vista includes no major end-user changes, it does include a few changes you might notice. In addition to the Instant Search changes mentioned previously, for example, Microsoft improved the built-in Disk Defragmenter utility so that you can now select which disk volumes (partitions) are defragged automatically, as shown in Figure 25.

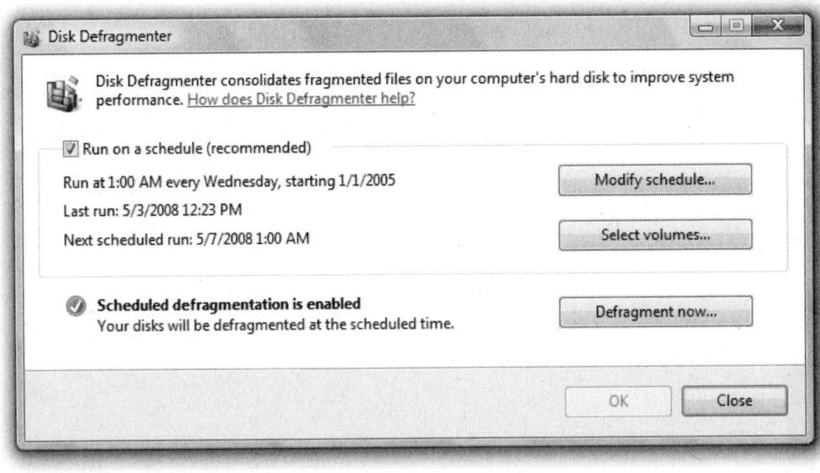

Figure 25: Disk Defragmenter is now more configurable than it was in the initially shipped version of Vista.

◆ **Administrative improvements:** Windows Vista SP1 includes a number of changes aimed at the system administrators who deploy, support, and maintain Vista-based systems. Local printing from a Windows Terminal Services session has been improved; there's a new version of the Network Diagnostics tool, available from the Diagnose and Repair link in Network and Sharing; and SP1 includes a number of Group Policy (GP) changes.

◆ **Support for new hardware and standards:** Windows Vista SP1 includes support for the extended FAT (exFAT) file system used in flash memory storage and consumer-oriented mobile devices, Secure Digital (SD) Advanced Direct Memory Access (DMA), EFI network booting on x64 PCs, the Secure Socket Tunneling Protocol (SSTP) remote access tunneling protocol, and DirectX 10.1, the latest version of Microsoft's multimedia and gaming libraries.

As you can see by reading through the preceding list, SP1 does not dramatically impact your day-to-day usage of Vista, though it does of course add many desirable low-level improvements. This is in keeping with Microsoft's traditional view of service packs, though nothing like Windows XP Service Pack 2, which was in many ways a major Windows update.

Windows Live and Microsoft's Online Services

A few years before Microsoft shipped Windows Vista, it began separately reevaluating the relationship between its PC operating system and the various online products and services it was then offering through its MSN brand. Executives at the company determined that they wanted to bring the company's Windows, online, and mobile experiences together in ways that were seamless but wouldn't run into any of the antitrust issues presented by previous integration strategies around Internet Explorer and Windows Media Player.

The result was Windows Live, a set of online products and services that extend the Windows user experience in exciting and unique ways. The sheer number of Windows Live services is somewhat daunting, and complicating matters is the fact that there are other Microsoft Live services, including Office Live, Games for Windows Live, and Xbox Live.

The most exciting development in the Live world, however, is Live Mesh, a new Microsoft platform that encompasses an Internet operating system (exposed as a Web-based desktop), your PC and Mac computer(s), and your mobile device(s).

cross ref   Microsoft's Live services are discussed in detail in Chapter 21.

Windows Live OneCare and Windows Home Server

While Windows Vista significantly enhances the home networking functionality in Windows, Microsoft has released other companion products that offer even more features. For example, the Windows Live OneCare subscription service combines antivirus, anti-spyware, and firewall security features with PC tune-up functionality and a first-class PC backup and restore service and can be installed on up to three PCs. OneCare also includes centralized multiple-PC management, monthly progress reports, online photo backup, and more.

Microsoft is also selling a Windows Home Server product through selected PC makers, providing centralized PC backup and restore, PC and server health monitoring, document and media sharing, and remote access.

cross ref   See Chapter 25 for more information about Windows Live OneCare and Windows Home Server.

And More

There's so much more: Microsoft's new Zune platform takes on the iPod and iTunes in ways that were impossible with Windows Media Player 11 (see Chapter 12). Windows PowerShell takes Windows Scripting and command-line work to a new, object-oriented future; see Chapter 24 for a complete rundown. And Microsoft's support for games in Windows Vista has gone online and taken on the Xbox 360 with Games for Windows Live. I examine this development in Chapter 16.

My Promise to You

I've barely scratched the surface of the changes you'll find in Vista compared with the capabilities of Windows XP. But as noted previously, Microsoft—and Windows Vista—isn't standing still. For this reason, no book, even one as comprehensive as I've tried to make this one, can cover it all. So join me online, at my SuperSite for Windows (**www.winsupersite.com**). There you'll find more Windows Vista information than you probably want—as well as an ongoing blog detailing errata and other changes for the book. In this way, *Windows Vista Secrets* is a living document, one that will be updated on an ongoing basis online.

See you on the Web!

Part I

Surviving Setup

Selecting the
Right Vista
Version

Chapter

1

◆ ◆

In This Chapter

Basic differences between the Vista versions

Which Vista versions you can safely avoid

Differences between the 32-bit and 64-bit versions of Vista

Determining the best Vista version for you

Choosing between the home and business editions

Choosing between Home Basic and Home Premium

Choosing between Vista Business and Vista Enterprise

Features available in all Vista versions

Choosing Vista Ultimate

◆ ◆

If you haven't purchased Vista yet—or you'd like to know whether or not it's worth upgrading to a more capable version of Vista—this chapter is for you. A step-by-step procedure leads you through the ins and outs of selecting the right version of Vista for you.

An Overview of All the Vista Versions

Back in 2001, life was easy: Microsoft released Windows XP in just two product editions, Windows XP Home Edition and Windows XP Professional Edition. The difference between the products was fairly obvious; and with its enhanced feature set, XP Pro was the more expensive version, as one might expect.

Over time, however, Microsoft muddied the waters with a wealth of new XP product editions. Three major product editions were added: Windows XP Media Center Edition, which received three major releases and one minor update between 2002 and 2005; Windows XP Tablet PC Edition, which received two major releases between 2002 and 2005; and Windows XP Professional x64 Edition, which took most of XP Pro's feature set and brought it to the x64 hardware platform. Other XP versions, such as XP Embedded and XP Starter Edition, can't really be considered mainstream products because they target specific usage scenarios and aren't broadly available to consumers.

Secret

Most PCs sold over the past decade are 32-bit computers based on Intel's x86 platform. While the industry was widely expected to make the jump to 64-bit computing at some point, that leap has come from an unexpected place: Intel's tiny competitor AMD developed the so-called x64 platform, which is essentially a 64-bit version of the aging x86 platform. x64-based PCs are completely compatible with x86 software; and though all PCs sold today are, in fact, x64-compatible, most PC operating systems (including Windows Vista) are sold in 32-bit versions for compatibility reasons. Even Intel is on board: Though the x64 platform was created by AMD, all of Intel's PC-oriented microprocessors are now x64-compatible as well.

Though not as technically elegant as so-called "native" 64-bit platforms such as the Itanium, x64 does provide all of the benefits of true 64-bit computing—including, most importantly, a flat 64-bit memory address space that obliterates the 4GB memory "ceiling" in the 32-bit world. For the purposes of this book, when I refer to 64-bit computing, I mean x64.

tip   You may occasionally hear Vista's versions referred to as SKUs, a term that stands for *stock keeping units*. I typically use the more common terms *product edition, version,* and *product version* throughout this book instead.

What follows is a review of the major Windows XP versions that Microsoft shipped between 2001 and 2006. In a moment, I'll compare these products with their corresponding Vista versions:

◆ Windows XP Starter Edition (less-developed countries only)

◆ Windows XP Embedded (sold in embedded devices only)

- ♦ Windows XP Home Edition
- ♦ Windows XP Home Edition N (European Union only)
- ♦ Windows XP Media Center Edition
- ♦ Windows XP Tablet Edition
- ♦ Windows XP Professional Edition
- ♦ Windows XP Professional Edition N (European Union only)
- ♦ Windows XP Professional Edition K (South Korea only)
- ♦ Windows XP Professional x64 Edition
- ♦ Windows XP for Itanium-based Systems

All Windows XP product versions, except Windows XP Professional x64 Edition, were available only in 32-bit versions.

For Windows Vista, Microsoft surveyed the market and came away with two observations. First, an experiment bifurcating the Microsoft Office product line into multiple product editions had proven enormously successful for the company. Second, customers were willing to pay a bit more for premium product versions, such as XP Media Center Edition, that offered extra features. Clearly, Microsoft's experiences over the past few years led directly to the situation we have with Windows Vista: The company has created six core Vista product editions, two of which can be described as premium versions. (If you include the so-called N and K editions (for the European Union and South Korea, respectively), there are actually nine product editions. If you count the 32-bit and x64 (64-bit) versions separately, since they are in fact sold separately for the most part, there are 17 product editions. Add the (PRODUCT) RED version of Windows Vista Ultimate—which is available only with select new PCs from Dell—and you've got 18. Here's the complete list:

- ♦ Windows Vista Starter
- ♦ Windows Vista Home Basic
- ♦ Windows Vista Home Basic (x64)
- ♦ Windows Vista Home Premium
- ♦ Windows Vista Home Premium N — European Union only
- ♦ Windows Vista Home Premium (x64)
- ♦ Windows Vista Home Premium N (x64) — European Union only
- ♦ Windows Vista Business
- ♦ Windows Vista Business K — South Korea only
- ♦ Windows Vista Business N — European Union only
- ♦ Windows Vista Business (x64)
- ♦ Windows Vista Business K (x64) — South Korea only
- ♦ Windows Vista Business N (x64) — European Union only
- ♦ Windows Vista Enterprise
- ♦ Windows Vista Enterprise (x64)
- ♦ Windows Vista Ultimate
- ♦ Windows Vista Ultimate (x64)
- ♦ Windows Vista Ultimate (PRODUCT) RED — Sold only through Dell on select machines

Secret

Microsoft originally planned an Itanium version of Windows Vista, which would run on high-end workstations. However, the company canceled this project during the beta process due to a lack of customer interest. Thus, the mainstream PC platform of the future is now secure: It will be 64 bits, and it will be x64, not Itanium.

tip

Notice anything else missing in that product lineup? That's right: There's no Embedded version of Windows Vista. Yet.

Confusingly, you also have to choose how you'll acquire Windows Vista. In addition to the most typical method—simply getting it with a new PC—you can purchase retail boxed copies of Windows Vista and other not-quite-retail versions of the software. It's confusing—but then that's why you're reading this chapter, no?

Here's my advice: Don't get bogged down in semantics or complicated counting exercises. With a little bit of knowledge about how these product editions break down and are sold, you can whittle the list down quite a bit very easily. Then you can evaluate which features are available in which editions and choose the one that's right for you based on your needs.

Understanding the Differences and Choosing the Right Version

The first step is to understand the differences between each Vista product edition. Then you need to understand the various ways in which you can acquire Windows Vista, either as a standalone product or as an upgrade to an existing version of Windows (including, confusingly, Windows Vista itself). Finally, you can weigh the various trade-offs of each option—features, price, and so on—and choose accordingly.

Step 1: Whittling Down the Product Editions List

I was really just having some fun at Microsoft's expense in the previous section; it's possible to categorize the Windows Vista product editions into four basic flavors. To do so, you need to temporarily forget about the differences between 32-bit versions and 64-bit versions (don't worry; I'll get to that) and just skip over the versions that aren't relevant. Once you do this, the following list emerges:

Windows Vista Home Basic

Windows Vista Home Premium

Windows Vista Business

Windows Vista Ultimate

This is a much more manageable list, but how did I arrive at it? After all, there were 18 product editions in the original list. It's time to take one more look, hopefully for the last time, at all those missing options.

Windows Vista Starter

You don't need or want Windows Vista Starter. It's that simple.

Windows Vista Starter is limited to 32-bit processors, supports only the basic Vista user interface, and addresses a limited amount of RAM. It's designed only as a loss leader to get Windows' pricing down to a level that's competitive in less-developed countries, where it can compete against low-cost PCs running the open-source Linux operating system.

More important, perhaps, Vista Starter is available only in a limited number of regions and cannot be purchased at retail, so it's a non-starter (I'm here all week, folks) for any mainstream or enthusiast Windows user.

Unless you're buying a PC in one of the few countries in which you can acquire Windows Vista Starter, you probably won't hear much more about this product; and if you are buying such a PC, your computing needs are pretty basic, so it's unlikely that you're ready for this book just yet.

The K and N Editions Aren't for You, Either

Whatever Vista versions are being offered in Korea (with a K moniker) or in Europe (with an N moniker), they're designed to satisfy the antitrust regulations and rulings in those locales, and you should ignore them also because these versions are more limited than the non-K and non-N Windows Vista versions sold in South Korea and the European Union (EU), respectively. In addition, they don't cost any less, so there's no reason to even consider them, even if you do live in these areas.

Consider the N editions of Windows Vista, which are sold only in EU markets. These products came about because of a 2004 EU ruling that required Microsoft to offer versions of Windows without the Windows Media Player included. The requirement for a separate version of Windows was intended to enhance competition in the market for media players, such as the downloadable RealPlayer application.

However, because Microsoft sells its N versions for the same price as its full-featured Windows versions, demand for the N versions never materialized. Until there's a big price difference, consumers will continue to treat N as "not interested." Ditto for the K versions.

You're Not the Enterprise

Windows Vista Enterprise is a special version of Windows Vista aimed at Microsoft's largest corporate customers. As such, it is very much like Windows Vista Business but with two main differences. One, it's available only through a corporate volume licensing subscription program. Two, it includes special licensing terms that allow you to run up to four more copies of the OS under a virtual machine on the same PC. Because of the unique way in which you must acquire this version, chances are good you won't be hunting around for Windows Vista Enterprise. That said, if you do get a PC from work with Windows Vista Enterprise on it, you're pretty much running a slightly souped-up version of Windows Vista Business.

64-Bit Versions of Windows Vista

The differences between 32-bit (x86) versions of Windows Vista and 64-bit (x64) versions are more complex. But here's the weird bit: Though virtually every single PC sold today is x64-compatible, virtually every single copy of Windows Vista that goes out the door on those new PCs is a 32-bit x86 version.

If you do manage to purchase a new PC with a 64-bit version of Windows Vista prein-stalled—and yes, they are out there if you look hard enough—that PC will come from the factory with all of the 64-bit hardware device drivers that are needed to support whatever add-ons and peripherals ship with the machine.

Consumers who are building their own PCs or adding Windows Vista to an existing PC have an additional issue to consider that is outside of the basic capabilities discussion covered in this chapter: Should you purchase a 64-bit version of Windows Vista? After all, 64-bit versions of Windows Vista can access far more RAM than 32-bit versions (up to 128GB as of this writing, compared to less than 4GB of RAM in 32-bit versions). In addition, 64-bit versions of Windows Vista are nominally more secure than 32-bit versions, as discussed in Chapter 8. Does that mean that 64-bit versions of Windows Vista are "better"?

Not exactly. Though 64-bit versions of Windows Vista are widely compatible with the hardware and 32-bit software that Windows users have been using for years, these products simply aren't as compatible as 32-bit versions of Windows Vista. For very many people, compatibility is the most important consideration when it comes to upgrading their PC, because they want everything they've been using to continue working. Moreover, few people need 4GB of RAM today, let alone more than that.

Here's my advice. Typical consumers should stay away from x64 versions of Windows for the lifetime of Windows Vista. There will be niggling hardware and software compatibility issues on Vista x64 because Microsoft requires hardware vendors to ship different drivers for the 32-bit (x86) and 64-bit (x64) versions of Vista. Guess which one is easier? Though hardware and software compatibility has already improved dramatically since Vista first shipped, typical users will be frustrated by the one or two incompatible applications or devices that are likely to appear. It's just not worth it. Not yet.

Put another way, if you have to ask—that is, if you're unsure whether you should be using Vista x64—then the answer is still the same: You shouldn't be running Vista x64. That said, Vista x64 is considerably more viable than it was when Vista first appeared; and it's moving quickly into the mainstream, though it's not quite there yet. Maybe by the next version of Windows.

For the coming year, gamers, digital-content creators, CAD-CAM workers, science and engineering users, and other power users who run into the 4GB ceiling in 32-bit versions of Windows are ideal candidates for Vista x64. These types of users understand the risks and limitations of the x64 platform and don't need my advice anyway. Enjoy the headroom.

Secret

Contrary to the conventional wisdom, 64-bit software isn't magically faster than 32-bit software. That said, 64-bit PCs running a 64-bit version of Windows Vista and native 64-bit software can often outperform 32-bit alternatives, but that's because you can add far more RAM to the 64-bit machine. Systems with massive amounts of memory just aren't as constrained and can operate to their full potential.

Windows Vista Ultimate (PRODUCT) RED

There are plenty of good reasons to consider Windows Vista Ultimate (PRODUCT) RED, as this version is part of the (PRODUCT) RED series of products, which helps the Global Fund combat AIDS in Africa. When you buy a (PRODUCT) RED product, you're helping others in need.

From a technology perspective, however, Windows Vista Ultimate (PRODUCT) RED is functionally identical to the "normal" versions of Windows Vista Ultimate, so readers of this book who have Windows Vista Ultimate (PRODUCT) RED will be as well-served as other Vista Ultimate users. Note that Windows Vista Ultimate (PRODUCT) RED cannot be purchased at retail (or online) as a standalone software package. It is sold only with specific PC models from the PC giant Dell.

Secret   If you're curious, Windows Vista Ultimate (PRODUCT) RED includes six unique (PRODUCT) RED–inspired wallpapers, a (PRODUCT) RED screen saver, two (PRODUCT) RED Windows Sidebar gadgets, and a (PRODUCT) RED–themed DreamScene animated background.

Step 2: Understanding the Differences between the Product Editions

Once you've narrowed the list down to the four contenders, it's time to evaluate them and understand which features are available in each product edition. There are various ways to present this kind of information, but tables, logically divided by category, are easy on the eyes and mind. Tables 1-1 through 1-10 list the five main Windows Vista product editions from which you can choose, and indicate which features are included with each.

Table 1-1: User Interface Features

	Home Basic	Home Premium	Business	Enterprise	Ultimate
Windows Vista Basic UI	Yes	Yes	Yes	Yes	Yes
Windows Aero UI ("Glass")	—	Yes	Yes	Yes	Yes
Windows Flip	Yes	Yes	Yes	Yes	Yes
Windows Flip 3D	—	Yes	Yes	Yes	Yes
Live Taskbar thumbnails	—	Yes	Yes	Yes	Yes
Instant search	Yes	Yes	Yes	Yes	Yes
Live content organization in Explorer windows	Yes	Yes	Yes	Yes	Yes

Table 1-2: Security Features

	Home Basic	Home Premium	Business	Enterprise	Ultimate
User Account Control (UAC)	Yes	Yes	Yes	Yes	Yes
Windows Security Center	Yes	Yes	Yes	Yes	Yes
Windows Defender	Yes	Yes	Yes	Yes	Yes
Windows Firewall	Yes	Yes	Yes	Yes	Yes
Internet Explorer 7 Protected Mode	Yes	Yes	Yes	Yes	Yes
Phishing Filter (IE7 and Windows Mail)	Yes	Yes	Yes	Yes	Yes
Windows Update (can access Microsoft Update)	Yes	Yes	Yes	Yes	Yes
Parental Controls	Yes	Yes	—	—	Yes

Table 1-3: Performance Features

	Home Basic	Home Premium	Business	Enterprise	Ultimate
Windows ReadyDrive	Yes	Yes	Yes	Yes	Yes
Windows ReadyBoost	Yes	Yes	Yes	Yes	Yes
64-bit processor support	Yes	Yes	Yes	Yes	Yes
Maximum RAM (32-bit version)	4GB	4GB	4GB	4GB	4GB
Maximum RAM (64-bit version)	8GB	16GB	128+GB	128+GB	128+GB
Physical processor support	1	1	2	2	2
Processor core support	Unlimited	Unlimited	Unlimited	Unlimited	Unlimited

Table 1-4: Reliability Features

	Home Basic	Home Premium	Business	Enterprise	Ultimate
Manual file backup and recovery	Yes	Yes	Yes	Yes	Yes

continues

Table 1-4: *(continued)*

	Home Basic	*Home Premium*	*Business*	*Enterprise*	*Ultimate*
Automatic backup	Yes, but not to a network location	Yes	Yes	Yes	Yes
Shadow Copies	—	—	Yes	Yes	Yes
System image backup and recovery	—	—	Yes	Yes	Yes
Encrypting File System (EFS)	—	—	Yes	Yes	Yes
Windows BitLocker Full Drive Encryption	—	—	—	Yes	Yes
Windows SuperFetch	Yes	Yes	Yes	Yes	Yes
Automatic hard disk defragmentation	Yes	Yes	Yes	Yes	Yes

Table 1-5: Internet Features

	Home Basic	*Home Premium*	*Business*	*Enterprise*	*Ultimate*
Internet Explorer 7	Yes	Yes	Yes	Yes	Yes
RSS support	Yes	Yes	Yes	Yes	Yes
Windows Mail	Yes	Yes	Yes	Yes	Yes

Table 1-6: Bundled Applications

	Home Basic	*Home Premium*	*Business*	*Enterprise*	*Ultimate*
Windows Calendar	Yes	Yes	Yes	Yes	Yes
Windows Contacts	Yes	Yes	Yes	Yes	Yes
Windows Sidebar	Yes	Yes	Yes	Yes	Yes
Games Explorer	Yes	Yes	Yes	Yes	Yes
Premium games	—	Yes	Yes	Yes	Yes

Table 1-7: Digital Media Features

	Home Basic	Home Premium	Business	Enterprise	Ultimate
Windows Photo Gallery	Yes	Yes	Yes	Yes	Yes
Themed photo slide shows	Yes	Yes	Yes	Yes	Yes
Windows Media Player 11	Yes	Yes	Yes	Yes	Yes
Windows Media Center	—	Yes	—	—	Yes
Windows Media Center HDTV and CableCard support	—	Yes	—	—	Yes
Xbox 360 Media Center Extender compatibility	—	Yes	—	—	Yes
Windows Movie Maker	Yes	Yes	—	—	Yes
Windows Movie Maker HD format support	—	Yes	—	—	Yes
Windows DVD Maker	—	Yes	—	—	Yes

Table 1-8: Networking Features

	Home Basic	Home Premium	Business	Enterprise	Ultimate
Network and Sharing Center	Yes	Yes	Yes	Yes	Yes
Improved wireless networking	Yes	Yes	Yes	Yes	Yes
Improved power management	Yes	Yes	Yes	Yes	Yes
Number of supported simultaneous peer network connections	5	10	10	10	10
Windows Meeting Space	View only	Yes	Yes	Yes	Yes
Improved file and folder sharing	Yes	Yes	Yes	Yes	Yes
Network Projector support	—	Yes	Yes	Yes	Yes
Presentation settings	—	Yes	Yes	Yes	Yes
Remote Desktop	Client only	Client only	Yes	Yes	Yes

continues

Table 1-8: *(continued)*

	Home Basic	Home Premium	Business	Enterprise	Ultimate
Join domain (Windows Server/SBS)	—	—	Yes	Yes	Yes
Offline files and folder support	—	—	Yes	Yes	Yes
IIS Web Server	—	—	Yes	Yes	Yes

Table 1-9: Mobility Features

	Home Basic	Home Premium	Business	Enterprise	Ultimate
Windows Mobility Center	Partial	Partial	Yes	Yes	Yes
Sync Center	Yes	Yes	Yes	Yes	Yes
Tablet PC functionality	—	Yes	Yes	Yes	Yes
Touch-screen support	—	Yes	Yes	Yes	Yes
Windows SideShow (auxiliary display support)	—	Yes	Yes	Yes	Yes

Table 1-10: Other Features

	Home Basic	Home Premium	Business	Enterprise	Ultimate
Windows Anytime Upgrade	Yes (to Home Premium or Ultimate)	Yes (to Ultimate)	Yes (to Ultimate)	—	—
Windows Ultimate extras	—	—	—	—	Yes
Speech recognition support	Yes	Yes	Yes	Yes	Yes
Accessibility settings and Ease of Access Center	Yes	Yes	Yes	Yes	Yes
Windows Welcome Center	Yes	Yes	Yes	Yes	Yes
XPS document support	Yes	Yes	Yes	Yes	Yes
Windows Fax and Scan	—	—	Yes	Yes	Yes

One big feature you don't get with Windows Vista Home Basic is the beautiful Windows Aero user interface, described in detail later in the book. If you want the absolute best graphical experience, don't pick Home Basic. That said, you might be surprised that the default Windows Vista Home Basic UI, called Windows Vista Standard, is pretty decent. You can find out more about this and other Vista UIs in Chapter 4.

Though 32-bit versions of Windows Vista "support" 4GB of RAM, they can access only about 3.1GB of RAM, even when a full 4GB of RAM is installed in the PC. This is because of a limitation in the way that 32-bit versions of Windows handle memory access. If you were to install an x64 version of Windows Vista on the same system, you would have access to the entire 4GB of RAM. 64-bit Vista versions have dramatically improved memory capacity, as noted in the preceding tables.

Regarding that 128GB address space on Windows Vista Business, Enterprise, and Ultimate, it's a moving target and could, in fact, go up in the years ahead. When Microsoft first shipped Windows Vista, a PC with 128GB was almost science fiction. It still is today, frankly, but as PC and workstation makers make ever more powerful machines, it's possible that one will eventually cross the 128GB-of-RAM barrier during Windows Vista's lifetime. If that happens, Microsoft will evaluate increasing the memory limit in x64 versions of Vista Business, Enterprise, and Ultimate.

With the exception of the Remote Desktop and Mobility Center features for portable PCs—both of which are limited in the Home versions—most of the features of Windows Vista are the same in all versions.

The home-oriented versions of Vista are more limited than the business versions in some ways, but they also include some unique multimedia functionality that's not available to Vista Business and Enterprise users. If the restrictions of a given version prevent you from using a feature you need in a more capable version, it's easy to upgrade Vista's Home and Business versions to Vista Ultimate. To do so, you can use the built-in Windows Anytime Upgrade applet (described later in this chapter and in Chapter 2).

Step 3: Making the Right Product-Edition Choice

Armed with the information in the preceding tables, you can think of Windows Vista as being divided into three basic product types:

♦ There are the consumer- or home-oriented versions, such as Windows Vista Home Basic and Home Premium. These products tend to include interesting digital-media functionality but not some of the more technically advanced reliability features, such as system image backup and recovery, EFS support, and domain support.

◆ The business-oriented versions of Windows Vista, including Windows Vista Business and Enterprise, include all of the business, reliability, and security features but are light in the digital-media arena (e.g., there's no Media Center, DVD Maker, Movie Maker, or so forth).

◆ On the high end, there's Windows Vista Ultimate, which very neatly combines all of the consumer-oriented features from Windows Vista Home Premium with all of the business and reliability benefits of Windows Vista Enterprise. Windows Vista Ultimate is, quite literally, a superset of all the other Vista product editions.

In any event, your options roughly break down between the consumer, business, and "über" versions of Vista, so you need to decide into which category you fall and then choose accordingly. The next sections help you break down these choices.

tip   Obviously, there is one other critical consideration here: price. For example, while Windows Vista Ultimate may seem like a best-of-both-worlds product, it also comes with premium pricing. Later in this chapter I'll describe the various ways in which you can purchase Windows Vista, and the cost of each version.

Choosing between Home Basic and Home Premium

Table 1-11 shows some of the features that differ between the Basic and Premium versions of Vista for home users. If you've decided that a Home version of Vista is all you need, Table 1-11 will help you decide which of the two available versions will best suit you. Note that Windows Vista Ultimate also supports all of Vista's Home features.

◆ **Home Basic**—Choose this if you don't need Media Center capabilities, the capability to burn DVDs, or any of the other features that come with Home Premium.

◆ **Home Premium**—Choose this if you have a Tablet PC (actually, it is hard to buy a Tablet PC that doesn't have at least Vista Premium installed on it) or if you want the more extensive multimedia features of the Premium version.

Table 1-11: Comparing Vista Home Basic and Home Premium

	Home Basic	Home Premium
Parental Controls	Yes	Yes
Windows Movie Maker	Yes	Yes
Themed slide shows	—	Yes
Windows Media Center	—	Yes
Windows Media Center—high-definition TV	—	Yes
Windows Media Center—CableCard support	—	Yes

continues

Table 1-11: *(continued)*

	Home Basic	*Home Premium*
Support for Media Center Extenders, including Xbox 360	—	Yes
Windows DVD Maker	—	Yes
Windows Aero user interface	—	Yes
Windows Tablet PC with touch-screen support	—	Yes
Windows SideShow	—	Yes
Windows Movie Maker HD	—	Yes
Backup of user files to a network device	—	Yes
Scheduled backup of user files	—	Yes
Network Projection	—	Yes
Presentation settings	—	Yes
New premium games	—	Yes
Windows Meeting Space	View only	Yes

Choosing between Vista Business and Enterprise

Table 1-12 shows the features present in the Business and Enterprise versions of Vista but not the Home versions, and the few features Enterprise has that Business doesn't. Note that Windows Vista Ultimate also supports all of Vista's business features.

◆ Both the Business and Enterprise versions, unlike the Home versions, support domain networking. This enables users to log on to a network server using Microsoft's Active Directory (AD) technology and share centrally managed resources.

◆ Enterprise supports a few additional features that might be crucial for your business. For example, BitLocker Drive Encryption enables you to securely encrypt files and folders. You can require users to have a physical token to decrypt and access these resources, protecting them from view if a PC is stolen or otherwise used by an unauthorized person.

Table 1-12: Comparing Vista Business and Vista Enterprise

	Business	*Enterprise*
Support for processors in two sockets	Yes	Yes
Shadow Copies	Yes	Yes
System image–based backup and recovery	Yes	Yes

continues

Table 1-12: *(continued)*

	Business	Enterprise
Encrypting File System	Yes	Yes
Desktop deployment tools for managed networks	Yes	Yes
Policy-based quality of service for networking	Yes	Yes
Windows Rights Management Services (RMS) client	Yes	Yes
Control over installation of device drivers	Yes	Yes
Network Access Protection Client Agent	Yes	Yes
Pluggable logon authentication architecture	Yes	Yes
Integrated smart card management	Yes	Yes
Wireless network provisioning	Yes	Yes
Domain join for Windows Server	Yes	Yes
Domain join for Windows Small Business Server	Yes	Yes
Group Policy support	Yes	Yes
Offline files and folder support	Yes	Yes
Client-side caching	Yes	Yes
Roaming user profiles	Yes	Yes
Folder redirection	Yes	Yes
Centralized power management via Group Policy	Yes	Yes
Windows Fax and Scan	Yes	Yes*
Internet Information Server	Yes*	Yes*
Small Business Resources	Yes	—
Windows BitLocker Drive Encryption	—	Yes
All 36 worldwide UI languages available	—	Yes
Simultaneous install of multiple UI languages	—	Yes
Subsystem for UNIX-based applications	—	Yes
Number of licenses for virtualized versions of the OS on the same hardware	0	4

*Feature is optional

Secret Windows Vista Enterprise was originally going to include a unique feature called Virtual PC Express. However, before Windows Vista was finalized, Microsoft decided to make its entire Virtual PC product line, which lets you run operating systems and applications in virtualized environments under a host OS, available free. Therefore, now you can download Virtual PC without cost, regardless of which version of Windows Vista you have. There are even separate versions for Vista 32-bit and 64-bit (x64) products. See www.microsoft.com/virtualpc.

Choosing Windows Vista Ultimate

Windows Vista Ultimate combines all of the features available in all of the other Vista versions, and does so at a premium price. The only compelling reason to pay extra to get Vista Ultimate is if you absolutely must have two features, one of which exists only in Home Premium (such as Windows Media Center) and the other of which can be obtained only in Business or Enterprise (such as domain login).

Windows Vista Ultimate also includes a few unique features of its own, the most prominent of which is Windows Ultimate Extras, a series of Windows Update–based downloads that add new features and expand on existing Vista technologies. To date, Microsoft has made games, animated desktops, and various enterprise-related features available only via Ultimate Extras.

Of course, if cost is no object, you might purchase Vista Ultimate just because you want everything Microsoft has to offer. If so—*enjoy!*

Purchasing Windows Vista

There are almost as many ways to purchase Windows Vista as there are Vista product editions. This can make acquiring Windows Vista somewhat complex, especially if you want to purchase a Setup disk and install the operating system on your own PC. Here are the ways in which you can acquire Microsoft's latest operating system.

With a New PC

The single best way to acquire Windows Vista is with a new PC from a major PC maker such as Dell, HP, or Lenovo. That's because PC makers spend huge amounts of time testing every hardware device that they sell in order to ensure that customers have the best possible experience.

One thing that has sullied this market, of course, is *crapware*, an industry practice whereby PC makers include useless or unwanted preinstalled applications on their pre-configured PCs. The good news is that this practice is slowly going away: Dell and other PC makers now offer new PCs without crapware, either free or for a small fee.

The cost of Windows on a new PC varies from PC maker to PC maker and from machine to machine. Generally speaking, a copy of some version of Windows Vista will be included in the price of virtually every PC sold today, and the actual cost to you will range from roughly $30 to $80. The cost of upgrading to more expensive Vista versions varies as well. My informal research (read: browsing the sites of PC makers online) reveals that you can typically move from Windows Vista Home Basic to Home Premium for less than $30, which is an excellent deal. The upgrade to Vista Business will typically set you back quite a bit more, around $100 to $130. The upgrade to Windows Vista Ultimate is about $125 to $150. (These additional costs are all based on a core system running Windows Vista Home Basic and can, of course, change over time.)

For example, Figure 1-1 shows Dell's "configurator" for a typical home PC.

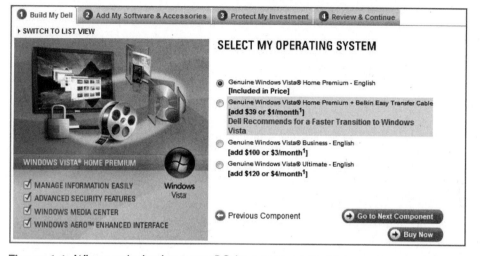

Figure 1-1: When you're buying a new PC, be sure to get the Vista version you really want.

As you'll see in a moment, the cost of upgrading to a better or more expensive Windows Vista version is almost always lower if you do it when you purchase the PC. Regardless of cost, however, it is always easier to upgrade during the purchase process because the PC maker will install and configure the OS for you.

Retail Boxed Copies

If you walk into an electronics superstore, the versions of Windows Vista you see are what's known as retail boxed copies of the software. You will see both *Full* and *Upgrade* versions of the software, and you should see versions of each for Windows Vista Home Basic, Home Premium, Business, and Ultimate. Here are the differences between the versions:

- ♦ **Full version:** A full version of Windows Vista (see Figure 1-2) can be used to perform a *clean install* of Windows Vista only. It cannot be used to upgrade an existing version of Windows to Windows Vista. Full versions of Windows Vista are more expensive than Upgrade versions.

- ♦ **Upgrade version:** An upgrade version of Windows Vista can be used to perform a clean install of Windows Vista or upgrade an existing version of Windows to Windows Vista. Upgrade versions of Windows Vista are less expensive than Full versions because you must be an existing Windows customer to qualify for Upgrade pricing. The Upgrade packaging for Windows Vista Home Premium is shown in Figure 1-3.

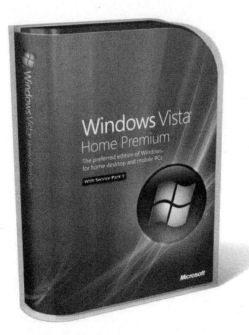

Figure 1-2: The retail packaging for Windows Vista includes a cool pull-out case.

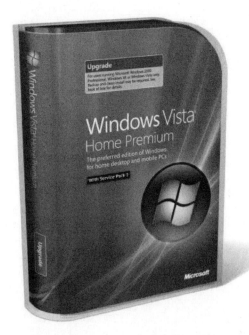

Figure 1-3: Note the prominent sticker on the Upgrade packaging.

Secret   Make sure you''re getting the latest version of Windows Vista when you purchase at retail. At the time of this writing that means a version that includes Service Pack 1, but I expect Microsoft to update its Vista retail packaging at least a few more times over the years.

That's the rub. Understanding how you qualify for an Upgrade version of Windows Vista can be somewhat confusing; and even then, it's not very clear when you can perform an in-place upgrade over an existing Windows version. Here are some guidelines.

Those Who Don't Qualify for an Upgrade Version of Windows Vista

If you are currently running any MS-DOS-based version of Windows—including Windows 95, Windows 98, Windows 98 Second Edition, or Windows Millennium Edition (Me)—or any version of Windows NT (3.x and 4.0), you don't qualify for any Upgrade version of Windows Vista. That means you need to grab a more expensive Full version instead. Because the Full versions of Windows Vista cannot be used to perform an in-place upgrade to Windows Vista, you need to back up all your documents and other data and your application settings, and find all your application install disks or executables so you can reinstall them after Vista is up and running.

Secret   Looking for an easy way to back up documents, settings, and other data and then restore it on Windows Vista? Good news: Windows Vista includes a tool for this purpose called Windows Easy Transfer.

Those Who Do Qualify for an Upgrade Version of Windows Vista

If you are running Windows 2000 or any mainstream desktop version of Windows XP—including Windows XP Home Edition, Professional Edition, Media Center Edition (any version), Tablet PC Edition (any version), or XP Professional x64 Edition—you qualify for an Upgrade version of Windows Vista.

That said, there are some limitations, depending on which Windows version you are running. Windows 2000 and Windows XP x64 users cannot upgrade to any Windows Vista version in place. These users will instead need to perform a clean install. (That is, they qualify for Upgrade pricing only.)

Those Who Do Qualify for an Upgrade Version of Windows Vista and an In-Place Upgrade (Sometimes)

If you're running any version of Windows XP except for x64 and you want to upgrade in place to Windows Vista, you can do so in some cases. The trick is understanding how different versions of Windows XP map to different versions of Windows Vista. For example, Microsoft will not let you upgrade from Windows XP Professional to Windows Vista Home Basic. Table 1-13 clarifies the in-place upgrade possibilities.

Table 1-13: Which Versions of XP Can Upgrade In-Place to Which Versions of Windows Vista

Windows Version	Vista Home Basic/N	Vista Home Premium	Vista Business/N	Vista Ultimate
Windows XP Home Edition	Yes	Yes	Yes	Yes
Windows XP Professional Edition	—	—	Yes	Yes
Windows XP Media Center Edition	—	Yes	—	Yes
Windows XP Tablet PC Edition	—	—	Yes	Yes

People with older Windows versions (9x, Me, NT) do not qualify for upgrade pricing, but Windows 2000 and XP x64 users do qualify for upgrade pricing—they just can't do an in-place upgrade. Instead, they need to use an Upgrade version of Vista to perform a clean install of the product. Confused?

Your decision regarding which version to purchase is also influenced by the cost difference of the more capable versions. In Table 1-14, you can see the current U.S. list prices for the different Vista versions. Pricing in countries other than the United States varies, but should roughly adhere to what is shown in Table 1-14. (Microsoft has already lowered the prices on certain Vista product editions once since the product became widely available, so you never know—this could change again.)

Table 1-14: U.S. List Prices for Different Vista Product Editions

Windows Vista Home Basic	
Windows Vista Home Basic Full	$199.00
Windows Vista Home Basic Upgrade	$99.95
Windows Vista Home Premium	
Windows Vista Home Premium Full	$239.00
Windows Vista Home Premium Upgrade	$129.00

continues

Table 1-14: (continued)

Windows Vista Business	
Windows Vista Business Full	$299.00
Windows Vista Business Upgrade	$199.00
Windows Vista Ultimate	
Windows Vista Ultimate Full	$349.00
Windows Vista Ultimate Upgrade	$219.00

Secret   Adding to the complexity here is that all retail versions of Windows Vista, except for Windows Vista Ultimate, are available only in 32-bit versions. If you want a 64-bit version of Windows Vista Home Basic, Home Premium, or Business, you can purchase the 32-bit version and then mail away for a 64-bit install disk. Windows Vista Ultimate includes both 32-bit and 64-bit installation disks.

OEM Versions

One of the biggest secrets in the software world is that Microsoft's operating systems are available from online retailers in special OEM versions (which come in just the Full SKU) that are aimed at the PC-builder market. These are the small "mom and pop"-type PC makers who build handcrafted machines for local markets. OEM packaging can be seen in Figure 1-4.

Secret   If you're buying a retail copy of Vista and you already own a previous version of Windows, such as XP, don't buy a full version of Vista. Find out what Microsoft's current requirements are to qualify for an upgrade version, which is much cheaper. To successfully load an upgrade version, you usually must be installing onto a machine that has the old version installed, or you must have the old version on a CD (which you insert briefly during the installation of the new OS as proof). Note, however, that you can in fact use an Upgrade version of Windows Vista to perform a clean install: you'll learn how in the next chapter.

Figure 1-4: Windows Vista OEM packaging
is pretty bare-bones.

OEM versions of Windows Vista differ from retail versions in some important ways:

They are dramatically cheaper than retail versions. As shown in Table 1-15, the OEM versions of Windows Vista are much cheaper than comparable retail versions. Note, however, that OEM pricing fluctuates somewhat, so the prices you see online could be a bit different.

They do not come with any support from Microsoft. Because PC makers support the products they sell directly, Microsoft does not offer any support for OEM versions of Windows Vista. This explains the cost differential, by the way.

You are not really supposed to buy them unless you're building PCs that you will sell to others. Technically speaking, OEM versions of Windows Vista are available only to those who intend to build PCs to sell. Furthermore, online retailers who sell OEM versions of Windows Vista are supposed to verify that you are a PC builder and/or sell the products with some kind of hardware. For this reason, you are sometimes asked to purchase a hardware tchotchske such as a USB cable when you purchase OEM software.

There's no box. This shouldn't matter too much, but you don't get the cool Vista retail packaging when you buy OEM. Instead, you pretty much get an install disk shrink-wrapped to a piece of cardboard, and a product key.

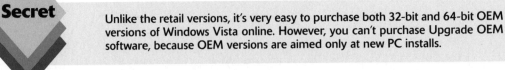

Secret

Unlike the retail versions, it's very easy to purchase both 32-bit and 64-bit OEM versions of Windows Vista online. However, you can't purchase Upgrade OEM software, because OEM versions are aimed only at new PC installs.

Table 1-15: U.S. List Prices for Different Vista OEM Product Editions

Windows Vista Home Basic	
Windows Vista Home Basic Full	$90.99
Windows Vista Home Premium	
Windows Vista Home Premium Full	$99.99
Windows Vista Business	
Windows Vista Business Full	$139.99
Windows Vista Ultimate	
Windows Vista Ultimate Full	$169.99

Depending on which version you're looking at, the savings are usually substantial. All of the OEM products (which are Full versions) are less expensive than the Upgrade retail versions of Vista. That said, OEM products cannot be used to upgrade an existing PC: They're for new installs only.

Secret

OEM versions of Windows Vista are sometimes sold in multi-OS packs. For example, you can purchase a three-pack of Windows Vista Ultimate if you'd like.

Windows Anytime Upgrade

Unlike previous versions of Windows, Vista provides an integrated capability to upgrade from a less powerful version to a more capable version at any time. You simply run the Windows Anytime Upgrade applet, select a source from which to purchase an upgrade license, and your PC is quickly enhanced with the more powerful version you've selected. Because of the way in which the Vista product line is designed, however, Windows Anytime Upgrade is available only in three Vista product editions:

♦ **Windows Vista Home Basic** can be upgraded to Windows Vista Home Premium or Ultimate via Windows Anytime Upgrade.

♦ **Windows Vista Home Premium** can be upgraded to Windows Vista Ultimate via Windows Anytime Upgrade.

♦ **Windows Vista Business** can be upgraded to Windows Vista Ultimate via Windows Anytime Upgrade.

Windows Anytime Upgrade is shown in Figure 1-5.

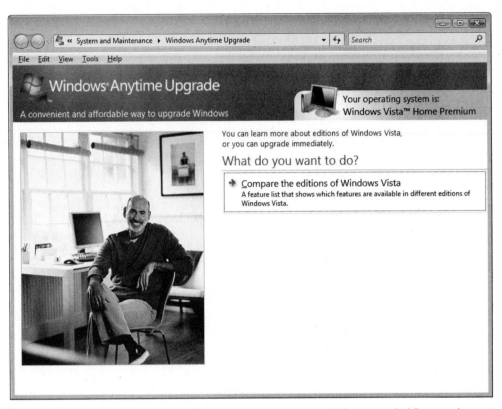

Figure 1-5: Windows Anytime Upgrade enables you to upgrade from certain Vista versions to other, more powerful versions.

Note that you cannot upgrade Vista Home Basic or Premium to Windows Vista Business or Enterprise. Likewise, there's no upgrade path from Vista Enterprise to Vista Ultimate. Purchasing a more capable version of Vista (Upgrade version) at retail and installing it over a lesser version is the only way to migrate in these cases.

Windows Anytime Upgrade is described in more detail in the next chapter.

Secret   There are other ways to acquire Windows Vista, actually. I mentioned previously that Microsoft sells subscription-based software through its volume licensing programs, for example. However, this book focuses on the ways in which individuals can acquire Windows Vista.

Summary

Windows Vista clearly offers a lot of options when it comes to picking a product version, but with a little know-how you will be able to make the right choice, one that matches both your needs and your budget. This chapter has provided what you need to know to match a Windows Vista version to your needs. Now you just need to figure out how much the upgrade is going to cost. Remember that it's often much cheaper to acquire a new Windows version with a new PC, so if you're going to be buying a new PC, be sure to get the right Vista version at that time. I cover this option in Chapter 2, along with other ways to install and upgrade to Windows Vista.

Installing or Upgrading to Windows Vista

Chapter
2

◆ ◆

In This Chapter

Acquiring Windows Vista with a new PC

Performing a clean install of Windows Vista

Upgrading to Windows Vista

Dual-booting with Windows XP and Windows Vista

Upgrading from one Vista version to another

Installing Windows Vista Service Pack 1

Slipstreaming service packs and other updates

Performing a clean install with an Upgrade version of Windows Vista

Delaying product activation

Installing Windows Vista on a Mac with Boot Camp and via virtualization

◆ ◆

So you want to install Windows Vista? Well, in this chapter I'll walk you through the many ways you can acquire Windows Vista, including a clean install, whereby Windows Vista is the only operating system on your PC; an upgrade, whereby you upgrade an existing version of Windows to Windows Vista, leaving all of your data, settings, and applications intact; and a dual-boot, whereby you leave Windows XP on your PC but install Vista to a different hard drive. You'll also learn about related topics, such as slipstreaming, delaying product activation, and—shocker—how to install Windows Vista on a Mac.

Taking the Easy Way Out: Acquiring Windows Vista with a New PC

The simplest way to get a working copy of Windows Vista is to buy a new PC. Stop laughing; I'm serious: Even though PC makers tend to fill their machines with oodles of useless utilities, add-on programs, and other sludge, the one thing you can always be sure of when you buy a new PC is that Windows Vista is going to work out of the box. That is, all of the hardware that comes as part of your new PC purchase will work without any additional effort on your part. In addition, you won't have to step through the various setup-related issues discussed later in this chapter. In fact, if you did purchase a PC with Windows Vista preinstalled, most of this chapter won't apply to you at all. You should be able to simply turn on your new PC and get to work.

Secret

One thing PC purchasers should know about is how to *restore* their system, returning it to the state it was in when new. Virtually all new PCs sold today include a means by which you can do this. Most of the time you can restore your PC using a special hidden partition on the system's hard drive. Other PC makers actually include a restore disk, or restore DVD, with the system. Check your documentation to be sure that you know how to restore your system if necessary. And when you're removing all of that junk that the PC maker installed on your previously pristine Windows Vista installation, be sure you don't remove anything you'll need to recover your system.

Interactive Setup

If you purchased a copy of Windows Vista on DVD at a retailer or online store (or "e-tailer," as I like to call them), you can install Vista using Microsoft's new Interactive Setup Wizard, which guides you through a series of steps required to get Vista up and running. There are three primary ways to install Windows Vista using Interactive Setup: a clean install, whereby Windows Vista will be the only operating system on the PC; an upgrade, whereby you upgrade an existing operating system to Windows Vista, replacing the old with the new; and a dual-boot, whereby you install Windows Vista alongside your old operating system and use a boot menu to choose between them each time you reboot. You'll look at all three methods in this chapter, in addition to a fourth and related installation method: a clean install using Upgrade media.

Clean Install

A *clean install* of the operating system is the preferred method for installing Windows Vista. Although it's possible to upgrade to Windows Vista from certain previous Windows versions (see the next section), this path is perilous and can often result in a Frankenstein-like system in which only some of your applications work properly. In my opinion, it's best to start with a clean slate when moving to a new operating system, especially a major release like Windows Vista.

caution Be sure to back up your critical data before performing a clean install. Typically, you will wipe out your PC's entire hard drive during a clean install, so any documents, e-mail, and other data will be destroyed during the process. Also, make sure you have all the installation files for the applications and hardware drivers you'll need to reinstall after Vista is up and running. I recommend copying them to a recordable disk or USB memory key or drive.

Step-by-Step: Windows Vista Interactive Setup

This section walks you through the entire Windows Vista setup process, using Microsoft's Interactive Setup Wizard. This application was completely overhauled for Windows Vista, and it's now much more streamlined, simplified, and faster-moving than the version used in Windows XP.

Follows these steps to install Windows Vista as a clean install:

1. Insert the Windows Vista DVD in your PC's optical drive and reboot the system. After the BIOS screen flashes by, you may see a message alerting you to press any key to boot from the CD or DVD. If so, press a key. Some systems, however, do not provide this warning and instead boot from the DVD by default.

Secret If your system does not boot from the DVD, you may need to change the system's boot order so that the optical drive is checked before the first hard drive. To do this, consult your PC's documentation, as each PC handles this process a little differently.

A black screen with a progress bar and the text "Windows is loading files" will appear, as shown in Figure 2-1.

2. Eventually, the screen displays a multicolored background and the initial setup window appears, as shown in Figure 2-2. Here, you can preconfigure the language, time and currency formats, and keyboard or input method you'll use during setup.

Figure 2-1: From inauspicious beginnings such as these come great things.

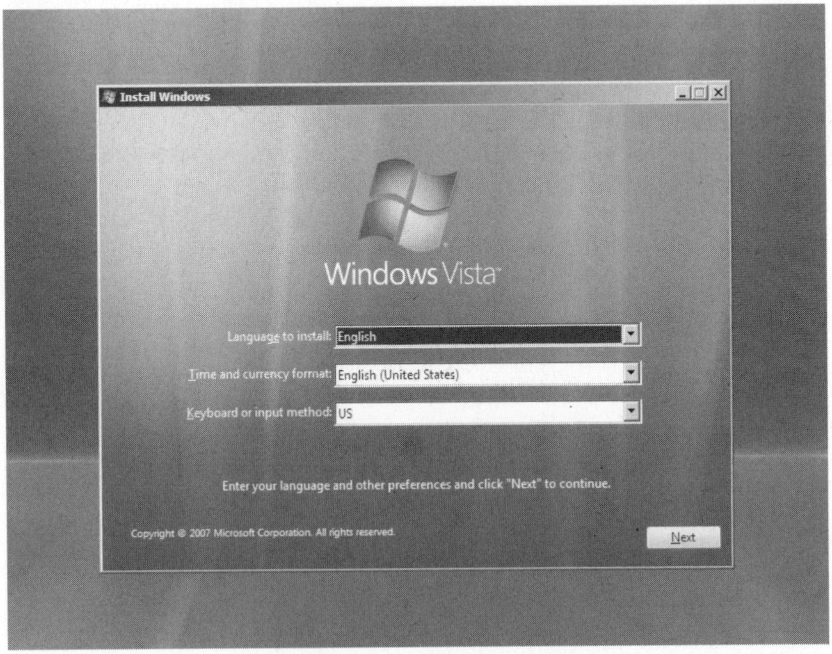

Figure 2-2: These settings apply only to setup, not the eventual Windows Vista installation.

Secret Microsoft changed the setup background image slightly for Service Pack 1, although this doesn't affect the setup experience per se. However, you may see a slightly different backdrop if you're installing the older, original version of Windows Vista and not the newer integrated version.

3. Click Next. The installation window appears, as shown in Figure 2-3. To continue with Interactive Setup, click Install Now.

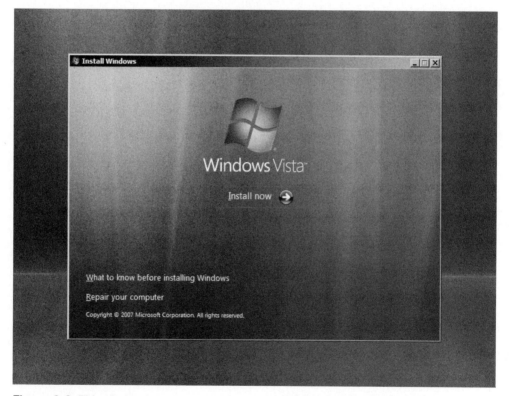

Figure 2-3: This window jump-starts setup and the Windows Vista recovery tools.

Secret This window also provides a way to access Windows Vista's new recovery tools. If you run into a problem with Windows Vista later, such as not being able to boot into Windows for some reason, you can boot your system with the Setup DVD and use these tools to help fix the problem.

4. In the next window (see Figure 2-4), enter your Windows Vista product key. This is a 25-digit alphanumeric string—in blocks of 5 separated by dashes—that you will find on a bright yellow product-key sticker somewhere in your Windows Vista packaging. You can also choose to have Windows Vista automatically activate for you.

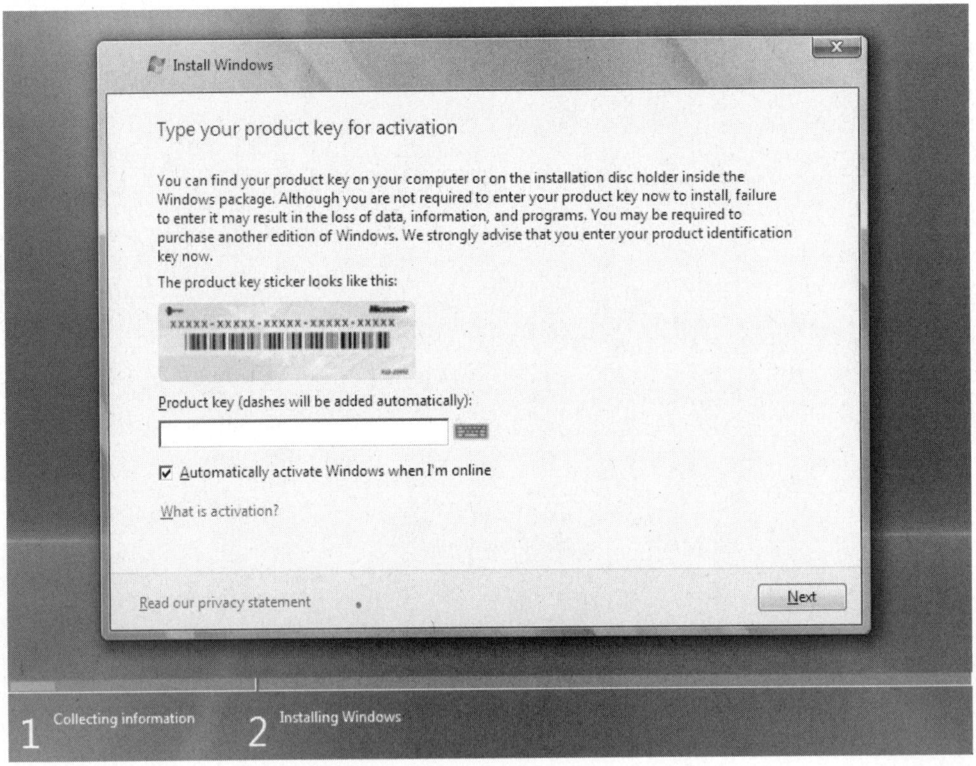

Install Windows

Type your product key for activation

You can find your product key on your computer or on the installation disc holder inside the Windows package. Although you are not required to enter your product key now to install, failure to enter it may result in the loss of data, information, and programs. You may be required to purchase another edition of Windows. We strongly advise that you enter your product identification key now.

The product key sticker looks like this:

XXXXX-XXXXX-XXXXX-XXXXX-XXXXX

Product key (dashes will be added automatically):

☑ Automatically activate Windows when I'm online

What is activation?

Read our privacy statement

Next

1 Collecting information 2 Installing Windows

Figure 2-4: Spread 'em. This is where Microsoft ensures you're genuine.

Secret

As it turns out, you do not actually have to enter your product key here. If you choose not to enter your product key, you are presented with the screen shown in Figure 2-5, where you must select the correct Vista product edition before proceeding.

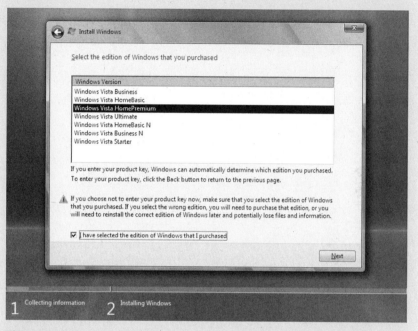

Figure 2-5: You're free to skip the product-key entry, but be sure to select the correct product edition if you do.

Secret

Do not lose your Windows Vista product key or give it away to anyone. Each Windows Vista product key is valid for exactly one PC. After you've installed Windows Vista and activated it—which ties the product key to your hardware—you won't be able to use this number again on another PC, at least not easily. Note, however, that you can reinstall Windows Vista on the same PC using this same product key. If for some reason you are unable to electronically activate Windows later, Vista will provide a phone number so you can do it manually.

5. In the next window (see Figure 2-6), you must agree to the End User License Agreement (EULA). Although very few people actually read this document, you should take the time to do so, as it outlines your legal rights regarding your usage of Windows Vista. If I understand it correctly, Microsoft exerts certain rights over your first born and your soul.

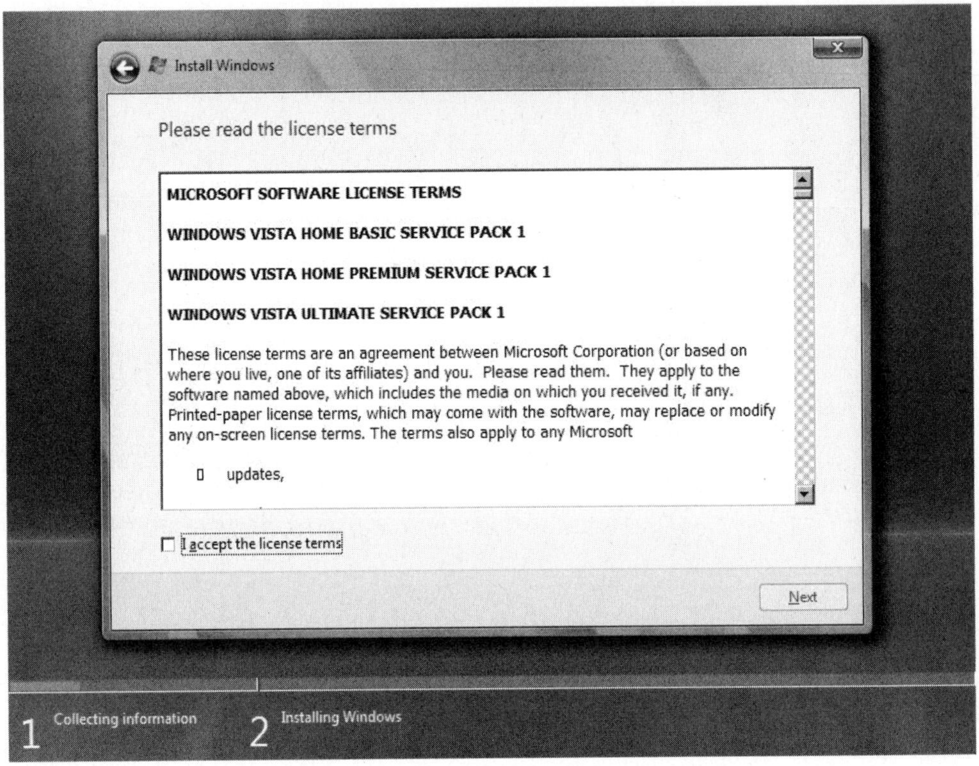

Figure 2-6: Sign over all your rights simply by clicking a single check box.

6. In the next window, select Custom (Advanced) as the install type and click Next.
7. Select the partition, or disk, to which to install Windows Vista. On a clean install, typically you will be installing Windows Vista to the only disk available, as shown in Figure 2-7.
8. Most users will see a link called More Options on this window. Clicking this link brings you to a screen where you can delete, format, or extend the current disk, if possible, or create a new partition if the hard drive is brand-new and unformatted. This window is shown in Figure 2-8.

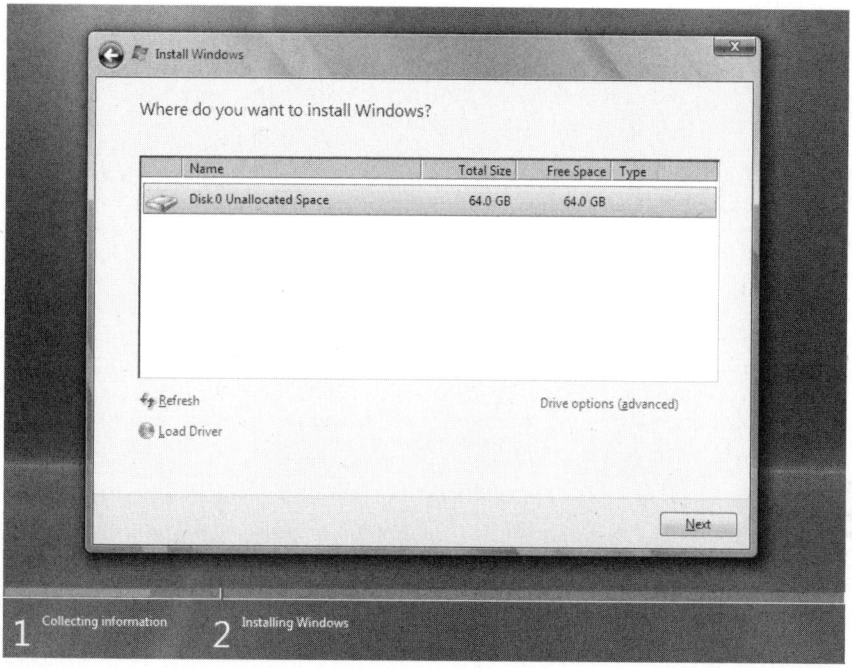

Figure 2-7: New to Vista setup is a more graphic disk configuration phase.

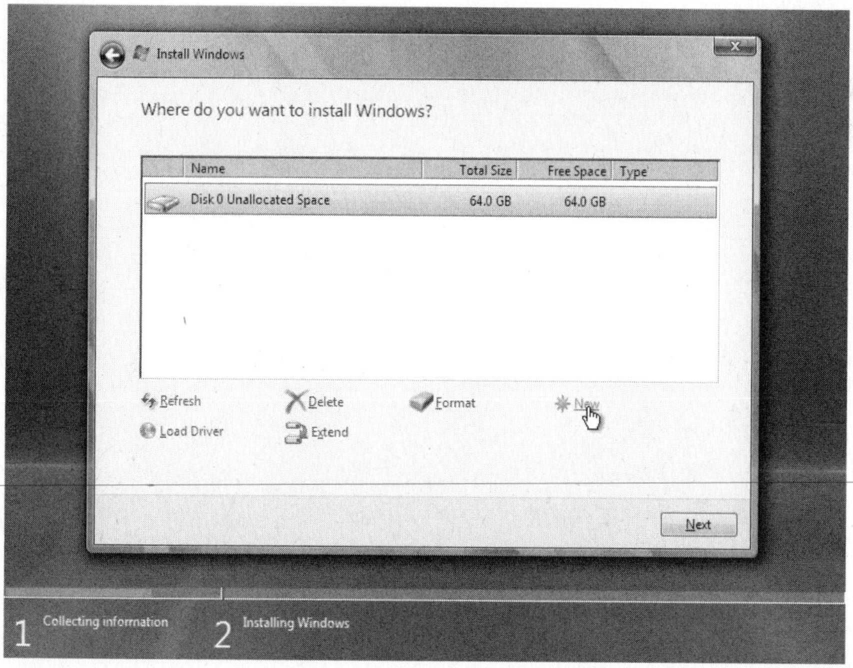

Figure 2-8: Here, you can perform various disk-related tasks, including resizing partitions.

Secret

If you are performing a clean install on a previously used machine, I advise you to format the disk during this step to ensure that none of the cruft from your previous Windows installation dirties up your new Windows Vista install. You don't actually need to format a new disk. If you attempt to install Windows Vista on an unformatted disk, setup will simply format the disk to its maximum capacity automatically.

9. After you've selected the disk and formatted it if necessary, you can walk away from your computer for 20–30 minutes, depending on your hardware. During this time, setup will copy the various files it needs for installation to the hard drive, expand the Vista image file from the DVD, install Windows Vista and any included software updates, and complete the installation by attempting to load drivers for your hardware. A screen like the one shown in Figure 2-9 will display during this entire process.

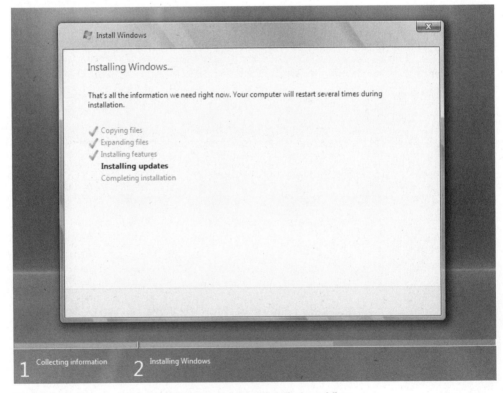

Figure 2-9: Grab a quick lunch while setup installs Windows Vista.

10. After a reboot or two, your PC will launch into the second, and final, interactive phase of setup. In the first screen, shown in Figure 2-10, you are prompted for a user name (typically a short name like *Paul* and not a full name like *Paul Thurrott*), a password, and a display picture. If you don't choose a picture, you get the flower by default. (You've been warned.)

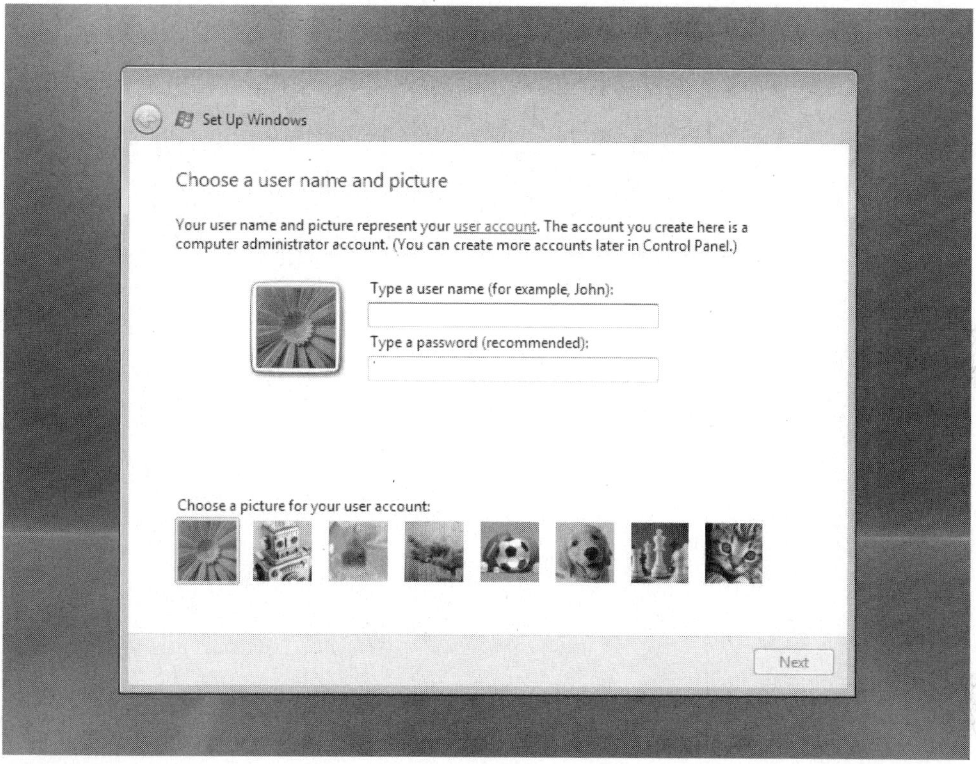

Figure 2-10: Specify the account you'll typically use in Windows Vista.

Secret

A few notes about this initial user account. Unlike Windows XP, Windows Vista does not create a visible administrator account automatically, for security reasons. Nor are you allowed to create up to five user accounts, as you were in XP. Instead, you can create a single user account during setup. That user account will be given administrator privileges. Subsequent user accounts—created in Windows Vista using the User Accounts Control Panel—are given limited user privileges by default, but that's easy enough to change. You'll learn how to create and modify user accounts in Chapter 9.

caution   Be sure to use a password, please. It's unclear to me why Microsoft even makes this optional, as using a strong password is one of the most basic things you can do to keep your system more secure.

11. Type a name for your PC and choose a desktop background (see Figure 2-11). By default, setup picks a PC name that is based on your user name. This isn't very creative, but you're free to change it.

Figure 2-11: Configure computer-related options here.

Secret   Setup provides you with only six potential background images for some reason. To change your background to another image or a solid color after setup is complete, right-click the Desktop, choose Personalize, and then Desktop Background. You'll find many more options there.

Secret

Setup doesn't let you specify a workgroup name or join an Active-Directory-based domain, as did the Windows XP setup routine. To change this after setup is complete, from the Start Menu, right-click Computer, and choose Properties. Then click the Change Settings link in the Computer Name, Domain, and Workgroup Settings section of the resulting window. The dialog box that appears is very similar to the one you're used to from Windows XP. In addition, as with Windows XP, you need to reboot after you've made a domain or workgroup change.

12. Choose whether to enable Automatic Updates, as shown in Figure 2-12. You should use the recommended settings, in which Windows automatically downloads and installs all updates. Alternately, you can choose to install only important updates or be prompted later.

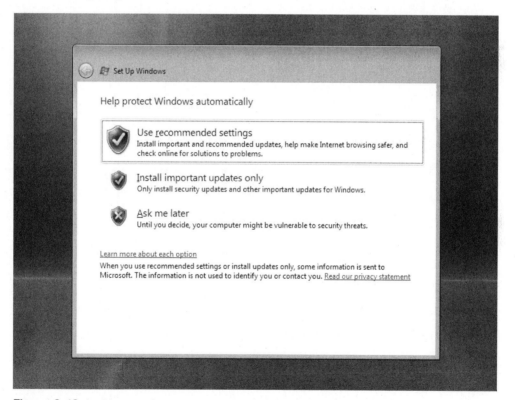

Figure 2-12: In this part of setup, you configure automatic updates.

Secret

This behavior is far more aggressive than the similar Setup screen that Microsoft added to Windows XP with Service Pack 2. Note that you can't choose to download but not install updates.

13. Configure the time zone, date, and time, as shown in Figure 2-13.

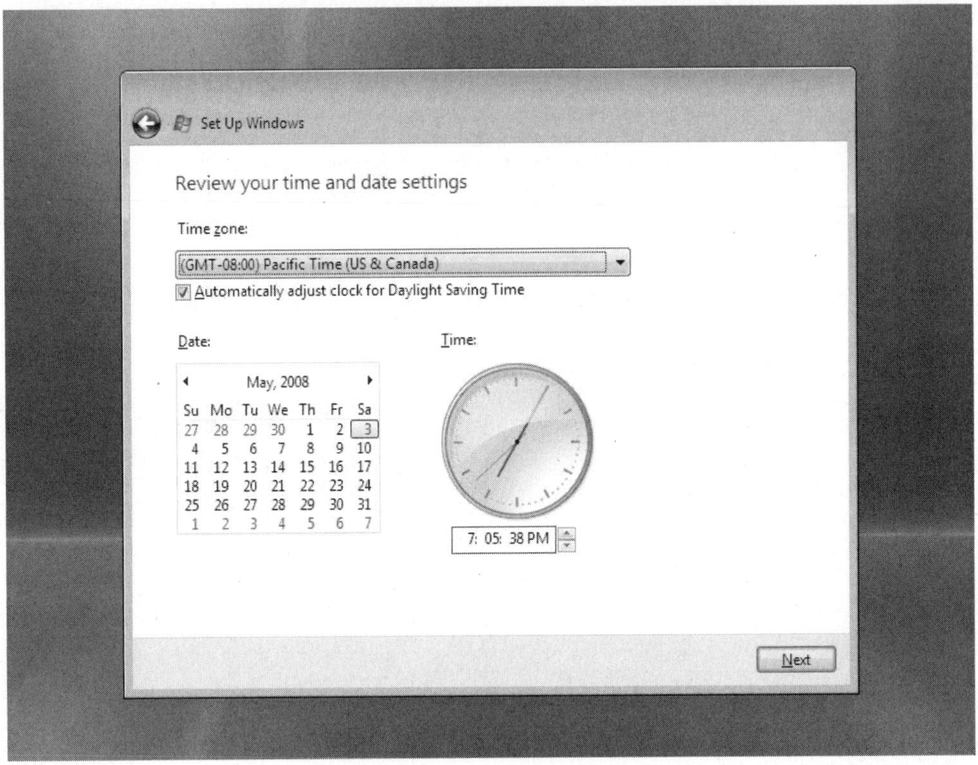

← 🗗 Set Up Windows

Review your time and date settings

Time zone:

(GMT-08:00) Pacific Time (US & Canada) ▼

☑ Automatically adjust clock for Daylight Saving Time

Date: Time:

◀   May, 2008   ▶

Su Mo Tu We Th Fr Sa
27 28 29 30   1   2 [3]
 4   5   6   7   8   9 10
11 12 13 14 15 16 17
18 19 20 21 22 23 24
25 26 27 28 29 30 31
 1   2   3   4   5   6   7

7: 05: 38 PM ▲▼

Next

Figure 2-13: Curious that the time zone defaults to Pacific Time.

Secret

Even if you're not particularly careful about setting the time correctly here, Windows Vista will eventually adjust to the correct time automatically because it is configured out of the box to synchronize with an Internet time server. That said, you should at least make an effort to ensure that the time is reasonably correct to avoid problems with this process.

14. If your network card is detected during setup and you're able to connect online, you'll see the network location dialog shown in Figure 2-14. From here, you can choose whether the network you're accessing is at home (and thus private), at work, or at a public location (such as a library, coffee shop, or airport). Windows configures networking appropriately in each case.

You are graciously notified when Interactive Setup is complete and you're ready to start (see Figure 2-15).

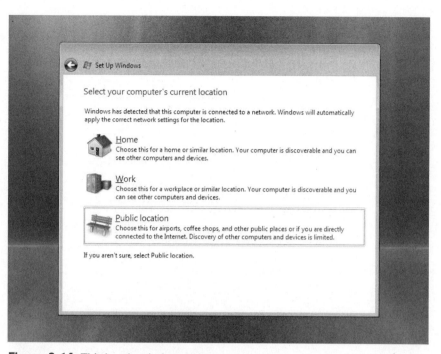

Figure 2-14: This handy window makes sure you are as secure as you need to be, depending on which type of network you're using.

Figure 2-15: The moment you've been waiting for.

Annoyingly, before the Windows Vista desktop appears, setup takes a final bow by testing your system's performance characteristics. You'll see what that means in the next section, but at this point you'll see a screen like the one shown in Figure 2-16. This process takes about 30 seconds to 2 minutes, depending on the speed of your PC. Trust me; it will feel like an eternity regardless.

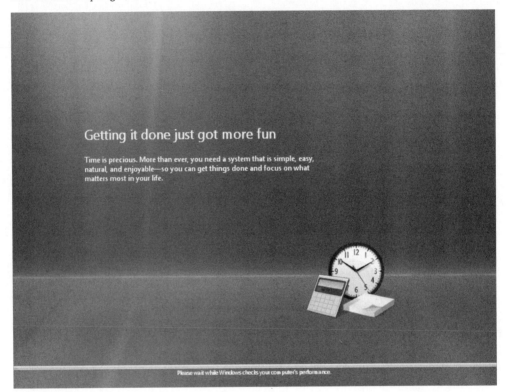

Figure 2-16: During the performance test, Microsoft displays a few small Windows Vista advertisements.

Post-Setup Tasks

With the performance test out of the way, setup finally quits, leaving you staring at your new Windows Vista desktop. A few things will occur in short order:

1. The Welcome Center window (shown in Figure 2-17) appears, providing you with a glimpse of your system details, performance rating, and a list of 6 to 12 tasks you might want to perform now that you're up and running. You can safely close this window, as I will guide you through all of the post-setup tasks you'll need to perform.

> **tip** If you do disable the Welcome Center, you can always access it at any time by navigating to All Programs ➪ Accessories ➪ Welcome Center in the new Start Menu.

Figure 2-17: The Welcome Center provides links to a lot of useful information and functionality.

Secret

The first time the Welcome Center appears, there's no indication that it's going to appear on your next reboot, but it will. From then on, however, the Welcome Center displays a Run at Startup option on the bottom of its window at startup. Clear this option if you want the Welcome Center to stop being so welcoming.

2. If your PC includes a network card (wireless or otherwise) that was properly detected and installed after setup, you will be prompted to configure that network connection. The dialog that appears will be identical to the one shown earlier in Figure 2-14.

3. Windows Sidebar appears on the right side of the screen. You can find out more about Windows Sidebar in Chapter 6.

Now it's time to finish configuring Windows Vista so you can begin using it. The first step is to check out your hardware driver: Ideally, all of the hardware connected to your

PC has been detected, and setup has installed drivers for each of your devices. To see whether this is the case, you need to open a tool called Device Manager. There are a number of ways to access the Device Manager, but the quickest is to select Search from the Start Menu, type **device,** and press Enter. This causes the Device Manager window to appear (see Figure 2-18).

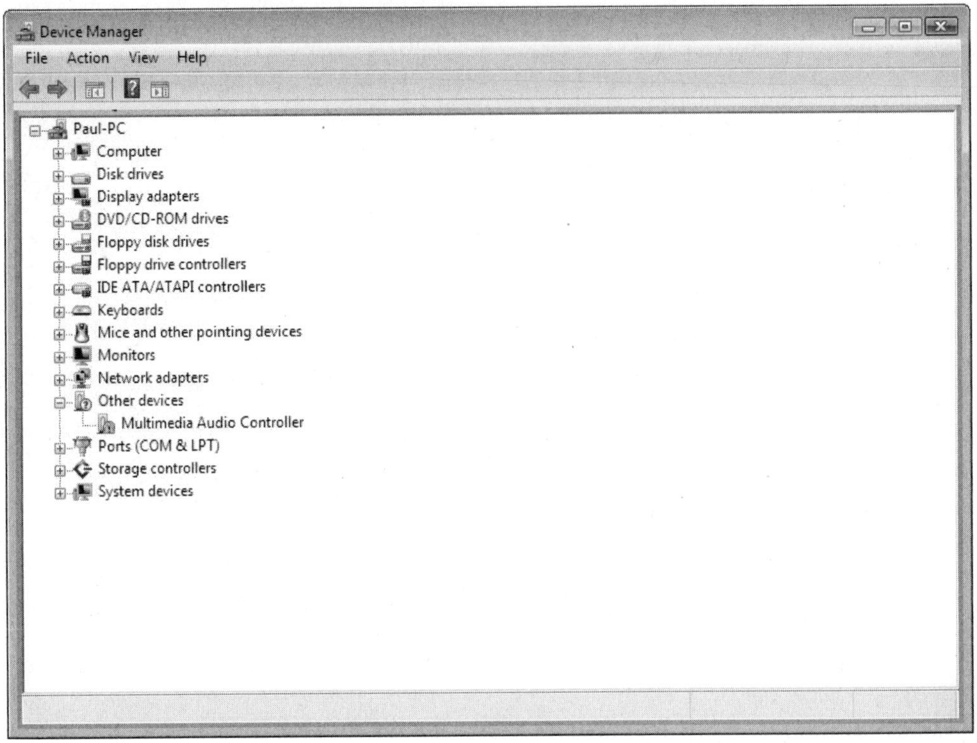

Figure 2-18: Device Manager tells you at a glance which hardware devices are connected and properly configured for your PC.

If any of the entries, or nodes, in the Device Manager tree view are open, displaying a device with a small yellow exclamation point, or *bang*, then you're going to need to install some drivers. There are four basic ways to install drivers in Windows Vista, listed here in reverse order of preference:

◆ **Automatically:** Right-click the unsupported device and choose Update Driver Software. Windows will search the local system, including any setup disks, to find the appropriate driver. In my experience this method almost never works, but it's worth trying.

◆ **Manually:** As before, you right-click the unsupported device and choose Update Driver Software. This time, however, you must supply the driver files via a setup disk or other means.

◆ **As an executable setup disk or download:** Many drivers come in self-contained executables whereby you run a setup routine just as you would for an application program. If possible, be sure to use a Windows Vista–compatible setup application: These should work just fine. However, Windows XP drivers often work as well, albeit with a little grumbling on the part of Windows Vista.

◆ **Using Windows Update:** This is the best way to install drivers, and it's the first place to visit if you discover that Windows Vista Setup didn't install all of your hardware. The hardware drivers found on Windows Update aren't always as up-to-date as those supplied directly from the hardware manufacturers. That said, Windows Update–based drivers have been tested extensively and should always be your first choice. Note that Vista will likely connect to Windows Update automatically if you have a configured network adapter, grabbing any device drivers it can, within minutes of booting into the desktop for the first time.

tip

To manually find drivers on Windows Update, open the Start Menu and choose All Programs ⇨ Windows Update. Click the Check for Updates link in the upper-left corner of the Windows Update application, as shown in Figure 2-19.

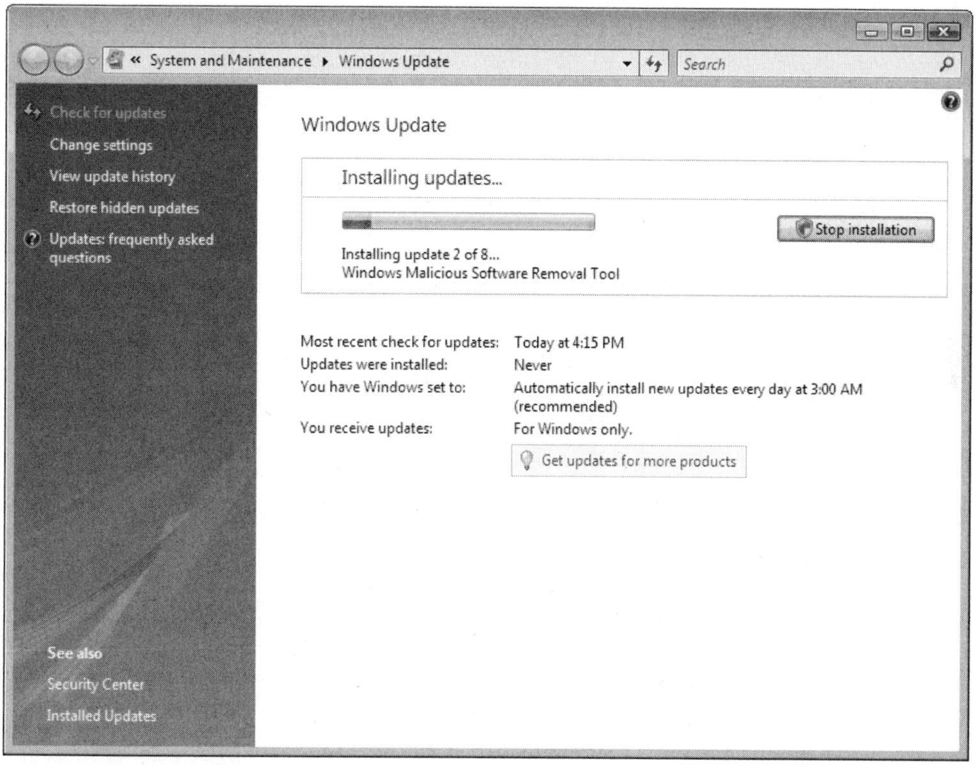

Figure 2-19: In Windows Vista, Windows Update can update your operating system, hardware drivers, and many Microsoft applications.

Repeat the preceding processes until all of your hardware devices are working. If you did run Windows Update during this time, you will likely have seen a number of Windows Vista product updates as well. You should install those updates before moving on to the next step.

Now it's time to install your applications. Install them one at a time and reboot if necessary after each install as requested. This process can often take a long time and is mind-numbingly boring, but you should have to do it only once.

With your applications installed, it's time to restore any data that you might have backed up from your previous Windows install; or, if you have installed Windows Vista to a brand-new PC, you can transfer user accounts, music, pictures, video files, documents, program settings, Internet settings and favorites, and e-mail messages and contacts from your old PC to Windows Vista using an excellent new Vista utility called Windows Easy Transfer. (From the Start Menu, select Search, type **easy,** and then press Enter.) This utility is a full screen wizard-like application (see Figure 2-20) that you can install and run on your previous OS as well.

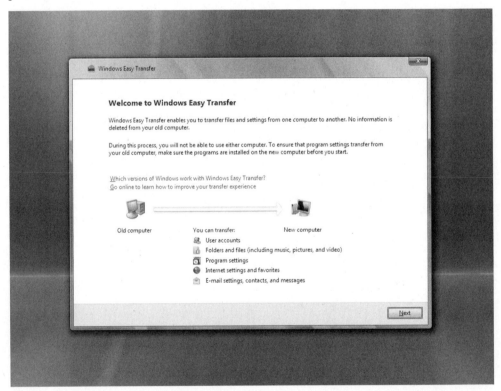

Figure 2-20: Windows Easy Transfer makes short work of transferring your old data, documents, and custom settings from Windows XP to Vista.

Upgrading

When I discuss upgrading to Windows Vista, I am typically referring to what's called an *in-place upgrade*. When you perform an in-place upgrade of Windows Vista, you replace your existing version of Windows with Windows Vista. An in-place upgrade, it is hoped, will bring with it all of your applications, documents, and custom settings. It is hoped.

The reality is that in-place upgrades often don't work as planned. For this reason, I don't recommend upgrading from your current Windows version to Windows Vista. If you simply must perform such an upgrade, behave as if you were doing a clean install just in case, and back up all of your crucial documents and other data ahead of time. That way, if something does go wrong you won't be stranded.

Before even attempting an upgrade, you should understand what kinds of upgrades are possible. Windows Vista ships in a wide range of product editions, most of which have direct relations in Windows XP. That said, only certain versions of Windows can upgrade to certain versions of Windows Vista. From a licensing perspective, only certain Windows versions are eligible for a Windows Vista upgrade. That is, you can't purchase and install an Upgrade version of Windows Vista unless you're using a supported Windows version now.

If you're running Windows 95, Windows 98 (or Windows 98 Second Edition), Windows Millennium Edition, or Windows NT 4.0, you are out of luck. You cannot purchase an Upgrade version of Windows Vista, and you cannot perform an in-place upgrade from your current operating system to any Windows Vista product edition. Instead, you must purchase the Full version of the Windows Vista product edition you want, and perform a clean install, as specified earlier in this chapter.

If you're running Windows 2000 or Windows XP Professional x64 Edition, you are eligible to purchase an Upgrade version of the Windows Vista product edition you desire. However, you cannot perform an in-place upgrade. Instead, you need to perform a clean install, as discussed previously, using the Upgrade version.

The only Windows versions that both qualify for a Windows Vista Upgrade version and can be upgraded in-place to Windows Vista are Windows XP Home, Professional, Media Center, and Tablet PC Editions. However, within this set of operating systems there are still some restrictions. To clarify your options, Table 2-1 summarizes which versions of Windows can be upgraded in-place to which Windows Vista versions.

Table 2-1: Which Versions of Windows Can Upgrade In-Place to Which Versions of Windows Vista.

Windows Version	*Vista Home Basic/Home Basic N*	*Vista Home Premium*	*Vista Business/ Business N*	*Vista Ultimate*
Windows 2000 Professional	No	No	No	No
Windows XP Home Edition	Yes	Yes	Yes	Yes
Windows XP Professional Edition	No	No	Yes	Yes
Windows XP Media Center Edition	No	Yes	No	Yes
Windows XP Tablet PC Edition	No	No	Yes	Yes
Windows XP Professional x64 Edition	No	No	No	No

Step-by-Step: Upgrading Windows XP to Windows Vista

If you're undaunted by the process of upgrading your copy of Windows XP to Windows Vista, in-place, then you've come to the right place. This section describes how it's done. Most of the process is virtually identical to the steps outlined for performing a clean install earlier in the chapter:

1. The first difference is that you will typically launch Windows Vista Setup from within Windows XP. Simply insert the Windows Vista Setup DVD into your PC's optical drive. The setup routine should auto-run, and you'll see the window shown in Figure 2-21.

Figure 2-21: When upgrading from Windows XP to Windows Vista, you will typically run setup from within Windows XP.

2. Click Install Now to continue. In the next step, you'll be asked if you want to go online to get the latest updates for installation. Always do so, because Microsoft continues to improve Windows Vista, and updates the setup process specifically. Setup will search for and download any updates.

3. Setup proceeds as it does during a clean install, and you enter the product key, agree to the EULA, and so on. When you get to the "Which type of installation do you want?" screen, it's time to step back a second and regroup. This is where we veer off into new territory.

4. Instead of choosing Custom, choose Upgrade. Setup first runs a compatibility check to determine whether any of your hardware or software will need to be reinstalled—or will work at all—after the upgrade is completed. After scanning your system, setup presents you with a Compatibility Report (see Figure 2-22). What you see here depends on how old and weather-beaten your system is. The more stuff you've installed, the greater the chance problems will occur.

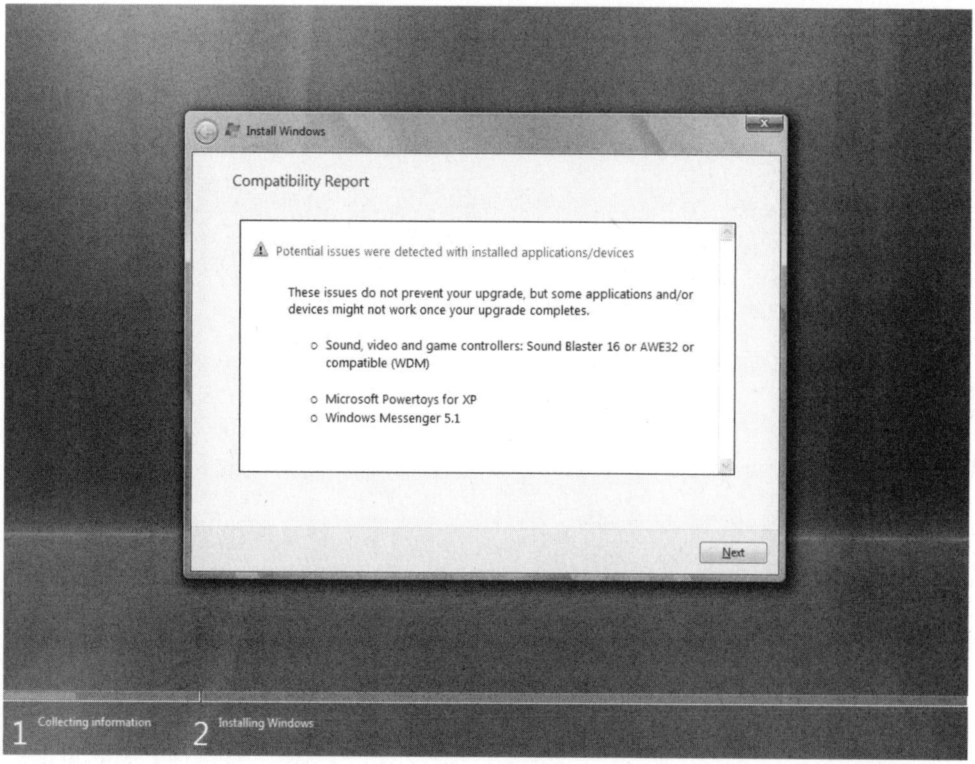

Figure 2-22: Cross your fingers: If you're lucky, nothing important will be unsupported in Windows Vista.

After that, setup will continue exactly as it does during a clean install. And I mean exactly: Unlike in previous Windows versions, Windows setup literally backs up your settings, data, and application information, performs a clean install of the operating system, and then copies everything back in a way in which it should all work as it did before. However, this is why the upgrade process is so dicey: If anything goes wrong, you've taken a perfectly usable Windows Vista install and mucked it up with all the garbage from your Windows XP install.

In any event, after setup is complete the system will reboot. Unlike other setup types, an in-place upgrade skips over a few steps, including those in which you configure your user name, password, display picture, desktop background image, and machine name, because you've presumably set up all of those options in your previous Windows version. Instead, setup jumps right to the Automatic Updates phase described in the "Clean Install" section of this chapter, and then the time and date settings (which, frankly, should have been configured correctly previously as well). After that, you click the Finish button (sorry, no "You're ready to start" message), and Windows setup tests your system performance and then loads the desktop, complete with the new Welcome Screen.

If everything goes well, you should be able to log on to your previously established user account and access a desktop that looks reasonably like the one you configured for Windows XP (see Figure 2-23).

Figure 2-23: Look familiar? This desktop was upgraded from Windows XP.

The big mystery, of course, is your data and applications. Spend some time testing each application to see if everything works. Figure 2-24 shows the Firefox Web browser, previously installed and configured in Windows XP, up and running just fine after an upgrade to Windows Vista.

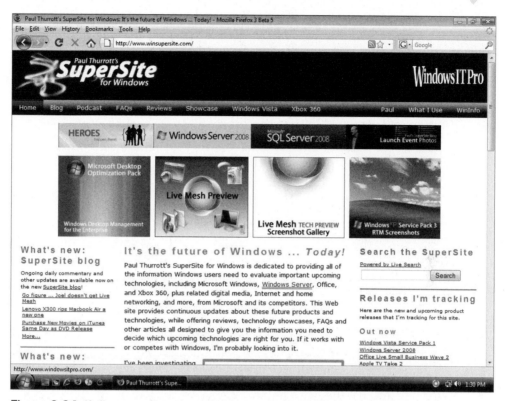

Figure 2-24: If all goes well, your previously installed applications should still work.

Because of the potential for problems, I recommend backing up any crucial data and settings before performing any operating-system upgrade.

Dual-Booting with Windows XP

With a radically different operating system such as Windows Vista, you may want to test the waters a bit before diving headlong into the future, or perhaps you need to run certain applications that still don't work properly in Windows Vista. Or you may be a software or Web developer, and you need to test your creations in both Windows XP and Windows Vista. Whatever the reasons, Microsoft has long supported the concept of *dual-booting*, whereby you install two or more operating systems on the same PC, choose between them using a boot menu when you turn on or reboot the PC, and then run one or the other.

tip   Windows NT 4.0, Windows 2000, Windows XP (all versions), and Windows Vista all support dual-booting natively. Although it's possible to dual-boot between most of these operating systems and an older Windows version such as Windows 98 or Me, DOS-based versions of Windows are no longer supported by Microsoft and therefore are not discussed here. If you need to run a legacy operating system, or a particular legacy application, I recommend a software virtualization environment such as Microsoft's Virtual PC 2007, which is designed specifically for Windows Vista.

I'm going to assume you already have Windows XP installed on your PC and that you want to add Windows Vista to the mix. I don't do this for my own benefit: Because Windows XP was developed years before Windows Vista and has no native understanding of Vista's boot loader and boot menu, it's simply better to install Windows XP first. Conversely, Windows Vista *was* designed with knowledge of XP's boot loader and boot menu, and therefore can safely be added to a PC after Windows XP.

Before proceeding, there are two major issues to consider:

     ◆ You need to add a second hard drive or partition to your computer into which you will install Windows Vista. You'll learn how to do this in the next section.

Secret   Do not, under any circumstances, try to install Windows XP and Windows Vista to the same partition or hard drive. While you might be able to pull this off, both operating systems use many identically named folders and you will run into problems.

     ◆ Decide how you are going to initiate the dual-boot install of Windows Vista. You have two options: One, while in Windows XP, insert the Windows Vista Setup DVD and begin setup from there. Two, reboot your system, boot from the Setup DVD, and begin setup that way.

Before looking at the difference, first you need to figure out how to make space for Windows Vista.

Secret   On a typical PC with two hard drives or partitions, one dedicated to Windows XP and one dedicated to Windows Vista, you will typically end up with XP on the C: drive and Windows Vista on the D: drive when you initiate the Windows Vista setup routine from within Windows XP. But when you reboot the system and boot with the Windows Vista Setup DVD, something magical occurs. After both operating systems are installed, Windows XP will be on C: and Windows Vista will be on D: while you're using Windows XP. But when you're using Windows Vista, the system will report that Windows Vista is on C: and Windows XP is on D:. This is vastly preferable to the former method because most people are used to seeing the operating-system partition located on the C: drive. For this reason, I recommend that you always install Windows Vista in a dual-boot scenario by booting the system with the Vista Setup DVD and launching setup from there.

Adding a Drive or Partition for Windows Vista

There are two ways to make space for Windows Vista on your existing PC. You can either add a second hard drive, using the new hard drive exclusively for Windows Vista, or you can *partition* your existing hard drive, creating two logical hard drives, or partitions—one for Windows XP and one for Windows Vista.

The former method is preferable because it doesn't require you to deal with messy partitioning software and potentially endanger whatever data you already have on the C: drive. Conversely, you do have to expend the effort to install the hard drive, which can be dicey with internal hard drives if you don't know your way around the innards of a PC. And, of course, some desktop PCs and most notebook PCs can't be upgraded to support an additional hard drive. In such cases, you'll need to partition the only hard drive you have.

If you're going to install a second physical hard drive, there's not much to say: Follow the manufacturer's instructions and you should be all set. Modern hard drives are quite capacious and shouldn't present any problems during setup.

If you're going to partition your existing hard drive, life isn't so simple. Most partitioning tools, such as the ones built into Windows XP and earlier, are *destructive partitioning tools*—that is, they literally destroy whatever was on the disk while partitioning. What you're looking for is a *non-destructive* partitioning tool, one that enables you to slice an existing hard drive or partition into two or more partitions while leaving all the data—and the operating system and applications—intact on the first.

Various commercial partitioning solutions are available. I use and recommend Norton PartitionMagic, which has always been reliable, but there are various free partitioning solutions out there as well. Just be careful: This is your data you're messing with, and you don't want the partitioning solution you use to accidentally make your hard drive inaccessible.

---

tip   Be sure to defragment your hard drive before partitioning in order to save time later (partitioning tools defrag for you as needed, but they aren't as efficient or fast as dedicated partitioning tools). Finally, make sure you create a partition with enough space on it to install Windows Vista. Microsoft specifies that Windows Vista requires 15GB of free space for the premium versions of the operating system (Home Premium and Ultimate), but keep in mind that you're going to want to install applications and so forth, so the more space you can spare the better.

---

caution   To make partitioning easier, preemptively name the new partition "Vista" or something similar, so you can easily recognize it during setup. You don't want to accidentally wipe out your XP install.

Step-by-Step: Installing Windows Vista in a Dual-Boot Setup

Assuming you have an additional free hard drive or partition, you can follow the steps outlined earlier in the "Clean Install" section when performing a dual-boot installation: Boot with the Windows Vista DVD, choose Install, enter your product key, agree to the EULA, and so on. You'll need to pay attention when setup reaches the screen that asks, "Which type of installation do you want?" This is shown in Figure 2-25.

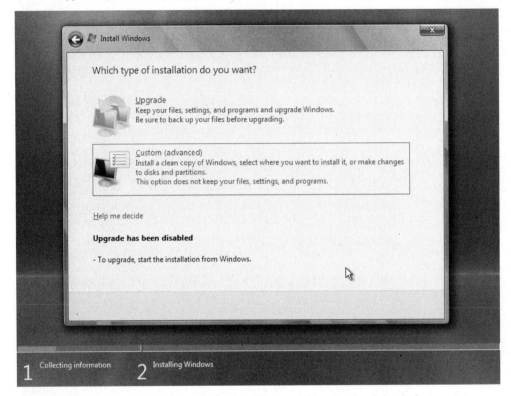

Figure 2-25: Heads up. In this phase of setup, be sure you make the right choices.

Choose the Custom (Advanced) install type and click Next. Then examine the next screen, which should resemble the one shown in Figure 2-26. Here, be sure to choose the empty partition that's been set aside for Windows Vista, and not your XP partition. If you followed my advice in the previous section, you gave this partition an easy-to-recognize name like Vista ahead of time.

At this point, setup will proceed again exactly as it does during a clean install. After Windows Vista is installed, however, you will notice one difference: When you reboot the PC, a boot menu like the one shown in Figure 2-27 appears, from which you choose between your previous operating system (Earlier Version of Windows) and Windows Vista.

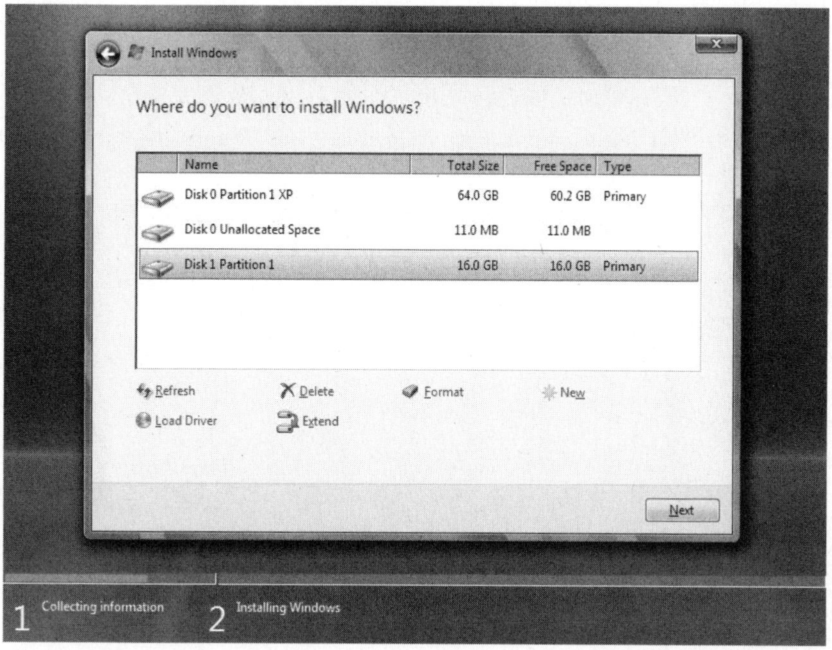

Figure 2-26: Careful: You want to choose the empty partition, not the XP partition.

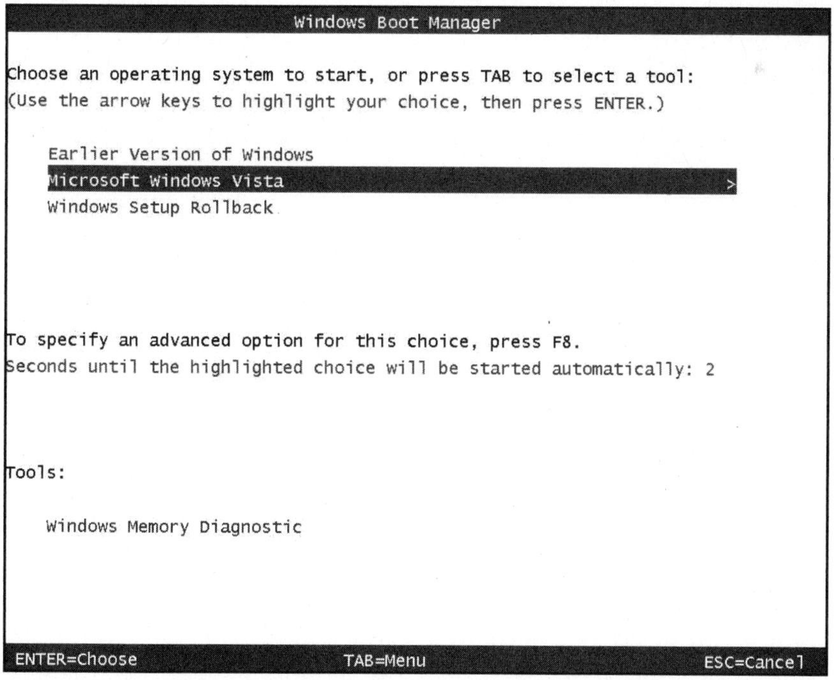

Figure 2-27: Microsoft's new dual-boot menu lets you choose between your previous operating system (typically some version of Windows XP) and Windows Vista.

You might notice that the boot menu uses a fairly lengthy 30-second countdown during which it waits for you to choose an operating system. That's a long time to wait; and if you're not using the time to make a choice, your system wastes a lot of time waiting to boot. Fortunately, if you think 30 seconds is too long, there's a way to change this behavior.

To do so, open the Start Menu in Windows Vista, right-click Computer, and choose Properties. This will display the new system information window, shown in Figure 2-28.

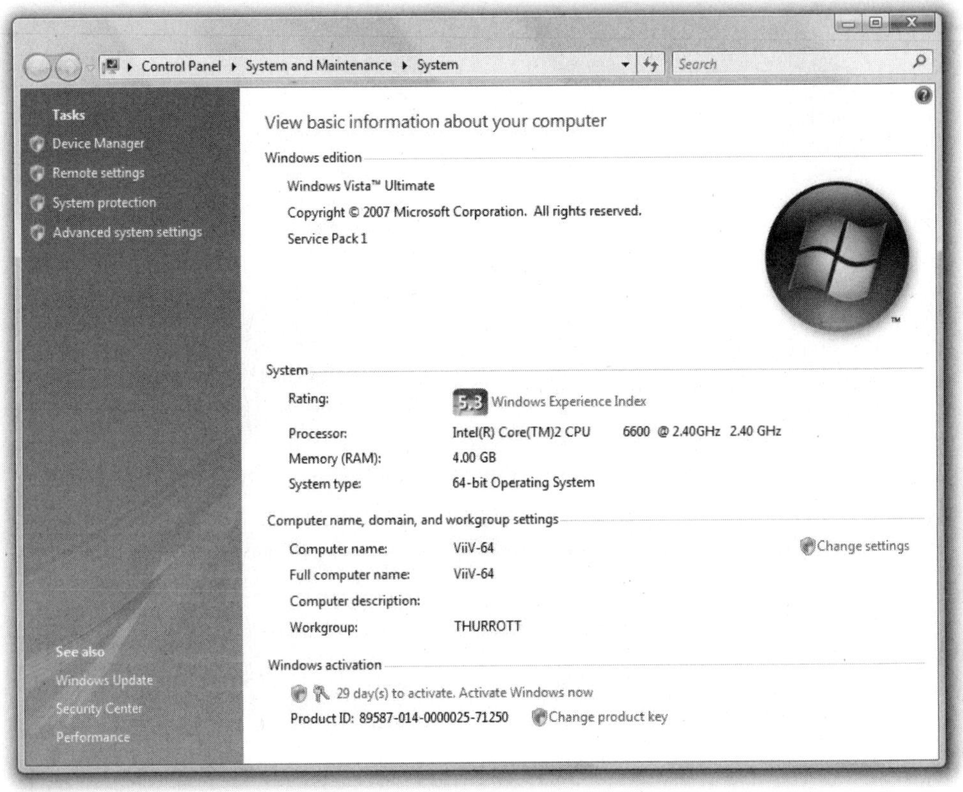

Figure 2-28: The default system information window is much more detailed than its counterpart in Windows 2000 or XP.

Now click the Advanced System Settings link in the Tasks list on the left side of the window. This will display the System Properties dialog, which is quite similar to the System Properties dialog from Windows XP. Navigate to the Advanced tab and click the button labeled Settings that appears in the Startup and Recovery section. This, finally, will display the Startup and Recovery dialog box, shown in Figure 2-29, where, yes, you can configure startup options.

Figure 2-29: It's buried deep, but this dialog box can be used to configure the boot menu and other boot options.

Here, you can make several choices, but the relevant ones are as follows:

◆ Determine which operating system is the default. Windows Vista is the default selection, by default.

◆ Determine how much time elapses while the boot menu is displayed before the system boots into the default operating system.

I typically set the timer to a small value like three seconds so that Windows Vista boots quickly but I have enough time to make a choice if I want to.

Secret

I've been referring to Windows Vista's dual-boot capabilities throughout this chapter, but in reality Windows Vista and previous NT-based Windows versions such as Windows 2000 and XP support *multi-booting*. That's right: With the right partitioning scheme, gobs of hard drive space, and plenty of time on your hands, you can configure your PC to boot between two, three, four, or more operating systems. Such a setup is conceptually interesting but of little use in the real world, at least for most people. As the saying goes, people who are dual-booting aren't getting anything done.

A better (and, yes, free) tool is available for configuring the Windows boot menu. Called NeoSmart EasyBCD (http://neosmart.net/dl.php?id=1), it offers several features that aren't accessible via the Startup and Recovery dialog in Vista, including the capability to change the names and order of the operating systems shown in the boot menu.

Upgrading from One Vista Version to Another: Windows Anywhere Upgrade

Microsoft offers a bewildering number of options when it comes to purchasing Windows Vista versions and upgrades, but one of the nicest additions to this panoply of choices is Windows Anytime Upgrade, an online service built into Windows Vista Home Basic, Home Premium, and Business editions. Windows Anytime Upgrade enables you to upgrade from one of those versions to a higher-end Vista version at a drastically reduced price. Which versions you can upgrade to and the cost of that upgrade depend on the version you're starting from.

For the first year or so that Windows Vista was on the market, Microsoft allowed users to electronically upgrade from one version of Windows Vista to another using Windows Anytime Upgrade. The company would send a product key to you via e-mail and you could use your existing Vista Setup DVD to perform the upgrade. This process, while convenient, proved too confusing for far too many users, so Microsoft discontinued electronic upgrades of Windows Vista in early 2008. The procedure in this book covers the new, revised version of Windows Anytime Upgrade.

Table 2-2 explains which Windows Anytime Upgrade choices are available, along with current pricing (in U.S. dollars).

Table 2-2: Windows Anytime Upgrade Choices and Pricing

Upgrade from...	...to Vista Home Premium	...to Vista Home Ultimate
Windows Vista Home Basic	Yes ($79)	Yes ($199)
Windows Vista Home Premium	—	Yes ($159)
Windows Vista Business	—	Yes ($139)

Pricing, as you can see, is heavily discounted over the traditional retail Upgrade cost. If you're running Windows Vista Home Basic, Home Premium, or Business, upgrading in this fashion is probably the way to go.

How It Works

You can access the Windows Anytime Upgrade application, shown in Figure 2-30, from the Control Panel (it's hidden in System and Maintenance) or by typing **anytime** in Windows Start Menu Search. (It's also available from the Welcome Center and from within the System window. Yes, Microsoft is very keen to get more of your money.)

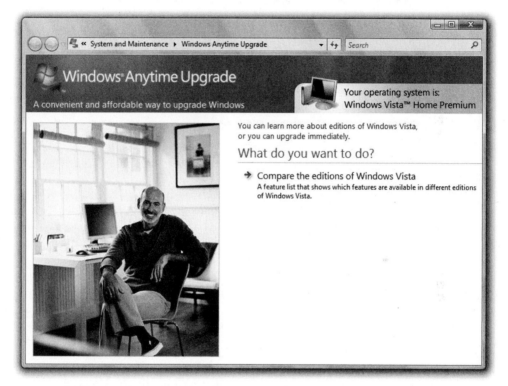

Figure 2-30: Windows Anytime Upgrade provides a way for you to upgrade from one version of Vista to another for less money.

When you click the Compare the Editions of Windows Vista link, you're redirected to Internet Explorer (or your Web browser of choice), which navigates to Microsoft's Windows Anytime Upgrade Web site, as shown in Figure 2-31.

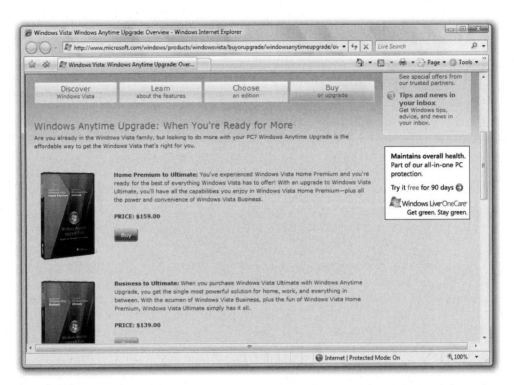

Figure 2-31: The Windows Anytime Upgrade Web site provides pricing and other information regarding your upgrade options.

This Web site presents the various Anytime Upgrade prices, as noted in Table 2-2, and a rundown of the various features in each Windows Vista product edition.

Purchasing is straightforward: Click the Buy button next to the Windows Anytime Upgrade option that's relevant to your situation (say, Business to Ultimate). IE will then navigate to a secure e-commerce site so you can make the purchase.

Secret

You can also purchase Windows Anytime Upgrade disks directly from online retailers such as Amazon.com. Indeed, because of occasional sales, you may want to shop around. To find these upgrade versions on Amazon, visit the site and then search for *Windows Anytime Upgrade*. Note, too, that Amazon.com and other e-tailers typically send your Windows Anytime Upgrade disk much more quickly than Microsoft does (the latter can take two to four weeks). So much for the "Anytime" part of this offer.

Upgrading with an Anytime Upgrade Disk

Once your Windows Anytime Upgrade package arrives in the mail, you can upgrade from one version of Windows Vista to another just as you would if you were upgrading from

Windows XP to Vista: Insert the Windows Anytime Upgrade disk into your PC's optical drive while Windows Vista is running and then run Setup (via AutoPlay or manually). As shown in Figure 2-32, the setup routine provided by this disk is identical to that of other retail Vista Full or Upgrade Setup disks.

Figure 2-32: The Windows Anytime Upgrade process proceeds like any other Vista Upgrade process.

Secret

Two important aspects of the Windows Anytime Upgrade process may not be obvious:

- **Use the right product key and Vista product edition:** On the setup screen titled Type Your Product Key for Activation, you can proceed in one of two ways: If you want to enter the product key right away you can do so, but you must enter the product key that came with your Windows Anytime Upgrade disk, not the one that came with your original version of Windows Vista. Alternately, you can choose to not enter the product key during setup. If you choose this option, then be sure to correctly identify which version of Vista you are upgrading to in the next step. For example, if you are upgrading from Windows Vista Business to Ultimate, choose Windows Vista Ultimate from the list of possible options.

- **Choose Upgrade, not Custom (Advanced):** On the setup screen titled Which Type of Installation Do You Want?, be sure to choose Upgrade.

For some reason, upgrading from one version of Windows Vista to another takes an astonishingly long time. Be prepared to leave your PC unattended for one to two hours.

Once Setup is complete, verify that you're now running the correct product edition by visiting the System window (from the Start Menu, right-click on Computer and choose Properties).

Secret   You have to activate Windows after any Anytime Upgrade, even if the system was previously activated. However, the standard 30-day grace period applies here, too. You can use the information in the section "Delaying Product Activation" later in this chapter to delay the activation up to 120 days if you'd like.

Installing Windows Vista Service Pack 1

Microsoft shipped the first Windows Vista service pack, Windows Vista Service Pack 1 (SP1), a little more than a year after it first made Windows Vista broadly available to consumers in January 2007. I discussed the major advances in SP1 in the "Read This First" chapter of this book, but most of this book assumes that you are updated with the latest Vista version. Therefore, this section highlights the ways in which you can upgrade if you're still running the original version of Vista.

Secret   You can tell which version of Windows Vista you're running by opening the System Properties window (from the Start Menu, right-click Computer and choose Properties) and examining the top section, Windows Edition. If you see a line that reads Service Pack 1, then you're up-to-date. Otherwise, you'll need to upgrade to Service Pack 1.

◆ **Automatic—Windows Update:** Most users will want to upgrade to Service Pack 1 automatically using the Automatic Updating functionality in Windows Update. You won't have to try hard to make this happen, as SP1 will show up as a recommended update and prompt you to install, as shown in Figure 2-33.

Windows Update–based installs offer another advantage. They are typically much smaller than the standalone installer, and thus install faster because Windows Update can intelligently detect exactly which components need to be updated and then download only those components.

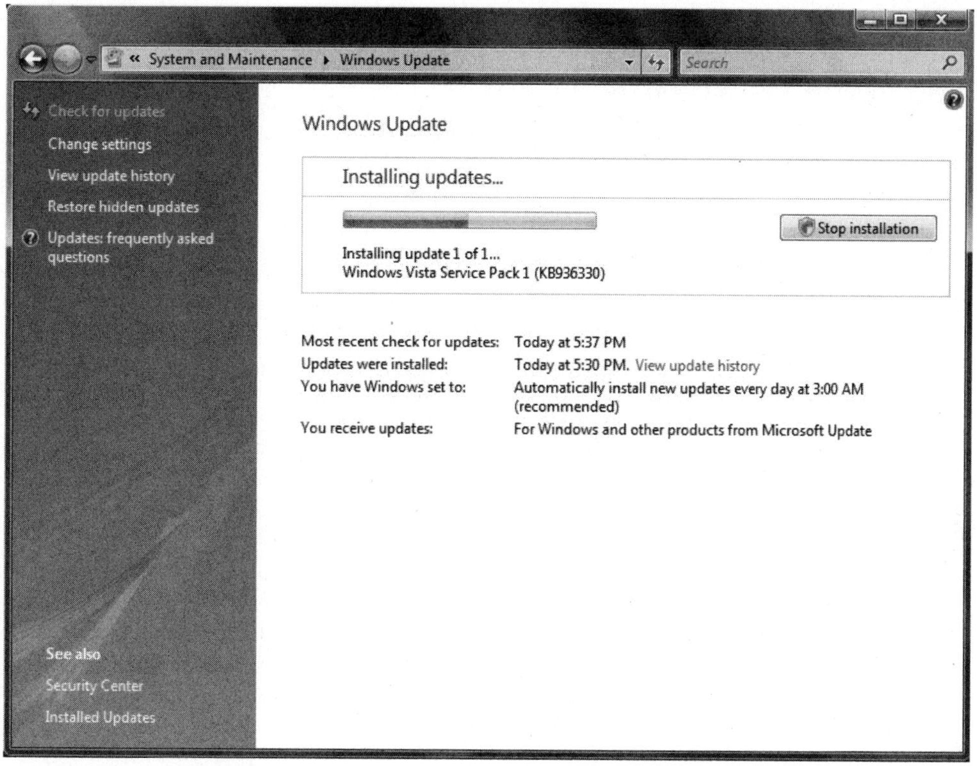

Figure 2-33: Automatically upgrading to Service Pack 1 via Windows Update is the way to go.

◆ **Manual—Download the standalone installer:** This is the brute-force install technique and is provided primarily for IT administrators who need to deploy SP1 to multiple PCs. There are two versions of the standalone installer, a 316MB version aimed at English, French, German, Japanese, or Spanish versions of Windows Vista, and a larger version for all languages. To find this update, search the Microsoft Downloads Web site (**www.microsoft.com/downloads/**) for KB936330, the Windows Vista Service Pack 1 Five Language Standalone, or for KB936330, the Windows Vista Service Pack 1 All Language Standalone installer. (This is a bit of an oversimplification. If you're running a 64-bit x64 version of Windows Vista, you'll need the x64 SP1 versions instead. Fortunately, the KB numbers are the same. Just add x64 to the search string to find the right files.)

The standalone installer setup process is wizard-based and very straightforward. It requires one reboot and is usually completed in less than half an hour.

Slipstreaming Service Packs and Other Vista Updates

In Windows 2000 and XP, Microsoft supported a way to integrate, or *slipstream*, service packs and other updates into a Windows install image so that its largest corporate customers would always have up-to-date installation sources. Otherwise, as each Windows version grew older, and more and more updates were shipped via Windows Update, these businesses would have to waste enormous amounts of time manually installing updates each time they installed the OS; and because these companies often need to mass-install Windows on hundreds or even thousands of PCs at one time, such a process was painful at best.

Microsoft is successful because it caters to businesses, not consumers; but as is so often the case with enterprise-oriented niceties, its Windows slipstreaming capabilities were subverted by enterprising tech enthusiasts who figured out how to slipstream service packs into Windows 2000 and XP and then create new bootable Setup disks that were always up-to-date with the latest fixes. I've published a number of slipstreaming guides on the SuperSite for Windows (**www.winsupersite.com**), including guides for Windows 2000 with Service Pack 2, and Windows XP with Service Packs 1, 2, and 3.

With Windows Vista, Microsoft promised an even simpler method of slipstreaming service packs and other updates. Vista, ostensibly, would enable IT administrators (and, yes, tech enthusiasts) to simply drag and drop updates into a special Update folder that could be created in the root of the Setup disk directory structure. It sounded like a wonderful feature. It still does.

Unfortunately, drag-and-drop slipstreaming—a capability Microsoft calls *offline updating*—never happened, at least not with the initially shipped version of Windows Vista. The reason is because Microsoft discovered a bug in Windows Vista's servicing stack. Therefore, with Vista Service Pack 1 (SP1), which shipped in early 2008, drag-and-drop slipstreaming is not possible. However, Microsoft has made changes to the Vista servicing stack and hopes to provide this functionality in the future.

Just as unfortunate perhaps is that the old method of slipstreaming service packs, which I so thoroughly documented on the SuperSite over several years, no longer works with Windows Vista either. That's because Microsoft has completely rearchitected the way that Windows Vista is deployed. The new system uses a single image file for deployment, whereas previous versions of Windows utilized thousands of tiny archived files. There are some serious advantages to Vista's new image-based deployment scheme, but they're of no use here.

So what's an enterprising Vista user to do? If you have an original version of the Windows Vista Setup DVD and you'd like to create a slipstreamed version of this disk that also includes Service Pack 1 (SP1), are you completely out of luck?

Of course not. Thanks to a handy and free third-party utility called vLite, or Vista Lite (**www.vlite.net/**), it's possible to efficiently slipstream Service Pack 1 (and other updates) into the original Vista Setup files and then create a bootable Setup DVD that enables you to install everything at once. vLite performs a number of other functions as well, but for purposes of this discussion I focus solely on the application's slipstreaming and disk-burning capabilities.

After downloading and installing vLite (see Figure 2-34), you must run it with administrative privileges (right-click the shortcut and choose Run as Administrator).

Figure 2-34: The free vLite utility can slipstream, or integrate, Windows Vista Setup files with SP1.

With your Windows Vista Setup DVD in the PC's optical drive, click the Browse button and navigate to the root of the optical drive. Select the correct Vista product edition from the list displayed in vLite's Images window and click OK. At this point, vLite will copy the files to a temporary location on your hard drive.

Now click the Next button. In the Task Selection screen, shown in Figure 2-35, you can choose from a number of tasks. Select Service Pack Slipstream and Bootable ISO from the list and click Next.

In the next dialog, shown in Figure 2-36, you need to supply vLite with a standalone version of the Windows Vista Service Pack 1 (SP1) updater. (See the previous section for details.) Once the file is downloaded, point vLite to the file by clicking Select. At this point, vLite undergoes a lengthy process whereby it combines the contents of the Vista Setup DVD with the updated files in SP1. Unfortunately, vLite isn't very good about communicating what it's doing. If you look in the lower part of the application window, you'll see text appear that says *Preparing*, and then *Extracting*, and then *Integrating*.

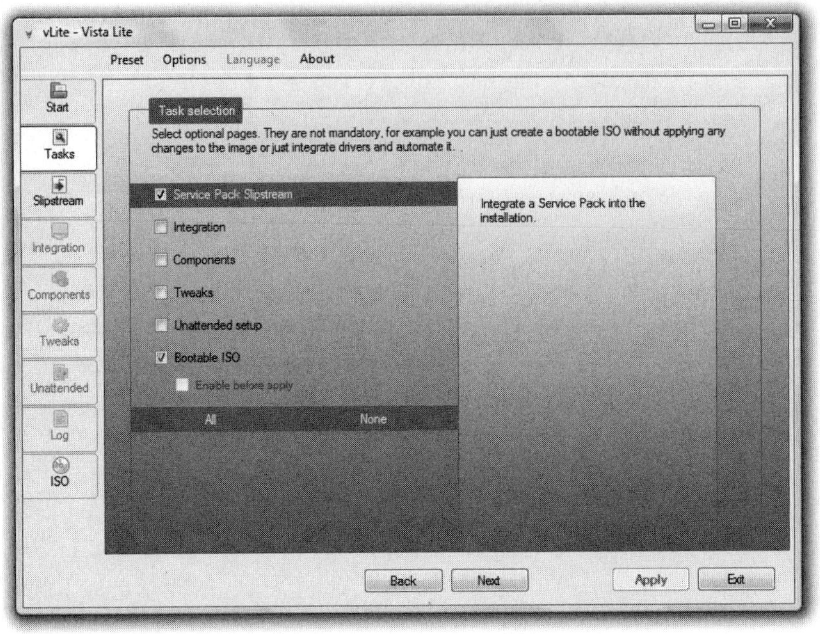

Figure 2-35: vLite offers a variety of Windows deployment options.

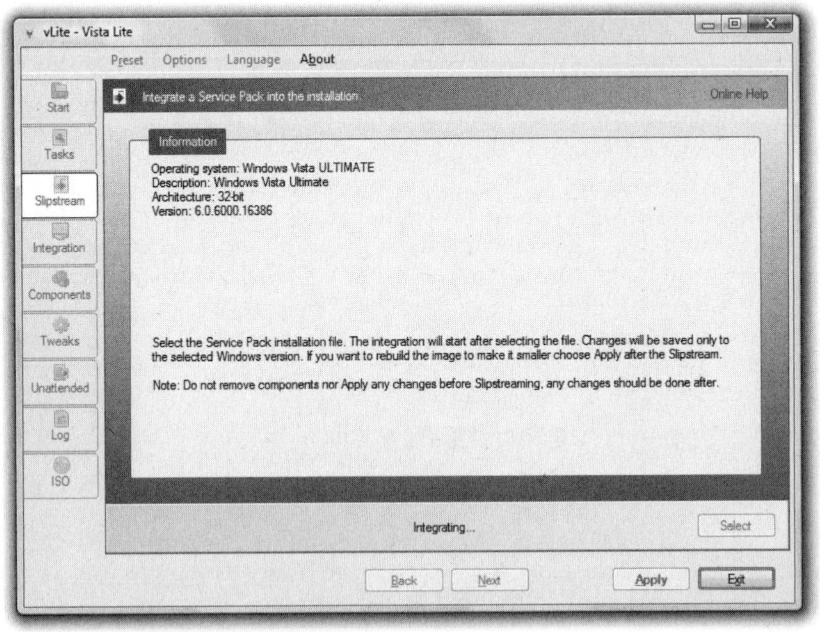

Figure 2-36: It's hard to tell, but vLite is busy integrating SP1 with the Windows Vista Setup files.

After a very long time—up to 90 minutes—vLite completes the integration process with a pithy *Finished!* message. Click Next to proceed to the ISO stage, in which you'll create a bootable integrated Setup disk. In the General section, select Direct Burn from the Mode drop-down list, as shown in Figure 2-37. Then click the Burn button to burn the disk.

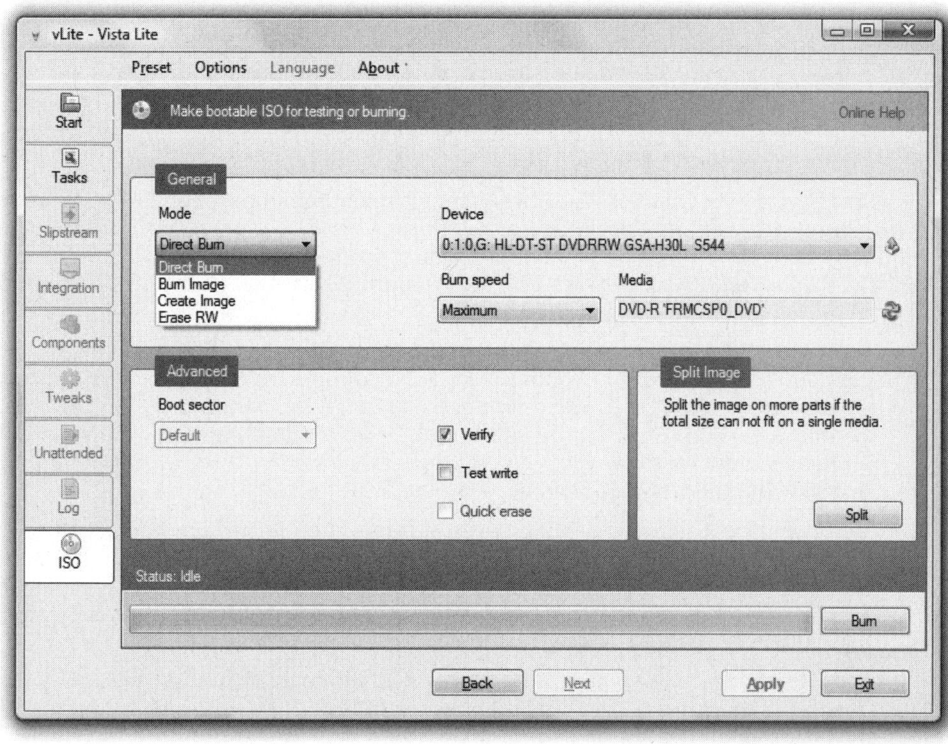

Figure 2-37: Switch from ISO to Direct Burn and you can burn your bootable disk.

When vLite has completed burning and testing your slipstreamed Setup DVD, you can use this disk to install Windows (with Service Pack 1) as you would had you purchased an integrated DVD at retail.

Secret

There is one difference, actually. Slipstreamed Setup disks created by vLite are specific to the Vista product edition you selected previously. For example, if you selected Vista Ultimate, you can install only Vista Ultimate with this disk.

Performing a Clean Install with an Upgrade Version of Vista

While most Windows Vista product editions are available in both Full and Upgrade versions, the differences between each aren't widely understood. The more expensive and seemingly more capable Full versions are designed to be installed only in a so-called "clean" install, as documented earlier in this chapter. That is, when you purchase a Full version of Windows Vista Home Basic, Home Premium, Business, or Ultimate, you're expected to install the software on a PC from scratch, and not upgrade an existing version of Windows to Windows Vista.

The Upgrade versions of Windows Vista, despite their apparently lower status, are in fact more powerful than the Full versions, because they can be used in different ways. Yes, you can use an Upgrade version of Vista to upgrade an existing version of Windows to Windows Vista, but you can also use an Upgrade version of Windows Vista to perform a clean install of the operating system.

The process for doing so, alas, is fairly convoluted. This wasn't always the case: In previous versions of Windows, you could boot a PC with the Upgrade Windows Setup disk and, at some point during setup, be prompted to insert the Setup disk from your then-older Windows version to prove that you qualified for Upgrade pricing. With that bit of legal maneuvering out of the way, you could then proceed with setup and complete a clean install using the Upgrade media.

Unfortunately, Microsoft disabled this upgrade compliance capability in Windows Vista, leading some to believe that it was now impossible to use Vista Upgrade media to perform a clean install. Microsoft's own support documentation says as much. In Knowledge Base article 930985, the company notes that "you cannot use an upgrade key to perform a clean installation of Windows Vista."

Fortunately, there are workarounds. One is documented by Microsoft and will likely be unacceptable to most users. The other is documented here and should work for just about anyone, though the process is admittedly a bit time-consuming.

Microsoft's Documented Method for Clean-Installing Vista with Upgrade Media

According to Microsoft, the only way to perform a clean install of Windows Vista using Upgrade media is to do so on a computer on which a previous version of Windows 2000, XP, or Vista is already installed. For this to work, you need to insert the Vista Upgrade disk while running the previous operating system, run Setup, and then choose Custom (Advanced) at the appropriate place during setup (as documented previously in this chapter).

This method is perfectly acceptable for users who wish to install Windows Vista in a dual-boot setup, as discussed earlier in this chapter. But if you want a cleaner system that's free of previous-OS detritus, there's a better way—a secret way.

Secret

Undocumented Method for a Clean Install of Vista with Upgrade Media

To perform a clean install of Vista with Upgrade media, you need to install Windows Vista once using the Upgrade Setup disk, but without entering your product key during setup. Then, once you've loaded the Vista Desktop for the first time, you can run setup again from within Vista and choose Upgrade (even though you'll be "upgrading" to the exact same version of Vista). Allow setup to complete a second time, and then you're good to go: You can enter your product key after the second setup routine is completed and activate Windows Vista successfully. These instructions work with both the original version of Windows Vista and the version that includes Service Pack 1.

Here are the complete instructions:

Step 1: Install Windows Vista

Boot your PC with the Windows Vista Upgrade DVD. After the preliminary loading screen, click Next to skip past the language preferences screen and then click the Install Now button to trigger Vista Setup. In the next screen, you are prompted to enter your product key, but leave the Product Key field blank, deselect the option titled "Automatically activate Windows when I'm online," and then click Next. Vista Setup will ask you whether you would like to enter your product key before continuing. Click No.

On the next screen, you'll be presented with a list of the Windows Vista product editions you can install. This list may vary from locale to locale, but you'll see options such as Vista Home Basic, Home Premium, Business, Ultimate, and some N editions. *Choose the product edition you actually own.* You'll be asked to verify that you've chosen the correct version. Do so and click Next. On the next screen, agree to the End User License Agreement (EULA) terms and click Next again.

On the next screen, you select the type of install. Choose Custom (Advanced), not Upgrade. Next, you choose the partition to which Windows Vista should be installed, and you can perform some basic disk-related tasks. If you're installing Windows Vista to a new PC, you can simply continue. Otherwise, you can format and partition the hard drive as needed before proceeding. I recommended formatting if a previous OS is installed.

Setup now continues as documented in the "Clean Install" section earlier in this chapter. (Refer to that section for a complete rundown of the process.) Once Vista is successfully installed and you are logged on, you'll be presented with your new Vista Desktop. Don't get too comfortable, however, as you're about to do it all again.

Step 2: Upgrade

If you try to activate Windows now, it will fail because you've performed a clean install of Vista and you have only an Upgrade product key. That means you have 30 days during which you can run this nonactivated version of Windows Vista, but why wait 30 days?

continues

continued

According to Microsoft, Upgrade versions of Vista support upgrading from "a compliant version of Windows, such as Windows Vista, Windows XP, or Windows 2000." Well, you just installed Windows Vista, so why not just upgrade from that install? That's right: You're going to upgrade the nonactivated clean install you just performed, which will provide you with a version of the OS that you can, in fact, activate.

To do this, just select Computer and double-click on the icon for the DVD drive that contains the Vista Upgrade media. Run setup again, this time from within Vista. Choose Install Now, and then Do Not Get the Latest Updates for Installation on the next screen. Then, in the now-familiar product-key phase, enter your product key. It's on the back of the pull-out Vista packaging. You can choose to automatically activate Windows when online; it's your choice. On the next screen, accept the Windows EULA.

Now choose the Upgrade option. Windows will install as before, though you might notice that it takes quite a bit longer this time. (Upgrade installs take up to 60 minutes, compared to 30 minutes or less with clean installs, and reboot at least one additional time.)

Because you've just completed an upgrade install, you won't be prompted to enter your user name and so forth (only the Automatic Updates and time zone screens are presented). Then you'll move to the setup performance check (again). When that's completed, enter the user name and password you created during the first install and log on to Windows.

Now that you've "upgraded" Vista, product activation will actually work. To activate Vista manually and immediately (unless you told it to do so during setup), from the Start Menu, right-click Computer and choose Properties. Then, at the bottom of the System window that appears, click the link titled Activate Windows Now.

Is this process legal? After all, anyone could purchase an Upgrade version of Windows Vista (thereby saving a lot of money compared to a Full version) and use it to perform a clean install even if they don't own a previous, compliant Windows version.

If you own a previous version of Windows, yeah, it is legal. If not, no, it isn't legal. It's that simple. From a technical standpoint, Microsoft designed Windows Vista to support upgrading from a previously installed copy of Windows 2000, XP, or Vista. It's not a hacker exploit but rather a supported process that was deliberately programmed into the setup routine. It's perfectly okay to do… as long as you are indeed a licensed user of a previous version of Windows. So go forth and upgrade. Legally.

Delaying Product Activation

Retail versions of Windows Vista must be activated within 30 days. Otherwise, the system slips into an annoying state in which it notifies you, every 60 minutes, that the system must be activated. Still, the 30-day grace period is useful, especially if you're just testing some things and want to make sure that your new install is working properly before you lock things down and tie your one product key to this particular PC.

That said, sometimes 30 days isn't enough, and if you want to extend this grace period, I've got some good news: Thanks to a barely documented feature aimed at Microsoft's corporate customers, it's actually possible to extend the activation grace period up to a total of 120 days. You just have to be a bit vigilant.

The key to extending the grace period is a command-line program in Windows Vista called Software Licensing Manager (SLMGR), which is actually a VBScript script named **slmgr.vbs**. (It can be found in c:\windows\system32 by default.) Using this script with the **-rearm** parameter, you can reset (or, in Software Licensing Manager lingo, "re-arm") Vista's 30-day activation grace period. This effectively resets the clock on the activation grace period back to a full 30 days whenever you run it.

Unfortunately, you can run this script successfully only three times, so it's theoretically possible to re-arm the product activation grace period to a total of 120 days (30 days of initial grace period plus three additional 30-day grace periods). That said, even the most careful of users will likely want to re-arm the grace period with a few days remaining each time, but you're still looking at over 100 days of non-activated Windows Vista usage.

You can view your current grace period in the System window. To do so, open the Start Menu, right-click the Computer icon, and choose Properties. The bottom section of this window, Windows activation, displays how many days you have until the grace period ends, and provides a link to activate Windows immediately, as shown in Figure 2-38.

Windows activation
 5 day(s) to activate. Activate Windows now
Product ID: 89587-014-0000025-71250   Change product key

Figure 2-38: Time to activate… or re-arm the grace period.

Here's how to re-arm the Windows Vista product-activation grace period:

1. Open the Start Menu, select Search, and type **cmd**.
2. Right-click the cmd shortcut that appears and choose Run as Administrator from the pop-up menu that appears. Windows Vista's command-line window appears.
3. Type the following text in the command-line window and press Enter when complete: **slmgr.vbs -rearm**.

   When the command is run successfully, a Windows Script Host window appears, noting "Command completed successfully. Please restart the system for the changes to take effect."
4. Click OK to close the Windows Script Host window and then restart the PC. When you reboot, reload the System window. As shown in Figure 2-39, the grace period has been reset to 30 days. Voila!

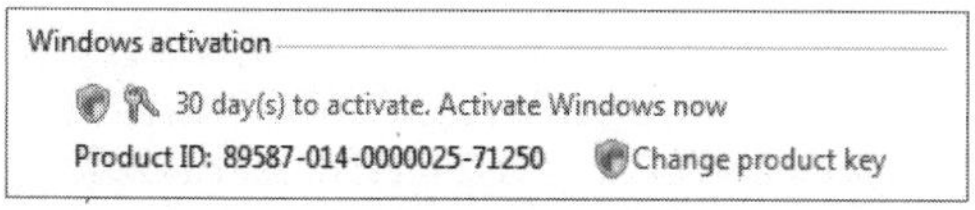

Windows activation
 30 day(s) to activate. Activate Windows now
Product ID: 89587-014-0000025-71250   Change product key

Figure 2-39: Happiness is a full 30-day grace period.

Secret

Software Licensing Manager isn't designed solely to extend the Windows Vista grace period. If you run **slmgr.vbs** from a Windows Vista command-line window without any parameters, you'll eventually be presented with the dialog in Figure 2-40, showing you the many possible options.

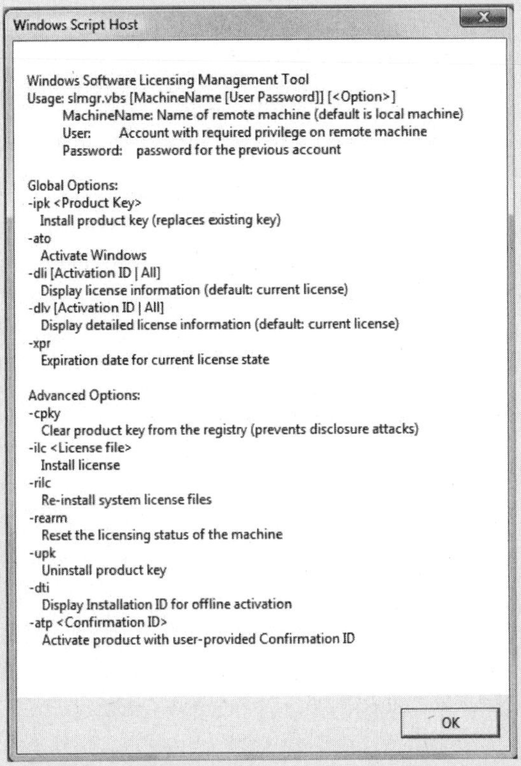

Windows Script Host ✕

Windows Software Licensing Management Tool
Usage: slmgr.vbs [MachineName [User Password]] [<Option>]
    MachineName: Name of remote machine (default is local machine)
    User: Account with required privilege on remote machine
    Password: password for the previous account

Global Options:
-ipk <Product Key>
   Install product key (replaces existing key)
-ato
   Activate Windows
-dli [Activation ID | All]
   Display license information (default: current license)
-dlv [Activation ID | All]
   Display detailed license information (default: current license)
-xpr
   Expiration date for current license state

Advanced Options:
-cpky
   Clear product key from the registry (prevents disclosure attacks)
-ilc <License file>
   Install license
-rilc
   Re-install system license files
-rearm
   Reset the licensing status of the machine
-upk
   Uninstall product key
-dti
   Display Installation ID for offline activation
-atp <Confirmation ID>
   Activate product with user-provided Confirmation ID

[OK]

Figure 2-40: The Software Licensing Manager performs a number of useful product activation–related services.

The most interesting of these include the following:

- **-ipk:** Enables you to change the Windows product key
- **-dlv:** Displays a detailed list of license information about your PC, including the Windows Vista product version and type (e.g., retail)
- **-ato:** Activates Windows Vista
- **-dti:** Activates Windows Vista offline, without an Internet connection

Installing Windows Vista on a Mac

When Apple switched its Macintosh computers from the aging Power PC architecture to Intel's PC-compatible x86 platform in 2006, the computing landscape was changed forever. No longer were PCs and Macs incompatible at a very low level. Indeed, Macs are now simply PCs running a different operating system. This fascinating change opened up the possibility of Mac users running Windows software natively on their machines, either in a dual-boot scenario or, perhaps, in a virtualized environment that would offer much better performance than the Power PC–based virtualized environments of the past.

These dreams quickly became reality. Apple created software called *Boot Camp* that now enables Mac users to dual-boot between Mac OS X and Windows XP or Vista. And enterprising tech pioneers such as VMware and Parallels have created seamless virtualization environments for Mac OS X that enable users to run popular Windows applications alongside Mac-only software such as iLife.

Now consumers can choose a best-of-both-worlds solution that combines Apple's highly regarded hardware with the compatibility and software-library depth of Windows Vista. Indeed, I've been using an Apple notebook running Windows Vista ever since Microsoft's latest operating system shipped publicly.

Secret

The differences between these two types of Windows-on-Mac solutions are important to understand. If you choose to dual-boot between Mac OS X and Windows using Boot Camp, you have the advantage of running each system with the complete power of the underlying hardware. However, you can access only one OS at a time and need to reboot the Mac in order to access the other.

With a virtualized environment such as Mac OS X, you have the advantage of running Mac OS X and Windows applications side by side, but with a performance penalty. In this situation, Mac OS X is considered the *host* OS, and Windows is a *guest* OS running on top of Mac OS X. Thus, Windows applications won't run at full speed. With enough RAM, you won't notice any huge performance issues while utilizing productivity applications, but you can't run Windows games effectively with such a setup. Note, too, that the Windows Vista Aero user experience is not available in today's virtualized environments, so you would have to settle for Windows Vista Basic instead.

Regardless of which method you use to install Windows Vista, be aware of a final limitation: You will need to *purchase* a copy of Windows Vista, as no Mac ships with Microsoft's operating system. This is a not-so-fine point that Apple never seems to point out in their advertising.

Dual Boot: Using Boot Camp

Boot Camp is a feature of Mac OS X and is configured via that system's Boot Camp Assistant. As shown in Figure 2-41, Boot Camp Assistant is available from the Mac OS X Utilities folder (Applications ➪ Utilities) and provides a wizard-based configuration experience.

Figure 2-41: Boot Camp helps you configure a dual boot between Windows and Mac OS X.

Boot Camp is available only in Mac OS X 10.5 "Leopard" or newer, and it supports only 32-bit versions of Windows XP and Vista.

The key to this wizard is the Create a Second Partition phase, where you can graphically resize the partition layout on the hard disk between Mac OS X and Windows, as shown in Figure 2-42. (Macs with multiple hard drives can be configured such that Mac OS X and Windows occupy different physical disks, if desired.)

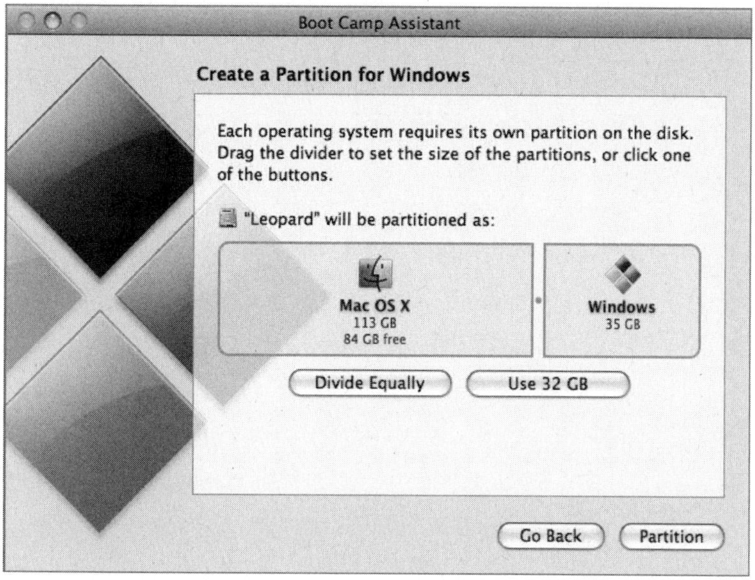

Figure 2-42: Drag the slider to resize the Mac and Windows partitions.

After that, Boot Camp prompts you to insert the Windows Vista Setup DVD and proceed with setup. From a Windows user's perspective, setup proceeds normally and Windows looks and acts as it should once installed. Be sure to keep your Mac OS X Setup DVD handy, however. It includes the necessary drivers that Windows needs to be compatible with the Mac's specific hardware.

Once you have Windows Vista up and running on the Mac, there are just a few Mac-specific issues you should be aware of:

- ◆ **Configuring Boot Camp:** When you install Windows Vista on a Mac using Boot Camp, Apple installs a Boot Camp Control Panel application, which you can access via Start Menu ⇨ Search by typing **boot camp**. This application helps you configure important functionality such as the default system to load at boot time (Mac or Windows).

  There's also a system notification tray applet that enables you to access the Boot Camp Control Panel and Boot Camp Help and choose to reboot into Mac OS X.

- ◆ **Switching between operating systems at boot time:** While you can choose the default operating system at boot time via the Boot Camp Control Panel application, or choose to boot into Mac OS X from within Windows by using the Boot Camp tray applet, you can also choose an OS on the fly when you boot up the Mac. To do so, restart the Mac and then hold down the Option key until you see a screen with icons for both Mac OS X and Windows. Then, use the arrow keys on the keyboard to choose the system you want and press Enter to boot.

- ◆ **Understanding Mac keyboard and mouse differences:** While Macs are really just glorified PCs now, Apple continues to use unique keyboard layouts and, frequently, one-button mice. As a result, you may have to make some adjustments when running Windows on a Mac. Table 2-3 lists some commonly used keyboard commands and explains how to trigger equivalent actions on a Mac.

Table 2-3: Windows Keyboard Shortcuts on the Mac

Windows Keyboard Shortcut	Apple External Keyboard	Built-In Mac Keyboard
Ctrl+Alt+Delete	Ctrl+Option+Fwd Delete	Ctrl+Option+Delete
Alt	Option	Option
Backspace	Delete	Delete
Delete	Fwd Delete	Fn+Delete
Enter	Return	Return
Enter	Enter on numeric keypad	Enter
Insert	Help	Fn+Enter
Num Lock	Clear	F6
Pause/Break	F16	Fn+Esc
Print Screen	F14	F11
Print active window	Option+F14	Option+F11
Scroll/Lock	F15	F12
Windows	Command	Command

Additionally, you can right-click items on a single-button Mac trackpad by holding two fingers on the trackpad and tapping the button. To scroll in a document or Web page, move two fingers on the trackpad simultaneously, either up or down.

Windows on Mac: Virtualization Solutions

If you'd prefer to join the ever-increasing ranks of Mac switchers—you traitor, you—you can still run Windows and, more important, Windows applications, from within Mac OS X. You do so via a virtualized environment such as VMware Fusion or Parallels Desktop, both of which fool Windows into running inside of a software-based PC that itself runs as an application under Mac OS X.

In the past, virtualized environments presented a number of huge issues, especially on the Mac. First, performance was abysmal, owing mostly to the underlying architectural differences between the PowerPC and Intel x86 platforms and the difficulty in translating running code between them. Second, virtualized environments have typically presented Windows and its applications as a sort of thing-in-a-thing, whereby the entire Windows environment would run inside a closed-off window that was quite separate and distinct from the Mac environment in which it was running. Moving back and forth between the Mac and Windows environments was jarring and difficult.

Modern virtualized environments—such as VMware Fusion and Parallels Desktop—have mostly overcome these issues. Thanks to the underlying Intel x86 platform now used by the Mac, virtualization offers better performance because there's no need to do on-the-fly code conversion. Yes, performance still suffers, but I think you would be surprised by how well Fusion and Parallels Desktop actually work.

More impressive, perhaps, both VMware Fusion and Parallels Desktop offer unique new usage modes that blur the line between the Mac and Windows desktops. VMware Fusion offers a feature called Unity that enables you to run a Windows application directly from the Mac Dock, switch between Windows and Mac applications using the Mac's Exposé window switcher, and drag and drop files between both systems. As shown in Figure 2-43, it's visually impressive and quite usable.

Figure 2-43: VMware Fusion enables you to run Windows and Mac applications side by side.

Parallels Desktop offers a similar feature called Coherence, which also integrates Windows applications into the Mac desktop experience. Shown in Figure 2-44, Coherence even supports copy and paste between Mac and Windows applications, and many other integration features.

VMware Fusion also offers an impressive bit of integration with Apple's Boot Camp functionality. If you've already installed Windows Vista in a dual-boot setup with Mac OS X using Boot Camp, Fusion will detect that Windows install and automatically enable you to access it as a virtualized environment from within Mac OS X. This, truly, is the best of both worlds, as you can choose to access Windows Vista natively via Boot Camp or virtualized from within Mac OS X using Fusion, all on the same machine.

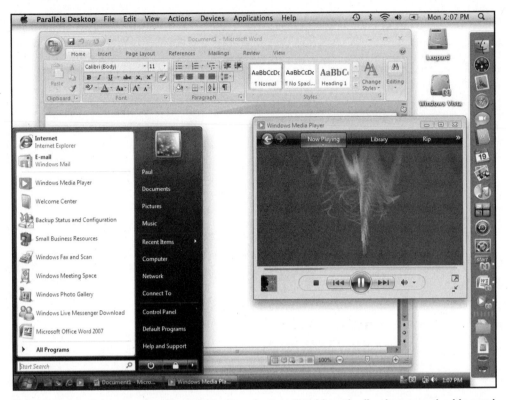

Figure 2-44: Coherence is a Parallels Desktop feature that blurs the line between the Mac and Windows environments.

You can find out more about VMware Fusion from the VMware Web site at **www.vmware.com/products/fusion**. Likewise, you can find out more about Parallels Fusion online at **www.parallels.com/products/desktop**.

Summary

Although Windows Vista setup is dramatically simpler than the setup routine used by Windows XP, there are still many options to understand and features you'll need to go back and configure manually after setup is complete. Depending on which Vista version you purchased and your needs, you can clean-install Vista as the sole OS on your PC, upgrade an existing Windows XP installation to Vista, or dual-boot between XP and Vista on the same machine. You can also use Windows Anytime Upgrade to upgrade from one version of Windows Vista to another, delay product activation from 30 days to 120 days, and slipstream service packs and other updates into your original Windows Vista Setup DVD. Users interested in getting the best of both worlds can even do the unthinkable: install Windows Vista on a Mac.

Hardware and Software Compatibility

♦ ♦

In This Chapter

Choosing not *to install Vista over an older operating system*

Recognizing when you may have to install Vista over an older OS

Using the Vista Upgrade Advisor to catch problems in advance

Taking action if the Vista Upgrade Advisor indicates that an updated driver "isn't available"

Resolving driver issues

♦ ♦

One of the biggest issues you'll face when moving to a new version of Windows—any version, not just Windows Vista—is compatibility. Whenever Microsoft changes the underpinnings of Windows as much as it did with Windows Vista, both hardware and software compatibility are going to suffer. That said, Microsoft claims that Windows Vista offers far better backward compatibility than did previous Windows versions, and it has the data to back up that assertion. However, all it takes is the loss of a single necessary hardware device or software application to turn any Windows upgrade into a disaster. In this chapter, I examine some of the compatibility issues you can run into when making the move to Windows Vista, and how you can troubleshoot them.

Hidden Perils of the Vista Upgrade

With all the new features and functionality provided by Windows Vista, you might be tempted to buy a retail version of the operating system and install it over your existing copy of Windows XP.

I don't recommend doing that, for the following reasons:

♦ Your old PC may not be up to the challenge of running Vista. You may need substantial investments in additional RAM, a more capable video card, a larger hard drive, or all of the above to get adequate performance from Windows Vista.

♦ Some of your hardware, such as printers and networking adapters, may not work at all after you install Windows Vista—unless you update the drivers they need to versions that are Vista-compatible.

♦ Even if you find that one or more of your drivers need to be updated, the vendor of your hardware may not make a Vista-compatible version available for months, years, or ever. (It's happened before with previous versions of Windows.)

♦ Some of the software that's installed and running just fine in Windows XP may not work properly once you've performed the upgrade.

♦ Finally, some software or hardware may never work in Vista. Companies do go out of business, after all.

Secret

Avoid Installing Vista over Windows XP

I recommend that you get Windows Vista preinstalled with your next new PC. This is the best way to acquire Vista. Another reasonable option, assuming you know what you're doing and have recent hardware, is to purchase a retail version of Windows Vista and then perform a *clean install* of the OS on your existing PC. I *don't* recommend that you install Vista over Windows XP.

Here's why. Installing Windows Vista on top of Windows XP may cause incompatibility problems that you might not be able to fix easily. When you buy a new PC with Windows Vista preinstalled, it's almost certain that the components in the PC will have been selected for their compatibility and will have the latest driver software. PC makers also support their products with Web sites that provide the latest known drivers. These sites aren't usually as up-to-date as they should be, but they will at least work. In general, you shouldn't consider installing Vista over Windows XP unless the following conditions are true:

• You need a feature of Vista that you can't add to XP.

continues

continued

- You need an application that requires Vista.
- You can't afford even the least expensive new PC that comes with Vista preinstalled.

Even if one of the preceding conditions is true, you may be better off backing up all of your old data to a CD/DVD or removable hard disk, formatting the old PC's hard drive, and doing a clean install of Vista. This avoids the possibility that some components of the old OS will hang around to cause conflicts. If you've never backed up and formatted a hard drive, however, don't try to learn how on any PC that's important to you.

If you do decide to install Vista over Windows XP, at least run Microsoft's Vista Upgrade Advisor, described in this chapter, to determine which drivers you may need to update first; and regardless of how you need to install Windows Vista, check out Chapter 2 first, which provides a thorough overview of the various ways in which you can get this system installed.

The Windows Vista Upgrade Advisor

To help you determine whether your current PC has the performance characteristics and hardware and software compatibility needed to avoid issues before upgrading or migrating to Windows Vista, Microsoft provides a handy tool called the Windows Vista Upgrade Advisor.

The Upgrade Advisor performs an analysis of your PC and is partly designed as a marketing tool, as it will recommend which version of Vista is right for your system. (Curiously, it almost always recommends one of the more expensive, premium versions.) The Upgrade Advisor also provides real-world benefit outside of Microsoft's needs: It will tell you which hardware devices and software applications need updates before they can work with Vista; and because the back end of the Upgrade Advisor application runs on Microsoft's servers, it always provides up-to-date information.

tip   The Windows Vista Upgrade Advisor can be downloaded from the Microsoft Web site. See www.microsoft.com/windows/products/windowsvista/buyorupgrade/ upgradeadvisor.mspx

Secret   While the Windows Vista Upgrade Advisor is primarily designed to help users of previous Windows versions discover whether their PC can be upgraded successfully to Windows Vista, it also has a secret second use: It can be run on Windows Vista and used to determine whether your PC is able to run a more-capable and -expensive version of Vista.

Using the Upgrade Advisor

The Windows Vista Upgrade Advisor is a simple wizardlike application, as shown in Figure 3-1.

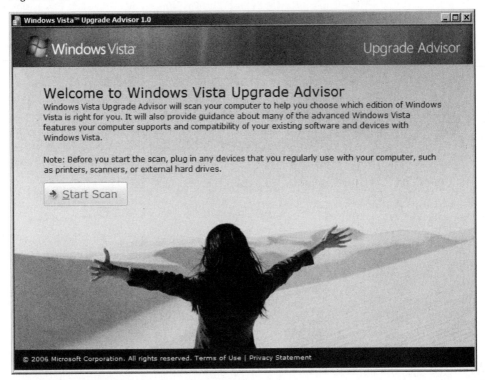

Figure 3-1: The Windows Vista Upgrade Advisor can be used to determine whether your PC has what it takes to compute in the 21st century.

The Upgrade Advisor is designed to test two different kinds of hardware compatibility:

◆ Whether your hardware is fast enough and modern enough to run Windows Vista satisfactorily.

◆ Whether your device drivers are compatible with Windows Vista.

The Upgrade Advisor's initial screen suggests that you should plug in any devices you may want to use with Vista. It's easy to forget some, but this is absolutely the right time to have them checked out, so here's a short list to jog your memory about the various devices you want to ensure are plugged into your PC and powered on before you start the Upgrade Advisor's system scan:

◆ Printers and scanners (make sure they're powered on not just plugged in).

◆ External hard disk drives, backup devices, and USB drives of all kinds.

◆ An extra USB hub that you seldom use—plug it in anyway to check it.

- ◆ Spare USB keyboards and mice that you may have forgotten.
- ◆ An iPod or other MP3 player, even if you seldom synchronize it to your PC.
- ◆ Headphones and other audio devices (they may require audio drivers that won't be tested unless the devices are jacked in to an audio port).

When you've checked for all of the preceding and you are satisfied that you've plugged in and turned on everything you might want to test, click the Start Scan button in the Upgrade Advisor to continue. Depending on the speed of your system, the scan can take anywhere from a minute or two to several minutes. As the scan progresses, Microsoft provides a handy marketing chart comparing the various retail versions of Windows Vista, as shown in Figure 3-2.

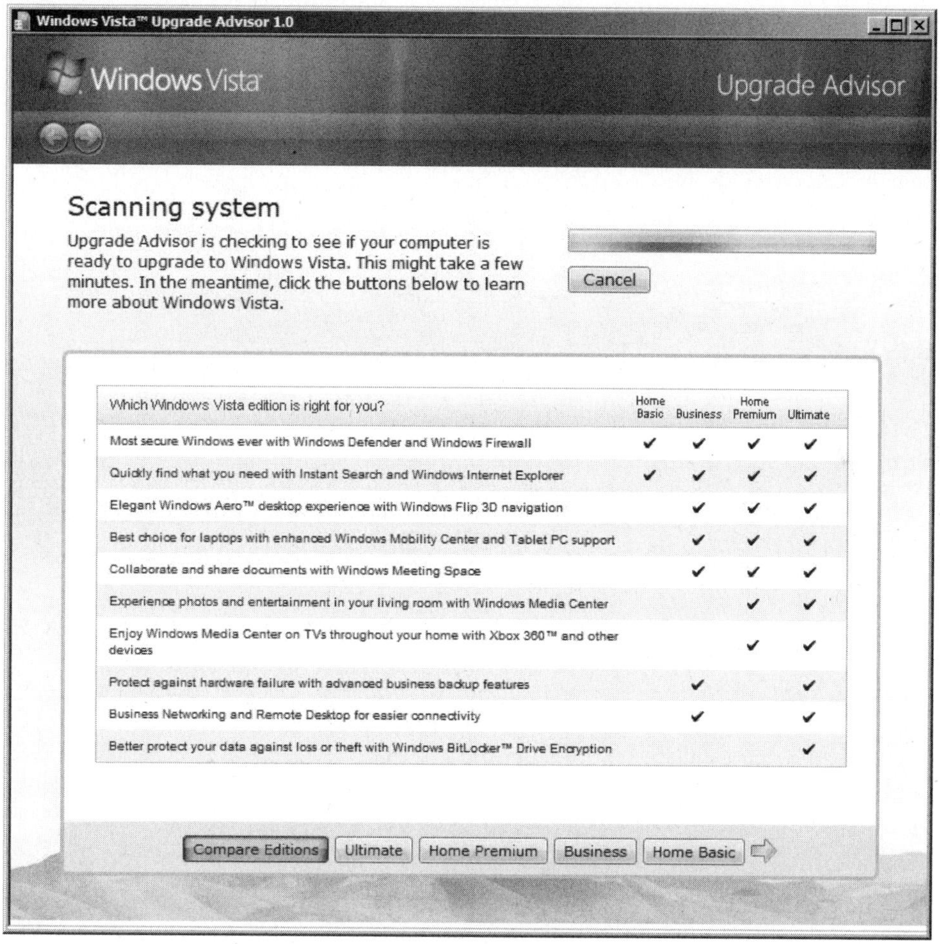

Figure 3-2: Hold your breath, as the moment of truth awaits.

Picking through the Results

The Upgrade Advisor tests three areas: The PC's hardware, to determine whether it meets the minimum Vista requirements; the various hardware devices attached to the system, to ensure that they all have compatible drivers; and the software applications.

When the test is complete, you will see a display like the one shown in Figure 3-3. Almost invariably, the Upgrade Advisor will tell you that your system is at least capable of running Vista's core experiences, which are the basic features required by all Vista product editions.

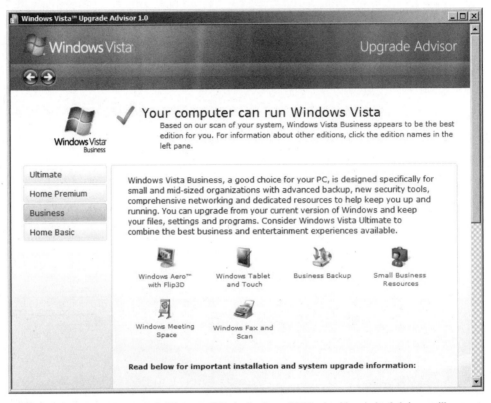

Figure 3-3: How did you do? On most PCs built since 2006, the Upgrade Advisor will report that the hardware can easily handle the core Windows Vista experiences. If a PC fails this test, don't even consider installing Windows Vista on the machine without some serious hardware upgrades.

Look below this message, however, and you may see some issues. As shown in Figure 3-4, many older XP-based PCs will have a number of problems to investigate.

Click one of the See Details buttons to get a more detailed report. As shown in Figure 3-5, the Upgrade Advisor provides separate views of the system (core PC hardware resources), devices, and programs (software applications), and provides a to-do task list so you know what to do before and after installing Windows Vista on that PC.

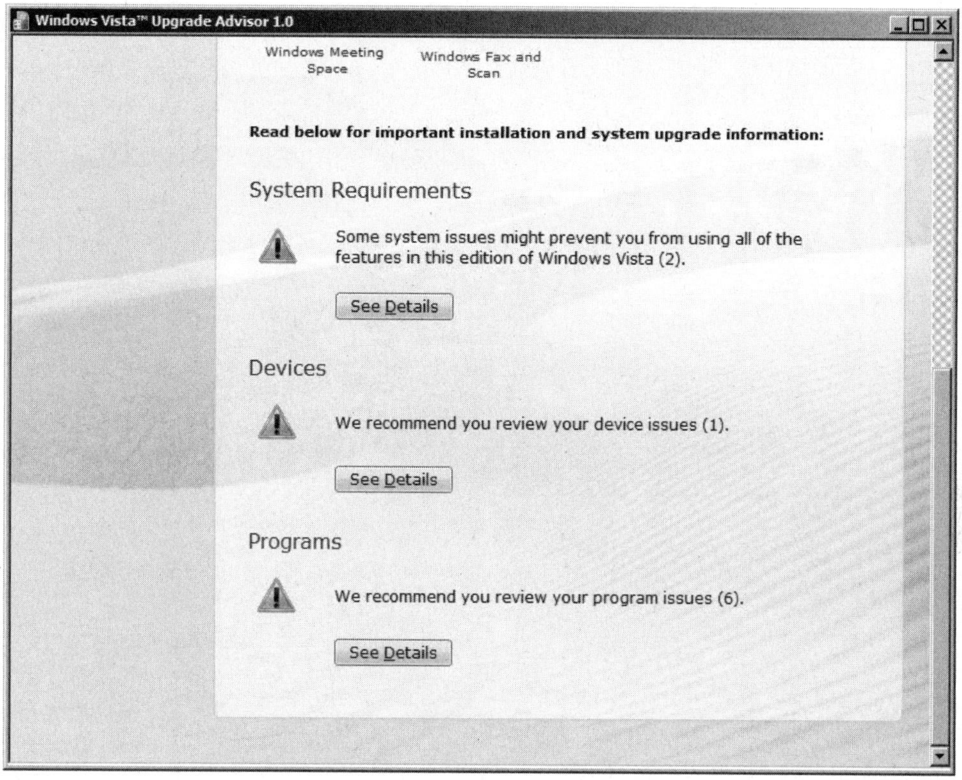

Figure 3-4: Many XP-era PCs will have a bit of upgrading ahead before they can be moved to Vista.

Depending on the age of your PC, the report could be a bit brutal. On a 2005-era IBM ThinkPad T43, for example, I was informed of the following issues:

- ◆ **System:** The Upgrade Advisor recommended upgrading both the video card and the RAM after installing Windows Vista. In the case of the RAM, that's good advice, as this particular system has only 512MB, the absolute minimum required by Vista. (I recommend 2GB.) The video card recommendation, however, is non-sensical: As this is a laptop, it's impossible to upgrade this component. The PC's CPU (a single-core Pentium M running at 1.86 MHz) and DVD drives were deemed acceptable.
- ◆ **Devices:** The pointing device on the ThinkPad would need to be updated with Vista-compatible drivers after installing the new OS, which is easy enough. All of the other attached devices are fine, the Upgrade Advisor reported.
- ◆ **Programs:** The Upgrade Advisor reported a surprisingly long list of "minor compatibility issues," including such applications as NetWaiting, an ATI video card utility, Windows Messenger, and a few others. None seem serious.

According to the provided task list, all of the updates I would need to make could occur after installing Windows Vista.

Figure 3-5: The Upgrade Advisor will provide a list of action items, if necessary, so you understand what you'll need to do before upgrading.

This report, of course, does highlight a potential pitfall of the Upgrade Advisor. The ThinkPad cited above is actually a horrible host for Windows Vista: The video chipset is woefully inadequate, as is virtually any single-core microprocessor; and while it's possible to upgrade the RAM to 2GB for a very reasonable $50 these days, the other hardware-related failings make this a nonstarter.

If you decide at this point to install Windows Vista on your own PC and it proves to be too slow for you, you can always upgrade your RAM, video board, and disk drive—possibly even swap out your motherboard for a new model—to improve the situation after the fact. However, you should have a reasonable concept of acceptable minimum performance. I discuss my minimum hardware recommendations for Windows Vista in Chapter 2.

Drivers That Lack a Vista-Compatible Version

If the Upgrade Advisor reports that a particular driver you need may not exist, the first place to start your search is the site of the hardware vendor. New drivers are released every day, so the one you need may have just come out and it's likely that the hardware maker will make them available long before they show up on Windows Update.

Smaller companies and those that no longer support a particular model of hardware may never spend the time to develop a Vista-ready driver. In that case, you may have no choice but to purchase newer hardware that does have a driver you can use in Vista.

Understanding Windows Vista Compatibility Issues

Any discussion of PC compatibility, of course, encompasses two very different but related topics: hardware and software. In order for a given hardware device—a printer, graphics card, or whatever—to work correctly with Windows Vista, it needs a working driver. In many cases, drivers designed for older versions of Windows will actually work just fine in Windows Vista. However, depending on the class (or type) of device, many hardware devices need a new Vista-specific driver to function properly on Microsoft's latest operating system.

Software offers similar challenges. While Windows Vista is largely compatible with the 32-bit software applications that Windows users have enjoyed for over a decade, some applications—and indeed, entire application classes, such as security software—simply won't work properly in Windows Vista. Some applications can be made to work using Windows Vista's built-in compatibility modes, as discussed below. Some can't.

A final compatibility issue that shouldn't be overlooked is one raised by the ongoing migration to 64-bit (x64) computing. Virtually every single PC sold today does, in fact, include a 64-bit x64-compatible microprocessor, which means it is capable of running 64-bit versions of Windows Vista. However, virtually all copies of Windows Vista that are sold are the more mainstream 32-bit versions of the system. I'll explain why this is so and how the situation will improve over time.

Secret

From a functional standpoint, x64 and 32-bit versions of Windows Vista are almost identical. I discuss cases where this is not true throughout the book. Readers interested in x64/64-bit computing should understand that only Windows Vista Ultimate comes with both 64-bit and 32-bit setup DVDs. Other Windows Vista versions typically include only the 32-bit version. If you'd prefer a 64-bit version of Windows Vista, Microsoft makes 64-bit setup DVDs available to existing Vista customers for the cost of shipping and handling. Details can be found inside any Windows Vista retail package.

Hardware Compatibility

One of the best things about Windows has been that you could go into any electronics retailer, buy any hardware device in the store, bring it home, and know it would work. Conversely, one of the worst things about any new version of Windows is that the previous statement no longer applies. I recall wandering down the aisles of a Best Buy in Phoenix, Arizona, over a decade ago when Windows NT 4.0 first shipped, with a printed copy of the Windows NT Hardware Compatibility List (HCL) in my hand. I needed a network adapter but had to be sure I got one of the few models that worked in the then new NT 4.0 system. (In the end, I bought the side model that was compatible.)

Windows Vista users face a similar problem today, though there are some differences. First, there's no HCL available anymore, at least not a public one, so you're a bit more on your own when it comes to discovering what's going to work. Second, Vista is already far more compatible with existing hardware than NT was back in the mid 1990s. Indeed, Microsoft claims that Windows Vista is actually more compatible with today's hardware than Windows XP was when it first shipped back in 2001. Based on my testing and evidence provided by Microsoft, I believe this to be the case, though overblown tales of Vista's compatibility issues burned up the blogosphere during its first year on the market.

I've tested Windows Vista over a period of years on a wide variety of systems, including several desktops (most of which use dual-core x64-compatible CPUs), Media Center PCs, notebook computers, Tablet PCs, and even two Ultra-Mobile PCs. Windows Vista's out-of-the-box (OOTB) compatibility with the built-in devices on each system I've tested has been stellar. (In this case, OOTB refers to both the drivers that actually ship on the Windows Vista DVD as well as the drivers that are automatically installed via Automatic Updating the first time you boot into your new Windows Vista desktop.) On almost all of these systems, Windows Vista has found and installed drivers for every single device in or attached to the system. So much for all those storied compatibility shenanigans.

How about those fears that Vista's high-end Windows Aero user interface requires hardware upgrades? Balderdash. On every single one of my systems, except for a 2002-era, first-generation Toshiba Tablet PC that was slow the day it came out of the factory, Windows Aero is enabled by default and works just fine. This even includes systems with integrated graphics, the very types of systems that were supposed to cause all kinds of problems.

Where you might run into hardware issues is with older scanners, printers, and similar peripherals. My network-attached Dell laser printer wasn't supported by Windows Vista–specific drivers until Service Pack 1 shipped. (It's really a Lexmark printer in disguise, so I was able to get it up and running just fine using Lexmark drivers previous to SP1.) Ditto with an older HP Scanjet scanner: It wasn't supported with Vista-specific drivers immediately in late 2006, but HP has since shown up with updated drivers that work just fine. An Epson photo printer has always worked just fine, and even uses Epson's bizarre configuration utility—though I've never had to install the software manually myself.

TV-tuner hardware? It just works. Zune? Done. Apple's iPods? They all work (even on x64 systems). Windows Media–compatible devices? Of course; they all connect seamlessly and even work with Vista's Sync Center interface.

Software Compatibility

I regularly use and otherwise test what I feel is a representative collection of mostly modern software. This includes standard software applications—productivity solutions and the like—as well as games.

I run a standard set of applications across most of my desktop and mobile PCs (see Chapter 7 for details). I've also tested numerous video games to see how they fare under the initially shipped version of Windows Vista, as well as Vista with Service Pack 1. The results were largely positive: Not only do most Windows XP-compatible applications and games work just fine under Windows Vista, many pre-Vista games also integrate automatically into Vista's new Games Explorer as well. Unless it's a very new game designed specifically for Windows Vista, you won't get performance information as you do with built-in games, but the game's Entertainment Software Ratings Board (ESRB) rating is enough to enable parents to lock kids out of objectionable video games using Vista's parental-control features. It's a nice touch.

**cross
ref**   See Chapter 16 for more information about gaming and Vista.

Software-compatibility issues in Vista are likely to appear with very old applications that use 16-bit installers and with classes of applications—especially antivirus, antispyware, and other security solutions—that need to be rewritten to work within Vista's new security controls. By mid 2007, compatibility issues with security software had all been resolved.

x64: Is It Time?

The one dark horse in the Windows Vista compatibility story is x64, the 64-bit hardware platform that we're all using today (though few people realize it). The x64 platform is a miracle of sorts, at least from a technology standpoint, because it provides the best of both worlds: compatibility with virtually all of the 32-bit software that's been created over the past 15 years combined with the increased capacity and resources that only true 64-bit platforms can provide.

When Windows Vista first debuted, x64 compatibility was a mixed bag. Hardware compatibility, surprisingly, was excellent, and virtually any hardware device that worked on 32-bit versions of Vista also worked fine on 64-bit versions. Software was another story. Too often, a critical software application simply wouldn't install or work properly on 64-bit versions of Windows, making these versions a nonstarter for most.

Time, however, truly heals all wounds. A huge number of compatibility issues were fixed over Windows Vista's first year on the market, and x64 versions of Windows Vista are now largely compatible, both from a hardware and software perspective, with anything that works with 32-bit versions of the system.

So, is it time? You're getting there. And if you're adventurous enough and technical enough, I think Vista x64 may be the right solution if you're hamstrung by the 4GB memory limit of 32-bit versions of Vista. That said, even Microsoft has been surprised by the slow uptick of 64-bit versions of Windows Vista, so much so that the company reversed course and announced that the next version of Windows, dubbed Windows 7, would ship in both 32-bit and 64-bit versions. Originally, Windows 7 was going to be 64-bit only.

Maybe it's not time after all.

Windows Vista Service Pack 1 Offers Better Compatibility

Thanks to the evolving nature of Microsoft's online software updating systems, today's Windows users can take advantage of ever-improving software and hardware compatibility. Instead of being stuck with whatever drivers and software-compatibility support that came in the box, Windows Vista users benefit from ongoing compatibility fixes that appear on Windows Update and are delivered automatically to users who need them. For users who purchase Windows Vista now that Service Pack 1 (SP1) is out, the situation is even better: All the updates that have shipped since Vista first appeared are included in this upgrade.

Antivirus is an obvious area where Windows Vista lagged behind at launch, though one might also make the argument that AV vendors were at fault. After all, they knew Vista was coming for years before it shipped. Regardless, within six months of Vista's release, all five major AV vendors had Windows Vista–compatible products on the market, compared to just three of five when Vista became generally available.

When trying to determine the success of Windows Vista's compatibility, consider the numbers. At the time of Vista's general availability in January 2007, over 1.5 million devices were Vista compatible. Less than a year later, it was over 2 million. Microsoft says that this figure represented about 96 percent of the devices on the market at the time. The company also notes that it was more ready with *ecosystem coverage*—that is, application and device support—with Vista than it was with any previous OS release, Today, Vista's compatibility with current hardware is closing in on an impressive 100 percent.

Secret

Do your part! Soon after installing Windows Vista for the first time, you'll be prompted to join Microsoft's Windows Customer Experience Improvement Program, shown in Figure 3-6. Don't ignore this offer: Participating in the program is painless and won't invade your privacy in any way. What it will do is make Windows better for everyone.

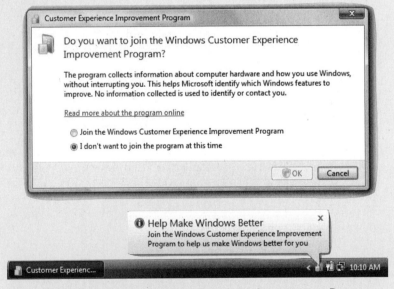

Figure 3-6: The Windows Customer Experience Improvement Program is an opt-in program through which you can help others help you.

Thanks to instrumentation that Microsoft added to Windows Vista, customers can optionally provide the company with feedback when things go wrong, as part of the Windows Customer Experience Improvement Program. This feedback has enabled the company to make fixes available at an unprecedented rate. More important, Microsoft is identifying the issues that are causing the most problems and fixing those first. Of the remaining 4 percent of incompatible devices, or about 70,000 devices, that existed at the start of 2008, 4,000 account for about 80 percent of the problems. Guess which ones Microsoft focused on first?

Microsoft tells me it will fix or create drivers for any device that generates 500 or more user reports, which further demonstrates the need to participate in the Customer Experience program. The only exception, of course, is drivers for devices that are no longer sold because the company that made them went out of business. Such devices will likely never be made compatible with Vista. As of the release of Service Pack 1, over 15,000 hardware devices have received the Certified for Windows Vista logo, a program aimed at helping consumers find Vista-compatible products. (This, by the way, explains the absence of a Hardware Compatibility List [HCL] these days.) Those looking for a seamless installation experience will be pleased to learn that the number of device drivers on Windows Update was up from about 13,000 at launch to over 54,000 with SP1, in addition to the 20,000 that ship on the Vista setup DVD.

Secret

Windows Vista SP1 also includes support for a number of new and up-and-coming hardware initiatives, including Unified Extensible Firmware Interface (UEFI) firmware on x64 systems, x64 Extensible Firmware Interface (EFI) network boot, Direct3D 10.1, the exFAT file system for flash-based devices, second-generation Windows Media Center Extenders, and so on.

How about software? Whereas the initially shipped version of Windows Vista supported about 250 logoed applications—that is, applications that were certified to be 100 percent compatible with Vista—as of the release of SP1, that number exceeded 2,500, over 10 times the original number. With SP1, 98 of the 100 top-selling applications at the time were compatible with Vista, while 46 of the top 50 online downloads were also Vista compatible.

Finally, Windows Vista SP1 also includes fixes for numerous incompatible enterprise applications that were deployment blockers during Vista's first year on the market. More specifically, Microsoft and its partners remediated over 150 enterprise application blockers, applications that previously prevented one or more corporations from upgrading to Vista.

Dealing with Software Incompatibility

Regardless of Windows Vista's compatibility successes, compatibility issues can still bite you when you least expect it. Fear not: There are ways to get around most software-incompatibility issues. You just have to know where to look.

Compatibility Mode

If you do run into an application that won't work properly in Windows Vista, first try to run it within a special emulation mode called *compatibility mode*. This enables you to trick the application into thinking it is running on an older version of Windows. There are two ways to trigger this functionality: automatically via a wizard, or manually via the Explorer shell. There's also a third related function, the Program Compatibility Assistant, which appears automatically when Windows Vista detects you're having a problem installing or using an application.

Let's take a look at all three.

Using the Program Compatibility Wizard

You'd think that using a wizard would be easier than manually configuring compatibility mode manually; and it would be if you could just find the wizard. Unfortunately, the Program Compatibility Wizard isn't available from the Windows Vista user interface. Instead, you have to trigger it from within Help and Support.

Here's how: Open the Start Menu and choose Help and Support. In that application's Search box, type Program Compatibility Wizard and press Enter. The first search result you'll see will be Start the Program Compatibility Wizard. This entry provides a link to start the wizard, which is shown in Figure 3-7.

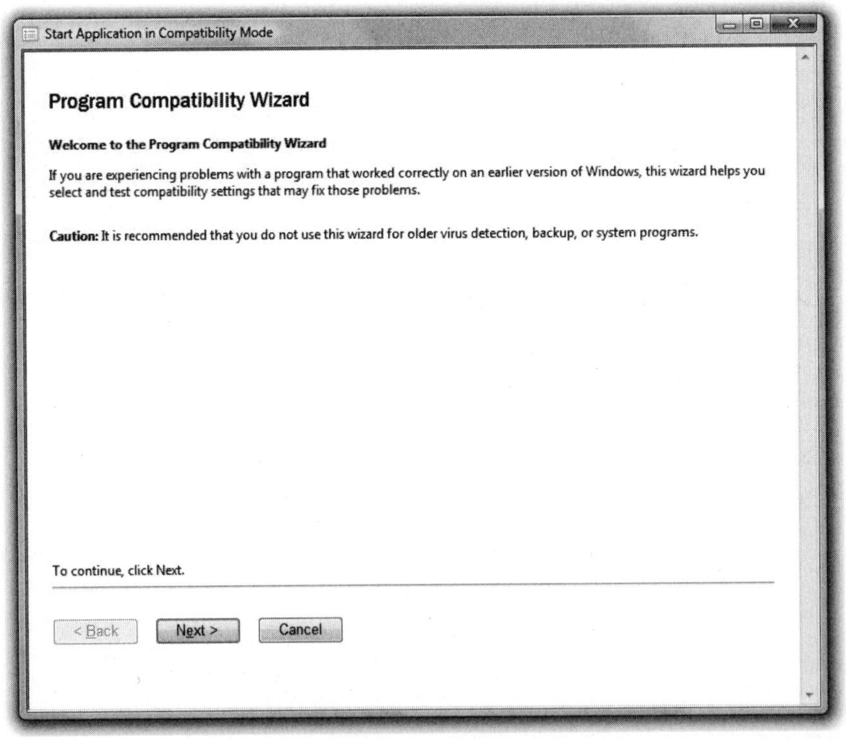

Figure 3-7: It's pretty well hidden, but the Program Compatibility Wizard might be just what you need to get that stubborn legacy application to run correctly in Windows Vista.

The admittedly bare-bones-looking Program Compatibility Wizard steps you through the process of identifying the application to run in compatibility mode and which settings you'd like to configure. These steps include the following:

- **Locating the application:** You can have the wizard automatically generate a list of potential applications, which includes applications already installed on the system as well as downloaded and optical-disk-based installer applications. Alternately, you can choose the installer in the optical (CD-ROM) drive or locate the application manually.

- **Select a compatibility mode:** Select which version of Windows you'd like to emulate for that one application. Possibilities include Windows 95, Windows 98/Me, Windows NT 4.0 (Service Pack 5), Windows 2000, Windows XP (Service Pack 2), and Windows Server 2003 (Service Pack 1). You can also choose not to use a compatibility mode.

- **Choose display settings:** You can choose from a variety of settings that might positively affect the application. These include using only 256 colors, using a 640 × 480 resolution, disabling Vista's visual themes, disabling desktop composition (which is responsible for the Windows Aero user interface), and disabling display scaling on high-DPI displays. These options can all be disabled independently.

- **Administrative privileges:** If the program must be run with administrative privileges, you can enable that functionality here.

Once you've configured things as you like, you can test-run the application to see how things work out. You can then either accept the configuration, go back and make changes, or just quit the wizard.

Enabling Compatibility Mode Manually

You don't actually have to hunt around for the Program Compatibility Wizard if you want to run an application in compatibility mode. Instead, find the executable (or, better yet, a shortcut to the executable, such as the ones you'll find in the Start Menu), right-click, and choose Properties. Then, navigate to the Compatibility tab, shown in Figure 3-8.

As you can see, this tab provides all of the options found in the wizard, but in a handier, more easily contained location. Just pick the options you'd like, click Apply, and test the application. Once it's working correctly, you can click OK and never bother with this interface again.

Compatibility mode is a great (if hidden) feature, but it's no panacea. Some applications will simply never run on Windows Vista, no matter what you do.

Secret   Compatibility mode should not be used to enable older security applications such as antivirus. These types of applications should be run only on the operating systems for which they were designed.

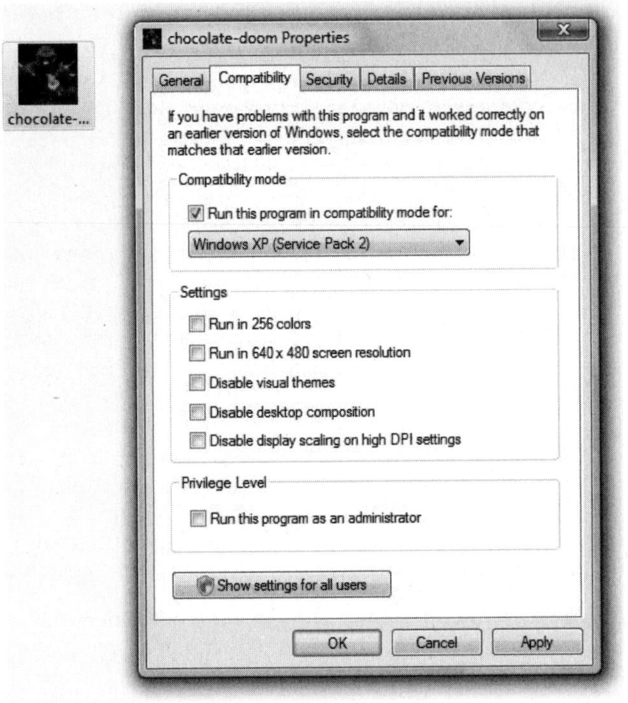

Figure 3-8: Any application can be run in compatibility mode.

Understanding the Program Compatibility Assistant

When Windows Vista detects that you're installing an application with a known compatibility problem or suspects that a just-completed application installation has not concluded successfully, it will offer to fix the problem. This functionality, called the Program Compatibility Assistant, occurs automatically, as shown in Figure 3-9. You're free to decline the offer if you believe the application ran correctly. There is no way to trigger it manually, as you can with program-compatibility mode.

Virtual PC

Virtual PC is a software solution that provides a virtual machine environment in which *guest* operating systems, with their own applications and services, can run separately and independently from the *host* environment, or physical PC. To the operating system and applications running in a virtual environment, the virtual machine appears to be a real PC, with its own hardware resources and attributes. These virtualized systems have no knowledge or understanding of the host machine at all.

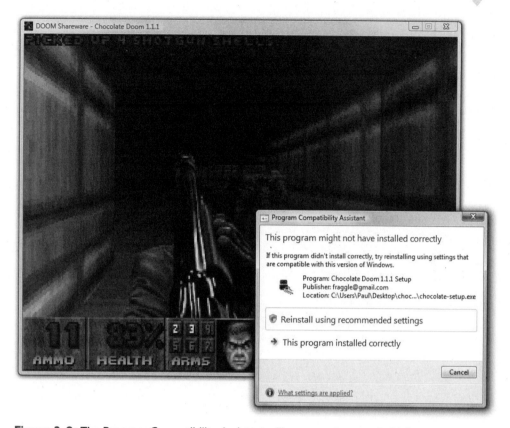

Figure 3-9: The Program Compatibility Assistant will pop up whenever it thinks you need help.

Though virtual machines cannot rival the performance of real PCs for interactive use—they're useless for graphically challenging activities such as modern, action-oriented games, for example—they are perfect for many uses. In fact, virtual machines are often used to test software in different environments, or test Web sites and Web applications with different browser versions.

For Windows Vista, virtualized environments such as Virtual PC—shown in Figure 3-10—play a special role. Because new versions of Windows are often incompatible with legacy applications, a virtual machine environment running an older version of Windows and those incompatible legacy applications can be quite valuable. Best of all, in such cases, users are often less apt to notice any performance issue because older operating systems tend to require fewer resources anyway.

Figure 3-10: Here, you can see Windows XP running inside Virtual PC on top of Windows Vista.

That said, for the best results, anyone utilizing Virtual PC to run an older operating system such as Windows XP along with whatever set of Vista-incompatible applications is well served to pack the host PC with as much RAM as physically possible. For typical PCs today, that means loading up with 4GB. Remember: You're running two operating systems and any number of applications simultaneously. That old Pentium 3 with 256MB of RAM just isn't going to cut it.

Using Virtual PC

If you want to run an incompatible application, Virtual PC should be considered your last option because of its high overhead and the confusion of running two Windows desktops side by side. The good news, however, is that Virtual PC itself is absolutely free. It used to be a paid, commercial product, and Microsoft initially planned to offer a version of Virtual PC only in the Enterprise version of Windows Vista as an enticement to corporations; but before Vista was finalized, Microsoft decided to make Virtual PC available as a free Web download for Windows users (**www.microsoft.com/virtualpc**).

Secret

Virtual PC is available in separate 32-bit and 64-bit versions. Make sure you download the correct version for your PC.

Secret Sadly, Virtual PC will not install on all versions of Windows Vista. Microsoft has artificially limited the installer so that it works only with Windows Vista Business, Enterprise, and Ultimate editions.

Virtual PC provides a very simple console window from which you can manage any virtual machine environments you create. The console displays any existing virtual machines (VMs) you've already set up, and provides access to common functions, such as individual VM settings, Virtual PC options, and the New Virtual Machine Wizard, which is used to create new virtual environments.

Shown in Figure 3-11, the New Virtual Machine Wizard can create new virtual environments using an existing virtual disk, or, more likely, by creating a new one from scratch. In the latter case, you install a new operating system just as you would normally, using the original setup CD or DVD, or an ISO image, which can be "mounted" so that it works like a physical disk from within the virtual environment.

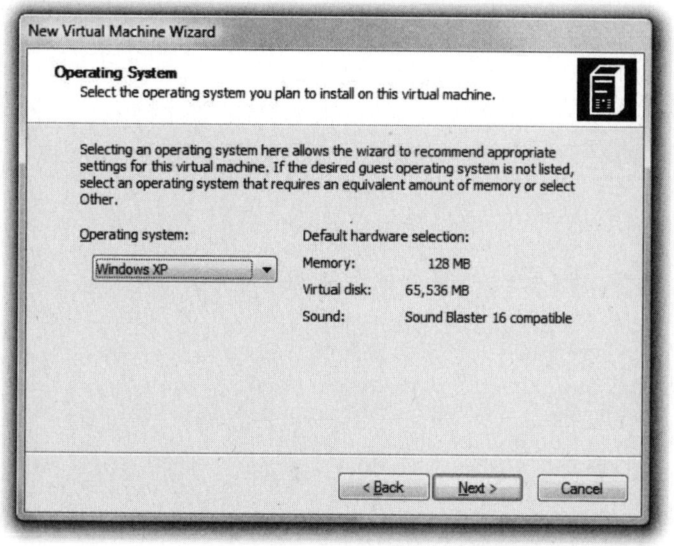

![New Virtual Machine Wizard screenshot showing Operating System selection page. Operating system: Windows XP. Default hardware selection: Memory: 128 MB, Virtual disk: 65,536 MB, Sound: Sound Blaster 16 compatible. Buttons: Back, Next, Cancel]

Figure 3-11: Virtual PC's New Virtual Machine Wizard helps you determine the makeup of the virtualized environment.

After determining the name and location of the virtual machine, you're prompted to select the operating system that the VM will contain. Virtual PC natively supports several different Windows versions, including Windows 98, NT Workstation, 2000, XP, and Vista. It also supports OS/2, Windows NT Server, Windows 2000 Server, Windows Server 2003, and Windows Server 2008.

Secret   Though Virtual PC is available in a 64-bit version, the product supports only 32-bit guest operating systems.

Noticeably absent from this list, incidentally, is any form of Linux. You can, in fact, try to install various Linux distributions in Virtual PC using an "other" OS option, but this install type has some limitations, chief among them a lack of integration with the host environment that supported guest operating systems receive. That said, many modern Linux distributions don't work correctly in Virtual PC unless you are capable of some serious tinkering. In this case, Google is your friend.

Secret   Virtual PC supports Windows Vista, but the emulated graphics subsystem utilized by this environment is not powerful enough to render the operating system's Windows Aero user interface. Therefore, if you choose to run Windows Vista in a virtual machine, you have to make do with the Windows Vista Basic user interface. The various Vista user interface types are described in Chapter 4.

After allotting some RAM to the virtual machine and choosing between an existing virtual hard drive (VHD) or a new one, you're off to the races, installing the older OS in the virtualized environment (see Figure 3-12).

In use, virtual machines are like slower versions of "real" PC installs. You can continue running guest operating systems in a Virtual PC window side by side with the host Vista system, or you can run the guest OS full-screen, making it appear as if your modern Vista-based PC has gone back in time. Virtual PC supports a variety of niceties for moving information back and forth between the host and guest operating systems, including cut-and-paste integration and the notion of a shared folder that exists in both systems so you can move files back and forth.

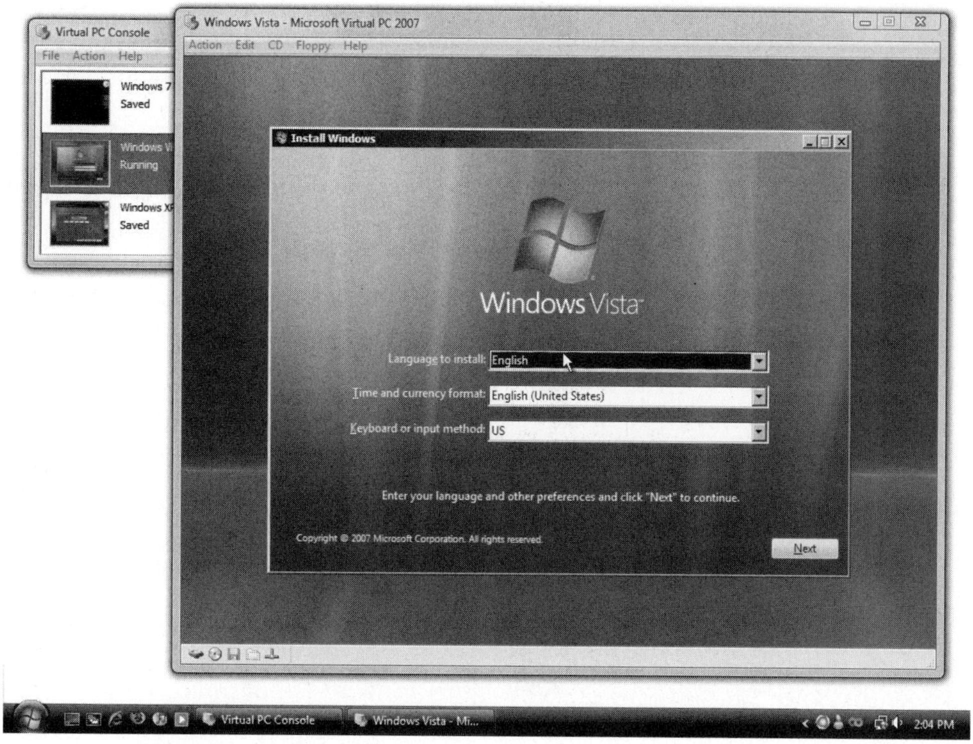

Figure 3-12: Installing a guest OS in Virtual PC.

Looking to the Future

As it stands today, Virtual PC is an interesting and, in many cases, desirable solution; but running a second operating system in a window, with its own set of applications and settings, can be confusing, and it's certainly not a viable long-term solution. Microsoft knows this, and it is evolving the virtual machine technology in Virtual PC in several important ways. These improvements, incidentally, indicate the way in which future versions of Windows will handle backward compatibility (and, I hope, make a chapter like this redundant for Windows 7 or beyond). Here's how the technology from Virtual PC is evolving:

◆ **On the server:** Microsoft created a server-based version of Virtual PC, naturally called Virtual Server, which allowed the company's largest corporate customers to consolidate aging NT-based servers into farms of virtualized environments. Virtual Server was a fine product, but it suffered from the same performance issues that Virtual PC faces. With Windows Server 2008, Microsoft created its first *hypervisor*-based virtualization solution, called Hyper-V. This technology runs closer to the metal than Virtual Server, so it offers much better performance and is more secure and easily maintainable. Despite utilizing a different architecture, however, Hyper-V is compatible with the same VHDs used by Virtual PC and

Virtual Server, ensuring that customers who adopted Microsoft's virtualization products early in the game could move their virtualized environments forward.

◆ **Application virtualization:** Microsoft purchased a company called SoftGrid and relaunched its application virtualization solution as Microsoft Application Virtualization. This software, initially aimed only at corporations, enables Microsoft customers to deploy applications in special virtualized packages. Instead of delivering an entire virtualized environment to end users, companies can deliver individual applications in a package, along with any required dependent files. These packages break the application/operating system lock and allow for some interesting scenarios, including the ability to run multiple versions of the same application on a single OS. Then, in 2007, Microsoft purchased another innovative company in the virtualization space called Kidarow. This acquisition gave Microsoft the final piece of the puzzle: the ability to combine the power of Virtual PC with the application independence of SoftGrid.

A combination of SoftGrid and Kidaro technologies will form the basis of Microsoft's compatibility story in future versions of Windows. Rather than bake backward compatibility into Windows as it has in Windows Vista and previous Windows versions, Microsoft will be able to move in completely new technical directions, secure in the knowledge that its virtualization platform will enable users to install virtually (sorry) any application that works on older versions of Windows. The key is packaging them into mini-virtualized environments that include only those parts of Windows XP, Windows 98, or whatever they need in order to run.

Virtual PC is just the start.

Summary

Windows Vista constitutes, in many ways, a break with the past, but that doesn't necessarily mean you have to make a break with your existing hardware or software just yet. Using Microsoft's Windows Vista Upgrade Advisor, you can determine whether your current PC is powerful enough to run Windows Vista and, if so, which of your existing hardware devices will work properly after the upgrade. After installing Windows Vista, however, you're not on your own. Service Pack 1 adds dramatic compatibility improvements; and features such as program compatibility, the Program Compatibility Wizard, and the Program Compatibility Assistant can force older Windows applications to run fine in Vista. If that doesn't work, there are always virtualization solutions, including Microsoft's free Virtual PC. Chances are good there's a way to make your existing devices work.

Part II

The Windows Vista User Experience

What's New in the Windows Vista User Interface

Chapter

4

◆ ◆

In This Chapter

Exploring the various Windows Vista user experiences

Understanding what you need to run Windows Aero

Examining the Windows Vista shell with Explorer

◆ ◆

Gazing upon Windows Vista for the first time, you will immediately be struck by how different everything looks when compared to older Windows versions such as Windows XP and Windows 2000. Now, windows are translucent and glass-like, with subtle animations and visual cues. This new interface leaves no doubt: Windows Vista is a major new Windows version, with much to learn and explore. In this chapter, you'll examine the new Windows Vista user interface, called Aero, and learn what you need to know to adapt to this new system.

Understanding the Windows Vista User Experience

When the first PCs hit the streets over 20 years ago, users were saddled with an unfriendly, nonintuitive user interface based on the MS-DOS command line and its ubiquitous C:\ prompt. Since then, computer user interfaces have come a long way, first with the advent of the mouse-driven graphical user interface (GUI) on the Macintosh and later in Windows, and then with the proliferation of Internet connectivity in the late 1990s, which blurred the line between local and remote content and led to the currently emerging era of "cloud computing," whereby PC-like user interfaces are available on the Web.

Microsoft has been at the forefront of the evolution of state-of-the-art computer GUIs for the masses over the years. Windows 95 introduced the notion of right-clicking on objects in the operating system to discover context-sensitive options; Windows 98 introduced a shell, Explorer, that was based on the same code found in the Internet Explorer Web browser; and Windows XP began a trend toward task-oriented user interfaces, with folder views that change depending on the content you are viewing or have selected.

In Windows Vista, the Windows user interface, or as Microsoft likes to call it, the Windows *user experience*, has evolved yet again. Assuming you are running a mainstream Vista product edition (Windows Vista Home Basic and Starter editions need not apply) and have the right kind of display hardware, you are presented with a translucent, glass-like interface that takes the Windows user interface metaphor to its logical conclusion. That's right: In Windows Vista, windows actually appear to be made of glass, just like real windows. (Unfortunately, you can also break Windows as easily as the real thing, a fact driven home by the wide range of electronic attacks we've all experienced over the years.)

At a higher level, however, it may be comforting to understand that much in Windows Vista has not changed since XP. That is, you still press a Start button (though it's now officially called the Start Orb, I'll continue to call it the Start button) to launch the Start Menu, from where you can perform tasks such as launch applications; access the Control Panel, networking features, and other related functionality; and turn off the system. A taskbar still runs along the bottom of the Windows Vista desktop, containing buttons for each open window and application, and a tray notification area still sits in the lower-right corner of the screen, full of notification icons and the system clock. The desktop still contains icons and shortcuts.

Windows still appear to float above this desktop, and all of your familiar applications and documents will still work, especially now that Service Pack 1 is available. The high-end Windows Aero user experience is shown in Figure 4-1.

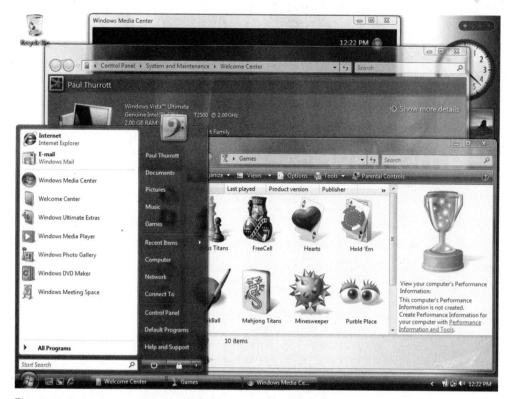

Figure 4-1: Windows Vista offers this high-end user experience.

Secret

What you see in Windows Vista depends largely on which version of Vista you're using, the hardware in your system, and your own personal preferences. More confusing, perhaps, is that you likely won't see options for all four of the user experiences Microsoft offers in Vista. However, the method you use for changing between these experiences is the same for all Vista product editions except for Starter Edition: You need to access the classic Appearance Settings dialog box, which will look familiar if you're used to previous Windows versions. To access this dialog box, right-click the Desktop and choose Personalize. Then, click the Window Color and Appearance link in the Personalization appearance and sound effects control panel window that appears. Finally, click the link titled "Open classic appearance properties for more color options." (Whew!)

This old-school dialog box enables you to switch between what Microsoft still calls, disconcertingly, *color schemes* (see Figure 4-2). Windows Aero is the high-end user experience, and the one you'll likely want (it's not available in Vista Home Basic or Starter). Windows Vista Basic is the simplest version of the new user interface, and it is available to all Vista editions, including Starter. Windows Vista Standard (not to be confused with the Windows Standard color scheme) is available only in Windows Vista Home Basic, so many readers won't see this option.

continues

continued

Windows Classic is available to all Vista editions, and all of the color schemes except for Windows Aero, Windows Vista Standard, and Windows Vista Basic actually utilize the Classic user experience.

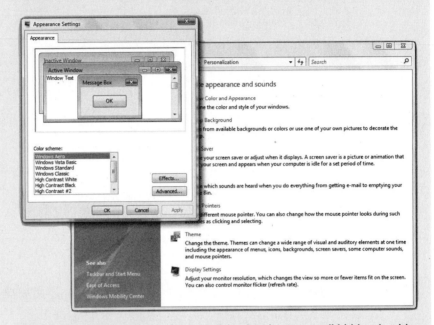

Figure 4-2: The Appearance Settings dialog box is pretty well hidden, but it's the secret to switching between various user experience types.

Table 4-1 summarizes the different user experiences and which product editions you need to access them.

Table 4-1: Which User Experiences Work in Which Windows Vista Product Editions

User Experience	*Available in Which Windows Vista Product Editions*
Windows Vista Classic	All
Windows Vista Basic	All
Windows Vista Standard	Home Basic only
Windows Aero	Home Premium, Business, Enterprise, Ultimate

There are other requirements for some of these user experiences, however. The following sections highlight the different user experiences that Microsoft has included in Windows Vista, and explain how and when you might see them.

Windows Classic

Like Windows XP, Windows Vista includes a user experience called Windows Classic that resembles the user interfaces that Microsoft shipped with Windows 95, 98, Me, and 2000. (It most closely resembles Windows 2000.) This interface is available on all Windows Vista product editions, including Starter Edition. Classic is included in Windows Vista primarily for businesses that don't want to undergo the expense of retraining their employees to use the newer user experiences.

Secret

Even though Microsoft markets Windows Classic as being identical to the Windows 2000 look and feel, in fact there are numerous differences. Therefore, users will still require some training when moving from Windows 2000 to Windows Vista and Classic mode, or will need to reconfigure various Windows Classic features so the system more closely resembles Windows 2000. For example, the Start Menu and Explorer windows still retain the layouts that debuted with Windows Vista, and not the styles you might be used to in Windows 2000, although you can fix this somewhat. To use the old Start Menu, right-click the Start button and choose Properties. Then, select the option titled Classic Start Menu, and click OK. It's a bit more complicated to use a Windows Explorer look and feel that is closer to that of Windows 2000. To do so, select Computer from the Start Menu and then press the Alt key to display the Classic menu (which is hidden by default in Windows Vista). Select Folder Options from the Tools menu to display the Folder Options dialog. Then select the option titled Use Windows classic folders and click OK. *Voilà!* Your system should now look a lot more like Windows 2000 (see Figure 4-3).

Figure 4-3: Windows Classic enables Vista users to enjoy the Windows 2000 user interface.

Secret

If you work in the IT department of a business that is considering deploying Windows Vista, you can actually roll out a feature called Classic Mode via Group Policy (GP) that does, in fact, configure Windows Vista to look almost exactly like Windows 2000. Classic Mode essentially combines the Classic user experience with the secrets mentioned previously.

Windows Vista Basic

Windows Vista Basic is the entry-level desktop user experience in Windows Vista and the one you will see on Windows Vista Home Basic or in other editions if you don't meet certain hardware requirements, which I'll discuss shortly. From a technological perspective, Windows Vista Basic renders the Windows desktop in roughly the same way as does Windows XP, meaning it doesn't take advantage of Vista's new graphical prowess and enhanced stability. That said, Vista Basic still provides you with many of the unique features that make Vista special, such as integrated desktop search—available via a search box in the upper-right corner of every Explorer window—and Live Icons, which show live previews of the contents of document files. The Windows Vista Basic user experience is shown in Figure 4-4.

Secret

Windows Vista Basic isn't as attractive as Windows Aero, but there are actually some advantages to using it. For starters, it offers better performance than Aero, so it's a good bet for lower-end computers. Notebook and Tablet PC users will notice that Vista Basic actually provides better battery life than Aero too, so if you're on the road and not connected to a power source, Vista Basic is a thriftier choice if you're trying to maximize runtime.

Conversely, Windows Vista Basic has a few major, if non-obvious, disadvantages. Because it uses XP-era display rendering techniques, Windows Vista Basic is not as stable and reliable as Aero and could thus lead to system crashes and even "blue screen of death" crashes because of poorly written display drivers. Aero display drivers are typically far more reliable, and the Aero display itself is inherently superior to that offered by Basic. Nor does Vista Basic enable you to use some unique Vista features, such as Flip 3D and taskbar thumbnails, that require Aero technologies.

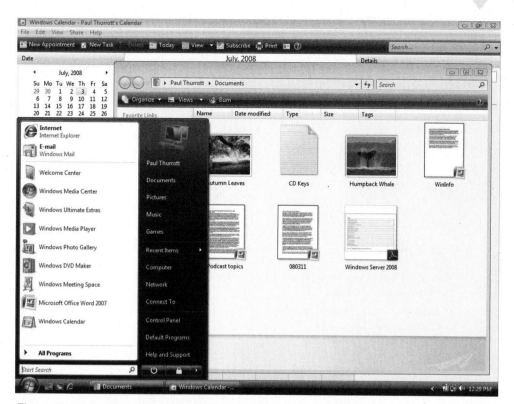

Figure 4-4: Even Windows Vista Basic is capable of displaying Live Icons.

Even if you are running Windows Aero, you may still run into the occasional issue that causes the display to flash and suddenly revert back to Windows Vista Basic. For example, some older applications aren't compatible with Windows Aero; when you run such an application, the user experience will revert to Windows Vista Basic. When you close the offending application, Aero returns. In other cases, certain applications that use custom window rendering will actually display in a Windows Vista Basic style, even though all of the other windows in the system are utilizing Aero. These are the issues you have to deal with when Microsoft makes such a dramatic change to the Windows rendering engine, apparently. The good news is that these glitches are significantly less common with Windows Vista and Service Pack 1 (SP1). Most modern Windows applications work just fine with Aero.

Windows Vista Standard

This oddball user experience is designed specifically for Vista Home Basic users and is an olive branch, of sorts, to those who have the hardware required to run Windows Aero but cannot do so because that user experience is not included in Home Basic.

Secret   Windows Vista Standard has the same hardware requirements as Aero, as described in the next section.

Vista Standard is essentially a visual compromise between Vista Basic and Windows Aero. That is, it features the look and feel of Windows Aero, minus the translucency effects. Under the hood, however, it utilizes the less-sophisticated display technologies utilized by Windows Vista Basic.

In addition to lacking Aero's transparency feature, Windows Vista Standard also dispenses with many other Aero features, such as Flip 3D and live taskbar thumbnails. Windows Vista Standard is shown in Figure 4-5.

Figure 4-5: Windows Vista Standard looks like Windows Aero, but without the translucency and Aero effects.

tip   If you are running Windows Vista Home Basic and would like to upgrade to Aero, you need to utilize Vista's unique Windows Anytime Upgrade service—available to Vista Home Basic and Home Premium customers—to upgrade to Windows Vista Home Premium or Ultimate Edition. I discuss Windows Anytime Upgrade in Chapter 2.

Windows Aero

Windows Aero is the premium user experience in Windows Vista and the one most users will want to access. It provides a number of unique features. First, Windows Aero enables the new Aero Glass look and feel in which the Start Menu, the taskbar, and all onscreen windows and dialog boxes take on a new glass-like translucent sheen. In Figure 4-6, you can see how overlapping objects translucently reveals what's underneath.

Figure 4-6: The Aero Glass effect provides a heightened sense of depth and a more professional-looking user experience.

Aero Glass is designed to move the visual focus away from the windows themselves and to the content they contain. Whether that effort is successful is open to debate, but it's certainly true that window borders have lost the vast, dark-colored title bars of previous Windows versions and provide a softer-looking and more organic-looking container around window contents. Compare Windows XP's My Computer window to Windows Vista's Computer window in Figure 4-7.

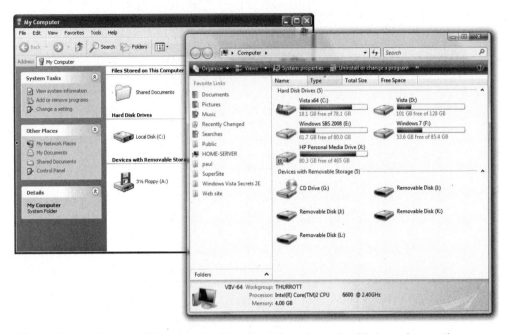

Figure 4-7: In Windows XP, too much of the visual focus is on the title bar, whereas the software window chrome in Windows Vista puts the focus on the contents of the window.

tip

When you have a lot of Aero windows open onscreen, it's often hard to tell which one is on top or has the focus. Typically, that window will have a bright red Close window button, whereas other windows will not.

When you utilize the Windows Aero user experience, you receive other benefits. Certain Windows Vista features, for example, are available only when you're using Aero. Windows Flip and Flip 3D, two new task-switching features, are available only in Aero. Windows Flip 3D is shown in Figure 4-8.

Secret

Windows Flip and Flip 3D are most typically accessed via keyboard shortcuts. The trick, of course, is that you have to know those shortcuts. To use Windows Flip, hold down the Alt key and press the Tab key to cycle between all of the running applications and open windows. To use Flip 3D, hold down the Windows key and press the Tab key to cycle between these windows.

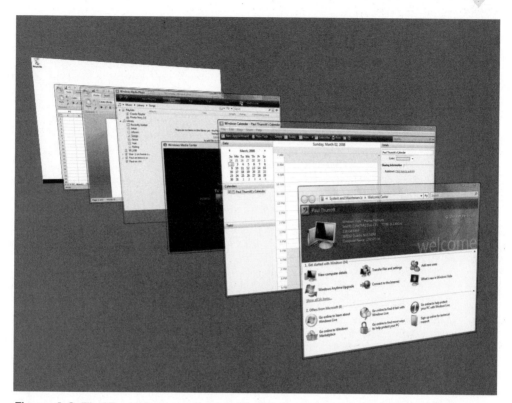

Figure 4-8: Flip 3D enables you to inspect all of the running tasks and pick the window you want.

Aero also enables dynamic window animations, so that when you minimize a window to the taskbar, it subtly animates to show you exactly where it went. This kind of functionality was actually first introduced in Windows 95, but it has been made more subtle and fluid in Windows Vista. Additionally, Aero enables *live taskbar thumbnails*: When you mouse over buttons in the taskbar, a small thumbnail preview will pop up, showing you the window without actually activating it first, as shown in Figure 4-9.

Figure 4-9: Live taskbar thumbnails make it possible to preview windows without maximizing them or bringing them to the forefront.

In addition to its obvious visual charms, Windows Aero also offers lower-level improvements that provide a more reliable desktop experience than you might be used to with previous Windows versions. Thanks to a new graphics architecture based on DirectX video-game libraries, Windows Vista can move windows across the screen without any of the visual tearing or glitches that were common in Windows XP. The effect is most prominent in windows with animated content, such as when you're playing a video in Windows Media Player (WMP). But it's not just about looks. Windows Aero is simply more reliable than the other user experiences. To understand why that's so, you need to examine Aero's strict hardware and software requirements.

Windows Aero Requirements

As noted earlier, you have to be running Vista Home Premium, Business, Enterprise, or Ultimate Edition in order to utilize Windows Aero. Windows Aero is not available in Vista Starter or Home Basic.

Next, your display adapter must meet certain technical requirements. That is, it must support DirectX 9.0 with Pixel Shader 2 in hardware and be supported by a new Windows Display Driver Model (WDDM) driver. The WDDM driver requirement is part of the reason why Aero is so much more reliable than other Vista user experiences: To become WDDM certified, a driver must pass certain Microsoft tests focused around making these drivers of higher quality.

Additionally, your graphics card must have enough dedicated memory (RAM) to drive your display. Table 4-2 explains how much video RAM you need to run Windows Aero at particular screen resolutions.

Table 4-2: Video RAM Needed to Drive Certain Resolutions

Video RAM	Display Resolution
64MB	Lower than 1280 x 1024 (fewer than 1,310,720 pixels)
128MB	1280 x 1024 to 1920 x 1200 (1,310,720 to 2,304,000 pixels)
256MB	Higher than 1920 x 1200 (more than 2,304,000 pixels)

Secret

Microsoft makes these requirements sound so difficult and complicated. In fact, virtually every single 3D graphics card on the market, as well as Intel's low-end Graphics Media Accelerator 950 integrated graphics chipset, is capable of running Windows Aero. In addition, most of today's graphics cards come with at least 128MB of RAM. Note, however, that most older integrated graphics chipsets, such as those found on most notebooks and Tablet PCs sold before 2005, are not compatible with Windows Aero. Furthermore, in order to obtain Aero on a system with integrated graphics, at least 512MB of system RAM must be available after the integrated graphics reserves whatever it needs.

Configuring Windows Aero

If you're not a big fan of the translucent glass effects provided by Windows Aero but would still like to take advantage of the other unique features and reliability offered by this user experience, take heart. Microsoft has nicely provided Aero with a handy configuration utility that enables you to fine-tune how it looks.

This functionality is available via the Personalization section of the Control Panel. The quickest way to get there is to right-click a blank area of the desktop, choose Properties, and then select Window Color and Appearance from the Personalization appearance and sound effects control panel. This window, shown in Figure 4-10, enables you to change various aspects of Aero's visual style.

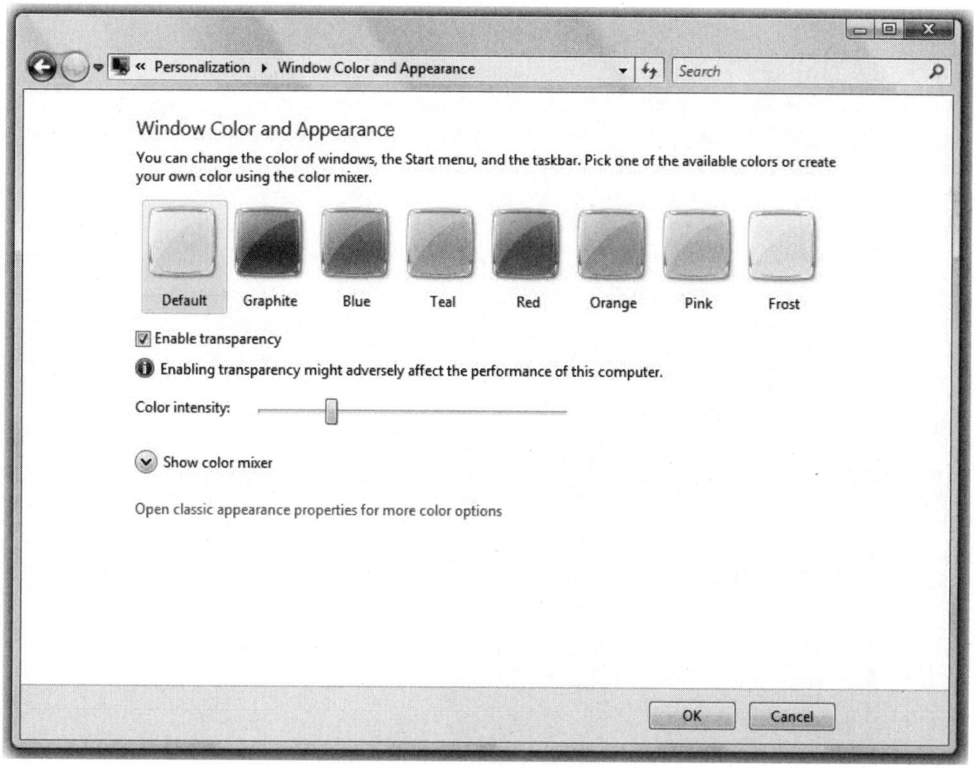

Figure 4-10: Change the color scheme or transparency of Aero windows with this utility.

First, you can pick between preset color options by selecting one of the color scheme swatches shown at the top of the window. Second, you can disable transparent glass (translucency) or vary the intensity of the translucency to meet your liking. Finally, you can expand the color mixer option and apply varying levels of color, saturation, and brightness to achieve just the look and feel you want. Click the Show Color Mixer option to expose the color mixer.

tip   In my experience, most of the preset color options just make Aero windows look dirty. The exception is Frost, which is very clean looking. You might also find some success with varying the intensity of the translucency effect or by just disabling it all together. Personally, after playing around with this feature a lot, I've finally left it with the default look and feel.

Exploring with the Windows Vista Explorer Shell

Regardless of which user experience you choose, you're going to notice a number of visual and functional changes as you begin navigating around Windows Vista. This section highlights the most important changes you should be aware of and helps you find some old favorites buried in the transition.

Start Menu

The Start Menu, shown in Figure 4-11, has been enhanced since Windows XP to make it easier to use and better looking. Like its predecessor, you access the Start Menu by pressing the Start Orb, which replaces the Start button in previous Windows versions and now resembles a rounded Windows flag. It no longer includes the word "Start." Presumably, most users understand how this button works by now.

Figure 4-11: The Windows Vista Start Menu.

Like the Windows XP Start Menu, the Vista Start Menu is divided vertically into two halves. On the left half is a list of your most recently used applications; on top of that, two application types—Web browser and e-mail—are pinned so that they're always accessible. On the right is a list of special shell folders and other system locations and tasks that you might need to access frequently.

You can modify the upper-left portion of the Start Menu in two ways. One, you can determine which Web browser and e-mail application appear in these special locations. To do so, right-click the Start button, choose Properties, and then click the Customize button in the Start Menu Properties dialog box. In the Customize Start Menu dialog box that appears, pick the Web browser and e-mail applications you prefer from the drop-down lists next to Internet link and E-mail link, respectively. Alternately, deselect either or both options if you don't want them to appear on the Start Menu.

You can also drag shortcuts to your favorite applications into this area and "pin" them permanently. To do so, select the shortcut you want to pin from the Start Menu and drag it up above the line that separates the Internet and E-mail links from the most recently used application list. To remove a shortcut from this area, right-click it and choose Remove from This List.

Accessing All Programs

At the bottom of the most recently used applications list, you'll see the familiar All Programs link. However, in Windows Vista, this link behaves quite differently from the All Programs link in Windows XP, which launches a cascading series of menus when clicked. Now, in Windows Vista, this link expands the Start Menu's All Programs submenu directly within the Start Menu itself. As with XP, you don't have to click the link to make that happen. Instead, you can simply mouse over it. In Figure 4-12, after hovering the cursor over All Programs, the submenu opens, replacing the most frequently used application list.

This change was made for a number of reasons. First, expanding All Programs inside the Start Menu eliminates the sometimes maddening pause that occurs in Windows XP when you click or mouse over the All Programs link. Second, many users found the cascading menu system used previously to be hard to navigate. How many times have you expanded submenu after submenu, only to inadvertently move the mouse cursor off the menu and cause the whole thing to disappear? It's happened to the best of us.

To navigate through the various submenus linked from All Programs, you simply have to click various folders. When you do so, the menu expands in place and scrollbars appear so you can move around within the menu structure. As shown in Figure 4-13, submenus that expand within the current view are easier to navigate than cascading menus.

Figure 4-12: No more fumbling with cascading menus.

Figure 4-13: With the new Start Menu, you never have to worry about losing your place.

Those more comfortable with the keyboard can easily navigate the new Start Menu as well. To do so, click the Windows key or the Ctrl+Esc keyboard shortcut to open the Start Menu. Then, press the up arrow key once to highlight All Programs. To expand All Programs, press the right arrow key. Then, use the arrow keys to navigate around the list of shortcuts and folders. Anytime you want to expand a submenu (indicated by a folder icon), press the right arrow key. To close or contract a submenu, press the left arrow key. To run the selected shortcut, press Enter.

Searching for Applications

One of the most important new features in Windows Vista is its integrated search functionality. Although you might think that this feature is limited only to finding documents and music files, you can actually use it for a variety of tasks; and depending on where you are in the Vista interface, those searches will be context sensitive. When you search from the Start Menu's useful new Search box, located on the left side of the menu underneath All Programs, you will typically be searching for applications. You can also use this feature to launch applications quickly, when you know their names. This is especially useful for applications such as the Reliability and Performance Monitor that are somewhat difficult to find elsewhere in Windows Vista.

The Search Menu's search feature isn't limited to searching applications. You can also use it to search Internet Explorer Favorites or History. You can also search the Internet or both the Internet and the local file system at the same time. To do so, type in a search query and then click either the Search the Internet or the Search Everywhere link that appears. Results from these searches will appear in separate windows (Internet searches in your default Web browser and computer/Internet searches in a Windows Explorer window). To find out more about searching the file system and constructing your own saved searches, please refer to Chapter 5.

Here's how it works. When you open the Start Menu and begin typing, whatever you type is automatically placed in the Search box. For example, suppose you want to run Notepad. You could always click the Start button, expand All Programs, expand Accessories, and then click the Notepad icon. Alternately, you could press the Windows key and just type **notepad**. As you type, applications that match the text appear in a list, as shown in Figure 4-14. When you see the application you want, use the arrow keys (or mouse cursor) to select it. Notepad will start normally.

The Start Search is even better than this. You don't have to type the entire name of an application. Instead, you can just start typing the first few letters. For example, on most systems, just typing **no** should be enough to display Notepad as the first choice in the found-programs list. That is, you could just type **no** and then press Enter to run Notepad. Try this shortcut with some favorite applications to see how little typing is actually required. The aforementioned Reliability and Performance monitor can be selected by simply typing **re**; and Device Manager comes up with a quick **de**. Nice!

Figure 4-14: The new integrated search feature makes short work of finding the application you want.

Secret

Microsoft thinks that this new search feature will replace the old Run command that appeared in previous versions of the Start Menu. (I think they're right, for whatever that's worth.) However, it's possible that some users will prefer to use the old Run command, which brings up a small dialog box and maintains a history of previously accessed commands. (I'm looking at you, Luddite.) Good news: You can turn it on. To enable the Run command in Vista's Start Menu, right-click the Start Orb, choose Properties, and then click the Customize button. Scroll down the list until you see the Run command option (the list is alphabetical) and then select it. Click OK and then OK again to see the Run command back where it used to be.

Accessing Special Shell Folders and System Locations

On the right side of the Start Menu is a list of commands that are vaguely similar to what appears on the XP Start Menu. However, many of the names have changed. For example, My Documents is now named Documents, My Pictures is now Pictures, My Music is now

Music, My Computer is now Computer, and My Network Places is now Network. There are some new items, too, as well as some missing items that were present in XP.

The first thing you may notice in this area is the addition of a new command, which has the same name as your user account. If you're logged on as Paul, for example, the first link on the right side of the Start Menu will also be named Paul. When you click this link, it opens a Windows Explorer window displaying the contents of your user folder, which is found in C:\Users*Your User Name*, by default, and contains folders such as Documents, Pictures, Music, and so on. It's unclear to me why you would ever need to access this folder, except in rare circumstances. (Here's one: Your Videos folder is available here and cannot be added to the Start Menu or easily accessed in any other way.) For this reason, you may simply want to remove it from the Start Menu and replace it with a more frequently needed command. Start Menu customization is covered in the next section.

The Games link is also new to Windows Vista. This opens the new Games Explorer, which provides access both to games that came with Windows and to those you might purchase separately.

cross ref   You'll examine Vista's Games functionality in Chapter 16.

tip   One feature some people might miss with the new Start Menu is the capability to quickly cause the system to shut down, restart, sleep, or hibernate using just the keyboard. In Windows XP, you could tap the Windows key, press U, and then U for shutdown, R for restart, S for sleep, or H for hibernate (the latter of which was a hidden option). Because of the new Start Menu Search feature in the Windows Vista Start Menu, these shortcuts no longer work, but you can still perform these actions with the keyboard in Windows Vista. Now, however, you have to tap the Windows key and then press the right arrow key three times to activate the Lock This Computer submenu, which links to the aforementioned options as well as to Switch User, Log Off, Lock, and, if you have a notebook computer with a docking station, Undock. The default option—that is, the one that is selected after you tap the right arrow key three times—is shut down.

And while I'm on this topic, notice that the Lock This Computer menu is, alas, a pop-up menu similar to the All Programs menu in Windows XP. Why Microsoft figured it was OK to kill pop-up menus in one place but add them back in another is a mystery.

Start Menu Customization

Although the Windows Vista Start Menu is a big improvement over its predecessor, you will likely want to customize it to match your needs. I've already discussed how you access this functionality: Right-click the Start button, choose Properties, and then click the Customize button. Table 4-3 summarizes the available options.

Table 4-3: Start Menu Customization Options

Start Menu Option	What It Does	Default Value
Computer	Determines whether the Computer item appears as a link or menu, or is not displayed. This was called My Computer in Windows XP.	Display as a link
Connect To	Determines whether the Connect To item appears. If you have a wireless network adapter, this item will trigger a submenu.	Enabled
Control Panel	Determines whether the Control Panel item appears as a link or menu, or is not displayed.	Display as a link
Default Programs	Determines whether the Default Program item appears. This item was called Set Program Access and Defaults in Windows XP with Service Pack 2. In Windows Vista, it launches the new Default Programs Control Panel.	Enabled
Documents	Determines whether the Documents item appears as a link or menu, or is not displayed. This was called My Documents in Windows XP.	Display as a link
Enable dragging and dropping	Determines whether you can drag and drop icons around the Start Menu in order to change the way they are displayed.	Enabled
Favorites menu	Determines whether the Favorites menu item appears.	Disabled
Games	Determines whether the Games item appears as a link or menu, or is not displayed.	Enabled
Help	Determines whether the Help item appears. This item launches Help and Support.	Enabled
Highlight newly installed programs	Determines whether newly installed applications are highlighted so you can find them easily.	Enabled
Local User Storage	Determines whether the User Name item appears as a link or menu, or is not displayed.	Enabled
Music	Determines whether the Music item appears as a link or menu, or is not displayed. This was called My Music in Windows XP.	Enabled
Network	Determines whether the Network item appears as a link or menu, or is not displayed. This was called My Network Places in Windows XP.	Enabled
Open submenus when I pause on them with the mouse pointer	Determines whether mousing over a submenu (like All Programs) will cause that submenu to open (or expand).	Enabled

continues

Table 4-3: *(continued)*

Start Menu Option	What It Does	Default Value
Pictures	Determines whether the Pictures item appears as a link or menu, or is not displayed.	Enabled
Printers	Determines whether the Printers menu item appears.	Disabled
Run command	Determines whether the Run command item appears.	Disabled
Search (no longer available with Service Pack 1)	Determines whether the Search item appears. This item launches a Windows Explorer search window. Note that the capability to enable this option is removed when Vista is upgraded to Service Pack 1.	Enabled in the original version of Vista; n/a with SP1
Search box	Determines whether the Start Menu's integrated search box appears.	Enabled
Search Communications	Determines whether the Start Menu's integrated search box searches for communications (e-mail, contacts, instant messaging messages).	Enabled
Search Files	Determines whether the Start Menu's integrated search box searches for files and, if so, whether to search all files or just the current users files.	Enabled
Search Programs	Determines whether the Start Menu's integrated search box searches for applications.	Enabled
Sort All Programs menu by name	Determines whether the All Programs submenu is organized alphabetically.	Enabled
System Administrative Tools	Determines whether the System Administrative Tools item appears on the All Programs menu, on the All Programs menu and the Start Menu, or is not displayed.	Disabled
Use large icons	Determines whether the left side of the Start Menu renders large icons. Otherwise, small icons are used.	Enabled

Advanced Start Menu Customization

One of the features of the Start Menu that's not immediately obvious is that it is composed of items from the following two different locations, both of which are hidden by default:

  ◆ **Within your user profile:** By default, C:\Users*Your User Name*\AppData\Roaming\Microsoft\Windows\Start Menu

  ◆ **Inside the profile for the Public user account that is common (or public) to all users:** Typically, C:\ProgramData\Microsoft\Windows\Start Menu

If you navigate to these locations with Windows Explorer, you can drill down into the folder structures and shortcuts that make up your own Start Menu, as shown in Figure 4-15. What's odd is that these two locations are combined, or aggregated, to form the Start Menu you access every day.

Secret It's much easier to access these folders by right-clicking on the Start button. To access your own private portion of the Start Menu, choose Open from the right-click menu. To access the Public portion of the Start Menu, choose Open All Users.

Why would you want to access these locations? Although it's possible to customize the Start Menu by dragging and dropping shortcuts like you might have done with Windows XP, doing so can become tedious. Instead, you can simply access these folders directly, move things around as you see fit, all while opening the Start Menu occasionally to make sure you're getting the results you expect. For example, you might want to create handy subfolders such as Digital Media, Internet, and Utilities, rather than accept the default structure.

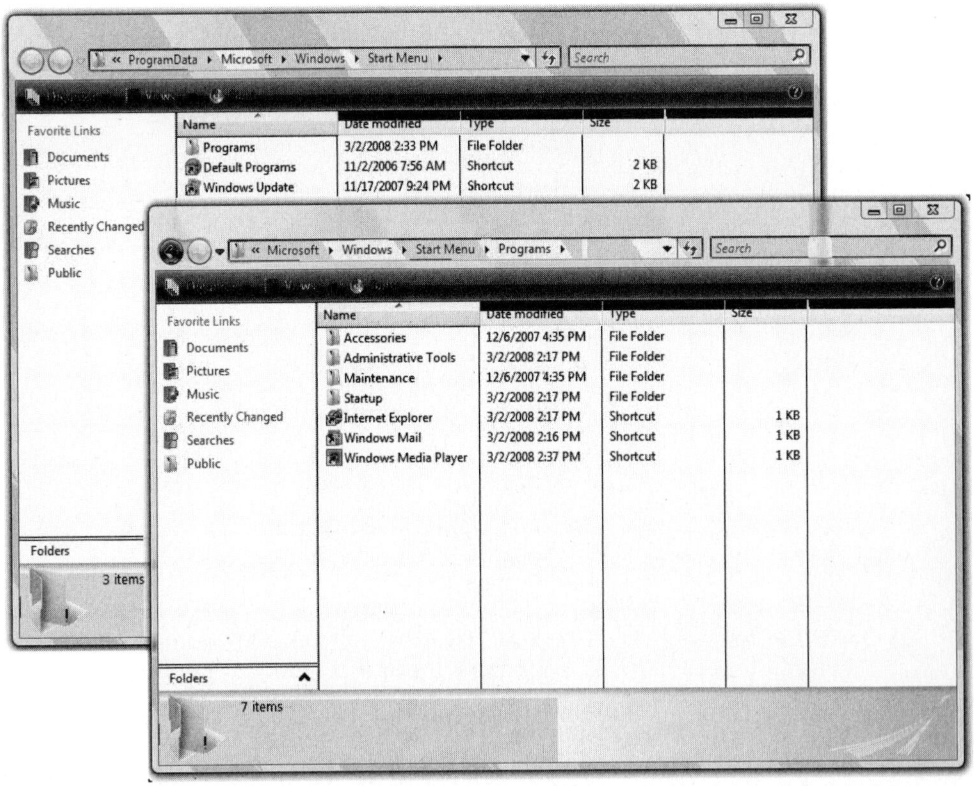

Figure 4-15: Fully customizing the Start Menu requires a bit of spelunking in two different folder structures.

Secret

Be careful when you customize the Start Menu this way. Any changes you make to the Public Start Menu structure will affect any other users who log on to your PC as well.

Desktop

At first glance, the Windows Vista desktop looks very similar to that of Windows XP. Well, looks can be deceiving. In fact, Microsoft has made some much-overdue and quite welcome changes to the Windows desktop, although of course with these changes comes a new set of skills to master.

For the most part, you access desktop options through the pop-up menu that appears when you right-click an empty part of the Windows desktop. In Windows XP, this menu has options such as Arrange Icons By, Refresh, Paste, Paste Shortcut, Undo, New, and Properties. In Windows Vista, naturally, this has all changed.

At the top of the right-click menu is a new submenu, called View, shown in Figure 4-16. This submenu enables you to configure features Windows users have been requesting for years: You can now switch between Large Icons, Medium Icons, and Classic Icons; you can select auto-arrange and alignment options; and you can hide the desktop icons altogether, as you could in XP.

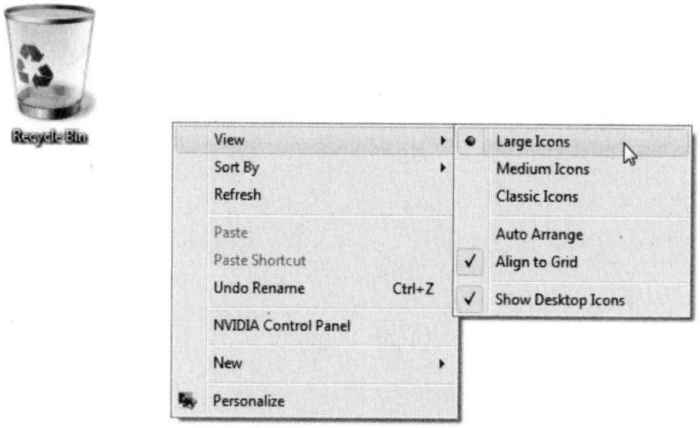

Figure 4-16: Something old, something new: Microsoft changes menus arbitrarily again, but in this case you get some new functionality.

The Sort By submenu is similar to the top part of the Windows XP Arrange Icons By submenu. Here, you get sorting options for Name, Size, Type (as in file extension), and Date Modified. The Refresh, Paste, Paste Shortcut, Undo, and New items all carry over from XP as well.

Those of you lucky enough to have Windows Vista Ultimate will see a unique option below Undo in this context-sensitive menu, assuming you have installed the Windows DreamScene Ultimate Extra, which enables you to replace the static desktop background with an animated movie. This option, Play DreamScene, enables you to start and stop the DreamScene desktop animation.

As with Windows XP, Windows Vista includes a New menu item in the Desktop properties menu that enables you to create new objects on the desktop. These objects include folders, shortcuts, and a variety of document types; the exact document types shown here vary from system to system, depending on which applications you've installed. Some of these document types are installed as part of Vista, such as Bitmap Image and Text Document, while others show up as part of a separate application install. The option Microsoft Office Word Document, for example, is installed with Microsoft Office or Word.

Secret

Most of these objects are pretty useless: When was the last time you needed to create an empty bitmap image on your desktop? They are relics from Windows 95, when Microsoft was pushing a then-new document-centric computing model that, frankly, never took off. That said, I find the New Folder option to be quite useful. My vote for most useless new object, however, has to go to New Shortcut. I'm reasonably sure that the only people on earth who ever actually created a shortcut using this method were the people who had to document this feature for a book they were writing. I'm astonished it's still available in Windows Vista.

At the bottom of the right-click menu is another new option, dubbed Personalize. This replaces the Properties option from XP and now displays the Control Panel's Personalization section when selected. From here, you can access a wide range of personalization options, only some of which have anything to do with the desktop.

Secret

One of the big questions you likely have, of course, is what the heck happened to the familiar Display Properties dialog box that's graced every version of Windows from Windows 95 to Windows XP? Sadly, that dialog box is gone, but pieces of it can be found throughout the Personalization Control Panel if you know where to look. Table 4-4 shows you how to find the different sections, or tabs, of the old Display Properties dialog box, which have been effectively scattered to the winds. It's unclear whether Windows Vista's approach is better, but if you're looking for XP Display Properties features, you really have to know where to look.

Table 4-4: Where to Find Old Display Properties Tabs in Windows Vista

Display Properties Tab	Where It Is in Windows Vista
Themes	Control Panel ⇨ Personalization ⇨ Themes
Desktop	Replaced by the new Desktop Background window, found at Control Panel ⇨ Personalization ⇨ Desktop Background
Screen Saver	Control Panel ⇨ Personalization ⇨ Screen Saver
Appearance	Control Panel ⇨ Personalization ⇨ Visual Appearance, and open classic appearance properties
Settings	Control Panel ⇨ Personalization ⇨ Display Settings

Secret

The Desktop tab of the Display Properties dialog box in Windows XP had a Customize Desktop button that launched a Desktop Items dialog box from which you could configure which icons appeared on the desktop and other related options. But in Windows Vista, the Desktop tab has been replaced with the new Desktop Background window, which does not provide a link to this functionality. To access the Desktop Icon Properties dialog box, as it's now known, right-click on an empty portion of the desktop and choose Properties. Then, from the Personalize appearance and sounds control panel that appears, click the "Change desktop icons" link in the tasks list on the left. Some functionality, however, is missing. You can no longer run the Desktop Cleanup Wizard or place Web items on your desktop, as you could in XP. However, the Start Search box comes to the rescue with Disk Cleanup: To run Disk Cleanup in Windows Vista, just open the Start Menu, type Disk Cleanup, and then tap Enter.

You can see other options in the Desktop properties menu, but these are not typically installed by Microsoft. For example, some graphics chipset makers install links to their own utilities and figure that the Desktop properties menu is the logical place to access those tools. Intel adds two menu options, Graphics Properties and Graphics Options, on systems using some of its embedded graphics solutions. These options are not part of Vista per se and vary from system to system.

Customizing How Windows Appear on the Desktop

Most Windows users are probably familiar with the fact that windows in, ahem, Windows can appear to float onscreen, be maximized to occupy the entire desktop, and be minimized so that they are hidden in a taskbar button. There's no need to belabor these obvious capabilities here: Windows in Windows Vista work pretty much like they always have.

There are a few differences, however, and some cool capabilities you might not be aware of. First, if you're running the Windows Aero user experience, you will notice that the window Minimize, Restore/Maximize, and Close buttons adopt a pleasant glowing effect when you mouse over them. The Minimize and Restore/Maximize buttons glow blue, indicating that clicking these buttons is a nondestructive act. The Close button, meanwhile, glows a menacing red color. The intent is clear: Click with caution.

Secret

Early versions of Windows featured something called the *window control button*, which was previously denoted by a small icon in the upper-left corner of most windows. In Windows Vista, these icons are gone, replaced by the same translucent-glass look that graces the rest of the tops of most Aero windows. Amazingly, the window control button still exists: It's just hidden, an archaic artifact from the Ghost of Windows Past. To see it, just click in the upper-left corner of most windows, including all Explorer windows. Ta-da! You'll see the old pop-up window with options such as Restore, Move, Size, Minimize, Maximize/Restore, and Close, as shown in Figure 4-17.

continues

continued

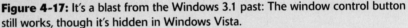

Figure 4-17: It's a blast from the Windows 3.1 past: The window control button still works, though it's hidden in Windows Vista.

You'll look at Windows Vista's Windows Explorer windows later in this chapter. For now, let's examine how you can arrange windows over the Vista desktop. Global window arrangement options are obscurely accessed via a contextual menu that appears when you click a blank area of the taskbar. (You will take a look at the taskbar in the next section.) These options are found on the taskbar because it's the one piece of onscreen real estate in Windows that's guaranteed to be visible, or at least accessible, regardless of what else is going on. You see four window arrangement options when you right-click an empty area of the taskbar:

◆ **Cascade Windows:** This incredibly unhelpful view style arranges all of the open windows on your desktop so that they visually cascade down from the upper-left corner of the desktop (see Figure 4-18). One gets the feeling that this feature was added in Windows 2.0, when Microsoft wanted to show off that its windowing system now supported overlapping windows, and was subsequently left as-is.

◆ **Show Windows Stacked:** If you are curious how multiple open but unmaximized windows would look onscreen side by side, select this option. It places the onscreen windows in a grid, with no overlapping edges (see Figure 4-19). As with the previous option, it's hard to imagine this view style having much use today.

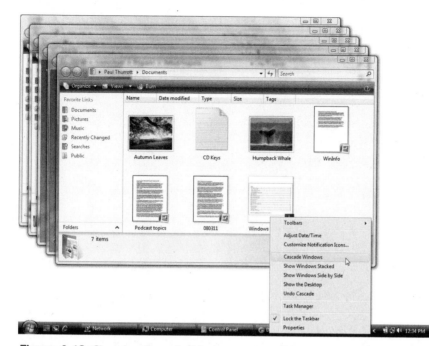

Figure 4-18: Choosing Cascade Windows causes all onscreen windows to line up diagonally from the top-left corner of the screen.

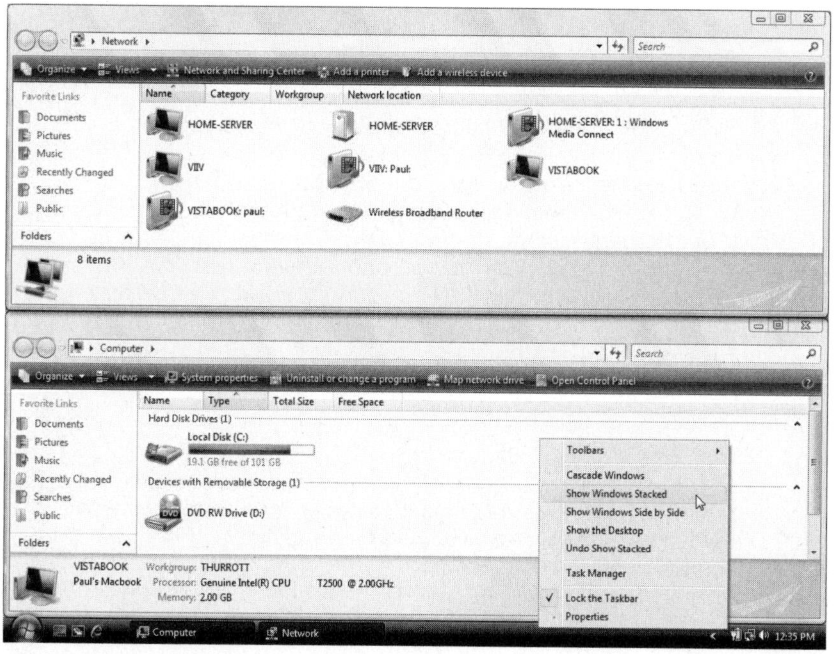

Figure 4-19: Stacked windows line up horizontally and will arrange in a grid if there are enough of them.

◆ **Show Windows Side by Side:** This one is slightly more interesting: Instead of a grid, open windows are arranged in vertical columns, side by side (see Figure 4-20). This view is especially useful if you want to copy a file between two Explorer windows.

Figure 4-20: In this view, windows are arranged side by side, vertically.

◆ **Show the Desktop:** Arranging windows is fun, but what if you want to see the desktop and it's covered with a tangle of windows? (You can be *too* productive, after all.) Microsoft has had a Show Desktop icon, found in the Quick Launch toolbar (described later in the chapter), for a while now, but Windows Vista provides several ways to hide all the onscreen windows and access the desktop immediately. In addition to the Show Desktop icon in the Quick Launch toolbar, there's a Show the Desktop option in the taskbar right-click menu, and you can now access the desktop via icons in the Windows Flip and Flip 3D task switchers, a feature that is brand-new to Vista.

While these aforementioned view styles are somewhat uninteresting as described, there is a little secret that makes them far more useful, especially the Show Windows Side by Side option. Suppose you want to display two windows side by side, but you have several open windows. Wouldn't it be nice to only change the display of those two windows and leave the other windows as they are?

continues

continued

Good news: It's possible. First, hold down the Ctrl key on your PC's keyboard and click the taskbar button of the first window you'd like to arrange. Notice that it remains depressed (as in pressed in, not suicidal). Now, hold down the Ctrl key again and click a second window's taskbar button. Repeat for as many buttons as needed. Then, right-click an empty area of the taskbar, or one of the selected taskbar buttons, and choose one of the three view styles described previously. Success! (See Figure 4-21.)

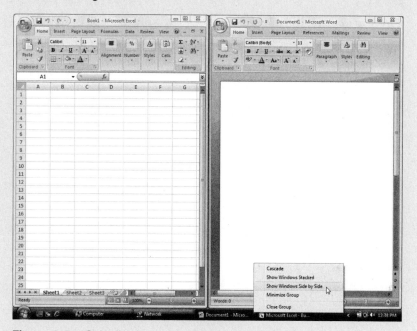

Figure 4-21: Ctrl+click to choose exactly which windows to arrange.

Taskbar

In Windows Vista, the system taskbar works similarly to the way it did in Windows XP. Every time you open an application or Explorer window, you will see a new button appear in the taskbar. When you click one these buttons, the selected window comes to the forefront. If that window was already at the forefront, then it is minimized. If you have numerous open windows from the same application—like you might with Internet Explorer—then the taskbar groups these buttons into a pop-up list, just like it did in Windows XP. When you right-click a taskbar button, you see a menu that is identical to that in XP.

Other features carry over from XP as well. When you right-click a blank area of the taskbar, you get a pop-up menu with links to enable toolbars, arrange desktop windows in various ways, show the desktop, access the Task Manager, toggle taskbar locking, and access the Taskbar and Start Menu Properties dialog box, from which you can configure various taskbar options (see Figure 4-22).

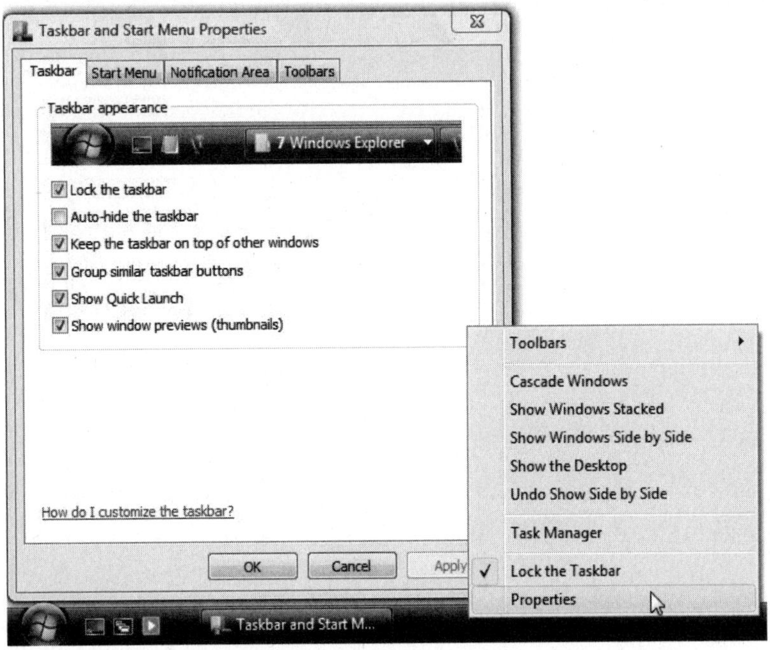

Figure 4-22: From here, you can customize certain taskbar features.

What's new is that you can get live thumbnail previews when you mouse over taskbar buttons (refer to Figure 4-9). To enable this feature, the option Show Thumbnails must be enabled, which it is by default. Note, too, that the notification area options have been moved to a new tab of this dialog in Windows Vista. You'll look at this feature later in this chapter.

Customizing the Taskbar

While most Windows users are probably familiar with the taskbar as it appears by default, this handy Windows feature can be configured in a number of ways, many of which dramatically change its appearance. This means you can make the taskbar work the way you want it to: You don't have to accept the taskbar as delivered by Microsoft.

> **tip** Most of the changes described in this section require you to "unlock" the taskbar. By default, the Windows Vista taskbar is locked so that you do not inadvertently move, resize, or change its layout. To unlock the taskbar, right-click a blank area of the taskbar and choose Unlock the Taskbar. Later, when you're done making changes, relock the taskbar so you don't mistakenly undo anything you've configured. Logically, this is done by right-clicking an empty area of the unlocked taskbar and choosing Lock the Taskbar.

By default, the taskbar occupies a single "line," height-wise, where by "line" I mean the height of one icon. With the taskbar unlocked, however, you can increase the height of the taskbar, thus increasing the number of lines it utilizes. To do this, position the mouse cursor over the top edge of the taskbar. Notice that the cursor changes from a pointer to a double arrow. To increase the size, hold down the mouse button and drag up. To decrease the height again, repeat those steps but drag down. You can increase the height of the taskbar from one line up to half the height of the screen. Of course, such a taskbar would make your system almost unusable. I recommend experimenting with a double-height taskbar first, as shown in Figure 4-23.

Figure 4-23: A double-height taskbar is particularly useful on high-resolution screens.

tip   As you increase the height of the taskbar, the system clock (described later in this chapter) changes to accommodate the additional space. At the default one line of height, the clock displays just the time. With two lines or more, however, the clock also displays the day of the week (e.g., Thursday) and the date.

You can also opt to hide the taskbar, an option that is particularly valuable on lower-resolution screens where pixel count is at a premium. When hidden, the taskbar essentially disappears, but it is still available by moving the mouse to the bottom edge of the screen; when you do so, the taskbar slides back up so you can access the Start Menu and other taskbar features. Move the mouse away again, and the taskbar slides back under the screen.

To hide the taskbar, you need to display the Taskbar and Start Menu Properties dialog: Right-click the Start Orb, select Properties, and then navigate to the Taskbar tab. Then, check the item labeled Auto-hide the Taskbar.

There are other useful options in this properties dialog. For example, you can enable and disable taskbar button grouping and live taskbar thumbnails via the option titled Show Window Previews (thumbnails).

Secret   Though the taskbar sits on the bottom of the Windows desktop by default, you can actually drag it to any of the other three screen borders if desired. To do so, unlock the taskbar and then simply use your finely-honed drag-and-drop skills to drag the taskbar to any screen edge, as shown in Figure 4-24. It can be on the top, bottom, left, or right side of the screen; and any other customizations work regardless of where the taskbar is found, so you can mix and match. I happen to think that a triple-height, auto-hid taskbar on the top of the screen is pretty ugly, but you might find it the pinnacle of productivity. Hey, it's your PC. Go nuts.

Figure 4-24: The taskbar can actually live on any screen edge.

As with previous versions of Windows, Microsoft also includes several additional toolbars that you can enable to appear within the taskbar. One of these taskbar toolbars, Quick Launch, has proven so popular that it's now enabled by default and filled with a few useful default icons, including Show Desktop, Switch between Windows (which actually triggers Flip 3D), and Internet Explorer. You can drag your own shortcuts into Quick Launch, resize it to meet your needs, or just get rid of it. You can also enable some other taskbar toolbars, such as Address (an IE-style Address Bar), Windows Media Player (described in Chapter 11), Links (also from IE), Tablet PC Input Panel (only available on Tablet PCs and Ultra-Mobile PCs running Windows Vista Home Premium, Business, Ultimate, or Enterprise editions; see Chapter 18), and Desktop (displays whatever icons are on your desktop). Some third-party applications, such as Apple iTunes, add their own taskbar toolbars, and if you're a real geek, you can make your own toolbar, by pointing the wizard that appears at a folder you'd like to access from the taskbar. Any icons in this folder appear in this new taskbar toolbar.

Some people find it useful to add multiple toolbars to the taskbar, but in my own experience I've found only the Quick Launch toolbar to be especially useful. I stock mine with a few icons I use regularly, such as iTunes and Firefox, but if you do find multiple toolbars useful, consider expanding the taskbar too so that each toolbar has enough space. You can also resize individual taskbar toolbars while the taskbar is unlocked.

---

tip   While not strictly a taskbar feature, you can also access Windows Vista's Task Manager from the taskbar. To display the Task Manager, right-click an empty area of the taskbar and select Task Manager from the menu that appears.

Notification Area and System Clock

Way back in Windows 95, Microsoft introduced a number of user interface conventions that still exist in Windows Vista. These include, among others, the Start button (now the Start Orb) and Start Menu, the taskbar, the Windows Explorer windows, and the notification area, which sits at the right end of the taskbar by default. You'll typically see two types of items here: the system clock and various notification icons. Some of these icons are installed by default with Windows, such as the volume control, the network icon, Safely Remove Hardware, and others. Other icons can be installed by third-party applications. For example, Windows Home Server and many security applications install tray icons.

tip Like the devil, the notification area goes by many names. When you see references to such things as the "system tray" or the "tray notification area," these are referring to the same place in the Vista UI: the notification area.

As the name suggests, the tray is designed for notifications and shouldn't be used as a taskbar replacement, although some developers try to use it that way for some reason (some applications inexplicably minimize to the tray, rather than to the taskbar as they should). Applications such as Windows Live Messenger and Microsoft Outlook, which need to alert the user to new instant messages, e-mails, or online contacts, also use the tray, and display small pop-up notification windows nearby.

Secret If you're not interested in a bunch of tiny icons cluttering up your notification area, you can do something about it. Some icons can be removed permanently, though this option varies from application to application: Try clicking or right-clicking the icon and seeing if there's an option to remove or hide the icon. If not, you might have to delve into the application's Options dialog (or similar configuration utility) and see whether there's a way to disable the notification icon from there. If all else fails, you can simply hide the icon from the Taskbar and Start Menu Properties window. Navigate to the Notification Area tab, click Customize, and you'll see lists of the icons that are currently displayed, as well as a separate list of icons that appeared in the past. Next to each icon is a user-configurable display behavior, which can be switched between Hide when Inactive, Hide, and Show. Click the behavior and choose Hide for each icon you'd like to hide. Hidden notification icons can be accessed by clicking the little white chevron to the left of the notification area; this expands the icon list to show the hidden icons.

Despite plans to remove the notification area and replace it with a Sidebar panel, Microsoft pretty much left this feature intact in Windows Vista. Not much has changed: You can now configure some notification area features—such as which system icons are displayed by default, and the display behavior of any notification icon on your system—from a new Notification Area tab in the Taskbar and Start Menu Properties dialog box, but that's about it.

Exploring the New System Clock

One thing that has changed demonstrably is the system clock. In Windows Vista, this feature is now dramatically better than its XP counterpart. At first glance, it's not obvious what has changed. The clock displays the time, as you'd expect; and if you mouse over the time display, a pleasant-looking balloon tip window appears, providing you with the day and date. So far, it's basically the clock in XP.

In Windows XP, however, you could access the system's Date and Time Properties dialog box by double-clicking the clock. This is changed in Windows Vista. Instead, you can single-click the clock to display a new pop-up window, shown in Figure 4-25, which provides a professionally formatted calendar and analog clock. There's also an option to display the new Date and Time Properties window.

Figure 4-25: Windows Vista includes a nice-looking calendar and clock display.

When you click Change Date and Time Settings, you'll see the new Date and Time properties window, shown in Figure 4-26. Here, you can configure options you'd expect, such as date, time, and time zone, but you can also configure additional clock displays, which is an excellent feature for travelers or those who frequently need to communicate with people in different time zones.

From the Additional Clocks tab of this dialog box, you can add up to two more clocks. Each clock gets its own time zone and optional display name. What's cool about this feature is the way it changes the clock displays. Now, when you mouse over the clock, you'll see a pop-up that lists data from all of your clocks, as shown in Figure 4-27.

Click the clock to see the nice display shown in Figure 4-28.

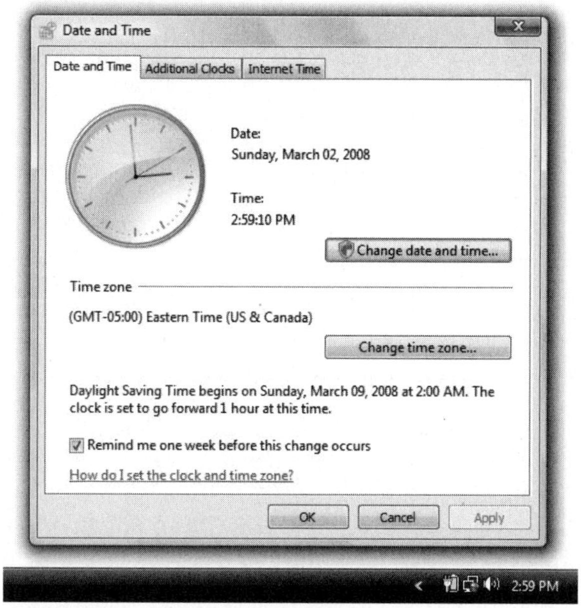

Figure 4-26: The Date and Time properties dialog box has been completely overhauled.

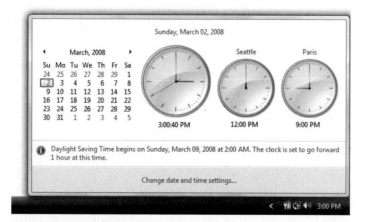

Figure 4-27: You can configure up to three clocks in Windows Vista.

Figure 4-28: This handy and speedy time and date display can also handle up to three clocks.

Windows Vista Explorer

No discussion of the Windows Vista user experience would be complete without a look at the ways in which Windows Explorer has evolved in this Windows release. Windows Explorer first appeared in Windows 95, replacing the many horrible manager programs (File Manager, Program Manager, and so on) that plagued previous Windows versions. It was a grand idea, but then Microsoft made the mistake of combining Internet Explorer with the Windows shell. Starting with an interim version of Windows 95, the Windows Explorer shell has been based on IE, and since then we've all suffered through a decade of security vulnerabilities and the resulting patches.

In Windows Vista, that integration is a thing of the past. Windows Explorer has been completely overhauled; and although it's arguably better than the Explorer shell in Windows XP, it's also quite a bit different. (It even loses a few features from the Windows XP shell, though it gains some unique new functionality.) Microsoft has also introduced some new terminology into the mix, just to keep you on your toes. For example, as My Documents is renamed to Documents in Windows Vista, Microsoft now refers to that window as the Documents Explorer. Likewise with all the other special folders: There are now Explorers for Pictures, Music, applications, devices, and other objects.

From a usability perspective, much has changed since XP. Let's examine a typical Explorer window, as shown in Figure 4-29. The menu bar is gone, replaced by a hidden Classic Menu, which can be dynamically triggered by tapping the Alt key. The main toolbar is also gone, replaced by back and forward buttons, the new enhanced address bar, and the new integrated search box.

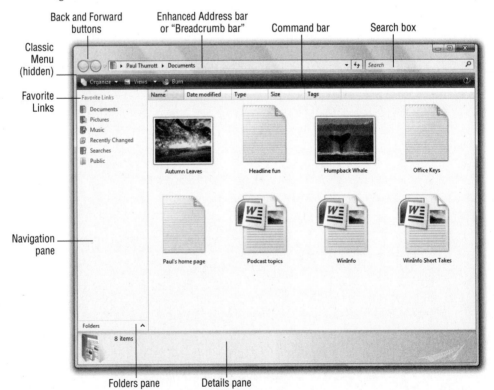

Figure 4-29: Like many user interface pieces in Windows Vista, Explorer windows have changed fairly dramatically.

Below those controls is a new user interface construct called the *command bar,* which includes context-sensitive commands and replaces the old task pane from Windows XP Explorer. In other words, the options you see in the command bar vary from window to window according to what's selected. On the bottom is a new Details pane, which also varies according to the current window and what's selected. Are you sensing a theme here?

In the center of the window is the Navigation pane with collapsing Folders view, a large icon display area, and, optionally, a Preview pane. (This latter pane was, for a time, referred to as the Reading pane. Trivia is my middle name.) The next few sections delve into what all of these features do.

Classic Menu

One of the guiding principles in Windows Vista is simplification. In previous Windows versions, virtually every system window and application included a top menu structure. In Windows Vista, however, these menus are typically either nonexistent or hidden by default. To display the menu in an Explorer window temporarily, simply tap the Alt key. (See Figure 4-30.)

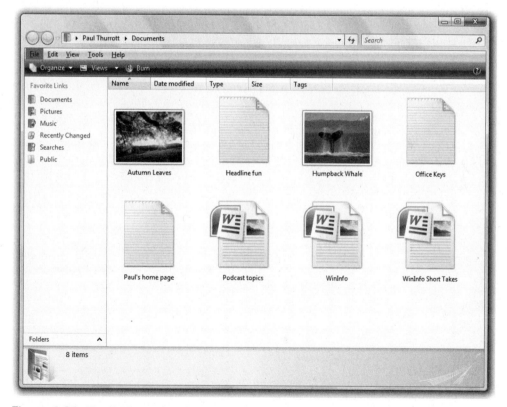

Figure 4-30: The Explorer menu, now called the Classic menu, is hidden by default in Windows Vista but can be displayed by tapping the Alt key.

Alternately, you can enable it permanently by choosing Folder Options from the Tools Menu, navigating to the View tab of the Folder Options dialog box, and enabling the option titled Always Show Classic Menus. There's precious little reason to do this, however. The menu just takes up valuable space.

tip   The Classic menus in Explorer are virtually identical to their XP counterparts. One major exception is the Favorites Menu, which does not appear in Vista because IE is no longer integrated with the Windows shell.

Enhanced Address Bar

For the first time since Windows 95, the address bar gets a major overhaul in Windows Vista. Now, instead of the classic address bar view, the address bar is divided into drop-down menu nodes along the navigation path, making it easier than ever to move through the shell hierarchy. This new interface is referred to as the *breadcrumb bar*, though I'm pretty sure there isn't a gingerbread house at the end with a witch living in it.

To see how it works, open the Documents window—sorry, the Documents *Explorer*—by clicking the Documents item in the Start Menu and observing the address bar. It is divided into three nodes: a folder icon, a node representing your user profile (Paul, in my case), and Documents. Each has a small arrow next to it, indicating that you can click there for a drop-down menu.

To navigate to a folder that is at the same level in the shell hierarchy as the Documents folder, click the small arrow to the right of your user name. As shown in Figure 4-31, a drop-down menu appears, showing you all the folders available inside your user account folder. You can click any of these to navigate there immediately. Note that doing this in XP requires two steps. First, you have to click the Up toolbar button; then you have to double-click the folder you want. That's progress, ladies and gentlemen.

To simply move back up a level, click the node to the left of the current location. In this example you would click the node denoted by your user name.

Secret   To see the classic address bar, simply click a blank area of the enhanced address bar. The breadcrumb bar disappears and the arcane, text-based address appears in all its colon and forward-slash beauty. To return to the safety of the breadcrumb bar, click elsewhere in the window.

Instant Search

Windows Vista has Start Menu Search, Internet Explorer search, a new Search window, and even an instant Search box in every Explorer window. This is useful because the instant Search box is context-sensitive. Sure, you could search your entire hard drive if you wanted, but what's the point? If you're in a folder and you know that what you're looking for is in there somewhere, maybe in one of the subfolders, then the instant Search box is the tool to use.

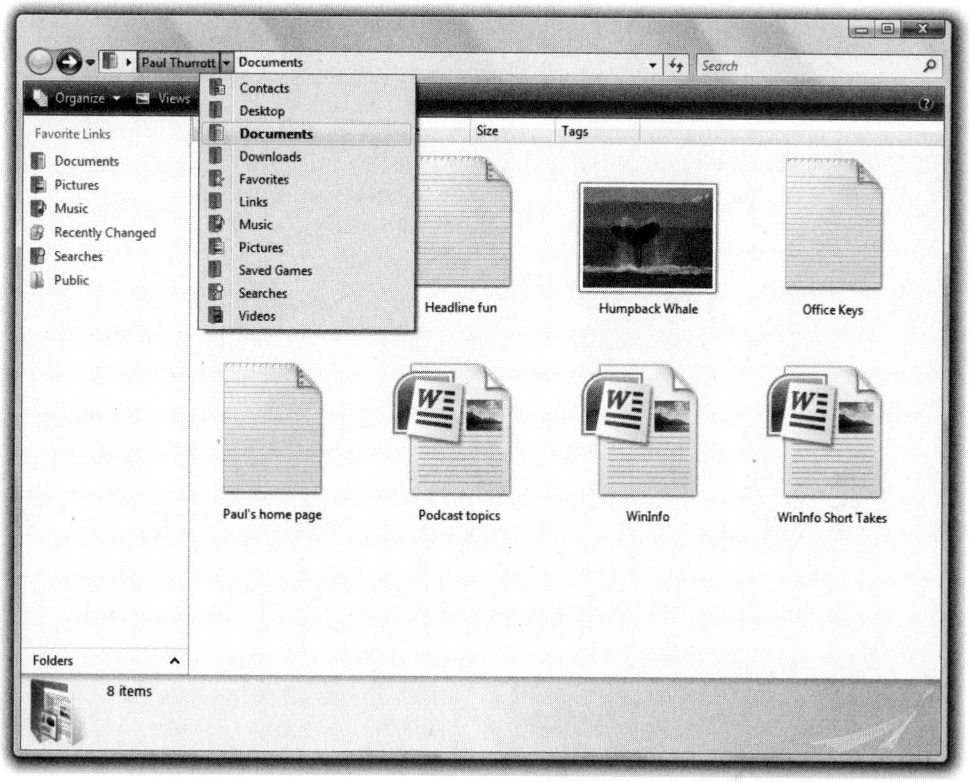

Figure 4-31: The new address bar makes it easy to move through the shell hierarchy.

To search for a document or other file in the current folder or one of its subfolders, just click the Search box and begin typing. Your results begin appearing immediately. When the search results list is complete, you can also click a link titled Search for *search query* in Index that enables you to search the entire hard drive.

cross ref   For more information about Windows Vista's Instant Search functionality, please see Chapter 5.

Command Bar

The new command bar combines the functionality of the toolbar and task panes from the Windows Explorer windows in Windows XP in a new, less real estate–intensive space. Like the task pane in XP, portions of the command bar are context-sensitive and change depending on what items you are viewing or have selected.

That said, the following portions of the command bar remain constant regardless of what you're viewing:

♦ **Organize button:** This appears in all Explorer windows and provides you with a drop-down menu from which you can perform common actions such as create a new folder; cut, copy, paste, undo, and redo; select all; delete; rename; close; and get properties.

♦ **Layout submenu:** This option enables you to determine which user interface elements appear globally in all Explorer windows. These elements include Classic Menus (off by default), Details Pane (on by default), Preview Pane (off by default), and the Navigation Pane (on by default).

♦ **Views button:** Use this option to change the icon view style for the current window. Unlike the Layout options, this option is configurable on a folder-by-folder basis.

The other options you see in the command bar vary according to view and selection. For example, Figure 4-32 shows how the command bar changes in the Documents window when you select a document file.

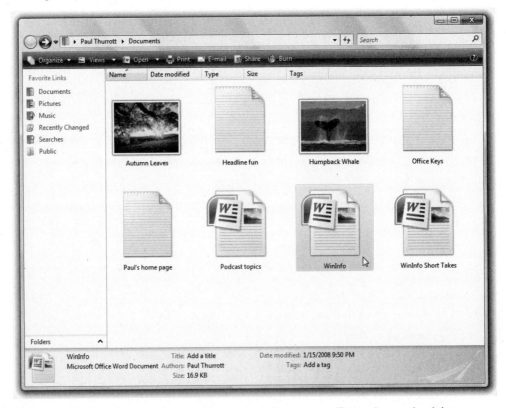

Figure 4-32: The command bar provides options that are specific to what you're doing.

Navigation Pane

On the left of every Windows Explorer window, by default, is a new area called the Navigation pane, shown in Figure 4-33. This pane features a list of common shell locations (e.g., Documents, Pictures, Music, and the like) as well as any saved searches that are relevant to the current view. For example, the Documents folder includes a search folder called Recently Changed that enables you to view only those documents that have recently been edited in some way.

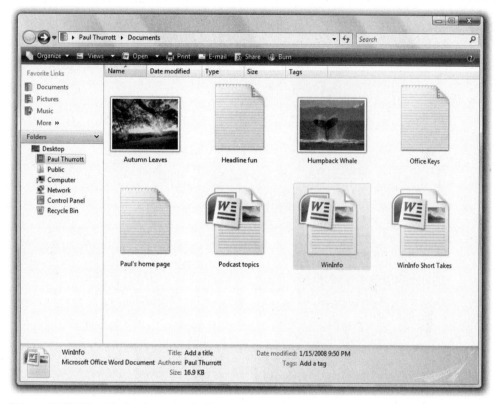

Figure 4-33: The Navigation pane includes the Favorite Links and Folders sections.

At the bottom of the Navigation pane is a small panel named Folders. If you click the small arrow to the right, the Folders pane expands into the Navigation pane, providing you with a traditional file explorer view. The Folders pane is Vista's answer to the old Folders pane from previous versions of Windows, but it works differently. Now, it's always visible onscreen as a link you can expand at will. Folders is a global option: If you enable it in one window, it appears in any future Explorer windows you open.

Live Icons and Preview Pane

In Windows Vista, document icons are "live" and can provide you with a rich preview of their contents depending on which view style you're using, as shown in Figure 4-34.

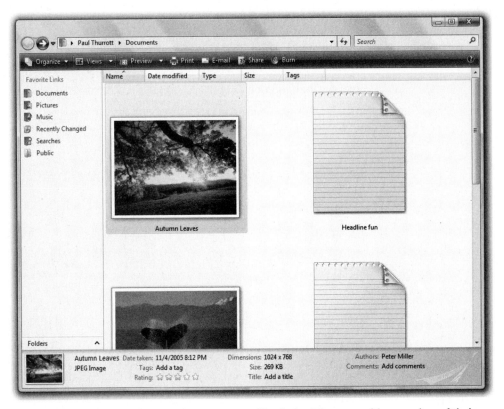

Figure 4-34: In Windows Vista, documents are "live," providing you with a preview of their contents.

But even when you're using one of the smaller view styles, you can get live previews. Simply enable the Preview pane (also a global option), and as you select individual documents, you'll see a preview in that pane, which is located on the right side of the window (see Figure 4-35).

Details Pane

By default, every Windows Explorer window includes a Details pane at the bottom that provides a list of properties about the currently selected file or document. Previously, you had to open the file's Properties sheet to view this information.

Secret

The Details pane is resizable. The bigger you make it, the more preview information you receive. (The reverse is also true.) Note that this feature is global—after you resize the Details pane, the setting is preserved in all subsequent Explorer windows.

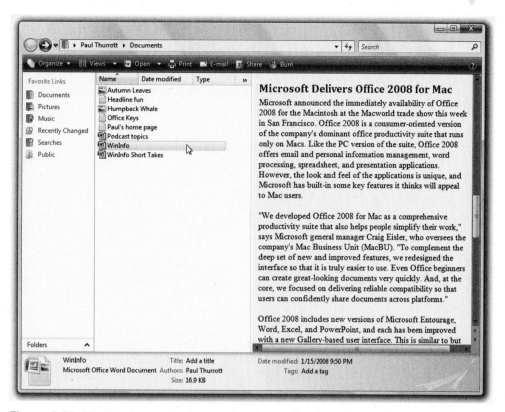

Figure 4-35: The Preview pane takes up a lot of space, but it can be used in lieu of actually opening a document in a separate application.

More to Come...

There's so much more to know about the Windows Vista Explorer, including various changes to the special shell folders, icon view styles, and saved searches. You'll look at all of those features in upcoming chapters.

Summary

Anyone who uses Windows Vista needs to deal with its user interface, which is both brand-new in many ways but also extremely familiar to anyone who has used Windows XP. Like its XP predecessor, Windows Vista features a Start Orb (button) and Start Menu, a taskbar, a notification area, and a desktop; but Vista goes beyond XP by improving each of these features while adding other unique features and new user experiences, such as Windows Vista Basic and Standard and Windows Aero.

Where's My Stuff? Finding and Organizing Files

◆ ◆

In This Chapter

Working with the Windows Vista file system

Understanding virtual folders

Finding the documents and files you want

Creating and using Search Folders

◆ ◆

W indows Vista includes an updated version of the Explorer file system that appeared in Windows XP. Like its predecessor, Windows Vista supports the notion of *special shell folders* where you can access such much-needed data files as documents, digital photos, digital music, and videos. However, Vista also adds a number of new Explorer constructs, such as *virtual folders* called Search Folders, which are confusing but powerful when used correctly. In this chapter you will explore the Windows shell and learn how to take advantage of the new features Microsoft added to Windows Vista.

Understanding Special Shell Folders

Most *Windows Vista Secrets* readers are probably familiar with basic computer file system concepts such as files, folders, and drive letters; but you may not realize that certain locations in the Windows shell—that is, Windows Explorer, the application with which you literally explore the contents of your PC's hard drives—have been specially configured to work with particular data types, and live in the shell hierarchy outside of their physical locations. In Windows XP and previous Windows versions, these locations were called *special shell folders*, and they included such things as My Documents, My Pictures, and My Music.

In Windows Vista these special shell folders still exist, but now most of them have different names and are accompanied by a number of new members. They're also in a different location: Whereas Windows XP placed user folders (which contain the special shell folders for each user) in C:\Documents and Settings*Your_User_Name* by default, Windows Vista uses the simpler C:\Users*Your_User_Name*, as shown in Figure 5-1.

These special shell folders are listed in Table 5-1.

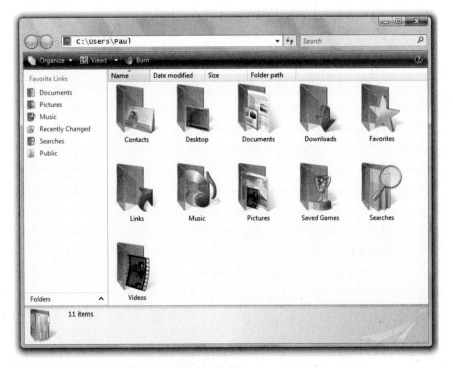

Figure 5-1: Windows Vista special shell folders.

Table 5-1: Special Shell Folders

Home	This special location is named after your user name. If you chose the user name Paul, for example, then your Home folder would be named Paul as well. (Case matters: If you enter **paul**, it will be paul and not Paul.) This folder is available as the top option on the right-hand, fixed part of the Start Menu. Although it was never particularly obvious, every user actually had a Home folder in previous Windows versions.
Contacts	A new addition to Windows Vista, Contacts acts as a central database for Vista's centralized contacts management, which is used by Windows Mail and can be used by any third-party application. You can examine Contacts in Chapter 20.
Desktop	This folder represents your Windows Vista desktop. Any folders, files, or shortcuts you place on the desktop appear in this folder too (and vice versa). There's one exception: If you enable certain desktop icons—such as Computer, User's Files, Network, Recycle Bin, or Control Panel—via the Desktop Icon Settings dialog, these icons will not appear in the Desktop folder.
Documents	A replacement for My Documents, this folder is specially configured to handle various document types, such as Word documents, text files, and the like. As with its predecessor, Documents is the default location for the Save and Save As dialog boxes in most applications.
Downloads	New to Windows Vista, this folder is the default location for files downloaded from the Web with Internet Explorer and other Web browsers, including Mozilla Firefox.
Favorites	A central repository for your Internet Explorer Favorites (or what other browsers typically call Bookmarks). The Favorites folder has been in Windows for several years. You can find out more about IE in Chapter 19.
Links	New to Windows Vista, this folder typically contains shortcuts to common shell locations. Its contents appear in the Favorite Links pane of Windows Explorer windows. Note that only shortcuts to folder and other shell locations appear in Favorite Links. If you copy a shortcut to a document here, for example, it will not appear in the list.
Saved Games	A new addition to Windows Vista, the Saved Games folder is designed as a place for Vista-compatible game titles to store saved game information. Vista and video games are covered in Chapter 16.
Pictures	A replacement for My Pictures. The Pictures folder is designed to handle digital photographs and other picture files and to work in tandem with other photo-related tools in Vista, such as Windows Photo Gallery and the Import Pictures and Videos Wizard. You can look at Vista's photo features in Chapter 13.
Music	A replacement for XP's My Music folder. The Music folder is designed to work with digital music and other audio files. If you rip music from an audio CD or purchase music from an online music service such as the Apple iTunes Store or Amazon MP3, those files are typically saved to your Music folder by default. You can discover more about digital music in Chapters 11 and 12.
Searches	New to Windows Vista, this folder contains built-in and user-created saved searches. You'll examine this functionality later in the chapter.
Videos	A replacement for My Videos. This folder is designed to store digital videos of any kind, including home movies. It also interacts with video-oriented tools in Vista, such as Windows Movie Maker and Windows DVD Maker. You can take a look at these OS features in Chapter 14.

Each of the special shell folders in Windows Vista shares certain characteristics. First, they are all *physical folders* in the sense that they are represented by a specific location in the Windows shell hierarchy. For example, your Home folder is now found at C:\Users*username* by default. Likewise, Documents can be found at C:\Users*username*\Documents.

tip

In Windows XP you had to run Windows Movie Maker once before the My Videos folder would appear. This is no longer the case in Windows Vista, where the new Videos folder is always available under each user's Home folder. However, as with XP, it's still impossible to add a link to the Videos folder to the right side of the Start Menu. The Videos folder, it seems, is still a second-class citizen in Microsoft's eyes.

You might notice that most folder names (Saved Games is a curious exception)—and indeed the names of the folders above each of them in the shell path—has been stripped of spaces. That is, each folder is now a single word (e.g., Documents instead of My Documents). That's because of a renewed commitment to shell scripting in Windows Vista, an environment in which it's simply harder to deal with spaces. (See Chapter 24 for more information about Vista's scripting capabilities.)

Finally, many of the special shell folders are represented somewhat differently in the Windows shell than are other folders, which you might think of as normal physical folders. The Documents, Favorites, Music, and Pictures folders are all colored blue-green now instead of the normal yellow folder color; and although you can create a folder almost anywhere you'd like in the Windows Vista shell—assuming you have the security credentials to do so—special shell folders are typically found only in their preset locations within the file system.

Secret

Advanced users can use the Registry Editor (**regedit.exe**) to change special shell-folder locations. (If you're not familiar with the Registry, this isn't the time to start. You can irreparably harm Windows via the Registry.) Using regedit, navigate to HKEY_CURRENT_USER\Software\Microsoft\Windows\CurrentVersion\Explorer\Shell Folders. You'll see a variety of special shell folders listed there, including Personal (Documents), My Music (Music), My Pictures (Pictures), and My Video (Videos). To change the location of one of these special folders, simply double-click in regedit and add the new location to the Value data field in the dialog that appears.

tip

You can see some of Vista's special folders in your Start Menu, but if you want a better idea of how they're laid out in the file system, simply launch Windows Explorer and enable the classic left-mounted folder hierarchy, which is now found in the bottom-left corner of the window.

In addition to the new special shell folders in Vista, there are also some differences in the way that preexisting special shell folders are organized now. For example, folders such as My Pictures, My Music, and My Videos were physically arranged below (and logically contained within) the My Documents folder in previous Windows versions; but in Windows Vista the new versions of these folders are found directly below each user's Home folder, alongside Documents. This won't affect typical users, who will likely access special shell folders like My Documents and My Pictures only from the Start Menu, but more advanced users will want to be aware of the changes.

tip
> The new Home folder layout is actually quite similar to that used by Unix and Linux systems, including Apple's Mac OS X. Vista even follows the same naming conventions these competitors utilize.

Visualization and Organization: How the Windows Vista Shell Works

In each Windows version, you can utilize several shell view styles, each of which presents the files and folders you're looking at in slightly different way. These view styles—and the ways in which you access and configure them—have changed dramatically in Windows Vista.

By comparison, Windows XP offered six Explorer view styles—Thumbnails, Tiles, Icons, List, Details, and, for folders containing digital pictures, Filmstrip. There were also ways you could arrange the files in folders, such as by name, type, or total size, or in groups, where icons representing similar objects would be visually grouped together. All of these options could be configured in a number of ways, including via buttons in the Explorer window toolbar, by right-clicking inside of an Explorer window, or from the View menu. Maddeningly, Windows XP would often forget folder view styles, either on a per-window or systemwide basis. This is one of the few areas in which Windows XP was inferior to its predecessors.

Secret
> Alas, Windows Vista can forget window positions, sizes, and view styles, too, though this is much less common than it was in XP. There's good news, however: You can make a simple Registry change to improve Vista's memory by allocating more system resources dedicated to remembering this information.
>
> Here's how you do it: Open the Registry Editor (regedit in Start Menu Search) and navigate to HKEY_CURRENT_USER\Software\Microsoft\Windows\Shell. Then, in the right pane of the Registry Editor window, right-click the value BagMRU Size and click Modify. The default for this value is 1388 (hexadecimal). Change it to a larger value, such as 20000 (decimal) and then click OK and exit the Registry Editor.

Once you upgrade to Vista, you'll have to relearn many of your shell skills because the user interface has changed so much. Microsoft has changed not only the layout of the Explorer window user-interface elements and menu items from which you configure view styles, but many of the view styles and arrangement options themselves.

In Windows Vista you can choose from seven view styles, as demonstrated in Figure 5-2 and described in Table 5-2.

Figure 5-2: The different view styles in Windows Vista.

Table 5-2: Explorer View Styles

Extra Large Icons	An absolutely gigantic view style that takes full advantage of Vista's nearly photographic-quality icons, which are rendered at 256 x 256 pixels.
Large Icons	Similar to the Windows XP Large Icons view, this view style provides 128 x 128 icons laid out in a conventional grid.
Medium Icons	A new style unique to Windows Vista, Medium Icons are similar in style to Large Icons, but smaller at 64 x 64 pixels.
Small Icons	A blast from the past: Small icons appeared in Windows 95, Windows 98, Windows Me, and Windows 2000, but were exorcised from Windows XP for some reason, much to the chagrin of many users. Rejoice; this option is back.
List	A columnar version of Small Icons view, with the same-size icons but a more linear look.

continues

Table 5-2: *(continued)*

Details	A columnar view style that uses the same icon size as Small Icons but presents them in a more regulated fashion. Details view is quite prominent in Windows Vista, in sharp contrast to previous Windows client versions.
Tiles	A relatively new view style—it debuted in Windows XP and is the standard view style for most Explorer windows in that Windows version—Tiles view presents information about each folder and file to the right of the icon, as with Small Icons and Details, but utilizes a much larger icon (it's the same icon used by Medium Icons view). Because of the extra space available, Tiles view can present more than just the icon's name. What you see depends on the file type. Microsoft Word documents, for example, include both the name of the file and the notation "Microsoft Word Document." Digital photos include the name and the date the picture was taken.

You can access these styles similarly to how you did so in Windows XP, via the Views button in an Explorer window toolbar, via the View submenu on the menu that appears when you right-click a blank area of the current Explorer window, or, if you have the Classic Menus option enabled, via the View Menu.

> **tip**   Unlike previous Windows versions, Windows Vista—finally—enables you to choose different icon view styles for the Desktop, as well as for normal Explorer shell windows. To access these view modes, right-click a blank area of your Desktop and choose View. You'll see three view styles here: Large Icons, Medium Icons, and Classic Icons. (Details, Extra Large Icons, Small Icons, and Tiles are not available on the Desktop. Maybe next time.)

Interestingly, these seven shell view styles are not your only view style options. You can also access intermediary view styles between each of those stock settings using a new slider control that appears when you click the small arrow on the right side of the Views toolbar button, as shown in Figure 5-3. This control enables you to fine-tune the look and feel of individual Explorer windows so you can create a view style that matches your preferences and system capabilities. For example, on a large widescreen display you might prefer larger icons, whereas a smaller notebook display might look better to your eyes in Details view. It's up to you.

Secret   You can also move the slider with the scroll wheel on your mouse if it's so equipped. Simply open the slide control by clicking the arrow as noted previously and then use the scroll wheel to find the view style you like.

Figure 5-3: You needn't be constrained by the six stock view styles; Vista enables you to select styles that fall somewhere between the presets.

Sorting the Vista View Styles

What else has changed? Well, you may recall that the Windows XP Details view provided columns by which you could sort the contents of the current window. In Windows Vista, every view style can be sorted by these columns, even if you can't see them. To see this in action, open a Windows Explorer window and repeatedly click the Views button. Each time you do so, the icon view style changes.

Secret

For some reason, clicking the Views button toggles only six of the seven available view styles. If you want to use Extra Large Icon view, you have to do a bit more work: Click the More Options button to the right of the Views button to display the Views drop-down menu and then select Extra Large Icons.

What remains is the list of column headings that you typically associate with Details view. The column headings you see vary from window to window, depending on the content. In the Document window you'll see column headings for Name, Data Modified, Type, Size, and Tags, but the Pictures folder has column headings for Name, Date Taken, Tags, Size, and Rating, as shown in Figure 5-4.

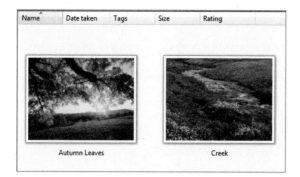

Figure 5-4: The available view styles vary depending on folder contents, and can be modified if you're particularly choosy.

These column headings aren't just for show. As with previous Windows versions (in which the column headings were available only in Details view), you can click any column heading in order to sort the currently viewed content by that criteria. For example, if you click the Name column heading, the folders and files in the current folder will be sorted alphabetically by name, from A to Z. If you click the Name column heading a second time, the sorting is reversed and the folders and files are listed from Z to A. Each column heading works in a similar fashion.

Another change is that the column headings now have a drop-down list box associated with each of them. These list boxes provide you with a wealth of sorting options. To trigger the list box you first need to find it. Mouse over a column heading (e.g., Name) and an arrow will appear on the right side of the column heading. If you click this arrow, the drop-down list box appears, as in Figure 5-5. The various gadgets and doohickeys you see in the list box might be confusing initially, so take a closer look.

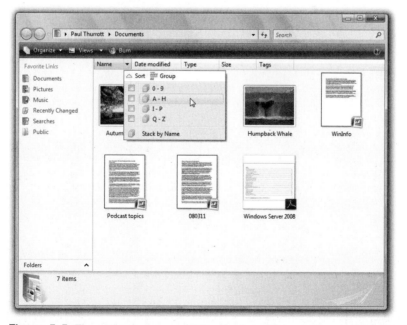

Figure 5-5: The sort columns are interactive too: Click one for more information.

At the top of the list box you will see two or three of the following options, depending on which column heading you choose:

♦ **Sort:** This works just like clicking the column heading normally does; it sorts the folders and files in the current window accordingly. However, it does provide a bit of a visual cue, which can be handy: If the little arrow to the left of Sort is pointing down, as shown in Figure 5-6, then clicking the Sort option will result in a reverse sort (e.g., Z to A in the case of the Name column heading). If the arrow is pointing up, the items are sorted normally (A to Z for Name).

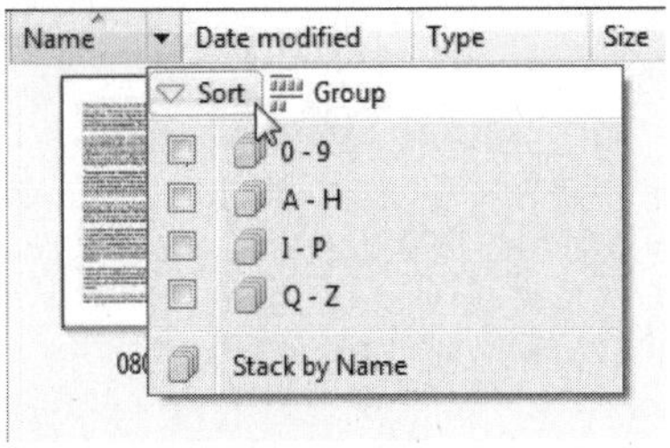

Figure 5-6: New sorting and grouping options ensure that your Explorer windows always reflect your preferences.

♦ **Stack:** This option is brand-new to Windows Vista, and Microsoft says it is the result of years of user-interface testing (which likely explains why it's so well hidden). According to Microsoft, as hard drives get bigger and bigger and users store more and more data on those drives, it's getting harder and harder to find the information you need. Stacks are one way to present a lot of information in a simpler fashion. Like most computer user-interface metaphors, "stack" comes from a traditional desktop, on which you might stack related papers together, creating a literal stack of documents. In the real world you might stack together documents for a specific trip, project, or other relationship. Now you can do so in Windows Vista as well. However, because Stacks don't actually appear in the current folder but instead open a search-results window, you'll examine this functionality more closely later in this chapter when you take a look at Vista's deeply integrated search features.

♦ **Group:** This enables you to group folders and files into related groups, as you would when using the Windows XP Tiles view, but now you can group files and folders regardless of the view style. (Well, almost: The Group option is disabled if the folder is in List view for some reason.) You can group by name, date modified, keywords, author, type, and other criteria, and your grouping options vary according to the contents of the folder you're currently viewing. In a typical folder full of documents the default is Date Modified, but you can choose other grouping types by right-clicking the current folder and choosing Group By and then the criteria you want.

tip   The Group option is most famous for its appearance in the default view of My Computer in Windows XP, which grouped tiled icons by type. Interestingly, this is exactly the same in Windows Vista, so open My Computer now to see how a grouped view can look. You can see an example in Figure 5-7. (Note that the types of items displayed in the Windows Vista version of My Computer are a bit different.)

Figure 5-7: Grouped tiles were such a hit in Windows XP that they're back as the default view for Computer in Windows Vista.

Below the Search box, what you see depends on the column heading you've clicked. For example, the Date Modified column heading includes a mini calendar control that enables you to specify a date or even a date range from which to filter the current folder (see Figure 5-8). Like the search functionality mentioned previously, the results of this filter are displayed in a new view that actually contains search results, described later.

Finally, at the bottom of the drop-down list box are several preset Stack settings, which also vary according to which column heading you've chosen. The Name column heading, for example, includes preset Stacks such as 0–9, A–M, and N–Z (the actual letter ranges you see reflect the names of the files and folders you're viewing). What's nice about these preset Stacks is that they're, ahem, stackable. That is, you can check any number of these preset Stacks to filter the view (which, yes, returns a search result). For example, you can filter the view to contain files and folders that begin (or end) with both numbers from 0–9 and letters A–M (see Figure 5-9).

Figure 5-8: Need to sort a group by date? Check out the cool calendar control.

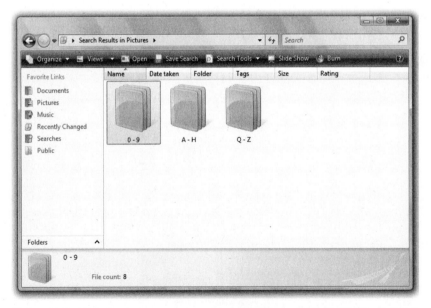

Figure 5-9: With Stacks, you can group related files and folders inside of virtual folders that can offer a bit of clarity in an otherwise-crowded folder.

Other column headings offer different preset Stacks. You might see Last Week and Today under the Date Modified heading, for example, or Paul and Unspecified under Author. As is often the case in Windows Vista, of course, the options available vary according to your particular system. That is, you won't see a Paul option unless one of the documents in the current folder was actually authored by someone named Paul.

Where Is It Now?

One of the challenges facing anyone moving to Windows Vista is that Microsoft changed the location of many user-interface elements, which might make it hard for you to navigate around the shell in some instances. Table 5-3 summarizes some of the changes you can expect to see, and how to work around them.

Table 5-3: Where to Find Common XP Shell Features in Windows Vista

My Documents	Renamed to Documents.
My Recent Documents	This Start Menu item was renamed to Recent Items.
My Pictures	Renamed to Pictures.
My Music	Renamed to Music.
My Video	Renamed to Videos.
My Computer	Renamed to Computer.
My Network Places	Renamed to Network.
Control Panel	Location and name unchanged from Windows XP.
Connect To	Unchanged from Windows XP.
Set Program Access and Defaults	Renamed to Default Programs and made part of the Control Panel. It can be found in Control Panel ➪ Programs ➪ Default Programs.
Printers and Faxes	Removed from the default Start Menu. Printers can be configured in Control Panel ➪ Hardware and Sound ➪ Printers. Faxing can be configured in the new Windows Fax application, which is found only in the Business and Ultimate editions of Windows Vista.
Help and Support	Location unchanged from Windows XP.
Search	In the originally shipped version of Windows Vista, the location of the Search item was unchanged from Windows XP. However, Microsoft removed this feature from the Start Menu beginning with Windows Vista Service Pack 1, a change discussed later in this chapter.
Run	Removed from the default Windows Vista Start Menu. To achieve a similar effect, type the name of an application into the Start Menu's Start Search text box. Alternately, you can customize the Start Menu to include the old Run item.

continues

Table 5-3: *(continued)*

Windows Explorer and Folders View	Rather than use separate My Computer and Explorer view styles, all shell windows in Windows Vista now incorporate an optional and expandable Folders panel in the bottom-left corner.
Explorer Menu System	This was renamed to Classic Menus and hidden by default, but you can view it by pressing the Alt key. To permanently enable the menu, click the new Configure This Explorer's Layout button and select Classic Menus.
Folder Options	Although Folder Options is still available from the Tools menu of the hidden Explorer menu (see the previous item), only the General and View tabs are available from the resulting dialog box. To access the File Types item, navigate to Control Panel ➪ Programs ➪ Default Programs ➪ Associate a File Type or Protocol with a Program. To access Offline Files, utilize the new Sync Center.
Explorer Status Bar	Replaced by the Details pane, which now sits at the bottom of all shell windows by default. Curiously, you can still enable the old status bar by tapping Alt and choosing Status Bar from the View menu.
Map/Disconnect Network Drive	This is still accessible via the Tools menu, which is hidden by default. Press the Alt key to view this menu (see Explorer Menu System, above).

Search Folders, Saved Searches, and Virtual Folders

Early in the several-year development life cycle of Windows Vista, Microsoft began talking up a new file-management system that's based on a new user-interface construct called a *virtual folder*. As the name suggests, a virtual folder is a special kind of folder that does not actually represent a physical location in the file system. You may recall that the constructs you call folders and special shell folders do, in fact, correspond to discrete locations in the shell namespace. That is, they are what you might call *real* or *physical* folders. Unlike real folders, virtual folders do not actually contain files and other folders. Instead, virtual folders contain *symbolic links*, or shortcuts, to real files and folders.

You might be surprised by how virtual folders are created: They're really just the physical embodiment of a file search. That's right: Virtual folders contain search results, presented in a way that is nearly indistinguishable from the display of a real folder. For this reason, Microsoft has elected to name virtual folders as Search Folders in Windows Vista; and Search Folders, naturally, contain saved searches.

Secret

Virtual Folders—A Short History Lesson

Let's step back a bit before diving too deeply into potentially confusing territory. In order to understand Vista's virtual folders, it's important to first understand the thinking that went into this feature; and because this is the ever-delayed Windows Vista I'm talking about, it might also be helpful to know about Microsoft's original plans for the Vista shell and virtual folders and compare those plans with what eventually happened.

continues

continued

Microsoft originally decided not to include in Vista a traditional file system with drive letters, physical file-system paths, and real folders. The software giant wanted to virtualize the entire file system so that you wouldn't need to worry about such arcane things as "the root of C:" and the Program Files folder. Instead, you would just access your documents and applications without ever thinking about where they resided on the disk. After all, that sort of electronic housekeeping is what a computer is good at, right?

This original vision required a healthy dose of technology. The core piece of this technology would be a new storage engine called WinFS (short for Windows Future Storage), which would have combined the best features of the NTFS file system with the relational database functionality of Microsoft's SQL Server products. As of this writing, Microsoft has been working on WinFS, and its predecessors, for about a decade.

Unfortunately, the WinFS technology wasn't even close to being ready in time for Windows Vista, so Microsoft pulled WinFS out of Vista and began developing it separately from the OS. Ultimately, it completely canceled plans to ship WinFS as a separate product. Instead, WinFS technologies will be integrated into future Windows versions and other Microsoft products.

Even though WinFS was out of the picture, Microsoft figured it could deliver much of that system's benefits using an updated version of the file system indexer it has shipped in Windows for years; and for about a year of Vista's development in 2004–2005, that was the plan. Instead of special shell folders such as Documents, users would access virtual folders such as All Documents, which would aggregate all of the documents on the hard drive and present them in a single location. Other special shell folders, such as Pictures and Music, would also be replaced by virtual folders.

Problem solved, right? Wrong. Beta testers—who are presumably more technical than most PC users—found the transition from normal folders to virtual folders to be extremely confusing. In retrospect, this should have been obvious. After all, a virtual folder that displays all of your documents is kind of useful when you're looking for something, but where do you save a new file? Is a virtual folder even a real place for applications that want to save data? And do users need to understand the differences between normal folders and virtual folders? Why have both kinds of folders?

With the delays mounting, Microsoft retreated from the virtual-folder scheme, just as it had when it stripped out WinFS previously. That's why the file system you see in Windows Vista is actually quite similar to that in Windows XP and previous Windows versions. That is, the file system still uses drive letters, normal folders, and special shell folders such as Documents and Pictures. If you're familiar with any prior Windows version, you should feel right at home in the Vista shell. (Likewise, if you've found the Windows file system to be a bit, well, lackluster, all the same complaints still apply in Vista.)

There's one major difference between Vista's file system and that of previous Windows versions, although it's not particularly obvious. Even though Microsoft has decided not to replace special shell folders with virtual folders in this release, the company is still shipping virtual-folder technology in Windows Vista. The idea is that users will get used to virtual folders now, and then perhaps a future Windows version will simply move to that system, and eventually we'll all reach some nerd-vana where all the silly file-system constructs used today are suddenly passé.

continues

continued

In short, virtual folders do exist in Windows Vista; they're just somewhat hidden. OK, they're *really* well hidden, maybe even devilishly well hidden. That makes them a power-user feature and thus, for readers of this book, inherently interesting. Most people won't even discover virtual folders and their contained shared searches. In fact, if you want to harness some of the most awesome and unique technology in Windows Vista, this is the place to start; the skills you learn now will give you a leg up when Microsoft finally gets around to retiring the current file system. It's only a matter of time.

Understanding Search Folders

Search Folders contain the saved results from a search query. They are built using Vista's indexing engine and stored in an XML file format that developers can easily access, modify, and extend. There are two types of saved searches: those built into the system itself and thus exposed automatically in the shell, and those that you build yourself. The following sections describe both kinds of saved searches.

Using Prebuilt Search Folders

Microsoft provides a small number of useful saved searches for you, and they're available as soon as you begin using Windows Vista. There are two ways to discover these saved searches:

◆ Open an Explorer window, which contains a single search folder, called Recently Changed, in its navigation pane by default.

◆ Navigate to the Searches folder, which is found in each user's Home folder (typically, C:\Users*username*\ Searches). The Searches folder is shown in Figure 5-10.

Table 5-4 lists the prebuilt Search Folders that Microsoft provides in Windows Vista.

Table 5-4: Prebuilt Search Folders

Recent Documents	Finds any document files you've accessed recently, including Word documents, text files, and locally saved HTML files
Recent E-mail	Finds any Windows Mail–based e-mail you've received recently
Recent Music	Finds any music files that you've played in Windows Media Player 11 recently
Recent Pictures and Videos	Finds any digital photos or videos you've viewed recently
Recently Changed	Finds data files of any kind that you've changed recently, including documents, music files, digital photos, and digital videos
Shared By Me	Finds folders that are configured as shared folders (and can thus be accessed by other people on your local network if networking is configured for that functionality)

Figure 5-10: The Saved Searches folder contains prebuilt and user-made Search Folders.

Secret

Although Search Folders appear and act like normal folders, they are actually specially formatted XML files that use a .search file extension. For example, the Search Folder named Attachments is actually a file named Attachments.search. If you want to edit one of these saved searches, simply right-click it in the shell and choose Open With ⇨ Notepad. **DANGER:** Be careful not to leave the check box named *Always Use the Selected Program to Open This Kind of File* checked (selected), however. If you do that, your Search Folders will revert to normal text files and won't work properly anymore and there is no simple way to get them back short of restoring a backup or reinstalling Windows Vista.

Looking at the Code for a Search Folder

Take a quick look behind a typical Search Folder called Shared by Me. If you open this saved search in a text editor such as Notepad, you'll see that it's composed of XML code, as shown in Listing 5-1.

Listing 5-1: Example Source Code from a Saved Search

```xml
<?xml version="1.0"?>
<persistedQuery version="1.0">
  <viewInfo viewMode="details" iconSize="16">
    <visibleColumns>
      <column viewField="System.ItemNameDisplay"/>
      <column viewField="System.DateModified"/>
      <column viewField="System.Keywords"/>
      <column viewField="System.SharedWith"/>
      <column viewField="System.ItemFolderPathDisplayNarrow"/>
    </visibleColumns>
    <frequentlyUsedColumns>
      <column viewField="System.Author"/>
      <column viewField="System.Kind"/>
      <column viewField="System.Size"/>
      <column viewField="System.Title"/>
      <column viewField="System.Rating"/>
    </frequentlyUsedColumns>
    <sortList>
      <sort viewField="System.SharedWith" direction="descending"/>
    </sortList>
  </viewInfo>

  <query>
    <conditions>
      <condition type="andCondition">
        <condition type="leafCondition" property="System.IsShared"
          operator="eq" value="true"/>
        <condition type="leafCondition" property="System.FileOwner"
          operator="eq" value="[Me]"/>
      </condition>
    </conditions>
    <kindList>
      <kind name="item"/>
    </kindList>
    <scope>
      <include knownFolder="{5E6C858F-0E22-4760-9AFE-EA3317B67173}"/>
      <include knownFolder="{DFDF76A2-C82A-4D63-906A-5644AC457385}"/>
    </scope>
  </query>

</persistedQuery>
```

You don't have to be a programming guru to understand what's going on here. There are a few main parts to the saved search file: **viewInfo** (which includes a single subpart called **sortList**) and **query**, the latter of which includes the **scope** and **visibleInList** subparts.

The **sortList** subpart in the **viewInfo** part clearly defines how the saved search will be displayed: by date modified in descending order. The **scope** subpart inside the **query** part is interesting: It specifies three folder locations that this query will search. Those huge strings of letters and numbers are known as a globally unique identifier (GUID). Each GUID identifies a unique location. When you create your own Search Folders (described later in this chapter), one or more scope subparts are used, and filled with normal shell location strings, such as C:\Users\Paul.

Editing a Search Folder

If you're an XML expert, you can manually edit any saved searches, including the ones that Microsoft ships with Windows Vista. Any text editor, including Notepad, enables you to change the contents of a saved search in addition to simply viewing them. However, this isn't necessarily a great idea unless you really know what you're doing. In fact, it's a perfectly horrible idea. A better idea is to use Vista's built-in user interface for creating your own search folders.

Creating Your Own Search Folders

Although the built-in saved searches can be handy, the real power of virtual folders is that you can make your own. As you use Windows Vista, you may find yourself occasionally performing the same search repeatedly. If that's the case, you can simply save the results as a Search Folder, which you can then access later as if it were a normal folder.

Like the built-in Search Folders, any Search Folder that you create yourself is dynamic, meaning it can change every time you open it (and cause its underlying search query to run). For example, if you create a Search Folder that looks for all Microsoft Word (***.doc** and ***.docx**) files, you may produce a search results list containing 125 matches; but if you add a new Word document to your Documents folder and reopen the Search Folder, you'll see that you now have 126 matches. In other words, Search Folders aren't static; they don't cease to be relevant after they're created. Because they literally requery the file system every time they're run—for example, when the folder is opened—saved searches always return the most up-to-date results possible.

Searching for Files

To create a Search Folder, you must first search your hard drive for some kind of file. In a simple example, you might look for any files on your hard drive that contain your full name. To do so, launch Windows Vista search by selecting WinKey+F. This displays the Search tool, as shown in Figure 5-11.

Secret

Don't have a Windows key on your keyboard? No problem: Just open the Start Menu and select F3.

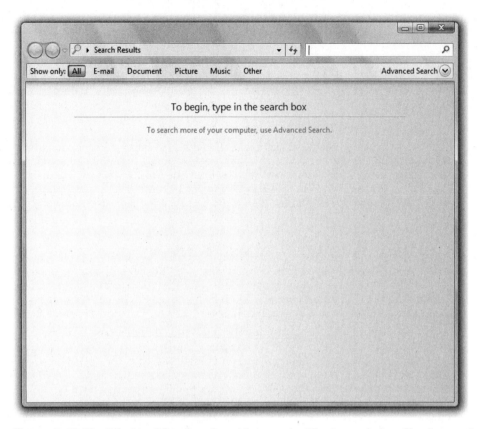

Figure 5-11: The Windows Vista Search tool is a standard Explorer window. Simply type the word or phrase you are looking for into the Search box.

Secret

In the originally shipped version of Windows Vista, Microsoft included a Search entry on the right side of the Start Menu. This entry is absent with the release of Service Pack 1 (SP1) and it cannot be added back via the taskbar and Start Menu Properties interface as you may expect. That's because Microsoft bowed to pressure from its competitors—specifically, Internet search giant Google—which complained that the integrated search functionality in Windows Vista made it too difficult to sell competing desktop search solutions such as Google Desktop Search. To appease Google and avoid a lengthy and potentially costly antitrust investigation, Microsoft agreed to make some changes to Windows Vista, essentially treating search like other so-called Windows "middleware" that can be replaced by users. There are a number of components to this change, but the obvious visual change is that the Start Menu's Search entry is now missing in action. (This change does not affect Start Menu Search, however, which is denoted by the "Start Search" box in the lower-left corner of the Start Menu.) For a lot more information about this change, please refer to my article, "Instant Search Changes to Windows Vista Service Pack 1," on the SuperSite for Windows: www.winsupersite.com/showcase/winvista_google_changes.asp.

Searching is context-sensitive. If you bring up the Search tool as described here, Windows Vista will search the most common locations where documents might be stored in the file system. (These locations are called *indexed locations* in Windows Vista. They are the file-system locations that are indexed, or kept track of, by the Instant Search indexer.) However, if you use the Search box in any Explorer window, Vista will search only the current folder (and its subfolders).

Not surprisingly, you can change the locations that Windows Vista indexes by default. Equally unsurprisingly, finding the user interface for this requires a bit of spelunking. Fortunately, I've done the dirty work for you: Just open the Start Menu and type **Indexing Options** (you should see it appear after just *ind*) and press Enter to display the Indexing Options control panel. A word of caution: Don't add too many file-system locations to the indexed locations list, and certainly not the whole hard drive, because doing so could adversely affect your PC's performance. The only compelling reason to change this setting is if you regularly keep your document files in a nonstandard location (that is, not the Documents, Music, or Pictures folders or other locations not found in your Users folder). To add a location to the indexed locations, click the Modify button and then the Show All Locations button in the Indexed Locations dialog that appears. In the next window, you can expand the locations—such as Local Disk (C:)—that appear in the Change Selected Locations list. As you expand the tree view, place a check next to any folders you want indexed.

tip
If you want the absolute best performance, consider moving the index to your fastest hard drive. To do this, open Indexing and Search Options and click the Advanced button. From the Advanced dialog box that appears, click Select New and choose a disk you know to be faster than the system disk. Close all the dialogs and reboot for the change to take effect.

In the Search window, select the Search box in the upper-right corner of the window (it should be selected by default) and begin typing your search query. As you type, Windows Vista queries the index of files contained on your hard drive and returns the results of your in-progress search in real time, as shown in Figure 5-12.

Figure 5-12: Instant Search truly is instant, assuming you're using the Search box. Here, search results are returned as you type.

This feature is called *as-you-type search* or *word-wheeling*. Contrast this with most search tools, in which you type a search query and then press Enter or a user-interface button in order to initiate the actual search. Vista can perform search queries as you type because the information it's looking for is instantly available due to indexing. On a typical PC, there's no performance penalty.

As Vista displays the search results, a green progress bar appears in the Search window's address bar. When the query is complete, the progress bar disappears.

Secret

Although you're probably familiar with file and folder searching using the Find function in previous Windows versions or a third-party tool such as Google Desktop or MSN Desktop Search, you may not be familiar with some commonly used wildcard characters, which can help fine-tune your searches. For example, the asterisk (*) stands for one or more letters, whereas the question mark (?) is used to represent any one letter.

Filtering the Search Results

A search query that is as general as your name can result in hundreds or thousands of hits, so it's more useful to filter the search results a bit to make the search more specific. You do this by using the Show Only toolbar in the Search window. Here you can specify which file types you'd like to search: All, E-mail, Documents, and some others.

When you specify a file type, such as Document, the search results list is trimmed down, often significantly, as shown in Figure 5-13.

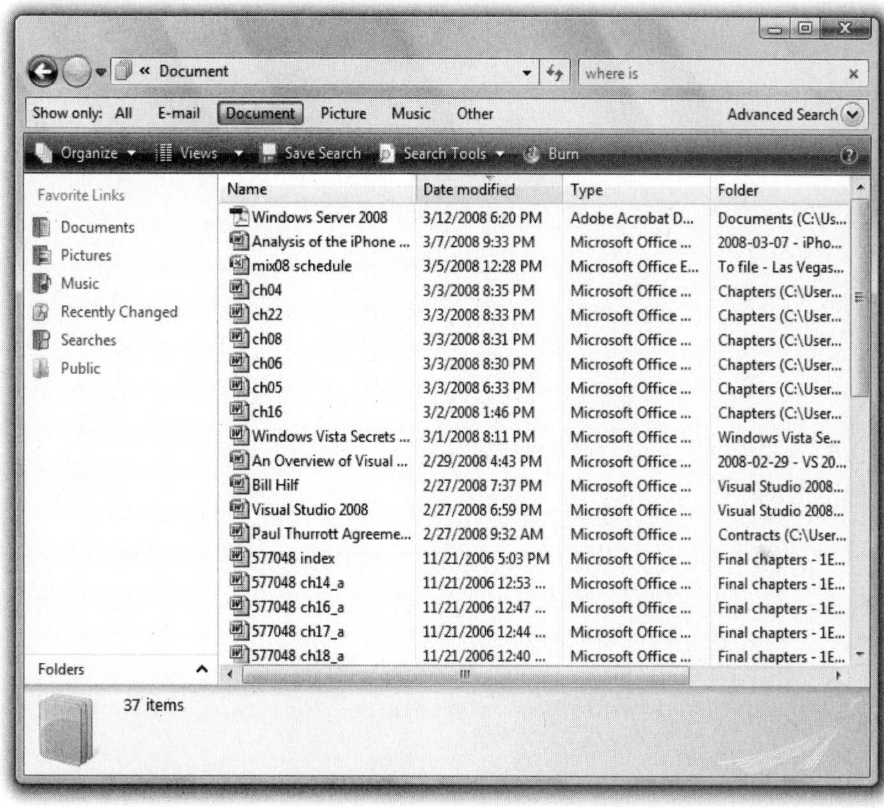

Figure 5-13: A filtered search results list is typically more relevant.

What happens when you want to display results that include two or more file types or perform even more powerful searches? By default Search looks in all indexed locations, but you can also force it to search all drives and devices, the current user's Home folder, or another location that you specify. For these types of searches, you need to access Advanced Search, as denoted by the Advanced Search button on the right of the toolbar. Click this button, which resembles a downward-pointing arrow, and you'll be presented with the Advanced Search pane, shown in Figure 5-14.

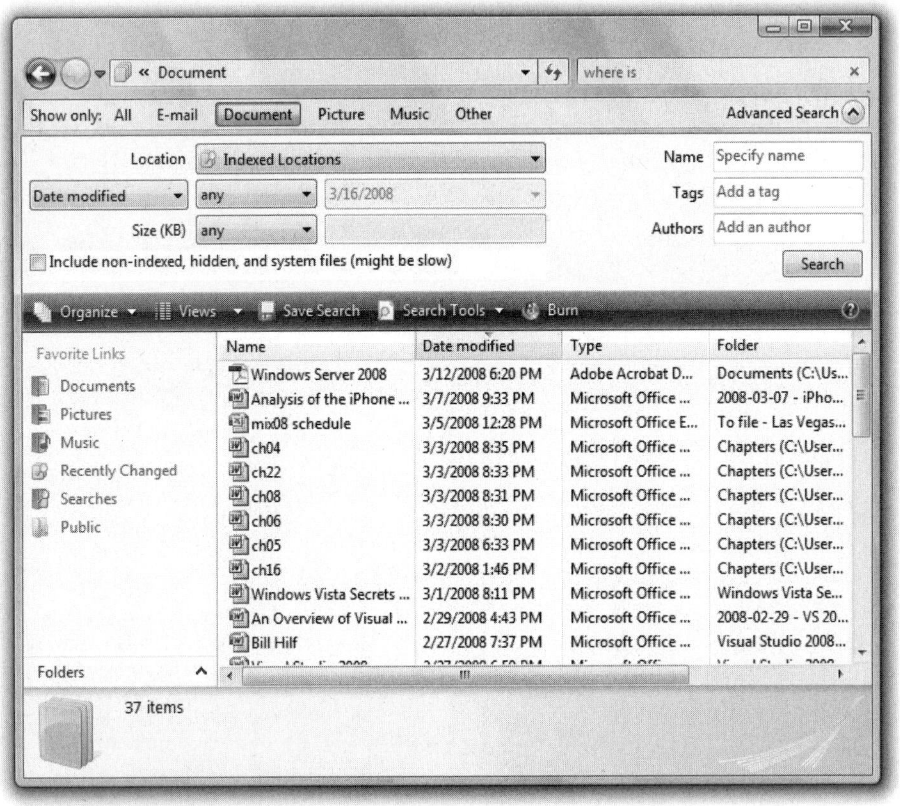

Figure 5-14: With the Advanced Search pane, you can highly fine-tune your searches.

With this pane, you can filter your search by a wide range of criteria:

◆ **Document type:** At the top of the Advanced Search pane is a row of boxes, labeled All, E-mail, Document, Picture, Music, and Other. Select a box to narrow down the options to specific document types. "Other" is the oddball. It shows results for such things as Outlook Appointments and Contacts (among others).

◆ **Location:** In this context, location refers to locations in the Windows Vista file system. The default option, of course, is Indexed Locations, but you can also choose between certain special locations (e.g., Everywhere or Computer), specific drives (as in drive letters, not physical disks), and other search locations, the latter of which brings up a Choose Search Locations dialog from which you can check any number of disparate locations from your system.

◆ **Date:** Here you can choose between Date, Date Modified, and Date Created, in each case specifying criteria such as any date (the default), the exact date (Is), Is Before, and Is After. For example, you might look for files that were created after a certain date or on an exact date.

♦ **Size:** This option enables you to specify the file size or file-size range to include in your search. The default, of course, is Any, which means that files of all sizes will be included in the search results. Other criteria include Is, Is Less Than, and Is Greater Than.

♦ **Name:** This option enables you to specify a filename or, using wildcards, a number of filenames. For example, I might type *thurrott* to search for all filenames including that word, or *thurrott OR mckiernan* to search for all filenames including either word. Searching for *paul AND thurrott* would return only those filenames that included both of those words.

♦ **Tags:** While the inclusion of metadata such as tags is unlikely to gain much traction in Windows Vista's lifetime outside of music and picture files, Microsoft has at least made it possible for users to add this additional information to each document, which can lead to speedier and more refined searches. For example, there's a Tags field in the Save As dialog of most Office 2007 applications, and the Windows Photo Gallery application in Windows Vista supports the tagging of photo files (using such terms as *Vacation*, *Family*, or whatever tags you may prefer). If you don't use a lot of tags yourself—and chances are good that you don't, as this feature is virtually invisible—this option won't be of much use; but tagging is a key tenet of the search-based file system that Microsoft had hoped to add to Windows Vista, so my guess is that you'll see a lot more of this stuff moving forward.

♦ **Authors:** Many applications support the concept of an author or authors each time a document file is created; and on any given PC, the default author is typically the person who registered or activated the copy of Windows you're using. As with tagging, Microsoft Office is a typical example of an application that utilizes this metadata: Each time a logged-on user runs an Office application for the first time, that user is prompted to enter his or her name and initials. This information is used as the Authors tag by default. (You can change this on a document-by-document basis.)

♦ **Include non-indexed, hidden, and system files:** Finally, you can force Instant Search to be anything but instant: It can search non-indexed, hidden, and system locations, which is both slow (because they're not indexed) and generally pointless (because most people don't store documents in the Program Files or Windows directories). Still, it's there if you need it.

Secret   Every shell location can be searched, including some that might not be obvious, such as the Recycle Bin. To search the Recycle Bin, simply open it, select the Search box, and begin searching.

Note that searches performed using the Advanced Search pane are *not* instant. To trigger an advanced search, you need to click the search button inside the pane. These searches can often take a while to perform, depending on which filters you've created.

Saving a Search

After you have created a search, especially a fairly complicated one that you may need to repeat, it's a good idea to save it. Curiously, there's no obvious way to do this. To save a search, press Alt to bring up the Classic Menu, and then select Save Search from the File menu, as shown in Figure 5-15. This displays a standard Save As dialog box, where you can provide a name for your saved search. Logically, by default saved searches are saved to your Searches folder (found under your user's Home folder), but you can change the location if you'd rather save a search to your desktop, the Documents folder, or another location. You can also drag any saved search to the Favorite Links section of the navigational pane in Windows Explorer so you can access it easily later.

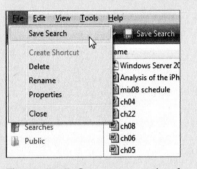

Figure 5-15: Save your searches for later using Vista's hidden Classic Menu.

Summary

Microsoft may have removed its WinFS technology from Windows Vista, but you'd never know it based on the amount of integrated search technology that is still built into the system. The integrated search functionality in Windows Vista is a huge improvement over the far more limited Find functionality in Windows XP, with numerous entry points in the OS, including every Explorer window, and intelligent results based on where the search was instigated. You can even search for applications, documents, and other objects directly from the Start Menu. Best of all, the Windows Vista search functionality includes one of the system's best power-use features: the capability to save searches as dynamic virtual folders that you can access repeatedly as if they were normal shell folders. It's no wonder that even innovative Apple copied this functionality from Microsoft. The deep OS integration in Apple's Mac OS X Spotlight feature was directly inspired by the integrated search work Microsoft first announced it would include in Windows Vista.

Using Windows Sidebar

Chapter

6

With the proliferation of local and global digital information since the advent of the public Internet, Microsoft has been working on ways to integrate the data you need most often in a seamless way with the Windows desktop. Early in the development of Windows Vista, the company created a feature called Windows Sidebar, which would sit on the edge of the PC display and provide a centralized and standardized area for Windows features, third-party applications, and Web services to provide notifications and alerts. Although the original Sidebar was scrapped partway through Vista's development, a new version of the Sidebar, based on Web standards and partially integrated with Microsoft's Live.com Web site (**www.live.com**) and the Sideshow feature on some portable computers and other devices, was eventually created. This chapter examines this new feature of the Windows shell and demonstrates how you can use the Sidebar to keep valuable information at your fingertips.

What Is Windows Sidebar?

Back when Microsoft shipped Windows 98, it added a debatably useful feature called Active Desktop that provided an HTML (Hypertext Markup Language) layer on top of the traditional desktop. Active Desktop was an attempt to capitalize on the then-emerging trend of users wanting to combine live data from the Web with their PC operating system. The term for this at the time was *push technology*. The idea was that although you could use a Web browser to manually find data on the Web, or *pull* data from the Web, a push-technology client like Active Desktop could *push* data to the user automatically with no interaction required.

Ultimately, users found Active Desktop to be confusing and undesirable, mostly because Microsoft and its partners used it as a front end for advertisements and other unwanted information; and although the feature was never really removed from Windows, it was deemphasized in subsequent Windows versions, such as Windows XP. As shown in Figure 6-1, however, it's still possible to add Web content to your XP desktop via Active Desktop if you really want to.

Active Desktop may have failed, but the underlying benefits of push technology are still valid today. You can see that this type of functionality still exists in such technologies as RSS (Really Simple Syndication), which in fact attempts to solve essentially the same problem as Active Desktop: Rather than force users to manually search for the content they want, that content is delivered automatically to them using a unique kind of client (in this case, an RSS client). One such RSS client is included in Windows Vista as part of Internet Explorer 7, discussed in Chapter 19.

In Windows Vista, Active Desktop is finally gone forever, but integrated push technology lives on with a brand-new feature called Windows Sidebar. Like Active Desktop, Windows Sidebar is available by default and is running when you start up your new Windows Vista–based PC for the first time. Moreover, it will keep on running unless you configure it not to do so, but Windows Sidebar solves one of Active Desktop's major problems by moving the main user interface off the desktop and to the side of the screen where it won't typically be hidden under your open applications and other windows. (If it is hidden by windows, you can optionally configure Windows Sidebar to appear "on top" of other windows.)

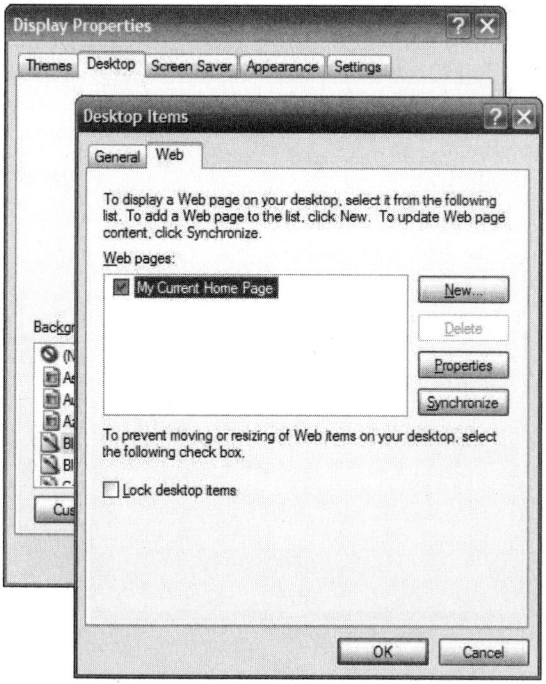

Figure 6-1: Like a vestigial tail, the Active Desktop feature lives on, largely unused, in Windows XP.

Secret

What, you say you don't want Windows Sidebar to appear on your screen every time you boot into Windows? Yes, you can disable this feature:

1. Locate the Windows Sidebar icon in the tray notification area to the left of the system clock in the taskbar. (You may need to click the chevron at the left of the notification area to expand it and display all of the available icons.)
2. Right-click the Windows Sidebar icon and choose Exit.
3. In the window that appears, clear the check box next to Start Sidebar when Windows Starts.
4. Click the Exit Sidebar button.

If you change your mind and would like to run Sidebar later, just use Windows Vista's new Start Menu Search feature to locate the Windows Sidebar shortcut. Open the Start Menu and type **Sidebar** to find it. Note that if you quit Sidebar while it is hidden, it will be hidden at the next startup as well.

Put simply, Windows Sidebar is a panel that sits at the edge of your screen and houses small *gadgets*, or mini-applications, each of which provides specific functionality, as shown in Figure 6-2. Gadgets typically connect to data somewhere, be it on your PC or on the Internet. Windows Vista ships with a variety of these gadgets, but you can download many more online; and if you're familiar with Web technologies such as HTML, DHTML (Dynamic HTML), and JavaScript, you can even build your own gadgets.

Figure 6-2: Active Desktop lives: Windows Vista's new Windows Sidebar feature enables you to access Web-based information from your desktop.

Because Windows Sidebar does occupy a small portion of vertical onscreen real estate, this feature is more useful for those with widescreen displays. That said, Windows Sidebar appears under other windows by default so that users with normal square-shaped screens can also use it. You'll examine this behavior in just a bit.

> **tip** If you are using a widescreen display, you may want to configure Windows Sidebar to appear on top of other windows, like the taskbar. That way it will always be onscreen, even when application windows are maximized.

Launching Windows Sidebar

Windows Sidebar should launch automatically when you boot into Windows Vista. If you disable the Windows Sidebar's autorun functionality, you'll have to go digging for it in the Start Menu. It's somewhat hidden in Start ➪ All Programs ➪ Accessories (see Figure 6-3). This is made all the more confusing because Microsoft has changed the way the Start Menu expands; instead of the submenu system employed in previous versions, the submenu expands and contracts in place right within the Start Menu now. A better way, as always, is to use Start Menu Search: Just open the Start Menu and type **side**; you should see Windows Sidebar as the top entry in the search results.

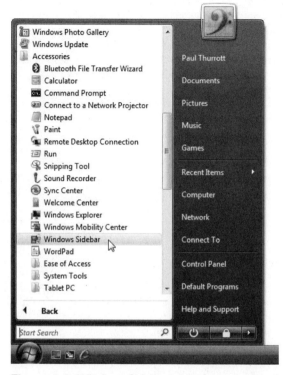

Figure 6-3: Windows Sidebar is buried pretty deeply in the Start Menu.

When Windows Sidebar starts, you'll see a subtle black shadow appear on the right side of the screen, as shown in Figure 6-4. Additionally, a nearly indiscernible Windows Sidebar icon appears in the tray notification area next to the system clock. Depending on how your system is configured, you should also see one or more gadgets, or mini-applications, displayed in the Sidebar itself.

Figure 6-4: At first you might think something is wrong with your display, but that's just Windows Sidebar subtly appearing onscreen.

tip
Microsoft configures Windows Sidebar in a standard way with only three gadgets, so you will see only these default gadgets if you install Windows Vista yourself. It's far more likely, however, that you will acquire Windows Vista with a new PC, and PC makers have a nasty habit of either disabling the Sidebar by default or, more frequently, spamming it up with a set of their own machine- or company-specific gadgets. I have yet to see a PC maker ship a useful, unique Sidebar with one of their machines. (If you do see such a thing, I'd love to hear about it. Drop me a line at thurrott@windowsitpro.com.) In short, the Sidebar on your own computer could very well have been modified extensively, which usually means that it will contain a bunch of weird gadgets, many of which you might not want. I'll show you how to get rid of them soon.

If you move the mouse cursor to the right side of your screen, the Windows Sidebar will fade into the foreground slowly, and you'll see that it is, in fact, a translucent panel of sorts, and not a screen defect. That shadow appears only when Windows Sidebar is configured to autohide, which it is by default. You'll learn more about this and other configuration options in the next section.

Configuring Sidebar

It's highly unlikely that you'll want to use Windows Sidebar in its default form, whether you installed Vista manually or just got a new PC. Thankfully, Windows Sidebar includes a number of configuration options. You can change the way this panel displays, where it displays, which gadgets it displays, and other related options; and, of course, you can determine whether it appears at all when Windows Vista first boots.

Configuring the Sidebar Display

Many Windows Sidebar features can be configured directly from the Windows Sidebar Properties dialog box. To access this dialog box, move the mouse over to the Sidebar, right-click, and choose Properties. As shown in Figure 6-5, this dialog box enables you to change how the Sidebar is displayed on your screen.

Secret

You can also access Windows Sidebar properties by finding the Windows Sidebar notification icon, right-clicking it, and choosing Properties.

Figure 6-5: The Sidebar Properties dialog box enables
you to configure Sidebar display features.

Using Sidebar Properties

Using this simple window, you can determine whether the Sidebar runs every time
Windows starts. This option is applicable on a user-by-user basis; disabling Sidebar auto-
start for one user will not prevent Sidebar from autostarting for other users.

You can also choose from several arrangement options. For example, the Sidebar can
appear under other windows (the default), or it can be displayed on top of other windows
as the taskbar does. If you opt to display the Sidebar on top of other windows, it appears as
a solid, glasslike panel and loses the subtle shadow and translucency effects. Additionally,
floating windows—applications, dialog boxes, and so on—will appear below the Sidebar.
Note an additional behavior associated with this mode, however: When you maximize
any window, that window will treat the innermost edge of the Sidebar as the new edge
of the screen. As shown in Figure 6-6, this can create a strange effect when both floating
and maximized windows are displayed with the Sidebar.

You can also configure the Sidebar to appear on the right or left of the screen (but not
on the top or bottom); and if you have multiple computer displays, you can choose which
monitor you want to use for the Sidebar. Figure 6-7 shows a multi-screen display in which
the Sidebar appears only on monitor 1, which is the rightmost monitor.

Figure 6-6: When the Sidebar is configured to appear in front of other windows, maximized windows treat the Sidebar as the edge of the screen (on the left), but floating windows can still display below it (on the right).

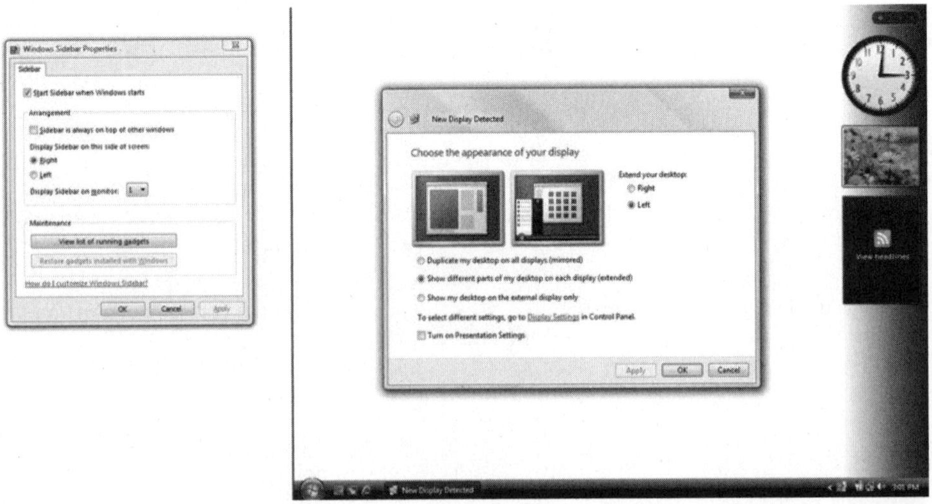

Figure 6-7: On a multi-monitor system, the Sidebar appears only on a single display.

Under the Maintenance section of the Sidebar properties are two options. View List of Running Gadgets enables you to examine which gadgets you've configured to run in the Sidebar. This option is useful because the resulting dialog displays a list of currently running gadgets, along with their version numbers and the name of the company or individual who created them. You can remove running icons from the Sidebar here (though there's an easier way you'll learn soon). Note that removing a gadget does not delete it from your system.

caution　Be careful not to install gadgets from sources you don't trust. Obviously, gadgets created by Microsoft will be safe, but it's possible that a malicious hacker may someday create a gadget designed to do horrible things to your PC. When it comes to anything that connects to the Internet, proceed with caution.

The option Restore Gadgets Installed with Windows is typically grayed out and thus unavailable. This button is enabled when you uninstall one or more of the default gadgets included with Windows Vista. If you mistakenly delete something useful, such as the Clock gadget, you can restore it with this button.

Other Sidebar Configuration Options

In addition to the Sidebar Properties dialog box, there are other ways you can configure various Sidebar features. For example, when you right-click the Sidebar surface, you'll see a number of options. To hide the Sidebar—not to be confused with autohide—select Close Sidebar. When you do this, the Sidebar disappears from the screen. To make it reappear, click (or right-click) the Sidebar icon in the tray and choose Open.

tip　Most of the menu options you see when you right-click the Sidebar are available from the Sidebar icon in the tray. (The one exception is Close Sidebar.) This duplication enables you to easily access various Sidebar features when the Sidebar is hidden or cannot be seen under other windows. The Sidebar icon's menu is available only when you right-click the icon. If you just click it, nothing happens.

Secret　If you use the Alt+Tab keyboard shortcut to task-switch between running applications and windows, and choose the option for Desktop, all of your running applications and other displayed windows will minimize or hide, including the Sidebar if it is configured to display underneath other windows. To redisplay the Sidebar, select another application or window from the task switcher. If the Sidebar is configured to always be on top of other windows, however, it won't disappear when you task-switch to the Desktop.

Adding Gadgets to the Sidebar

The Sidebar isn't particularly interesting by itself. That's because Windows Sidebar is really just a container for gadgets, and it is these gadgets that make the Sidebar truly useful. To add gadgets to the Sidebar, click the Add Gadgets button at the top of the Sidebar, which resembles a plus mark. (Alternately, right-click the Sidebar, or the Sidebar icon, and choose Add Gadgets.) This causes the Add Gadgets window to appear, as shown in Figure 6-8. This window provides you with a number of built-in gadgets, which you can add directly to the Sidebar surface.

Figure 6-8: With Add Gadgets, you get a menu of gadgets from which to choose.

To add a gadget to the Sidebar, either double-click the gadget in Add Gadgets or simply drag and drop a gadget onto the Sidebar surface, as shown in Figure 6-9. You can also change the order in which gadgets appear on the Windows Sidebar by dragging them up and down.

Secret

You can add multiple copies of any gadget to the Sidebar if you'd like. This is handy for certain gadgets, such as the Clock, each instance of which can be set to a different time zone, and Weather. I use multiple copies of the Weather gadget to keep track of the weather in both Celsius and Fahrenheit; I'm hoping that by keeping these gadgets next to each other, I'll slowly learn to subconsciously translate between the two temperature types. Hey, it's a theory.

Figure 6-9: You can drag gadgets around
just like you do files on the Windows desktop.

Secret

What happens if you add too many gadgets? After all, the Sidebar is only so big.
If you add enough gadgets, the Sidebar will open a second pane and enable Next
Pane and Previous Pane buttons at the top of the Sidebar. To switch between the
panes, simply click these buttons.

Looking at the Built-In Gadgets

Table 6-1 summarizes the gadgets that ship with Windows Vista.

Table 6-1: Built-In Windows Sidebar Gadgets

Gadget		What It Does
Calendar		Provides a handy onscreen calendar with both day and month views. Note that there is no Settings window for Calendar. It's designed to tell you the date and day of the week only.
Clock		A clock that can be configured to show the time in any time zone or city worldwide, or just use the current system time. Clocks can be named, and you can choose among eight different clock styles. You can also choose whether to enable the second hand.

continues

Table 6-1: *(continued)*

Gadget		What It Does
Contacts		A gadget-based version of Windows Contacts. It links only to Windows Contacts and not to other contacts databases. You can switch between a full contacts list and a details view of an individual contact. There's even a search bar. As with Calendar, Contacts has no Settings window. What you see is what you get.
CPU Meter		A set of gauges that tracks the load on your PC's microprocessor and RAM, using percentage only. There is no Settings window for this gadget.
Currency		A simple currency converter. It's handy if you want to see how poorly the U.S. dollar is doing today against the Euro. There is no Settings window for this gadget.
Feed Headlines		An RSS client that integrates with the RSS feeds to which you've subscribed in Internet Explorer. You must click the View Feeds button before it displays the results of any feed. To view more information about a particular feed, click the feed, and Feed Headlines expands past the Sidebar with a larger text view. To view the actual feed or Web page in Internet Explorer, click the headline in the expanded window. (See Chapter 19 for more information about RSS feeds.) The Feed Headlines Settings window enables you to configure which of IE 7's RSS feeds to display and how many headlines are displayed at a time.
Notes		A cute little note pad, similar to a sticky note, perfect for jotting down reminders. The Settings window for this gadget enables you to pick the font used for notes, and which of six colors to use for the virtual pad of paper.
Picture Puzzle		Remember those little handheld tile games in which you move tiles around until the picture displayed on the front of the tiles is complete? Well, here it is in gadget form. You can choose from 11 pictures, enable a timer, and click a small button to see what the finished picture is supposed to look like.
Slide Show		A photo-slideshow gadget with a host of options. You can pick the folder from which to obtain the pictures (the default is the Public Pictures folder), the amount of time to display each image, which of 15 transitions to use, and whether the pictures should be shuffled. While the gadget is running, you can also mouse over its surface to access a small controller overlay with Previous, Play/Pause, and Next buttons, as well as a View button that displays the current picture in Windows Photo Gallery.
Stocks		An electronic stock ticker that integrates with Microsoft's MSN Money Central to provide constant stock-price updates. By default, this gadget displays the Dow Jones Industrial Average, the NASDAQ composite, and the S&P 500 index, but you can add and remove stock symbols as you see fit.

continues

Table 6-1: *(continued)*

Gadget		What It Does
Weather		A weather gadget that can be configured for any town and can display the temperature in Fahrenheit or Celsius. Note that you can search by town/city name (e.g., Paris, France) or by zip code (e.g., 02132).

Some of these gadgets are obviously just for fun, but some are truly useful, especially for serious multi-taskers. I especially appreciate the Clock and Weather gadgets, which can be used in multiple instances for different locations, and the Calendar.

Configuring Gadgets

When you have one or more gadgets displayed on the Sidebar, you'll probably want to configure them in some way. Some gadgets offer no customization per se, but many expose their customizable features via a Settings window. The way you access this information is identical for any gadget. If you move the mouse cursor over a gadget, you'll see one or more small user interface items appear in the top-right corner of all the gadgets, as shown in Figure 6-10: a small close button (resembling an x), which is always present, and, possibly, a small wrench. This second item appears only on gadgets that offer some form of customization.

Figure 6-10: When you mouse over a gadget, you'll see some new UI components appear around the edges.

If you click the close button, the gadget will close and disappear from the Sidebar without any warning dialog box; but if you click the wrench, the gadget will display its Settings window. Each gadget displays a different set of Settings options. Figure 6-11 shows the Settings options for the Clock gadget.

In addition to configuring individual gadgets, you can also rearrange gadgets on the Sidebar surface using your well-developed drag-and-drop skills. Simply grab a gadget with the mouse and move it up and down the Sidebar surface until it's positioned where you want it. Note that this feature works best when there are several gadgets. If you have only a few gadgets displayed on the Sidebar, they will be arranged only at the top of the Sidebar. You cannot arbitrarily move them down onto unused portions of the Sidebar's bottom area. If you try to, the bottom-most gadget will simply slide right back up so that it is on the bottom of the stack of gadgets.

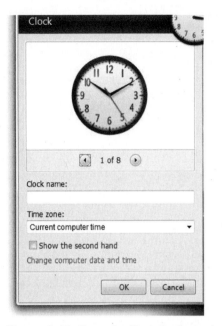

Figure 6-11: From the Clock Settings window, you can select a clock name, the time zone, and optionally show the clock's second hand.

To access common gadget options, you can right-click any gadget. This displays a pop-up menu from which you can control the opacity, or translucency, of the gadget (20, 40, 60, 80, or 100 percent, where 100 percent is the default), and access other options. (Confusingly, a gadget's Settings window is accessed via the Options menu.)

Moving Gadgets to the Windows Desktop

Surprisingly, you can also move gadgets directly to the Windows Desktop if you'd like, making the Sidebar and its gadgets work a lot more like the old Active Desktop. To do so, simply drag and drop a gadget from the Sidebar onto an empty area of the Windows desktop, as shown in Figure 6-12.

Figure 6-12: Sidebar gadgets aren't locked into the Sidebar. You can put them on the Desktop as well. Here you can see a Desktop-based gadget on the left and a Sidebar-based gadget on the right.

tip You can also move a gadget to the desktop by right-clicking it in the Sidebar and choosing Detach from Sidebar.

When you drag a gadget onto the desktop in this fashion, you'll notice that it actually grows a bit bigger than it was when displayed on the Sidebar itself.

Secret Many gadgets also offer additional functionality when dragged onto the Desktop. The best example of this is the Weather gadget. When displayed on the Windows Sidebar, this gadget presents the current temperature along with a small graphic depicting the current conditions. However, when you drag it to the Desktop the Weather gadget shows additional information, including the current day's high and low temperatures and a three-day forecast. To move a gadget back to the Sidebar, simply drag and drop the Sidebar. Alternately, you can right-click a floating gadget and choose Attach to Sidebar.

Secret If you move gadgets to the Desktop, the Sidebar still needs to be running in order for them to display. However, you can close (really, hide) the Sidebar if you'd like. When you do so, floating gadgets will still appear. However, if you quit the Sidebar, the floating gadgets will disappear from the Desktop as well.

You can also add gadgets to your Desktop by opening the Add Gadgets dialog box and dragging a gadget from there directly to the Desktop, and not to the Sidebar.

Gadgets remember where you left them. If you have some gadgets on the Desktop and some others on the Sidebar and you quit the Sidebar and then restart it, each of the gadgets will reappear exactly where you left it. (This includes multiple monitor setups as well, which is nice.) Additionally, the Sidebar remembers how it was configured when you quit. If you quit the Sidebar while it is hidden, it will start up next time hidden as well.

tip You might be wondering if there is any easy way to access floating gadgets that have been hidden by other application windows. There is, assuming the Sidebar is visible: Simply right-click the Sidebar (or click the Sidebar tray icon) and choose Bring Gadgets to Front. This will display any floating gadgets on top of your other windows.

tip Gadgets floating on the desktop can also be configured to permanently float above all other windows if needed. Simply right-click the gadget you'd like to see on top of other windows and select Always on Top from the menu that appears.

Removing Gadgets

To remove a gadget from the Sidebar or desktop, simply right-click it and choose Close Gadget. Alternately, mouse over the gadget and click the small close button that appears. This does not delete a gadget from your system, of course. You can re-add any removed gadgets later from the Add Gadgets window.

Secret

Advanced Sidebar-Configuration Options

Although the Sidebar configuration user interface is fairly complete, there are a few things you can't easily do. Behind the scenes, however, the Windows Sidebar utilizes special configuration files named **settings.ini** to determine all of its configuration possibilities. If you don't mind taking a small risk by editing these files with a text editor such as Notepad, you can perform various configuration tasks that are impossible with the standard Sidebar UI. Before you make changes, be sure to back up any files you'll be editing. You'll also want to quit the Sidebar before editing these files.

There are two versions of **settings.ini**. The first is devoted to systemwide configuration options and default settings, and is located in C:\Program Files\Windows Sidebar by default. If you right-click this file and choose Edit, you'll see the contents of this file, which should resemble the following (obviously, the details vary on a system-by-system basis):

```
[Root]
SettingsVersion=00.00.00.01
SidebarShowState=Imploded
SidebarDockedPartsOrder=0x1,0x2,0x3,
Section0=1
Section1=2
Section2=3
[Section 1]
PrivateSetting_GadgetName=%PROGRAMFILES%\windows sidebar\gadgets\Clock.
gadget
PrivateSetting_Enabled=true
[Section 2]
PrivateSetting_GadgetName=%PROGRAMFILES%\windows sidebar\gadgets\
SlideShow.Gadget
PrivateSetting_Enabled=true
[Section 3]
PrivateSetting_GadgetName=%PROGRAMFILES%\windows sidebar\gadgets\
RSSFeeds.Gadget
PrivateSetting_Enabled=true
loadFirstTime=defaultGadget
```

A second version of the Sidebar **settings.ini** file is available for each user. This file is located in C:\Users\[*your user name*]\AppData\Local\Microsoft\Windows Sidebar by default. This file has a similar structure, but will typically be much longer depending on how much you've configured Windows Sidebar. Here's an example of what the first section of this file could look like:

```
[Root]
SettingsVersion="00.00.00.01"
```

continues

continued

```
SidebarShowState="Imploded"
SidebarDockedPartsOrder="0x1,0x2,0x3,0x8,0x5,0x6,0x7,0x9,"
Section0="1"
SidebarAutoStart="true"
SidebarDockedPartsPage1="8"
OneTimeRemoveGadgetMessageShown="true"
Section1="2"
Section2="3"
PickerPosX="482"
PickerPosY="313"
Section3="5"
Section4="6"
Section5="7"
Section6="8"
OneTimeExitMessageShown="false"
SidebarDockSide="2"
SidebarAlwaysOnTop="false"
SidebarDockMonitor="0"
OneTimeHideMessageShown="true"
[Section 1]
PrivateSetting_GadgetName=%PROGRAMFILES%\windows sidebar\gadgets\Clock.
gadget
PrivateSetting_Enabled=true
SettingsExist="True"
clockName=
themeID="5"
timeZoneIndex="-1"
secondsEnabled="False"
PrivateSetting_GadgetTopmost="false"
PrivateSetting_SidebarDockedState="Docked"


[Hashes]
...
```

Take a look at a few of these settings. The **SidebarShowState** option is set to Imploded in the code example. This means that the Sidebar will be displayed normally, and not in front of other windows. **SidebarDockSide** is set to 2, which is the right side of the screen. If you change this number to 1, the Windows Sidebar will be displayed on the left.

In addition to the options shown here, there are a few other undocumented options. For example, if you'd like a certain gadget to never appear in the Add Gadgets windows, you could simply find the gadget in C:\Program Files\Windows Sidebar\Gadgets and delete it, but what if you wanted it to be available to other users? In this case you could simply add a line like the following to your user's version of **settings.ini**:

```
PickerDefaultPackageSkipList=SlideShow.Gadget,worldClock.Gadget
```

continues

continued

This particular code would only make the Clock gadget unavailable. Obviously, there are many more settings possibilities. It's also likely that an enterprising software developer will come up with a TweakUI-style application that provides the same functionality. Stay tuned to my Web site, the SuperSite for Windows, for any breaking news in this regard: **www.winsupersite.com**.

Finding New Gadgets

In order to make it easy for users to find new gadgets that will run on both the Windows Sidebar and the Desktop, Microsoft has created a Web community called Windows Live Gallery (**http://gallery.microsoft.com**). Actually, this community is designed for users of all kinds of gadgets, including those that run on the Windows Live Web sites, Windows Live Messenger, Windows Live Toolbar, Windows Sideshow, as well as Windows Sidebar. To find gadgets that run specifically on Windows Vista's Sidebar feature, use this URL: **http://vista.gallery.microsoft.com/**.

Microsoft has basically created three different gadget environments to date: the Sidebar and the Windows Vista desktop, Live.com and various other Windows Live Web sites, and Windows Sideshow, an external display that is beginning to appear on new notebook computers, Tablet PCs, and other devices.

Secret

Unfortunately, the three environments are not entirely compatible, so you can't just create one gadget that works in all three. If you wanted a gadget that would display your e-mail, for example, you would need different versions for Sidebar, Windows Live, and Sideshow. That said, gadgets for all three environments could be built using the same HTML, DHTML, and JavaScript technologies and could share some code.

On the Windows Live Gadgets Web site, shown in Figure 6-13, you can find galleries of downloadable gadgets, information for developers who would like to make their own gadgets, forums for providing gadget feedback, and other information.

Windows Live Gadgets includes a wealth of information and documentation about building gadgets that work in any or all of the supported environments. If you are a developer, you'll appreciate the fact that the Sidebar is essentially a graphic script-hosting environment: All of your skills writing Web applications and Web sites are transferable to gadget design and development.

There are other online resources for Sidebar gadgets as well. The aforementioned Live .com Web portal (**www.live.com**) offers some Sidebar gadgets, although most of that site's gadgets are obviously designed for Live.com, not Sidebar; and there are many, many third-party gadget sites on the Web. There are Google search gadgets, dictionaries, and virtually everything imaginable out there.

tip

One question I'm asked fairly often is which Sidebar gadgets I regularly use. Yes, I really do use Windows Sidebar, and I always configure it with the same gadgets, all but one of which ship with Vista: Clock, Calendar, and Weather, with two instances of Clock (one for where I am at the time and one for Paris, a city I visit frequently), and two instances of weather (one Fahrenheit, one Celsius, both pointed at the same location). The only third-party gadget I use is called Multi-Meter (Dual Core). This gadget is similar to Vista's built-in CPU Meter but (in my opinion) more attractive. More important, it provides separate readouts for each processor core; and on the dual-core systems I've been using since Vista first shipped, this is interesting information to me.

Figure 6-13: Windows Live Gadgets is a Web community for finding Sidebar gadgets.

Where Have I Seen This Before?

Although Windows Sidebar is a new feature that's unique to Windows Vista, you may already know that mini-applications called gadgets or something similar have been around since the earliest days of computers. Back when PCs lacked graphics cards and were constrained to just 640K of RAM, Terminate and Stay Resident (TSR) mini-applications provided the same basic functionality as today's gadgets (minus the Web connections, of course), enabling users to run small utilities and even personal information-management applications alongside WordPerfect, dBASE, and Lotus 1-2-3. Even the earliest Macintosh computers supported a suite of mini-applications called Desk Accessories, which provided such utilities as calculators and text editors on a system that, technically speaking, could not multi-task.

More recently, a wide range of gadget-type environments have cropped up, and it would be irresponsible to suggest that Microsoft wasn't influenced in some ways by these tools. Environments such as Stardock's DesktopX (**www.stardock.com/products.asp**) were among the first to provide handy Web-connected utilities that run on the Windows desktop. A Mac tool called Konfabulator (**http://widgets.yahoo.com/**) was such a hit that Yahoo! purchased it, and Apple included a pretty obvious copy of it in Mac OS X, which it calls Dashboard. You'll look at two major Windows Sidebar alternatives in the next section.

Secret

Earlier Sidebar Iterations

If you followed the development of Windows Vista, you might be familiar with earlier versions of something called Windows Sidebar that were quite different from the Sidebar found in the finished product. Early on, Microsoft had hoped to replace Vista's system notification area, which dates back to the release of Windows 95 in 1995, with a feature called the Windows Sidebar. This early version of the Sidebar would have been the system's central location for alerts and notifications, and it included such things as a clock, a search box, a synchronization center, a media player, and a list of contacts. It might have even replaced the Windows taskbar, as evidenced by early prerelease versions of Windows Vista, which went by the code name Longhorn.

The original version of the Sidebar was influenced by work done at the MSN business unit at Microsoft, which had created an Internet client called MSN Premium that included a feature called Dashboard. Like the original Sidebar, Dashboard sat at the edge of the screen and included a list of contacts, a clock, and other useful at-a-glance information. The idea was to take this sort of functionality and make it part of the underlying operating system.

So, what happened? When Windows Vista's development schedule veered wildly out of control in 2004, Microsoft decided it was time to start over from scratch, so it dumped a number of features that were not considered core to the success of this release. Sidebar was among the projects that were cut. About a year later, however, Microsoft created the Platforms Incubation Team in order to foster an environment where smaller Windows applications could be developed quickly and updated regularly. This team resuscitated Sidebar and is responsible for the Windows Sidebar you see in Windows Vista today, including the decision to utilize Web standards instead of Vista-specific technologies that would have been more difficult for developers to learn. They also created the Windows Calendar application, discussed in Chapter 22, and, go figure, the Hold 'Em card game that's part of Ultimate Extras.

Exploring Sidebar Alternatives

As noted previously, a number of Microsoft competitors have created alternatives to Windows Sidebar. These systems are sometimes designed to be cross-platform—that is, they run on non-Windows systems such as Mac OS X. They also run on previous versions of Windows, such as Windows XP. Most of these products are also free, so while they don't offer the advantage of shipping inside of Windows, they're easy enough to obtain online.

All of these environments share the same basic principles, although each has its own differences, advantages, and limitations. The question, of course, is whether any of these alternatives outshine Windows Sidebar enough to consider installing them on Windows Vista.

I'll state right up front that I don't think so. Assuming you're even interested in using gadgets, the way that Sidebar integrates into Windows and is supported by such a wide-ranging set of third-party gadgets outweighs any small advantages that other environments might have. Installing yet another gadget-type environment would bring little advantage, but would clutter up your desktop in an unnecessary way. Chances are good that if you need a particular kind of gadget, there's one available for Windows Sidebar, and ultimately that is likely the biggest consideration any potential user should entertain.

Yet alternatives do have some advantages. I've chosen to focus on two here because they're both widely used and offer deep integration features with the two most popular online services currently available, Google and Yahoo!. If you're a heavy user of Google products such as Google Search, Gmail, and Google Calendar, Google Desktop may very much be of interest; and if you're a big Yahoo! fan, that company's Yahoo! Widgets provides a compelling Sidebar alternative. The next sections take a look.

Google Desktop

Google Desktop is Google's desktop search product, but it has evolved over the years to include far more than just desktop search. Indeed, given the integrated Instant Search functionality that's now available in Windows Vista, desktop search is barely a reason to even consider Google Desktop anymore. Even Google recognizes this reality: By default, Google Desktop is no longer preconfigured to index the PC when installed on Windows Vista.

What makes Google Desktop special, in my opinion, are its Google Gadgets and Sidebar features. (Sound familiar?) As with Windows Sidebar, Google Desktop provides a very familiar panel, which can be docked to either side of the screen and can hold several gadgets. It's just like Windows Sidebar from a usability perspective.

However, because this is Google, the Google Desktop Sidebar comes with a host of Google-made gadgets that integrate with the many Google online services that are currently available. If you're a big Google user, as I am, this may put Google Desktop over the top; because while it offers clock, calendar, weather, and notes gadgets just like Windows Sidebar, Google also provides gadgets for Gmail, Google Calendar, Google Video, Google Talk, and other Google services. There are even gadgets for popular non-Google services such as eBay, Twitter, and Wikipedia. Moreover, in my experience, developers have taken to Google's gadgets much more obviously than they have to those for Windows Sidebar. That suggests that Google Desktop users may have an easier time finding useful new gadgets in the future than Windows Sidebar users.

Shown in Figure 6-14, Google Desktop can be configured to look and function very much like Windows Sidebar.

Google Desktop can be downloaded from the Google Web site at **http://desktop .google.com/**.

Figure 6-14: Google Desktop provides its own sidebar and gadgets.

Yahoo! Widgets

Give Yahoo! a bit of credit: Not only is its Yahoo! Widgets tool arguably among the first of the desktop gadget tools—it's based on the Konfabulator engine that has been around for several years—but it also does things its own way. Unlike Google Desktop, Yahoo! Widgets doesn't look and act almost exactly like Windows Sidebar. Yes, Yahoo! Widgets offers mini-applications, called widgets instead of gadgets, which can live directly on the desktop or be docked on a sidebar-like panel, called a Widget Dock, on the side of the screen. And yes, these widgets often integrate with online services to provide such things as stock quotes, weather, and other timely information.

The similarities end there, however. Yahoo!'s widgets are unique-looking and, dare I say, are generally better-looking than the gadgets offered by Microsoft and Google. For one thing, they're more consistent: Unlike Microsoft or Google gadgets, Yahoo! widgets are all sized identically when docked, resulting in a cleaner look. (They are different sizes when undocked, or floating on the desktop, however.) You can also choose between available widgets directly from within the Yahoo! Widget Gallery, part of Yahoo! Widgets. That is, you won't be shuttled off to your Web browser to find other utilities as you are with both Windows Sidebar and Google Desktop.

I also like how Yahoo! handles widget overflow. If you have too many widgets to fit on the dock, you can scroll down the list to access hidden widgets; with Windows Sidebar you have to switch left to right between entire sets of gadgets. Unlike Windows Sidebar, the Yahoo! Widget Dock can be docked to any edge of the screen, not just the left and right sides. In addition, if you have two monitors, the Dock can extend across both screens if desired.

Yahoo's product is, of course, linked heavily to Yahoo's own online services. So if you're a Yahoo! kind of person, you'll appreciate integration with Yahoo! services such as Yahoo! Mail, Yahoo! Calendar, Yahoo! Finance, and Flickr. In addition, like Google's service, Yahoo! Widgets seems to be well supported by developers, and you can find a wide range of third-party widgets out there as well. It's also available for the Mac, if you're into that kind of thing.

Yahoo! Widgets is like the quirkier, cooler, younger sibling of Windows Sidebar, as you can see from Figure 6-15.

Yahoo! Widgets can be downloaded from the Yahoo! Web site at **http://widgets.yahoo.com/**.

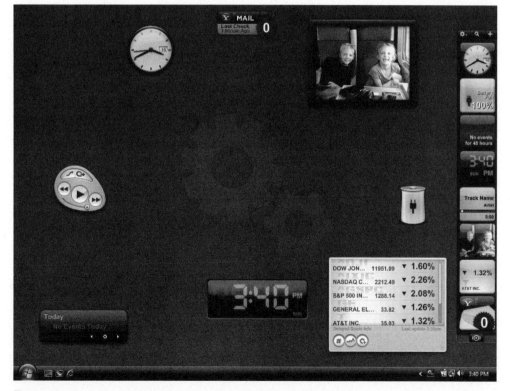

Figure 6-15: Yahoo! Widgets has a style all its own and may appeal to hip, younger users.

Summary

Windows Sidebar is a highly visual and obvious change in Windows Vista. Whether it's something you're going to want to leave running on your PC depends on your own preferences, of course. I think that Windows Sidebar can be a valuable addition to your desktop if you're using a widescreen display, are a natural multi-tasker, and find a handful of gadgets that you simply can't live without. However, some Windows Vista users will simply be unimpressed. For those users, it's not particularly easy, but you can at least turn it off. You can also examine a number of Sidebar alternatives from Microsoft's competitors, each of which provides its own gadget-like utilities.

Personalizing and Configuring Windows Vista

Chapter
7

◆ ◆

In This Chapter

◆ ◆

Windows Vista is the most comprehensively capable version of Windows yet created, with an unprecedented collection of useful application software and a technically impressive user interface. Of course, Windows Vista is just software, so it's not perfect; and depending on your needs or wants, you may prefer to customize Windows Vista to make it your own and to have it provide a more comfortable environment for your day-to-day work. This chapter presents a collection of ways to personalize and customize Microsoft's latest operating system.

Virtually any time you see words like *personalize* and *customize*—or, heaven forbid, *tweak*—used together with Windows, you can expect Microsoft's most controversial tool, the Registry Editor, to raise its ugly head. Well, I'm not going down that road. Life is too short to waste any entire chapter of this book—not to mention hours of your life—teaching you how to spelunk around the archaic and arcane depths of Windows' bowels. Sure, you'll see a handful of references to the Registry Editor in this book—in this chapter even— but only when no simpler alternatives are available. And just as you don't need to know how an internal-combustion engine works in order to drive a car, there are ways to make Vista your own without resorting to an ancient tool like the Registry Editor. You're going to customize Windows Vista the smart way!

The Windows Vista User Interface

Although Microsoft improved the Windows user interface in ways both subtle and pro-found in Windows Vista, that doesn't mean it's perfect out of the box. Everyone's needs and wants are different, and fortunately Microsoft has engineered Windows Vista in such a way that you can configure the system to your preferences. This section describes some of the ways in which you can tame the Windows Vista UI and make it your own.

Customizing the Start Menu

As discussed in Chapter 4, the Windows Vista Start Menu is an evolution of the Start Menu that debuted in Windows XP, and it offers a much smarter interface for interacting with the applications, documents, and other content on your PC than did the Start Menus from previous Windows versions.

As shown in Figure 7-1, the Windows Vista Start Menu is divided into a number of logical areas, each of which covers specific functionality.

These areas include the following:

♦ **Pinned items:** Found at the top-left corner of the Start Menu, this area contains shortcuts that are permanently displayed regardless of how often you use them. Shortcuts for your default Web browser and e-mail application are displayed by default.

♦ **Most Recently Used (MRU) list:** Here, taking up the majority of the left side of the Start Menu window, is a list of the applications you use most frequently. The algorithm Microsoft uses to determine this list is decidedly hokey, because it gives precedence to an application you just used instead of one you use regularly, every single day. Maybe they'll get it right in Service Pack 2.

♦ **All Programs:** This link reveals the All Programs list, a combination of the shortcuts stored in your user profile's Start Menu folder structure and the Public account's Start Menu folder structure. Unlike in Windows XP, the All Programs list appears inside of the Start Menu window instead of popping up in a separate, hard-to-navigate cascading menu.

Figure 7-1: The Vista Start Menu: Serviceable, yes,
but in need of a makeover.

 ◆ **Start Search:** Arguably the single greatest Windows Vista feature of all, and
    easily the best feature of the new Start Menu, Start Menu Search enables you to
    quickly and easily find any application, shortcut, document, e-mail, contact, or
    other searchable object. It's magic, and I love it.

 ◆ **User picture:** Here you will see the user picture you configured when you created
    your user account. It changes to different system icons as you mouse over the links
    on the right side of the Start Menu.

 ◆ **Links:** This is a list of important system locations that Microsoft thinks you will
    need regularly. These include such things as special shell folders (Documents,
    Music), Recent Items (a list of recently accessed documents and other objects),
    common shell locations (Computer, Network), configuration settings (Control
    Panel, Default Settings), and Help and Support.

 ◆ **Sleep/Shutdown:** On the bottom right of the Start Menu, you'll see two buttons,
    the rightmost of which includes a cascading pop-up menu with various power-
    management and shutdown-related options. These two buttons are configured
    differently by default depending on your system's power-management capabilities.
    (They can be modified, as discussed in Chapter 17.)

Most Start Menu customizations occur via the Taskbar and Start Menu Properties dialog, shown in Figure 7-2. You can display this window by right-clicking the Start button
(sometimes annoyingly called the *Start Orb* in Windows Vista) and clicking Properties. A
related dialog, Customize Start Menu, is displayed by clicking the Customize button.

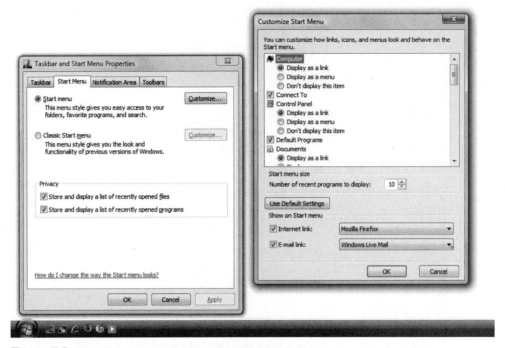

Figure 7-2: Start Menu customization typically starts here.

The Windows Vista Start Menu is full-featured, but it's still not configured optimally by default. Here are some of my favorite Start Menu tweaks.

Pinning Your Favorites, Unpinning the Others

For some reason, Microsoft decided that your default Web browser and e-mail application deserve special treatment, and shortcuts to these two applications are *pinned* to the top-left corner of the Start Menu by default in Windows Vista (just as they were in Windows XP, incidentally). You don't have to settle for that. Indeed, not only can you optionally disable the display of one or both of these shortcuts, you can pin any application shortcut—actually, any shortcut at all—to this section. Here's how:

◆ **Disable the Web browser link and/or e-mail link:** Open the Customize Start Menu dialog. On the bottom, you'll see two options in the Show on Start Menu section: Internet link and e-mail link. You can use this interface to configure which applications are your default Web browser or e-mail application, but you can also uncheck these options to remove those links from the Start Menu altogether. I generally remove the e-mail link because I use a Web-based e-mail solution (Gmail).

◆ **Pin applications you really do want to use:** Instead of Microsoft's arbitrary use of the pinned items section of the Start Menu as a place to access Internet features, you can place shortcuts there to applications you really do use all the time. To do so, open the Start Menu and drag a shortcut from your most recently used (MRU) or All Programs list up to the pinned-items section, as shown in Figure 7-3.

♦ **Unpin applications you don't want:** If you pin one too many shortcuts to the pinned items area, you can remove—or "unpin"— them. To do so, open the Start Menu and right-click the shortcut you'd like to remove. Then choose Unpin from the Start Menu. (Alternatively, you can choose Remove from This List, which also removes the shortcut from the MRU list, at least temporarily.)

Figure 7-3: Make the pinned-items area of the Start Menu your own.

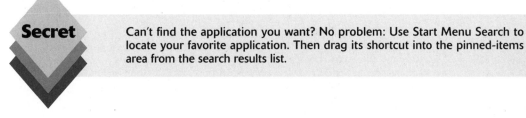

Secret

Can't find the application you want? No problem: Use Start Menu Search to locate your favorite application. Then drag its shortcut into the pinned-items area from the search results list.

Changing Your Logon Picture

Microsoft supplies a paltry 12 user pictures you can choose from, and only a pathetic eight of those are available if you configure the account during initial setup. Instead of using Vista's built-in images, why not use a favorite photograph or other image? Here's how: Open the Start Menu and click on the user picture at the top right of the Start Menu. This causes the User Accounts window to open. Click the link titled Change Your Picture, and you'll see the interface shown in Figure 7-4.

Figure 7-4: You don't have to settle for Vista's built-in account pictures.

Click the Browse for More Pictures link and then use the standard Open File window that appears to find a favorite photo.

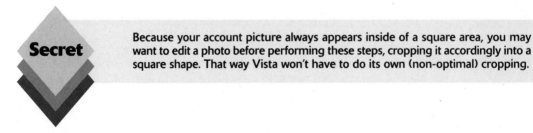

Secret

Because your account picture always appears inside of a square area, you may want to edit a photo before performing these steps, cropping it accordingly into a square shape. That way Vista won't have to do its own (non-optimal) cropping.

Adding, Configuring, and Removing Start Menu Links

Microsoft's options for Start Menu links—those important system locations shown on the right side of the Start Menu—are serviceable, but there's always room for improvement. To configure which items appear in the list—and remove the links you don't want while adding back those you do—open the Customize Start Menu window. There's a list at the top of this window that enables you to configure which links appear and, in many cases, *how* they appear; some links can appear as cascading submenus instead of standard buttons that launch separate windows. Here are the Start Menu links you can configure from this UI:

♦ **Computer:** Can be displayed as a link, as a menu, or disabled. This item is displayed as a link by default.

♦ **Connect To:** Can be enabled or disabled. This item is enabled by default.

♦ **Control Panel:** Can be displayed as a link, as a menu, or disabled. This item is displayed as a link by default.

♦ **Default Programs:** Can be enabled or disabled. This item is enabled by default.

♦ **Documents:** Can be displayed as a link, as a menu, or disabled. This item is displayed as a link by default.

♦ **Favorites menu:** Can be enabled or disabled. This item is disabled by default.

♦ **Games:** Can be displayed as a link, as a menu, or disabled. This item is displayed as a link by default on Windows Vista Home Basic, Home Premium, and Ultimate. It is disabled by default on Windows Vista Business and Enterprise.

♦ **Help:** Can be enabled or disabled. This item is enabled by default.

♦ **Music:** Can be displayed as a link, as a menu, or disabled. This item is displayed as a link by default.

♦ **Network:** Can be enabled or disabled. This item is enabled by default.

♦ **Pictures:** Can be displayed as a link, as a menu, or disabled. This item is displayed as a link by default.

♦ **Printers:** Can be enabled or disabled. This item is disabled by default.

♦ **Run:** Can be enabled or disabled. This item is disabled by default.

♦ **System administrative tools:** Can be displayed as a link, as a menu, or disabled. This item is displayed as a link by default.

For the most part, the defaults are acceptable. You can safely remove Default Programs, as you're unlikely to need it very often. If you're using a desktop PC with just wired networking, then the Connect To link is worthless, too. One thing you might want to experiment with is changing some links into menus. As shown in Figure 7-5, the effect is quite interesting. Some love it, some don't.

Additionally, this section of the Customize Start Menu window provides a few options that aren't related to the Start Menu Links area, though they're no less important. Key among them is Highlight Newly Installed Programs, which can be enabled or disabled. This item is enabled by default, but I strongly recommend disabling it, as the effect when enabled is annoying.

Figure 7-5: Certain Start Menu links can be configured as menus.

Using the Classic Start Menu

Old-timers may enjoy using the Classic Start Menu, which is reminiscent of the Start Menu from Windows 2000 and other outdated Windows versions. It even adds back a few Windows 2000-era desktop icons, as shown in Figure 7-6.

I'm not a big fan of the Classic Start Menu, because you lose so many great features from the Vista version, not the least of which is Start Menu Search, but if you do go this route be sure to check out the Customize Classic Start Menu options shown in Figure 7-7. There's a lot there to tweak.

Paul   Network   Internet Explorer   Control Panel

Figure 7-6: The Classic Start Menu is aptly named.

Figure 7-7: The Classic Start Menu is also highly customizable.

Cleaning Up the Tray Notification Area

While the tray notification area was originally designed with noble intentions, the proliferation of crapware and rampant abuse of the tray by even well-meaning applications has rendered this lonely backwater of the UI an unwelcome place indeed. On most users' systems, the tray notification is overrun with tiny icons, all vying for your attention (many of which, incidentally, don't even provide useful notifications of any kind, which was the purpose of this area to begin with). A typical Windows tray area resembles Figure 7-8.

Figure 7-8: Admit it; you've seen a tray notification area just like this.

You can reclaim your tray notification area, however. To do so, right-click a blank area of the taskbar and choose Properties to display the Taskbar and Start Menu Properties windows. Then navigate to the Notification Area tab, which provides an interface for hiding inactive icons (which is enabled by default but can do only so much) and for toggling the display of system icons such as the clock, the volume control, the network icon, and the power icon. What you're looking for, however, can be found when you click the Customize button. This displays the Customize Notification Icons window, shown in Figure 7-9.

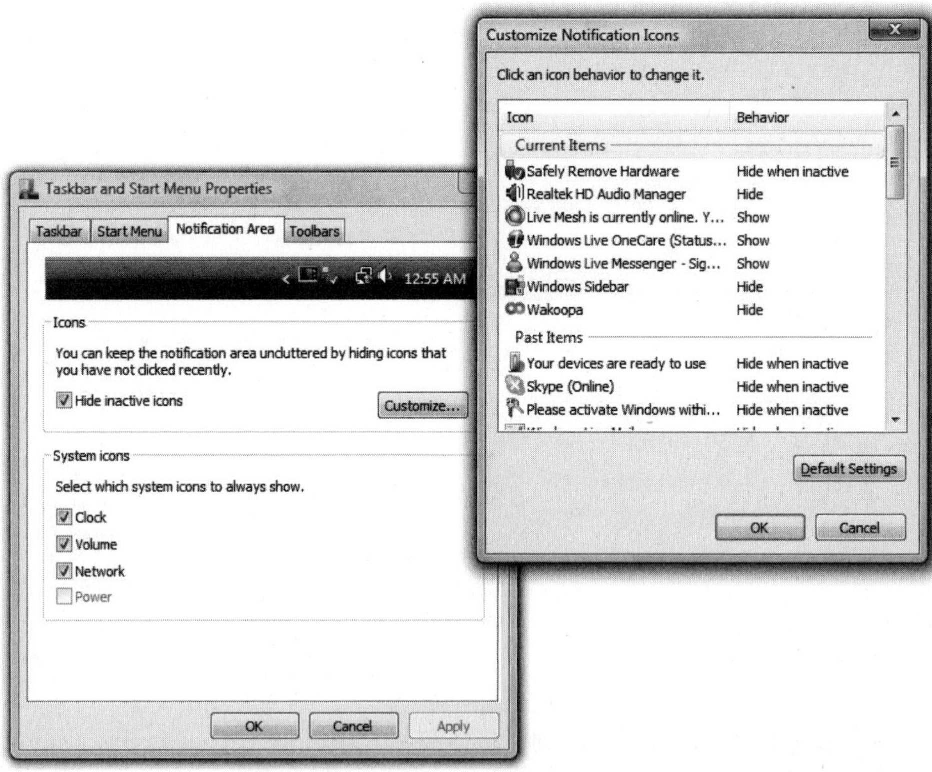

Figure 7-9: From this simple interface, you can hide those tray icons you never want to see.

The interface here is simple: Each icon that is currently displayed in the tray ("current items"), as well as every icon that's previously been displayed ("past items")—and thus could come back to haunt you again later—can be configured with one of three settings: Show, Hide, and Hide When Inactive. The default for all tray icons is Hide When Inactive, but I prefer to manually set useful icons (e.g., Live Mesh, Windows Live Messenger, and Windows Live OneCare) to Show, and set useless icons (e.g., Windows Sidebar) to Hide.

tip

I know what you're thinking, and you're right. Hiding icons in this fashion doesn't do anything to address a bigger and very real problem: These applications are starting up automatically and running in the background, taking up valuable resources. If you're looking for something a little more Draconian, check out the section "Making It Faster: Performance Tweaks," later in this chapter, where I show you how to prevent applications from running every time you boot up.

Configuring Folder Options

Although the version of Windows Explorer found in Windows Vista is quite a bit different from that found in Windows XP, some things haven't changed much at all. One of these things is Explorer's Folder Options functionality, which is typically accessed via the (hidden, in Vista) Tools menu. (You can also access Folder Options directly via Start Menu Search; just type **folder**.) The Folder Options dialog, shown in Figure 7-10, presents three tabs that are chock-full of configurable goodness.

Figure 7-10: Folder Options hasn't changed much since Windows XP, which is fine, as it's still very useful.

On the default General tab, you'll see options that broadly affect all Explorer windows. For example, you can switch between Windows Vista-style folders and Windows Classic folders, or back to Windows 95-style navigation, and enable the capability to open each folder in its own window.

Things really get interesting on the View tab. As shown in Figure 7-11, this tab provides a massive number of settings, so it's easy to get lost.

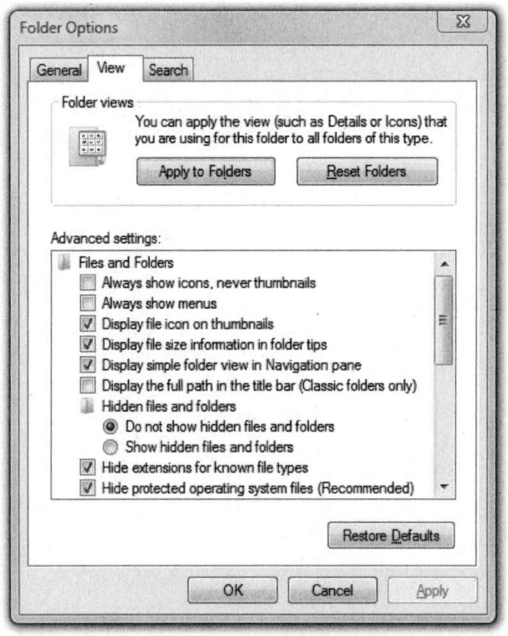

Figure 7-11: Virtually anything you'd like to configure about Explorer windows happens right here.

Some of the key settings you can configure here include the following:

◆ **Hidden Files and Folders:** By default, hidden files and folders are hidden.

◆ **Hide Extensions for Known File Types** and **Show Drive Letters:** In a long-standing bid for simplicity, Microsoft is working to at least hide things that confuse people, such as drive letters and file extensions. You can re-enable the display of file extensions, however, and you can hide the display of drive letters.

◆ **Hide Protected Operating System Files (Recommended):** There are hidden files, and then there are *hidden* files. Protected operating systems are the latter, and they are replaced automatically by Vista if you try to delete them, so Microsoft just hides them to avoid any confusion.

◆ **Remember Each Folder's View Settings:** This is enabled by default but Windows Vista, like XP before it, can often "forget" folder view settings. You'll look at this case explicitly in the next section.

◆ **Use Check Boxes to Select Items:** This feature is covered in Chapter 18 because it's enabled by default on Tablet PCs (and Ultra-Mobile PCs) but disabled by default on all other systems.

◆ **Use Sharing Wizard:** When you right-click a folder and click Share, Windows Vista utilizes the File Sharing Wizard, a feature covered in Chapter 10. If you disable this option, you'll see the folder's Properties window opened to the XP-style Sharing tab. I prefer the latter, frankly.

Forcing Explorer to Remember Window Settings

One of the most annoying problems with Windows XP is that its version of Windows Explorer has a difficult time remembering the customizations that users applied to windows. You spend a lot of time configuring a window to look a certain way, but then the next time you open it, everything you did is gone, replaced by some default look and feel.

Microsoft was aware of this problem and pledged to fix it in Windows Vista; and sure enough, Vista does do a better job of remembering customized window settings. Unfortunately, as with XP, Windows Vista *still* loses windows settings on occasion—and I speak from experience when I say that it's as irritating as ever.

There are two basic steps you can take to correct this problem if it occurs on your PC:

1. **Reset folder views:** The least painful and destructive method is to use the built-in UI in Windows Vista to reset all custom folder views to their default and then reapply your custom settings. To do this, open Folder Options, navigate to the View tab, and click the Reset Folders button. The effect should be immediate.

2. **Increase the cache size for folder views.** Windows Vista allocates a certain amount of storage space to custom folder views. If you exceed this capacity, Vista will literally start forgetting some folder views. Fortunately, you can increase the cache size. To do so, open the Registry Editor (from Start Menu Search, enter **regedit**) and navigate to HKEY_CURRENT_USER\Software\Microsoft\Windows\Shell. Then, in the right pane, right-click on BagMRU Size and choose Modify from the pop-up menu. In the window that appears, select Decimal in the Base section and then type **20000** (or a similar figure that's bigger than the default value of 8192) in the Value Data field. Click OK and then close the Registry Editor. You'll need to reboot or at least log off and log on again for the changes to take effect.

Replacing Vista's Compressed Folders with Something Useful

Microsoft has included ZIP compression compatibility in Windows for a while now courtesy of an incurably lame feature called Compressed Folders. This feature is still present in Windows Vista, but it's horrible, so I replace it with a worthier alternative. My choice is WinRAR (**www.rarlabs.com/**), which can also work with the more efficient RAR compression format as well as older formats such as CAB, ARJ, and TAR. WinRAR is shown in Figure 7-12.

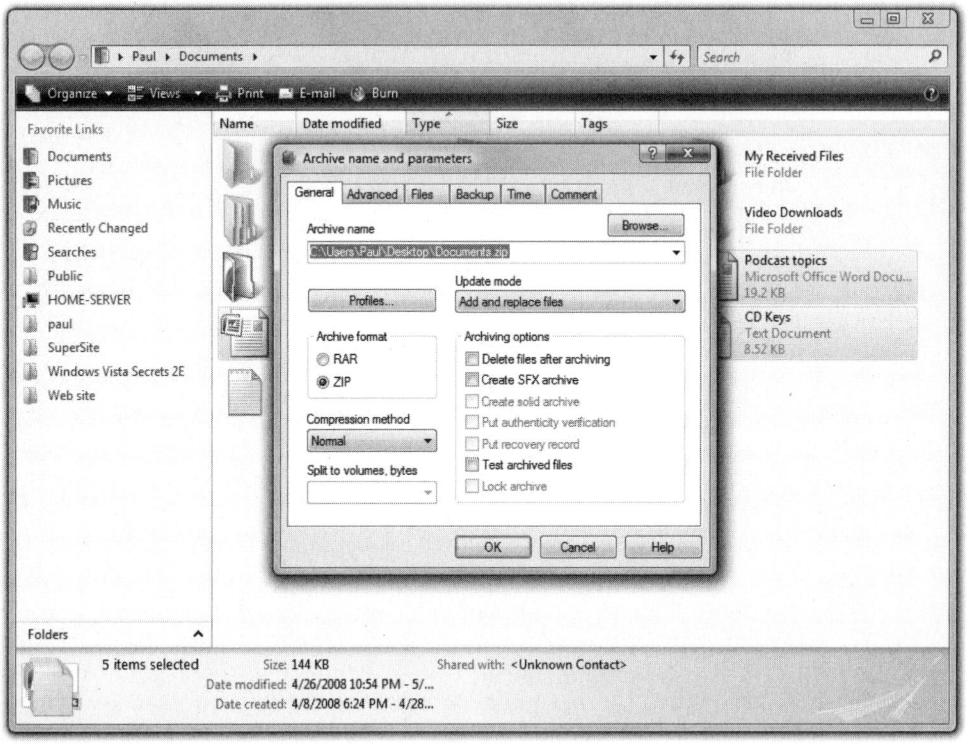

Figure 7-12: WinRAR is an awesome compression utility and far superior to Compressed Folders.

WinRAR isn't the only compression game in town. Other alternatives to consider include PKZIP for Windows (**www.pkware.com**), WinZIP (**www.winzip.com/**), and SecureZIP (**www.securezip.com**).

Replacing the User Interface

I happen to believe that Windows Vista's user interface is a tremendous improvement over those of both its predecessor, Windows XP, and various competing operating systems such as Mac OS X. You may not agree. If that's the case, you might consider one of the utilities out there that enable you to replace the standard Window Vista UIs with new skins, some of which are quite attractive. The best of the lot is Stardock WindowBlinds, which offers custom UI skins with configurable color schemes (see Figure 7-13).

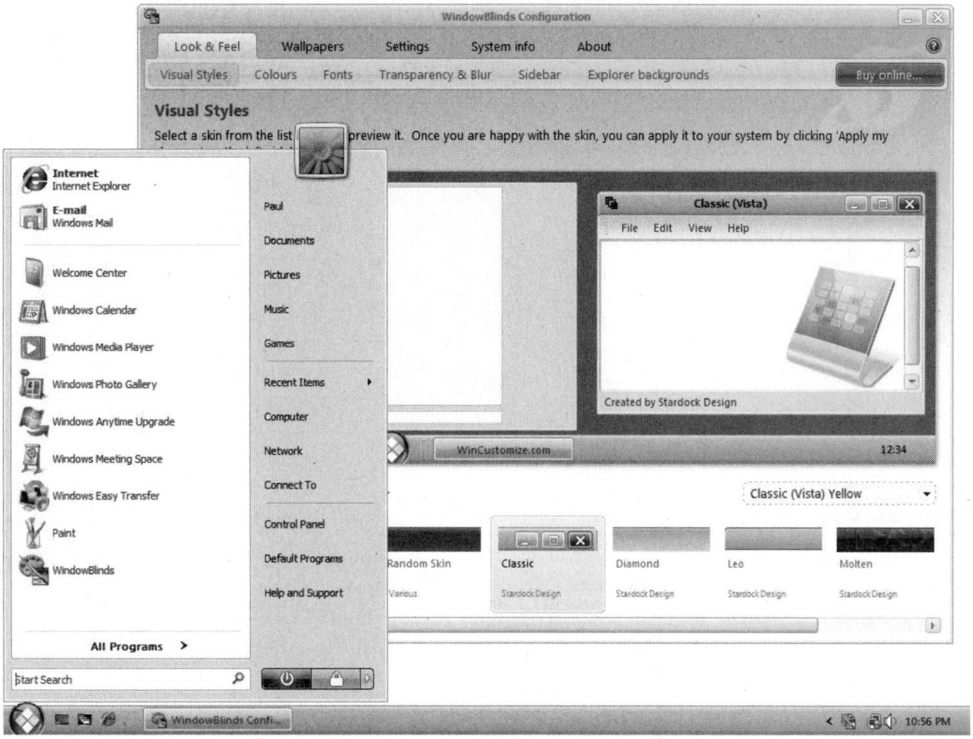

Figure 7-13: Tired of the stock Windows UI? WindowBlinds is the tool for you.

Branding Windows Vista like a PC Maker

This one is just good old-fashioned fun: If you've ever purchased a new PC, you've probably noticed that the PC maker has customized the System Properties window with their logo and other information. Well, you can customize this information yourself. There are two ways to handle this. You can muck around in the Registry, which is time-consuming and difficult, or you can simply use the wonderful freeware utility called WinBubble (**http://unlockforus.blogspot.com**), shown in Figure 7-14.

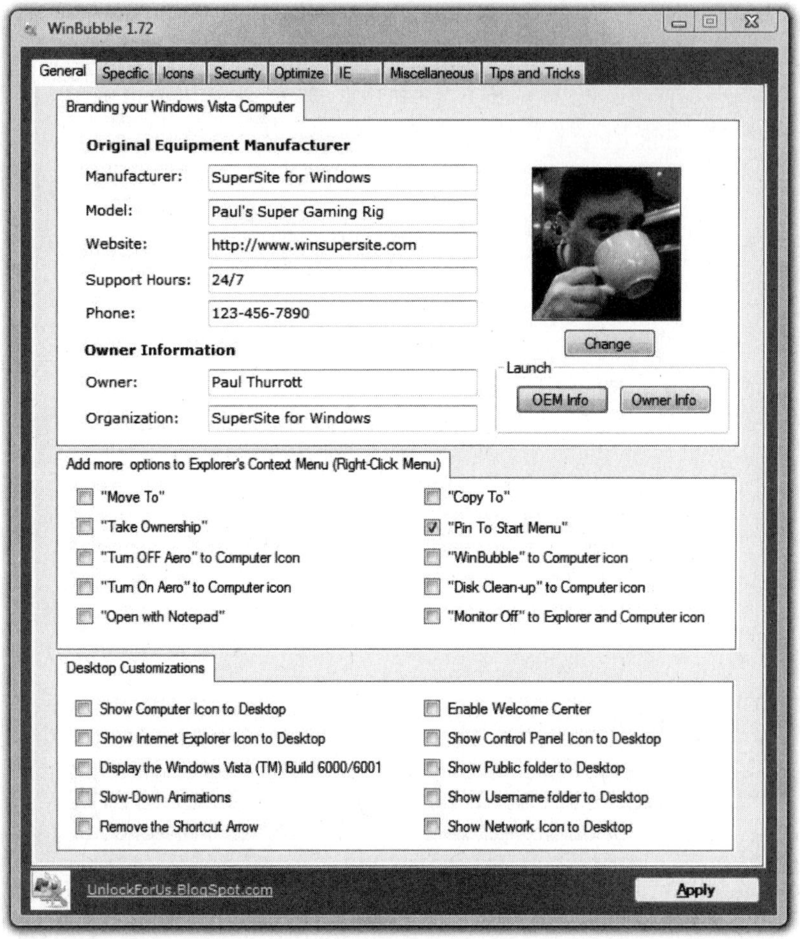

Figure 7-14: WinBubble provides a number of tweaking features, including the capability to modify the OEM branding.

Once you apply the changes, check out the System Properties window to see the havoc you've wrought (see Figure 7-15). Neat, eh?

> **tip**
>
> In case it's not obvious, WinBubble can also be used to *remove* branding, so if you purchased a PC and want to get rid of that HP logo in the System Properties window, this is a great way to do so.

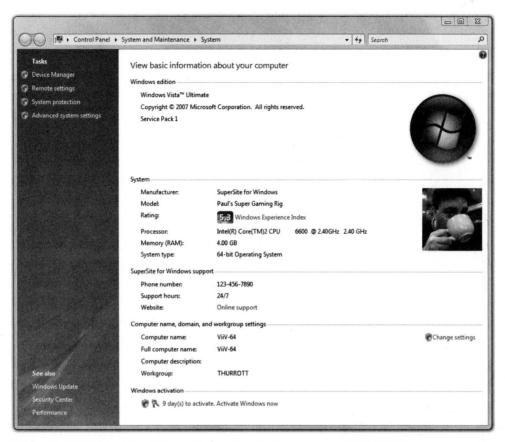

Figure 7-15: A customized System Properties window, courtesy of WinBubble.

Secret

WinBubble does a *lot* more than just help you change the branding. In fact, this handy utility is, I believe, the Vista tweaking tool that's closest in spirit and functionality to Microsoft's long-admired TweakUI. Microsoft never made a version of TweakUI for Windows Vista for some reason, but it doesn't matter: WinBubble fills that gap quite nicely.

Making It Faster: Performance Tweaks

One of the biggest complaints about Windows Vista, especially from those upgrading from Windows XP, is that the new system doesn't perform as speedily on the same hardware. Truth be told, Windows Vista works just fine if you operate the system with reasonable hardware specs. Regardless of the performance attributes of your PC, faster is always better. In this section, I'll show you some ways you can make Windows Vista run more efficiently.

Taking Out the Trash

While I do recommend buying a new PC with Windows Vista preinstalled to get the best experience, the truth is that many PC makers seem to go out of their way to screw up what should be a happy experience. They do so by loading down their new PCs with extensive collections of largely useless utilities, a practice that's gotten so out of hand that the industry has adopted the term *crapware* to describe it. Fortunately, there are a few things you can do to avoid crapware. First, you can purchase PCs only from those PC makers that offer no crapware, such as Dell. Or you can simply not worry about it and download a wonderful free utility called the PC Decrapifier (**www.pcdecrapifier.com**), which automates the removal of trialware and other annoying crapware that PC makers tend to preinstall (you know, for your convenience).

The PC Decrapifier, shown in Figure 7-16, is free for personal use and highly recommended if you're looking for that new-PC smell. However, be sure to uncheck any items you do want to keep, as some of the so-called crapware that PC Decrapifier finds might actually be useful.

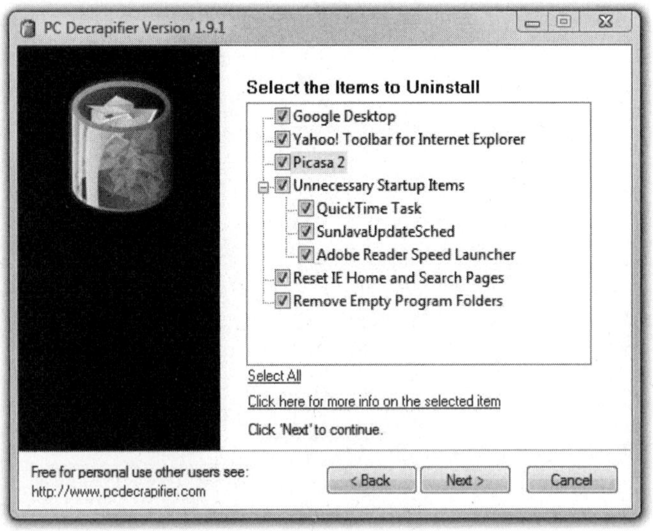

Figure 7-16: The PC Decrapifier will help you clean the junk off your PC.

tip	The PC Decrapifier works perfectly well on any PC, not just new PCs. In fact, it's a great tool for automating the cleanup of a PC you've been using (and abusing) for a long time.

Making It Boot Faster

Throughout the years, all Windows versions have shared a common problem: they degrade in performance over time and boot more slowly the longer the computer is used. Microsoft addressed this gradual sludgification somewhat in Windows Vista, and compared to Windows XP there are certainly some improvements. For example, unlike XP, it's actually possible to take a year-old Windows Vista install, clean some things up, and get it back in tip-top shape. With XP, you'd eventually be forced to reinstall the entire OS in order to regain lost performance.

Boot-up speed, of course, is a primary concern. In order to speed the time it takes for your PC to return to life each time you sit down in front of it, there are a number of steps you can take:

♦ **Remove unwanted startup items:** Over time, as you install more and more software on your computer, the number of small utilities, application launchers, and, most annoyingly, application *prelaunchers* (which essentially make it look like those applications start more quickly later because large chunks of them are already pre-loaded) that are configured to run at startup multiply dramatically. There are several ways you can cull this list, but the best one is a hidden feature inside Windows Defender, the antispyware utility that's built into Windows Vista. (What's a start-time optimizer doing in Windows Defender, you ask? Well, Windows Defender is based on a product Microsoft purchased that once included a number of cool PC utilities, and this one was apparently deemed good enough to keep it included in the product.)

To cull the list of startup applications, open Windows Defender (Start Menu Search, and enter **defender**) and click the Tools link in the toolbar. Then click Software Explorer to see the interface shown in Figure 7-17.

Before attempting to make any changes, you must click the button Show for All Users. After dealing with the User Account Control prompt that appears, you can scan the list on the left side, looking for any suspicious or unwanted startup applications. As you click each option, the right side of the application will provide information about the selection. You can also remove or disable unwanted items. Success!

♦ **Do a little cleanup:** There is a number of things you can clean up on your PC that will have mild effects on performance. One of the more effective is Vista's hidden Disk Cleanup tool (Start Menu Search, and type **disk clean**), shown in Figure 7-18. This little wonder frees up hard drive space by removing unused temporary files. (Free hard drive space is important for keeping virtual memory running optimally. Virtual-memory optimization is covered in just a bit.)

Figure 7-17: One of the best features of Windows Defender is hidden and unrelated to the product's core functionality.

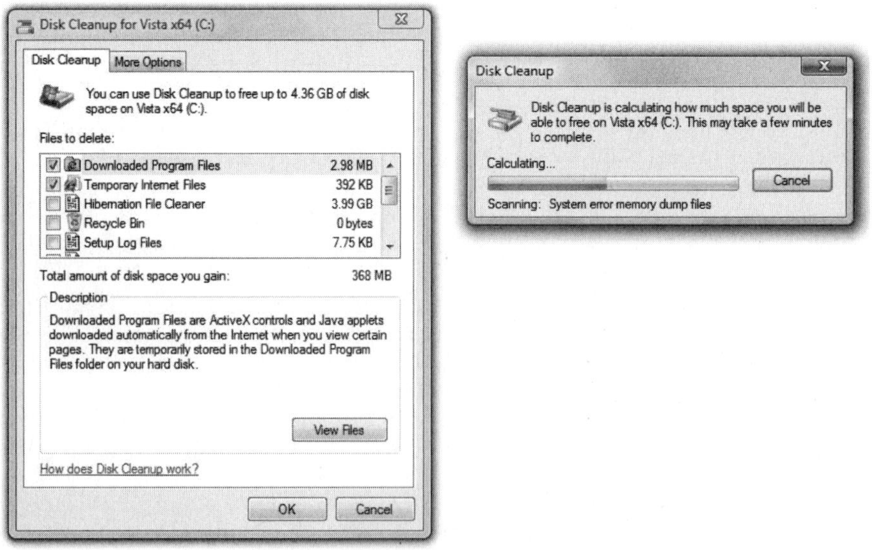

Figure 7-18: The Disk Cleanup utility can clear out unneeded files.

Secret You can automate Disk Cleanup using another hidden Vista utility, the Task Scheduler. This process is documented in Windows Vista's Help and Support: Search for *Schedule Disk Cleanup* to learn more.

◆ **Don't shut down the PC:** This one may seem obvious or even humorous, but think about it: Why are you shutting down the PC anyway? Windows Vista supports advanced power management states, including Sleep and Hibernation, and these states enable your PC to "shut down" and "power on" far more quickly than actual shutdowns and power-ups. I examine Vista's power-management functionality in Chapter 17, but don't be thrown by the chapter title: The power-management information there applies to both desktop PCs and mobile computers.

Secret You can also automate various PC-cleanup activities with tools such as Windows Live OneCare, which is discussed in Chapter 25. This comprehensive PC-health solution also includes a nice start-time optimizer.

Using Vista's Performance Options

Windows Vista uses an advanced desktop composition engine and provides a number of subtle but pleasing UI animations by default. Some of this stuff, frankly, is a bit much; and all of it takes its toll on the performance of your PC. Fortunately, the operating system also includes a number of configurable performance options. They're *really* hard to find but it's worth it if you have an older PC and have noticed some slowdowns with Windows Vista.

To access Windows Vista's Performance Options, you need to jump through a number of hoops: Open the Start Menu, right-click on Computer, and choose Properties. Then, in the System window that appears, click the Advanced system settings link in the Tasks list on the left. In the System Properties window that appears, navigate to the Advanced tab and click the Settings button in the Performance section. Once you've gone through all that, you'll see the window shown in Figure 7-19.

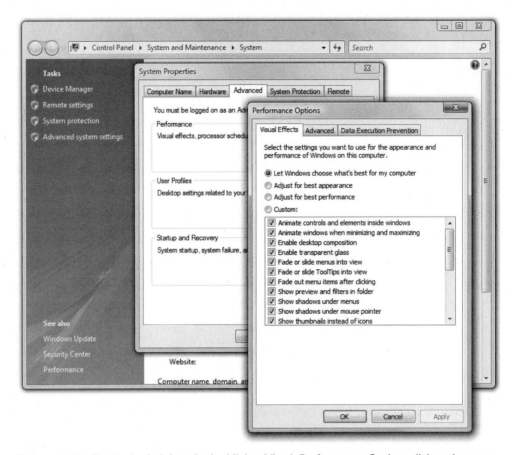

Figure 7-19: They're buried deep in the UI, but Vista's Performance Options dialog gives you fine-grained control over the look, feel, and performance of your PC.

Here you can choose between three automated settings (Let Windows Choose What's Best for My Computer, Adjust for Best Appearance, and Adjust for Best Performance). Alternately, you can click the Custom option and then enable and disable any of the 20 user-interface-related options that appear in the custom settings list. Most of these options should be self-explanatory, and many appeared in previous versions of Windows, but a few Vista-specific options are worth highlighting:

◆ **Enable desktop composition:** This is the core Windows Vista display engine. If you disable this feature, you'll lose Windows Aero and its related glass effects and will be forced to use the less attractive, less reliable Windows Vista Basic user interface. However, on systems with very low-end video cards, Windows Vista Basic will often perform faster than Windows Aero.

◆ **Enable transparent glass:** This option configures the translucency effects you see in the Windows Aero interface. Disabling this feature is equivalent to unchecking the Enable Transparency check box in the Window Color and Appearance control panel and results in a slight performance boost.

◆ **Use visual styles on windows and buttons:** Disabling this feature causes Vista to revert to the ancient-looking Windows Classic user interface. It will dramatically increase the performance of your PC at the expense of attractiveness and reliability.

Secret

Don't fall into a common trap and assume that Windows Aero universally makes your PC slower. That's not the case at all: Because Aero offloads much of the computation required for generating the display from the PC's microprocessor to the graphics processor, or GPU, in your video card, running Aero will actually result in *faster* performance, at least on systems with modern 3D video cards. Furthermore, because Windows Aero is far more reliable than other display modes, your system will be more reliable overall if you use Aero. Don't believe the haters, people.

Monitoring Performance and Reliability

Windows has had a Performance Monitor since the earliest days of NT, but with Windows Vista, Microsoft debuts an amazing new utility, the Reliability Monitor, which tracks the overall reliability of your PC over time, ever since the first day you booted up into Windows Vista. Both utilities are now part of a combined Reliability and Performance Monitor tool (Start Menu Search, and type **relia**), which is shown in Figure 7-20.

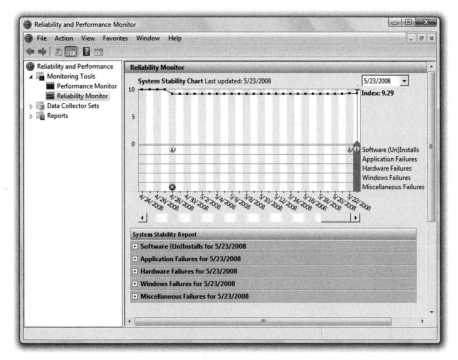

Figure 7-20: Another hidden wonder of Vista: the Reliability Monitor.

The Reliability Monitor assigns a reliability rating to your PC on a scale from 1 to 10, where 1 is horrible and 10 is perfect. Out of the box, Vista gets a perfect 10, but from there on out it's all downhill: Any glitch, any application, hardware, or Windows failure, will cause the reliability rating to plummet. Meanwhile, days with no problems are barely rewarded, with only a slight bump. If anything, I think Vista's being too hard on itself.

Consider Figure 7-21. Here you see a decidedly different reliability picture, a PC on which multiple applications have failed, repeatedly, over a period of time. The reliability rating is a sad 3.76, its lowest score yet over a month and a half of use.

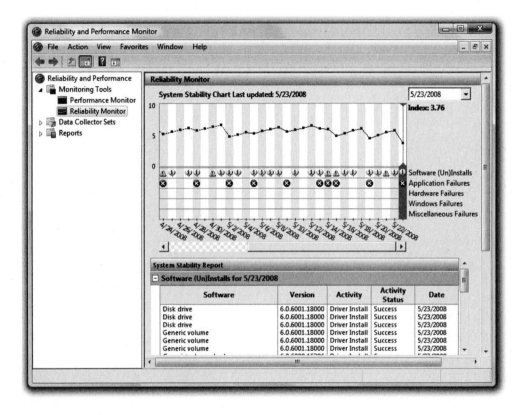

Figure 7-21: Ouch. Windows Vista is painfully honest about unreliable systems.

What went wrong with this disaster of a PC? I must be miserable using that machine, right? Not exactly. The Reliability Monitor shown in Figure 7-21 is from my daily-use desktop PC. I do use this machine to test a wide range of software, and many of the application failures are related to beta versions of Mozilla Firefox (and most of those failures had to do with using incompatible browser add-ons). You can see individual problems by clicking on dates and viewing what went wrong, as shown in Figure 7-22.

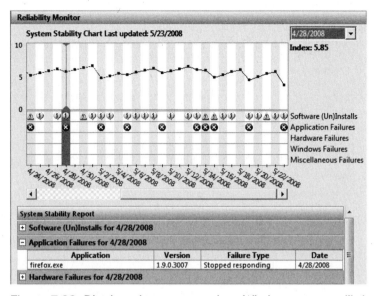

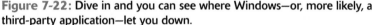

Figure 7-22: Dive in and you can see where Windows—or, more likely, a third-party application—let you down.

That's what's beautiful about the Reliability Monitor. It gives you a place to see exactly what is causing the problems. Then you can take steps to fix those problems. (In my case, this simply meant waiting for Mozilla to ship the final version of Firefox 3 so the add-on makers could update their products for the new version.)

This illustrates why I think the Reliability Monitor is a bit harsh. Over the six-week period shown, my PC was actually quite reliable—and it certainly never crashed, froze, or blue-screened.

Making Menus Faster

While Windows Vista has reduced the number of menus you'll run into, especially in the Start Menu, once you start hunting around the UI, you'll find a great number of menus. There's the embedded menu that pops up inside the Start Menu when you mouse over the All Programs link, for example, as well as the Recent Items link, which opens a pop-up menu by default. These and other Vista menus are designed with a built-in display delay of 400 milliseconds so that they don't open immediately, but you may want them to open faster, or even immediately. Fortunately, it's an easy fix.

The trick is a single Registry key, found in HKEY_CURRENT_USER\Control Panel\Desktop. It's named MenuShowDelay, and if you're comfortable lurking around the Registry with the Registry Editor, go nuts. Otherwise, you can simply use the free WinBubble (**http://unlockforus.blogspot.com**) utility described earlier in the chapter. Using this tool, navigate to the Optimize tab, and you'll see an option titled Menu Show Delay. Simply change its value from 400 to something smaller if you'd like the menus to display more quickly; or change the value to 0 to make them appear immediately. Then click Apply, log off, and log back on to see how much faster they are.

Improving Vista's Memory

A long time ago, in an operating system far, far away, the PCs of a bygone era had woefully inadequate amounts of RAM, and the versions of Windows used back then would have to regularly swap portions of the contents of RAM back to slower, disk-based storage called *virtual memory*. Virtual memory was (and still is, really) an inexpensive way to overcome the limitations inherent to a low-RAM PC; but as users ran more and more applications, the amount of swapping would reach a crescendo of sorts as a magical line was crossed and performance suffered.

Today, PCs with 2 to 4GB of RAM are commonplace, so manually managing Windows Vista's virtual memory settings is rarely needed. That said, you can do so if you want, though you'll have to navigate through a stupefying number of windows to find the interface:

1. Open the Start Menu, right-click on Computer, and choose Properties.
2. In the System window that appears, click the Advanced System Settings link in the Tasks list on the left.
3. In the System Properties window that appears, navigate to the Advanced tab and click the Settings button in the Performance section.
4. In the Performance Options dialog that appears, navigate to the Advanced tab and click the Change button. (Whew!)

You'll be rewarded with the Virtual Memory dialog shown in Figure 7-23.

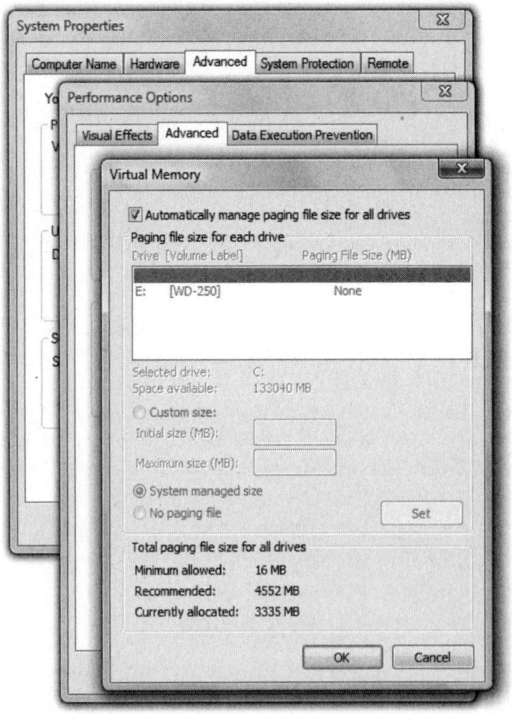

Figure 7-23: This might just be the furthermost region of the Windows Vista UI: Virtual Memory.

By default, Vista is configured to automatically maintain and manage the paging file, which is the single disk-based file that represents your PC's virtual memory. Vista will grow and shrink this file based on its needs, and its behavior varies wildly depending on how much RAM is on your system: PCs with less RAM need virtual memory far more often than those with 4GB of RAM (or more with 64-bit versions of Vista).

While I don't generally recommend screwing around with the swap file, Vista's need to constantly resize the paging file on low-RAM systems is one exception. The problem with this behavior is that resizing the paging is a resource-intensive activity that slows performance. Therefore, if you have less than 2GB of RAM and can't upgrade for some reason, you might want to manually manage virtual memory and set the paging file to be a fixed size—one that won't grow and shrink over time.

To do this, uncheck the option titled Automatically Manage Paging File Sizes for All Drives and select Custom Size. Then determine how much space to set aside by multiplying the system RAM (2GB or less) by 2 to 3 times. On a PC with 2GB of RAM, for example, you might specify a value of 5120 (where 2GB of RAM is 2,048MB, times 2.5). This value should be added to both the Initial Size and Maximum Size text boxes to ensure that the page file does not grow and shrink over time.

Secret

Optionally, you can put the paging file on a separate hard disk (a physical hard disk, not just a second partition) for better performance.

Using ReadyBoost

Another way to improve performance on systems with 2GB or less of RAM is to use a new Windows Vista feature called *ReadyBoost*. This technology uses spare storage space on USB-based memory devices such as memory fobs to increase your computer's performance. It does this by caching information to the USB device, which is typically much faster than writing to the hard drive. (Information cached to the device is encrypted so it can't be read on other systems.)

There is a number of caveats to ReadyBoost. The USB device must meet certain speed characteristics or Vista will not allow it to be used in this fashion. Storage space that is set aside on a USB device for ReadyBoost cannot be used for other purposes until you reformat the device; and you cannot use one USB device to speed up more than one PC. (Likewise, you cannot use more than one ReadyBoost device on a single PC.)

In my testing, ReadyBoost seems to have the most impact on systems with less than 1GB of RAM, and it clearly benefits notebooks more than desktops, as it's often difficult or impossible to increase the RAM on older portable machines.

When you insert a compatible USB device into a Windows Vista machine, you will see a Speed Up My System option at the bottom of the Auto Play dialog that appears, as shown in Figure 7-24. When you select this option, the ReadyBoost tab of the Properties dialog of the associated device will appear, enabling you to configure a portion of the device's storage space. It recommends the ideal amount based on the capacity of the device and your system's RAM.

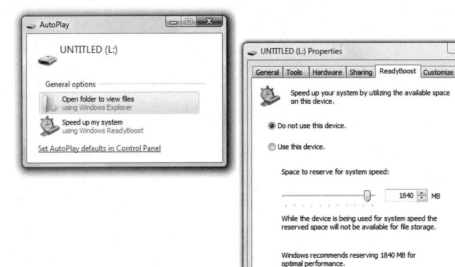

Figure 7-24: ReadyBoost provides an inexpensive and simple way to boost performance on low-RAM PCs.

Obviously, ReadyBoost won't work unless the USB memory key is plugged into your PC. This can be a bit of a hassle because you need to remember to keep plugging it in every time you break out your portable computer. Still, ReadyBoost is a great enhancement and a welcome feature, especially when a PC would otherwise run poorly with Windows Vista.

Adding More RAM

This final tip may seem a bit obvious, but Windows Vista is a resource hog, and it will steal whatever RAM you throw at it. More than any version of Windows before it, Windows Vista wants and requires as much RAM as you can possibly put in your PC. My advice here is simple: 2GB of RAM is the minimum for a happy Windows Vista PC, and most PC users would be better off with more. If your PC can support 4GB of RAM, upgrade to 4GB. Memory is inexpensive these days, so cost is rarely an issue.

Secret

Microsoft says that 32-bit versions of Windows Vista support up to 4GB of RAM (while 64-bit versions support quite a bit more). While this is technically true, 32-bit versions of Windows are actually limited in their support of RAM because of its underlying architecture. Therefore, even on systems with a full 4GB of RAM, 32-bit versions of Windows Vista can really access only about 3.12GB to 3.5GB of RAM, depending on your configuration. In the initially shipped version of Windows Vista, the System window would accurately portray how much RAM it could access, but this confused (and probably infuriated) those who paid for and installed 4GB of RAM, so with Service Pack 1 (SP1), Vista now reports that your PC has 4GB installed, even though it can't use all of it.

The obvious question is whether you should even bother upgrading to 4GB of RAM when your 32-bit version of Vista can't actually address almost 1GB of that storage space anyway. The answer is an unqualified yes, for two reasons. First, you'd have to really go out of your way to upgrade a PC to 3GB of RAM instead of 4GB, and the cost differential would be minimal. Second, who says you're always going to be using a 32-bit version of Windows? You may decide in the future to go the 64-bit route. When that happens, you'll be happy you went for the full 4GB of RAM instead of saving a few pennies to no good end.

For the record, I max out the RAM on every single PC I use because the costs are so minimal and the effect in Windows Vista is extremely positive. You just can't overstate how important more RAM is to Windows Vista.

Summary

Windows Vista supports a wide range of configuration options and other tweaks, and only some of them are found in this chapter. Throughout the book, I provide advice and tips about configuring and personalizing various aspects of the OS as well; but with a system as vast and complicated as Windows Vista, there's always more to be done, and entire books could be (and have been) written solely about optimizing, customizing, and otherwise tweaking Windows. Hopefully, this chapter gives you some idea of the kinds of things you can do to make Windows Vista a truly personalized experience.

Part III

Security

Vista Security
Features

♦ ♦

In This Chapter

Using Windows Security Center to monitor the health of your PC

Using tools such as Windows Defender, Windows Firewall, and Windows Update to keep your PC secure

Browsing the Web securely with Internet Explorer 7

Preventing physical loss with BitLocker Drive Encryption

Getting the best security with an x64 version of Windows Vista

♦ ♦

Although highly visual features such as the Windows Aero user interface and Windows Sidebar are obvious changes to Windows Vista, some of the more important, if less obvious, changes in this new operating system occur under the hood. For example, Microsoft completely rearchitected Windows Vista to be more componentized, a change that enables more efficient updating and servicing. The biggest under-the-hood improvement to Vista, of course, involves security changes. Whereas Windows XP had to be changed dramatically in Service Pack 2 (SP2) to be more secure, Windows Vista was designed from the outset to be as secure as possible, building off and expanding on the work the company first did in XP SP2. In this chapter, you examine the new security features in Windows Vista that will affect you in day-to-day use.

Security and Windows Vista

It's been a tough decade for Windows users. As Microsoft's operating system entered the dominant phase of its existence, hackers began focusing almost solely on Windows, as that's where all the users are. As a result, various Windows versions have suffered through a seemingly never-ending series of electronic attacks, security vulnerabilities, and high-profile malware breakouts.

In 2003 Microsoft halted development of its major operating system and application products and began an internal review of its software-development practices. The company reexamined the source code to its then-current projects and developed a new software-engineering approach that is security-centric. Now the software giant will not release any software product that hasn't undergone a stringent series of security checks. Windows Vista is the first client operating system shipped that has been developed from the get-go with these principles in mind. That is, it has been architected to be secure from the beginning.

Is Windows Vista impenetrable? Of course not. No software is perfect; but Windows Vista is demonstrably more secure than its predecessors. And although Windows users will no doubt face awesome security threats in the future, Microsoft at least has the lessons it learned from the mistakes of the past to fall back on. Many people believe that the security enhancements in Windows Vista will prove to be a major reason many users will upgrade to this version. This is completely valid.

Secret

I want to expose one myth right now: While proponents of UNIX-based systems like Apple Mac OS X and Linux like to tout the supposed security benefits of their systems over Windows, the truth is that these competitors benefit primarily from *security by obscurity*. That is, so few people use these systems relative to Windows that hackers don't bother targeting the minority operating systems. Consider this: In 2007, the installed base of Windows-based PCs exceeded 1 billion, but the maker of the number-two OS, Apple, claims just 25 million users. That's right, only 2.5 percent of the Windows user base is using the number-two most frequently used OS on earth. Hackers may be evil but they're not dummies: They know where the numbers are.

This isn't a partisan attack on Mac OS X or Linux. Both are fine systems, with their own particular strengths; and as far as security by obscurity goes, it's certainly a valid enough reason to consider using OS X or Linux instead of Windows. It's one of the reasons I use Mozilla Firefox instead of Internet Explorer: In addition to various features that Firefox offers, the browser is hacked a lot less often than IE simply because fewer people use it.

Windows Vista's security features permeate the system, from top to bottom, from the high-profile applications, applets, and control panels you deal with every day to the low-level features most Windows users have never heard of. This chapter highlights most of Vista's new security features, starting with those you will likely have to deal with as soon as you begin using Microsoft's latest operating system. First, however, take a look at the number-one thing Windows Vista users need to do to thoroughly secure their system.

Securing Windows Vista in Just Two Steps

Out of the box, Windows Vista includes antispyware functionality in the form of *Windows Defender,* a two-way firewall in Windows Firewall; a hardened Web browser (IE 7); and automatic updating features that keep the system up-to-date, every day, with the latest security patches. Also included is a new User Account Control (UAC) feature, covered in the next chapter, which protects administrator-class accounts in ways that were impossible with previous Windows versions while making Standard account types far more usable. It would seem that Vista comes with everything you need to be secure.

Sadly, that's not quite the case. First, Microsoft makes it too easy for users to opt out of one of the most important security features available in the system. In addition, one glaring security feature is missing from Vista. You'll want to make sure you correct both of these issues before using Vista online. Fortunately, doing so takes just two steps:

1. **Enable automatic updating:** If you set up Windows Vista yourself, one of the final setup steps is configuration of Automatic Updates, the Windows Update feature that helps to ensure your system is always up-to-date. However, Automatic Updates can't do its thing if you disable it, so make sure at the very least that you've configured this feature to install updates automatically. (Optionally, you can enable the installation of recommended updates as well, but these are rarely security-oriented.) I can't stress this enough: This feature needs to be enabled. If you're not sure how this is configured, run Windows Update and click Change Settings in the left side of the window. Make sure the option Install Updates Automatically (Recommended) is selected.

2. **Install an antivirus solution:** Many new PCs are preinstalled with security suites from companies such as McAfee and Symantec. While I happen to feel that these suites are better than nothing, they're also a bit bloated and perform poorly in my own tests. (They also tend to replace Vista's built-in security features, which is unnecessary.) I prefer standalone antivirus solutions for this reason. There are many excellent options, including ESET Antivirus, which in my own tests has proven to do an excellent job with minimal system impact. You can find out more about ESET Antivirus from the ESET Web site: **www.eset.com**.

Security in Windows Vista starts with this simple rule: Leave all the security settings on at their defaults and install an antivirus solution. That said, a full understanding of what's available in Windows Vista from a security standpoint is, of course, beneficial. That's what this chapter is all about.

Now it's time to take a closer look at Vista's security features.

Secret

While commercial antivirus solutions are generally more effective, you may be surprised to discover that you can get a perfectly good antivirus solution free, which is perfect for budget-minded students and other individuals. The best free antivirus solution I've used is AVG Anti-Virus Free Edition. It's not quite as light-weight as ESET Antivirus, but it's close, and not as bloated as those unnecessary security suites. Best of all, did I mention that it is free? You can find out more about AVG Anti-Virus Free Edition from the AVG Technologies Web site: http://free.avg.com.

Windows Security Center

When Microsoft shipped Windows XP Service Pack 2 (SP2) in the wake of its 2003 security-code review, one of the major and obvious new features it added to the operating system was the Security Center, a dashboard or front end of sorts to many of the system's security features. In Windows XP SP2, the Security Center was designed to track the system's firewall, virus protection, and Automatic Updates features to ensure that each was enabled and as current as possible. If any of these features were disabled or out-of-date, the Security Center would warn the user via a shield icon in the notification area near the system clock, or via pop-up warning balloons.

In Windows Vista, the Security Center has been dramatically updated in order to support new security features in this Windows version. Shown in Figure 8-1, Vista's Security Center looks superficially similar to the XP SP2 version, but there's actually a lot more going on there once you begin examining its new functionality.

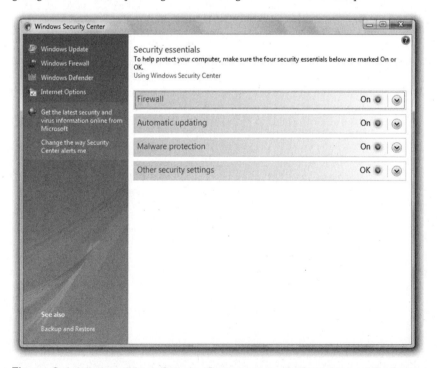

Figure 8-1: Windows Vista's Security Center now tracks far more security features.

The basic way that Windows Security Center works hasn't changed. The Security Center still tracks certain security features and ensures that they're enabled and up-to-date. If they're not, the Security Center displays its shield icon and alerts you via pop-up balloons. As shown in Figure 8-1, however, the Security Center now tracks far more security features than before. Here's what the Security Center is monitoring:

◆ **Firewall:** The Security Center ensures that Windows Firewall is enabled and protecting your PC against malicious software that might travel to your PC via a network or the Internet.

◆ **Automatic updates:** Like Windows XP, Windows Vista includes an Automatic Updates feature that can automatically download and install critical security fixes from Microsoft the moment they are released. The Security Center ensures that Automatic Updates is enabled.

◆ **Malware protection:** Although Windows Vista doesn't ship with any antivirus protection, the Security Center still checks to ensure that an antivirus service is installed and up-to-date. Modern antivirus solutions are designed to integrate with Windows Security Center so that the system can perform this monitoring function. New to Windows Vista is Windows Defender, Microsoft's antispyware and antimalware tool. Windows Security Center also ensures that Windows Defender is enabled, active, and using up-to-date spyware definitions.

◆ **Other security settings:** New to Windows Vista, the Security Center ensures that Internet Explorer 7 is configured in a secure manner. If you change any IE security settings, Security Center will warn you constantly about this issue. The Security Center also ensures that the User Account Control (UAC) technology, also new to Windows Vista, is active. Described more fully in Chapter 9, User Account Control is one of the many security technologies in Windows Vista designed to ensure that the system is running with minimum exposure to electronic threats.

If all of the features that the Security Center is monitoring are enabled and up-to-date, you won't ever see this feature unless you manually navigate to it. (You can find the Security Center in Control Panel ➪ Security ➪ Security Center, or via Start Menu Search.) However, if one or more of these features are disabled, misconfigured, or out-of-date, the Security Center will provide the aforementioned alerts. It will also display its displeasure with red highlighted sections in the main Security Center window. In such a case, you can expand the offending section and resolve the issue using a button provided. For example, if you disabled User Account Control, you'll see a Turn It On Now button that when selected will immediately enable that feature and return your system to a more secure state.

---

tip   If you install Windows Vista yourself, you will see a red Security Center icon in the notification area of the taskbar. This is because Windows Vista doesn't ship with any antivirus solution: To make this alarm disappear, install a third-party antivirus solution.

One new Security Center feature in Windows Vista enables you to configure how the Security Center alerts you when a security feature is not working properly. Open the Security Center and click the link titled Change the Way Security Center Alerts Me to see the dialog box shown in Figure 8-2. This way, you can optionally disable the pop-up alerts if you'd like.

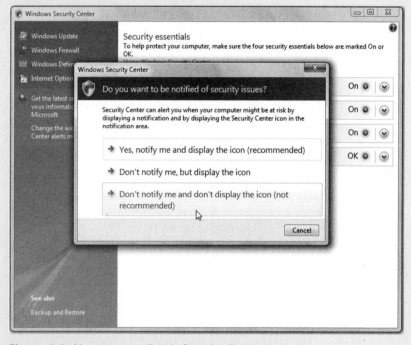

Figure 8-2: Now you can disable Security Center pop-ups.

The Security Center also provides handy links to the various security features it monitors, including Windows Update, Windows Firewall, Windows Defender, and Internet Options.

Windows Security Center has been subtly updated in Windows Vista Service Pack 1 (SP1), though the changes won't be immediately obvious to users. Under the hood, Microsoft has changed this feature so that competing security suites, such as those from Symantec and McAfee, can actually replace the Security Center with their own dashboards. Technically, this shouldn't happen unless the competing product provides *all* of the functionality of Windows Security Center. You're most likely to see this if you purchase a new PC from a major PC maker that includes a trial version of a security suite or if you're a Symantec or McAfee customer and you install one of their security suites on top of Windows Vista. In such a case, the built-in Windows Security Center feature may not be available. Presumably, whatever product you've installed will do as good a job as Windows Security Center.

Windows Defender

Over the years, hackers have come up with new and inventive ways to attack PCs. Recently, spyware, one of the most pervasive and difficult forms of malware yet invented, has become a serious issue. For this reason, Windows Vista includes an integrated antispyware and antimalware package called Windows Defender. Unlike some security products, you won't typically see Windows Defender, as it's designed to work in the background, keeping your system safe; but if you'd like to manually scan your system for malware or update your spyware definitions, you can do so by loading the Windows Defender application, available through the Start Menu.

tip Windows Defender does occasionally show up as an icon in the system notification area. This generally happens when the tool has been unable to download new definitions, the files it uses to ensure that its antispyware database is up-to-date. In such a case, you can click the Windows Defender icon and trigger a manual download of the latest updates.

Shown in Figure 8-3, Windows Defender has a simple interface. You can trigger a malware scan, view the history of Defender's activities, or access various tools and options.

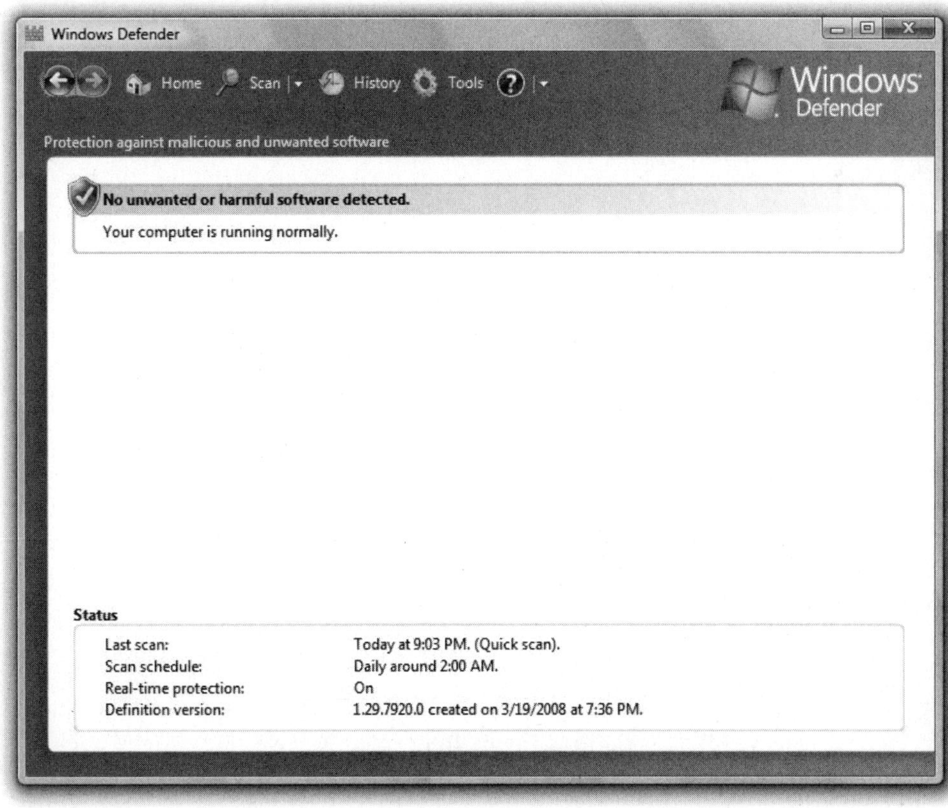

Figure 8-3: Windows Defender runs silently in the background and works well. What more could you ask?

Secret

Security researchers almost unanimously agree that no one antispyware product is enough to completely protect your PC from malware attacks. For this reason, you should always run at least two antispyware products at the same time.

tip

Windows Defender is also available for Windows XP. If you have other XP-based PCs, you might want to consider downloading Windows Defender for those systems as well.

Secret

Web Secret

One of the best features in Windows Defender is hidden a bit in the application's user interface. The Software Explorer—found in Tools ➪ Software Explorer—lists the applications that run at startup (you can also change the display to list currently running applications, network-connected applications, and other features). Best of all, you can actually remove or disable startup applications. In previous versions of Windows, you would use the System Configuration utility (**msconfig. exe**) for this functionality; System Configuration is still available in Windows Vista, but Windows Defender's Software Explorer feature is arguably a better solution because it provides so much information. You can even use it to prevent the System Configuration utility from running at startup, which can be useful. Chapter 7 covers Software Explorer in more detail.

Windows Firewall

When Microsoft first shipped Windows XP in 2001, it included a feature called Internet Connection Firewall (ICF) that could have potentially thwarted many of the electronic attacks that ultimately crippled that system over the ensuing several years. There was just one problem: ICF was disabled by default, and enabling and configuring it correctly required a master's degree in rocket science (or at least in computer science security). Microsoft wised up and shipped an improved ICF version, renamed as Windows Firewall, with Windows XP SP2. Best of all, it was enabled by default. Sure, it broke tons of applications at first, but now, years later, most Windows applications know how to live in a firewall-based world.

In Windows Vista you get an even better version of Windows Firewall. Unlike the XP SP2 version, the version in Windows Vista can monitor certain outbound network traffic as well as inbound network traffic; and because it's integrated so deeply into the system, it can prevent Windows components from sending data out over the network if they're not designed to do so. This should prevent problems that arise when certain Windows components are replaced by malicious code.

Secret

There's some confusion about how Windows Firewall is configured in Windows Vista. Although it is indeed enabled to monitor both inbound and outbound network traffic, it is configured differently for each direction. Windows Firewall, by default, is configured to block all incoming network traffic that is not part of an exception rule, and to allow all outgoing network traffic that is not blocked by an exception rule. This means that Windows Firewall is secure by default. It integrates with the other security features in Windows Vista to ensure that your system is as safe as possible, certainly a lot safer than what was possible in Windows XP.

The Windows Firewall user interface is simplicity itself. Shown in Figure 8-4, Windows Firewall is initially configured to block any unknown or untrusted connections to the PC that originate over the network. You can enable exceptions to this behavior on the Exceptions tab. Typically you just leave it alone, of course.

> 🛡 Windows Firewall   🗕 🗖 ✕
>
> 🛡 Turn Windows Firewall on or off
>
> 🛡 Allow a program through Windows Firewall
>
> **Windows Firewall**
>
> Windows Firewall can help prevent hackers or malicious software from gaining access to your computer through the Internet or network.
>
> How does a firewall help protect my computer?
>
> 🛡 Windows Firewall is helping to protect your computer
>
> Windows Firewall is on.   🛡 Change settings
>
> Inbound connections that do not have an exception are blocked.
>
> Display a notification when a program is blocked: Yes
>
> Network location: Private network
>
> What are network locations?
>
> See also
> Security Center
> Network Center

Figure 8-4: Windows Firewall.

Secret

The Windows Firewall interface is quite similar to that found in Windows XP with Service Pack 2, even though much has changed under the hood; but Microsoft also includes a second, secret interface to its firewall that presents far more options. Called Windows Firewall with Advanced Security, you can access it via the also hidden Administrative Tools that ship with all mainstream Windows Vista versions. To find it, navigate to Control Panel and turn on Classic View. Then select Administrative Tools ⇨ Windows Firewall with Advanced Security. As shown in Figure 8-5, the tool loads into a Microsoft Management Console (MMC).

Figure 8-5: Windows Firewall with Advanced Security.

Here, you can inspect and configure advanced firewall features, such as inbound connection rules and outbound connection rules, and so on. This tool is almost identical to the one Microsoft ships with Windows Server 2008 and should be of interest to advanced users and, of course, IT administrators who need to centrally manage hundreds or thousands of Vista installations. The latter market, of course, is who Windows Firewall with Advanced Security is really aimed at.

Secret

As good as Vista's firewall is, you should absolutely use a third-party firewall instead if you're using a security software suite. In such cases, the security suite will typically disable Windows Firewall automatically and alert Windows Security Center that it is now handling firewalling duties. In contrast to antispyware applications, never run two firewalls at the same time, as they will interfere with each other. If you're not running a third-party security suite, Windows Firewall works just fine: It's all you're likely to need from a firewall.

Windows Update

In previous Windows versions, Microsoft introduced a Web-based service called Windows Update that provided software updates to Windows users. That service has since been superseded by Microsoft Update, which also provides updates to many other Microsoft software products; but Windows Update lives on in Windows Vista, albeit in a brand-new form.

As shown in Figure 8-6, Windows Update is now a client application that you can access from the Start Menu. From here, you can check for and install new updates, hide updates you don't want to be alerted about anymore, and view the history of updates you've already installed. You can also click a link to enable Microsoft Update functionality, enabling Windows Update to download and install updates for other Microsoft applications, such as Microsoft Office and various Windows Live products.

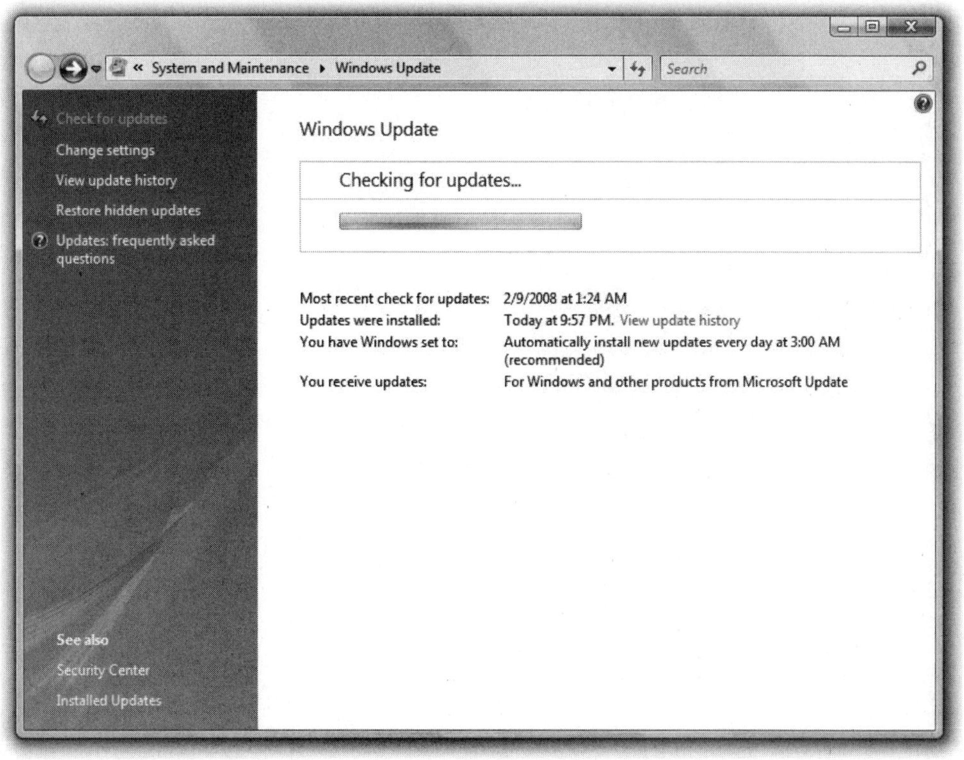

Figure 8-6: Windows Update is reborn in Windows Vista as a client-side application.

Users of Windows Vista Ultimate can also access Windows Ultimate Extras from Windows Update (see Figure 8-7). These extras include exclusive applications and services that run the gamut from games (Hold 'Em) to enterprise-oriented add-ons for the Windows BitLocker feature described later in this chapter. Windows Ultimate Extras appear in Windows Update whenever new updates are available for download.

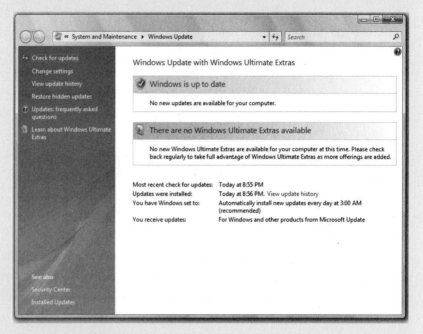

Figure 8-7: In Windows Vista Ultimate, Windows Update is used to download Ultimate Extras as well.

Curiously, Windows Vista doesn't offer any direct links to Automatic Updates, the Windows feature that automatically downloads critical security fixes. That is, you can't access Automatic Updates from its old location in the System Properties dialog box as you could in Windows XP. That's because Automatic Updates has been more tightly integrated with Windows Update. Configured when Windows Vista is first set up, Automatic Updates provides automatic updating services for Windows Update, just as the old Automatic Updates tool did. To configure automatic updating, open Windows Update and click the Change Settings link. The window shown in Figure 8-8 will appear. This window also enables you to configure whether Windows Update will connect to the Microsoft Update service, which provides updates for Microsoft applications, as well as Windows itself. You can also specify whether to automatically install recommended (that is, nonsecurity) updates.

continues

continued

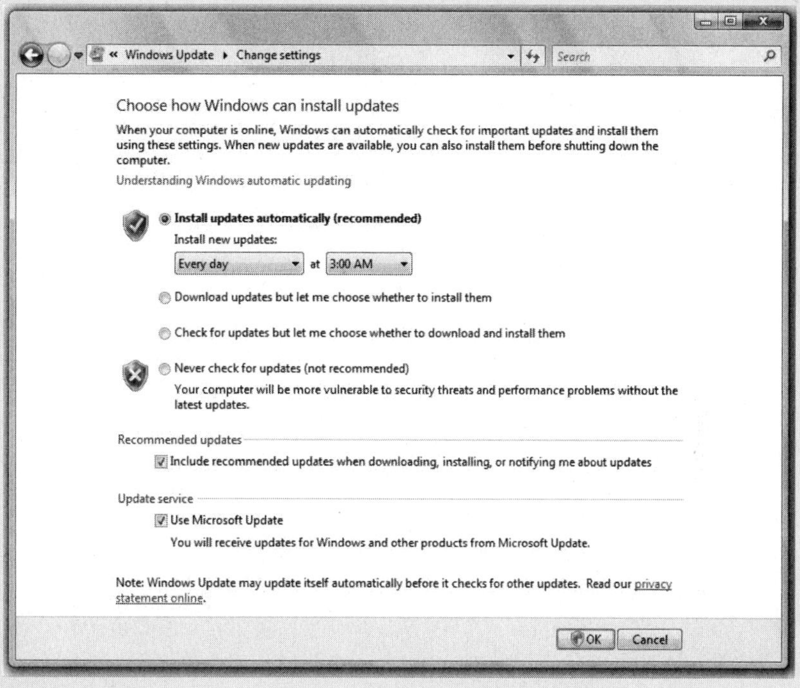

Figure 8-8: Automatic updating is now a feature of Windows Updates, not a separate tool.

User Account Security Features

Windows Vista includes two major technologies that help protect different types of user accounts from outside threats. Dubbed User Account Control and Parental Controls, these technologies are discussed in Chapter 9.

Internet Explorer 7 Security Features

The version of Internet Explorer 7 packaged with Windows Vista includes a number of advanced security technologies that make this the safest version of IE yet. In this section you'll examine the many security features Microsoft added to Internet Explorer 7. These features were absolutely necessary: Ever since Microsoft integrated Internet Explorer with the Windows shell beginning in the mid 1990s, Internet Explorer has been a major avenue of attack against Windows. With Windows Vista, finally, Microsoft has decoupled IE from the Windows shell and introduced advanced security controls that make IE safer.

cross
ref   Chapter 19 covers the functional aspects of Internet Explorer 7.

tip   Internet Explorer 7 is available to Windows XP users too, so you may be wondering whether this browser is really a benefit of Vista, or if the new security features it offers are in fact available to a much wider audience. As it turns out, the Windows XP version of IE 7 does offer some important security improvements over its predecessors, including some of the technologies discussed here; but as is often the case with security features that are present in both XP and Vista, the Vista version includes unique functionality that makes this newer OS more secure, overall, than XP. IE 7 Protected Mode, for example, is unique to Windows Vista.

ActiveX Opt-In

Initially developed as a lightweight version of COM (Component Object Model)—executable code modules designed to be small and fast enough to work over the Internet—Microsoft's ActiveX technology has been maligned by security experts as being one of the most insecure technologies created in the past 20 years. ActiveX controls litter literally every Windows system in existence, and hundreds of thousands of them are available online. Unfortunately, some of the controls—which can take various forms, such as browser helper objects, toolbars, and so on—are malicious and designed to hurt PCs.

In previous Internet Explorer versions, Microsoft didn't differentiate between ActiveX controls that were designed expressly for the Web—such as the Adobe Reader add-on—and those that were designed to be used locally on the PC only (Microsoft still includes many such controls with Windows). With Internet Explorer 7, a new feature called *ActiveX Opt-In* automatically disables entire classes of ActiveX controls, including those that were not designed specifically for use over the Internet. Now, when you visit a Web page that tries to activate an ActiveX control on your system, the Internet Explorer 7 Information Bar prompts you so you can decide whether or not to proceed, as shown in Figure 8-9.

If you know a particular control is safe, the Information Bar lets you enable the control and proceed.

Protected Mode

Available only in Windows Vista, Internet Explorer Protected Mode ensures that Internet Explorer 7 runs with even lower security privileges than a standard user account. This is a huge improvement over the way IE 7 works in, say, Windows XP. On that system, IE runs in the context of the user account of the current user, which is typically an administrator-class account with wide-open access to everything on the system. In Windows Vista, IE 7 always runs in a special low-privilege mode that is below that of both administrators and standard users; and it does so regardless of what kind of user is currently logged on.

cross
ref   See Chapter 9 for information on the standard user account type.

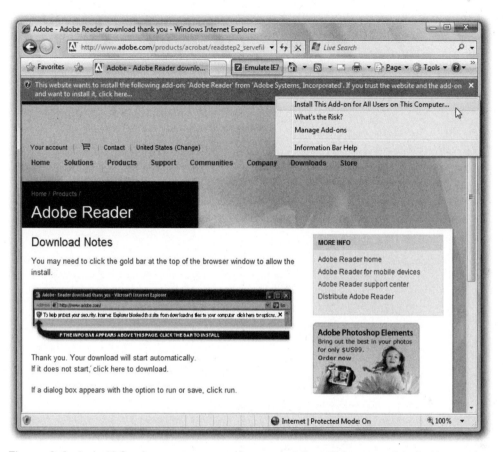

Figure 8-9: ActiveX Opt-In protects you against potentially malicious use of ActiveX controls.

This important feature ensures that automated electronic attacks cannot succeed against Internet Explorer 7, and because the browser is restricted from accessing any part of the user's hard drive other than the Temporary Internet Files folder, Internet Explorer is effectively sandboxed from the rest of Vista. As a result, should an attack succeed somehow, any malicious code that is injected into the system will find itself in a location that is isolated from the rest of the file system. Furthermore, the code will simply be deleted when Vista reboots. IE is significantly safer than it used to be.

> **tip**   You can ensure that IE is running in Protected Mode by viewing the IE status bar. You should see text that reads "Protected Mode: On." Protected Mode is configured in the Security tab of the Options dialog (see Figure 8-10).

🌐 Internet | Protected Mode: On   🔍 100% ▼

Figure 8-10: It's subtle, but important: This text means you're browsing safely.

Secret

Protected Mode is enabled by default in all Internet Explorer security zones except for Trusted Sites. That is, IE will be running in this more secure mode while browsing sites on the Internet and the local intranet, as well as while browsing sites you've marked as restricted. Trusted Sites are, by definition, sites that you have specifically marked as trusted, so these sites are accessed using a less-elevated security level.

Fix Settings for Me

In the past, it was sometimes necessary to temporarily change Internet Explorer's security settings in order to run a certain Web application or access certain online features; but once you did that, it was hard to figure out what you needed to do to restore Internet Explorer back to its default state. If you are forced to change Internet Explorer 7's security settings in a way that lowers Vista's security prowess, the browser will begin prompting you with its Information Bar. Then you can access a simple new feature called Fix Settings for Me to return IE to its default security settings.

Shown in Figure 8-11, this feature simply requires you to click the Information Bar and select Fix Settings for Me. You'll be prompted with a confirmation dialog box, and Internet Explorer reverts to its default settings. It's easy and effective.

Figure 8-11: Fix Settings for Me enables you to back away from an insecure Internet Explorer 7 setup.

tip	As times goes on, the need to temporarily override IE 7's security features in order to access specific sites will be less and less common. ***I don't advise ever doing this, actually.***

Phishing Filter

Internet Explorer 7 includes an integrated Phishing Filter that can help prevent you from being a victim of identity theft. These so-called phishing attacks are described in Chapter 20 because this type of attack is most commonly launched via an e-mail solution.

tip	Amazingly, the Phishing Filter is optional in Internet Explorer 7. I cannot stress this strongly enough: Enable this feature the first time you run Internet Explorer 7 (you'll most likely be prompted). If you didn't do so and would like to enable it now, click the Tools button in the IE command bar and select Phishing Filter ➪ Phishing Filter Settings. Confusingly, this displays the Advanced tab of the Internet Options dialog. In the Settings list, scroll down to the Security section and ensure that the option titled Turn on Automatic Web Site Checking is checked.

Delete Browsing History

In previous Internet Explorer versions it was difficult to delete various data related to Web browsing, such as temporary Internet files, cookies, Web history, saved form data, or saved passwords. In IE 7 all of this information can be deleted from a single dialog, either individually or all at once. Shown in Figure 8-12, Delete Browsing History is available from the Tools button in the IE command bar.

Figure 8-12: Delete Browsing History is a godsend for the security-conscious and truly paranoid.

Other Internet Explorer Security Features

The list of Internet Explorer 7 security features is vast, although you won't likely run into most of them unless you're truly unlucky. IE 7 integrates with Windows Defender to provide live scanning of Web downloads to ensure that you're not infecting your system with spyware, and it integrates with Vista's parental controls (see Chapter 9) to ensure that your children are accessing only those parts of the Web you deem safe. IE 7 also provides International Domain Name (IDN) support so that hackers can't construct malicious Web sites that mix character sets in order to fool unsuspecting users. In addition, various low-level changes prevent cross-domain or cross-window scripting attacks.

Secret

Should Internet Explorer 7 somehow be compromised, there's even a way out. A new Internet Explorer mode called Add-ons Disabled Mode loads IE with only a minimal set of add-ons so you can scrub the system of any malicious code. You can access this mode by navigating to All Programs ⇨ Accessories ⇨ System Tools ⇨ Internet Explorer (No Add-ons) in the Start Menu. Alternately, use Start Menu Search to find Internet Explorer (No Add-ons).

BitLocker Drive Encryption

In Windows XP and previous NT-based versions of Windows, Microsoft offered a feature called Encrypting File System (EFS) that enabled users to encrypt important folders or files. This prevents thieves from accessing sensitive data should your computer be physically stolen: If the thief removes your hard drive and attaches it to a different computer, any encrypted files cannot be read even if the thief figures out a way to access the hard drive's file system. EFS has proven to be a popular feature with IT administrators, the security-conscious, and roaming executives with laptops.

tip

NT-based versions of Windows include Windows NT 3.x and 4, Windows 2000, Windows XP, Windows Server 2003, Windows Vista, and Windows Server 2008. Older versions of Windows, such as Windows 95, 98, and Millennium Edition (Me), were based on less sophisticated and less secure DOS code.

EFS is still present in Windows Vista and works as before, but it's been augmented by a new technology called BitLocker. Like EFS, the new BitLocker feature in Windows Vista enables you to encrypt data on your hard drive to protect it in the event of physical theft, but BitLocker offers a few unique twists:

- ◆ BitLocker is full-disk encryption, not per-file encryption. If you enable BitLocker, it encrypts the entire hard disk on which Windows Vista resides, and all future files that are added to that drive are silently encrypted as well.

- BitLocker has been enhanced in Windows Vista Service Pack 1 to allow for full-disk encryption of nonsystem partitions as well, so in addition to encrypting the entire hard disk on which Vista is installed, you can now optionally encrypt any other partitions.

- BitLocker protects vital Windows system files during bootup: If BitLocker discovers a security risk, such as a change to the BIOS or any startup files (which might indicate that the hard drive was stolen and placed in a different machine), it will lock the system until you enter your BitLocker recovery key or password (discussed shortly).

- BitLocker works in conjunction with new Trusted Platform Module (TPM) security hardware in some modern PCs to provide a more secure solution than is possible with a software-only encryption routine. BitLocker may not be theoretically impregnable, but in most real-world scenarios, no hacker will defeat a BitLocker-protected PC.

Secret

BitLocker is available only to users of Windows Vista Enterprise and Ultimate editions. Users of other Vista versions need to use EFS to manually encrypt individual folders (and, by extension, their contents) instead.

There isn't a heck of a lot to configure for BitLocker. It's either on or it's not, and you either have TPM hardware or you don't: If your system does have TPM hardware, BitLocker will use it. Otherwise, you must use a USB memory drive as a startup key. This key is physically required to boot the system. If you don't have the key, or you lose it, you will need to enter a recovery password to access the drive instead. Here's where things get tricky: You can print out the recovery password and store it in a safe place, such as a physical safe or safety deposit box, or you can store it on a different computer in a text file, perhaps in an encrypted folder or encrypting ZIP file. However you store the recovery password, you can't lose it. If you lose both the startup key (either in the TPM hardware or on a USB memory key) and the recovery password, then the data on the BitLocker-protected hard drive is gone forever. There is literally no other recovery option available. Microsoft Support can't help you.

Still undaunted? You enable BitLocker by navigating to the BitLocker Drive Encryption tool in the Control Panel (Control Panel ⇨ Security ⇨ BitLocker Drive Encryption). Shown in Figure 8-13, BitLocker is straightforward. To enable it, simply click the Turn On BitLocker option.

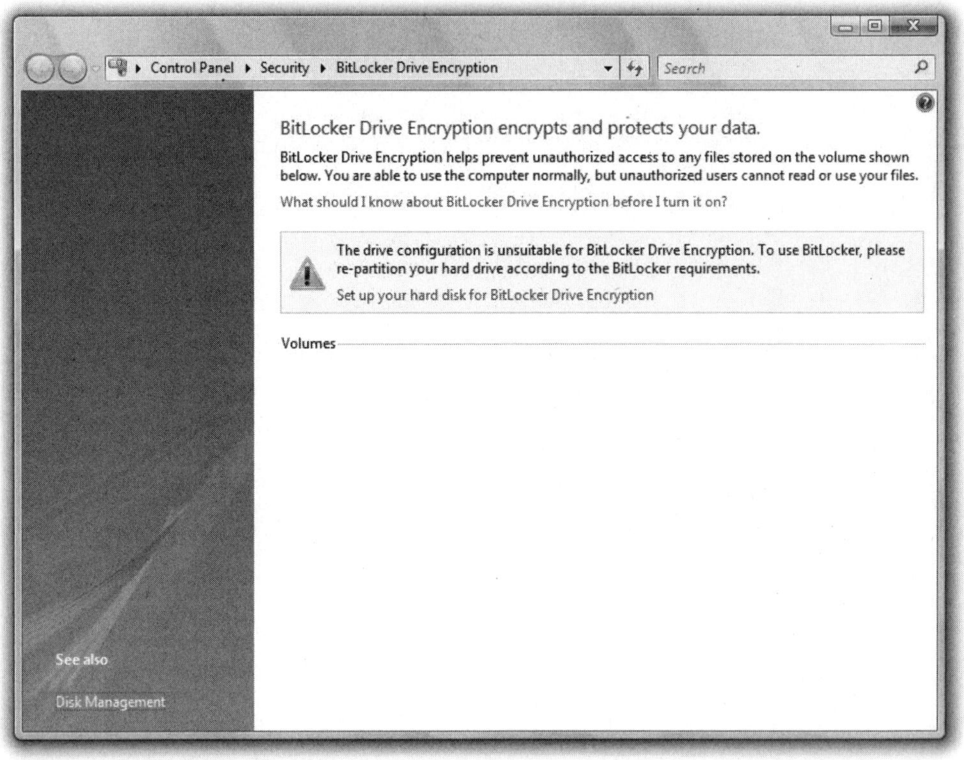

> BitLocker Drive Encryption encrypts and protects your data.
>
> BitLocker Drive Encryption helps prevent unauthorized access to any files stored on the volume shown below. You are able to use the computer normally, but unauthorized users cannot read or use your files.
>
> What should I know about BitLocker Drive Encryption before I turn it on?
>
> ⚠ The drive configuration is unsuitable for BitLocker Drive Encryption. To use BitLocker, please re-partition your hard drive according to the BitLocker requirements.
>
> Set up your hard disk for BitLocker Drive Encryption
>
> Volumes
>
> See also
>
> Disk Management

Figure 8-13: BitLocker is an exceedingly easy feature: It's either on or off.

Secret

Okay, I've oversimplified things. There's not much to configuring BitLocker if your hard drive is already partitioned correctly for this feature. Frankly, that's a big if: BitLocker requires at least two partitions on your primary hard drive, one for the system and one, called the active drive, that's reserved for BitLocker (but is not encrypted). This BitLocker active drive has to be 1.5GB or more in size. Both partitions must be formatted with NTFS. If you've already installed Windows Vista and didn't partition the drive correctly to accommodate BitLocker, you're pretty much out of luck. Vista doesn't offer any way to automatically repartition the drive for BitLocker, so you'll have to fumble around with Vista's Disk Management tool (Start Menu Search ➪ Computer Management) or a third-party partitioning tool that can nondestructively change the size of an existing partition.

Fortunately, there's a solution, but it's available only to Windows Vista Ultimate users. (Why Microsoft's volume license customers can't access this tool with Windows Vista Enterprise is beyond me.) Called the BitLocker Drive Preparation Tool, it's one of those elusive Windows Ultimate Extras tools, so you need to download and install it from Windows Update before you can use it.

continues

continued

BitLocker Drive Preparation, shown in Figure 8-14, is exactly the tool that Microsoft should have included in Vista to begin with: It examines your system, determines how the hard drive needs to be repartitioned in order to accommodate BitLocker, and then, get this, actually makes the changes for you automatically. Moreover, it's nondestructive, so it won't harm whatever data might already be residing on the C: drive. What a concept.

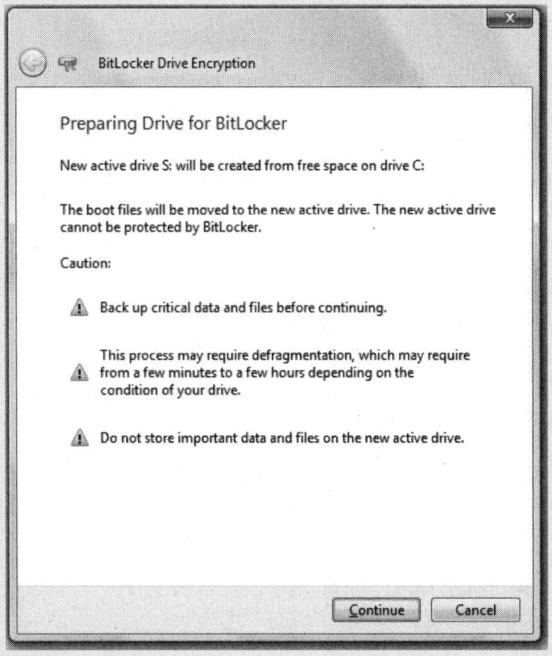

Figure 8-14: BitLocker Drive Preparation is a magic tool, but it's available only to Vista Ultimate users.

If you have the appropriate TPM hardware, BitLocker will save its encryption and decryption keys in that hardware. Otherwise, you are prompted to insert a USB memory key, which you'll need to insert in the machine every time it boots up. Optionally, you can also create a startup key or PIN to provide an additional layer of protection. The PIN is any number from 4 to 20 digits. The startup key and PIN can be enabled only the first time you enable BitLocker.

When BitLocker is enabled—a process that takes quite a bit of time, incidentally, because it must encrypt the contents of the drive—you don't have to do much in terms of configuration. You'll see a new Manage Keys link in the BitLocker Drive Encryption control panel, and you can create a recovery password from there. If you choose to print the password, be sure to save it in a safe place. Seriously.

Low-Level Security Features

Windows Vista includes a vast array of low-level security features. One of the most dramatic is *service hardening.* Because of the modular architecture of Windows Vista, the system has been created in such a way that the components that make up the system are as isolated from and independent of each other as possible.

Furthermore, Microsoft has gone over each of these components to ensure that they are running under the lowest possible security privileges. This protection extends to the system services that run silently in the background.

There's also a new feature called Address Space Layout Randomization (ASLR) that randomly loads key system files in memory, making them harder to attack remotely. This is a security technique that's been employed by UNIX-based systems for some time.

While none of these features are particularly configurable, it's fair to say that Windows Vista is the most secure Windows version ever made, thanks to the sum of these and many other security enhancements.

Secret

To get the absolute best security with Windows Vista, you can run one of the x64 versions of the operating system. (See Chapter 1 for information about choosing between x64- and x86/32-bit versions of Windows Vista.) That's because the x64 versions of Windows Vista include a few unique security features that are not available or as effective in the 32-bit versions of the operating system:

- A hardware-backed version of Data Execution Protection (DEP) that helps prevent buffer-overflow-based attacks.
- x64 drivers must be digitally signed, which suggests (but doesn't ensure) that x64 drivers will be more stable and secure than 32-bit drivers, which are often the cause of instability issues in Windows.

Of course, x64 versions of Windows Vista have their own compatibility issues, with both software and hardware. The trade-off is yours to make: better security and reliability or compatibility.

Summary

Although much is made of Vista's new user interface and other highly visible features, its new security features are, beyond a doubt, the number-one reason to consider upgrading to this new operating system. Although it's possible to duplicate many of the end-user features in Windows Vista on Windows XP, Vista's many security improvements are available only to those who upgrade to the latest Windows version. Security isn't something that's easy to sell, per se, and various vulnerabilities will still crop up over time; but make no mistake: Vista's security improvements are as dramatic as they are important. Vista is vastly more secure than Windows XP can ever be.

Users, Accounts, and UAC

Chapter

9

◆ ◆

In This Chapter

Understanding the types of user accounts you can create in Windows Vista

Using User Account Control to protect your system

Configuring User Account Control

Turning off User Account Control

Applying and configuring Parental Controls for your children

How Parental Controls work and how you can override their settings

◆ ◆

By now most Windows users are probably familiar with the notion of user accounts and how each user on a PC can have his or her own individual settings, documents, and other features. In Windows Vista, Microsoft has simplified the user account types down to just two, and has locked them down to make the system more secure. Thanks to new features such as User Account Control and Parental Controls, Vista is far more secure than previous Windows versions, but it's also possible to modify Vista's user-related security features to achieve a comfortable middle ground between the utmost in security and usability. This chapter describes these new features and explains how they can be put to the best possible use.

<table>
<tr><td>note</td><td>Windows Vista user accounts include a variety of obvious functionality that is not covered here explicitly because this book focuses on secrets, those features that are brand-new to Vista and/or so well hidden you'd never normally know about them. So, yes, you can add cute pictures to your user account; add, change, and remove passwords; and even change your account type, but you can do much more than that. This chapter looks at the new stuff that makes user accounts so much better in Windows Vista.</td></tr>
</table>

Understanding User Accounts

Starting with Windows XP, Microsoft began to push PC-based user accounts to consumers. That's because XP, unlike previous consumer-oriented Windows versions (such as Windows 95, 98, and Me), was based on the enterprise-class Windows NT code base. NT originally was developed in the early 1990s to be a mission-critical competitor to business operating systems such as UNIX. Previously, consumer Windows products such as Windows 95 and Windows Me were based on legacy MS-DOS code and provided only the barest possible support for discrete and secure user accounts because those systems were designed for single users only.

Eventually, however, Microsoft began moving the two products together. Windows XP, released in 2001, was the first mainstream NT-based Windows version, and this product marked the end of the DOS-based Windows line. Windows Vista, like Windows XP, is based on the NT code base, which means that versions of Vista are being marketed to both individuals and businesses, and that Vista will retain—and even enhance—the paradigm of each user having his or her own user account for accessing the PC. Therefore, it's worth discussing how user accounts have changed in Windows Vista compared to Windows XP.

First, however, a short review may be in order. When you installed or configured Windows XP for the first time, you were prompted to provide a password for the special administrator account and then create one or more user accounts. Administrator is what's called a *built-in account type*. The administrator account is typically reserved for system housekeeping tasks and it has full control of the system. Theoretically, individual user accounts—that is, accounts used by actual people—are supposed to have less control over the system for security reasons. In Windows XP, that theory was literally a theory. Every user account you created during XP's post-setup routine was an administrator-level account, and virtually every single Windows application ever written assumes that every user has administrative privileges. This resulted in an ugly chicken-or-egg situation that has caused several years of unrelenting security vulnerabilities because malicious code running on a Windows system runs using the privilege level of the logged-on user. If the user is an administrator, so is the malicious code.

In Windows Vista, everything has changed. Yes, you still create user accounts; and, it is hoped, with passwords. (Why Microsoft still doesn't require this is beyond me.) And you still log on to the system to access applications, the Internet, and other services, as you did in Windows XP. But in Windows Vista, user accounts—even those that are graced with administrative privileges—no longer have complete control over the system, at least not by default. Microsoft, finally, is starting to batten down the virtual hatches and make Windows more secure. Although there are ways to counteract these preventive measures, the result is a more secure operating system than previous Windows versions, one that hackers have found and will continue to find more difficult to penetrate. The following sections look at what has changed.

Creating the Initial User Account

When you install Windows Vista for the first time or turn on a new computer that has Windows Vista preinstalled from a PC maker, you will eventually run into the so-called out-of-box experience (OOBE), whereby Vista prompts you for a few pertinent bits of information before presenting you with the Windows desktop for the first time. Unlike with XP, an administrator account is not created by default. Instead you are prompted to create a different user account during the OOBE, and while that account is granted administrative privileges, remember that this privilege isn't as all-powerful as it was in XP. You'll see why in just a moment.

Secret

One feature that's missing from Windows Vista, incidentally, is that it's no longer possible to create up to five user accounts during Vista setup, as it was in XP setup. You can create only a single user account while configuring Windows Vista for the first time, so if you want to create more accounts, you have to do that after you log on; and those accounts, by default, are not created with administrative privileges unless you change the settings (a process described fully in just a moment).

Understanding Account Types

Windows Vista, unlike XP, supports just two account types:

- **Administrator:** This is (almost) exactly what it sounds like, and is basically the same as the administrator account type in Windows XP. Administrators have complete control of the system and can make any configuration changes they want, though the method for doing so has changed somewhat since XP.

- **Standard user:** A standard user can use most application software and many Windows services. Standard users, however, are prevented from accessing features that could harm the system. For example, standard users cannot install applications, change the system time, or access certain Control Panel applets. Naturally, there are ways around these limitations, discussed in a bit.

Microsoft would like most people to run under a standard user account; and although this would indeed be marginally safer than using an administrator account, I can't recommend it. That's because Microsoft has actually locked down the administrator account in Windows Vista, making it safer to use than ever before. More important, perhaps, you'll ultimately find an administrator account to be less annoying than a standard user account. To find out why that's so, you need to examine a new security feature in Windows Vista: User Account Control.

User Account Control

No Windows Vista feature is as controversial and misunderstood as User Account Control, or UAC. Tech pundits have screamed far and wide about this reviled feature, spreading mistruths and misunderstandings and generally raising a lot of ruckus about nothing. If these pundits would just calm down long enough to actually use User Account Control for longer than a single afternoon, they'd discover something very simple: It's not really that annoying, and it does in fact increase the security of the system. Indeed, I would argue that User Account Control is one of the few features that really differentiates Vista from XP, because there's no way to add this kind of functionality to XP, even through third-party add-on software. User Account Control is effective; it really does work.

Great, but what is it exactly? In order to make the system more secure, Microsoft has architected Windows Vista so that all of the tasks you can perform in the system are divided into two groups, those that require administrative privileges and those that don't. This required a lot of thought and a lot of engineering work, naturally, because the company had to weigh the ramifications of each potential action and then code the system accordingly. What they arrived at is a decent technical compromise; and although some of the security controls in Windows Vista will likely cause fits in certain circles, many users will understand that they're in place to keep the system more secure and will learn to live with them. Anyone who has ever been bitten by a worm, virus, Trojan, or other bit of malicious code should gladly and willingly accept the new restrictions.

Here's how it works. Every user, whether configured as a standard user or an administrator, can perform any of the tasks in Windows Vista that do not require administrator privileges, just as they did in Windows XP. (The problem with XP, from a security standpoint, of course, is that *all* tasks are denoted as not requiring administrative privileges.) You can launch applications, change time zone and power-management settings, add a printer, run Windows Update, and perform other similar tasks. However, when you attempt to run a task that does require administrative privileges, the system will force you to provide appropriate credentials in order to continue. The experiences vary a bit depending on the account type. Predictably, those who log on with administrator-class accounts experience a less annoying interruption.

Standard users receive a User Account Control credentials dialog box, as shown in Figure 9-1. This dialog box requires you to enter the password for an administrator account that is already configured on the system. Consider why this is useful. If you have configured your children with standard user accounts (as, frankly, you should, if you're going to allow them to share your PC), then they can let you know when they run into this dialog box, giving you the option to allow or deny the task they are attempting to complete.

Figure 9-1: Standard users attempting to perform admin-level tasks are confronted by the User Account Control credentials dialog box.

Administrators receive a simpler dialog box, called the User Account Control consent dialog box, shown in Figure 9-2. Because these users are already configured as administrators, they do not have to provide administrator credentials. Instead they can simply click Continue to keep going.

Figure 9-2: Administrators receive a less annoying dialog box.

Secret By default, administrators using Windows Vista are running in a new execution mode called Admin Approval Mode. This is why you see consent dialog boxes appear from time to time even though you're using an administrator-type account. You can actually disable this mode, making administrator accounts work more like they did in XP, without any annoying dialog boxes popping up. However, understand that disabling Admin Approval Mode could open up your system to attack. If you're still interested in disabling this feature, or disabling User Account Control, you will learn how at the end of this section.

Secret Conversely, those running with administrative privileges who would like Windows Vista to be even more secure—and really, why aren't there more people like you in the world?—can also configure the system to prompt with a User Account Control credentials dialog box (which requires a complete password) every time they attempt an administrative task. This option is also discussed shortly.

The presentation of both User Account Control dialog boxes can be quite jarring if you're not familiar with the feature or if you've just recently switched to Vista. If you attempt to complete an administrative task, the screen will flash, the background will darken, and the credentials or consent dialog will appear somewhere onscreen. Most important, the dialogs are modal: You can't continue doing anything else until you have dealt with these dialog boxes one way or the other.

Secret The screen darkening and modal nature of the UAC prompts indicate that Vista has moved into the so-called *secure desktop*, which is a special, more secure display mode that Microsoft also uses during logon and when you access the Ctrl+Alt+Del screen. It's possible to configure UAC to work without the secure desktop, but this is not recommended because UAC dialogs could be spoofed by malicious hackers. You'll examine various UAC configuration options later in this chapter.

For the record, there's actually a third type of User Account Control dialog box that sometimes appears regardless of which type of user account you have configured. This dialog box appears whenever you attempt to install an application that has not been digitally signed or validated by its creator. These types of applications are quite common, so you're likely to see the dialog box shown in Figure 9-3 fairly frequently, especially when you're initially configuring a new PC.

By design, this dialog box is more colorful and "in your face" than the other User Account Control dialog boxes. Microsoft wants to ensure that you really think about it before continuing. Rule of thumb: You're going to see this one a lot, but if you just downloaded an installer from a place you trust, it's probably okay to go ahead and install it.

User Account Control

⚠ An unidentified program wants access to your computer

Don't run the program unless you know where it's from or you've used it before.

    Combined-Community-Codec-Pack.exe
    Unidentified Publisher

To continue, type an administrator password, and then click OK.

    Paul
    Password

⌄ Details   [OK]   [Cancel]

User Account Control helps stop unauthorized changes to your computer.

Figure 9-3: This dialog box (colorful onscreen) appears whenever you attempt to execute an application installer from an unknown source.

The behavior of User Account Control has led some to describe this feature as needlessly annoying. However, Windows Vista isn't even the first OS to use this type of security feature: Mac OS X and Linux, for example, have utilized a UAC-type user interface for years now; and unlike with other systems, User Account Control actually becomes less annoying over time. That's because most UAC dialog boxes pop up when you first get Windows Vista. This is when you'll be futzing around with settings and installing applications the most; and these two actions, of course, are the very actions that most frequently trigger User Account Control. The moral here is simple: After your new Vista PC is up and running, User Account Control will rear its ugly head less and less frequently. In fact, after a week or so User Account Control will be mostly a thing of the past. You'll forget it was ever there.

Secret

Disabling User Account Control

Okay, you don't believe me. Well, as a sign of the trust I have in *you,* I'm actually going to tell you how you can completely disable User Account Control. I don't recommend this; but as I mentioned earlier, many people are going to be annoyed by User Account Control despite its good intentions, and they're going to want to simply disable it. As it turns out, there are several methods for disabling User Account Control. I'll describe two here.

Method 1: Using the User Accounts Control Panel

To disable User Account Control just for the current user, access the User Account control panel. The easiest way is to open the Start Menu and type **user accounts** into Start Menu Search. Then, click the link titled Turn User Account Control On or Off, as shown in Figure 9-4. Ironically, you need to clear a User Account Control dialog to acces this option.

continues

continued

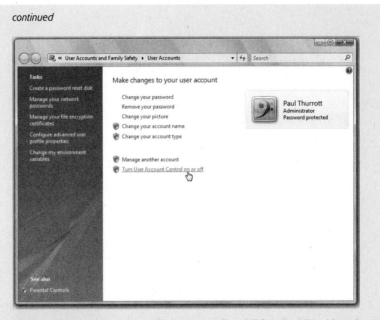

Figure 9-4: Wait a second. There's actually a UI for disabling User Account Control?

In the next window that appears (see Figure 9-5) simply uncheck the box next to Use User Account Control (UAC) to Help Protect Your Computer. Click OK. Two things will happen immediately.

Figure 9-5: It doesn't get much simpler than this, but actually there's a catch.

continues

continued

First, a dialog will appear warning you that you must restart your computer in order to apply the change you just made. UAC will remain on until you do this. Second, the Windows Security Center will flash a dangerous-looking warning balloon indicating that this change is dangerous. Additionally, the red Security Center shield icon will appear in your system tray. (See Figure 9-6.) This icon will remain there until you do one of two things: fix the problem (that is, turn UAC back on) or configure it to stop bothering you.

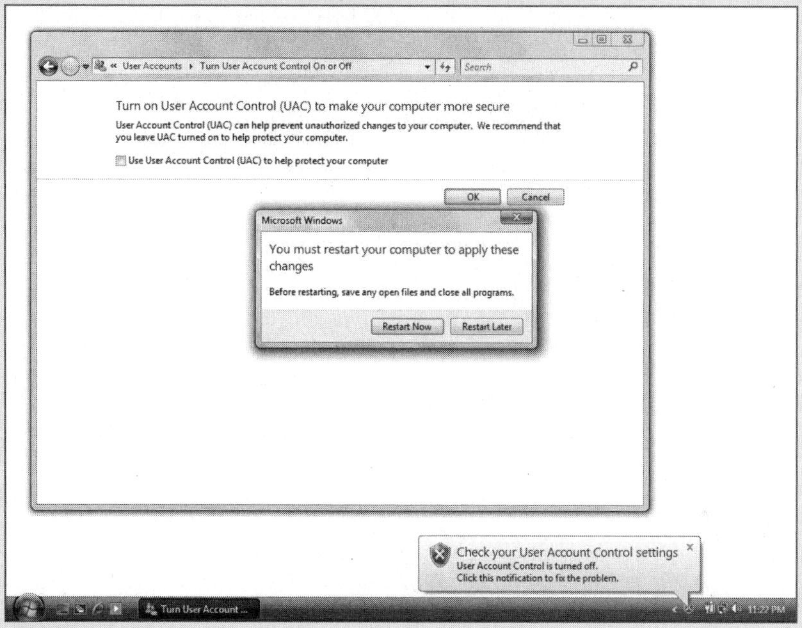

Figure 9-6: Windows Vista doesn't like it when you mess around with User Account Control.

You're getting into a gray area here because I've already warned you to leave User Account Control on, but in for a foot, in for a mile, as they say. If you're dead set against leaving User Account Control on, you may as well get rid of that annoying shield icon. To do so, double-click it to display the Windows Security Center (which has a red highlighted section explaining why it's upset). Then click the link on the left of the application titled Change the Way Security Center Alerts Me. In the dialog that appears, shown in Figure 9-7, select Don't Notfiy Me, and Don't Display the Icon (Not Recommended). The dialog will disappear, as will the shield icon. However, Security Center will still retain its red color.

If you later change your mind, you can reenable User Account Control in a variety of ways. The easiest is to open the Security Center and click the Turn It On Now button next to User Account Control. This change is immediate and does not require a reboot.

continues

continued

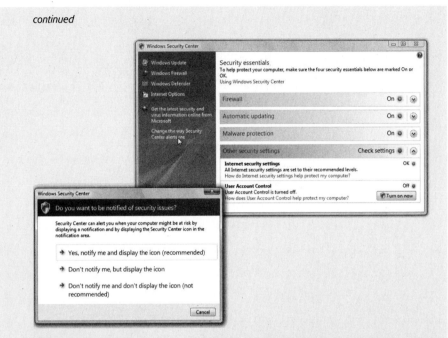

Figure 9-7: I don't recommend choosing door number three unless you back up regularly and are convinced you know what you're doing.

Method 2: Achieving a Happy Middle Ground with TweakUAC

The problem with disabling User Account Control, in my opinion, is that you lose too much. In addition to the notifications, a number of other useful Vista security features disappear when you disable UAC, including Internet Explorer Protected Mode (see Chapter 8). Fortunately, there's a way to get most of the benefits of User Account Control but without the annoying pop-ups, assuming you're running with an administrator-class account (and almost everyone using Vista will be doing so). It's called User Account Control "quiet" mode. Configuring this feature is a bit of a hassle (you'll see why in the next section), but fortunately there's a wonderful (and free) third-party utilty called TweakUAC (www.tweak-uac.com) that enables you to use this mode. (It also enables you to turn off UAC all together.) Here's how it works.

When you run TweakUAC, you'll see three options, as shown in Figure 9-8: Turn UAC off Now, Switch UAC to the Quiet Mode, and Leave UAC On.

These options are self-explanatory, but it's the middle one that interests us. This puts UAC into quiet mode. No more pop-ups. Unfortunately, Windows Security Center will still throw a fit, so use the instructions in the previous section to disable Security Center's annoying red shield icon if it irritates you.

continues

continued

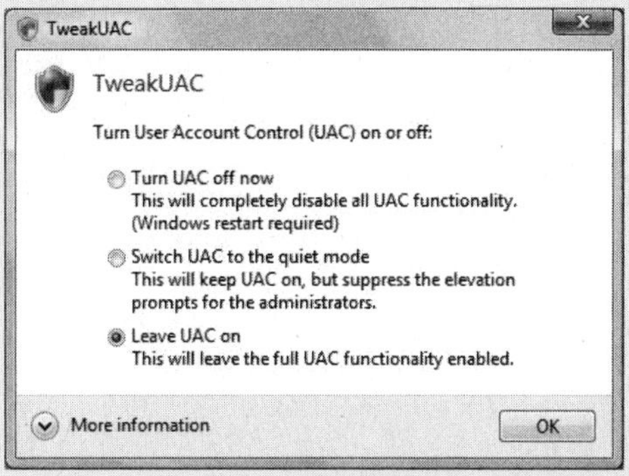

Figure 9-8: TweakUAC takes the multitude of User Account Control options that are available and presents the three most frequently needed options.

Configuring User Account Control

Secret

If you're the tweaker type and are running Windows Vista Business, Enterprise, or Ultimate, Microsoft makes a number of User Account Control settings available through the hidden Local Security Settings management console. To launch this console, open the Start Menu and type **secpol.msc** in Start Menu Search. (You have to type the entire command for it to work.) This displays the administrative console shown in Figure 9-9.

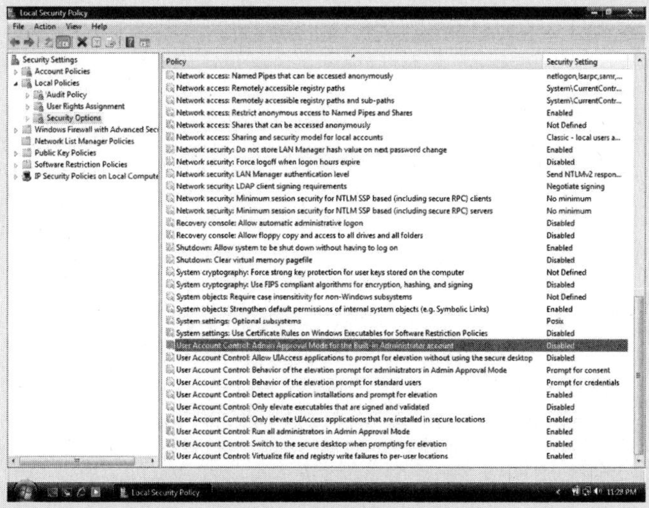

Figure 9-9: The Local Security Policy management console enables you to configure various security features, including User Account Control.

continues

continued

To access the User Account Control options, expand the Local Policies and Security Options nodes in the tree view under Security Settings in the left pane of the management console. When you do so, the right pane will be populated with a list of security options. Scroll to the bottom, where you will see several security options related to User Account Control. Table 9-1 highlights these settings and explains what each one does.

tip   The Local Security Policy management console should be used only on PCs that are not centrally managed by a Windows Server–based Active Directory (AD)–based domain. Unless you work for a large company, it's unlikely that your PC is centrally managed in this way.

Table 9-1: User Account Control Features That Can Be Customized

Security Option	What It Does	Default Setting
Admin Approval Mode for the built-in administrator account	Toggles Admin Approval Mode for the built-in administrator account only. When Admin Approval Mode is off, UAC is said to be in "quiet" mode.	Disabled
Allow UIAccess applications to prompt for elevation without using the secure desktop	Determines whether properly installed applications that need to be run with administrative privileges can prompt for elevation without entering the secure desktop. "UIAccess" applications are applications that are installed in "trusted" shell locations such as the Windows directory or the Programs Files directory.	Disabled
Behavior of the elevation prompt for administrators in Admin Approval Mode	Determines what type of prompt admin-level users receive when attempting admin-level tasks. You can choose between a consent dialog box, a credentials dialog box, and no prompt.	Prompt for consent
Behavior of the elevation prompt for standard users	Determines what type of prompt standard users receive when attempting admin-levels tasks. You can choose between a consent dialog box, a credentials dialog box, and no prompt.	Prompt for credentials
Detect application installations and prompt for elevation	Determines whether application installs trigger a User Account Control elevation dialog box	Enabled
Only elevate executables that are signed and validated	Determines whether only signed and validated application installs trigger a User Account Control elevation dialog box	Disabled

continues

Table 9-1: *(continued)*

Security Option	What It Does	Default Setting
Only elevate UIAccess applications that are installed in secure locations	Determines whether only properly installed applications can be elevated to administrative privileges.	Enabled
Run all administrators in Admin Approval Mode	Determines whether all admin-level accounts run in Admin Approval Mode, which generates User Account Control consent dialogs for admin-level tasks. When Admin Approval Mode is off, UAC is said to be in "quiet" mode.	Enabled
Switch to the secure desktop when prompting for elevation	Determines whether the Secure Desktop environment appears whenever a User Account Control prompt is initiated by the system.	Enabled
Virtualize file and registry write failures to per-user locations	Determines whether User Account Control virtualizes the Registry and file system for legacy applications that attempt to read from or write to private parts of the system. Do not disable this option.	Enabled

To change a setting, double-click it. Just select the option you want (Enabled or Disabled for most of the UAC-related features) in the resulting dialog and then click OK.

Secret If you're running Windows Vista Home Basic or Home Premium, you need to edit the Registry to achieve these UAC changes. You can learn how at my SuperSite Blog at the SuperSite for Windows: http://tinyurl.com/3foy3q.

Secret As is always the case with User Account Control, changing most of these options will trigger a spaz attack from Windows Security Center. That is, it will display a warning dialog regularly going forward and leave a red shield icon in the tray notification area unless you disable the way in which the Security Center warns you of problems. On the flip side, if you revert any of these options to their default (read: desired) values, the Security Center warnings will disappear immediately.

Parental Controls

Although Windows XP was the first version of Windows to make user accounts truly usable, Windows Vista is the first to make them safe for children. Now it's possible to apply Parental Controls to your children's accounts to keep them away from the bad stuff online and off, and give you peace of mind that was previously lacking when the kids got on a computer. Vista's Parental Controls are available on a per-user basis, and you might be surprised by how well they work.

Secret   Parental Controls are available in Windows Vista Home Basic, Home Premium, and Ultimate, but not Business or Enterprise.

Configuring Parental Controls

To set up Parental Controls, you first need to configure one or more user accounts as standard user accounts; these are the accounts you'll configure for your children.

Secret   Parental Controls cannot be applied to an administrator-class account. They can be applied only to standard users. In addition, there's another limitation. While it's technically possible to configure Parental Controls on a system in which one or more administrators do not have passwords, doing so would be folly. Parental Controls rely on the controlled accounts (your kids' accounts) not having access to administrator accounts. If one or more administrator-class accounts do not have passwords, your kids will be able to bypass any controls you set up. Thus, be sure that any administrator-class accounts on the PC have passwords.

Then, from an administrator account, you can configure Parental Controls. To do so, just type **parental** in Start Menu Search to locate and access the Parental Controls application. Then select the user to which you'd like to add Parental Controls. You will see the User Controls dialog, shown in Figure 9-10.

tip   You can configure Parental Controls on only one account at a time. If you have three children to whom you'd like to apply identical Parental Controls, unfortunately you will have to repeat these steps for each of your children's accounts.

Figure 9-10: Parental Controls enable you to configure various restrictions for your children.

By default, Parental Controls are not enabled for any standard user accounts. When you do enable Parental Controls by checking the option titled On, Enforce Current Settings, you can configure the features discussed in the following sections.

Activity Reporting

When this feature is enabled, your children's Parental-Control-related activity is recorded and presented to you periodically in report form. The reports are available from this Parental Controls window and include such things as top 10 Web sites visited, most recent 10 Web sites visited, logon times, applications run, instant-message conversations, link exchanges, Webcam usage, audio usage, game play, file exchanges, SMS messages, e-mails received and sent, and media (audio, video, and recorded TV shows) played. An empty sample report is shown in Figure 9-11, giving you an idea of the amount of information that is collected.

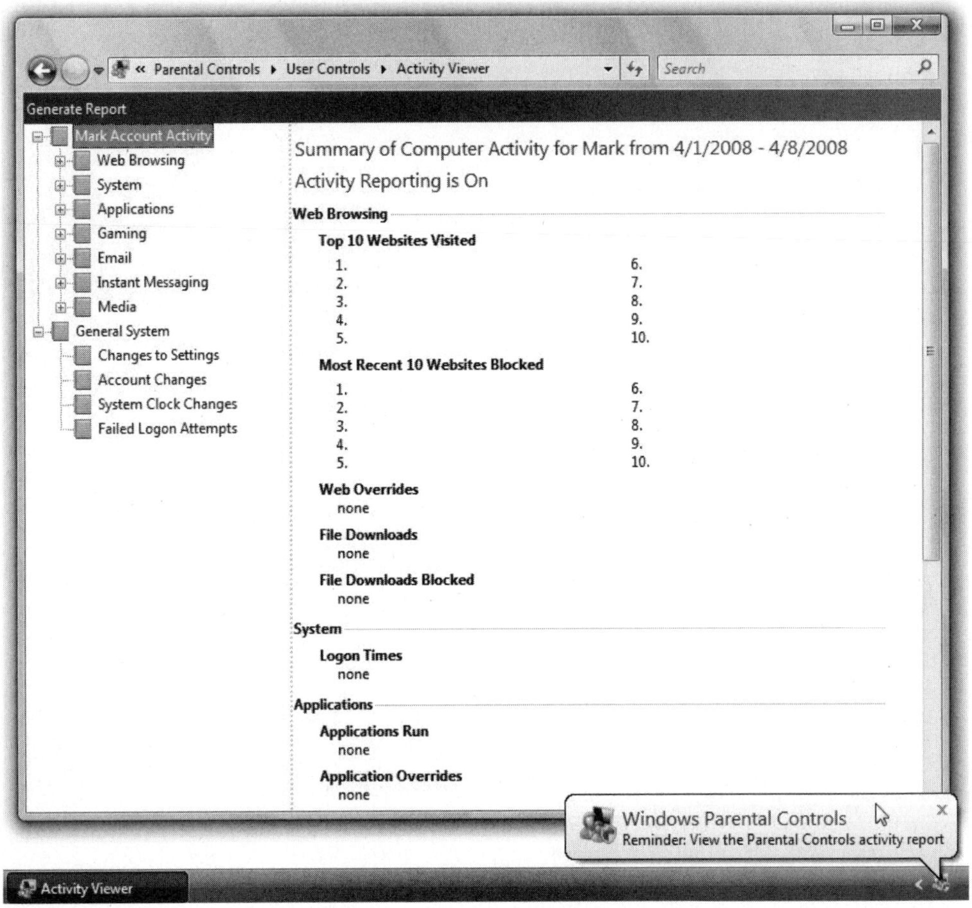

Figure 9-11: With Parental Controls, you can view reports that summarize your children's recent activities on the PC.

Reports are available for each standard user account. There's also a different report type, called General System, that logs such things as when Parental Controls settings, accounts, or the system clock are changed, or when users fail to log on correctly because of entering an incorrect password (or when attempting to log on during a time period that is forbidden because of Parental Controls).

Windows Vista Web Filter

The Web Restrictions Parental Controls determine what Web content your children can access. As shown in Figure 9-12, Web Restrictions controls give you fine-grained control over Web access.

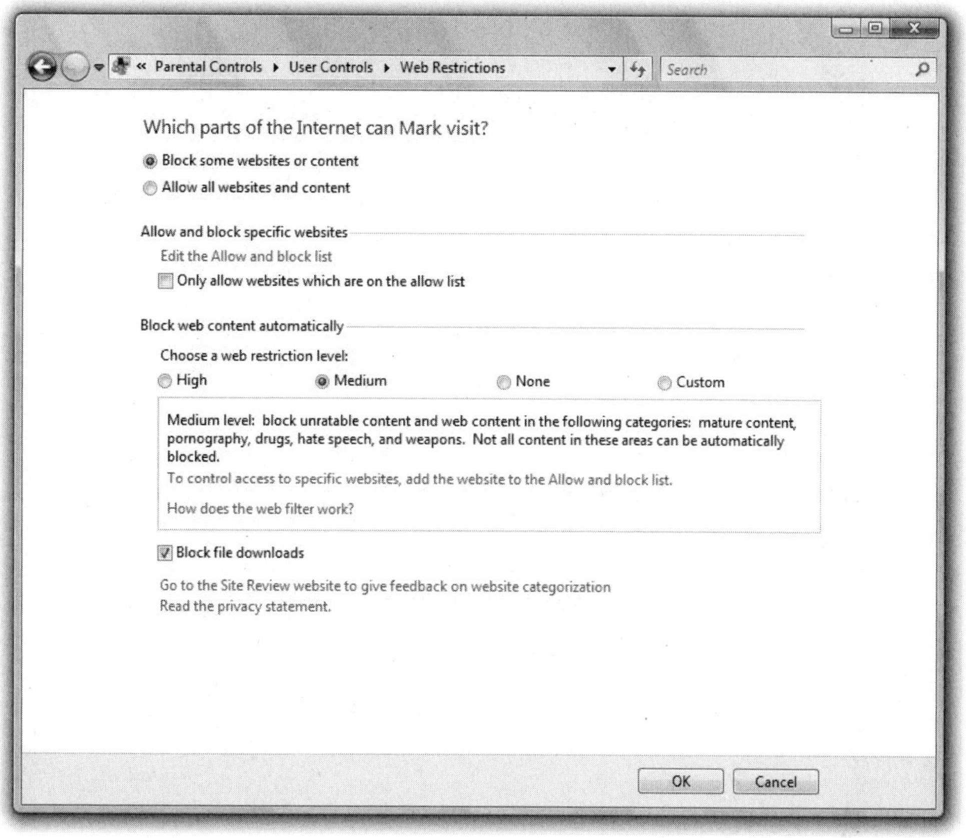

Figure 9-12: Windows Vista's Web restrictions will keep your children safe online.

You can block Web content using plain English Web restriction levels such as High, Medium, None, or Custom. If you choose Custom, you can determine exactly what kind of Web content you'd like to block. Blockable subject matter includes pornography, mature content, sex education, hate speech, bomb making, weapons, drugs, alcohol, tobacco, gambling, and unrated content. You can also configure very specific Allow and Block lists, whereby you list specific URLs you're either okay with or don't ever want allowed (see Figure 9-13). If you're really worried about the Web, you can block all Web sites except those you explicitly allow. Finally, you can also completely block all file downloads.

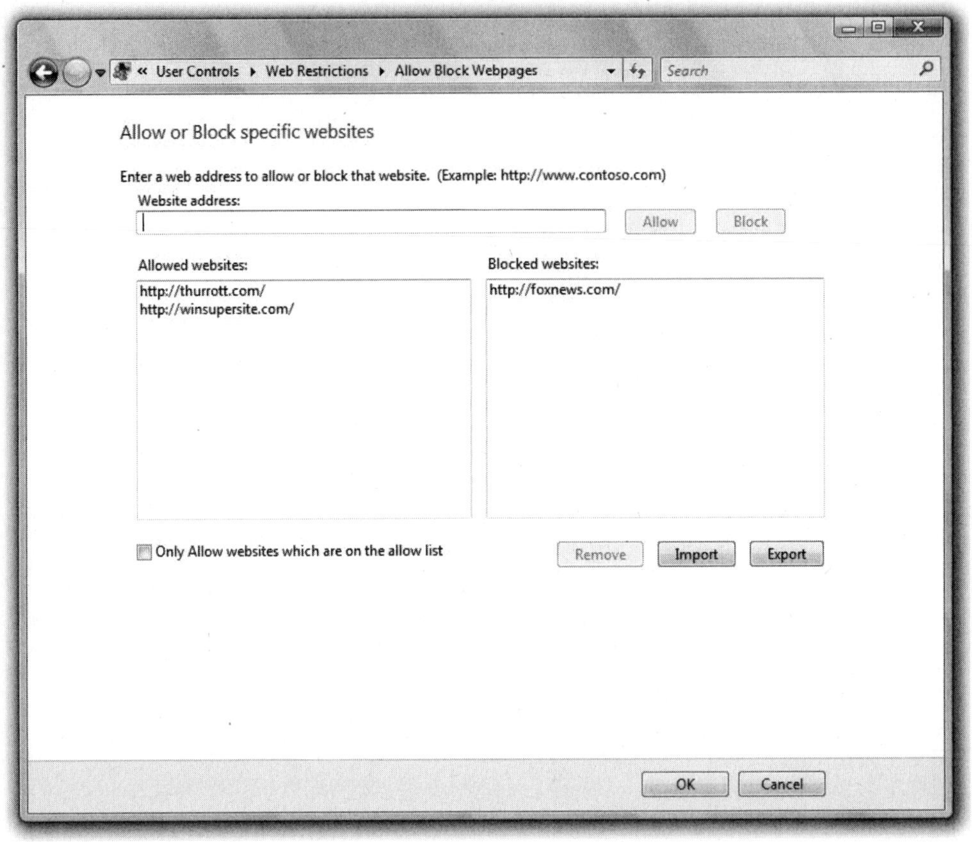

Figure 9-13: Talk about fine-grained: You can allow or block specific Web sites if you want.

Time Limits

This is one of my favorite Parental Controls because it's so obvious and graphical. The Time Restrictions Parental Controls provides a graphical grid that enables you to configure exactly when your kids can use the computer. By default Windows Vista users can use the PC on any day at any time, but by dragging your mouse around the grid shown in Figure 9-14 you can prevent your children from using the computer at specific hours, such as late at night or during school hours.

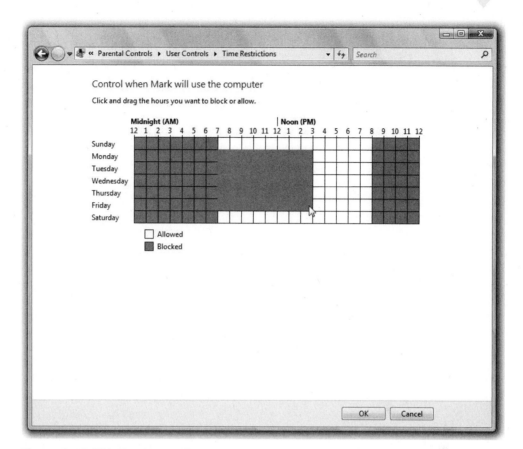

Figure 9-14: This simple and effective interface helps you configure when your kids can and cannot use the PC.

Games

The Game Restrictions Parental Controls specifies whether your children can play games on the PC and, if so, which games they can access. By default standard account holders can play all games. Of course, you can fine-tune that setting using the screen shown in Figure 9-15, which appears when you click Set Game Ratings.

Figure 9-15: With the games restrictions, you can control which games your kids play.

Here you can set acceptable game ratings using the Entertainment Software Ratings Board's (ESRB) rating system, blocking or allowing games with no rating. Additionally, you can block games based on content, using a surprising range of content types, including unrated online games, alcohol and tobacco reference, alcohol reference, animated blood, blood, blood and gore, cartoon violence, comic mischief, crude humor, drug and alcohol reference, drug and tobacco reference, drug reference, edutainment, fantasy violence, and about 200 others. It's a long list.

Finally, you can also block or allow specific games, which is surprisingly helpful because many Windows games do not digitally identify their ESRB rating. The nice thing about this UI, shown in Figure 9-16, is that Parental Controls sees which games are already installed on the system and enables you to supply a Caesar-style yea or nay.

Control specific games Mark can and can not play

Allowed Ratings:
E10+ - EVERYONE 10+, T - TEEN, Ao - ADULTS ONLY, E - EVERYONE, Ec - EARLY CHILDHOOD, M - MATURE
Denied Descriptors: None

Title/Rating	Status	User Rating Setting	Always Allow	Always Block
Chess Titans E	Can play	◉	○	○
FreeCell E	Can play	◉	○	○
Hearts E	Can play	◉	○	○
Hold 'Em T: Simulated Gambling	Can not play	○	○	◉
InkBall E	Can play	◉	○	○
Mahjong Titans E	Can play	◉	○	○
Minesweeper E	Can play	◉	○	○
Purble Place E	Can play	◉	○	○
Solitaire E	Can play	◉	○	○
Spider Solitaire E	Can play	◉	○	○

Figure 9-16: Use this dialog to block or allow specific game titles.

Allow and Block Specific Programs

This final setting, Application Restrictions, enables you to manually specify applications that you do or do not want your child to use. By default standard users can access all of the applications installed on the system. However, using the interface shown in Figure 9-17, it's possible to fine-tune what's allowed. If you don't see an application in the list, click Browse to find it.

Secret

One of the most unique features of Windows Vista's Parental Controls is that they aren't limited to use with children. Indeed, many security-conscious users will find that it's worth setting up a standard user account for themselves, applying various Parental Controls to it, and then using that account for their normal PC operations. Why would you want to do such a thing? Well, for starters, you might want to protect yourself from some of the nastier things that happen online. It's something to think about.

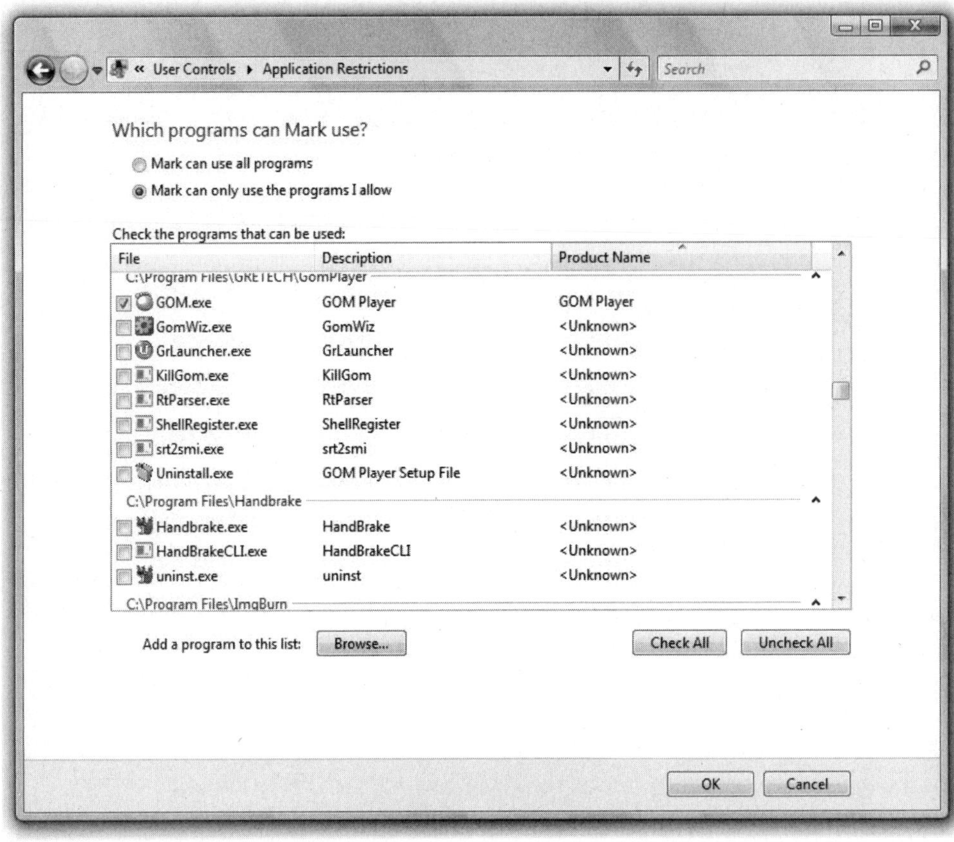

Figure 9-17: From this list, you can choose the applications your children can access.

Running as Standard User with Parental Controls

You may be wondering what the experience is like running a standard user account to which Parental Controls have been applied. For the most part, it's just like running a standard account normally, but certain actions will trigger Parental Controls blocks, depending on how you've configured Parental Control restrictions. For example, if the user attempts to log on to the system during a time period in which the parent has restricted that, he or she will be prevented from doing so, as shown in Figure 9-18.

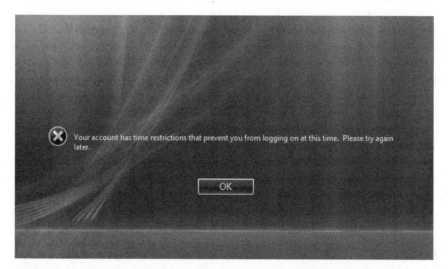

Figure 9-18: Sorry, Johnny: Your parents say it's too late to be computing.

Similarly, if you try to run an application that is not explicitly allowed by Parental Controls, you will see the dialog box shown in Figure 9-19.

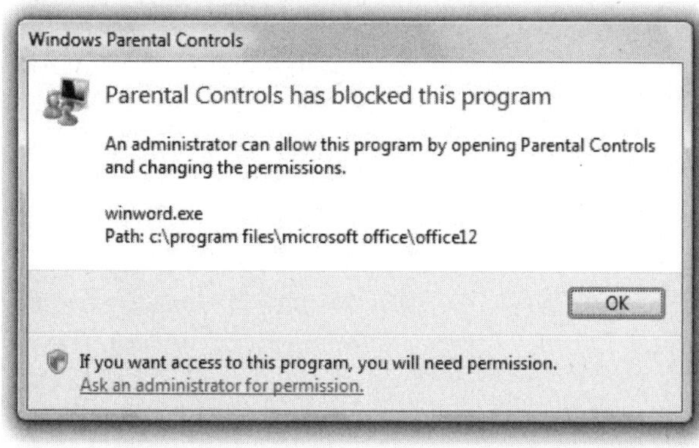

Figure 9-19: Sorry, but this application is being blocked by Vista's Parental Controls.

Note that you can ask for permission to run individual blocked applications. When you choose this option, the User Account Control credentials dialog box appears (see Figure 9-20), giving parents a chance to review the action and then decide whether to give their permission.

Figure 9-20: If parents are around, they can okay blocked activities.

The Web experience is similar. If you use Internet Explorer to browse to a type of site that is forbidden via Parental Controls, IE will display the page shown in Figure 9-21. Again, you can click the Ask an Administrator for Permission link to get an override. When you do so, the User Account Control credentials dialog box appears.

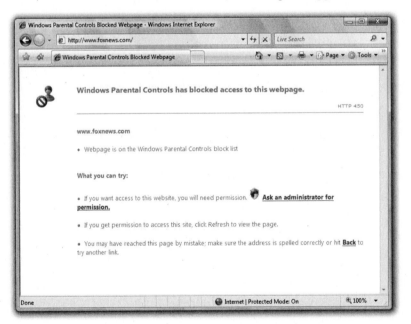

Figure 9-21: Web restrictions work in a similar manner thanks to Parental Controls integration with Internet Explorer 7.

If a Web download is attempted when Web downloads are restricted by Parental Controls, the dialog box in Figure 9-22 appears. In this case there is no administrator override: Downloads have been explicitly restricted with Parental Controls.

Figure 9-22: When downloads are prevented, there's no way to get an override.

Secret

Although Windows Vista's Parental Controls features are excellent, you may want to investigate two related Microsoft services: Windows Live OneCare (see Chapter 25), which proactively ensures that Vista's security settings are configured correctly at all times, a boon for childrens' PCs; and Windows Live Family Safety (see Chapter 21), a free online service for managing and monitoring your children's Web browsing habits.

Incidentally, some other activities are simply blocked as well and thus can't be overridden. If you specifically block a game or application, for example, even a parent can't unblock it on the fly, as shown in Figure 9-23. Instead you have to make a configuration change in Parental Controls, back in your own account.

Figure 9-23: Programs that are specifically blocked can't be overridden.

Summary

Windows Vista, for the first time, makes it possible for users to run the system in more secure ways, thanks largely to advances in the way that user accounts are handled. Although features such as User Account Control will often seem annoying, the alternative is worse, as evidenced by the past half-decade of Windows security vulnerabilities. Vista's Parental Controls, meanwhile, finally extend a measure of safety to your children, whether they're using local applications or browsing the Web.

Windows Vista Networking

◆ ◆

In This Chapter

Some Vista networking technologies that debuted in Windows XP SP2

Differences between Windows XP and Vista networking

New Windows Vista networking features

Understanding network locations

Working with the Network and Sharing Center

Using Network Maps

Connecting to networks

Setting up connections and networks

Managing network connections

Sharing folders, printers, and media libraries

◆ ◆

W indows networking has come a long way since the days of Windows 95. Back then, the big news was the move to 32-bit computing, but Windows networking was still largely a heterogeneous affair, with Windows 95 supporting a confusing mix of networking technologies, including Banyan, LAN Manager, Novell NetWare, IPX/SPX, and a then-emerging dark horse called TCP/IP, which forms the underlying foundation for the Internet. Since then, the industry—and Windows along with it—has embraced TCP/IP-based networking as the de facto standard, and support for staples of the previous decade of networking—things such as dial-up networking or Microsoft's workgroup-oriented NetBEUI protocol—have either been removed from Windows entirely or depreciated in anticipation of future removal.

Today, networking is all about TCP/IP, wireless, WAN, and Ethernet connections, and pervasive connectivity; and Windows Vista is right there, as was its Windows 95 predecessor at the time, supporting all of the new and emerging networking technologies that are relevant now and in the future. If you made the transition from earlier versions of Windows XP to Windows XP with Service Pack 2 (SP2), you're already pretty far down the road to understanding how networking has improved in Windows Vista, as that update brought with it a number of Vista-era networking-related improvements. But even Windows XP with SP2 can't hold a candle to Vista's networking prowess. In this chapter I'll show you why that's the case and how you can best take advantage of Vista's networking capabilities.

Windows XP with SP2: First-Generation Vista Networking

Windows XP is fondly remembered today, but in fact the initially shipped version of that operating system was probably the most insecure product Microsoft has ever shipped. That wasn't obvious at the time, of course, but during the first year of XP's release, hackers launched an unprecedented number of electronic attacks on the system, causing Microsoft to halt new-OS development for about nine months so that it could devise its Trustworthy Computing initiative and apply the security principles it learned during this process to its products. The first product to ship after this period was Windows XP Service Pack 2 (SP2), which included a number of security technologies that Microsoft had originally intended to ship first in its next OS, now called Windows Vista.

Before moving on to what's new in Windows Vista, I want to look at the security technologies Microsoft introduced in XP SP2 to see how they compare to their Vista counterparts. Why look at security in a chapter about networking? When you think about it, many OS security features are directly related to networking because the most common way for hackers to attack a PC is electronically, over the network; and with pervasive broadband Internet connections becoming increasingly common, understanding these technologies is critical for anyone using a Windows PC today:

◆ **Automatic Updating:** Beginning with Windows XP with SP2, Windows users received a full-screen advertisement for Automatic Updating, the Windows Update-based service that automatically keeps your Windows PC up-to-date with the latest critical security updates. Microsoft also began using subfile patch-management technologies, keeping the download sizes to a minimum and speeding updates. Figure 10-1 shows how the automatic updating invitation varies between Windows XP and Vista.

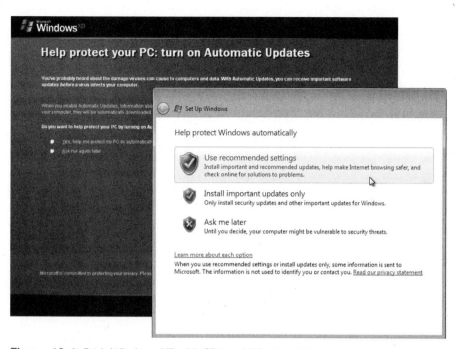

Figure 10-1: Both Windows XP with SP2 and Windows Vista prompt you to configure Automatic Updating before booting into the desktop for the first time.

◆ **Windows Firewall:** While the originally shipped version of Windows XP did in fact ship with firewall software, it was disabled by default and most Windows software was written to assume that no firewall existed. Because firewalls are designed to control the network traffic coming in and going out of your PC, this type of software is key to preventing unwanted software—such as viruses and other malware—from performing dangerous actions and potentially enabling a hacker to remotely control the PC. Figure 10-2 shows the differences between the Windows Firewall in Windows XP and Vista.

cross ref   Chapter 8 covers Windows Firewall.

◆ **Windows Security Center:** In XP SP2, this dashboard monitors the state of the firewall, antivirus, and automatic updating functionality installed on the computer and ensures that they're running and up-to-date. (The Vista version has been dramatically improved to monitor other security features, including antispyware, User Account Control, and Internet Explorer 7's antiphishing feature, among others. You can see the differences between the two versions in Figure 10-3.)

cross ref   Windows Security Center is covered in Chapter 8.

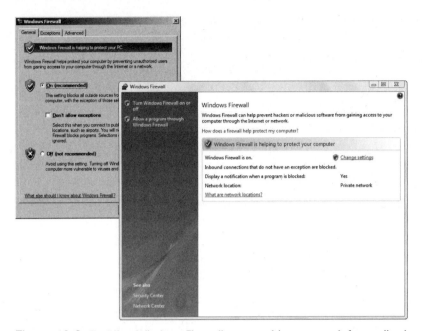

Figure 10-2: Enabling Windows Firewall meant a bit more work for application makers but much better security for end users.

Figure 10-3: Windows Security Center handles many more security controls in Vista than it does in XP.

⬥ **Internet Explorer:** IE 6 was dramatically improved in SP2 with a new pop-up blocker, protection against so-called "drive-by" downloads, a new Manage Add-ons applet, and other security-oriented features. Manage Add-ons was significantly enhanced in Windows Vista's IE 7, as shown in Figure 10-4.

cross ref Chapter 19 looks at Internet Explorer in detail.

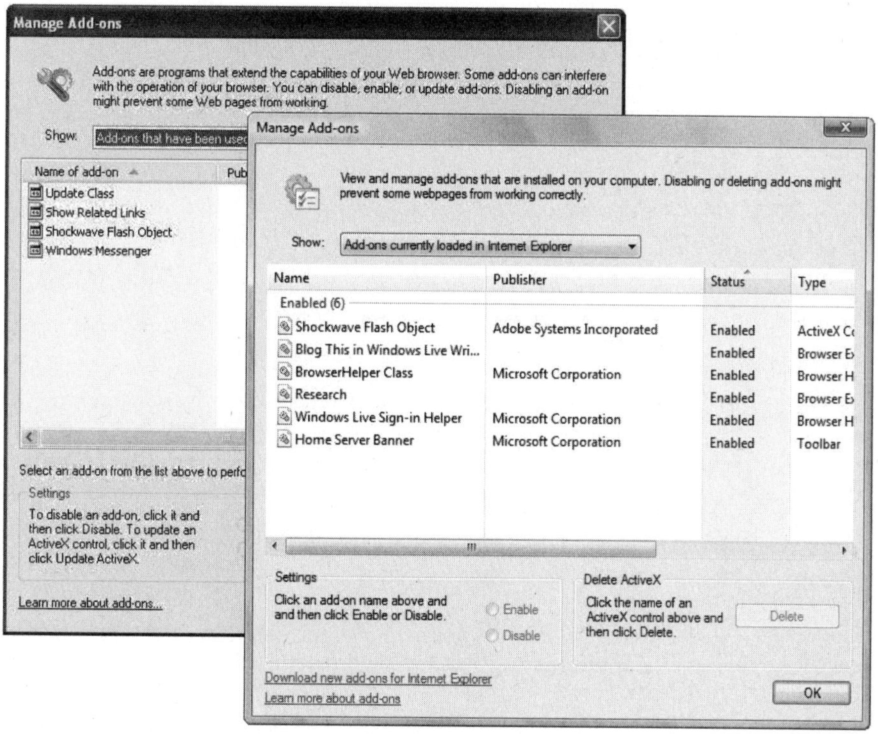

Figure 10-4: Internet Explorer 6 and 7 both feature pop-up blockers and a way to manage add-ons.

⬥ **Attachment blocking:** Both Outlook Express (e-mail) and Windows Messenger (instant messaging) were upgraded with blocking functionality for unsafe attachments. Today, both products have been upgraded significantly and moved into the Windows Live initiative.

cross ref Outlook Express' two successors, Windows Mail and Windows Live Mail, are covered in Chapter 20. You can find out about Windows Live Messenger, the successor to Windows Messenger, in Chapter 21.

◆ **Wireless networking:** In the originally shipped version of Windows XP, wireless networking configuration was almost nonexistent. If there was a wireless network nearby, the system would simply connect to it, security be damned. Microsoft changed this behavior slightly in Service Pack 1, adding a block that prevented automatic connections to insecure networks. In SP2, Microsoft applied several Vista-era touches, including a new Wireless Connection application and a simple Wireless Network Setup Wizard. Things are even simpler in Windows Vista, as shown in Figure 10-5.

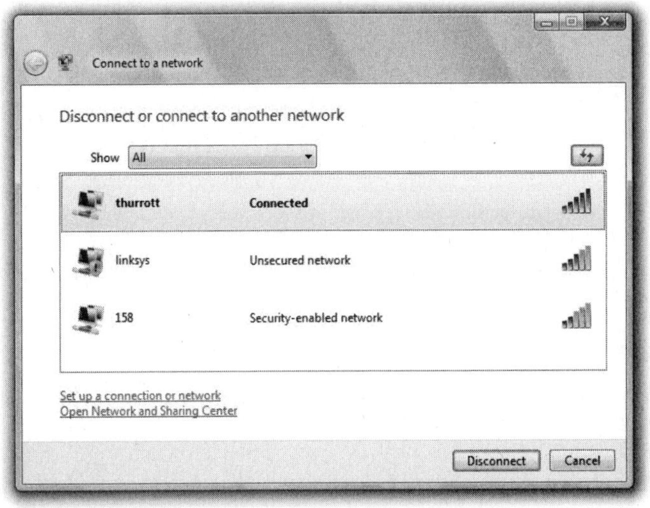

Figure 10-5: Wireless networking became more secure and simpler in Windows XP SP2. It's even better in Windows Vista.

Windows XP with Service Pack 2 was a tough upgrade because the security improvements broke a lot of existing applications, causing headaches with users, IT administrators, and application developers. However, these security changes were necessary and have made the transition to Windows Vista that much easier.

What's New in Windows Vista Networking

Moving forward to Windows Vista, the focus from a networking standpoint was to make things as simple as possible while keeping the system as secure and reliable as possible as well. At a low level, Microsoft rewrote the Windows networking stack from scratch in order to make it more scalable, improve performance, and provide a better foundation for future improvements and additions. Frankly, understanding the underpinnings of Vista's networking technologies is nearly as important as understanding how your car converts gasoline into energy. All you really need to know is that things have improved dramatically under the hood.

Secret

In addition to standard IP-based networking, the Windows Vista networking stack also supports the next-generation IPv6 (IP version 6) network layer. (The current version has been retroactively renamed to IPv4.) The big advantage of IPv6 is that it provides a much larger address space than IPv4. IPv6 provides 128-bit IP addresses, compared to 32-bit addresses in IPv4. The IPv6 address space isn't four times as large as that of IPv4, as you might assume, however; it is, in fact, quite a bit bigger. Whereas IPv4 supports 2^{32} IP addresses (approximately 4 billion IP numbers), IPv6 supports 2^{128} addresses, or about 340 quadrillion unique addresses.

That said, IPv6 is still a bit futuristic. There are no mainstream implementations of the technology anywhere yet; but when it happens—and invariably, the Internet itself will have to make the switch—Windows Vista will be ready.

Here are some of the major end-user improvements that Microsoft has made to Windows Vista networking:

♦ **Network and Sharing Center:** In previous versions of Windows, there wasn't a single place to go to view, configure, and troubleshoot networking issues. Windows Vista changes that with the new Network and Sharing Center, which provides access to new and improved tools that take the guesswork out of networking.

♦ **Seamless network connections:** In Windows XP, unconnected wired and wireless network connections would leave ugly red icons in your system tray, and creating new connections was confusing and painful. In Vista, secure networks connect automatically and an improved Connect To option in the Start Menu provides an obvious jumping-off point for connecting to new networks.

♦ **Network Explorer:** The old My Network Places explorer from previous versions of Windows has been replaced and upgraded significantly with the new Network Explorer. This handy interface now supports access to all of the computers, devices, and printers found on your connected networks, instead of just showing network shares, as XP did. You can even access network-connected media players, video game consoles, and other connected device types from this interface.

♦ **Network Map:** If you are in an environment with multiple networks and network types, it can be confusing to know how your PC is connected to the Internet and other devices, an issue that is particularly important to understand when troubleshooting. Vista's new Network Map details these connections in a friendly graphical way, eliminating guesswork.

♦ **Network Setup Wizard:** If you're unsure how to create even the simplest of home networks, fear not: Windows Vista's improved Network Setup Wizard makes it easier than ever thanks to integration with Windows Rally (formerly Windows Connect Now) technologies, which can be used to autoconfigure network settings on PCs and compatible devices. This wizard also makes it easy to configure folder sharing (for sharing documents, music, photos, and other files between PCs) and printer sharing.

♦ **Folder and printer sharing:** The model for manually sharing folders between PCs has changed dramatically in Windows Vista, but Microsoft has intriguingly retained an alternate interface that will be familiar to those who are adept at setting up sharing on XP-based machines. I'll show you why this type of folder sharing is, in fact, easier to set up than Vista's new method. Printer sharing, meanwhile, works mostly like it did in XP.

The following sections cover these features and other new Vista networking features.

Network Locations

If you already have a wired or wireless home network (or, more typically, a home network that features both wired and wireless connection types) or you bring a Vista-based mobile computer to a new networking environment (such as an Internet cafe, coffee shop, airport, or similar location), you will run into one of Windows Vista's best new features: the Set Network Location wizard. Shown in Figure 10-6, this wizard takes the guesswork out of connecting to a network by providing clear explanations of the different ways in which you can make the connection.

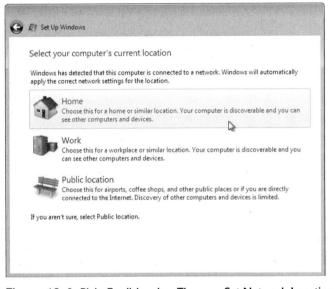

Figure 10-6: Plain English rules: The new Set Network Location wizard makes it easy to configure a network connection securely.

This wizard also appears when you're installing Windows Vista for the first time (as described in Chapter 2). It can appear during the final stages of setup if your network adapter was correctly found and configured and there are networks with which to connect. Otherwise, you'll see it when you boot into the Windows Vista desktop for the first time.

This wizard is the model of simplicity, though arguably it could be even simpler (I'll explain that in just a bit). It offers three options:

◆ **Home:** Used for your home network or other trusted network type. When connected to such a network, your computer will be *discoverable*, meaning that other computers and devices on the network will be able to "see" your PC and, with the appropriate credentials, access any shared resources your PC may be providing. Additionally, you will be able to discover other PCs and devices connected to the network.

◆ **Work:** Used for your workplace or other trusted network type. As with the Home location, a network configured for the Work location provides discoverability of network-based PCs and devices.

Secret

Given the apparent similarities between Home and Work, there must be some difference between the two, right? Microsoft wouldn't create two different network locations that were, in fact, exactly the same, would it? Actually it would (and did): From a functional standpoint, Home and Work are in fact identical. The only difference between the two is the icon used to denote each network location type: The Home location features a friendly-looking home icon, whereas the Work location is denoted by a more industrial-looking office building.

Why have two different locations when a single "Home or Work" location would have achieved the same goal? Keep in mind that the point of the Set Network Location wizard is to make things easy on people. To the average consumer, Home and Work are obvious options, whereas a combined "Home or Work" might cause a bit of wasted time.

⬥ **Public location:** This is used for any Public network connection, especially Wi-Fi connections you might run into at the aforementioned cafes, coffee shops, airports, and similar locations. With a Public location type, you're assumed to need Internet access and little else: Network discoverability is kept to a minimum, and software on your system that might normally broadcast its availability—such as shared folders, printers, and media libraries—are kept silent.

Secret

Behind the scenes, the Set Network Location wizard is, in fact, working with just two location types, one of which covers both Home and Work and one that represents the Public location. Interestingly, Microsoft even goes so far as to give these "true" location types different names. So Home and Work are, in fact, really of type Private, and Work is really of type Public. Further confusing matters, you can display these location types in the Network Location wizard if you run it manually from the Network and Sharing Center (described in more detail in the next section). To see this, open the Start Menu, right-click Network, and choose Properties. Then click the Customize link next to the name of your network. Now, you'll see the Set Network Location as it really is, as shown in Figure 10-7.

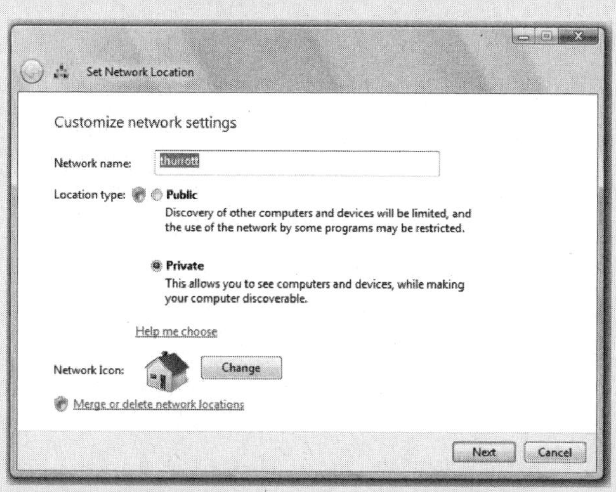

Figure 10-7: The Set Network Location wizard isn't so friendly if you launch it from the bowels of the Network and Sharing Center.

Setting the network location is generally a "set it and forget it" affair. Windows Vista will remember the unique setting you configure for each network you connect to and then reapply those settings when you reconnect. This is especially handy for mobile computers. When you're at home or work, Vista ensures that your network location type is Private; but when you connect to the Internet at a coffee shop you may frequent, the location type will be set to Public.

Secret

Truth be told, Windows Vista actually does support three network location types, but the third is for networking domains based on Microsoft's enterprise-oriented Active Directory technologies. Because most people don't have Active Directory domains in their homes, I don't examine this network location type too closely in this book. Instead I focus on so-called "workgroup" computing, or what the rest of the industry calls *peer-to-peer networking*. In domain-based networking, all of the security and configuration settings are maintained on central servers, whereas in workgroup computing environments, PCs are islands of functionality and each maintains its own set of users and shared resources.

Secret

While Windows Vista does utilize workgroup-type networking by default, the notion of workgroups is now depreciated and will likely be replaced in the next Windows version. Put more simply, in Windows XP and previous versions of Windows, you could automatically connect to shared folders on other computers only when they were in the same workgroup—that is, on the same network (or IP subnet). This is no longer true in Vista. In fact, you could configure every single PC in your home with a different workgroup name and you'd still have no issues sharing information between them. The only time workgroups are relevant in Vista is when your home network has both Vista-based PCs and PCs that are based on older Windows versions. In such a case, you should configure the workgroup name to be identical on all PCs. You do this in a similar manner to how it is done in Windows XP: From the Start Menu, right-click Computer, choose Properties, and then click the Change Settings link next to Computer Name, Domain, and Workgroup Settings.

What's the real difference between Private and Public network locations? (Or, if you like, Home/Work locations and Public locations?) In both location types Windows Firewall is on, but configured somewhat differently. Network discovery is on while connected to Private networks, but off for Public networks. Sharing of folders, printers, and media is on by default in Private networks, but off in Public networks.

Once you've connected to a network, you'll see a Network icon appear in the tray notification area. (This icon was called a "connectoid" in previous Windows versions.)

This icon can have three states:

　◆ **Connected with local and Internet access:** In addition to being able to connect to resources on the local network, you are also connected to the Internet. This icon type is shown in Figure 10-8.

Figure 10-8: This is what you're looking for: A healthy network connection.

　◆ **Connected with local access only:** You are connected to the local network but do not have Internet access, as shown in Figure 10-9.

Figure 10-9: This icon means you won't be connecting to the Internet.

　◆ **Disconnected:** I noted previously that Windows Vista, unlike XP, doesn't leave stranded disconnected network tray icons littered around your tray notification area. Here is the exception: If you're connected to a network and that connection is severed—perhaps because the gateway or switch sitting between your PC and the network has been disconnected—and there are no other networks to which you can connect, you will see the notification icon shown in Figure 10-10.

Figure 10-10: Houston, we have a problem.

You'll learn more about network troubleshooting later in the chapter.

Network and Sharing Center

Most people will simply boot up Windows Vista for the first time, configure the network location for a Home, Work, or Public location, and go about their business; but Microsoft provides a handy new front end to all of the networking-related tasks you'll ever have to complete in Windows Vista. It's called the Network and Sharing Center, and as shown in Figure 10-11, it is indeed a one-stop shop for all your networking needs.

You can access the Network and Sharing Center from a variety of locations. The most obvious is via the tray notification area Network icon discussed in the previous section. Just click it once and then click the Network and Sharing Center link in the pop-up window that appears. I prefer the Start Menu approach: Open the Start Menu and type **sharing** in Start Menu Search.

However you enable this utility, the Network and Sharing Center provides a wealth of configurable networking information, as outlined in the following sections.

Figure 10-11: The Network and Sharing Center is brand-new to Windows Vista.

Network Map

Displayed at the top of the Network and Sharing Center window is a simple network map depicting the basic relationship between your computer, the local network to which you're connected, and the Internet. This display varies a bit depending on whether you're connected via a wired or wireless network, as shown in Figure 10-12. For wired networks, on the top, the network name is rather arbitrary (and something you can rename from within the Network and Sharing Center). With wireless networks, shown on the bottom, the network name represents the actual name that was given to the wireless network (yes, you can rename wireless networks too, though this is less obvious or desirable).

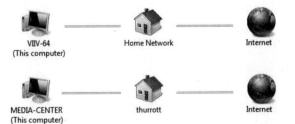

Figure 10-12: A basic Network Map for wired (top) and wireless (bottom) networks.

The Network and Sharing Center can also display a more detailed network map that shows you a topographical view encompassing other PCs and devices on your home network. You can see this map by clicking the link titled View Full Map. As shown in Figure 10-13, this map can be quite full indeed.

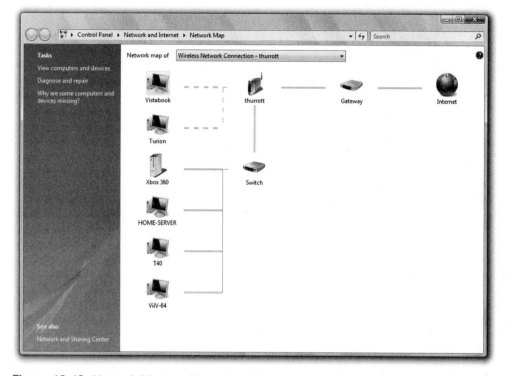

Figure 10-13: Network Map provides a visual representation of your home network.

Connected Networks

Below the basic network map is a list of one or more connected networks. In Figure 10-14, for example, you can see a computer that has two active network connections, one wired and one wireless.

Each connected network (not be confused with network connections, which are described later) has various configurable properties. These properties are typically accessed via the Customize link that accompanies each connected network listing, though wireless connections also have a special Disconnect link that enables you to quickly disconnect from that network.

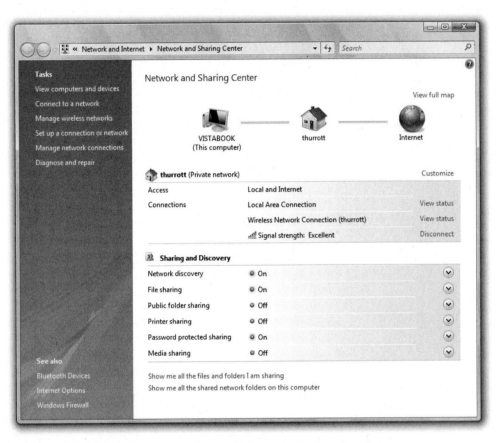

Figure 10-14: You can be connected to multiple networks simultaneously.

When you click the Customize link, you'll see the Set Network Location dialog described earlier in the chapter. From here you can configure the following properties:

- **Network name:** This is typically set to a generic *Network* for wired connections. Wireless connections utilize the actual name of the wireless network. That said, you can change the name of either. (Changing the name of any network here changes only the way you reference the network from within Vista. It doesn't actually change the name of a wireless network, for example.) This setting cannot be changed unless the location type is Private.

- **Location type:** Here you can choose between the previously discussed Public and Private network location types.

- **Network icon:** Windows Vista provides a generic network icon, but you're free to change it to a different icon. This can be helpful for identifying connected networks at a glance. I typically change the icon for my home wired network to a home icon, while I use a different icon for wireless networks. The network icons display next to each connected network name in the connected networks list in the Network and Sharing Center. This setting cannot be changed unless the location type is Private.

Sharing and Discovery

In this section of the Network and Sharing Center, you can view and configure a number of properties related to network discovery and sharing. Note, however, that Vista's network location functionality autoconfigures these settings accordingly. This interface gives you an opportunity to override Vista's default settings.

The following settings are available:

- ◆ **Network discovery:** It's on by default in Private networks and off by default in Public networks.
- ◆ **File (folder) sharing:** This refers to file shares you have explicitly set up yourself. I describe how to do this toward the end of the chapter. File sharing is on by default in Private networks and off by default in Public networks.
- ◆ **Public folder sharing:** Windows Vista includes a special Public folder structure that's not associated with any of the users configured on the PC. This gives you a safe place from which to share files without having to manually create folder shares under your own user profile. Public folder sharing is off by default.
- ◆ **Printer sharing:** If printer sharing is enabled, people who can discover your PC on the network will be able to print to printers you have shared. Printer sharing is on by default in Private networks and off by default in Public networks. Printer sharing is covered later in the chapter.
- ◆ **Password protected sharing:** As with the Set Network Location wizard, this is one of Vista's best and most underheralded features. By default, password protection is enabled so that even when you have enabled file sharing, users who discover your PC on the network must first authenticate with a valid user name and log on before they can actually access any shared resources. You can disable this, but it's not recommended.
- ◆ **Media sharing:** This feature determines whether other PCs and devices on the network can access your shared media library, which is typically set up through Windows Media Player 11 (see Chapter 11) or Windows Media Center (see Chapter 15). It's on by default in Private networks and off by default in Public networks.

At the bottom of the Network and Sharing Center window are two other links related to sharing and discovery:

- ◆ **Show me all the files and folders I am sharing:** This launches a search folder called Shared By Me, which contains all of the folders you are sharing and their contents, as shown in Figure 10-15. (Search folders are covered in Chapter 5.)
- ◆ **Show me all the shared network folders on this computer:** This presents a more traditional view of the folder shares configured on your PC.

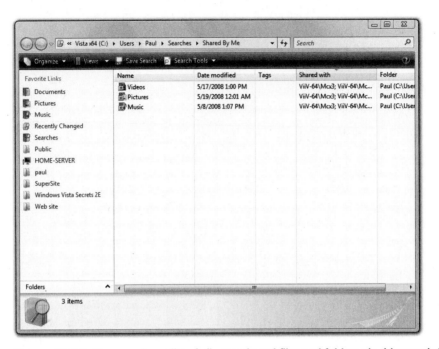

Figure 10-15: You can view a list of all your shared files and folders via this search folder.

View Computers and Devices

Clicking this link, which is found in the Tasks list on the left side of the Network and Sharing Center, launches the Network Explorer, shown in Figure 10-16. This is also the view you receive when you click Network in the Start Menu. Compared to the My Network Places view, Network is quite an improvement.

From the Network Explorer, you gain access to the following:

◆ **Discovered computers:** These are computers on the local network that offer folder and printer shares. You should be able to connect to any PCs on a Private network, but only the local PC on a Public network. If you double-click on a discovered computer, you'll see a list of the folder and printer shares available on that system, as shown in Figure 10-17.

◆ **Media devices:** This includes digital media–oriented hardware devices, such as Xbox 360 video game consoles, Media Center Extenders, and other digital media receivers, as well as any shared media libraries on Windows-based PCs. Each of these items behaves a bit differently. For example, if you click a shared media library, Windows Media Player 11 will load and display the shared library. Double-click a Media Center Extender and Windows Media Center will launch, enabling you to configure connectivity between the two. And if you double-click an Xbox 360 or other digital media receiver, Windows Media Player will launch and present its Media Sharing interface so you can configure sharing with that device.

Figure 10-16: Vista's Network Explorer connects to far more than just folder shares.

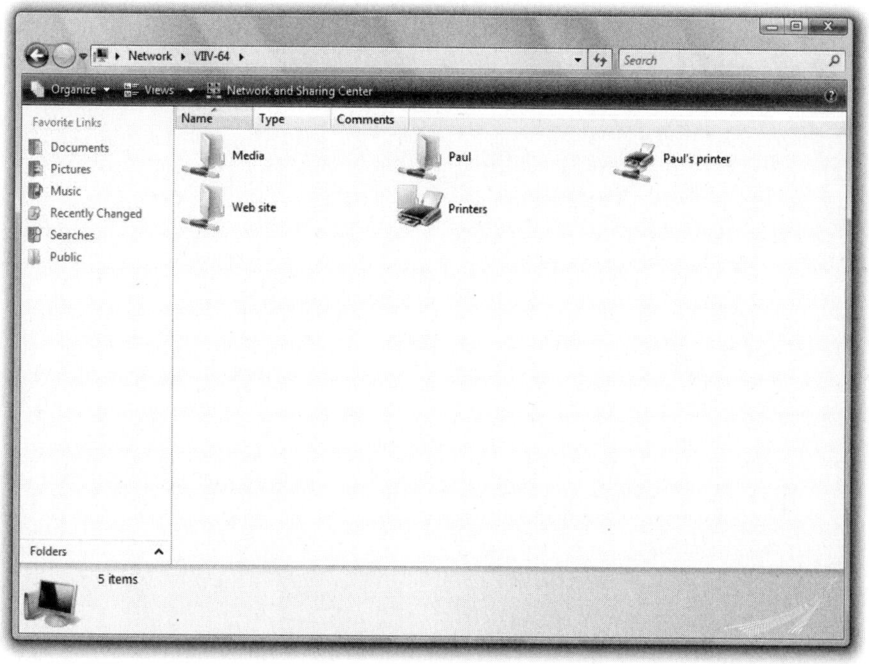

Figure 10-17: You can navigate into discovered PCs to see which shared resources are available.

◆ **Network infrastructure:** Your broadband router will show up here as long as it's compatible with modern networking technologies such as Universal Plug and Play (UPnP). Double-clicking this icon usually loads the device's Web-based management console, which varies from manufacturer to manufacturer.

◆ **Other devices:** When Network Explorer detects other network devices but can't correctly identify them, it places them in the Other Devices category and provides a generic icon. Zune media sharing (Chapter 12) causes such an icon to appear, as does Windows Home Server (Chapter 25).

Connect to a Network

This second link in the Network and Sharing Center's Tasks list triggers the Connect to a Network wizard, which can also be triggered via the Connect To item in the Start Menu. What you see here depends on whether your PC is configured with a wireless networking adapter.

Wired-Only Connections

If you're connected to a wired (Ethernet-based) network and do not have a wireless networking adapter in your PC, you'll see the rather unhelpful version of the Connect to a Network wizard shown in Figure 10-18. This window appears when you're already connected to a network and there are no other available networks with which to connect. Essentially, you're just offered a variety of related links.

> **tip** The wizard tries to autodetect any available networks, but you can continue to attempt to connect to a network if you're sure there's one available that Vista hasn't found. To do so, click the link titled "Set Up a Connection or Network." When you do, you'll be presented with the version of the Connect to a Network wizard that's described in the section "Set Up a Connection or Network" later in the chapter.

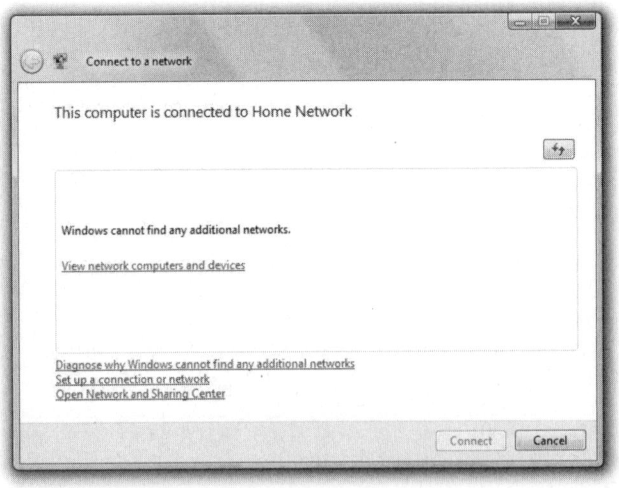

Figure 10-18: You're already connected, and no other networks are available.

Wireless Connections

For those with a wireless network adapter (including users with both wired and wireless connections), the Connect to a Network wizard typically presents many more options. As shown in Figure 10-19, you will often see a list of available wireless networks, including any to which you are already connected.

Figure 10-19: With a wireless adapter, you'll usually see more connection options.

Here you can view the list of available networks, sorted by connection strength, and perform a number of related actions:

♦ **Connect:** You can attempt to connect to any available wireless networks by double-clicking the appropriate entry in the list. Note that protected wireless networks—those for which a passcode have been configured—require you to correctly authenticate before you can connect.

♦ **Diagnose:** If your existing wireless connection is not working correctly, you can try to diagnose the problem. To do so, right-click the connected network and choose Diagnose. Windows Vista will launch its Network Diagnostics wizard, shown in Figure 10-20. This tool will step you through the process to determine what the problem is and help you correct it.

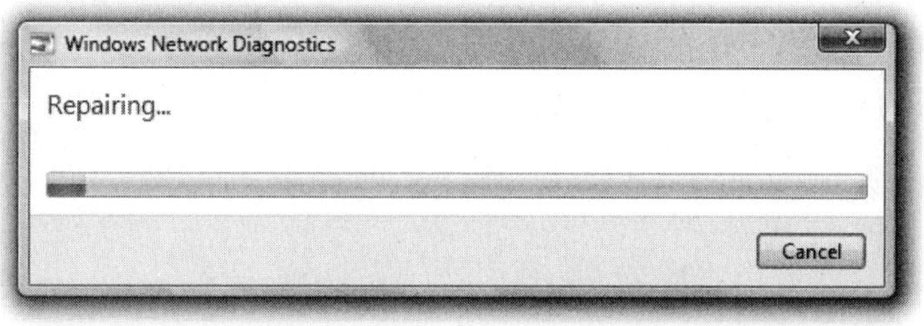

Figure 10-20: Windows Vista features wonderful networking-troubleshooting tools.

Secret

As noted previously, Windows Vista's networking stack is dramatically improved over those in previous Windows versions; but even Vista can't overcome the limitations and problems caused by home networking equipment and service providers. I've found that many connection problems are caused by either the balkiness of the networking hardware I use or my service provider. In the former case, resetting the hardware gateway/switch often solves connection problems, while resetting the PC's network adapter can sometimes help as well: Choose Reset the Network Adapter from the Windows Network Diagnostics wizard to attempt that fix. If the problem is the service provider, sometimes all you can do is call and complain.

tip

Note that this applies only to wireless networks. If you need to diagnose a wired network, you need to access the Diagnose and Repair option found in the Tasks list of the Network and Sharing window.

◆ **Disconnect:** If you'd like to disconnect from the current network, select it from the list and click the Disconnect button.

◆ **Redetect available networks:** To force Windows Vista to search for more wireless networks, click the little Refresh button that appears at the top right of the list of available networks.

◆ **Filter the list:** To display only certain types of available networks, use the Show drop-down list box. Your options are All (the default), Dial-up and VPN, and Wireless.

◆ **Get more information:** To see a quick overview of the connection properties of the currently connected network, mouse over it in the list. As shown in Figure 10-21, a balloon window appears, providing you with more information about the connection, including the friendly name of the wireless network (which you can change as documented previously in the chapter), the signal strength, the security type, the radio type (802.11b, 802.11g, 802.11n, and so on), and the SSID (the "real" name of the wireless network).

◆ **Get even more information:** While the information described in the previous bulleted point is helpful, you can dive even deeper. To do so, right-click the connected wireless network and choose Properties. From this view you can change such information as the security type (none, WPA2-Personal, and so on), the encryption type, the passcode (or as Vista calls it, the security key), and, via the Connection tab, whether you automatically connect to this network whenever it is in range.

◆ **Get status information and make changes:** There is yet another way to get even more information about a wireless connection. Right-click the connected wireless network and choose Status. This will display the Status dialog shown in Figure 10-22. From here you can view information about the status of your connection (including a very detailed list that appears when you click the Details button), access the Properties dialog discussed in the previous section, disable the wireless hardware, or launch the Windows Network Diagnostics wizard.

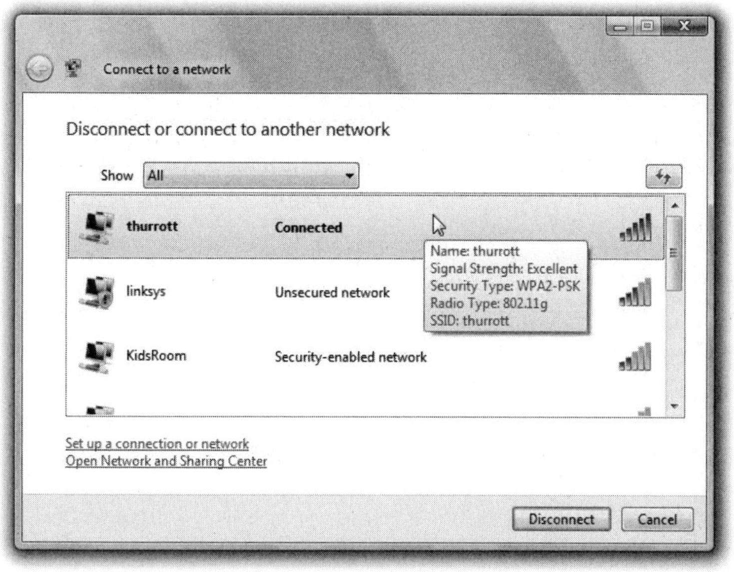

Figure 10-21: Get quick connection information by mousing over a connected network.

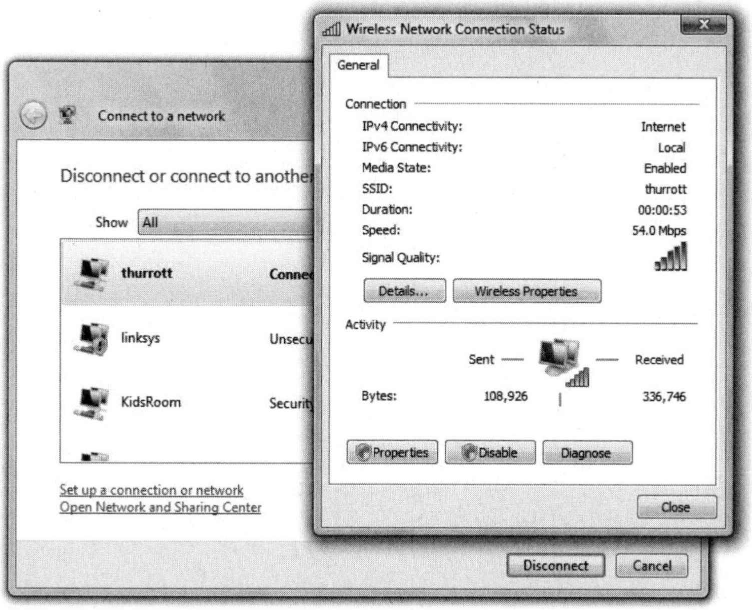

Figure 10-22: The Wireless Network Connection Status dialog provides a wealth of information about the connection status of your wireless card.

The Wireless Network Connection Status dialog is an excellent place to look if you're having trouble with your connection. In such cases, I usually head into Status ⇨ Details and view the IPv4 IP address. If it's set to 169.x.x.x, then I know something is wrong. The 169 address range is automatically provided by Windows Vista when there is no connectivity, and in such cases you will be unable to reach the Internet. From here you can head to the Diagnose button and have Windows Vista fix the problem.

Set Up a Connection or Network

The Set Up a Connection or Network link launches the Set Up a Connection or Network wizard, shown in Figure 10-23. This wizard is a handy front end to all of the network connection types you can create in Windows Vista.

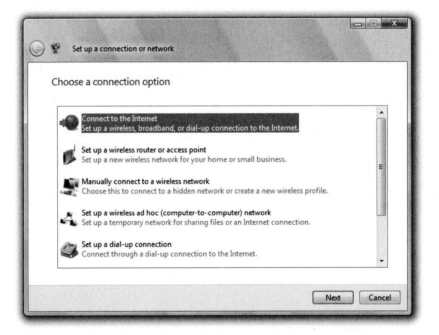

Figure 10-23: Need to set up a network connection? This is the place to be.

Your options here are many, but Microsoft breaks them down to four obvious subsets:

◆ **Connect to the Internet:** Choose this if you need to set up a wireless, wired, or dial-up connection to the Internet. Generally speaking, you will almost never need to use this option, but there are two exceptions. One, you may have a DSL or similar broadband connection type called PPPOE (called Point-to-Point Protocol over Ethernet) that requires you to actually enter a user name and password before you can get online. Two, you're using a wireless network (though this option will simply launch the Connect to a Network wizard discussed previously).

♦ **Set up a wireless router or access point:** Here Windows Vista will step you through the process of configuring a wireless router or access point, but also configure related settings that might be of interest to multi-PC households or home-based businesses, including file and printer sharing (examined later in this chapter). The wizard will detect your network hardware and settings and then forward you to the networking hardware's Web-based configuration. Of course, this varies from device to device.

♦ **Manually connect to a wireless network:** This connection type is available only on wireless networks. It provides an alternative to the Connect to a Network wizard that is especially useful when you need a network connection that does not broadcast its SSID (and is thus normally "invisible"). As shown in Figure 10-24, you'll need a bit more information than is normally the case, including the name (SSID) of the network, the security and encryption types, and the security key (passcode).

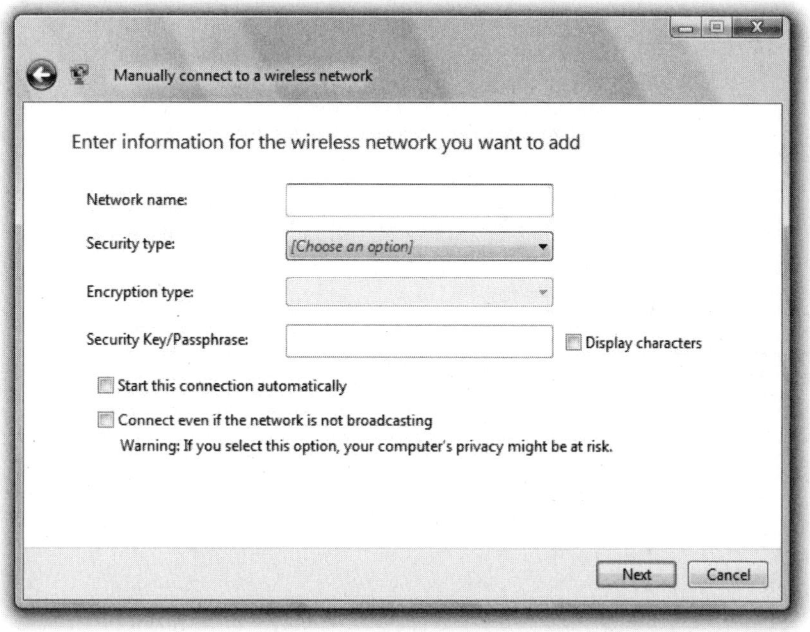

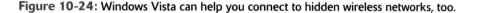

Figure 10-24: Windows Vista can help you connect to hidden wireless networks, too.

♦ **Set up a wireless ad hoc (computer to computer) network:** This option provides a way to set up a temporary peer-to-peer (P2P) network between two closely located PCs with wireless adapters. Why might you want to do such a thing? It can be a handy way to share files or even a (wired) Internet connection. Note, however, that creating such a network disconnects you from any traditional wireless networks.

◆ **Set up a dial-up connection:** The 1990s are calling: If you're stuck in dial-up hell (that is, you need to connect to a dial-up Internet connection via a telephone line and computer modem), this option will get you started. Note that traditional dial-up services such as AOL and NetZero often provide special software and don't require you to use this sort of interface.

◆ **Connect to a workplace:** Choose this option if you need to create a VPN (virtual private network) or direct-dial connection to your workplace. Some businesses require a VPN connection so that any connections between your PC and the corporate network are electronically separated from the public Internet, and thus somewhat protected from snooping. You either need a VPN connection or you don't; and if your company doesn't explicitly configure your PC for this feature or provide their own custom VPN software solution, they will provide instructions on how to get it to work.

◆ **Connect to a Bluetooth personal area network (PAN):** This connection type is available only on PCs with Bluetooth hardware. It provides access to Windows Vista's Bluetooth Personal Area Network Devices dialog, shown in Figure 10-25. A Bluetooth PAN is a special kind of ad hoc or P2P network that is typically created to facilitate file sharing between a PC and a Bluetooth-capable device, or between a small collection of Bluetooth-capable devices (such as smartphones, Palm devices, and the like). Note that not all Bluetooth-capable devices support PAN functionality, however.

Figure 10-25: Vista's Bluetooth capabilities are best suited for device interoperability.

Secret

If you wanted to, you could actually create a PAN between two or more Bluetooth-equipped Windows Vista-based PCs. This would enable you to share files using the Bluetooth File Transfer Wizard and view and edit PAN properties via the Network and Sharing Center, as shown in Figure 10-26. That said, Bluetooth connections are pretty slow and require the devices to be very close to each other. You're almost certainly better off sharing files over a traditional network, a temporary ad hoc (P2P) network, or via a USB storage device.

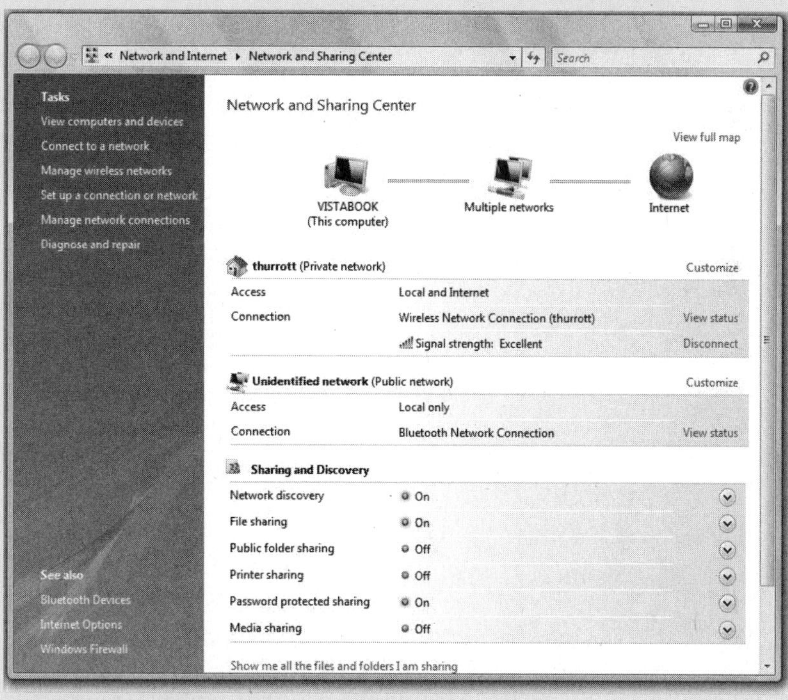

Figure 10-26: Bluetooth PANs show up in the Network and Sharing Center just like other networks.

Managing Network Connections

One of the big changes between Windows XP and Vista is what happens when you right-click the Network link in the Start Menu (called My Network Places in XP) and choose Properties. In XP, this launches Network Connections, a Windows Explorer view of the various networking devices in your PC. In Vista, of course, doing this launches the Network and Sharing Center, a much more comprehensive resource for all your networking needs.

What if you really do want to access your network connections for some reason? In Vista, you do this by first launching the Network and Sharing Center and then selecting the Tasks link titled Manage Network Connections. As in XP, the Explorer location that opens is called Network Connections, and the functionality it provides is virtually identical (see Figure 10-27).

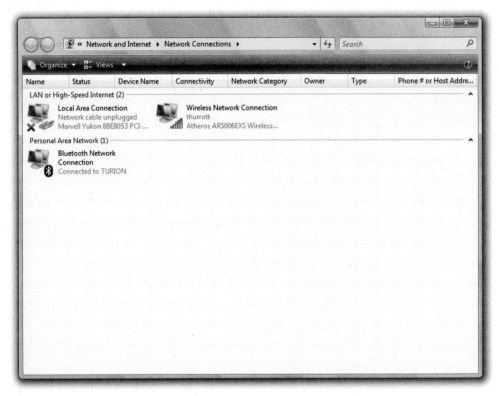

Figure 10-27: Vista's Network Connections works just like the XP version.

The big difference is that the visible network connection options—shown when you select a particular network connection—appear in the Explorer window's toolbar instead of in a Network Tasks pane. The options are the same:

◆ **Disable this network device:** Clicking this will disable the device hardware and disconnect you from any connected networks.

◆ **Diagnose this connection:** This launches the Windows Network Diagnostics wizard.

◆ **Rename this connection:** This option enables you to rename the connection from the bland but descriptive defaults Microsoft chooses (e.g., Local Area Connection and Wireless Network Connection).

◆ **View status of this connection:** This launches the connection status window, which was described previously.

◆ **Change settings of this connection:** This option brings up another blast from the past, the old Network Connection Properties dialog, from which you can view and configure the various network types, protocols, and other networking technologies supported by the connection. As shown in Figure 10-28, this dialog hasn't changed much since Windows 95.

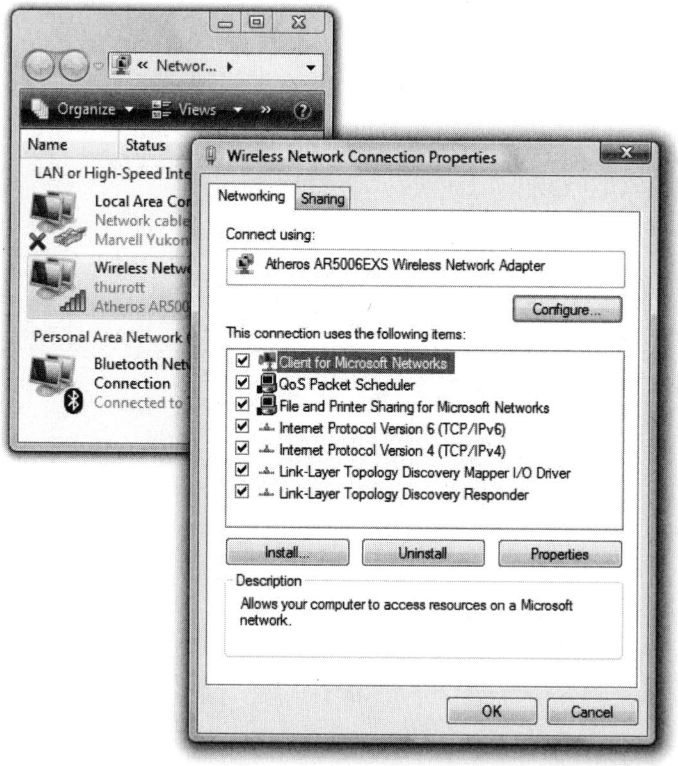

Figure 10-28: Proof that the good old days weren't really that good.
Windows networking used to mean actually configuring these options manually.

You may also see a View Bluetooth Network Devices option if your PC has Bluetooth capabilities. Finally, note that you can right-click a connection to access many of these options.

Secret

Because previous versions of Windows didn't provide a handy front end to all of the system's networking features, accessing Network Connections used to be a common activity. However, thanks to the Network and Sharing Center, this is no longer the case. Therefore, while these options are all still available, chances are good you will almost never need to navigate this far into the UI for any reason.

Diagnosing and Repairing

This final link in the Network and Sharing Center simply launches the Windows Network Diagnostics wizard, discussed previously in the chapter.

Sharing Between PCs

Generally speaking, networking is designed to facilitate two things: a connection between your PC and the outside world—including other PCs as well as the Internet—and sharing resources between your PC and the outside world. For the latter case, Microsoft has been building sharing features into Windows for years in the form of shared folders, shared printers, and shared media libraries, and these features are even easier to use in Windows Vista than they were in XP.

Secret

By default, Windows Vista is configured so that folder sharing requires password protection. For example, if you configured a user named Paul with the password 123 on a computer named PC-A and have likewise configured a user named Paul with no password (or a different password) on a computer named PC-B, the user Paul on PC-B won't be able to access any folders shared by Paul on PC-A unless he provides the appropriate logon information when prompted. To bypass this issue, it's best to use passwords for all accounts on all PCs, and use the same password when you configure identically named accounts on different PCs.

Sharing Folders

In Windows Vista, as in Windows XP, you can share individual files, but it often makes more sense to share folders. Then any files you place inside those shared folders will be shared with others. This is much easier to manage than individual file shares.

Windows XP supports two methods for sharing folders. The first, *simple file sharing*, was aimed at overcoming the complexities of the previous method, called *classic file sharing*. However, I find XP's simple file sharing to be a bit *too* simple. In fact, it's so simplistic that it's almost broken because it offers only two permission levels: Full Control and Read Only. (Unfortunately, it's also the only way to share files in XP Home Edition.) Classic file sharing in XP is unchanged from previous NT-based versions of Windows, including Windows 2000, and is more flexible but more complex.

Moving forward to Windows Vista, Microsoft supports two sharing methods again, though the names have changed. Now you have sharing and advanced sharing. Unlike the simple file sharing from Windows XP, standard sharing involves a decent wizard that walks you through the process of sharing a folder. Advanced sharing is Vista's interface for what used to be called classic file sharing.

Sharing a Folder: The Wizard-Based Approach

Microsoft's wizard-based approach to folder sharing is simple enough. Navigating with Windows Explorer, locate and select the folder you'd like to share on your home network. Then click the Share option in the Explorer toolbar (or right-click the folder and choose Share). The File Sharing wizard, shown in Figure 10-29, will appear.

In the first stage of the wizard, you set the permission level for each user configured on the system, and remove those users to whom you do not wish to give access. By default, you are configured with owner permissions while all other users are configured with co-owner permissions.

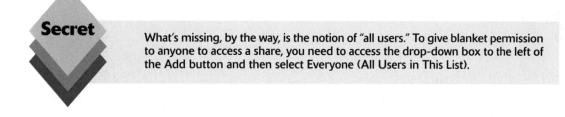

Figure 10-29: Vista's File Sharing wizard provides a more fine-grained approach to sharing than did XP's simple file sharing.

Secret

What's missing, by the way, is the notion of "all users." To give blanket permission to anyone to access a share, you need to access the drop-down box to the left of the Add button and then select Everyone (All Users in This List).

The following permission types are available:

◆ **Owner:** This is essentially admin-level permissions, and you are free to view, add, edit, or delete any shared file, as well as configure or remove the folder share.

◆ **Co-owner:** Users with this permission level can view, add, edit, or delete any shared file.

◆ **Reader:** Users with this permission level can view shared files but not add, edit, or delete them.

◆ **Contributor:** Users with this permission level can view or add shared files, but can edit or delete only files that they have contributed.

Once you're done configuring permissions, click the Share button and you're good to go. To change sharing permissions or stop sharing the folder, select it again, choose Share, and then choose the appropriate option from the File Sharing wizard, which will now resemble Figure 10-30.

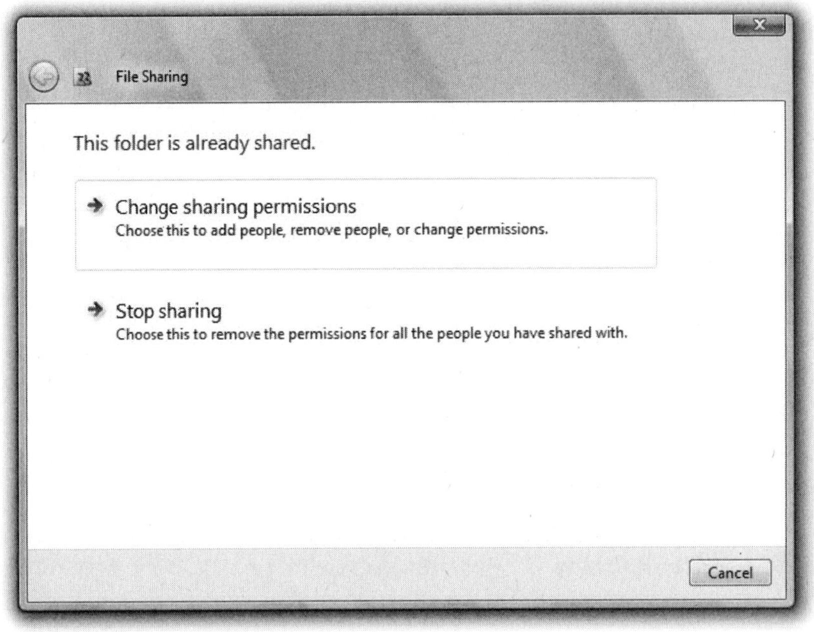

Figure 10-30: The File Sharing wizard can also be used to reconfigure or stop sharing.

Advanced Sharing

The File Sharing wizard works well enough, but if you've been sharing folders with Windows for a while now, as I have, you may actually be more comfortable with Vista's alternative sharing UI, which very closely resembles classic file sharing from Windows XP. To access this interface, locate the folder you'd like to share, right-click, and choose Properties. Next, click the Sharing tab, shown in Figure 10-31.

If you click the Share button, you'll see the now-familiar File Sharing wizard. Instead, click Advanced Sharing. This launches the Advanced Sharing dialog, which is very similar to the Sharing tab of a folder's Properties window in Windows XP (when classic file sharing is enabled, as it is by default in Windows XP Professional). The Advanced Sharing dialog, shown in Figure 10-32, assumes you know what you're doing, but it's very easy to use.

To share a folder this way, select the option titled Share This Folder. Then, accept or edit the share name and click the Permissions button to display the Permissions dialog. From here you can set the permission level for users and groups. By default, only the Everyone group, which represents all user accounts on the system, is present, but you can click Add ⇨ Advanced ⇨ Find Now to choose other users and groups individually if needed. Click OK when you are done.

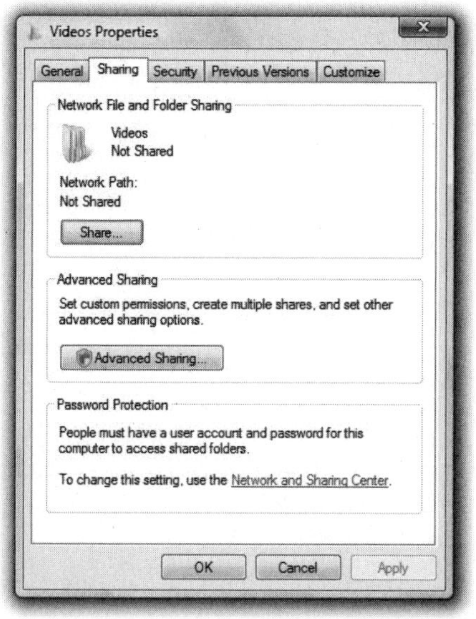

Figure 10-31: Like XP, Vista offers two ways to share folders: Sharing for Dummies (the wizard) and Advanced Sharing.

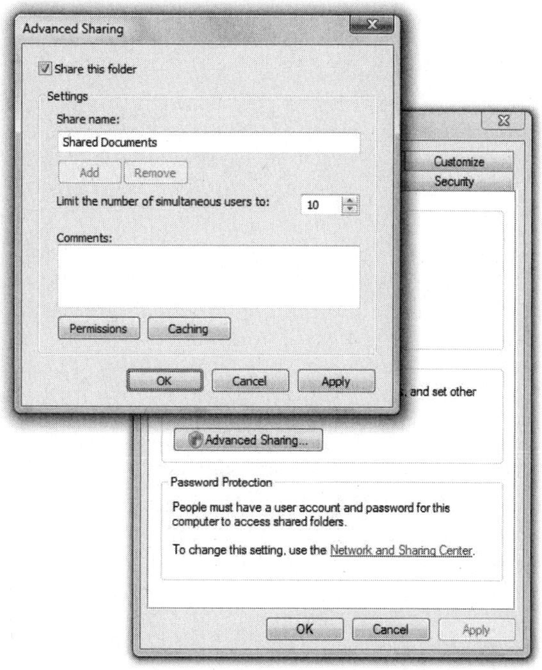

Figure 10-32: If you don't mind getting your feet wet, Advanced Sharing is the way to go.

Secret   Advanced Sharing provides a number of features that aren't available via the File Sharing wizard. One is a limit on how many people can be connected simultaneously to the share. Consumer-oriented versions of Windows Vista, such as Vista Home Basic and Home Premium, are limited to 5 simultaneous connections, while other Vista versions—Business, Enterprise, and Ultimate—are limited to 10. You can reduce the number of connections to a given folder in the Advanced Sharing window. (You cannot, however, raise the limit beyond 5 or 10, depending on which version of Windows Vista you're using.)

Secret   Another unique feature of Advanced Sharing is the capability to configure folder caching, which determines whether connected users can cache the contents of shared folders locally for use offline. You access this functionality via the Caching button in Advanced Sharing.

While some people will no doubt have very specific sharing needs, most simply want to open up a portal from which they can share files with others or with other PCs. In this case, Advanced Sharing is actually quite a bit quicker than the wizard.

Public Sharing

In addition to the traditional sharing methods already mentioned, Windows Vista supports the concept of public sharing, whereby the entire Public folder structure (found in C:\Users\Public) is shared by default with all users configured on the PC (and it's shared so that all users have full control). Public sharing is enabled by default, so you don't have to do anything special to make it work.

Public sharing is particularly interesting if you have multiple users who regularly log on to the same PC and wish to make certain documents, photos, music files, and other files available to all users. Simply place them in Public Documents, Public Photos, Public Music, or anywhere else within the Public folder structure.

Sharing Printers

While network-attached printers are becoming more common these days, many people still use printers that are directly connected to an individual PC, typically by a USB cable. In such cases, it's nice to be able to print to that printer from other PCs on the home network. Although you could temporarily unplug these printers and plug them into a different machine, an easier way is available. You can share these printers so that other PCs on the network can access them.

Secret

For this to work, the PC to which the printer is connected must be turned on, and not asleep, in hibernation, or shut down. You don't need to leave it logged on with a particular user account, however.

Unlike with folder sharing, Windows Vista doesn't provide a printer sharing wizard, so you just need to know where to look. To share a printer, navigate to the Printers folder in the Control Panel (use Start Menu Search, and type **printers**), select the printer you'd like to share, and then click the Share button in the toolbar (or right-click it and choose Sharing).

This launches the Printer Properties dialog, with the Sharing tab selected, as shown in Figure 10-33.

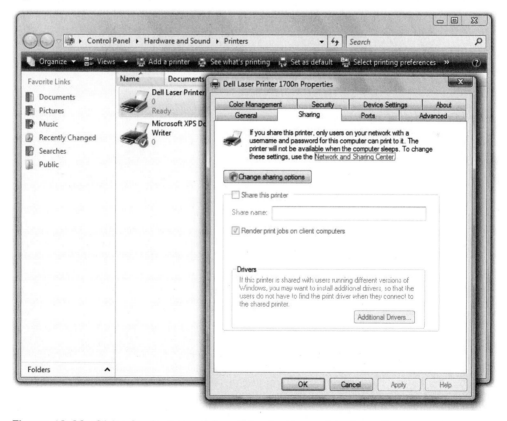

Figure 10-33: Click a few buttons, and you'll be sharing a printer in no time.

Now click Change Sharing Options. This changes the Share tab, providing you with a link to share the printer. Select that check box, view (and potentially edit) the share name, and click OK.

There are two ways to configure this shared printer on a different PC in your network:

◆ **Via Printers:** Navigate to the Printers folder and select Add a Printer from the toolbar. In the Add Printer wizard, select Add a Network, Wireless, or Bluetooth Printer. The wizard will search for available printers and eventually display the shared printer, as shown in Figure 10-34. Click Next and wait while the printer is configured. Finally, complete the wizard and you will be able to use the printer.

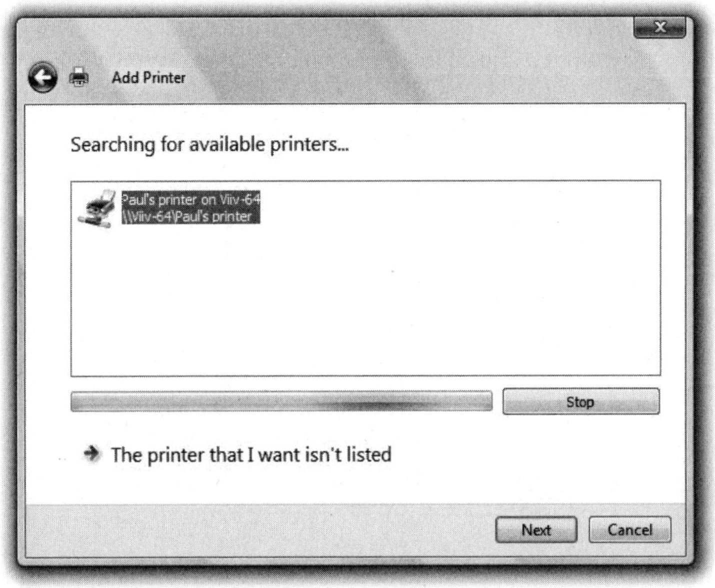

Figure 10-34: Shared printers typically appear automatically.

◆ **Via Network:** Navigate to the Network folder and then the PC that is sharing a printer. There you'll see an icon representing the shared printer, as shown in Figure 10-35. Double-click this icon and it will be added to your list of available printers. However, you have to visit the Printers folder if you wish to make this your default printer.

Secret

While it's not common, you can also configure permissions on shared printers. Doing so, of course, is not obvious. To limit access to a printer, launch the printer's Properties window and then navigate to the Security tab. This interface offers settings for printing, managing printers, managing documents, and special permissions, all of which can be applied on a user-by-user basis.

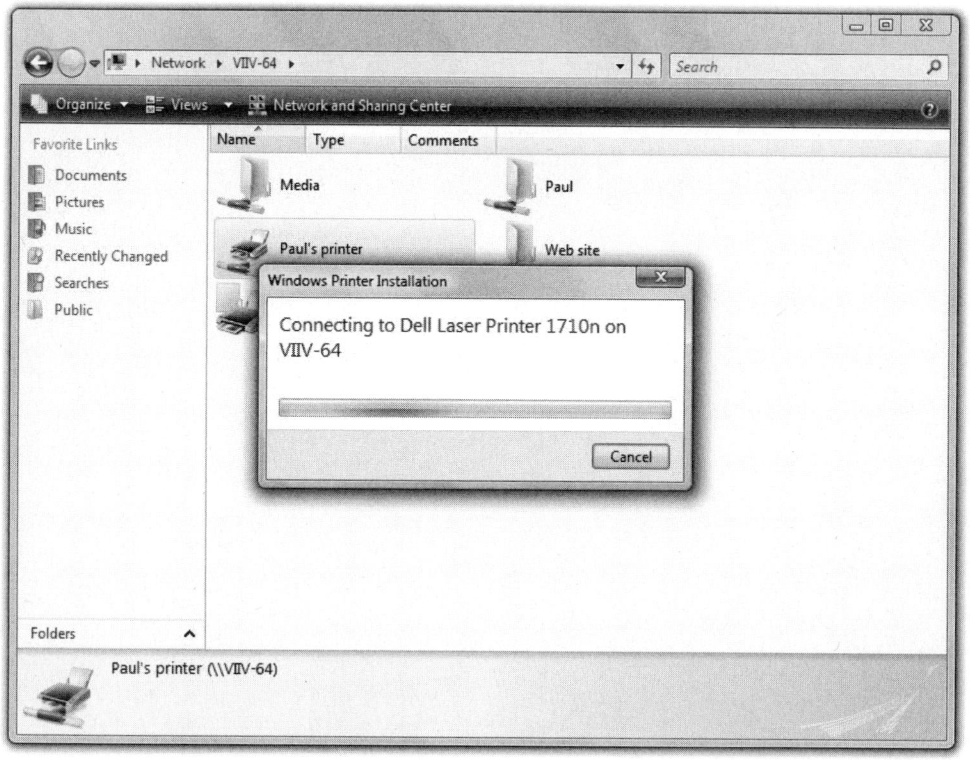

Figure 10-35: Shared printers can also be accessed in the Networks folder structure.

Sharing Media Libraries

Windows Vista also makes it easy to share media libraries—digital music, videos, and photos—between PCs and with compatible devices, using a technology called Windows Rally (formerly Windows Connect Now). Chapter 11 covers this functionality.

Summary

Windows Vista offers the simplest yet most powerful networking functionality of any Windows version to date, with everything you need to create and connect to home networks and the Internet. While all of the features available in Windows XP are still available in Windows Vista, they've all been updated and enhanced and wrapped into a stunningly complete new user interface called the Network and Sharing Center. Whatever your networking need, Windows Vista has you covered.

Part IV

Digital Media and Entertainment

Windows Media Player

In This Chapter

Using Windows Media Player

Understanding the new visual user interface

Working with digital music, photos, videos, and recorded TV

Ripping and burning CDs

Synchronizing with portable media devices, including the iPod

Sharing your media library with other PCs, devices, and the Xbox 360

Accessing online music services

Exploring Windows Media Player alternatives

ive Microsoft a little credit: When it launched its first all-in-one digital media player—Windows Media Player 7, with Windows Millennium Edition (Me) in 2000—the company made it clear that this product would be about more than just music. Today, Windows Media Player 11, the version that ships with Windows Vista, is dramatically improved, with support for music, videos, photos, recorded TV shows, streaming Internet media, and more. It really is an all-in-one solution for virtually all of your digital media needs—well, with one major exception: Windows Media Player 11 doesn't natively support Apple's dominant iPod, the best-selling portable MP3 player on the planet. In this chapter, you'll learn how to get the most of Windows Media Player 11. You'll even learn how to make it work with the iPod.

> **note**   Microsoft is so taken with Apple's iPod that it has emulated that product with its own Zune platform, which includes portable media player devices, Zune PC software, and online services. In fact, Zune directly competes in many ways with Windows Media Player, offering an alternative to the program that Microsoft ships with Vista. For this reason, the next chapter covers Zune separately.

Media Player Basics

As in the other chapters, this chapter assumes you're familiar with basic operations in Windows and its many bundled applications. Microsoft has included a very simple media player in Windows for over a decade, and a full-featured, all-in-one player since Windows Me, so it's likely you're at least passingly familiar with this all-in-one jukebox solution.

That said, Windows Media Player 11 can be fairly complicated if you don't understand what it's doing, so this section examines this new Media Player and its core functionality before moving on to more complex topics.

Setting Up Windows Media Player 11

The first time you launch Windows Media Player 11, you're forced to step through a quick wizard that enables you to configure various options, as shown in Figure 11-1. Don't click Next here, however, as doing so will configure Windows Media Player using some presets that might have undesired consequences. Instead, carefully read through the options that Microsoft presents. It's possible to configure these options after the fact, of course, but it's better to do so now, as you'll see in a moment.

> **Secret**   On the first page of the wizard, you're asked to choose between Express and Custom setup options. ***Always*** choose Custom. Express may be quicker, but it doesn't give you access to the most important Windows Media Player 11 configuration options, and instead chooses defaults that benefit Microsoft, not you.

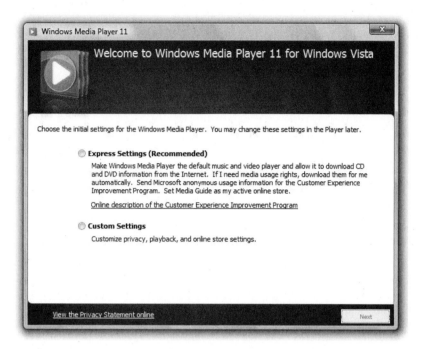

Figure 11-1: Be sure to read through the options here very carefully; don't just accept the default values.

Secret

In the initially shipped version of Windows Vista, Microsoft offered access to an online music service called MTV URGE. Since that time, however, Microsoft and MTV have gone their separate ways. URGE is still available, but it's now part of RealNetworks' Rhapsody online service. Windows Media Player can still be configured with various other online music services, as described later in this chapter.

After you choose Custom, you are presented with the window shown in Figure 11-2, which is very similar to the initial dialog box presented by Windows Media Player 10, the previous version of this software (which was made available to Windows XP users). Here, you pick various privacy options.

In the Enhanced Playback Experience section, weigh the second option very carefully. If you have a finely crafted media library, in which you've lovingly downloaded and applied album art for all of your ripped music files, you will definitely want to clear the check box titled Update My Music Files by Retrieving Media Information From the Internet. If you don't, you will find that over time your media library becomes a jumbled mess, as Media Player changes your nicely formatted music files to match what a third-party library on the Internet says are the correct song, album, and artist names, often with disastrous results.

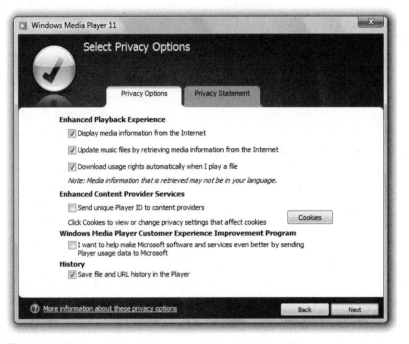

Figure 11-2: Thanks to near-constant lawsuits, Microsoft cares very much about your privacy.

Conversely, if you're just starting out and intend to use Windows Media Player 11 to rip your CDs to the PC, leave this option checked: Users who are less precise with their music files—most people, probably—will actually benefit from this service.

The other options should be self-explanatory, and none are as potentially destructive as the option just discussed. You can leave the other options at their defaults.

A second tab in this section of the setup process provides links to two online privacy statements. These statements explain Microsoft's stance on user privacy with regard to the data it collects via Windows Media Player and other applications. It's not as scary as it sounds.

When you click Next, you're presented with a window that is new to Windows Media Player 11. It enables you to place Media Player shortcuts on the Desktop and Quick Launch toolbar, respectively, as shown in Figure 11-3. If you think either of those shortcuts will be valuable, check the appropriate boxes and continue. (The shortcut link in the Quick Launch toolbar option is selected by default.)

The next window, shown in Figure 11-4, is also new to Windows Media Player 11. Here, you can choose to make Windows Media Player 11 the default music player for all of the media types it supports, or you can choose the exact file types that it will play.

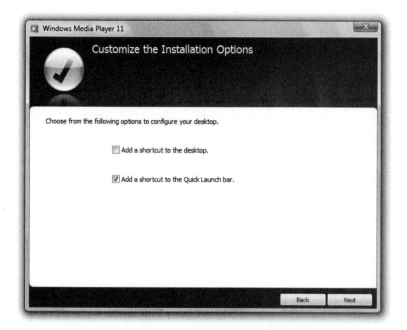

Figure 11-3: I recommend using at least one of these shortcuts. You'll be surprised how often you need to access Windows Media Player.

Figure 11-4: Be careful here: The options are really between utter simplicity and mind-numbingly confusing.

It may not be obvious, but this phase of setup is aimed at experts, and most users should simply choose the first option, Make Windows Media Player 11 the Default Music and Video Player. Of course, if you have strong feelings about using a different media player for specific file types, you can choose the second option, but understand that you'll need to deal with Vista's horrible and unfriendly Set Program Associations utility, shown in Figure 11-5. (Chapter 7 covers this utility more closely.) Here, you can configure which media file types will be associated with Windows Media Player 11.

Figure 11-5: In previous Windows versions, this information was buried in the system and configured directly through Windows Media Player.

Secret

What you see here varies according to which media player software is installed on your PC. If you or your PC maker has installed other media player solutions, such as Apple QuickTime Player, Apple iTunes, Microsoft Zune, RealNetworks RealPlayer or Rhapsody, and the like, certain file types may be configured to work with different applications. Again, this is a power-user feature, so unless you really know what you're doing, your best bet is to choose the Select All option and then click Save.

continues

continued

These settings are configured on a user-by-user basis, so if multiple users are configured on the same PC, everyone can select different media player applications and associate digital media file types with whatever applications they prefer. For example, you may choose to use Windows Media Player while your children might like iTunes instead. Everyone can make different choices without affecting the other users on the machine.

If you don't choose to alter the file types that are associated with Windows Media Player here, fear not: You can do it later. To do so, open the Start Menu and click Default Programs. Then, in the Set Default Programs window that appears, select Windows Media Player from the list on the left. Then select either Set the Program as the Default, which will assign all possible defaults to Windows Media Player, or Choose Defaults for this Program, which will bring you to the view shown earlier in Figure 11-5.

Finally, as shown in Figure 11-6, you are asked whether you'd like to configure an online store, although no online stores are actually offered. Instead, you can choose to configure the Media Guide, which is a Microsoft informational service, not a store; or you can opt not to configure a store at all.

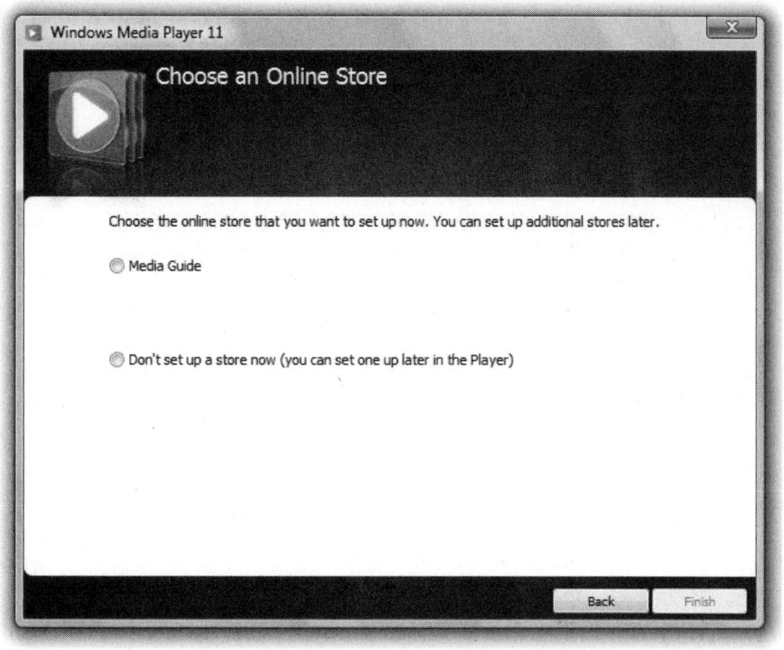

Figure 11-6: Where did all the stores go? The market has moved on since Windows Vista first arrived.

Secret   This was where MTV URGE was previously offered, but because that service is no longer available via Windows Media Player, you're presented with a rather bland set of options instead. You can configure other online music stores later.

tip   Unlike with URGE, you can still configure the Media Guide if your PC is not connected to the Internet.

That's it; you're done. Once you click the Finish button, you're presented with the actual Windows Media Player user interface.

Understanding the Windows Media Player 11 User Interface

Shown in Figure 11-7, Windows Media Player 11 is a dramatic departure from previous Windows Media Player versions, with a more visual media library view that relies heavily on album art and photo and video thumbnails. (This explains the player's desire to connect to the Internet to retrieve media information, by the way.) In addition, Windows Media Player 11 adopts the Windows Vista look and feel, with glasslike window borders and the new black-and-blue color scheme that Vista reserves for media applications.

tip   Windows Media Player 11 ships with a small selection of sample music and video content, which I use for the examples in this part of the chapter. This enables you to get started with the player even if you don't have any content of your own.

Compared to its predecessors, Windows Media Player 11 offers several improvements and changes. First, the player no longer uses a hokey, pseudo-rounded window that doesn't quite work correctly (maximize Windows Media Player 10 in Windows XP to see what we mean by this). Instead, Windows Media Player 11 looks and acts like many other Windows Vista applications. Second, the toolbar has been enhanced with back and forward buttons (arrows), which enable you to easily move between the Media Player options provided along the rest of the toolbar: Now Playing, Library (the default view), Rip, Burn, and Sync. (A sixth, somewhat segregated item, relates to the online stores you may have configured for Windows Media Player. By default, this reads as either Media Guide or Online Stores, but you'll look at this functionality later in the chapter.)

[Windows Media Player screenshot — window titled "Windows Media Player" with toolbar tabs: Now Playing, Library, Rip, Burn, Sync, Media Guide. Navigation breadcrumb: Music ▸ Library ▸ Songs. Left pane shows Playlists, Create Playlist, Library (Recently Added, Artist, Album, Songs, Genre, Year, Rating), paul on vistabook. Right pane lists albums: Aaron Goldberg — Worlds — 7 — OAM's Blues — 4:26 — Aaron...; Aisha Duo — Quiet Songs — 11 — Despertar — 5:07 — Aisha...; 17 — Amanda — 4:06 — Aisha...; Habib Koite & Bamada — Muso Ko — 1 — I Ka Barra (Your Work) — 5:00 — Habib...; 9 — Din Din Wo (Little Child) — 4:45 — Habib...; Karsh Kale — Realize — 2 — Distance — 5:27 — Karsh K...]

Figure 11-7: It's not your father's media player: Windows Media Player 11 is highly graphical, with rich views of your music, photos, and videos.

Here's how the back and forward buttons work in Windows Media Player. If you're in the media library (denoted by a highlighted Library toolbar button) and click the Rip toolbar button, for example, you'll find yourself transported by the Media Player music ripping option. Now, you can press the back button to return to the previous option you visited (i.e., Media Library). If you do navigate back to the media library, you can subsequently click the forward button to return to the Rip option again. In other words, these buttons work just like their equivalents in Internet Explorer and the Windows shell. Figure 11-8 demonstrates how it works.

Secret

At one time, Microsoft hoped to establish a standardized UI convention whereby every single Windows Vista application utilized this style of navigation. Over time, however, it became clear that UI navigation wasn't always required and that in certain application types, such as wizards, prominent forward buttons are non-intuitive. Long story short: You'll see these UI elements only in certain places in Windows Vista, and typically only where they truly make sense.

Figure 11-8: Follow the progression as the user first navigates to Rip, uses the back button to return to Library, and then uses the forward arrow to return to Rip.

Speaking of the right side of the toolbar, this area has been cleaned up substantially this time around. Windows Media Player 10 had Music, Radio, Video, and Online Stores buttons. Now, there is just an Online Stores button (which might read as Media Guide depending on how you configured the player during setup).

Dig a little deeper and you'll see another new bit of user interface right below the toolbar: a breadcrumb bar on the left side of the player that helps you navigate through the various media libraries you'll access in Windows Media Player 11, including Music (the default), Pictures, Video, Recorded TV, and Other Media. On the right side are separate buttons for layout and view options, the new Instant Search box (another staple of the Vista user interface), and a button for toggling the player's optional List Pane, which appears on the right side of the window when enabled. The next sections discuss what each of these features does.

Using the Category Button and Breadcrumb Bar

In Windows Media Player 10 (and 7, 8, and 9, for that matter), Microsoft divided your media library by media type using an expanding tree view that many users found difficult to use, especially users with large media libraries. Regardless of your experience, however, the tree view was simply lousy because it made it too easy to get lost. Windows Media Player 11 does away with this, replacing the tree view with a simpler breadcrumb bar (similar to what is used in the Windows Explorer address bar) that is triggered by the Category button. If you click this button you can choose between the various media types Media Player supports, as shown in Figure 11-9, and view only that part of the media library you need.

Figure 11-9: Media Player isn't just about music: You can enjoy other content as well.

By default, you will be in Music view, since most people use Windows Media Player to play music. Notice that the breadcrumb bar to the right of the Category button enables you to dive into your media library in various ways. For example, by default, the music portion of your media library displays your content by songs. You can change this view by clicking on the various nodes in the breadcrumb bar. Suppose you wanted to view just the albums, and not the individual songs. To do so, click the arrow next to Library in the breadcrumb bar and select Album, as shown in Figure 11-10.

Figure 11-10: Media Player's Media Library view can be changed in a multitude of ways to match your preferences.

What you see in the breadcrumb bar depends on which section of the media library you are viewing. For example, music has options for albums, artists, songs, and genres, whereas video has options for all video, actors, genre, and rating.

The advantage to the breadcrumb bar in Windows Media Player, like that in Windows Explorer, is that it's much easier to move arbitrarily around your media libraries without having to navigate up and down a messy tree view control. For example, if you're viewing your music albums, as shown earlier in Figure 11-10, and suddenly want to look at your digital movies, you can just click the Category button and select Videos. You're in.

Layout Options

The Layout Options button enables you to configure various parts of the Windows Media Player 11 user interface. These parts include the Navigation pane, which is the list of information found on the left side of the player (enabled by default); the List pane, which was a prominent part of the Windows Media Player 10 interface but is off by default in Windows Media Player 11; and the Classic Menus, which are off by default, as they are in so many Windows Vista applications.

Secret

To access the Windows Media Player 11 menu system without enabling Classic Menus, simply press the Alt key at any time. Alternatively, right-click any empty spot in Windows Media Player's black toolbar button. Either way, you'll see a pop-out version of the Media Player menu appear, as shown in Figure 11-11.

Figure 11-11: No need to enable Classic Menus: The Windows Media Player menu is always available if you just know where to look.

Typically, you're going to want to leave the Navigation pane on. This is a handy place to access the topmost (well, rightmost) items in the Media Player breadcrumb bar without having to drop down a menu. The List pane will likely be of interest in two main scenarios. First, if you're a big fan and user of previous Windows Media Player versions, you're probably used to the way those media players used temporary and saved playlists as the main way to interact with your music collection, so you'll find the List pane to be both usable and logical; but the List pane is useful in other situations. If you're going to create a saved playlist or burn some songs to an audio CD, for example, the List pane can act as a handy holding area for the tracks you want to include.

If you enable Classic Menus, you'll see a top-mounted menu structure similar to that found in previous Windows Media Player versions. My advice is still to skip out on Classic Menus, and enjoy the uncluttered simplicity of the Media Player interface.

View Options

Like the Layout Options button, the View Options button triggers a pop-out menu, but this one includes just a few options, all of which are related to the way the current media library view is displayed. There are three options here: Icon, Tile/Expanded Tile (depending on the content being viewed), and Details.

In Icon view, the media library displays each item as an icon. Albums appear as they do in a real music store, with colorful and easily recognizable cover art. Artists and other groups appear as *stacks,* as shown in Figure 11-12, when there is more than one contained item. For example, if you have two or more albums by Collective Soul ripped to your hard drive, the Collective Soul icon will display as a stack, not a standard square icon, the latter denoting a single album.

Figure 11-12: Stacks denote that the icon contains other items that can be represented by their own icons.

Stacks are cool because they are immediately obvious. They look just like a stack of paper on your desk, or, in this case, a stack of CD cases. You'll see a lot of stacks in both the Genre and Year views in the Music portion of the media library. When you drill into a stack—by double-clicking it—you typically see a standard icon view. For example, navigating into the Collective Soul stack mentioned previously reveals a display of CDs by that band, as shown in Figure 11-13.

Figure 11-13: Inside a stack, you'll see the contained items.

In Tile view, items display in a manner similar to the Tiles view in Windows Explorer. (Why there is a slight name discrepancy is beyond me, but it's fair to say that Microsoft isn't famous for consistency.) That is, you will see an icon for each item—CD art in the case of music—and related textual information to the right. Each item in this view style is considered a tile consisting of an icon and its related information. In some views, such as the Songs view in Music, Tile is replaced by an alternative view called Expanded Tile, which provides even more related textual information—a list of songs, in this case—as shown in Figure 11-14.

Tile view is nice if you have a lot of screen real estate or think you might occasionally want to edit song ratings, which is one of the bits of related info displayed on each tile.

In Details view, the media library behaves like it did in previous Windows Media Player versions (and, incidentally, as it does in Apple's popular iTunes program): as a textual list of information. This interface, which seems to be modeled after 20-year-old MS-DOS database applications like dBASE III+, is utilitarian, but it also performs a lot faster than the more visual Icon and Tile/Expanded Tile views. Therefore, if you have a slower computer, a massive music collection, or a low-resolution display, this might actually be your best bet. It will certainly provide the best performance.

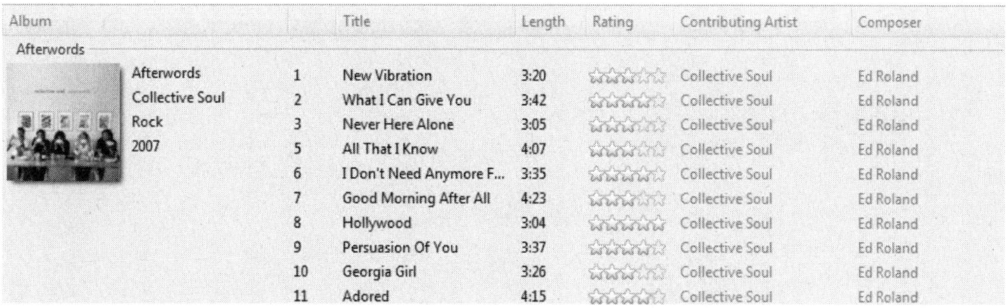

Album			Title		Length	Rating	Contributing Artist	Composer
Afterwords								
	Afterwords		1	New Vibration	3:20	★★★★★	Collective Soul	Ed Roland
	Collective Soul		2	What I Can Give You	3:42	★★★★★	Collective Soul	Ed Roland
	Rock		3	Never Here Alone	3:05	★★★★★	Collective Soul	Ed Roland
	2007		5	All That I Know	4:07	★★★★★	Collective Soul	Ed Roland
			6	I Don't Need Anymore F...	3:35	★★★★★	Collective Soul	Ed Roland
			7	Good Morning After All	4:23	★★★★★	Collective Soul	Ed Roland
			8	Hollywood	3:04	★★★★★	Collective Soul	Ed Roland
			9	Persuasion Of You	3:37	★★★★★	Collective Soul	Ed Roland
			10	Georgia Girl	3:26	★★★★★	Collective Soul	Ed Roland
			11	Adored	4:15	★★★★★	Collective Soul	Ed Roland

Figure 11-14: Expanded Tile view provides even more information about each item.

> **tip**
>
> Depending on what you're viewing, some view styles will not be available. For example, in the Songs view in Music, you can only choose Expanded Tiles view and not Icon or Details. Of course, why would you ever want to view songs in Icon mode?

Instant Search

In keeping with one of the biggest selling points of Windows Vista, Windows Media Player 11 includes an Instant Search box so you can quickly find the content you want. Annoyingly, the Search box in Windows Media Player 11 is instant: As you type in the name of an artist, album, song, or other media information, the Media Library view is filtered in real time. In other words, it doesn't wait for you to press Enter; it searches as you type.

> **Secret**
>
> Instant Search is context sensitive. If the media library is currently viewing songs in Music, it will search for songs that match your search query; but if you're viewing artists, it will search artist names instead. If you aren't interested in Media Player trying to outthink you, however, you can apply your search to other criteria—like the entire library—by clicking the drop-down arrow to the right of the Instant Search box and picking the option you want. You'll see options such as Library, Artists, and Albums, as shown in Figure 11-15.

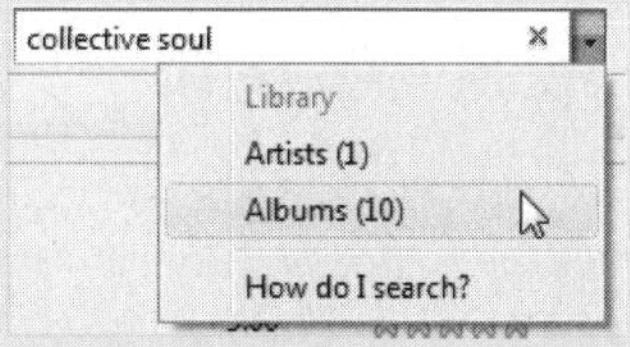

Figure 11-15: Instant Search works well in Windows Media Player and can be used to quickly find particular items in even the biggest media libraries.

List Pane

To the right of the Instant Search box is a small right-pointing arrow that enables you to toggle the List pane, described previously. When the List pane is active, the arrow is still there, so you can turn it off again easily. The List Pane is shown in Figure 11-16.

Figure 11-16: How the mighty have fallen. In previous Media Player versions, the List pane was a major focal point of the UI, but now it's sort of an afterthought.

Keyboard Shortcuts for Media Player Navigation

If you're a keyboard jockey, you'll appreciate that Windows Media Player includes a wealth of keyboard shortcuts related to navigating around the Media Player user interface. These shortcuts are summarized in Table 11-1. Note that not all shortcuts will work at all times; their availability depends on what's going on in Windows Media Player at the time.

Table 11-1: Keyboard Shortcuts for Navigating around Windows Media Player 11

Navigation Operation	Keyboard Shortcut
Navigate backward to the previous Media Player experience (identical to pushing the back button)	Alt+left arrow
Navigate forward to the previously accessed Media Player experience (identical to pushing the forward button)	Alt+right arrow
Switch to normal mode	Ctrl+1
Switch to skin mode	Ctrl+2
Switch to Artist view (in Music), All Pictures (in Pictures), All Video (in Video), All TV (in Recorded TV), or Other Media (in Other Media)	Ctrl+7
Switch to Artist view (in Music), Keywords (in Pictures), Actors (in Video), Series (in Recorded TV), or Folder (in Other Media)	Ctrl+8
Switch to Artist view (in Music), Date Taken (in Pictures), Genre (in Video), or Genre (in Recorded TV)	Ctrl+9
Select the Instant Search box (in Library view only)	Ctrl+E
Display Windows Media Player Help	F1

Playing Music and Other Media

As with previous Windows Media Player versions, you can easily select and play music in the media library; but the range of options you have for doing so has increased in this version, and Microsoft has finally put some frequently needed playback options, such as Shuffle and Repeat, right up front where they belong.

To play a single song in Media Player, simply double-click the item in a Media Library view. It will begin playing immediately. To play a complete album, double-click the album's cover art. Simple, right? Most items work this way in the media library.

Secret There are, of course, exceptions. You can't play a stack of items by double-clicking it, for example. Instead, doing so simply opens the stack and displays the items it contains. If you want to play a stack, right-click it and choose Play.

At the bottom of the Media Player interface is the new universal media playback control, which is centered in the application window and provides simple access to the most frequently used playback features (see Figure 11-17).

Figure 11-17: The new universal media playback control puts the most frequently used playback buttons up front and center.

These are, from left to right, Shuffle, Repeat, Stop, Previous, Play/Pause, Next, Mute, and a volume slider. These controls should be self-explanatory, but what might not be obvious is how you trigger these features, plus other playback controls, using the keyboard. These keyboard shortcuts are explained in Table 11-2.

> **tip** The first two buttons, Shuffle and Repeat, are actually toggles, so they can be selected or deselected. When selected, the functionality is enabled.

Table 11-2: Keyboard Shortcuts for Controlling Media Playback in Windows Media Player 11

Playback Operation	Keyboard Shortcut
Start or pause playback	Ctrl+P
Stop playback	Ctrl+S
Stop playing a file and close it	Ctrl+W
Toggle Repeat (audio files only)	Ctrl+T
Navigate to the previous item or chapter	Ctrl+B
Navigate to the next item or chapter	Ctrl+F
Toggle Shuffle	Ctrl+H
Eject optical disk (CD or DVD)	Ctrl+J
Toggle the Classic Menus in Full mode	Ctrl+M
Fast forward	Ctrl+Shift+F
Change playback to fast play speed	Ctrl+Shift+G
Change playback to normal speed	Ctrl+Shift+N
Change playback to slow play speed	Ctrl+Shift+S
Rate the currently playing item as zero stars (not rated)	Ctrl+Windows key+0
Rate the currently playing item as one star	Ctrl+Windows key+1
Rate the currently playing item two stars	Ctrl+Windows key+2
Rate the currently playing item three stars	Ctrl+Windows key+3
Rate the currently playing item four stars	Ctrl+Windows key+4

continues

Table 11-2: *(continued)*

Playback Operation	Keyboard Shortcut
Rate the currently playing item five stars	Ctrl+Windows key+5
Toggle Mute	F8
Decrease the volume	F9
Increase the volume	F10

Finding and Managing Your Music

If you already have a bunch of CDs that you've ripped to the PC, music you've purchased from an online store, or other digital media content, and you want to make sure you can access it easily from Windows Media Player, then take a moment to tell Media Player where that content is. By default, Windows Media Player monitors certain folders for content, including the current user's Music folder, the All Music folder, the current user's Pictures folder, the All Pictures folder, the current user's Videos folder, the All Videos folder, and, if you are using Windows Vista Home Premium or Ultimate editions, the Recorded TV folder. You can add other folders to this watch list as well.

Finding Your Music

You can speed media detection by telling Windows Media Player to manually search for media. This can also be helpful when you've chosen to store media in a nonstandard location.

To do this, click the small arrow below the Library button in Windows Media Player 11 and select Add to Library from the resulting drop-down menu (see Figure 11-18). This displays the Add to Library dialog box, where you can manually find media and add other folder paths to the list of folders that Media Player monitors.

Figure 11-18: The Add to Library dialog specifies where Windows Media Player looks for content.

Secret   You can also trigger the Add to Library dialog at any time by pressing F3.

By default, Add to Library displays in a super-simplified view style. Click the Advanced Options button to display the complete dialog box, shown in Figure 11-19.

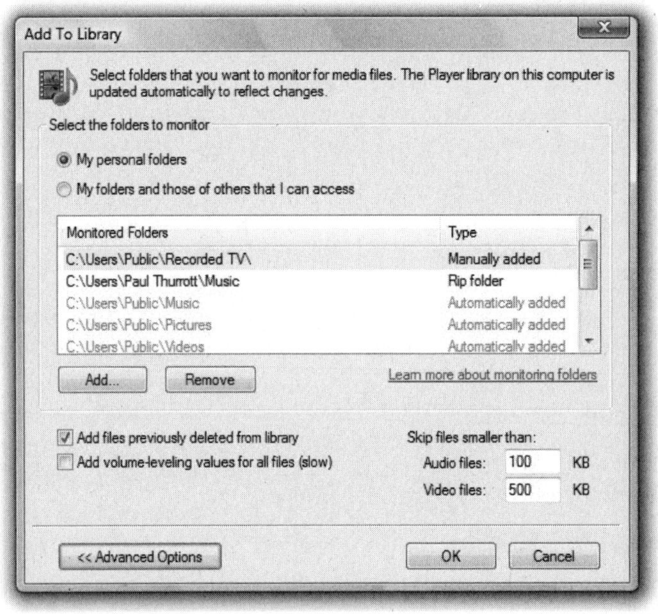

Figure 11-19: With Advanced Options shown, Add to Library provides more options, including a list of monitored folders.

To add nonstandard folder locations to the monitored folders list, click the Add button. Note that you can choose to add volume-leveling information to each imported file, which slows the importing process but ensures that each media file plays back at a consistent volume level. This can be hugely important if you often shuffle songs from different sources.

Secret   While you can add as many folders to the Monitored Folders list as you'd like, you cannot remove certain preset folders. These folders are denoted by type Automatically Added and are grayed out.

When you click OK, Media Player will manually search its monitored folders list for new media. An Add to Library by Searching Computer dialog appears. Note that this process can be quite lengthy, depending on the number of locations Windows Media Player must search and the number of media items it finds. You must manually close the Add to Library by Searching Computer window when searching is complete.

If you want to manually add songs to the media library, you can also select them in Windows Explorer and simply drag them into Windows Media Player's media library. Behind the scenes, Windows Media Player will not add those folder locations to its monitored folders list, but will only add the dragged media to the media library.

Table 11-3 highlights the keyboard shortcuts used for managing the media library.

Table 11-3: Keyboard Shortcuts for Finding and Organizing Media in Windows Media Player 11

Media Management Operation	Keyboard Shortcut
Create a new playlist	Ctrl+N
Open a file	Ctrl+O
Edit media information on a selected item in the library	F2
Add media files to the library	F3
Refresh information in the panes	F5
Specify a URL or path to a file	Ctrl+U

Secret

Managing Your Music

As you add music to your collection, you may discover that Windows Media Player's reliance on album art as a visual means for quickly finding your music is a liability, as some music won't have the correct cover art. Instead, you'll just see a black square. If this happens, fear not: It's easy to add album art to your blanked-out music. There are two ways, manual and automatic.

To manually add music to your blanked-out albums, search the Web or browse to a Web site such as Amazon.com using your Web browser and then search for each album, one at a time. The Amazon.com Web site is an excellent repository of album art: Simply click the See Larger Image link that accompanies each album and then drag the image from the Web browser onto the blanked-out image in Windows Media Player, as shown in Figure 11-20. Voilà! Instant album art. (You can copy and paste to apply album art: Just use the Windows copy functionality from Explorer and then right-click the album cover in Windows Media Player and choose Paste Album Art from the pop-up menu that appears.)

continues

continued

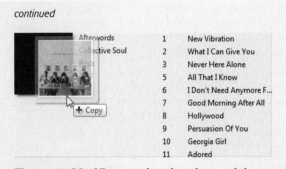

1	New Vibration
2	What I Can Give You
3	Never Here Alone
5	All That I Know
6	I Don't Need Anymore F...
7	Good Morning After All
8	Hollywood
9	Persuasion Of You
10	Georgia Girl
11	Adored

Figure 11-20: Album art is only a drag and drop away.

The manual approach works well if you only have a few missing bits of album art, but if you have multiple missing pieces of album art, you'll want to use a more automated method. There are many ways to do this, but Windows Media Player actually includes a Find Album Info feature that, among other things, helps you add missing album art. To trigger this feature, navigate to an album that's missing album art in the Media Player media library, right-click the offending album, and choose Find Album Info. This displays the Find Album Info window. Find Album Info is pretty simple: Choose the album from the available selections and you're off and running. Note that this tool has a huge disadvantage: It works on a track-by-track basis, even when you select an entire album. That's not automated enough.

Instead of Find Album Info, try another right-click option, Update Album Info (unless, of course, you don't want Microsoft messing with your carefully massaged media files, in which case you've probably skipped over this section anyway). Update Album Info is totally automated: If the online database that Microsoft licenses for Media Player has your album correctly listed, you should see the album art appear pretty quickly.

If neither of Microsoft's automated methods works, it's time to take matters into your own hands and try a third-party utility. One such solution is Art Fixer, which scans your media library and looks for missing album art. The application then runs through each album missing art, one at a time, and presents possible solutions. Pick the one you want and move on. You can download Art Fixer without cost at **www.avsoft.nl**.

Playing with Photos, Videos, and Recorded TV Shows

In keeping with its name, Windows Media Player is about more than just music. You can also manage and access other digital media content, including photos and other pictures, videos, and recorded TV shows. For the purposes of Windows Media Player, "recorded TV shows" refers to files that are stored in Microsoft Digital Video Recording (dvr-ms) format. This is the format used to record TV shows with Windows Media Center, covered in Chapter 15, but you don't need to use Windows Media Center to access these recorded TV shows; they play fine in Windows Media Player as well. (You do, however, need Media Center to *record* TV shows, of course, along with TV tuner hardware.)

Accessing Photos with Media Player

Unlike its predecessor, Windows Media Player manages your photo collection by default (in Windows Media Player 10, you had to manually enable this functionality). To access your photo collection, click the Category button (remember, it's under the back button) and choose Pictures. This will put the media library in All Pictures view, shown in Figure 11-21. By default, you will see all photos.

Figure 11-21: Windows Media Player in Pictures view.

Secret   Unless you've manually searched for media as described in the previous section, Windows Media Player won't populate its pictures library until you navigate to it for the first time. Therefore, the first time you access this view, you might have to wait a few seconds while your photos load into the player.

When you double-click a photo in Pictures view, Media Player switches to Now Playing and displays the image in a slideshow with the other pictures around it, as shown in Figure 11-22. You can use the standard Media Player navigational controls to move through the playlist, shuffle the order, and so on. You can also click the back button to return to the media library.

Figure 11-22: It's not the optimal way to view photos, but Windows Media Player can be used in a pinch.

Media Player's support of photos isn't fantastic, and you should probably use Windows Photo Gallery—described in Chapter 13—to manage your photos instead, because that application includes decent editing tools and is optimized for this task. However, there's a reason Media Player supports photos: You can synchronize them with a portable device and enjoy them on the go. You'll look at Windows Media Player 11's support for portable media devices later in this chapter.

Secret

There are many other reasons to use Windows Photo Gallery instead of Windows Media Player, at least for photos. Case in point: While you can set the speed of photo slideshows in Photo Gallery, slideshows using Windows Media Player are always stuck at the same speed (5 seconds per picture). Moreover, unlike Photo Gallery, there's no way to change the theme or the type of the slideshow. That said, Windows Media Player is decidedly better than Photo Gallery when it comes to videos, even though Photo Gallery does technically support videos as well as photos.

Playing Videos and DVD Movies

Because of its history as an all-in-one media player, Windows Media Player 11 is an excellent solution for managing and playing videos that have been saved to your PC's hard drive. These movies can be home movies you've edited with Windows Movie Maker (see Chapter 14) or videos you've downloaded from the Internet. Windows Media Player also makes an excellent DVD player.

Secret As with Windows XP, Microsoft doesn't make it particularly easy in Windows Vista to access your Videos folder, which is where you'll typically store your digital movies; like Windows XP, you can't add a shortcut to the Videos folder directly to the right side of the Start Menu. Instead, you need to open your user folder (the first link on the right side of the Start Menu) and then open the Videos folder from there. Yes, it's dumb.

You access digital videos in Media Player by choosing Video with the Category button. Videos display as large thumbnails in the media library by default; double-clicking them, of course, plays them.

tip You can make video playlists, which is actually pretty useful. Just open the List pane and drag over the videos that you want in a new playlist.

Out of the box, Windows Media Player 11 supports a wide range of popular video formats, including MPEG-2, Windows Media Video (WMV) and WMV-HD, and AVI. Unfortunately, Media Player lacks support for a few popular formats, notably DivX and XViD, which are growing increasingly popular online, and QuickTime, Apple's near-ubiquitous format for movie previews. Fortunately, there are ways around these limitations. To add support for the popular DivX and XViD formats, you can simply download files from the Web that will add support for these formats. The free version of DivX is available from the DivX Web site (**www.divx.com/**), whereas XViD codecs can be downloaded from **www.xvid.org/**.

Secret Dealing with QuickTime format is a bit trickier. Sure, you could download Apple's free QuickTime Player, or pony up $30 for QuickTime Pro, but neither of these enable you to play back QuickTime content in Windows Media Player 11 or Windows Media Center. To gain this functionality, you need to turn to QuickTime Alternative, which is available on the Free Codecs Web site (**www.free-codecs .com/download/QuickTime_Alternative.htm**). This excellent bit of software enables you to play QuickTime files in Media Player, Media Center, and even your Web browser. Did I mention it's free?

Secret

Another route to consider is an all-in-one codec pack. The one I use and recommend is called the Combined Community Codec Pack, or CCCP. It is free, updated regularly, and includes a stunning range of media codecs, including Ogg, MPEG-4/H.264, Xvid, DivX, AC3, and many, many others. You can find CCCP and more information at **www.cccp-project.net/**.

In previous versions of Windows Media Player, you needed to download a $10 DVD decoder in order to add movie DVD playback functionality to the player. In Windows Media Player 11, this is no longer an issue: For the first time, you can now play DVD movies in Media Player without having to go to the pain and expense of finding and purchasing extra software. That's because Microsoft has included this functionality in Windows Media Player, free. DVD playback is shown in Figure 11-23.

Figure 11-23: For the first time, you can play DVD movies in Windows Media Player without purchasing additional software.

Note that Windows Media Player changes a bit when you are watching a DVD movie. The universal media playback control drops the Shuffle and Repeat buttons, which don't make sense in the context of DVD movie playback, and picks up a new DVD button. When you click this button, you'll see the menu shown in Figure 11-24. This provides you with quick access to the root and title menus of the DVD and enables you to access other DVD features, such as languages, captions, and angles.

Figure 11-24: The DVD menu provides access to features that are specific to DVD movies.

tip   Note that the time display to the left of the DVD button can be toggled between three views: time elapsed (the default), time elapsed and total play time, and total play time. To toggle between these views, just click the time display. Each time you click, the time display changes.

Regarding DVD navigation—that is, the process of selecting items from menus in the DVD movie you're watching—you will typically want to use the mouse, as keyboard control seems to be unreliable. To navigate DVD menus with the mouse, just move the mouse pointer over items in the menu and watch for selection graphics to appear (these vary from DVD to DVD). You can trigger a selected item by tapping the primary mouse button.

Secret

Instead of spending money on a third-party DVD playback application, you might want to invest in something that's even more useful: software that makes the DVD playback experience demonstrably better. It's called Slysoft AnyDVD, and this little wonder provides a wealth of features, including the following:

- Removes region code limitations so you can play back DVDs from outside your country or region
- Prevents DVDs from launching annoying PC-based software automatically
- Allows you to skip directly to the main DVD menu or the start of the actual movie, bypassing those annoying previews and other junk that movie makers always put at the beginning of DVDs
- Bypasses DVD encryption so you can "rip" a DVD to your hard drive and watch the movie without the disk

AnyDVD isn't free, but I think it's worth it. You can find out more from the Slysoft Web site: **www.slysoft.com/**. I discuss this application a bit in Chapter 14 as well, where I describe DVD ripping techniques.

Playing Recorded TV Shows

If you're using a Media Center PC, or a PC running Windows Vista Home Premium or Ultimate edition and a TV tuner card that's connected to a TV signal, you have the capability to record TV shows (discussed in Chapter 15). TV shows recorded with Windows Media Center are aggregated by Windows Media Player 11 as well, and appear in the media library when you select Recorded TV from the Category button. Recorded TV works just like any other videos, as shown in Figure 11-25, but it occupies a lot of disk space, due to Microsoft's use of an inefficient video codec.

As with videos, recorded TV shows are shown in a nice thumbnail icon view by default. If you already have Media Center on your PC, why would you want to access these shows in this fashion? Actually, there are a few reasons.

First, you might want to synchronize your recorded TV content with a portable device so you can access these shows at your convenience—during the morning commute, on a plane, or in other mobile situations. As you might expect, that's indeed the primary reason this content type shows up in Media Player. But what about users with laptops? You might have Media Center on your desktop PC or Media Center PC, but if you're running a different Vista version (or a previous version of Windows) on your notebook computer, you can use Windows Media Player to access that content: Just copy the shows you want to watch to your notebook, take them on the road, watch them, and then delete them when you're done.

Secret

Seriously, delete them. Media Center content takes up massive amounts of hard drive space. Thirty minutes of recorded TV takes up almost 2GB in Vista's version of Media Center. Yikes. Thankfully, you can convert these files into smaller versions using Windows Movie Maker. You'll learn how in Chapter 14.

Figure 11-25: Recorded TV shows are like videos, except that they're humongous files.

As you might expect, Windows Media Player supports a wide range of keyboard shortcuts related to videos, DVDs, and Recorded TV shows, as shown in Table 11-4.

Table 11-4: Keyboard Shortcuts for Video in Windows Media Player 11

Video Operation	Keyboard Shortcut
Zoom the video to 50 percent of its original size	Alt+1
Display the video at its original size	Alt+2
Zoom the video to 200 percent of its original size	Alt+3
Toggle display for full-screen video	Alt+Enter
Return to full mode from full screen	Esc
Rewind	Ctrl+Shift+B
Toggle captions and subtitles on or off	Ctrl+Shift+C
Fast forward	Ctrl+Shift+F
Change playback to fast play speed	Ctrl+Shift+G

continues

Table 11-4: *(continued)*

Video Operation	Keyboard Shortcut
Change playback to normal speed	Ctrl+Shift+N
Change playback to slow play speed	Ctrl+Shift+S
Rate the currently playing item as zero stars (not rated)	Ctrl+Windows key+0
Rate the currently playing item as one star	Ctrl+Windows key+1
Rate the currently playing item two stars	Ctrl+Windows key+2
Rate the currently playing item three stars	Ctrl+Windows key+3
Rate the currently playing item four stars	Ctrl+Windows key+4
Rate the currently playing item five stars	Ctrl+Windows key+5

Ripping CDs to the PC

If you haven't yet copied your audio CD collection to the PC, Windows Media Player 11 makes doing so as painless as possible. Understand, however, that *ripping* a CD collection—as those in the know call the copying process—can be quite time-consuming, especially if you have a large CD collection. Before you can get started, you need to make a few configuration changes.

Secret

Configuring Media Player to Use the Right Audio Format

To configure Windows Media Player 11 for CD ripping, open the Rip menu by clicking the small arrow under the Rip toolbar button and then choose More Options, as shown in Figure 11-26.

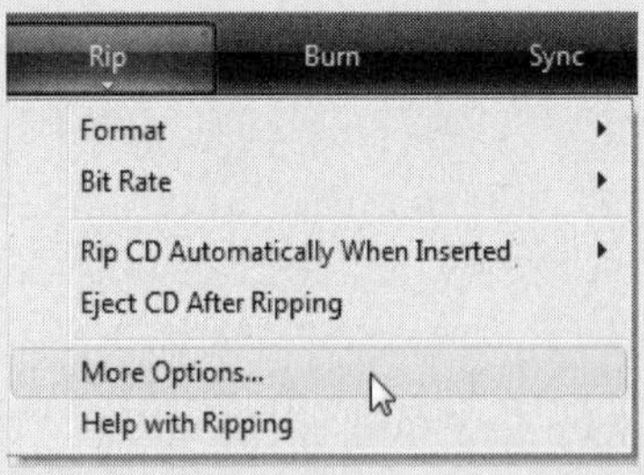

Rip	Burn	Sync

Format   ▶
Bit Rate   ▶

Rip CD Automatically When Inserted   ▶
Eject CD After Ripping

More Options...
Help with Ripping

Figure 11-26: Under each toolbar button is a tiny link that exposes a hidden pop-up menu.

This displays the Rip Music tab of the Media Player Options dialog box, as shown in Figure 11-27.

continues

continued

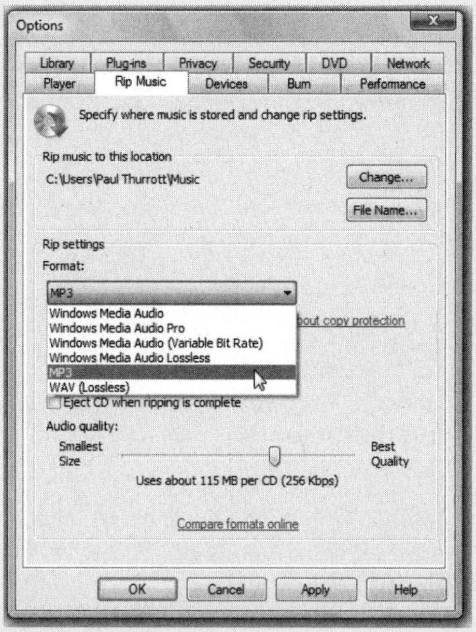

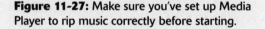

Figure 11-27: Make sure you've set up Media
Player to rip music correctly before starting.

There is a number of options here, but I am primarily concerned with Rip settings, which determine the file format Media Player will use for the music you
copy. By default, Media Player will rip music to Microsoft's proprietary Windows
Media Audio (WMA) format. I cannot stress this point enough: Do not—ever—
use this format.

Here's the deal: WMA is a high-quality audio format, and much more desirable
from a technical standpoint than competing options such as MP3 or Advanced
Audio Coding (AAC), the format Apple uses for its own music. However, because
WMA is not supported on some of the most popular music devices on the planet
(including the iPod), I advise against storing your entire collection in a format
that could be a dead end in a few years (and is potentially incompatible with the
device you're using right now).

Instead I recommend the MP3 format, which is a de facto audio standard supported by every single audio application, device, and PC on the planet. No, MP3 is
technically not as advanced as WMA, or even AAC for that matter, but that's OK.
Thanks to today's massive hard drive sizes, you can simply encode music at a high
bit rate. The higher the bit rate, the better the quality. (And, not coincidentally,
the bigger the resulting file size, but who cares? Storage is cheap.)

Here's how you should configure Windows Media Player 11 for ripping CDs.
First, choose MP3 from the Format drop-down list box. Then, using the Audio
quality slider, change the quality setting so that it is three-quarters of the way
up the scale (256 Kbps) or higher. The highest setting, 320 Kbps, is even better,
but you might not notice a difference between the two.

Secret

Prior to Windows Media Player 10, Microsoft did not include integrated MP3 creation capabilities in its media players, but this functionality is now included at no extra cost, as with DVD viewing capabilities.

Ripping Music

To rip, or copy, an audio CD to your PC, simply insert the CD into one of your PC's optical (CD, DVD) drives. An Auto Play dialog box is displayed, asking you what you'd like to do. Dismiss this dialog box immediately: Instead of choosing Rip Music from CD—which is one of the options shown in the Auto Play dialog box—you will want to first ensure that Media Player has correctly identified the disk.

Secret

You can completely disable Auto Play, or just disable it for audio CDs, if you think you're smart enough to remember that you just inserted a disk and don't need to be reminded by Windows. If this is the case, open the Start Menu and type **Auto Play** to locate the Auto Play control panel. In the window that appears, navigate to the first option, Audio CD, and choose Take No Action, or whatever option you prefer. To turn off Auto Play universally, uncheck the box titled Use Auto Play for All Media and Devices.

In Media Player, click the Rip button. The CD you've inserted should appear. Examine the disk name, artist name, genre, date, and each track name to ensure that they are correct. If anything is wrong—and chances are good something will be wrong given the quality of the online service Microsoft uses for this information—you can edit it now before the music is copied to your computer. To edit an individual item, right-click it and choose Edit.

To edit the entire album at once, right-click any item and choose Find Album Info. This displays the Find Album Information window, shown in Figure 11-28, which compares a unique identifier on the CD with a Web-based database.

If you find a match for the CD you've inserted, select it, click Next, and then confirm that you chose the correct album.

When everything is correct, click the Start Rip button (hidden near the bottom right of the Windows Media Player window) to begin the copy process. Under the Rip Status column, you'll see progress bars for each song that mark the progress of the CD copy. This is shown in Figure 11-29.

Figure 11-28: Windows Media Player can look up your CD online and, it is hoped, find a match.

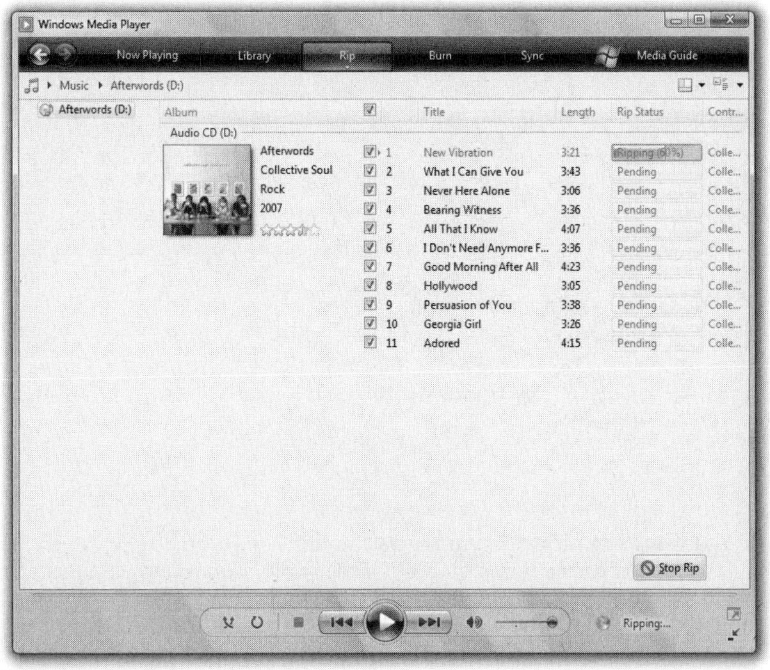

Figure 11-29: Windows Media Player provides you with an ongoing status update as you rip a CD to the hard drive.

Secret By default Windows Media Player 11 copies music to your Music folder. First it creates a folder named for the group, and then underneath that it will create a folder named for the album. Inside of the album folder, you'll find the individual files that make up each of the tracks in the copied album. You can change the location where Media Player stores your songs, and the template used to name each file, in the Rip pane of the Windows Media Player Options dialog box. For most people, the default values are just fine.

Burning Your Own Music CDs

When you have a lot of your music on your PC, you're going to want to listen to it in various ways. On the PC, you can create custom playlists of songs you really like; if you have a Media Center PC, you can even interact with these playlists using a remote control, your TV, and (if you're really on the cutting edge) a decent stereo system. If you want to take your music collection on the road with you, there are other options. You can synchronize music with a portable device, as described in the next section, or you can create your own custom mix CDs, using only the songs you like. These CDs can be played in car stereos, portable CD players, or any other CD players.

As with CD ripping, you're going to want to configure Media Player a bit before you burn, or create, your own CD. To do this, open the Burn menu, shown in Figure 11-30, and make sure that Audio CD, and not Data CD or DVD, is selected.

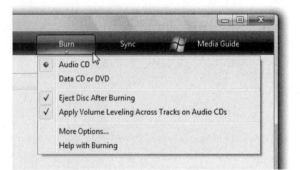

Figure 11-30: This hidden menu provides quick links to options related to CD burning.

You can also click More Options from this menu to access the Burn tab of the Windows Media Player Options dialog.

Secret You won't normally need to access the Burn tab, with one possible exception: If you notice that your created disks aren't playing properly in your CD player, you can turn down the burn speed of your CD/DVD burner, which might result in more reliable disks.

Secret

If you have a CD or DVD player that can play back data CDs or data DVDs, that option will enable you to create disks with far more music. For example, a typical audio CD can contain about 80 minutes of music maximum, but a data CD—with 700MB of storage—can store 10 times that amount. DVDs are even larger. Check with your CD player or DVD player's instructions to see if it is compatible with data disks.

When you're sure that you're set up for audio CD creation, insert a blank CD. Windows will display an Auto Play dialog box with two options by default: Burn a CD (using Windows Media Player) or burn files to disk (using Windows). You can choose the first option or dismiss the dialog box and navigate to the Burn experience in Windows Media Player by clicking the Burn button. When you do so, Media Player displays the List pane and creates an empty Burn List, which is a temporary playlist into which you can copy music to be burned to disk (see Figure 11-31).

Figure 11-31: The elusive List pane appears when it's time to burn a disk.

To add music to this list, navigate through your music collection and drag the songs you want on the disk over to the List pane.

Secret Can't see any music listed in the main pane? Click on the Library toolbar button to display your music library and then select a grouping (Album, Songs, whatever). Then click Burn again. Now you should have your music listed in the center of the application window and your blank Burn List on the right.

At the top of the List pane, Media Player provides a handy progress bar and time limit gauge so you can be sure that your Burn List isn't too long to fit on the CD. Fill up the Burn List with as much music as you'd like, making sure that you don't exceed the time limit. When you're ready to create the disk, click the Start Burn button at the bottom of the List pane. When you do so, the Burn experience appears, and Media Player begins burning the disk, as shown in Figure 11-32.

Under the Status column, you'll see progress bars appear next to each song as they're burned to disk. CD burning moves along pretty quickly, especially on a modern optical drive.

Figure 11-32: Burn, baby, burn: Media Player's Burn experience makes short work of custom mix CDs.

Synchronizing with Portable Devices

Although the iPod gets all the press these days, a popular family of Windows Media Player–compatible portable players offers better features and functionality than Apple's devices, and often at a better price. Although it's not possible here to describe every single non-Apple device available, mostly because new devices enter the market almost every month, what you're looking for, generally, is a portable device that's made for Windows Vista. Of course, that's most devices.

Secret

Devices that are compatible with Windows Media Player 11 used to be labeled as *PlaysForSure*-compatible. PlaysForSure was a Microsoft marketing campaign aimed at educating consumers about which devices work seamlessly with Windows Media Player. Unfortunately, Microsoft killed this program, replacing it with the semi-related and preexisting "Made for Windows Vista" logo program. There's just one problem: Most of these devices work just fine with Windows XP and Windows Media Player 10 as well. Therefore, most vendors no longer use this logo. Generally, most Windows-compatible devices work just fine with Windows Media Player, including those made by companies such as Creative, iriver, Samsung, and SanDisk. Even Sony is starting to come around: Though its devices were previously compatible only with its own proprietary software, newer Sony devices work just fine with Windows Media Player as well. When in doubt, check the box or do some research first. Microsoft lists compatible devices on its Web site: **www.microsoft.com/windows/windowsmedia/devices/**.

Using Windows Media–Compatible Devices

If you do go the Windows Media route, you'll find that setup and configuration are simple: Just plug the device into your Windows Vista–based PC and wait a few seconds while Vista automatically downloads and installs the correct driver, as shown in Figure 11-33.

Figure 11-33: Say what you will about Vista compatibility, but portable devices are usually configured correctly and automatically.

Next, launch Windows Media Player 11 and get to work. You can synchronize music with all portable devices, and photos, movies, and recorded TV shows with many of them. What you can do is determined by the capabilities and capacity of the player you select.

For those with light needs—a few hundred songs but no photos or videos—a 1GB to 2GB flash-based device should work just fine. Even some of these small players are stepping up with video and photo support, so look for crisp-color screens, even at the low end.

For the ultimate in portable entertainment, you'll want a device with a large color screen and a massive hard drive. With enough storage space, you'll have no problems storing all the photos, home movies, and recorded TV shows you want to watch.

Whichever device you choose, configuration is largely hands-free and occurs behind the scenes. If you plug the device in while Media Player isn't running, you will see an Auto Play dialog box that enables you to choose between different options, including synchronizing with Windows Media Player. You can choose that, or close the dialog box and manually launch Windows Media Player.

When you launch Windows Media Player 11, you should see the player listed at the bottom of the Navigation pane, as shown in Figure 11-34, and the current player in the List pane on the right of the window. This Navigation pane entry enables you to navigate through the media in your players in the same way you would media on your PC.

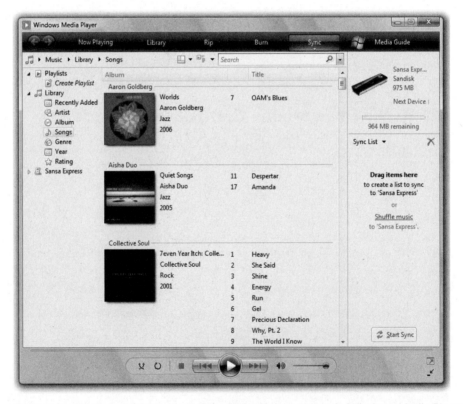

Figure 11-34: Compatible connected portable devices appear in Windows Media Player's Navigation pane.

That's pretty interesting, and it enables you to manually manage the content you're carrying around with you, but where Media Player really shines when it comes to devices is in its ability to automatically synchronize content between the player and the device. Synchronizing is about more than just copying media to the device. It's about ensuring that the media on your device is always what you want and always up-to-date.

Synchronizing with a Portable Device

You handle all of your device synchronization through the Sync experience in Media Player, which logically enough is accessed through the prominently displayed Sync button in the application's toolbar. Technically, there are two kinds of synchronization: Sync (or what I think of as "true sync") and Shuffle. You will typically use Sync when you have a large-format portable device (that is, one with multi-gigabytes of storage, most likely hard drive–based). Shuffle is aimed at smaller players on which you can't possibly fit all of your music collection, but you'd like to get a sampling.

To set up a device for Sync, select it in the Navigation pane and then click the Sync toolbar button. Next, open the Sync menu (by clicking the small arrow below the Sync button) and choose the device name in the list and then Set Up Sync. This launches the Device Setup window, shown in Figure 11-35, from where you will configure which media files you want synchronized with the device.

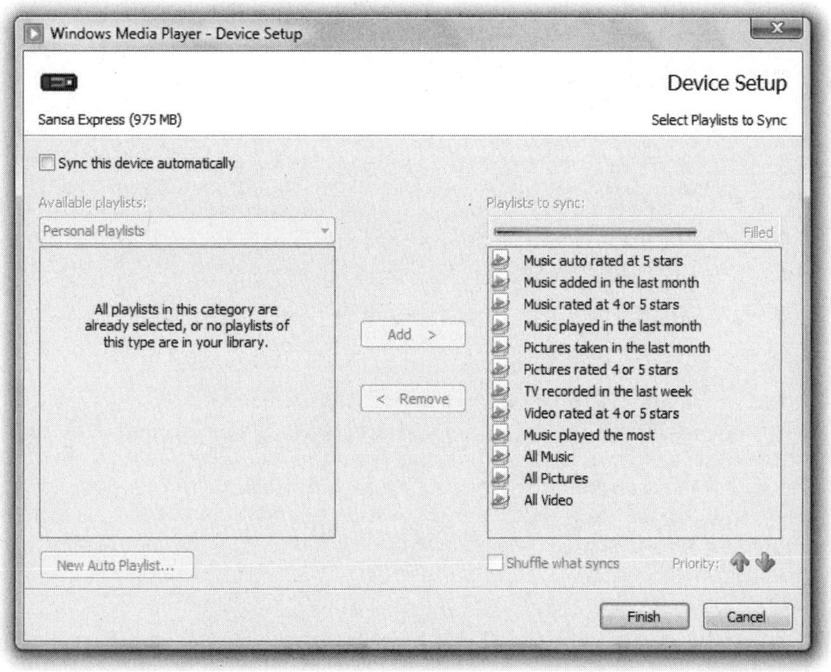

Figure 11-35: If you know what you're doing, choose Sync and let your media fly free.

From this interface, you can do a few things. You can set up automatic synchronization, and, depending on the capabilities of your device, sync all of your music, photos, and videos accordingly. If the device is too small to hold all of that content, Media Player will pick which content to sync, based on criteria like ratings and so forth. (This is essentially what Shuffle does.)

Secret   Don't worry about multigigabyte video files clogging up your portable device. Windows Media Player uses a technology called *transcoding* to copy large video files (and even, optionally, high-quality music files) into smaller versions that are tailored to your device. I examine this capability in the next section.

If you're the type of person who makes a lot of hand-crafted playlists, you can use the Device Setup window to ensure that only the music you care about is synchronized with the player. Just select the playlists you want copied to the device and then those playlists, as well as the music contained in each, will be copied over. It's all up to you.

Secret   One final point about Sync: I mentioned earlier that synchronization was about more than just copying. Here's why that's true. If you configure a portable device to synchronize with certain playlists, or even, for example, your entire music library, the content on the device will be updated every time you make a change to those playlists or libraries. Therefore, if you rip a new CD to your PC and then connect the device to the PC, and that device is synchronized with your entire music library, that new content will silently and automatically be copied to the device. Likewise, if you add (or remove) a song from a playlist that is synchronized with a device, the next time you connect the device, its music library will be updated to reflect the changes you made on the PC. Maybe Bill Gates was on to something when he started talking about the "magic of software" after all.

Using Shuffle

If you're using a small-capacity device, typically one that is based on Flash RAM and contains only a few gigabytes or less of storage space, you might want to configure the device to Shuffle, rather than Sync. In Shuffle mode, the entire contents of the device are replaced with a random selection of songs from your music library, so you always have a fresh set of tracks each time you connect the device and reshuffle it. You can also manually change the track list on the device by opening the Sync menu and choosing Shuffle *[device name]*.

---

tip   Shuffle isn't the answer for many people, however. If you have a wide selection of music types in your media library, you might find it a bit jarring as your player moves from, say, classical Mozart to hard rock Van Halen to new age David Lanz. Indeed, many people use smaller Flash-based players while working out, and it's likely that such people will want a particular kind of music on their players. (David Lanz is hugely talented, but he just doesn't make good workout music.) Be sure you know what you're doing before picking Shuffle.

Whichever sync type you choose, Windows Media Player uses a Sync Results view to show the progress of file copying, as shown in Figure 11-36. After all of the files you've chosen have been synced to the device, you can unplug it, pop in the headphones, and rock out.

Figure 11-36: During sync, Windows Media Player shows the status of each file it's copying.

Managing a Portable Device in Windows Media Player

Primarily, most of your PC-to-portable device interactions will involve synchronizing content between the two (and charging the portable device, which occurs while it's connected to the PC via a USB cable). However, there are a number of ways you can configure portable devices in Windows Media Player 11, and some of these options are important if you want to get the most out of your devices.

To change the name of your device as it appears in Windows Media Player, open the Sync menu and choose the current device name followed by Advanced Options. In the Sync tab, you can rename the device. If you're not using the Shuffle option, you can also use this interface to specify various synchronization options, such as how much space on the device you'd like to reserve for file storage. (Many portable devices have enough capacity that they make for excellent general-purpose file storage devices as well as media players.)

In the Quality tab of the same dialog box, you can control how Media Player transcodes music, videos, and recorded TV that is synchronized with the device. The issue here is simple: A 19GB video file might look great on your PC, but few portable devices are capable of HDTV-quality video and surround sound. Therefore, rather than waste valuable storage space on your device, Windows Media Player can make copies of these content types that are smaller and more in line with your player's capabilities.

tip Transcoding can be quite time consuming, so Windows Media Player does it in the background. If you often take your device along for the morning commute, it might be a good idea to leave Media Player on overnight so it can transcode and synchronize any new content.

You can separately configure how Media Player transcodes music and videos/recorded TV. By default, Media Player will automatically transcode content as required, or, if you feel very strongly about file size and quality, you can manually choose how the player will handle these media types.

Secret Audiophiles can actually use this feature to ensure that Media Player does not transcode music to lower-quality files, ensuring that what they hear on their music player is at the same quality level as the original recordings.

You can also access some portable device options from the Devices tab of the Windows Media Player Options dialog. The quickest way to access this dialog is to choose More Options from the Sync menu. In this dialog, you can select the device you'd like to configure and then click the Properties button to display the Properties dialog described previously. Alternately, you can click the Advanced button to display the File Conversion Options dialog box, shown in Figure 11-37. This dialog box enables you to choose advanced transcoding options, such as whether video and audio files are converted in the background (which is recommended) and where Media Player stores temporary files.

Figure 11-37: You can really micromanage the transcoding functionality of Media Player if you'd like.

Using an Apple iPod with Windows Media Player 11

Secret

You can't use an iPod natively because Microsoft knows that if it did the engineering work to make it happen, Apple would simply launch an antitrust lawsuit. Given this limitation, you might think that getting an iPod to work with Windows Media Player 11 is a non-starter, but as it turns out, an enterprising third-party company, Mediafour (**www.mediafour.com/**), makes an excellent solution called XPlay that adds iPod compatibility to Windows Media Player. XPlay makes the iPod work just like any other portable music device in Windows Media Player.

What about content purchased from Apple's online store, the iTunes Store? After all, Apple offers an unparalleled number of digital songs and albums, TV shows, movies, audio books, music videos, and other content from the iTunes Store. Unfortunately, because most of this content is protected in some manner with Digital Rights Management (DRM) technology and encoded in Media Player–unfriendly formats, there's no easy answer; indeed, to date, no one has provided a way to deprotect video content sold via iTunes. But music is a bit simpler. Apple offers some music in nonprotected AAC format. This music won't work in Windows Media Player, but you can use Apple's desktop-based iTunes software to convert it to MP3 format, which works fine. The protected songs, also sold in AAC format, are a bit more problematic: You'll have to burn the songs to CD and then manually re-rip them back to the PC in MP3 format. Aside from the sheer effort involved, this method isn't particularly elegant because Apple's low-quality 128 Kbps AAC tracks aren't great source material: The resulting MP3 files will likely be hissy, tinny, or otherwise thin sounding. My advice is to avoid purchasing music from iTunes and choose a better solution, such as the Amazon MP3 store, described later in this chapter.

Sharing Your Music Library

One of the nicest features of Windows Media Player is its *media sharing* functionality. This feature enables you to share your Media Player 11–based music library with other PCs running Windows Media Player 11, various Media Connect–based devices, and Microsoft's multimedia game machine, the Xbox 360.

tip

If you want to share your media library with one or more PCs, Windows XP works just fine, too. Just make sure that all of the PCs are running Windows Media Player 11.

Why would you want to do that? Well, many homes have two or more PCs these days, so it makes sense to save some disk space and utilize your Wi-Fi (or wired) home network to access music, photos, and videos that are stored on other PCs. In one typical scenario, you may have a desktop PC with a large hard drive on which you store all of your media content. Using a wirelessly equipped notebook, you can easily access that content from elsewhere in the house; or you can access that content using a network-attached device such as a media receiver or Xbox 360, neither of which offers a lot of local storage.

Secret

Share and Share Alike:
Setting Up Your PC for Sharing

Before you can share your media library content, you have to do some configuration. First, the PC must be connected to your home network, and you must have already configured the PC's network connection to access your network as a private network. If you haven't done this, here's the quickest way.

Right-click the network connection icon in the system tray and choose Network and Sharing Center. Then, in the Network and Sharing Center window that appears, click Customize below the network map and next to your home network (which will typically have a name like *Network*). In the Set Network Location dialog box that appears, choose Private for location type and click Next. Then click Close. (Make sure you do this for your home network only, and not for any public networks you might visit.)

Please note that you need to repeat this process on any other Windows Vista–based PCs with which you'd like to share media libraries. This step isn't required for Windows XP.

Next you need to configure Windows Media Player 11 for sharing. To do so, open the Media Player, open the Library menu (by clicking the small arrow below the Library toolbar button), and choose Media Sharing. This will display the Media Sharing dialog box shown in Figure 11-38.

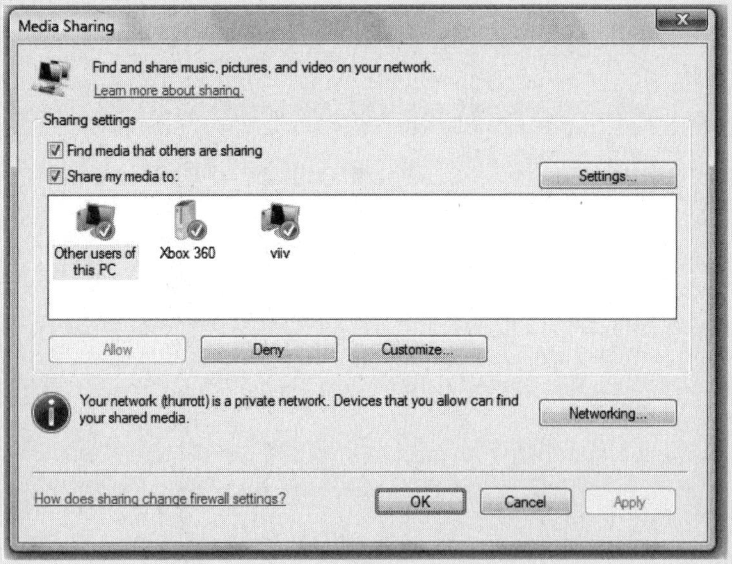

Figure 11-38: Here you configure the PCs and other devices with which you will share digital media content.

continues

continued

In Media Sharing, select the check box Find Media that Others are Sharing if you'd like to find other shared music libraries on your home network. If you want to share the music library on the current PC, select the Share My Media check box, and then examine the icons that represent the various PCs and devices that you can share with. Select each in turn and click the Allow button for the devices with which you'd like to create sharing relationships. As you allow devices, a green check box will appear on their icons, as shown in Figure 11-39 (without the color, of course).

Figure 11-39: Who and what you share with is completely up to you.

If you'd like to specify the type of content you want to share, click the Settings button. You can choose between music, pictures, and videos, and choose whether to filter via star ratings or parental ratings.

Connecting to a Shared Music Library with Windows Vista

When you've shared a music library on one PC, you'll be prompted to set up sharing on any other Windows Vista PCs you have in the house. As shown in Figure 11-40, you'll be prompted to establish a sharing relationship with the PC that is sharing content.

Figure 11-40: When a PC begins sharing media over the network, you'll be prompted to establish a sharing relationship.

To establish this relationship, you can click the balloon window. However, the window fades away pretty quickly (presumably because it's annoying). If this happens, you can still set up sharing: The sharing icon remains in the tray notification area. Right-click this icon to set up sharing (Open), disable future notifications, or Exit (which allows future sharing notifications to display). Alternately, simply double-click the icon to set up sharing.

In the Windows Media Player Library dialog box that appears, you can choose to Allow or Deny the other PC's request to access your shared media. You can also click a Shared settings button to access the Media Sharing dialog described in the previous section.

After you've established a connection with a shared media library, you'll see it appear in the Windows Media Player's navigation pane, as shown in Figure 11-41. You can expand and contract the list under the PC's name just as you would your own library, search for and access media, and play music and video files.

Figure 11-41: Shared media libraries appear in the Navigation pane and can be accessed similarly to your own media library.

There are some limitations, of course. You can't change the contents of shared media libraries, burn them to CD or DVD, or perform any other actions that might potentially violate the media owner's rights. And sharing is, of course, a two-way street: In order for you to access media on a shared media library, a user on the other PC has to allow sharing to your PC first.

Secret

You don't need two PCs to set up sharing because two users on the same PC can also share media with each other on the same PC. Configuration is identical to sharing between PCs; just select the Other Users of this PC icon in the Media Sharing window to set it up.

Connecting to a Shared Music Library with Xbox 360

With Xbox 360 game consoles now found in tens of millions of homes worldwide, Microsoft has found a perfect way to share PC-based music libraries with a device that is probably connected to the best TV display and stereo system in the home. Thankfully, the process is simple:

1. After you've configured Windows Media Player 11 to share its media library, ensure that your Xbox 360 is connected to the home network, and then turn it on. You will see a Found Windows Media Center Extender balloon window, but you can ignore this for now (unless you're using your Windows Vista–based machine as a Media Center PC; in that case, check out Chapter 15 for more information).

2. You will also see a balloon window appear for sharing with the Xbox 360. Double-click this icon and click Allow in the resulting dialog box. Alternatively, access the Media Sharing dialog box described earlier and make sure the Xbox 360 is configured to allow sharing.

3. Access your Xbox 360 and navigate to the Media blade, as shown in Figure 11-42. This part of the Xbox 360 user interface enables you to interact with PC-based digital media, connected portable devices (e.g., iPods and other MP3 players), and even external hard drives with stored digital media files. Right now, of course, you are just concerned with sharing media content from a Windows Vista–based PC.

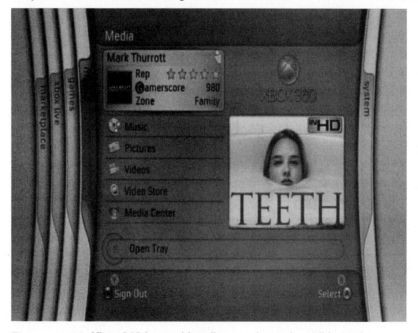

Figure 11-42: Xbox 360 is a multimedia powerhouse in addition to its more pedestrian video game playing capabilities.

4. To play shared music, select the Music option to display the Music page. Then select the name of your Vista-based computer from the source list on the left. (You'll also see options such as Console, Current Disk, and Portable Device.) If this is the first time you've done this, Xbox 360 will need to download Windows Media Connect, which is the same software many devices use to stream media from Windows Vista–based PCs. After this download is completed, Xbox 360 will automatically connect to PCs that are sharing media libraries. Just select the correct PC from the list to continue.

Now you can access your PC's media library using a simple menu that consists of albums, artists, saved playlists, songs, and genres (see Figure 11-43). Xbox 360 also includes a decent media player for playing back this content.

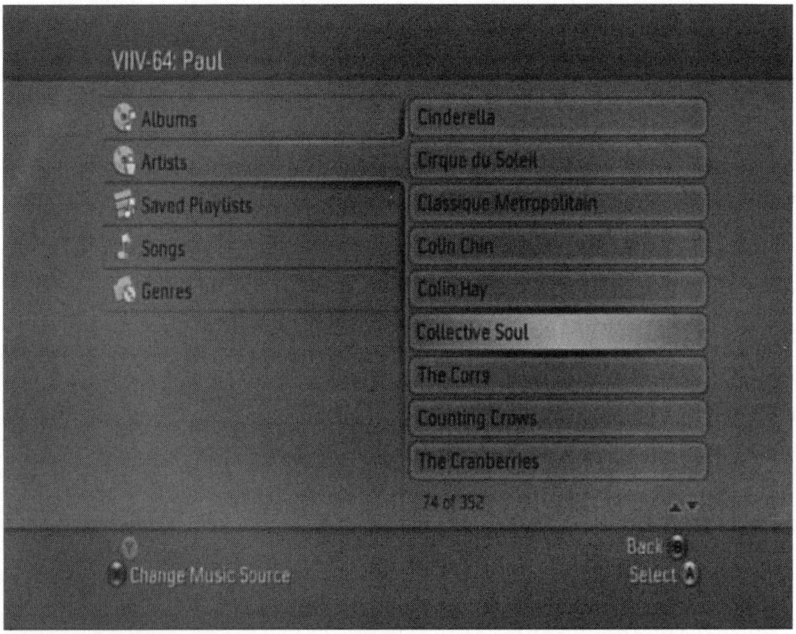

Figure 11-43: PC-based content is accessed via a text-based menu on the Xbox 360.

As you might expect, photos and videos are accessed in a similar manner.

Secret

If you attempt to access photos or videos from an Xbox 360 or other Windows Media Connect device and receive a "No photos found," "No videos found," or similar message, then you're not sharing any content of this type. To add photo or video content to Windows Media Player, you can either add it via Windows Photo Gallery (see Chapter 13) or use the Find Media steps described earlier in this chapter (press F3) to manually search folders that include photo and video content.

Secret

The Xbox 360 isn't the only electronics device that can access digital media content on your Vista-based PC over the home network. A variety of hardware makers, such as D-Link, Linksys, and others, sell so-called digital media receivers, which are simple set-top boxes that bridge the gap between your home stereo and TV and your PC. Sony's PlayStation 3 (PS3) also offers Xbox 360–like media connectivity functionality, also using Microsoft Windows Media Connect technology. Increasingly, it's getting easier and easier to access your content regardless of where you are.

Accessing Online Music Stores

Although Apple's iTunes Music Store is the current market leader, a host of Windows Media–compatible online music services are also available, and these services all work pretty nicely from within Windows Media Player 11. One service, however, stands out among all the rest, because it sells unprotected MP3 music exclusively, a service even Apple doesn't offer. Unprotected MP3 is important because this format is the most compatible across all the devices, PCs, and software you use, both today and tomorrow. In addition, it works just great with Windows Media Player 11. It's called Amazon MP3, and I take a look at this one first.

Amazon MP3

At a very basic level, online music services all perform the same functions. They provide music for sale (so-called *a la carte downloads,* whereby you can purchase individual songs or albums) or, in some cases, provide subscription music services, which enable you to access all of the service's music, on a number of PCs and even portable devices, for a monthly or yearly fee. Music services also typically offer editorial content—ways to discover new music or find out additional information about your favorite artists and albums. They often supply custom playlists, and other content. Amazon MP3, which, as the name suggests, is part of the Amazon.com online retailing site, is actually fairly bare bones, in keeping with Amazon's policy of keeping things simple. That is, the service is offered only via the Web. There's no deep integration with Windows Media Player, as was the case with many previous online music services, and there's no download-able media management application (though Amazon does offer a very simple PC-based song downloader, as you'll soon see). What you get is access to millions of unprotected MP3 tracks, either individually or within prepackaged digital albums, using Amazon's familiar interface.

Accessing Amazon MP3

To see Amazon MP3 in action, open Internet Explorer or your favorite Web browser and navigate to **www.amazonmp3.com/**. Shown in Figure 11-44, this part of Amazon's site should be immediately familiar if you're a frequent visitor.

Figure 11-44: Amazon MP3 combines the convenience of Amazon's e-commerce site with a millions-strong collection of unprotected MP3 songs.

You can browse Amazon MP3 in several ways. The service highlights new and notable albums, top songs and albums, and editor's pick selections, and you can browse via genre, album price range (there's a surprisingly good selection of low-cost MP3 albums available), and via a variety of promotions. This being Amazon, of course, one of the best ways to find content is to use the site's integrated search functionality. If a particular song or album isn't available digitally, Amazon offers you a chance to purchase it in a more traditional (albeit less instantly gratifying) CD-based format.

Purchasing Music from Amazon MP3

When you've found an album you might be interested in, you'll see some surprising niceties. As with more traditional online music stores, Amazon MP3 offers 30-second previews of each song, accessed from directly within the Web browser. Just click the little play button next to any song name, as shown in Figure 11-45, to get a preview.

Amazon also offers a wealth of customer reviews, its patented one-click ordering capability, and links to related music, including music that was purchased by people who also purchased the album you're currently viewing.

Figure 11-45: You won't need to launch a separate application to get song previews.

To purchase an album, click the button labeled Buy MP3 Album (or Buy MP3 Album with 1-Click). Alternately, you can purchase individual tracks by clicking the Buy MP3 button found next to each track name. Amazon provides a handy Amazon MP3 Downloader application that you can install on your PC, which you'll be prompted to do the first time you purchase a song or album. This application manages music downloads from the service. More important, it integrates with Windows Media Player (or, if you prefer, Apple iTunes), automatically adding any music you purchase from Amazon MP3 to your Windows Media Player–based media library.

Because it offers some configuration options, you may want to manually download the Amazon MP3 Downloader before purchasing any music. To do so, navigate to the Amazon MP3 store and click Getting Started. Then locate the link for downloading the Amazon MP3 Downloader and then download and install the application. Next, open the Start Menu and type **Amazon MP3 Downloader** to manually launch the application. (It will later launch automatically whenever you download music from Amazon.) From this application, select File ➪ Preferences. You'll see the dialog shown in Figure 11-46.

In the Media Library section, choose Add It to Windows Media Player from the drop-down list box so that songs downloaded from the service are automatically added to Windows Media Player. Then click OK and you're good to go.

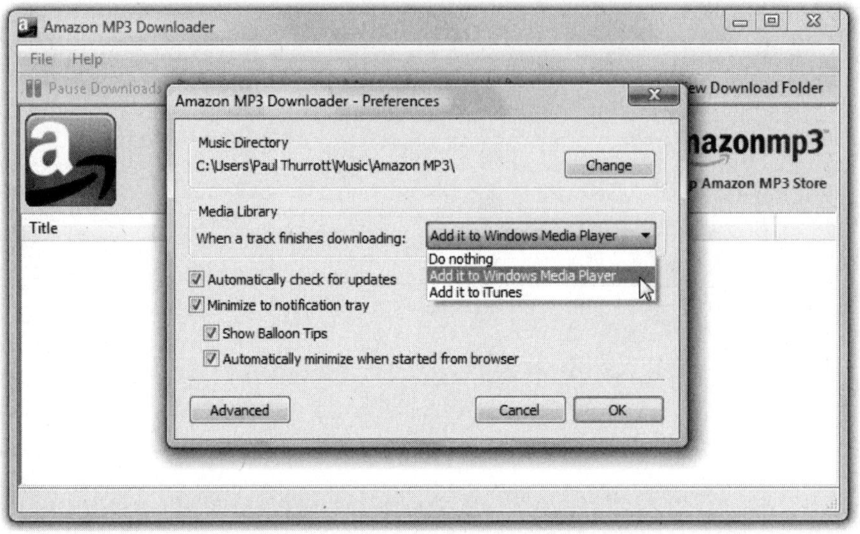

Figure 11-46: Amazon MP3 integrates with either Apple iTunes or Windows Media Player.

Now, when you purchase songs or albums from Amazon MP3, you don't have to worry about any management issues: They'll be downloaded directly to your Music folder (under an Amazon MP3 subfolder) and added to your Windows Media Player media library. *Voilà!*

Other Windows Media Player 11–Compatible Music Stores

Although URGE is pretty exciting, it isn't the only online music service game in town. To access other services that are compatible with Windows Media Player 11, you have to dig a little bit: Open the Online Services menu (by clicking the small arrow below the URGE button in the Media Player toolbar) and choose Browse All Online Stores. This will present you with options to install support for other services. It isn't possible to cover them all here, but a few do stand out, described in the following sections.

Audible.com

Audible.com, now owned by Amazon, offers over 40,000 audiobooks and other content, including newspapers. There's not much Windows Media Player integration here. Basically, what you get is the plain vanilla Audible.com Web page, loaded inside the Media Player. If you're interested in listening to Audible audiobooks on a portable player, you should ensure that the device is compatible: Audible maintains a useful database of devices that work and can help you download correctly formatted audiobooks.

eMusic

Like Audible, eMusic loads a basic version of its Web site inside Windows Media Player, but eMusic tackles a decidedly different market than Audible. This service focuses on low-cost unprotected MP3 music, and it offers billions of tracks. The catch is that most of these tracks are from no-name independent groups that you've probably never heard of. On the other hand, the tracks are cheap. Some eMusic songs can be had for as little as 33 cents. Furthermore, eMusic offers a subscription service—for a monthly fee, you can download a set number of songs.

Movielink

Movielink rents and sells digital video content, including TV shows and movies, both big budget and independent. The selection is somewhat sparse, at least compared to your local Blockbuster, but it's not horrible. As with other video services, Movielink encodes its films with DRM—in this case, Windows Media DRM, which is completely compatible with Windows Media Player and most Media Player–compatible portable video devices, but not much else. Note that if you do purchase a movie or TV show from Movielink, you can't edit it using the techniques discussed in Chapter 14.

MusicGiants

MusicGiants is a high-end music service with a twist: Its songs are all encoded in a perfect, pristine format known as *lossless*. This type of music is compressed, as are virtually all digital music files, but in a way in which none of the original quality is lost. MusicGiants utilizes the lossless version of Windows Media Audio (WMA) and markets it as High Definition (HD) Music, in order to cash in on the current craze surrounding HDTV. Normally, I wouldn't recommend purchasing any WMA-encoded music, but because MusicGiant's tracks are lossless, you can burn them to CD and then re-rip them back to the computer using a more compatible format, such as MP3, without a huge loss in quality. If you're an audiophile, this is the service for you.

Napster

The predecessor to Napster was the original file-sharing phenomenon and the reason why peer-to-peer (P2P) networking solutions still have such a bad name. The current version of Napster shares only the name with its predecessor, however. Today's Napster is a more traditional music service, offering both "a la carte" downloads of individual songs and albums and a subscription service that enables you to access any of the company's millions of songs for as long as you're paying. A Napster To Go service extends this offer to dozens of compatible portable audio devices. Unlike the other services, Napster requires a small software download, though you're also free to access the service via your Web browser.

Frankly, if you're new to the online music service market, Amazon.com is the best choice, thanks to its compatibility and Windows Media Player integration; but if you already have an account at Napster or another service, they're all still available—if somewhat deprecated—in Windows Media Player 11.

Secret   You can switch between any of the Media Player–compatible online music services at any time. After you've installed and configured any of the music services that are available from within Windows Media Player 11, you can simply open the Online Services menu and pick the service you'd like to use. You'll see an entry for each configured service.

Other Online Music Stores

As good as it is, Windows Media Player isn't the home of all online music stores. The most popular, *Apple iTunes Store,* is accessed via that company's PC software, offering music, movies, TV shows, music videos, audiobooks, podcasts, and other content, including iPod games. Apple's service has proven hugely popular with consumers largely because of its tie-in with iPods and the iPhone. In truth, it's a decent application in its own right, but the Windows version suffers from performance and stability issues.

www.apple.com/itunes

If you're more the subscription music kind of fan, the *Rhapsody* service might be of interest. As with Napster To Go, this service provides access to millions of tracks for a monthly fee, and it's compatible with a wide range of portable devices. Unlike Napster, however, Rhapsody must be accessed via a proprietary RealNetworks application, which I find a bit bizarre and hard to use.

www.rhapsody.com

Finally, as mentioned earlier, Microsoft has followed in the footsteps of Apple and created a separate digital music platform called *Zune* that closely mimics the iPod/iTunes ecosystem. Microsoft's contribution to this market isn't just a copycat, however; the Zune portable players, PC software, and online services all offer features and functionality that's nowhere to be found on the iPod or iTunes, and because it's from Microsoft and likely the future of the company's digital media efforts, Zune is covered in its own chapter, Chapter 12.

www.zune.net

Windows Media Player Alternatives

While at one time it seemed as if Microsoft's simple inclusion of Windows Media Player in Windows would be enough to catapult that software to ubiquity, a funny thing happened on the way to that imagined future: It never happened. Sure, Windows Media Player is indeed still the most popular media player software on earth, but the gap is closing, and fast, with Apple's iTunes, thanks to that software's tie-in with the iPod, a portable media player family so popular that it revived Apple's financial fortunes. As it turns out, iTunes isn't the only viable Windows Media Player alternative around; depending on your needs, you may find one or more of these alternatives compelling. Remember: There's no need to limit yourself to a single media player. Different players provide different services, and you may find that installing two or more of these options makes the most sense; all of the media players mentioned here are free or at least are offered in free versions.

Secret

The best reason to have a few different players floating around on your PC is compatibility: While it's possible to download software that makes Windows Media Player compatible with different audio and video formats, it's often far easier and less problematic to simply download a more compatible player. Apple's media players, for example, excel at playing back the increasingly common H.264 video format, a derivative of MPEG-4 that is notoriously unfriendly with Windows Media Player.

Apple iTunes

It's impossible to discuss Windows Media Player and media players in general without at least a passing reference to Apple iTunes, the fastest-growing media player on the market today. Compared to Windows Media Player, iTunes is a resource hog and runs more slowly, but it's natively compatible with iPods and iPhones and will always be the first to work with Apple's latest devices. But there's another great reason to buy into the Apple ecosystem: Only iTunes offers such a full range of purchasable (and, in the case of movies, rentable) content through the iTunes Store, which you access directly from within the iTunes PC application. Apple iTunes is free, and you can use it without an iPod. It's a credible all-in-one challenger to Windows Media Player, despite its flaws.

www.apple.com/itunes

Apple QuickTime Player and QuickTime Pro

In addition to iTunes, Apple also provides its QuickTime Player software, which is a far simpler media player that's geared largely to video playback. It's especially well suited to MPEG-4 formats such as H.264, which is becoming increasingly popular. QuickTime is a prerequisite for iTunes and is free, but a commercial version called QuickTime Pro offers simple video editing features.

www.apple.com/quicktime

GOM Player

If you're not an Apple fan or you merely want a simple and fast video player that can play H.264 movies, plus those encoded in a host of other formats, including DivX, XviD, FLV1, AC3, OGG, MP4, H.263, and others, GOM Player is a great choice. It's small, fast, and free, and the player will help you automatically find any required codecs if it runs into a video file it can't normally play. This player can't replace Windows Media Player—it's really just for video playback—but it's a great tool to have in your arsenal just in case.

www.gomplayer.com

Media Player Classic

Before Microsoft created the all-in-one version of Windows Media Player whose latest version you know and love today, the company included a far simpler version of Windows Media Player in older Windows versions. Some still miss that old player, so a free version, called Media Player Classic, is now available from the open-source community. Despite its simple UI, Media Player Classic does a lot more than the software on which it is based. It can be used to play DVD movies, and supports a variety of video codecs (including QuickTime and RealVideo). As with many of these other players, the emphasis here is on video and simplicity.

http://sourceforge.net/project/showfiles.php?group_id=205650&package_id=245753

Microsoft Zune

As noted frequently throughout this chapter, Microsoft's Zune platform is covered in detail in Chapter 12, but note here that the Zune PC software can be used to manage music and video libraries, just like Windows Media Player, and you don't have to buy a Zune device to take advantage of this elegant and interesting (if overly simple) software. If you find Windows Media Player to be a bit complex and you aren't interested in syncing with a Windows-compatible portable media device, Zune may be of interest. It also represents a serious attempt by Microsoft to completely rethink the concept of media player software, so despite many surface similarities to Windows Media Player, it's really quite different, and in a fun way. It's also natively compatible with the H.264 video format, which is increasingly important.

www.zune.net

RealNetworks RealPlayer

Once a mainstay in every PC user's digital media toolbox, RealNetworks' RealPlayer has fallen on hard times. Like Windows Media Player, RealPlayer started out as a much simpler bit of software, aimed in this case mostly at streaming Web audio and video, but it evolved over time into a formidable all-in-one media player. Today's RealPlayer comes in free and paid (Plus) versions, but both provide a plethora of functionality and compatibility, not to mention some unique new features, which is why RealPlayer is still interesting today: If you enjoy all those YouTube-type videos that are so popular these days, you may be interested in knowing that RealPlayer enables you to download Web videos—like those from YouTube—to your hard drive, so you can enjoy them offline.

www.realplayer.com

VLC Media Player

As with GOM Player, VLC Media Player is small, fast, and free, offering a simple video player alternative that's compatible out of the box with a wide range of video formats. Unlike GOM Player, however, VLC Media Player can also be used with various Web-based video streams, so it's a viable alternative to QuickTime and other solutions that act as front ends to videos you stream rather than download.

www.videolan.org/vlc

WinAmp

When Microsoft first began working on the all-in-one version of Windows Media Player almost a decade ago, the big media player online was WinAmp, a hackerific and quirky free download. Today, WinAmp is owned by AOL, and the player itself has adapted to the times by adopting many of the all-in-one features that made Windows Media Player so popular. But the quirkiness remains, and that's part of the appeal of WinAmp. While I can't personally get too excited by this product, I know a lot of people who still rely on it and love its unique design. WinAmp works in a completely different way than Windows Media Player, but it offers many of the same features. If you're looking for a true alternative to Windows Media Player, this may just be it.

www.winamp.com

Summary

Windows Media Player 11 is the most full-featured version of Media Player yet, with a simpler and more visual user interface, awesome media-sharing capabilities, and integration with some of the most exciting online music and video services ever offered. You can even make Windows Media Player 11 work with Apple's stunning iPod. There are plenty of free competitors out there, but many Windows Vista users will find everything they need right there in Windows Media Player. If not, you might want to check out Microsoft's Zune, which you can take a closer look at in the next chapter.

Zune: A Digital Media Alternative

Chapter
12

◆ ◆

◆ ◆

Microsoft surprised everyone in late 2006 by introducing its Zune digital media platform, an integrated set of software, services, and hardware that competes both with market leader Apple and with its own older digital media initiative, the Windows Media Player–based PlaysForSure. The first Zune didn't really take the world by storm, but a second-generation platform released a year later is much more impressive and provides a look at the future of Microsoft's digital media platform. This chapter examines the Zune platform, including the Zune PC software, the Zune Marketplace online store, the Zune Social Web-based community, and various Zune portable media devices, including the Zune 4, 8, 30, and 80.

> **tip**
>
> OK, Microsoft's Zune platform isn't designed specifically for Windows Vista—it runs on Windows XP as well—and it's not included in the box with Windows Vista like most of the features and products discussed elsewhere in this book. So why include an entire chapter about a software, hardware, and services player that essentially competes with what is included in Windows Vista? As I'll explain in a bit, whereas Windows Media Player is a nod to the past, Zune is Microsoft's digital media mulligan, an attempt at a do-over. If the company could bundle Zune in Windows, it would; but because of heightened antitrust regulations around the word, Microsoft is instead keeping Zune separate, much in the same way that it's pulled various Windows Live services out of Windows. I cover those services in Chapter 21. I'm covering Zune here because it's an important product that extends Vista's capabilities in useful and exciting ways. Zune, like Vista, *is* the future.

Why Zune?

Over the past decade, Microsoft has found that translating its success in operating systems into other markets isn't always a sure thing. Yes, its Microsoft Office productivity suite is a blockbuster success, and its enterprise-oriented Windows Server products aren't too shabby either, but these products are all obviously related. And Microsoft's Windows, Office, and Windows Server products are, in fact, responsible for almost all of the company's revenues.

That's the problem. Success has eluded most of Microsoft's other products, including its digital media products, its Xbox video game business, and its Live and MSN online services. In each case, Microsoft's dominance in operating systems and office productivity software hasn't helped it expand successfully into other markets.

What's surprising about Microsoft's failure in the digital media market is that it actually does bundle its excellent Windows Media Player software with Windows, and it's done so for several years now. Despite this, Apple has taken a dominant position in the market with its iPod and iPhone portable devices, its iTunes PC software and iTunes Store online service, and related products such as the Apple TV set-top box. Apple's success is well-deserved—its products are routinely highly rated and are, in fact, almost universally excellent—but it has caused Microsoft's competing solution, based around Windows Media Player, to first falter and then fail in the market.

That solution, which was once called PlaysForSure, sought to duplicate Microsoft's experiences in the PC market. Microsoft created the software based on its Windows Media platform, consisting of Windows Media Player, Windows Media and Audio formats, Windows

Media DRM (Digital Rights Management) for content protection, and much more. However, the company relied on a variety of hardware partners to design, ship, and market a set of competing portable devices and hardware, much like different PC makers make PCs. It also relied on a second set of partners to create online services for music, movies, and other content, all built on Windows Media.

It sounded like a great idea, but it wasn't really a great idea because Microsoft couldn't control the entire process. Even though it might introduce new platform features, it had to wait for the hardware makers and services to implement support, and when Apple came along with a centralized solution, controlled and designed by a single company, consumers took note. Today, PlaysForSure is essentially dead in the sense that you won't see PlaysForSure logos on any products at your local electronics retailer. Sure, numerous portable devices (made by companies such as Creative, Samsung, Sandisk, and others) still work just fine with Windows Media Player and online services such as Amazon Unbox, CinemaNow, and Napster, but the PlaysForSure ship has sailed, people, and the biggest indication that that's true is the fact that Microsoft, the originator of PlaysForSure and its underlying Windows Media platform, has moved on to something else, something called Zune.

Secret

To be fair to Windows Media, the platform has a lot of life left in it, and as you discovered in Chapter 11, Windows Media Player is, in particular, an excellent bit of software. According to Microsoft, it intends to co-develop both Windows Media and Zune, though the PlaysForSure logo program has been discontinued and rolled into the more nebulous Designed for Windows Vista logo program (which, to my knowledge, few device makers and services have embraced with any particular gusto). Moreover, Microsoft is indeed improving its Windows Media Player software with new versions, which will appear in the future and in the next version of Windows after Windows Vista. All that said, Microsoft is throwing considerable resources at Zune and will improve this platform dramatically in the years ahead. If you're a gambler, this is the obvious pick.

Zune 1.0

To the cynical, Microsoft's Zune platform is a fairly transparent copy of the Apple play-book. As with Apple's iTunes platform, Zune is centrally controlled by a single team, in this case from Microsoft. Like Apple's platform, Zune includes PC software for organizing and playing music and other content, accessing an online store, and managing compatible portable devices. Put another way, Zune is a closed platform, as is Apple's. The Zune devices work only with the Zune PC software, and the Zune PC software can't be used to manage any non-Zune devices. The advantages of this kind of solution are tighter integration between hardware and software and, in the case of Zune, a growing set of online services.

It's nice when it works out that way, but whereas Apple has gotten almost everything right with its iPod, iTunes, and related solutions, Microsoft has stumbled a bit as it tries to find its way. Today's Zune is a dramatic improvement over the first iteration, and no doubt future versions will be even better, but the Zune is an evolving platform. As such, it has as many deficits as advantages.

Microsoft shipped the first Zune version in late 2006. There was a single Zune hardware device, the since-renamed Zune 30, which came in a classic iPod form factor and included a 30GB hard disk for storage. The Zune hardware was decent if unexceptional, but the first Zune software—shown in Figure 12-1—was almost comically bad. It was essentially a rebranded version of Windows Media Player with a weird gray skin. Zune's online store, Zune Marketplace, was accessed via this software interface.

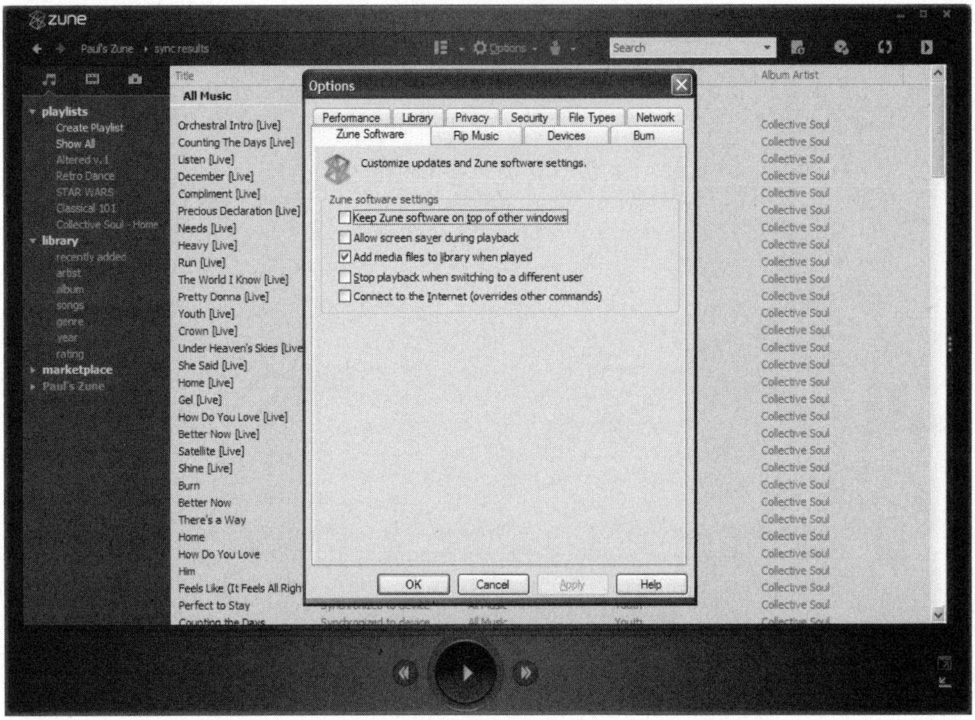

Figure 12-1: The first Zune software was just an ugly skin on top of Windows Media Player.

Was it successful? I guess that depends on how you define successful. Microsoft sold about 1.5 million Zune 1.0 devices in its first year on the market, just a tiny fraction of the number of iPods that Apple sold during the same time period; but Microsoft can and did accurately claim that this level of sales was enough to catapult the Zune to the number two position in the market for hard-drive-equipped MP3 players (behind, yes, the iPod—way behind). Just by entering this market, even with a decidedly lackluster product, Microsoft was able to immediately outsell all of the PlaysForSure and non-Apple competition. That's actually not too shabby.

Zune 2.0

The less that's said about Microsoft's first version of Zune, the better. For the second iteration of the Zune platform, Microsoft set its sights considerably higher and the results were predictably more favorable. There are more devices, new device capabilities (all of which, amazingly, were ported back to the original Zune device), new PC software, a completely redesigned Zune Marketplace, a completely new Zune Social online community service, and even new hardware accessories (which, yes, will also work with older Zunes), if you're into that kind of thing.

This chapter closely examine all of these changes—except for those new hardware accessories, sorry. First, however, allow me to present the best Zune secret of all.

Secret   You don't need to buy a Zune device to use the Zune software, Zune Marketplace, or Zune Social. The Zune software is freely available to anyone running Windows XP or Windows Vista, as are the online services. That means you can very easily check out Microsoft's alternative digital media platform without first plunking down hundreds of dollars on a portable device.

By itself, the Zune PC software is an excellent alternative to Windows Media Player, so we'll look at that first.

Media Player Alternative: A Look at the Zune PC Software

Anyone with Windows Vista or Windows XP can download and install the Zune PC software. It's free and is in many ways a better media player than Windows Media Player 11, which ships as part of Vista. Is Zune good enough to make you forego other media players? I don't think so. Zune is missing a few commonsense features that most readers will find necessary, but its cool design and tight integration with online services and Zune devices is sure to win many people over. The following sections take a closer look.

Finding and Installing Zune

Like Apple, Microsoft no longer bundles its digital media software with its devices. Instead, it directs users to the Zune Web site (**www.zune.net**), where they can download the latest version of the Zune PC software. This is a smart move because Microsoft, again like Apple, updates their software fairly regularly. (Not providing an install disk also enables Microsoft to create smaller and more eco-friendly Zune packaging. You know, just like Apple.)

In addition, as is true with iTunes, you don't need a device to take advantage of most of this player's features. It works just fine as a standalone media player. You may find it taking the place of Windows Media Player for many of your day-to-day digital media playing needs.

The Zune Web site, shown in Figure 12-2, is kind of a mess, but from here you can do a number of things, including download the Zune software, which is what I'm going to focus on here.

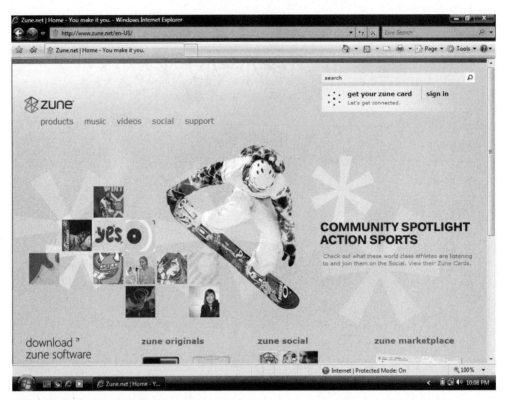

Figure 12-2: When it comes to Zune marketing, there's sometimes a gap between what's really hip and what Microsoft thinks is hip.

When you do navigate to the Zune software download page, you have two options: Sign Up and Download or just Download. The former option steps you through a wizard that creates what's called a Zune tag for you. This Zune tag, which is tied to a Windows Live ID (typically a hotmail.com or live.com e-mail address) can be valuable, especially if you want to take advantage of Zune's so-called social features. It is also a necessity if you ever plan to purchase music or other content from Zune's online store, Zune Marketplace. However, you don't need to configure a Zune tag just to use the Zune PC software, so we can skip that for now. You'll look at Zune tags and related issues later in the chapter.

Secret

Make sure you download the correct version of the Zune software. Microsoft makes separate 32-bit (x86) and 64-bit (x64) versions available. If you're unsure, you almost certainly need the 32-bit version, but you can find out in the System Properties window (Start Menu Search and enter **System**) whether you're running a 32-bit or 64-bit version of Vista.

Installing Zune is fairly straightforward. The setup application presents a simple wizard that installs the software and gets you up and running quickly without reboots. When setup is complete, you'll be confronted with the screen shown in Figure 12-3. You can customize settings at this point or jump right into the player. I strongly recommend taking the time to customize settings. As with Windows Media Player, it's not wise to accept Microsoft's default settings.

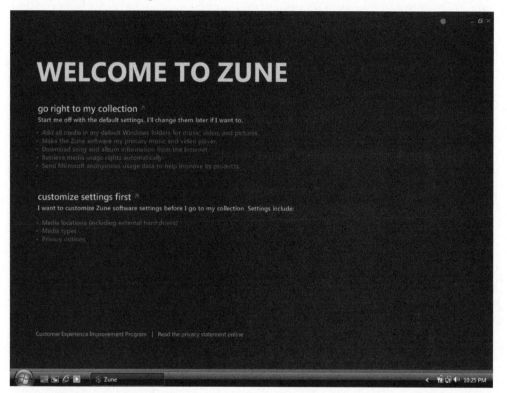

Figure 12-3: Never accept the defaults from Microsoft. Customizing is key to making Zune work the way you want it to.

If you do skip the customization step here, you can always customize the Zune PC software settings later by clicking the Settings link in the upper-right corner of the Zune application window. In fact, even if you do customize settings right away, you should visit the link later, as Settings offers more options than what are exposed in the original wizard.

Configuring the Zune Software

If you opted to customize settings first, the Setup wizard moves into a three-step phase whereby you can configure collection, file type, and privacy settings. The first entry, Collection, refers to the media collection that you organize and enjoy in the Zune PC software. As shown in Figure 12-4, you can configure Monitored Folders, just like in Windows Media Player, as well as related options, such as whether Zune should automatically update missing album artwork. Leave this option checked, as Zune is particularly good at replacing missing artwork.

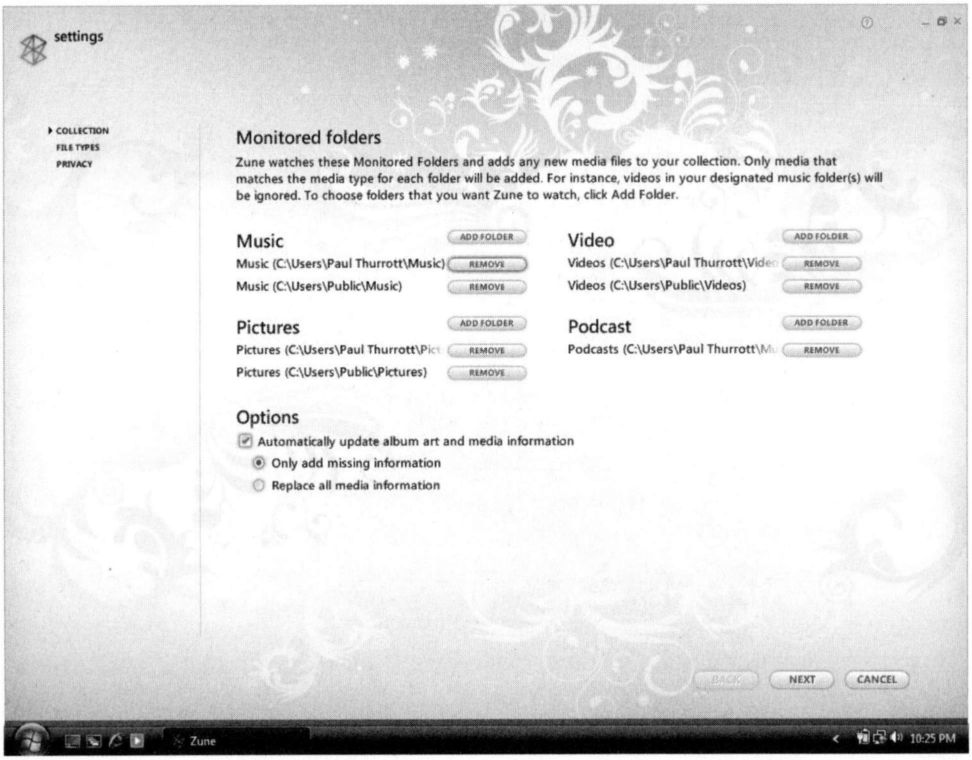

Figure 12-4: Monitored Folders determines where Zune looks for content.

Unlike Windows Media Player, Zune enables you to remove default locations such as your Music, Pictures, and Videos folders from the Monitored Folders list. I've never understood why this wasn't possible in Windows Media Player; after all, many users prefer to locate media in other locations and forego Microsoft's default folder structure.

In the next step of the wizard, you determine the file types for which Zune will be the default player. Zune's format compatibility is an interesting combination of Windows Media Player and Apple iTunes. It supports Microsoft formats such as WMA and WMV, open formats such as MP3 and JPEG, but also Apple-friendly formats such as MPEG-4, H.264, and AAC.

Secret What Zune can't do, unfortunately, is play any protected content purchased from the iTunes Store, so most music and all TV shows, movies, and audiobooks purchased from iTunes are still incompatible with Zune.

Until you're ready to commit to Zune full-time, you may want to unselect all the formats presented by the wizard, retaining their current default players. Later, when you've grown comfortable with Zune, you can decide whether to switch, just use it for certain file types, or dump it altogether.

Secret How do you change these settings later? You can always access Zune's Settings dialog, of course, but Windows Vista includes a handy Default Programs applet that works even better. Just open the Start Menu and select Default Programs. Then, in the window that appears, choose Set Your Default Programs. Then, from the list that appears, select Zune (and/or other media player applications) and configure accordingly. For example, if you'd like Zune to be the default player for every file type with which it is compatible, you can select Zune from the list and then click the link titled Set This Program as the Default. To use Zune for only certain file types, click Choose Defaults for This Program Instead.

In the wizard's next step you can choose whether you want to automatically and silently participate in Microsoft's Customer Experience Improvement Program. I recommend doing so. Microsoft uses the anonymous data it collects to improve its software, and the results of this program have had enormously positive impacts on software as diverse as Windows, Office, and Zune.

Once that's done, the setup wizard ends and you're dumped into the Zune player's main user interface. (If you already have content on your PC, it's copied into Zune's media library. You'll look at that in the next section, however.) First, click the Settings link in the upper-right corner of the application window. This provides the three settings areas configured earlier, but it also includes a number of others, as shown in Figure 12-5.

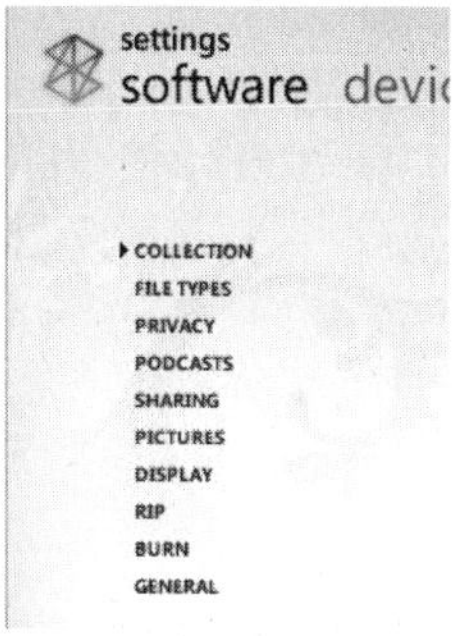

settings
software devi

▶ COLLECTION
FILE TYPES
PRIVACY
PODCASTS
SHARING
PICTURES
DISPLAY
RIP
BURN
GENERAL

Figure 12-5: The Zune setup wizard provides only some of the options you can configure in Zune.

These additional settings include the following:

◆ **Podcasts:** Podcasts are the Internet's answer to radio, although they are pre-recorded audio files, not live streams. More important, podcast support is one of many advantages that Zune has over Windows Media Player. Unlike the bundled media player that comes in Vista, Zune actually understands and works natively with podcasts, enabling you to subscribe and listen to these unique content types in logical ways. In the Podcasts settings, you determine how many episodes of each podcast to keep and how they will be ordered for playback.

◆ **Sharing:** The Sharing settings pane includes options for standard PC-to-PC media sharing as well as sharing between the Zune PC software and Xbox 360 video game consoles. You will look more closely at this functionality later in the chapter.

◆ **Pictures:** This simplistic settings pane provides just a single option: the length of time each photo will display during a photo slide show.

◆ **Display:** Display settings enable you to customize the Zune application window with any of six possible background designs and configure onscreen animations and video enhancements.

◆ **Rip:** Rip settings offer a simple front end for various options related to CD ripping. Key among these, of course, is the format used. Zune defaults to WMA for some reason, but you should change this to 256 Kbps MP3 or higher for maximum compatibility and reasonable quality.

◆ **Burn:** Burn settings are, of course, dedicated to Zune's CD and DVD burning capabilities. The application can burn audio CDs and data CDs or DVDs. You can also configure whether the disk is ejected on burn completion, and the burning speed.

◆ **General:** The General settings pane includes a few fairly innocuous options, but one is quite important: Media Folder determines where Zune stores content that is generated through the Zune software, including ripped CDs, Zune Marketplace purchases, and subscribed podcasts. By default, the application uses a folder named Zune, which is located under your Music folder. If you'd like to change this (you might even consider just using the Music folder, for example), here is the place to do it.

When you're done configuring these various options, click the OK button. You'll be returned to the main application view.

Using Zune

The Zune user interface, shown in Figure 12-6, is a breath of fresh air compared to more staid digital media applications like Windows Media Player and, especially, Apple iTunes. This is by design. After basing the first version of its Zune PC software on Windows Media Player, Microsoft went back to the drawing board and built its Zune 2.x software from the ground up as a brand-new application. The result is visually stimulating and, frankly, kind of pretty. It is, however, lacking a few of the power-user features you may have come to expect from Windows Media Player. That's what happens when you start from scratch, I guess.

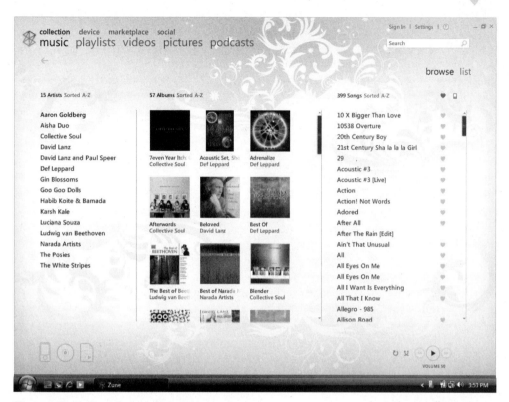

Figure 12-6: Zune is attractive and easy to use.

Secret   You may be interested to know that the Zune 2.x user interface was created by the same visual designers at Microsoft who were responsible for the UI of Windows Vista's Windows Media Center. This team's year-long involvement with Zune, in fact, helps explain why the follow-up to Windows Media Center, code-named Fiji, has been delayed. Presumably, they're back to work on Fiji now that Zune 2 has shipped.

Zune utilizes a single application window and typically uses a columnar display to present content in different, visual ways. There are four main UI zones, or parts, in Zune:

♦ **Collection:** This default view shows the collection of media you have on your PC and are managing with Zune. It is in turn divided into subzones such as Music, Playlists, Videos, Pictures, and Podcasts. Each represents content that is stored locally on your PC. I will examine the Zune's Collection zone throughout this part of the chapter.

◆ **Device:** This view pertains to any Zune device (or devices) you own and have linked to this particular PC's collection. It is divided into subzones such as Status, Music, Playlists, Videos, Pictures, and Podcasts. I will look at this zone and how Zune devices work at the end of the chapter.

◆ **Marketplace:** This view connects to Microsoft's online store and presents Zune Marketplace. There are currently three subzones—Music, Podcasts, and Downloads—though I expect more to be added in the future. I describe Zune's online services later in this chapter.

◆ **Social:** Here you can access your Zune tag/Windows Live ID/Xbox 360 Gamertag Inbox, which is much like e-mail but not nearly as useful. Don't worry; I'll explain this later in the chapter as well.

First, however, it's time to take a look at the main reason so many people are interested in Zune: digital music.

The Zune User Experience

Regardless of where you are in the Collection view, a few common elements are available. The Collection, Device, Marketplace, and Social links are common to all parts of the Zune UI, as are the Sign In, Settings, and Help links in the upper-right corner of the application window. On the bottom is a series of three icons on the left (see Figure 12-7).

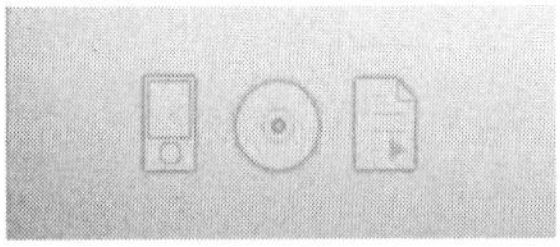

Figure 12-7: Inscrutable? Maybe.
Useful? You bet.

These are, from left to right, as follows:

◆ **Device:** If you have a Zune portable device, you can access its sync status and other information from this first icon.

◆ **Disk:** From here you can access Zune's disk play, rip, or burn functionality. You can also drag songs here to create a burn playlist, which is used to create a custom audio CD.

◆ **Playlist:** This icon enables you to create new playlists, access existing playlists, and add songs to the current playlist.

What you see in the bottom center of the application window depends on what's going on. If you're not playing any content, adding media, or performing other tasks, it is empty. When you're playing back some kind of content, you'll find a playback timeline with the name of the media, the elapsed time, and the remaining time, as shown in Figure 12-8.

Collective Soul

1:52   -1:51

Figure 12-8: This timeline appears only
when you actually play content.

Finally, on the bottom right of the application window, you'll see the playback controls shown in Figure 12-9. These controls include what you would expect: Play/Stop, Previous, and Next, as well as Repeat and Shuffle toggles. A final curious-looking pink icon launches Zune's amazing Now Playing view, which I'll examine shortly.

VOLUME 50

Figure 12-9: Zune's playback controls include the usual suspects plus one that's not so familiar.

If you mouse over the Volume text below the playback controls, you'll get a volume slider that you can use to adjust the playback volume.

Enjoying Music

In the Music view you get a three-pane look at your music collection (see Figure 12-10). On the left is a textual list of artists, which can be sorted alphabetically or in reverse alphabetical order. In the center, widest pane, are your albums, in graphical album art splendor; these can be sorted alphabetically, in reverse alphabetical order, by release year, or by date added. On the right is a list of songs. These are sorted alphabetically, in reverse alphabetical order, by track number, or by rating.

Figure 12-10: The Music experience provides an attractive three-pane view.

Secret

Sorting these columns in not obvious, but here's how it works: If you mouse over any of the three column headings, the heading name will be highlighted in gray. To change the sort type, just click this heading. It will toggle through each available option as you click.

Suppose you want to drill into your music collection. If you select an artist from the left-most Artists pane, the middle and right panes change to reflect this choice, as shown in Figure 12-11. For example, when I select Collective Soul in my own collection, I see whatever Collective Soul albums I own in the middle Albums pane, and on the right, in the Songs pane, there's a list of all of the Collective Soul songs in my collection.

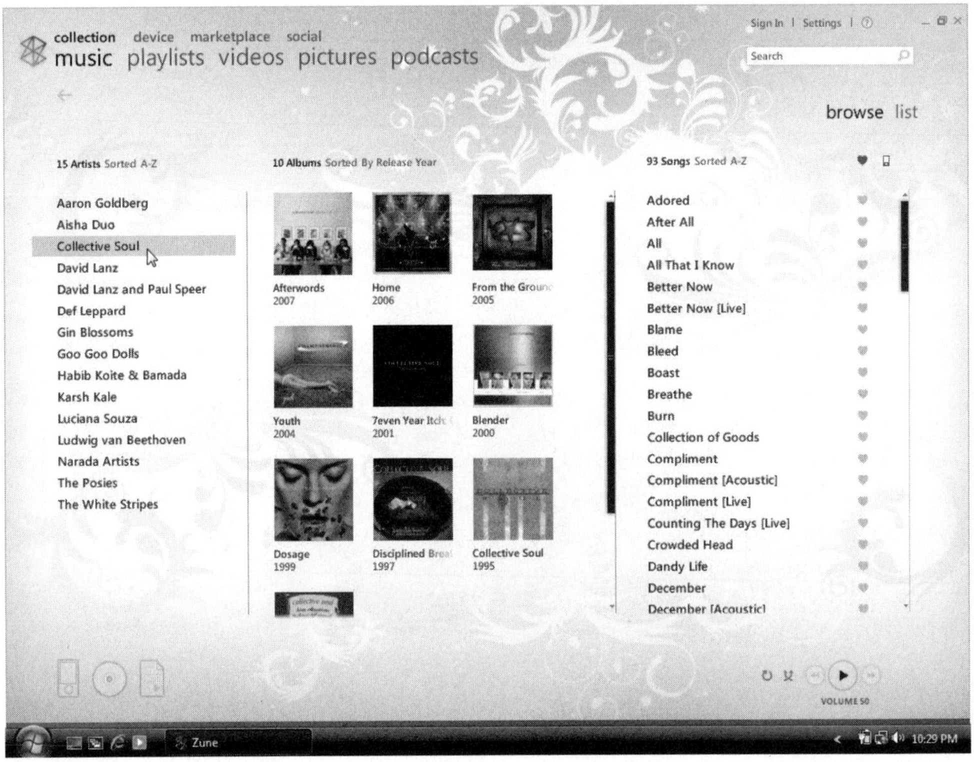

Figure 12-11: Filtering the view to a single artist.

You can drill down further, of course. If you select an individual album in the Albums pane, that album becomes selected and the Songs list is constrained to only those songs in the selected album, as shown in Figure 12-12.

To play an album or song just double-click the item. The first song in the album (or the individual song you selected) will begin playing immediately. Meanwhile, a few things change in the Zune UI. The playback timeline appears, a small Now Playing icon appears next to the currently playing song in the Songs pane, and the Play button changes to Pause.

This is probably a good time to point out Zune's amazing Now Playing screen. You enable it by clicking the pink Now Playing button to the right of the Next button in the playback controls area. Alternately, you can click the Now Playing icon to the left of the currently playing song in the Songs pane. Either way, the Zune player UI switches to Now Playing mode, shown in Figure 12-13.

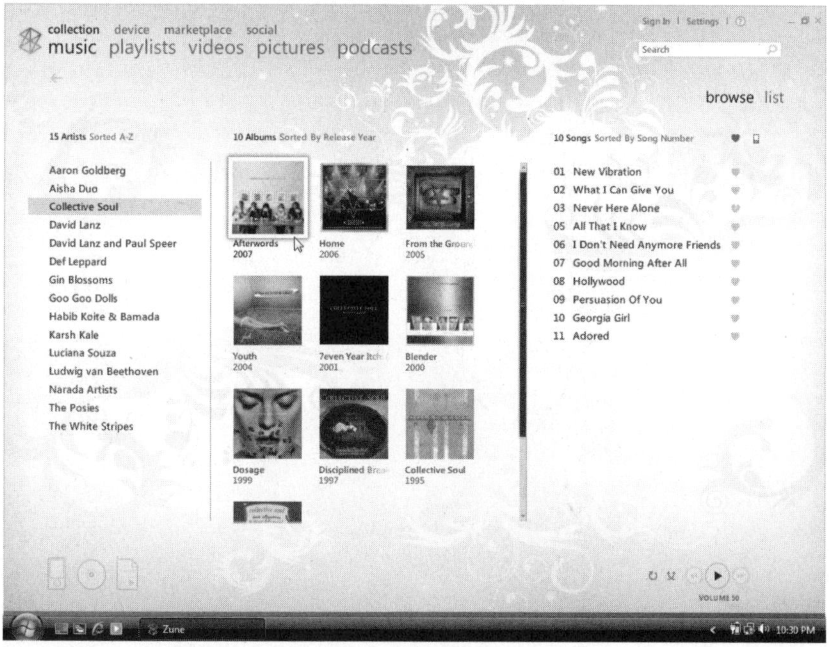

Figure 12-12: Filtering the view to a single album.

Figure 12-13: The Zune Now Playing mode is particularly impressive looking.

There's some information about the currently playing song over a cool backdrop made up of your collection's album art. In addition, temporarily, you'll also see the current playlist (what's displayed in the Songs pane), the playback timeline, and the playback controls. When you move the mouse off these elements they fade away, as shown in Figure 12-14.

Figure 12-14: Stop moving the mouse and most of the onscreen fluff disappears.

To close Now Playing, click the Exit button in the bottom right corner of the player window.

Rating Content

While media players such as Windows Media Player and Apple iTunes support a ratings system whereby each song (or other content) can be rated on a scale from 1 to 5 (or from 0 to 5 if you consider no rating a 0), Microsoft has simplified this to the bare minimum in Zune. Instead of five stars, you can assign three different ratings:

- ◆ **Unrated:** In this case, the item has not been rated.
- ◆ **I Don't Like It:** This rating is reserved for songs and other items you specifically do not like.
- ◆ **I Like It:** This rating, of course, applies to songs and other content you enjoy.

What's interesting about the Zune rating system is that if you've already rated songs in either Windows Media Player or iTunes and then later install Zune, the Zune PC software will import your existing ratings and convert them to Zune-friendly values. Songs you've rated as 3 to 5 stars will be given the "I Like It" rating. Songs you've rated as 1 or 2 will receive "I Don't Like It." Unrated songs, of course, remain unrated.

Finally, Zune also uses cute little heart icons to represent each rating. The I Like It rating is a solid heart, while the I Don't Like It rating, humorously, is represented by a broken heart. Unrated songs get no heart. Each icon option is shown in Figure 12-15.

Figure 12-15: Zune offers simpler ratings with cute icons.

To set or change ratings, just click the heart icon next to each song in the Songs pane. Each time you click, the rating will toggle to the next available value. (You can also right-click songs and choose an appropriate rating from the context menu that appears. This method works for rating multiple songs simultaneously, though of course each will be assigned the same rating.) You cannot rate an entire album by right-clicking it in the Albums pane.

Secret

As with Windows Vista itself, it's useful to remember that right-clicking throughout the Zune user interface can reveal some interesting features and options. The old adage is as relevant here as ever: When in doubt, right-click.

Working with Playlists

With most media players, including Windows Media Player and iTunes, rating songs is important because these ratings can be used to create automated playlists of songs that you can then use to create custom audio CDs or sync back to a portable device. For example, it's very easy to create a so-called smart playlist in Windows Media Player that includes only your very favorite songs (that is, those with 5-star ratings). And that's exactly the type of playlist one might like to sync back to whatever portable player one is using. Obviously.

Well, not to Microsoft. One of the things that got lost in the shuffle when the company re-architected its Zune PC software from scratch is that it no longer supports smart playlists that automatically update themselves as more content is added to the collection and/or rated. Instead, Zune only supports standard, manually created playlists. They're not as good as smart playlists, but they're still a powerful tool, and they can and should be used to create lists of songs you're going to burn to CD or copy to a Zune portable device.

Here's how they work. The songs listed in the Songs pane are basically a temporary playlist. This temporary playlist changes as you select different items in the Artists and Albums panes, and when you actually start playing a selection of songs, it becomes the Now Playing playlist. This, too, is temporary in that it's not saved to disk or synchronized with any portable players. It's ephemeral, existing in the Zen-like now.

Zune provides a number of ways to formally construct a playlist that has a name and is saved to disk, including the following:

◆ **The Playlists icon:** In the bottom left of the Zune application window is a Playlists icon. (The icon resembles a dog-eared sheet of paper with a Play symbol on it.) If you mouse over this icon, a pop-up menu appears. It has two options by default: Create Playlist and Now Playing. If you create other playlists, they'll appear in the list as well, so everything in this list other than Create Playlist is there so that you can make it the current playlist. If you click the Playlists icon, the Zune UI will send you to the Playlists sub-area in Collections.

◆ **Collection ⇨ Playlists:** From this sub-area you can create new playlists or view or edit any playlists you may have already created. If you do have one or more playlists, this view resembles Figure 12-16.

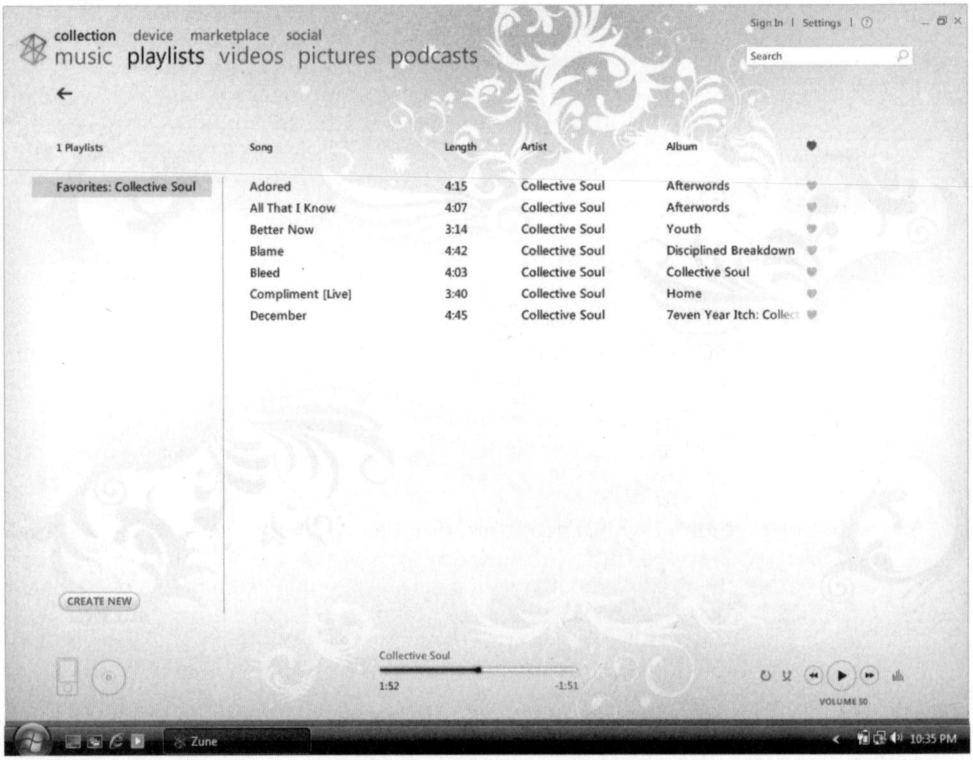

Figure 12-16: Zune doesn't support smart playlists, but you can still get a lot of use out of manual playlists.

◆ **Right-click:** A better way to interact with playlists is through the Zune software's right-click context menus. If you find some songs you'd like to add to a new or existing playlist, just select them, right-click, and choose Add to Playlist. When you do so, the Choose a Playlist dialog appears, shown in Figure 12-17. From here, you can select an existing playlist or click the Create New button to create a new playlist.

CHOOSE A PLAYLIST

Collective Soul

New songs

The Corrs

OK   CANCEL   CREATE NEW

Figure 12-17: From here, you can assign selected songs to particular playlists.

◆ **Drag and drop:** One of the more unexpected ways in which you can interact with playlists is similar to the right-click method except that you have to do a bit of work first. That is, you must mouse over the Playlists icon and either create a new playlist or select an existing playlist from the pop-up menu that appears; in either case that will become the active playlist. Then, you can find content in the Artists, Albums, or Songs pane that you'd like to make part of that playlist, select it, and drag it over to the Playlist icon (see Figure 12-18).

From the Playlists subzone, you can add items to the Burn list to burn them to a CD or DVD, in much the same manner as described above; drag and drop works just fine using the Disk icon you'll see there, as does the right-click menu. You can also use these methods to sync playlists to a device.

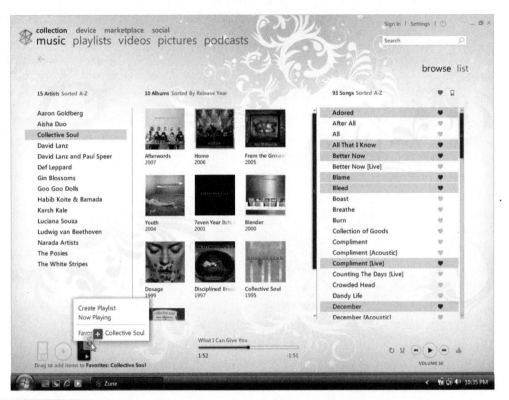

Figure 12-18: Content dragged onto the Playlists icon is added to the active playlist.

Working with Videos

Like Windows Media Player, Zune supports playing back various types of movies. There are some key differences between the two, however, including the following:

◆ **Windows Media Player has a more flexible UI:** WMP supports full, compact, skins, mini-player, and a true full-screen playback mode for videos. Zune is far less configurable. It has a nice-looking full-screen mode (Now Playing), but it's not truly full screen in that it doesn't even hide the Windows taskbar, as shown in Figure 12-19.

◆ **They support different video formats:** While there's some overlap—both Windows Media Player and Zune play nonprotected WMV files, for example—video format support differs in important ways between each player. For example, Windows Media Player can play DRM-protected WMV videos from services such as CinemaNow and MovieLink, which Zune cannot. More important, perhaps, WMP can play DVD movies: Zune can't. Zune isn't a completely lost cause, however: It handles MPEG-4 and H.264 movies just fine, formats that are increasingly common thanks to the iPod. (That said, Zune can't play DRM-protected videos purchased from the iTunes Store.)

Figure 12-19: It looks nice, but Zune's full-screen playback mode isn't really full screen.

The takeaway from all of this is that Zune cannot replace Windows Media Player when it comes to PC-based video playback. Instead, video support in the player seems to be there largely to facilitate synchronization with Zune devices.

tip   Syncing video with Zune devices works just like syncing music.

Organizing Pictures

Zune's support of pictures is likewise lackluster and seems to be oriented more toward device synchronization than actual PC playback. In this way the Zune software is much like Windows Media Player. It offers only basic picture viewing functionality, with simple slideshows. That said, the Zune does present folders of photos in a very visual way. As shown in Figure 12-20, folders of photos utilize a thumbnail and a large photo count within the Zune player.

Zune's slideshow also works within the pseudo full-screen mode that's provided for videos, as shown in Figure 12-21.

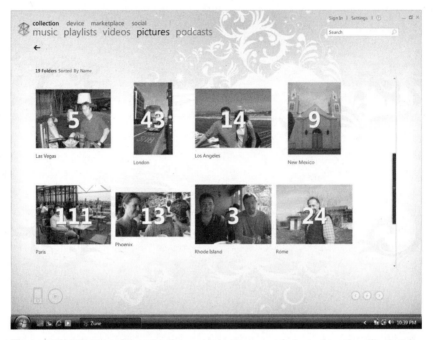

Figure 12-20: Zune doesn't offer much in the way of photo functionality, but its presentation of folders of photos is highly visual.

Figure 12-21: Photo slideshows utilize whatever playlist is currently playing for a full multimedia experience.

tip   Syncing photos with Zune devices works just like syncing music.

Radio in the 21st Century: Enjoying Podcasts with Zune

As the Internet's answer to radio broadcasts, podcasts are an awesome diversion, with topics ranging from the expected tech nonsense to travel, food, celebrity gossip, and more. In other words, it's just like radio but that's from a content perspective. The problem with podcasts is that in order to enjoy them effectively, you need a software client that can work with the underlying technologies that distribute and manage these recordings. (Perhaps not surprisingly, podcasts rely on a form of the RSS technologies discussed in Chapter 19.)

Windows Media Player is not such a client. While you can of course play podcast files with Windows Media Player—they are typically delivered as standard MP3 files, after all—this software has no understanding of the infrastructure that is used to post new podcast episodes. Thus, it is impossible to subscribe to podcasts with Windows Media Player.

Zune has no such problem. In fact, one of the major new features of the Zune 2 platform is that it's completely compatible with podcasts, so you can subscribe to podcasts with Zune and sync them with your Zune device if you have one.

First, you might want to configure how the Zune PC software handles podcasts. This is done via the Podcasts section in Zune Settings, as shown in Figure 12-22. Here, you can determine how many episodes you want to keep of each podcast (three is the default, but you can keep as few as one at a time or as many as all of them) and how the podcast episodes will be ordered (newest episodes first or oldest episodes first). Unfortunately, these settings are universal. You can't configure them differently for individual podcasts.

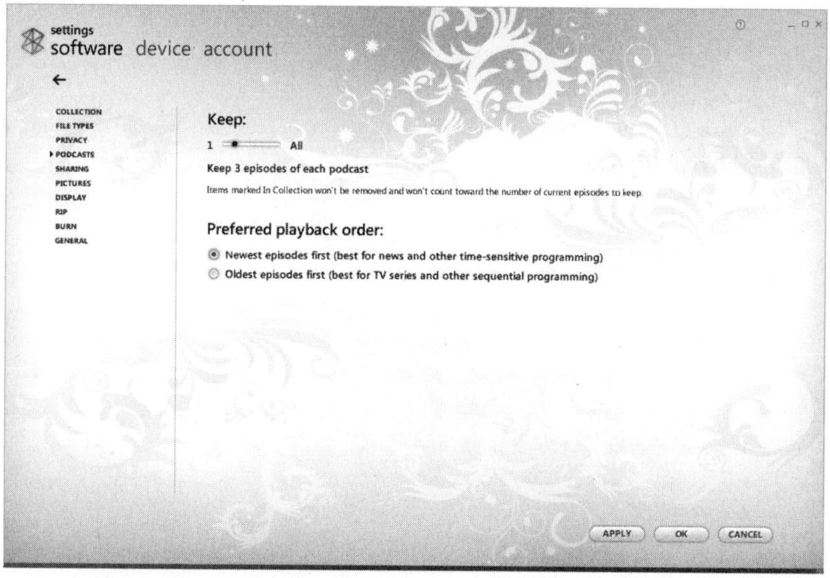

Figure 12-22: Before subscribing to any podcasts, you should configure how Zune handles podcast subscriptions and playback.

To subscribe to a podcast, you have two options. First, you can search podcasts via Zune Marketplace, which I discuss later in this chapter. As far as podcasts go, Zune Marketplace has a great selection and its integrated search tool and genre-browsing capabilities make finding the right podcasts short work. A typical podcast entry in Zune Marketplace is shown in Figure 12-23. As you can see, you can easily download an individual episode to try it out, or click the Subscribe button to begin receiving new episodes automatically.

Figure 12-23: Now there's a handsome devil.

A less well known method of subscribing to podcasts is via a standard RSS feed. To subscribe to a podcast this way, you need to visit the podcast's Web site in a Web browser and copy the URL for its RSS feed to your clipboard. Then, open the Zune PC software and navigate to Collection ⇨ Podcasts. In the lower left corner of the player is an Add a Podcast button. Click this button and then paste the RSS feed URL into the dialog that appears, as shown in Figure 12-24.

SUBSCRIBE

Enter the URL of the podcast you want to add, then click Subscribe.

http://leoville.tv/podcasts/ww.xml

(SUBSCRIBE)   (CANCEL)

Figure 12-24: It's low-tech, but this works too.

To test this, use a random podcast RSS feed URL such as, oh, say, **http://leoville.tv/podcasts/ww.xml**. You'll thank me someday.

Sharing Zune

If you're *really* living the digital media lifestyle, you might want to share the content in your Zune collection with other devices around your home, including PCs, digital media receivers, and the Xbox 360. Not surprisingly, this is all very possible.

Sharing with PCs and Other Windows Media Devices

Windows Vista already includes integrated digital media sharing features, and those features (described in the previous chapter) continue to work just fine if you choose to use the Zune PC software to manage your music. That's because Zune integrates with this underlying technology and shares, by default, the same monitored folders and media folders as Windows Media Player and Windows Media Center. As long as you've correctly configured media sharing as outlined in Chapter 11, it will work fine if you choose to use Zune instead of Windows Media Player.

Secret

Here's a shocker: This sharing ability extends even to DRM-protected music that you've purchased from Zune Marketplace.

Sharing with the Xbox 360

Zune also supports an optional media sharing feature that's aimed at the Xbox 360. If you have one of these devices and think you may want to stream music, movies, and other content from your Zune media library, you'll need to enable this functionality first. To do so, navigate to Settings ➪ Sharing. What you see should resemble Figure 12-25.

Click the button labeled Enable Media Sharing with Xbox 360. (It's actually labeled ENABLE MEDIA SHARING WITH XBOX 360 for some reason, but no matter.) Once you have done this, you can configure a few other sharing options, such as the name that will identify your media collection to the Xbox 360, which media types to share (music, video, and pictures are available, but only music is selected by default), and whether you want to share your media library with any nearby Xbox 360 or would prefer to specify a particular console. (The Zune-based PC and Xbox 360 must, of course, be on the same home network for the sharing feature to work.)

On the Xbox 360, media sharing is handled via the Media blade, just as it is for any other shared PC-based media libraries. To find your Zune, navigate to Zune and then choose Music. Click the blue X button on the Xbox 360 controller to choose a music source. You might see any number of sources depending on how many PCs and media libraries are available on your home network. In general, your Zune-based PC should be represented twice, once for the Media Connect/Windows Media Player–based library, and once for Zune. These entries take the form

MACHINE-NAME: User-Name

MACHINE-NAME: Zune-Collection-Name (Zune)

where the top entry is a Media Connect shared library and the bottom one is a Zune shared library. On my notebook computer named VISTABOOK, for example, I see the following entries:

VISTABOOK: Paul Thurrott

VISTABOOK: Paul's Zune (Zune)

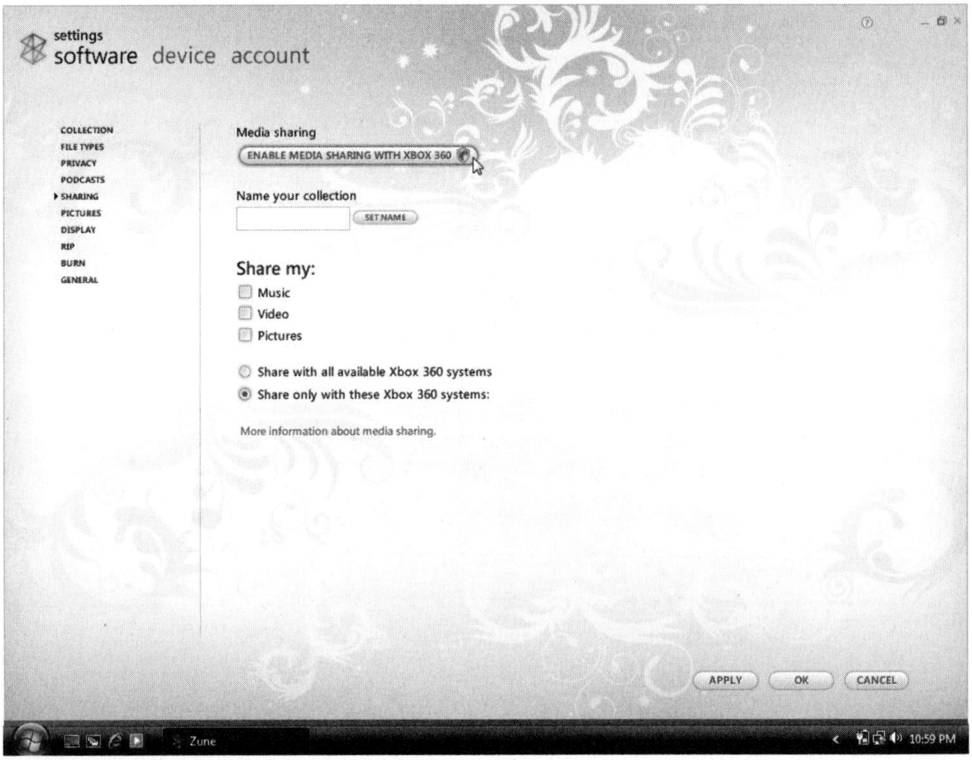

Figure 12-25: From this screen you can determine whether Zune will share its media library with one or more Xbox 360s in your home.

Both entries have the machine name as VISTABOOK. The top one uses the name with which I log on to Windows because it's a Media Connect share. The bottom one uses the name "Paul's Zune" because that's the name I configured in the Settings ➪ Sharing screen in the Zune UI on that machine. Both shares are on the same PC and both could theoretically be pointing to exactly the same content (or not, depending on how you chose to configure monitored folders in each). In addition, differing file format compatibility could lead to slightly different library content, even if they are pointing to the same file locations.

After you're connected, you can browse and play media from the Zune library just as you would from a Media Connect share. You can even do some things that aren't possible from within the Zune PC software, such as browse by genre.

World Wide Zune: A Look at the Zune Online Services

With the first version of the Zune platform, Microsoft created its Zune Marketplace, an online store that sold only music, and then only music that was protected by Microsoft's Windows Media DRM (Digital Rights Management) technologies. This limited the appeal of Zune Marketplace to the 17 or so people who bought the first-generation Zune devices. Clearly, some tweaking was in order.

For the second-generation Zune, Microsoft has significantly enhanced Zune Marketplace and added a second Zune-oriented online service, modeled on Xbox Live, called Zune Social. While Zune Marketplace is still accessed solely through the Zune PC software (much as the iTunes Store is typically accessed via the PC-based iTunes software), Zune Social is accessible via the Web. Additionally, Zune Marketplace has been updated in some significant ways that make the service more interesting to people who are interested in using the Zune software but don't want to buy a Zune device.

In this section, I'll examine both Zune Marketplace and Zune Social.

Zune Marketplace

As one of just four top-level menu items in the Zune PC software, Zune Marketplace offers an extremely rich and visual user interface. Shown in Figure 12-26, Zune Marketplace is designed to be more friendly and appealing than Apple's iTunes Store (shown in Figure 12-27). It certainly is that, which isn't hard to achieve given the ugly, busy UI that Apple employs.

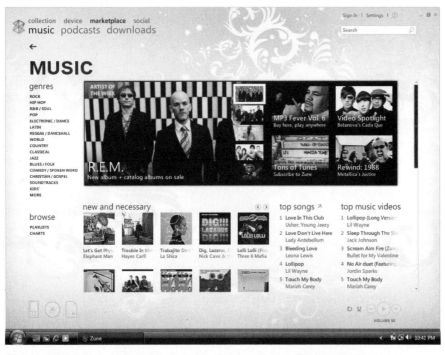

Figure 12-26: Zune Marketplace is open, airy, and visually appealing.

Figure 12-27: Contrast Zune Marketplace with the iTunes Store, a service so busy it's like the MySpace of online retailers.

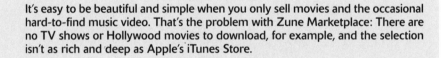

Secret

It's easy to be beautiful and simple when you only sell movies and the occasional hard-to-find music video. That's the problem with Zune Marketplace: There are no TV shows or Hollywood movies to download, for example, and the selection isn't as rich and deep as Apple's iTunes Store.

The layout of Zune Marketplace mirrors that of the PC software interface. You start in the Music section of the service—currently, there are only two other sections, Podcasts and Downloads—and are presented in a columnar view. If you're familiar with the Zune PC software you'll feel right at home in Zune Marketplace.

Browsing the Zune Online Store

When it comes to finding music online, of course, discoverability is key. One of the biggest failings of the iTunes Store is that it's not a friendly place to browse around and discover new music. Microsoft is seeking to avoid this problem by providing a more visual experience where discovering new music is appealing and obvious.

Music, as you might expect, is at the center of the Zune experience. This is for practical reasons: The vast majority of portable media device buyers are interested in music above all else; hence, that is pretty much all Zune Marketplace sells. (For now. Microsoft will no doubt begin selling TV shows and renting movies via Zune Marketplace soon, possibly by the time you read this.) In this area, Zune Marketplace does a reasonable job. There are several top-level genres, curiously ordered not alphabetically but rather in what is presumably some editorialized list according to user preference: Rock, Hip-hop, R&B/Soul, Pop, Electronic/Dance, Latin, Reggae/Dancehall, World, Country, Classical, Jazz, Blues/Folk, Comedy/Spoken Word, Christian/Gospel, Soundtracks, and Kids. Via a "More" option, you can access an additional five subgenres: Avant-Garde, Easy Listening, Miscellaneous, New Age, and Seasonal. There is also a separate two-item Browse list below Genres that includes links for Microsoft-created playlists and top-seller charts.

In the so-called "above the fold" area, Zune Marketplace promotes featured content, "New and Necessary" albums, top songs, top music videos, top albums, and top playlists, the latter of which are made by editors in Microsoft's Zune organization. Below that are Dig Deeper links for emerging artists, older content, and so on.

Secret Microsoft now sells two kinds of music, which is confusing. Most tracks are available in DRM-encoded WMA files, which I do not recommend purchasing: These tracks cannot play in iPods and will be difficult to effectively archive and move forward to new PCs and devices. A minority of the tracks sold on Zune Marketplace are in DRM-free MP3 format, however. These types of tracks are highly desirable because they are compatible with virtually all PCs, devices, and software. Unfortunately, unlike Apple and other services, Zune Marketplace doesn't offer a separate section where you can just browse DRM-free tracks. I'll show you how to differentiate between WMA and MP3 tracks in Zune Marketplace in just a bit.

Unfortunately, there isn't a way to dig very deeply into the Marketplace. For example, if you click the Playlists link under the Browse heading on the Zune Marketplace front page, you'll navigate as expected to a Playlists page. One of the few lists here is Top Playlists which includes only five items. There's no way to go further: Five items are all you get, suggesting that these aren't just the top five, they're the only five.

Secret Obviously, there are more than five playlists, but Microsoft doesn't do a good job of organizing and presenting them. To dig deeper, skip the Dig Deeper links and check out the Genres list on the left. These links don't actually connect you with the master genre pages, they connect to genre-specific playlists (which often use the term *mixtapes* despite the fact that audio tape became obsolete about 200 years ago). Sure enough, there are plenty of playlists in there, if you just know where to look.

Where Zune Marketplace really shines is its artists pages. (A typical page is shown in Figure 12-28.) These pages are far better-looking than anything in iTunes, and they offer more useful information.

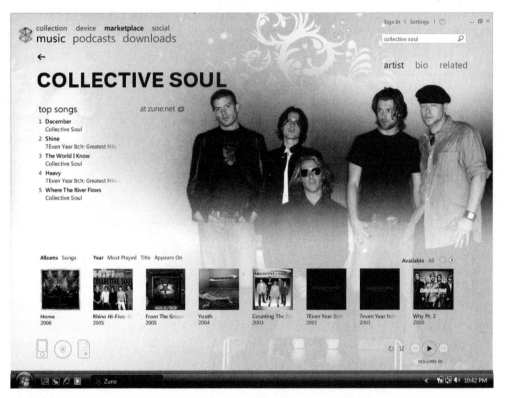

Figure 12-28: The nicest thing about Zune Marketplace is the individual pages for artists.

For example, in addition to cool edge-to-edge graphical designs, you can get (often very detailed) biographical information, along with numerous photographs for top bands, and huge lists of related bands. You can switch between a graphical view of all available music from that band, and a subset of only that content you can actually purchase there. Many of the artist bios are like short novels, extending far below the lower edge of the application window and including numerous photographs.

Secret

In case you're wondering, this biographical information is not created by Microsoft. In fact, Apple licenses exactly the same artist bios in its iTunes Store. Missing from Apple's site is the other information, including the photos.

Zune Marketplace also offers excellent ways to find music that is similar to the artists you already know and love. Each artist page includes a list called Influenced By, which includes the bands that influenced the artist you're currently exploring. A Related Artists list is typically even longer, with numerous entries. A third list, Related Genres, provides yet another jumping-off point. It's an impressive store for music lovers.

Finding Music and Music Videos

Like most online music stores, Zune Marketplace offers various ways to find content. You can browse via the methods described previously or you can use the handy Search box to search for artists, albums, songs, or podcasts. Search works much like Instant Search in Vista, with just one difference. It's not instant, so you have to press Enter to trigger the search.

With regard to finding content in Zune Marketplace, two obvious issues arise. First, while Zune Marketplace does indeed sell music videos, the store does nothing to make them easy to find. There isn't a Music Videos store section as there is for Podcasts, for example. Instead, music videos are just found in the music section. Have fun looking for them. Here's one tip: There is a Top Music Videos list on the front page of the Zune store. This list only links to five videos, but if you select one, you'll be brought to the page for that video. This page will contain a list of related videos, though they tend to be from the same artist.

Another related issue is that while Microsoft does sell some songs in MP3 format, most of the content on the service is still sold in DRM-protected WMA format. I can't stress this enough: Don't waste your money or time on DRM-protected tracks; if you're going to shop at Zune Marketplace, you're going to want to stick with MP3 tracks.

Finally, there is no way to display only MP3 songs, or more easily find MP3 songs on Zune Marketplace. Therefore, you're going to have to waste a lot of time looking around and hoping you come across MP3 tracks. Incidentally, MP3 tracks on Zune Marketplace are accompanied by a small MP3 icon so you know what you're getting.

Secret   A better solution, of course, is to shop at stores that offer only unprotected MP3 files. My favorite is Amazon MP3 (**www.amazonmp3.com/**).

Podcasts

Microsoft was roundly criticized for its utter lack of support for podcasts in the first version of its Zune platform. They've clearly taken this criticism to heart in version two, as podcasting is a first-class citizen this time around. Via the prominent Podcasts menu, you can access a basic collection of podcasts, but one that admittedly falls far short of the selection available at iTunes.

Secret   Almost all podcasts are distributed in DRM-free MP3 format, regardless of where you find them. This means you can use the best tool for the job. For example, even if you're a Zune device owner who uses the Zune PC software and accesses Zune Marketplace regularly, you can still download podcasts with iTunes. They'll sync right up with the Zune device and work just fine.

To be fair, the podcast section on Zune Marketplace has grown over time as users and podcasters have made suggestions; and, of course, you can manually subscribe to any podcast using an RSS-type URL via the Zune PC software as well. Finally, give Microsoft credit for actually calling them podcasts and not something lame like Zunecasts. You know they thought about it.

Spending Points: Purchasing Music Online

Zune Marketplace isn't ideal for a number of reasons. It lacks non-audio commercial content such as TV shows and movies; there are no audiobooks; and much of the music that's available for sale is in undesirable DRM-protected WMA format. Nor is there any easy way to find those songs that are in MP3 format. It's a mess.

However, the single biggest problem, in my opinion, is that Microsoft makes it very difficult to purchase content online. They don't accept payment in the currency of the country in which you live. Instead, they use a bizarre electronic currency called Microsoft Points that seems designed to make Microsoft rich in the same way that Richard Pryor purloined leftover subpenny transactions in *Superman III*.

No, I'm not kidding.

Instead of U.S. dollars or euros or whatever currency is legal tender where you live, Microsoft uses this Microsoft Points system because it can avoid the huge number of credit card transaction fees it would be forced to pay if it let you buy songs one at a time using a credit card. (Ignore for a moment that Apple and every other online store allows just that.) Here's how it works: Instead of buying content online, you buy blocks of Microsoft Points. The cost of these points varies from region to region, but in the United States they break down as shown in Table 12-1.

Table 12-1: Microsoft Points vs. Reality

Points	Cost (US$)
100	$1.25
500	$6.25
1000	$12.50
2000	$25.00
5000	$62.50

When you purchase a block of Microsoft Points, they're applied to your Windows Live ID, so you can use them on Zune Marketplace (to buy music) or on Xbox Live, via an Xbox 360, to purchase Xbox Live Arcade titles, video rentals, and other items. Sticking with the Zune Marketplace discussion for now, as you purchase songs online, your pool of available points is depleted. Therein lies the problem with Microsoft Points: There's no actual way you'll ever evenly spend the points you've purchased. You're essentially giving Microsoft an interest-free loan.

Here's why: Individual songs on Zune Marketplace are 79 Microsoft Points (which is equivalent to 99 cents, the same price that Apple charges for a single song), but 79 doesn't divide equally into 100, 500, 1000, 2000, or 5000. Therefore, no matter what you buy, there will always be points left over. Points that you paid Microsoft for. Money that is now in Microsoft's bank account and not yours, accruing interest.

My advice here is very simple. Don't buy content from Zune Marketplace, even if you are a huge believer in the Zune vision and think that the Zune devices are next to godliness. You're wasting your money.

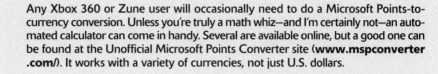

Secret Any Xbox 360 or Zune user will occasionally need to do a Microsoft Points-to-currency conversion. Unless you're truly a math whiz—and I'm certainly not—an automated calculator can come in handy. Several are available online, but a good one can be found at the Unofficial Microsoft Points Converter site (**www.mspconverter .com/**). It works with a variety of currencies, not just U.S. dollars.

Zune Pass: An All-You-Can-Eat Subscription Service

Okay, there is one exception to the preceding rule, which applies only to song purchasing. In addition to the dubious song purchasing plan that Microsoft invented to slowly siphon every last cent out of your wallets, the company has also created a Zune subscription service called Zune Pass. This service could actually make a lot of sense for you if two things are true. One, you're still young or interested enough to want to discover new music on an ongoing basis. Two, you own or are going to purchase a Zune device in addition to using the Zune PC software.

Here's the deal: Zune Pass costs $14.95 a month in the United States. Frankly, this is a little steep, and Microsoft isn't offering special deals if you sign up for several months or one year at a time, but this $14.95 buys you ongoing access to all of the several million DRM-protected songs that Microsoft sells via Zune Marketplace. As long as your subscription is active, you can download and listen to any protected song they offer, both in the PC-based Zune software and on your Zune portable media player.

As with anything that sounds too good to be true, there are some caveats. As noted previously, this subscription service doesn't extend to the DRM-free MP3 tracks Microsoft sells. You can't burn any of these downloaded songs to CD. The subscription covers music only, not music videos. And as soon as your subscription lapses—poof!—any songs you've downloaded are gone.

If you're old and crusty like me, this may not seem like a good deal, but if you're young and have constantly evolving musical taste, Zune Pass may be just what the doctor ordered. Over time, you will discover more and more new music and find out what you really like. By the time your tastes settle down, you may be ready to start buying certain music.

Zune Social

The second Zune-oriented online service is called Zune Social. It's basically a duplication of much of the Xbox Live service but for Zune users. That is, it's essentially an online identity that is tied to a Windows Live ID account—giving others access, in this case, to your musical preferences. (By comparison, the Xbox Live service provides online access to your game playing.) It also provides other related services, such as an inbox for receiving, well, Zune messages.

Zune Social can be accessed in two ways. In the Zune PC software you can click the prominent Social link to access your Zune Inbox (which is identical to your Xbox 360 Inbox if you linked that to the same Windows Live ID as well). This is shown in Figure 12-29.

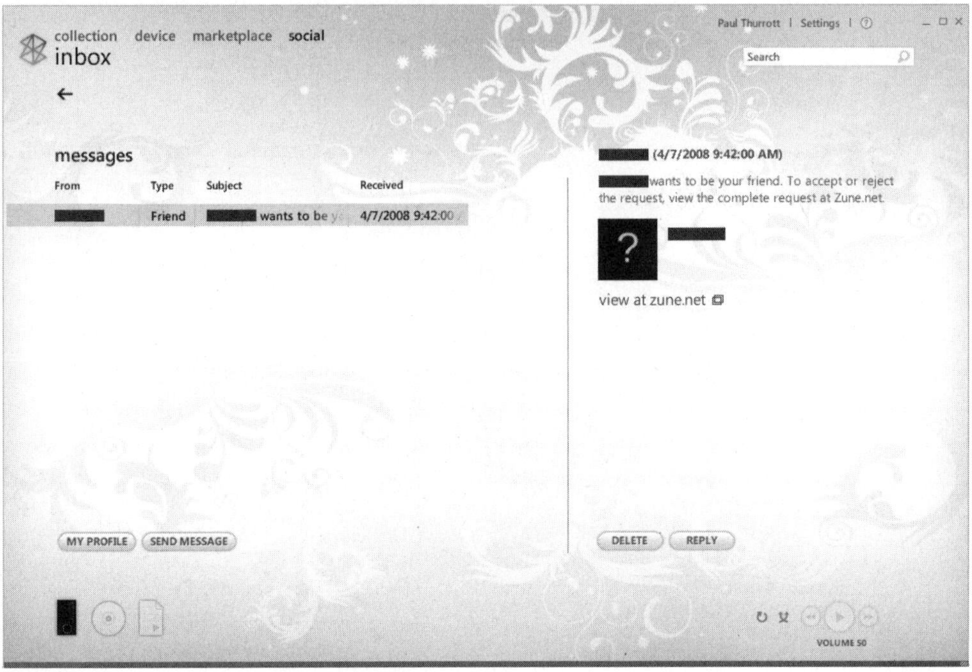

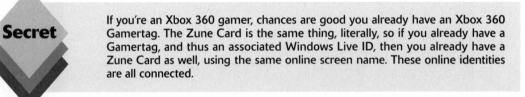

Figure 12-29: The only social bit in the Zune software is your Inbox.

This Inbox is particularly weak, and it's unclear why Microsoft even made it part of the PC software. Yes, you can read messages from this interface, but if you want to reply to a message or write a new message, you have to do so from the Web, which is the second place where Zune Social is accessed.

Secret

If you're an Xbox 360 gamer, chances are good you already have an Xbox 360 Gamertag. The Zune Card is the same thing, literally, so if you already have a Gamertag, and thus an associated Windows Live ID, then you already have a Zune Card as well, using the same online screen name. These online identities are all connected.

Secret

What's silly about this system as it's currently implemented is that cross-service integration is a bit weak. If someone sends you a message from their online Zune Card, for example, you won't be able to read that message from within the Xbox 360 dashboard or online at Xbox.com. Instead, you can only read it from within the Zune PC software or online via Zune.net. The reverse, of course, is also true. Presumably, these service entry points will become more integrated—and thus, ironically, more social—over time.

The Web-based version of Zune Social, found at **http://social.zune.net/**, offers a more complete look at what Microsoft is trying to accomplish: making the act of listening to digital music, which is today very much a solitary experience, into a more social experience.

At the heart of this system is the Zune Card, which is analogous to the Xbox Gamertag. This virtual card, which is currently tied to the Zune.net Web site but can also be embedded in other Web sites online, tracks what you're listening to in the Zune software and devices and displays that information for others to see.

To understand how this works, take a look at Figure 12-30, which shows a typical Zune Card. It's pretty graphical, with album art displays and three basic views. The default view, Home, displays the album art for the songs you've most recently played.

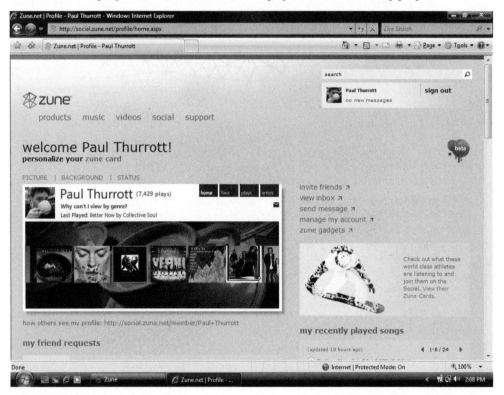

Figure 12-30: On the Zune Social Web site, others can view your Zune Card and check out your musical tastes.

On the groaningly named Favs view, you can see those albums and songs that have been played frequently or specifically marked by the user as being favorites. Another view, Plays, shows recently played songs in order. There's also an Artists view.

Clearly, Zune Social has the makings of a Facebook-style community, and I can envision some people rallying around similar music just as they do with video games now on Xbox Live. Personally, this is a tough sell, as I'm over 40 and don't troll the Internet (or, for that matter, brick-and-mortar stores) looking for others with similar musical tastes, but as I so often discover these days, I'm not exactly the target market here either. The idea is a good one. What it needs is a bigger market of users, sharing information about music with each other.

Secret If you're freaking out about the privacy implications of this service, worry no more: Everything I've described here is opt-in. You can decide who sends you messages, who can see your friends list, and who can discover what music you've been listening to. (Each option can be configured as everyone, friends only, or blocked.)

Zune to Go: Using Zune Devices

The Zune PC software is free: You can download it, check it out, and dump Windows Media Player entirely if you'd like. Ditto for Zune Marketplace and Zune Social: While you do have to link your Zune tag to a Windows Live ID, both services can at least be accessed for free. Of course, you'll need to spend some money if you want to buy music at Zune Marketplace.

The biggest investment you're going to make on the Zune platform will come about when and if you decide to go all in and snag a Zune portable media player. These devices, which compete with various Apple iPod models, are not inexpensive. They're high-quality, competitive devices, and if you like what you've seen with the Zune software and services, something tells me you're going to enjoy the Zune hardware too.

The current generation of Zune hardware is the second that Microsoft has offered in the market. Whereas the first-generation Zune platform included just a single hardware device—the 30GB Zune 30 player (see Figure 12-31), the second generation expands into a more complete product lineup. Interestingly, Microsoft didn't actually replace its Zune 30 player with a new model. Instead, it augmented that player with other new models and added new capabilities that are available on all players, old and new.

The new players start with two ultra-portable devices that utilize 4GB and 8GB of flash storage instead of heavier, bigger, and slower hard disks. Dubbed the Zune 4 and Zune 8, respectively, these devices come in a variety of colors, but color and storage capacities aside, they're all otherwise identical (see Figure 12-32).

On the high end, Microsoft has added a new 80GB hard drive–based mode, the Zune 80, shown in Figure 12-33. This player is available only in black and is roughly the same size as the Zune 30, but is thinner and features a larger, nicer-looking screen.

Secret More Zunes are on the way, according to Microsoft, as are Zune software capabilities for Windows Mobile–based phones. By the time you read this, the Zune ecosystem will likely have grown somewhat.

Figure 12-31: Microsoft still sells the Zune 30 and has augmented it with new Zune 2.0 capabilities.

Figure 12-32: The Zune 4 and Zune 8 utilize flash storage and offer a small form factor.

Figure 12-33: The Zune 80 is Microsoft's premium digital media player.

Choosing a Zune

Pricing for the Zune lineup is similar to that of Apple's iPod lineup. At the time of this writing the Zune 4 is about $150, while the Zune 8 comes in around $180. Zune 30 pricing has dropped dramatically since the new Zune 2.0 devices first shipped, so shopping around pays off. They ostensibly retail for about $200. Meanwhile, the Zune 80 retails for about $250.

If you are in the market for a new Zune, my advice is to skip the Zune 30: It doesn't include some of the newer Zune hardware features discussed in this chapter, and it's slightly bulkier and heavier than the other models. It's also the model most likely to become obsolete first.

Secret

If you purchase a Zune 4, 8, or 80 online through Microsoft's Zune Originals service (**http://zuneoriginals.net/**), you can choose from over 40 custom, laser-engraved artwork designs and add your own text. These designs are applied to the back of the device. Zune Originals is not available for the Zune 30, yet another reason to forego this model.

Because the software-based functionality on all three Zune models is identical, any decision about models should come down to the following:

◆ **Form factor:** The Zune 4 and Zune 8 will appeal to those who have less content and value small size over capacity. If you're going to use a Zune while exercising, for example, a Zune 4 or 8 is ideal from a form factor perspective.

◆ **Capacity:** While a Zune 80 might seem like overkill from a capacity perspective, this is the device to have if you intend to load up with videos and large photo collections in addition to more typical audio content. Few people have tens of gigabytes of music, but video adds up very quickly.

◆ **Price:** Like other high-quality electronic devices, Zunes are fairly expensive. If you can't afford a Zune 80—or just don't want to drop $250 on what is essentially a digital bauble, the lower-end Zunes are also quite nice. Sometimes, simply meeting your budget is the most obvious and important factor of all.

Link Your Zune: Installing and Configuring the Player

Whichever Zune you purchase, the process for connecting it to your PC and synchronizing the device with the Zune PC software is nearly identical. First, ensure that you have the latest version of the Zune PC software installed, using the instructions from earlier in this chapter to get it up and running and, preferably, connected to a Windows Live ID. After removing the Zune from its packaging, connect it to the PC with the included USB cable (which, sadly, is specially made for the Zune, so you can't just use any old USB cable) and then follow these steps:

1. Wait while Windows finds and then installs the drivers needed to interact with your Zune. This process, shown in Figure 12-34, is automatic and should conclude quickly. Once the drivers are loaded, the Zune PC software will appear.

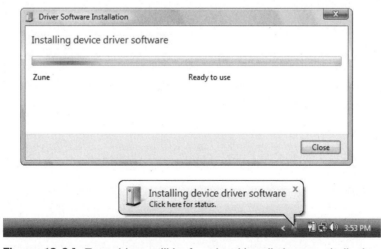

Figure 12-34: Zune drivers will be found and installed automatically the first time you plug in the device.

2. The setup process will begin. Chances are good you'll need to install a Zune firmware update before you can continue, as shown in Figure 12-35. This firmware, which is referred to as the "Device software" in the Zune PC software setup wizard, is the software on the device that provides the device's user interface and other functionality. The firmware update process is mandatory: Zune won't let you continue until the device's firmware is up-to-date.

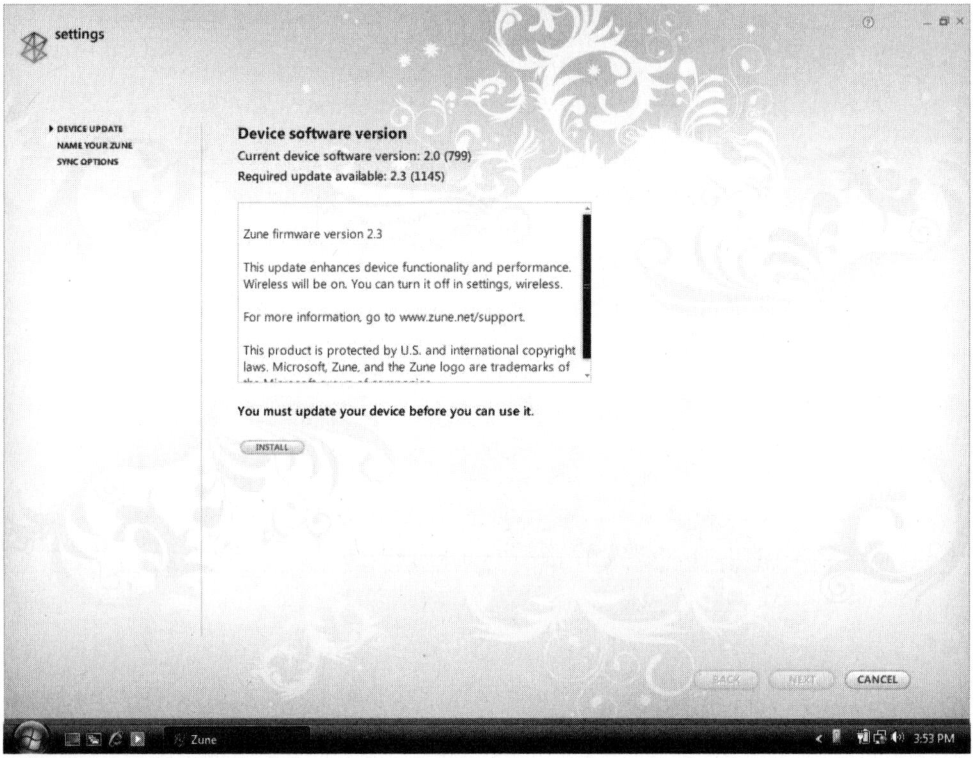

Figure 12-35: You will typically have to update the Zune firmware before configuring the device for synching with your PC.

3. Once that process is complete—it will take a minute or so and require a number of quick device reboots—Zune will indicate that the Zune device is up-to-date. Click Next in the bottom right corner of the application window to continue with setup.

4. In the next phase of setup, shown in Figure 12-36, you supply a friendly name for the device (something like *Paul's Zune*) and determine whether you want to link the Zune to your Zune tag/Windows Live ID. If you've already begun using the Zune PC software and have established a Zune tag, there's no reason not to link it with the device now. That said, you can link the device to your Zune tag anytime.

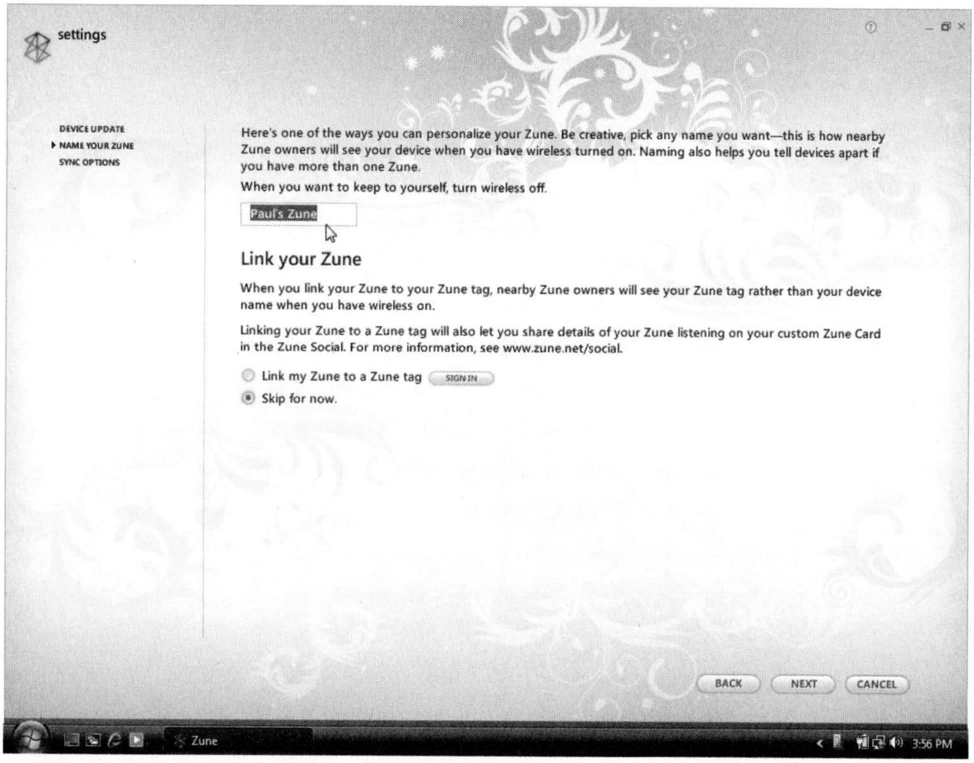

Figure 12-36: This time it's personal.

5. In the final and most crucial phase of the setup wizard, shown in Figure 12-37, you determine how the Zune syncs with your media library. There are separate entries for music, video, pictures, and podcasts, and in each case you can only choose between Sync All and Let Me Choose. How you sync depends on a number of factors, including the size of your media collection and the capacity of your device. For example, if you have 30GB of music, you can't just "Sync All" with a Zune 8 because that device has only 8GB of storage. Because this is a big decision, we'll examine it further in the next section. For now, just select Let Me Choose for each media type and then click Finish to complete the wizard.

6. At this point, the Zune PC software displays the main screen (Collection ⇨ Music), which is a bit surprising, but if you look in the lower-left corner of the application window, you'll see a colored Zune icon—that matches the color and Zune device you purchased, by the way—that's lit up and synchronizing, as shown in Figure 12-38. You can watch the synchronization progress via the percentage text under the device icon.

Figure 12-37: Zune's synchronization options are perhaps a bit too simplistic.

Figure 12-38: It's subtle, but the Zune PC software will trigger whatever sync options you set up in the wizard.

7. Click the Zune device icon to display the Device Status screen (Device ➪ Status) shown in Figure 12-39. From here you can see an almost life-size device icon (again, in the correct color and style) with Just Added, Now Syncing, and Syncing sections that, together, give you an idea of how well the synchronization process is going. There's also a Total Space Used graph on the bottom that indicates how much of the device's storage space is used.

Secret

The Total Space Used graph is interactive: As you mouse over the various segments of the graph, it will tell you how much space each type of content—music, pictures, podcasts, and videos, as well as reserved space—uses individually.

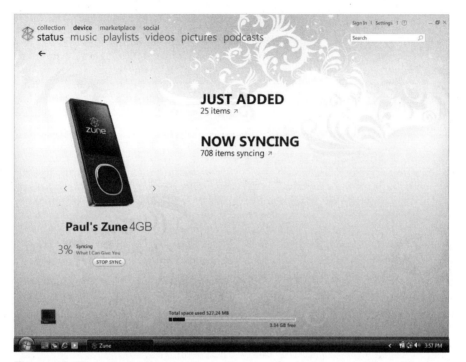

Figure 12-39: In Device Status, you can see how sync is going and find out how much of the device's capacity is utilized.

You can sit and watch the device fill up with content (if you configured it to sync) or simply begin using any other part of the Zune PC software UI. You can also do other things while the device syncs, including shop in Zune Marketplace.

Secret   This one is kind of fun: Microsoft includes content on the Zune. This means you can actually view photos, watch movies, and listen to music on your new Zune before you even get it home and sync it with your computer. That's not to say you're going to enjoy any of this stuff, but it's an unusually generous preload.

Secret   Speaking of the content included with the Zune, one additional thing you should be aware of is that the Zune will not sync it back to your PC by default, so if you'd like to back it up, you should do so. Here's how: In the Zune PC software, navigate to Device and then Music, Videos, Pictures, and Podcasts in turn. In each of these sections, select the preloaded content, right-click, and choose Copy to My Collection. This content will then automatically sync back to the PC. Music and podcasts are copied to your Music folder, while pictures are copied to your Pictures folder and videos are copied to your Videos folder.

To Sync or Not to Sync, That Is the Question

Okay, you've just purchased a new Zune device and you obviously want to get some content on there, and fast. The question is, how are you going to make that happen? The Zune PC software offers two basic options for synchronizing your media library with your Zune device, and these options are independently set across the four basic content types (music, video, pictures, and podcasts) that the Zune platform supports today. That is, you can automatically sync all content (Sync All) or you can manually sync on certain content (Let Me Choose).

Choosing a Sync Strategy

Let me be very clear about this choice: If you can do it—that is, if the capacity of your device is large enough to handle the size of your media library—the Sync All option is much simpler and better implemented in the current Zune software. (I'll explain why this is so in just a moment.) That said, you may not want all of certain content types to sync with your device. For example, while a Zune 4 or Zune 8 is perfect for enjoying music and podcasts, its tiny screen makes it more difficult to enjoy pictures. And as for videos, forget about it.

Here are some basic rules for choosing how to sync:

◆ **If the device has enough storage, choose Sync All:** If you can get every last song, picture, video, and podcast from your media library onto the device, do so. A Zune 80 should be enough storage for all but the most demanding users. Sync All is easier.

◆ **Unless you have specific needs, choose music first:** Choose music at the expense of other nonaudio content. Today's Zune is simply optimized for audio. In this case, you might choose Sync All for music only and then manually sync only the video, picture, and, optionally, podcast content you really want.

◆ **Understand what you're getting into with manual sync:** The Zune's manual sync functionality is a bit harder to manage. There is a single place in the Zune UI to see what you're syncing to a particular device, but it's not clear. This is a real shortcoming if you're not detail oriented, so I want to spend just a moment more on it before moving on to one of the Zune's most exciting innovations: Wireless sync.

Manual Sync

Suppose, for whatever reason, you've decided (or been forced) to manually sync content from your Zune media library to your device. My thoughts and prayers are with you.

Here's how it works, using music as an example. As you navigate around your music library in the Zune PC software, you'll notice that you can manually sync artists, albums, and even individual songs with your device. To manually sync an artist, album, or individual song (or songs) you need to right-click one or more of those items and choose Sync with *device* (where *device* is the name of your Zune device) from the pop-up menu that appears (see Figure 12-40).

When you choose this kind of synchronization, whatever content you've selected is copied to the device immediately, and the Zune creates something called a *Sync Group,* which is a collection of items that are synced together as a whole. In the Songs column, you'll see a tiny On Device icon (in the shape of a Zune device) appear next to each song that is synced with the device.

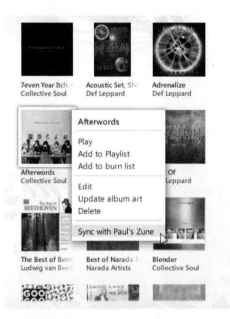

Figure 12-40: Manually syncing artists and albums isn't exactly intuitive.

Secret

When you right-click individual songs in the Songs column, you'll see an additional option that's not available when you click artists or albums: Never Sync with *device*. This provides you with some fine-tuning, so even if you choose to automatically sync everything by a particular artist, for example, you can manually exclude certain songs.

The problem with manual sync, of course, is that it's obvious where you go to see and manage what you're syncing. As you navigate around your music collection, tagging individual artists, albums, and songs for sync, the list of synced items is growing ever larger. You'll see those little On Device icons sprouting up here and there. How do you manage this mess?

As it turns out, this information is managed from within the Device section of the Zune PC software. This makes sense when you think about it, because it's certainly possible to own two or more Zune devices and configure sync differently for each. Therefore, to see which songs you're syncing, navigate to Device ⇨ Music. You'll see a screen similar to the one shown in Figure 12-41.

Figure 12-41: You can manage manual sync from within the Device area of the Zune PC software.

To stop synching particular artists, albums, or songs, just right-click as appropriate. What you will see varies according to which items you've chosen to sync and then which items you're choosing here in the UI. For example, say you've chosen to sync all music from the band Collective Soul. The way you did that was to right-click Collective in the Artist list in Collection ⇨ Music and choose Sync to *device*. Okay, so now you navigate to Device ⇨ Music and you want to remove some items. Here are the options:

- **Right-click on the artist name:** If you right-click on the artist name in the left-most column, called Sync Groups, you see an option titled Delete Sync Group. If you select this, Zune will stop synching music from this artist and will immediately remove all of the music that was previously synced to the device. (Obviously, the music will remain on your PC and in your Zune media library.)

- **Right-click on an individual album that's within a sync group:** You can delete individual albums from the device by choosing Delete from *device*. When you do this the album is deleted from the device only. More important, it is removed from the Sync Group as well (in this case, all music by Collective Soul), so when you sync the device in the future, music from that album will no longer be synced.

- **Right-click on an individual song that's within a sync group:** You can also delete individual songs from the device by choosing Delete from *device*. As with albums, the song is deleted from the device and removed from the Sync Group.

If you navigate back to Collection ⇨ Music, you'll see that songs you have removed from Sync Groups have a small "Excluded" icon next to them instead of an On Device icon.

It's also worth pointing out that Sync Groups aren't always as clear-cut as an individual group. As you sync more and more content to your devices, a number of Sync Groups will appear, some of which are more arbitrary collections of music. And, of course, you'll have Sync Groups that comprise other content types such as podcasts, pictures, and video.

In any case, as you can see, manual sync is a lot of work. It's not so bad if you want to sync only a couple of items of a particular content type, but it can quickly get out of hand if you start adding more and more items. Auto Sync is the way to go if possible.

Wireless Sync

The type of synchronization I've been discussing thus far is very similar to the way that you would sync iPods, iPhones, and other portable digital media devices, but the Zune offers a fairly unique feature, called wireless sync, that enables you to synchronize content over your wireless home network.

Wireless sync works with all Zune models, including the older Zune 30, and requires a 802.11b/g Wi-Fi wireless network. (The PC can be connected via wired Ethernet.) Obviously, this kind of sync is slower than a USB tether, especially if you're stuck using the older, slower, and generally less desirable 802.11b variant. It's not particularly battery-friendly either. For this reason, Zune devices will not automatically sync wirelessly with your PC-based Zune library unless the device is powered somehow (either by a dock or a USB sync cable that's plugged into electric power with an optional Zune power adapter).

You can, however, trigger a manual wireless sync via the device. To do so, however, you must first configure the device for wireless sync using the Zune PC software. After ensuring that the device is connected to the PC via USB—you can't configure this feature otherwise—navigate to Settings ⇨ Device and then choose Wireless from the list of options. You'll see a screen like that shown in Figure 12-42. Click Set Up Wireless Sync to continue.

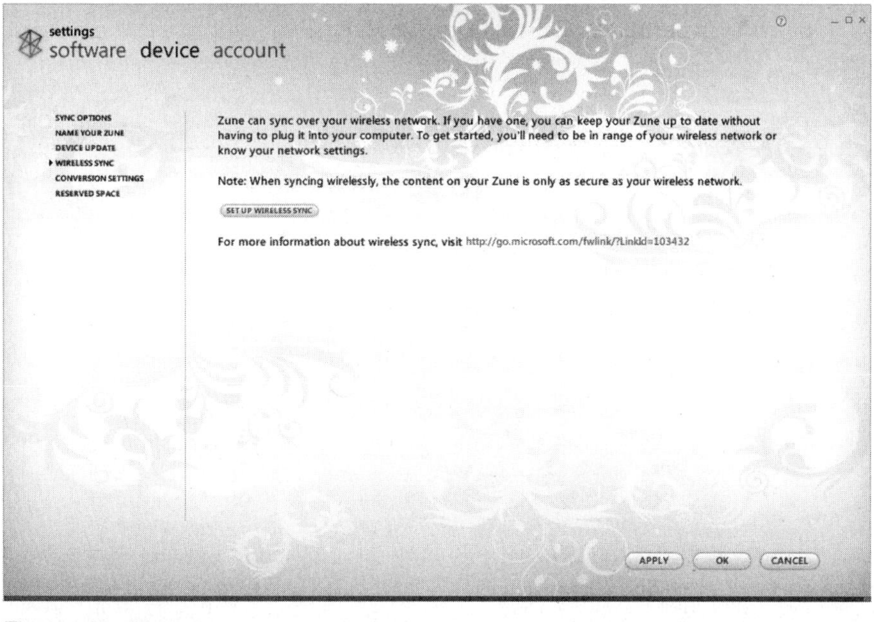

Figure 12-42: Before you can wirelessly sync with your Zune device, you must configure this feature in the Zune PC software.

At this point, the Zune software will search for available wireless networks. If you're connected to a wireless network already, Zune will ask you if you'd like to use that network for wireless sync. If not, you can choose the appropriate wireless network from a list. Click Finish and Zune will connect to the wireless network and configure the device accordingly.

Secret

Can't connect? Zune has certain requirements for wireless networks, including compatibility with a limited range of wireless security technologies. These include open networks with no encryption (which, obviously, you would never do), WEP (64-bit or 128-bit key), WPA-PSK (TKIP), WPA-PSK (AES), WPA2-PSK (AES, not supported on Zune 30), and WPA2-PSK (TKIP, not supported on Zune 30). For more information and wireless sync troubleshooting tips, please visit the Microsoft Web site: **http://go.microsoft.com/fwlink/?linkid=103432**.

Once that's completed, perform a normal, wired sync with the device. Then unplug it from the PC to test wireless sync. On the device, navigate to Settings ⇨ Wireless, and select Sync Now. The device will connect to your wireless network, connect to your PC, and perform a sync, albeit a bit slowly.

Aside from rampant abuse of battery power, why might you find wireless sync desirable? First, many people are now in the habit of charging their digital devices in a central location, perhaps using one of those charging stations you may have seen. This way, when they head off to work in the morning, everything is charged, ready, and accessible. By enabling wireless sync you can charge your Zune along with your smart phone and other devices, and not worry about carting it over to the PC every couple of days to sync manually.

Second, and an arguably more interesting use for this technology, is home entertainment. Many people keep a digital media device dock next to their home theater so they can use this device with the best stereo in the house. (Note that because the Zune 4/8 doesn't support video out, this scenario would only include audio content such as music and podcasts with these particular devices.) If you keep your Zune by the home theater with an AV dock, you can ensure that it's always up-to-date, as it will be silently syncing back to the PC in the other room while it's docked.

Finally, many users simply forget to sync. Enabling wireless sync means that all you have to do is charge the device within range of your wireless network (typically almost anywhere in your home) and it will sync automatically.

Updating Zune

As with any electronic device, make sure your Zune is always up-to-date. That's because Microsoft often ships updates, both for the Zune's PC-based software and for the firmware that runs on the device itself. (For whatever its worth, Microsoft also updates Zune Marketplace and Zune Social regularly, but because those updates occur in the cloud, you don't have to do any work to stay up-to-date.)

The Zune PC software should alert you periodically when new updates are available. However, you can manually check for software updates by navigating to Settings ⇨ Software ⇨ General. Then click the Check for Updates button in the Software Updates section.

Likewise, the Zune PC software should periodically alert you when updates are made available for whatever Zune device(s) you own. To manually check for a firmware update, plug in the device and then navigate to Settings ⇨ Device ⇨ Device Update in the Zune PC software.

tip   The Zune 4/8, Zune 30, and Zune 80 all use slightly different versions of the Zune firmware, so Microsoft makes different updates available for each of these devices.

Secret   One feature that's not obvious is that you can restore your Zune device in various ways. If you just want to erase the content on the device and start over, you can do so from within the Zune PC software, but if you want to literally restore the Zune to factory condition—that is, with the firmware version that originally came on the device—you need to do that directly from the Zune itself. The process is somewhat complicated, but is described in Microsoft Knowledge Base Article 927001 (**http://support.microsoft.com/kb/927001/en-us** in the United States). Note that restoring your Zune in this fashion will not restore the music, photo, and video content that originally came on the device, so be sure to back that up before restoring the device. You can back up Zune-based content—that is, copy it back to the PC—by navigating to Device ⇨ Music (or Device ⇨ Videos or Device ⇨ Pictures) in the Zune PC software, right-clicking the content, and choosing Copy to Collection.

Summary

Microsoft's Zune platform may not ship with Vista, but as with the company's Windows Live products and services, it extends Vista in fun and interesting ways and is an important step toward Microsoft's future platforms. The Zune PC software and services are free and available to all Vista users, even those who choose not to purchase a Zune portable media device. Those who do opt to buy into the Zune platform fully—by purchasing a Zune device and, perhaps, subscribing to Zune Pass—will discover a highly integrated digital media platform that, yes, takes a page from the Apple playbook but does so in a decidedly Microsoft way. Put simply, Zune is an excellent opportunity to see the future of Microsoft's digital media platform…today.

Enjoying Digital Photos

❖ ❖

In This Chapter

Using the Pictures folder to store digital photos

Playing photo slideshows from the shell

Using the new Windows Photo Gallery to organize your picture collection

Customizing how your pictures are displayed in Photo Gallery

Adding metadata such as tags, captions, and ratings to your pictures

Importing pictures from a camera, memory card, scanner, or data disk

Editing pictures with Windows Photo Gallery and third-party applications

Sharing pictures with others in a variety of ways

Upgrading to Windows Live Photo Gallery

❖ ❖

Windows XP took a task-based approach to digital media files, enabling you to manage digital photos, music, and videos directly in the Explorer shell. In Windows Vista, that's all changed. Although some digital media tasks are still possible from the shell, Microsoft now provides discrete applications for managing these files. For digital photos (and videos, as it turns out), the new Windows Photo Gallery application provides a handy front end to many of the tasks you need to accomplish.

In this chapter, you'll examine the many ways in which the Windows shell has changed in Windows Vista with regard to digital photos, and then take an extensive look at the new Windows Photo Gallery. You'll also learn about Windows Live Photo Gallery, an optional new version of Windows Photo Gallery that Microsoft makes available as a free download online. Windows Live Photo Gallery offers everything that Windows Photo Gallery offers plus some unique additional functionality.

Using the Pictures Folders

Like so many other conversations about Windows Vista, when discussing how this system handles digital photos it's instructive to first recall how these tasks were handled in Windows XP. Several years ago, when Windows XP first shipped, Microsoft imbued the system with a number of task-centric user interface elements that made it fairly easy to work with digital media files directly in the Explorer shell. For example, the My Pictures special shell folder provided several picture-specific tasks, such as Get Pictures From Camera or Scanner, View as a Slide Show, and Order Prints Online, among others. Windows XP also included a number of picture-specific folder views, such as Filmstrip, which made viewing pictures from Explorer reasonably pleasing. The Windows XP My Pictures folder is shown in Figure 13-1.

Other operating systems, such as Mac OS X, offer fewer shell-based digital photo management features, but Mac users have come to love the iPhoto digital photo management application, and on Windows, applications such as Google's Picasa have proven hugely popular with users. For this reason, Microsoft retreated from the task-centric user interfaces it developed for Windows XP and has instead created the iPhoto-like Windows Photo Gallery application for Windows Vista, which is described later in this chapter.

Of course, you may be wondering at this point whether there are any picture management capabilities left in the Windows Vista shell. It's a valid question with a complicated answer. Yes, you can still manage digital photos in Windows Vista's Explorer shell, but a few things have changed, including the following:

♦ The My Pictures folder has been replaced by the more succinctly named Pictures folder, and instead of being a subfolder of My Documents (itself now renamed to Documents), Pictures now sits alongside Documents in your user folder (typically in C:\Users*Your User Name* by default).

♦ The shell-based picture capabilities have been revamped rather dramatically in Windows Vista. The Filmstrip view is gone, although Vista's shell does include a decent selection of view styles, all of which provide thumbnail images of pictures in those types of files. (There's also an optional Preview pane that offers Filmstrip-like functionality.) Some of the task-centric stuff is still there in slightly altered form: If you select a picture file, for example, you'll see options for Preview, Slideshow, Print, E-mail, and Share appear in the folder's toolbar.

Let's take a closer look at these changes.

Figure 13-1: With Windows XP, digital photo management occurred directly in the Explorer shell, not within a separate application.

Where Is It Now?

Table 13-1 summarizes some of the picture-related changes you can expect to see in the Windows shell, and how to find similar features in Windows Vista.

Table 13-1: Where Common Picture-Related Features Are in the Windows Vista Shell

Feature	Where It Is in Windows Vista
Web Publishing Wizard (accessed via the Publish This Folder/Picture to the Web option in the File and Folder tasks area)	Missing in action. Microsoft no longer offers a direct way to publish pictures to the Web in Windows Vista. Instead, Microsoft would prefer you to use its Windows Live services, such as Windows Live Spaces, to publish photos online. This service is discussed in Chapter 21.
Share this folder	Replaced by a new Share toolbar button that launches the File Sharing Wizard.

continues

Table 13-1: *(continued)*

Feature	Where It Is in Windows Vista
Get pictures from camera or scanner	Missing, but the AutoPlay dialog box still appears whenever you plug in a digital camera or insert a memory card into a PC-connected memory card reader. Now you typically acquire pictures from a camera or scanner with Windows Photo Gallery.
View as a slide show	Replaced by the Slide Show toolbar button. Windows Vista offers dramatically better Explorer-based photo slideshows than does Windows XP.
Order prints online	You must now launch Windows Photo Gallery to access this functionality.
Print this picture/print the selected pictures	Replaced by a new Print toolbar button.
Set as Desktop background	You can launch Windows Photo Gallery to access this functionality. Alternatively, you can still right-click a picture and choose Set as Desktop Background From the Menu that appears.
E-mail this file/e-mail the selected items	Replaced by a new E-mail toolbar button.
Preview picture	Replaced by a new Preview toolbar button that offers enhanced functionality thanks to an attached drop-down menu from which you can choose which application to use to preview the selected image.
Edit picture	Missing, but if you select an application from the new menu attached to the Preview button, which includes editing functionality (e.g., Paint or Windows Photo Gallery), you can edit the picture that way.
Shell-based photo and photo folder views	Mostly missing. Now you should use Windows Photo Gallery and its organizational view styles to view your photo collection in a variety of different ways.

Where Are the Pictures?

In Windows XP, Microsoft expected people to organize their photos in the My Pictures folder. This hasn't changed too much in Windows Vista: Now, Microsoft expects that most users will store their photos in their Pictures folder, and then manage and edit them in Windows Photo Gallery. However, with more people building simple home networks and enabling multiple users to create their own user accounts on single PCs, the concept of public folders—that is, folders that can be accessed by any user logged onto the PC—is gaining acceptance in Windows Vista as well.

This feature was accessed via the All Users pseudo-account in Windows XP. In that system, an All Users folder was found in C:\Documents and Settings alongside each of the folders for actual user accounts. In Windows Vista, the layout has changed but the idea is the same. Now the Documents and Settings folders has been renamed to Users, and the All Users pseudo-account has been replaced by Public, which is represented by a folder structure containing data that is shared by all users who log on to the local machine. The Public folder contains its own Pictures folder, logically called Public Pictures. If you save pictures to this folder, they will be accessible to everyone who uses the PC.

> **tip** The availability of a Public Pictures folder is interesting for a couple of reasons, but one of the main reasons is because Microsoft provides several sample pictures in Windows Vista, which are accessible through the Public Pictures folder. To find them, access the Sample Pictures shortcut in your Pictures folder, which points to C:\Users\Public\ Public Picture\Sample Pictures. As shown in Figure 13-2, this folder contains numerous beautiful background images that are suitable for your Desktop or enjoying in other ways.

Figure 13-2: Windows Vista comes with a number of high-quality sample pictures.

In fact, these aren't the only sample images found in Windows Vista. Microsoft also provides a wide range of other high-quality, high-resolution images, intended for use as Desktop backgrounds. If you know where to find them, you can make copies in the Public Pictures folder (or any other folder) and access them more directly. To do so, navigate to C:\Windows\Web\. You'll notice a folder called Wallpaper. Right-click the folder and choose Copy. Then navigate to Public Folders, right-click a blank area of the window, and choose Paste. The Wallpaper folder contains several subfolders, each containing pictures in different categories, such as Black and White, Light Auras, Paintings, Textures, Vistas, and Widescreen. Most of them are quite stunning.

Organizing Photos with the Windows Vista Shell

In the Pictures and Public Pictures folders, and in any other folder that contains picture files, you can organize pictures in various ways. The Views toolbar button enables you to cycle through various shell view styles, including some—such as Extra Large Icons and Large Icons—that are particularly nice for viewing a folder full of pictures, as shown in Figure 13-3. (Note, however, that you can only access Extra Large Icons by clicking the More options button next to Views and selecting Extra Large Icons from the list. If you simply toggle through the various views with the Views button, Extra Large Icons will never come up.)

Figure 13-3: Some of the Windows Vista view styles are particularly nice when used with pictures.

In Windows Vista and for the first time in Windows, you can now view picture thumbnails on the Desktop. Previously, this functionality was available only in traditional folder windows. That said, the Windows Desktop icons are still limited to three view styles only: Large, Medium, and Classic.

Additionally, you can use the organizational capabilities of Windows Vista to view pictures in a wide variety of new ways. As described in Chapter 5, Windows Vista includes new file organizational features such as Stacks and Groups, which can be quite handy when used in conjunction with Picture files.

To sort a folder of pictures, right-click a blank area of an open folder and choose Sort By. This triggers the submenu shown in Figure 13-4, enabling you to choose from a variety of sorting options, including Name, Date Modified, Date Taken, and others. For the most part, these options are straightforward, although the Tags and Ratings options are described in the context of Windows Photo Gallery later in the chapter.

Figure 13-4: Use Windows Vista's file sorting options to organize your pictures in various ways.

The Group and Stack options are somewhat more impressive. In the same pop-up menu described above, you can choose Group By and then Name, Date Modified, Date Taken, Tag, Size, or Rating, and choose whether to group in ascending or descending order. For example, you might choose to group by Tags, which would alphabetize the list of pictures and segregate them into groups like those shown in Figure 13-5. If you check the Descending option the list will sort in reverse order.

Figure 13-5: Group By enables you to segregate the current view into logical groups.

tip

You may have noticed there's also a More option in the Group By submenu. If you click this option you'll be treated to a Choose Details dialog box that actually enables you to choose which items will appear in that submenu. That means you can remove some of the default options and add such esoteric Group By options as Type, Dimensions, and more. The list is quite extensive, and of course many of the options apply only to non-picture files. Furthermore, this list can be customized on a folder-by-folder basis.

Secret

To remove a group view, simply choose a Sort option using that same pop-up menu. That will have the effect of canceling out the grouping. It's unclear why there isn't a simple None option in the Group By submenu.

To access Windows Vista's interesting Stack feature, you follow a similar path: Choose a blank area of the current window, right-click, and select Stack By followed by Date Modified, Date Taken, Tag, Size, or Rating. Stacked views can be quite nice. If you choose to stack the Sample Pictures by Rating, for example, you'll see three stacks representing the pictures, which are rated as 3 Stars, 4 Stars, and 5 Stars, as shown in Figure 13-6. You can traverse each stack as if it were a real folder: For example, the 3 Stars stack (which is really a virtual folder) contains each sample picture that Microsoft rated as 3 Stars.

Figure 13-6: Stacks, a new UI element in Windows Vista, enable you to organize files by category as if they were virtual stacks of paper.

Secret

If you're familiar with the virtual folder capabilities of Windows Vista, you'll recognize the Group and Stack displays as in-place searches that can be saved for later use. (Otherwise, please refer to Chapter 5 for more information.) That means you can save these views as *saved searches* and access them later whenever you want. To save a Stack By view, simply click the Saved Search button in the window's toolbar. For example, you might create a virtual folder called Favorite Pictures that is populated only with photos that have been rated with 4 or 5 stars.

To view information about a picture, hover over a picture file with your mouse; a pop-up window appears. What you see in this pop-up depends on the type of picture it is. For photos you've taken yourself with a digital camera, you typically see the type, date taken, rating, dimensions, and size information. Scanned images display type, rating, dimensions, and size information only. Meanwhile, other images simply display their type, dimensions, and size. This latter display is pretty much the least information a picture can supply to Windows Vista because type, dimension, and size are common to all images. The other information is presented if provided by the underlying photo. This information, called *metadata*, varies from file to file.

The Details pane at the bottom of the Explorer window is also populated with a variety of unique information in addition to what is shown in the pop-up. These features are shown in Figure 13-7. Note that the Details pane almost always shows more information than the fly-over pop-up.

Figure 13-7: In Windows Vista, selected images cough up their deepest secrets.

Secret

To get even more information, or metadata, about a picture file, including such esoteric data as the make and model of the camera used to take the image, the F-number, the ISO speed, and other information, right-click an image, choose Properties, and navigate to the Details pane.

Viewing Photos in Windows Vista

To simply view an image in Windows Vista, double-click it or select it and click the Preview button in the window's toolbar. This launches the Photo Gallery Viewer application, which is similar to, but more powerful than the Windows Picture and Fax Viewer application from Windows XP. Shown in Figure 13-8, Windows Photo Gallery Viewer contains all of the picture-specific features found in Windows Photo Gallery, but none of the organizational features. Put another way, Photo Gallery Viewer is designed for working with single images only, whereas Windows Photo Gallery is aimed at managing your entire collection, or library, of digital images.

Figure 13-8: Photo Gallery Viewer is like Windows Photo Gallery Lite.

What are the differences between the Windows XP Picture and Fax Viewer and the Windows Vista Photo Gallery Viewer? Table 13-2 shows you where to find Picture and Fax Viewer features in Photo Gallery Viewer.

Table 13-2: Where Picture and Fax Viewer Features Can Be Found in Windows Vista Photo Gallery Viewer

Windows XP Picture and Fax Viewer	Windows Vista Photo Gallery Viewer
Previous Image	Previous button in navigational toolbar

continues

Table 13-2: *(continued)*

Windows XP Picture and Fax Viewer	Windows Vista Photo Gallery Viewer
Next Image	Next button in the navigational toolbar
Best Fit	Not available; use Change the Display Size slider instead
Actual Size	Not available; use Change the Display Size slider instead
Start Slide Show	Play Slide Show button in the navigational toolbar
Zoom In	Replaced by Change the Display Size slider in the navigational toolbar
Zoom Out	Replaced by Change the Display Size slider in the navigational toolbar
Rotate Clockwise	Rotate Clockwise button in the navigational toolbar
Rotate Counterclockwise	Rotate Counterclockwise button in the navigational toolbar
Delete	Delete button in the toolbar
Print	Print button in the toolbar
Copy To	Replaced by the Copy option, accessed via the File button
Edit	Open button in the toolbar (also enables you to choose which application to use)
Help	Help button in the toolbar

In addition to the functionality you were used to in Windows XP, the Photo Gallery Viewer includes a number of other unique features, which you'll examine more closely later in the chapter.

Customizing a Picture Folder

In Windows XP you could customize picture folders in a variety of ways. This functionality, alas, is largely missing in Windows Vista because Microsoft moved the picture organizational features into Windows Photo Gallery Viewer. You may recall that you could customize a picture folder in two ways in XP: Pictures (best for many files), which would present the folder in Thumbnail view, and Photo Album (best for fewer files), which would present the folder in Filmstrip view.

Unfortunately, Filmstrip view was removed in Windows Vista. Now there is only one picture-related folder customization option: Pictures and Videos. Accessing this option is the same as it was in Windows XP: Right-click a blank area of an open folder (or right-click a folder icon) and choose Customize This Folder. This causes the folder's Properties dialog box to appear, with the Customize tab displayed, as shown in Figure 13-9.

Figure 13-9: In Windows Vista, the folder customization options have been somewhat scaled back.

Secret

If you really miss Filmstrip view, as I do, you can check out a similar, albeit more unwieldy, folder view in Windows Vista and see if it will meet your needs. Called the Preview pane, you enable it by clicking the Organize button in the current window's toolbar and then choosing Layout ⇨ Preview Pane. As shown in Figure 13-10, the Preview pane occupies the right side of the window and shows an automatic preview of the currently selected file, much like the old Filmstrip view.

Figure 13-10: Enabling the Preview pane in folders that contain images gives you an effect similar to that of the old Filmstrip view.

Playing Photo Slideshows from the Shell

One of the neatest if underappreciated new features in Windows Vista is its ability to launch attractive photo slideshows directly from the Explorer shell. Just navigate to a folder full of pictures, or any folder that's been customized with the Pictures and Videos template, including the Pictures folder, and you will see a toolbar button called Slide Show. Click this, and Windows Vista prepares a full-screen photo slideshow, as shown in Figure 13-11.

Figure 13-11: Photo Gallery Slide Show offers impressive-looking slideshows on capable PCs.

Because this slideshow feature, called Photo Gallery Slide Show, utilizes the underlying, hardware accelerated Aero features in Windows Vista, there are a few caveats. First, performance can be somewhat abysmal, particularly startup performance, especially if you're trying to trigger a slideshow on a folder with too many photos. (Note that Photo Gallery Slide Show will include any photos that are found in subfolders within the current folder.)

Second, Photo Gallery Slide Show supports a variety of themes, some of which are quite attractive, but not all of these themes are available on all systems. Those with Windows Vista Home Basic or Business will see only two basic slideshow options. Those with Windows Vista Home Premium or Ultimate running on a lower-end PC with integrated graphics will see five themes. However, those with Windows Vista Home Premium or Ultimate running on a decent PC with 3D graphics hardware will have a choice of several themes. All of these themes are available from the Themes button on the floating navigational control that appears onscreen during slideshow playback if you move the mouse around.

You will see two basic slideshow themes in any version of Vista:

◆ **Classic:** An old-fashioned slideshow with no panning or zooming effects. Transitions are non-existent and new images simply pop onscreen.

◆ **Fade:** This is similar to Classic except that new images fade in as the previous image fades out.

Windows Vista Home Premium or Ultimate users get the following additional themes:

◆ **Pan and Zoom:** Inspired by the default slideshow in Windows Media Center, this slideshow animates images across the screen, panning and zooming each image.

◆ **Black and White:** This is similar to Classic except that the images are shown in grayscale and utilize a fade effect.

◆ **Sepia:** This is similar to Classic except that the images are shown in a sepia color scheme and utilize a fade effect.

If you're running Windows Vista Home Premium or Ultimate and your PC utilizes 3D graphics hardware, you have several additional themes, including Album, Collage, Frame, Glass, Spin, Stack, and Travel. Each is attractive and worth investigating. The travel theme is shown in Figure 13-12.

Figure 13-12: Photo Gallery Slide Show provides various themes based on the version of Vista you're running and your PC's capabilities.

If you click the gear icon in the floating navigation bar in Photo Gallery, a variety of configuration options appear, including three speed-related options (Slow, Medium, Fast), Shuffle, Loop (repeat), and Mute.

Secret

That last option is interesting because it suggests that there's some sort of integrated music playback option, a typical feature of most photo slideshow options. This is misleading and then some. Unfortunately, there's no way to automatically jump-start a soundtrack for your slideshows with Photo Gallery Slide Show. Instead, you're expected to manually start playing the music of your choice and then start the slideshow. If you select the Mute option in Photo Gallery Slide Show, it will globally mute any audio playback on your PC.

Click the Exit option in the floating navigational toolbar to end a slideshow. You can also press the Esc key to end a slideshow.

Managing Pictures with Windows Photo Gallery

If you were a fan of the shell-based photo management features in Windows XP, you might be somewhat disappointed that Microsoft removed a lot of that functionality from Windows Vista. But fear not: Those features—and many more—are now available in the new Windows Photo Gallery. This easy-to-use application provides a single location from which you can organize, edit, and share your digital memories, and in an interesting twist, Windows Photo Gallery can manage both photos and videos, despite its name. It doesn't, however, provide video-editing features. For that, you must use Windows Movie Maker, which is described in Chapter 14.

Examining the Photo Gallery User Interface

Windows Photo Gallery is available from the All Programs section of the Start Menu. (Just search for *windows photo* using Start Menu Search.) The application follows the increasingly familiar Windows Vista digital media application style, with a simple, black, top-mounted toolbar, a translucent bottom-mounted navigational control, and no visible menus, as shown in Figure 13-13.

tip

If you're familiar with Microsoft's now discontinued Digital Image Suite product line, you might note that Windows Photo Gallery looks quite similar to Digital Image Suite Library. That's by design: Windows Photo Gallery offers a compelling subset of the features in Digital Image Suite, but provides users with more advanced needs with an obvious up-sell.

Figure 13-13: Windows Photo Gallery is simple but full-featured.

The Windows Photo Gallery user interface is divided into just a few main sections. Between the toolbar and navigational control are two areas, or panes, by default: a View By pane on the left that specifies which photos you will view, and a Thumbnail pane that displays the pictures in the current view. There is also a button for choosing a Thumbnail view and a Search box for fine-tuning the current view.

| tip | Windows Photo Gallery displays other panes under certain conditions. If you view a single image with the application or click the Info button in the toolbar, a right-mounted Info pane appears, providing information about the current picture. When you choose to edit an image, an Edit pane appears with various editing options. And another pane, called Table of Contents, can also be made to appear between the View By and Thumbnail panes. This pane provides a list of all the groups displayed in the Thumbnail pane, and is obviously most useful if you've grouped the view in the Thumbnail pane view. To enable the Table of Contents, select Table of Contents from the button for choosing a Thumbnail view, which is located above the Thumbnail pane and next to the Search box. The Table of Contents pane is shown in Figure 13-14. |

Figure 13-14: In Windows Photo Gallery you can enable a Table of Contents pane to help you navigate through large image libraries.

Secret

Picture Files: Where and Which Ones?

You may be wondering how Windows Photo Gallery aggregates the picture files found on your PC. Does it search your entire PC for content? Actually, no. Instead, it looks in four locations by default: your Pictures and Videos folders and the Public Pictures and Public Videos folders. You can add photos manually to the Windows Photo Gallery library. To do so, simply drag them from the shell into the Windows Photo Gallery Thumbnail view. However, you may simply want to add your own folders to the Windows Photo Gallery list of watched folders. You'll learn how in the next section, but if you're familiar with the concept of Windows Media Player monitored folders, the theory here is similar.

What about picture file type support? Obviously, Windows Photo Gallery supports common image file types such as JPEG, (non-animated) GIF, PNG, TIFF, and Bitmap. Of course, newer digital cameras support various RAW file types, which are uncompressed, and Microsoft had pledged to support RAW files in Windows Vista. Unfortunately, Windows Photo Gallery cannot edit RAW images out of the box, but if you install a compatible Windows Imaging Component (WIC) driver from a camera maker, Windows Photo Gallery enables you to edit RAW images and export them to JPEG. It cannot save edits directly to any RAW image.

Changing How Your Digital Memories Are Displayed

Windows Photo Gallery is a fairly versatile application. In the View By pane, you can choose to filter the view of photos and videos by various criteria. The top option, or node, is called All Pictures and Videos. This option enables you to view all of the photos and videos you have in the Pictures, Public Pictures, Videos, and Public Videos folders.

If you want to filter the view down a bit you can expand and contract the various nodes found in the View By pane. For example, if you expand All Pictures and Videos you'll see subnodes for Pictures and Videos. Choosing one of those will filter the Thumbnail pane to show only the selected content. Other nodes in the View By pane include Recently Imported, Tags, Date Taken, Ratings, and Folders.

tip
The Folders node provides you with a close approximation to the old XP-style shell management. When you expand this node, you'll see a cascading set of folders representing the folders that Windows Photo Gallery watches for new content.

Secret
Although it's not obvious at all, you can actually add or remove folders from the list of folders that Windows Photo Gallery watches. To add a folder, simply navigate to that folder in an Explorer window and then drag it over to the Folders node. To remove a folder, including one of the default folders, right-click it inside the Windows Photo Gallery View By pane and choose delete. When you delete a folder in this manner, you are also deleting the original, so you are also deleting the actual pictures as well. In other words, be very careful.

As is often the case with any tree control–type user interface, the View By pane can grow beyond the bounds of the application window quite easily, especially if you have a large image library with many folders or tags. In such a case, the View By pane adopts an ugly but useful scrollbar so you can still access all of your pictures.

Grouping and Arranging in Photo Gallery

The Thumbnails pane supports a number of organizational features that will be familiar to you if you've spent time playing around with similar features in the Windows shell (as described earlier in this chapter). To access the various organizational features, just click the square Thumbnail view button next to the Search box. The menu that appears enables you to choose between the following three view styles, and by grouping and arranging options, you can toggle the optional Table of Contents pane:

◆ **Thumbnails:** This view style is displayed in Windows Photo Gallery by default. It presents the images in your picture library in a manner similar to Large Icons view in Explorer, except that only the thumbnails are displayed; there are no picture names cluttering up the display.

◆ **Thumbnails with Text:** This view is almost identical, but adds a text line below each thumbnail. The text you see varies according to which option is selected in the Thumbnail view button's Arrange By option. The default is Date Modified, so that's likely what you will see unless you've changed the selection.

◆ **Tiles:** This view is perhaps the most useful. Shown in Figure 13-15, the Tiles view style provides a listing of the name, the date modified, size, dimensions (resolution), rating, and a caption for each thumbnail. (Note that you can't see as many pictures at once because each thumbnail is accompanied by so much text.) This view style is, of course, very similar to the Tile view style in Windows Explorer.

Figure 13-15: In Tiles view you can see and edit important metadata information.

Secret

Much of the information shown in Tiles view can be edited. To edit the name, date modified, rating, or caption for any picture, simply click the appropriate value. These features are covered in the next section.

Secret

Though there is no obvious thumbnail resizing tool, similar to the slider available in the Views toolbar button pop-up menu in Explorer windows, you can, in fact, resize image thumbnails in Windows Photo Gallery. The trick is to use a mouse with a scroll wheel. To resize thumbnails, hold down the Ctrl key on the keyboard. Then, while still holding down the key, scroll up with your mouse's scroll wheel to make the thumbnails bigger. Conversely, scroll down to make them smaller. This method works with all view styles: Thumbnails, Thumbnails with Text, and Tiles.

Secret

To reset the thumbnails to their default size, use the Ctrl+0 keyboard shortcut. Alternately, click the Reset Thumbnails to Default Size button in Windows Photo Gallery's navigational control, as shown in Figure 13-16.

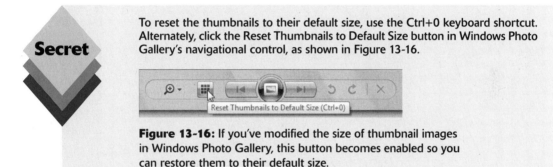

Figure 13-16: If you've modified the size of thumbnail images in Windows Photo Gallery, this button becomes enabled so you can restore them to their default size.

As with Windows Explorer windows, you can group information shown in Windows Photo Gallery's Thumbnails view by a variety of criteria, including Auto, Date Taken, Month Taken, Year Taken, Time Taken, File Size, Image Size, File Type, Rating, Folder, Tag, Camera, or None, in either ascending or descending order. This feature works identically to its shell-based cousin: When grouping is enabled, pictures are segregated into visual groups. For example, if you group by Year Taken you will see groups such as 2006, 2005, and so on, as shown in Figure 13-17.

The Sort By option determines the order in which pictures will be arranged within groups or, if you have Group By set to None, within the entire view. You can choose between Date Taken, Date Modified, File Size, Image Size, Rating, Caption, and File Name, and can of course sort in ascending or descending order. Again, this works identically to the way the Sort By option works in Explorer windows, except that here certain unique photo-related sorting options are presented as well.

If you'd like, you can also enable a unique feature called the Table of Contents, which is an optional pane that provides a list of all the groups displayed in the Thumbnail pane. The Table of Contents is interesting if you are using the Group By feature and have an awful lot of pictures. That's because the Table of Contents acts like the Table of Contents in a book, enabling you to jump from group to group quickly. For example, suppose you have grouped by Year Taken. The Table of Contents pane lists the name of each year for which you have one or more photos. Additionally, small blue bars below each year name visually hint at the number of pictures for each year. As you click year names in the Table of Contents, the Thumbnail pane scrolls down to display the corresponding group, as shown in Figure 13-18. In addition, as it scrolls, a hazy blue box appears in the Table of Contents, visually showing you which portion of your pictures you're currently viewing.

Figure 13-17: Don't be afraid to customize the Windows Photo Gallery display so that it matches your preferences.

Figure 13-18: It ain't pretty, but the Table of Contents is useful if you need to move quickly through a lot of pictures.

Secret The Table of Contents display varies according to how you've grouped photos. If you group by Month Taken, for example, the Table of Contents displays months. Similarly, if you group by Rating, the Table of Contents will consist of ratings.

Adding Tags, Ratings, and Captions to Your Pictures

Although the Table of Contents feature is nice, if difficult to find, you're probably going to want a more elegant way to filter the view of your photo collection. For example, what if you want to see just your vacation pictures? Or pictures that contain family members? Or any other criterion that might be important to you?

Windows Photo Gallery offers a number of ways to help you filter your photo display so that you can see just the photos you want. Of course, you have to do a bit of work to make these features useful. If you're really into digital photography, however, you may agree it is worth the effort.

The first of these features is called *tags*. Tags are unique labels that you can apply to pictures to help identify which ones are related. By default, every picture in Windows Photo Gallery is not tagged, though photos you acquire from a digital camera or scanner with this software are, in fact, automatically tagged. However, you can create your own tags and then apply them to multiple pictures. You can also apply multiple tags to each picture. Tags can be as detailed or generic as you want, but many users will be well served by tags such as Family, Vacation, Personal, Work, Home, and so on.

To create a tag, expand the Tags node in the View By pane. Then, click the Create a New Tag node, which is the top node in the list of tags. When you do so, an edit box appears, enabling you to create your own tag. Give it a name and press Enter. You might want to repeat this process until you've created all the relevant tags you can think of.

To add tags to your pictures, select the picture or pictures you'd like to tag, then drag them to the tag name in the View By pane (see Figure 13-19).

You can also drag pictures to multiple tags if you'd like. For example, some pictures might end up being tagged as Family, Vacation, and Personal.

tip You can also add tags via the Info pane. To do so, select a picture or set of pictures and click the Add Tag link in the Info pane. The new tag will be added to both the pictures and the list of available tags.

To remove a tag, select the picture or pictures you'd like to remove, then right-click the tag name in the Info pane and select Remove Tag, as shown in Figure 13-20.

Figure 13-19: Tagging doesn't get any easier than this: Use your existing drag-and-drop skills to add metadata to your digital photos and other images.

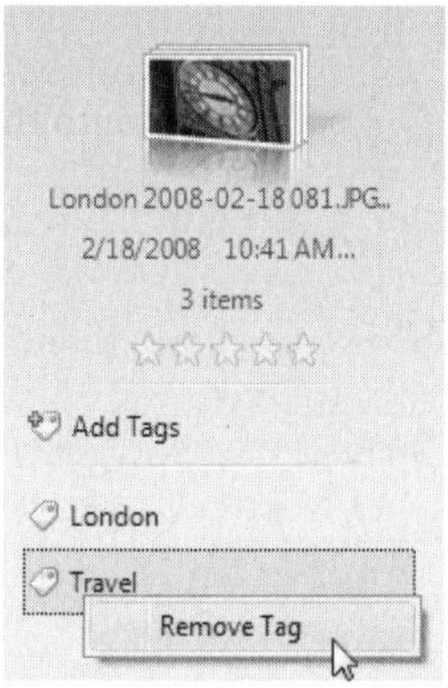

Figure 13-20: Tags can be viewed and removed from the Info pane.

After you've applied tags to your pictures, you can start filtering the view by this information. In the View By pane, simply select the tag you want and the Thumbnails view will change to display only those pictures with that particular tag.

Secret

> To display a view that includes more than one tag, Ctrl+click each tag name you want in the View By pane. *Voilà*—a custom view style.

Another way to filter your images is to apply *ratings* to your pictures, on a scale from one to five stars. To add a rating to a picture, you must first enable the Info pane. (Click the Info button in the toolbar if the Info pane is not visible.) Then select the image you'd like to rate, select and click the line of stars you see in the Info pane. To give a picture a four-star rating, for example, click the fourth star, as shown in Figure 13-21.

Figure 13-21: Ratings provide a way for you to grade your pictures.

As you can probably guess by now, you can select multiple images and apply ratings to all of them simultaneously. You can also rate images via drag-and-drop with the tags feature discussed previously. Just select one or more photos and then drag them onto the rating you'd like to apply. To remove ratings, just drag them to the Not Rated rating.

Finally, you can optionally create a unique *caption* for each of your pictures. These captions are simply descriptive text labels, so you can be creative. You might add text such as "Doesn't Dad look surprised here?" or "Bob finally made it to the top of the mountain!" It's up to you.

To add a caption to a picture or group of pictures, select one or more pictures and then click in the Add Caption or Click to Edit Caption area at the bottom of the Info pane. Add any text you'd like.

Secret

> Captions are limited to 255 characters, so you technically can't add *any* text you'd like.

note

Tags, captions, and ratings are what is known as *metadata,* which is simply data about data. Put another way, metadata is information that summarizes or explains the context of the underlying object, which in this case is a picture. Other files, including documents, music files, and video files, can all contain metadata as well.

More important, perhaps, tags, ratings, and captions travel with the underlying pictures. That is, they're not limited to or specific to Windows Photo Gallery. If you use Windows Photo Gallery to rate a picture with five stars, for example, that rating will appear in Windows Media Player 11 or other applications that are compatible with this kind of metadata. Likewise, if you change the rating, tag, or caption for a picture inside of Windows Media Player, that change will be reflected in Windows Photo Gallery.

Secret

Thanks to improvements to Windows Explorer in Windows Vista, you can also add or edit metadata directly from the shell. To do so, select one or more image files in Explorer and then note the Tags, Rating, and Title entries in the Details pane. (The Title entry is the same as Caption in Windows Photo Gallery. Ah, the consistency of Microsoft software products.) You can edit these items directly from this location if you like.

Searching for Pictures in Photo Gallery

Adding metadata such as tags, ratings, and captions is nice for filtering the current view, but you can also use these and other metadata to search for specific pictures from within Windows Photo Gallery in the same way that you search for documents and other files in Windows Explorer.

tip

Not coincidentally, this metadata also factors into shell-based searches as well as from within Windows Vista. When you add metadata to a digital media file, it can be used from virtually anywhere, assuming the application or service is aware of such information.

To search for pictures in Windows Photo Gallery, simply type a search phrase into the Search box located to the right of the square Thumbnail button. If you tagged certain pictures with a tag such as "vacation," for example, you could use that phrase to find all your vacation pictures, but you can also search for text in file names and captions. In Figure 13-22 you can see a filtered view that includes the results of a search.

Figure 13-22: Searching in Windows Photo Gallery is similar to searching in the Windows Vista shell.

Secret

As with shell-based searches, searching via Windows Photo Gallery is instantaneous, so you will see search results appear as you type. By default, Photo Gallery searches in the current view, so if you've customized or filtered the view in any way, that will affect the search results. To search your entire photo library, click the See Other Options drop-down arrow to the right of the Search box and choose Search All Items in Photo Gallery from the drop-down menu that appears.

Importing Pictures into Photo Gallery

If you already have pictures on your PC, you can add them to Windows Photo Gallery by copying them into watch folders, adding their containing folders to Photo Gallery's watch folder list, or by dragging them directly into the application window. What if you need to import new pictures via a digital camera, memory card, picture CD or DVD, or scanner? Like Windows XP, Windows Vista supports image acquisition via all of these sources.

Secret

Curiously, the photo import functionality in Windows Photo Gallery is horribly broken in that it is not as full-featured as that in Windows XP. In Windows XP you can actually choose which pictures to import from the camera or memory card. Using Windows Photo Gallery, you simply import every single picture. There's no way to pick and choose, but I've got good news: Microsoft fixed this feature in its follow-up to Windows Photo Gallery, called Windows Live Photo Gallery. This and other unique features of Windows Live Photo Gallery are discussed at the end of this chapter because they offer a superset of the functionality in Windows Photo Gallery. However, understand that I'm documenting how photo acquisition works with Windows Photo Gallery in this section because it's a feature that's included with every copy of Windows Vista. Nonetheless, you should use Windows Live Photo Gallery instead, if only because its photo acquisition features are so much better. You've been warned!

When you plug in a compatible camera (via USB) or memory card (via a memory card reader), the Windows Auto Play function kicks in by default, asking you what you'd like to do. The default option, Import Using Windows, runs a simple wizard that steps you through the process of acquiring your pictures.

tip

If you don't see the Auto Play dialog box appear for some reason, you can open My Computer, right-click the appropriate device, and choose Open Auto Play. Alternately, from within Windows Photo Gallery you can simply click the File toolbar button and choose Import from Camera or Scanner from the pop-up menu that appears.

What you see depends on whether you're importing from analog (scanner) or digital (camera or memory card) sources.

Importing Images with a Scanner

While the world has pretty much transitioned to digital photography, many people still have older photos and other paper-based content that they want to digitize and add to their digital photo collections. Devices called *scanners* have been designed for just this purpose, and you probably won't be surprised to discover that Windows Vista offers first-class support for scanners via its Windows Photo Gallery application.

To digitize a photo or other image with a scanner, click File on the Windows Photo Gallery toolbar and then select Import from Camera or Scanner from the drop-down list that appears. If your scanner is connected to the PC and properly configured it should appear in the resulting dialog, shown in Figure 13-23.

Once you click Import, the New Scan wizard appears, shown in Figure 13-24. From here you can configure a bewildering series of scanning options.

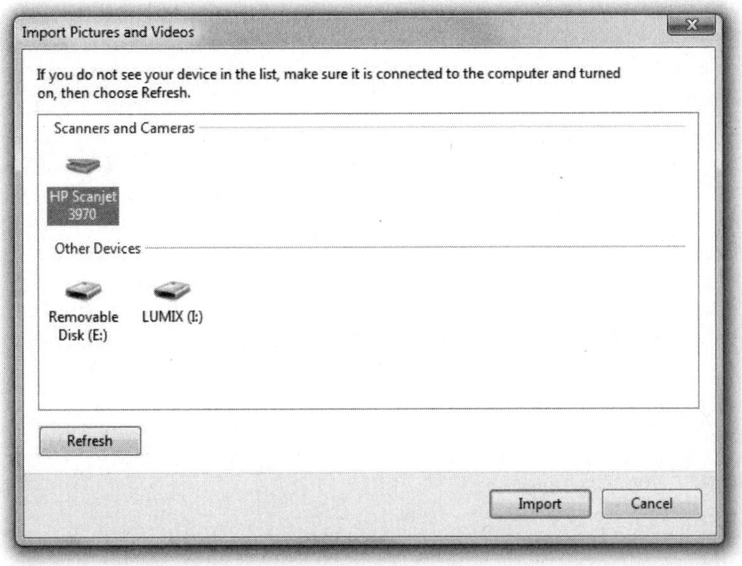

Figure 13-23: Scanners show up alongside cameras and other digital image sources in Windows Photo Gallery.

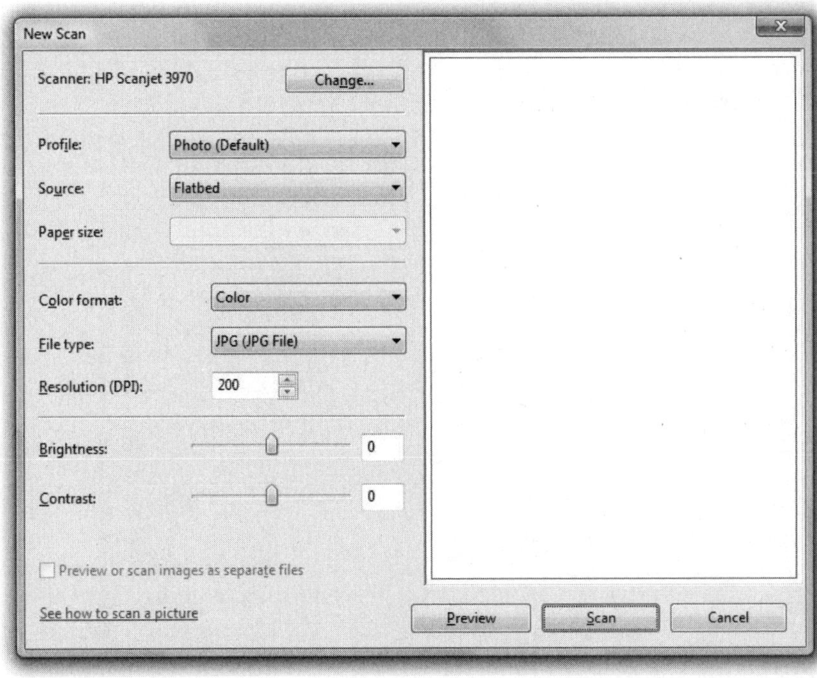

Figure 13-24: Here is where you configure your scanner and prepare for scanning.

A few of these options are quite important:

◆ **Profile:** Make sure this is set accordingly. That is, use Photo (Default) for your photos and Documents for your documents.

◆ **Source:** Typically you'll be using a flatbed scanner for photos, but some scanners support other scanning methods, including slide and negative scanners.

◆ **Color Format:** Here you can choose between Color, Grayscale, and Black and White. You'll almost always want to use Color, but for black-and-white photos choose Grayscale, not Black and White. You will typically use Black and White only for documents.

◆ **File Type:** Most of the time you'll want to go with the default (JPG, for JPEG) if you're scanning photos, but there are other options available, all of which are of higher quality than JPG. Choose TIF for documents.

◆ **Resolution:** The default resolution here, 200 DPI (dots per inch), is pretty low. Depending on the capabilities of your scanner, select a higher value (I use 600 DPI, for example), which results in a higher-resolution image; you can edit this image and resize it as needed. It's better to start off with a bigger source image and then downsize as needed.

There are also Brightness and Contrast sliders. Ignore these and use the photo-editing features of Windows Photo Gallery to edit the scan later.

Because most scans do not occupy the entire flatbed area, arrange the photos or other documents you wish to scan on the scanner and then click the Preview button. As shown in Figure 13-25, Windows Photo Gallery will do a preliminary scan so you can crop accordingly, using the markers.

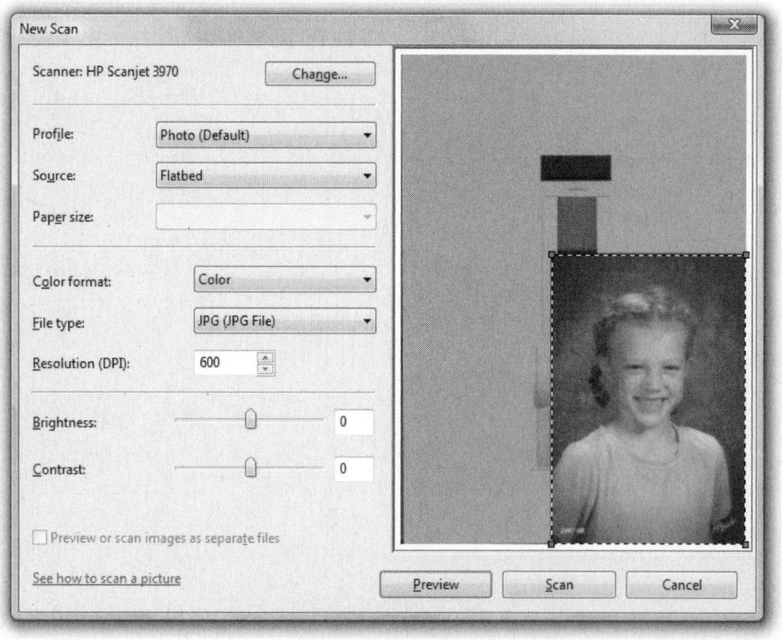

Figure 13-25: Once you've previewed a scan, you can use the onscreen guides to crop for the final scan.

After you've cropped as needed, click the Scan button to perform the actual scan. Windows Photo Gallery will scan the image and prompt you to provide a tag for the image. This is optional, but the tag is also used to name the photo file that's created, as well as the folder that contains it. For example, if you scan an image and then supply the tag "Celtics ticket," Windows Photo Gallery will, by default, create a file called Celtics ticket.jpg inside a folder named Celtics ticket that exists under your Pictures folder.

Because scanning is more art form than science, chances are good you're going to want to make some edits before the rough scan can be considered a final image. You can use Windows Photo Gallery or your favorite photo-editing application to make these edits. You get a look at Windows Photo Gallery's photo-editing features later in this section.

Importing Images from a Digital Camera or Memory Card

In the first step of the Image Import wizard, you can add a new tag or select an existing tag from a drop-down list. (If you'd like to add more than one tag, you need to do so later in Windows Photo Gallery.) Next, click Import, and optionally choose to delete the original files from the camera or memory card.

When the import process is complete, Windows Photo Gallery loads with the Most Recently Added node displayed so you can see, organize, and edit your new pictures as needed.

---

tip   Behind the scenes, a lot of other things have happened. First, the Image Import wizard created a folder inside of Pictures that is constructed from the date plus the tag name you supplied earlier. For example, if the date is May 29, 2006 and you used the tag "Bob's Office," you'll see a folder called 2006-04-29 Bob's Office inside of Pictures. Each photo inside of that folder is named accordingly—i.e., Bob's Office 001, Bob's Office 002, and so on. Meanwhile, the Bob's Office tag has also been added to the list of tags found inside of Windows Photo Gallery. You can now apply this tag to other pictures if you want, or add other tags to the pictures you just imported.

You can change a variety of options related to importing pictures via the Windows Photo Gallery Options dialog box. To access this dialog box, click the File toolbar button and then choose Options. The Import tab, shown in Figure 13-26, provides a number of options you can change, including the folder to which imported pictures should be copied, the name that the wizard generates for the new pictures and containing folder, and so on. You can also click a link to revert to the system default settings.

 **Secret**   You can access the options for the photo import functionality by accessing the File menu in Windows Photo Gallery and choosing Options. Then navigate to the Import tab.

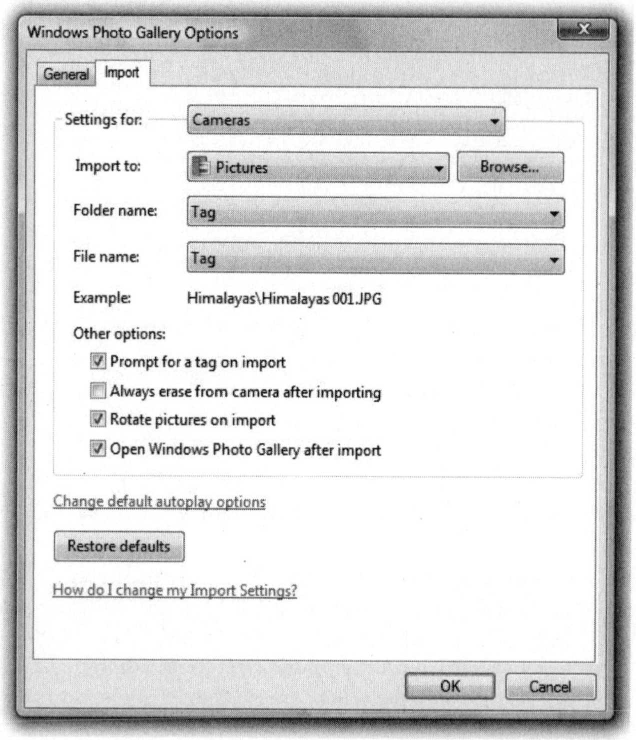

Figure 13-26: In Windows Vista, picture acquisition is controlled from inside Windows Photo Gallery.

Editing Pictures

When you double-click an image in Windows Photo Gallery, the application switches into its Viewer mode, which is what you see when you open image files directly from the Windows shell. In Viewer mode, Photo Gallery replaces the View By and Thumbnail view panes (and the Table of Contents, if it's displayed) with a simpler display consisting only of the image you're viewing and the Info pane. In this view, you'll often want to click the Fix button to display the application's image-editing functions.

Editing Photos with Windows Photo Gallery

This is a big change from Windows XP, which doesn't offer much in the way of editing functionality beyond the very basic facilities of Windows Paint. When you preview an image and click the Fix button in Windows Photo Gallery, the display changes, replacing the Info pane with the Edit pane, and providing a list of image-editing features, as shown in Figure 13-27.

Figure 13-27: The editing features in Windows Photo Gallery enable you to perform several popular photo-editing tasks.

The Windows Photo Gallery image-editing features are as follows:

◆ **Auto Adjust:** This tool evaluates the picture and performs a variety of changes based on the needs of the image. Basically, it's a best-guess estimate of what needs to be fixed; although it's often a decent try, you'll want to carefully evaluate the changes before committing them to the file.

Secret

Fortunately, Windows Photo Gallery applies any changes you make to a copy of the original photo and archives the original photo on disk, at least by default. You can change this functionality so that the original versions of altered files are automatically moved to the Recycle Bin (via the Options dialog, which you can find via File ⇨ Options), but I don't recommend this. Because of the compressed nature of JPEG images in particular, resaving digital photos can result in dramatic quality reduction. Be careful not to resave JPEG images too often; if you're going to edit a JPEG file, edit and save it once.

tip

If you don't like what Auto Adjust does to your picture, click the Undo button at the bottom of the Info pane. If you've performed multiple operations, this button will pop-up a menu that enables you to choose which operations to undo, or you can Undo All changes you've made.

Secret

The Undo button provides multiple levels of undo, so if you commit a number of changes, you can access its pop-up menu, shown in Figure 13-28, to undo specific changes or multiple changes all at once.

Figure 13-28: Everyone makes mistakes.

◆ **Adjust Exposure:** Unlike Auto Adjust, this doesn't provide a single-click solution. Instead, when you click this option, the Info pane expands to display slider controls for Brightness and Contrast, as shown in Figure 13-29. Move these sliders to the left or right to adjust these properties until you're happy with the results.

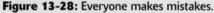

Figure 13-29: Adjust Exposure provides access to Brightness and Contrast sliders.

◆ **Adjust Color:** This is also a little more involved. When you select this option another new area expands in the Info pane, where you can use sliders to adjust the temperature, tint, and saturation of the photo.

◆ **Crop Picture:** This tool enables you to crop the current picture in order to change its aspect ratio if needed, or simply edit out parts of the picture that are uninteresting. A Proportion drop-down box (see Figure 13-30) enables you to specify how you want the picture cropped.

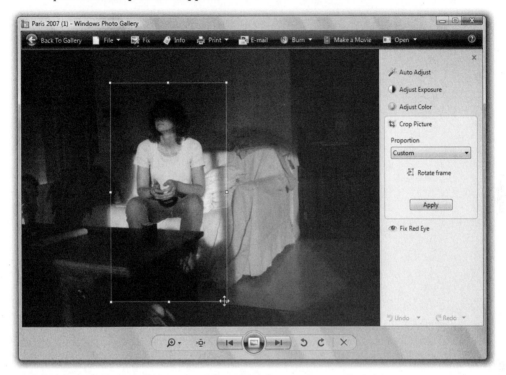

Figure 13-30: The Crop Picture function provides a variety of ways for you to highlight the important parts of a picture.

After you have picked a proportion, you can use the onscreen guide lines to select the portion of the image you would like cropped.

tip Because cropping a picture can often result in a dramatically different final image, you may want to copy, or duplicate, a picture before cropping it, just in case. To do so, select the image you want to crop and then choose Duplicate from the File button's drop-down menu.

◆ **Fix Red Eye:** Red-eye correction is one of the most often needed features in any photo-editing package, and fortunately the one in Windows Photo Gallery works pretty well. Simply click this option and then draw a rectangle around each of the eyes you want to correct in the current picture, as shown in Figure 13-31. When you release the mouse button, Windows Photo Gallery attempts to remove the red eye. It's usually pretty successful, but you may need to try a few times to get it just right.

Figure 13-31: Everyone appreciates a little red-eye removal.

Secret

They're not well documented, but there are some handy keyboard shortcuts you can use while editing pictures with Windows Photo Gallery. For example, you can zoom in on a picture by pressing Ctrl (or Alt) and the + key at the same time, and zoom out with Ctrl (or Alt) and the - key. Normally, when you're zoomed in, you can move around the picture using the small hand cursor; but in certain editing tasks, such as Crop Picture and Fix Red Eye, the cursor changes for other purposes, preventing you from navigating around a zoomed picture. To return temporarily to the hand icon for these edits, hold down the Alt key and move around with the mouse. Then release the Alt key and the cursor will return to the way it was before. By the way, Ctrl+0 zooms the picture back to its default zoom level (whereby the picture fills the entire viewing area).

Secret

Another great reason to use Windows Live Photo Gallery instead of Windows Photo Gallery is that it includes additional photo-editing features. Again, you can take a look at Windows Live Photo Gallery's unique additional features at the end of this chapter.

Editing with Other Applications

Although the basic editing features in Windows Photo Gallery should satisfy many people's needs, there are many other photo-editing solutions out there, and you may want to use them to edit your photos instead, especially if your needs aren't addressed by Windows Photo Gallery (or Windows Live Photo Gallery). A number of alternatives are available, including desktop applications Adobe Photoshop Elements and Google Picasa, which you can access directly from within Windows Photo Gallery, which is pretty handy.

Secret

There's also an increasingly impressive collection of Web-based photo-editing solutions, such as Adobe Photoshop Express (**www.photoshop.com/express/**) and Picnik (**www.picnik.com/**). Sadly, neither integrates with Windows Photo Gallery in the same way as Windows-based applications—at least not yet.

To do so, use the Open button on the Windows Photo Gallery toolbar. If you don't have any photo-editing applications installed in Windows Vista, you will simply see Windows Paint listed in the resulting drop-down menu when you click this button. But if you installed a third-party application it should appear in the list as well, as shown in Figure 13-32. This way, you can edit a photo in the application you like the most, while still using Photo Gallery's excellent management capabilities to perform other photo-related tasks.

Figure 13-32: You're not stuck with the useful but limited photo-editing features of Windows Photo Gallery.

tip If your application doesn't appear in the Open drop-down menu, you can add it easily enough: Simply select Choose Program from the Open drop-down menu then choose the program from the list, or click the Browse button to find it on your hard drive. When you've accessed a program in this fashion, it will be added to the Open drop-down list.

Sharing Photos with Others

Although you may find the process of managing, organizing, and editing photos to be somewhat tedious, there is of course a wonderful payoff: Once you've created an extensive photo library containing your most precious memories, you can then share those photos with your family, friends, and others in a stunning variety of ways. You can think of Windows Photo Gallery as the means to an end: For the most part, you'll use this application for the nitty-gritty management work, and then use its sharing features to spread the wealth.

Enjoying Photos on Your Own PC

Before delving into the various ways you can share your digital memories with others, let's examine a few ways you can enjoy your photos on your own PC. First, you can use any picture as a Desktop background. There are a multitude of ways to do this, but one of the best things you can do is duplicate a favorite picture in Windows Photo Gallery and then use the application's Crop feature to crop it to the exact resolution (or aspect ratio) of your screen. That way you won't have to worry about stretching the picture in any way on your Desktop.

Windows Vista also enables you to use animated photo slideshows as a screen saver. To access this functionality, open the Control Panel and navigate to Appearance and Personalization. Then choose Change Screen Saver from the Personalization section.

> **tip** There's a handy way to navigate to this location if you're already using Windows Photo Gallery: Just select File ⇨ Screen Saver Settings.

In the resulting dialog box, choose Photos from the Screen Saver drop-down menu. Next, click Settings. As shown in Figure 13-33, this dialog box enables you to choose which pictures to use in your screen saver, along with various other related options. You can click Preview in the Screen Saver Settings window to see how your new screen saver looks.

> **Secret** The Windows Vista Photos screen saver doesn't just work with photos; it uses videos as well, so you can also mix home movies into your slide show, if you're into that kind of thing.

Printing Pictures and Order Prints

If you want to share pictures with others, one of the most obvious ways is to create traditional paper-based prints. These can be wonderful gifts, and while the digital revolution is in full swing, not everyone has a PC or always wants to enjoy pictures only with their computer. There are two ways to create picture prints in Windows Vista. You can print pictures on your own photo printer, if you have one, or you can order prints online.

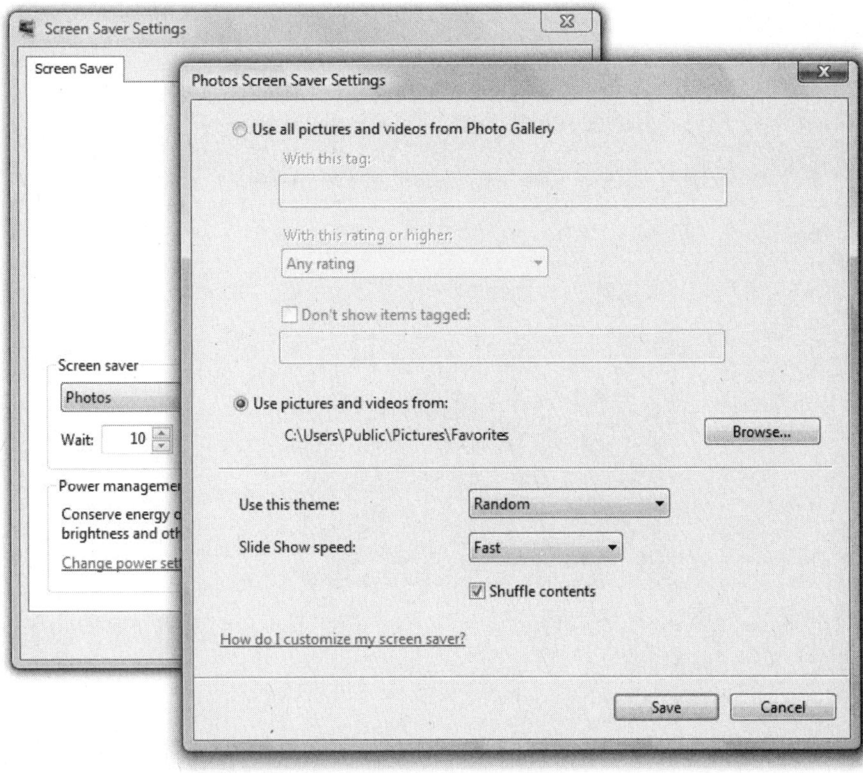

Figure 13-33: One of the coolest ways to personalize your system is to use your own photo as a screen saver.

To print pictures yourself, open Windows Photo Gallery, select the picture (or pictures) you'd like to print, click the Print button in the toolbar and then choose Print from the drop-down menu. This action launches Windows Vista's excellent Print Pictures wizard, which is depicted in Figure 13-34.

From this deceptively simple wizard you can customize the print job in a variety of ways, choosing what size prints to create, which printer to use, and a number of other options.

To order prints from an online photo service, select a group of photos and then choose Order Prints from the Print button's drop-down menu. This launches the Order Prints wizard, which provides a handy front end to various online printing services that have arrangements with Microsoft. Give it a second: The list of approved services sometimes takes several seconds to load (and requires an Internet connection, of course).

tip   You don't have to settle for the options Microsoft provides. Bypassing the Order Prints function in Windows Photo Gallery, you can use Internet Explorer or another Web browser to discover, sign up for, and order prints from any number of Web-based photo printing services. You can also bring a digital camera memory card into many pharmacies and photo-printing retail kiosks and print photos from there.

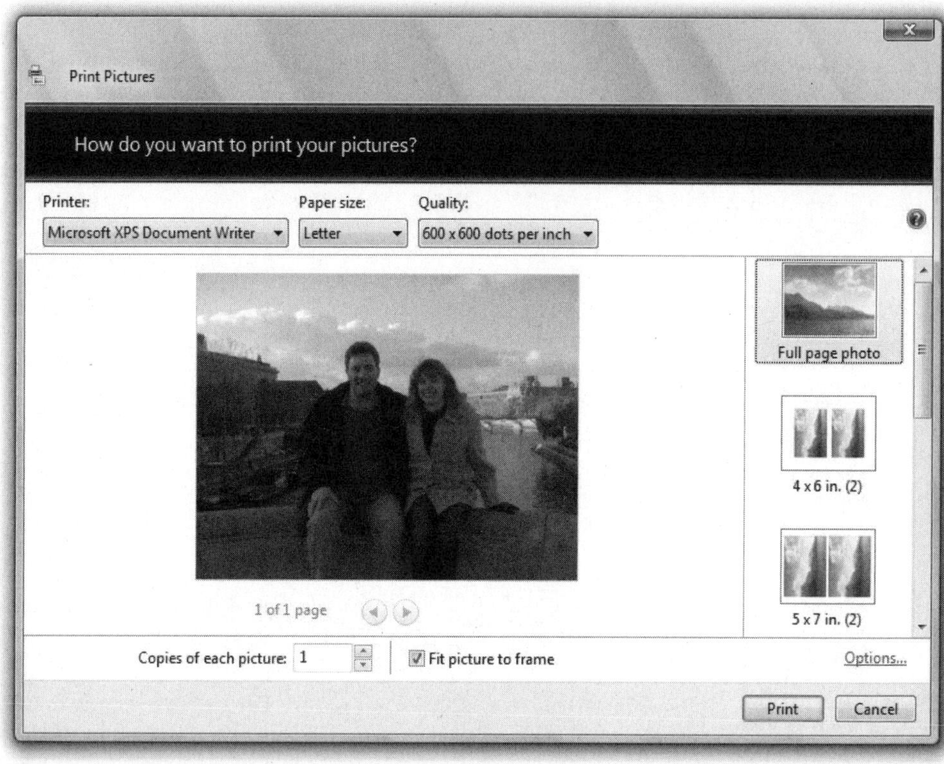

Figure 13-34: You may be surprised by how many options you have for printing photos in Windows Vista.

Secret

One obvious feature that's missing from Windows Photo Gallery is the capability to create photo books, which make great gifts or excellent keepsakes of family vacations and other events. Several online services are dedicated to helping you make your own books, but my two favorites by far are My Publisher (**www.mypublisher.com/**) and Blurb (**www.blurb.com/**).

Getting Creative: Adding Photos to Movies, DVDs, and Data Disks

Windows Photo Gallery also offers basic integration features with Windows Move Maker, Windows DVD Maker, and Windows Vista's integrated CD and DVD burning capabilities to help you create movies of your photo slide shows, or data disks full of your favorite pictures.

To create a digital movie of your favorite photos, select the photos you want in Windows Photo Gallery and then click the Make a Movie button on the toolbar and select Movie. Windows Movie Maker will launch and import all of the selected photos into a new project, as shown in Figure 13-35, which you can then edit into a finished movie. Chapter 14 covers Windows Movie Maker's movie-editing capabilities—including how you can use this tool to make movies of photos.

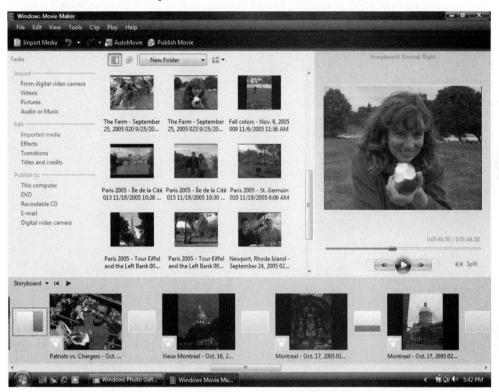

Figure 13-35: With Windows Movie Maker, you can turn a string of photos into a compelling animated home movie.

To add a similar slide show to a DVD movie, select the photos as before and then click the Burn button on the toolbar and select Video DVD. This will import the pictures into Windows DVD Maker, shown in Figure 13-36, which enables you to create DVD movies. Windows DVD Maker is also covered in Chapter 14.

If you want to create backups of your photo gallery or share pictures with others electronically, Windows Photo Gallery also enables you to create data disks, in either CD or DVD format. Again, click the Burn button on the Windows Photo Gallery toolbar, but this time choose Data Disk from the resulting drop-down menu. You'll be prompted to insert a blank CD or DVD disk into your recordable optical drive (see Figure 13-37), and then Windows Vista uses its integrated disk-burning capabilities to copy the photos onto the disk.

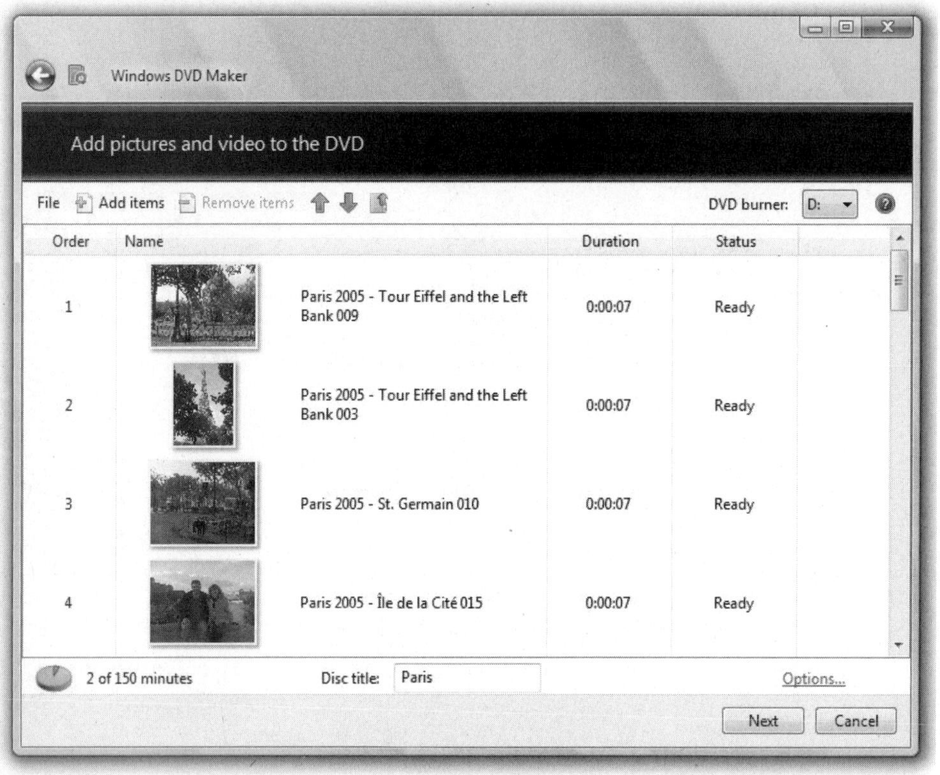

Figure 13-36: Windows DVD Maker enables you to distribute your favorite photos via a DVD movie.

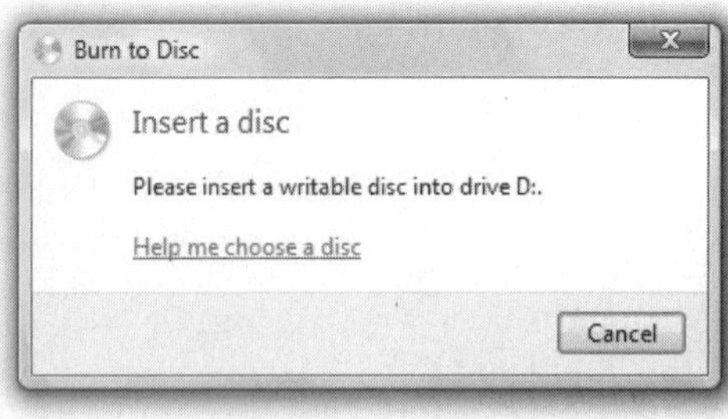

Figure 13-37: OK, it's not pretty, but if you're looking for a way to back up your photos to DVD or CD, Windows Photo Gallery has you covered.

Sharing through E-mail

If you'd like to send a picture or a group of pictures to other people, you can use the built-in e-mail sharing capabilities of Windows Photo Gallery. First, select the pictures you'd like to send, and then click the E-mail button in the toolbar. The Attach Files dialog, shown in Figure 13-38, will appear. Here you can choose how or whether to resize your images for transit, which is likely a good idea as many of today's digital photos are quite large. Several picture size options are available, including Smaller (640 × 480), Small (800 × 600), Medium (1024 × 768, which is the default), Large (1280 × 1024), and Original Size.

After your selection, click Attach and a new e-mail message will appear in Windows Mail (see Chapter 20) or whatever e-mail application you've specified as the default.

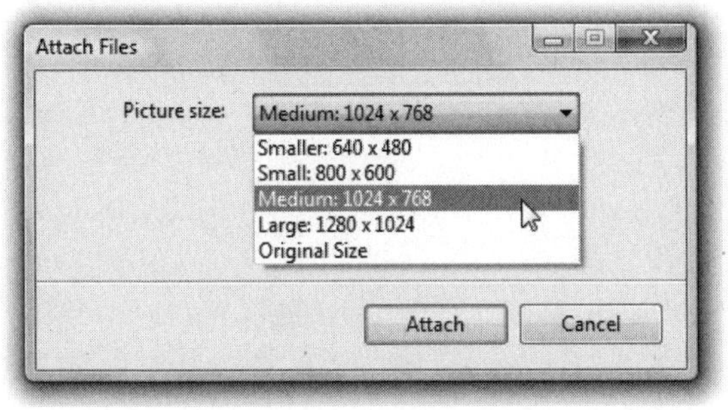

Figure 13-38: The Picture Size drop-down menu enables you to choose from various preset sizes.

Network-Based Library Sharing and Portable Device Syncing

Using new functionality in Windows Vista, you can also share your photo library with other Windows Vista–based PCs on your home network and synchronize with a compatible portable device. Links to both of these options are available via the File button's drop-down menu, but because these features are actually exposed through Windows Media Player 11 and not Windows Photo Gallery, I discuss this functionality in Chapter 11.

Using Photo Gallery to Manage Digital Videos

Although the name Windows Photo Gallery suggests that this application is suitable only for pictures, it can also be used to manage digital videos. This makes sense: Today, most digital cameras and many cell phones include video recording capabilities, and I would guess that short videos created on these devices are already far more common than video shot with traditional video cameras.

Videos can be viewed in Windows Photo Gallery by selecting All Pictures and Videos or Videos from the View By pane, or one of the other video-related nodes (see Figure 13-39).

Figure 13-39: Videos, too, can be organized in Windows Photo Gallery.

By default, videos appear as thumbnails that provide a glimpse into the contained movie. If you double-click a video in Windows Photo Gallery, the application switches into a special video preview mode so you can watch the movie, as shown in Figure 13-40. (Conversely, when you open a movie file from the Windows shell, it typically opens in Windows Media Player 11.) Note that in this mode, the application's navigational control changes to add Play and Stop buttons, like a video player.

Even though the Windows Photo Gallery toolbar doesn't change when you view videos or video previews, some options simply aren't available with videos. For example, the Fix menu returns the simple message "Video files can't be edited using Photo Gallery" if you try to access it.

---

tip   As with photos, Windows Photo Gallery only parses certain folders when it wants to find video content. These folders are your Videos folder (typically found in C:\Users\ *your user name*\Videos, by default) and the Public Videos folder. However, you can manually add videos from other locations by simply dragging them into the Windows Photo Gallery Thumbnail View pane.

Videos are fully compatible with the tag, rating, and caption metadata types that are utilized by pictures. This means that you can easily add this information to your videos, filter the view, and search for specific video content just as you do with pictures. Again, this makes sense given that most of the videos you have on your PC have likely come from a digital camera.

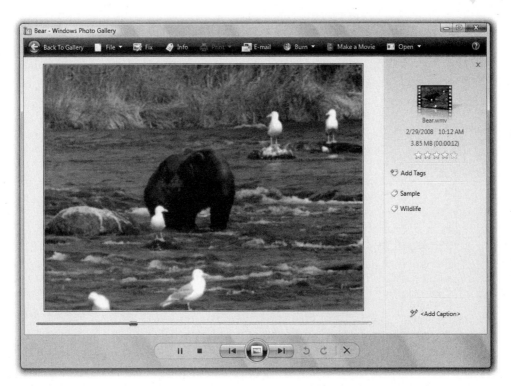

Figure 13-40: Videos that happen in Windows Photo Gallery stay in Windows Photo Gallery.

Upgrading to Windows Live Photo Gallery

One of the problems with tying applications like Windows Photo Gallery to Windows releases is that they can typically only be updated every few years. To combat this problem, Microsoft has moved development of two Windows Vista applications—Windows Mail and Windows Photo Gallery—into its Windows Live group, which creates online services and Windows applications that tie in to online services. (Microsoft calls this its "Software + Services" strategy.) The idea is simple: By making these applications available online, Microsoft can update them much more frequently.

Since shipping Windows Vista to consumers in early 2007, Microsoft has shipped a number of Windows Live offerings, but one of the more comprehensive is its Windows Live suite of applications, which includes Windows Live Messenger (instant messaging), Windows Live Hotmail (Web-based e-mail), Windows Live Photo Gallery (an updated version of the Windows Photo Gallery application from Windows Vista), Windows Live Writer (an excellent blog editor), Windows Live Spaces (an online blog service), Windows Live Events (an e-vite–type online service for event planning and celebration), Windows Live Mail (a replacement for the Windows Mail application in Windows Vista), Windows Live SkyDrive (an online storage service), Windows Live Family Safety (an online service that helps parents protect their children online), Windows Live Toolbar (an add-on for Internet Explorer), and others. You can find the full list at **www.windowslive.com/**. Yeah, it's pretty comprehensive.

In my opinion, Windows Live Photo Gallery is the most intriguing application in the Windows Live suite. It's unusual, but not unique, in that it is one of the few Windows Live applications that is an upgrade for, and replacement of, an application that ships as part of Windows Vista. (The other is Windows Live Mail, which replaces Vista's Windows Mail.)

Secret

Windows Live Photo Gallery works in Windows XP, too, which is neat, as its predecessor was Vista-only. This is true of Windows Live Mail as well.

At a Glance: Determining Which Application You're Using

As you might expect, Windows Photo Gallery and Windows Live Photo Gallery are quite similar. (After all, Windows Live Photo Gallery is simply an updated version of Windows Photo Gallery.) That said, there are some visual changes in addition to the functional changes I discuss in a moment. Comparing the toolbars for each application, as shown in Figure 13-41, you can see the most obvious of these changes.

Figure 13-41: You can tell just by looking at them next to each other that Windows Photo Gallery (top) and Windows Live Photo Gallery (bottom) are a bit different.

First, whereas Windows Photo Gallery sports a black toolbar, the Windows Live Photo Gallery toolbar is sea green (although you can't see this in the black-and-white screenshot). This is actually somewhat surprising. Most Windows Live applications have configurable color schemes, but Windows Live Photo Gallery is unique, at least at the time of this writing, in that you're stuck with the default color.

And whereas the Windows Photo Gallery toolbar buttons are centered horizontally in the application window, those of Windows Live Photo Gallery are flush against the left side of the application window. Some of the toolbar buttons are different, too: Windows Live Photo Gallery adds a new Publish button (described shortly) and consolidates the contents of the old Burn and Make a Movie buttons with a new Make button.

Finally, Windows Live Photo Gallery has a prominent Sign In button to the far right of its toolbar. This button enables you to sign in to your Windows Live ID (previously your Passport account), part of Microsoft's online services initiative. Because your Windows Live ID provides you with single sign-on access to other Windows Live services, this is a convenience, but an optional one. You absolutely don't have to sign in to use most of Windows Live Photo Gallery's features.

In short, Windows Live Photo Gallery expands on its Vista-based predecessor in interesting and useful ways, but because it is otherwise identical to Windows Photo Gallery, I'll just discuss the additional features you get by upgrading to this free product.

Simpler Photo Selection

While it's possible to select multiple pictures in Windows Photo Gallery using the familiar Ctrl+click method, doing so can be error prone, so Microsoft has borrowed an optional selection feature from the Windows Explorer shell for Windows Live Photo Gallery: the capability to select multiple items using check boxes. To see this in action, mouse over a photo thumbnail in Windows Live Photo Gallery; you'll see a small empty check box to the top left of the thumbnail. If you click this box a check mark appears inside and the item is selected. To select multiple items, simply check the boxes next to whatever images you want selected, as shown in Figure 13-42.

Figure 13-42: Windows Live Photo Gallery supports a new thumbnail selection model.

Secret

In the Windows shell, the capability to select multiple items with check boxes is enabled in the Folder Options dialog. To find this option in any Explorer window, press Alt to display the Classic menu, choose Folder Options from the Tools menu, and then navigate to the View tab and choose Use Check Boxes to Select Items in the Advanced Settings area. This selection style is actually enabled by default in Windows Vista if the system detects it is running on a Tablet PC, Ultra Mobile PC (UMPC), or other system for which a pointing device such as a pen or stylus is used. That's because it's hard to Ctrl+select when using a stylus.

New View Styles

One surprising omission in Windows Live Photo Gallery is that the square Thumbnail view button (found to the left of the Search box in Windows Photo Gallery) is missing. How the heck are you supposed to select a view style if this button is missing?

Apparently, Microsoft assumes everyone has gotten more sophisticated in the past year. Rather than provide this functionality via a conveniently located and easily discoverable button, they've hidden it in a right-click menu. Yu can change the view style, along with other thumbnail display options, by right-clicking an empty area of the Thumbnail pane and choosing View from the pop-up menu that appears. When you do so, prepare for a shock: Whereas Windows Photo Gallery offered just a paltry three view styles (Thumbnails, Thumbnails with Text, and Tiles), Windows Live Photo Gallery offers many more, including Thumbnails, Thumbnails with Date Taken, Thumbnails with Date Modified, Thumbnails with File Size, Thumbnails with Image Size, Thumbnails with Rating, Thumbnails with Caption, Thumbnails with File Name, and Details. Most of these views work as you might expect, but one, Details, is worth noting. This option replaces the old Tiles view and provides a lot of information attached to each image, as shown in Figure 13-43. Note that it's nothing like Details view in the Explorer shell at all, despite the name.

Figure 13-43: The new Details view delivers nice thumbnails with plenty of information about each photo.

Secret   The new Details view is full featured: You can edit the rating and caption (but not tags) metadata right next to each photo's thumbnail.

As with Explorer windows in Windows Vista, Windows Live Photo Gallery adopts a handy set of grouping columns, regardless of the view style. Unlike the shell, however, you can't configure which columns you get: You're stuck with the default columns of Name, Date, Rating, and Type.

tip   Regardless of which view style you choose, the resizing secret from Windows Photo Gallery still works: Just hold down the Ctrl key and use your mouse scroll wheel to resize the thumbnails.

Photo Stitching

If you've ever vacationed in a scenic spot, you've probably engaged in an age-old photographic ritual: taking a series of panoramic shots, moving from one side to the other, as you pan around to take in the entire (ahem) vista. The problem is, when you get home and copy those pictures to the computer, they're all disjointed and it's not clear that they fit together at all. High-end photography tools such as Photoshop have long offered a way to stitch these photos back together again into a single widescreen shot; now Windows Live Photo Gallery offers this functionality as well.

The trick, of course, is to find two or more shots that can be visually connected in this fashion. Once you've done that, select them in Windows Live Photo Gallery, click the Make toolbar button, and choose Create Panoramic Photo from the drop-down menu that appears. Windows Live Photo Gallery will composite the photos and then prompt you to save the resulting combined image, using a standard Windows Save As dialog box that's been renamed to Save Panoramic Stitch. Select a name and location for the resulting file and click the Save button to save the results.

At this point, Windows Live Photo Gallery will commit the newly stitched photo to disk, leaving the originals as is, and will display the new photo. As shown in Figure 13-44, the stitching effect is usually seamless.

The one task you'll have to perform with stitched panoramic photos is trimming off some excess black space in order to arrive at a normal, rectangular image. Just click the Fix toolbar button and then use the Crop photo tool in the Edit pane to do so.

Figure 13-44: This panoramaic photo was made by stitching three separate photos together.

Adjust Detail/Sharpen Photo Fix

Speaking of the Edit pane, you'll notice a few changes and improvements here as well in Windows Live Photo Gallery. First, all of the tools have been de-capitalized since Windows Photo Gallery, so Auto Adjust becomes Auto adjust, and so on. One tool, Crop Picture, has been renamed, to Crop photo. Best of all, Windows Live Photo Gallery adds a new editing tool, Adjust detail. (Note that for the purposes of this book, however, dialog box options appear in the text in title-case form, e.g., Adjust Detail tool.)

When you click on Adjust Detail in the Edit pane, you'll see a Sharpen slider appear, as shown in Figure 13-45. Sliding this bar to the right increases the sharpness of the picture. This effect can be quite appealing, depending on the photo. Just be careful not to go too far with it, as over-sharpened pictures tend to be a bit stark-looking.

QuickTime Movie Support

It may seem curious for Microsoft to add support for an Apple movie format, QuickTime, to Windows Live Photo Gallery. After all, Microsoft and Apple compete in various digital media markets. But this decision was quite pragmatic: Microsoft added QuickTime compatibility because so many digital cameras these days include the capability to create short videos in this format. If you have such a camera, Windows Live Gallery will be even more useful to you.

Figure 13-45: New to Windows Live Photo Gallery is an Adjust Detail tool, which enables you to increase the sharpness of a photo.

Dramatically Improved Photo Acquisition

I complained earlier in this chapter that the photo acquisition capabilities in Windows Photo Gallery were seriously lacking compared to similar functionality in Windows Vista's predecessor, Windows XP. Well, Microsoft listened: One of the best aspects of Windows Live Photo Gallery is that the photo acquisition feature has been dramatically enhanced. In fact, it's so good that you should use this tool to import photos from cameras and other digital sources, even if you decide to use another application to perform other digital image activities. (The scanner acquisition capabilities are largely unchanged since Windows Photo Gallery.)

Configuring Windows Live Photo Gallery for Importing Photos

To see the difference, plug a digital camera into your PC via USB or insert a memory card into a memory card reader. As shown in Figure 13-46, new Windows Live Photo Gallery options have been added to the list of Picture options, alongside the older options for Windows Photo Gallery (and, possibly, any third-party applications you or your PC maker may have installed).

Figure 13-46: Now you can choose to import or view photos with Windows Live Photo Gallery instead of Windows Photo Gallery.

Secret

To ensure that Windows Live Photo Gallery is the default choice for importing photos, open the Start Menu and choose Default Programs. Then, in the Default Programs control panel, select the link titled Change AutoPlay Settings. Next, in AutoPlay, find the Pictures option and change it to Import Pictures and Videos Using Windows Live Photo Gallery.

In the Import Photos and Videos dialog that appears, you'll be told how many new photos and videos were found and given three options:

♦ **Review, organize, and group items to import:** This is the option you should choose every time you import photos using Windows Live Photo Gallery. You'll examine this process in the next section, but first you have some configuration changes to make.

♦ **Import all items now:** If you prefer for Windows Live Photo Gallery to import your photos in one giant, mindless batch—you know, as Windows Photo Gallery does—then this option is what you're looking for. My advice is simple: Don't ever use this option, even if you believe you only have a single event's worth of photos on your camera or memory card.

♦ **More options:** This link opens the Import Settings dialog, which is also available from within Windows Live Photo Gallery by selecting File ➪ Options from within the application and then navigating to the Import tab of the resulting dialog. Examine this dialog at least once before importing any photos because you're almost certainly going to want to change the way in which photos are organized on your hard drive once their imported. The Import Settings dialog is shown in Figure 13-47.

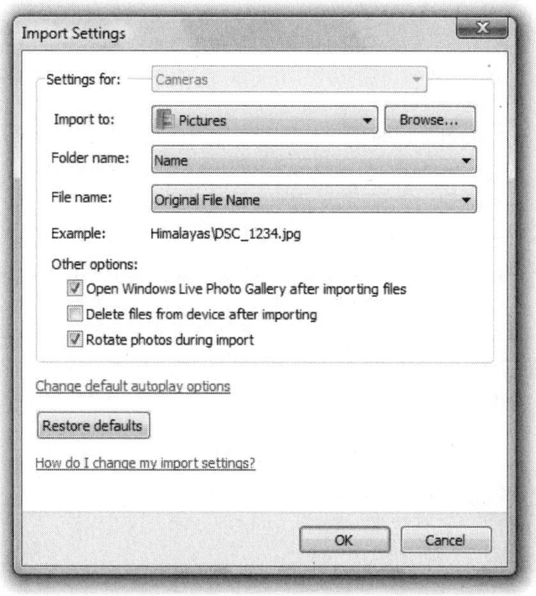

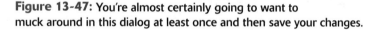

Figure 13-47: You're almost certainly going to want to muck around in this dialog at least once and then save your changes.

There's a lot going on here, but most of it can be divided into two simple categories: where your photos will be imported to and how they will be named when copied to disk. By default, photos are imported to a subfolder under your Pictures folder. The folder name they're saved to can be one of several options, the default of which is Name, meaning the name you supply while importing photos. But you may want to use one of the other options, which include Date Imported + Name, Date Taken + Name (the one I choose), Date Taken Range + Name, Name + Date Imported, Name + Date Taken, or Name + Date Taken Range.

You have similar options for naming individual photos, including Name, Original File Name (curiously, the default option), Original File Name (Preserve Folders), Name + Date Taken (the one I choose), and Date Taken + Name.

As you modify the choices for folder and file naming, the Import Settings dialog provides a preview of the type of folder structure and files it will create. For example, my chosen settings result in an example such as *2008-07-01 Himalayas\Himalayas 2008-07-01001.jpg*.

Other options are available as well: You can choose whether to open Windows Live Photo Gallery after importing files (selected by default), whether to delete the original files from the camera or memory card after they're imported (not selected by default), and whether to automatically rotate those photos that need to be rotated (selected by default). I happen to leave all three selected, but this is a matter of personal preference.

Importing Photos with Windows Live Photo Gallery

Once Windows Live Photo Gallery is correctly configured, you can begin importing photos. As noted in the previous section, you should always choose the first option in Import Photos and Videos: Review, Organize, and Group Items to Import. That's because when you do so, the application groups your photos intelligently by event and creates folders accordingly, although you can still edit the groups as desired. It's really well done.

Once you select this option and click Next, you'll see the second section of this wizard, with photos grouped according to date and time (see Figure 13-48).

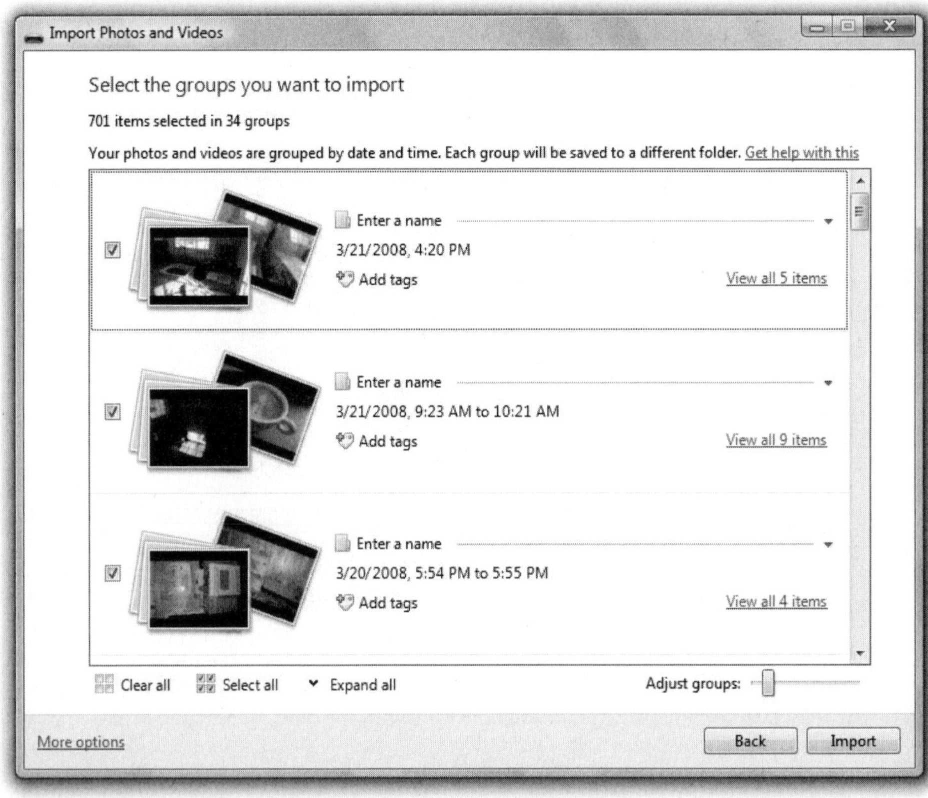

Figure 13-48: Finally, a way to determine exactly which photos to import and how they'll be grouped in folders on disk (and, logically, within Windows Photo Gallery and Windows Live Photo Gallery).

Here you can choose which photos to import, using the check boxes on the left and the handy Clear All and Select All buttons; and adjust the grouping using a simple slider (in which sliding to the left lowers the amount of time between groups and sliding to the right increases the time). More important, you can provide a name for each group and tag each group as you see fit. You can also click a View All Items link next to each group to ensure that they're grouped exactly the way you want, as shown in Figure 13-49. (You can also contract each group again by clicking anywhere in the area above the photo previews.)

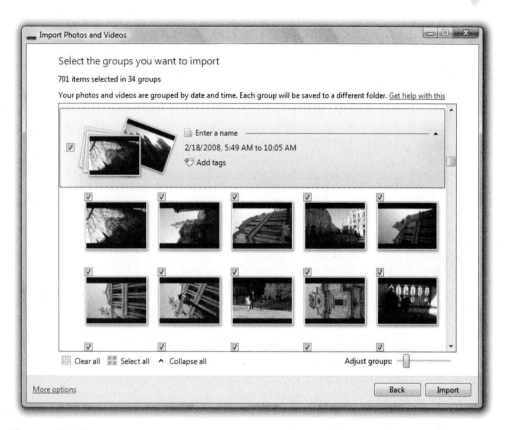

Figure 13-49: You can expand each group to see which photos will be included.

> **tip**
> If you don't have enough room in the Import Photos and Videos window, you can resize the window accordingly. Just grab the lower-right corner of the window with the mouse cursor and resize away.

Once you've named, tagged, and grouped everything to your heart's content, click the Import button. Windows Live Photo Gallery will import the photos you've selected to the hard drive and into your Windows Live Photo Gallery and Windows Photo Gallery photo libraries.

> **tip**
> Even if you chose not to delete files as they're imported in the Import Options dialog previously, you can choose to do so on-the-fly every time you import photos: The import window also includes a check box for this purpose.

Integration with Windows Live Services and Third-Party Services

As you might expect of a Windows Live application, Windows Live Photo Gallery offers unique integration points with other Windows Live online services. Perhaps more impressive, it also offers some integration with non-Microsoft online services. It's time to examine this integration.

I mentioned previously that Windows Live Photo Gallery enables you to log on to your Windows Live ID account using a handy Sign In link in the upper-right corner of the application. This is entirely optional (as are the other Windows Live integration features), but if you do use a Windows Live ID you might find it convenient to automatically log on each time you use Windows Live Photo Gallery. Doing so gives you access to the other services with which this application integrates, meaning you won't have to manually log on later.

Most new integration points are accessible via the new Publish toolbar button, from which you can access the following features:

◆ **Publish on Windows Live Spaces:** Any selected photo(s) will be published to your Windows Live Space, a Microsoft-hosted blog service (**http://spaces.live.com**). Unlike other companies, Microsoft doesn't actually offer a separate photo-only online storage service. Instead, users are expected to store their photos online via Windows Live Spaces. (This feature requires you to log on with your Windows Live ID first.)

◆ **Publish on MSN Soapbox:** Any selected video(s) will be published to MSN Soapbox, Microsoft's answer to YouTube (**http://soapbox.msn.com**). The Publish wizard that appears enables you to provide a title and description, add a limit of five tags, and select a category and permission level (public or hidden). This is shown in Figure 13-50. (This feature requires you to log on with your Windows Live ID first.)

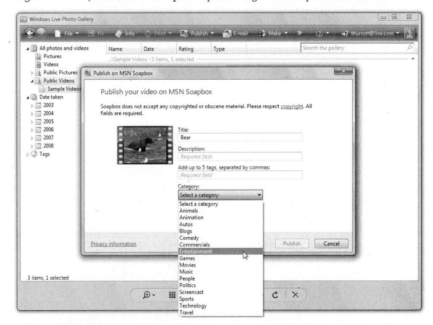

Figure 13-50: Want to share your videos with the world, or at least the small subset of the world that's heard of Soapbox? This is the way.

◆ **More Services:** This is, perhaps, the most interesting option because it's the gateway to non-Microsoft services. At the time of this writing, access is available to only once service—the Flickr photo-sharing site—but I'm told that Microsoft plans to add more services in the future. (This feature requires you to authorize Windows Live Photo Gallery to access your Flickr account first.)

Summary

Although Windows Vista completely steps back from the shell-based photo-management functionality that was provided in Windows XP, the new Windows Photo Gallery application more than makes up for it. Windows users now have an obvious place to manage, edit, share, and otherwise enjoy digital photos (and videos). Windows Photo Gallery is one of the better end user additions to Windows Vista; Windows Live Photo Gallery, an update to Windows Photo Gallery that's available free online, is even better, offering additional functionality and fixing a few problems of its predecessor.

Digital Videos and DVD Movies

Chapter 14

J ust a few short years ago, the notion of consumers using PCs to edit their home movies into professional-looking productions was science fiction, but then Apple came along with iMovie and proved that not only was it possible but that high-quality video-editing tools could be done elegantly and in a user-friendly fashion. At that time, Microsoft had just released its first Windows Movie Maker tool, a crippled Windows Me application that was aimed only at the low end of the market. Today, in Windows Vista, Microsoft has a variety of tools for managing, viewing, editing, and publishing digital video of all kinds. You can even edit TV shows, removing commercials, and make your own movie DVDs. Moreover, because this is a PC with a rich ecosystem of third-party applications, it's possible to perform other relevant tasks in Vista as well, including duplicating DVDs and "ripping" DVD movies to the hard drive. You can even duplicate and rip copy-protected DVDs if you know where to look. This chapter delves into all of that.

Managing Digital Movies with Windows Vista

Like Windows XP before it, Windows Vista provides several ways to manage, view, and otherwise enjoy digital movies. You may recall that Windows XP included a special shell folder called My Videos. Actually, you will be forgiven for not remembering that—in Windows XP the My Videos folder was curiously deprecated when compared to its My Documents, My Music, and My Pictures siblings. It didn't appear on the Start Menu by default and couldn't be added later. In fact, My Videos didn't even appear in the Windows XP shell until you started Windows Movie Maker for the first time.

In Windows Vista the situation is only marginally different. The My Videos folder has been replaced by the new Videos folder, in keeping with Microsoft's new shell folder naming scheme. It's no longer a special shell folder, and it's not located in the file system inside of Documents, as before. Instead, it sits under your Home folder (C:\Users*Your user* by default) alongside Documents, Music, Pictures, and other commonly needed folders. However, it still doesn't appear on the right side of the Start Menu for some reason, and once again there's no way to make it appear there.

So how do you get to the Videos folder, you ask? In Windows XP you could simply open My Documents and there it was. In Vista, the easiest way is to open your Home folder, which is represented by your user name in the upper-right corner of the Start Menu. When you click that link the Home folder opens in its own window, as shown in Figure 14-1. Inside, you'll see the Videos folder.

In addition to Videos, Windows Vista maintains another folder for videos called Public Videos. (This was called Shared Videos in Windows XP and was in a different location.) Public Videos, as you might expect, is located inside the directory structure for the Public user account and is shared between all of the users configured for the current PC. Sadly, there's no easy way to find it. You have to manually navigate to C:\Users\Public\Videos (by default) to find this folder.

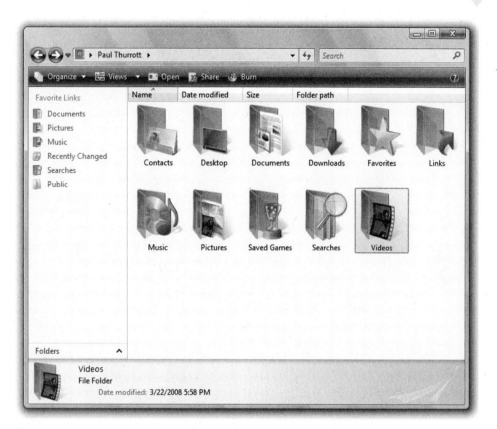

Figure 14-1: You'll find the new Videos folder inside your Home folder.

tip   There's also a Sample Videos folder that includes a set of short sample videos provided by Microsoft. You can find a shortcut to this folder in your Videos folder, but the actual folder is located in C:\Users\Public\Videos\Sample Videos by default.

Secret

Because of the proliferation of digital cameras with video capabilities, you will very likely find videos scattered around inside your Pictures folder. When you copy pictures from a digital camera to Windows Vista (or to previous versions of Windows), any videos on the camera will be copied to the same location, which is typically a subfolder under Pictures. Thankfully, you can use Windows Vista's Instant Search feature to find these videos: Open the Pictures folder and type **video** in the Search box in the upper-right corner of the window. In addition to any photos with the word *video* in their title, you may find several movie files as well. In Figure 14-2 you can see some of these movies grouped by type. Typical movie types include Movie Clip, QuickTime Movie, Video Clip, and Windows Media Audio/Video file.

Figure 14-2: Look, ma! There are videos in my Pictures folder.

Secret

If you'd like a handy way to access these hidden videos from one location in the Windows shell, you can create a Search Folder, which I discuss in detail in Chapter 5, and save it inside your Videos folder. That way you always have a convenient way to access all of those disparate and hidden video files.

With all these different locations for finding digital videos, you might wonder what Microsoft was thinking. Although I could never claim to offer any insight along those lines, I can tell you that video management, like that of music and photos, has changed dramatically in Windows Vista. Although it's still possible to navigate around the Windows shell and double-click movies to play them in Windows Media Player or another software tool, Microsoft actually expects that most of its users will instead use dedicated applications to manage and view digital movies. You get a chance to look at them all in the next few sections.

Watching and Managing Movies with Windows Photo Gallery and Windows Live Photo Gallery

The primary movie management tool in Windows Vista, believe it or not, is called Windows Photo Gallery. Why Microsoft didn't choose to name it Windows Photo and Movie Gallery is unclear, but the fact remains that you can organize and manage (and even play) virtually all of the digital video on your system with this tool. Although I describe this application in detail in Chapter 13, it may be worth a short side trip here to discuss how it works with digital movies specifically.

tip Microsoft has released an updated version of Windows Photo Gallery, called Windows Live Photo Gallery, and made it available as a free download from the Web. While this new application is discussed in Chapter 13 too, note that from a movie management perspective, Windows Photo Gallery and Windows Live Photo Gallery are almost identical. There's just one big difference, and it may put this application over the top for you: Unlike Windows Photo Gallery, Windows Live Photo Gallery works with movies stored in Apple's QuickTime format as well. From here on out, any discussion of Windows Photo Gallery refers to both Windows Photo Gallery and Windows Live Photo Gallery unless otherwise noted.

By default, Windows Photo Gallery enables you to manage photos and videos together, and it's designed to search the Pictures, Videos, Public Pictures, and Public Videos folders for video (and photo) content by default. (You can manually configure Windows Photo Gallery to search other locations as well; see Chapter 13 for more information.) When it comes to video, all the metadata application information works equally well with movies as it does with photos. That is, you can add tags, ratings, and captions to movies, just as you can with photos.

If you want to work only with movies in Windows Photo Gallery, select the Videos entry under All Pictures and Videos in the application's View By pane. Now you will see only videos in the Thumbnails pane, as shown in Figure 14-3. (Windows Live Photo Gallery handles this slightly differently for some reason: You need to click on particular folder names, such as Videos and Public Videos, to see all of the videos on your system with this application.)

As you mouse over individual videos, a pop-up window displays, showing a larger thumbnail and other information about the file, including its name, size, rating, and the date and time it was created. You can see this effect in Figure 14-4.

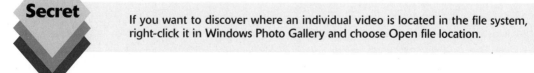

Secret If you want to discover where an individual video is located in the file system, right-click it in Windows Photo Gallery and choose Open file location.

Figure 14-3: Even video files are displayed with nice thumbnail images in Windows Photo Gallery.

Figure 14-4: Nice flyover effects give you more information about individual videos.

To play a video, simply double-click it. Curiously, videos opened in Windows Photo Gallery play in Windows Photo Gallery—and not in Windows Media Player, as you might expect. This is undesirable for a few reasons, but the most obvious is that the video playback pane in Windows Photo Gallery is only as large as the application window, which is often larger than the original video, causing blurry resizing effects. As shown in Figure 14-5, Windows Photo Gallery isn't the optimal place to play video files.

Figure 14-5: You can play videos in Windows Photo Gallery, but it's better suited for just managing the files.

From this window you can add ratings, tags, and captioning metadata if you so desire. You can also edit the file's creation date and time data. What you can't do is edit the movie—clicking the Fix toolbar button just displays an unhelpful message. My advice is to use Windows Photo Gallery to manage videos only, but to use Windows Media Player, described in the next section, for playback. I discuss editing digital movies later in this chapter as well.

Secret

If you're wondering whether you can play movies in Windows Media Player from within Windows Photo Gallery, the answer is a qualified yes. To trigger Windows Media Player playback from Windows Photo Gallery, don't double-click a video thumbnail. Instead, select the video file you'd like to play and then choose Open ⇨ Windows Media Player from the application's toolbar. (Alternately, right-click the video file from within Windows Photo Gallery and choose Open With ⇨ Windows Media Player from the pop-up menu that appears.) The real question, of course, is whether you can make Windows Photo Gallery be the default player from within Windows Media Player. The answer, sadly, is no.

Watching and Managing Movies with Windows Media Player

Most people think of Windows Media Player as a music player, but in fact Windows Media Player can also work with video and photo content as well. (As you'll see in Chapter 11, however, Windows Media Player only handles these types of content so that they can be synchronized with portable media players.) This capability isn't new to Windows Media Player 11, the version that Microsoft ships with Windows Vista. However, because videos do play natively in Windows Media Player 11, you might want to manage videos, to some degree, in the player too. Like Windows Photo Gallery, Windows Media Player 11 is configured to automatically monitor certain folders for digital media files, and those locations include, by default, your Videos folder and the Public Videos folder. No surprise there.

To configure Windows Media Player to display only videos, select Video from the Categories button, as shown in Figure 14-6.

Figure 14-6: Yes, that little doohickey is the key to some important Media Player functionality: picking the type of media to display.

As shown in Figure 14-7, the Media Player display will change to show only video thumbnails.

Figure 14-7: Windows Media Player is just one of many places in Windows Vista from which you can manage digital movie files.

From here you can play, rate, and rename individual videos, but that's about it. You can't add tags from within Windows Media Player, for example. Typically, you use this application to simply play videos. That's Windows Media Player's strong suit, and you can use the player's various controls to change the size of the video, display it using a nice full-screen mode, or even minimize the player to the system taskbar and watch it there while you get work done.

Secret   One nice side effect of Windows Media Player's capabilities is that you can actually create temporary or saved playlists of videos. That way you can trigger a collection of videos to play in order or randomly. It's not possible to do that from the shell or within Windows Photo Gallery; if you save the playlist, you can access it from Windows Media Center, described in the next section.

Watching and Managing Movies with Windows Media Center

Windows Media Center is, of course, the premium environment in Windows for enjoying digital media content such as photos, music, movies, and, yes, even live and recorded TV shows. But Media Center—discussed in detail in Chapter 15—isn't just for people with expensive home theater setups. There's no reason you can't use Media Center with a mouse and keyboard on your desktop PC or notebook. In fact, you may find it quite enjoyable to do just that.

Secret   Because it is a premium feature, Windows Media Center is not available in all Windows Vista product versions. You have to be using Windows Vista Home Premium or Windows Vista Ultimate to get Windows Media Center.

As shown in Figure 14-8, Windows Media Center is a seamless, home theater–like application that works best full screen but can absolutely be enjoyed in a floating, resizable window alongside your other applications if you feel like doing a bit of multi-tasking.

To use Media Center to manage your digital movies, navigate to Pictures + Videos in the Start page and then choose Video Library. The first time you enter this area, Media Center will ask if you'd like to choose other folders to watch for videos. If you've already configured either Windows Photo Gallery or Windows Media Player to watch particular folders, or you intend to only use the default folders for video content, you can select No; in that case, Windows Media Player uses the same database of watch folders as those other two applications.

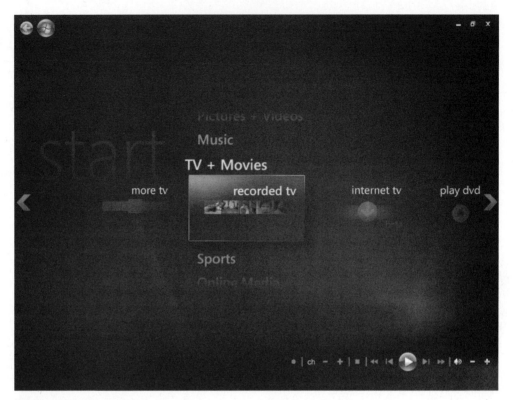

Figure 14-8: Windows Media Center is a nice graphical front end to a variety of digital media experiences.

If you choose Yes, Media Center will walk you through its Library Setup wizard. From here you can easily add other folders to monitor for video content.

Video Library, shown in Figure 14-9, provides a horizontally oriented grid of videos through which you can navigate by either name or date. To watch a video, simply select it.

Secret

Although Windows Media Center offers tag-based navigation for music and photos, it does not do so for videos. To navigate your video collection by tag, you need to use Windows Photo Gallery.

Figure 14-9: In Media Center, videos include graphical thumbnails, making for a highly visual navigation experience.

In a related vein, you can't tag, rate, or add captions to videos in Media Center only. Essentially, Windows Media Center simply offers a high-end place for video consumption. If you want to interact with videos, you'll need to look elsewhere.

tip   As noted previously, Windows Media Center also works with live and recorded TV content. Although this content is technically digital video, I discuss this in more detail in Chapter 15, and later in this chapter in the discussion about editing and republishing recorded TV content.

Secret

Using Movies as Your Desktop Background

This is going to sound crazy—and let's be honest here for a moment, it *is* kind of crazy—but if you have the right version of Windows Vista, you can actually utilize certain videos as an animated Desktop background. Once you've digested that one, let me explain how it works. First, you have to be running Windows Vista Ultimate. This version of Windows Vista includes access to Microsoft's Windows Ultimate Extras, a collection of additional Vista features that are available only in Vista Ultimate. (The differences between each Vista version are found in Chapter 1.) Next you download and install Ultimate Extras via Vista's Windows Update service, and one of those extras is a cool little tool called Windows Dreamscape. This utility enables you to use a video (or, as Microsoft notes, even a slideshow of your favorite pictures) as your Desktop background instead of the typical static background. Most videos aren't particularly well suited for this purpose, but Microsoft provides a collection of interesting animated videos you can sample. To find them, right-click on the Desktop and choose Personalize. Then, select Desktop Background, and from the Location drop-down in the next window choose Windows DreamScene content. A typical DreamScene is shown in Figure 14-10.

Figure 14-10: Windows DreamScene enables Windows Vista Ultimate users to replace the static Desktop background with something a bit more animated. It's hard to see here, but this isn't a still image but rather an animated movie file.

continues

continued

The fun thing about DreamScene is that it works with virtually any video file, assuming it's encoded in the MPEG-2 (MPG) or Windows Media Video (WMV) formats. (You also need video hardware that's capable of displaying the Aero user interface, which by the time you read this will be all PCs on the market.) That means you could conceivably use a video you've recorded with your digital camera or video camera as an animated Desktop background. To test this, navigate to the location of a compatible video file with Windows Explorer. Then, right-click the video and select Set as Desktop Background. As shown in Figure 14-11, your video replaces the old background image. Talk about interactive vacation movies!

Figure 14-11: You can even use your own home movie as a Desktop background.

Obviously, most home movies are not steady enough to be used as a background, and you may very well discover that the shaky nature of such video is more distracting than enjoyable, but it's certainly worth checking out.

Editing Digital Video with Windows Movie Maker

Windows Movie Maker is Microsoft's tool for creating and editing digital videos. You can import a variety of digital media types into the application, including home movies, photos, music and other audio files, and even recorded TV shows. Then, using simple editing techniques along with professional transitions and effects, you can create complete videos that can be shared with others through PCs, e-mail, the Web, digital video tape, or—in conjunction with Windows DVD maker, described at the end of this chapter—DVD movies.

Secret

You may have heard of something called Movie Maker HD (where HD stands for high definition, as in HDTV). Technically, Movie Maker HD is not a separate version of Movie Maker, but rather a description of features that Movie Maker gains in certain Windows Vista product versions. All versions of Windows Vista include Movie Maker, but only the versions in Windows Vista Home Premium and Ultimate can import from and publish to HD video sources. You need a fairly high-end PC to manipulate such video, of course; but such powerful PCs are becoming more and more common.

Windows Movie Maker is a relatively straightforward application, assuming you're comfortable with video editing (and heck, who isn't?). Even for the uninitiated, Windows Movie Maker is pretty easy to use. You just need to know your way around.

Starting Windows Movie Maker

Typically, you start Windows Movie Maker by launching its shortcut from the Start Menu. (Type **movie** in Start Menu Search to find it quickly.) Windows Movie Maker is also available from elsewhere in Windows Vista. As noted in Chapter 13, you can trigger Windows Movie Maker from the Windows Photo Gallery and Windows Live Photo Gallery applications if you want to create a movie of a photo slideshow, for example.

Secret

In increasingly rare cases you may get an error message when you try to launch Windows Movie Maker. If you see an error dialog like that shown in Figure 14-12, then your PC is not powerful enough to run the Vista version of Windows Movie Maker.

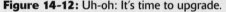

Figure 14-12: Uh-oh: It's time to upgrade.

continues

continued

You have two options here. One, you could upgrade your PC to a DirectX 9–compatible video card. This is a very inexpensive option for most desktop PCs. However, most portable computers do not have upgradable video hardware. The second option, which isn't obvious at all, is to download Windows Movie Maker 2.6 from the Microsoft Web site. This older version of Windows Movie Maker was originally designed for Windows XP, but Microsoft now offers it to Windows Vista users with low-end hardware. You can use the following URL, or visit the Microsoft Download Center and search for Windows Movie Maker 2.6 for Vista.

**www.microsoft.com/downloads/details.aspx?FamilyID=
d6ba5972-328e-4df7-8f9d-068fc0f80cfc&displaylang=en**

The version of Windows Movie Maker covered in this chapter is 6.0, not 2.6, as this is the version that ships with Windows Vista. Most readers of this book are probably not running Windows Vista on ancient hardware and will thus never see that message. All this said, Windows Movie Maker 2.6 isn't horrible and does offer many of the features found in version 6.0. What it's lacking, primarily, are the Auto Movie and DVD export features found in Windows Movie Maker 6. Windows Movie Maker 2.6 is shown in Figure 14-13.

Figure 14-13: Windows Movie Maker 2.6 is available to Vista users with low-end video hardware.

Understanding the Movie Maker User Interface

Windows Movie Maker is divided into three basic areas from top to bottom: The menu and toolbar at the top, the panes section in the middle, and the Storyboard/Timeline area at the bottom. As shown in Figure 14-14, these areas are clearly delineated.

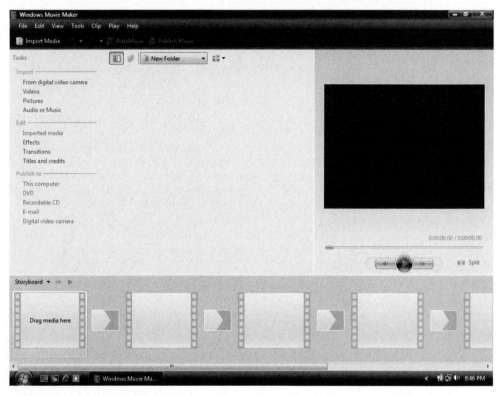

Figure 14-14: Windows Movie Maker takes digital media content in and spits out finished video after a bit of fine-tuning.

Because the menu and toolbar area are similar to other Windows applications, most of the discussion here focuses on the other two parts of the Movie Maker user interface, which are unique to this application.

In the center left of the application window, you'll see the Tasks pane, which you can use to literally step through the tasks needed to bring a custom video production to life. In the center is the Imported Media pane, in which you collect shortcuts to digital media files on your PC that will be used in the current project. On the right is the Preview pane, where you can preview your video creation as it is developed. These panes are shown in Figure 14-15.

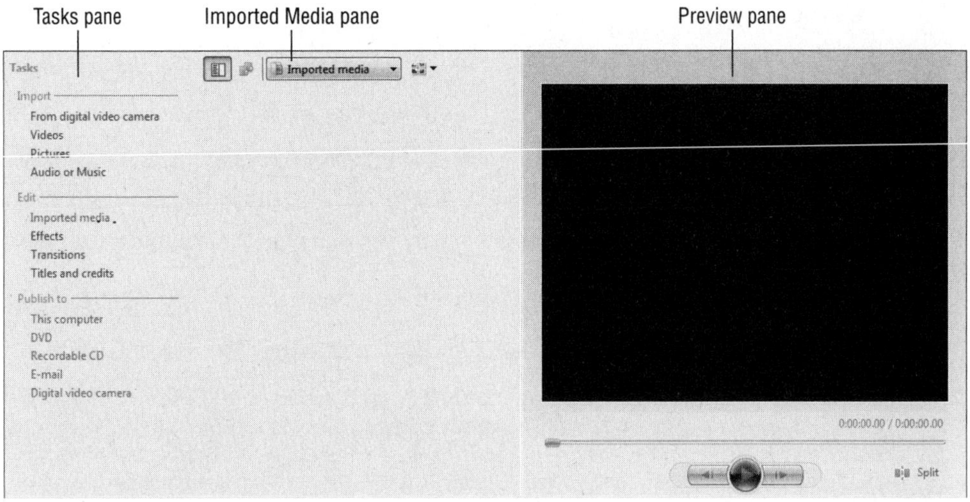

Tasks pane   Imported Media pane   Preview pane

Figure 14-15: The Tasks, Imported Media, and Preview panes dominate the Windows Movie Maker application.

> **tip**
>
> Note that the Preview pane is resizable, so you can alternatively increase the size of the video pane and decrease the size of the Imported Media pane, and vice versa, as necessary. The Storyboard/Timeline pane at the bottom holds the edited version of the current video project and can operate in two modes. Storyboard mode, which is the default, displays the digital media files that make up your video project in sequential order, and it presents small user interface slots for video effects and transitions, giving you a nice overview of the bits and pieces that make up the project. The Storyboard is shown in Figure 14-16.

Figure 14-16: The Windows Movie Maker Storyboard pane.

In Timeline mode, shown in Figure 14-17, you see a more literal representation of the video project, presented in a time-based display that is perfect for fine-tuning details of the presentation, such as timing. This is the mode you'll use to trim audio and video clips. I recommend staying in Timeline mode for all but the simplest video projects.

Figure 14-17: Timeline mode provides a more detailed representation of the video you're creating.

Importing Digital Media into a Project

To start a new project in Windows Movie Maker, you first need a collection of shortcuts to digital media files that will be used in your final video. Windows Movie Maker can import a variety of video, audio, and picture files, and these files can be assembled however you like in your project's storyboard or timeline. Table 14-1 highlights the formats you can use with Windows Movie Maker.

Table 14-1: Media Formats Supported by Windows Movie Maker

Movie formats	.ASF, .AVI, .DVR-MS, .M1V, .MP2, .MP2V, .MPE, .MPEG, .MPG, .MPV2, .WM, .WMV
Audio formats	.AIF, .AIFC, .AIFF, .ASF, .AU, .MP2, .MP3, .MPA, .SND, .WAV, .WMA
Picture formats	.BMP, .DIB, .EMF, .GIF, .JFIF, .JPE, .JPEG, .JPG, .PNG, .TIF, .TIFF, .WMF

Secret

The MS-DVR format is new to this version of Windows Movie Maker. This is the format Microsoft uses for its Media Center recorded TV shows. That's right: You can use Movie Maker to edit TV shows, so if you'd like to save a movie or show you've recorded, or edit out the commercials or the dead time at the beginning and end of the recording, you can now do so.

There is one caveat to this capability, however. Shows recorded on certain channels, such as HBO and Cinemax, cannot be edited (or, for that matter, copied to a PC other than the one on which it was recorded). That's because these shows are protected by so-called Broadcast Flag technology, which television stations can use to restrict copying. Currently, this technology is used mostly on pay cable channels in the U.S. market, but it will become increasingly common as digital video recording (DVR) solutions such as Media Center and TiVo become more prevalent.

Secret

What about files you can't import? While it's impossible to cover every contingency, I'd like to raise a few issues here. First, some files simply can't be imported, no matter what you try. These include such things as music, movies, or TV show episodes you've purchased from an online service such as Apple iTunes, Amazon Unbox, or Movielink. These files are protected to prevent intellectual property theft, and are thus specifically designed to prevent you from editing them in Windows Movie Maker or similar applications. When you try to import such a file, you see the error message shown in Figure 14-18.

Figure 14-18: Protected and incompatible movie files can't be edited in Windows Movie Maker.

Another obvious source for video content is DVD movies. After all, wouldn't it be cool to include portions of your favorite movies in your own video creations? Maybe so, but Windows Vista doesn't include any way to acquire content from DVD movies, whether they're protected (as are Hollywood-created DVD movies) or not (as are most homemade DVD movies). Before you can use content from a DVD movie in Windows Movie Maker, you need to copy that content to your hard drive in a format that Windows Movie Maker understands. I explain how to do this later in the chapter.

Finally, you may have a number of movies on your hard drive in common video formats, like Apple QuickTime, that won't work in Windows Movie Maker. As long as these files are unprotected—as they will be if you created them yourself, perhaps with your digital camera—then you can simply convert these files from QuickTime or whatever format they may be in, to a format that Windows Movie Maker understands. In the case of QuickTime, you can use the Export function in Apple's QuickTime Player Pro (which isn't free, alas) to export movies in AVI format, as shown in Figure 14-19. AVI files work just fine in Windows Movie Maker.

continues

continued

Figure 14-19: QuickTime files aren't exactly friendly when it comes to Microsoft applications, but you can convert them into a compatible format.

To import a movie, photo, or music file into Movie Maker, click the Import Media button on the Movie Maker toolbar, choose Import Media Items from the File menu, or simply drag the files into the Imported Media pane from any Explorer window. Likewise, if you want to import content from a digital video camera, select Import from Digital Video Camera from the File menu and step through the wizard.

tip Remember that digital video imported from your digital still camera can be obtained using the normal Import wizard that appears when you connect the camera to your Windows Vista PC. These videos are located in your Picture folder, in whatever folder you created during import.

Figure 14-20 shows a variety of media types located in the Movie Maker Imported Media pane, including a JPEG photo, an MP3 music file, and a WMV movie file.

Figure 14-20: After you've assembled the pieces that comprise your video, it's time to start editing.

Secret

When you import content into Windows Movie Maker, you're only telling Windows Movie Maker where to find that content. In other words, Movie Maker doesn't make a copy of the content, it only displays a shortcut to the original content. If you were to delete or move a file that Windows Movie Maker needs for a video project, it won't work properly anymore.

Editing a Recorded TV Show or Movie

The simplest way to make a movie is just to grab any bit of media—be it music, picture, or video, though of course video works best—and take it to the storyboard. Then, you can press Play in the Preview pane and watch your simple, unedited creation play through to completion. Typically, however, you're going to want to make something a bit more sophisticated, so for this section I'll assume that you have a recorded TV show you'd like to edit. You will want to remove the dead space at the beginning and end of the show, edit out any commercials, and then save the show back to your hard drive in a high-quality format that is compatible with Windows Vista PCs, portable devices, and digital media receivers. Later you'll even write this show to DVD so you can watch it on any standard DVD player.

tip If you don't have a recorded TV show, perhaps because your PC isn't connected to a TV signal through a TV tuner card, fear not. You can use one of the sample recorded TV shows included with Media Center, or a sample video file that ships with Windows Vista. Or grab some of your own home video footage. It's up to you.

note By default, recorded TV shows are stored in C:\Users\Public\Recorded TV. There's no Recorded TV folder under a normal user account's Home folder because recorded TV shows are shared by all users on the PC.

Navigate to the Recorded TV folder and import a recorded TV show or one of the samples that Microsoft provides in C:\Users\Public\Recorded TV\Sample Media. It's time to start editing. You'll need to put Windows Movie Maker into a mode that's designed for this and then import some video. It's time to jump right in.

Working with the Timeline

First, put Windows Movie Maker in Timeline mode: Click the Storyboard button in the upper-left corner of the Storyboard pane and choose Timeline from the drop-down menu that appears. Movie Maker will now resemble Figure 14-21.

Drag the Recorded TV show (or movie) you want to edit from the Imported Media pane down into the Video well in the timeline. When you do so, Movie Maker will resemble Figure 14-22. The TV show or video will fill up the Video pane out to the length of the actual video.

If you're editing a recorded TV show, the first step is to remove the unrelated content at the beginning of the show. Press the Play button to play through this content and find the beginning of the bits you'd like to save. You can skip ahead, pause, and rewind to the beginning of the timeline as required. After you've found the exact moment at which the actual show begins, click Pause. If you can, try to make this pause point occur right when the image fades to black or just a hair before the actual video starts.

tip You can use the small Zoom Timeline In icon at the top of the Timeline pane (it looks like a small magnifying glass with a plus sign on it) to visually "zoom into" the timeline and more precisely position where you want to split the clip.

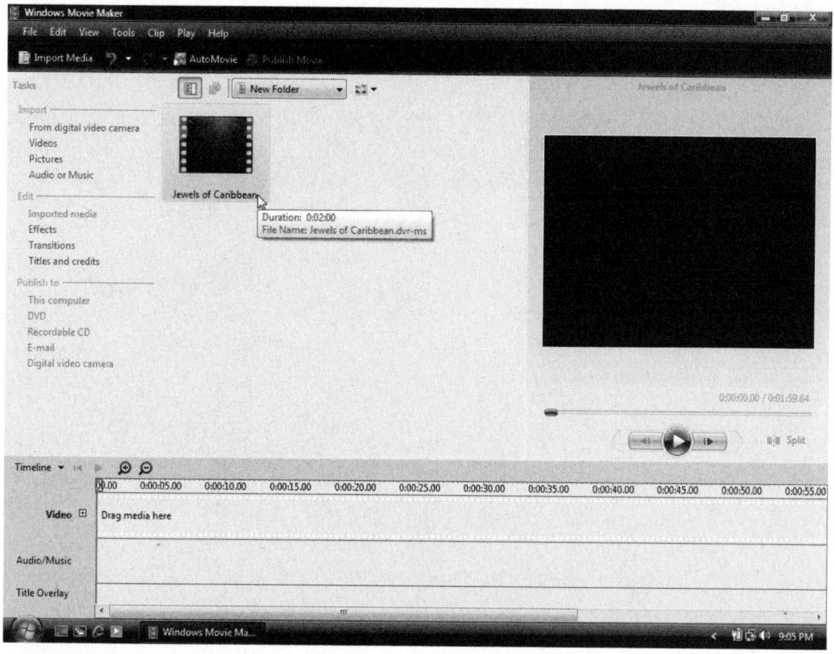

Figure 14-21: In Timeline mode you can fine-tune the various video, audio, and title elements that make up your movie.

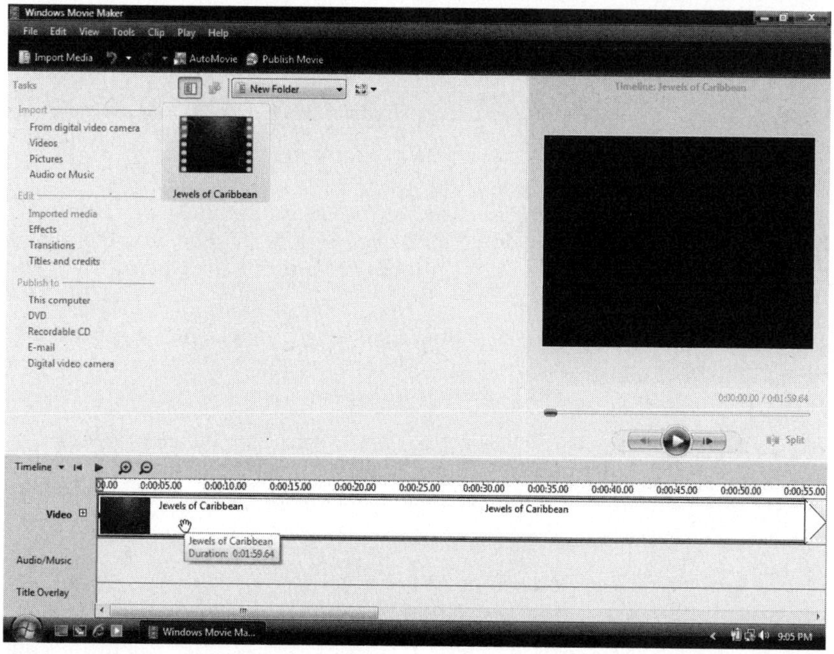

Figure 14-22: With your TV show or movie in the timeline, you can see how much time it occupies and prepare for edits.

Now click the Split button, which is located just below the video preview in the Preview pane. This will create a break point in the video, as shown in Figure 14-23, effectively dividing the video portion of the timeline into two sections.

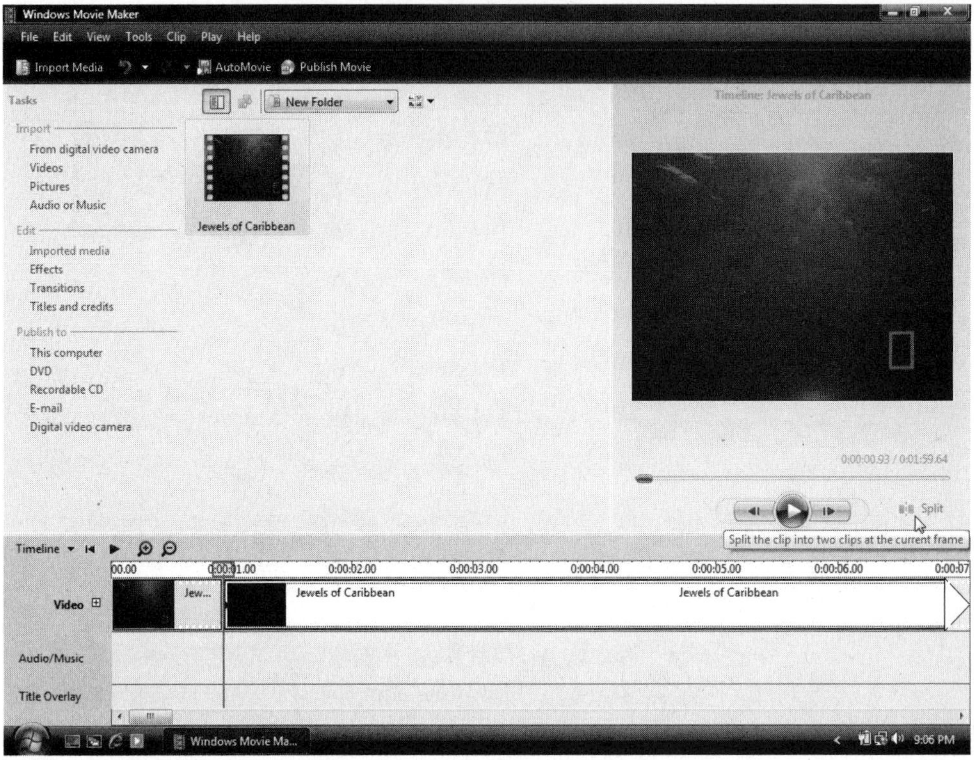

Figure 14-23: Trim off the unwanted beginning part of the video.

To trim the unwanted beginning portion off the video, select the first video segment, which will now be highlighted in white, and click Delete. When you do so, the remainder of the video—the clip that was to the right of the split or break point—will slide left so that it starts at the beginning of the timeline.

Now trim the end of the TV show or video. Using the blue pill in the scrubber bar below the video preview in the Preview pane, move forward through the remaining video until you can pinpoint where you'd like the ending to be.

tip   You can actually make more precise edits if you navigate through the video using the green positional bar in the timeline, especially if you zoom in first using the Zoom Timeline In icon.

As before, use the Split button to trim off the end of the video. Then select this ending video clip in the timeline and click Delete to remove it from the timeline.

Secret To remove commercials from recorded TV shows, use a similar technique to locate the beginning and end of each commercial block and then remove that clip from the timeline. It may take a bit of time, but you can certainly remove any extraneous video you don't want with just a little effort.

Secret You can also combine two separate video clips if you'd like to work with them as a single unit. To do so, select the first clip. Then, while holding down the Ctrl key, select the second clip. Now choose Combine from the Clip menu. In order for this to work, both clips must be right next to each other.

Fade In and Fade Out

One of the simplest edits you can make is to add Fade In and Fade Out effects to a clip. In the case of the TV show I just edited, I removed video from both the beginning and the end of the original video. This can be a bit jarring, so Windows Movie Maker includes a very simple way to visually (and audibly) fade into the current clip when it starts and then fade out when it ends.

To add these effects, right-click the current clip in the timeline and select Fade In. Then, right-click again and choose Fade Out. Each time you add an effect like this to a clip, a small star icon in a gray square appears in the clip, as shown in Figure 14-24.

When you play back the edited clip in the Preview pane, you'll see that these effects hide the jarring nature of the cuts you previously made. Success.

Cross-fade

Movie Maker supports a third simple fade effect that you can create entirely from within the timeline. Say you want to smooth the transitions between two clips (maybe where you exorcised commercials in a recorded TV show). In this case, it doesn't make sense to fade out the first clip and then fade in the second, because it would take too much time. Instead, drag one video clip over an adjoining video clip, as shown in Figure 14-25, to make them smoothly transition into each other using a cross-fade effect.

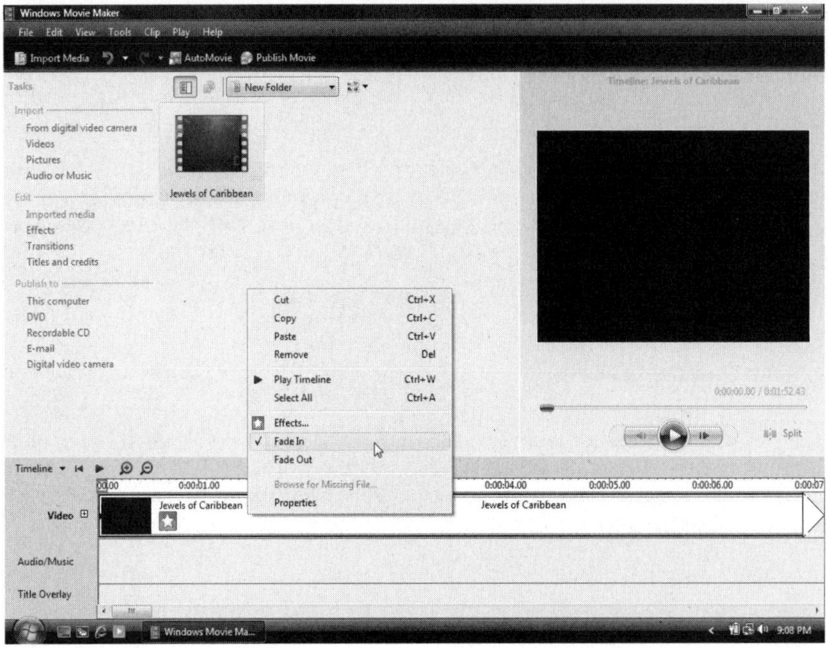

Figure 14-24: You can easily add Fade In and Fade Out effects without resorting to the more complicated Effects feature.

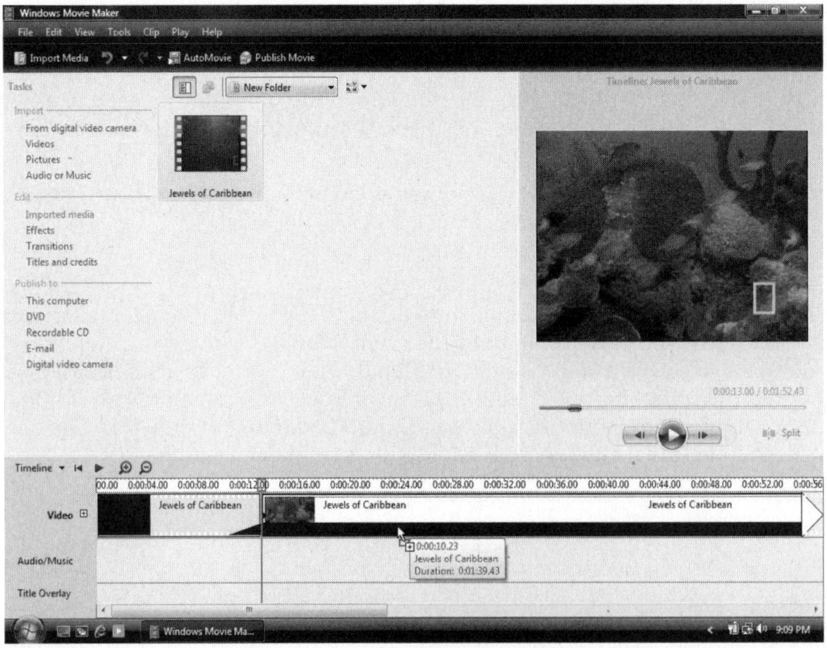

Figure 14-25: You can use your drag-and-drop skills to create cross-fade transitions in the timeline.

Adding Transitions and Effects

Fade In, Fade Out, and Cross-fade are nice, but Windows Movie Maker also supports many other *transitions* and *effects*. These include a huge collection of video transitions that are inspired by the transitions you see every day in TV shows and movies. To access these transitions, click the Transitions link in the Edit portion of the Tasks pane. The Imported Media pane will "transition" into the Transitions pane and present you with numerous transition options, as shown in Figure 14-26.

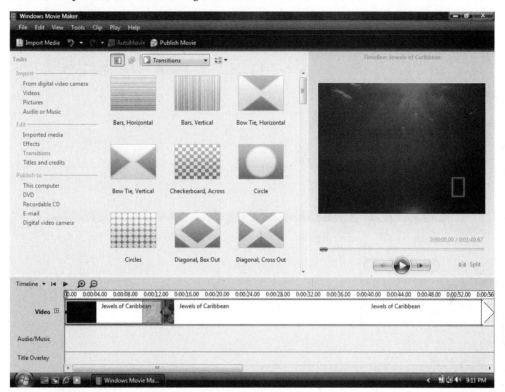

Figure 14-26: Don't be too aggressive with transitions, as they can be visually jarring, exactly the opposite effect that you're trying to achieve.

To add a transition to your video, locate a split between two video clips in the timeline. Then find the transition you want in the Transitions pane and drag it down to the timeline, below the split between the two clips you just located in the Transition well, as shown in Figure 14-27. (This well appears the first time you add a transition.)

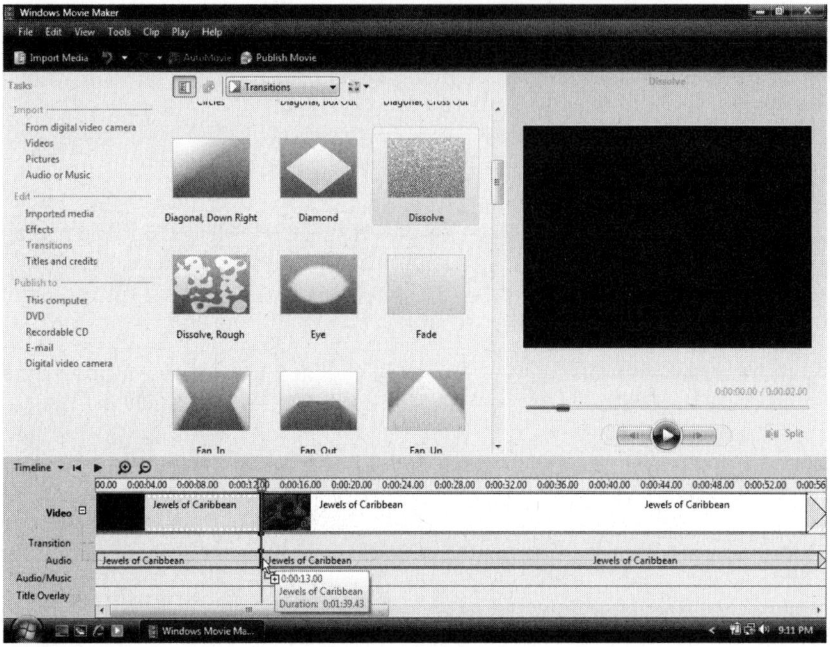

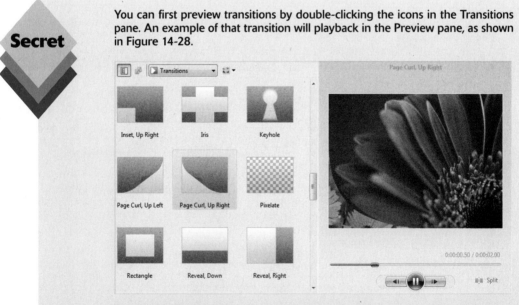

Figure 14-27: Adding transitions is a simple drag-and-drop affair.

Secret

You can first preview transitions by double-clicking the icons in the Transitions pane. An example of that transition will playback in the Preview pane, as shown in Figure 14-28.

Figure 14-28: You don't have to commit a transition to your edited video to see what it looks like. Instead, see a sample preview first.

When you add a transition to the timeline, it appears in the timeline well below the video, in the Transition well. To remove a transition, right-click it and choose Remove.

You can also add special effects to your videos, although these too should be used judiciously. Video effects range from blurring, brightness changes, and various fades to color and hue changes and zooms. To see which effects are available, select the Effects link in the Edit portion of the Tasks pane, as shown in Figure 14-29.

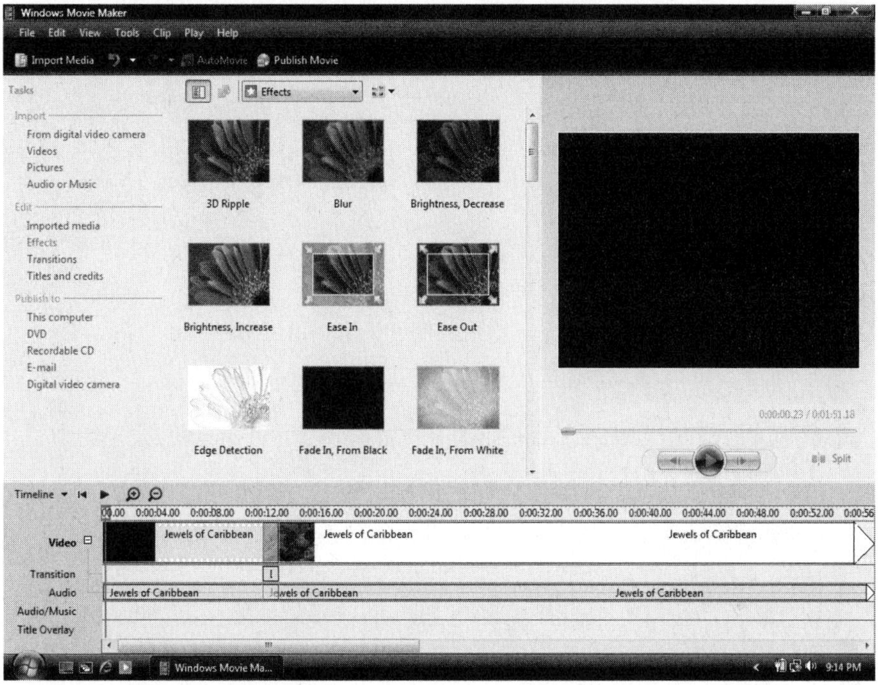

Figure 14-29: As with transitions, you're given a wide range of effects with which to play. Practice moderation if possible.

Unlike transitions, effects are added directly to a video clip, not between video clips. Pick the effect you want—after double-clicking it to preview it in the Preview pane—and then drag it to a video clip in the timeline. Preview your changes in the Preview pane.

When you add an effect to a video clip, you'll see a small star icon in a gray square appear on the clip, just as you do with the Fade In and Fade Out effects. Unfortunately, it's not quite as easy to remove an effect as it is to remove a transition, although it basically just involves an extra step, because you can apply more than one effect to any video clip.

Secret

Technically, you can even reapply multiple copies of an effect to any video clip. For example, if you added the Sharpen effect to a clip but found that it wasn't quite sharp enough, you could add it again to make it even sharper.

To remove an effect, right-click the clip in question and choose Effects. Then, in the resulting Add or Remove Effects dialog shown in Figure 14-30, select the effect or effects you don't want and then click the Remove button.

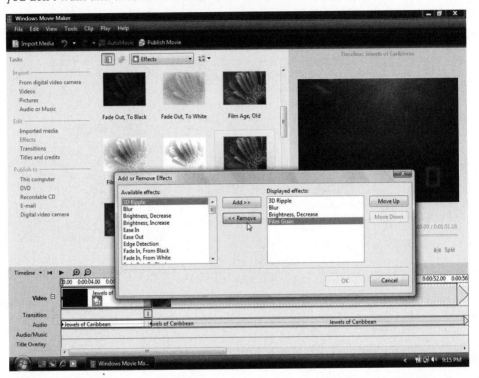

Figure 14-30: Effects are stackable: You can apply multiple effects to a single video clip and later remove the ones you don't want.

Adding Titles and Credits

Finally, you can add titles and credits to your video. Titles are typically added at the beginning of a video or clip, whereas credits are typically titles that appear at the end of a movie. Titles can be added anywhere through a movie as needed. For example, if you edited a movie of your vacation to Hawaii, you could add titles at various points to describe where each scene occurred. As with transitions and effects, you want to balance your use of titles so that they don't overpower the movie, but good titles are useful for providing context.

To add a title to the beginning of your movie, click the Titles and Credits link in the Edit portion of the Tasks pane. This option behaves differently than most Movie Maker tasks. As shown in Figure 14-31, the application switches into a unique Titles and Credits mode, where you can add titles at the beginning of the movie, before the selected clip, or on the selected clip. You can also choose to add credits at the end of the movie.

Pick Title at the beginning. Then enter the title you'd like to use in the provided text boxes. As you type, the titles you enter will be previewed in the video preview window in the Preview pane, as shown in Figure 14-32.

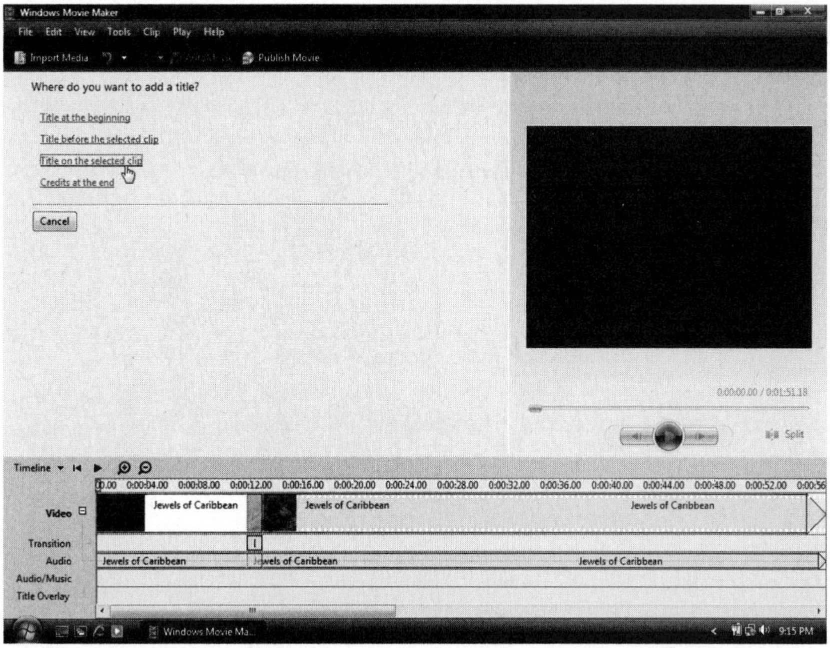

Figure 14-31: Movie Maker provides a variety of options for adding text over the video.

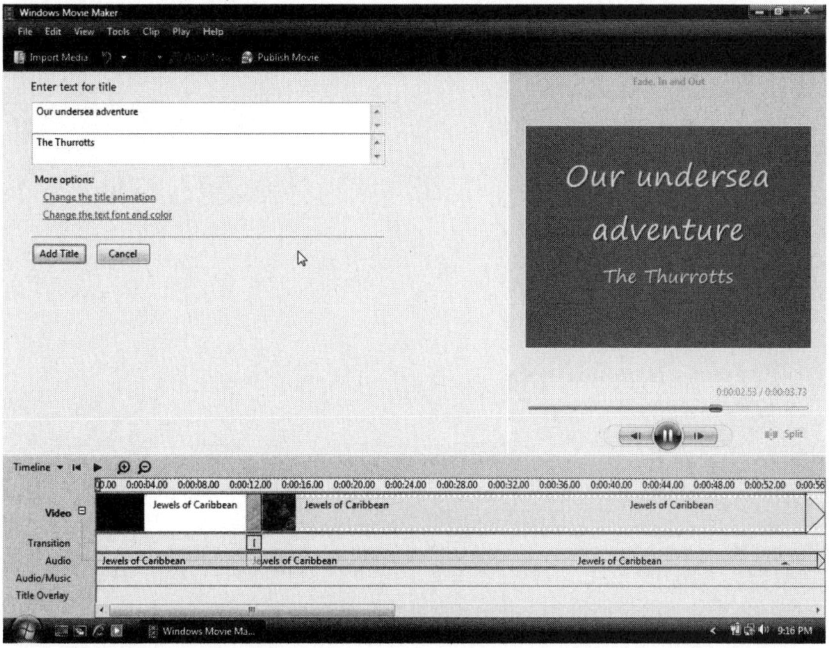

Figure 14-32: Edit your title in real time and then apply it to the video when you're happy with the results.

Under the More Options link are two more title-related options you can configure:

- ◆ **Change the title animation:** By default, Movie Maker uses a simple Fade, In and Out animation for the title, but you can choose among a surprising number of animations, so check out the full list, part of which is shown in Figure 14-33. Each time you select a new animation type, it is previewed in the Preview pane.

- ◆ **Change the text font and color:** You can also configure the font used for the title, including the font style, color, transparency, size, and other options, as shown in Figure 14-34. When you combine these options with the title animation options shown previously, you can see that this process can become overwhelming pretty quickly. Still, the variety of title types here is pretty impressive.

When you're done, click the Add Title button and the title will be added before the beginning of the video in the timeline. Click Play to watch your masterpiece.

Be sure to experiment with the various title types. While the first two options provide a title over a solid background color, the third option, Title on the Selected Clip, is perhaps the most useful. This applies a title directly over the video, which is usually the effect you want, as shown in Figure 14-35.

Again, experiment and have fun.

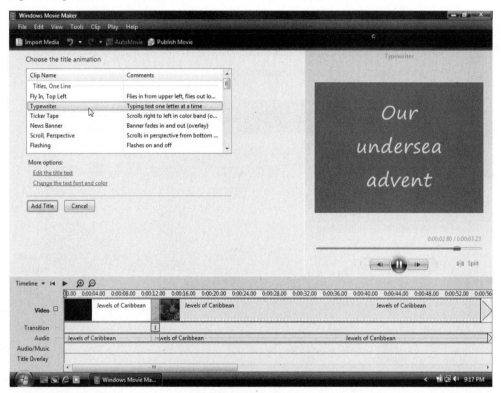

Figure 14-33: Don't get stuck with the default title animation. There are plenty to choose from.

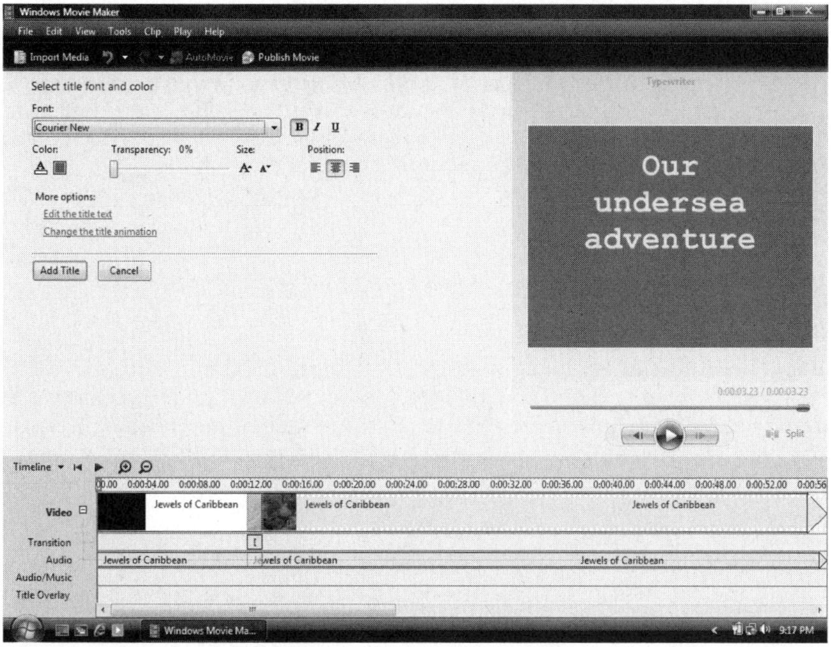

Figure 14-34: Edit the title font to your heart's content.

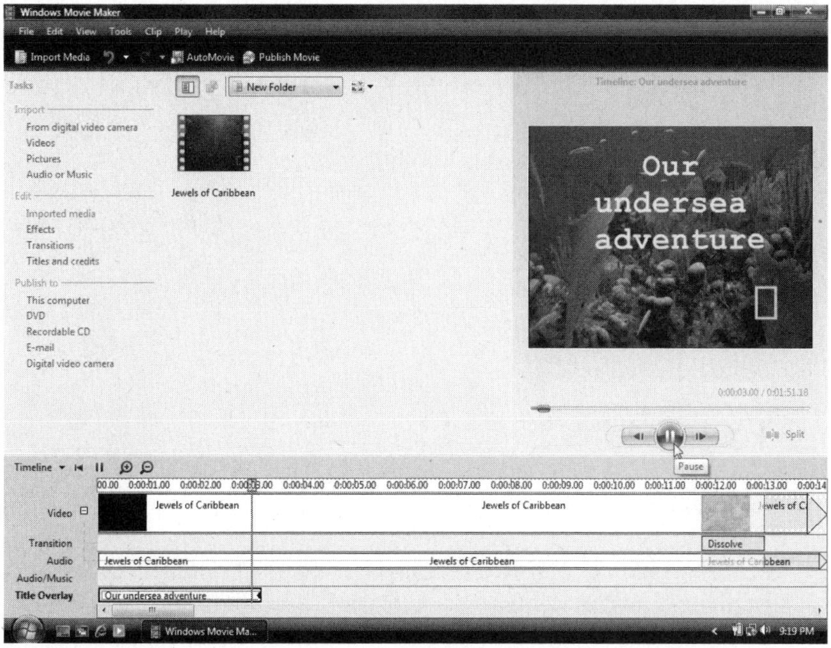

Figure 14-35: How professional: an animated title on top of moving video.

Secret Titles are deleted just like video clips. Select them in the timeline, press Delete, and they're gone forever. That said, Windows Movie Maker remembers the font and animation style you previously selected, so if you inadvertently chose the wrong title type, it will be easy to redo the title.

Sharing Your Movies

The whole point of editing a home movie, TV show, or other video is to watch it and, preferably, share it with others. Fortunately, Windows Movie Maker includes a multitude of ways to share your completed videos. All of these options are located in the Publish To section of the Tasks pane. When you select one of these options, Windows Movie Maker will usually instantiate a version of the Publish Movie wizard. Alternately, you can simply click Publish Movie in the Movie Maker toolbar. When you do so, you see the version of the wizard shown in Figure 14-36. This wizard will guide you through the type of movie publishing you selected.

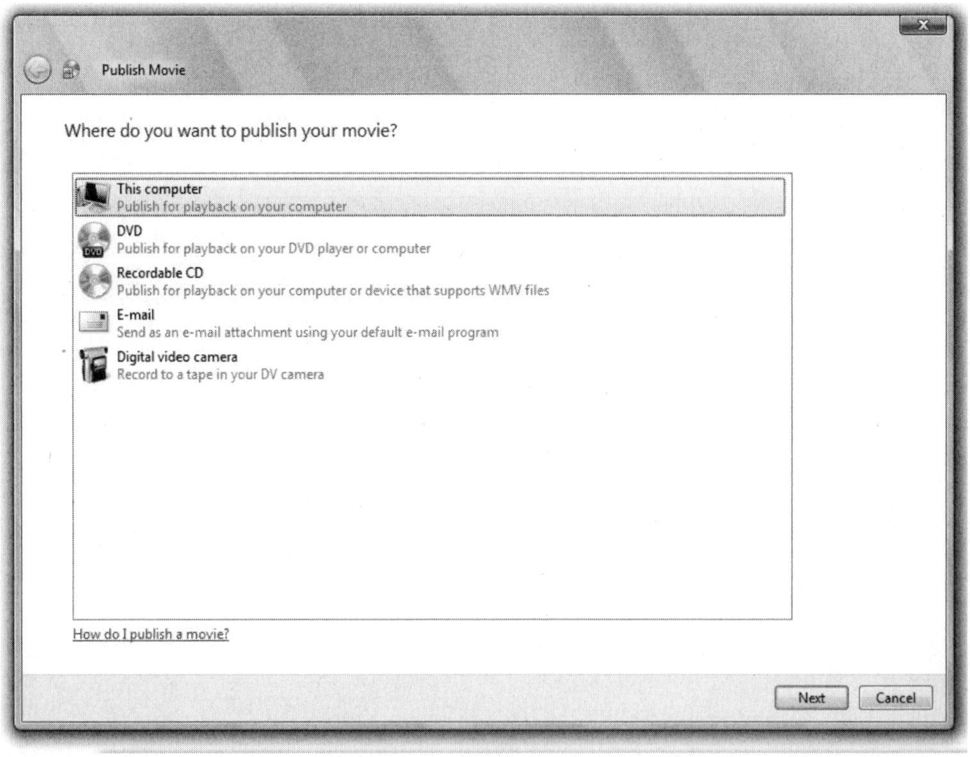

Publish Movie

Where do you want to publish your movie?

This computer
Publish for playback on your computer

DVD
Publish for playback on your DVD player or computer

Recordable CD
Publish for playback on your computer or device that supports WMV files

E-mail
Send as an e-mail attachment using your default e-mail program

Digital video camera
Record to a tape in your DV camera

How do I publish a movie?

Next   Cancel

Figure 14-36: The Publish Movie wizard is typically the last thing you'll see when working with Windows Movie Maker.

Secret

There is one exception. When you choose DVD from the Publish To portion of the Tasks pane, a new application will launch, as described later.

Publishing to the PC

If you'd like to save your edited movie as a digital video file that can be viewed on a PC, a Media Center PC, a portable media device, a PDA or smartphone, or another device, choose the This Computer option. Windows Movie Maker can publish movies to two different formats:

- ◆ **AVI (Audio Video Interleave):** This format offers very high quality and is very compatible but requires a lot of disk space.
- ◆ **WMV (Windows Media Video):** This format can be configured for a variety of quality levels and resolutions, but typically takes up less disk space than AVI. Unfortunately, WMV isn't very compatible with non-Microsoft solutions. For example, Apple's digital media products such as the iPod, iPhone, and iTunes software are incompatible with WMV.

So how do you decide which format to use?

If you're working with a home movie that was shot with a digital camcorder, you should typically save a copy of the edited movie in the AVI format for archival purposes, but the WMV format makes a lot more sense for distribution.

If you're editing a recorded TV show, save the edited file to WMV. This file will be dramatically smaller than the DVR-MS original and can offer similar visual quality.

If you intend to enjoy the file on a PC, portable media device, digital media receiver, or other device, go with WMV after ensuring that the device is WMV compatible. If it isn't, then save to AVI and use a third-party application (such as QuickTime Player Pro) to convert that file into a format with which the device is compatible, such as H.264.

Okay, now it's time to create that movie.

In the first phase of the Publish Movie wizard you'll be asked to give the movie a name and choose a location to which to publish it (the Videos folder by default). Next, you can choose the quality level and resolution of the final video, as shown in Figure 14-37. In this phase of the wizard, you can choose between Best Quality (which annoyingly varies according to the performance characteristics of your PC), a special file size, or you can choose from a long list of settings.

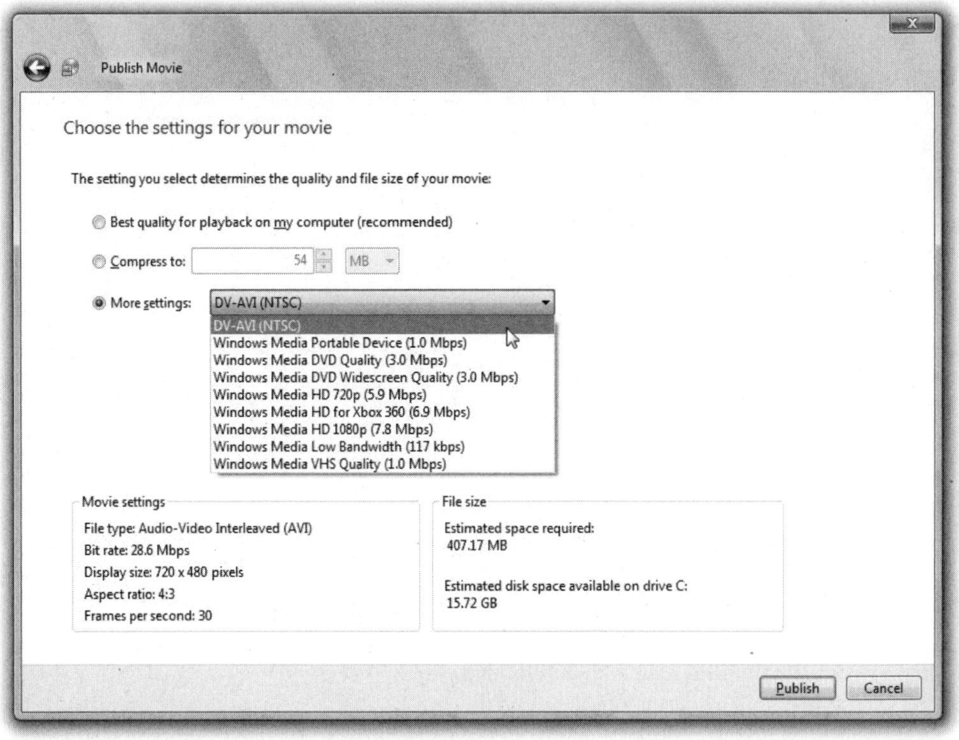

Figure 14-37: In the settings portion of the Publish Movie wizard you determine the quality, resolution, and file size of the resulting video.

What you see for that third option depends on which version of Windows Vista you're using. All versions of Windows Vista support the settings types described in Table 14-2.

Table 14-2: Video Settings Supported by All Versions of Windows Vista

Setting	Type	Bit Rate	Resolution	Aspect Ratio	Frames Per Second (FPS)	Storage Space Required for 30 Minutes of Video
DV-AVI	AVI	28.6 Mbps	720 x 480	4:3	30	6.44GB
Windows Media Portable Device	WMV	1.0 Mbps	640 x 480	4:3	30	234MB
Windows Media DVD Quality	WMV	3.0 Mbps	720 x 480	4:3	30	688MB

continues

Table 14-2: *(continued)*

Setting	Type	Bit Rate	Resolution	Aspect Ratio	Frames Per Second (FPS)	Storage Space Required for 30 Minutes of Video
Windows Media DVD Widescreen Quality	WMV	3.0 Mbps	720 x 480	16:9	30	688MB
Windows Media Low Bandwidth	WMV	117 Kbps	320 x 240	4:3	15	27MB
Windows Media VHS Quality	WMV	1.0 Mbps	640 x 480	4:3	30	241MB

If you're running Windows Vista Home Premium or Ultimate, you will see additional HD video modes as well. Note that it doesn't make much sense to save a low-quality video in HD format. That is, you should only save an edited HD video in an HD format. Table 14-3 shows the additional HD formats that Vista Home Premium and Ultimate provide.

Table 14-3: HD Video Settings Supported Only by Windows Vista Home Premium and Ultimate

Setting	Type	Bit Rate	Resolution	Aspect Ratio	Frames Per Second (FPS)	Storage Space Required for 30 Minutes of Video
Windows Media HD 720p	WMV	5.9 Mbps	1280 x 720	16:9	30	1.36GB
Windows Media HD for Xbox 360	WMV	6.9 Mbps	1280 x 720	16:9	30	1.58GB
Windows Media HD 1080p	WMV	7.8 Mbps	1440 x 1080	16:9	30	1.8GB

You don't have to be a high school AV geek to understand that bigger and better quality video types require more PC processing power and dramatically more storage space, especially for HD video. The big question is, which video setting should you use?

That all depends, of course, on your source video. A general rule of thumb is to save your edited video in a format that is equivalent to, or of lower quality, than the original video. Otherwise, you're needlessly wasting space.

Secret

Understand that you can save your edited video multiple times. You can save one version in AVI format for backup purposes, another in WMV DVD quality for viewing on your Media Center PC, and yet another in WMV Low Quality for distribution on the Web. Of course, this would require more time and patience than most people have.

Once you've chosen a format, click the Publish button and sit back and wait. It takes enormous amounts of time to publish video to the hard drive, especially when you're working with HD content.

When the publishing process is complete, the wizard provides you with an opportunity to view your creation. As shown in Figure 14-38, the video plays back in Windows Media Player.

Figure 14-38: If you chose a nice balance between size and quality, the resulting video should look good in Windows Media Player.

Publishing to DVD or CD

If you want to publish your edited movie directly to DVD, Windows Movie Maker will prompt you to save the current project (as described later in the chapter) and will then open Windows DVD Maker (also covered later in this chapter).

Publishing to recordable CD is another story. Whereas a typical recordable DVD has space for 4.7GB or 9.4GB of content (or 1 or 2 hours of digital video, respectively), most CDs only contain about 700MB of storage space. Thus, the quality of the resulting video will generally not be as high as what is possible with a true DVD movie, unless the edited video is very short.

There's another difference between DVD movies and CDs. Video CDs are not the same as DVDs: Instead of creating a standard DVD movie disk that can play in any DVD player or PC, when you create a movie CD, you're essentially copying a digital video to a CD, much in the same way that you might copy such a file to a hard disk or USB memory card. Therefore, you can choose among the same video settings discussed in the previous section. The resulting disk will play on some DVD players, but should work on all modern PCs.

Publishing for E-mail Distribution

If you'd like to send your edited video to others via e-mail, Windows Movie Maker assumes that the resulting file should occupy 10MB or less of disk space so that it will be delivered properly by most e-mail services. You're not given any way to edit the size of the file. There's another difference too: After the wizard is done creating the movie, two options appear, as shown in Figure 14-39. You can play the movie (in Windows Media Player) or save a copy of it to the computer. That last bit is interesting because it indicates that Movie Maker wouldn't normally save this version of the file locally.

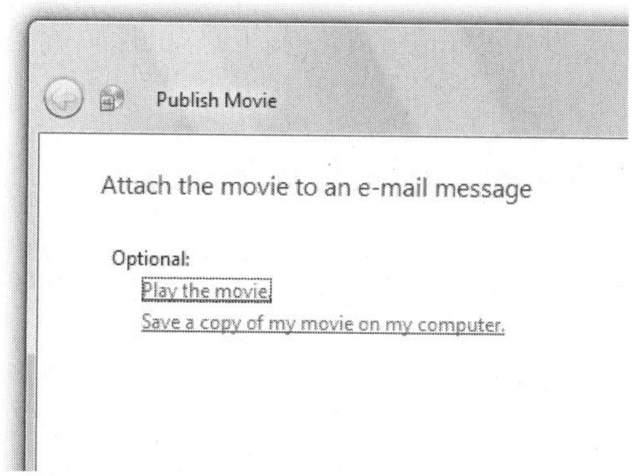

Figure 14-39: With the e-mail option, Movie Maker chooses the size and quality and you choose whether to save a copy locally.

When you click Attach Movie, a copy of the e-mail–compatible movie is added to a blank e-mail message in your default mail application.

Writing Back to a Digital Video Camera

If you acquired a home movie via digital video camera or have a digital video camera lying around, it makes sense to copy a perfect digital version of your edited video back to tape. Why? Well, in addition to providing you with a perfect backup of your movie, using a video tape for this purpose will save hard disk space. To do so, simply insert a blank video tape into your camcorder, connect the camera to the PC via a FireWire (IEEE 1394) cable, and start the wizard.

Secret

Note that publishing a movie to digital video in this fashion can be quite slow: It require one minute of copying time for every one minute of edited video.

Secret

Sharing Your Movies on the Web

While Windows Movie Maker's sharing options are pretty comprehensive, Microsoft somehow managed to miss what is perhaps the single most popular sharing option available today: Web sharing. Web sites such as YouTube are incredibly popular these days, so much so that even Microsoft has gotten into the game with a video-sharing service called MSN Soapbox. But there's no way to share your videos directly from Windows Movie Maker. No problem: Getting a video you created in Windows Movie Maker to the Web isn't that hard if you know what you're doing.

The trick is to ensure that your videos aren't larger (from a file size perspective) or longer, time-wise, than what is allowed by the service. Each online video service is a bit different. According to YouTube, they accept videos that are 1GB in size or smaller and 10 minutes long or less. They can handle formats such as .WMV, .AVI, .MOV, and .MPG, though YouTube will ultimately transcode whatever you upload into H.264 MPEG-4 with MP3 audio. MSN Soapbox is even more accommodating: They accept formats such as AVI, ASF, WMV, MOV, MPEG 1/2/4, 3GP, 3G2, DV, QT, DivX, and Xvid. Like YouTube, MSN Soapbox is going to transcode whatever you upload, so the higher the quality the better.

These limitations aren't overly restrictive if you're uploading a handmade home video; because both support WMV format, that's a logical starting point, as WMV is one of the two major formats supported by Windows Movie Maker.

Here's the secret: All you have to do is ensure that the video you output with Windows Movie Maker comes in below the upper limits of the video service you choose to utilize. In the Publish To section of Windows Movie Maker, choose This Computer. Then, in the settings portion of the Publish wizard, select the option Compress To. If the size listed there is smaller than 1GB (1024MB), that's what you want to use. If it's bigger, change it to 1024MB and click Publish. Then upload your video to the Web. It's that easy.

Saving and Working with Projects

Before moving on to the wonderful world of DVD movies, I should make one final point about Windows Movie Maker. Each time you copy material into the Movie Maker timeline or storyboard and begin editing, you should save your progress as a Windows Movie Maker project. That way, you can come back later, as you would with an unfinished Word document, and make additional changes.

To save a Windows Movie Maker project, simply choose Save Project from the File menu. By default, projects are saved to your Videos folder, but you're free to save them wherever you'd like. You can reopen saved projects at any time, naturally enough, by selecting File ⇨ Open Project.

Secret A Windows Movie Maker project is basically just a file that points to the various digital media files you're accessing, along with whatever edits, transitions, effects, and titles you've made in the timeline or storyboard. The project does *not* contain any videos, photos, music files, or other content. If you move these files around in the file system or delete them, Windows Movie Maker will not be able to use them in a saved project later.

Creating DVD Movies with Windows DVD Maker

Windows Vista, for the first time, includes an application for *burning*, or creating, DVD movies. As you might expect from a first effort, Windows DVD Maker isn't a terribly sophisticated application, so the quality and variety of DVD movies you can make is fairly limited. On the plus side, DVD Maker does deliver the most commonly wanted DVD-making features, and, as you might expect, it's especially well-suited for beginners. So if you've never made a DVD movie, take heart. This is a great place to begin.

Secret DVD Maker is only available to users of Windows Vista Home Premium and Windows Vista Ultimate. If you have a different Vista version, you need to upgrade to one of these versions in order to use Windows DVD Maker. Alternately, you could purchase one of the many third-party DVD maker applications on the market. Note that any third-party package will be more sophisticated, but also more complex, than Windows DVD Maker.

Secret

There are actually several ways to start DVD Maker:

- From within Windows Photo Gallery, you can select a group of photos or videos and then select Burn ⇨ Video DVD from the toolbar.

- From within Windows Movie Maker, you can choose DVD from the Publish To portion of the Tasks pane.

- If you saved a DVD Maker project previously, you can double-click that project's icon in the shell and pick up where you left off.

- Or you can simply find Windows DVD Maker in the Windows Vista Start Menu and launch the application manually, then add content to an empty project as you go.

The last approach will gain you the skills necessary to explore the other options, so I'll examine Windows DVD Maker as a standalone application here, but its integration with Windows Photo Gallery and Windows Movie Maker can and should be explored as well.

To start Windows DVD Maker, open the Start Menu and locate the Windows DVD Maker shortcut in the All Programs group. (Again, Start Menu Search works wonders: Search for **dvd** to find Windows DVD Maker quickly.)

Secret

Even if you're using Windows Vista Home Premium or Ultimate, it's possible that you won't be able to run this application. Like Windows Movie Maker, Windows DVD Maker requires a certain type of video hardware, and while most readers likely meet this minimum requirement, you might not find yourself in this group. You'll know you're in trouble if you see the error dialog shown in Figure 14-40.

Figure 14-40: No DVD Maker for you.

Unlike with Windows Movie Maker, however, you have only one option if you see this error message while trying to run Windows DVD Maker. You have to upgrade your video hardware. That's because Vista is the first version of Windows to ship with DVD Maker. There's no older version to fall back on. That said, you could always avail yourself of the many third-party DVD-making solutions out there, but a better investment would be an inexpensive video card, as it would benefit your system in many other ways as well.

Windows DVD Maker, shown in Figure 14-41, is a simple wizard-based application that steps you through the process of adding content and menus to your eventual DVD movie.

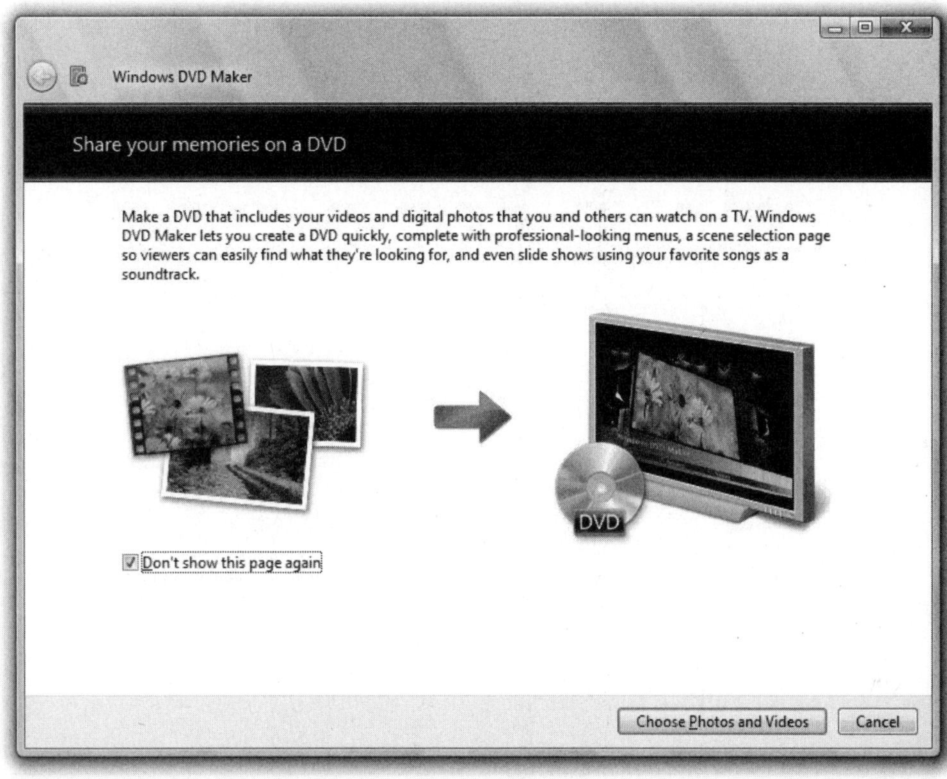

Figure 14-41: No frightening user interfaces here. DVD Maker is the definition of simplicity.

Secret

Like Windows Movie Maker, Windows DVD Maker works with something called a *project*—that is, a file you can save and reload later describing the DVD you're making. Unlike Windows Movie Maker, there is no obvious way to save a project while you're compiling your DVD. However, if you look closely, you'll see a single menu item, File, in most of the Windows DVD Maker screens. When you click this menu, you'll see options for saving, loading, and making new projects. You can also save your project by clicking the more prominent Cancel button. This will close Windows DVD Maker, but the application will prompt you to save the current project first. (Well, you have to use a "Start" button to shut down the system, so in Microsoft's world this is all perfectly logical.)

note   DVD Maker projects are saved in your Videos folder by default.

Only one instance of DVD Maker can be running at a time.

Adding Photos and Videos to Your DVD Project

As noted previously, Windows DVD Maker is a wizard-based application in which you move through a limited set of steps and end up, it is hoped, with a nice-looking DVD movie that will play on virtually any DVD player. In the first step of the wizard, shown in Figure 14-42, you add the content you want on the DVD.

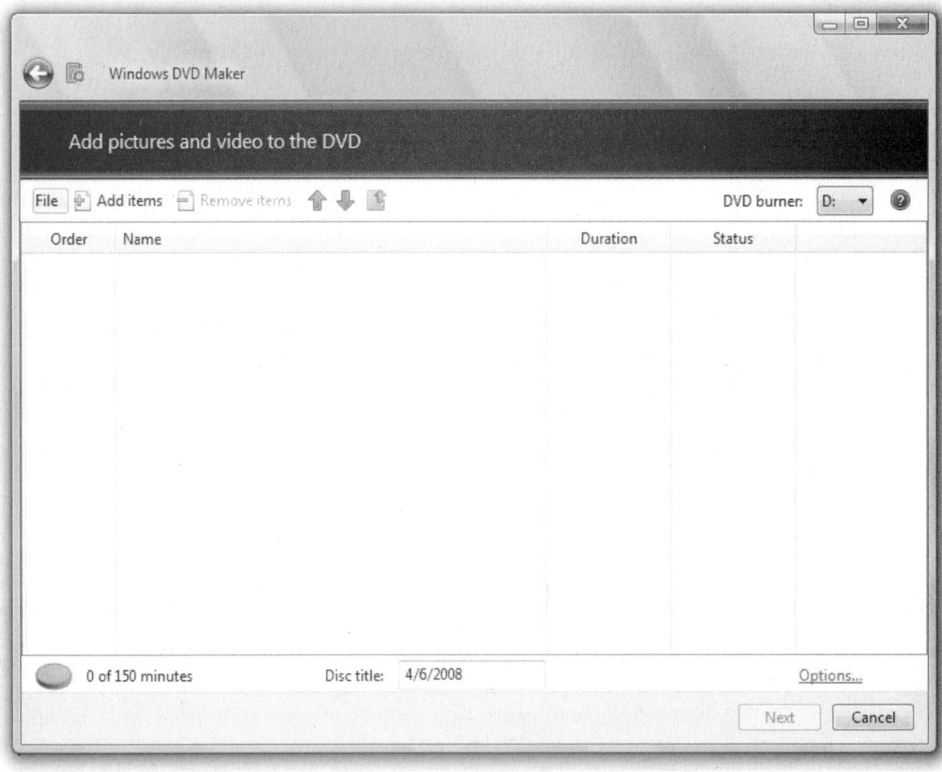

Figure 14-42: Every Windows DVD Maker project starts with this blank slate.

This content consists of pictures and video. You can drag items to the DVD Maker application using your standard drag-and-drop skills, or you can click the Add Items button, next to the File menu, to display a standard Vista File Open dialog. Use this dialog to navigate to the content you want on your DVD movie.

note If I can vent for a moment, the more I think about it, the more obvious it becomes to me that Windows DVD Maker, while adequate for the job at hand, is a mess from a user interface perspective. There's no true menu structure, per se, just a single File menu jammed into the upper-left corner of the application window. You can add items to the current project in two different ways, one obvious and one hidden. The application's options are configured via an HTML-like Options link that sits in the lower-right corner of the window—that is, except for the DVD burner, which for some reason is always available in the upper-right corner of the first phase of the wizard. (Meanwhile, DVD burning speed is configured in the Options dialog.) Moreover, while it features a prominent Internet Explorer–like Back button in the upper-left corner, Next is a more typical Windows-type button that sits, you guessed it, in the lower-right corner.

This application deserves a special place in the User Interface Hall of Shame. It looks and works nothing like any other Windows Vista application. When you add videos to a Windows DVD Maker project, they appear in the wizard as you might expect. Pictures are a little different. If you drag one or more image files into Windows DVD Maker, the application creates a folder called Slide Show, as shown in Figure 14-43. From this point on, any photos you add to the project are added to this one folder and displayed as an animated slideshow in the finished DVD.

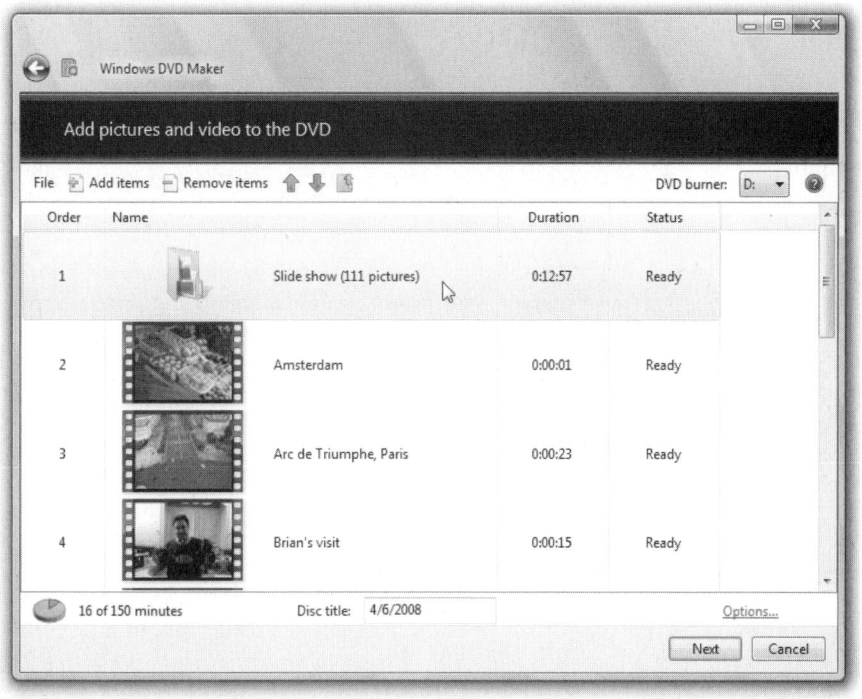

Figure 14-43: The Slide Show folder contains any pictures you add to your DVD project.

Secret

You can't have two or more photo slideshows on a single DVD. Only one is allowed.

Secret

You also cannot add videos to the Slide Show folder. If you try to add a video, it will be added to the root of the project instead.

Secret

You can navigate inside the Slide Show folder in Windows DVD Maker if you'd like. To navigate back out to the root of the DVD, click the small Back to Videos toolbar icon, shown in Figure 14-44.

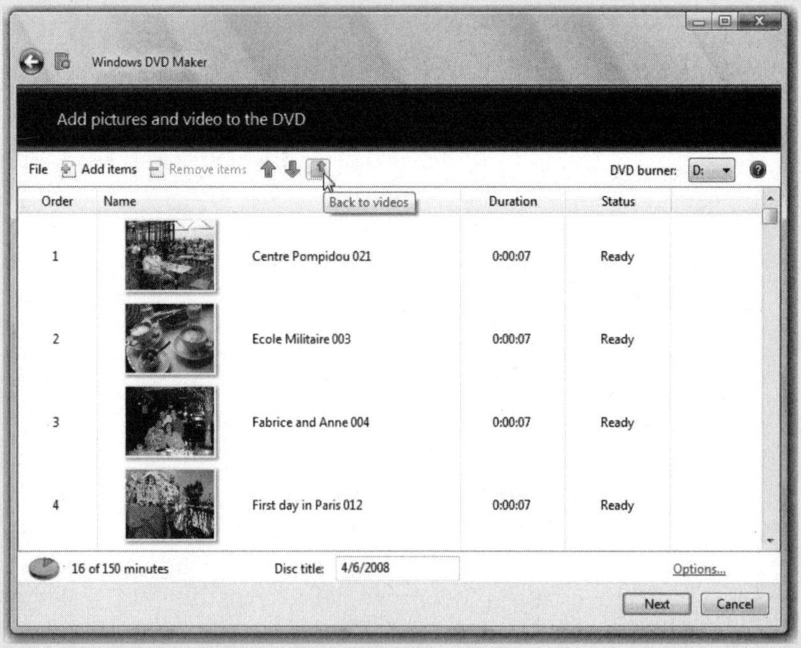

Figure 14-44: Yet another nearly hidden user interface feature. This one enables you to escape from the Slide Show folder.

To remove a video, a picture, or the Slide Show folder, select it in Windows DVD Maker and click the Remove Items button. Alternatively, click Delete or right-click the item and choose Remove.

About DVD Storage Issues and Formats

One issue you should be concerned about is how much content will fit on the DVD. Windows DVD Maker works with standard recordable DVDs, so the storage capacities are based on the media you use. With a standard *single-layer* recordable DVD, you can store up to 60 minutes of video. With a standard *dual-layer* recordable DVD, you can store up to 120 minutes of video.

Another issue, of course, is that there are several recordable DVD types out there. To create a DVD movie that will work in virtually any DVD player in the world, use write-once DVD-R or DVD+R media. Both work well, though DVD+R seems to have won the format wars and is more common, while DVD-R offers better compatibility with older DVD players if that's an issue. Avoid rewriteable DVD formats, such as DVD+RW or DVD-RW, because they won't work with most standalone DVD players (though they're fine for testing and PC-based use). If you see the acronym DL used, that describes dual-layer, a technology that doubles the capacity of a recordable DVD's storage space. You might also be constrained by the capabilities of your DVD writer. If your hardware is only compatible with, say, DVD+R, then obviously you need to use DVD+R recordable disks, but if you have a multiformat DVD writer, it's your choice; you can use four different recordable DVD formats: DVD+R, DVD+RW, DVD-R, and DVD-RW.

Arranging Content

When you've added two or more items to your Windows DVD Maker project, you can start thinking about the order in which they will appear on the final DVD movie. Although DVD Maker doesn't offer a huge selection of DVD menu layout options, you can reorder items. You'll notice that the list of videos and photo slideshows in the wizard has an explicit order, as noted by the Order column heading. You can easily reorder items in the following ways:

◆ **Drag and drop:** Using the skills you've no doubt honed over the years in Windows, simply grab an item in the list and drag it to the position in the order you'd like it to appear.

◆ **Move Up and Move Down buttons:** In the Windows DVD Maker toolbar are two arrow-shaped buttons representing *move up* and *move down* that enable you to reorder the selected item as indicated. This is shown in Figure 14-45.

◆ **Right-click method:** You can also right-click any item and choose Move Up or Move Down from the resulting pop-up menu.

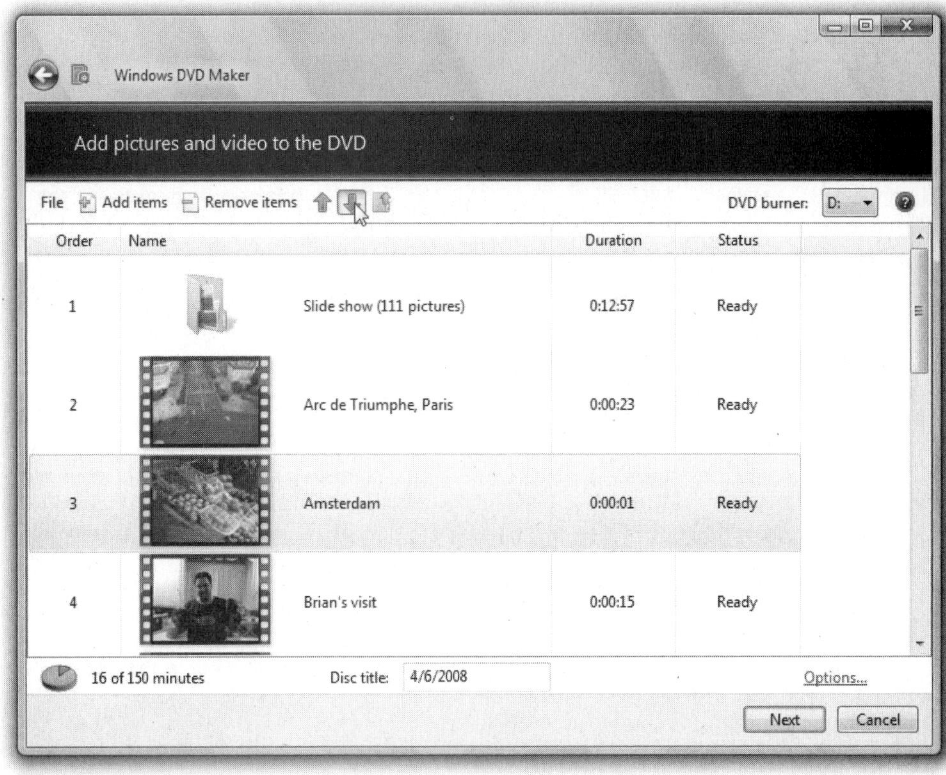

![Windows DVD Maker screenshot showing the "Add pictures and video to the DVD" window with a content list including a slide show and three video items, and a disc title field set to 4/6/2008.]

Figure 14-45: While customization is limited, you can at least change the order of items.

Previewing Content

If you'd like to play a video or preview a photo that's in your DVD Maker project, simply double-click that item. Videos play back in Windows Media Player by default, whereas photos are previewed in Windows Photo Gallery.

Secret   Note that you cannot "play" the Slide Show folder. You can only open the folder and view the files inside, one at a time.

Naming Your DVD Movie

Under the content list of this initial window you'll see a small and easily missed text box called Disk Title. By default it's set to the current date in *M/D/YEAR* format, where *M* is a one- or two-number representation of the month (e.g., 1), *D* is a one- or two-number representation of the day (e.g., 30), and *YEAR* is a four-number representation of the year (e.g., 2007).

You will want to change this title to something descriptive, because it will be used on the DVD's menu as the title of the DVD movie. A home movie DVD, for example, might be called *Our Summer Vacation* or similar.

Secret

You can pick whatever title you want, but only 32 characters are allowed.

Understanding DVD Movie Options

In keeping with the Salvador Dali–like user interface minimalism of Windows DVD Maker, you access the application's DVD Options dialog box via a small Options link in the lower-right corner of its window (and not via a Tools ⇨ Options menu as you might expect). When you click this link the DVD Options dialog box opens, shown in Figure 14-46. Note that these options are related to the DVD you're creating and not to the Windows DVD Maker application per se.

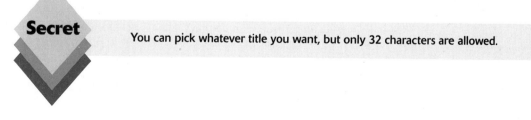

Figure 14-46: DVD Options enables you to configure a small number of settings related to the DVD you're creating, not to the application itself.

The following options are available:

- ◆ **DVD playback settings:** You can configure your DVD movie to play its content in one of three ways:
  - • **Start with DVD menu:** Indicates that your DVD will behave like a typical Hollywood DVD and will display a DVD menu on first start.
  - • **Play video and end with DVD menu:** Causes the DVD movie to play through the DVD content first and then display the menu only after the content is complete.
  - • **Play video in a continuous loop:** Simply plays the DVD content repeatedly, in a loop. Users can still access the DVD menu, however, by pressing the Menu button on their DVD remote control or player.
- ◆ **DVD aspect ratio:** Enables you to configure whether the DVD's video playback and menu display in a 4:3 aspect ratio (which is not really square per se but is certainly close to square) or in wide-screen 16:9 aspect ratio. The choice you make here should be based on the aspect ratio of the screen on which you think the DVD will be accessed, and on the aspect ratio of the content you're using. Today, most video content is still created in a 4:3 aspect ratio despite the widespread use of wide-screen displays. That said, most television sets sold today are now wide-screen. The choice is yours, and you can certainly make a version of the DVD in both formats just to see the differences, though that will be time consuming.
- ◆ **Video format:** Enables you to choose whether the DVD will be created in the NTSC or PAL video format. Choose the format that is used in your locale. For example, the NTSC format is correct for the United States, but PAL is used in countries such as France and Ireland.
- ◆ **Other DVD settings:** In the bottom of the DVD Options dialog, you can set options for the DVD burner speed and the location where the application will store its temporary files during the DVD creation process. Typically, you will want to leave the DVD burner speed at the fastest setting, but if you run into problems burning DVDs, you can change it to a slower speed. This will increase the amount of time it takes to create your DVD movie but results in a more reliable burn experience. Most users will want to leave the temporary file location setting untouched; but if one of your hard drives is faster or has much more space available, you can use this setting to change the location where temporary files are stored and, possibly, speed up the DVD creation process.

Secret

You will need a hard drive or partition with at least 5GB of free space in order to create a single-sided DVD movie. Dual-layer (DL) DVDs require at least 10GB of hard drive space.

Secret

Do not attempt to create a DVD movie on a hard disk that is slower than 5,400 RPM. Faster drives—7,800 RPM and 10,000 RPM, for example—running on modern hard-drive interfaces (SATA, or Serial-ATA, instead of IDE/ATA, for example) will get better results.

Working with DVD Menus

After you select the content to be included on the DVD movie and set the DVD options, you can move on to the next step in the Windows DVD Maker wizard and select a menu style. As shown in Figure 14-47, this second and final step in the wizard can be skipped altogether if you like the default menu style: Simply click Burn and off you go.

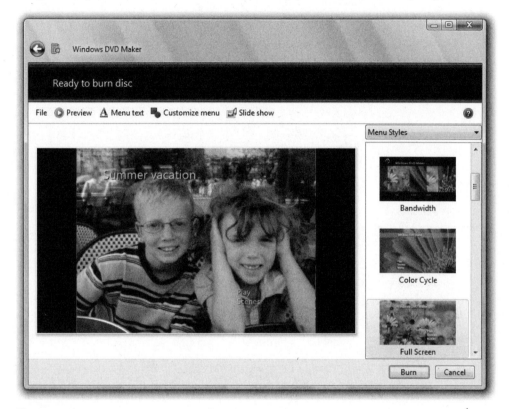

Figure 14-47: In the curiously named Ready to Burn Disk stage of the DVD Maker wizard, you can pick menu styles.

Secret

When you click the Next button to move to the second phase of the DVD Maker wizard, you will notice that there is no corresponding Back button. That's because Windows DVD Maker adheres to a silly new Windows Vista application style: A graphical Back button is illogically located in the upper-left corner of the application window. It resembles the Back button in Internet Explorer (that is, it's a blue arrow). Why it's not next to a similar Next button is unknown.

It makes sense to spend a bit of time here and experiment with the built-in menu styles, as you might not be too excited by the default option. Besides, there are a number of other things you can do here, including previewing the DVD, changing the menu text, customizing the menu, and adding music to and changing options for the photo slideshow. You'll look at those options in the next section.

Along the right side of the application window is a list of menu styles, each presented with a visual thumbnail to give you a rough idea of how it will appear in your DVD. Windows DVD Maker includes roughly 20 DVD menu styles. To select and preview a different menu style, simply select it in the list. After churning for a few moments, the DVD menu preview will change to reflect your selection, as shown in Figure 14-48.

Figure 14-48: Windows DVD Maker includes a decent selection of menu options.

Each menu style is quite different. Some offer an animated video preview running behind the menu text, while others offer multiple video previews running simultaneously, or even animated menu text that flies in from the sides of the screen. Be sure to experiment here.

Changing Other DVD Options

To fully configure your DVD movie and appreciate what effect the various DVD menu options will have on the finished product, you need to preview the movie and access the other options that are available in this step of the wizard.

Previewing the DVD Movie

Even if you don't think you'll need to make any changes, always preview your DVD before committing it to disk. You do so by clicking the Preview toolbar button, which brings up a Preview Your Disk view with a virtual DVD player, complete with DVD controls such as Menu, Play, Pause, and so on (see Figure 14-49).

Figure 14-49: While previewing your DVD movie, you can see how it will behave and look in a real DVD player.

Here, you might discover that the font used for the menu text is ugly, that you made a bad decision about how the menu appears, or that you want to change to a different menu style all together. To make any changes, click OK (or the Back button) and get back to work.

Secret

Yes, you can also go back from the Ready to Burn Disk phase to the first step of the DVD Maker wizard. The application will remember the settings you configured regardless of which direction you go in the user interface.

note Each "scene" in the DVD menu correlates to a video or photo slideshow you imported into the Windows DVD Movie Maker project.

Changing the Menu Text

To change a variety of options related to the DVD menu text, click the Menu text button. Here, as shown in Figure 14-50, you can change the font (including color and bold and italic attributes, but not, curiously, the size), the disk title, and the text used for the Play, Scenes, and Notes links. You can also write a block of descriptive Notes text that will appear on a subpage of the main DVD menu.

Figure 14-50: Here, you can change a variety of menu text options and add an optional block of Notes text.

Secret   By default, the Notes link and corresponding Notes text will not appear. You have to add the text first. You can add up to 255 characters in the Notes block. The previews on the right side of the window show you what the optional Notes page will look like—and, of course, you can also see it in the DVD preview described previously.

Customizing the Menu

To customize the appearance of the DVD menu, click the Customize menu toolbar button. For some reason, you can change some font properties here again, duplicating the functionality of the menu text options described in the previous section. However, the rest of the disk menu options shown here are unique, as shown in Figure 14-51. You can change the videos that display in the foreground and background (the layout and appearance of which vary from menu style to menu style), the audio that plays over the menu (curiously, you can't make it silent, however; it will default to the audio in the selected video clip instead), and the style of the menu links or buttons.

Figure 14-51: In addition to picking general menu styles, you can also configure various aspects of the DVD menu layout and presentation.

Secret

The video and audio used in the DVD menu don't even have to be related to the media files you chose for inclusion in the DVD movie itself. For example, you could select two movies and a photo slideshow for the DVD, and separate third and fourth movies for the title if you want.

If you make enough changes or want to reuse the customizations you made, you can actually save them as a brand-new style. When you do this, a new entry called Custom Styles is added to the drop-down above the list of menu styles on the right side of the application window. Now you can choose between Menu Styles and Custom Styles.

Configuring the Photo Slideshow

If you've included a photo slideshow in your DVD movie, you can customize it by clicking the Slide Show button in the DVD Maker toolbar. In the Change Your Slide Show settings dialog, shown in Figure 14-52, you can add one or more songs (music files) to the slideshow, alter the length of time each photo displays, choose a transition type (Cross-fade is the default), and decide whether to use pan and zoom effects, which provide a welcome bit of animation to the slideshow.

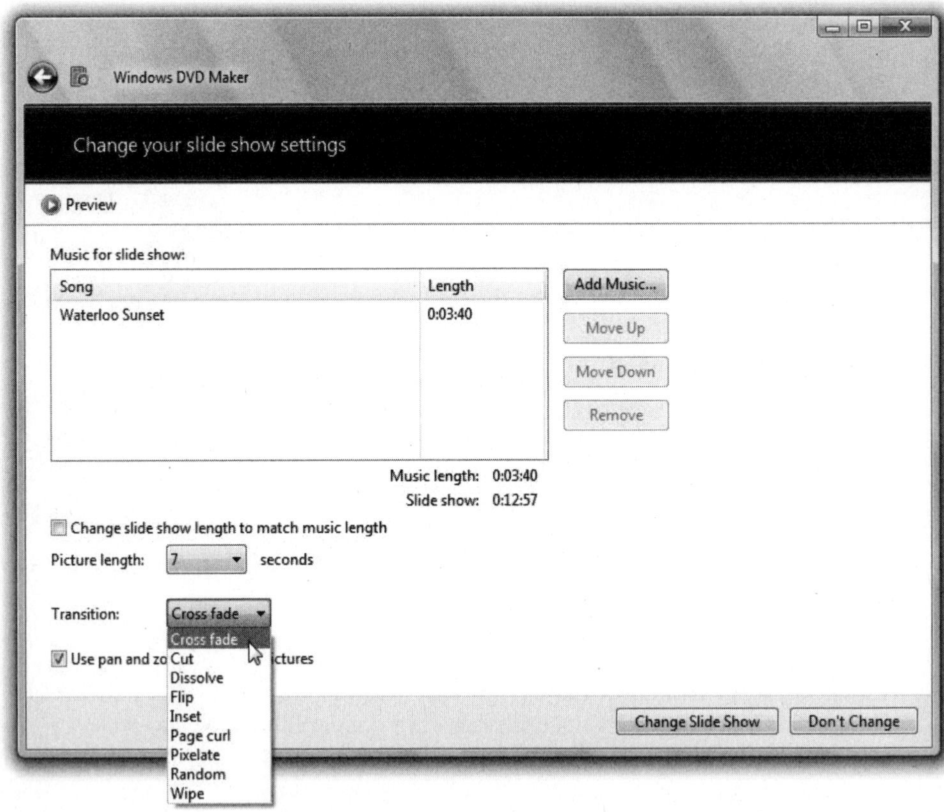

Figure 14-52: Here you can configure a nice range of options for your photo slideshow.

tip   Adding music and animation effects to a photo slideshow dramatically improves its effectiveness, so spend some time playing around with these options.

Writing the Movie to Disk

When you're satisfied with the DVD movie, it's time to burn it to disk. Click the Burn button to proceed.

If there is no writeable DVD in the drive, Windows DVD Maker will prompt you to insert one. Use the lowest-capacity disk possible (4.7GB for one hour or less of video), as those disks tend to be less expensive than the dual-layer versions. That said, a dual-layer (DL) disk will work just fine if that's all you have.

If your PC does not have a DVD burner Windows DVD Maker will tell you that a DVD burner is required and recommend that you connect one before continuing. Optionally, you can save the project instead and install a DVD burner later.

Secret

What you can't do easily is copy the DVD Maker project to a different PC with a DVD burner and then create the DVD there. That's because the project will look for the content needed to create the DVD in file paths relative to where they were on the original PC. In order to make this work, you would have to copy the content for the project to the same locations on the second PC as they were on the first.

After you've inserted a blank recordable DVD in the drive, DVD Maker will begin the creation process. This can be extremely lengthy, depending on the amount of content you've included. While DVD Maker is creating the DVD, the application window closes and a small Burning dialog appears in the lower-right corner of your screen, charting its progress.

When the DVD is completed, Windows DVD Maker ejects the DVD drive tray so you can go try it in a DVD player. You're also prompted to create another copy of the disk if you'd like. Click Close to cancel that option and return to the main DVD Maker application.

The Final Frontier: Duplicating and Copying DVDs

While it's likely that you have at least some video content of your own, most home video tends to be short or at least short-lived. Many people have had the same basic experience: Excited by the start of a family or relationship, you purchase an expensive video camera, eager to document your lives as if anyone, let alone you, were particularly interested in watching most of the video you eventually shoot. Video cameras tend to gather dust in a closet, so you move on to digital cameras and even cell phones and smart phones, many of which now offer low-quality to decent-quality video capabilities in addition to their more common still-picture functionality. But even that tends to be a low-impact hobby: Most of the video I've taken with my digital camera, for example, has been created by mistake. I meant to take a still shot, but the camera dial had turned to the video setting while in my pocket. As I result, I have dozens of five-second-long videos on which you can hear me in the background muttering about what went wrong. Its compelling footage, let me tell you.

While I have no doubt that some of you out there will become dedicated videographers, most people enjoy an entirely different kind of video far more often than your own home movies, whether they were taken accidentally or on purpose. You rent and purchase DVD movies, for example, and, increasingly, high-definition (HD) Blu-ray movies. You watch movies and TV shows on TV and enjoy On Demand rental content. You watch short video clips on YouTube and other Web sites. And a small minority of users even purchase and rent TV shows and movies electronically, using services such as Apple iTunes, Amazon Unbox, CinemaNow, MovieLink, and others.

Wouldn't it be nice to get some of that content on your PC or portable media devices so you could enjoy it on the road, while commuting, at the gym, or in other situations when it's not convenient or possible to be sitting on your couch watching TV, or sitting in front of your Internet-connected PC? Sure it would, and you can make it happen.

Some of the scenarios just listed are more problematic than others, but I'll focus on DVD movies here because these shiny, silver disks are, by far, the most common way most of us enjoy video entertainment. That said, it's worth at least a short side trip first to look at what's going on with these other entertainment types:

◆ **Blu-ray:** As of this writing, the ability to create a DVD version or PC-playable file from a Blu-ray movie is somewhat of a pipe dream, though hackers are working on it. A bigger issue, from a PC perspective, involves Blu-ray playback. If you have a Blu-ray optical disk drive on your PC, you also need a variety of hardware that is *HDCP (High-bandwidth Digital Content Protection)* compatible. That is, Windows Vista has been engineered in such a way that your video card, sound card, monitor, and other hardware must all be HDCP compatible before you can play back that Blu-ray movie you legally purchased. The reason is because Blu-ray movies are essentially perfect digital copies of the original film, and Hollywood is understandably anxious to prevent consumers from illegally copying these perfect digital copies and giving them to friends. To be fair, any new PC purchased from 2007 on, especially those that come with Blu-ray optical drives, should be fully HDCP compatible. But that doesn't help those who purchased PCs before then or built their own PCs. In the end, consumers have a lot of work to do to ensure they can view Blu-ray content on their PCs.

Secret

Alternately, you could simply purchase a wonderful software product called AnyDVD HD. Available from Slysoft (**www.slysoft.com/**), AnyDVD HD enables you to watch Blu-ray movies on a non-HDCP-compliant PC. It also performs a number of other useful Blu-ray related jobs, including removing BD+ copy protection and region codes from Blu-ray disks, meaning you can watch international Blu-Ray movies, a huge plus for movie buffs. AnyDVD HD also includes all of the other excellent features from the standard AnyDVD utility, which I examine more closely in just a bit.

◆ **Recordable TV content:** Windows Vista already includes all the software tools you need to record TV shows from a variety of sources, including cable TV and HD sources such as HD cable and over-the-air (OTA) HD. I examine this functionality, which is part of the Windows Media Center software, in Chapter 15.

♦ **YouTube videos:** Online video entertainment sites such as YouTube are quite popular, but while YouTube and other sites make it easy to enjoy videos online, what they don't offer is a way to download your favorite videos so you can enjoy them offline.

Secret

To download unprotected copies of YouTube and other online videos to your hard drive, check out the free RealNetworks RealPlayer media player (**www .realplayer.com/**).

♦ **Content from online services:** Apple iTunes, Amazon Unbox, and others rent movies and sell movies and TV shows in various formats. Fortunately, these movies arrive as PC-friendly video files, so you should have no problem accessing them offline on a portable computer. Different services are compatible with different portable devices and digital media receivers, however. Apple's files are compatible only with its own hardware, including iPods, iPhones, and Apple TVs. Meanwhile, all of the other services have standardized on Microsoft's Windows Media Video (WMV) format, so these files should be compatible with any Windows-compatible devices that aren't made by Apple. Note, however, that all of this content is copy-protected, and as of this writing there's no way to remove that copy protection and use this content in your own projects. Some services do, however, allow you to burn purchased movies to DVD.

Now it's time to take a look at the two biggest missing features in Windows Vista when it comes to digital video: duplicating DVD movies and ripping, or copying, DVD movies to PC-compatible video files.

Duplicating DVD Movies

From a fair-use perspective, it should be possible to make a backup copy of your legally purchased DVD movies, assuming you're doing so for archival purposes and will not be distributing those copies, or the originals, to others outside your immediate family. This is a bit spurious from a legal standpoint, I think, but there is one reason I've backed up a few DVD movies myself, and it has nothing to do with archiving. I travel a lot for work, and like many people, I like to bring along DVD movies for those otherwise wasted hours on planes and in hotel rooms. However, I don't want to subject expensive DVD purchases to the rigors of travel. I'm thinking of a particularly maddening experience on a cross-country flight in which a few of my DVDs were actually cracked thanks to an overzealous fellow passenger jamming his too-large bag into a too-small storage compartment directly on top of my bag.

You'd think that Windows Vista would offer some sort of basic DVD backup utility, even if it were designed to only function on that tiny percentage of unprotected (that is, home-made) DVDs that are out there—but it's not there. Vista includes ways in which you can burn data DVDs and create DVD movies, but it's surprisingly light when it comes to DVD backup. You'll have to look elsewhere.

I've come across several excellent DVD backup utilities, and chances are good that your PC came with one of them. The Nero Ultra Edition suite (**www.nero.com/**) and Roxio Easy Media Creator (**www.roxio.com/**) are popular PC bundles; and of course you can purchase these huge and sometimes confusing digital media suites on your own if you're looking for that kind of thing. I tend to prefer simpler solutions. For example, SlySoft's CloneDVD (**www.slysoft.com/en/clonedvd.html**) is an excellent and inexpensive way to back up entire DVDs or just the parts of a DVD you want. That's literally all it does, and it does it well. CloneDVD is shown in Figure 14-53.

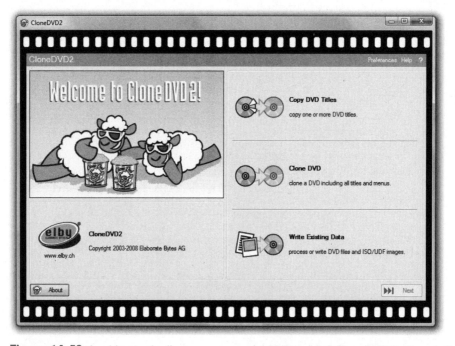

Figure 14-53: Looking to duplicate a commercial DVD movie? CloneDVD is the solution.

Secret

What all of these solutions lack is a way to back up commercial, Hollywood-type DVDs. That's because these DVDs come with a form of copy protection that prevents such copying. In order to bypass this protection, you'll need something such as SlySoft AnyDVD (or AnyDVD HD: **www.slysoft.com/en/anydvd .html**), which I strongly recommend. AnyDVD removes the encryption from DVD movies, enabling you to back up Hollywood movies. It removes the DVD region coding from DVD movies, so you movie buffs can enjoy DVD movies that are purchased outside of your locale. But AnyDVD isn't just about bypassing copy protection. In fact, other features make this tool of interest to anyone who enjoys DVD movies regularly on a PC. It prevents the automatic launching of not-so-friendly "PC-friendly" software on video DVDs. It also enables you to skip annoying trailers and other baloney that movie companies force on us, letting you jump directly to either the main movie or the DVD's title menu. And it does this automatically: Pop in a disk and AnyDVD will do its thing under the hood. This is one of the best utilities I've ever purchased.

Ripping DVDs to the PC

While duplicating a DVD may be of limited interest, ripping (or copying) a DVD movie to your hard drive, much in the same way that you rip songs from an audio CD to your hard drive in MP3 format, is probably more interesting to a wider audience. This also enables you to leave the master DVD copies of your movies safe at home while you travel or commute. It also means you don't have to travel with a bunch of disks, disks that aren't exactly the most battery-efficient thing to watch when traveling on battery power.

There are two major problems with ripping DVDs:

♦ First, you need a tool such as the aforementioned SlySoft AnyDVD because Hollywood DVD movies are copy-protected and designed so that they cannot be copied to your PC.

Secret

To be fair to Hollywood, however briefly, there is a growing generation of dual-use DVD disks out there that include both the standard DVD movie (which works on all DVD players, of course, including those in PCs) and so-called Digital Copy versions, which come in both iTunes- and Windows Media-compatible versions. The Windows Media Digital Copy version of these movies is a protected WMV file you can copy to your PC's hard drive and then to a compatible portable device. The first Digital Copy–compatible DVD movie, "Family Guy Blue Harvest," debuted in early 2008. As of this writing, there aren't that many Digital Copy DVDs, but if this format takes off, it could answer a lot of the complaints about fair use and DVD movies.

♦ Second, you need to determine which tool you want to use to rip DVD movies, as Windows Vista doesn't include anything. On a related note, you have to settle on a video format for those ripped files. (In the music field, this is simple: MP3 is the universal standard for audio files and it is the most compatible with software and devices. Video, alas, is a bit trickier.)

Ripping DVDs in Windows Media Video Format

If you're going to stick with the Windows Media world—that is, PC software such as Windows Media Player and Windows Media Center, Windows Media–compatible portable devices (or Zunes; see Chapter 12), and digital media receivers such as the Xbox 360 and various Media Center Extenders—then you should obviously be ripping your DVD movies into WMV format. In this case, you have an excellent option: SlySoft CloneDVD mobile (**www.slysoft.com/en/clonedvd-mobile.html**). This software can rip DVD movies into a variety of formats, including WMV. It also offers a surprising array of quality options, so be sure to check the technical specifications of the portable device you'll be watching these movies on before ripping. (The exact resolution of the finished movie varies depending on the aspect ratio of the source movie, but you can choose between such resolutions as 320 × PNG, 480 × PNG, 640 × PNG, 720 × PNG, 852 × PNG, and 720 × 480 (NTSC TV), where PNG can vary.)

Follow these steps to rip a commercial DVD movie to your hard drive in WMV format:

1. Insert a DVD movie into your optical drive.
2. Launch CloneDVD mobile. As shown in Figure 14-54, this wizard-based application supports a number of video formats (DivX, WMV, and so on) and comes with presets for numerous devices, e.g., the Xbox 360, PlayStation 3, Apple iPod and iPhone, Microsoft Zune, and many, many others.

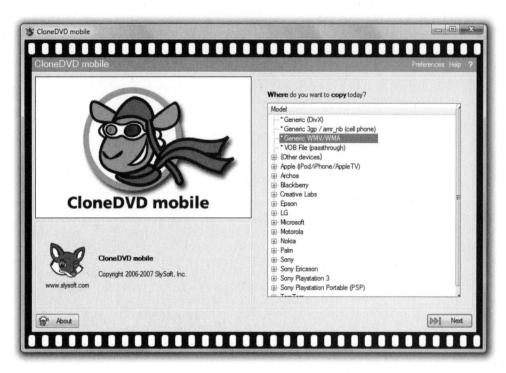

Figure 14-54: CloneDVD Mobile enables you to rip DVDs into digital video files on your PC.

3. Choose Generic WMV/WMA from the list of possible options in the first part of the wizard and then click the Next button.

4. In the next phase of the wizard, you have to choose the VIDEO_TS folder on the DVD. To do so, click the small Browse button on the right and then navigate to the DVD movie in the dialog that appears, expanding the tree view if necessary to select the VIDEO_TS folder, as shown in Figure 14-55. Next, click OK.

5. After you have selected the VIDEO_TS folder, CloneDVD Mobile will present a list of the video tracks available on the DVD and will preview the selected track in the Preview tab. Generally speaking, the main DVD movie you want will be the longest video on the disk. Select it, ensure that it's correct using the Preview tab, and then click Next.

6. In the Audio and Subtitle Settings phase of the wizard, you can choose which audio stream to use (English by default in the U.S.) and whether you want subtitles hard-coded onto the movie (and if so, which language to use). Click Next when you've made the appropriate selections.

7. Finally, in the Output Method dialog, shown in Figure 14-56, you choose options such as the resolution, video quality, and, perhaps, zoom settings. These options are very important, so you'll need to choose wisely.

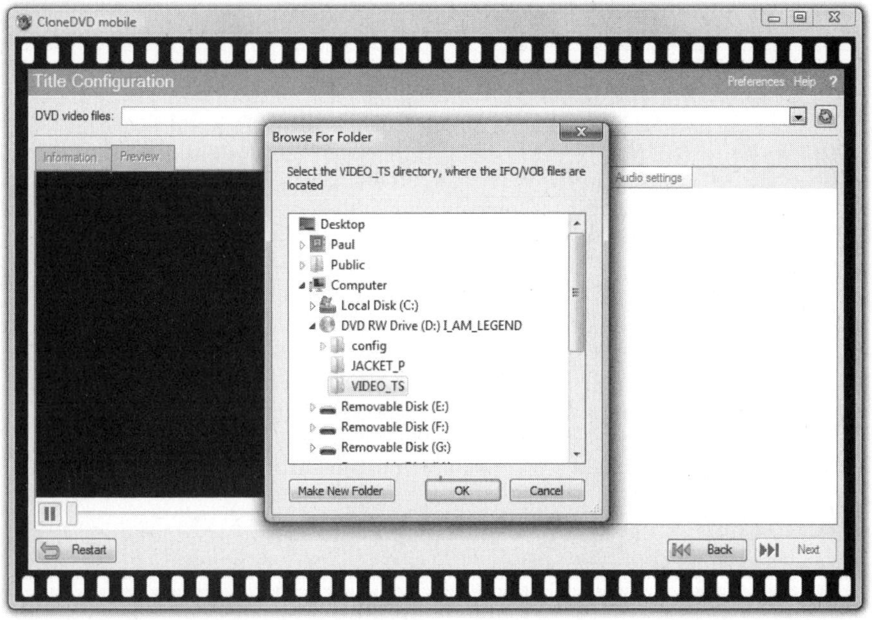

Figure 14-55: The key to a successful DVD rip is locating the VIDEO_TS folder structure on the DVD movie disk.

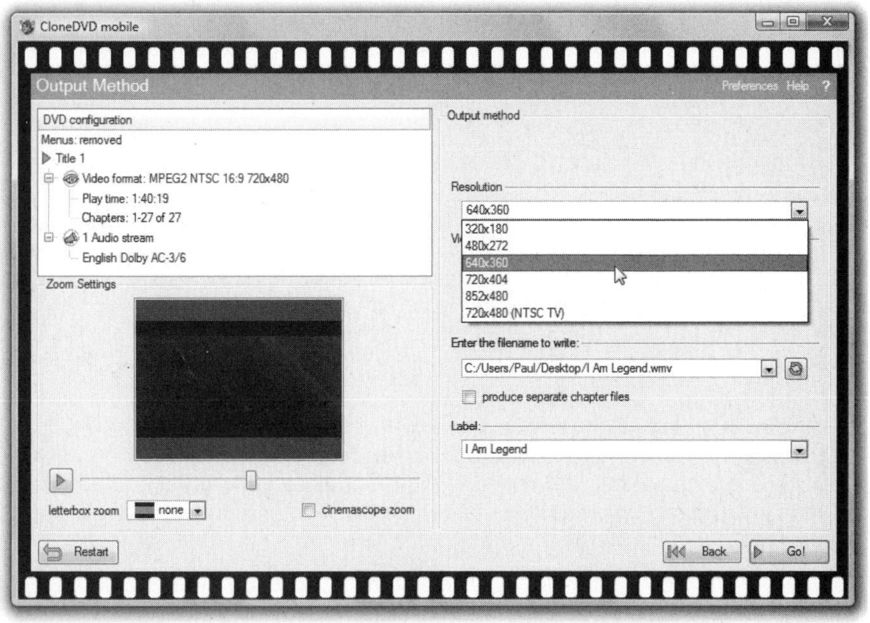

Figure 14-56: Here is where you determine the quality (and thus the size) of the resulting video.

In the Resolution drop-down, you'll see a variety of options (which, again, depend on the actual aspect ratio of the original movie). Roughly speaking, the higher the resolution, the better the video will look, up to a certain point, and the larger the resulting file will be. Remember that it doesn't make sense to create digital videos that are larger than the source material: DVDs are always 720 ⇨ 480 or less, so you should ignore the 852 × PNG option for the most part. Finally, you'll want to ensure that the video you create will work on your portable device. If it's too big, then Windows Media Player will have to transcode it before copying it to the device, a process that can be time consuming. In my experience, videos that are 640 × 480 and below offer a good compromise between quality, size, and compatibility.

8. Select a resolution (typically 640 × 480 or less) and then click the Default button next to the Quality slider. (You can slide this to the right for better-quality video, though these files will also be larger.) Then, provide a label for the video (something like *Name of the Movie* instead of VIDEO_DVD or whatever). Typically, you will want to leave the Zoom settings alone, but you can experiment with the Letterbox Zoom and Cinemascope Zoom settings to see how they change the resulting video.

9. Click Go when you're ready to encode, or create, the video. A Save As–type dialog will appear, enabling you to name the video file and pick a location where it will reside on the hard drive. Videos are typically stored in the Videos folder, as you know, but you're free to create it virtually anywhere.

The amount of time this encoding process takes depends on the performance characteristics of your PC. Generally, it should take 50 to 100 percent of the length of time it would take to actually watch the movie if performed on a modern PC with decent 3D video hardware.

Once you've created a movie in this fashion, you can copy it to another PC, a portable device, or a digital media receiver (including the Xbox 360), or use it in Windows Movie Maker or Windows DVD Maker projects.

Ripping DVDs in H.264 format

If you're more in the Apple camp, you should focus on the H.264 format, which is a modern version of the MPEG-4 standard. H.264 videos are high quality and compatible with iPods, iPhones, the Apple TV, the Xbox 360, Microsoft's Zunes, and a limited range of other devices, so be sure to check for compatibility. On the PC, H.264 also works fine with Apple QuickTime and iTunes, and with free media player software such as GOM Player (**www.gomlab.com/**) and VLC Media Player (**www.videolan.org/vlc/**). Note that H.264 video is incompatible, however, with Windows Movie Maker and Windows DVD Maker.

To rip to H.264 format in Windows Vista, you have a variety of options. You can use the aforementioned CloneDVD or the very similar Nero Recode, which is part of the Nero Ultra Edition suite (**www.nero.com/**). Both of these tools work similarly, but for H.264 I prefer the open-source Handbrake tool (**http://handbrake.fr/**), which has wonderful presets for iPods and other Apple devices. (Note that the Apple iPod presets work just fine with Microsoft's Zune devices too.)

Here's how you can rip a commercial DVD movie to your hard drive in H.264 format:

1. Insert a DVD movie into your optical drive.

2. Launch Handbrake. (Note that this application should be run with administrative privileges.) This application is shown in Figure 14-57.

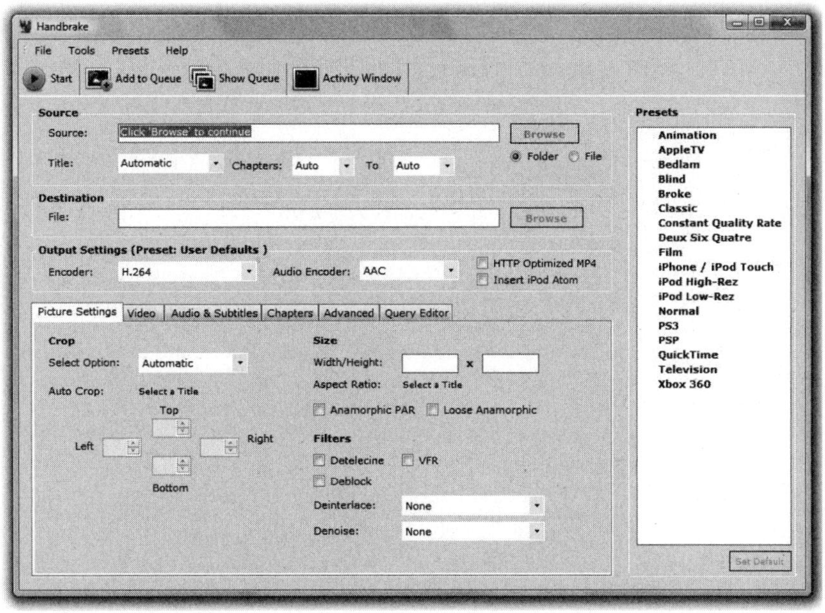

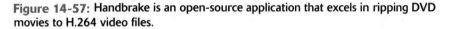

Figure 14-57: Handbrake is an open-source application that excels in ripping DVD movies to H.264 video files.

3. Choose the VIDEO_TS folder on the DVD. To do so, click the Browse button in the Source section of the Handbrake application. Then navigate to the DVD movie in the dialog that appears, expanding the tree view if necessary to select the VIDEO_TS folder. Click OK. Handbrake presents a Reading Source dialog while it gets information about the DVD movie.

4. Once this process is complete, you can choose the correct movie on the DVD via the Title drop-down menu, shown in Figure 14-58. Generally speaking, the main DVD movie you want will be the longest video on the disk. Select it.

5. Click the Browse button next to the File text box in the Destination section. In the Save As dialog that appears, navigate to the location on the disk to which you'd like to save the resulting file. Then give it a plain English name and click Save. (Optionally, you can choose between the mp4 and iPod-friendly m4v file extensions in the Save As Type field, though both should work interchangeably.)

6. Select a preset. I generally choose the iPod Hi-Res preset, which encodes videos at 640 ⇨ PNG, offering the greatest compatibility between iPods, iPhones, the Apple TV, and the PC. (Note that choosing a higher resolution could cause compatibility problems because Apple doesn't support automatically transcoding video, as does Windows Media Player.) You can choose optional video settings by clicking the Video tab. For example, you can enable two-pass encoding to obtain a higher-quality video file, though such files will also take longer to rip (twice as long, in fact).

7. In the Picture Settings tab, make sure Automatic is selected under the Crop section. This ensures that the movie is cropped to the correct aspect ratio.

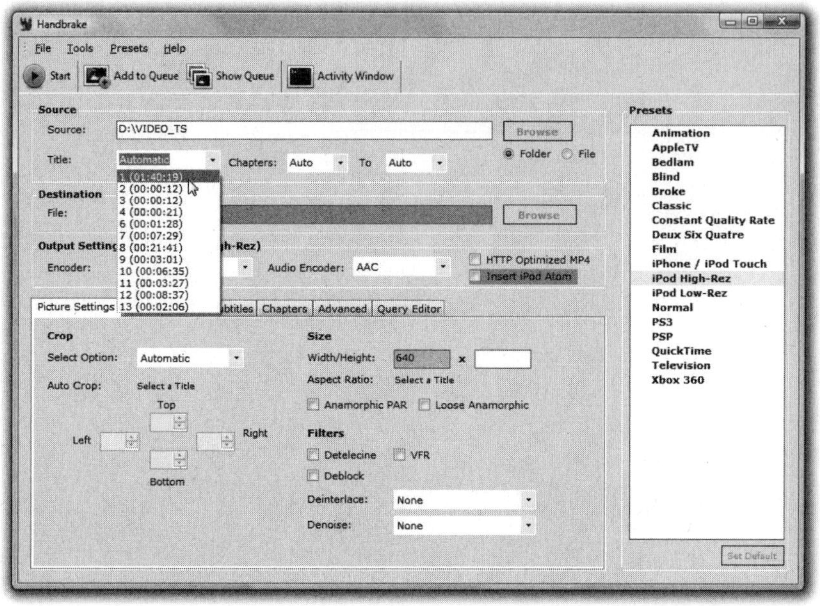

Figure 14-58: Sometimes you'll have a number of movies to choose from.

8. Finally, make any other changes you might need. For example, you can visit the Audio & Subtitles tab to change the audio track or add subtitles.

9. Click the Start button to begin encoding.

H.264 video encoding, like that of WMV, is very much dependent on the performance characteristics of your PC. That said, H.264 encoding is generally much slower than WMV encoding. The resulting files should be of similar or better quality when ripping with similar settings, however.

Once you've created a movie in this fashion, you can copy it to another PC, an Apple or Zune portable device, or a digital media receiver (including the Xbox 360 and Apple TV). What you can't do, of course, is use it in Windows Movie Maker or Windows DVD Maker projects. If this is a problem, you can use Apple QuickTime Player Pro to convert the movie into AVI format.

Summary

The digital video capabilities in Windows Vista are vastly superior to those offered in Windows XP. You can manage your digital movie collection in a variety of ways, including the Windows shell, Windows Photo Gallery, Windows Media Player, and Windows Media Center. You can use Windows Movie Maker to edit and distribute your home movies, recorded TV shows, and other video-related content, including HD content, and can output the results in HD-compatible glory if you're so inclined. Using Windows DVD Maker, you can even publish movies and photo slideshows to standard DVD movies that will work in virtually any DVD player in the world, and if you don't mind spending a bit of money and making the effort, you can even back up commercial DVDs and rip them to disk as unprotected digital video files.

Vista in the Living Room: Windows Media Center

Chapter

15

◆ ◆

In This Chapter

Understanding how Media Center has evolved over the years

Seeing how Media Center has changed in Windows Vista

Configuring Windows Media Center extensively

Touring the new user interface

Accessing the Media Center TV, movie, photo, and video experiences

Extending Media Center into other rooms with Xbox 360 and other extenders

Synchronizing Media Center with portable devices

Using Media Center to burn your own CDs and DVDs

◆ ◆

Although Microsoft was criticized for taking so long to bring Windows Vista to market, the truth is that the software giant wasn't idle during the several year wait between Windows XP and Windows Vista. One of the most innovative technologies Microsoft added to Windows during this time period is Windows Media Center, a wonderful, remote control–accessible front end to all of your digital media content, including live and recorded TV shows, and digital videos, photos, and music. Media Center is equally at home in your living room, bedroom, or home office. In Windows Vista, the Media Center environment has been improved with added functionality and a nicer user interface. It's also available in two mainstream versions of the operating system instead of being relegated to a single, special version of the OS. Thus, it will reach a far wider audience than it did previously. This chapter takes a detailed look at Microsoft's digital media solution for the living room, Media Center.

A Short History of Media Center

In January 2002, shortly after the release of Windows XP, Microsoft announced that it was working on software, then code-named Freestyle, that would extend the reach of Windows into the living room. Freestyle, which was eventually renamed to Windows XP Media Center Edition, was really just Windows XP Professional with a Media Center application and various Media Center–related services added on top. Media Center, the application, was and is a user interface designed for use with a remote control (although it works fine with a mouse and keyboard too). This is what Microsoft calls the *ten-foot user interface* (compared to the mouse and keyboard interface, which is referred to as the *two-foot interface*.)

The original Media Center version included all of the basic features you've come to associate with Media Center in the intervening years. It supported a simple menu-based user interface with options for recording TV, watching live TV, controlling cable set-top boxes via a so-called IR blaster, and enjoying digital media experiences such as music, pictures, videos, and DVD movies (see Figure 15-1). Windows XP Media Center shipped as a special new version of Windows in October 2002 and was available only with select Media Center PCs, a new generation of media-capable computers that, it was hoped, consumers would purchase and use in their home theater setups. The software was well received by reviewers, but it didn't sell very well because Media Center PCs were relatively expensive, and setting up TV tuner cards to work with cable signals was (and, sadly, still can be) difficult.

The second version of Windows XP Media Center Edition, code-named Harmony, shipped a year later as Windows XP Media Center Edition 2004. This version was also available only with new PCs, and added support for FM radio tuner cards, online services, and functionality that Microsoft had previously left to the two-foot experience, such as CD ripping. As you might expect, the product also included various UI and performance improvements as well.

In late 2004, Microsoft shipped the most extensive Media Center update yet, Windows XP Media Center Edition 2005, code-named Symphony. This version sported dramatic user interface improvements, including a scrolling main menu, a much simpler setup experience, vastly improved TV picture quality with fewer MPEG-2 compression artifacts, and support for up to three TV tuners, one of which can be an over-the-air (OTA) HDTV tuner. Microsoft also added support for Media Center Extenders, hardware devices that resemble set-top boxes and enable you to access the Media Center experience remotely via your home network to other TVs in the house: That way, you can watch a live TV show on one TV, with an Extender, and watch a recorded TV show on a different TV, using the Media Center PC. Media Center 2005 supported up to five Extenders, depending on the hardware capabilities of the system. Microsoft also shipped Media Center Extender software for its Xbox video game console, which enabled that device to be used like a dedicated Media Center Extender.

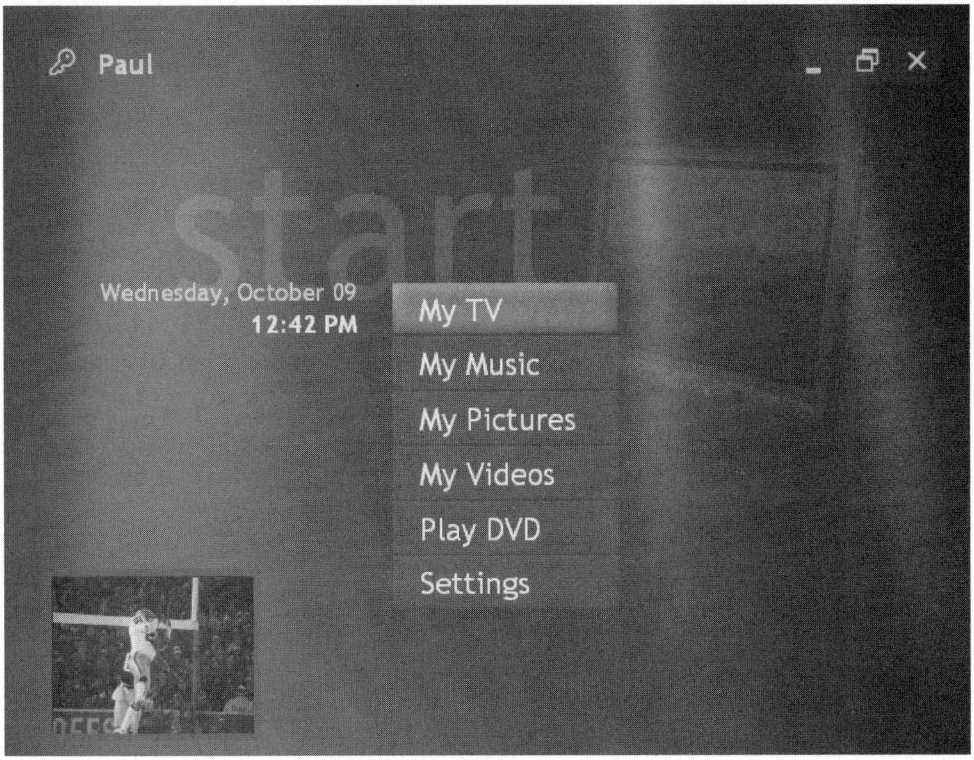

Figure 15-1: The original Windows XP Media Center Edition

Although late 2005 didn't see a major Windows Media Center release, Microsoft did ship a Media Center update that year, ignominiously named Windows XP Media Center Edition 2005 Update Rollup 2 (UR2). This free update to Media Center 2005 added support for the Xbox 360 and its built-in Media Center Extender functionality, a feature called Away Mode that enabled newer Media Center PC models with modern power management features to move quickly between on and off states that more closely resemble TV sets than PCs; DVD changer support; a new DVD burning utility; and support for up to four TV tuners (two of which can be standard definition, and two of which can be OTA HDTV tuners). UR2 also added a wonderful new video Zoom feature that helps make 4:3 TV pictures look better on wide-screen displays, support for digital radio, and various bug fixes and performance improvements. Windows XP Media Center Edition 2005 UR2 is shown in Figure 15-2.

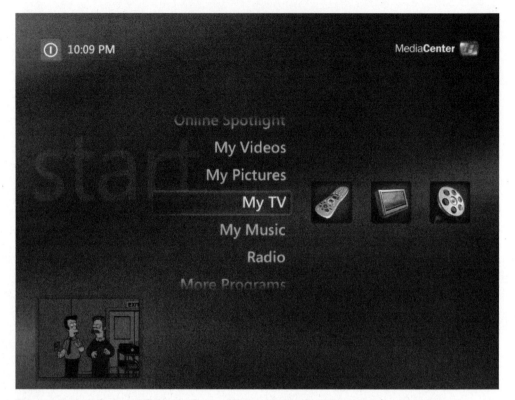

Figure 15-2: Windows XP Media Center Edition 2005 with UR2 was fast, stable, and clean looking.

Aside from the actual products that were rolled out over these years, Microsoft made some of its biggest improvements to Media Center from a marketing standpoint. Although the Media Center software was never released as a standalone add-on for all Windows users, Microsoft dropped the price of this XP version and stopped requiring PC makers to ship it only with new PCs that included TV tuners. Thus, over the years, Media Center quickly became one of the best-selling versions of Windows XP, and it's now installed on millions of PCs worldwide. Many Media Center users don't use the TV functionality at all, in fact, but use the software just to enjoy digital media. Today, Windows Media Center is a mature product that's benefited greatly from years of user feedback and continual improvements.

Media Center in Windows Vista

With Windows Vista, Microsoft has made some big changes to Media Center. First, the software is no longer available only in a single special Windows Media Center product. However, you still can't purchase Windows Media Center separately from Windows. Instead, you obtain Windows Media Center with two different Windows Vista product editions: Windows Vista Home Premium and Windows Vista Ultimate.

If you're using Windows Vista Home or Business editions, you can upgrade to a Media Center–compatible version of Windows Vista by using the Windows Anytime Upgrade functionality, discussed in Chapter 1.

The second and less obvious change is that the version of Media Center that ships with Windows Vista is only a half-realized version of where Microsoft hopes to take Media Center in the future. That is, while much of the Media Center interface has changed dramatically in Windows Vista, many of the subpages you'll navigate through while using this system have not really changed since Windows XP Media Center Edition 2005, aside from a few theme changes to make these pages look more like the Vista version. These weird throwbacks to XP Media Center 2005 appear throughout the chapter, but keep in mind that Microsoft will be releasing an update to Media Center, called Windows Vista Media Center Feature Pack 2008 (and it is hoped by the time you read this), that will complete the transition to the new user interface. At this point, how the update will be delivered is still a mystery. Currently, this Media Center update is code-named "Fiji."

From a high-level standpoint, Media Center has been upgraded in Windows Vista to be more intuitive and obvious. If you're used to previous Media Center versions, the changes will be a little jarring; but Microsoft hopes the new UI will help users find the content they want more quickly, with less navigating (and remote control button pushing). At a low level, Media Center has been architected to be more scalable, so that Microsoft's partners can more easily extend Media Center to do more. It is hoped that this results in more and better online experiences, applications, and other software that works both with and within Media Center.

Third, Media Center also now supports a technology called CableCard, which enables specially manufactured Media Center PCs to directly control cable systems without a jury-rigged IR blaster and cable set-top box. What CableCard does is replace a cable box with a card that is plugged directly into the computer. It's a great idea, especially for anyone who's had to suffer through the performance issues incurred by IR blasting.

Sadly, Windows Media Center's support for CableCard cannot be added after the fact, nor can it be added to a PC that you have built yourself. CableCard support can only be provided by a major PC maker at the time you purchase your PC. That's because Hollywood is freaked out by the notion that users now have access to pristine, perfect digital copies of their HD movies and television shows. Therefore, it has created a copy protection scheme that ensures that digital content is protected from theft. This scheme is present in Windows Vista. If it weren't, CableCard and other HD technologies (such as support for HD Blu-Ray disks) simply wouldn't work. Unfortunately, the Draconian nature of Hollywood's control over this content makes it a lot harder on consumers. Go figure.

Finally, there's a fourth major change. The version of Media Center in Windows Vista will not work with first-generation Media Center Extender devices, including the software-based version that shipped for the original Xbox. Instead, you need to use an Xbox 360 or a new lineup of second-generation Extender-enabled devices, including set-top boxes, televisions, and DVD players. You'll examine Media Center's Extender capabilities later in this chapter.

Secret

Microsoft doesn't like to talk about it, but several features have been removed from Media Center in Windows Vista, and first-generation Extender support is only the beginning. In this version, Windows Messenger and MSN Messenger integration was removed because the Messenger interfaces no longer ship as part of the operating system. (Thanks a lot, U.S. Department of Justice!) Caller ID has also been removed, a feature that enabled users to connect their phone line through the PC; when a phone call arrived, the Caller ID information would pop up onscreen so you could decide whether to pause TV or whatever before getting off the couch to grab the phone. Fortunately, numerous kinds of Caller ID add-ons for Media Center are available online. One such solution is Vista Caller-ID, and it's free: www.vistacallerid.com/.

Configuring Media Center

Before you do anything in Media Center, you should configure it to work with your PC's display and sound system, your Internet connection, and, if present, your TV signal. Unlike any other Windows Vista feature, Media Center configuration is a bit time-consuming and requires you to be prepared in advance. Unless you've done this before, plan to spend about an hour configuring Media Center for the first time.

When you first launch Media Center, you will see a Media Center–style dialog box—as shown in Figure 15-3—asking you whether you'd like to configure these features via an Express or Custom method. You can also optionally choose to run setup later.

Express Setup will utilize the default settings. Generally speaking, I do not recommend allowing Microsoft to configure any of its software with the company's default settings, so my advice is to not choose the Express Setup option. If you do choose Express setup, Media Center will be configured to download media information from the Internet and perform other Internet-based tasks you may not approve of.

If you choose Custom Setup—which roughly corresponds to the setup experience used by previous Media Center versions—you will need to step through the Media Center setup wizard manually. Though it is a bit time-consuming, I recommend you choose this option: Even if you ultimately choose the options Microsoft would have configured for you automatically in Express options, at least this way you know exactly what happened.

tip Media Center actually enables you to skip the configuration stage and configure Media Center settings later. To do so, click the Setup Later button.

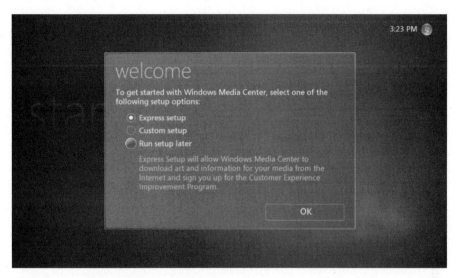

Figure 15-3: Media Center's notification dialog boxes aren't really separate windows, but rather part of the underlying display. However, you still need to deal with these alerts before doing anything else in Media Center.

Running the Setup Wizard

To configure Media Center in a more personalized fashion than is provided by Microsoft's default settings, choose Custom Setup in the Media Center Welcome dialog described in the previous section. This launches the Media Center setup wizard, which runs in full-screen mode, as shown in Figure 15-4.

Figure 15-4: Media Center setup will guide you through many of the configuration tasks you should complete before using this interface.

The wizard steps you through the various options Media Center needs to run correctly, including your Internet connection (which includes a Join Wireless Network Wizard if you utilize a wireless connection), whether you'd like to join Microsoft's Customer Experience Program to help the company improve Media Center, and so on. All of these steps are explained as you continue through this section.

There are two sections to Windows Media Center setup: Required and Optional. In the Required section, the setup wizards walks you through the process of configuring those features that are required in order for Windows Media Center to function properly. You will encounter the following configuration tasks in the Required section:

- ♦ **Privacy statement:** Microsoft is serious about your privacy. I know this because I read their privacy statement. You should too.

- ♦ **Customer Experience Improvement Program:** Here, the wizard asks if you'd like to join Microsoft's Customer Experience Program (Help Improve Windows Media Center). What Microsoft is really asking you is whether you'd like to have your computer automatically send anonymous reports about Media Center performance and reliability to the company over the Internet. In general, this is a wise option to enable because your Media Center experience will be aggregated with that of other Media Center users around the world to help find and fix issues with the software; but if you're a privacy hound and not particularly trusting of Microsoft, you may want to simply choose No Thank You and move on.

- ♦ **Enhanced Playback:** Right after the Customer Experience Program phase, you'll see a Get The Most From Windows Media Center screen. Here, you are asked whether you'd like to let Media Center connect automatically to the Internet to automatically download music information, album art, and other data. In Chapter 11, I recommend being very careful about allowing Microsoft to do this, and that advice applies here as well: If you have carefully crafted your ripped CD meta-data, you might want to select No here. If, however, your digital media files are in need of some help—that is, you don't have album art associated with each of your ripped CD albums—then you should choose Yes. Media Center's interface is very visual in Windows Vista, and it works better when it can display graphical representations of your digital media.

After this, you'll be told that the required components have been set up. I know what you're thinking: That wasn't so bad. True, but the Optional Setup section, shown in Figure 15-5, is more difficult, so we'll look at these customizations far more closely. In this section of setup, you configure your tuners, TV signal and program guide (if your PC has one or more TV tuners installed), and your display, speakers, and media libraries. My advice here is simple: If you are going to be using Media Center at all, especially for watching and recording TV, you need to take the time to go through each of these steps.

Secret

You will only see the first Optional Setup item, Configure the TV Signal, if Windows Media Center detects that you have TV tuner hardware installed on your PC. In Figure 15-5, this option does not appear because this particular PC doesn't have a TV tuner card.

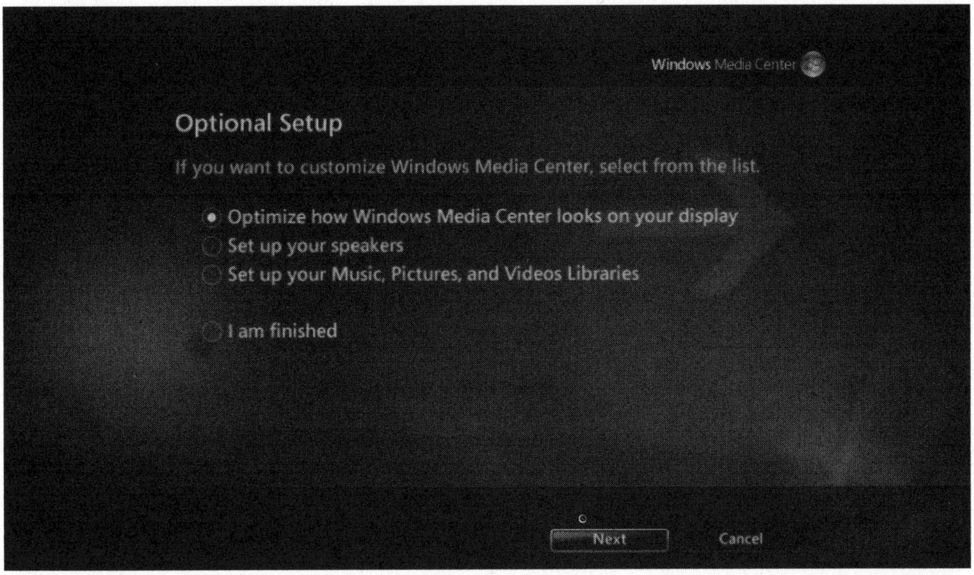

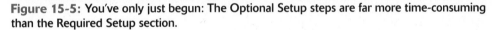

Figure 15-5: You've only just begun: The Optional Setup steps are far more time-consuming than the Required Setup section.

Configuring TV

If your PC includes at least one TV tuner card that is connected to a TV signal of some sort, refer to your Media Center PC's or TV tuner card's documentation for information on setting up the required hardware. Then you can configure Media Center to access and record televisions shows as follows:

1. Configure the TV signal. The wizard will initially ask you to confirm the region in which you live (United States, in my case). At that point, Media Center downloads TV setup options that are specific to your region.

Secret

In case it's not obvious, yes, that means you must have a live Internet connection in order to configure TV support within Media Center. In fact, Media Center relies on an Internet connection to keep its program guide, through which it displays the available TV shows at any given time, up-to-date. Although it's possible (but not advisable) to turn off the PC's Internet connection after you have configured its TV features, you absolutely must be connected to the Internet to complete this part of setup.

2. Choose between automatic and manual TV signal configuration. In my experience, automatic configuration works best when you're connected to a TV signal via a cable set-top box and are using IR blasting to control the box's channel changing functionality. (IR blasting is a method of transmitting, or "blasting," remote control signals to the cable box via a threadlike cable that runs from the PC's TV

tuner card to the front of the cable box; it enables a Media Center PC to emulate the cable box's remote control and send control signals to the box.) Conversely, manual configuration works better for a direct TV connection, whereby a coaxial cable plugs into the wall and connects directly to your TV tuner card (i.e., there is no set-top box). Because the manual method always works and requires more thought, I cover that here. Choose the *I Will Manually Configure My TV Signal* option, and then click Next.

3. In the next screen, you choose what type of TV signal you receive: Cable, Satellite, or Antenna. If you choose Cable or Satellite, you're asked whether you have a set-top box. If you do, setup will walk you through a series of steps in which you configure the system to control your set-top box so that you can change channels, raise and lower the volume, and perform other actions from within Media Center while using the Media Center remote control. If you don't have a set-top box, you can simply skip that part.

4. After configuring the system to use a set-top box, choose whether to use the program guide, which provides always-updated TV program listings that are specific to your cable system. Because the program guide requires Media Center to connect to Microsoft servers, you must okay this option. Unlike some of the other Media Center options, this one is a no-brainer: If you are going to use Media Center for TV, then you should absolutely enable this feature. You'll look at the program guide later in this chapter.

5. Now configure Media Center to work with your particular TV system. After you enter your zip code (in the United States), Media Center downloads a list of TV providers that match the type of TV signal you selected earlier. Pick the one that matches the service you receive and then Media Center will download the program guide for that service.

Secret Media Center downloads about two weeks' worth of program guide data at a time. The first time you do this, it takes a few minutes; but in the future, the guide download occurs in the background, and you won't even be aware it's happening. This enables the program guide to always be up-to-date.

Configuring the Display

In the Display Configuration phase, you optimize Media Center for your display. Media Center natively supports the following display types:

- ◆ **PC Monitor:** For a CRT monitor connected via a VGA cable
- ◆ **Built-In Display:** For a notebook computer
- ◆ **Flat Panel:** For a flat-panel monitor connected via a VGA or DVI cable
- ◆ **Television:** For any type of TV connected via composite, S-video, DVI, VGA, HDMI, or component cable
- ◆ **Projector:** For a dedicated projector connected via composite, S-video, DVI, VGA, HDMI, or component cable

Choose the correct display type, as shown in Figure 15-6.

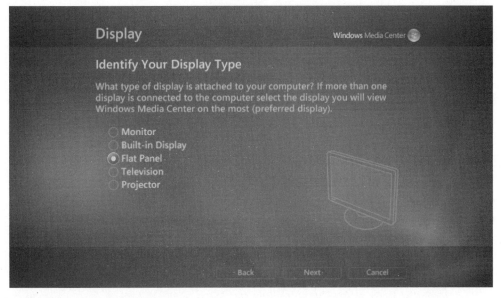

Figure 15-6: Media Center natively supports several display types and optimizes its display based on what you choose here.

Next, choose the correct connection type based on how your system is physically connected to the display, as shown in Figure 15-7. Consult your Media Center PC's documentation if you're not sure which display and connection types are employed. This step is important, because Media Center attempts to optimize the video output based on your selection.

Figure 15-7: Again, the choice you make here is very important because Vista optimizes its display based on it.

Secret

Ensure that you're using the highest-quality connection type. In rough order of quality, from worst to best, the options are composite, S-Video, VGA, Component (YPbPr) DVI, HDMI. If you're using a built-in display, such as that on a notebook computer, you really don't have any options.

After you've chosen the display and connection types, the wizard prompts you to choose the Display Width (really, the aspect ratio) of your display. You have two options: Standard (4:3) and Widescreen (16:9). Again, if you're not sure what to choose here, consult your display's documentation (or just look at the display—standard screens are basically square, whereas wide-screen displays are just that, wide-screen.) The wizard then checks the system and prompts you about the resolution of the display, as shown in Figure 15-8.

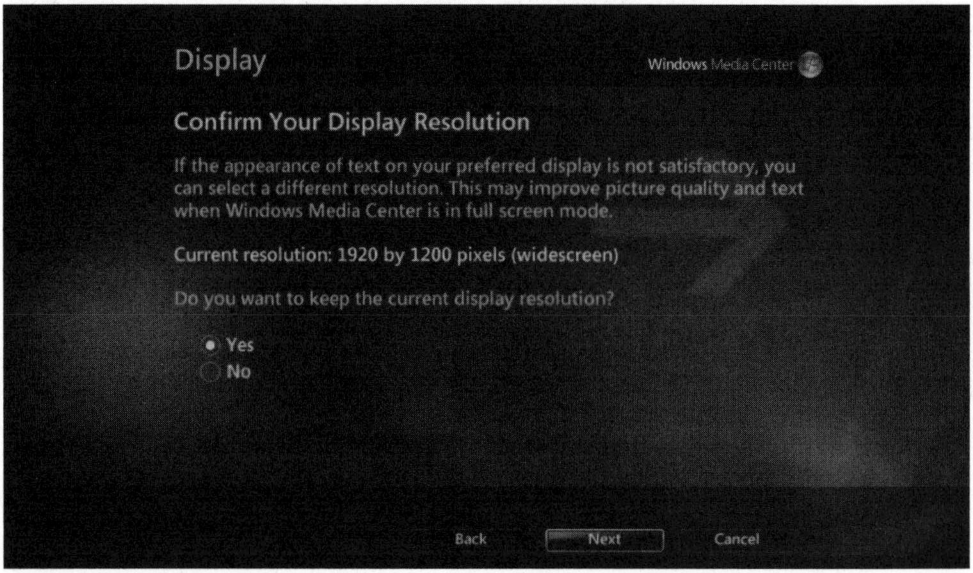

Display   Windows Media Center

Confirm Your Display Resolution

If the appearance of text on your preferred display is not satisfactory, you can select a different resolution. This may improve picture quality and text when Windows Media Center is in full screen mode.

Current resolution: 1920 by 1200 pixels (widescreen)

Do you want to keep the current display resolution?

• Yes
◦ No

Back   Next   Cancel

Figure 15-8: In general, you should ensure that Media Center is using the highest resolution supported by your display.

You can accept the value it provides (which you should do if it is correct) or select No. If you choose the latter option, you will be presented with a list of possible display resolutions, based on the capabilities of your display and whether you're using a wide-screen aspect ratio.

tip

On a high-end HDMI-based HDTV display, for example, you might see options such as 1920 x 1200, 1080p (59.95Hz), 1680 x 1050, 1440 x 900, 1360 x 768, and so on. Try to choose the highest resolution your display supports in order to get the best picture quality.

Next, you can optionally configure your display's controls, including calibrating the display's onscreen centering and sizing, aspect ratio, brightness, contrast, and RGB color balance. These controls are less important on VGA, DVI, and HDMI connections, but analog connections such as composite and S-Video often benefit from some fine-tuning. If you're using Media Center on a PC display, simply click Finish This Wizard. Otherwise, you might want to take the time to fine-tune the display.

Configuring Sound

In the next part of the Optional Setup section of Media Center setup, you can configure a number of options related to the speakers that are attached to your Media Center PC.

First, you'll be asked to configure the speaker connection type, as shown in Figure 15-9. This is a fairly technical question, and one that varies considerably from system to system, so you may, unfortunately, need to consult your PC's documentation to make the right choice. (Or, you may be a stereo geek—not that there's anything wrong with that.)

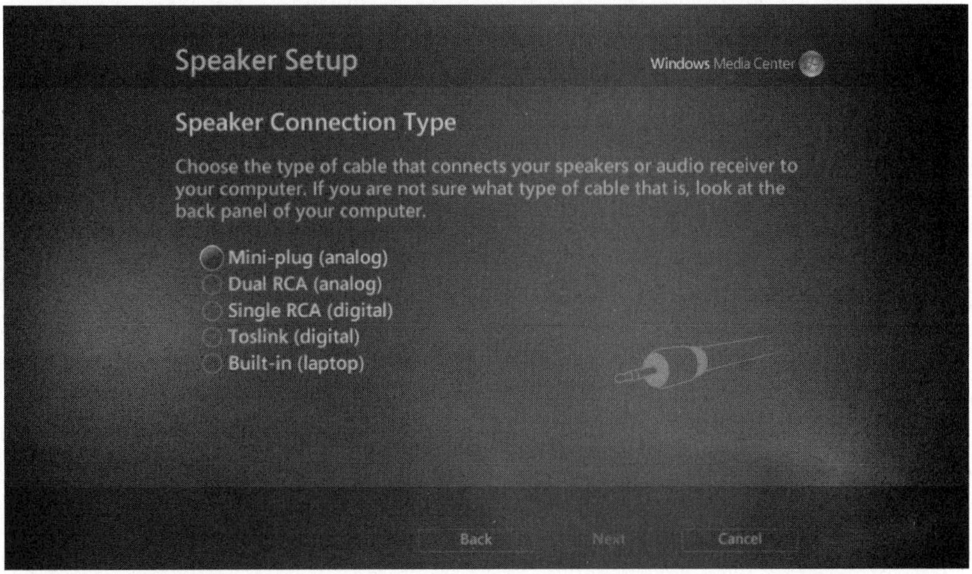

Figure 15-9: Time to reach for the documentation? Most Vista users probably have no idea how to answer this question.

Next, you'll configure the number of speakers. Vista's version of Media Center supports three speaker configurations: two speakers (stereo), 5.1 surround sound (two front speakers, two rear speakers, and a center speaker), or 7.1 surround sound (two front speakers, two rear speakers, two side speakers, and a center speaker). Choose the configuration that most closely matches your hardware and click Next.

In the Test Your Speakers dialog, shown in Figure 15-10, click Test to test the speakers and ensure that everything works as expected. If you don't hear the test sound in some or all of the speakers, the wizard will help you troubleshoot the problem.

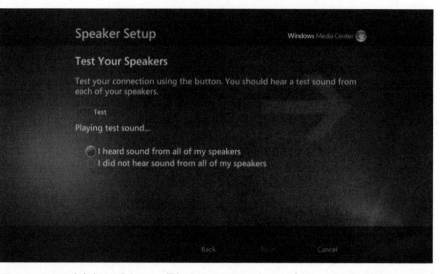

Figure 15-10: It is hoped that you'll hear a number of tones from each of your connected speakers.

Media Center's speaker setup is quite a bit more limited than the speaker configuration options you get in Windows Vista's Control Panel. There, you can configure stereo, quadraphonic, 5.1 surround, and 7.1 surround speaker setups. You can reach this Control Panel in various ways, but the most obvious is to right-click the volume icon in Vista's tray notification area, select Playback Devices from the menu that appears, and then select your speakers in the resulting dialog and click Configure. As shown in Figure 15-11, this Control Panel also enables you to test individual speakers separately.

Figure 15-11: Both Media Center and Windows Vista have their own ways to configure sound.

Configuring Your Digital Media Libraries

In the next phase, you can configure which folders Media Center monitors to fill your Music, Pictures, and Videos libraries with content. By default, Windows Media Center monitors the same folders you configure as Monitored Folders in Windows Media Player, discussed in Chapter 11, so if you already configured Monitor Folders in Windows Media Player, there may be no reason to do it here as well.

That said, some users will choose to use Media Center instead of Windows Media Player; and though the process of setting up Monitored Folders in Media Center is a bit different due to its wizard-based design, the results are the same.

Secret
Folders you configure as Monitored Folders in Windows Media Player are watched by Media Center as well; but the reverse is also true: If you configure Media Center to watch certain folders, those changes will be reflected in Windows Media Player too.

Secret
Intriguingly, Media Center offers an option that's lacking in Windows Media Player with regard to Monitored Folders: You can configure Media Center to stop monitoring default folders such as C:\Users*Your User Name*\Music, C:\Users*Your User Name*\Pictures, and C:\Users*Your User Name*\Videos.

When you're done stepping through the Optional Setup section, select I Am Finished and then click Next. Media Center indicates that you're done and provides yet another button (this time labeled Finish) to click. Unfortunately, you're not really done.

Configuring Media Center Features after Setup

After you're done configuring Windows Media Center with the setup wizard, you'll be presented with the Media Center menu system, or, as I like to call it, Start screen (see Figure 15-12).

You can examine the finer points of this user interface in the next section. For now, I want to discuss how you can configure Media Center further after completing the setup wizard. Some of the configuration information you'll see directly corresponds to features you configured in the wizard (or even runs part of the wizard in some cases); but you can access many more Media Center features from outside the wizard. For this reason, it's important to step through the Media Center Settings functionality to ensure that the system is configured exactly the way you want it.

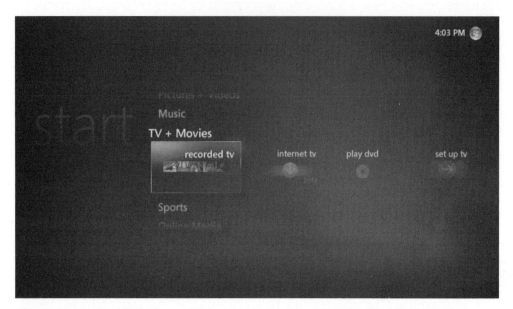

Figure 15-12: The Media Center Start screen is your home base for all of Media Center's experiences.

You can access Settings from virtually anywhere in Media Center, but the simplest method is to navigate to the Start screen (press the green Start button on the screen or on the Media Center remote, or select Alt+Home) and then scroll up the main menu to Tasks. Click the Settings link, on the left. Shown in Figure 15-13, Settings includes links to several major areas.

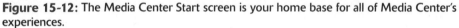

Figure 15-13: From here, a world of customization.

There's little need to walk you through each and every feature here. Instead, in the Secrets boxes that follow, I highlight options that are new to Windows Vista, those options that contain unlikely benefits, and the options you should absolutely consider changing.

Secret

General

The General Settings screen is shown in Figure 15-14. If you are using Media Center as the main interface to your TV in the living room, do the following:

1. Navigate to General ⇨ Startup and Window Behavior.
2. Select the Windows Media Center Window Always On Top option.
3. Select the Start Windows Media Center When Windows Starts option.
4. Disable Show Taskbar Notifications, because you'll likely never see the Windows taskbar anyway.

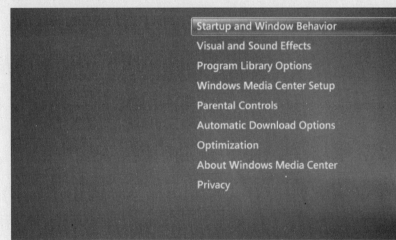

Startup and Window Behavior

Visual and Sound Effects

Program Library Options

Windows Media Center Setup

Parental Controls

Automatic Download Options

Optimization

About Windows Media Center

Privacy

Figure 15-14: Here, you configure Media Center options that apply throughout the Media Center interface.

Have kids? Use the Parental Controls feature to access a suite of excellent ratings-based controls that will prevent your children from viewing TV shows, DVD movies, or movies that you object to. You input a four-digit code to unlock these shows for yourself. Parental controls can be found in General ⇨ Parental Controls.

Keep your system optimized: In Settings ⇨ General ⇨ Optimization, you'll find one of Windows Vista's funniest (or saddest, depending on your perspective) features. It claims to "optimize" Windows Media Center every day at a set schedule (usually 4:00 a.m.). What does this optimization do, exactly? It reboots the PC. Yes, you read that right.

If you need to rerun setup, or just part of setup, you can do so from within the General Settings section. Just click Windows Media Center Setup and then choose from Set Up Internet Connection, Set Up TV Signal, Set Up Your Speakers, Configure Your TV or Monitor, or Run Setup Again.

TV

If you're hearing impaired, you can enable Closed Captioning, significantly improved in this version, in TV ⇨ Closed Captioning. Closed Captioning can be on, off, or on when muted. Naturally, the quality of the captioning depends on the content creators, who, unfortunately, have no federal requirements regarding accuracy.

Pictures

Be sure to closely examine the options in Picture Settings. You may want to enable Show Pictures in Random Order for better slide shows; and consider changing the transition time from 12 seconds to something smaller, like 5 seconds. You can also optionally enable captions, which is really only useful if you've named your photographs logically (e.g., "Day at the beach 06") instead of accepting the camera defaults (e.g., P0000537).

Library Setup

If you skipped the Library Setup portion of Optional Setup described earlier, or simply want to add or remove monitored media folders, you can do so now.

A Somewhat New User Interface

Okay, enough with the configuration already. Now it's time to take a look at the Windows Media Center user interface. Prior to Windows Vista, Media Center presented most of its menus using lists of text that were formatted to be readable on TV displays. In keeping with the more visual style of Windows Vista, however, the new Media Center version is more graphical and takes better advantage of the onscreen real estate offered by wide-screen displays such as HDTV sets. This interface may be a bit jarring if you're used to using previous Media Center versions, but newcomers should be able to adopt the new user interface fairly easily.

The main Media Center menu, or Start screen, was shown earlier in Figure 15-12. From here, you scroll up or down to access top-level Media Center experiences such as TV + Movies, Music, Pictures + Videos, Tasks, Online Media, and Sports. You can also scroll left and right to access sub-options within each top-level experience. For example, if TV + Movies is selected, you can move left and right to access options such as More TV,

Recorded TV, Live TV, Guide, Movies Guide, Play DVD, and Search. (If TV is not configured, you might see a Setup TV option as well, as shown in Figure 15-15.)

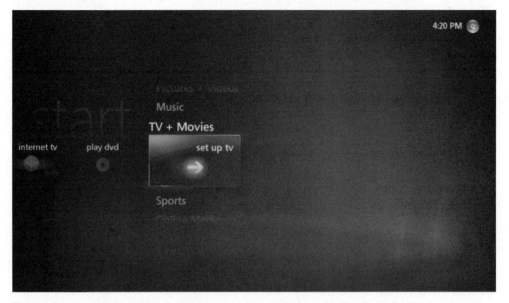

Figure 15-15: It takes a bit of getting used to, but Windows Media Center's menu system
scrolls both up and down and left and right.

You will run into these types of horizontally scrolling menu options throughout the Media
Center interface, so it's a good idea to get used to them by experimenting with the Start
screen. How you navigate through the interface depends on whether you're using the
keyboard, a mouse, or a Media Center remote control (which you might have received with
your PC). Each can be used to navigate through the Media Center interface. Table 15-1
summarizes how you access the most common Media Center navigational options with
each controller type.

Table 15-1: How to Get It Done in Windows Media Center

Media Center action	Keyboard	Mouse	Remote Control
Open Windows Media Center or return to the Windows Media Center Start screen.	Press the Windows key+Alt+Enter.	Select Media Center from the Start Menu or click the Media Center logo while in Media Center.	Click the Start button.
Close Windows Media Center.	Press Alt+F4.	Select Shutdown and then Close from the Start screen.	Select Shutdown and then Close from the Start screen.
Select the highlighted option.	Press Enter.	Click the highlighted option.	Click OK.

continues

Table 15-1: *(continued)*

Media Center action	Keyboard	Mouse	Remote Control
Go back to the previous screen.	Press Backspace.	Click the Back button.	Click Back.
Go to the first item in a list.	Press Home.	Scroll to the top of the list with the mouse's scroll wheel.	Press the Page Up button until you reach the top of the list.
Go to the last item in a list.	Press End.	Scroll to the bottom of the list with the mouse's scroll wheel.	Press the Page Down button until you reach the bottom of the list.
Move left.	Press the left arrow.	Move to the left side of the menu and click the left arrow that appears; or, press left on a tilting scroll wheel-equipped mouse.	Click the Left button.
Move right.	Press the right arrow.	Move to the right side of the menu and click the right arrow that appears; or, press right on a tilting scroll wheel-equipped mouse.	Click the Right button.
Move up.	Press the up arrow.	Move to the top of the menu and click the up arrow that appears; or, scroll up on a scroll wheel-equipped mouse.	Click the Up button.
Move down.	Press the down arrow.	Move to the bottom of the menu and click the down arrow that appears; or, scroll down on a scroll wheel-equipped mouse.	Click the Down button.
Toggle full-screen mode.	Press Alt+Enter.	Click the Maximize button.	n/a

Secret

The four-way menu navigation isn't unique to Windows Media Center. Microsoft first used this navigational paradigm in its software for Portable Media Centers, but more recently you can see it used in the software that powers Microsoft's Zune portable media players. Chapter 12 covers the Zune platform.

One feature you can access only with the mouse is the new controls overlay that appears when you move the mouse around while Media Center is enabled. Shown in Figure 15-16, these controls provide you with access to the Back and Start buttons in the top-left corner of the display, and a nice set of playback controls perfect for music, TV, videos, or other multimedia content in the bottom-right corner.

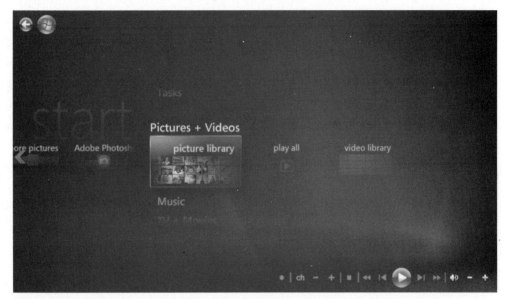

Figure 15-16: Media Center's new overlay controls are elegant-looking and easy to use.

Previously, I mentioned that some of the screens in Media Center were new to this version while others are carryovers from Windows XP Media Center Edition 2005. You might be wondering what actually changed.

The Start screen is all-new in the Windows Vista version of Media Center. When TV, video, or a DVD movie is playing (but not, oddly, a photo slide show) and you return to the Start screen, the Start screen is overlaid on the video, as shown in Figure 15-17. Previously, the video playback would be seen in a small picture-in-picture (PIP)-type window in the lower-left corner of the screen.

What's odd is that many subpages revert to the old way of doing things. For example, if you access the Details information for a playing video, TV show, or other movie content (by right-clicking the screen and choosing Video Details or Movie Details, or clicking the More Info button on the Media Center remote), the video pops into a tiny PIP window in the lower-left corner of the screen and isn't overlaid by the rest of the Media Center display, as shown in Figure 15-18.

You'll find inconsistencies like this throughout Media Center. Remember, Microsoft has only partially realized its vision for the next-generation Media Center. Future updates will use the video overlay style in all Media Center screens. For now, only two places use this overlay: The Start page and the Program Guide.

Figure 15-17: New to Vista: Movies and TV shows can be overlaid by the Start screen.

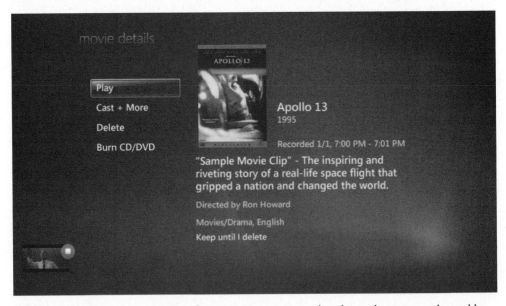

Figure 15-18: Blast from the past: Some screens revert to the picture-box approach used by previous Media Center versions.

Exploring the Media Center Experiences

Media Center offers a rich and exciting way to access live and recorded television shows and movies, digital photos, home videos, digital music, and other digital media content, and it works equally well on a notebook, your desktop PC, or via an HDTV display in your living room. This section examines the various digital media experiences offered by Media Center.

TV and Movies

The television experience sits up front and center in Windows Media Center, although it's likely that many Windows Vista users will not have a TV tuner card installed in their system, let alone one that is connected to and controlling their TV source (cable, satellite, or whatever). That's too bad: Although much of Media Center is exciting, its TV capabilities are the most impressive and quite superior to competing digital video recording (DVR) solutions such as TiVo. It's time to take a look.

Live TV

Assuming you went through the Set Up TV Signal wizard described earlier in this chapter, you should be able to click the Live TV button on your remote (or select Live TV from the TV + Movies entry on the Media Center Start screen) and begin watching live TV immediately. Using your remote, you can change channels, view a program guide (see the section "TV and Movie Guides" later in this chapter), pause, rewind, and restart live TV, and perform all the other actions you'd expect from a normal television.

> **tip**
>
> One caveat: If you're using an IR blaster to control your cable box or satellite dish, you may notice that some operations, such as changing channels, are quite a bit slower than they were when you accessed these devices directly. That's because Media Center (like other DVR solutions) employs a technique called IR blasting. That is, it has to translate the commands you press on the remote, send the control codes for the device via IR, and then wait while the device performs whatever action you requested. Because of this delay, you won't be able to quickly move through the channels to see what's on. No big loss, however: The integrated Program Guide and recording functionality largely eliminates this need.

One very cool feature of the TV, movie, and video experiences in Media Center is that playing content will continue to play in the background of the screen if you navigate back to the Start screen or the program guide. The effect is somewhat stunning. To return to Live TV, press Back or the Live TV button.

Recorded TV

Live TV is fine...for the twentieth century. As you begin using Media Center, you'll quickly discover that it's so much better to record television and then watch it at your own convenience. Doing so has three big benefits when compared to live TV:

- ◆ You can skip over commercials and watch just the show itself.
- ◆ You can pause live TV if interrupted by the phone or some other annoyance.
- ◆ You can watch the show on your schedule, not that of the TV networks. Forget must-see TV. You can watch what you want, when you want.

Like live TV in Media Center, you can, of course, pause, rewind, and fast forward recorded TV.

There are many, many ways to record TV shows in Media Center, but the best way is to use Media Center's search capabilities to locate the shows you want. Then you can configure it to record individual shows (such as when you want to record a movie or see what a particular TV show is like) or a series (for popular shows like *Lost* or *The Office* where you don't want to miss a single show).

1. To search for a show to record, navigate to the Start screen, select TV + Movies, and then Search. (It's *waaaaay* over on the right.) As shown in Figure 15-19, you'll see a variety of ways to search, including by title, keyword, categories, movie actor, or movie director.

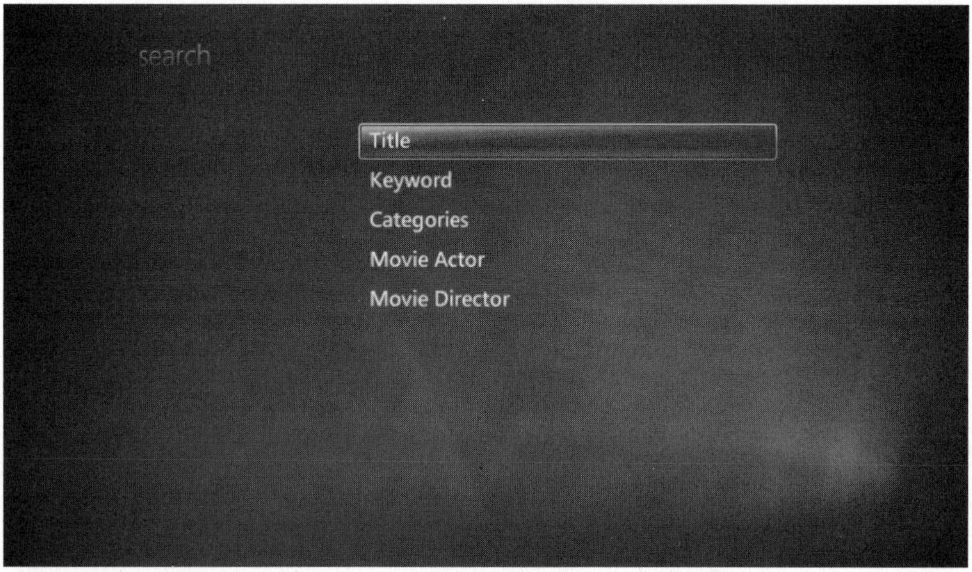

search

Title
Keyword
Categories
Movie Actor
Movie Director

Figure 15-19: Media Center's searching functionality has improved dramatically in Windows Vista.

2. For TV shows, the title is often the way to go. Choose Title and then begin typing the name of the show until you see the one you want (see Figure 15-20).

tip   Some popular syndicated shows, such as "The Simpsons," are on multiple times a day on multiple channels. Newer shows, meanwhile, that are running for the first time, are usually on less frequently and only on one station. Note one exception to this rule: Many TV providers now supply two versions of local TV stations, one in standard definition and one in high definition (HD). Typically, it's advisable to record HD shows on the HD version of the station on which it appears, and vice versa.

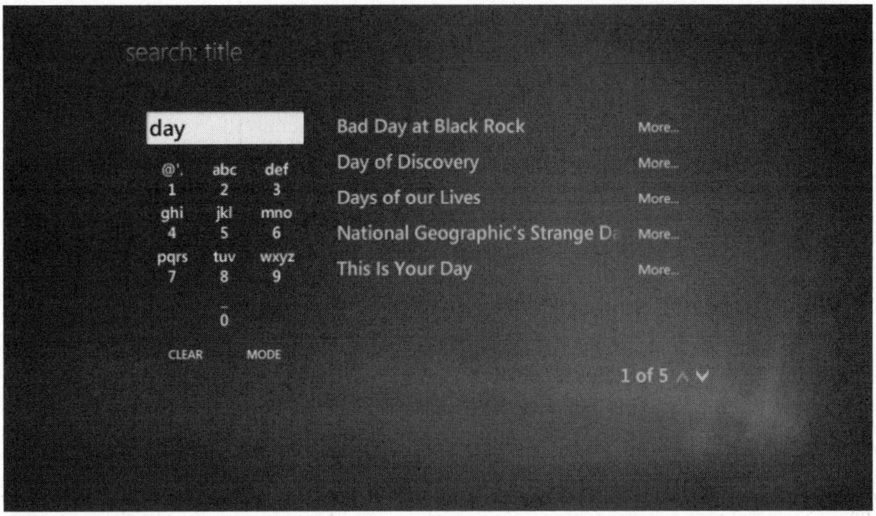

Figure 15-20: Keep typing until you've whittled the search results down to a manageable list.

3. Select the show name from the list and you'll be taken to a screen showing all of the times that show is on.

   • To record an individual show, select it from the list and click the Record button on your remote. (Alternatively, right-click the show title and choose Record.) You'll see a red circle appear next to the show, indicating that the show will record.

   • To record a series, press the Record button twice (or right-click and choose Record Series). As shown in Figure 15-21, multiple red circles will appear next to the show, and possibly next to other episodes shown in the list.

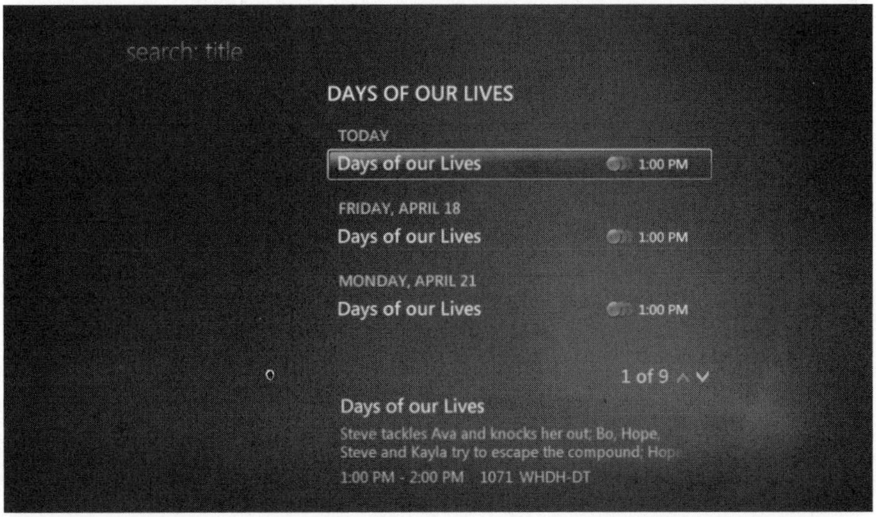

Figure 15-21: When you record a series, you'll see this unique recording graphic.

For series recordings, ensure that you're recording exactly what you want. To do this, right-click one of the episodes that is marked with multiple red circles, and then choose Series Info (or select and click More Info on the remote). On the Series Info screen, you'll see the list of episodes that is currently scheduled to record. Click Series Settings to configure how the series will record.

On the Series Settings screen, you can choose when the recording will stop (on time, or some number of minutes after it is scheduled to end); which recording quality level to use (always choose Best); how long to keep each episode (until space is needed, until I watch, until I delete, and so on); how many recordings to keep at a time; which channels to record from; when to record; and which types of shows to record (first-run only, or first-run and rerun). You will want to spend some time configuring these options, both in general (via TV in Settings) or for individual shows. For example, if you know that a particular show always runs three minutes late, be sure to configure it to record late in Series Settings.

tip You can view and configure various recorded TV shows and features from the Recorded TV screen. Just choose View Scheduled to see a list of shows that will be recorded in the future, to view all of the series you're recording, and to see a list of the shows you recorded in the past.

TV and Movie Guides

Media Center has always provided a free program guide, which shows you a listing of the shows available on your TV provider. You can use this guide to view what's currently showing and what's coming up. It's also a handy way to find shows to record: If you happen to get a high-quality HDTV station, for example, you can scroll through the timeline on just that station and see what's coming up, marking shows and movies to be recorded as you go.

tip To discover more about an individual show, select it in the guide and choose More Info. To watch a show that is currently on, simply select it. You can also filter the guide to show only the types of shows you want to see: To do that, click the Guide button while in the guide (or click the Categories bar at the left of the guide) and then select Most Viewed, Movies, Sports, Kids, News, or Special (see Figure 15-22). This is a great feature for anyone (such as sports fans) who wants to filter out the programming chaff and be left with only those shows that interest them.

Although Media Center's program guide is nothing new, there is a new Movies Guide in this version that's worth exploring. It replaces the Movies functionality from Media Center 2005; that feature was pretty cool, but it was buried deep in the My TV section of the user interface. The Movies Guide provides a handy front end to all the movies that are available now and in the near future on your cable system or other TV source. Shown in Figure 15-23, this feature is hugely graphical, using DVD box art to help you visually navigate through the list of available options.

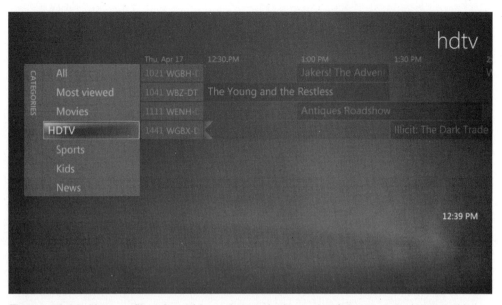

Figure 15-22: You can filter the guide to show only the types of shows you're interested in.

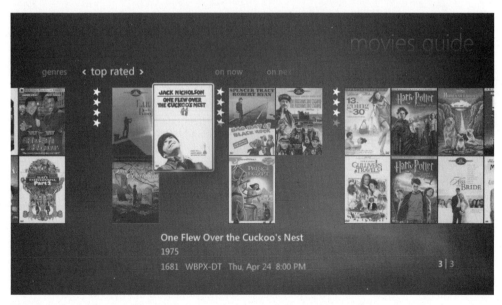

Figure 15-23: The Movies Guide is a great way to find movies to watch or record.

DVDs

As you might expect, Media Center is an excellent DVD player too, offering virtually all of the functionality of a standalone DVD player, as shown in Figure 15-24. When you insert a DVD movie into the PC while Media Center is running, it will start immediately. From there, you can use the DVD button on your remote to return to the DVD's main menu, or the remote-based or onscreen playback controls to control playback.

Figure 15-24: Media Center is also a first-rate DVD player.

Whether you're watching TV, a movie, a video, or a DVD, be sure to experiment with Media Center's excellent Zoom feature, which cycles between four different zoom modes: Normal (1), Zoom (2), Stretch (3), and Smart (4). Users with wide-screen displays will want to check out Smart zoom, because it intelligently zooms standard-definition 4:3 content in such a way that it fills the entire screen without making people onscreen look stretched.

Media Center will also benefit from the SlySoft AnyDVD software (www.slysoft.com/) recommended in Chapter 14. Using this software, you can cause playing DVD movies in Media Center to jump directly to the title menu or even the start of the movie, bypassing all that junk that Hollywood studios put on the beginning of disks these days.

Pictures and Videos

In previous versions of Media Center, Picture and Videos were separate experiences. For some reason, Microsoft has lumped them together in Windows Vista, which I think is a mistake, as pictures (typically digital photos) and videos (which can be home movies or any kind of digital video) are two entirely different things.

Opinions aside, they're represented together now under the Pictures + Videos menu off the Start screen. You'll see two main items there, Picture Library and Video Library, as well as a few other options such as Play All and More Pictures.

Pictures

The Pictures experience in Windows Media Center is accessed via the Pictures Library item in the Start screen. As shown in Figure 15-25 it's sorted by name by default and includes nice-looking thumbnails of the subfolders and pictures contained in your Pictures folder. You can choose to sort the library by date, if desired, or run a slide show of all of your pictures from this screen.

Figure 15-25: The new Pictures experience is even more graphical than its predecessor, with horizontally scrolling content.

When you navigate into a folder that contains individual photos, you'll see that the options remain the same: You can navigate horizontally through the collection of pictures, sort by name or date, or start a slide show.

---

tip   You should really change some of those slide show settings. For example, you might want the pictures to display randomly, or you might decide that the default display time of 12 seconds is quite a bit too long.

Secret

To access the hidden Pictures options, right-click (or press the More Info remote button) on any selected photo or folder. You'll see a number of options, including Burn (covered later in this chapter), View Small, Library Setup, and Settings.

- View Small will change the thumbnail images to smaller icons, which may make it easier to find content when many files are being displayed.
- Library Setup brings you to the watch folder wizard discussed previously in "Configuring Your Digital Media Libraries" earlier in this chapter.
- The Settings option navigates you to Media Center Settings. Here, you can choose Pictures and modify how slide shows work, as shown in Figure 15-26.

Save	✓ Show pictures in random order
Cancel	✓ Show pictures in subfolders
	☐ Show caption

Show song information during slide show:
- ● At beginning and end of song
- ○ Always
- ○ Never

Transition type:
- ● Animated

3 of 7 ∧ ∨

Figure 15-26: Be sure to change the settings for slide shows before launching one.

Videos

The Videos experience in Windows Media Center is inconveniently accessed via the Video Library item in the Pictures + Videos section of the Start screen. Video Library is sorted by folders by default (or date taken, optionally) and includes nice-looking thumbnails of the subfolders and movies contained in your Video folder. When you click on a video, it begins playing immediately (see Figure 15-27). You can use the onscreen controls (in two-foot mode) or the playback controls on your remote control to pause, fast forward, and perform other playback-related functions.

Secret

Curiously, there are no video-related options in the Media Center Settings screen. Despite this, you can right-click anywhere in Video Library and choose Settings. From there you can set various settings for other Media Center features, but not videos.

Figure 15-27: Videos behave much like TV shows, and offer the same controls.

Music

Media Center's Music experience is accessed via the Music item in the Start screen. From here, you can access the Music Library (that is, the songs and albums you've purchased online or ripped from CD to your hard drive) or Radio, which enables you to access Internet-based radio stations.

The Media Center's Music Library organizes the digital music you're storing on your PC in an attractive, horizontally organized way, using album art information to identify each item. By default, Music Library is organized by album, as shown in Figure 15-28.

Figure 15-28: The Music Library album view is graphical and fun to navigate, especially if you have a lot of music.

Unlike other Media Center experiences, you can choose to view your music in a wide variety of ways, including by artist, genre, song, playlist, composer, year, or album/ artist. What's interesting here is that some of these views—such as Artist, shown in Figure 15-29—are displayed in a textual, not graphical, format.

Figure 15-29: Sadly, other parts of the Music experience aren't so graphical.

As with other parts of the Media Center interface, you can navigate around, dive right in, and play any music at any time; but with the concept of the Now Playing list, you can also add music, on-the-fly, to a temporary playlist. To do so, right-click an item and choose Add to Queue, as shown in Figure 15-30. In this way, you can construct a playlist for an event, such as a party, or to later synchronize with a portable device.

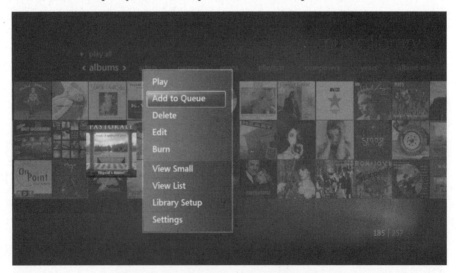

Figure 15-30: The Media Center Queue is like an on-the-fly, "Now Playing" playlist.

The first time you add music to the queue/Now Playing list, it begins playing immediately and you'll see a thumbnail of the current song's album art appear in the lower-left corner of the screen, as shown in Figure 15-31.

Figure 15-31: The currently playing song appears in the lower-left corner of the Media Center display.

To access the Now Playing list, click this thumbnail. Now Playing is shown in Figure 15-32.

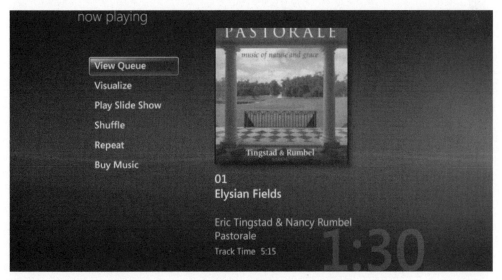

Figure 15-32: The full-screen view of the Now Playing list is attractive as well.

The default view shows only the current song, but you can also click the View Queue button to see a list of all the songs in the Now Playing list.

After you've collected a selection of music you like, you might want to save it as a permanent playlist. To do so, click View Queue and then click Save As Playlist. You can also change various playback options from this screen, including shuffle and repeat.

Secret

One of the coolest features of Media Center is its capability to play photo slide shows that are accompanied by music. To do this, play some music. Next, navigate into your photo library and choose the photos you'd like to view. This is a fantastic way to enjoy pictures from a recent vacation, birthday party, or other family event. As shown in Figure 15-33, you'll see nice overlays describing the current song as it begins and ends. Underneath that: your photo animated slide show.

"Better Now"
Collective Soul
Youth (2004)

Figure 15-33: One of the most enjoyable Media Center experiences: a photo slide show accompanied by music.

Accessing Windows Media Center Away from the PC

Beginning in late 2004 with Windows XP Media Center Edition 2005, Microsoft and a handful of its hardware partners began shipping devices (or, in the case of Microsoft's solution, a software add-on for the original Xbox) called Media Center Extender. These Extenders (again, aside from the Xbox software) were set-top boxes, much like DVD players or cable boxes, which you would place on or near a TV somewhere in your house.

They could then connect wirelessly if you had a wireless network, or via Ethernet cabling to your home network and thus to your Media Center PC. The idea is that Extenders can literally extend the reach of your Media Center, its stored multimedia content, and even live TV to other TVs around your home.

It was a good idea in theory. Unfortunately, the first-generation Media Center Extenders weren't very good in practice. They were expensive, for starters, and lacked key features such as built-in DVD players. (This was important because DVD content can't be extended from the PC to an Extender for copyright reasons.) In addition, because they were based on low-end, Windows CE–based chipsets, the Extenders were not capable of rendering some of Media Center's nicer graphical effects. I don't think many Extender users missed some of the user interface–based animations per se, but Extenders were incapable of animating photos and transitions during photo slide shows. It was all rather inelegant.

With the version of Windows Media Center in Windows Vista, Microsoft has eliminated the first-generation Media Center Extenders, so if you have a hardware Extender or an Xbox with Microsoft's Media Center Extender software, they won't work with Windows Vista. Instead, you need to get an Xbox 360—which includes second-generation Extender software—or a second-generation Extender device. The Xbox 360 is powerful enough to render the graphical effects that first-generation Extenders could not, so you get the full Media Center experience; and while second-generation Extender hardware is still pretty low-rent compared to an Xbox 360, and thus lacks some of the animation features of Media Center, these devices are still decent all-around solutions. Instead of empty boxes with Extender chipsets built in, it's now possible to get Extender functionality in certain DVD players, TV sets, and other devices.

Because the Xbox 360 video game console is so much more prevalent than dedicated Extender devices and probably always will be, I focus on the Xbox 360 here; but using a device-based Extender is almost identical, although, of course, the Xbox 360 can play blockbuster video games as well.

Using an Extender isn't the only way to get content from your Media Center out into the world. This section also examines how you can use Media Center to interact with portable devices and to burn your own audio CDs and movie DVDs.

Using an Xbox 360 or Media Center Extender

The Xbox 360 is an interesting synthesis of video gaming, online services and communities, person-to-person interaction, and multimedia. It is, in other words, everything the first Xbox was plus a whole lot more. While it doesn't make sense to cover the Xbox 360 in depth here, suffice it to say that Microsoft's latest video game console is actually a multifunction device with impressive nongaming capabilities in addition to its core features.

If you do have an Xbox 360 (or have just purchased a Media Center Extender–capable device of any kind), connecting it to your Media Center PC is relatively straightforward. You'll want a 100 Mbps wired home network for best performance, especially if you intend to stream live or recorded TV; but a 54 Mbps wireless network (802.11g or 802.11a) should suffice as well, assuming you're not doing a lot of other high-bandwidth networking activity while using the Extender.

tip   An 11 Mbps 802.11b network is completely inadequate for this functionality. However, note that most Media Center Extenders also work with 802.11n wireless networks. This type of wireless network is vastly superior to even 802.11g and performs pretty well even with HD video content. The Xbox 360 does not support 802.11n.

Your Xbox 360 includes instructions on connecting the device to your home network. Assuming you're up and running—you should be able to log on to the free Xbox Live service, for example—you're ready to link the Xbox 360 to your Media Center. To do so, ensure that Windows Media Center is running on your Windows Vista PC. Then, turn on the Xbox 360, being sure to eject whatever game DVD happens to be in the tray. On the Xbox 360, navigate to the Media blade and select Media Center. The Xbox 360 provides some basic information about Media Center functionality and instructs you to click the Windows Media Center button onscreen. Do so.

If the two machines are connected to the same network, you will see a Windows Media Center Extender dialog box appear in Media Center, as shown in Figure 15-34. Click Yes to begin the setup process.

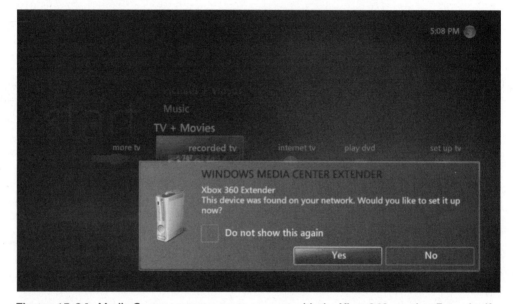

Figure 15-34: Media Center prompts you to connect with the Xbox 360 or other Extender if it can detect it.

At this point, a wizard will walk you through the process of configuring the Xbox 360 (or other Extender) to work with your Media Center PC. Note that the Xbox 360 and other Media Center Extenders can be configured to work with only one Media Center PC at a time. (However, each Media Center PC can connect to up to five different Extenders.)

The only tricky part of this Extender setup process is that you need to enter an eight-digit *setup key* in the Media Center setup wizard to link the two machines. When Media Center prompts you for this key, walk over to the Xbox 360 with pen and paper so you can write down the number displayed on the Xbox 360/Extender. Then, return to the PC and enter the setup key to continue, as shown in Figure 15-35. Click Next to continue.

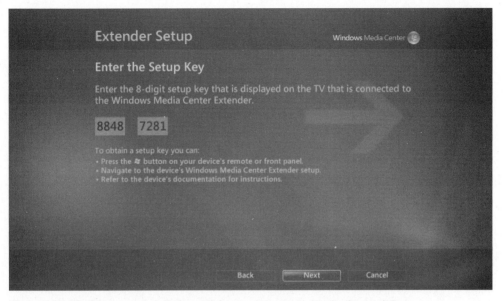

Figure 15-35: The setup key links an Extender to a single Media Center PC.

At this point, the Extender setup wizard prompts you to allow it to make changes to the Vista firewall and some system services that enable the PC and the Extender to communicate over the network. You are then prompted to navigate through the following steps.

In the Extender Media Settings, you are asked whether you would like to see your media folders on the Extender, as shown in Figure 15-36. Typically, you want to answer Yes to this question, as the Media Center experience would be pretty uninteresting on the Extender if it couldn't see your media files.

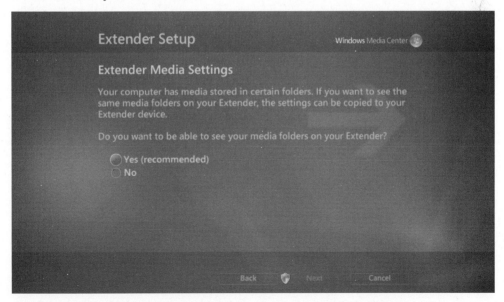

Figure 15-36: The setup key links an Extender to a single Media Center PC.

At this point, the wizard makes a number of changes to your system, as shown in Figure 15-37. This process can take a few minutes, as part of the configuration is locating and identifying all of your media.

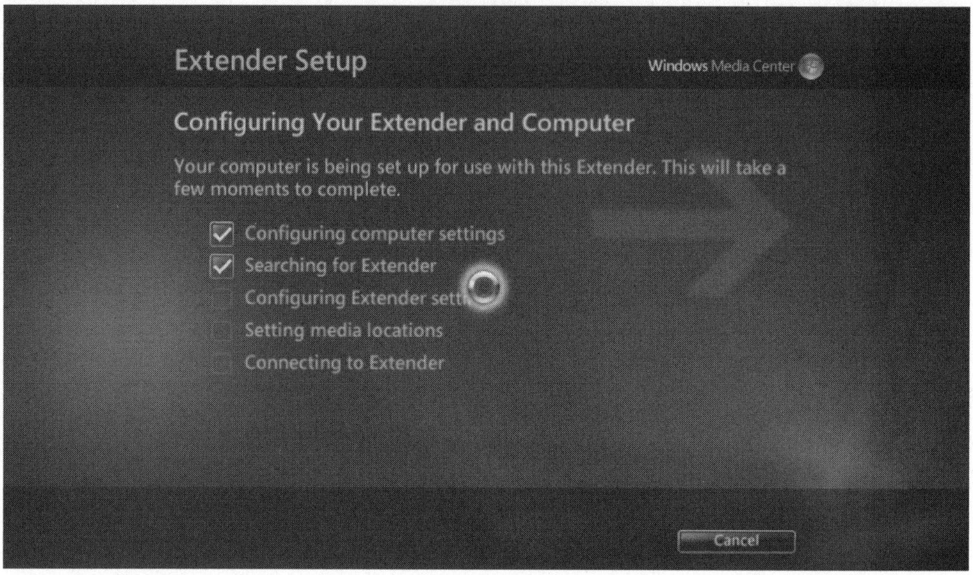

Extender Setup   Windows Media Center

Configuring Your Extender and Computer

Your computer is being set up for use with this Extender. This will take a few moments to complete.

☑ Configuring computer settings
☑ Searching for Extender
    Configuring Extender sett
    Setting media locations
    Connecting to Extender

Cancel

Figure 15-37: Give it a few seconds, and you'll be ready to enjoy your content on a TV elsewhere in the house.

Meanwhile, notice on the Xbox 360 that the screen has changed to a black "Contacting Windows Media Center" display. Once the "Connecting to Extender" portion of Configuring Your Extender and Computer is completed on the PC, you will see the familiar Media Center experience appear on the Xbox 360 (or Extender).

From that point, using Media Center Extender via the Xbox 360 should be virtually indistinguishable from using it on the PC, albeit with a possible lag time due to network slowness. You can use the Xbox 360's hand controller as a remote control, or you can purchase an Xbox 360 Media Remote—several are available.

You can even use a Media Center PC remote with the Xbox 360, and I've found this to be the best solution, as these remotes tend to be more full-featured than the ones offered specifically for the Xbox 360. To use a Media Center PC remote with the Xbox 360, you need to configure the machine first: Navigate to the System blade and choose Console Settings ⇨ Remote Control. From this user interface, choose All Channels (which enables you to use both Media Center PC remotes and Xbox Media Remotes).

Secret

A few quick if obvious points about Extenders. If you are using an Xbox 360 as an Extender, then the visual experience should be identical to that on your Windows Vista PC, with a few exceptions. For example, you can only run the Media Center experience full screen, and you'll never see the control overlays that appear when you move the mouse around on the PC version. On dedicated Extender hardware, the visual experience is largely similar to that on the Xbox 360, except that some of the more subtle animation effects are missing. For example, the Start screen background doesn't subtly animate as it does on the Xbox 360 and PC. Instead, it's a static bitmap.

In addition, some Extenders include a DVD drive or are themselves embedded in other hardware, such as an HDTV display. In these cases, the hardware may have other non-Extender capabilities that may be of interest. These experiences occur outside of the Media Center environment, however. Consult your documentation for details.

After configuring an Xbox 360 or other Extender for use with Media Center, you can visit Settings ⇨ Extenders to add other Extenders, configure a single Extender-related option (whether notifications are displayed when an Extender is connected), and view information about the Extenders that are already connected, as shown in Figure 15-38. From here, you can tune the network for best performance—which I recommend—and reconfigure, disable, or uninstall an Extender.

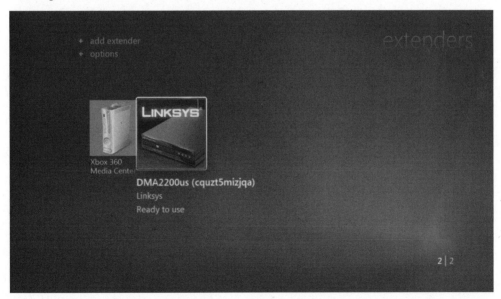

Figure 15-38: Media Center Extenders are configured through Settings ⇨ Extenders. Here, you can see two Extenders: an Xbox 360 and a dedicated Extender.

tip

Note that the Xbox 360 and other Media Center Extenders will make an appearance in the Network location in the Windows Vista shell after you've configured them to work with Windows Media Center, as shown in Figure 15-39. If you double-click the Xbox 360 Media Center Extender or Extender device icon, Media Center will load and attempt to reconfigure the Extender. You can cancel this if you did so by mistake.

Figure 15-39: Configured Media Center Extenders also show up in Vista's Network applet.

Secret

When you configure any Media Center Extender device, Windows will silently create a new user account, with a name like Mcx1, which is used by the Extender to access your PC's media resources. Mcx1 will appear in the User Account control panel, but you shouldn't try to change it in any way, because doing so will break the connection between the Extender and Media Center. Put simply, these accounts are configured automatically and should be ignored.

Synchronizing with Portable Devices

If you're using a portable MP3 player or other portable multimedia device, you may want to synchronize it with your digital media content using Windows Media Player, as discussed in Chapter 11. This is the recommended approach if the system you're using is a typical PC, where you interact with the machine using the mouse and keyboard while sitting at a desk.

If, however, you utilize Windows Media Center via a remote control in your living room, bedroom, or other non-home office location, you might want to use Media Center to synchronize with a portable device instead; and, as you might expect, Microsoft supports this scenario fully.

To synchronize content between Media Center and a portable device, plug in the device and ensure that it's fully supported by Windows Vista. That is, if Windows Vista doesn't automatically recognize the device and install drivers, you might have to visit the device maker's Web site and download and install the drivers manually. This is rare, however. Most portable media devices work fine with Windows Vista, and automatically.

Secret   Note that while the process described in this section applies to virtually all portable media devices, it does not apply to Apple's iPod, iPhone, and other Apple devices. These devices are not natively Media Center compatible. I discuss how you can make an Apple device work better with Windows Media Player, and thus with Media Center as well, in Chapter 11.

Secret   Nor does the process described in this section apply to Microsoft's own Zune. Currently, there's no way to directly link a Zune device with Windows Media Center, unfortunately. Instead, you need to use the Zune PC software, as described in Chapter 12.

When that's done, launch Media Center and navigate to Settings ➪ Sync from the Start screen (see Figure 15-40).

Media Center will pop up an alert asking if you'd like to synchronize media content with the device. When you click the Yes button, the Manage List window appears, shown in Figure 15-41. From this window, you can specify which content from your Media Center PC will be synchronized with the device. By default, the Manage List screen displays a list of the built-in playlists, such as Music Rated At 5 Stars, Music Added In The Last

Month, and so on. (If you've been using the system for some time, you may have created your own playlists. These will appear here as well.) It also includes links for All Music, All Pictures, and All Video, none of which are advisable unless you have a particularly capacious device.

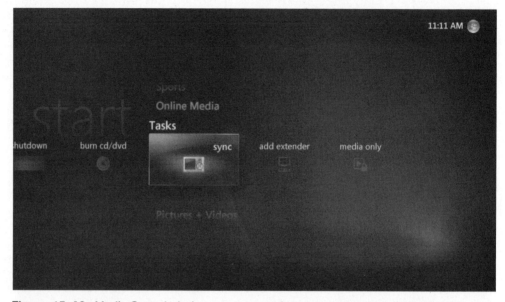

Figure 15-40: Media Center's device management features are accessed via Settings.

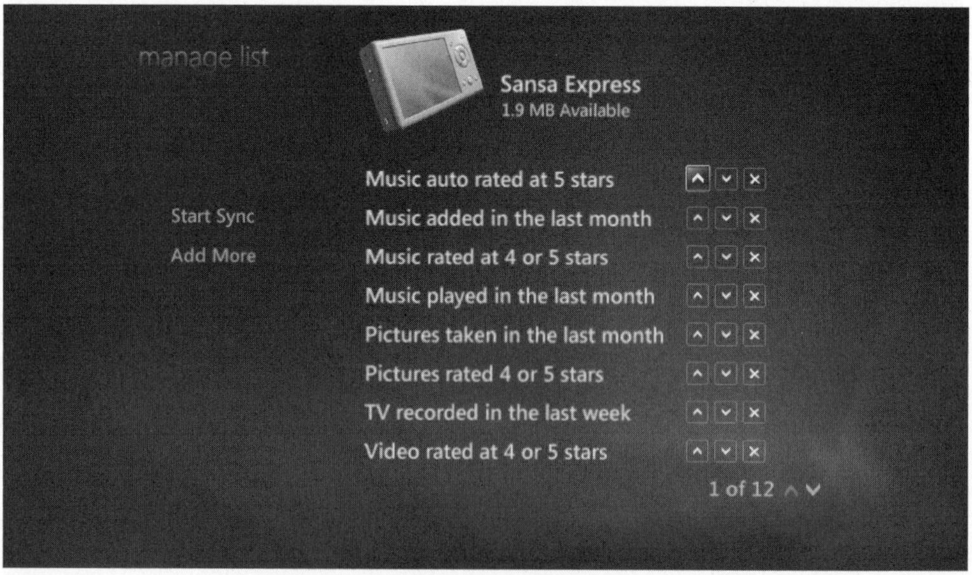

Figure 15-41: The Manage List window determines which content is synchronized with a device.

As with much of its other functionality, Media Center shares playlists with Windows Media Player. Therefore, any playlists you create in Windows Media Player will appear here in Media Center. The reverse is also true: Playlists you create in Media Player appear in Windows Media Player too.

For many people, those options will not be exactly what they're looking for. The alternative is to exit out of this screen and create custom playlists that will hold the content you would like copied to the device. Alternately, you can click the Add More option on the left side of the Manage List window and navigate through a list of content, checking the types you'd like synchronized.

Depending on your needs, you might want to simply remove all of the playlists shown in the Manage List window (by pressing the small delete button, shaped like an x, to the right of each item). Then, you can use Add More to add only the content you want, or create your own custom playlists. It's up to you.

When you've determined which content to synchronize, press the Start Sync option. A Sync Progress dialog box will appear while the content is synchronized between the PC and device. You can do other things in Media Center while this happens: Just click the OK button to move along. When the sync process is completed, a Sync to Device notification appears.

What if you have more than one portable device? When you select Sync from the Settings menu, you'll be presented with a screen that enables you to choose which device to access.

Secret

When you synchronize a device with Media Center, that device is added to the Windows Vista Sync Center as well, and you'll see a new icon in the system tray that enables you to open Sync Center, shown in Figure 15-42, or perform various synchronization-related activities right from the Windows shell. When you unplug the device, the Sync Center icon disappears (unless other synchronizable devices are attached).

continues

continued

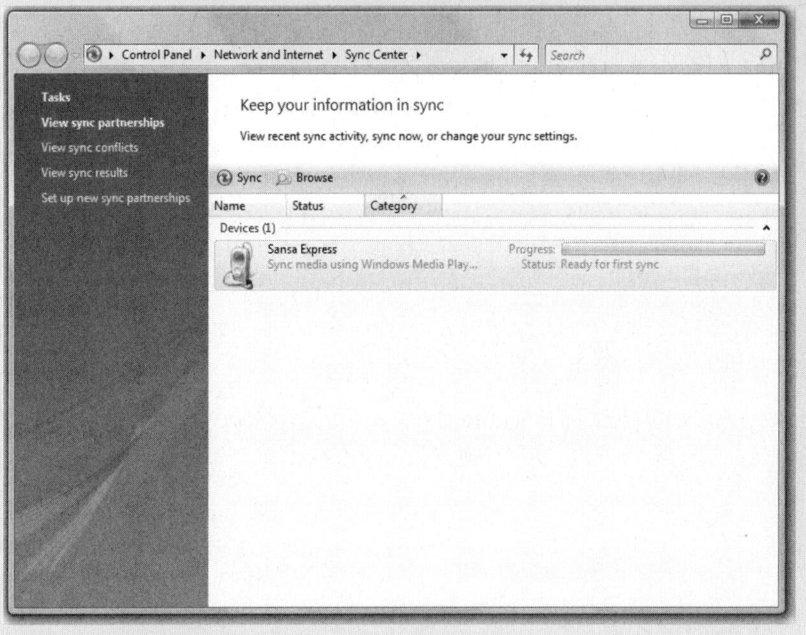

Figure 15-42: Sync Center is a centralized location in Windows Vista for managing portable devices of all kinds, including PDAs, phones, and MP3 players.

Burning a DVD Movie or Music CD

Windows Media Center also includes native CD and DVD burning capabilities. This means that you can create your own audio CDs, data CDs (containing pictures, photos, TV shows, or whatever), DVD movies (typically of TV shows), or DVD data disks.

Creating an Audio CD

To create an audio CD, follow these steps:

1. Select an artist, album, playlist, genre, or song list from within Media Center's music library, right-click it (or press the More Info button on the remote) and choose Burn. As shown in Figure 15-43, you will be prompted to insert media if you haven't already done so.

2. Choose Audio CD in the next screen and then provide a name for the CD (Media Center will default to the name of the media you previously selected).

Figure 15-43: Various collections of music can be written to disk from Media Center, enabling you to enjoy your favorite tunes on the go.

Secret

Although it's possible you may want to recreate a CD you already ripped to the hard drive, it's more likely that will you want to create what's called a *mix CD*, a CD of various content that you've hand-picked. For this reason, it's much easier to create a playlist first, add the songs you want to it, and then start the audio CD creation process when you're done. Be mindful of the limits of a typical CD, which can store about 80 minutes worth of music.

3. In the next screen, Review & Edit List, click Add More and repeat the preceding steps until you've filled the CD or added everything you want.
4. Click Burn CD. Media Center will make sure you want to proceed and then burn the CD.

Assuming you used write-once media (that is, not a rewriteable CD), the resulting CD should work fine in any CD player, including in-car, home, and portable CD players.

Creating a Data CD or DVD

To create a data CD or DVD—that is, a disk that contains the underlying media files, one that will not play back in a normal CD or DVD player, follow these steps:

1. Select an item in the appropriate Media Center experience, right-click (or press the More Info button on the remote), and choose Burn (for pictures, videos, and music) or Burn CD/DVD (for recorded TV).

2. If you haven't already inserted compatible writeable optical media, Media Center will prompt you to do so. In this example, assume you insert a blank CD-R.

3. In the next screen, choose Data CD (not Audio CD) and then click Next.

4. Pick a name for the disk; Media Center will auto-select the name of the media you initially selected as the default.

5. In the next screen, Review & Edit List, click Add More and repeat the preceding steps until you've filled the CD or added everything you want.

6. Click Burn CD. Media Center will make sure you want to proceed and then burn the CD. Because CDs are relatively small, from a storage perspective, burning a CD does not take a lot of time.

For the most part, the resulting CD will work only in a computer.

Secret   However, many car and home CD players are now compatible with MP3 and WMA formats. If this is the case, you can use this functionality to create a data disk of music files, and it should play just fine in such a player.

Creating a DVD Movie

To copy a recorded TV show to a DVD movie, follow these steps:

1. Open Recorded TV (in TV + Movies ⇨ Recorded TV) and select the movie you'd like to copy to DVD.

2. Right-click (or press the More Info button on the remote) and choose Burn CD/DVD.

3. If you haven't already inserted compatible writeable optical media, Media Center will prompt you to do so.

4. In the next screen, Media Center asks whether you prefer a Data DVD or a Video DVD. Select Video DVD and click Next.

5. Pick a name for the DVD movie; Media Center will auto-select the name of the TV show as the default, as shown in Figure 15-44.

Secret   Note that you can only add videos and Recorded TV to DVD movies from Media Center in this fashion. If you want to add a photo slide show, you need to use Windows DVD Maker, which is covered in Chapter 14. Photos can be added only to data DVDs from within Media Center.

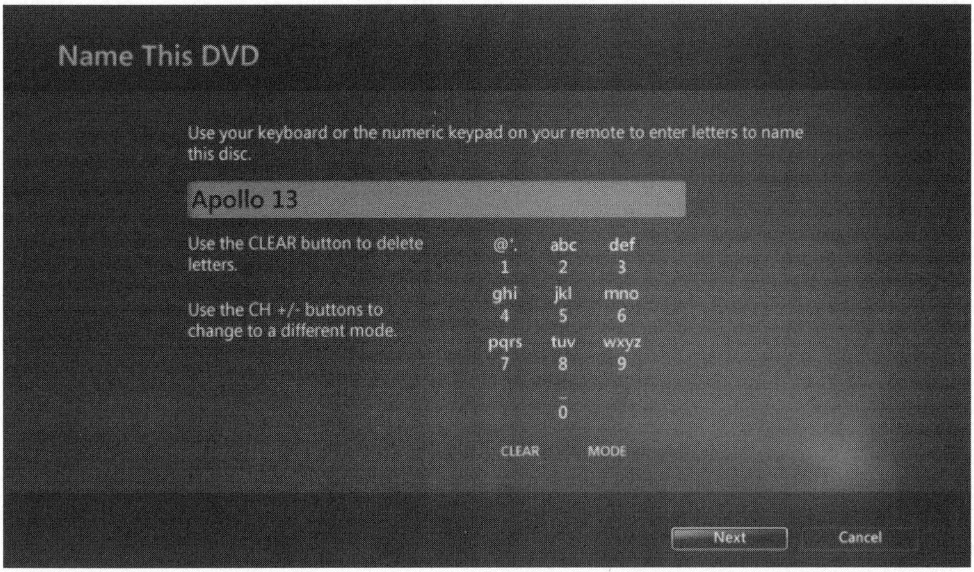

Name This DVD

Use your keyboard or the numeric keypad on your remote to enter letters to name this disc.

Apollo 13

Use the CLEAR button to delete letters.

Use the CH +/- buttons to change to a different mode.

@'. 1	abc 2	def 3
ghi 4	jkl 5	mno 6
pqrs 7	tuv 8	wxyz 9
	⁻ 0	
CLEAR	MODE	

Next   Cancel

Figure 15-44: Media Center tries to guess which name you want for the DVD movie.

6. In the next screen, Review & Edit List, you can perform a number of actions. If the TV show you selected is the only one you want on the DVD, then simply click Burn DVD to commit the movie to disk. Otherwise, click Add More and repeat the preceding steps.

Secret

Some recorded TV shows cannot be burned to DVD. For example, shows on pay stations such as HBO and Cinemax are referred to as *protected content* in Media Center. That means Microsoft is respecting the so-called broadcast flag technologies these channels are using to protect the content. The result is that HBO (which owns Cinemax too) and other channels have made the decision that they don't want users copying their content. This means that you can't copy a Media Center–recorded version of an HBO show to a portable device or other PC either, incidentally. It just won't work.

tip

If you select too much content, Media Center will warn you that the TV shows (or videos) must be burned at a lower-quality level in order to fit everything on the disk. You can choose to remove a TV show or video or accept the lower quality.

7. When you do finally set about actually burning the DVD, be prepared for a wait. DVD burning takes a long time, especially for video content. A...really...long...time.

tip

You can do other things in Media Center when a DVD is burning, but the burning process will take even longer in such a case. You've been warned.

When the DVD is completed, it should work just fine in any DVD player, including the set-top box you probably use on your TV, portable DVD players, in-car DVD players, and laptops.

Summary

Windows Media Center is a wonderful environment for enjoying digital photos, music, videos, TV shows, and other digital media content. If you're lucky enough to be using this system via a Media Center PC or any Xbox 360's Media Center Extender functionality, that's even better—the best features of Media Center come to life when accessed via an HDTV set and remote control. But Media Center isn't just for TVs. Even on a more pedestrian portable computer, Media Center provides a highly visual way of enjoying digital media content. For many users, this program will be reason enough to upgrade to Windows Vista Home Premium or Ultimate.

Having Fun: Games and Vista

♦ ♦

In This Chapter

Discovering the games that Microsoft supplies with Windows Vista

Utilizing the new Games special shell folder

Installing and configuring other games

Utilizing game controllers and other game-related hardware

Taking advantage of Games for Windows Live

♦ ♦

A lthough the experts may extol the many productivity enhancements in Windows Vista, the truth is we all need to relax sometimes. Fortunately, since the earliest versions of Windows, Microsoft has included a number of games with its operating system, from classics such as Minesweeper and Solitaire to lamented lost titles such as Pinball 3D. In Windows Vista, Microsoft has provided users with a totally refreshed and modernized set of game titles, as well as a centralized Games special shell folder that aggregates all of your game titles and related hardware devices, such as game controllers. In this chapter, you can have a bit of fun, Windows Vista style.

Games Included with Windows Vista

If you were a fan of Minesweeper, FreeCell, or any of the classic games from Windows past, get ready for a fun surprise: In Windows Vista, many of these games have been completely overhauled with new graphical treatments that take advantage of the underlying 3D graphics capabilities of Microsoft's latest operating system. Here are the games that ship with Windows Vista.

Chess Titans

What it is: A 3D chess game (see Figure 16-1).

Available in Windows Vista Home Premium, Business (optional install), Enterprise (optional install), and Ultimate.

Figure 16-1: Chess Titans.

FreeCell

What it is: A variation of the Solitaire card game, sometimes called Klondike (see Figure 16-2).

Available in Windows Vista Home Premium, Business (optional install), Enterprise (optional install), and Ultimate.

Figure 16-2: FreeCell.

Hearts

What it is: A classic card game; a variation of whist (see Figure 16-3).

Available in Windows Vista Home Premium, Business (optional install), Enterprise (optional install), and Ultimate.

Hold 'Em

What it is: A Texas Hold 'Em card game (see Figure 16-4).

Available in Windows Vista Ultimate (optional install, part of Windows Ultimate Extras).

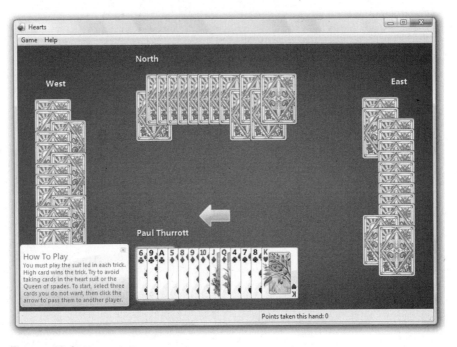

Figure 16-3: Hearts.

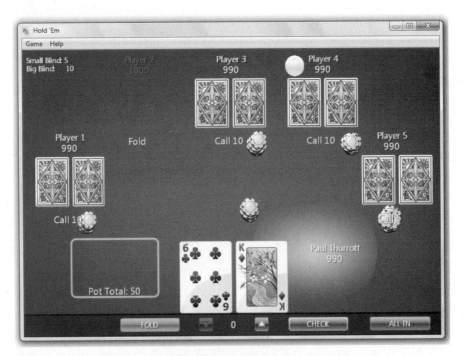

Figure 16-4: Hold 'Em, an Ultimate Extra exclusive.

InkBall

What it is: A Tablet PC-based game in which you use the stylus to push onscreen balls into holes in a maze (see Figure 16-5).

Available in Windows Vista Home Premium, Business (optional install), Enterprise (optional install), and Ultimate.

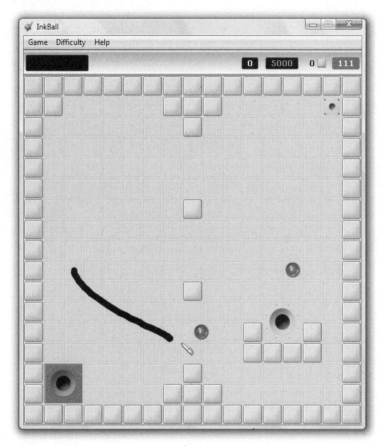

Figure 16-5: InkBall.

Mahjong Titans

What it is: A curiously addictive Chinese tile game (see Figure 16-6).

Available in Windows Vista Home Premium, Business (optional install), Enterprise (optional install), and Ultimate.

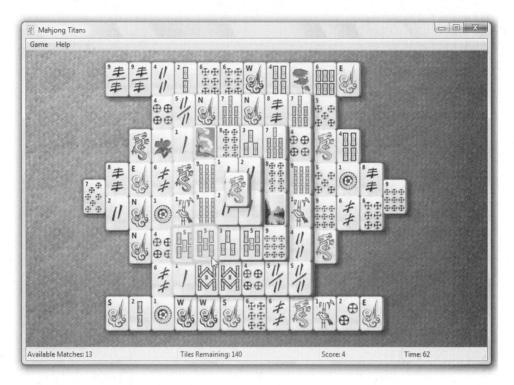

Figure 16-6: Mahjong Titans.

Minesweeper

What it is: An old favorite, updated for Windows Vista, in which you must uncover all of the spots on a grid that do not include a hidden bomb (see Figure 16-7).

Available in Windows Vista Home Premium, Business (optional install), Enterprise (optional install), and Ultimate.

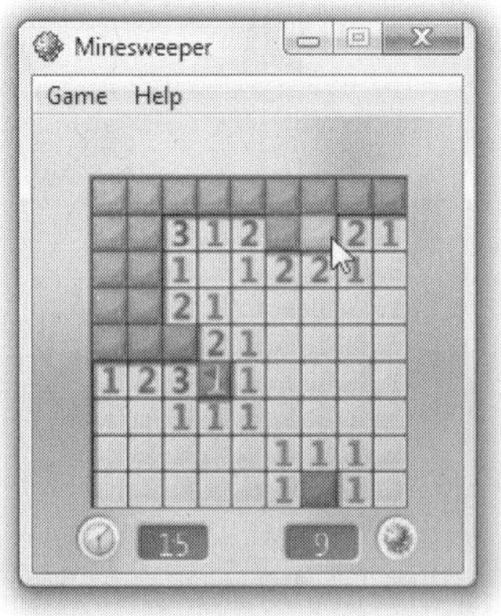

Figure 16-7: Minesweeper.

Purble Place

What it is: A children's game that is new to Windows Vista (see Figure 16-8).

Available in Windows Vista Home Premium, Business (optional install), Enterprise (optional install), and Ultimate.

Figure 16-8: Purble Place.

Solitaire

What it is: The classic single-player card game in which you try to rearrange a shuffled deck of cards (see Figure 16-9).

Available in Windows Vista Home Premium, Business (optional install), Enterprise (optional install), and Ultimate.

Spider Solitaire

What it is: A two-deck variant of Solitaire (see Figure 16-10).

Available in Windows Vista Home Premium, Business (optional install), Enterprise (optional install), and Ultimate.

Figure 16-9: Solitaire.

Figure 16-10: Spider Solitaire.

Using the Games Folder

Although the built-in games were relegated to the All Programs portion of the Start Menu in previous Windows versions, Windows Vista now includes a special shell folder called Games, which it has elevated to a position on the permanent, rightmost side of the main Start Menu display, as shown in Figure 16-11.

Figure 16-11: Apparently, games are as important in Windows Vista as the computer and the network. Yeah, you bet they are.

When you select this option, you're shown the Games special shell folder, as referenced in Figure 16-12. Games is a handy front end to the games that are included with Windows Vista as well as a number of other game-related features, including third-party games you install yourself, game hardware, parental controls, and other tools.

As you select any of the built-in game titles, a large version of the game's icon, its recommended and required performance rating, and its Entertainment Software Rating Board (ESRB) rating are displayed in the Preview pane, which is found on the right side of the Games window. (You'll take a look at performance ratings later in this chapter.)

Figure 16-12: The Games special shell folder.

tip Depending on how you've installed or acquired Windows Vista, you may see additional games in the Games folder. For example, PC makers often include their own selection of game titles; and if you've upgraded from Windows XP, many of the games you previously installed in that system should show up here as well.

To launch a game, simply double-click its icon or select the icon and click the Play toolbar button. As shown in the figures earlier in this chapter, the games included with Windows Vista are significantly more attractive than the games in previous Windows versions.

As a special shell window, Games is customized in certain ways. The toolbar includes links to Games options, game-related tools, and Vista's parental controls, which provides a way for parents to restrict which games their children can play (among other related functionality; see Chapter 9 for more information about parental controls). If you select a game from the list of available titles, the toolbar will change to include a Play menu and, in most cases, a Community and Support button that links to the Web site of the company that made the game. (Oberon Games supplied the updated game titles in Windows Vista.) You will examine these features in the next few sections.

Some of the options mentioned previously appear only for built-in games. If you select a game you installed previously, for example, you will see a Play menu, but not the Community and Support button.

Game Updates and Options

Various Games options can be configured via the Set Up Games Folder Options dialog, which you can access via the Options button on the toolbar in the Games folder. Shown in Figure 16-13, this dialog enables you to configure the few options that are directly related to Games.

Figure 16-13: Here, you can determine how the Games folder behaves.

These options include whether Windows Vista should download information about the games you've installed and whether it should list the most recently played games.

If you're a big game player, note that the sort column in the Games folder includes Last played, which enables you to sort the games in the folder in the order they were most recently played. This way, the games you play most often will always be first. You can also do neat things such as use Vista's new Explorer sorting options to group the games by such criteria as Rating or even Required Windows Experience Index.

Rating Your System's Performance

One of the more interesting features in Windows Vista is the new Performance Information and Tools functionality. Using a simple interface, you can let Windows Vista test your system, determine its overall performance rating on a scale from 1 to 5.9 (at this writing, anyway; Microsoft says it will raise the uppermost possible scores over time), and then get advice about ways to improve performance. This tool isn't just useful for game playing, but it should be quite interesting to gamers and anyone else who wants to ensure that their system is running as efficiently as possible.

To access this user interface, click the Tools button and then choose Performance Information and Tools from the drop-down menu. (Alternately, you can find this tool in Control Panel ➪ System and Maintenance ➪ Performance Information and Tools.) Shown in Figure 16-14, this Control Panel gives you an idea of how fast your overall system is and rates individual components such as processor, memory, graphics, gaming graphics, and primary hard disk.

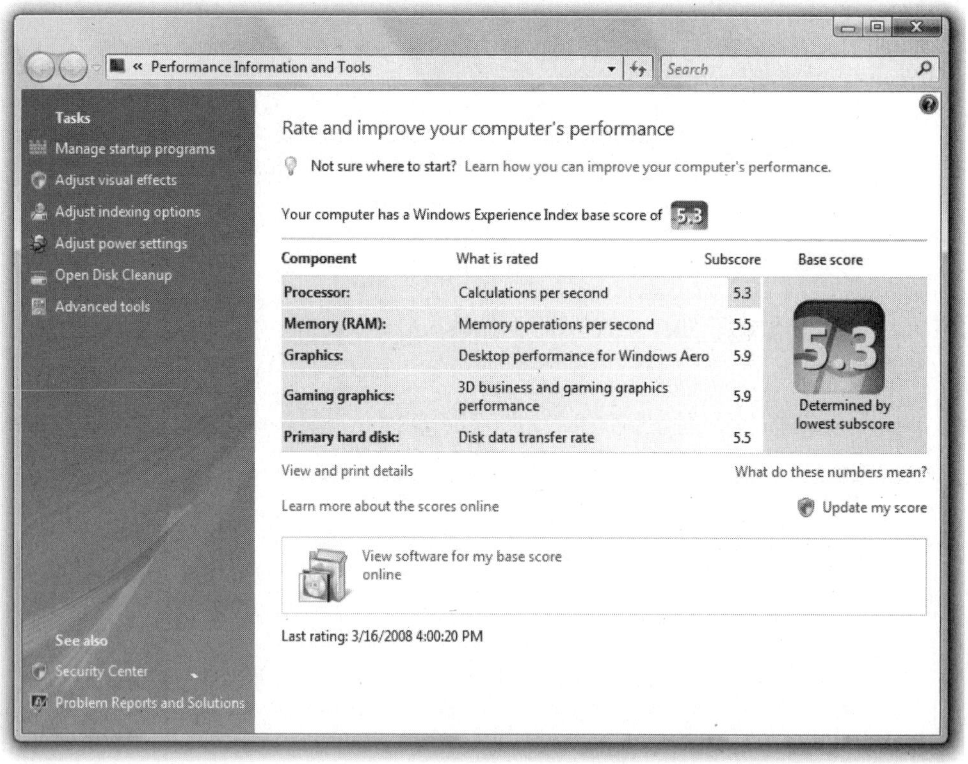

Figure 16-14: Performance Information and Tools puts your system to the test.

Typically, your PC's performance is tested and given a rating during initial setup. However, if you don't see a score—called the Windows Experience Index, or WEI—or perhaps if you'd like to retest the system because you've made a hardware change, you will see a button titled Rate This Computer. Press the button to run the test, which takes a few minutes and then returns a score. If you've already run the test, you can click the link titled Refresh Now to run the test again at any time.

> **tip**
>
> Based on the scores your PC and individual components receive, you may want to make some upgrades. For example, a score below 4 in any one category should be a warning sign to any dedicated gamer. There's also a performance issues section that lists a number of general issues that could affect overall system performance. You can scan the list and click any that you'd like to fix. This will cause a Solutions dialog box to appear, which steps you through the process needed to fix the problem. Serious gamers are going to want scores in the 5s.

Managing Your Game Controllers and Other Game-Related Hardware

In addition to working with actual games, you can manage your game-related hardware from the Games folder as well. If you click the Tools button in the toolbar, you'll see several items in the drop-down menu that are related to hardware gaming:

◆ **Hardware:** This option launches the Hardware and Sound Control Panel, from which you can perform such tasks as access configuration information for printers, audio devices, mouse, scanners and cameras, keyboard, and other hardware devices. Hardware and Sound is shown in Figure 16-15.

Figure 16-15: Hardware and Sound is a handy front end to all of your hardware devices.

tip This is also a handy place to access the Windows Device Manager, which can tell you whether you need updated drivers for any of your hardware devices. You'll see Device Manager in the list of options in the Hardware and Sound Control Panel.

◆ **Display Devices:** This option launches the Display Settings dialog box, shown in Figure 16-16. What you see here depends largely on your hardware, but the dialog generally includes information about the displays and video cards attached to your system, and screen resolution and color depth.

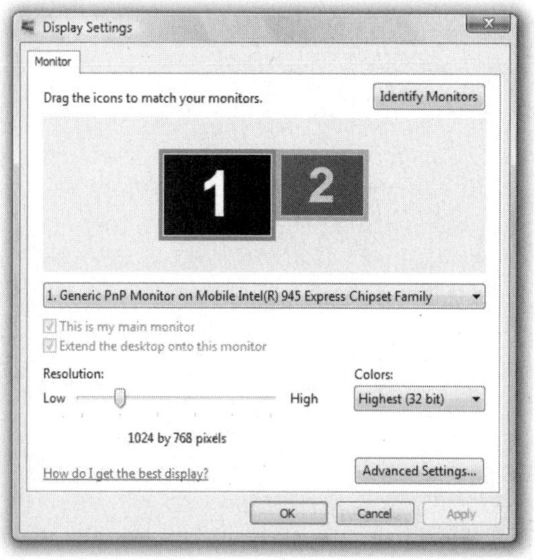

Figure 16-16: From Display Settings, you can access configuration information about your display devices, screen resolution, and color depth.

◆ **Input Devices:** This option launches the Game Controllers dialog, which provides access to configuration information about any game controllers, such as the Microsoft Xbox 360 Controller for Windows, that you may have attached to your PC. The Game Controllers dialog is shown in Figure 16-17.

tip Many people play PC-based video games with the mouse and keyboard instead of a joystick or Xbox-style hand controller. You can access the properties for both of these devices from the Hardware and Sound Control Panel described previously.

◆ **Audio Devices:** This option launches the Sound dialog, which provides access to the new sound device customization features included in Windows Vista, including subwindows for hardware such as your speakers. The Speakers Properties dialog is shown in Figure 16-18.

◆ If you double-click an audio device in the list, you can delve into its unique abilities. For example, the Volume Control playback device enables you to configure how many speakers you have attached to the PC, various default volume levels, and much more.

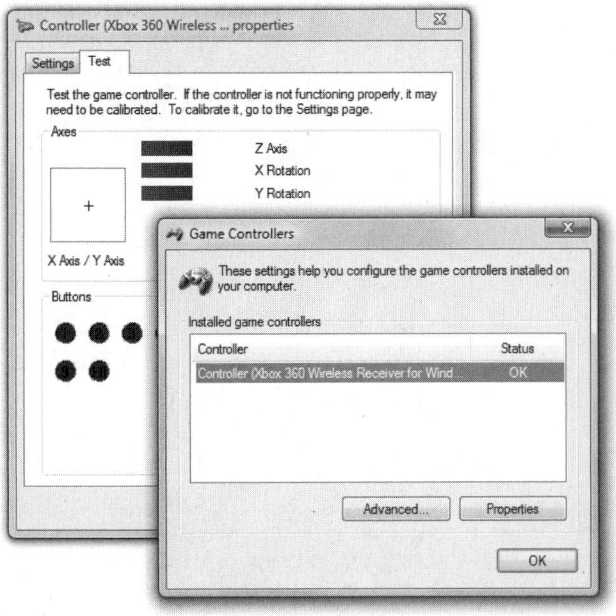

Figure 16-17: Game Controllers enables you to configure settings for your gaming controllers.

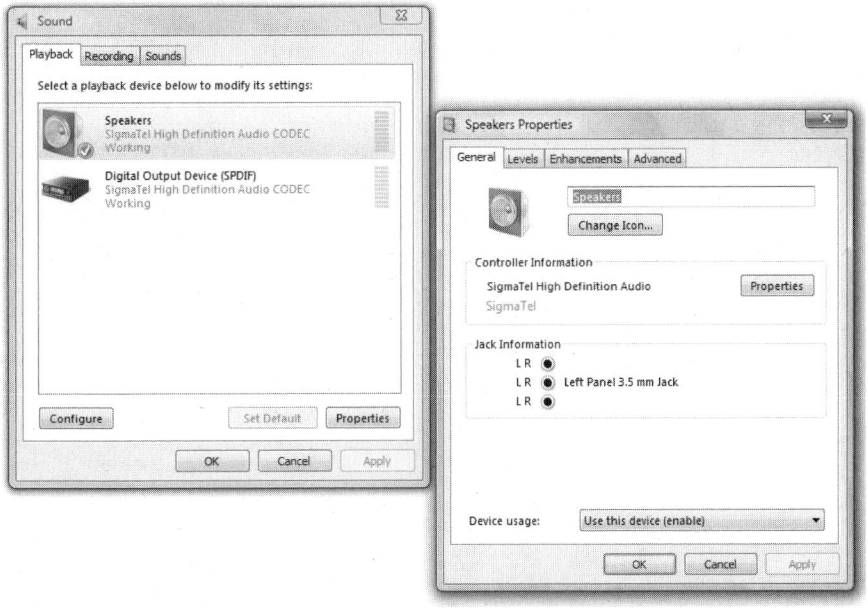

Figure 16-18: Windows Vista features new ways to interact with your sound hardware.

There are also links for Firewall and Programs and Features, as follows:

◆ **Firewall:** This entry is important because some games require specific network ports to be open so that you can play against other people online.

◆ **Programs and Features**: This is the Control Panel applet that is your primary interface for uninstalling or changing applications.

Installing and Playing Third-Party Games

Windows Vista's built-in games are attractive and even occasionally addictive, but real gamers will want to install their own games. One of the big questions with Windows Vista concerns compatibility: How compatible will this system be with the mammoth Windows software libraries out there? This question is particularly problematic for games, because they tend to take more advantage of low-level hardware features that are typically hidden from within Windows.

Secret

The other big gaming-related question, of course, is whether the latest version of Windows—in this case, Windows Vista—measures up, performance-wise, with its predecessor (in this case, Windows XP). In the case of the originally shipped version of Vista, the answer was no. However, with the advent of Windows Vista Service Pack 1 (SP1) and the passage of time, most gamer-related hardware drivers have improved to the point where the performance differences between Vista and XP are minimal. Besides, Vista also provides unique gaming-related features you can't get in XP, such as Vista-specific games (e.g., *Halo 2*) and Vista-specific technologies such as DirectX and Direct3D 10.x.

Using Legacy Games with Windows Vista

In my testing of fairly recent and even several-year-old game titles (hey, someone has to do it), I've found Windows Vista to be reasonably compatible with so-called legacy game titles. In some cases, such as Valve's epic *Half-Life 2*, which is a modern 3D shooter, there's no work to be done at all: You simply install the game as before—albeit with the occasional User Account Protection (UAP) silliness. (See Chapter 9 for more information.)

Other games, especially older games, require a bit of prodding. In some cases, Windows Vista includes compatibility information about certain problematic game titles. For example, when I initially installed Microsoft's classic *Halo: Combat Evolved*, I was presented with the dialog shown in Figure 16-19. Halo has known compatibility issues with Windows Vista. Fortunately, these issues have since been resolved. I expect this to be the case with most popular game titles.

Secret

This isn't a problem for *Halo 2*, which was released exclusively for Windows Vista. That's right, you need Windows Vista to run *Halo 2*.

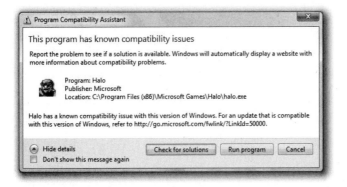

Figure 16-19: Microsoft knows there are issues running certain games on Windows Vista and tries to help.

Secret

Adding Games to the Games Folder

Although this isn't documented anywhere, it's quite possible to add games you've installed on your PC to the Games special shell folder, so you can access them as you do the built-in games. Presumably, next-generation game titles will do this automatically so that they can integrate more closely with the games-related infrastructure Microsoft created in Windows Vista.

To add a third-party game title to the Games folder, simply drag a shortcut to the title into the folder. As shown in Figure 16-20, legacy games such as *Halo* and *Half-Life 2* can be added directly to Games. Many games are added automatically, however, so check before dragging and dropping.

Figure 16-20: You can also add your own games to the Games folder.

If you expand the See Details widget on this dialog, you'll discover that *Halo* developer Bungie (then a subsidiary of Microsoft) released a Vista-compatible patch. The dialog provides a link to download that patch so you can get back to the game.

tip Any games in the Games folder, including built-in games and third-party games, can be customized, but in very limited ways. If you look at the Play button in the Games toolbar, you'll see that it has a drop-down menu associated with it, with one option: Customize. Click this option and the Customize dialog is displayed (see Figure 16-21).

This enables you to create numerous shortcuts for a single game title. This is handy for several reasons. For example, some games come with different shortcuts for launching single-player and multiplayer versions of the game, so this would be an obvious place to add a shortcut for the secondary version, which you could then access from the Play button's drop-down list. Other games enable you to add command-line options to access special game features. As any dedicated gamer knows, these options can often be used to unlock new features or even cheat.

Figure 16-21: With the Customize dialog, you can create multiple launch points for each game.

Secret

Problems with x64 Versions of Windows Vista

If you think the process of installing and playing older games in Windows Vista is difficult, then you'll want to avoid the x64 versions of Windows Vista for a while. If you purchase a copy of Windows Vista Ultimate at retail and install it on x64-based hardware—that is, a PC that includes an AMD or Intel microprocessor that includes the 64-bit x64 processor instruction set—you will be able to install either the 32-bit or 64-bit version of Windows Vista. (Other Vista versions provide an opportunity to switch to the x64 version via a mail-in offer.) My advice is simple: With very few exceptions, you want to install the 32-bit version, not the x64 version, of Windows Vista.

continues

continued

Here's why. Although the x64 versions of Windows Vista enable you to use more than 4GB of RAM, very few people will ever need that much during the lifetime of this OS version. Moreover, the downsides to x64 are daunting. First, the x64 versions of Windows Vista cannot utilize any of the thousands of 32-bit device drivers out there, so you have to make sure that you have a 64-bit driver for each and every hardware device you are, or will be, using. Currently, there are still plenty of instances where 64-bit drivers aren't—and maybe never will be—available.

Second, software compatibility is more problematic in the x64 versions of Windows Vista. Although Microsoft tried to engineer these versions of the OS to run 32-bit software—that is, virtually every single bit of Windows software produced before 2007—many software packages refuse to install or run. And yes, you guessed it, games are among the worst offenders. If you're a gamer, you will want to stick with the normal 32-bit Vista versions.

That said, some games will work fine in the x64 versions of Windows Vista, and some game makers are actually creating special x64 versions of their game titles so early adopters can experience next-generation computing. Over time, of course, this situation will get better and better; but for now, I believe that x64 is just too problematic for most Windows users. You've been warned.

Downloading More Games for Windows Vista

In addition to the games that come with Windows Vista, the vast library of legacy game titles out there, and the unique Windows Vista game titles that developers will be creating, there's one more avenue for adding games to Windows Vista: Microsoft will be offering a variety of entertainment-related downloads via both Windows Updates and, for Ultimate Edition users, the unique Windows Ultimate Extras.

Shown in Figure 16-22, Windows Ultimate Extras is a special benefit of using the most advanced Windows Vista edition. Ultimate Edition users have access to a number of special features via this interface, including unique applications. One of these applications, Hold 'Em, is a game.

Secret

Microsoft has seriously deemphasized Windows Ultimate Extras since first announcing the feature, and the company has had trouble delivering on the few Extras it has already promised. Beginning with Service Pack 1, the descriptions of Ultimate Extras are far more vague than they were in the initially shipped version of Vista, and it's unclear what kind of support this feature will have going forward.

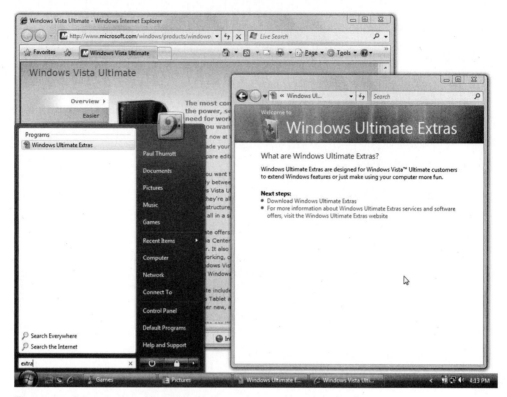

Figure 16-22: Windows Ultimate Extras includes the game Hold 'Em.

Games for Windows Live

Separate from its PC gaming initiatives, Microsoft has been promoting its line of Xbox video game consoles since 2001. In late 2005, the company significantly raised the bar with the release of its second-generation Xbox 360 console, featuring unparalleled graphics power and connectivity, and ushering in a new era of video gaming. In some ways the biggest leap forward that Microsoft made with the Xbox 360, however, was the massive set of improvements it made to the system's online service, Xbox Live. Xbox Live, in addition to providing a way for Xbox-based gamers to face off in multiplayer matches, also offers movie and TV show downloads, instant messaging functionality, and other features. It's the most full-featured online service for any console, by far.

Xbox Live has been so successful that it has colored how the company approaches other similar online endeavors. In the years since the launch of the Xbox 360, Microsoft has used its successes with Xbox Live as a model for such things as the Zune Marketplace, an online store that supports Microsoft's digital media players (see Chapter 12) and now a new initiative called Games for Windows Live.

Games for Windows Live is an attempt to replicate the success of Xbox Live on the PC, literally, and provide interconnectivity between Windows-based gamers and Xbox 360-based gamers. Because it is both modeled on and tied directly to Xbox Live, it should come as no surprise that Games for Windows Live is very much like Xbox Live. That said, it's still fairly immature compared to Xbox Live and is lacking some key features. It also has some troubling problems that suggest that Games for Windows Live will never really take off in the same way as Xbox Live has on Microsoft's consoles.

Here's what's happening.

Xbox Live on Windows: What Needs to Happen

Xbox Live customers each have a *Gamertag,* which is associated with a Windows Live ID (formerly called a Passport account; see Chapter 21 for more information). This Gamertag includes a reputation (or Rep, scored from one to five stars), a Gamerscore (the total number of Achievement points collected in all the Xbox 360 games the gamer has played), and other data. Gamers can access the list of games they've played, with Achievements broken down by game. (They can access other players' Gamertags too.) Each Gamertag has associated lists of messages (similar to e-mails), friends (like contacts), and players (other gamers they've faced off against online). Also included are various settings, related to game types, the Dashboard, and other aspects of the Xbox 360 experience.

The reason the Xbox Live Gamertag system works so well on the Xbox 360 is that Microsoft has made the underlying Xbox Live service so thoroughly integrated across the system. If you're in a game of *Gears of War 2* or watching a live or recorded TV show via the Xbox 360's Media Center Extender functionality (see Chapter 15), your friends can see what you're up to, even if they're playing *Rainbow Six Vegas 2* or just browsing the downloadable content on Xbox Live Marketplace, Microsoft's online store.

The trick is bringing this experience to Windows users. Here, Microsoft has only been partially successful.

The Games for Windows Live Experience

Sadly, the integrated nature of Xbox Live is exactly what Microsoft got wrong with Games for Windows Live. On the Windows side, Microsoft has done nothing to make Live as ubiquitous as Xbox Live is on the Xbox 360. Nor has Microsoft done much to integrate Live into Microsoft's instant messaging application, Windows Live Messenger, the obvious linking point between the two services. You can access your Xbox Live-based friends list from Messenger, via the Xbox 360 tab, but you can't access other Xbox Live data, such as stored messages or Achievements, from that client. Moreover, you can't even access any Xbox Live/Games for Windows Live info from the Games Explorer in Windows Vista. Nope, Games for Windows Live is most incredibly a disconnected experience in Windows. Strictly speaking, you can only access the service from the very limited selection of games that are currently compatible with Games for Windows Live.

In other words, you're really only participating in Games for Windows Live when you're playing a compatible game, which amounts to a very small selection of titles. Most game developers today are forgoing the Games for Windows Live program and simply doing their own thing—or they're signing up for the less inclusive "Games for Windows" logo program instead. These games supply some of the benefits of Games for Windows Live (discussed shortly) but none of the online capabilities. That's not to say that you can't play these games online, but that these games aren't tied into Microsoft's Live network in any way.

Clearly, a better way to handle this would be for Microsoft to create a pervasive Games for Windows Live client, available via Games Explorer and Windows Live Messenger and elsewhere in Windows, which could be accessed both inside and outside of Live-compatible game titles. Alas, as you don't have that kind of seamless experience here, let's examine just what you do get.

Boot up a Live-compatible title such as *Halo 2* for Windows Vista, *Gears of War* for Windows, or *Hour of Victory* for Windows, and you can access the Live service by pressing the Home button on your keyboard, as shown in Figure 16-23.

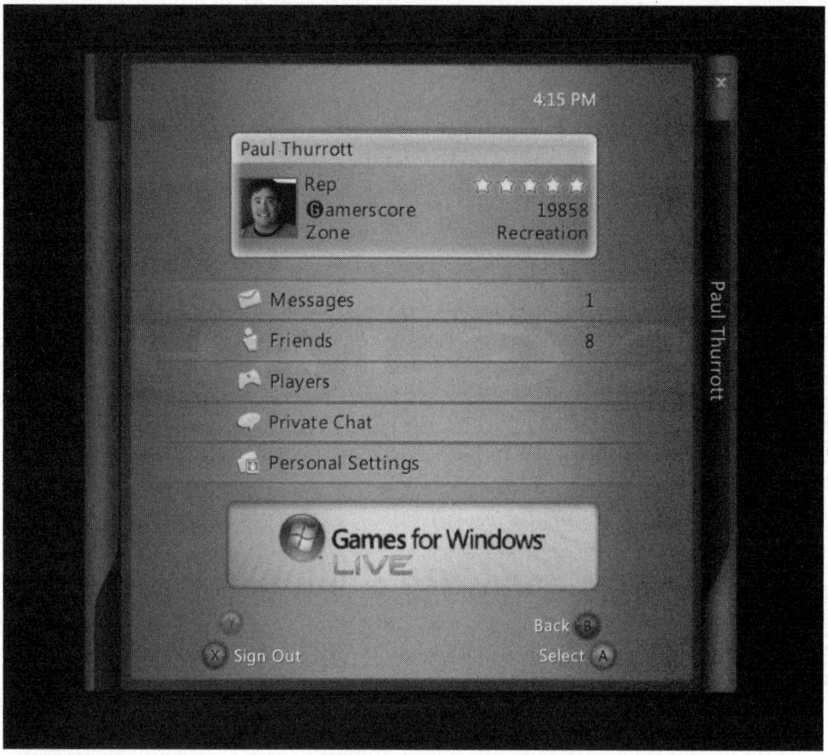

Figure 16-23: The Live experience in Windows requires a compatible game. It supplies a subset of the functionality Xbox 360 users are familiar with.

As you can see, this is a reasonable facsimile of the Xbox Guide, which you access on the Xbox 360 when you press the Xbox button on the controller. From here, you can access your Gamertag's Gamer Profile, as shown in Figure 16-24; your Messages, Friends, and Players lists; a Private Chat area for one-on-one voice conversations; and Personal Settings, which includes Online Status, Voice, and Notifications only. (On the Xbox 360, you also get Vibration, Themes, Active Downloads, and Shut Down, most of which are specific to the Xbox 360 console.)

As with the 360's Xbox Dashboard, virtual Xbox 360 controller buttons appear throughout the UI, so you know which buttons to press to perform different actions. (The red B button is typically Back, for example.) However, on Windows, you can also press the corresponding keyboard key (e.g., the *b* key) to perform the same actions, which is handy and logical, especially for those without Xbox 360 controllers.

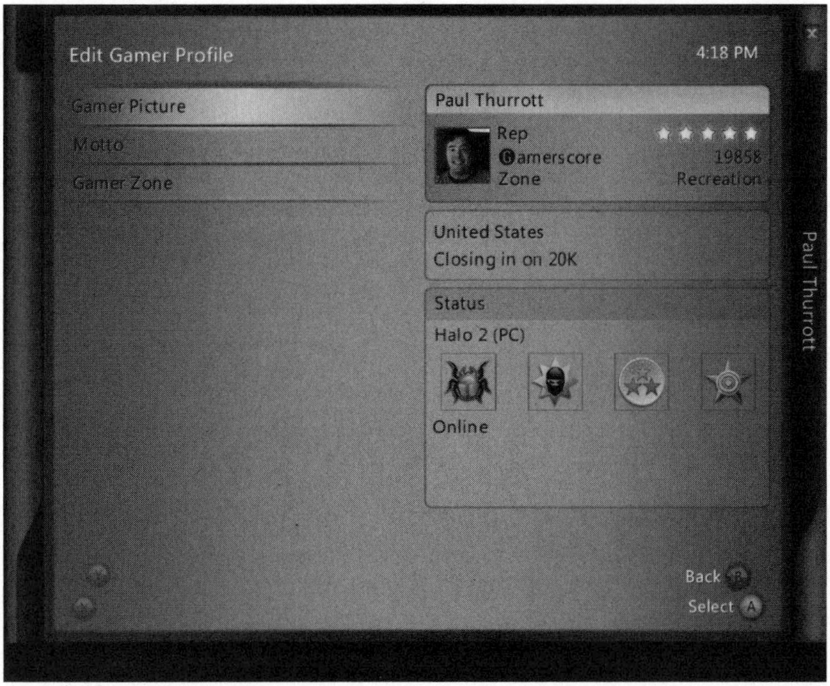

Figure 16-24: Your Gamer Profile provides information about you that is accessible to others on Live.

Basically, the Games for Windows Live experience appears to be designed for just a few basic tasks, including the following:

◆ **Accessing and modifying information associated with your Gamertag:** You can view your Gamerscore, Rep, and other related info, access overall and individual game Achievements (see Figure 16-25), and so on. Account management occurs outside the client: If you access this option, you'll be presented with an IE window.

◆ **Messages:** Here, you can access messages sent through the Xbox Live/Games for Windows Live network. These message are e-mail-like in nature, as shown in Figure 16-26, but can include audio and video messages in addition to normal text messages (the latter of which are limited to 255 characters). You can create new text and audio messages from the client, but you cannot create video messages. You can send and approve Friend requests as well.

Secret

Okay, you can actually access some of these messages from Microsoft's Web-based interface as well, found at www.xbox.com. Note that some messages sent from older Xbox games can only be accessed from within those games.

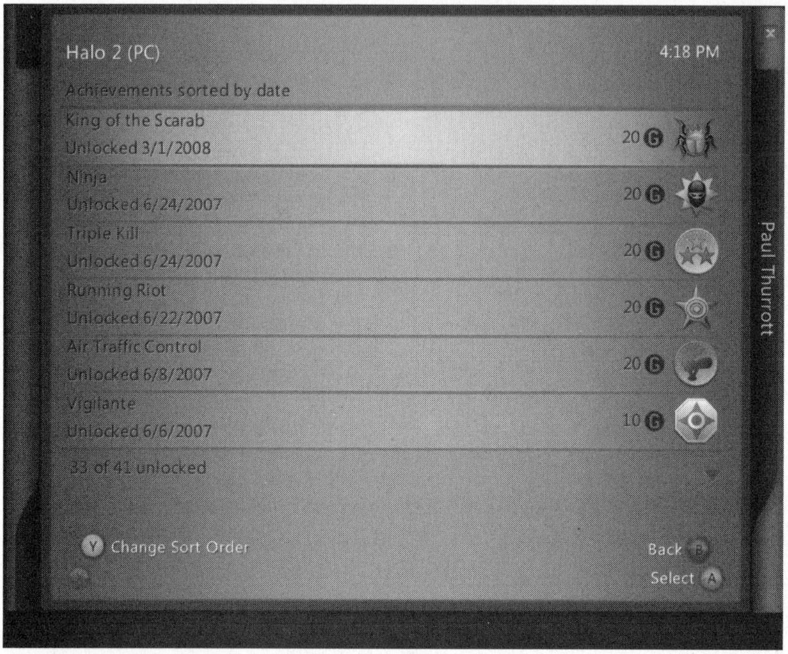

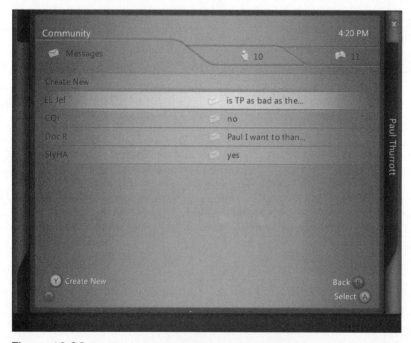

Figure 16-25: You can look up all of your game Achievements, whether they occurred on the Xbox 360 or on Windows.

Figure 16-26: It's like e-mail, but you can only access and send these messages from an Xbox 360 or a Games for Windows Live compatible game.

◆ **Friends:** This is the list of people with whom you have created online relationships. As with the Xbox 360, this list is ordered with those who are currently online at the top, followed by the remainder of your Friends list in alphabetical order. You can see what your online Friends are up to (which game they're playing, or other Xbox 360 experiences they're enjoying, such as Windows Media Center or browsing the Xbox Dashboard).

◆ **Players:** This is the list of Xbox Live/Games for Windows Live users with whom you've competed recently online. As with the Friends list, players who are currently online appear at the top of the list. All the normal functions are available, so you can submit a player review, file a complaint, mute them, send a message or invite them to a private chat, or send a Friend Request.

◆ **Private Chat:** Here, you can engage in up to five separate one-on-one audio chats with Friends and other players. This requires an Xbox 360 controller with an attached headset, or you can use any Windows-compatible microphone.

◆ **Personal Settings:** In this submenu, you can configure your Online Status (Online, Away, Busy, or Appear Offline); your Voice options (playback and recording volume, plus access to sound hardware and a Mute Microphone option); and Notifications (even more limited than on the 360—you can toggle Show Notifications and Play Sound only).

As with Xbox Live, there are two levels of the Live service, and if you're an Xbox Live member already, all your rights and capabilities transfer over automatically to Games for Windows Live, so users who opted for the free Xbox Live Silver membership can access a single Gamertag with an associated Gamer Profile, Gamerscore, and Friends list, single-player game Achievements, private text and audio chat, and PC-only multiplayer gaming. For about $50 a year, you can upgrade to Xbox Live Gold, which gives you all the functionality from the Silver membership plus multiplayer matchmaking capabilities with those in your Friends list, TrueSkill Matchmaking for finding players online who better match your own abilities, multiplayer Achievements, and cross-platform game play. Currently, cross-platform game play, whereby an online multiplayer game can mix and match PC and Xbox 360 gamers is limited to a rather lousy game called *Shadowrun*. It's unclear when or if more of these cross-platform games will appear.

If you're an Achievements hound, you may be interested to know that some Xbox 360 games have been ported to Games for Windows Live, enabling you to effectively play the same game twice, once on Xbox 360 and once on Windows, and double up on the Achievements. Currently, games such as *Gears of War, Hour of Victory* (EU only), *Kane & Lynch: Dead Men, The Club, Universe at War, Viva Piñata*, and others offer this possibility. In addition, an original Xbox blockbuster, *Halo 2*, has been ported to Windows, providing Achievements for the first time. There's never been a better time to rack up Achievements points.

Looking at the big picture, it's hard to escape the notion that Microsoft has delivered the absolute minimum here: Games for Windows Live provides a single online identity with a unified contacts list that combines people you communicate with on the Xbox 360 and the PC. So much other obvious functionality is missing in action. For example, there's no way to change a Gamertag picture to any picture you can access from the PC; and you can't access the tremendous Xbox Live Marketplace from the PC at all, though Microsoft is arguably working toward some of this functionality in its related Zune Marketplace (see Chapter 12). There are no downloadable games, especially the popular Xbox Live Arcade titles. And Microsoft is going to have a hard time convincing third parties to come on board when Games for Windows Live games can't offer the best online features unless their customers pay $50 a year for Xbox Live Gold. Most PC games offer free online play today or charge their own feeds for monthly subscriptions. I have a hard time imagining these companies ever embracing Microsoft's proprietary sandbox.

In any event, Games for Windows Live is here, and if you're a dedicated gamer, it's still worth looking into.

Summary

There's no doubt about it: Windows Vista is the ultimate operating system for gamers, and arguably a better destination than even the Xbox 360 or Sony's Playstation 3, thanks to the wide variety of compatible game titles and the never-ending march of PC innovations. With its array of nicely spiffed-up built-in games, parental controls aimed at helping keep children away from inappropriate games, stellar support for gaming hardware, and a handy Games explorer that works nicely with third-party games, Vista has it all. And if you own Windows Vista Ultimate, you can look forward to some extra perks in this category as well: There's a unique Texas Hold 'Em game that's only available via this service. Finally, Microsoft is also working to port its Xbox Live service to Windows in the form of Games for Windows Live. So far, it's not that impressive, but Microsoft has a way of plugging away at things until they get it right. So stay tuned: The best is yet to come.

Part V

Mobility

Vista to Go: Windows Vista Mobility Features

Chapter

17

❖ ❖

In This Chapter

Managing the Windows Vista user interface settings for optimal performance and battery life

Discovering new power management features

Creating and using your own power plans

Utilizing the new Windows Mobility Center

Exploring new features aimed at presentations

Accessing files and folders while disconnected from the network

Holding ad hoc meetings with others over your own wireless network

Using Windows SideShow

❖ ❖

W indows Vista is the ultimate version of Windows for users on the go. Whether you use a notebook computer, Tablet PC, or Ultra-Mobile PC, you won't get a better mobile experience than what's available in Microsoft's latest desktop operating system. This time around, Microsoft has fortified Windows with new user interface, power management, and presentation capabilities, along with a suite of mobile-oriented applications and utilities that tie it all together. You'll learn about each of these features in this chapter.

Windows Vista on the Road

Over the years, Microsoft has steadily improved Windows to better take advantage of the unique hardware features and capabilities offered by portable computers such as notebooks, laptops, and Tablet PCs (including a smaller new generation of tablet devices called Ultra-Mobile Personal Computers, or UMPCs). For the most part, using Windows Vista on a notebook computer or other portable PC is just like using it on a desktop PC. That is, a notebook computer can do anything a desktop PC can, and Windows Vista doesn't offer a limited feature set when you're using a portable PC. In fact, if anything, Windows Vista offers more functionality on portable PCs than it does on desktop computers. That's because certain Vista features really only come to life when they're used on a portable PC.

Given this, you may want to approach Windows Vista a bit differently when using a notebook computer. Certain operating system features, such as the user interface or power management plan you select, can affect both performance and battery life when you're not connected to power, for example. Vista also includes special presentation, security, and networking features that are often specific to portable computers, or at least work somewhat differently when you're using a portable PC. Windows Vista also includes certain software applications, such as Mobility Center, that are available only on portable computers.

tip	In this chapter, I use terms such as *portable PC, portable computer, notebook, laptop,* and even, occasionally, *Tablet PC* to describe mobile computers running Windows Vista. For the most part, these terms are largely interchangeable in the context of this chapter unless specifically stated otherwise.

Working with the Vista User Interface

One of the most obvious improvements in Windows Vista is the Windows Aero user interface, discussed in Chapter 4. Windows Aero offers several unique features compared to the other UI options available in Windows Vista, including translucency, various special effects, and even access to certain Windows features, such as the Windows Flip 3D application-switching utility. Conversely, Windows Aero is more hardware intensive than other display modes and can thus result in poorer battery life than the other user interface options. Your decision whether to use Windows Aero—shown in Figure 17-1—depends on how you feel about battery life, performance, and usability.

Figure 17-1: Windows Aero is gorgeous-looking but can drain a notebook's battery more quickly than other Windows Vista user interface options.

Before getting to that, however, you should also be aware that many portable computers—especially those made before 2008—simply don't include enough graphical processing power to even run Windows Aero. If this is the case, you will typically see the Windows Vista Basic user interface instead. There's also an option called Windows Standard that offers an enticing middle ground between the beauty of Windows Aero and the power management thriftiness and performance of Windows Classic, the low-end user interface that is designed to resemble the user interface from Windows 2000.

Depending on your hardware, your choice might already be made: If you install Windows Vista on a portable PC, and the user interface is set as Windows Vista Basic and not Windows Aero, then you're out of luck: Your system is not capable of displaying Vista's highest end user interface.

Secret

It *is* possible that your mobile computer can handle Windows Aero even if Windows Vista Basic appears by default. There is a chance that Windows Vista simply didn't install the latest driver for your display hardware. Before sinking into despair, consult the documentation for your notebook, find out exactly which display hardware it uses, and then visit Windows Update via the Start Menu to obtain the latest driver and see if that makes a difference. Alternately, visit the hardware maker's Web site; sometimes the vendor offers drivers directly to consumers as well.

Secret

If you're not the kind of person who reads documentation, Windows Vista offers a few utilities that can help you determine which display hardware your system is utilizing. The first is called System Information (type **System Information** in Start Menu Search). Under the System Summary list on the left, choose Components ⇨ Display. You can also try the DirectX Diagnostic Tool (**dxdiag** in Start Menu Search): You'll see information about your display device on the Display tab of this application, shown in Figure 17-2.

DirectX Diagnostic Tool

| System | Display | Sound 1 | Sound 2 | Input |

Device

Name: Mobile Intel(R) 945 Express Chipset Family
Manufacturer: Intel Corporation
Chip Type: Intel(R) GMA 950
DAC Type: Internal
Approx. Total Memory: 256 MB
Current Display Mode: 1024 x 768 (32 bit) (60Hz)
Monitor: Generic PnP Monitor

Drivers

Main Driver: igdumd32.dll
Version: 7.14.0010.1409 (English)
Date: 1/2/2008 5:48:34 PM
WHQL Logo'd: n/a
DDI Version: 9Ex

DirectX Features

DirectDraw Acceleration: Enabled
Direct3D Acceleration: Enabled
AGP Texture Acceleration: Enabled

Notes

• No problems found.

| Help | | Next Page | Save All Information... | Exit |

Figure 17-2: You can find out about your display hardware using the DirectX Diagnostic Tool, a hidden Windows feature.

tip

In order to run Windows Aero, you need a DirectX 9–compatible video card with 64MB or more of discrete graphics RAM, depending on the resolution of your display (64MB is adequate for a 1024 x 768 display, but you need 128MB or more for higher resolutions). Newer integrated graphics chips—the types that share RAM with the system and are more common on notebooks—are now capable of displaying Aero.

Assuming your machine is powerful enough to display Windows Aero, you might still want to opt for the Windows Vista Basic user interface, because of its thriftier power management. However, Windows Aero is more stable and reliable than other user interfaces because of the way it interacts with the underlying system and required signed drivers from hardware makers. Like all trade-offs, the decision is not an easy one. My advice is to test how your particular system behaves on battery power while using both user interfaces. If the battery life difference between the two is negligible, go with Windows Aero.

To change the user interface, right-click the desktop and choose Personalize from the resulting pop-up menu. This displays the Personalization Control Panel window. The first option, Window Color and Appearance, enables you to choose between user interface types. If you click this option and see the dialog shown in Figure 17-3, then you're running Windows Vista Basic, and there's no way to enable Windows Aero short of contacting the notebook maker and finding a Vista-capable driver.

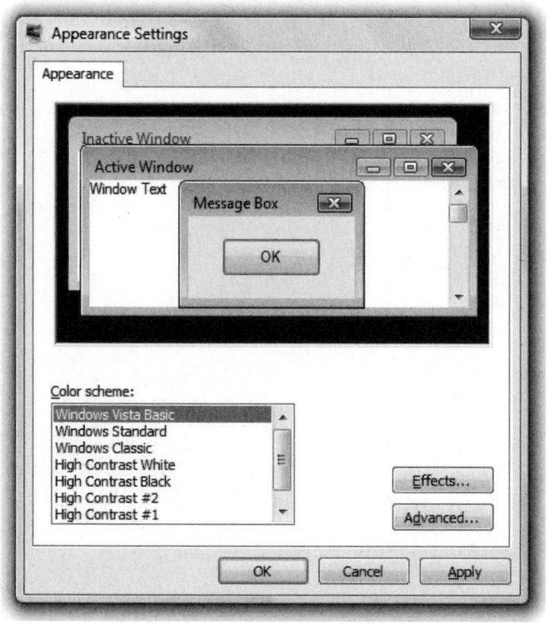

Figure 17-3: If you see this dialog, you're running Windows Vista Basic.

If, however, you see the window shown in Figure 17-4, then you're running Windows Aero, the high-end user interface.

From here, you can make two changes that affect the performance and battery life of Windows Vista:

◆ You can turn off Windows translucency by unchecking the Enable Transparency option. Translucency is a fun feature, but it doesn't really aid productivity, so this is an obvious candidate for change.

◆ The second option is to use Windows Vista Basic instead of Aero. To do so, click the *Open classic appearance properties for more color options* link at the bottom of the window. This will display the dialog shown earlier in Figure 17-3. Select the Windows Vista Basic option (and not the confusingly named Windows Standard option, which is actually a color scheme for Windows Classic) to invoke Windows Vista Basic.

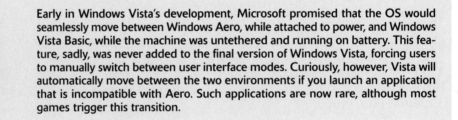

Figure 17-4: This window signifies that you're running Windows Aero.

Power Management

Although even desktop-based computers running Windows Vista support various power management features, this functionality is much richer and varied on portable computers, which is why I'm discussing it in this chapter. Windows Vista's power management functionality can be accessed throughout the user interface in various ways, but the easiest way to understand power management in Vista is to realize that it comprises three basic areas: a new system notification battery meter icon, a new Power Options Control

Panel, and a newly simplified set of power management plans. This section examines each of these features.

Updated Battery Meter

Mobile computing users are quite familiar with the battery meter that has resided in the tray notification area since Windows 95. This handy icon has been significantly updated in Windows Vista and can appear in various states, which change the look of the icon. The state you see depends on whether the machine is connected to a power source, and how well the battery is charged. Table 17-1 summarizes the various icon types you can expect to see.

Table 17-1: Windows Vista Battery Meter States

Icon	State	What It Means
	Charged, plugged in	The battery is completely charged and the system is plugged into a wall outlet.
	Charging, plugged in	The battery is charging while the system is plugged into a wall outlet. (This icon is animated.)
	On battery power	The battery is discharging because the system is operating on battery power.

Secret

Although the new battery meter now offers far more functionality than before, you may find it a bit bewildering. That's because the new battery meter offers a completely different experience depending on how you decide to interact with it. Here are the various actions you can perform with the battery meter:

• **Mouse-over:** If you move the mouse cursor over the battery meter, it will display the pop-up window shown in Figure 17-5. This pop-up window summarizes the state of the battery and the currently used power plan. It is a view-only window; you can't click on it to access more information. For that, you need to use one of the following options instead.

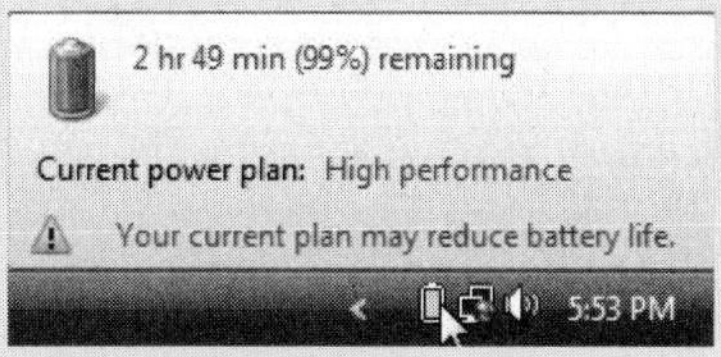

> 2 hr 49 min (99%) remaining
>
> Current power plan: High performance
>
> ⚠ Your current plan may reduce battery life.
>
> ‹ ▯▯◁» 5:53 PM

Figure 17-5: This handy pop-up provides you with an at-a-glance look at the state of power management for your system.

continues

continued

- **Single-click:** If you click the battery meter icon once, you'll see the larger and interactive pop-up window shown in Figure 17-6. This pop-up window provides the same information as the mouse-over pop-up, but it also enables you to select from one of three preset power plans (discussed in the next section) and access other power management–related OS features. (Note that the plans shown in the figure are Microsoft's defaults: PC makers often replace at least one of these power plans with their own custom plan, so what you see here may vary.)

Figure 17-6: This pop-up offers a wealth of power management functionality in a relatively small space.

- **Right-click:** If you right-click the battery meter, you'll see the pop-up menu shown in Figure 17-7. From this menu, you can access Power Options (discussed later in this chapter), Windows Mobility Center (also discussed later in this chapter), or click an option curiously titled Show System Icons, which brings up the Notification Area tab of the Taskbar and Start Menu Properties dialog. From here you can turn off the battery meter (identified as Power) if you'd like. My advice: Leave it on if you're using a mobile computer.

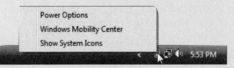

Figure 17-7: This pop-up menu offers a way to access the Windows Vista mobile and power management features.

Secret

If you're running a desktop PC, the Power tray notification icon is unavailable, and there's no way to enable it via the Taskbar and Start Menu Properties dialog; but that doesn't mean you can't change the power management settings on a desktop PC. To access Vista's Power Options, just open the Start Menu and type **power options** in Start Menu Search.

tip Curiously, if you double-click the battery meter, nothing happens.

Power Plans

Microsoft has simplified the power plans in Windows Vista. These power plans are used to manage your PC's use of its power resources, both while attached to power and while running on battery. Three preconfigured power plans are included in a stock installation of Windows Vista, but you can modify each of them to suit your needs, and you can even add your own power plans.

tip Confusingly, your PC maker might make its own machine-specific power plans as well, so if you purchased a notebook with Windows Vista preinstalled, you might see additional plans listed. You can edit any plans, however, including those made by Microsoft or your PC maker, and create your own plans.

The three built-in power plans are discussed in the following sections.

Balanced

This default plan balances power management between power consumption and performance. It does this based on how you're using the computer at the time. If you begin playing a game or accessing Vista's multimedia features, Windows Vista automatically ratchets up the processor speed to make sure you don't experience any slowdowns. Similarly, if you're just browsing the Web or reading text documents, Vista will slow the processor down as much as possible, conserving battery power.

 **Secret** By default, with the Balanced power plan, your system's microprocessor will be running at about 65 percent of its maximum performance. Based on need, Balanced allows the processor to use as little as 5 percent of its maximum performance and as much as 100 percent. This is true when the system is either running on battery power or plugged in, so don't think that using Balanced in some way prevents your computer from working at its full potential. If you need the processing power, you'll get it.

While plugged into a power source, the Balanced power plan turns off the display and hard disk after 20 minutes of inactivity. After 60 minutes of inactivity, the computer will go to sleep. Under battery power, Windows will turn off the display after five minutes of inactivity, and will turn off the hard drive after 10 minutes of inactivity. Windows puts the PC to sleep after 15 minutes of inactivity while on battery power.

In my experience, Balanced is the optimal power plan to use for portable machines of all kinds.

Power Saver

This plan sacrifices performance for better battery life. It should be used only by those with light computing requirements or those who are trying to maximize uptime while on the road. I often switch to Power Saver mode when I'm on a flight and I need to maximize battery life in order to get some writing done. However, because Power Saver adversely effects system performance, you won't want to use this mode while watching a DVD or digital movie or playing a game.

By default, with the Power Saver power plan, your system's microprocessor will be running at about 40 percent of its maximum performance. Based on need, Power Saver allows the processor to use as little as 5 percent of its maximum performance, but only as much as 50 percent. (This is true whether the system is running on battery power or plugged in.) Unlike Balanced, Power Saver truly is a compromise: In the interests of maximizing battery life, Power Saver will never allow your processor to reach its full performance potential. This is a problem only because it does so even while the system is plugged into a power source.

Here's how Power Saver affects your power management settings. Even when plugged in, Windows Vista aggressively decreases the processor speed and display brightness. After 20 minutes of inactivity Windows turns off the display and hard drive, and then puts the computer to sleep after an hour.

On battery power, Power Saver is even more aggressive. Windows Vista will turn off the display after three minutes and the hard drive after five minutes. Then, Windows will put the PC to sleep after 15 minutes of inactivity.

Power Saver is also the only power plan to use what Microsoft calls an *adaptive display*. That is, if you've configured your system to use the Windows Aero user interface and you switch to battery power while using the Power Saver plan, Windows automatically switches the display to Windows Standard, removing translucency and other Aero effects. Once you plug in the system again, the Aero effects return automatically. Power Saver does this because certain Aero effects are unduly taxing on the system from a power management perspective.

High Performance

The High Performance plan provides the highest level of performance by maximizing the system's processor speed at the expense of battery life. This plan is aimed at those who spend most of their time playing modern video games or working in graphic-intensive applications. This is the default power plan for all desktop PCs.

Yes, you guessed it: Under the High Performance plan, Vista provides 100 percent of your CPU's processing power, all the time.

Under the High Performance plan, Windows Vista will turn off the display and hard drive on a plugged-in PC after 20 minutes of inactivity, but the computer is never put to sleep. On battery power, the PC's display and hard drive are turned off after 20 minutes, as before, but the computer is put to sleep after one hour.

Secret

Desktop PCs utilize power plans as well, and though High Performance is the default, it may not be the best option, especially if you're concerned about the environment and saving energy. Instead, I recommend manually switching your desktop PC to Balanced. Windows will be more aggressive about putting the system to sleep and your PC will use less power (and thus, draw less energy) in normal use. Of course, if you need the full power of the processor—e.g., for a game or graphics application—Balanced will let you have it. This plan is the best of both worlds.

Scanning through the power plans, it's likely that you'll find a plan that at least somewhat matches your expectations, but you don't have to accept Microsoft's default settings. You can easily modify any of the existing plans, and even create your own power plans. You'll look at those possibilities in the very next section.

Power Options Control Panel

Windows Vista's power options are, go figure, configured via the Power Options Control Panel applet, which is available in Control Panel ➭ Mobile PC ➭ Power Options on a note-book computer, or Control Panel ➭ Hardware and Sound ➭ Power Options on a desktop PC. (Just type **power options** into Start Menu Search to get there quickly, regardless of what kind of PC you have.) Shown in Figure 17-8, this Control Panel initially presents a selection of the three power plans mentioned previously. (Again, you may see different options if your PC maker decided to configure its own custom plan.)

There's a lot more going on here, however. On the left of the window are a number of power management–related tasks. If you're using a mobile computer of any kind, navigate through each of these options to ensure that your system is configured exactly the way you want it. These options are interesting to desktop PC users as well.

tip

Some of the options listed here are available from the Mobile PC or Hardware and Sound page in Control Panel as well.

Requiring a Password on Wakeup

The first option, *Require a password on wakeup,* varies a bit depending on your system's capabilities, and there's a lot more going on here beyond the password option hinted at in the link. On a typical desktop PC, this Control Panel page resembles what is shown in Figure 17-9.

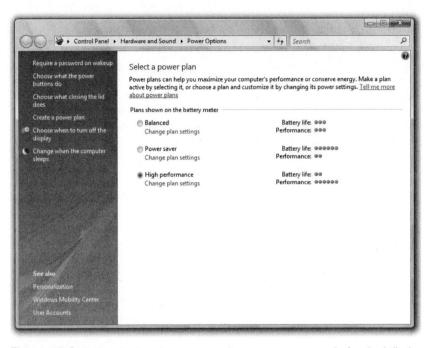

Figure 17-8: Power Options is your central management console for the Windows Vista power management features.

Figure 17-9: Desktop PCs don't have many power management options related to hardware features.

But when you view this page on a typical notebook computer, you'll see the options shown in Figure 17-10. These options are directly related to the additional hardware buttons and features included with mobile computers.

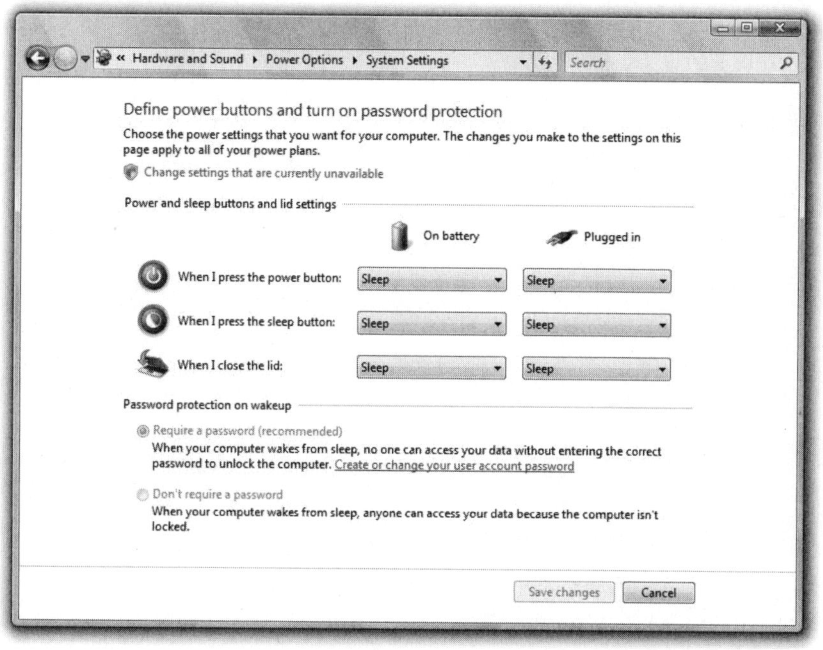

Figure 17-10: Notebook computers and other mobile PCs offer power management options related to the lid and other hardware features.

Here, you can modify how Windows Vista reacts when you press the PC's power button; press the sleep button; or, on portable computers configured with a lid-based display, when you close the lid. Each of these options has different settings for when the system is operating on battery power versus plugged in.

Complementing the *Require a password on wakeup* option described earlier, this dialog also includes a single wakeup-related option that determines whether you need to log on again each time the system wakes up after being in the sleep state. By default, Windows Vista does require you to log on again to unlock the computer as a security measure. I strongly advise leaving this feature enabled, especially if you're a mobile computer user who often accesses the PC on the road.

Secret

If you do decide to change the *Require a password on wakeup* option, you may very well discover that the options *Require a password (recommended)* and *Don't require a password* are grayed out and thus unavailable for editing. No problem: To change this option, click the link titled *Change settings that are currently unavailable*. You'll see a small Windows shield icon next to it, indicating that this choice will trigger a security-oriented User Account Control (UAC) prompt—for your protection, of course.

Returning to the Power Options display, the following additional options are available on the left side of the window.

Choose What the Power Buttons Do

Humorously, this option triggers the same display described previously. The top half of the dialog relates to this option.

Choose What Closing the Lid Does

This option, which is available only on portable computers with a lid, also brings you to the same dialog described previously. Why three different options all land on the same display is a question best saved for the UI wizards at Microsoft.

Create a Power Plan

When you click this option, you're brought to the Create a Power Plan page, a short wizard you can use to create your own power plan:

1. First, choose the preset power plan—Balanced, Power Saver, or High Performance— that you would like to base your plan on (see Figure 17-11). Give the plan a name and click the Next button.

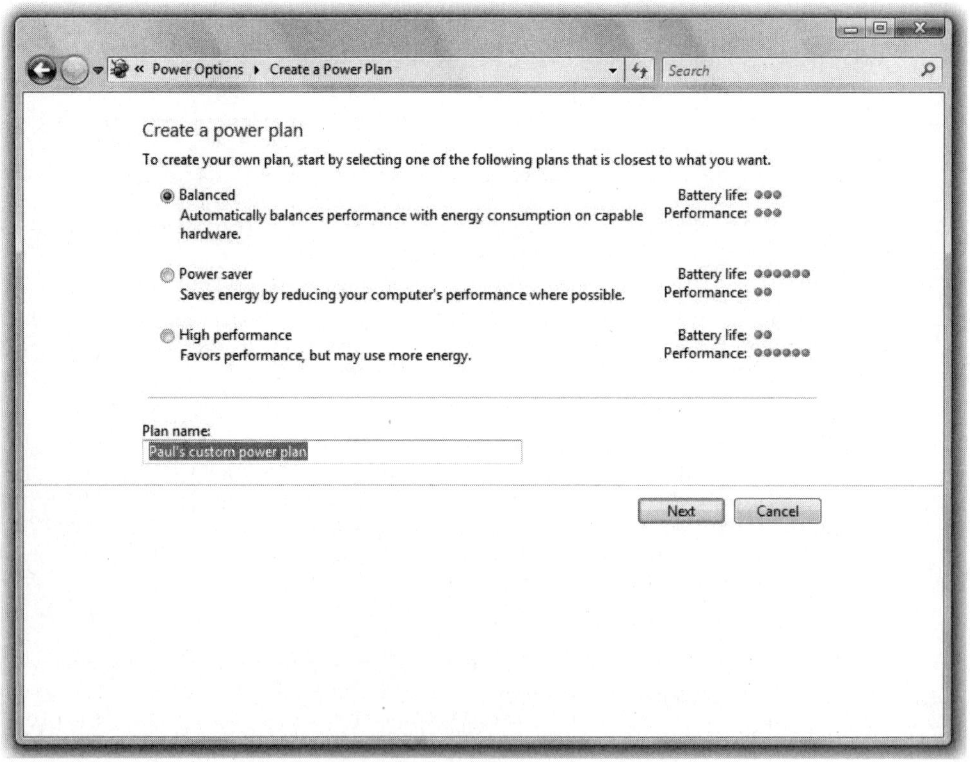

Figure 17-11: New power plans are modeled after one of the existing plans.

2. In the next step of the wizard, shown in Figure 17-12, specify when the system will turn off the display and put the system to sleep, on both battery power and when plugged in. (Desktop PC users will see only a single option for each, as these PCs are always plugged in.)

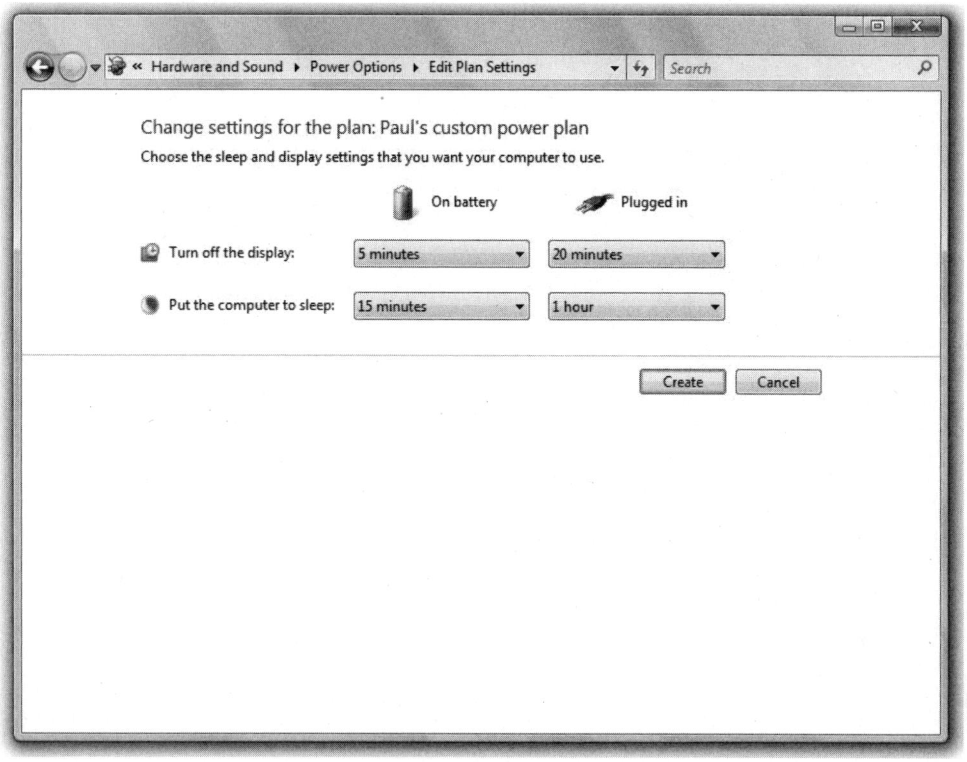

Figure 17-12: Curiously, you don't get options for turning off the hard disk.

3. Click the Create button to create your plan, which will be added to the list of available plans, as shown in Figure 17-13. Annoyingly, it replaces one plan in the so-called Preferred plans list, though that plan is still available in the less impressive-sounding Additional Plans section.

This is all well and good, but the short wizard you just used doesn't really provide access to all of the power management options you can configure; and isn't that the point of this exercise—to create a custom power plan that exactly matches your needs and desires?

To modify your custom plan (or an existing preset plan for that matter), click the Change Plan Settings link below the plan name. This brings you to a dialog that resembles the second phase of the wizard just described, but with one difference: There's now a Change Advanced Power Settings link. Click that link to modify other settings. Doing so opens the Advanced Settings dialog, shown in Figure 17-14.

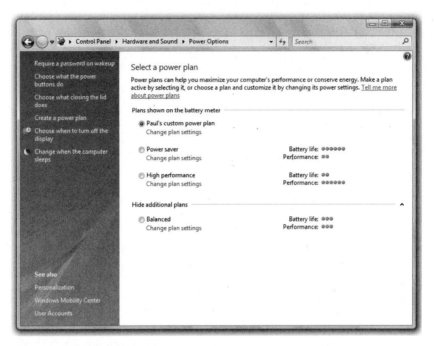

Figure 17-13: Custom power plans replace the plan on which your plan was based, but the old default plan is still available.

Figure 17-14: Use this rather complicated dialog to handcraft your power plan using every single power management option available to Windows Vista.

The Power Options Advanced settings window is, by nature, confusing. The window itself is not resizable, so it provides only a postage-stamp-sized view of the many power management features you can customize. More problematic, you have to expand nodes in a tree control—arguably the worst PC user interface element of all time—to find all the options. Nonetheless, it's worth the trouble.

Here are the power management options available via this dialog:

◆ **Additional settings:** Here, you configure whether the system requires a password when it wakes from sleep. (Portable PCs divide this option into two sub-options: one for when the system is plugged in and one for when it's attached to a power source.) The default option is Yes for both, and you should leave them alone unless you're interested in playing Russian Roulette with private data stored on your PC.

◆ **Hard disk:** Use this option to configure the hard disk to wind down after a period of time to preserve power. (As with many settings, portable PCs have separate options for battery and power.) On battery, you want this time to be reasonably low, maybe 10 minutes, but you should also configure a desktop PC or power-attached portable PC to wind down the hard drive after a short time period as well, if only to conserve power consumption.

◆ **Wireless Adapter Settings:** This option may seem fairly esoteric, but it can affect the performance of your wireless card (a common feature in portable PCs) and the PC. This feature is of interest only to portable PC users. By default, under most power management plans, the wireless adapter is set to run with maximum performance. The only exception is the Power Saver plan, on battery power: In this mode, the wireless adapter is configured to run under maximum power-saving mode, which conserves power by lowering the effectiveness of the wireless radio. You can configure this option as follows: Maximum Performance, Low Power Saving, Medium Power Saving, and Maximum Power Saving. Frankly, this might be too fine-grained for most people, and I've had little success determining what effects each state really has on power management and performance overall. Given this, my recommendation is to leave this setting at its default, based on which power plan you based your own plan on.

◆ **Sleep:** This section supports three options: Sleep after, Allow hybrid sleep, and Hibernate after. The first and third are straightforward, but the middle option might be confusing. Newer PCs support a new type of Sleep mode called Hybrid Sleep, which enables the machine to appear to turn off and on almost immediately, like a consumer electronics device. If you have a PC manufactured after mid-2006, it might support this feature, so experiment with enabling Hybrid Sleep. If it works well, use this instead of Hibernation, as Hybrid Sleep is essentially a replacement for that older form of power management. Otherwise, you might want to enable Hibernation, which was a major power management feature in Windows XP. Hibernation is faster than turning on and off the PC, but much slower than Sleep or Hybrid Sleep. It also preserves the state of the system so you can get up and running with your applications more quickly.

◆ **USB settings:** Your PC can optionally turn off select USB devices when it enters certain power management states. This can improve battery life, as USB devices, like mice, storage devices, cameras, and other devices, draw power from the PC. However, it also prevents you from using these attached devices. Suspended USB devices will wake up again once the system is plugged in to a power source.

◆ **Power buttons and lid:** What you see here varies according to the hardware capabilities of your PC, but you can usually draw the distinction neatly between desktop PCs and portable PCs. Desktop PCs typically see two options: Power button action and Start Menu power button, whereas portable PCs will see two additional options: Lid close action and Sleep button action. Power button action determines what happens when you press the hardware On/Off switch on the PC (this can be configured separately for battery power and plugged in). Options include Do nothing, Sleep, Hibernate, and Shut Down. Lid close action behaves similarly, but refers to what happens when the lid of a portable computer is shut: You can choose between the same four options. If your PC has a dedicated Sleep button (as do many portable machines), the Sleep button action provides the same configurability, but for that particular button. The Start Menu power button is unique: This specifies what happens when you click the power button in the Start Menu, shown in Figure 17-15. This button invariably triggers Sleep in each of the three preset power management plans.

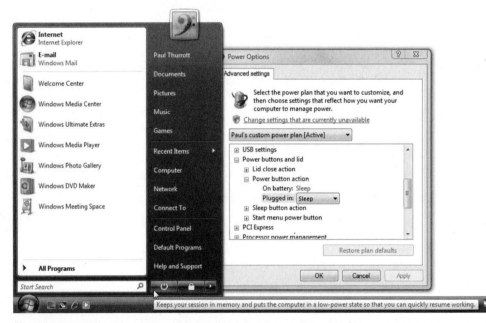

Figure 17-15: The Start Menu power button is fully configurable; you just need to know where to look.

◆ **PCI Express:** This option should typically not be changed. On a desktop PC, it should be set to Off so that hardware expansion cards attached via the PCI Express bus are always available. On portable PCs, it is set to Maximum Power Savings or Moderate Power Savings, depending on the power plan and whether the system is running on battery power.

◆ **Processor power management:** This setting has some of the biggest impacts on performance and battery life and should be carefully chosen. This option enables you to fine-tune how much processor power is used under certain states. Earlier in this chapter, I described how the default power plans affect processor performance, and you should use that as a guideline. Note, however, that you will likely be disappointed with the system's performance while doing multimedia tasks if 100 percent of the processor's performance isn't available.

◆ **Search and indexing:** Windows Vista's integrated search functionality is wonderful, but it can be a real drag on system performance, especially when it is indexing content. To minimize the impact on your system, especially consider reducing the load that search and indexing can exert on battery power. The settings here match the names of the default power plans (High Performance, Balanced, and Power Saver), so consider simply leaving them at their default values, based on whichever plan you're editing.

◆ **Display:** Here, you can specify how quickly Windows Vista turns off the display, which is pretty straightforward, and configure the adaptive display, which can be set to on or off. If you're trying to wring as much battery life out of the machine as possible, I recommend turning the adapter display on, but only for battery power.

◆ **Windows DreamScene settings:** If you're using Windows Vista Ultimate and have downloaded the optional Ultimate Extra called Windows DreamScene, you'll see a related power management option listed here. That's because Windows DreamScene replaces your static desktop background with an animated video, a change that can be visually appealing (if distracting) but power management unfriendly. There are two options: Power Saver (for portable PCs) and High Performance (for desktop PCs). Under the Power Saver option, animated Windows DreamScene backgrounds are disabled while on battery power. While disabled, you'll see a still frame from the animation; plug the machine back in and the video continues as before. It's pretty seamless.

◆ **Multimedia settings:** One of the nicest features of Windows Vista is that it makes it very easy to share media such as music, videos, and photos from PC to PC. However, when you're running on battery power, media sharing can be resource intensive and thus exacerbate energy consumption, so you may want to curtail media sharing on battery power. Available options include Allow the computer to sleep, Prevent idling to sleep, and Allow the computer to enter Away Mode. The first two are self-explanatory, and portable computers should always be allowed to enter Sleep mode while on battery power. The final option, however, might be confusing. Away Mode is a new power management option, related to media sharing and the Media Center feature in Vista, that enables background media tasks, such as Media Center recording of TV shows and media sharing, to occur in the background even while the system otherwise appears to be asleep. This mode thus provides most of the power management benefits of Sleep while still allowing media sharing to occur.

Secret

Away Mode actually debuted in Windows XP Media Center Edition 2005 Update Rollup 2 (UR2), the last major Media Center update before Vista shipped, but it's been enhanced in Windows Vista. The important thing to remember is that Away Mode cannot be invoked unless this power management setting is explicitly changed to Allow the computer to enter Away Mode. In Vista, Away Mode is used by Windows Media Center Extenders connecting to the PC (see Chapter 15) and media sharing (Chapter 11).

◆ **Battery:** This option, available only on portable PCs, determines how the system battery is configured to warn you or perform certain actions at specific times, such as when the battery is low or critically low. Options include critical battery action (what happens when the battery life falls to a "critical" level), low battery action (what happens when the battery life falls to a "low" level), low battery notification (whether the system informs you of the transition into this state), low battery level (at what percentage of full the battery is considered "low"), and critical battery level (at what percentage of full the battery is considered "critical").

◆ **Third-party power management settings:** Many hardware makers have created their own advanced power management settings, which can be exposed to the user via this Control Panel and configured accordingly. For example, display card maker ATI has an ATI Graphics Power Settings option that helps you configure how ATI Mobility Radeon graphics products impact overall power consumption.

Secret

To use the option Never for many of the options described above, type in **0** (the number zero). This will change automatically to Never.

Choose When to Turn Off the Display

This option triggers the same dialog previously described.

Change When the Computer Sleeps

This option also triggers the same dialog described previously in the "Requiring a Password on Wakeup" section.

Deleting a Power Plan

If you created a custom power plan and aren't happy with it, you can delete it, though the process isn't straightforward. To delete a power plan, open Power Options and ensure that the power plan you want to delete isn't the active (selected) power plan. Then, click the link titled Change Plan Settings under the name of the plan you'd like to delete. You will see a Delete This Plan link in the window that appears. As shown in Figure 17-16, click this link to delete the plan.

Secret

You cannot delete any of the built-in power plans.

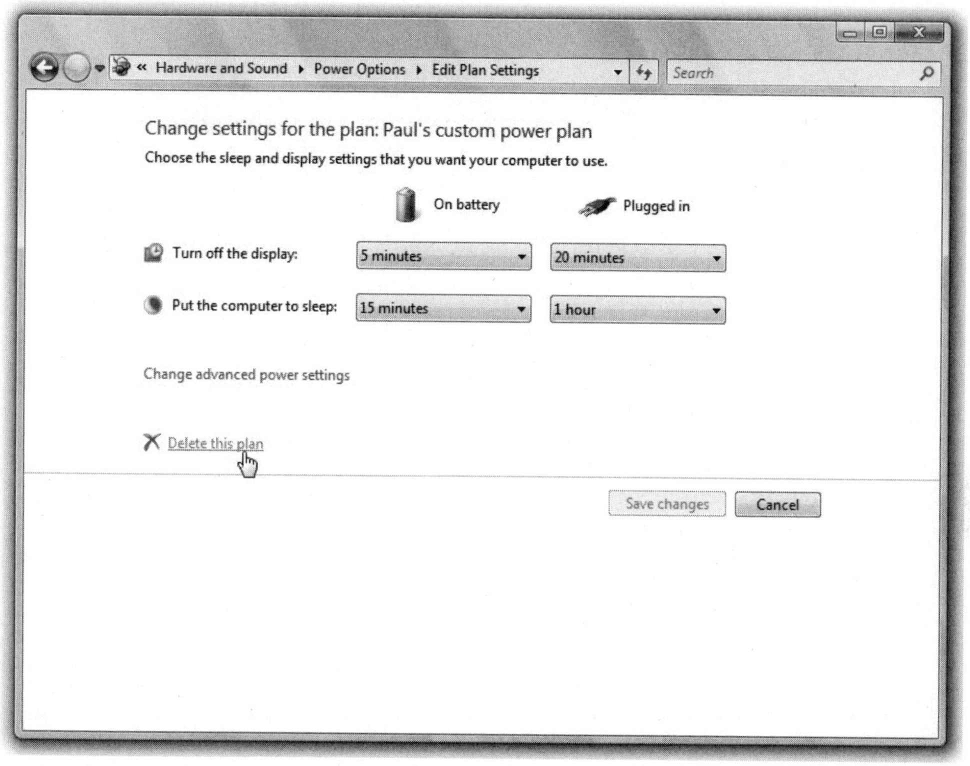

Figure 17-16: You have to select another plan first, but once you do, any custom power plan can be deleted.

Windows Mobility Center

If you've ever owned a mobile PC, you've probably marveled (and not in a good way) at the cruddy utility applications that PC makers seem compelled to ship with their hardware. Microsoft feels your pain. In Windows Vista, for the first time, the software giant has taken the first steps toward creating a centralized management console called Windows Mobility Center for all of this functionality, and it has preloaded this dashboard with all of the utilities a mobile user could want. Best of all, PC makers are free to extend Mobility Center with their own machine-specific mobile utilities. I can't guarantee these products are any good, but at least they're easily located in this new centralized management console.

Shown in Figure 17-17, Windows Mobility Center is available only on mobile computers. You won't see it on desktop PCs.

Secret

The secret keyboard shortcut Windows Key+X also starts Mobility Center.

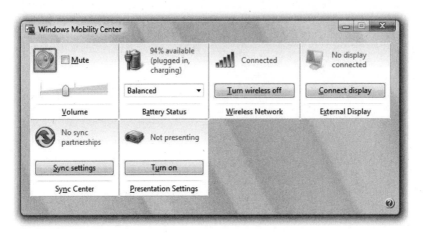

Figure 17-17: Windows Mobility Center looks nothing like any other Windows Vista applications.

You start Mobility Center by finding it in the Start Menu or by typing **mobility** into Start Menu Search, which is quite a bit faster.

Secret

Okay, you can actually enable Windows Mobility Center on desktop PCs if you really want to, though to do so you need to do a bit of Registry hacking. Here's how: Open the Registry Editor (regedit.exe) and navigate to HKEY_CURRENT_USER ➪ Software ➪ Microsoft ➪ MobilePC. Next, add a new key called MobilityCenter. Inside this key, add a new DWORD (32-bit) value with the name RunOnDesktop and a value of 1 (00000001). Now reboot and you will find that Mobility Center is available, albeit without some of the portable PC-oriented files that are discussed in this chapter.

Curiously, Windows Mobility Center in no way resembles any of the other applications that Microsoft bundled with Windows Vista. Instead, a set of mobile-related options are arrayed in cubes across an unadorned window that cannot be resized or formatted in any way. These options, which vary according to the capabilities of your PC, can include Brightness, Volume, Battery Status, Wireless Network, External Display, Sync Center, and Presentation Settings.

Basically, each of these cubes launches a setting that mobile PC users need fairly often. Click the icon in the Volume cube, for example, and the Sound Control Panel appears. Alternately, you can set or mute the system volume from directly within Mobility Center.

Secret

With one exception, all of the options available in Mobility Center are available elsewhere in the Windows Vista user interface. That one exception is Presentation Settings, covered in the next section.

tip Remember that you might see additional cubes here that were installed by your PC maker.

Presentations A-Go-Go

Although not a particularly glamorous lifestyle, many mobile users cart their notebooks around the globe, set them up in an unfamiliar location, and attempt to give a presentation using Microsoft PowerPoint or a similar presentation package. Notebooks are perfect companions for such users because of their portability; but until Windows Vista, they weren't particularly accommodating if the presentation was conducted on battery power—thanks to various power management settings, the presentation could disappear as the display was shut down or the machine went to sleep. In Windows Vista, Microsoft has added two major features related to giving presentations, one of which solves the problem just mentioned.

Presentation Settings

An obscure but useful feature, Presentation Settings enables you to temporarily disable your normal power management settings and ensures that your system stays awake, with no screen dimming, no hard drive disabling, no screen saver activation, and no system notifications to interrupt you. In other words, with one click of the mouse (well, a few), you can set up your mobile PC to behave exactly the way you want it to while giving a presentation.

To enable Presentation Settings, run Mobility Center as described in the previous section and click the projector icon in the Presentation Settings cube. The Presentation Settings dialog is shown in Figure 17-18.

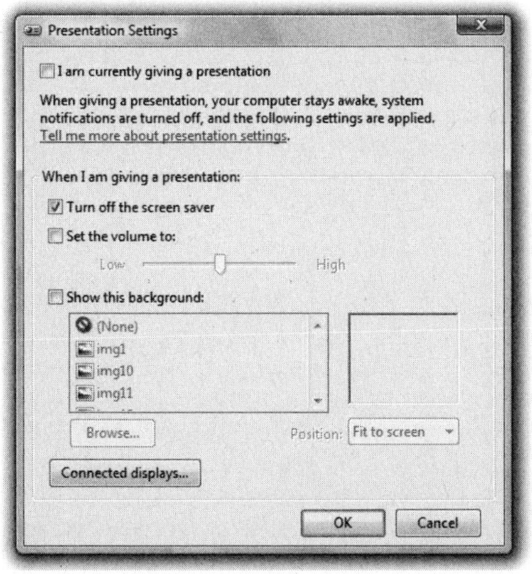

Figure 17-18: Presentation Settings is a boon to anyone who's had to struggle with Windows getting in the way of a presentation.

Select the *I Am Currently Giving a Presentation* option to enable Presentation Settings. Optionally, you can turn off the screen saver (the default), turn off the system volume, and temporarily change the desktop background. Presentation Settings also provides a handy way to configure connected displays, including network projectors.

> **tip** You can also enable Presentations with a single click by clicking the Turn On button in the Presentation Settings cube in Windows Mobility Center. Regardless of how you enable this feature, the Presentation Settings cube will change to read Presenting, and the projector icon will change to an On state.

Using a Network Projector

If you're going to show a presentation via a modern network-based projector, Windows Vista includes a Connect to a Network Projector utility that automatically configures firewall settings and searches for nearby projectors. To run this utility, find Connect to a Network Project in Start Menu ➪ All Programs ➪ Accessories. You can search for a projector automatically or enter the projector's IP address.

Other Mobile Features

In addition to the major new mobility-related features mentioned previously, Windows Vista ships with a host of other technologies that benefit mobile workers. This section highlights some of these features and explains how you can best take advantage of them.

Offline Files and Folders

In Windows XP, Microsoft introduced a feature called Offline Files and Folders that enables mobile users to mark network-based files and folders so that they will be cached (stored) locally, using space on the mobile computer's hard drive. When the mobile PC is connected to the network, the local and remote versions of the files and folders are synchronized so that they are always up-to-date. When users work away from the network—which can be a corporate network based on Active Directory or just a simple wireless home network—they can access these remote resources even when in a disconnected state, just as if they were connected.

Offline Files and Folders is a wonderful idea, and it's been made even better in Windows Vista. It works almost exactly as before, as you'll see here, but now Windows Vista uses Delta Sync technology, first developed by Microsoft's Windows Server team, to speed synchronization. Delta Sync works on the subfile level: If a user changes part of a document, for example, only the changed parts of the document need to be synced to the server. Previously, the entire document would need to be synchronized. This bit of software wizardry is far more efficient than bulk file copies, although I can't really understand how it works under the hood.

To set up Offline Files and Folders for the first time, use the new Network Explorer to navigate to a location on your network that contains files or folders you'd like to cache locally. Then, right-click the items you'd like to cache and choose Always Available Offline. When you do so, the Always Available Offline dialog (shown in Figure 17-19) is displayed, and you can synchronize the content to your hard drive.

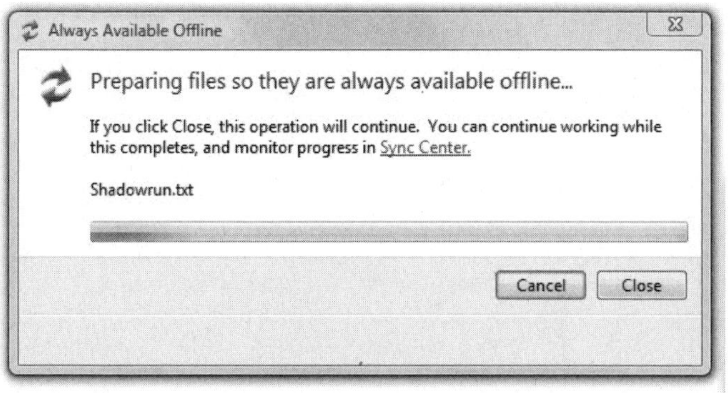

Figure 17-19: You can configure network-based data to be available even when you're not connected to the network.

When the synchronization is complete, you'll see a small sync icon overlay appear on top of the lower-left corner of the folder or file you just synced. This icon overlay indicates that the item is available offline.

tip To remove this association, right-click again and uncheck Always Available Offline.

In Windows XP, Offline Files and Folders were managed via the Folder Options window. In Windows Vista, you manage these relationships in the new Sync Center, which is shown in Figure 17-20. The Sync Center is used to manage relationships between Windows Vista and portable devices (such as PDAs and smartphones) as well as offline files and folders. It does not, however, manage relationships with network-based media devices, such as other PCs, Xbox 360s, and Media Center Extenders. No, I don't know why.

Regardless of how many network-based files and folders you make available offline, you will only see one item, Offline Files, in the main Sync Center display. If you double-click this item, you can dive into the partnership detail, and see separate items for each network share that contains shared files and folders. You can also click the Sync button to manually synchronize with the server, or click Schedule to view and manage the sync schedule. The schedule is managed via a simple wizard-based application that enables you to schedule synchronization at specific times or in response to certain events, such as when you log on or lock Windows, or when your computer is idle.

If you take your system on the road and modify network-based files and folders, they will be synchronized with the server when you return. Should there be any conflicts—such as what can occur when a file is edited both on the server and in your local cache, you are given the opportunity to rectify the conflict in a variety of ways, most of which are nondestructive.

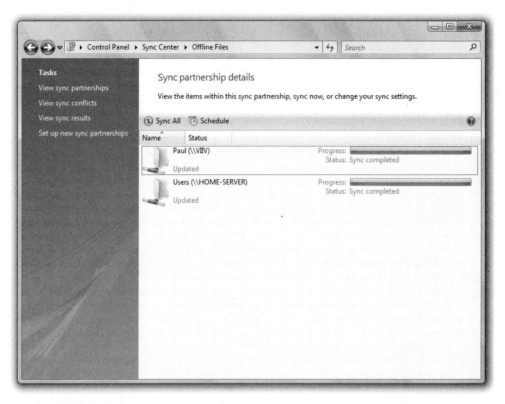

Figure 17-20: Sync Center is an almost one-stop shop for Windows Vista's relationships with other devices and network-based files and folders.

Windows Meeting Space

In a nod to the peer-to-peer technologies that have been sweeping across the PC industry since the Napster phenomenon of a decade ago, Windows Vista includes a new peer-to-peer service called Windows Meeting Space that is oriented toward collaboration, not stealing music. (Presumably, any technology can be used for good or evil.) Windows Meeting Space enables you to share documents, applications, or your entire desktop with other network-equipped Windows Vista users near you, and can automatically set up an ad hoc network if no wired or wireless network is available.

Secret

To use this ad hoc network, however, each user needs to have a Windows Vista–equipped machine with a properly configured wireless card. Meeting Space is most often used by notebook users for this reason, and it's useful when coworkers meet in a coffee shop, airport, hotel, and so on, to collaborate, even when there's no wireless network (or when the network in question requires a usage fee).

To start Windows Meeting Space, you need to first configure the new People Near Me service of Windows Vista, which helps Vista identify other users near you—both physically and on the same network subnet—that meet the technical qualifications of Meeting Space. The first time you run Meeting Space, you'll be prompted to configure People Near Me with your name and various other options, as shown in Figure 17-21.

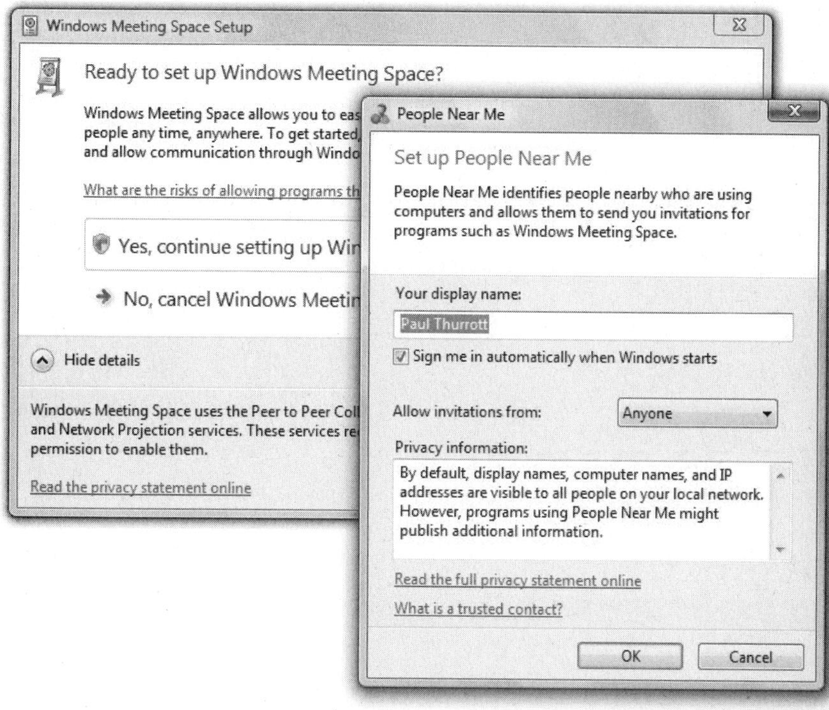

Figure 17-21: People Near Me is the Windows Vista feature that helps Windows Meeting Space find other people with whom to collaborate.

After People Near Me is configured, you'll be presented with the main Windows Meeting Space application window, shown in Figure 17-22. This window enables you to start a new meeting or find other meetings in progress nearby.

To start a new meeting, click Start a New Meeting. Then, provide a name, passphrase, and, optionally, other meeting-related options as prompted. A new Meeting Space will be shown, with panes for sharing applications or the desktop, people nearby, and handout downloads (see Figure 17-23).

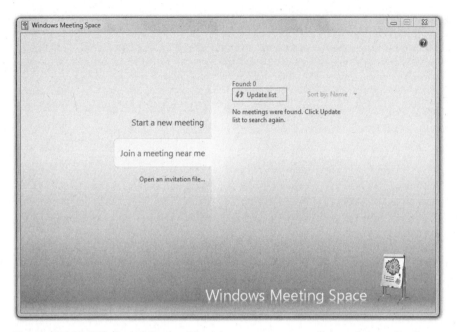

Figure 17-22: Windows Meeting Space is a peer-to-peer collaboration application.

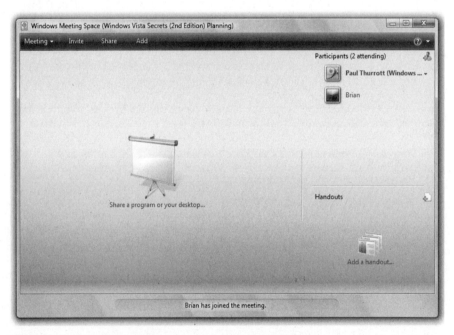

Figure 17-23: Virtual meetings can get as busy as physical meetings, with multiple participants and a lot of work.

From here, the person who started the meeting—called the *meeting presenter*—can share applications or his or her entire desktop, and the display will be remotely routed to each participant (maximize the window for best results). You can also pass electronic notes to one another, as with an instant messaging (IM) application, and participants can copy documents into the Handouts well so that other users can download them.

Windows SideShow

A new generation of Tablet PCs and notebook computers—and, Microsoft says, even other devices such as TV sets and remote controls—include a new kind of auxiliary display that enables you to access certain information on the computer, even when it's asleep. These auxiliary displays are initially most interesting on mobile computers, and they are available in color and black-and-white versions.

Here's how they work: Auxiliary displays access a feature in Windows Vista called SideShow to display small gadgets, similar to those used by the Windows Sidebar (see Chapter 6), that provide limited access to various applications and services in Windows. You'll see a Windows Media Player gadget that enables you to play music in your Windows Media Player 11 media library, and an e-mail gadget that helps you read e-mail. All of these gadgets work when the laptop's lid is closed, they require very little power, and they come on instantly. Although Microsoft ships a number of gadgets of its own, you can expect third parties to come up with their own gadgets as well, especially those companies that make and sell SideShow-equipped devices.

The bad news about Windows SideShow is that you need very specific hardware to access this feature. You can't add on an auxiliary display, at least not elegantly, to a mobile PC. Therefore, you need to get a brand-new mobile device with an integrated auxiliary display in order to experience it for yourself. At the time of this writing, almost two years after Vista first shipped, auxiliary displays are still very rare.

Improved Support for Tablet PC Hardware

If you're using a Tablet PC computer (a notebook computer that typically comes in one of two form factors: a convertible laptop or a true slate-type tablet) or a notebook computer with Tablet PC–like hardware, such as a touch screen, digitizer screen with stylus, or a compatible external writing pad, Windows Vista includes a wide range of functionality related to handwriting recognition, pen-based input, and the like. I discuss these features in the next chapter, which is devoted entirely to Tablet PCs and other computers that have Tablet-like hardware, such as Ultra-Mobile PCs, or UMPCs.

Secret

Although this book focuses on the tools that Microsoft ships with Windows Vista, note that the company also offers some interesting free tools for Windows Vista users via its Web site. The most notable of these, from a mobility perspective, is SyncToy. According to Microsoft, this fascinating little application helps you copy, move, rename, and delete files between folders and computers quickly and easily. And while that's a very generic description, the beauty of this tool is that it enables you to synchronize the contents of a folder on one computer with the contents of a folder on another computer, so it's a great synchronization tool for people who usually use a desktop PC at home or the office but have to frequently travel with a portable PC as well. You can find out more at www.microsoft.com/downloads/. Just search for **SyncToy**.

Summary

There's no doubt about it: Windows Vista is the most capable and feature-packed operating system yet created for mobile computers. Thanks to new features such as Windows Mobility Center; Presentation Settings; network projector support; Windows Meeting Space and People Near Me; and massive changes to power management; Windows Vista will keep any mobile computer humming along nicely with a wide range of new and improved functionality. And if you're lucky enough to be using an innovative Tablet PC or Ultra-Mobile PC (UMPC), your mobility options are even more impressive. You'll take a look at Vista's unique support for these new PCs types in the next chapter.

Using Tablet PCs and Ultra-Mobile PCs

Chapter
18

◆ ◆

In This Chapter

History of the Tablet PC, the Ultra-Mobile PC, and Microsoft's pen-enabled software

Discovering the changes to Tablet PC functionality Microsoft made in Windows Vista

Using and configuring Tablet PC features

Entering handwritten text with the Tablet PC Input Panel

Using Flicks and other gestures

Controlling your computer with speech recognition

Understanding Tablet PC–related changes to the Windows shell

Accessing Tablet PC utilities such as the Snipping Tool, Windows Journal, and Sticky Notes

Working with Ultra-Mobile PCs

◆ ◆

During the life cycle of Windows XP, Microsoft shipped two versions of that OS that were targeted specifically at Tablet PCs, a new type of mobile computer based on notebooks that added digitized screens and pens for a more natural style of interaction. Tablet PCs flopped, but Microsoft's software was, for once, widely heralded for its high quality. With Windows Vista, Microsoft has made the Tablet PC capabilities available to a far wider range of PCs and has lifted the restrictions on how users acquire these capabilities. It's now possible to get Tablet PC functionality in most mainstream versions of Windows Vista, and on a wide range of hardware types, including a new generation of tiny mobile devices called Ultra-Mobile PCs, or UMPCs.

A Short History of the Tablet PC

In mid-2002, Microsoft released the first version of Windows XP that was specifically targeted at a new generation of pen-based notebook computers called Tablet PCs. Logically named Windows XP Tablet PC Edition, this software wasn't, of course, the first to try to combine pens (or, really, styluses) with PCs. Indeed, as long ago as the late 1980s, innovative companies such as Go, Apple, and Palm were leading the way to a future of more ergonomic and natural interactions with computers. Even Microsoft got into the game in the early 1990s with a short-lived (and overhyped) product called Pen Windows that, frankly, amounted to nothing.

Tablet PCs, however, were (and still are) different. First, they were mainstream computers with added functionality such as displays with built-in digitizers that could not only sense pen input, but also in many cases even understand when the tip was pressed down harder or lighter. Second, they originally came in two form factors, though more are now available. The first was called a *tablet,* although it's also sometimes referred to as a *slate design.* These machines did not include integrated keyboards and trackpads, but were instead intended to be used primarily via the pen. You could, of course, attach keyboards, mice, and even auxiliary displays to these machines, typically via USB. A typical slate-type Tablet PC is shown in Figure 18-1.

Figure 18-1: Slate-type Tablet PCs do not include integrated keyboards and pointing devices but instead require the use of a pen, or stylus.

The second Tablet PC type, and the one that continues today as the mainstream Tablet PC design, is called a *convertible laptop*. Shown in Figure 18-2, these machines look just like regular laptops, but with one difference: The screen can be swiveled around and rotated back onto the keyboard, giving the machine a temporary slate-like form factor. In this way, a convertible laptop can be used like a regular notebook computer—with a keyboard and trackpad—or like a slate-type Tablet, via the pen.

Figure 18-2: Convertible Tablet PCs have proven to be the most popular design because they can be used like a normal notebook computer when needed.

First-generation Tablet PCs didn't exactly take off in the market. There are many reasons for this, but for once Microsoft wasn't to blame. In fact, the initial version of Windows XP Tablet PC Edition was surprisingly solid. It was based on Windows XP Professional, and thus could do everything that XP Pro could. It supported a variety of screen digitizer types, could perform decent handwriting recognition, could switch the display between landscape and portrait modes on-the-fly (to better simulate writing on a pad of paper), and included some worthwhile software, such as a Windows Journal note-taking application, a Sticky Notes utility, a game, and an add-on pack for Microsoft Office that gave it better Tablet capabilities. All in all, it was an excellent release. Windows XP Tablet PC Edition is shown in Figure 18-3.

Why did Tablet PCs fail in the market? For starters, they were too expensive. Partly to offset research and development costs, and partially to help pay for XP Tablet PC Edition, which carried a premium over other XP editions, PC makers priced first-generation Tablet PCs too high. The machines were also woefully underpowered, with anemic Pentium III Mobile processors. Battery life, too, was horrible, negating the advantages of the platform. Many users who might have otherwise been interested in the ultimate mobile companion gave up given the prices, performance, and battery life.

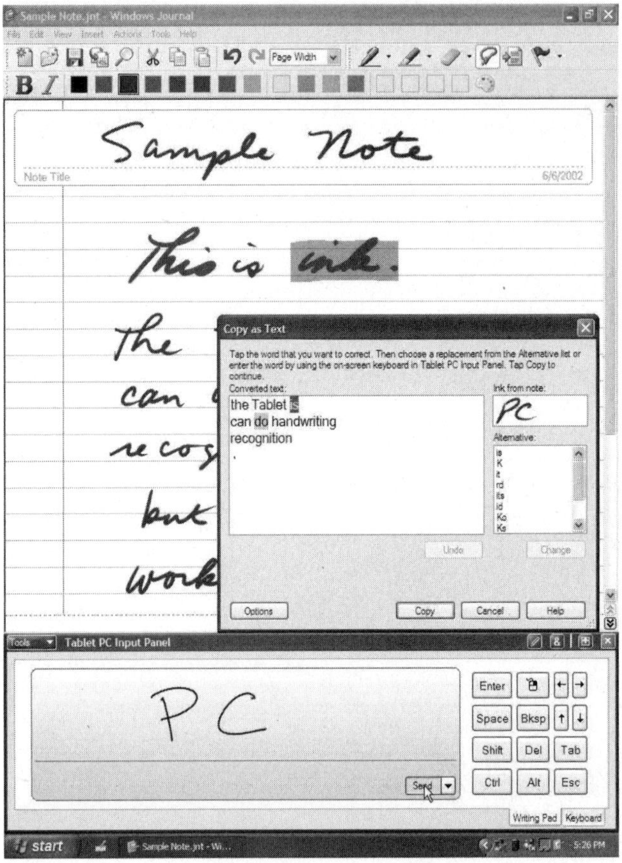

Figure 18-3: Microsoft's original Tablet PC operating system was surprisingly good, but it floundered in the market.

Microsoft trudged on, thanks in part to the involvement of Bill Gates, the company's co-founder and then the chairman and chief architect of the software firm. Gates was convinced that Tablet PCs were the future, and in late 2004 the company shipped its second version of Windows XP aimed at Tablet PC hardware. Dubbed Windows XP Tablet PC Edition 2005, this software benefited from the release of Intel's Centrino platform and Pentium-M microprocessors, which offered notebook makers dramatically better performance and battery life. New Tablet PC designs showed up, with both larger and smaller form factors, giving customers more options. In addition, prices came down. Now it's possible to get a Tablet PC for little more than a comparable notebook. Some PC makers even include Tablet capabilities as an add-on option.

Windows XP Tablet PC Edition 2005 added a new version of the Tablet PC Input Panel (TIP), a pop-up window that is used to translate handwriting into non-Tablet-enhanced applications. The new TIP included real-time recognition, so handwriting was translated on-the-fly, giving you the option to correct as you wrote, rather than after a line of text was entered. XP Tablet PC Edition 2005 was also contextually aware, meaning the system could filter its handwriting recognition library based on what you were doing in order to achieve better results. For example, if you are entering script into a text field that accepts only numbers, the OS will only test your handwriting against numbers, not its entire library of characters. Windows XP Tablet PC Edition 2005 is shown in Figure 18-4.

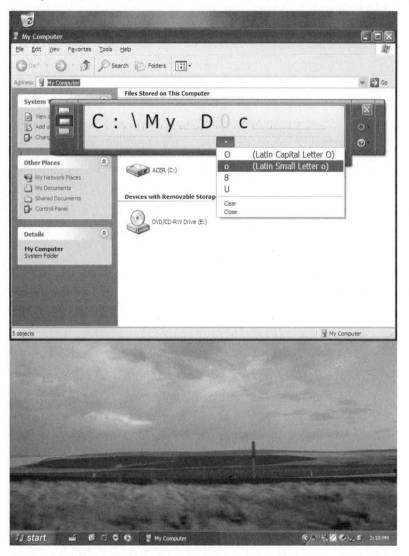

Figure 18-4: Windows XP Tablet PC Edition 2005 offered many improvements over its predecessor, including an enhanced TIP.

Like its predecessor, Windows XP Tablet PC Edition 2005 was technically excellent; unfortunately, also like its predecessor, it failed to make much of a dent in the market, despite a seemingly endless market, including students, factory floor workers, roaming sales people, doctors, and many others who would benefit from this platform. Part of the reason for this continued lackluster success was that customers couldn't use just any PC with XP Tablet PC Edition 2005: You had to purchase a system with that software prein-stalled. You couldn't use any digitizer, like the millions of available pen input systems out there, typically in use by graphic designers. And it didn't support touch-screen interaction: You either interacted with the system via a pen/stylus, or you used the more conventional keyboard and mouse interface common to other PCs.

All these issues were addressed in Windows Vista. Indeed, the Tablet PC features in Windows Vista are the best yet.

Tablet PC Capabilities in Windows Vista

For Windows Vista, Microsoft has decided to open up the market for Tablet PC functional-ity dramatically. There is no Windows Vista Tablet PC Edition. Instead, users automati-cally get Tablet PC functionality if they use Windows Vista Home Premium, Business, Enterprise, or Ultimate editions with a PC that includes compatible hardware such as a screen-based digitizer or touch screen. That's right, you don't even need a true Tablet PC. More to the point, many Tablet PC features work even if you're just using a keyboard and mouse, although of course such systems are only marginally interesting.

One point that's as important today as it was when Microsoft offered Tablet PC–based versions of XP is that these systems are full-fledged PCs. The operating system isn't scaled back or stripped down in any way, and all of the software you've come to know and love works just fine, as it would on "normal" PCs. This is probably more obvious now that there's no longer a Tablet PC version of Windows. But if you're worried that you're losing anything by going with a Tablet, fear not: Tablet-based computers are like a superset of a more pedestrian PC. They do more, not less.

Secret

In addition to pulling the Tablet PC features into mainstream versions of Windows Vista, Microsoft has also stopped selling Media Center–specific versions of Windows with Vista as well, so users who run Windows Vista Home Premium or Ultimate have an interesting "best of both worlds" capability. They can uti-lize the Media Center and Tablet PC functionality of Windows together on the same PC. With Windows XP, this would have required two different operating systems and, likewise, two very different PCs. Windows Media Center is covered in Chapter 15.

Using a Tablet PC

In Windows Vista, using the system's integrated Tablet PC functionality is virtually iden-tical to the way it worked in Windows XP Tablet PC Edition, but naturally with a few enhancements. Windows Journal, Sticky Notes, and the Tablet PC Input Panel (TIP) all make it over with some functional improvements, as does the Snipping Tool, a favorite Tablet PC download that Microsoft used to provide separately. This section examines how the Tablet PC functionality has improved in Windows Vista.

tip   These Tablet PC features apply, for the most part, to Ultra-Mobile PCs, which are dis-cussed later in this chapter. UMPCs are essentially small form-factor Tablet PCs with touch-screen support.

Configuring Tablet PC Features

Before using your Tablet PC or tablet-equipped PC with a stylus or other pointing device, you should probably take the time to configure the Tablet PC functionality that's built into Windows Vista. If you have Tablet hardware, you'll see a few items in the shell that aren't available on non-Tablet hardware, including a handy way to select multiple items with a pen, a few new tray notification icons that appear over time, and the same reordering of Control Panel items that one sees when using Windows Vista with a notebook computer. With the exception of that last item, you'll examine these features throughout this chapter.

Tablet PC features are configured via the Control Panel, through the Tablet PC Settings option in Mobile PC. This dialog, shown in Figure 18-5, includes four tabs that help you configure the system for tablet use.

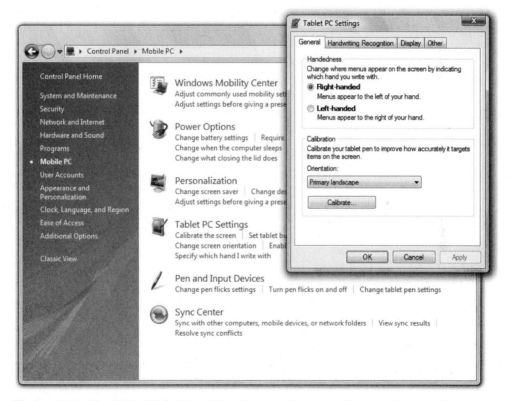

Figure 18-5: The Tablet PC Settings dialog box is an important first stop for any tablet user.

Secret

If you're using a non-Tablet system, the Tablet PC features are found in a different location: Control Panel ➪ Hardware and Sound ➪ Tablet PC Settings. Yes, that's correct: You'll see Tablet PC Settings on any Vista-based PC.

Using Tablet PC Settings

In the General tab, you configure the Tablet PC for right- or left-handed use and determine the screen orientation (portrait or landscape). This tab also provides a link to Microsoft's Digitizer Calibration Tool, which is used to ensure that the pen hits the screen on target. Anyone who's used a Pocket PC will recognize this tool, shown in Figure 18-6. You launch the tool by clicking the Calibrate button.

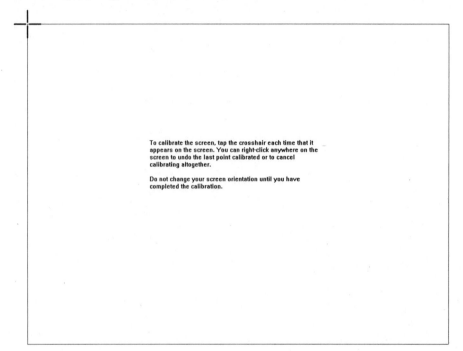

To calibrate the screen, tap the crosshair each time that it appears on the screen. You can right-click anywhere on the screen to undo the last point calibrated or to cancel calibrating altogether.

Do not change your screen orientation until you have completed the calibration.

Figure 18-6: The Digitizer Calibration Tool helps you configure your pen for accuracy.

Secret The Digitizer Calibration Tool only supports calibrating integrated digitizers. It will not work with an external digitizer. If you're using an external digitizer, it should have come with software to help you calibrate the pen.

In the Handwriting Recognition tab, shown in Figure 18-7, you configure two tools that help you personalize the system's handwriting recognition. These are the Handwriting Recognition Personalization tool and Automatic Learning.

The Handwriting Recognition Personalization tool helps you improve the system's handwriting recognition results by stepping you through a wizard in which you provide examples of your handwriting.

Figure 18-7: Here, you can specify whether Vista's handwriting recognition is personalized for you.

Secret

You can trigger Tablet PC pen training in a variety of ways, but the simplest is to use Start Menu Search. Just open the Start Menu, type **pen**, and then select Tablet PC Pen Training from the list that appears. Tablet PC Pen Training, shown in Figure 18-8, is a critical tool for anyone new to the pen-based features of Windows Vista.

Figure 18-8: If you're new to pen-based computing, this is an ideal first stop.

Automatic learning, meanwhile, is an opt-in (and recommended) Tablet-based service that gathers information about the words you use regularly, and how you write them, and then skews the system's handwriting recognition so that it can be more accurate and attuned to both your writing style and word usage.

Secret

While the personalized recognizer is available on all Vista-based PCs, automatic learning is available only on Tablet PCs (including Ultra-Mobile PCs), so if you visit this location on a non-Tablet PC, you'll see a message to that effect, and the Automatic Learning section of the Handwriting Recognition tab is grayed out.

In the Display tab, shown in Figure 18-9, you configure the default screen orientation from a selection of four possible options: primary landscape, secondary portrait, secondary landscape, and primary portrait. You can also change the order in which these orientation options are implemented when you press the hardware-based screen orientation button that is found on many Tablet PCs.

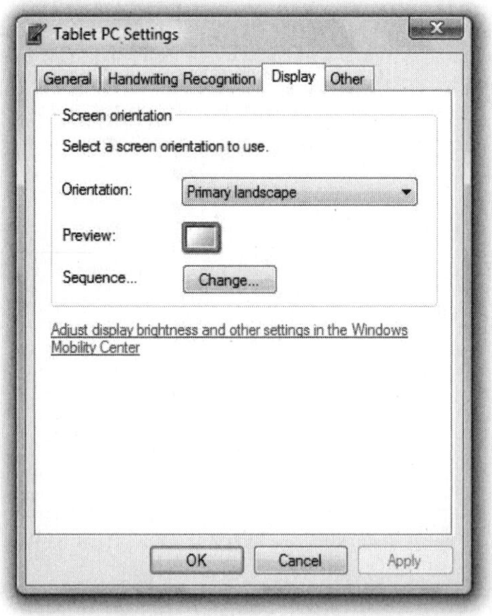

Figure 18-9: Use the Display tab to configure the screen orientation and which views the system chooses when you push your Tablet's screen orientation button.

Consider a typical slate-style Tablet PC device, on which the display takes up most of the surface of the front of the device. On such a machine, you could conceivably view the screen in any of the four configuration options, depending on how you're holding it. The primary landscape and primary portrait modes are the two modes that you'll use most often, based on the button layout on the device, your left- or right-handedness, and the ways that feel most comfortable to you. The secondary portrait and secondary landscape modes are less frequently used modes.

Most users will likely just need two screen orientation types, especially if they're using a convertible laptop-style Tablet PC. In normal laptop mode on such a device, when the user is accessing the system through the keyboard and mouse, the screen would be in a horizontal view. This would be primary landscape. But when the screen is rotated so that the system is accessed like a tablet, using the stylus, this would be primary portrait (or perhaps secondary portrait depending on the user and the layout of the device's hardware controls). In this case, you might want to configure primary landscape for the first and third locations in the orientation sequence, and primary portrait for positions two and four.

On the Other tab, there's a link to Pen and Input Devices, which is a separate Control Panel applet. On Tablet PCs and UMPCs, there's also a link to the Table PC Input Panel Options Control Panel. You'll look at this last tool later in the chapter. The Other tab is shown in Figure 18-10.

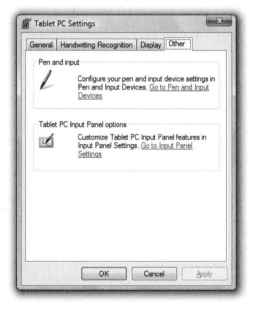

Figure 18-10: You'll find two options here only if you're using a Tablet PC.

tip   You could separately navigate to Pen and Input Settings on a Tablet PC with Start Menu Search: Open the Start Menu, type **pen and**, and then tap Enter. You can find the Tablet PC Input Panel Options elsewhere as well: Open the TIP as described later in this chapter and then choose Options from the Tools menu.

Using Pen and Input Devices Settings

The Pen and Input Devices dialog, shown in Figure 18-11, also offers a variety of tabs, each of which provides configuration options related to the stylus, or pen, you're using with the system.

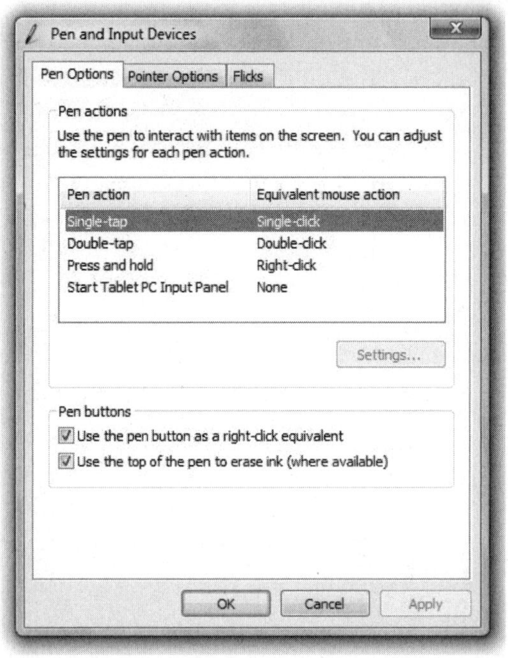

Figure 18-11: Here is where you can configure options related to your stylus and Tablet PC hardware.

The Pen Options tab enables you to configure what different pen actions and Tablet PC buttons do. By default, a single-tap is the equivalent of a single-click with a mouse button, for example; whereas a double-tap, naturally, emulates a mouse double-click. You can also configure press and hold (right-click by default, although some Tablet PC styli actually include a dedicated pen button that acts as a right-click button in conjunction with a tap) and the Start Tablet PC Input Panel button, which is found on some Tablet PCs.

In the Pointer Options tab, you can configure whether Vista's new dynamic feedback for Tablet PCs is enabled, as well as a few other pointer-related options. Dynamic feedback is an excellent bit of new functionality in Windows Vista, and it's designed to provide visual feedback whenever you perform a pen action—such as a single-tap, double-tap, pen button press, or right-click (pen button press plus a tap). Each of the visual feedback types are circular in nature, and are shown in Figure 18-12.

In the Flicks tab, you can configure various options related to Flicks, which are discussed later in the chapter. Flicks are one of the major new features in the Windows Vista version of the Tablet PC software, so hang around—I'll get to that.

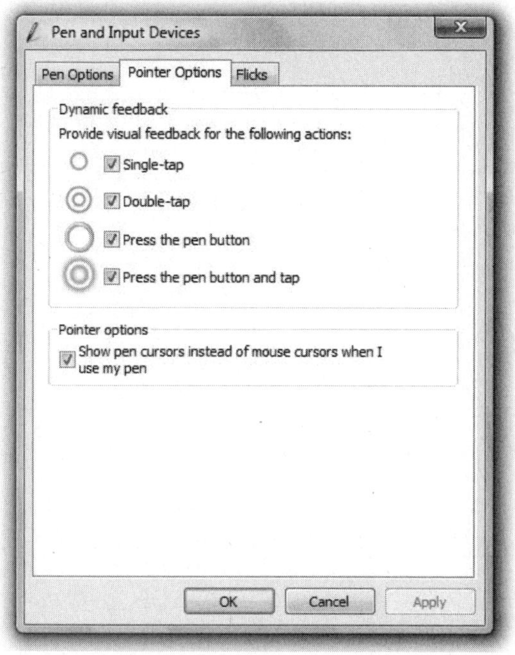

Figure 18-12: In Windows Vista, you can be sure a
pen action occurred thanks to dynamic feedback.

Secret Tablet PCs and UMPCs with a touch screen have a fourth tab in the Pen and
Input Devices dialog called Touch. Because this feature is more common on
Ultra-Mobile PCs, I examine this last option at the end of the chapter.

Tablet PC Input Panel

Back in the original version of Windows XP Tablet PC Edition, the Tablet PC Input Panel,
or TIP, was typically docked to the bottom of the screen, just above the taskbar, and you
toggled its display by clicking a TIP icon next to the Start button. In Windows XP Tablet
PC Edition 2005, Microsoft enhanced the TIP by enabling it to pop up in place, where
you needed it. That is, if you wanted to input some text into the address bar of an Internet
Explorer window, for example, you could tap the address bar with the pen and the TIP
would appear in a floating window right under the tap point. That way, you wouldn't

have to move the pen up and down across the entire screen in order to enter text or other characters.

That said, the TIP could still be manually launched by clicking that special icon next to the Start Menu; and the TIP in Windows XP Tablet PC Edition 2005 was a pretty big bugger, occupying a large swath of onscreen real estate.

These issues are now fixed in Windows Vista. Instead of a special taskbar button, the TIP is now always accessible, but mostly hidden, on the edge of the screen. As shown in Figure 18-13, only a small portion of the TIP is visible by default.

Figure 18-13: The TIP stays out of the way until you need it—really far out of the way.

If you're not even sure you're seeing the TIP, you can mouse over it (using either mouse or pen/stylus). When you do so, the TIP peeks out just a bit more, as shown in Figure 18-14.

Figure 18-14: It's not shy, per se, but the TIP needs some encouragement before it will display itself completely.

To activate the TIP, simply click it with the pen or stylus. The TIP will then appear in the center of the screen, as shown in Figure 18-15.

Figure 18-15: An activated TIP is a happy TIP.

So what does the TIP do? The TIP is designed to help you interact with applications that aren't natively Tablet PC aware. (That is, virtually every single application on the planet.) Therefore, if you want to enter a URL in the Internet Explorer address bar, search for an application in Windows Vista's Start Menu Search, or perform similar actions, the TIP does all the work. It enables your pen to work with any application.

What's nice about the TIP is that you don't really have to worry about where it is on the desktop, or whether it's enabled. Just tap a text-entry area in any application, even those not made by Microsoft, using the pen or stylus that came with your Tablet. When you do, you'll see a mini-TIP pop-up appear, as shown in Figure 18-16.

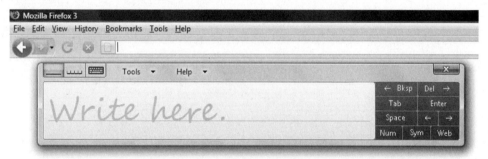

Figure 18-16: The TIP is available anytime you need it.

To see (and use) the full TIP, just tap this mini-TIP. As shown in Figure 18-17, you'll then get the full TIP, exactly where you need it.

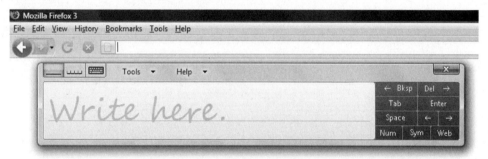

Figure 18-17: The TIP is a bridge between applications of the past and the way in which everyone will interact with computers in the future (at least according to Bill Gates).

Compared to the TIP in previous versions of Windows XP Tablet PC Edition, The Windows Vista TIP offers very similar functionality with a slightly reworked user interface. The Quick Launch icons for the Writing Pad (the default), Character Pad, and On-Screen Keyboard modes have been moved to the top of the window, next to the Tools and Help menus. The TIP's three different modes are shown in Figure 18-18.

The right side of the TIP, which includes buttons for frequently needed actions, has been dramatically simplified. If you've used a Tablet PC before, you'll have no problems using the new TIP.

Figure 18-18: The TIP can work like a continuous writing pad, a writing pad in which you enter one character at a time, or an onscreen keyboard.

Secret

In the previous version of Microsoft's Tablet PC operating system, the TIP included dedicated buttons for Web shortcuts such as http://, www., and so on. These can now be accessed through the new Web button, which expands to show these and other related options, as shown in Figure 18-19. Likewise, the Sym button expands to show various symbols (!, @, #, and so on), while the Num button expands to show numbers. The Web button expands automatically when you select the address bar in Internet Explorer 7.

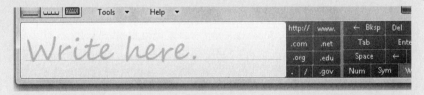

Figure 18-19: When you tap the Web button, a new menu of Web-oriented shortcuts appears.

To close the TIP (which really just returns it to its near-hidden location on the side of the screen), just tap the Close window button.

If you want to return the TIP to its previous behavior of docking at the top or bottom of the screen, click the Tools button and choose the appropriate option: Dock at Top of Screen or Dock at Bottom of Screen. The default (and new) behavior is called Float.

Be sure to spend some time meandering around the TIP's Options dialog, shown in Figure 18-20. The TIP supports an amazingly rich collection of configurable options, including such things as to which side of the screen it docks, whether it's configured for left- or right-handed users, and how the Writing Pad and Character Pad recognize handwriting (as you write, the default; or after you pause).

Figure 18-20: The TIP supports a rich array of configurable options.

Finally, while Windows Vista does enable handwriting recognition personalization by default so that the system learns your handwriting style as it goes, you could and probably should take the time to engage in a little handwriting recognition training if you think you're going to be using a pen to interact with Vista regularly. There are various ways to trigger this training, but one handy place is right in the TIP: Click Tools ➪ Personalize Handwriting to launch the Handwriting Personalization wizard, shown in Figure 18-21.

tip
As always, Start Menu Search comes to the rescue if you want to find Handwriting Personalization quickly: Just open the Start Menu, type **personalize** and tap Enter.

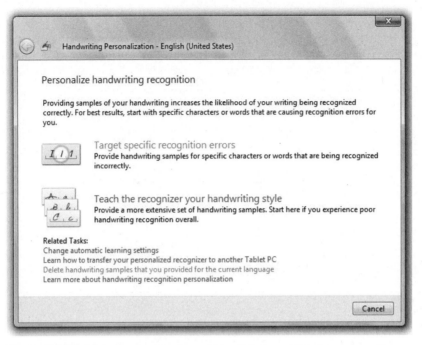

Figure 18-21: Make it your own by teaching Windows Vista how you write.

Flicks and Gestures

Flicks, called "gestures" in other pen-based systems, are special quick movements you can make with a Tablet PC stylus over the digitizer to navigate quickly or launch shortcuts for commonly needed functionality such as copy and paste. With a flick, you literally flick the pen in a certain way to cause an action.

Secret　Windows Vista also supports a related type of gesture called a Touch Flick, which enables you to perform similar actions using your finger on special touch-screen displays.

There are two types of flicks: navigational and editing. Navigational flicks include such things as scroll up, scroll down, back, and forward. Editing flicks include cut, copy, paste, delete, and undo. Flicks occur when you flick the pen in any of eight directions: up, down, left, right, and the diagonal positions between each.

You configure flicks via the Flicks tab of the Pen and Input Devices dialog (which again, can be accessed by typing **pen and** in Start Menu Search). Additionally, you will likely see a Pen flicks icon in the system tray on most Tablet PC systems, as shown in Figure 18-22. This handy icon provides quick access to current Flicks settings when clicked and offers a handy pop-up menu when right-clicked.

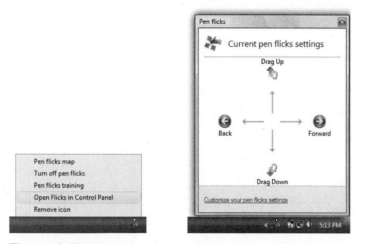

Figure 18-22: Two views of the Pen Flicks tray icon: when right-clicked (left) and clicked (right).

Returning to the Flicks tab of the Pen and Input Devices Control Panel, shown in Figure 18-23, from here you configure whether Flicks are available, what types of Flicks are available, and how sensitive the digitizer will be to recognizing Flicks.

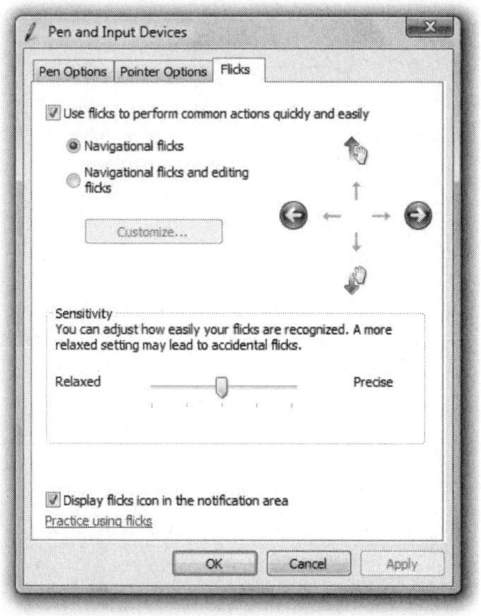

Figure 18-23: Flicks are customized via a lonely tab in an obscure dialog.

This particular feature varies according to each system, based on the sensitivity of the digitizer and pen combination.

Secret

In addition to pen sensitivity, you will see an option for touch sensitivity on this tab if your Tablet PC or UMPC includes a touch-enabled screen. This is shown in Figure 18-24.

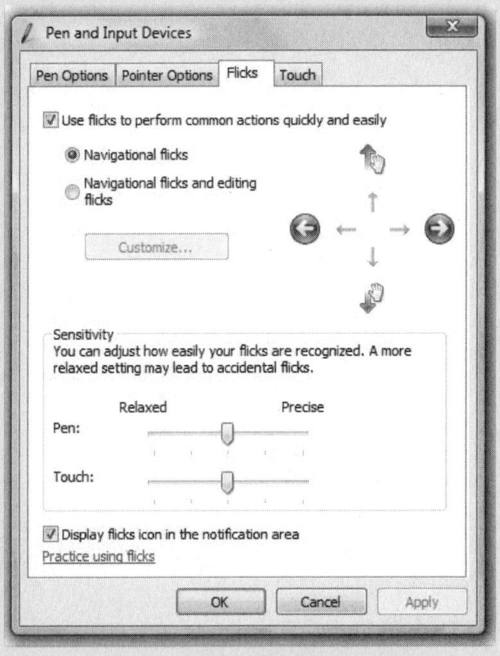

Figure 18-24: Touch-enabled screens get an additional touch sensitivity option.

By default, only navigational flicks are available where flicking left and right triggers back and forward actions, respectively, while flicking up and down enables you to scroll within documents. To enable both navigational and editing flicks and then customize the settings, select *Navigational flicks and editing flicks* and then click the Customize button. This launches the somewhat intimidating Customize Flicks dialog, shown in Figure 18-25.

The sheer number of options available to each flick can be somewhat daunting, though Microsoft does supply some commonsense defaults. To see which options are available, just click the drop-down box next to any flick, as shown in Figure 18-26.

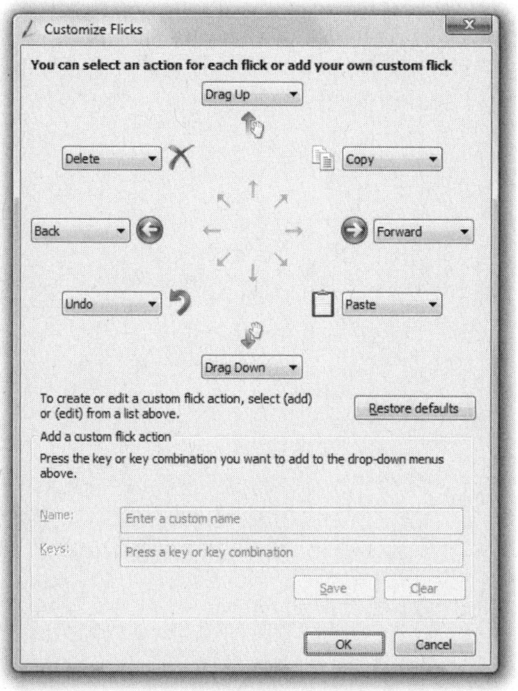

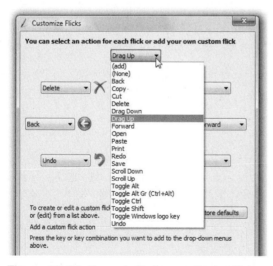

Figure 18-25: Customize Flicks enables you to specify what each of the eight possible Flicks can do.

Figure 18-26: If you do find yourself using flicks, you'll have plenty of options to pick from.

tip   The Practice Using Flicks link at the bottom of the Flicks tab of the Pen and Input
       Devices dialog provides a link to a handy Pen Flicks Training application, shown in
       Figure 18-27, that will help get you up to speed with this productivity-enhancing fea-
       ture pretty quickly.

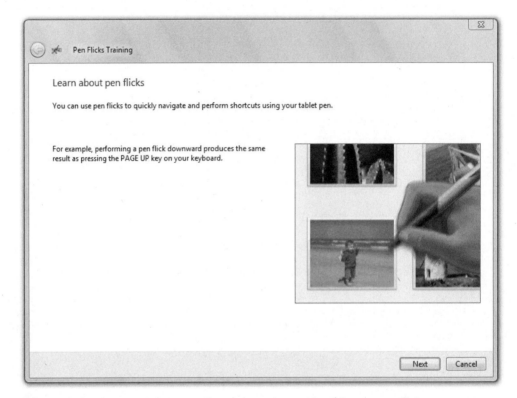

Figure 18-27: Pen Flicks Training helps you practice and learn how to use flicks.

Secret   Microsoft has supported gestures on its Windows Mobile operating system for
              quite some time, and much of the functionality you see in Flicks comes directly
              from that work.

Password Hiding on Logon with Pen

In the Windows XP Tablet PC Editions, you could log on to the PC using a stylus and the TIP in onscreen keyboard mode: All you had to do was tap your password with the stylus. The problem was that each key in the onscreen keyboard would be highlighted as you tapped, so someone looking over your shoulder could steal your password relatively easily.

In Windows Vista, Microsoft has implemented a small but important security change: As you tap the onscreen keyboard on the TIP during logon, the keys are no longer highlighted. Your password is safe—or at least as safe as it can be—from prying eyes, although it's a little disconcerting to tap the virtual keyboard and not get any feedback at all.

Secret Microsoft also uses this technique whenever you need to enter a password in a secure Web page.

-))

Secret ## Voice Control

One of the biggest promises with the original Tablet PC operating system was that Microsoft would one day extend the more natural user interaction techniques it was offering for that system with the ultimate in human/PC interaction: voice control. Successfully parodied in *Star Trek IV*, voice control has long been an unattainable goal for PC users. Today, a small fraction of the population is able to put up with the training time required to make third-party voice control systems even remotely usable; but Microsoft has been working on its speech-recognition technologies for several years now and you can see the fruit of its labors in Windows Vista.

tip That said, Windows Vista's voice control features are still passable at best. To enable speech recognition, navigate through Control Panel to Ease of Access and then Speech Recognition Options (see Figure 18-28). You need to perform several steps to make this work. First, you have to enable speech recognition. Then you have to set up your microphone for optimal performance using a simple wizard. Next, Microsoft has a nice speech tutorial and speech reference card to help you understand how the system works. Finally, there is a training wizard that you should spend some time with to make the system work better for you and your particular speech patterns.

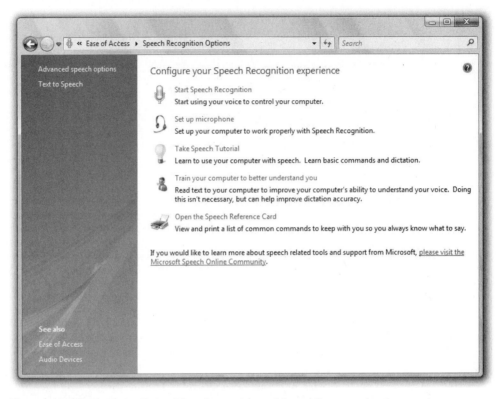

Figure 18-28: From the Control Panel, you can enable, configure, and train speech recognition so that you can control the system with your voice.

Shell Changes for Tablet PC Users

One thing you'll probably notice right away is that Windows Vista displays a new user interface element by default when it detects Tablet PC hardware on your system. It's a small check box that's available next to virtually every shell item, including the desktop's Recycle Bin and every icon in Computer and the other Explorers that appears when you move the mouse cursor over the item. (It also works in any shell view style.) In addition, it's available in the Start Menu.

Shown in Figure 18-29, this check box makes it easier to select multiple items in the shell using a pen. Otherwise, you'd have to drag a selection box around, which can be difficult with a pen.

Secret

Windows Vista users without Tablet PC hardware can turn this feature on if desired. (Conversely, Tablet PC users can turn it off.) To do so, you need to find the Folder Options dialog. (The easiest way is to use Start Menu Search, of course—just open the Start Menu and type **folder options**.) Navigate to the View tab and check the Use Check Boxes to Select Items option.

Figure 18-29: Windows Vista offers a fairly elegant way to multi-select items with a pen.

In addition to the check boxes, you'll see a few other small changes on a system with Tablet PC hardware. For example, the Welcome Center includes a link to Tablet PC training, a Pen Flicks icon appears over time in the tray notification area of the taskbar, and the Control Panel includes a top-level Mobile PC item that provides quick links to notebook and Tablet PC–based options. In addition, of course, you'll see the edge of the TIP sticking out on the left side of the screen by default, waiting for your pen to activate it.

> **tip** Oddly, many Tablet PC–oriented features are installed by default even on non-Tablet systems. You'll see entries for a number of these features and related applications throughout the Start Menu and Control Panel on normal desktop and notebook computers.

One of the more disconcerting changes that will affect most users with Tablet PC hardware is that menu items in Explorer and various applications expand to the left of the mouse cursor (see Figure 18-30), instead of to the right, as is usually the case.

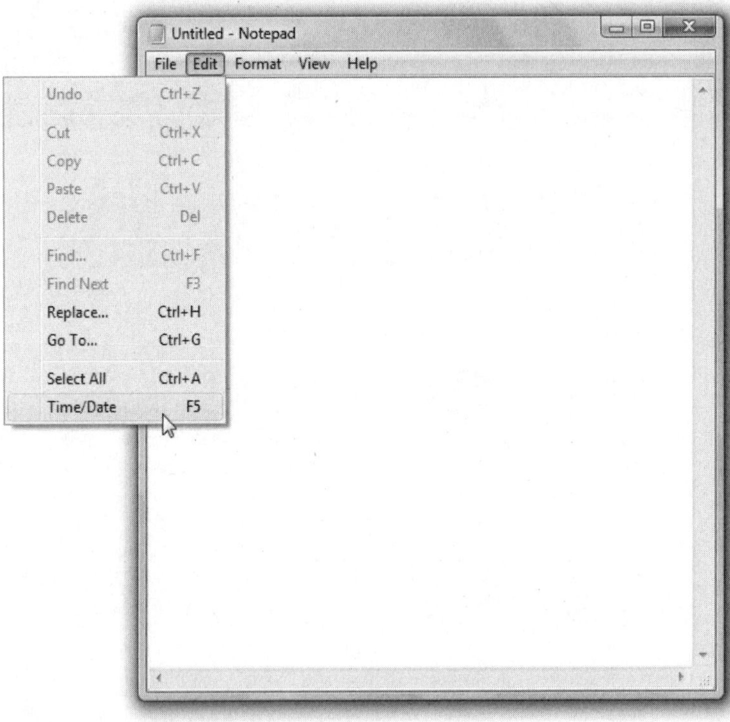

Figure 18-30: Righties will see pop-up menus on the left on Tablet PCs, which can be somewhat disconcerting.

This effect is visible only when you've configured the system's Tablet PC functionality for right-handed use. (If you configured it for left-handed use, the menus appear on the right as usual with other Vista PCs.) This is because users would otherwise cover up the menu with their hand while tapping around with the stylus. By having the menu pop up on the left, Microsoft can ensure that your hand won't cover what you need to see.

Revisiting Some Old Friends

Windows XP Tablet PC Edition was always well supported with a group of fun accessories, or mini-applications, that enable users to use the pen in fun and unexpectedly productive ways. Microsoft includes three of these accessories in Windows Vista, and they're all worth a look.

Snipping Tool

The Snipping Tool is a Windows accessory aimed at Tablet PC users that enables you to circle any area of the screen and copy the encircled image to the system clipboard. You can then paste the image into e-mail messages or any other document, and annotate it with your own handwritten notes. The Snipping Tool is particularly well suited to copying information from Web pages, but it works well with just about anything.

The Snipping Tool is launched via the Start Menu (just type **snip** or look for Snipping Tool in All Programs ⇨ Accessories). When you first launch the application, it assumes you want to grab a screen capture, or *snip*, right away; but you can cancel that operation by clicking the Cancel button. Then, you can more closely examine this useful utility's user interface and uncover its surprisingly rich feature set. The Snipping Tool is shown in Figure 18-31.

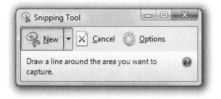

Figure 18-31: The Snipping Tool can be used to capture arbitrary parts of the screen.

If you just click the New button, the entire screen will fade, enabling you to drag the pen (or the mouse) around the screen to capture a given area, as shown in Figure 18-32; or, you can click the small arrow next to the New button to choose other capture types, including free-form snip (the default when using a pen), rectangular snip (the default when using a mouse), window snip (to capture a single window), or full-screen snip (to capture the entire screen).

Figure 18-32: While snipping the screen, the Snipping Tool fades everything so the clippers are front and center.

When you've captured a portion of the screen, or the entire screen, that image is hidden in the Windows clipboard as an image. You can then paste that image into any application that supports images, including a Word document or Microsoft Paint. The Snipping Tool also opens an edit window that enables you to save the image to disk in various image formats, send the snip via e-mail, or, more interestingly, add your own handwriting-based comments to the snip (see Figure 18-33).

Figure 18-33: The Snipping Tool enables you to annotate snips with your own handwriting and then send them via e-mail, save them to disk, or copy them to the clipboard.

note The Snipping Tool first debuted as a PowerToy for Windows XP Tablet PC Edition. Microsoft shipped an updated version of the tool in the Experience Pack for Tablet PC in 2005. You can see this heritage in the design of the applet's window buttons, which are still curiously XP-like.

Secret If you need to regularly take screenshots, the Snipping Tool is only marginally easier to use than the built-in Windows screen-capture utilities, which enable you to copy either the contents of the entire screen to the clipboard at any time by pressing PrtScn (Print Screen) or the contents of the top-most window by pressing Alt+PrtScn. If you need something more elegant than that, you should use a dedicated screen-capture utility, such as the excellent TechSmith SnagIt (www.techsmith.com/), which I use and recommend.

Windows Journal

Windows Journal is a simple note-taking application that debuted in the first version of Windows XP Tablet PC Edition. Shown in Figure 18-34, Windows Journal works only with handwriting and cannot be used to take notes with the keyboard. It remains an excellent way to get accustomed to Tablet PC usage, especially if you're a beginner.

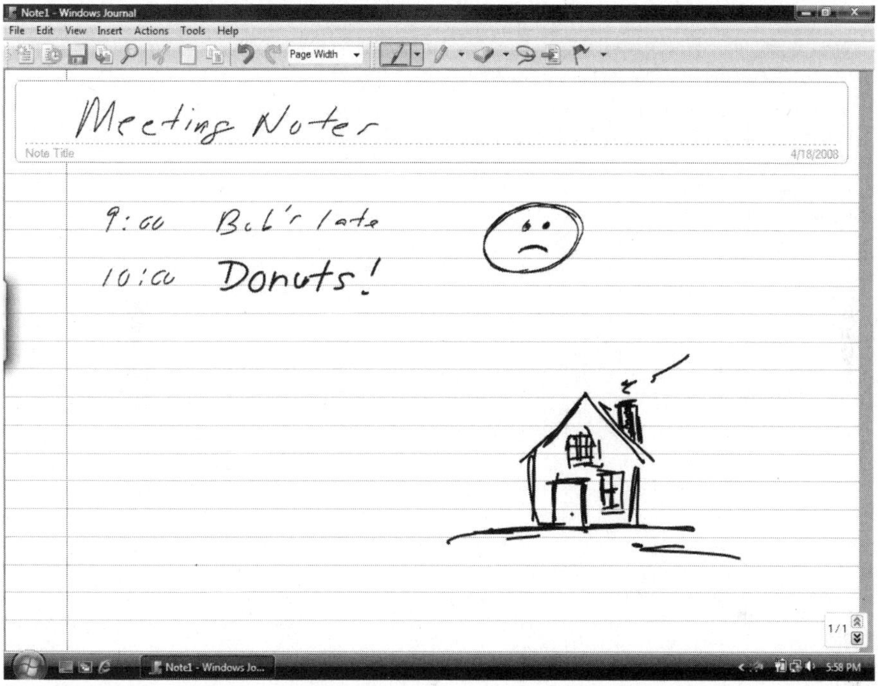

Figure 18-34: Windows Journal is designed for anyone who wants to take handwritten notes.

Windows Journal defaults to a college-ruled notebook look and feel, but you can change the style using Journal's stationery and template features. Stationery is a combination of paper size (such as 8.5″ by 11″), line style (college ruled, wide ruled, and so on), and other characteristics; or you can choose from preset templates such as Blank, Dotted Line, Memo, and others. To define the default look and feel of your notes, visit Tools ⇨ Options ⇨ Note Format.

note   Curiously, you can draw in Windows Journal using the mouse if you want, although the results are rarely inspiring.

tip   Microsoft also sells an excellent and full-featured note-taking application called OneNote, which you can purchase as part of the inexpensive Microsoft Office Home and Student Edition 2007. OneNote supports both pen- and keyboard-based note taking, as well as audio and video recording that can be synchronized with notes. It is much more sophisticated than Windows Journal and has been updated far more frequently.

Sticky Notes

Shown in Figure 18-35, Sticky Notes is a Windows Vista accessory that any user can use to create short handwritten or voice notes. The application resembles a small stack of yellow notes, just like the paper-based sticky notes they're meant to represent. Sticky Notes is designed for a Tablet PC, and indeed, you'd need such a device for the handwritten note portion, but anyone can use Sticky Notes to create voice notes.

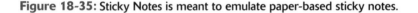

Figure 18-35: Sticky Notes is meant to emulate paper-based sticky notes.

Working with Ultra-Mobile PCs

In late 2005, Microsoft launched an online viral marketing campaign for something called Origami, which was later revealed to be part of its Ultra-Mobile PC, or UMPC, initiative. UMPCs are basically touch-screen-capable ultra-small form factor mobile computers, sort of sub-sub-notebooks that eschew traditional keyboards and pointing devices in favor of a smaller, highly portable form factor. They're larger than a PDA but smaller than the smallest slate Tablet PC, though they typically incorporate the full feature set of true Tablet PCs as well.

> **tip**
>
> Don't confuse Ultra-Mobile PCs (UMPCs) with Ultra Low-Cost PCs (ULCPs) a new generation of sub-$500 computers. Many ULCPs are notebook computers, such as the Asus EeePC or Intel Classmate, but they are not UMPCs.

Origami 1.0

The first generation of UMPC devices ran Windows XP Tablet PC Edition and was criticized for being somewhat pointless, a solution to a problem no one had; but Microsoft had a vision of a very specific portable computing experience that would utilize a seven-inch screen and weigh less than three pounds. With the first-generation UMPC, the company targeted tech enthusiasts—which helps explain the viral marketing campaign—but that proved to be a mistake. The devices sold poorly when they hit the market in early 2006.

The UMPC form factor, not surprisingly, has been at the center of some heated debates. Because it is too large to place in a typical pocket (like a smartphone or PDA), but too small to contain a usable keyboard (at least by traditional mobile PC standards), the UMPC occupies an interesting but perhaps dubious segment of the market. It's just unclear whether customers are really looking for a device that's larger than a cell phone but smaller than a subnotebook.

What Microsoft was doing with the UMPC at a software level, however, was interesting. The company had created a touch-enabled software front end to Windows XP called the Origami Experience and had configured Windows to be optimized for both the capabilities and limitations of the devices at the time. This provided customers with not only the familiar Windows user experience but also some unique capabilities that were specific to the UMPC platform. Think of it this way: Microsoft was pushing an ultra-mobile touch user interface years before Apple entered the market with the iPhone, and they'll never get any credit for it at all.

A Vista Origami

For the second go-round, Microsoft fine-tuned the software, based it on Windows Vista, and worked with a new generation of more efficient hardware. It can still be performance-challenged, thanks to the limitations of the ultra-low-voltage (ULV) processors that are typically used to power such devices, but various hardware makers and Microsoft have worked in concert to create more interesting solutions that will appeal to a wider audience. And somewhat surprisingly, UMPCs are heading to the enterprise now as well. It's a potentially compelling solution for those who need to work and connect on the go.

The primary advantage of a UMPC compared to a smartphone or PDA, of course, is that it's a real PC. It runs real Windows software, albeit somewhat slowly, and it can do so in even the most cramped situations, such as a typical airline's coach seat. The battery life is fantastic, and much better than anything I've seen from traditional business notebooks, especially if you're running typical application software. (Battery life during media playback is mediocre, in my experience.)

Compared to a Tablet PC, of course, a UMPC is much more compact and portable, which should appeal to a number of user types, including students, women, and traveling salespeople.

Thanks to a variety of innovative hardware designs, you'll see interesting keyboard and pointing device solutions. For example, the Samsung Q-series UMPCs, shown in Figure 18-36, feature an impressive and tiny smartphone-like thumb keyboard, split in half such that there are keys on each side of the screen. Holding the device with two hands, as you would naturally, the keys are right where your thumbs are, and work just like the keyboard on the smartphone you're probably already using. I wouldn't want to type an article or book chapter on that keyboard, but it's great for e-mail, Web browsing, document editing, and other light editing tasks, and is certainly much better than an onscreen virtual keyboard (which is also available courtesy of Vista's Tablet PC functionality, of course). When you're back at the office, you can plug into USB keyboards and mice, and even an external screen, and have a desktop-like experience, albeit a fairly slow one.

Figure 18-36: Some UMPCs feature innovative built-in keyboards for typing on the go.

A Tour of the UMPC Software

While the underlying operating system on a UMPC is a stock version of Windows Vista Home Premium, Business, or Ultimate with full Tablet PC capabilities enabled, Microsoft has added a number of UMPC-specific software solutions to the mix as well, and of course various PC makers also supply their own device-specific utilities. Before I get to that, however, you're probably curious what the UMPC/Vista interface looks like. As shown in Figure 18-37, it's basically Windows Vista...but on a low-resolution screen, typically 1,024 × 600 or less.

Figure 18-37: UMPCs utilize Windows Vista, so they're immediately familiar, but they generally offer lower-resolution screens than a typical portable computer.

Here are some of the software applications you can expect to see on a UMPC.

Touch Settings and Touch Options

The Touch Settings application is enabled when you're using a touch-capable screen or device such as a UMPC. Shown in Figure 18-38, it's a full-screen application that enables you to optimize and customize the touch settings on the PC.

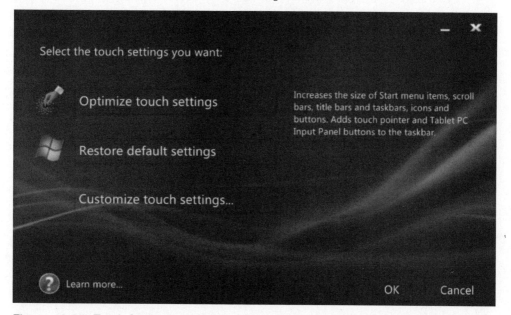

Figure 18-38: Touch Settings is a UMPC-specific application that enables you to customize the Windows Vista UI for the unique needs of the device and its touch-capable screen.

The key to using this application is skipping the first option, *Optimize touch settings,* which optimizes only a few of the possible onscreen elements. Instead, choose *Customize touch settings,* which provides you with a second screen where you can choose between a wide range of optimization settings. These include optimizing Internet Explorer; the Start Menu; scrollbars; window title bars and the taskbar; opened items; the Tablet PC Input Panel; and the Touch pointer (covered next). If you optimize enough of these settings, your system will look quite a bit different, as shown in Figure 18-39.

One of the less obvious features you can enable through Touch Settings is the touch pointer, which complements the onscreen keyboard in the TIP with an onscreen mouse. Shown in Figure 18-40, the touch pointer appears when you tap anywhere on the screen. To emulate a normal mouse click, just tap the left button of the virtual mouse. To emulate a right-click, tap the right button.

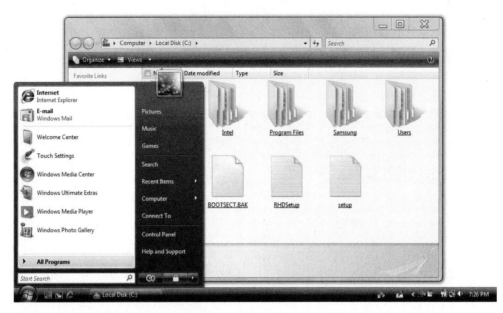

Figure 18-39: Whoa! When optimized, onscreen elements look awkward, but they're easier to tap with your fingers.

Figure 18-40: The touch pointer does for mouse clicks what the TIP does for keyboard input.

In addition to Touch Settings, note that touch-enabled PCs, like Ultra-Mobile PCs, have an extra tab, called Touch, in the Pen and Input Devices dialog that's specifically related to touch features. Shown in Figure 18-41, this tab enables you to configure whether touch settings and the touch pointer are enabled, along with various touch actions.

The Origami Experience

The Origami Experience is the poster child of the UMPC world, a unique Microsoft application that combines the simplicity and basic look and feel of Media Center with a touch-enabled interaction scheme. While it's geared primarily toward entertainment—three of the four most prominent options in the initial UI are related to music, video, and pictures—it can also be used as a straightforward program launcher. The Origami Experience is shown in Figure 18-42.

The Origami Experience interface is colorful, obvious, and easy to use. There are quick link buttons on the top for task switching (that is, Windows Flip), battery life, and wireless signal, but most of the screen is occupied by large, colorful icons that are easy to look at and, more important, easy to tap with your finger. Yes, the Origami Experience can be used with a mouse and keyboard, of course, but it's really geared for touch screens.

Figure 18-41: Touch settings are spread all over the OS, unfortunately.

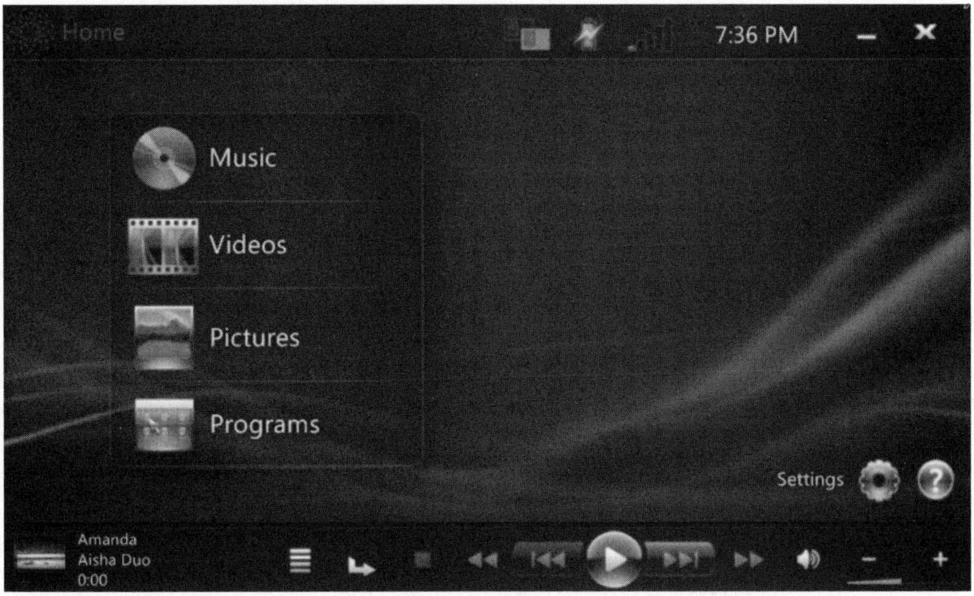

Figure 18-42: It's like Media Center Lite, perfect for small form factor PCs.

The Music experience offers nice views that include Now Playing (see Figure 18-43) and Library (see Figure 18-44), both of which sport large, finger-friendly icons and controls.

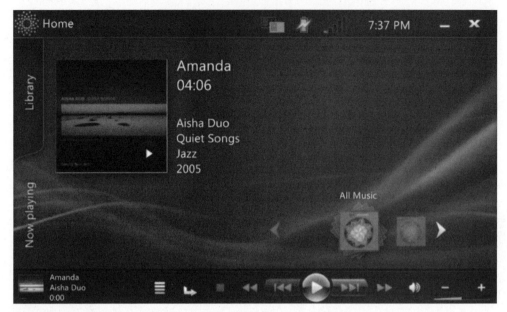

Figure 18-43: Similar to Windows Media Player, the Now Playing view offers a look at the current song.

Figure 18-44: In Library, you can easily access all of the music content stored on the device.

As you might expect, Videos and Pictures offer similar experiences, with both Now Playing and Library views in both.

Aside from music, video, and pictures, Origami provides a fourth option, Programs, which opens to reveal five subcategories: Connect, Communicate, Entertainment, More Programs, and Tools (see Figure 18-45).

Figure 18-45: The Origami Experience offers finger-based access to non-entertainment applications too.

Of course, once you launch any of the applications displayed within these groups, you're popped out of the Origami Experience. This is somewhat jarring but understandable, as Microsoft couldn't replace the entire Windows UI. That said, there are some inconsistencies: The Sudoku game (see Figure 18-46) appears within Origami Experience but not in the Vista Games Explorer for some reason—despite the fact that Sudoku is a standalone game that does not run from within the Origami Experience.

Microsoft says that the Origami Experience isn't just about a new user interface or enabling touch access to most operating system functions. Instead, this environment is optimized for what the company calls *quick interactions*. This is different from the typical Windows user interface paradigm, where you're typically multi-tasking and getting a number of things done in tandem. In the Origami Experience, the expectation is that you're typically doing just one thing, or performing a single task while also playing music. It's a new interaction method that's essentially single-tasked by design. This makes sense both for the devices that will typically run this system and for the limitations of the underlying hardware.

Another way to view the Origami Experience is via a consumption/management perspective. For example, you won't manage your music collection or import CDs to the hard drive from within the Origami Experience. Instead, you continue using Windows Media Player (or Windows Media Center) for those tasks; but the Origami Experience is a very simple UI for *consuming* content, such as music. In this way, it's very much like the first version of Media Center, which, since then, has evolved to include some management and acquisition functionality, as discussed in Chapter 15.

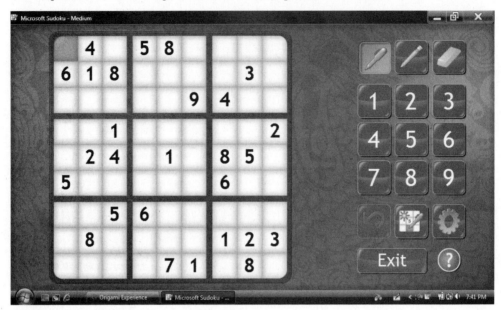

Figure 18-46: Sudoku, a cool touch-enabled game.

Dial Keys

Microsoft's take on the virtual keyboard for Ultra-Mobile PCs is called Dial Keys (see Figure 18-47). Dial Keys utilizes two crescent-shaped virtual half-keyboards that appear in the lower-left and lower-right corners of the screen. (The standard Tablet PC-style virtual keyboard is also available, of course.)

The idea here is that you'll be holding a (typically) keyboardless UMPC in your hands and these two half-keyboard crescents will appear where your hands are, providing easy access to typical capabilities. In real-world use, feedback on this feature has been mixed according to Microsoft. Some users absolutely love it, while others prefer the tactile feel of a real keyboard. For this reason, many UMPC makers are building small keyboards directly into their devices as well.

Touch-Enabled Games and Entertainment Applications

Most UMPCs ship with a selection of Tablet- and touch-enabled games such as InkBall and Sudoku. There's also a version of Microsoft Reader, the company's eBook reader, shown in Figure 18-48, which is designed specifically for Ultra-Mobile PCs. This version of Reader is particularly nice and stretches the width of the page across the entire screen.

Figure 18-47: Dial Keys is the new onscreen virtual keyboard designed especially for UMPC devices.

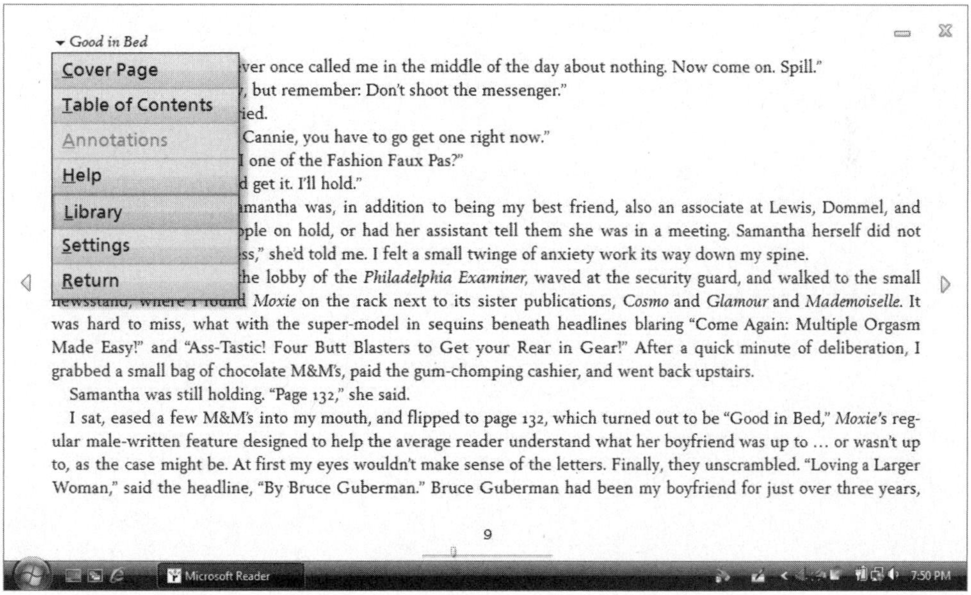

▾ *Good in Bed*

Cover Page

Table of Contents

Annotations

Help

Library

Settings

Return

...ver once called me in the middle of the day about nothing. Now come on. Spill."

..., but remember: Don't shoot the messenger."

...ied.

...Cannie, you have to go get one right now."

...I one of the Fashion Faux Pas?"

...d get it. I'll hold."

...mantha was, in addition to being my best friend, also an associate at Lewis, Dommel, and ...ple on hold, or had her assistant tell them she was in a meeting. Samantha herself did not ...ss," she'd told me. I felt a small twinge of anxiety work its way down my spine.

...he lobby of the *Philadelphia Examiner*, waved at the security guard, and walked to the small newsstand, where I found *Moxie* on the rack next to its sister publications, *Cosmo* and *Glamour* and *Mademoiselle*. It was hard to miss, what with the super-model in sequins beneath headlines blaring "Come Again: Multiple Orgasm Made Easy!" and "Ass-Tastic! Four Butt Blasters to Get your Rear in Gear!" After a quick minute of deliberation, I grabbed a small bag of chocolate M&M's, paid the gum-chomping cashier, and went back upstairs.

Samantha was still holding. "Page 132," she said.

I sat, eased a few M&M's into my mouth, and flipped to page 132, which turned out to be "Good in Bed," *Moxie*'s regular male-written feature designed to help the average reader understand what her boyfriend was up to ... or wasn't up to, as the case might be. At first my eyes wouldn't make sense of the letters. Finally, they unscrambled. "Loving a Larger Woman," said the headline, "By Bruce Guberman." Bruce Guberman had been my boyfriend for just over three years,

9

Microsoft Reader

Figure 18-48: Microsoft Reader, enhanced specifically for the UMPC.

Summary

As with Windows Media Center, Microsoft has taken the Tablet PC functionality it developed during the lifetime of Windows XP, enhanced it, and made it available to far more users in Windows Vista. Whether you have a traditional Tablet PC, a convertible laptop, a PC with a touch-based screen, an Ultra-Mobile PC (UMPC), or even a normal desktop or notebook computer, there's a Tablet PC feature in Windows Vista that's sure to delight. It is hoped that as this technology goes more mainstream, more people will become comfortable with this alternative form of computer interaction that could yet change the world.

Part VI

Internet and Networking

Browsing the Web

Chapter
19

In This Chapter

Understanding the new Internet Explorer 7 user interface

Working with tabbed browsing and Quick Tabs

Searching the Internet

Optimizing the Internet Explorer 7 display

Printing information you find on the Web

Become more efficient with Internet Explorer 7's keyboard shortcuts

Discovering and mastering the new RSS features

Looking to the future with Internet Explorer 8

Understanding your Web browser alternatives

W indows Vista features a brand-new and much-improved version of the Internet Explorer Web browser called Internet Explorer 7. As with previous Windows versions, Internet Explorer 7 is integrated into Windows Vista, although Microsoft offers a free download of Internet Explorer 7 for Windows XP as well. However, here's one reason to upgrade to Windows Vista: The version of Internet Explorer 7 found in Microsoft's latest operating system is actually much more secure than the XP version and even offers a few unique features. This chapter examines Internet Explorer 7; a new freely downloadable upgrade called Internet Explorer 8; and some Web browser alternatives you may want to use instead.

What Happened

To say that Internet Explorer has an ignoble history is perhaps an understatement. Originally conceived as a minor add-on for Windows 95 and one that did not ship in the initial version of that Windows release, Internet Explorer later became the linchpin of Microsoft's strategy for competing in the dot-com era, and, not surprisingly, the subject of antitrust legal battles that continue to this day.

The problem, legally and technically, is that Microsoft *integrated* Internet Explorer directly into Windows. This intermingling of Windows and Internet Explorer code began with Windows 98, and Microsoft designed the system in such a way that Internet Explorer could not be easily removed from the operating system. Integrating its immature Web browser with Windows led to years and years of security problems. Some of these were so severe that Microsoft was eventually forced to delay the release of Windows Vista simply so that it could ensure that its Internet Explorer–riddled operating systems were shored up with additional defenses.

Worst of all, after Microsoft won the browser wars in the early 2000s, displacing competitors such as Netscape and Opera, the company lost interest in Internet Explorer and stopped active development of the browser. It even briefly considered removing Internet Explorer from Windows Vista altogether, relegating its Web browsing duties to the Explorer shell, which as you probably know is simply based on Internet Explorer code anyway.

Then a wonderful thing happened. A scrappy group of upstarts from The Mozilla Foundation (since renamed to The Mozilla Corporation) took the vestiges of the software code from Netscape's browser and reconstituted it as a small, lean, and powerful browser named Firefox. Roaring out of the gate in 2004, Firefox quickly began seizing market share from Internet Explorer, thanks to its unique new features and functionality. Suddenly, Microsoft was interested in updating Internet Explorer again. It's amazing what a little competition can do.

Starting with the Service Pack 2 (SP2) version of Windows XP, Microsoft reestablished its Internet Explorer team and began working actively on new features. Although the version of Internet Explorer 6 that appeared in Windows XP SP2 was focused largely on security, a future version, Internet Explorer 7, would include a huge number of functional improvements, aimed at closing the gap with Firefox and giving Microsoft's customers reasons not to switch. For the first time in several years, Internet Explorer is a compelling Web browser again, and it's likely that many Windows Vista users will want to use this product to browse the Web and access other Web-based content.

Secret

Truth be told, I still use, prefer, and recommend Mozilla Firefox over Internet Explorer, although the latest Internet Explorer versions do indeed include a number of new and interesting features that should satisy the needs of most users. I examine Mozilla Firefox later in this chapter.

Basic Internet Explorer Usage

Although it's unlikely that *Windows Vista Secrets* readers are unaware of basic Internet Explorer features, many of you may have moved along to Mozilla Firefox or other browsers over the past few years. If that's the case, this section will serve as a nice refresher.

Starting Internet Explorer

Click the Internet Explorer icon at the top of the Start Menu to start Internet Explorer, which is shown in Figure 19-1. You can also start Internet Explorer by clicking the Internet Explorer icon in the Quick Start toolbar, which is visible by default in Windows Vista.

Figure 19-1: Internet Explorer 7.

Secret

In previous versions of Windows you could type a Web address (i.e, URL) in the address bar of any Explorer window and press Enter to change the Explorer window into an instance of Internet Explorer. This no longer works the same way in Windows Vista: Now, when you type a Web address into an Explorer address bar and press Enter, a new Internet Explorer window opens.

Secret

Depending on which version of Windows Vista you're using, you will see two or three different icons for Internet Explorer in the Start Menu hierarchy. In 32-bit versions of Vista, you will see two icons: one simply labeled *Internet Explorer* and the other named *Internet Explorer (No Add-ons)*. I explain the differences between these versions later in this chapter. Users of 64-bit/x64 versions of Windows Vista will see a third Internet Explorer icon. This version, *Internet Explorer 64-bit*, is a true 64-bit version of Microsoft's browser. However, it is not the Internet Explorer version you will typically use because the default 32-bit version is more compatible with the wide range of browser add-ons available online. There is no functional advantage to using the 64-bit version of Internet Explorer, but because of the add-on compatibility issues, there are some functional disadvantages.

New Link, New Window...or New Tab

If you want to open a new window when you jump to a new site, hold down the Shift key when you click the link. (If you prefer, you can right-click the link and then click Open In New Window to do the same thing without using the keyboard.) You'll then be able to see both the target site and the source page in different Internet Explorer windows. You can also choose to use Internet Explorer's new tabbed browsing feature instead, which is described in more detail later in the chapter, but you can open links in a new tab by holding down the Ctrl key while clicking the link. (Alternately, you can right-click the link and select Open In New Tab.)

Managing Downloads from the Internet

Like previous versions of Internet Explorer, Internet Explorer 7 does not provide a download manager. Instead, it provides only basic functions for downloading files from Internet servers. Each time you click a link to download a file with Internet Explorer, you get a new download dialog.

Secret

Given this limitation, it will come as no surprise that a variety of enterprising developers have created download managers for Internet Explorer. My favorite comes with a free add-on called IE 7 Pro (www.ie7pro.com).

Edit on the Internet Explorer Toolbar

Unlike previous Internet Explorer versions, Internet Explorer 7 doesn't include an Edit button on its command bar by default. (This button is used to open the current page in your text or HTML editor of choice.) If you don't see the Edit button and wish you did, here's how to get it back:

1. Click the Tools button in the Internet Explorer toolbar, which Microsoft has renamed the command bar.
2. Select Toolbars ⇨ Customize.
3. In the Customize Toolbar dialog, shown in Figure 19-2, select Edit from the Available Toolbar Buttons field on the left and then click the Add button.

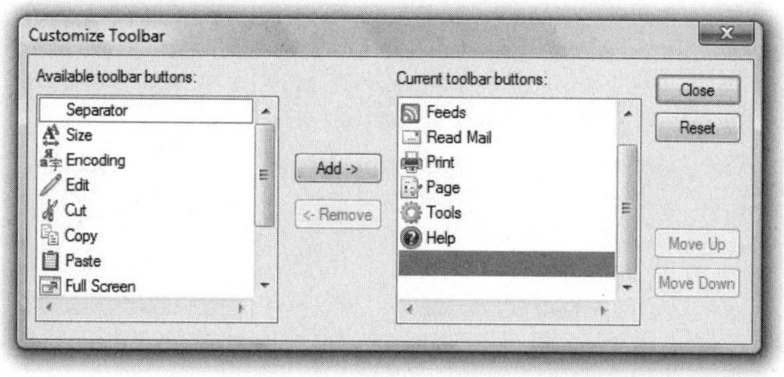

Figure 19-2: You can customize which buttons Internet Explorer displays in its command bar.

4. Click Close.

Secret

This might be a good time to customize the command bar regardless of your interest in the Edit button. You will most likely see a few buttons you'll never use—Research comes to mind—and a few to which you might like ready access (such as Read Mail and Size).

The Complete AutoComplete

Internet Explorer has an autocomplete feature that helps you complete your entry in the address bar as soon as you type in the first few letters. For example, type **www.appl**, pause for a few seconds, and you'll get a drop-down list of sites you have previously visited that start with **www.appl**, including **www.apple.com/**, as shown in Figure 19-3. Even if a long list of URLs that start with the same letters that you've typed appears, you can easily use your mouse or arrow keys to scroll to and highlight an entry in the list, and then press Enter or Tab to jump to the site. This feature works much like Start Menu Search.

Figure 19-3: Internet Explorer's address bar includes autocomplete functionality.

If you press Alt+D to select the address bar and then Alt+down arrow (or F4) when the address bar is active, Internet Explorer displays a drop-down list of complete addresses you've recently typed in the address bar. This is a totally different list from the autocomplete drop-down list; it is the same list that appears when you click the down arrow at the right end of the address bar (see Figure 19-4).

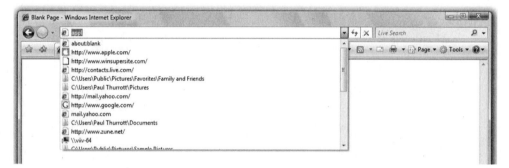

Figure 19-4: You can also view all of the Web addresses you've recently accessed.

To enable or disable autocomplete, choose Tools ➪ Internet Options, click the Content tab, and click the Settings button in the AutoComplete section. In the AutoComplete Settings dialog, you can choose whether to use AutoComplete for Web addresses, forms, or user names and passwords.

> **tip**
>
> You can save time when typing Web addresses by having Internet Explorer automatically preface your entry with **www.** and end it with the suffix **.com**. Just type the domain name in the address bar and then select Ctrl+Enter. For example, type **windowssecrets**, select Ctrl+Enter, and you get www.WindowsSecrets.com. This is different from actually searching on the Internet for the address; see the "Autosearch for a Web Address" section later in this chapter for more information.

Finding Web Sites

Want to find a specific Web site, or text from a specific Web page? In an Internet Explorer window, click the address bar, type **find**, **search**, or **?**, type a space, and then type the name of the company or organization whose site you want to find. If the name has a space in it, forget typing the **find**, **search**, or **?**, and just put double quote marks around the name. You can also just type in any word to initiate the search function.

This automatically starts a search for the company, word in a Web page, or organization on Live.com.

Autosearch for a Web Address

Internet Explorer will automatically search on the Internet for a Web address if you ask it to. Type a fragment of an address in the address bar and press Enter, and Internet Explorer will treat the fragment as a search term. After a minute or two, you'll see a list of URLs containing the text you typed.

You can choose to turn this feature off or change how it functions by taking these steps:

1. Click Tools ➪ Internet Options.
2. Click the Advanced tab and scroll down to Search from the Address Bar.
3. Select the option that you prefer—Do Not Search from the Address Bar or Just Display the Results in the Main Window (the default)—and then click OK.

> **tip** It isn't the default, so you might miss it: Internet Explorer will not put in placeholder borders for images yet to be downloaded. If you want this feature turned on so that the text can wrap around the images as yet unseen, you can turn it on in the Internet Options dialog. Choose Tools ➪ Internet Options, click the Advanced tab, and scroll down to Multimedia. Mark the Show Image Download Placeholders check box, and then click OK.

Copy and Paste Links

Wherever there's a hot link, there's a way to cut and paste it. If you receive an e-mail message in Windows Mail that contains a link, you can, of course, just click it to invoke an Internet Explorer window (if it's a link to a Web site or an FTP address).

You can right-click a link and click Copy Shortcut, and then paste this URL into the address bar, into a text file, onto the Desktop—whatever you like. You can also click Add to Favorites instead of Copy Shortcut.

Right-click a Web page name in your History Explorer bar, and you can click Copy or Add to Favorites. You can do the same with a Web page name in search results displayed in the Search Explorer bar.

Toggling Internet Explorer between Full-Screen Mode and Restore

Open Internet Explorer and tap the F11 key. If you weren't before, you are now in full-screen mode. If you were maximized before, pressing F11 again will get you back there. Full-screen mode, shown in Figure 19-5, covers even the taskbar, and features an autohide main toolbar.

Figure 19-5: IE's full-screen mode.

Secret

If you want the main toolbar to always appear while in full-screen mode, right-click the small black area below the Minimize, Restore, and Close window buttons and uncheck Auto-Hide from the menu that appears.

Favorites and Offline Web Pages

A URL (Uniform Resource Locator) is a unique identifier for a Web page or other resource on the Internet. Windows maintains a list of URLs for your favorite sites. Your *favorites* are actually shortcuts stored in the Favorites folder. They're accessed from the traditional Favorites menu—which is hidden by default in the Windows Vista version of Internet Explorer 7—or via the new Favorites Center, described later in this chapter.

You can store whatever you like in the Favorites subfolders, but I suggest limiting what you put in these folders to shortcuts (either to URLs or to other folders or documents). You can put copies of URL shortcuts on your Desktop and start your Internet Explorer by clicking a shortcut's icon.

To create a shortcut to your favorites, open an Explorer window and navigate to Favorites in your Home folder. Right-drag and drop your Favorites folder onto your Desktop. Choose Create Shortcut(s) Here.

Secret

If you use multiple PCs, managing different Favorites lists on each of your PCs might be a bit of a hassle. Microsoft has a solution, albeit it in a non-obvious place. Its Windows Live Toolbar includes a feature that enables you to aggregate your favorites in an online storage area. That way, you can access all of your favorites from any PC, as long as you've installed this toolbar in Internet Explorer. You can find out more about this toolbar in Chapter 21.

URL Shortcuts

Internet Explorer keeps track of Web sites using shortcuts to URLs. These shortcuts have an extension of **url** instead of the standard **lnk** extension for Windows shortcuts.

URL shortcuts store more information about the URLs than just their name and location values. Internet Explorer uses this additional information to help you manage your short-cuts and view Web sites offline. You can see this information by right-clicking a URL shortcut in Windows Explorer and choosing Properties.

You can create a URL shortcut to a Web site just by displaying the site in an Internet Explorer window and clicking the new Add to Favorites button.

If you would rather put the shortcut directly on the Desktop, right-click an area on the Web page that doesn't include a graphic or a link to another location and choose Create Shortcut from the context menu. You can also drag the icon at the left end of the address bar to the Desktop to create a shortcut to the Web page.

tip

To create a shortcut to a link (a jump to another URL) in a Web page, drag the link to the Desktop. You can later click this shortcut to open an Internet Explorer window and go to the indicated location on the Web.

tip

You don't have to put URL shortcuts in the Favorites folder or one of its subfolders. If you do, then the shortcuts are accessible from the Favorites Center, but you are free to put them wherever you like. You can create many folders of URL shortcuts, and place shortcuts to these folders on your Desktop.

Saving Graphics from the Web to Your PC

If you want to save a Web-based graphic that you are viewing in Internet Explorer, right-click it, choose Save Picture As (sometimes you will see Save Background As, as well), and then give it a path and a name. If you don't save a graphics file as you're viewing it, you can save it later from the cache. When Internet Explorer first downloads a graphics file, it automatically caches (saves) it in the Temporary Internet Files folder. You can find the file in this folder and save it permanently by copying it to another location.

If you want to turn a graphic in a Web page into wallpaper on your desktop, right-click the graphic and choose Set As Wallpaper.

Saving Complete Web Pages

Saving a Web page as an HTML file in Internet Explorer usually saves only the text and layout of the page—the graphics are saved separately as links. However, Internet Explorer does have the ability to save a Web page as a single document. The MIME HTML (**.mht**) file format incorporates both the graphics and the HTML text on a Web page into one file. The graphics are encoded using MIME (and Uuencoding), so everything is stored in e-mail-capable, 7-bit ASCII text characters, but Internet Explorer can decode the file on-the-fly and display the graphics.

This feature greatly expands the power of the Internet. If a document is displayed as one Web page, you can download it and all of its associated graphic files, and save everything in one very convenient document. If you do this, then you don't have to save the document as an offline page to keep it readily available.

There's only one problem with MHT-style Web archives: They only work with Internet Explorer. If you choose to utilize an alternative Web browser such as Mozilla Firefox, MHT files will continue to open in Internet Explorer.

To save a Web page in this format, merely tap the Alt key to enable the Internet Explorer menu and then click File ➪ Save As, and choose Web Archive, Single File in the Save As Type field. This secret isn't hidden, but it sure is powerful. It turns the Web into something that you can actually use as a publishing arena.

You can see the entire underlying text file if you open a file with an mht extension in WordPad. If you click View ➪ Source in Internet Explorer when viewing an mht file, you'll only see the HTML code and not the encoded graphics that are in fact there in the file.

Internet Explorer also enables you to save a document as a complete Web page (click File ⇨ Save As, and choose Web Page ⇨ Complete in the Save As Type field). In this case, the graphic files are not included in the HTML source text. Instead, Internet Explorer creates a subfolder in which it saves the downloaded graphics files. It rewrites the saved Web page to reference the graphics files in this subfolder, and enters the Web page's URL as a comment at the top of the page. These types of documents will typically open fine in other browsers, including Firefox. Indeed, Firefox uses a similar mechanism for saving "complete" Web pages.

Finally, you can also save Web pages as a Webpage type, which includes only the text of the page along with links to the online graphics. If you choose this option and view a saved page while offline, you'll see just the text. However, if you are online, the graphics will load as normal.

Turning Your Favorites into a Web Page

The Favorites menu and submenus are fine for starters, but sometimes it is a bit of a drag to search repeatedly through all these menus. How about creating a single Web page of all your favorites? Or separate Web pages for different subsets of favorites?

Internet Explorer includes the Import/Export Wizard, which can export your favorites or cookies. It writes them to your disk in a format that Netscape, Mozilla Firefox, and other browsers can read. You can also use the wizard to import cookies and favorites from other browsers. The wizard writes out your favorites as an HTML file, which makes it easy to look through your favorites with Notepad and edit them if you like. You can also use the HTML file as a page in Internet Explorer, from which you can easily jump to any site on your list.

Choose File ⇨ Import and Export to run the Import/Export Wizard. As shown in Figure 19-6, this wizard offers a number of interesting functions, including the aforementioned capability to export Favorites. It's also been updated to support unique Internet Explorer 7 features discussed in the next section.

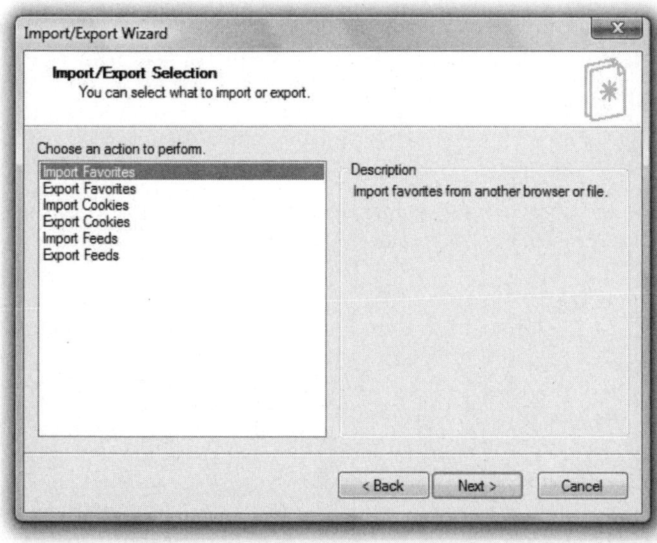

Figure 19-6: The Import/Export Wizard is a vital tool for moving between different Web browsers.

Internet Explorer 7 Is Not Your Father's Web Browser

If you're familiar with Internet Explorer 6 or previous Internet Explorer versions, you might be in for a shock when you first start Internet Explorer 7: Gone is the simplicity of the Internet Explorer you know, replaced with a more complicated user interface that mimics the look and feel of the Windows Explorer shell while providing ever-larger areas of onscreen real estate for all its new features. Shown in Figure 19-7, Internet Explorer 7 is quite a bit busier-looking than its predecessors, especially when you enable the Classic Menu.

Figure 19-7: Something old, something new: Internet Explorer 7 is clearly a new Internet Explorer, but you may find it difficult to find features you were used to.

What has changed in the Internet Explorer 7 user interface? First, the menu bar is hidden and renamed to Classic Menu, similar to what happened with the menu bar in the Explorer shell and many other Windows Vista applications. Microsoft says that it disabled the Classic Menu to reduce the clutter, but I think you'll agree that the Internet Explorer 7 user interface is still quite a bit more cluttered than that of Internet Explorer 6.

> **tip**
> If you don't like this design decision, you can temporarily cause the Internet Explorer 7 Classic Menu to appear by pressing the Alt key once. Alternately, you can simply click the new Tools Command Bar icon and select Toolbars ⇨ Classic Menus to enable this menu all the time. This is how Internet Explorer 7 is configured in Windows XP.

Various user interface elements have also been moved around to conform to the new Windows Vista common user interface style. The Back and Forward buttons are prominently featured in the upper-left corner of the window next to the top-mounted address bar, for example. The main toolbar, now called the *command bar*, is now located way over to the far right of the window, causing the Home button to be located quite far from its previous location, which is sure to frustrate those who have committed the location of this commonly needed button to memory.

tip	You can easily resize the command bar if you want in order to see all of its buttons. First, ensure that the toolbars are not locked by navigating to Tools ➪ Toolbars and unchecking Lock the Toolbars (this option is unchecked by default). Then, you can drag the command bar left and right to resize it. If you make the command bar too short, a double chevron will appear at the right, indicating that you can reach the rest of its options via a drop-down menu, as shown in Figure 19-8.

Figure 19-8: Hidden command bar options can be accessed via this handy drop-down menu.

The Command Bar

Love it or hate it, the new command bar houses some of Internet Explorer's most commonly needed functionality. Table 19-1 explores the options you'll see, from left to right, in this toolbar. All of these features are described in more detail later in this chapter.

Table 19-1: Default Internet Explorer 7 Command Bar Buttons

Command Bar Button	What It Does
Home	Navigates the browser back to your home page (or home pages, as the case may be). This button includes an optional drop-down menu as well, which enables you to change your home page(s) and add and remove home page(s).
Feeds	Provides a handy front end to the new support of RSS feeds in Internet Explorer
Print	Provides printing facilities that are dramatically improved compared to previous Internet Explorer versions

continues

Table 19-1: (continued)

Command Bar Button	What It Does
Page	This button launches a drop-down menu that provides access to options related to Web pages, such as zoom and text size.
Tools	This button launches a drop-down menu that provides access to options related to the Web browser itself, including security feature configuration, Internet options, and which toolbars are displayed. Tools is similar to the Tools menu in the Classic Menu, but lacks certain options, such as Windows Update.
Help	This button launches a drop-down menu that is similar to the Help menu item in the Classic Menu.

As discussed earlier in this chapter, you can also customize which buttons appear in the Internet Explorer 7 command bar.

Table 19-2 summarizes the optional buttons you can add to the Internet Explorer 7 command bar. You can also add one or more *separators*, which visually separate command bar buttons. Most of these features are described later in this chapter.

Table 19-2: Optional Internet Explorer 7 Command Bar Buttons

Command Bar Button	What It Does
Size	Toggles the font size of the text in the current browser window between preset sizes, including Largest, Larger, Medium (the default), Smaller, and Smallest
Read Mail	Adds a button to launch Windows Mail, or your default e-mail application
Encoding	Provides a drop-down menu that enables you to select from the various language and locale display modes that are available on your system. Typically, you will leave this at its default value, Unicode (UTF-8), unless you are browsing the Web in an area of the world that uses right-to-left text or other text encoding methods.
Edit	Opens the currently displayed Web page in your default Web page editor application
Cut	Cuts the currently selected text from the address bar and places it on the Windows clipboard
Copy	Copies the currently selected text from the address bar or Web page and places it on the Windows clipboard
Paste	Pastes the contents of the Windows clipboard at the cursor position
Full Screen	Toggles the Internet Explorer 7 Full-Screen mode.

> tip
>
> If you install software that adds a button to the Internet Explorer toolbar, that button will be added to the right side of the command bar now. For example, Windows Live Messenger installs a Messenger button, and Microsoft Office (2003 and newer) installs a Research button (and, if you've installed OneNote, a Send to OneNote button). You might see other similar buttons, depending on which software you've installed. Likewise, if you upgrade from Windows XP to Windows Vista, any buttons that were added to Internet Explorer 6 will show up in the Internet Explorer 7 command bar. You can remove these buttons via the Customize Toolbar dialog described previously.

Where Is It Now?

Hundreds of millions of people accustomed to Internet Explorer 6 may be asking this question. Despite IE's widespread use, Microsoft made some startling changes to the way Internet Explorer 7 works. With that in mind, Table 19-3 should help Internet Explorer 6–savvy users find their way around the new interface.

Table 19-3: Where Common Internet Explorer Features Moved in Internet Explorer 7

Feature	Where It Is Now
File menu	Now called the Classic Menu and hidden by default. Press the Alt key to display this menu.
Back button	Now located in the upper-left corner of the browser window
Forward button	Now located in the upper-left corner of the browser window to the right of the Back button
Stop button	Moved to the right of the Refresh button
Refresh button	Moved to the right of the address bar
Home button	Moved to the command bar
Search button	Replaced by a new Search box found in the top-right of the browser window
Favorites button	Replaced by the Favorites Center. The icon for Favorites Center is a yellow star and is found below the Back button.
History button	Missing in action. You can access the browser history by displaying the Favorites Center, however.
Mail button	Replaced by the optional Read Mail command bar button and the Send This Page option on the Page button's pull-down menu
Print button	Now located in the command bar
Edit button	Missing in action. To edit a Web page, enable the Classic Menu by pressing Alt and then choose Edit from the File menu.

continues

Table 19-3: *(continued)*

Feature	Where It Is Now
Go button	Missing in action. To load a Web page whose address you've typed into the address bar, simply press Enter.
Status icon ("throbber")	In previous versions of Internet Explorer, an Internet Explorer E logo or Windows logo in the upper-right corner of the browser indicated progress while a Web page was loading. In Internet Explorer 7, this has been replaced by a standard progress bar, which is located in the middle of the status bar at the bottom of the browser window.
Address bar	Now located in the top row of controls in the browser window to the right of the Forward button
Information bar	Hidden by default, but still located at the top of the Web page display area
Status bar	Still located at the bottom of the browser window. The status bar in Internet Explorer 7 behaves similarly to the status bar in previous Internet Explorer versions.

New Internet Explorer 7 Features and Functionality

After you get over the new look of Internet Explorer you will discover that Microsoft has added a lot of new functionality to this release. Indeed, Internet Explorer is arguably the most dramatic upgrade in the history of Microsoft's Web browser. This section covers the biggest changes.

Managing Your Favorite Web Sites with Favorites Center

In previous versions of Internet Explorer, the Favorites folder provided a place in the system where you could save links, or shortcuts, to your favorite Web sites. Favorites were typically accessed in Internet Explorer via the Favorites menu. This tradition has changed somewhat in Internet Explorer 7. Now, Favorites are more easily and obviously accessed via a new Favorites Center, which is basically an Explorer bar that can be triggered to appear on the left side of the browser window. You trigger the Favorites Center, shown in Figure 19-9, by clicking the yellow star icon.

tip   The Favorites menu still exists in Internet Explorer 7, but you have to display (or permanently enable) the Classic Menu in order to see it. To do so, tap the Alt key and choose Favorites.

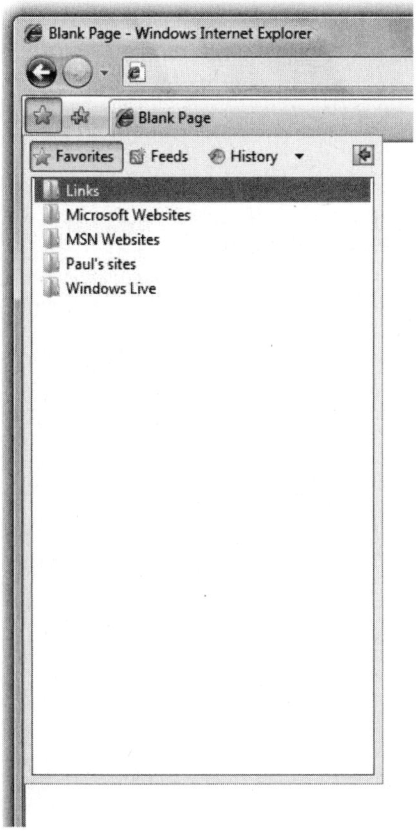

Figure 19-9: The new Favorites Center provides a holding pen for your Favorites, browser history, and subscribed RSS feeds.

By default, the Favorites Center appears in Favorites view, which displays your favorite Web sites in a menu-like list; but don't be concerned that Microsoft simply duplicated the functionality of the old Favorites menu and moved it to a new location in order to fool you. The Favorites Center includes far more functionality than the old Favorites menu.

> **tip** The Favorites Center appears as a floating panel of sorts by default, but you can attach, or pin, it to the browser window by clicking the Pin button, which looks like a small door with a green arrow on it. Curiously, to close the Favorites Center when pinned, you need to click the Close Favorites Center button, which looks like a small black x.

To see what this means, enable the Favorites Center and mouse over the various folders and shortcuts shown in the list. If you mouse over a folder, a small blue arrow appears. If you click this arrow, you will open all of the shortcuts in that folder in their own tabs. (See the next section for more information about tabbed browsing if you don't understand what this means.) Naturally, if you click a shortcut, that shortcut will open in the current browser window; and if you click a folder, the view will expand to show you the contents of that folder, as shown in Figure 19-10.

Figure 19-10: The Favorites Center provides a more full-featured hub for your favorite Web sites.

In addition to containing links to your favorite Web sites, the Favorites Center also includes views for History (your browser history) and something called Feeds. You might think of the Favorites Center as the front end to the memory of Internet Explorer 7. Here's how these two new buttons work:

◆ **Feeds:** Contains RSS feeds to which you've subscribed. (You'll examine RSS feeds in detail later in this chapter.)

◆ **History:** Shows you the Web pages you visited in the past. When you click this button, a drop-down menu enables you to organize the list by various criteria and search your history for a previously viewed page.

To add the Web page you're currently viewing to your Favorites list, click the new Add to Favorites button, which is found just to the right of the Favorites Center button. (It resembles a star with a green plus sign on top of it.) This button enables the menu shown in Figure 19-11, and from here you can add the current page to Favorites and perform a few other related functions.

Figure 19-11: Internet Explorer 7 makes adding a new favorite more obvious.

Navigating the Web with Tabbed Browsing

Tabbed browsing is a feature that optionally enables users to open new Web pages within the frame of a single browser window, and access each individual page via a series of visible tabs. This feature has been available in other Web browsers for years, and Internet Explorer was the last major browser to add the feature. Now that Microsoft has finally caught up and added this crucial bit of browsing functionality to Internet Explorer 7, Internet Explorer is no longer a second-class Web citizen.

If you haven't had the opportunity to use tabbed browsing, chances are good you'll appreciate the feature, especially if you tend to open a lot of Web documents in different windows. Because you can now optionally open new Web documents in a tab contained within a single browser window, you have fewer windows to manage and less clutter on your Desktop.

Here's how tabbed browsing works. By default, Internet Explorer opens with a single document loaded, as before; but now, each document Internet Explorer displays is contained within a tab. The top of the tab—the part that looks like an actual tabbed file folder—is found near the top of the browser window, below the address bar and to the right of the Favorites Center and Add/Subscribe buttons. If you choose to never deal with tabs per se, Internet Explorer essentially acts as it did before; you will merely see that single tab near the top of the window.

The beauty of tabbed browsing, however, is that you can open multiple tabs, which are essentially child windows of the main browser window. To open a new tab, click the New Tab button, which is the gray square-shaped object to the right of the rightmost tab, as shown in Figure 19-12. When you mouse over this little tab, an icon appears, indicating what will happen if you click it.

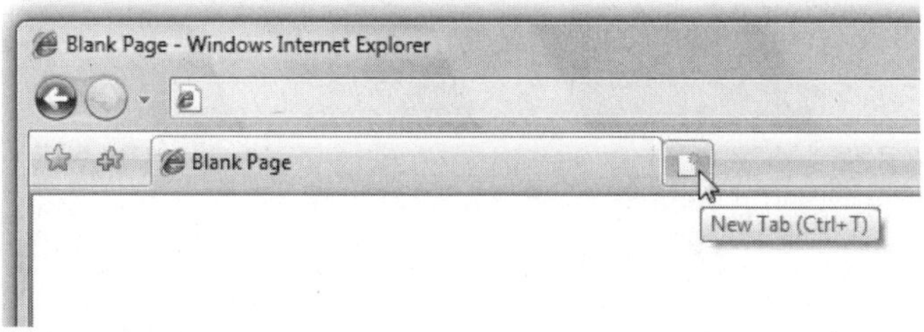

Figure 19-12: To open a new tab, click the New Tab button.

Secret

Although this isn't documented, you can also open a new tab by double-clicking the blank area to the right of the New Tab button.

By default, the new tab will open to a "Welcome to tabbed browsing" blank page and you're good to go: You can enter a Web address and navigate there, go directly to your home page, or perform any other similar navigational tasks. However, there are better ways to open a new tab. You can use the Ctrl+T keyboard shortcut, for starters. This will open a new tab in a manner similar to clicking the New Tab button.

Alternately, suppose you're doing a Google search and you want to open links to certain search results in new tabs. (This is actually a great use for tabbed browsing.) To open a link in a new tab, you can right-click the link and choose Open in New Tab, or Ctrl+click the link (that is, hold down the Ctrl key on your keyboard while you click it). You can also click the middle mouse button to open a new tab as well.

This method is particularly effective when you have a list of hyperlinks that you want to open, all at the same time. You can simply move down the list, Ctrl+clicking as you go, and then casually examine each tab in order.

That last item brings up an interesting issue: How do you navigate between tabs? You may recall that you can navigate between open windows in Windows using the Alt+Tab key combination (or, starting in Windows Vista, the new Flip 3D function, which is toggled by using the Windows Key+Tab key combination). In Internet Explorer 7, you can select an individual tab by clicking its tab button, but you can also use various key combinations to select tabs. To cycle through the available tabs, use the Ctrl+Tab key combination. Or, to move in reverse order, try Ctrl+Shift+Tab.

To close a tab, click the Close Tab button, which appears as a small x on the tab button of each tab; or use the Ctrl+W keyboard shortcut. Note that Internet Explorer prompts you now if you attempt to close the entire browser window if two or more tabs are open: As shown in Figure 19-13, closing down multiple tabs (that is, open documents) with a single mouse click could be disastrous, so this is a nice feature.

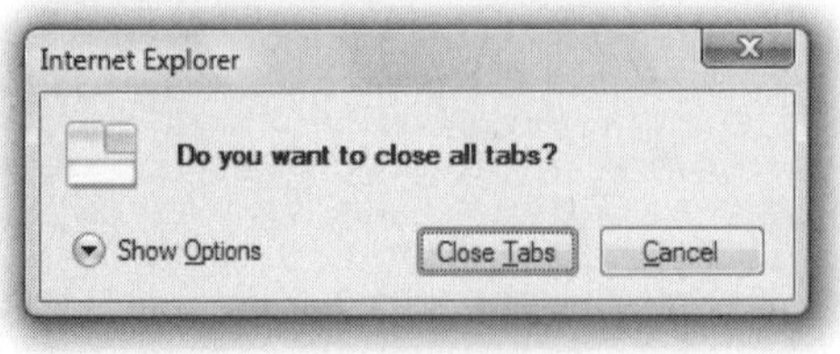

Figure 19-13: Internet Explorer 7 will warn you if you attempt to shut down a browser window with two or more open tabs.

Quick Tabs

Although other browsers have had tabbed browsing functionality for years, Internet Explorer 7 is the first to utilize an innovative new tabbed browsing feature called Quick Tabs. Quick Tabs are a visual way of managing the open tabs you have in any Internet Explorer 7 window, and it's likely that you'll be quite taken with it. In fact, it's so nice-looking that other browser makers rushed to copy it for their own products, an interesting about-face.

To understand why Quick Tabs is so cool, you'll have to open a number of Web pages in different tabs in Internet Explorer 7. When you are displaying two or more tabs in an Internet Explorer browser window, you'll notice that a new icon appears next to the Favorites Center and Add to Favorites icons. This icon enables you to use Quick Tabs; it resembles four squares. When you click the Quick Tabs icon, the document contained in each tab will be tiled in a thumbnail view within the main browser window, as shown in Figure 19-14.

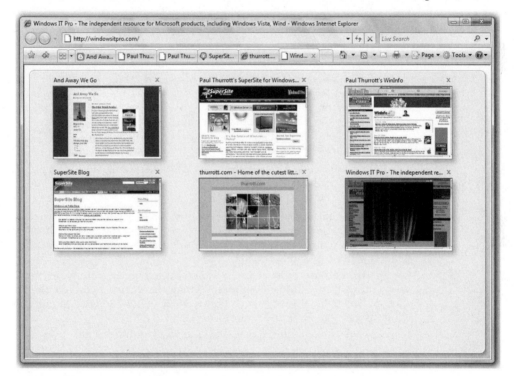

Figure 19-14: Quick Tabs enables you to quickly and visually determine which documents are loaded in each tab.

To select a particular tab from this display, simply click any of the thumbnails. That page will jump to the front and Internet Explorer will return to its normal display. You can also click the Quick Tabs icon again to return to the normal browser display.

Finally, the Quick Tab icon also provides a drop-down menu. When you select this menu, you'll see a list of the available documents, as shown in Figure 19-15. You can jump to a particular tab by selecting any of the options, and the currently displayed tab is displayed in bold type.

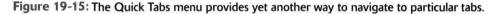

Figure 19-15: The Quick Tabs menu provides yet another way to navigate to particular tabs.

Using Multiple Home Pages

You may recall that previous Internet Explorer versions enabled you to specify any Web document as your home page, the page that is displayed when the browser is launched. Starting with Internet Explorer 7, you can now assign multiple documents as your home page, and each document opens in its own tab. This concept is similar to that of a *tab set*, which is portrayed in the Favorites menu or Favorites view of the Favorites Center as a folder full of links. Therefore, your home page can be a single page, like before, or it can be a folder full of links, or a tab set.

There are a number of ways to assign multiple Web documents as your home page, but you must first load each of the documents you want into Internet Explorer. Then, perform either of the following actions:

◆ **Use the Tools button:** Click the Tools button and select Internet Options to display the Internet Options dialog. In the Home page section at the top of the General tab, click the Use Current button. All of the open documents in the current browser window will be added to the list.

◆ **Use the Home button:** Next to the Home button on the command bar is a small arrow indicating a drop-down menu. Click this arrow and then choose Add or Change Home Page. As shown in Figure 19-16, a new Add or Change Home Page window will appear, with three options.

Pick *Use the current tab set* as your home page and then click OK.

Figure 19-16: This new window enables you to quickly change your home page.

You can also come back later and add or remove documents from the list. To add a document while keeping all of the other documents, first load the document you want to add. Then, select all of the Web address in the browser's address bar and copy it to the clipboard (by clicking Ctrl+C or right-clicking and choosing Copy). Next, select Tools ➪ Options, and click inside the list of Web addresses shown in the Home Page section of the General tab. As shown in Figure 19-17, you can edit this list as if it were any text file. Paste the contents of the clipboard into a new line of the list to add it to the list of home pages.

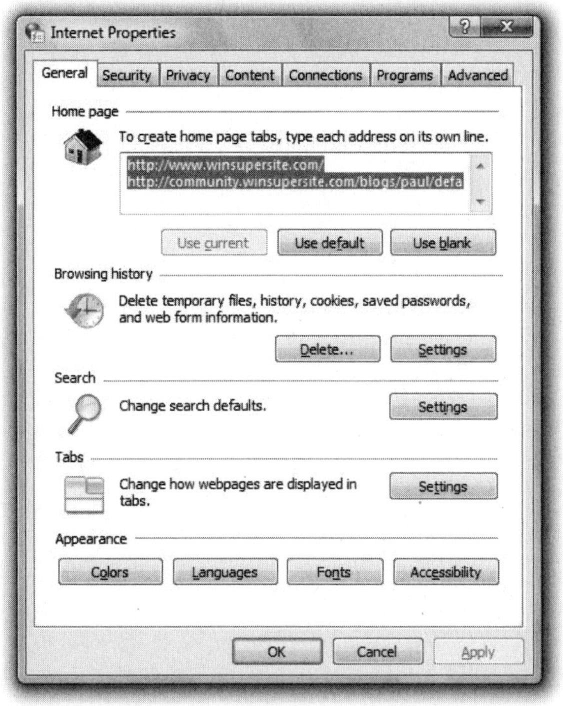

Figure 19-17: You can easily add and remove Web documents from your list of home pages.

You can delete particular home pages in a similar fashion. Simply open the Internet Options dialog and edit the list, removing the pages you no longer want.

Integrated Web Search

In previous versions of Internet Explorer, Microsoft built in very basic Web search features, as documented earlier in this chapter; but the company has been busy advancing the state of the art in Web search in other products released since Internet Explorer 6, including a variety of MSN and Windows Live toolbars, its MSN Search and Windows Live Search services, and its index-based desktop search technologies, which are included in Windows Vista. In Internet Explorer 7, Microsoft has finally added integrated Web search functionality to its browser as well. It's pretty obvious, too: A new Search box sits prominently in the top-right corner of the browser window, to the right of the address bar and Refresh and Stop buttons. What's not obvious is how powerful this feature is and how easily it can be configured to your needs.

Before getting to that, think about how Web search worked in Internet Explorer 6. Basically, you could navigate to a Web search engine, such as Google (**www.google.com**) or, if you were savvy enough, you could utilize the autosearch feature to search the Web directly from the address bar. In Internet Explorer 7, you don't have to know about this secret because the Search box is built right into the browser and is displayed by default. To search in Internet Explorer 7, simply select the Search box, type a search query, and tap Enter (or press the Search button, which resembles a magnifying glass). The Search box displays the name of the default search provider—again, MSN Search by default—in light-gray text just so you know what it will use.

Secret

If you're a keyboard maven like me, you can also jump directly to the Web Search box by tapping Ctrl+E. I'll highlight other IE 7 keyboard shortcuts later in the chapter.

Specifying a Different Search Provider

While I'm sure the software giant would prefer otherwise, you don't have to use Microsoft's search engine. If you're a Google fan, for example, you can use Google instead, or any other search engine you prefer. To select Google as the default search provider, click the Search Options button (the small arrow to the right of Search) and select Google if it's available. Now, all of your searches—including autosearch from the Internet Explorer address bar—will use Google instead of MSN Search.

If Google isn't in the list, open the Search Options menu and select Find More Providers. Internet Explorer will navigate to Microsoft's Search Providers Web site (**www.microsoft .com/windows/ie/searchguide/**), where you can pick from a list of search engines, as shown in Figure 19-18.

Under Web Search, click the link titled Google. Then, in the Add Search Provider dialog that appears, check the option titled *Make this my default search provider* and then click the Add Provider button. The Live Search text in the Web Search box should change to Google. If it doesn't, select Google from the Search Options menu.

Using Find in Page

In addition to searching the Web, the Internet Explorer 7 search functionality also enables you to search the text within a currently loaded document. This is handy when you search the Web for a specific term and then load a page that contains the text, but is quite long. Instead of reading the entire document, you can search within the document for your search string. This feature is called Find in Page.

To access Find in Page, you must first load a Web document. This can be something you searched for, or it can be any Web page anywhere on the Web. Then, select Ctrl+F to open the Find dialog, shown in Figure 19-19.

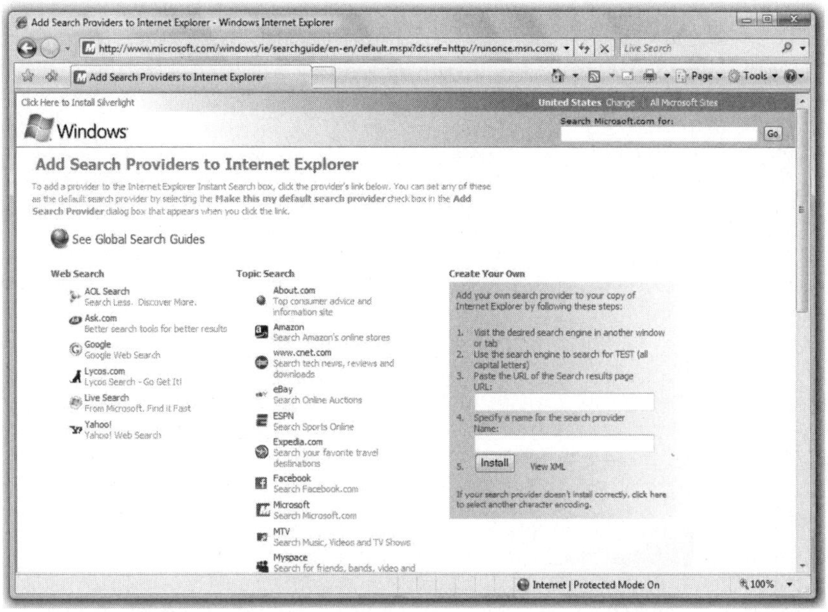

Figure 19-18: Don't get stuck with Windows Live Search. From here you can choose Google, Yahoo!, or any other search engine you prefer.

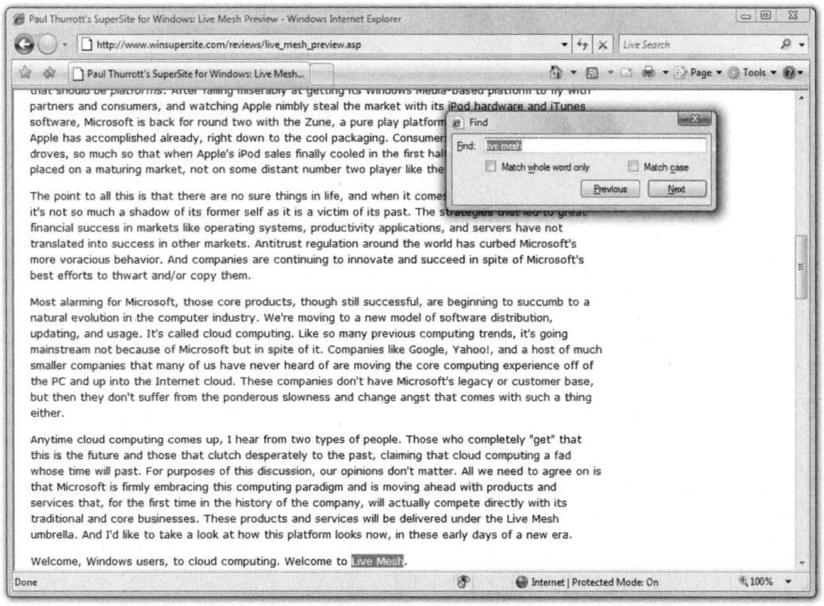

Figure 19-19: The Find dialog offers old-fashioned in-page searching capabilities.

Enter a search string in the Find box and click Enter to find it. You can keep tapping Enter repeatedly to find further instances of the search text. As you tap Enter, each repetition of the search string on the page is highlighted in turn, helping you find what you're looking for.

Find in Page is a decent feature, but it could be improved in a number of ways. The Windows Live Toolbar for Internet Explorer, discussed in Chapter 21, includes one such improvement: When this toolbar is enabled, every instance of a search term can be highlighted at once, making it even easier to find what you're looking for.

However, I think there's a better way to search within Web pages. As I mention later in the discussion about Mozilla's alternative browser, Firefox, that product features a superior Find toolbar, subtly located at the bottom of the browser window. This toolbar offers a number of advantages over the Find in Page dialog, which, among other things, can block the very text you're trying to read. Not surprisingly, several free add-ons provide this functionality to Internet Explorer. My favorite is IE 7 Pro (**www.ie7pro.com/**), shown in Figure 19-20. When this add-on is installed, Internet Explorer search is taken to the next level.

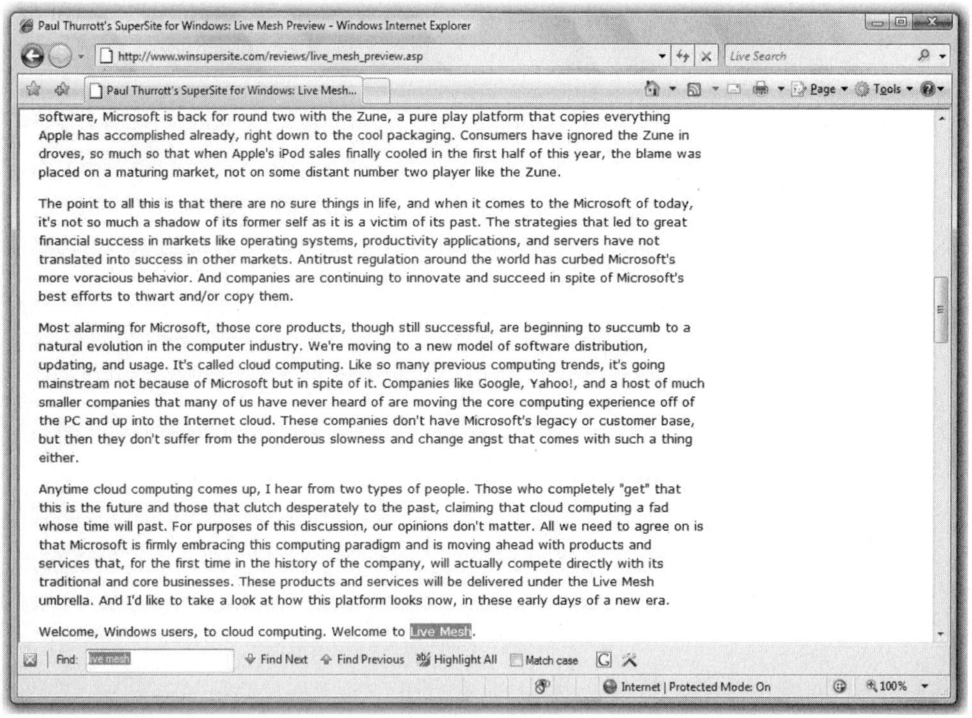

Figure 19-20: You don't need to switch to Firefox to get superior Find in Page functionality. Just download IE 7 Pro.

Working with the Internet Explorer 7 Display

In previous versions of Internet Explorer, the way text was displayed in the browser depended on various factors, including whether you had enabled ClearType (in Windows XP only), a display mode that triples the vertical resolution of text via a technology called *subpixel rendering.* Most people find ClearType to be hugely beneficial on LCD displays, but many complain that it makes text look fuzzy on older CRT-type monitors.

Secret   In Internet Explorer 7, ClearType is always enabled by default; but if you find that the display is blurry on your monitor, you can turn it off. To do so, open Internet Options and navigate to the Advanced tab. In the Settings list, scroll down to the Multimedia section. Then, deselect the option titled *Always Use ClearType for HTML* and restart the browser. Problem solved.

Configuring Text Size and Page Zoom

Before Internet Explorer 7, Microsoft's browsers offered only rudimentary text-sizing capabilities. Although you would typically view the text in a given Web page at 100 percent magnification, Internet Explorer also offered a Text Size option that enabled you to navigate between options such as Largest, Larger, Medium (the default), Smaller, and Smallest. These options still exist in Internet Explorer 7, and if you're happy with them feel free to continue using them. However, they're hidden by default, as the Internet Explorer menu is hidden. To display the menu, tap the Alt key and select Text Size from the View menu.

That said, you're going to want to skip the Internet Explorer Text Size options and utilize the new Page Zoom feature instead. Unlike the Text Size options, Page Zoom works by retaining the underlying design of the Web page you're viewing. That is, it doesn't just increase or decrease the size of text, which often blows away the underlying layout design. Instead, Page Zoom intelligently zooms the entire page display, including both graphics and text, thereby improving the readability of the text and retaining wonderful graphical image quality as well.

The Page Zoom user interface is located in the bottom-right corner of the browser window, at the far right of the status bar. There, you'll see a small magnifying glass icon with the text *100%* next to it (by default). When you click the small arrow to the right of this icon or text, a pop-up menu appears, as shown in Figure 19-21, from which you can choose various zoom amounts.

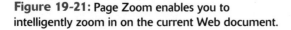

Figure 19-21: Page Zoom enables you to intelligently zoom in on the current Web document.

You can also simply click the Page Zoom icon to jump between preset page zoom values of 100 percent, 125 percent, and 150 percent. The graphics look quite good as they're resized, but the text is simply phenomenal-looking. No matter how much you zoom in, the text looks impressive, as shown in Figure 19-22.

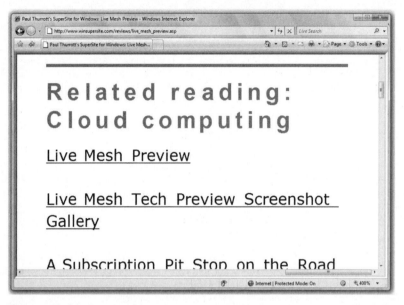

Figure 19-22: People with vision problems will appreciate the way Page Zoom makes text appear crisply and clearly.

Browsing in Full-Screen Mode

Like its predecessors, Internet Explorer 7 supports a full-screen browsing mode in which Internet Explorer covers the entire display, including the Windows Vista taskbar. To enable full-screen mode, tap F11 or choose Full Screen from the Tools menu. By default, full-screen mode even hides the Internet Explorer toolbars, so you can literally use the entire system display to read the current Web page, as shown in Figure 19-23. (It does not, however, hide the status bar.)

---

tip   To display the Internet Explorer toolbars in full-screen mode, simply move your mouse to the top of the screen. The toolbars will slide in with an animated effect.

Figure 19-23: You can still display the toolbars in full-screen mode.

Printing

Anyone who has tried to print a Web page with Internet Explorer knows how poorly that feature works. Well, take heart: Microsoft has done more than fix printing in Internet Explorer 7, removing problems that existed in previous versions, such as the way that the rightmost third of most page printouts would simply disappear off the side of the page. Now, in Internet Explorer 7, printing is actually a positive experience. It's been thoroughly overhauled.

You access most printing features directly through the Print button, which is found in the Internet Explorer command bar. If you just click the Print button, Internet Explorer will print the currently displayed Web page using your default printer. (You can also select Ctrl+P to immediately print the current page.)

However, the Print button also offers a drop-down menu, shown in Figure 19-24, from which you can access additional functionality, including Print Preview and Page Setup. Both are dramatic improvements over previous Internet Explorer versions.

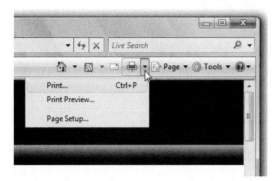

Figure 19-24: Printing has gotten a lot more sophisticated with IE 7.

Using Print Preview

When you select the Print Preview option from the Print button drop-down menu, you'll see the Print Preview display shown in Figure 19-25. From here, you can switch between portrait and landscape display modes, access the Page Setup dialog, and perform other printing-related tasks.

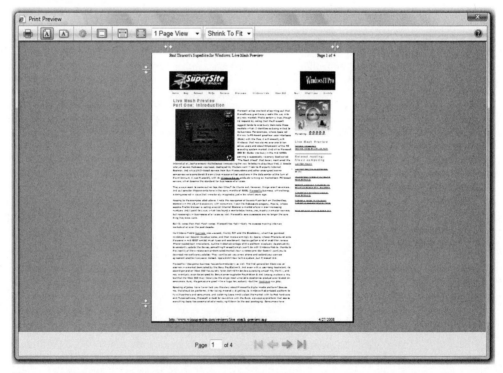

Figure 19-25: The Internet Explorer 7 Print Preview feature is a big improvement over Internet Explorer 6.

The biggest change from Internet Explorer 6 is that you can now easily toggle whether each page includes footer and headers. To see how this works, click the Turn Headers and Footers On or Off button (it's the fifth one from the left) and see how it changes the display in Print Preview. You can also display the pages to print in various ways. For example, you can display an entire page in the window, fit the display to the width of the window, or even display multiple pages, as shown in Figure 19-26.

When you're ready to print, click the Print button at the bottom of the Print Preview window; or click Close to return to Internet Explorer.

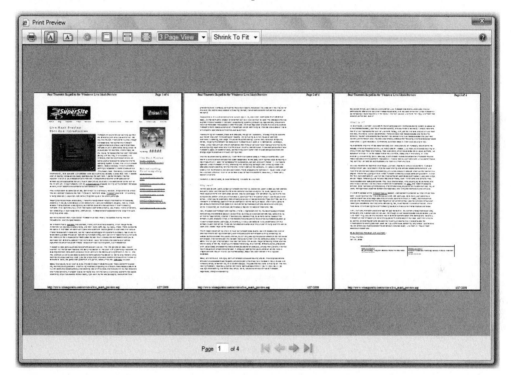

Figure 19-26: A multiple-page preview in Internet Explorer 7.

Secret

Another truly amazing feature is that you can print, and print preview, only the content you've selected in a Web page. That is, you don't have to print an entire Web page. Instead, you can print text that you've selected, or highlighted.

To see how this works, open a Web document and select some text. Then, choose the Print Preview option from the Print button drop-down menu. When the Print Preview window appears, you'll see a new Select Content drop-down menu in the middle top of the window, shown in Figure 19-27. Open the drop-down list and choose *As selected on screen*. Now, only the selected text is ready to print.

continues

continued

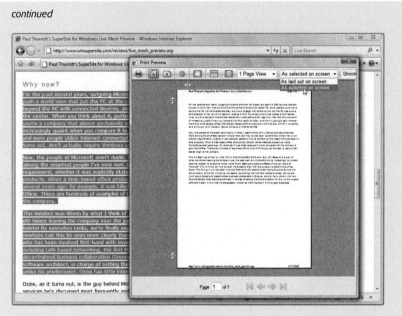

Figure 19-27: With IE 7, you can print only those parts of a Web page you want.

Using Page Setup

If you want even more control over how your Web pages will print, you can use the Page Setup dialog. This dialog can be accessed in two ways: through the Page Setup button in the Print Preview toolbar, or through the Page Setup option in the Print button's drop-down menu. This dialog, shown in Figure 19-28, enables you to configure the paper size and source, the margin sizes, and the text strings used to configure the header and footer display.

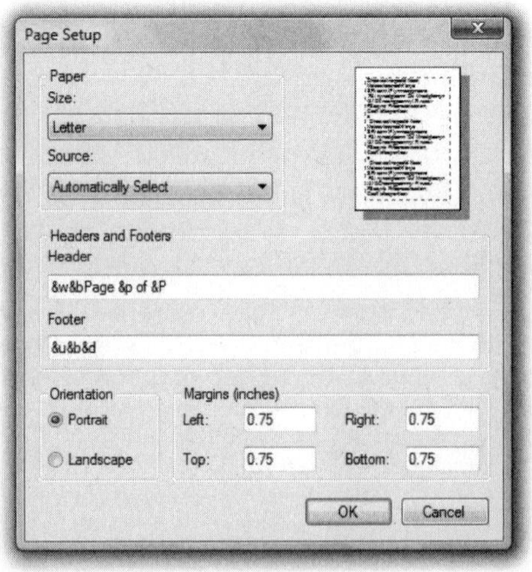

Figure 19-28: Change various printing options through the Page Setup dialog.

By default, the Header text string is set to **&w&bPage &p of &P**, which looks like gobble-dygook until you realize that each of those characters has meaning. The **&** character is used to denote a header or footer *variable,* so **&w** is a variable, which happens to stand for window title. The full range of header and footer variables is shown in Table 19-4.

Table 19-4: Page Setup Header and Footer Variable Values

Variable	Value
Window title	&w
Page address (URL)	&u
Date in short format	&d
Date in long format	&D
Time	&t
Time in 24-hour format	&T
Current page number	&p
Total number of pages	&P
Right-aligned text (following **&b**)	&b
Centered text (between **&b** and **&b**)	&b&b
An ampersand character (**&**)	&&

tip In previous versions of Internet Explorer, you had to use the Page Setup dialog to remove headers and footers from the printout. This method still works, though the Print Preview method described previously is simpler and quicker. To remove the header completely, simply select the Header text box and delete all of the text.

Covering Your Tracks

Yes, it was possible in previous IE versions to perform housekeeping tasks such as removing temporary Internet files and cookies, and deleting your browser history and saved form data and passwords; but it was also difficult and time-consuming. Internet Explorer 7 now offers an incredibly handy front end for doing this all with just two clicks of your mouse button. The feature is called Delete Browsing History, and it's a nifty addition to Microsoft's browser.

To access Delete Browsing History, open the Tools menu and choose Delete Browsing History. Shown in Figure 19-29, the resulting window enables you to delete the aforementioned items either individually or all at the same time using the Delete All button. It's a one-stop shop for covering your tracks.

Figure 19-29: Delete Browsing History is one of the best new features in Internet Explorer 7.

Here's what each of the options means.

◆ **Temporary Internet Files:** These are downloaded files that have been cached in your Temporary Internet Files folder, including Offline Favorites and attachments stored by Microsoft Outlook.

◆ **Cookies:** These are small text files that include data that persists between visits to particular Web sites.

◆ **History:** This is the list of Web sites you've visited with Internet Explorer and the Web addresses you've typed in the Windows Vista Run dialog.

◆ **Form data:** This is information that has been saved using Internet Explorer's autocomplete form data functionality.

◆ **Passwords:** These are passwords that were saved using Internet Explorer's auto-complete password data functionality.

Understanding and Using RSS

Although much of the World Wide Web is based on a rather passive system whereby users manually browse to the Web sites they would like to visit, a new type of Web technology, alternatively named *Really Simple Syndication* or *Rich Site Summary,* but usually referred to by the abbreviation RSS regardless, has turned that paradigm on its head and changed the way many people consume Web-based information. In keeping with this sea change, Internet Explorer 7 supports RSS, enabling Windows Vista users to access Web-based content in both traditional and more leading-edge ways.

RSS is basically a data format, based on XML, designed for distributing news and other Web-based content via the Internet. Content that is available via RSS is said to be published in RSS format, while applications (such as Internet Explorer) that can access RSS content are said to subscribe to that content.

What makes RSS different from traditional Web browsing is that RSS applications periodically poll the content publishers to which you've subscribed, so if you subscribe to the

RSS *feed*, as such a link is called, for a particular Web site, that feed will be updated on your local machine periodically, assuming you have an Internet connection. Most good RSS applications, including Internet Explorer 7, enable you to specify how often feeds are updated. Some feeds, obviously, are updated more often than others.

Secret

You won't be surprised to discover that I have a number of RSS feeds for my most frequently published sites. These two will be of interest to *Windows Vista Secrets* readers:

SuperSite for Windows: www.winsupersite.com/supersite.xml

SuperSite Blog: http://community.winsupersite.com/blogs/paul/rss.aspx

The Internet Explorer RSS functionality is exposed in a number of ways. The Internet Explorer 7 command bar has a prominent orange Feeds button, which provides an obvious front end to this technology. The Feeds button is grayed out if you are currently visiting a Web page with which no RSS feed is associated, however, so you must visit a site with an RSS feed to discover how it works.

Viewing an RSS Feed

As an example, take a look at my SuperSite for Windows Web site (**www.winsupersite .com**). Because this site has an RSS feed, the Internet Explorer Feeds button is orange. To view the feed, simply click the button. Internet Explorer will switch to its new Feeds view, which displays the content of the SuperSite for Windows feed (in this case) in the vaguely pleasant, if bland, style shown in Figure 19-30.

Figure 19-30: Internet Explorer 7 feed reading page.

Secret

Some Web sites include two or more RSS feeds. If so, you can display the list of available feeds by clicking the small arrow at the right of the Feeds button (see Figure 19-31). Then, simply choose the feed you want. This feature is sometimes visible when sites support different types of feeds too. For example, in addition to RSS, some sites support a similar type of feed called Atom.

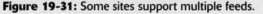

Figure 19-31: Some sites support multiple feeds.

In the Feeds view, you can perform various actions, including searching the feed for specific text using the Search box in the upper-right corner of the page, or sorting by date (the default) or title. The SuperSite for Windows feed publishes only the title and a small abstract for each article it lists; if you want to view a full article, you must click on the title of the article you'd like to read. Some feeds publish entire articles directly in the feed, so you don't have to manually visit the main Web site; and some sites, such as the SuperSite Blog, offer categories, so the Feeds view displays those on the right, enabling you to filter the view by category, as shown in Figure 19-32.

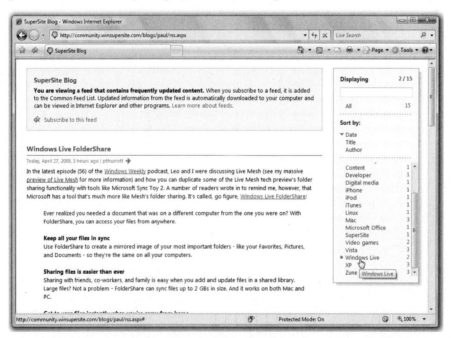

Figure 19-32: You can easily sort the Feeds view using a variety of methods.

Subscribing to an RSS Feed

In the Feeds view, you're essentially just browsing the Web as before, albeit through a nonstandard display; but the real power of RSS feeds is realized when you subscribe to feeds. To subscribe to the SuperSite for Windows feed, you simply click the *Subscribe to this feed* link at the top of the page. When you do so, the Subscribe to This Feed dialog appears, as shown in Figure 19-33. Here, you can edit the name of the feed (as it will appear in your browser only) and where it will be created (the Feeds folder, by default).

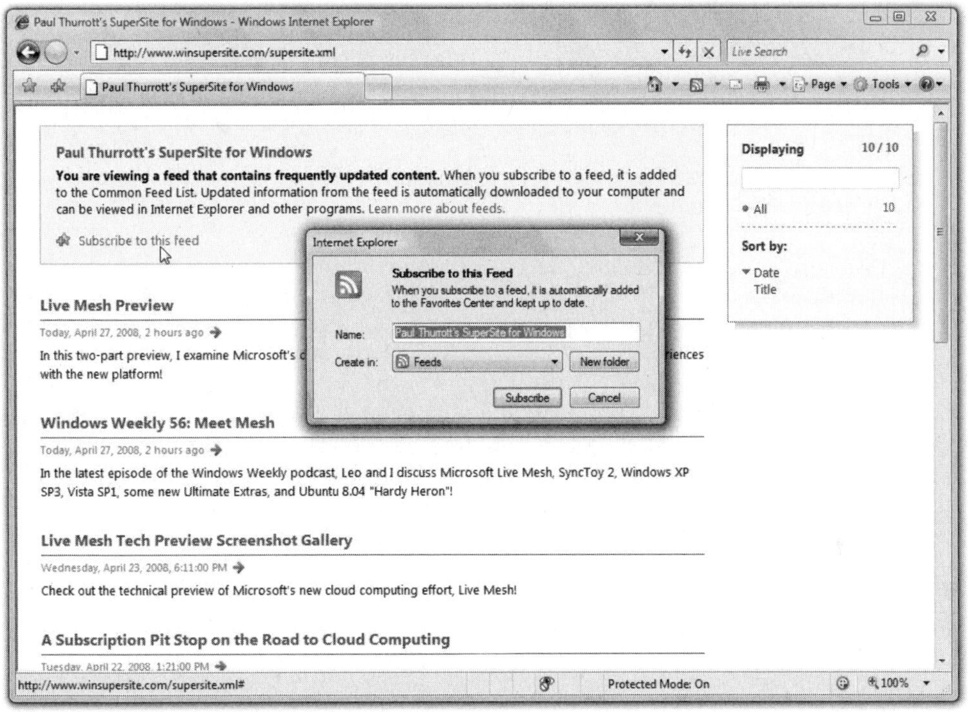

Figure 19-33: When you subscribe to an RSS feed, it is stored in a Favorites-like database.

When you've subscribed, the Feeds view changes to indicate that you've successfully subscribed to the feed, adding a new View My Feeds link. Additionally, you may see an alert noting that automatic feed updates are turned off. If you see this alert, then your RSS subscriptions will not be updated automatically. To enable this functionality, click the Turn On Automatic Feed Updates link.

Managing RSS Feeds

Internet Explorer treats RSS subscriptions much like Favorites. However, RSS subscriptions are not stored in your Favorites folder. Instead, they are stored in a special database that is based on the RSS platform technologies built into Windows Vista.

You access your subscribed feeds through the Favorites Center. You may recall from the discussion earlier in this chapter that Feeds, like Favorites and History lists, are saved in this browser memory store. If you open the Favorites Center, you'll see that Paul

Thurrott's SuperSite for Windows has been added to the Feeds list, which is shown in Figure 19-34.

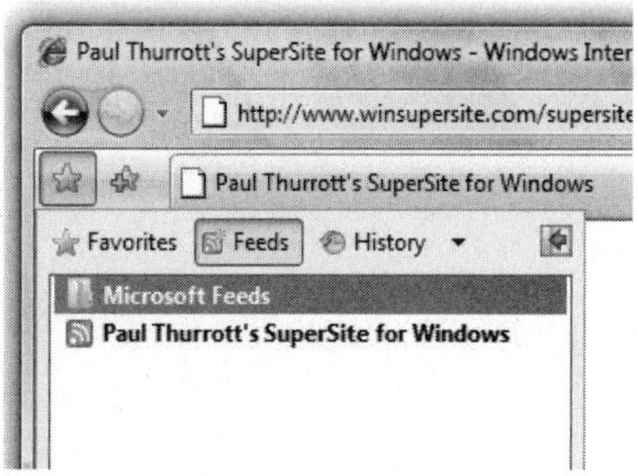

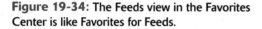

Figure 19-34: The Feeds view in the Favorites Center is like Favorites for Feeds.

As with your Favorites list, you can do a few interesting things with RSS feeds in the Favorites Center. When you mouse over a feed in the list of subscribed feeds, a small refresh icon appears. If you click this icon, the feed is manually updated if there is any new content to download. If you simply click the feed name, the feed will be displayed in the feed reading page as you'd expect.

To configure how an individual feed is updated and archived, you can right-click it in the Feeds list and choose Properties (or, from the Feeds view of an individual feed, click the View Feed Properties link shown on the right side of the window). Either way, you'll see the Feed Properties window, shown in Figure 19-35.

Figure 19-35: You can configure individual feed properties from this window.

Here, you can configure how often the feed is updated, whether or not to automatically download attached files (disabled by default for security reasons), and when to begin archiving the feed.

You can also view and change feed properties globally. To do so, open the Internet Options window and navigate to the Content tab. Then, click the Settings button in the Feeds section. In the Feed Settings dialog, shown in Figure 19-36, you can configure settings that apply globally to Internet Explorer's feeds functionality.

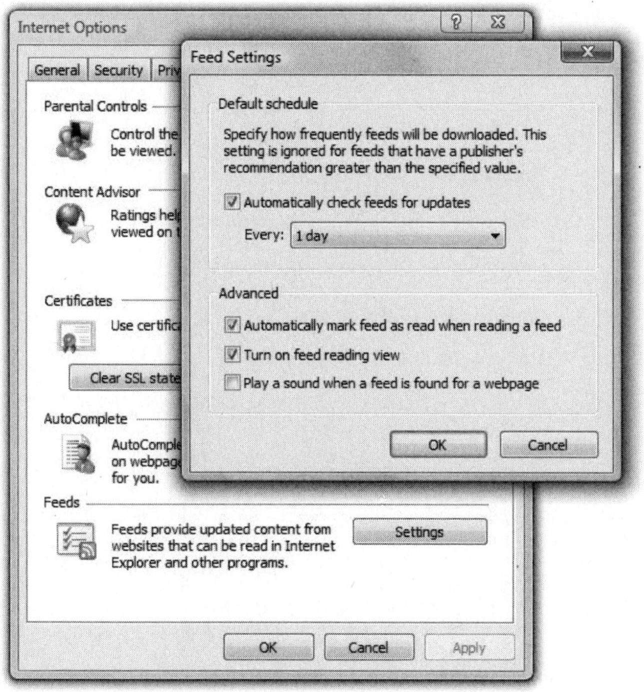

Figure 19-36: Global feeds settings are available via Internet Options.

RSS Is a Platform

One of the more interesting things about the RSS support in Internet Explorer 7 is that it's based on a much wider RSS platform that is available to any application running in Windows Vista. This means that third-party applications can access the RSS feeds you've subscribed to in Internet Explorer and provide you with even more advanced functionality. To see an example of what's possible, check out the RSS Feeds gadget for the Windows Sidebar, examined in Chapter 6, and the Feeds functionality in Windows Live Mail, covered in Chapter 20.

Internet Explorer 7 Keyboard Shortcuts

Keyboard shortcuts make it possible to navigate the Internet Explorer user interface without having to move your hand away from the mouse. Internet Explorer 7 supports virtually all of the keyboard shortcuts supported by Internet Explorer 6, but it also adds a slew of new shortcuts related to new functionality in this version. Table 19-5 summarizes the Internet Explorer 7 keyboard shortcuts.

Table 19-5: Internet Explorer 7 Keyboard Shortcuts

Keyboard Shortcut	What It Does
Alt+left arrow key	Navigate to the previous page.
Alt+right arrow key	Navigate to the next page.
Esc	Stop the current page from loading.
F5 or Ctrl+R or Ctrl+F5	Refresh (reload) the current page.
Alt+Home	Go to your home page.
Alt+D	Select the address bar.
Ctrl+Enter	Automatically add **www** and **.com** to what you typed in the address bar.
Spacebar	Scroll down the Web page.
Shift+spacebar	Scroll up the Web page.
Alt+F4	Close the current window.
Ctrl+D	Add the current page to your Favorites list.
Alt+N	Select the information bar.
Shift+F10	Open the context menu for the currently selected item.
Shift+mouse click	Open the link in a new window.
Ctrl+mouse click	Open the link in a new background tab.
Ctrl+Shift+mouse click	Open the link in new foreground tab.
Ctrl+T	Open a new tab.
Alt+Enter	Open a new tab from the address bar.
Ctrl+Tab	Switch between available tabs.
Ctrl+Shift+Tab	Switch between available tabs in the opposite direction.
Ctrl+W	Close the current tab (or current window if no tabs are open).
Ctrl+x (where x represents the number of the tab, as numbered from 1 to 8)	Switch to a particular tab.

continues

Table 19-5: *(continued)*

Keyboard Shortcut	What It Does
Ctrl+9	Switch to the last tab.
Ctrl+Alt+F4	Close other tabs.
Ctrl+Q	Open Quick Tabs.
Ctrl+(+)	Zoom the page by 10 percent.
Ctrl+(-)	Decrease the page zoom by 10 percent.
Ctrl+0	Zoom to 100 percent (normal view).
Ctrl+E	Navigate to the Toolbar Search box.
Alt+Enter (from the Search box)	Open Search in a new window.
Ctrl+Down Arrow (from the Search box)	Display the search provider menu.
Ctrl+H	Open the Favorites Center to the History view.
Ctrl+I	Open the Favorites Center to the Favorites view.
Ctrl+J	Open the Favorites Center to the Feeds view.

In addition to these handy keyboard shortcuts, Internet Explorer 7 also supports a few helpful mouse actions, which are like shortcuts you can trigger with the mouse. These actions are detailed in Table 19-6.

Table 19-6: Internet Explorer 7 Mouse Actions

Mouse Action	What It Does
Click the middle mouse button	Open the link in a new tab.
Click the middle mouse button on the tab	Close a tab.
Double-click the empty space to the right of the New Tab button	Open a new tab.
Ctrl + mouse wheel up	Zoom the page by 10 percent.
Ctrl + mouse wheel down	Decrease the page zoom by 10 percent.

Secret

Note that other browsers support a much wider range of these mouse actions, which are typically called *mouse gestures,* or simply *gestures,* outside of Microsoft. Fortunately, some intrepid developers have released a handy plug-in for Internet Explorer 7 that adds far more mouse actions to the browser. Head over to The Code Project (www.codeproject.com/atl/MouseGestures.asp) if you think this will enhance your productivity.

cross ref   This is Internet Explorer I'm talking about, so you might be wondering where you can find a discussion of Internet Explorer 7 security features. Have no fear: Internet Explorer 7 includes a huge number of security-related features, and they're all covered in Chapter 8.

To the Future with Internet Explorer 8

Secret   As I write this book, Microsoft is busy working on a new version of its venerable Web browser. Imaginatively named Internet Explorer 8, this browser is currently available only in very early beta form. Thus, you should consider this section a preview only, as much will likely change between the time I write this and the time you read it. For the absolute latest information about Internet Explorer 8, check my Web site, the SuperSite for Windows (www.winsupersite.com).

Looking at the Internet Explorer 8 developer preview release, I see two major new features vis-à-vis Internet Explorer 7: Activities and WebSlices.

Activities

Several years ago, Microsoft developed a user interface feature called Smart Tags that it planned to incorporate into Office XP and Internet Explorer 6, part of Windows XP. Smart Tags were added to Office XP as planned and they still exist today in subsequent versions of that product, as shown in Figure 19-37; but the company's plans to include Smart Tags in IE 6 were scuttled after Web developers and users complained long and hard about the feature, which many saw as anti-competitive. Therefore, IE 6 shipped without Smart Tags, and the feature, presumably, was dropped for good.

Not so fast: In Internet Explorer 8, Smart Tags are back, renamed Activities; and to prove they are not exclusionary or anti-competitive, Microsoft has stocked even beta versions of Internet Explorer 8 with a number of Activities that are made by its competitors.

Like the Smart Tags they so clearly replace, Activities provide Web pages with contextual menus that provide additional information via Web services that lead readers to new locations. The contents of these contextual menus vary according to what is selected on the page and which Activities are available in the user's browser. In other words, the functionality is not provided by the underlying Web site at all. It is provided by the browser via this new feature.

Activities are certainly interesting and useful; they also enable users to completely bypass whatever facilities the Web site itself has provided. For example, you might use the Internet Explorer 8 Activities feature to find a Yahoo! Map for a selected address on a Web page; but that page may supply its own map, one that you have now chosen to bypass. My guess is that this feature will cause the same consternation among Web developers that Smart Tags did several years ago. What may offset these complaints is that many Activities are now created by Microsoft's competitors, and many more are sure to follow; with Smart Tags, the default tags were all Microsoft-specific, raising privacy and exclusivity concerns.

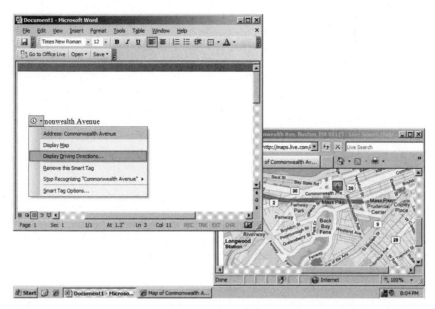

Figure 19-37: Smart Tags passed muster in Office, but users worried that IE-based Smart Tags would be too intrusive.

Now it's time to see how this feature works. If you select a word or any other text in a Web page in IE 8 Beta 1, a small green Smart Tag appears. Click this tag to display the menu shown in Figure 19-38, loaded with Activities that may (or may not) apply to the selected text.

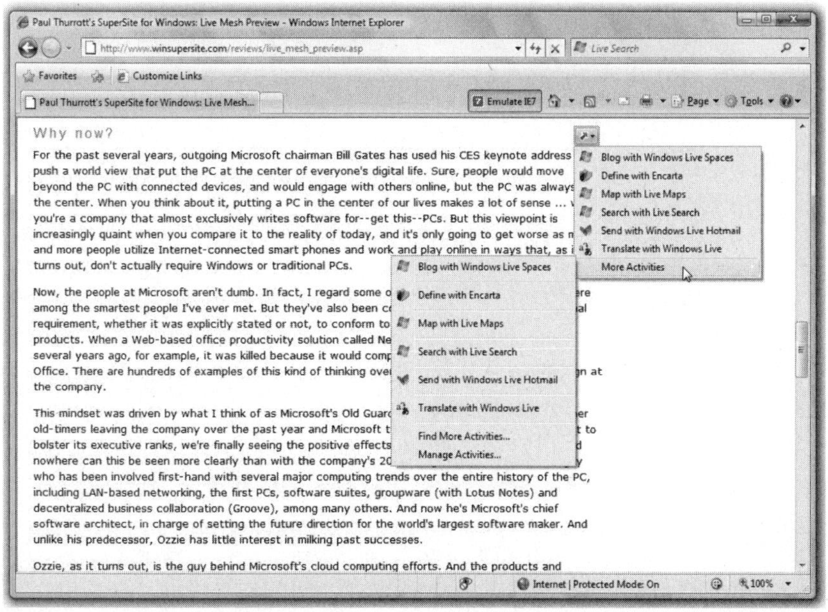

Figure 19-38: Activities enable Internet Explorer 8 to extend the capabilities of Web sites in ways the site author(s) never envisioned—or perhaps wanted, for that matter.

What you will see, of course, depends on what's selected—because the Activities list is contextual—and on which Activities are loaded in your browser. By default, Internet Explorer 8 ships with several Activities, including Define with Encarta, Map with Live Maps, and Translate with Windows Live; but you can also visit a Web page to add new Activities from Microsoft and companies such as eBay, Facebook, and Yahoo! (see Figure 19-39). The process of adding Activities is much like adding search providers in IE 7.

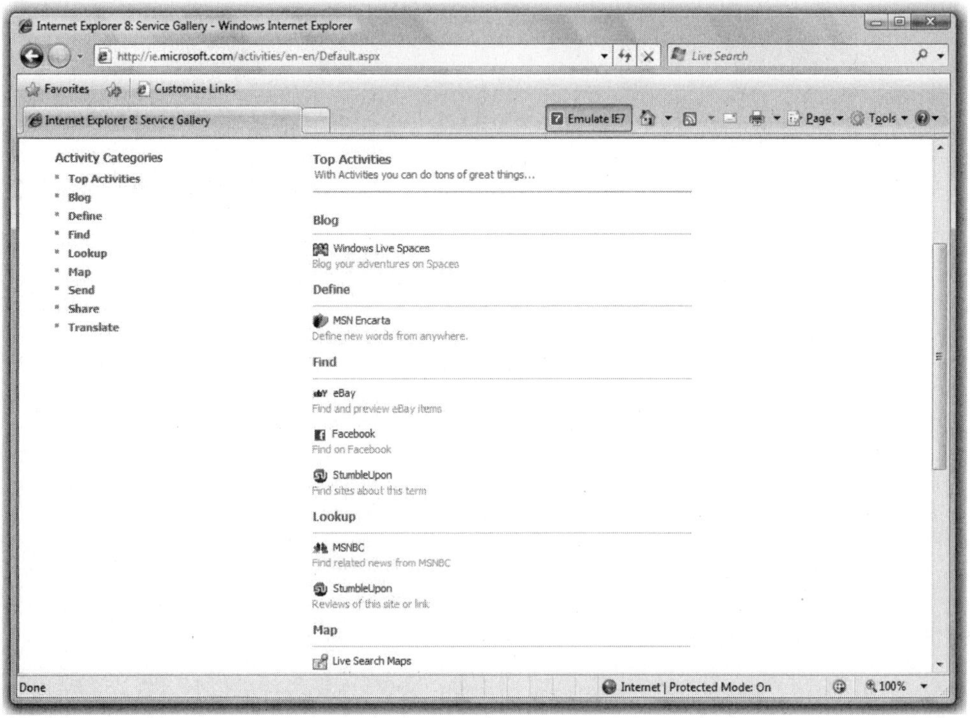

Figure 19-39: More Activities are made available via the Web.

What might one do with Activities? You can highlight an individual word and get a definition. You can select a full address and get a map. You can highlight a word in a foreign language and get a translation. By design, most Activities trigger a small pop-up window, but many also provide a link so you can load the information in a separate window or tab.

You can also use Activities to send information from a Web page to another location, triggering a Google search, perhaps, or blogging about the selected text in Windows Live Spaces.

WebSlices

The other major new Internet Explorer 8 feature, WebSlices, provides a way for Web sites to easily enable readers to "subscribe" to information in a manner that is simpler and more obvious than the RSS feeds functionality described earlier in the chapter. In sharp contrast to Activities, WebSlices requires some support from the underlying page. That is, to enable this feature, a Web developer specifically has to add some code to a Web page's underlying HTML code. Fortunately, it's not much code, and given the point of this feature, it's not the type of thing you'll be sprinkling liberally around a site anyway.

Developers can mark a portion of a Web page as a WebSlice, which can then be automatically monitored for changes and saved as mini-Favorites in the new Internet Explorer 8 Favorites Bar (which, in this release, exists between the main toolbar and the Tabs/command bar). A weather-oriented Web site might mark the forecast portion of a page as a WebSlice, so that any user who subscribed to this slice could then view just the updated forecast at any time. Pre-built WebSlices are already available for Facebook friends' status updates, eBay item monitoring, and MSN news headlines. Expect more in the future.

Unlike RSS feeds, which are typically saved somewhat like IE Favorites, but in the Feeds list, WebSlices are normally saved to the new Favorites Bar, which is enabled and displayed by default. When you save a WebSlice, an RSS Feed-like dialog appears, and then the new slice appears in this toolbar, as shown in Figure 19-40.

Figure 19-40: WebSlices live in the new Favorites Bar.

When you click the link to the slice, a new page will load, as shown in Figure 19-41. Sometimes you see the information in a pop-up window. To get more information, click on the item you're viewing.

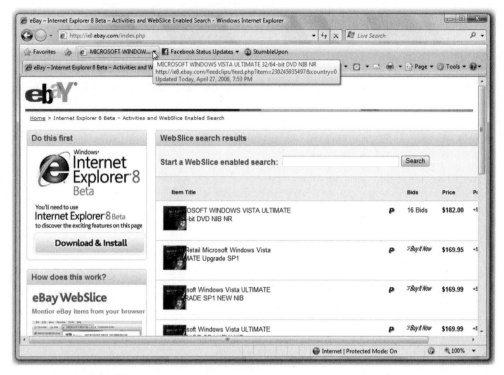

Figure 19-41: WebSlices can appear in pop-ups or in the full browser window.

It's unclear at this time whether WebSlices will ever gain the same support and traction as RSS feeds. Yes, it's simpler than an RSS feed, both conceptually and practically, but I can see open standards purists being up in arms over what will likely be seen as Microsoft subverting existing content subscription methods. We'll have to see how the feature evolves and whether enough sites implement it before we can have an intelligent debate on the issue. In any case, I do like the visual nature of WebSlices; and Microsoft has made the specifications for WebSlices available to one and all via the Creative Commons license, so other browser makers can implement this feature, too.

Other New Features in Internet Explorer 8

While Microsoft is sure to add other major new features in Internet Explorer 8 before its final release, at this early stage only a few other features stand out.

Microsoft is again changing the way that you interact with browser add-ons (or plug-ins) in Internet Explorer—there is an attractive new Manage Add-ons dialog in this release, shown in Figure 19-42. Now, add-ons are segregated by type—Toolbars and Extensions, Search Providers, and Activities—and you can easily filter the view by currently loaded, all add-ons ever used, those that run without permissions, and downloaded ActiveX controls.

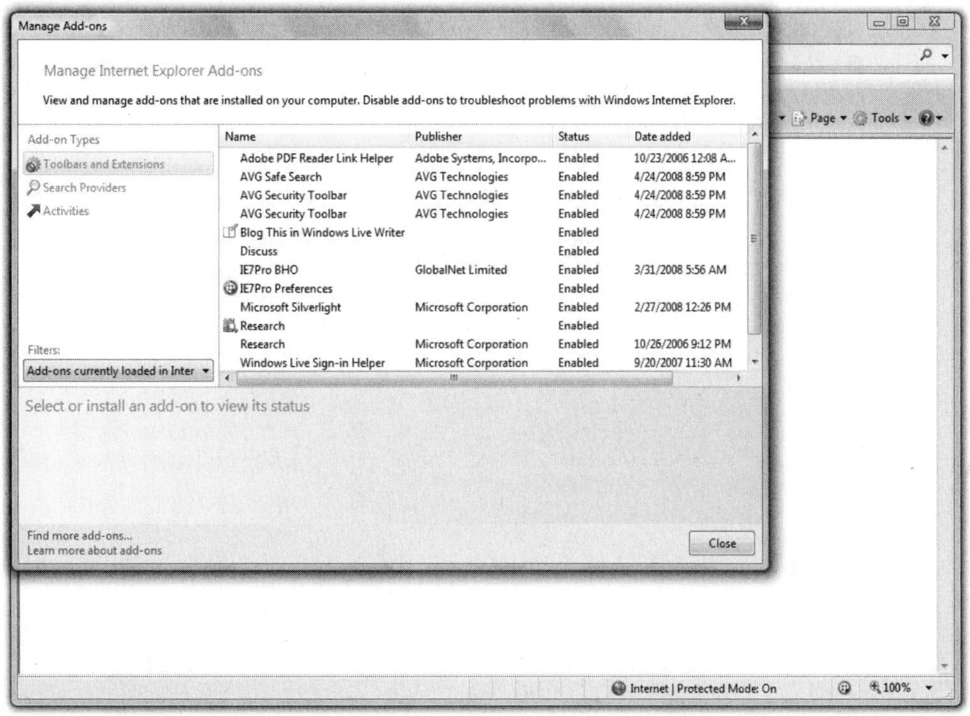

Figure 19-42: Manage Add-ons is being substantially overhauled in IE 8.

In the beta version of Internet Explorer 8, the address bar supports a new domain name highlighting feature. This is designed to help people understand when they're being spoofed, but it makes me think I have eye problems. If you load a URL such as **www. microsoft.com/windows/ie/ie8/welcome/en/default.html**, most of the URL will be grayed out, but the domain name part (**microsoft.com**) will appear in black and be thus emphasized (i.e., it appears as **www.microsoft.com**/windows/ie/ie8/welcome/en/default.html.)

Also on the security front, Microsoft is adding a new Safety Filter feature to IE 8. The Safety Filter is basically an expansion of the Phishing Filter from IE 7 that adds additional protection against evolving threats. According to Microsoft, it analyzes the full URL string loaded into Internet Explorer 8 and provides more granular protection than was possible with the Phishing Filter, leading to greater protection against more targeted and sophisticated attacks.

Developer-Oriented Changes

In addition to the features noted previously, Microsoft has made numerous developer-focused improvements to the browser in Internet Explorer 8. While much of this information is quite technical, it's worth noting that Microsoft will render the Web in a standards-based mode that's far closer to the way other browsers behave, such as those discussed in the next section, and much less like IE 7 and previous IE versions. Microsoft is also supporting modern Web standards such as HTML 4.01 and CSS 2.1

Web Browser Alternatives: Mozilla Firefox and Apple Safari

While Microsoft has made huge gains in Internet Explorer 7, and appears to be making similar advances in its next browser, the company's decision to essentially halt browser development during the several years after it shipped Internet Explorer 6 created an opening for other browser makers. In that time period, a major Internet Explorer competitor arrived in the form of Mozilla Firefox; and since then, iPod and Mac maker Apple has released its own browser, Safari, which is based on the same Web rendering engine used in its popular iPhone mobile solution. Both browsers offer users viable alternatives to Internet Explorer, so I'd like to discuss them briefly here.

Mozilla Firefox

Mozilla's free Firefox browser is small, fast, and powerful; and it's arguably even more secure than Internet Explorer. In fact, this is the browser I use daily, and I recommend that others do so as well. It's shown in Figure 19-43.

Figure 19-43: Mozilla Firefox is my favorite browser and the one I recommend to readers.

From a functional standpoint, Firefox offers virtually every feature found in Internet Explorer 7 (indeed, some of IE 7's features were lifted straight from Firefox), so you'll see features such as tabbed browsing support, inline search, RSS feed support, pop-up ad blocking, phishing protection, a Clear Private Data interface that mimics IE's Delete Browsing History, and a search engine manager.

Where Firefox shines, however, is in the features it exposes that can't be found in Internet Explorer. These include, but are not limited to, the following:

- **A rich add-ons ecosystem:** In my opinion, this is the number one reason to choose Firefox over Internet Explorer. Firefox is supported by an unprecedented number of extensions and themes. Extensions are essentially browser add-ons that extend the functionality of Firefox in some way. Themes enable you to change the entire Firefox user interface. IE does support a number of browser add-ons, of course, but Firefox's support is much deeper, and IE has nothing like the Firefox themes feature. You're pretty much stuck with what Microsoft gives you. You can find out more about Firefox add-ons via the Mozilla Web site (**https://addons.mozilla.org**).

- **Download manager:** Unlike Internet Explorer, Firefox sports a full-featured download manager that, among other things, enables you to pause and restart downloads. IE has nothing like it. Firefox's download manager is shown in Figure 19-44.

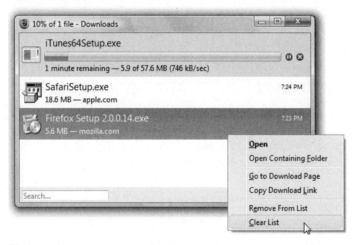

Figure 19-44: Every browser should have a download manager as good as the one in Firefox.

- **Spell Checking:** If you regularly make posts to blogs or otherwise use forms online, Internet Explorer leaves you hanging when it comes to spell checking. Firefox, however, supports integrated spell checking, helping to ensure that you don't make any silly spelling mistakes.

- **Tab reordering:** Both Firefox and Internet Explorer 7 support tabbed browsing, but only Firefox enables you to change the order of the tabs using your drag and drop skills, as shown in Figure 19-45.

Figure 19-45: You can reorder tabs in Firefox by dragging them left and right.

◆ **Find in Page:** As discussed previously, Microsoft's browser uses an old-fashioned Find dialog for locating text within a page. Mozilla, meanwhile, innovated with the more subtle Find toolbar, shown in Figure 19-46, which makes it much easier to find text.

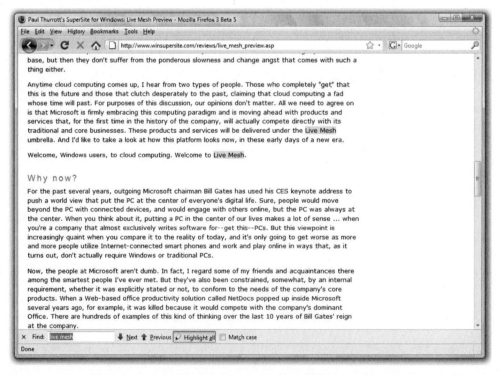

Figure 19-46: Firefox's Find toolbar is more capable than IE's Find in Page function, and it won't cover up the text you're looking for.

◆ **Session Restore:** If Firefox crashes while you're working or you're forced to reboot even though you have a bunch of browser windows open, no problem: The Session Restore feature will bring back all of the browser windows and tabs you were using the next time you open Firefox.

◆ **Automated updating, including all add-ons:** While Internet Explorer is updated via the Windows Update/Microsoft Update/Automatic Updates mechanisms, that's not the case with any of the browser add-ons you might have installed in Microsoft's browser. With Firefox, the browser and all add-ons are updated automatically through a centralized updating mechanism that runs, by default, each time you start the browser. With Firefox, you're always up-to-date.

For more information and the free download, please visit the Mozilla Web site (**www. mozilla.com**).

Apple Safari

Apple introduced its Safari Web browser, shown in Figure 19-47, on the Mac platform years ago, but its decision to ship a Windows version in 2007 came as quite a surprise. Since that first release, Apple has regularly updated Safari for Windows; and as a result, it's a viable Internet Explorer competitor today. Like Firefox, Safari is free.

Figure 19-47: Apple's Safari started off as a curiosity but has developed into a credible IE competitor.

Like Firefox, Safari sports a number of features that you'll find on the other browsers, including tabbed browsing, integrated bookmarks, pop-up blocking, RSS feed support, and the like. However, it also offers some unique features that you won't find on either Internet Explorer or Firefox, including the following:

✦ **Performance:** While my real-world experiences aren't quite so dramatic, Apple claims that Safari is almost two times as fast as Internet Explorer 7 or Firefox.

✦ **Superior Find in Page:** While Safari offers a Firefox-like Find toolbar, Apple turns it up a notch by automatically highlighting all instances of your search text on the page simultaneously, while dimming the rest of the page (see Figure 19-48). The result is the best implementation of Find in Page I've ever seen.

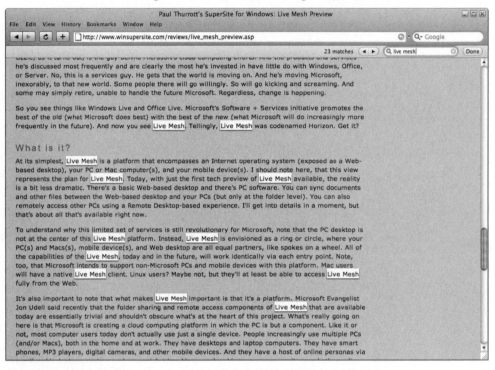

Figure 19-48: There's no doubt about it: Safari's Find in Page feature is the best yet.

✦ **SnapBack:** This unique Safari feature helps you return to the original search results page when you've found yourself navigating too far from those results (and who hasn't gotten lost in the Web like this?) SnapBack is exposed as an orange icon that appears in the Search field. No matter how far you've wandered, just click this icon and you'll be snapped back to your previous search results page.

✦ **Forms autofill:** While many browser add-ons for Firefox and Internet Explorer add a forms autofill feature, Safari includes it by default. This means it can automatically fill in such commonly needed data as your address, phone number, and e-mail address, and can do so in a safe manner.

◆ **Resizable text areas:** Have you ever tried to enter data into a text area in a form but felt constrained by the small size of that control? Safari comes to the rescue by enabling you to resize text area controls on any Web site, giving you the room you need, as shown in Figure 19-49.

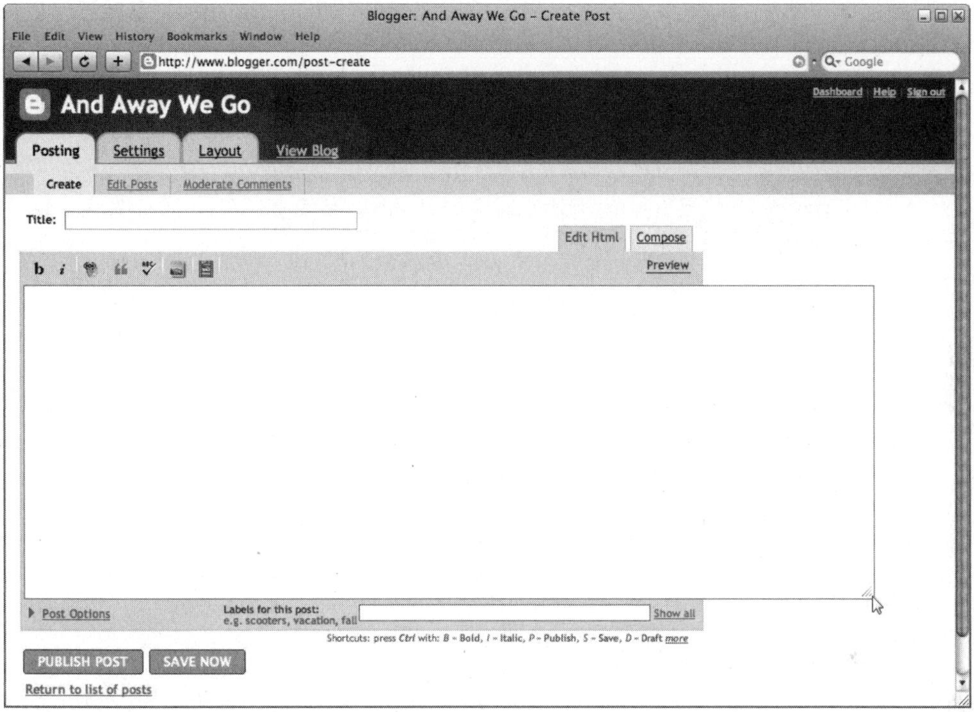

Figure 19-49: Safari enables you to resize text areas, giving you more room to enter text.

◆ **Gorgeous text and graphic rendering:** The best reason I've seen to use Safari, frankly, is its text and graphics rendering capabilities. I don't know how Apple does it, but text and graphics in Safari just look better than they do in Firefox or IE, and they seem to pop right off the page.

You can find out more about Safari, and snag the free download, from the Apple Web site (**www.apple.com/safari/**).

All that said, Safari isn't a slam dunk like Firefox. Unlike Mozilla's browser, Safari isn't supported by a rich ecosystem of browser add-ons. In fact, there are almost no Safari add-ons at all. And unlike Firefox, the Safari UI is almost completely noncustomizable. This is a problem because the default Safari user interface looks like a Mac application, not a Windows Vista application.

I prefer Mozilla Firefox over either Internet Explorer or Safari, but you can't go wrong with any of these browsers. The choice, as they say, is yours.

Summary

Internet Explorer 7 is a huge advance over previous versions, with major functional advances. Although you can debate whether the user interface changes make Internet Explorer 7 more difficult to use, it's hard to argue with the other features Microsoft has added—tabbed browsing and Quick Tabs, Favorites Center, integrated Web search, the browser's vastly improved text display and printing functionality, and its history-hiding techniques are all wonderful advancements. Internet Explorer 7 integration with RSS is also a positive sign: This standards-based Web technology is sweeping across the Internet, enabling everything from blogs to podcasts. For once, Internet Explorer is as capable and usable as its competition. That said, IE competitors such as Mozilla Firefox and Apple Safari offer unique features that may make a switcher out of you yet. However, Microsoft isn't standing still: By the time you read this, it should have already released its next browser, Internet Explorer 8.

Managing E-mail and Contacts

Chapter

20

◆ ◆

In This Chapter

The new Windows Mail features

Finding and managing the new Windows Mail storage engine

Upgrading to Windows Live Mail

Utilizing Web mail and other unique Windows Live Mail features

Managing contacts and contact groups with Windows Contacts and Windows Live Contacts

Importing contacts from your previous Windows version and between Windows Contacts and Windows Live Contacts

◆ ◆

When Microsoft shipped Windows 95, e-mail was a corporate tool but just a curiosity to the wider computer user base. Today, e-mail is a pervasive presence in many people's lives, both personal and professional, and one of the main activities that people perform with computers and other computerized devices, whether they're online or not. For years, Windows has been saddled with an almost universally loathed e-mail client called Outlook Express. Unfortunately, that e-mail client carries through to Windows Vista, albeit with a new name: Windows Mail. On the flip side, Microsoft has since updated Windows Mail to a much improved new version called Windows Live Mail, which addresses most of the shortcomings of Windows Mail. Moreover, Windows Vista introduces a dramatically improved contacts management system, based on XML technology, called Windows Contacts. You'll learn about all of these e-mail and contacts management solutions in this chapter.

Windows Mail Basics

In previous versions of Windows, Microsoft offered a bare-bones e-mail and newsgroup client called Outlook Express. The name suggested that Outlook Express was somehow a smaller, less functional version of Microsoft's premier e-mail and personal information management (PIM) client, Outlook, although the two applications are in fact not related. Oddly, Outlook Express includes certain functionality that was never included in Outlook—primarily support for USENET newsgroups—whereas Outlook, of course, includes numerous features not found in Outlook Express, including Exchange Server support, calendaring and tasks, and more.

tip   I'm often asked in which versions of Windows Vista readers can find Outlook or Microsoft Office. These applications are not part of any version of Windows but are instead sold separately. I believe the confusion arises because most people obtain new Windows versions with new PCs, and those PCs often come with a version of Office as well. For the record, you can purchase Outlook as a standalone application or as part of various versions of the Microsoft Office suite of applications. Or, you can save a lot of money and simply use Windows Live Mail for e-mail and contacts management, and Vista's Windows Calendar for scheduling and tasks. These solutions are all free to Windows Vista users, unlike Outlook (or Office). In Windows Vista, Outlook Express has been replaced by a new mail client called Windows Mail, shown in Figure 20-1. Given the new visual façade of this application, you're forgiven for believing that Microsoft has finally replaced the lackluster Outlook Express with something better. Unfortunately, that's not the case. Windows Mail is nothing more than a minor upgrade to Outlook Express, presented with a warmed-over UI that's only somewhat updated to look a bit like other Windows Vista applications. In fact, Windows Mail is actually missing a few features from Outlook Express. It's a sad state of affairs.

Windows Mail is one of those programs that many people use without ever realizing its full potential. One reason for this is that most people tend to use it as is—without bothering to consider all of the configuration possibilities that are available. In the following sections you'll learn how to use Windows Mail and make it better fit your needs.

Figure 20-1: Déjà vu—Windows Mail is really just a new name for a warmed-over version of Outlook Express.

Secret

While the user interface in Windows Live Mail, discussed later in this chapter, is somewhat different from that of Windows Mail, this information applies to Microsoft's newer e-mail client as well.

Configuring Windows Mail: A Few Quick Tips for Getting Started

To use Windows Mail with your e-mail account, you need to get the names of the SMTP and POP3/IMAP servers at your Internet service provider (ISP), as well as your e-mail address and e-mail password, your account name (user ID), and your logon password. If this is the first time you're running Windows Mail, you'll be prompted for this information in a wizard. If you've canceled this wizard previously, however, you can always add e-mail account information later: In the Windows Mail window, choose Tools ➪ Accounts, and then Add ➪ E-Mail Account to start configuring your Internet mail account.

By default, Internet Explorer uses Windows Mail as the mail tool when you click an e-mail address while viewing a Web page. If you want to use another e-mail client (such as Microsoft Outlook or Mozilla Thunderbird), you can change this default behavior. To do so, right-click the Start button, choose Properties, and then click Customize. In the bottom of the Customize Start Menu dialog, click the E-mail link button to pick the default client.

To read the articles (also called *messages* or *postings*) in USENET newsgroups online, you need to connect to a news server. Your ISP may maintain a news server, but Windows Mail is already preconfigured with a newsgroup account called Microsoft Communities that provides access to Microsoft's public product support newsgroup server. You can also connect to other news servers.

To connect to a news server, choose Newsgroup Account in the New Account wizard.

Changing Windows Mail Options Right Away

The default configuration for Windows Mail isn't optimal, especially for the first-time user. I suggest that you make the following changes before using Windows Mail to read or write any e-mail messages:

♦ Choose Tools ➪ Options. Click the Read tab, and mark the Automatically Expand Grouped Messages check box. Now you won't have to click the plus symbol repeatedly to follow a conversation thread, at the slight cost of seeing multiple entries in a thread that you might not be particularly interested in. Optionally, uncheck the top option, *Mark messages read after displaying for 5 seconds,* unless you prefer this behavior.

♦ On the Signatures tab, enter at least a rudimentary signature—your name at least—or other information that you want to appear at the bottom of every e-mail message or newsgroup message you send. You can make additional signatures and get more elaborate, as discussed later in this chapter, but I suggest that you don't get carried away.

♦ To automatically associate a particular signature with a mail or news account, highlight it in the Signatures list and click the Advanced button. In the Advanced Signature Settings dialog, check all the accounts for which this signature is to be the default. For these accounts only, doing so will override the general default signature setting.

♦ Make sure that the Send Messages Immediately check box in the Send tab (Tools ➪ Options) is marked if you work online or want to have messages sent as soon as you finish writing them. If you work offline, clear this check box and choose Tools ➪ Send and Receive when you're ready to send your mail. You can also just click the Send and Receive button in the Windows Mail toolbar to send mail from your outbox to the mail server.

♦ If you are browsing the Internet online and click an e-mail address on a Web page to send a message, that message will not be sent right away unless the Send Messages Immediately check box is marked. Instead, it remains in your outbox until you click the Send and Receive button in Windows Mail.

♦ In the Spelling tab, make sure that the top option, *Always check spelling before sending,* is checked.

More Windows Mail Features

The Windows Mail window is divided into three panes. The Message List pane (the one on the top right) lists the message headers, and the Preview pane (the one on the bottom right by default) displays the contents of whatever message you have selected in the message header pane. You can arrange these two panes either horizontally or vertically. To do so, choose View ➪ Layout ➪ Below Messages or Beside Messages (actually below or beside message headers).

By default, Windows Mail displays its folders in a large pane on the left, called the Folder List. Unlike its predecessor, Outlook Express, however, Windows Mail does not display the contents of your address book in a pane on the lower left. Unfortunately, there's no way to enable this old feature because Windows Vista utilizes a new shell view, called Windows Contacts, for managing your e-mail contacts.

When you single-click a message header, you can view its contents in the Preview pane. This works just fine most of the time. If you want to view a message in a new (and bigger) window, double-click the message header. If you want to get rid of the Preview pane and only view messages in separate message windows, choose View ➪ Layout and clear the Show Preview Pane check box. Typically, you'll want to leave the Preview pane open, however.

tip If you want news messages to appear in the Preview pane as soon as you select them, choose Tools ➪ Options, click the Read tab, and make sure the *Automatically Download Message When Viewing in the Preview Pane* option is selected. When this option is turned off, you have to press the spacebar after selecting a message to display its contents in the Preview pane.

If you don't like the column order in the Message Header pane, drag the gray column header buttons to the desired position. You can also change the width of the columns by resting your mouse on the spacer line between column header buttons and dragging to the right or the left. To sort your messages by a particular column (such as the Subject column), click the column header button. To sort by the same column in reverse order, click the button again. To add or remove columns, right-click the column header and choose Columns, and then check or clear the boxes for the columns you want to display.

tip If you're using the Preview pane to view your messages, you can get a little extra room by hiding the header bar at the top of the Preview pane. To do this, choose View ➪ Layout ➪ Show Preview Pane Header. The trade-off is that you lose the capability to quickly open or save attachments by clicking the paper-clip button in the header bar. For this reason, you should leave the header on.

If you right-click the Windows Mail toolbar and choose Customize, you can change its content and appearance. The toolbar gets a lot bigger and more readable if you make the icons bigger (choose Large Icons from the Icon Options list) and take out the text under the buttons (choose No Text Labels from the Text Options list). You can also get rid of the toolbar altogether by choosing View ➪ Layout, and then clearing the check mark next to Toolbar. The Customize Toolbar dialog that makes all this possible is shown in Figure 20-2.

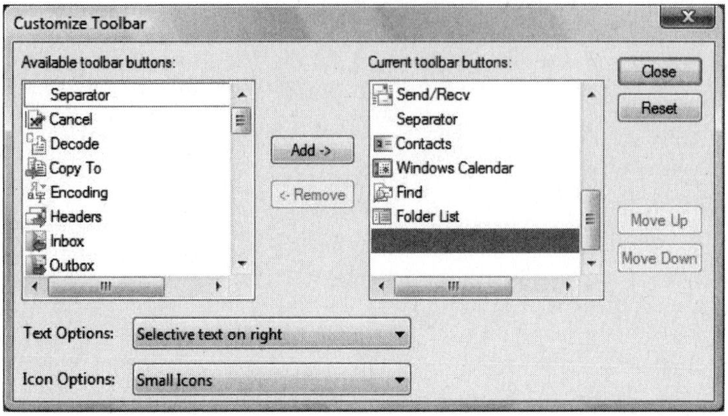

Figure 20-2: You don't have to accept the default Windows Mail toolbar layout.

Sadly, Microsoft removed the popular Outlook bar in this version, so that's no longer an option.

The Folder bar, shown in Figure 20-3, is a thick gray stripe under the toolbar that lists your current message folder and identity. When the Folder List pane is not displayed, you can use the Folder bar to verify which folder you're in and navigate to another. Click the name of the current folder in the Folder bar to display a drop-down folders list. The folders list works similarly to the Folder List pane, in that you can right-click folders in it, and use it to drag and drop.

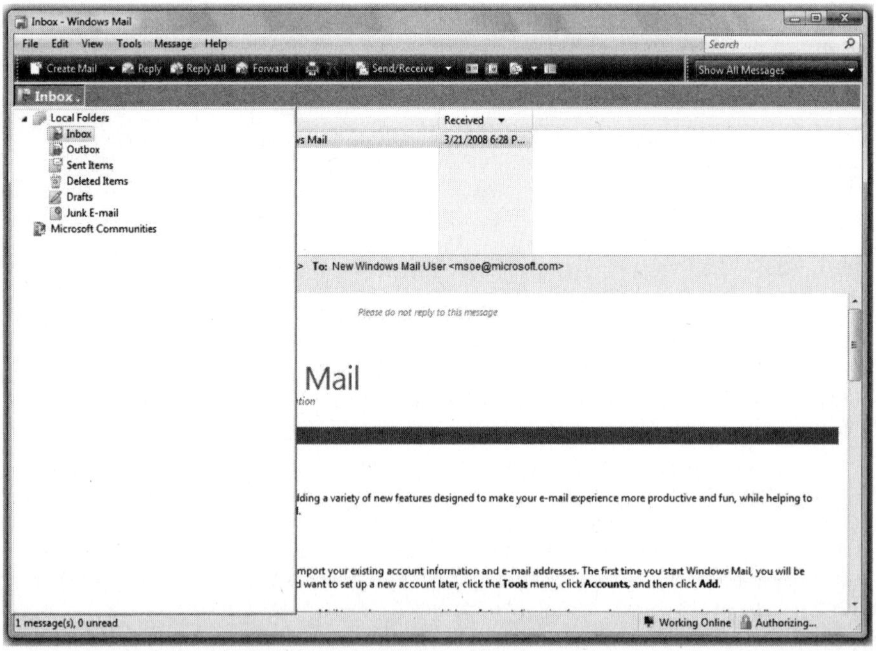

Figure 20-3: The Folder bar is an optional UI component that can be used with, or in place of, the folders list.

You may decide not to display the Folder List pane, and to use the folder list instead. This gives you a wider Preview pane and makes it easier to read messages without opening them. To turn off the Folder List pane, click the close window button in the upper-right corner of the pane—or choose View ⇨ Layout ⇨ Clear Folder List, and then click OK.

If you prefer to display the Folder List pane, you might find that the Folder bar takes up too much real estate in your Windows Mail window. To turn the Folder bar off, choose View ⇨ Layout, and clear the Folder Bar check box. If you do this, you may want to put the Folder List button on your toolbar so you can toggle the Folder List pane on and off without using the Folder bar.

Working Online or Offline

If you have a broadband Internet connection, you can work online all the time without thinking about it; but if you want to compose e-mail offline, such as when you're on a plane, you sometimes need a way to use communications applications such as Windows Mail and Internet Explorer without them constantly trying to access Internet-based servers.

For example, when you move from your inbox to a news folder, Windows Mail attempts to connect to that news server if you are working online. This might also happen when you highlight the header of an e-mail message that links to a Web site. If you just want to look at the messages without connecting, first switch to working offline. This setting is global for all of your applications that use it, so if you are offline in Internet Explorer, you are also offline in Windows Mail.

To change your work online/work offline setting manually, choose File ⇨ Work Offline. In addition, Windows Mail offers two other ways to both see and change your current state. One is an Offline button that you can add to your mail or news toolbar. When you are working offline, it appears to be depressed. The button's icon and text show you what will happen if you click it, *not* your current state. Some might find this confusing.

Secret

More convenient than the toolbar button is the status bar at the bottom of the Windows Mail application window. Not only does the status bar clearly indicate the current online/offline state, but you can toggle it on and off with a simple double-click. Best of all, it's visible all the time by default.

Using a Nondefault Mail or News Account

If you have set up more than one mail account, when you start a new mail message you will see a From field at the top of the New Message window displaying your default mail account. Likewise, when you reply to a mail message, the From field in your reply will display the account to which the original message was sent, but give you the option to change the account from which your reply is sent. News messages prompt you with a dialog to choose the account to use as well.

It's easy to choose a different mail account or news server for your message. Click the down arrow to the right of the From (or News Server) field in the message header and select from the list of active accounts. When a message is in the outbox, you can look in the Account column to see which account it will use. (If you don't see that column, right-click a column header, click Columns, mark the Account check box in the Columns list, and then click OK.)

Secret

Dragging and Dropping to a Windows Mail Message

If you want to send a new message containing some text from another message or document, all you have to do is drag and drop. Windows Mail must be open for this to work, but it can be minimized as follows:

1. Highlight the text that you want to send. If the text is in a Windows Mail message, you can highlight it in either the message window or the Preview pane. If it's in another document, such as a text file or a Microsoft Word document, highlight it there.

2. Drag and drop the highlighted text onto any message folder except the outbox. If Windows Mail is minimized, hover over its taskbar button until it opens. If the Folders pane is not displayed, hover over the folder name on the Folder bar until the Folders list appears. Drop onto a mail folder for mail, or onto a news folder for news. A New Message window appears containing only the text you highlighted. No header information appears in the new message, and no quote characters are included.

Using Windows Mail with E-mail

Windows Mail operates in mail mode by default, but you can switch between e-mail views by selecting different mail folders in the Folder List pane.

Handling Multiple E-mail Accounts

If you have multiple e-mail accounts, you can check for new messages on any single account manually. Just choose Tools ⇨ Send and Receive, and then choose the account from the submenu that appears. You can choose which e-mail accounts are polled when you click the Send and Receive button (which does the same thing as Tools ⇨ Send and Receive ⇨ Send and Receive All). Just click Tools ⇨ Accounts, highlight a mail account, click the Properties button, and mark or clear the *Include This Account When Receiving Mail or Synchronizing* check box. This also works when specifying which accounts Windows Mail polls automatically.

Replies to your messages will still go to your stated e-mail address (the reply address you indicate in the General tab of each account's Properties dialog) even though you don't necessarily send your e-mail through the SMTP server at your e-mail address location.

Choosing Which Account to Send Your Messages Through

If you have multiple e-mail server accounts, the New Message dialog enables you to choose which account the message will be delivered through. This is true even if you are replying to a message that may have been delivered through a different account. Each account has a specific SMTP outgoing mail server. To associate a specific account with a message, use the drop-down menu button at the right end of the From field.

If you don't specify an account, then Windows Mail sends the message through your default mail server account. Because each account can have a separate Internet connection, and because you can stack mail in your outbox, it is possible to click the Send and Receive button and have Windows Mail evoke multiple ISPs and send out mail through each of them.

New Mail Notifications

You can have your computer play a sound when your mail arrives. To do this, choose Tools ➪ Options, click the General tab, and select the *Play Sound When New Messages Arrive* check box. This only makes sense if you have marked *Check for New Messages Every [   ] Minute(s)* in the same tab.

Windows Mail must be running for the sound to play.

Secret

To pick the sound to play, right-click the volume icon in the Windows Vista system tray and choose Sounds. Then, in the Program list, scroll down to New Mail Notification. Click Sounds to pick a default sound, or click Browse to find another sound file you'd like to use.

Leaving Mail on the Server

If you are using a POP3 account and traveling, you might want to leave mail messages on your mail server until you get back, even though you want to read them now. That way, you can download them to your office computer when you return. (IMAP users should *always* leave their mail on the server; in a way, that's the point of IMAP.)

To do this, choose Tools ➪ Accounts, highlight your mail server, click the Properties button, select the Advanced tab, and enable the *Leave a Copy of Messages on Server* check box.

Converting Mail

You can import Exchange, Outlook, Outlook Express 6, and Windows Mail messages into Windows Mail format. In Windows Mail, just choose File ➪ Import and then Messages.

Reading and Managing Messages

E-mail differs from other types of messages in several ways, but one of the most significant is the ease in composing and sending messages electronically. This ease contributes to the absolute flood of messages that many people send and receive on a regular basis. Fortunately, Windows Mail offers several ways for you to deal with all of these messages—as you'll see in the following sections.

Did You Receive the Message?

When you send an important letter the old-fashioned way, you can ask the post office to notify you when the letter is delivered. It's possible for e-mail to work similarly, minus the friendly postal carrier. That is, you can ask to be notified when someone opens a message you have sent. In the New Message window, select Tools ⇨ Request Read Receipt. You can set this globally for all messages you send by choosing Tools ⇨ Options ⇨ Receipts and enabling *Request a Read Receipt for All Sent Messages*. Before you select this check box, however, consider carefully whether you really want to clutter your inbox with all those receipts.

If you receive a message with a receipt request, Windows Mail will ask whether you want to send a receipt. You can set it to Always Send a Read Receipt or Never Send a Read Receipt by marking the appropriate box on the Receipts tab of the Tools ⇨ Options dialog. If you decide to always send a receipt, you will probably want to make an exception for mailing lists by marking the Always Send a Read Receipt check box.

If you frequently send or receive digitally signed messages, it can be very helpful to verify that the message arrived free of security errors. You set the behavior for secure receipts separately from the nonsecure kind, using the same Tools ⇨ Options ⇨ Receipts dialog.

Choosing Your Columns

You can choose which columns to display in the Message pane. To do so, right-click any column header button and click Columns (or choose View ⇨ Columns). In the Columns dialog, mark the columns you want to see and clear those you don't. Use the move up button and the move down button to set the order in which columns appear (or you can drag the column header buttons to position them). Each message folder can have different column settings.

For example, if you find that the Flag column isn't useful and is just taking up space, you can turn it off. Although you will still be able to flag a message, you won't see the icons in the Message pane and will be unable to sort by flag.

tip If you have more than one incoming mail account, you might want to view the Account column. That way, you can easily see where a message came from without bothering with message rules. The Account column can also be very helpful in your outbox.

Composing and Sending Messages

You can associate a new e-mail message with a specific account at the time that the message is composed. This is especially helpful if you have multiple users with different accounts on the same computer:

1. Open a New Message window by clicking Message ⇨ New Message.
2. Click anywhere in the From field to display a list of your accounts.
3. Select the mail account you want to use when sending the message.

Using the Drafts Folder

The Drafts folder is a place to keep messages that you're not yet ready to send. When you are composing a message and you choose File ➪ Save, your unfinished message is automatically stored in the Drafts folder. If you close a New Message window without sending the message and click Yes when asked if you want to save it, the message will be stored in Drafts. To finish editing a message stored in the Drafts folder, double-click the message to open it. When you click the Send button, Windows Mail moves it from the Drafts folder to the outbox.

Quoting in Replies and Forwards

When you reply to an e-mail message, it's helpful if you can distinguish the text you write from the message text you are replying to. In plain-text messages, the standard is to place a > symbol in front of each quoted line of text. Fortunately, Windows Mail does this by default, but to configure related functionality, follow these steps:

1. Choose Tools ➪ Options in the Windows Mail window, and click the Send tab.
2. Make sure that the Include Message in Reply check box is enabled (this is the default). If this option is deselected, your replies will be much harder to understand because they will not include a copy of the original message.
3. On this same tab, click the Plain Text Settings button under Mail Sending Format. Make sure *Indent the Original Text with [ ] When Replying or Forwarding* is marked. Windows Mail no longer lets you use a character other than > at the beginning of each line of quoted text.
4. Click OK.

So far, so good; but this kind of quoting only works as long as you are replying to a message sent using plain text. Messages sent using MIME/Quoted Printable (such as HTML-formatted messages) don't insert line endings, so there are no line beginnings for Windows Mail to mark with >. Instead, the text is formatted in paragraphs. Even if you tell Windows Mail to reply in plain text, it will still not place a > at the beginning of quoted lines if they weren't originally composed in plain text. Instead, quoted HTML text is indented with a vertical bar along its left side.

Secret

There is a downside to marking Indent Messages on Reply, however, if you like to intersperse replies with quoted text to simulate a conversation. If you insert your reply after a section of quoted text, the new text is also indented with the vertical bar. To get rid of the indent and the bar, first place your insertion point in the quoted text where you want to insert your reply text and press Enter—this inserts a line break. Then, with your insertion point in the new paragraph, click the Paragraph Style toolbar button and click Normal. Even though the drop-down list shows that the current paragraph is already Normal, this will work. Your new text will be flush left and will not have a vertical bar.

Messages Formatted in HTML

Windows Mail formats your e-mail messages and newsgroup posts using HTML by default. Choose Tools ➪ Options, and click the Send tab to override the default setting for the current newsgroup post or e-mail message. Just choose Format in the New Message window, and click Rich Text (HTML) or Plain Text. If you're using HTML, you get a formatting toolbar that enables you to choose the font, font size, font color, and so on.

> **tip**
> **Many newsgroup and e-mail clients aren't able to display HTML-formatted text. If they can't, your correspondents will see the HTML tags embedded in the plain text of your messages—which they might not appreciate.**

Frankly, HTML e-mail is generally obnoxious. My advice is to use plain text for both e-mail and newsgroup messages. That said, you either want to use HTML mail or you don't.

If you do use HTML e-mail, you can configure Windows Mail to automatically start a new blank message with your chosen background color, background image, font, and margins. You can choose from among the existing stationery files, create new stationery, create stationery that is just a background color, or download new stationery from Microsoft.

To pick a default stationery type, choose Tools ➪ Options ➪ Compose, mark the Mail or News check box under Stationery, and click the Select button. You get to preview the stationery before you select it. After you have chosen a stationery type, clicking New Mail or New Post will open a New Message window with that stationery already included.

> **Secret**
> **Press Ctrl+F2 to confirm that the source code of the HTML e-mail file that Windows Mail uses to create the stationery has been inserted into your new message, including the name of the associated GIF file. In addition, at the top of this HTML view of your message, you'll find a reference pointing to the folder that holds the stationery's image file.**

If you want to create a message with something other than the default stationery, click the down arrow to the right of the New Mail or New Post button. You can pick something else or choose no stationery at all.

Attachments

To save an attachment to a message you have received, double-click the message header in the message header pane to display the message in a separate window. Then drag and drop the attachment icon from the Attach field into a folder or onto the Desktop. You can also right-click the attachment icon and click Save As.

To save an attachment without opening a separate message window, click the message header and then click the paper-clip icon in the upper-right corner of the Preview pane (the Show Preview Pane Header check box must be marked in the View ➪ Layout dialog). A menu listing the names of the attachments in the message appears. Click the name of the attachment you want to open. If you instead choose Save Attachments from this menu, you can browse to a folder to save more than one at a time.

You can also just highlight the message header and choose File ➪ Save Attachments.

New Features in Windows Mail

Okay, enough E-mail 101. It's time to take a look at some of the few new features Microsoft added to the Windows Vista version, Windows Mail. If you don't use Outlook Express, there's no reason to start now. There are much better e-mail clients out there, including Microsoft Outlook, and if you're looking for a solution that handles both e-mail and news-groups, Microsoft has shipped an updated and much improved version of Windows Mail called Windows Live Mail that is considerably more feature-packed than Windows Mail. You'll look at that solution later in this chapter.

That said, there are some new features and secrets to be found in Windows Mail too.

Slightly Updated User Interface

The first thing you'll notice when you fire up Windows Mail is that it's been updated subtly to conform to the new Windows Vista application look and feel. It still includes a classic menu bar, but the old bulky toolbar has been replaced by a smaller blue toolbar similar to those found in other Vista productivity applications such as Windows Calendar. That said, the user interface of Windows Mail is almost identical to that of Outlook Express. A new Contacts button in the toolbar replaces the old Contacts panel from Outlook Express, and various icons used throughout the Windows Mail user interface have been refreshed to be more Vista-like. But that's about it: Even the Windows Mail menu structure is virtually identical to that of its predecessor, with very few exceptions. This just isn't a brand-new application, let alone a major update.

Of course, if you are a dedicated Outlook Express user, that's probably good news. There's not a lot of relearning to do if you've upgraded to Vista.

No More Support for Web Mail

The biggest change in Windows Mail, unfortunately, is a bit of bad news. That is, support for Web-based e-mail services, including Microsoft's own Hotmail (including Windows Live Hotmail and MSN), has been eliminated. In Outlook Express, you could choose between POP3, IMAP, and HTTP mail server types; the latter was used for Web mail accounts. In Windows Mail, that last option was eliminated. Only POP3 and IMAP accounts are now supported.

Secret   In mid-2008, Microsoft ended support for Web mail from Hotmail and MSN in Outlook Express as well, citing the obsolete nature of the technologies needed to keep it working. Therefore, now Outlook Express users are out of luck too.

Why, you ask? After reassessing its Web mail strategy during the development of Windows Vista, Microsoft began evolving Hotmail into a new service called Windows Live Hotmail, which has both free and paid versions. Not coincidentally, the company is also offering a new downloadable e-mail client that is designed expressly for this new service. Called Windows Live Mail, this client offers support for Web mail accounts, including Hotmail and MSN. Microsoft's advice is to use this client, and not Windows Mail, if you need to access Web mail accounts. Coincidentally, my advice mirrors Microsoft's: Windows Live Mail is a better e-mail client than Windows Mail for a variety of reasons, and you should seriously consider using it instead of Windows Mail regardless.

tip   Windows Live Mail Desktop is covered at the end of this chapter.

Secret   Note that most Web mail services provide their customers with access to their e-mail accounts via the POP3 and/or IMAP protocols that Windows Mail supports, so you should still be able to access many Web-based e-mail services with Windows Mail. For example, Gmail offers support for both POP3 and IMAP to all customers. Yahoo!, by comparison, only does so if you pay for a Yahoo! Plus account.

Secret   My personal preference, incidentally, is for Google's free Gmail service. Gmail offers oodles of storage, and is fully compatible with Windows Mail (and Outlook and Windows Live Mail) even though it's technically a Web mail service. If you spend some time with Gmail's Web interface, you may never bother with a desktop e-mail application again: It's clean, fast, and easy to use. Check out www.gmail.com.

Web Instant Search

Like much of Windows Vista, Windows Mail is integrated with the operating system's instant search functionality. This means that Windows Mail picks up a handy instant Search box in the upper-right corner of the main application window. To search the current view—be it an e-mail folder or an online newsgroup—simply select the Search box and start typing. Searching is instantaneous, as it is in the Windows Vista Explorer shell, so it will begin filtering down the list as you type. In addition, instant search will search across all applicable criteria, including sender, subject line, and e-mail or newsgroup body.

Secret

Interestingly, the old Find toolbar button from Outlook Express is still available in Windows Mail. Why would you need Find when Windows Mail includes instant search? Actually, there are some good reasons. When you click Find, you'll see the Find Message dialog shown in Figure 20-4. This dialog enables a very fine-grained search; you can specify exactly the person, subject, or message you're looking for. More important, perhaps, you can also specify *where* to look using the Browse button. Unlike instant search, Find isn't limited to the current folder view.

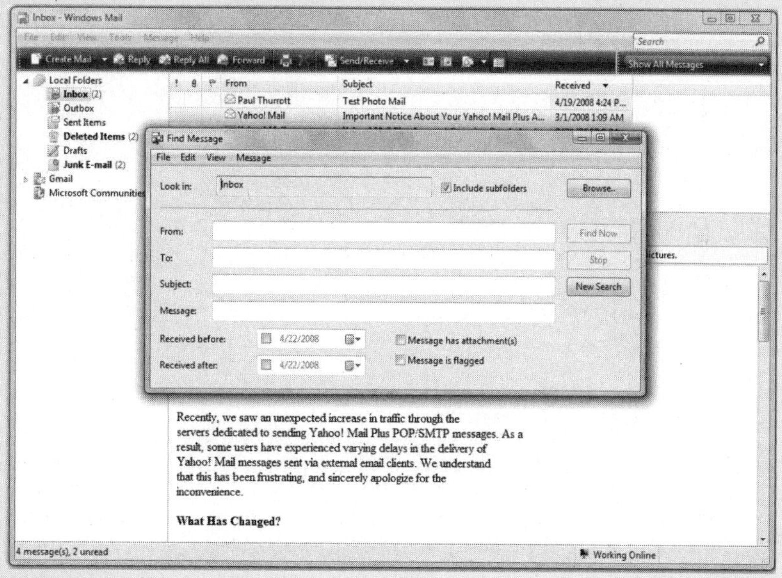

Figure 20-4: Find Message isn't as elegant as instant search, but it helps you look for what you want where you want.

Secret

You can also search your Windows Mail–based e-mail from Start Menu Search. As shown in Figure 20-5, e-mail is one of the default locations that's searched when you search from here. You'll see it under the Communications heading in the Start Menu Search results list.

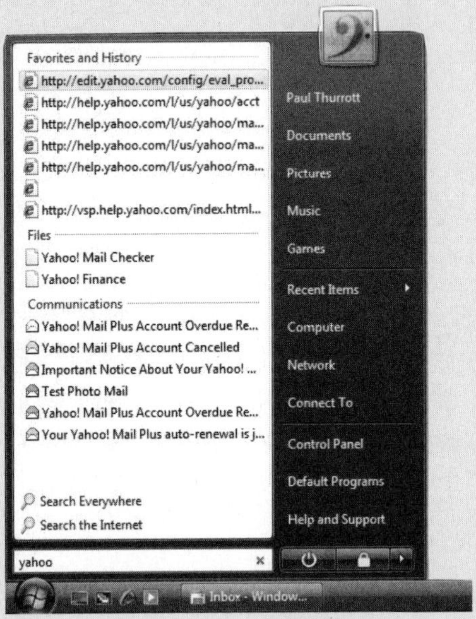

Figure 20-5: Thanks to deep integration within Windows Vista, you can search for e-mail directly from the Start Menu.

Contacts Integration

Whereas Outlook Express integrated with the Windows Address Book used in previous Windows versions, Windows Mail naturally integrates with the new Contacts store found in Windows Vista. I examine Contacts at the end of this chapter, but you can access Contacts from within Windows Mail through the aforementioned toolbar button, from the Tools menu, or by selecting Ctrl+Shift+C. Contacts is shown in Figure 20-6.

Automatic Spell Checking

Unlike its predecessor, Windows Mail includes built-in automatic spell checking. To get this functionality in Outlook Express, you had to have installed Microsoft Word or any other part of the Microsoft Office suite. That said, the Windows Mail spell checker is a bit less functional than the one included with Word or Office: It cannot suggest replacements for misspelled words on-the-fly, but instead offers suggestions only when you try to the send the mail (see Figure 20-7).

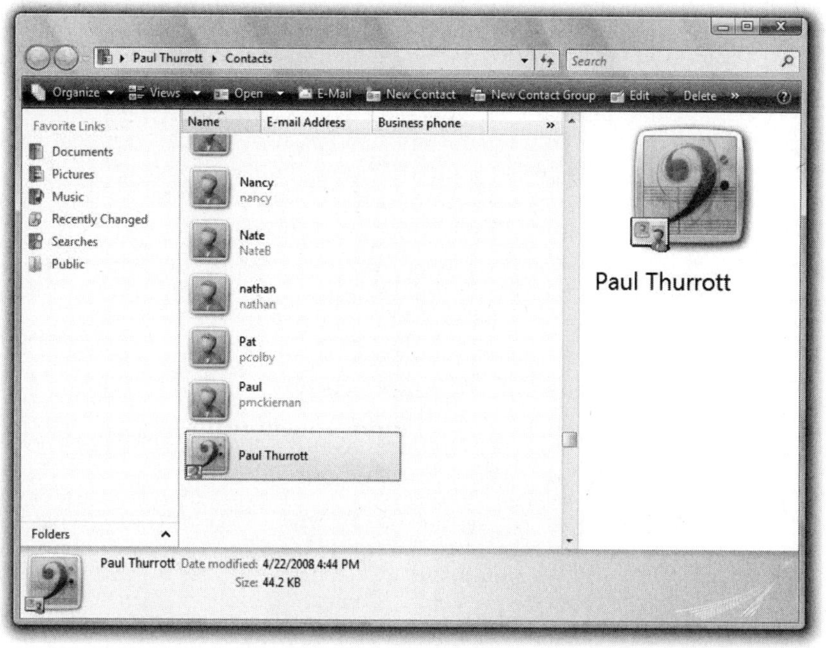

Figure 20-6: Windows Contacts is the new contacts management utility in Windows Vista.

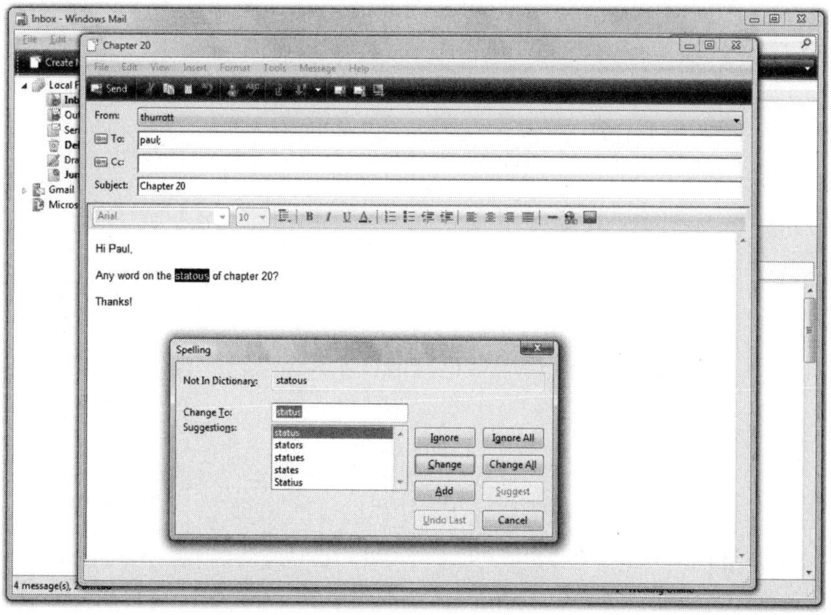

Figure 20-7: Windows Mail has spell checking, yes, but not on-the-fly spell checking.

No More Identities

Because Outlook Express was first designed to work with Windows 95 and subsequent consumer Windows products that had no real concept of individual user accounts, it used a construct called *identities* to enable users to create two or more pseudo-user accounts within the application. You could use identities in various ways. First, multiple users accessing Outlook Express from the same PC could maintain separate identities so that their e-mail accounts wouldn't co-mingle. Second, individual users could set up multiple identities within Outlook Express in order to separate them.

Identities no longer exist in Windows Mail. Now, users are expected to maintain their own user account, each of which has a separate desktop, configuration settings, and so forth.

cross
ref

See Chapter 9 for more information about user accounts.

Secret

If you upgrade an older computer to Windows Vista and were using Outlook Express with multiple identities, Windows Mail will run a wizard the first time it's launched that enables you to import identities into your user account. You can run this wizard, shown in Figure 20-8, on each account to ensure that the correct identities are matched to the correct user accounts in Vista.

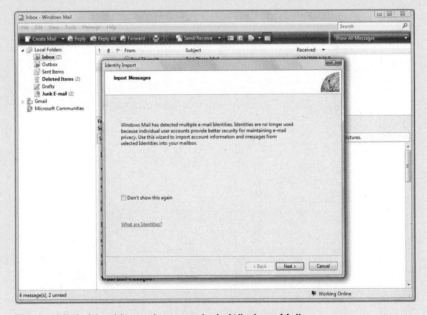

Figure 20-8: Identities no longer exist in Windows Mail.

New Mail Storage

Windows Mail, finally, uses an entirely new storage engine for e-mail that is more reliable and offers better performance than that used by Outlook Express. Anyone who's been frustrated by Outlook Express's antiquated storage engine—typically noticed when the application slows to a crawl when accessing large e-mail folders or newsgroups—should appreciate this change.

Secret

On a related note, it's now much easier to move the Windows Mail storage around in the file system because Windows Mail keeps everything—its e-mail and newsgroup folders, account information, and settings—in a single, easily accessible folder. Now, when you move the Windows Mail storage folder, everything else moves with it. This also makes Windows Mail much easier to back up. All of the Windows Mail data files can now be found in C:\Users*User Name*\AppData\Local\Microsoft\Windows Mail by default. To back this up, simply copy this folder to a different location, such as a rewriteable optical disk or removable hard drive. If you are backing up Windows Mail, back up your contacts as well. Contacts are stored in C:\Users*User Name*\Contacts by default.

Secret

If you do want to move the Windows Mail storage folder to a new location, it's actually quite simple.

1. Navigate to Tools ➪ Options ➪ Advanced, and click the Maintenance button (see Figure 20-9).

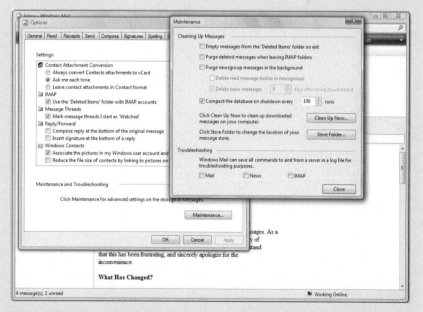

Figure 20-9: The Maintenance dialog enables you to change the location where you store your Windows Mail e-mail.

continues

continued

2. Click the Store Folder button.

3. In the Store Folder dialog, click the Change button and browse to the new location.

Unlike Outlook Express, the new Browse for Folder dialog in Windows Vista enables you to create a new folder as well, so you don't have to do that ahead of time as you did previously. Windows Mail moves all of your data to the new location automatically after you shut down the application.

tip   Registry buffs should be aware that Windows Mail's Registry structure has changed as well, so if you've been using a favorite set of Registry scripts for Outlook Express, beware: They won't work anymore in Windows Mail.

Security Features

In keeping with the push for better desktop security in Windows Vista, Windows Mail picks up a couple of useful features that make it marginally safer than Outlook Express. The first is a new Junk Mail filter, which is very similar to the Junk Mail filter found in Microsoft Outlook. You can access Junk Mail options from the Junk E-mail Options dialog, shown in Figure 20-10.

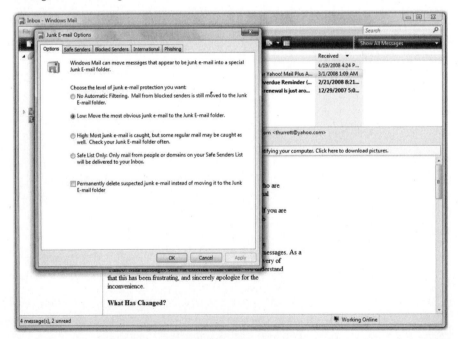

Figure 20-10: Finally, Windows Mail picks up one of the more useful features of Outlook.

Here, you can choose a level of automatic junk e-mail protection and set up Safe Senders, Safe Recipients, and Blocked Senders lists. There's also an International tab for automatically blocking mail written in languages you don't understand, and e-mail from certain top-level domain names. If you're familiar with junk e-mail protection in Microsoft Outlook, you'll be right at home here.

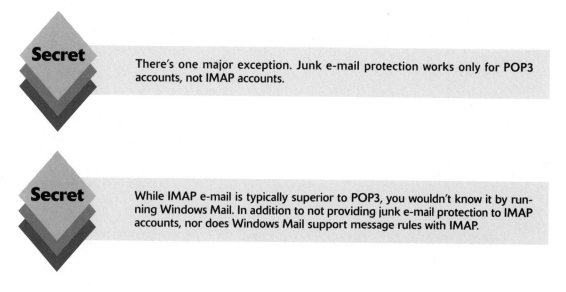

Secret
There's one major exception. Junk e-mail protection works only for POP3 accounts, not IMAP accounts.

Secret
While IMAP e-mail is typically superior to POP3, you wouldn't know it by running Windows Mail. In addition to not providing junk e-mail protection to IMAP accounts, nor does Windows Mail support message rules with IMAP.

In addition to its Junk Mail feature, Windows Mail also includes a phishing filter, which can prevent certain e-mail-based scams. Here's how a phishing (pronounced like *fishing*) attack works. A malicious user sends out junk e-mail to random recipients that appear to come from a bank, online retailer or auction site, or other trusted institution with which you might do business. These e-mails, which are often written in such a way to suggest that there might be something wrong with an account you have, try to get you to click embedded links and visit malicious Web sites. These Web sites are also masquerading as legitimate locations. They try to get you to provide valid logon information that you might use at the actual institution and then use this information for identity theft. Each year, millions of people fall victim to phishing scams.

To help prevent this, Microsoft has added antiphishing technology to both Internet Explorer 7 and Windows Mail in Windows Vista. In Windows Mail, the phishing filter is on by default. You can view two phishing filter options from the Phishing tab of the Junk E-Mail Options dialog if you're curious, but my advice here is simple. Don't turn this feature off under any circumstances.

Windows Live Mail: The Next Generation

Okay, I've said a lot in this chapter about Windows Mail because it is included free with Vista, and I'm reasonably sure that millions of dedicated Outlook Express users out there will simply begin using its replacement when they upgrade to Windows Vista. Fair enough. I've warned you about Windows Mail's failings.

I will offer this one last bit of advice, however: Microsoft has further upgraded Outlook Express/Windows Mail into a brand-new application called Windows Live Mail. It's available free from the Web as part of the Windows Live suite discussed in Chapter 21. Windows Live Mail offers all of the functionality of Windows Mail and then some, and you should seriously consider using it instead of Windows Mail regardless of whether you're an old Outlook Express fan. Windows Live Mail rights virtually everything that is wrong with Windows Mail.

As with Windows Live Photo Gallery, which builds off the Windows Photo Gallery application found in Windows Vista, Windows Live Mail is a next-generation e-mail client that builds off of Vista's Windows Mail. Thus, Windows Live Mail is now the very latest client in the Outlook Express family of e-mail applications. That said, Windows Live Mail is dramatically better than Windows Mail or Outlook Express, and unlike my feelings about those applications, I don't have many reservations about using Windows Live Mail. It's a great application.

The most impressive thing about Windows Live Mail is that it looks and acts almost nothing like Windows Mail, despite the common technical heritage. As shown in Figure 20-11, Windows Live Mail is both attractive and visually distinct from Windows Mail. It also offers nice integration points with various Windows Live services, which can be a plus if you're a fan of Microsoft's online work.

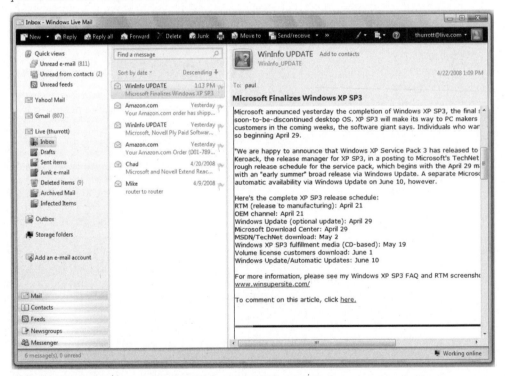

Figure 20-11: Despite its Outlook Express underpinnings, Windows Live Mail is pretty impressive work.

Windows Live Mail is designed to work primarily with Microsoft's Windows Live Hotmail and MSN e-mail services; and while the application does work particularly well with those services, it works just fine with any POP3 or IMAP e-mail account as well, just like Windows Mail. In fact, one of the best uses of Windows Live Mail is to access two or more e-mail accounts simultaneously from the same place.

Installing Windows Live Mail

Though Microsoft doesn't make this obvious, Windows Live Mail can in fact be downloaded independently, even though the company promotes it as part of a wider Windows Live suite, which includes other Windows Live products and services. Because I cover the Windows Live suite in Chapter 21, it makes sense to cover just the Windows Live Mail installation here.

You can trigger and install the Windows Live Mail download by visiting the Windows Live Mail Web site (**http://get.live.com/wlmail/overview**) instead of the main Windows Live Web site (**www.windowslive.com**). Once there, simply click the Get It Free button. When you do so, you'll be prompted to run or download the Windows Live Installer (WLinstaller.exe), assuming you're using Internet Explorer. (Some other browsers require you to download the file first and then execute it locally.) Choose Run. Once the install finishes downloading, it will run (after a brief UAC security prompt) and present the simple interface shown in Figure 20-12.

Figure 20-12: The Windows Live installer runs directly from the Web.

Click Accept to continue. In the first phase of the Windows Live Installer, you'll be presented with two options. In the first, you're asked to make MSN Home your Internet Explorer home page. In the unlikely event that you actually want to do that, feel free to leave it checked. Otherwise, uncheck this option. The second option regards Microsoft's customer experience program: The company collects anonymous data about your installation experience only so that it can improve the product in the future. I recommend leaving this option checked. Click Install when you're ready.

After a bit of churning, the Windows Live Installer begins installing Windows Live Mail. As shown in Figure 20-13, this installer can also be used to install a number of other Windows Live products, including Windows Live Messenger, Writer, Toolbar, Photo Gallery, and Family Safety. However, because you launched the installer from the Windows Live Mail page, you are installing only that tool and one required subcomponent—the Windows Live Sign-in Assistant.

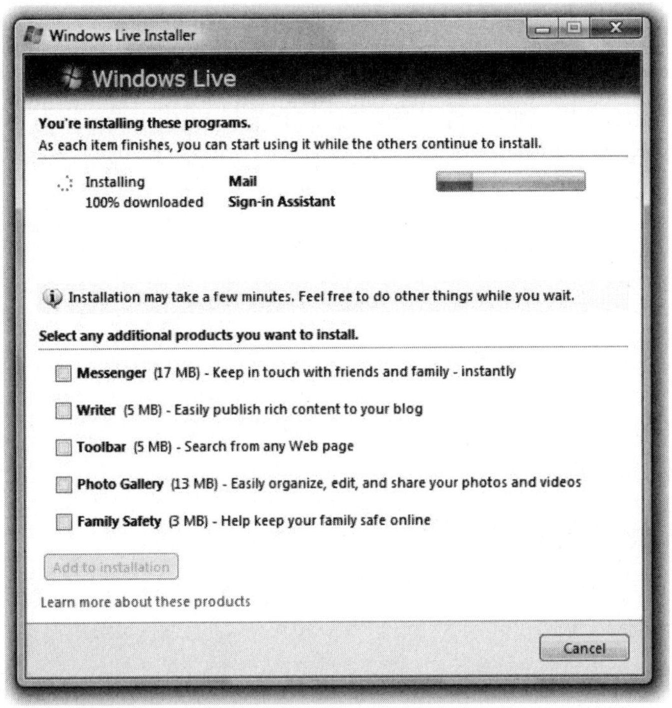

Figure 20-13: The Windows Live Installer can be configured to install just one product or any number of available Windows Live products and services.

That said, you are also free to install the other available products by checking the boxes next to each option. You can learn more about these products in Chapter 21.

Click the close button to close the Windows Live Installer. When you do so, Windows Live Mail starts up and prompts you to add an e-mail account, as shown in Figure 20-14. Not surprisingly, Hotmail- and MSN-based e-mail addresses are the easiest to configure: All you need is your e-mail address, password, and name.

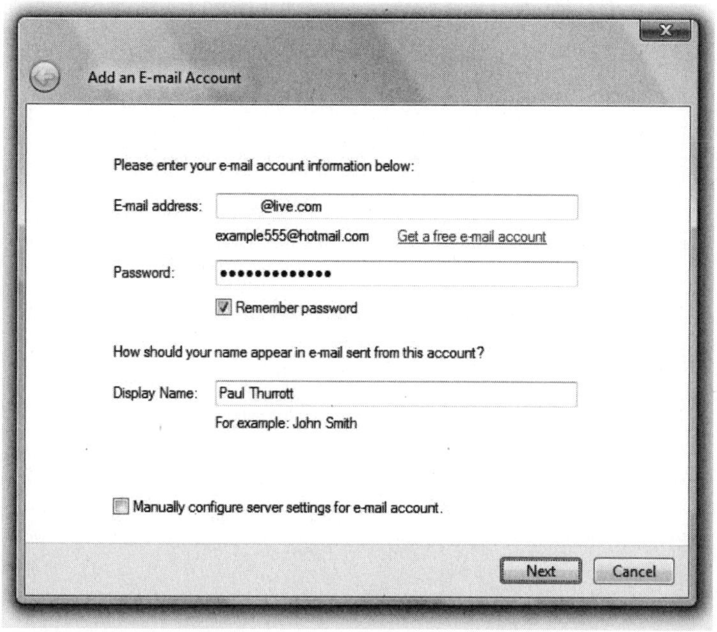

Figure 20-14: Unlike POP3 and IMAP accounts, Windows Live ID-based e-mail accounts can be set up with a minimum of configuration.

Assuming you have a Windows Live ID, and thus a Hotmail-type account, you should enter that information now. If you don't, be ready with the logon information required for your POP3- or IMAP-based e-mail account, as the information in the next section will make more sense if you've fully configured at least one e-mail account.

Understanding the Windows Live User Interface

Compared to Windows Mail, Windows Live Mail offers a fresher look and feel—and one that is far more customizable to boot—but it also adopts the more modern three-pane view that Microsoft first debuted in its business-oriented Outlook application. Shown in Figure 20-15, the Windows Live Mail user interface includes five main areas:

- ◆ **Toolbar:** Unlike Windows Mail, Windows Live Mail hides its toolbar by default, resulting in a more streamlined look. As with other Windows Vista applications, you can tap the Alt key to temporarily access the Windows Live Mail menu bar. You can also display the menu bar permanently if you so desire.

- ◆ **Folder pane:** This leftmost pane includes Quick views (essentially prebuilt stored searches that you might frequently need); storage folders, both local and remote, for all of the e-mail accounts you've configured; and Shortcuts, a list of buttons that link to Windows Live Mail experiences such as Mail, Contacts, (RSS) Feeds, (USENET) Newsgroups, and (Windows Live) Messenger.

- ◆ **Message pane:** This middle pane includes the instant search box and the message list, which varies according to which e-mail, RSS, or newsgroup folder you're currently viewing.

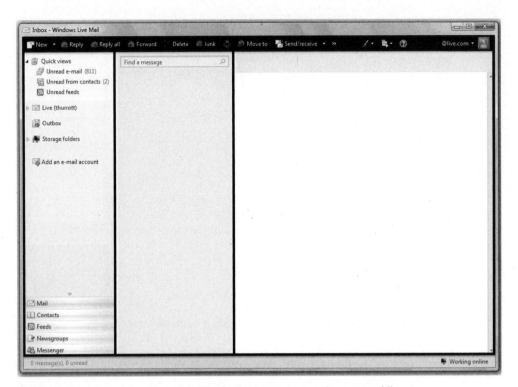

Figure 20-15: Windows Live Mail, like Outlook, presents a three-pane UI.

Secret

Windows Live Mail also supports an optional and confusingly named pane called the Active Search pane. This is a leftover from the days when Microsoft envisioned sponsoring this free product with paid advertisements, and it is not, as its name suggests, related to searching for e-mail. Instead, Active Search presents a columnar list of Internet-based advertising. There is absolutely no good reason to turn this thing on.

◆ **Reading pane:** This rightmost pane is shown to the right of the Message list by default, creating the application's three-pane look. However, if you prefer to make Windows Live Mail look more like Outlook Express or Windows Mail, you can move the Reading pane below the message list.

Changes to the Toolbar

Aside from the different layout, there are other differences between Windows Live Mail and its Vista-based predecessor. For example, whereas the drop-down menu attached to the Create Mail toolbar button in Windows Mail is oriented specifically to different types of stationery-based e-mails, the menu attached to Windows Live Mail's New button reveals a more diverse set of options. You can create new e-mail and Photo Mail (discussed later in the chapter), but you can also trigger an instant message (via Windows Live Messenger), mobile text message, or blog entry (using Windows Live Writer, described in Chapter 21). You can also create new contacts and folders (local or remote) from this menu.

On the Windows Live Mail toolbar, a Move to Junk Mail button is prominently available, enabling you to easily dispatch selected e-mails to the Junk Mail folder. This is much improved over the Junk Mail system in Windows Mail, which doesn't offer a simple way to mark individual messages as junk.

Whereas Windows Mail contains toolbar-based links to Vista applications such as Windows Contacts and Windows Calendar, Windows Live instead offers various links throughout the UI to different Windows Live services. Windows Live Contacts is accessed via the Contacts shortcut in the Folder pane, and, as mentioned previously, there are ways to access Windows Live Messenger and Writer directly from Windows Live Mail. The more central connection with Windows Live, however, comes via the Windows Live sign-in mechanism in the upper-right corner of the application window. Shown in Figure 20-16, this area varies greatly depending on whether or not you're logged on to your Windows Live ID.

Figure 20-16: If you haven't configured a Windows Live-based e-mail account, this menu doesn't do very much.

There are two other UI options in the Windows Live Mail toolbar worth discussing. At the far right of the toolbar, but to the left of the Windows Live ID button, are two unique buttons. The first, Color Scheme, enables you to change the colors of Windows Live Mail, a capability that is present in most downloadable Windows Live applications. The second, Show Menu, doesn't actually display the classic application menu but rather presents a short menu of options of its own, as shown in Figure 20-17.

Figure 20-17: The Show Menu button provides a mini-menu of its own.

The Layout option enables you to determine which UI pieces are visible in the Windows Live Mail application and, in some cases, where they are located. The Layout dialog, shown in Figure 20-18, expands and contracts as you select individual options.

Figure 20-18: Various elements of the Windows Live Mail UI are highly configurable.

Options, of course, opens the Windows Live Mail Options dialog, which is almost identical to the Options dialog in Windows Mail, and perhaps the best indication that these applications share a common heritage. There is one major exception: Whereas Windows Mail utilizes a Security tab to provide customizable virus protection, image downloading, and secure mail options, Windows Live Mail makes that part of a separate Safety Options dialog (also available via the Show Menu button). Safety Options, shown in Figure 20-19, includes settings related to junk mail filtering, safe and blocked senders, antiphishing, and more.

Secret

There are some minor differences in the options available to each application as well. Most are related to differences in the focus of each application. For example, Windows Mail contains options that pertain to Windows Contacts, as Windows Mail utilizes a separate application for managing contacts, whereas Windows Live Mail has integrated Contacts functionality. Meanwhile, the Windows Live Mail Options dialog presents a number of settings related to Windows Live services integration, as that is a primary feature of this application. Beyond these obvious changes, there are a few hidden gems. Windows Live Mail, for example, sports a custom dictionary that can be edited and supports as-you-type spell checking.

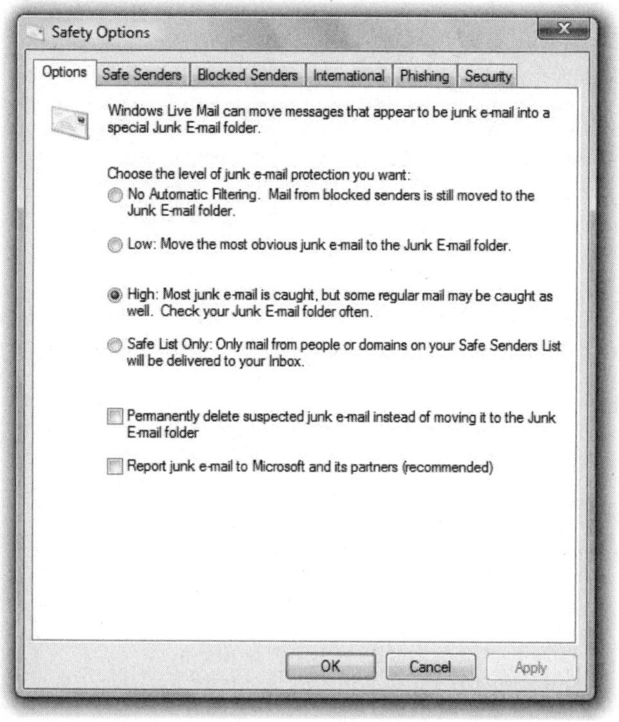

Figure 20-19: The Safety Options dialog replaces the Junk Mail Settings window from Windows Mail.

Finally, you can use the Show Menu button to customize the Windows Live Mail toolbar and toggle the permanent display of the application's Classic Menu.

Changes in the Folder Pane

In the leftmost pane in the application, called the Folder pane, you'll see a few major improvements. Whereas the Windows Mail Folders List is just that—a literal listing of local and remote folders—the Windows Live Mail Folders pane contains a number of different elements. They're laid out in a more attractive fashion—that is, without using a single tree view as in Windows Mail—but there's also additional functionality.

At the top of the Folders pane is a Quick Views section that includes three custom views by default: Unread e-mail, Unread from contacts, and Unread feeds. These views aggregate all of the e-mail, from all of the accounts you've configured, into a single view—so if you want to see all of your unread e-mail, regardless of the source, here's a great way to do so.

Below that you'll see separate folder structures for your remote e-mail accounts (which vary according to account type and which folders are available on each server) and local folders, which are called *storage folders* in this release. Naturally, you can drag and drop e-mail messages between them, including between different accounts and local folders.

At the bottom of the Folder pane is a new Shortcuts area, which is inspired by a similar UI element in Microsoft Outlook. Basically, it's a box with five buttons, most of which change the view in Windows Live Mail. By default, you're in the Mail view, but other options include Contacts (which opens in its own window and is described later in this chapter), Feeds (for RSS feeds, also covered later in the chapter), Newsgroups (as with Windows Mail, for USENET newsgroups), and Messenger (which launches or changes the focus to the Windows Live Messenger instant messaging application).

Changes in the Messages Pane

The central pane, Message Header pane, has two main sections by default: an instant search box where you can search the contents of your e-mail folders, and a message list, which shows the contents of the currently-selected folder.

In Windows Mail, the search box is found in the upper-right corner of the application window but it works in basically the same way with one major exception: Windows Live Mail enables you to filter search results by account, which is handy when you have several configured.

The Windows Live Mail Messages list works much like the similar feature in Microsoft Outlook, and not like the one in Windows Mail; and that's true even in you configure Windows Mail to work in a three-column view, with the Reading pane next to the Message list instead of below it. As shown in Figure 20-20, Windows Live Mail looks great configured this way, whereas Windows Mail does not.

Accessing RSS Feeds

As discussed in Chapter 19, Windows Vista includes compatibility with RSS feeds, an automated way of subscribing to frequently updated content online. (RSS is variously expanded to Real Simple Syndication or Rich Site Summary, depending on who you talk to.) This compatibility comes courtesy of technology that's integrated into Internet Explorer, Microsoft's Web browser. This makes some sense, because most users typically discover RSS feeds as they browse Web sites online, but there's some debate about whether the browser is really the best place to read, or *consume*, RSS feeds. Some argue, for example, that the e-mail client is the logical place for reading RSS feeds. After all, this application is already used to read content that is delivered on an ad hoc schedule.

Fair enough. Without picking a winner in this debate, I will at least point out that Microsoft is straddling both sides of the fence, because in addition to the Web-based RSS functionality in Internet Explorer, the company also provides access to RSS feeds in its two best e-mail clients, Microsoft Outlook (part of Office and generally aimed at business users) and Windows Live Mail (which is decidedly consumer oriented).

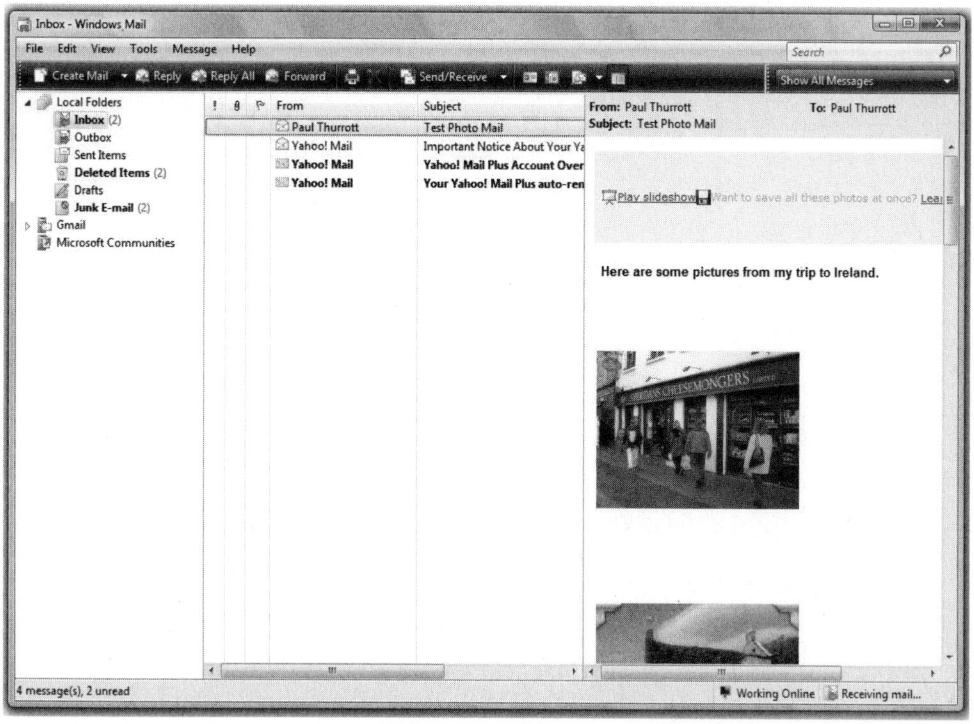

Figure 20-20: Unlike its predecessor, Windows Live Mail was designed to work in a three-column view.

Secret

RSS compatibility in Microsoft Outlook and Windows Live Mail shares another similarity: They both require you to have installed Internet Explorer 7 (which is provided as part of Windows Vista) or higher. That's because IE is still the ideal way to discover new feeds; but now you have a choice regarding where to enjoy that content, depending on your habits: You can do so in the browser, using the IE features discussed in Chapter 19, or you can use your favorite e-mail client.

Any RSS feeds to which you've subscribed in Internet Explorer appear automatically (and immediately, if both applications are open) in Windows Live Mail. RSS feeds are accessed via the Feeds link in the Shortcuts section found in the bottom-left corner of the application window. As shown in Figure 20-21, subscribed feeds look like e-mail messages in Windows Live Mail. This is both familiar and useful, as you can now utilize the application's e-mail-oriented features, like instant search, on subscribed content as well.

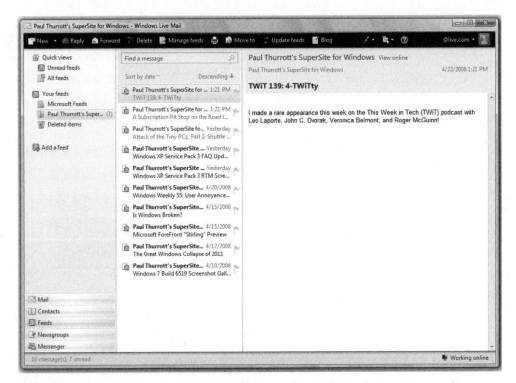

Figure 20-21: In Windows Live Mail, individual posts from RSS feeds resemble e-mail messages.

RSS feeds displayed in Windows Live Messenger provide only the content in each feed, so if the feed you're viewing provides only an abstract of each post and not the entire post, you can click a View Online link in the top of the Reading pane to view the entire post. When you click this link, the post opens in your preferred Web browser.

RSS feeds are managed via a handy Manage Your Feeds dialog, shown in Figure 20-22. You can find this utility by navigating into the Feeds interface in Windows Live Mail and then clicking the Manage Feeds toolbar button. (It's also available via the hidden Tools menu.)

While you will typically find and subscribe to new RSS feeds via Internet Explorer, this window enables you to manually add new feeds via a copy-and-paste mechanism.

Secret   And yes, you guessed it: Any RSS feeds you manually subscribe to in Windows Live Mail are visible and accessible via the RSS functionality in Internet Explorer's Favorites Center as well. That's because the underlying RSS storage engine is actually part of IE.

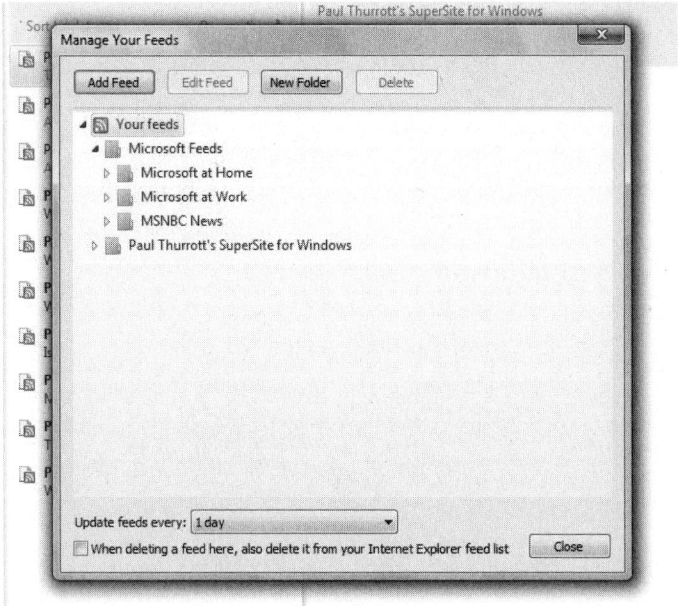

Figure 20-22: Manage Your Feeds helps you configure RSS feed settings and manually subscribe to new feeds.

Manually subscribing to RSS feeds isn't particularly enticing, but the real reason you should be interested in this window is that it provides a way to customize how often feeds are updated. The default is daily, which is fine for some feeds, but woefully inadequate for feeds from news sites, blogs, stock updates, and other sources that will update frequently throughout the day. If you're going to use RSS feeds at all, I recommend upping the frequency of feed updates. I've set it to update every 15 minutes, which is the shortest possible interval.

Using Photo Mail

While e-mail purists may balk at any talk about HTML e-mail, stationery, emoticons, and any other graphical flourishes that can't easily be transmitted via plain text, I've got a news flash for you—well, two actually. First, a huge segment of the computer-using public is quite taken with these colorfully presented and formatted e-mail messages. Second, and perhaps more important, even if you do consider yourself to be above such silliness, probably have parents, children, grandparents, or friends who might not share your geeky computer etiquette; and those people may very well enjoy seeing a nicely formatted e-mail full of family photos or other images.

Enter Photo Mail, one of the cooler new features of Windows Live Mail. Photo Mail addresses one of the biggest issues with today's e-mail solutions: It's hard to send a bunch of photos to others via e-mail in a way that's attractive and works with virtually any e-mail client on the other end. That's too bad—probably almost everyone you know has e-mail access, and there isn't a better way to send some pictures of the kids to grandma, or vacation photos to friends at work, and so on. Photo Mail is a good idea.

As you might expect given the name, Photo Mail enables you to select one or more pictures, place them attractively in an e-mail—and not as an indecipherable attachment—and then apply other HTML mail elements such as stationery, different layouts, emoticons, and the like. This section describes how it works.

First, click the down arrow next to the New button in the Windows Live Mail toolbar and select Photo e-mail (see Figure 20-23). As it turns out, you can actually construct a Photo Mail out of a normal e-mail message, but choosing this option gets you off on the right foot.

Figure 20-23: You can send a boring old e-mail, or you can send a new and improved Photo Mail!

A New Message window will open, as with any e-mail message you begin in Windows Live Mail; but on top of this window is an Add Photos dialog (see Figure 20-24). This dialog enables you to select one or more photos (using Ctrl+click or your other selection skills) and then place them in the e-mail using the Add button. What's interesting about this dialog is that you can keep adding photos in batches; it won't close until you click the Done button.

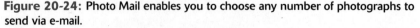

Figure 20-24: Photo Mail enables you to choose any number of photographs to send via e-mail.

When you do click Done, the Add Photos window disappears, and you'll see that Windows Live Mail has formatted the photos into an attractive grid layout, like the one shown in Figure 20-25, and provided some room at the top so you can type a message.

Figure 20-25: By default, Photo Mail messages are formatted in a simple grid with medium-size thumbnails.

Also showing is an additional Photos pane, which provides access to some interesting capabilities:

♦ **Add more photos:** This will redisplay the Add Photos window so you can add even more photos.

♦ **Borders:** You can choose between seven different photo borders: matting, wood frame, instant photo, metal corners, pushpin, spotlight, and brushed edges. Some of these—including matting, wood frame, metal corners, and pushpin—also let you pick from a selection of customizable colors. As you apply borders and border colors, the photos change to match your selection (see Figure 20-26).

Note that you can Ctrl+click or otherwise arbitrarily select photos in the e-mail message to apply different borders and/or border colors to different photos. If you want to remove a border, simply select the photo(s) and reclick the border option.

Figure 20-26: Photo Mail supports a wide range of border types and colors.

◆ **Photo adjustments:** You can autocorrect the brightness and contrast of the photos, convert them to black-and-white, or rotate them. The first two effects are applied to all photos simultaneously, unless you select one or more photos. Rotation can only be applied on a photo-by-photo basis, or to a selection of photos, not to all photos at once.

◆ **Resizing options:** You can opt to send low-quality images (roughly 512K each), medium-quality images (1MB), or high-quality images (5MB or less). Medium is the default, but if you opt for high-quality, only thumbnails will be sent via e-mail; the full-size photos are uploaded to Microsoft's servers.

Secret

You must be signed into a Windows Live ID to send high-quality photos. That's because the high-quality versions are actually uploaded to your Windows Live Spaces blog (see Chapter 21) and linked to from the e-mail.

Secret If you do log on to your Windows Live ID and enable high-quality photos, you are limited to sending 500 photos via Photo Mail per month and to uploading 500MB of photos to your Spaces account.

On the right side of this Photos pane is some information about the estimated upload time (which can be substantial for big Photo Mail messages) and the total size of the upload.

But wait, there's more. In addition to the photo formatting tools visible in the Photos pane, several other capabilities are present:

◆ **Drag and drop photo layout:** You can actually drag photos around inside the e-mail body, as shown in Figure 20-27, to visually reorder them.

Figure 20-27: Use your desktop skills to move photos around in Photo Mail.

◆ **Replace individual photos:** If you would like to replace an individual photo from the layout, just double-click it. The Add Photos window will appear, where you can choose another.

◆ **Add captions:** To add captions below a photo, just select a photo and then click in the area titled *Click here to add text*.

◆ **Choose different layouts:** The default grid-like layout you're presented with is only one of nine prebuilt layout types. Click the Layout button, as shown in Figure 20-28, to view all the potential styles, and experiment.

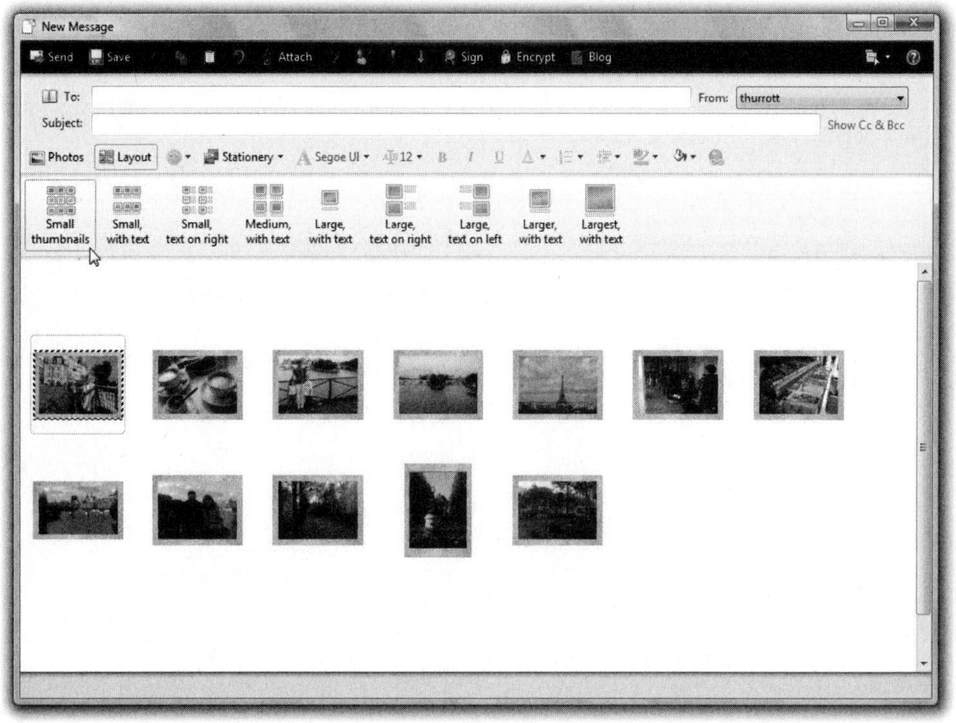

Figure 20-28: A variety of layout types are also available.

◆ **Use stationery and emoticons:** While I'm not positive that graphical emoticons are necessarily the way to go, the addition of a decent stationery via the Stationery button isn't a bad idea. Each stationery type is a template with a custom background image, unique text fonts and styles, and custom margins. A typical stationery, applied to a Photo Mail message, is shown in Figure 20-29.

You get the idea: Photo Mail is meant to be colorful and fun. Express yourself.

Figure 20-29: Finally, go nuts with some HTML effects.

Managing Contacts

If you're familiar with e-mail, chances are good you're equally at home with the concept of a contacts list or address book. Essentially a database, your own contacts list is a way to store information about the people with whom you regularly correspond, typically by e-mail, but increasingly in other ways, including via instant messaging solutions (such as Windows Live Messenger, discussed in Chapter 21) and social networking services (such as Facebook and MySpace).

This section examines Microsoft's two primary contacts management systems: the Windows Vista feature known simply as Windows Contacts, and Windows Live Contacts, Microsoft's cloud-based contacts management service. You can manage Windows Live Contacts online or via the Windows Live Mail application just discussed. More important, perhaps, you can move contacts back and forth between Windows Live Contacts and Windows Contacts as long as you know the secret. I'll show you how.

Contacts in Windows Vista

Unlike e-mail, the system for managing contacts in Windows has changed dramatically with Windows Vista. In previous Windows versions, Microsoft utilized an application called Windows Address Book (WAB) to handle contacts. WAB was a simple application, and it integrated nicely with Outlook Express, the Windows Mail predecessor. However, few other applications took advantage of WAB, so in Windows Vista, a new Windows Contacts mechanism has been architected to expose new technologies that developers are theoretically more likely to embrace. Indeed, Microsoft expects Windows Contacts to eventually replace all other personal contact storage systems used in Windows, whether they're made by Microsoft or other companies.

Secret   Under the hood, Windows Contacts utilizes a well-respected and widely used open technology called XML (Extensible Markup Language). XML is also used in many other places within Windows Vista. For example, the system's integrated support for RSS utilizes XML technology.

To the user, Windows Contacts is typically accessed through the new Contacts special shell folder, sometimes called the Contacts Explorer, which is specially formatted for managing contacts. You can also access this folder through the Start Menu as Windows Contacts. The Contacts Explorer is shown in Figure 20-30.

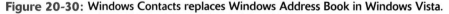

Figure 20-30: Windows Contacts replaces Windows Address Book in Windows Vista.

If you upgraded to Windows Vista from a previous Windows version (or ran the Windows Easy Transfer utility) and were using WAB for contacts, you should see all of your contacts in the new Contacts folder. Otherwise, Contacts will contain just one entry, which is set aside for your Windows user account.

Secret

If you don't see buttons such as New Contact, New Contact Group, Import, or Export in the Windows Contacts toolbar, you need to customize the look and feel of this Explorer so that it works correctly. To do so, right-click a blank area of the window and choose Customize This Folder. Then, in the Contacts Properties dialog that appears, choose Contacts from the list of possible folder type templates at the top and click OK.

Adding a New Contact

To add a new contact to Windows Contacts, simply click the New Contact toolbar button. This brings up a blank Contact Properties window, shown in Figure 20-31, which is roughly analogous to a similar window in the old WAB application.

Figure 20-31: In Windows Vista, Contacts are stored using an XML back end.

One feature that's new this time around is that you can add a picture to each contact. To do so, click the picture well in the upper-right corner of the Properties window and select Change Picture from the drop-down menu. You can then browse to the picture you want. Pictures are a nice way to customize your contacts. In Figure 20-32, you can see how a few photos really spice things up, especially if you experiment with the Contacts Explorer's view styles and choose one of the more visual styles.

Figure 20-32: A more visual interface to your friends, family, and co-workers.

Viewing and Editing Contacts

The Preview pane is not enabled by default in the Contacts Explorer, but you may want to enable it because you can select individual contacts and preview much of their information on-the-fly, without opening each one in a separate window. This is shown in Figure 20-33.

tip If the Reading pane is not enabled, you can enable it by clicking the Organize button in the Contacts toolbar and selecting Layout ⇨ Reading pane.

To edit a contact, simply double-click it. This displays the Contact Properties window described in the previous section, where you can change any of the contact's properties.

Figure 20-33: The Preview pane is a nice addition to Windows Contacts.

Organizing Contacts

If you have enough contacts, you might want to organize them into logical collections called *contact groups*. To do this, you must first create a group. For example, you may want to place your family members in a group called Family. Here's how you do it:

1. Make sure the Contacts Explorer is open and no contacts are selected.
2. Click the New Contact Group button in the Contact Explorer toolbar. This brings up the Contact Group Properties dialog, shown in Figure 20-34.

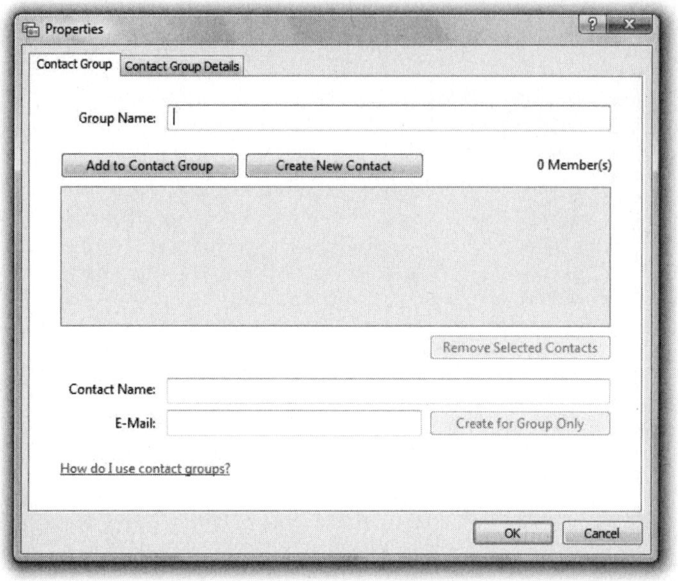

Figure 20-34: Here, you can create a logical group to contain related contacts.

3. Pick the contacts you want to add to the group by pressing the Add to Contact Group button, or simply press OK to create the group and then drag and drop the appropriate contacts into the group.

4. To view the contents of a group, double-click it. The Contact Group Properties dialog will display whatever contacts happen to be part of that group, as shown in Figure 20-35.

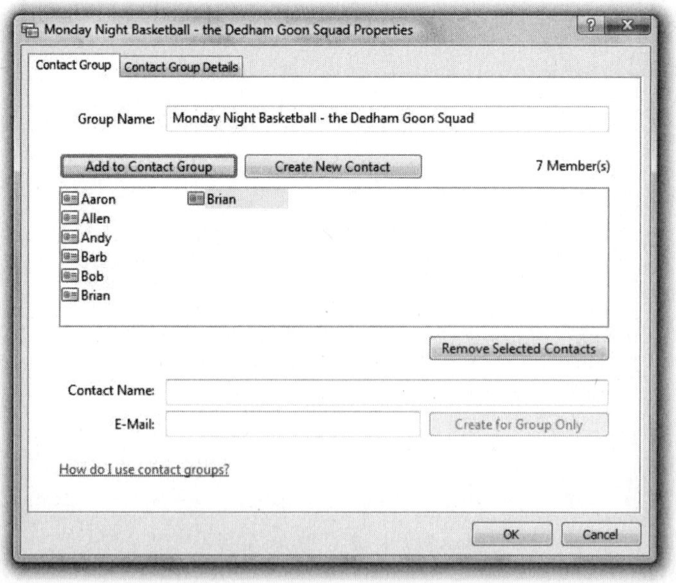

Figure 20-35: Contact Groups enables you to filter your contacts into logical groups.

Secret

Any contact can be a member of one or more contact groups, so you might think of a contact group as a container that holds shortcuts to contacts, rather than actual contacts. If you delete a contact group, you won't delete the contacts it contains.

tip

Contact groups can be accessed as a group in applications that utilize Windows Contacts, such as Windows Mail. For example, if you created a contact group called Family, you could address an e-mail to Family, and it would be sent to every contact in that group.

Windows Live Contacts: Your Contacts in the Clouds

Windows Contacts is a big improvement over the Windows Address Book, but it's still a local Windows application with lists of contacts that must be individually managed on each PC you own. If you are part of a multi-PC household, or spend a lot of time online, it might make sense to consider an Internet-based (or "cloud-based") contacts solution. These solutions exist once, online, and are managed by others. The nice thing about them is that they can be accessed from multiple PCs at any time. And anytime you make a change to the contacts list, those changes are made universally, no matter from where or how you access the contacts.

There are plenty of online contacts management systems, but because this is a book about Windows Vista, this section focuses on Microsoft's solution, called Windows Live Contacts, as its part of the company's online efforts to extend Windows. Essentially a component of Windows Live Hotmail, described in Chapter 21, Windows Live Contacts is a true cloud-based service. It also happens to work very well with Windows Live Mail, the desktop e-mail client introduced earlier in this chapter. It's time to take a look at how you can use this service online and locally, using Windows Live Mail.

Secret

Personally, I think an online contacts service is the way to go. That way, if you use multiple PCs, upgrade your PC, buy a new PC, or do any of the other things that PC users typically do, you never have to worry about blowing away your one contacts list by mistake. Online contacts services, such as Windows Live Contacts, are highly reliable and are managed elsewhere, which is exactly what most people are looking for; and Windows Live Contacts' integration with various Microsoft products, such as Windows Live Mail, makes it a winner in my book. In fact, it's the service I use to manage my own contacts.

Online, Windows Live Contacts is accessed directly via **http://contacts.live.com**, which resolves to an incredibly complicated URL and directs you to the Contacts component of Windows Live Hotmail (formerly called simply Hotmail). As shown in Figure 20-36, Windows Live Contacts presents a logical three-pane view, with access to contacts groups on the left, individual contacts in the middle pane, and a details pane on the right that provides information about the currently selected contact.

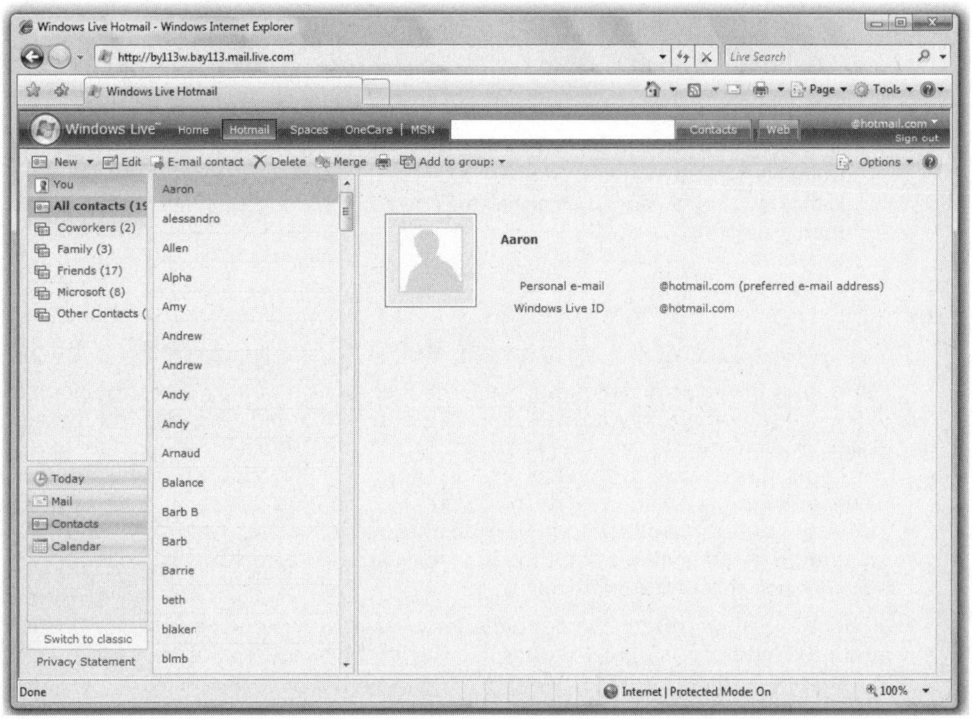

Figure 20-36: The Windows Live Contacts Web service looks and works much like a desktop application.

Secret

One oddity of Windows Live Contacts is that there is quite obviously a place for a photograph or other image in each contact's details view, but there's no way to add a picture. Microsoft tells me this is by design: Users of its Windows Live services are free to add their own display picture to their own contacts card, via Windows Live Contacts, Windows Live Messenger, and other entry points to the Windows Live Contacts infrastructure. Fair enough; but this doesn't explain why Windows Live Contacts users are unable to use their own images, especially for those contacts that aren't part of Windows Live. It is hoped that this will be changed in the future.

For many people, accessing Windows Live Contacts via its Web interface will likely be enough; but Microsoft provides an even nicer interface to this contacts list via Windows Live Mail. You access this functionality via the Contacts button in the Shortcuts list in the lower-left corner of the main Windows Live Mail application window. Shown in Figure 20-37, the local version of Windows Live Contacts is attractive, and looks and works just like Windows Live Mail.

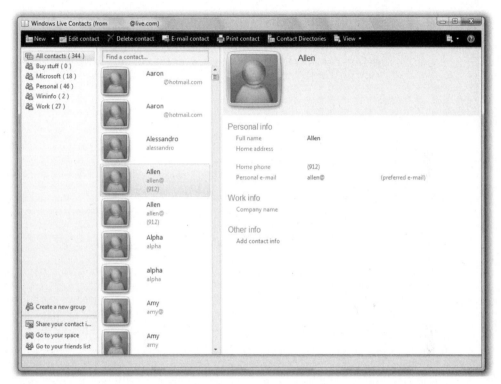

Figure 20-37: Looking for something a little more integrated? Check out Windows Live Contacts in Windows Live Mail.

What's amazing about this application is that what you're seeing is an automatically synchronized version of your online contacts list, so if you make any changes to a contact or group locally, those changes are reflected online immediately and automatically. (The reverse is also true.)

Secret

This means, among other things, that you can work with your master contacts list offline if necessary.

As you might expect of a Windows Live application, one of the hallmarks of Windows Live Contacts is that it integrates with other Windows Live services. When you select a contact who is also in your Windows Live Messenger friends list, you can choose to send that contact an instant message, view their Windows Live Spaces blog, or access the Space-based Friends Explorer, which helps you find, yes, friends of friends.

Secret   While Windows Live Mail supports multiple e-mail accounts, you can only manage contacts from a single source at a time. Windows Live Mail will use your default e-mail account as the source for the contacts list it displays when you click the Contacts button.

Importing and Exporting: Moving Contacts between Windows Live and Windows Contacts

Both Windows Contacts and Windows Live include import and export capabilities so you can copy contacts to and from these contact storage engines. In Windows Contacts, this functionality is almost completely identical to the fairly weak import and export features in Outlook Express. If you find that the import options aren't good enough, here's a secret: You can also import WAB contacts by exporting them from Outlook Express in Windows XP (or previous Windows versions) to a new WAB file. Then, copy the WAB file to Windows Vista and double-click it. The contacts will be imported into Windows Contacts.

If that doesn't work, try using the Windows Easy Transfer program to copy your old contacts from your previous operating system to Windows Vista Windows Contacts.

In the Web-based version of Windows Live Contacts, you can find contacts import and export functionality in the Options menu. Windows Live Mail supports importing from Microsoft Outlook, Outlook Express, Windows Contacts, a different Windows Live Hotmail account, Yahoo! Mail, and Gmail. You can export to a CSV (comma-separated value) file, which is compatible with most contacts databases, including Windows Contacts.

In the desktop version of Windows Live Contacts, you can import from the Windows Address Book (WAB), individual business card (VCF) files, Microsoft Outlook, Windows Contacts/Windows Address Book, and a CSV file. This application also supports exporting to VCF and CSV file types.

Secret   The import and export contacts functionality in Windows Live Contacts is hidden: Tap the Alt key to display the classic menu and then open the File menu to display the Import and Export options.

Summary

Although Windows Mail is largely a disappointing upgrade over its Outlook Express predecessor, this application does, at least, include a few interesting new features, including a phishing filter, automatic spell checking, and better performance, so it's worth a look if you're a die-hard Outlook Express user only. Others will find better features and functionality in Windows Live Mail, the dramatically updated version of Windows Mail that Microsoft now offers for free download from the Web. The new Contacts functionality in Windows Vista, meanwhile, is similar to its predecessor but accessible through a new shell-based user interface that is both easy to use and attractive. Between these solutions, virtually any user should find what they need for managing e-mail and contacts online; and if you combine them with the Windows Calendar feature discussed in Chapter 22, you have the makings of a full-featured personal information management solution that rivals even expensive commercial solutions such as Microsoft Outlook.

Turning It Up a Notch with Microsoft's Live Services

Chapter
21

◆ ◆

In This Chapter

Accessing Windows Live services that Microsoft promotes in Windows Vista

Establishing an online persona with Windows Live ID

Utilizing e-mail online with Hotmail

Blogging with Windows Live Spaces

Planning and immortalizing events with Windows Live Events

Storing files online with Windows Live SkyDrive

Downloading and installing Windows Live products with the Windows Live suite

Communicating with others online with Windows Live Messenger

Extending Internet Explorer with the Windows Live Toolbar

Creating a Web portal and searching the Web with Live.com

Take your first steps toward cloud computing with Live Mesh

◆ ◆

I n late 2005, about a year before it completed development of Windows Vista, Microsoft announced that it was radically changing its online strategy to better compete with Google, Yahoo!, and other companies. Microsoft's new strategy, called Software + Services, is simple: Because it already dominates the operating system market with Windows, it no longer needs to take the technically dubious (and antitrust unfriendly) tack of bundling online services directly in Windows, as it did in the past. Instead, Microsoft's online services are combining capabilities from both desktop software and online services to deliver the best possible user experience. More to the point, Microsoft can build off the success of Windows without unnecessarily taking advantage of its market power. Yes, most of its services will work best with Windows, and some will actually require Windows, but none will ship directly in the box with Windows.

It may seem like a subtle distinction; but after a decade of antitrust problems both in the United States and around the world, Microsoft is finally doing the right thing, both for the company itself and its customers. Previously, most of Microsoft's online services were developed through its MSN division, which used to develop the company's Internet access services. Now, however, that work has all been brought into the Windows Division; and not so surprisingly, the online services are now being marketed with the Windows Live brand, along with related Live services that bear brands such as Office Live and, yes, MSN.

Secret

You might not be surprised to discover that the various Windows Live services and desktop products are simply updated or new versions of products and services that were once being developed by MSN and were once branded with the MSN name. That is indeed exactly what happened.

note

Microsoft's Live services also includes a brilliant set of online services for gamers called Xbox Live.

When Microsoft announced its strategy to enhance the Windows product line with a set of online products and services under the Windows Live umbrella, it wasn't clear exactly what form the resulting software would take. Since then, however, Microsoft has shipped an impressive number of Live products and services, almost all of which are updated regularly. Staying on top of all these products and services would almost be a career in and of itself.

Because the Live services are being updated so frequently, it doesn't make sense to provide an in-depth look at every single one of them. Instead, what I'll do here is discuss the Live services that Microsoft is promoting directly in Windows Vista, along with those Live products and services that I think are the most interesting and useful to Vista users. You might be surprised by what's out there: Microsoft offers a comprehensive line of online products that enhance Windows Vista in various ways. These products and services, in effect, extend the capabilities of Windows Vista and make it a more valuable operating system.

Windows Live and Windows Vista

With previous versions of Windows, Microsoft bundled a few predecessors to its Live services, most notably the Windows Messenger instant messaging client, directly in the OS. With Windows Vista, that's no longer the case. Instead, Microsoft is subtly promoting Windows Live services in Windows Vista in two key areas.

First, a variety of Windows Live services are advertised in the Offers from Microsoft section of the Windows Vista Welcome Center, as shown in Figure 21-1. Because this window is displayed the very first time you boot into Windows Vista, and then again by default every time you reboot, millions of customers from around the world will be tempted to download and install some of these products. Fortunately, most of the Windows Live offers are for free, high-quality products.

Figure 21-1: There are no Windows Live products or services in Windows Vista per se, but Microsoft does go to great lengths to advertise them.

This window provides generic-sounding links to various Windows Live services. In actuality, they point to very specific products, such as the Windows Live suite, Windows Live Toolbar, Windows Live Search, Windows Live Home, Windows Live OneCare, and Windows Live Family Safety, all of which are covered in this chapter.

Second, Microsoft includes a shortcut in the default Windows Vista Start Menu called Windows Live Messenger Download. When clicked, this shortcut opens Internet Explorer 7 and navigates to the download page for Microsoft's instant messaging (IM) application. There is also an identical shortcut in the All Programs portion of the Start Menu.

Secret Annoyingly, if you do choose to install Windows Live Messenger via either one of these shortcuts, the shortcut for installing the product remains on your system. You can, of course, manually delete it by right-clicking it and choosing Delete, and then wading through the inevitable User Account Control (UAC) silliness that ensues any time you do something even remotely dangerous.

In addition to the Windows Live services mentioned previously, the Windows Vista Welcome Center also includes other offers from Microsoft, "Go online to Windows Marketplace" and "Sign up online for technical support":

Secret You could see other offers here as well, as Microsoft allows PC makers to add their own entries in the Welcome Center, just as they do with the Start Menu and Windows Desktop.

- Windows Marketplace, shown in Figure 21-2, is Microsoft's shopping and download site, from which you can purchase hardware and software for your Windows Vista–based PC. It has developed into an interesting destination, especially because much of the software it offers can actually be downloaded immediately, for instant gratification. (That is, you don't have to wait for an installation disc to arrive in the mail.) Additionally, Windows Marketplace offers a feature called Digital Locker, which maintains copies of any software you purchase digitally. If you ever need to download and reinstall something again, no problem—Digital Locker keeps a copy for you.

- The second option opens Internet Explorer and navigates to the Microsoft Help and Support Web site (**http://support.microsoft.com/**). From here, you can get guided help, visit the product solution center for Windows Vista, or submit support requests. It's a good place to visit if more traditional support options—such as the Vista help files, this book, or the geek teenager down the street—can't answer your questions.

Figure 21-2: Windows Marketplace showcases hardware and software that's compatible with Windows Vista.

Secret

Other support options are available to you as well, of course. For example, you might use Windows Mail or Windows Live Mail to visit Microsoft's product support newsgroups. There, you can get peer-to-peer support (from other Windows users and Microsoft MVPs) or even responses from the Microsoft engineers that frequent the groups. To access these newsgroups in Windows Live Mail, simply click the Newsgroups shortcut in the lower-left corner of the application window and then click on Microsoft Communities in the Quick Views area. And, of course, I maintain my own Windows-oriented Web site, Paul Thurrott's SuperSite for Windows (www.winsupersite.com).

Going Online and Learning about Windows Live

The shortcut titled "Go online and learn about Windows Live" opens Internet Explorer and brings you to a pared-down version of the Windows Live web site (**http://get.live.com/**) that includes information only about Microsoft's top-level Windows Live services, such as Windows Live Search (a Google competitor), Live.com (a Web portal), Windows Live Expo (an eBay competitor), Windows Live Messenger (instant messaging), Windows Live Mail (the Hotmail replacement), Windows Live Spaces (blogging), and Windows Live OneCare (a comprehensive PC safety product).

Secret   There are, of course, far more Windows Live products and services available to Windows Vista users. For the full lists, check out the Windows Live Ideas Web site (http://ideas.live.com/), which includes both beta (prerelease) and completed products and services.

Windows Live Services That Make Windows Vista Better

Microsoft is now promoting its Windows Live offerings specifically as value-added services that enhance your Windows Vista experience with free, familiar, and secure ways to connect and share with others. Marketing baloney aside, there's some truth to this, though, of course, Microsoft's lengthy list of available Windows Live products and services—not to mention the products and services that fall under other Live services product families— makes it hard to keep them all straight. In this section, I focus on a hand-picked list of Windows Live products and services that I believe truly do make Windows Vista better. You're free to pick and choose among them, of course.

Tying It All Together: Windows Live ID

Why you want it: It's needed to access many other Windows Live products and services.

Type: Online service

Alternatives: None

Though Microsoft doesn't explicitly market Windows Live ID, this important service sits at the middle of all of the company's Live products and services—including, yes, its Xbox Live and Zune Marketplace/Zune Social services. That's because Windows Live ID is Microsoft's central single sign-on service, and any Microsoft online product or service that requires a logon of some kind will require a Windows Live ID.

While the name Windows Live ID is unusual, you may be more familiar with the service's previous name, Passport. Microsoft dropped the name Passport when it changed to the Live branding it's now using, but the purpose is still the same. So, too, is the way in which you acquire a Windows Live ID: You typically do so by signing up for a Microsoft online service, such as Hotmail or Windows Live Messenger, which requires a logon. However, you don't have to do it that way. In fact, if you know you're going to be interacting with various Windows Live (and other Microsoft Live) services going forward, you can simply sign up for a Windows Live ID first. Here's how you do it.

Simply navigate to **http://login.live.com/** with Internet Explorer and click the link titled *Sign up for an account*. Yes, you're free to use the browser of your choice, but I've found that Microsoft's online services still work best with the company's own browser, so it's best to step through the original sign-up process with IE instead of Firefox or whatever other browser you may use.

Your Windows Live ID will be an e-mail address of some kind. Note that you are free to use an existing e-mail address as your Windows Live ID (like **paul@thurrott.com**), or you can create a new Windows Live ID using one of Microsoft's domains (typically hotmail. com or live.com). When you create a new Windows Live ID using Microsoft's domains, the company will also set up a free Windows Live Hotmail e-mail account for you (see the next section for details). This isn't the case when you use an existing e-mail address.

Because Hotmail is one of the services I'll be discussing in this chapter, I will assume you endured the lengthier process of creating a Windows Live ID using one of Microsoft's domains; but the process for adding a Windows Live ID to an existing e-mail account is similar, and simpler. During sign-up, you'll be asked to choose an e-mail address and password, and enter some basic account information.

Once the account is created, you are directed to Windows Live Account Services, where you will see that you are signed in to your new account. At that point you can access any of the Live services described in this chapter: When prompted to log on, do so with your newly created Windows Live ID.

Windows Live Hotmail (Hotmail) and Windows Live Contacts

Why you want it: One of the most pervasive and successful online services ever created; you get a free account with your Windows Live ID.

Type: Online service

Alternatives: Google Gmail (**www.gmail.com**), Yahoo! Mail (**http://mail.yahoo.com**)

Significantly upgraded in 2007, Windows Live Hotmail—more commonly referred to simply as Hotmail—is now a modern and mature Web mail service. It offers desktop application–like capabilities through its Web-based interface. It features excellent Windows and Windows Mobile integration hooks, and can be accessed from Microsoft's popular Outlook e-mail client.

For hundreds of millions of people worldwide, Hotmail is a big part of what it means to be online, connected, and communicating with other people. Of course, Hotmail also accommodates the various ways and places in which people now want to access e-mail. That is, many people now want to access e-mail constantly, whether they're at work, at home, or, with a new generation of mobile devices, on the go. Microsoft has Hotmail-based solutions for all of these scenarios. Home users can, of course, access the Web-based Hotmail service or access Hotmail through Outlook 2003 and 2007 via free Connector software or the Windows Live Mail client discussed later in this chapter.

Here are the features that I think are most important in the new Windows Live Hotmail.

User Interface

From a look-and-feel perspective, Windows Live Hotmail closely resembles a desktop e-mail application such as Outlook, as shown in Figure 21-3. There's a toolbar at the top, with all the expected options, such as New, Reply, Forward, Delete, Check Mail, and so on. There's also an Outlook-like three-pane view, with a folder list, e-mail list, and Reading pane displayed horizontally as you move your eye from left to right across the page.

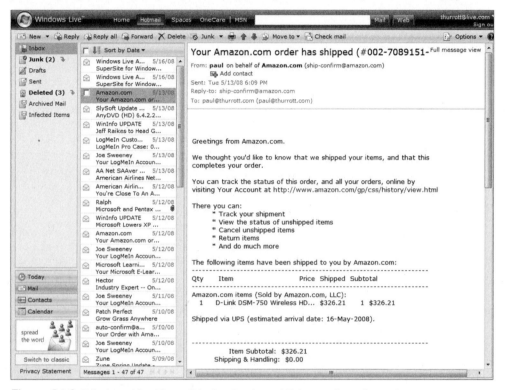

Figure 21-3: Windows Live Hotmail is the dominant Web e-mail service today.

This three-pane default view is the so-called "full" view. If you're a Hotmail old-timer and prefer the traditional Hotmail look and feel, Microsoft also offers a "classic" view, shown in Figure 21-4, that looks more like the old Hotmail. It's sort of a halfway house between the old MSN Hotmail and the new full view.

Secret   Classic view is an excellent choice for those with slow Internet connections. It will also be forced on you if you attempt to access the service from a nonsupported browser.

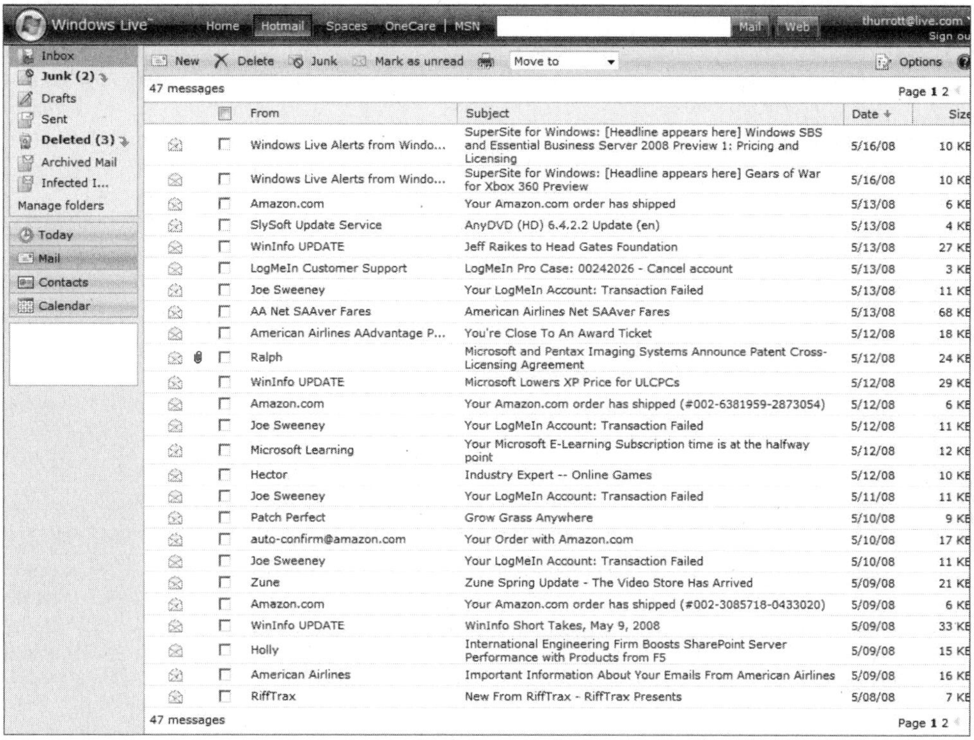

Figure 21-4: Windows Live Hotmail offers a classic view for Hotmail old-timers.

One important part of the Hotmail user interface is the Reading pane, which works like similar features in Microsoft Outlook and Windows Live Mail (discussed later in the chapter). This pane, which can be displayed on the right, on the bottom, or disabled all together, enables you to view e-mail as you navigate from message to message in the e-mail list, without having to open a separate window or, as is more typical with Web mail, navigate to a new page. The result is an e-mail application-like experience.

Microsoft also provides some basic color themes so you can personalize the Hotmail experience somewhat. In addition to the standard blue-green Windows Live look, there are also blue, red, black, silver, pink, green, purple, and orange themes. I don't find many of these particularly attractive, personally: A few available colors are a nice start, but they're only a start.

Security Features

If you're familiar with some of the security features Microsoft has added to Windows Vista features, such as Internet Explorer 7 (see Chapter 19) and Windows Mail (see Chapter 20), then you won't be surprised by the security advances in Windows Live Hotmail. There's a new safety bar—similar to the information bar in Internet Explorer 7—that displays color-coded alert flags for e-mails that Hotmail finds suspicious. This provides a nice visual cue about the safety level of the e-mail. For example, you'll see a yellow safety bar if an e-mail with embedded images, links, or attachments arrives from a source that's not in your contacts list or safe senders list; and you'll see a red safety bar when a potentially fraudulent e-mail, such as a phishing e-mail, arrives.

Hotmail now automatically scans all e-mail attachments. This scanning is free and works regardless of whether you've configured a similar AV scanner on your desktop computer.

Hotmail also sports pervasive junk mail controls with automatic reporting and user-controlled block and allow lists for fine-tuning e-mail filtering. Overall, the level of protection is just about exactly right and what you'd expect from a modern Web mail solution.

Productivity Enhancements

Windows Live Hotmail provides every user with at least 5GB of storage space (though that figure could rise by the time you read this). Microsoft's policy here is simple: It will increase that amount in the future as needed in order to ensure that storage space is never a differentiator between Hotmail and other services. That's a big deal, because it means that virtually all e-mail users could manage all of their e-mail via Microsoft's servers if they wanted to.

When you compose a new e-mail message, Windows Live Hotmail provides automatic address completion functionality, which is handy. The recommended addresses are drawn from your contacts list as well as the list of e-mail addresses from which you've received e-mail.

In another e-mail application-like feature, Hotmail provides automatic inline spell checking with suggested corrections, just like the desktop-based Windows Live Mail product: You'll see a squiggly red line under potential misspellings, and when you right-click that word, a list of corrections appears. You can also add words to your Hotmail dictionary via this right-click menu, or just choose to ignore the notation. Unfortunately, there's no grammar checker.

You can also drag and drop e-mail items (but not folders, not even for reordering), much like a desktop application. If you want to drag an e-mail message from the Inbox to the Deleted folder, for example, you just click and hold and then and drag it on over, as shown in Figure 21-5.

Hotmail also supports multi-selection, so you can select multiple e-mail messages, contiguously or not, and drag them to new locations, or right-click and perform actions such as Mark As Read, Delete, and the like.

Windows Live Hotmail provides full-text searching of e-mail from a prominent Search box in the toolbar that also enables you to optionally search the Web. E-mail searches are returned in a temporary Search Results folder and appear inline in Windows Live Mail just like the Inbox. (If you do choose to search the Web, Windows Live Mail opens a new browser window and forwards your request to the Live.com search engine.)

E-mail composition includes all the HTML e-mail niceties you'd expect, with various font and font styles, text justification, bulleting, indenting, and so forth. You can easily insert hyperlinks from the toolbar, as well as a cool new feature called a Search Link: Simply highlight some text in your message, click the Search Link button, and you'll create a hyperlink that will search Live.com for the selected text.

Another hidden feature is the Photo Upload tool: When you are ready to attach a file in an e-mail message in Hotmail, you'll see two options in the pop-down menu: File and Photo. As expected, File will display a Choose File dialog from which you can navigate in your system to find the file you'd like to attach. If you choose Photo, you'll see the Photo Upload tool, which loads in the browser window and enables you to graphically navigate through pictures in a single folder and select the ones you'd like to add, as shown in Figure 21-6.

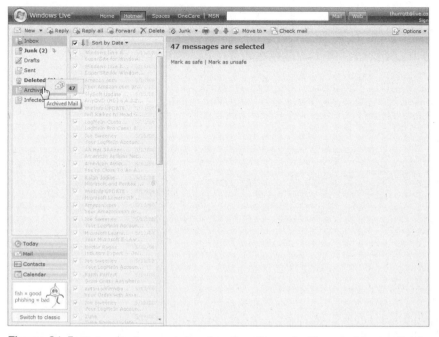

Figure 21-5: Hotmail's drag-and-drop functionality works like a desktop application.

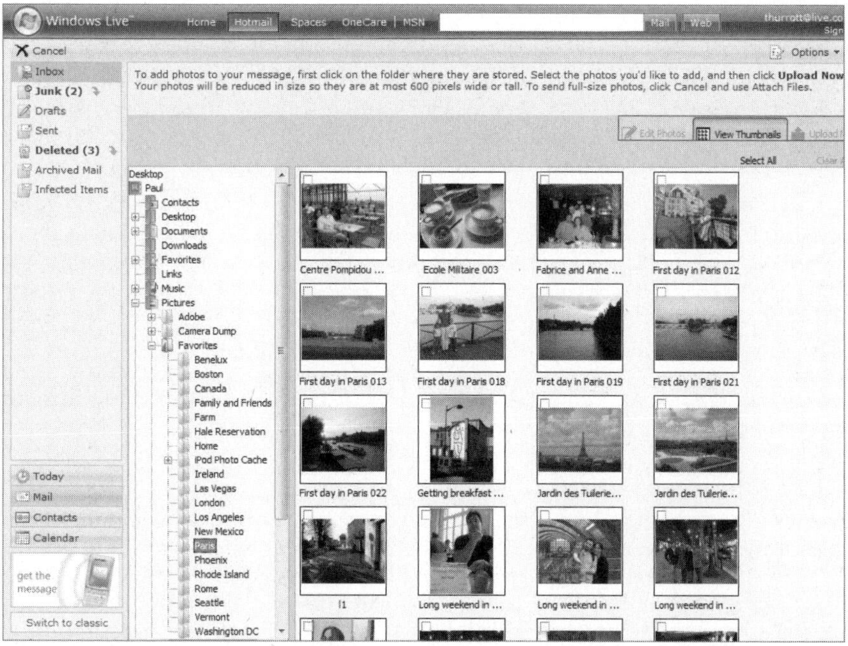

Figure 21-6: Windows Live Hotmail includes a sophisticated photo-attachment system.

As you mouse over individual photos in the tool, you can select them for inclusion and rotate them in two directions. If you click a photo, the tool moves into Edit mode, from which you can perform other operations related to contrast, brightness, cropping, and the like. It's no Photoshop, of course, but it's a nice feature.

Once you've selected all the photos you want, click the Upload Now button and resized versions of the images are added as attachments to your e-mail. By default, larger photos are resized so that they're no more than 600 pixels in the largest dimension. Thumbnail versions in the actual e-mail are no larger than 320 pixels.

Secret

The Photo Upload tool requires IE. If you're using Firefox or another full-view-compatible browser, you'll see only the File option, in which case you can simply attach photos as you would any file. Note that these files aren't automatically resized, so be careful if you're sending photos in this way.

Windows Live Contacts

Windows Live Contacts has been upgraded along with the Hotmail e-mail component and sports a number of new features, including Contacts/Web searching, one-click contacts addition, and so on. Windows Live Contacts integrates with both Hotmail and Windows Live Messenger, Microsoft's instant messaging client (described later in the chapter). If one of your Messenger contacts updates his or her personal information, for example, those changes are reflected across all Windows Live Contacts–compatible products and services, so you'll see the changes in your Contacts list in Hotmail as well.

Windows Live Hotmail also integrates nicely with various portable devices, especially Windows Mobile–based smart phones. Here, Microsoft is delivering on its "software plus services" mantra in a major way, because accessing Hotmail via a mobile device is, of course, the ultimate example of anywhere/anytime information access.

There are actually many different levels of smart device integration that enable you to access your Hotmail e-mail and contacts (and some other Windows Live services) when you're away from a PC. You can get SMS notifications on your smart phone each time a Hotmail-based e-mail arrives; you can utilize a mobile Web version of Hotmail via your smart phone's Web browser; or, if you have a Windows Mobile client, you can access the new Windows Live for Mobile, which includes an integrated client with Windows Live Hotmail, Messenger, Spaces, and Contacts integration. It's part of Windows Mobile 6 and newer, of course, but Windows Mobile 5 users can download the client directly to their device as well.

Windows Live Calendar

Windows Live Calendar, like Windows Live Contacts, ships as a component of Windows Live Hotmail. However, unlike Windows Live Contacts and Hotmail, Windows Live Calendar is on a separate development path and was still in beta when this book was revised. As such, you have to access the service from a separate URL (**http://calendar .live.com**) and put up with what is, currently, an unfinished product. Eventually, I expect Windows Live Calendar to rival the feature set of Google Calendar and provide an interesting online companion for Vista's Windows Calendar, examined in Chapter 22.

Windows Live Spaces

Why you want it: This is a super-simple way to create a personalized home page, connect with friends online, and share photos.

Type: Online service

Alternatives: Blogger, TypePad, WordPress

Windows Live Spaces (**http://spaces.live.com/**) is Microsoft's blogging solution—software that enables anyone to publish a personal Web site, complete with photos and interactive content, easily and without any technical knowledge. Spaces has proven quite popular— by some metrics it's actually the most popular blogging software in the world—and it certainly does provide a friendly and welcome environment with professional-looking page design and nice integration with other Windows Live services. A typical Windows Live Spaces blog is shown in Figure 21-7.

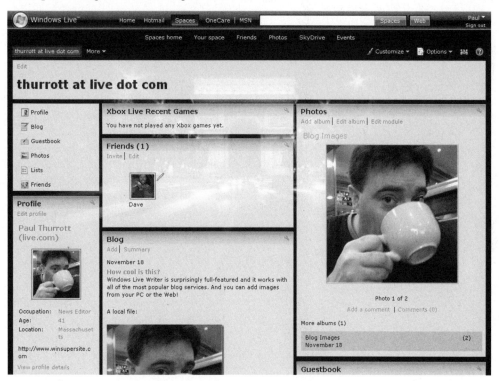

Figure 21-7: Windows Live Spaces enables anyone to create their own Web site.

Windows Live Spaces provides most of the services that typify blogs. That is, it provides a simplified, nontechnical way to post textual blog entries online, perfect for beginners. It provides syndication services, enabling content from personal Spaces to be subscribed to from news aggregators and other RSS-compatible applications and services such as Internet Explorer 7. It excels at creating lists of items, perfect for a blogroll or similar list of links; and it enables others to post comments to Spaces.

Windows Live Spaces goes beyond stock blogging features, adding functionality that I think many casual users and consumers will find exciting. It offers a highly customizable user interface, albeit one that exists clearly within the Windows Live site "style." It includes excellent photo uploading and slide show features (and can be used almost exclusively for sharing photos). It integrates Windows Live Messenger (see below) so that you are notified when your friends and other contacts update their own Spaces. In addition, in a nice nod to power users, it even enables you to post blog entries via a mobile phone or e-mail.

If Windows Live Spaces has a weak link, it's that you cannot create one at your own custom Web address, or URL. Instead, you must use Microsoft's more convoluted **spaces.live.com** addressing scheme. It is hoped that Microsoft will address this issue in a future update.

Windows Live Events

Why you want it: It provides a simple way to plan a party or other event, send electronic invitations, and share memories when it's over.

Type: Online service

Alternatives: Evite (**www.evite.com/**)

Built as an offshoot of Windows Live Spaces, Windows Live Events is an Evite competitor that does its inspiration one better: In addition to providing an excellent interface for planning parties and other events and sending electronic invitations to those events, Live Events adds something fairly unique: the capability to enable guests to return to the site after the event is over and share their memories. These memories can take the form of photo galleries and discussion boards. It's a surprisingly personal type of service, one that can turn a one-time event into a gift that keeps on giving.

Shown in Figure 21-8, Windows Live Events provides an interface for inviting guests to an event, sharing photos taken at the event, chatting online with guests both before and after the event, and customizing the event's site in various ways.

Figure 21-8: Windows Live Events makes it easy to plan events and reminisce about the good times later.

Windows Live SkyDrive

Why you want it: It offers 5GB of free online storage, and drag-and-drop uploading.

Type: Online service

Alternatives: XDrive (**www.xdrive.com/**)

Windows Live SkyDrive (**http://skydrive.live.com/**) is Microsoft's first foray into the "storage in the cloud" concept, though the software giant likes to refer to this service as a USB memory key in the sky. However you look at it, SkyDrive is an interesting solution for backing up files that you'll need to access later; and because it's on the Web, you'll be able to get to those files from any Internet-connected PC.

With SkyDrive, shown in Figure 21-9, you can create public and private folders and files, which you can then lock down or open to others on a folder-by-folder basis.

Figure 21-9: Windows Live SkyDrive is an online storage service.

Integration with other Windows Live services means you can very easily create a folder full of files, for example, which is shared only with very specific people in your Windows Live Contacts database. Beyond that, you can also configure individual users as readers or editors, enabling you to specify who can optionally add and change files as well.

If SkyDrive has a real fault, it's that there is no way to increase the storage allotment. My guess is that Microsoft will eventually move to a yearly subscription fee for more storage as part of a "SkyDrive Pro" service, or perhaps by aggregating the storage available across all of its Live services. For now, those with headier storage requirements—such as users who want to back up digital photos—will need to look elsewhere, such as Google Picasa Web or Flickr. But SkyDrive is an excellent backup solution—so excellent, in fact, that I used it regularly during the writing of this very book to ensure that every one of my chapters was safe and sound in an offsite—way offsite—backup.

Windows Live Suite

Why you want it: It provides a single downloadable version of Microsoft's best Windows Live applications.

Type: Suite of Windows applications

Alternatives: Google Pack (**http://pack.google.com/**)

Travel writer Rick Steves likes to refer to a favorite European destination as a "cultural bouillabaisse," and this moniker might equally be applied to Microsoft's Windows Live suite, a quirky collection of unique Windows applications that can improve your Windows Vista experience in interesting ways. The Windows Live suite arose out of a need to aggregate the various downloadable software applications that Microsoft offers via Windows Live. It did this for two reasons. One, these applications are integrated in various ways and thus work better together. (That said, you are free to download only those parts of the suite you actually want or need.) Two, it's simpler to provide access to these applications via a single installer. Otherwise, you'd have to hunt around the Web to find the applications you wanted.

The Windows Live suite (**http://get.live.com**) provides access to five downloadable applications, all of which are discussed in this chapter. These include Windows Live Mail (an e-mail application that replaces Vista's Windows Mail), Windows Live Messenger (an instant messaging and person-to-person communications tool), Windows Live Photo Gallery (a photo management and editing solution that replaces Vista's Windows Photo Gallery), Windows Live Writer (a surprisingly powerful blog editor), and Windows Live Toolbar, an Internet Explorer add-on that makes it easy to access Windows Live services from your favorite browser.

The suite's integrated installer, shown in Figure 21-10, enables you to choose which Windows Live applications you'd like to install.

Figure 21-10: The various applications in the Windows Live suite can be installed together via a single installer.

Windows Live Mail

Why you want it: This is a surprisingly solid e-mail application that aggregates multiple accounts, including those from Hotmail.

Type: Windows application

Alternatives: Mozilla Thunderbird, Microsoft Outlook

As noted in Chapter 20, Windows Vista includes a new mail client named Windows Mail that is really just Outlook Express from Windows XP with a new name and a few features removed. Well, there's a new mail client in town, and if you're slumming around with Windows Mail for some reason, you might want to give it a shot. It's called Windows Live Mail, and although it's based on the same technical underpinnings as Windows Mail (i.e., it's really just an upgraded version of Outlook Express as well), it does offer one killer feature that's sorely lacking in Windows Mail: It can access the Web-based Hotmail and Windows Live Mail services.

Figure 21-11 shows Windows Live Mail in action.

If you want to learn more, no problem: Windows Live Mail is fully explored in Chapter 20.

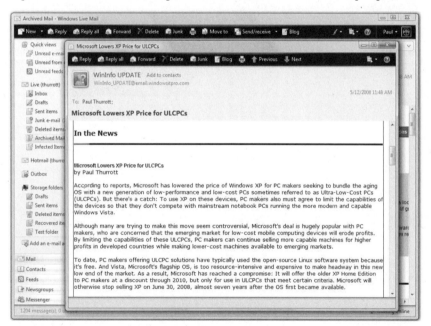

Figure 21-11: Windows Live Mail Desktop is based on the same technologies as Windows Mail, but offers many more features.

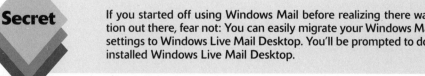

Secret

If you started off using Windows Mail before realizing there was a better solution out there, fear not: You can easily migrate your Windows Mail accounts and settings to Windows Live Mail Desktop. You'll be prompted to do so after you've installed Windows Live Mail Desktop.

Windows Live Messenger

Why you want it: It's an excellent way to communicate with others around the world via text, audio, or video chat.

Type: Windows application

Alternatives: AOL Instant Messenger, Skype, Yahoo! Messenger

Windows Live Messenger replaces MSN Messenger as Microsoft's mainstream instant messaging (IM) application. In truth, the term "instant messaging" doesn't really do this application justice. Although it can indeed be used to hold text-, audio-, and video-based chats online with your friends, co-workers, and other contacts, Windows Live Messenger is blurring the line with telephone-like functionality thanks to its integration of Voice over IP (VoIP) technologies. That means you can make long-distance and international phone calls via Windows Live Messenger for a small fraction of what you're probably being charged by the phone company. It might be time to invest in a PC headset. Windows Live Messenger is shown in Figure 21-12.

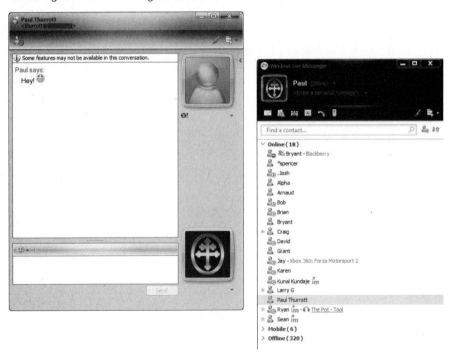

Figure 21-12: Windows Live Messenger offers IM functionality and can be used to make PC-to-phone calls.

Secret

Windows Live Messenger can also be used to communicate with friends using Yahoo! Messenger, a competing instant messaging application.

Windows Live Photo Gallery

Why you want it: It's a superb update to the Windows Photo Gallery application included with Windows Vista.

Type: Windows application

Alternatives: Google Picasa, Adobe Photoshop Express

Windows Vista ships with an excellent photo viewing, editing, and management solution called Windows Photo Gallery; but because Vista was the first version of Windows to include this application, and Microsoft wanted to provide updates in a timelier manner than every three years alongside the next Windows version, the company is now providing a free upgrade to Windows Photo Gallery on the Web. Dubbed Windows Live Photo Gallery, this application is shown in Figure 21-13.

Figure 21-13: Windows Live Photo Gallery is a nice upgrade for Vista's built-in Windows Photo Gallery.

Windows Live Photo Gallery provides several important improvements to Windows Photo Gallery and is a must for anyone using Vista's built-in application. These improvements include a dramatically better photo importer, new editing tricks, a cool new photo panorama function, and integration with various online services, including Windows Live Space and even non-Microsoft services such as Flickr. Windows Live Photo Gallery is such a big deal, in fact, that it is covered exhaustively in Chapter 13.

Windows Live Writer

Why you want it: It's the ultimate blog editor.

Type: Windows application

Alternatives: None

While every blogging solution available offers a Web form of some sort where aspiring bloggers can post their writings and other blog items, such forms are relatively primitive. Enter Windows Live Writer, a superb blog editor that works with Windows Live Spaces, yes, but also with virtually every other blog service on earth.

Shown in Figure 21-14, Windows Live Writer features an attractive user interface and an amazingly complete feature set. I've tested Writer with Windows Live Space, Blogger, and Community Server, and the results are fantastic.

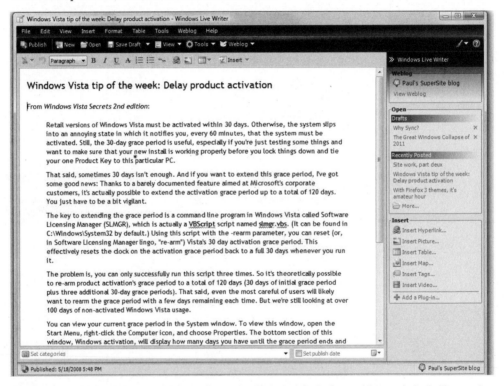

Figure 21-14: Windows Live Writer adopts the look and feel of your blog so it feels like you're editing right on the Web.

Windows Live Writer works with common blog features such as categories and includes inline spell checking; hyperlink, image, photo, and video insertion capabilities; and awesome text-editing features. You can even upload images to Google's Picasa Web service, in addition to Windows Live Spaces. Writer is an impressive little niche application that many people are going to find quite advantageous. It's that good.

Windows Live Toolbar

Why you want it: You're a heavy user of IE and Microsoft's Live services.

Type: Windows application

Alternatives: Google Toolbar, Yahoo! Toolbar

Anyone who's used Internet Explorer is probably familiar with the notion of helper toolbars that include such things as integrated search boxes, pop-up blockers, and a variety of other useful features. Given how advanced Internet Explorer 7 is—it includes, by default, both an integrated Search box and a pop-up blocker, for example—you might think that these toolbars would be a thing of the past. That, alas, is not true; and while the Googles and Yahoo!s of the world are still offering their own brands of Internet Explorer–compatible toolbars, Microsoft has one, too. Not surprisingly, it's called Windows Live Toolbar.

Windows Live Toolbar, shown in Figure 21-15, includes numerous potentially useful features, such as smart menus that enable you to find any location on a map simply by highlighting the address on a Web page. There's a form-fill function that saves commonly typed Web form information (name, address, telephone number, and so on), sparing you from having to manually enter that data repeatedly. The toolbar also integrates with a number of useful Windows Live online services, giving you one-click access to such things as Windows Live Spaces (blogging) and Windows Live Mail.

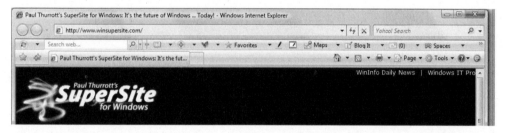

Figure 21-15: The Windows Live Toolbar integrates with Internet Explorer 7 and adds a number of useful features.

Why would you want such a thing? Toolbars like the Windows Live Toolbar are aimed at heavy users of a particular Web services company, so if you have bought into Microsoft's online vision—which is absolutely okay, by the way—the Windows Live toolbar might be useful to you. I happen to use Firefox and several Google online services—Gmail, Google Calendar, Picasa Web, and so on—but I still refrain from using the Google toolbar for Firefox.

The real appeal to the toolbar, frankly, isn't what is installed by default, but rather what you can add to it: Microsoft and its partners offer a wide variety of toolbar buttons that extend the toolbar, and thus the browser itself, in very interesting ways. One excellent example is the Windows Live Favorites button, which enables you to save your Favorites up in the cloud, in a single place, rather than maintain different Favorites collections on each PC. That's a nifty feature. Whether it's worth the download is your call.

Windows Live OneCare

Why you want it: Microsoft's security suite also includes centralized PC management features.

Type: Windows application

Alternatives: Norton 360

There's probably a great joke just waiting to be told about the operating system company whose buggy products inspire a multibillion-dollar security tools market only to see the OS company enter that market with a security solution designed to protect users from problems caused by vulnerabilities in its own products. Let that one sink in for a second and then get Windows Live OneCare, Microsoft's desktop security solution, which is excellent. Here's what you get.

Windows Live OneCare, shown in Figure 21-16, is a subscription offering that ostensibly costs $50 a year, but in reality can be had for much, much less (think half off or more) from various electronics retailers, both online and offline. It covers up to three PCs in your home, so you can install OneCare on multiple machines; and it provides a bevy of services, including antivirus and antispyware protection, a two-way firewall that's more capable than the one included with Vista, nice wizard-based file backup and restore functionality, multi-PC management, and free technical support via phone, e-mail, or online chat, 24 hours a day, 7 days a week.

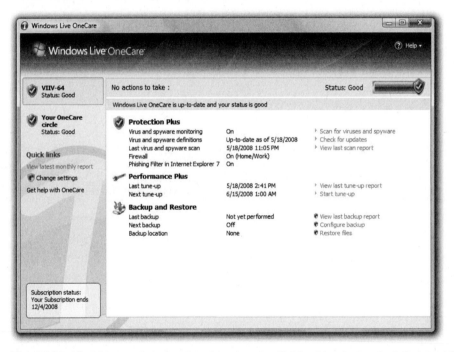

Figure 21-16: Windows Live OneCare is a complete PC health solution for Windows Vista.

Windows Live OneCare runs continually in the background, monitoring your system, and ensuring that it's always up-to-date. It also runs regular PC tune-ups, to ensure that the system is running at top speed. Overall, Windows Live OneCare is an excellent addition to Windows and is highly recommended. In fact, it works so well with Windows Vista that I've dedicated half of Chapter 25 to this intriguing companion product.

The only thing missing from Windows Live OneCare, and it's a curious omission, frankly, is e-mail antispam protection. Microsoft responds that most of its customers are already protected from spam via services provided by their e-mail provider (Google Gmail, Hotmail or Yahoo!, and so on), their Internet service providers (ISPs), or their e-mail clients. True enough, if you choose to use the company's Hotmail service, you do get a certain level of protection against spam, assuming you don't mind using the Web-based client. Not surprisingly, however, security suites from McAfee, Norton, and Zone Alarm all offer e-mail antispam capabilities.

A Few Other Windows Live Services

In addition to the several Windows Live products and services that Microsoft promotes from within Windows Vista, the company offers a wide range of other Windows Live services, which you can examine and download online at your leisure. Here are a few of the more valuable Windows Live services you may want to check out.

Live.com

Why you want it: It provides a customizable online search engine and Web portal.

Type: Online service

Alternatives: Google, Yahoo!

Microsoft's Web portal, Live.com (**www.live.com/**), shown in Figure 21-17, looks like a simple search page.

Figure 21-17: Live.com offers Web search but is also highly customizable.

Live.com may look simple, but it's highly customizable. You can add a number of dynamic content panes containing news, sports, or entertainment headlines, weather, stock quotes, and even your Hotmail e-mail. When you do so, Live.com transforms into the more personal experience (at **http://my.live.com**) shown in Figure 21-18.

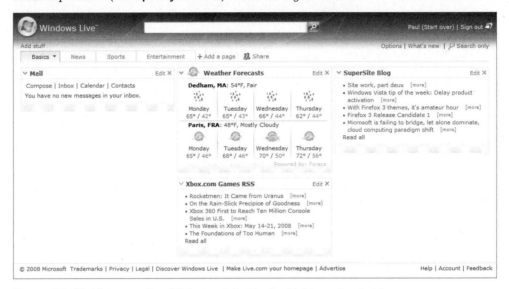

Figure 21-18: Live.com offers Web search but is also highly customizable.

But wait, there's more. In addition to the Spartan Live.com Web site and more personalized version, Microsoft also offers a third Live.com portal called Windows Live Home (**http://home.live.com/**). This portal provides access to a wide range of your personalized Live products and services, including Hotmail, Windows Live Calendar, Windows Live Messenger, Windows Live Contacts, Windows Live Spaces, Windows Live Events, Windows Live SkyDrive, OneCare, MSN, Office Live, and Family Safety, among others. Sounds like it would be awfully cluttered, no? Well, check out the picture of transcendent bliss in Figure 21-19. Windows Live Home is actually a pretty clean portal.

Although Google has become so popular that the term *Google* is now used both as the company's name and as a verb to describe searching the Web (as in, "I need to Google Windows Vista to find out more about it"), it's not the only game in town. Live.com, with its Windows Live Search, is now the default search service in Windows Vista's version of Internet Explorer 7, and the company hopes that this exposure will help it convince users to give the service a chance. Give it a shot. The customization options are quite interesting.

Secret

Like the Windows Sidebar (see Chapter 6), my.live.com can be customized with gadgets, small software programs that provide much more interactivity than is commonly associated with Web pages. Live.com gadgets are created similarly to Windows Sidebar gadgets, so many developers will create gadgets that work in both places. To discover gadgets for Live.com (or the Sidebar), visit Windows Live Gallery (http://gallery.live.com).

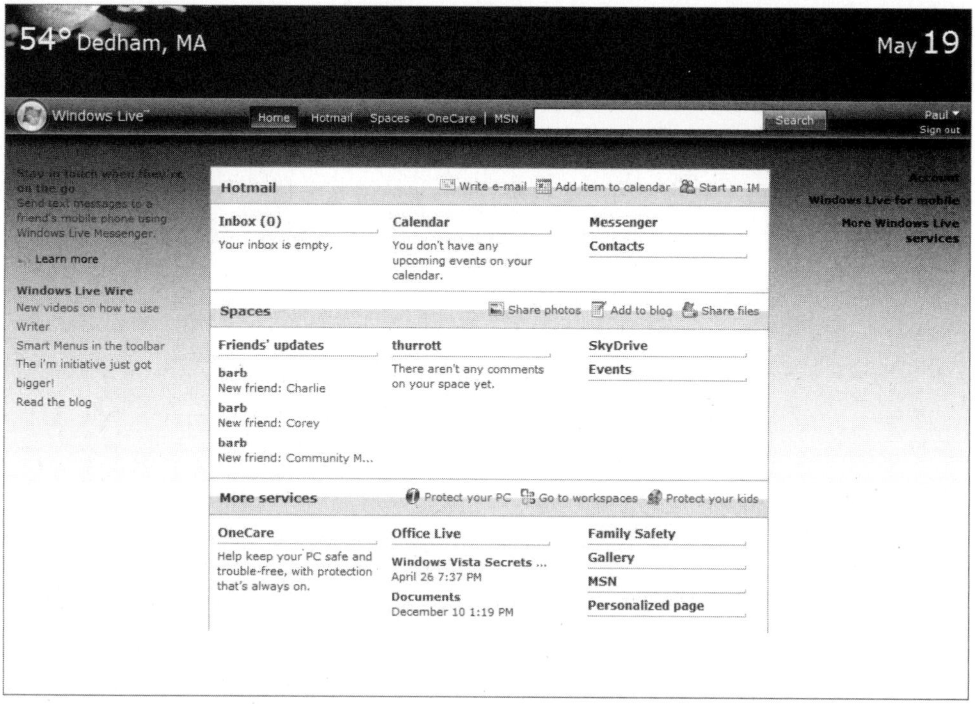

Figure 21-19: The surprisingly clean-looking Windows Live Home.

Windows Live OneCare Safety Scanner and Windows Live OneCare Family Safety

Why you want it: It offers decent PC security for people not interested in paying for a Microsoft subscription.

Alternatives: AVG Free Edition

Although Microsoft does offer a Windows Live OneCare subscription product (mentioned earlier in this chapter), the company's customers told it that it would need to protect nonsubscribers online if it expected them to access its various Windows Live services. Therefore, Microsoft has extended the OneCare brand into a variety of other free services, including an online virus scanner (the Windows Live OneCare safety scanner at **http://safety.live.com** and the Windows Live OneCare Family Safety service at **http://fss.live.com**, which provides Web filtering and contacts management for parents concerned about keeping their children safe online. The Windows Live OneCare safety scanner is shown in Figure 21-20.

Unlike the safety scanner, Windows Live OneCare Family Safety requires a small download. More important, it also requires that you and your children all have Windows Live IDs; but the extra effort may well be worth it. With this Web-based service, you can monitor your children's activities online, and protect them from undesirable content and online predators. What the heck—it's absolutely free.

Figure 21-20: The Windows Live OneCare safety scanner provides free safety scans from the Web.

Beyond Windows Live

While the name Windows Live can and should suggest a connection with Windows, Microsoft is busy creating a number of other online services and products that it has branded in a curious number of ways. This section briefly highlights some non-Windows Live online services that you should be aware of.

Live Mesh

Why you want it: It offers free remote access and PC-to-PC document synchronization services.

Type: Online service/Windows application

Alternatives: None

Live Mesh is an evolving new Microsoft platform that encompasses an Internet operating system (exposed as a Web-based desktop), your Vista-based PC(s), and your mobile device(s). It enables you to sync documents and other files between the Web-based desktop and your PCs (but only at the folder level). You can also remotely access other PCs using a remote desktop-like experience. Microsoft says it will add other services in the future, and of course developers are racing to take advantage of this new "cloud computing" platform as well.

At a conceptual level, what's most interesting about Live Mesh is that the PC desktop is not at the center of this emerging platform. Instead, Live Mesh is envisioned as a ring or circle, whereby your PC(s), mobile device(s), and Web desktop are all equal partners, like spokes on a wheel (see Figure 21-21).

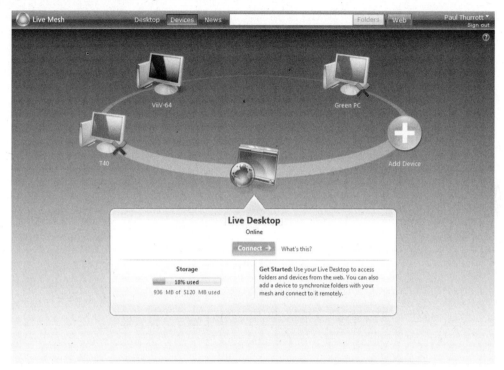

Figure 21-21: Live Mesh is conceptually a circle of connected PCs, devices, and a Web-based desktop.

All of the capabilities of the Live Mesh, today and in the future, will work identically via each entry point. Note, too, that Microsoft intends to support non-Microsoft PCs and mobile devices with this platform. Mac users will have a native Live Mesh client. Linux users? Maybe not, but they'll at least be able to access Live Mesh fully from the Web-based desktop, which is shown in Figure 21-22.

In short, Microsoft is creating a cloud computing platform in which the PC is but a component. Like it or not, most computer users today don't typically use just a single device. People increasingly use multiple PCs (and/or Macs), both in the home and at work. They have desktops and laptop computers; they have smartphones, MP3 players, digital cameras, and other mobile devices. In addition, most users have a host of online personas via e-mail and instant messaging services, social networking memberships, e-commerce sites, and other online communities. Users manage these disparate components separately and with great complexity and difficulty.

Figure 21-22: The Live Mesh Web desktop.

This situation is similar to what it must have been like being one of the first automobile owners 100 years ago. Back then, you had to have extensive technical knowledge about the vehicle to use and maintain it. Today, that market has evolved and matured such that most car owners simply use their vehicles without needing to understand how they work. Computing, too, must mature in the same fashion, and it must do so while meeting the ever-increasing needs of a mobile and interconnected user base.

With Live Mesh, Microsoft seeks to bridge the gap between all the currently disconnected devices, computers, and Web services now used. And though a Web-based desktop sits conceptually on the Live Mesh ring, you use the Web as a hub of sorts for authentication and connections. Naturally, Microsoft utilizes Windows Live ID for this purpose. This provides individual users with a way to collect the list of computers and devices they're using, of course, but it also provides the infrastructure for sharing between users. If you want to do something very simple, such as provide a way for others you trust to access the contents of a shared folder, Live Mesh makes it both possible and seamless.

Live Mesh, alas, is an evolving platform, and much about it will change between the writing and reading of these words. That said, Live Mesh offers two basic features today: document synchronization and remote desktop access. They're worth exploring briefly.

Live Mesh Document Sync

Every time you create a folder in the Web-based Live Mesh Desktop, Live Mesh creates a special blue shortcut to that folder on the desktop of each connected PC. The first time you click this shortcut, you're presented with a Synchronize Folder dialog that enables you to set up synchronization for the folder. The default synchronization option will be changed to *When files are added or modified.* If you accept this option, you can optionally (and preferably) relocate the local version of the folder and move on with life. If, however, you choose to change the sync type back to *Never with this device,* then the shortcut disappears from the PC desktop.

Assuming you do want to sync the folder between your local PC and the Live Desktop (and, potentially, other devices), the icon will change from a special blue shortcut to a special blue folder and the window will open. As with folders viewed from the Live Desktop, locally synced Live Mesh folders also include the Live Mesh Bar on the right, as shown in Figure 21-23. There's one major difference, however: On the PC, you can minimize but not close the Live Mesh Bar if you'd like.

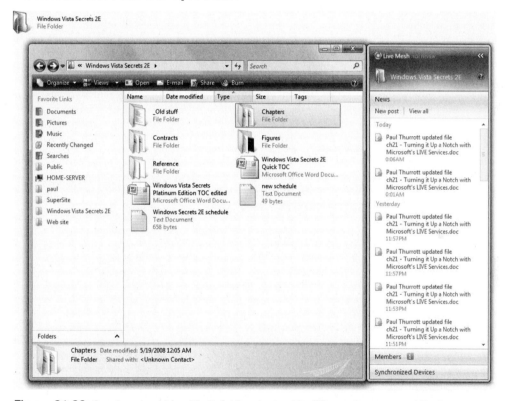

Figure 21-23: Synchronized Live Mesh folders look a bit different from normal Explorer windows.

The most important thing to note about locally accessed synchronized folders, of course, is that you can drag and drop content into them; and because they're automatically synchronized, any files and folders you copy into these folders on your PC are synced back to the Web-based Live Desktop and to any other devices with which you've configured synchronization. Because folder sync occurs on a folder-by-folder basis, you need to manually configure each Live Folder to sync to each device. This can be done via the Live Desktop or individually on each PC.

Live Mesh folder synchronization has proven to be fast and reliable—so much so, in fact, that I've begun using this mechanism to synchronize the contents of this book between my various PCs. As I worked on the chapters locally, via various desktop PCs and notebook computers, the book files (typically, Word documents and image files) were synchronized automatically, both up to the Internet cloud (the Live Desktop) and to whatever other PCs I'd added to my Live Mesh. Live Mesh folder sync is an instant backup solution combined with instant access to the very latest versions of the files no matter which PC I'm using.

Live Mesh Remote Desktop

Live Mesh also includes a handy remote access feature called Live Mesh Remote Desktop. To access this feature, open the Live Mesh menu, either on your local PC or from within Live Desktop, find the PC you'd like to remotely control, and then click the appropriate Connect to Device link. Live Mesh will open a Remote Desktop-type window, complete with a unique Live Mesh Bar that includes remote desktop-oriented functionality such as Send Ctrl+Alt+Del, Hide desktop on remote device, and Show desktop as actual size. These options are shown in Figure 21-24.

By default, the remote desktop is scaled to fit the confines and resolution of the window, though you can use the aforementioned option to change that and scroll around within a truly windowed view of the remote desktop.

Figure 21-24: Live Mesh Remote Desktop enables you to remotely access PCs connected to your Mesh.

Secret

The Remote Desktop feature in Windows Vista requires Vista Business, Ultimate, or Enterprise: Home versions need not apply. This is a problem with the remote access feature in Windows Home Server, described in Chapter 25, because that feature relies on Remote Desktop functionality. Thus, Microsoft's "Home" server can't provide remote access to "Home" versions of Windows. Armed with this knowledge, you may assume that Live Mesh Remote Desktop will work only on non-Home versions of Windows, but that's not the case: Live Mesh Remote Desktop works fine with both Windows Vista Home Basic and Home Premium.

MSN

Why you want it: You can't get enough of celebrities, movies, or music.

Type: Online service

Alternatives: Yahoo!, iGoogle

Started in 1995 as a traditional online service aimed at the current giants in the online world at the time—you remember America Online and CompuServe, right?—the Microsoft Network, or MSN, evolved over the years to address the ever-changing Web landscape. Today, MSN is no longer at the crux of Microsoft's online strategy—that would be Live—but it's still kicking around as the entertainment-oriented Web portal, shown in Figure 21-25.

Figure 21-25: MSN lives on as a celebrity-driven Web portal.

While most of the former MSN services have jumped ship to Windows Live, a few remain under the MSN brand, including MSN Radio (**http://radio.msn.com/**), an online radio station portal; MSN Soapbox (**http://soapbox.msn.com/**), a video-sharing site similar to YouTube; and MSN Money (**http://money.msn.com/**), among a few others.

Summary

This chapter examined some of Microsoft's many Live products and services, which extend Windows Vista with a number of useful Web-based capabilities, including instant messaging, PC safety and security, e-mail, and much more. With Windows Live services, you can communicate with friends, co-workers, and loved ones, publish your thoughts and photos to Web sites, and keep your PC running securely and smoothly. Unlike previous Microsoft online services, the Windows Live services integrate with Windows only when you choose to install them: They aren't simply provided for you whether you need or want them or not. In addition to Windows Live, Microsoft provides several other services under its Live Mesh, MSN, and Office Live brands. Chances are good that if you'd like to do something online, Microsoft has you covered.

Part VII

Home Office/Power User

Managing Your Schedule with Windows Calendar

Chapter 22

A
lthough operating systems such as Linux and Mac OS X have offered calendaring applications for years, Microsoft has historically sold such functionality as part of its Office and Works productivity suites instead of adding it directly to Windows. Starting with Windows Vista, however, Windows users are finally getting a first-class calendaring solution as part of their favorite operating system. Dubbed Windows Calendar, this application provides attractive and full-featured calendaring options, including tasks functionality, the capability to subscribe to remote calendars, and even a way to publish your own calendars for others to use. This chapter examines this interesting and useful new Windows application.

Understanding PC Calendaring

If you've ever used the Calendar component in Microsoft Outlook, shown in Figure 22-1, then you're familiar with the notion of PC-based calendaring and scheduling. Microsoft Outlook is an extremely powerful tool, enabling you to create and manage appointments, meetings, and other events, as well as tasks and other time-based schedules. For all its strengths, however, Microsoft Outlook isn't perfect. First, you must pay a hefty sum for Microsoft Outlook unless you get a version along with other Microsoft Office applications when you purchase a new PC. Second, Outlook is designed to work primarily with Microsoft Exchange–based servers. Although it's possible to use Outlook as an individual, it's not ideal, and even the latest Outlook version offers only very simple methods for sharing calendaring information with other people.

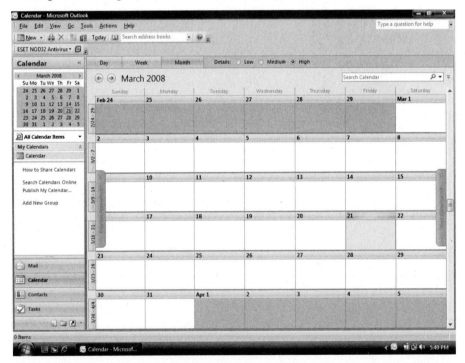

Figure 22-1: Yes, it's full-featured and powerful, but Microsoft Outlook is also expensive.

Meanwhile, standards-based Web calendars have been gaining in popularity for the past few years, and these solutions offer features that are much more applicable to individuals than what Outlook offers. Best of all, most of these Web-based calendars are free. For example, Apple Computer supplies users of its Mac OS X operating system with a calendar application called iCal that integrates very nicely with Web standards for calendaring, making it possible for iCal users to share calendars with family and friends from around the world. The Mozilla Corporation, which makes the popular Firefox Web browser, is developing its own calendar application called Sunbird, offering similar functionality to Windows and Linux users. Alternatively, if you'd prefer to work directly on the Web, you can use a calendaring solution such as Google Calendar, shown in Figure 22-2.

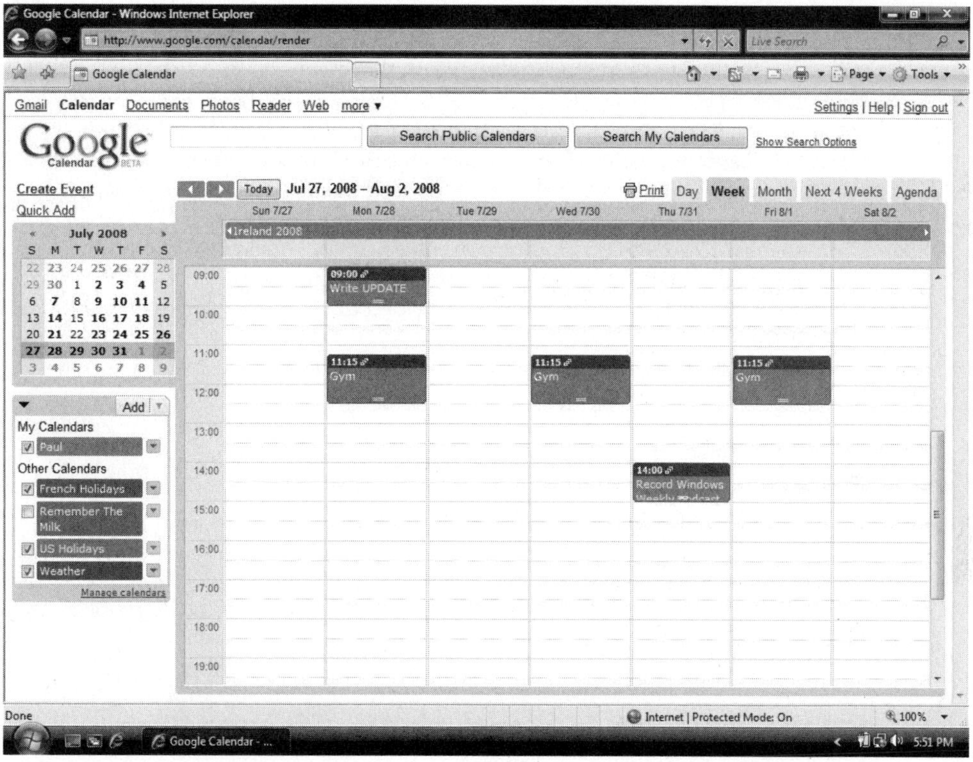

Figure 22-2: Google Calendar runs via any Web browser but requires you to be online.

Standards-based calendar applications offer a number of useful features. First, you can create discrete calendars in categories such as Personal, Work, Gym, or any categories you choose and overlay them as needed on the same calendar view to see how your entire schedule plays out. You can share calendars with others, via a publish and subscribe mechanism that enables you to superimpose your own calendars visually with remote calendars, overlaying these on one another and your own calendars. Using this functionality you could, for example, find a night when both you and your spouse were free to have dinner at a restaurant together, or compare your son's soccer schedule with your own weekend plans to make sure you can get to the game.

Because these standards-based calendars are becoming so popular, many organizations and individuals publish their own schedules on the Web so that other individuals can subscribe to them. If you're a fan of the Boston Red Sox or any other sports team, you can subscribe to their schedule and always be alerted when a game is coming up. There are calendars out there for all kinds of events, including regional holidays, concerts, and the like; and these calendars can be superimposed on your own calendars within these calendaring applications.

There's more, of course. Standards-based calendars also typically support lists of tasks, which can be assigned days and times for completion and checked off as they are completed. You can print calendars in attractive styles, and use them as paper-based personal information managers during your work week or on trips. All of this is possible without having to deal with an expensive, centralized server. The Internet's enterprising denizens have gotten their hands on calendaring and rescued it from the shackles of Microsoft Exchange.

> **tip**
>
> When I refer to standards in regard to calendaring, I'm referring to the iCal, or iCalendar, standard, which specifies "interoperable calendaring and scheduling services for the Internet." Rather than extend proprietary solutions such as Outlook to the Internet, the iCal standard proposes that all calendars should use a single, open standard for interoperability purposes. It's a great idea and works well in the real world. You can find out more about the iCal format on the IETF Web site (www.ietf.org/rfc/rfc2445.txt).

Exploring Windows Calendar

Microsoft isn't blind to this change in how people are interacting online via standards-based calendars. That's why Windows Vista includes a standards-based calendar application, Windows Calendar. If you're familiar with competing solutions such as Apple iCal or Mozilla Sunbird, Windows Calendar will seem very familiar. It works with the same standards-based calendaring format, and it can publish and subscribe to the same sources as those solutions. However, because Windows Calendar is built into Windows Vista, it will soon become the predominant calendaring solution for individuals worldwide. For this reason, I expect standards-based calendaring to become truly mainstream during the lifetime of Windows Vista.

> **tip**
>
> Obviously, Microsoft isn't giving up on its Exchange Server and Outlook product lines. For a quick understanding of how these solutions are differentiated, think of it this way: Exchange and Outlook are tools for business users, whereas Windows Calendar is for individuals such as consumers, soccer moms, and your grandparents. Put simply, Windows Calendar is for *people,* not businesses. Tellingly, Microsoft has also developed a consumer-oriented calendaring service on the Web, called Windows Live Calendar, which conforms to iCal standards and doesn't integrate at all with Exchange. Even Microsoft is getting the message when it comes to calendaring, albeit slowly.

Understanding the Windows Calendar Interface

Windows Calendar can be found in the All Programs portion of the Start Menu (use Start Menu Search to find it quickly). When you launch Windows Calendar for the first time, you are presented with a standard daily calendar view, and you'll see that Windows Calendar has created its first calendar for you, which is named after your user name (e.g., *Paul's Calendar*. Figure 22-3 shows this default view.

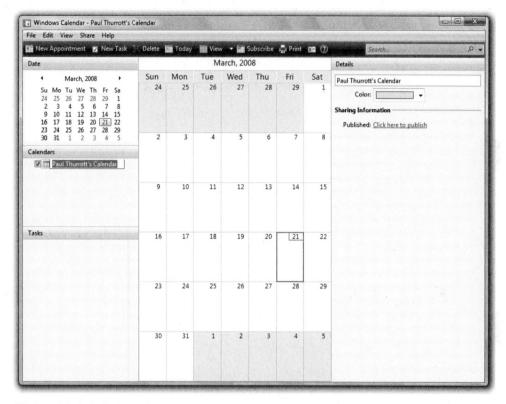

Figure 22-3: Windows Calendar shares many similarities with other standards-based Internet calendars but is presented in a clean, Vista-like user interface.

The Windows Calendar user interface is divided into a number of logical areas. On the top is a menu bar and toolbar. (Yes, that's right: Unlike most Vista applications, Windows Calendar features an old-fashioned menu bar.) Below that are three areas, or panes, all of which are displayed by default, though two are optional. On the left is the Navigation pane, which enables you to select between different calendars and tasks. In the center of the application window is the current calendar view, which is set to Day view by default. On the right is the Details pane. This pane varies according to what's currently selected inside Windows Calendar. By default, the current calendar is selected in the Navigation pane, but you might select other items, such as an appointment or a task. When you do so, the Details pane changes appropriately.

Understanding Windows Calendar Lingo

Because there are so many calendar applications out there, you might be confused about some of the language Microsoft uses to describe the various items associated with Windows Calendar. Table 22-1 summarizes these items.

Table 22-1: Common Items in Windows Calendar

Windows Calendar Item	Definition
Calendar	A collection of appointments that makes up your schedule. You can have different calendars for different purposes and intermingle or overlay them within the Windows Calendar user interface.
Group	A logical grouping of related calendars. Also called a Calendar Group.
Appointment	A meeting or other event. Appointments can have specific starting and ending times or be all-day or multi-day events. For example, a meeting typically has static start and end times, whereas a vacation could be created as a multi-day event.
Task	A to-do item that typically needs to be completed by a specific day and time
Publish	A method by which a calendar is distributed electronically so that it might be shared with others or viewed online
Subscribe	A method by which a remote published calendar is displayed locally within Windows Calendar and is updated automatically as changes are made to the original

Working with Calendars and Groups

The first time you launch Windows Calendar, you'll see that it has created a default calendar for you with the name *[User name's] Calendar* (where *User name* is obviously replaced by the logon name of the current user). Each calendar gets its own name and color, and you can change either. For some people, this single calendar may be enough, but others may want to create different calendars for the different types of events they confront each day. Microsoft has also added the capability to create calendar groups, called *Groups*, within which you can collect related calendars if desired.

Take a look at some of the ways in which you might organize your calendars within Windows Calendar. As stated previously, the default calendar you get just by running Windows Calendar might be suitable for you, but some users will want to organize things differently, and there are certainly many advantages to using different calendars. First, because each calendar is assigned a unique color, appointments for each calendar will stand out visually. Second, because you can arbitrarily hide and show individual calendars, it's possible to simplify the calendar view as needed, which can be handy when publishing or printing calendars. The important thing to remember is that Windows Calendar supports virtually any level of customization when it comes to calendar management. For example, you can use Windows Calendar to do any of the following:

♦ **Change the name of the default calendar:** Just select the name of the calendar in the Details pane as you would when renaming a file in Windows Explorer and type a new name, as shown in Figure 22-4.

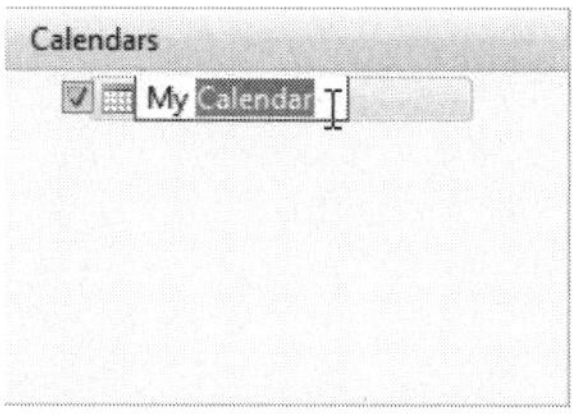

Figure 22-4: Renaming a calendar is simple:
Just select the name in the Details pane and start typing.

♦ **Change the calendar display color:** Click the Color drop-down bucket in the Details pane and choose from one of the 12 available colors. Alternately, click More Colors to bring up the color picker and choose from any color Windows can display.

♦ **Create a new calendar:** Open the File menu and choose New Calendar. A new calendar will appear in the Calendars list inside the Navigation pane. Because the default name is New Calendar, you'll want to change that: Simply start typing to give it a new name. If the name becomes deselected for some reason, click the new calendar name in Calendars and then select the name in the Details pane and begin typing.

♦ **Create calendar groups:** You can use a calendar group to logically group related calendars. For example, you might create a group called Personal and lump calendars such as Home, Health, and Vacations in it; or you might have a work group within which you would create calendars called Meetings, Work Trips, or whatever.

To create a calendar group, select File ➪ New Group from the menu. Calendar groups appear in the Calendars section of the Navigation pane as small folders. By default, groups will be empty. You can drag existing calendars in and out of groups, but if you want to create a new calendar inside of an existing group, you can do that, too: Simply right-click the group folder and then choose New Calendar from the menu that appears. Figure 22-5 shows how one might organize a large number of calendars and groups.

Secret

Although Windows Calendar is pretty accommodating when it comes to organizational styles, one thing you can't do is create a calendar group within another calendar group. Windows Calendar allows only a single level of groups.

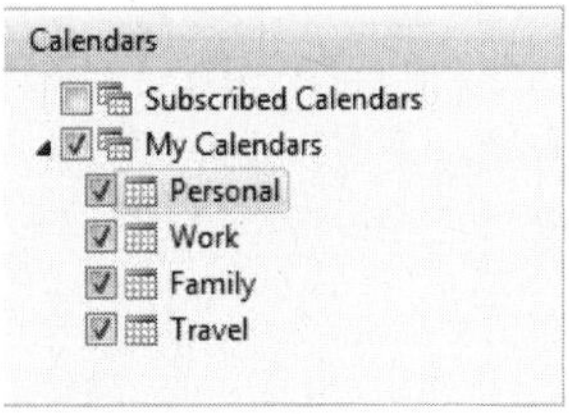

Figure 22-5: If you're really systematic, Windows Calendar will reward you with fine-grained control over calendar organization.

Secret

Here's one excellent use for groups. Later in this chapter, I discuss ways in which you can subscribe to calendars that have been published online by organizations and individuals. I recommend creating groups for these subscribed calendars in order to keep them separate from your personally created calendars. For example, you might create a group called Subscribed Calendars, Sporting Events, or whatever is appropriate.

Understanding Calendar Views and Navigation

Windows Calendar supports the following four basic view styles:

◆ **Day view:** Presents a top-down view style segregated into 30-minute slices, as shown in Figure 22-6.

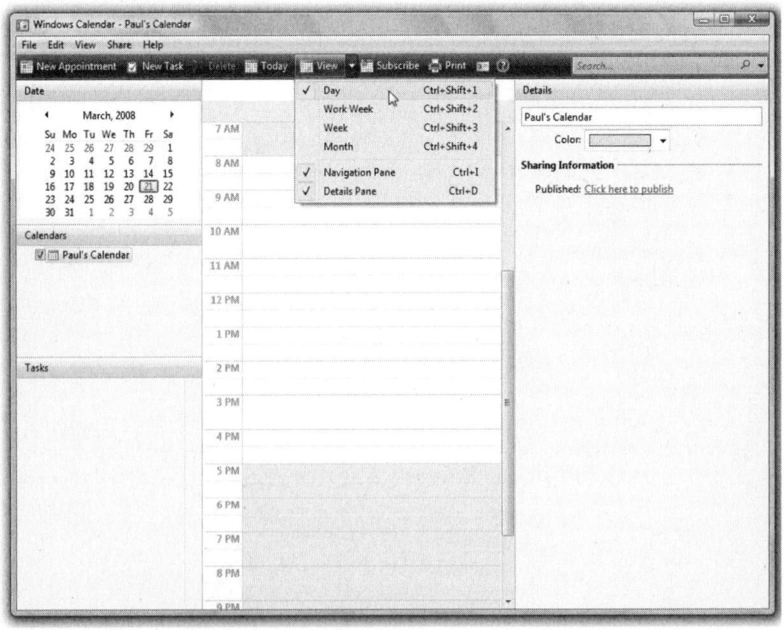

Figure 22-6: Windows Calendar's Day view.

◆ **Work Week view:** Divides the display into five columns, one for each day of the work week (Monday through Friday). As with Day view, the view is segregated into 30-minute slices of time from top to bottom, as shown in Figure 22-7.

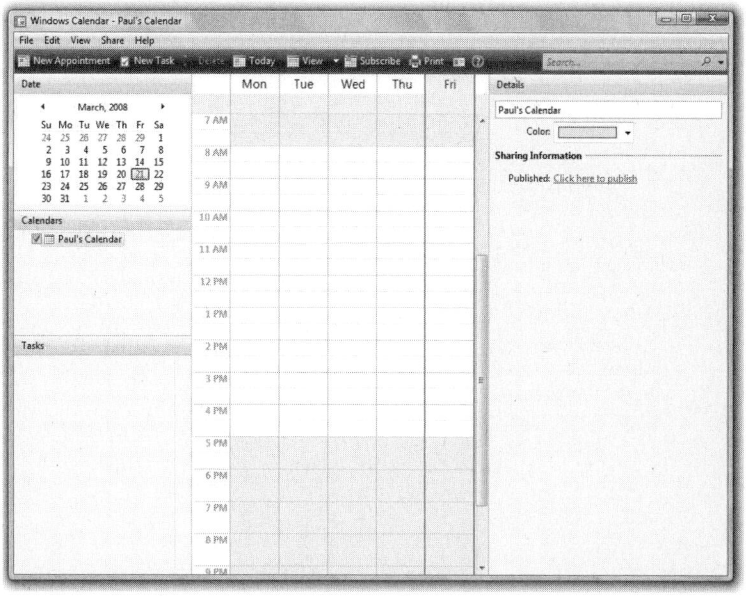

Figure 22-7: Work Week view displays just one work week at a time.

◆ **Week view:** This view, shown in Figure 22-8, divides the display into seven columns, one for each day of the week (versus five for Work Week view) As with Day view, the view is segregated into 30-minute slices of time from top to bottom.

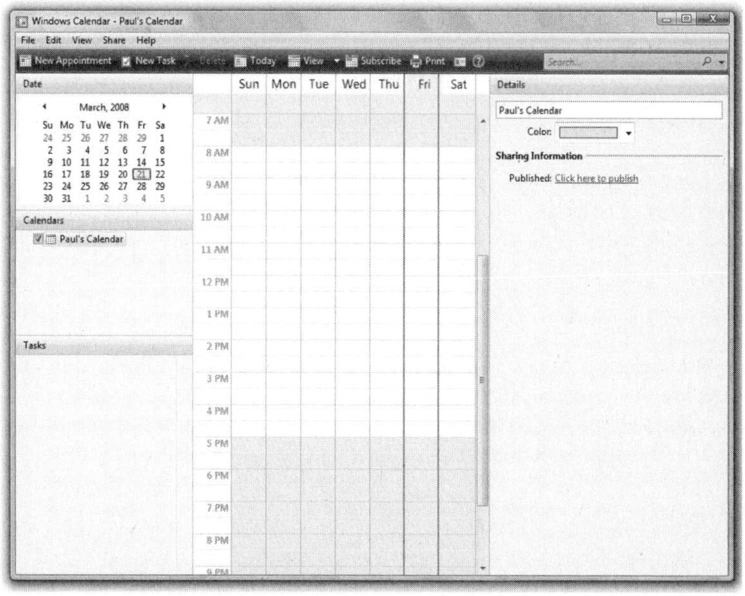

Figure 22-8: Windows Calendar's Week view.

◆ **Month view:** The central pane of Windows Calendar is divided into a standard monthly calendar view, where each day of the month is denoted by a square shape (see Figure 22-9).

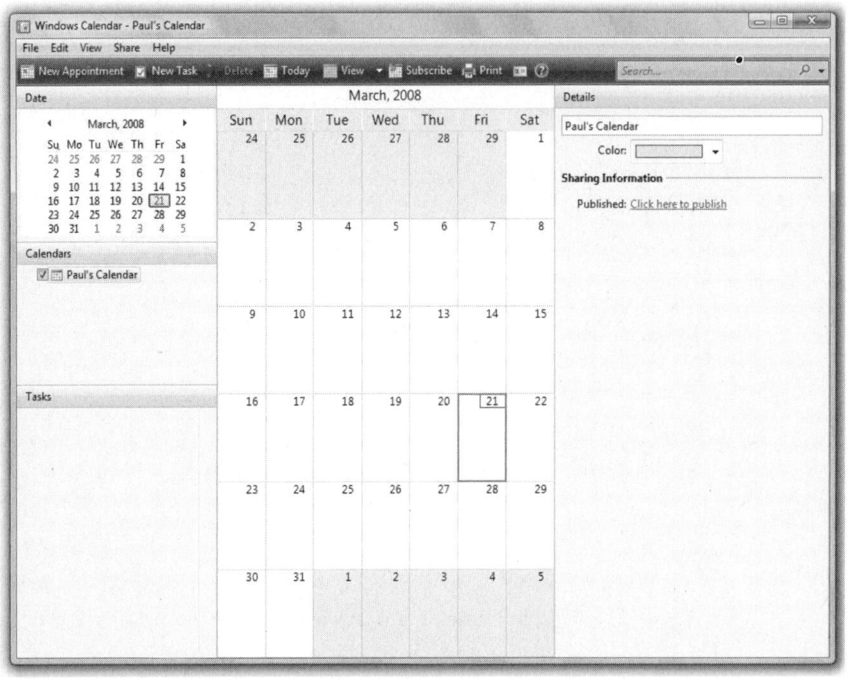

Figure 22-9: Windows Calendar's Month View.

In Work Week view, Week view, and Month view, the currently selected day is demarcated by bold blue lines. By default, this day is set to the current day. If you select other days for various reasons and want to return to the default display, click the Today button in the Windows Calendar toolbar. When you do so, the current day is selected.

tip If jumping directly to today isn't exactly what you're looking for, you can also cause Windows Calendar to jump to any date you choose. To do so, select the View menu (not the View toolbar button) and then Go to Date. Then, in the resulting dialog, simply pick the date you want as well as the view style you'd like displayed.

tip The little calendar found in the Date section of the Navigation Pane can be used to view different months without changing the main calendar view. If you look at this little calendar, you'll see small arrows to the left and right of the month name. Click them to navigate back and forth, respectively, from month to month.

Hiding and Viewing Calendars

If you've configured a number of calendars, you may sometimes want to hide certain calendars in the main calendar view. Notice that each calendar and group has a check box next to its name in the Calendars section of the Navigation pane. When a calendar or group is checked, appointments contained within that calendar will display normally within the main calendar view, using the color that's been assigned to the containing calendar; but when you uncheck a calendar or group, those items will be hidden.

Configuring Windows Calendar

Windows Calendar offers a variety of configuration options. You can hide the Navigation and Details panes, although I don't recommend doing so because they're useful and often needed. To do so, select View from the Windows Calendar menu or click the small arrow next to the View button in the Windows Calendar toolbar. From either menu, you can toggle both the Navigation and Details panes (you can toggle these panes via the View menu) and perform other tasks. The View button's pop-down menu is shown in Figure 22-10.

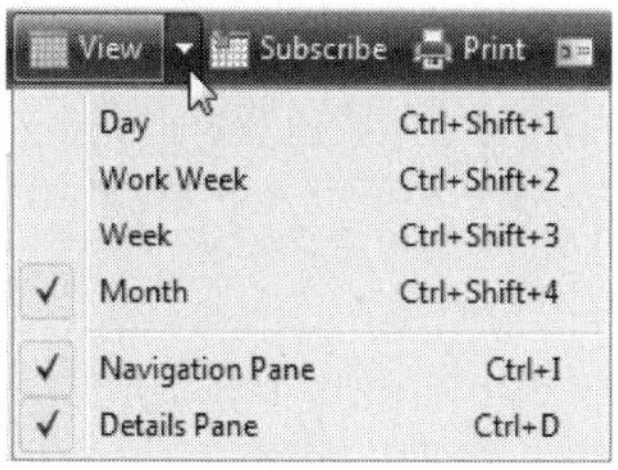

Figure 22-10: The View button enables you to configure the display layout.

To access other Windows Calendar options, you need to visit the application's Options dialog (select File ⇨ Options in the menu bar; there's nothing like consistency). The Options dialog is shown in Figure 22-11.

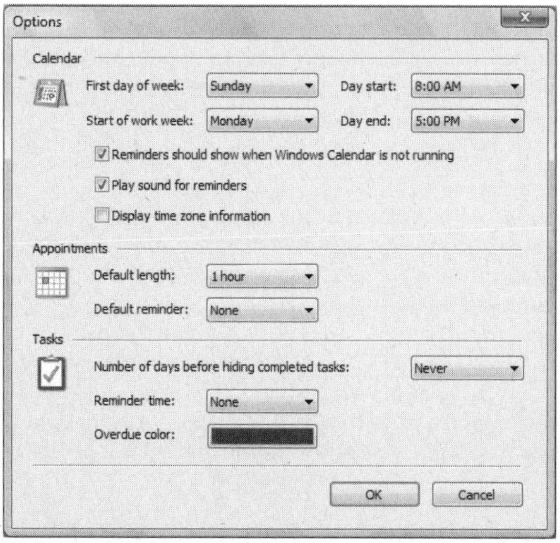

Figure 22-11: Most of Calendar's options are configurable via this simple window.

A number of calendar-related options are available from this interface. You can configure the first day of the (full) week as well as the start of the work week (typically Sunday and Monday, respectively). You can determine when the day starts (8:00 a.m., by default) and ends (5:00 p.m., by default), which is handy for the non-Month views; in these views, nonwork hours are shown in gray while work hours are white. There are also two options related to reminders:

◆ You can enable reminders even when Windows Calendar is not running, which is recommended if you want to be alerted to upcoming events.

◆ You can also optionally choose to play sounds when reminders appear, which can be handy if you're near the computer but not looking at the screen.

Finally, you can choose whether to display time zone information.

Secret

Microsoft's handling of time zones is notably bad, but this isn't just an issue in Windows Calendar. By default, if you create a number of appointments for, say, a business trip and then actually travel to a new time zone and change Vista's system clock to match the new time zone, all of the appointments you've created in Windows Calendar will be skewed by the number of hours separating the time zones. This is silly, but by displaying time zone information, you can overcome this issue by specifying appointments in both the correct time and time zone. Appointments are covered in the next section, but my advice here is simple: If you travel at all, enable Windows Calendar's time zone display and use it.

The Options dialog also includes sections for configuring appointments and tasks, options covered later in this chapter.

Working with Appointments

Within each calendar you use in Windows Calendar, you create various *appointments*. An appointment is an event that occurs on a specific date or over a range of dates. Appointments can have static beginning and ending times—e.g., a meeting that runs from 9:00 a.m. to 10:00 a.m.—or be all-day events. Appointments also have other characteristics. For example, you might create an appointment for an event that occurs repeatedly, such as a birthday or anniversary. You can also choose to be alerted when specific appointments are coming up.

There are various ways to create a new appointment in Windows Calendar, but how you do so matters little because you can change any appointment details during the creation process. For example, suppose you want to schedule a meeting for 9:00 a.m. next Monday. One way to do so would be to select the appropriate calendar and then navigate to the specific date in Day view. Then, position the mouse cursor over the time at which you'd like the appointment to begin, and double-click to start creating the new appointment. As shown in Figure 22-12, two things happen when you do this. First, a new appointment appears within the center calendar view and the name of the appointment is highlighted. Second, information about the new appointment appears in the Details pane.

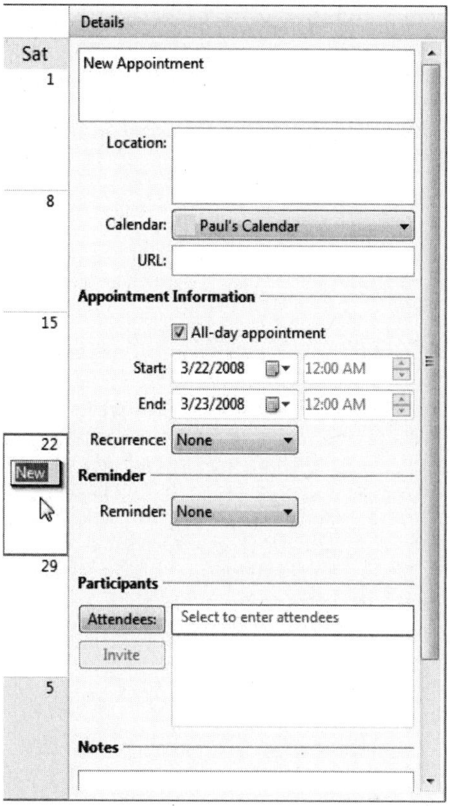

Figure 22-12: Creating a new appointment in Windows Calendar.

Examining Appointment Details

You can edit the following characteristics of the appointment:

◆ **Title:** This is how you identify an appointment. You can use any title you'd like, such as *Meeting with Sarah, Paul's birthday,* or *Flight to Paris.*

◆ **Location:** As with the title, this entry can contain any text value (e.g., *Phone,* for phone calls; *Meeting Room 133; American Airlines Flight 133;* or whatever. Go nuts, it's your calendar.

◆ **Calendar:** This is a drop-down list box where you specify the calendar to which the appointment will be attached. If you use multiple calendars, you can drop down the list and pick the appropriate calendar.

◆ **URL:** If a Web address is associated with the appointment, you can enter it here.

◆ **Appointment Information:** Use this section to specify the starting and ending times (and days) or whether it's an all-day event. You can also specify whether the appointment repeats. If it does, you can choose between Every Day (as shown in Figure 22-13), Weekly, Monthly, Yearly, or Advanced. If you select the latter option, the Recurrence dialog appears, where you can fine-tune its repetition characteristics. If you chose to enable time zones, and you should, you'll also see time zone drop-down lists associated with the starting and ending times of your appointment. By default, the time zone for each is set to the system's current time zone, but you can change this—for example, if you know that the appointment refers to a meeting or event that will take place in a different time zone.

Figure 22-13: Use Recurrence to set up how often an appointment repeats.

◆ **Reminder:** If you'd like Windows Calendar to pop up a reminder dialog at a specified interval before an appointment, this drop-down box enables you to configure that. Allowable reminder times include 0, 5, 15, and 30 minutes; 1, 2, and 4 hours; 1, 2, and 4 days; 1 and 2 weeks, or On date, which triggers a reminder at the start of the day of the appointment. When the Reminder dialog, shown in Figure 22-14, does appear, you can "snooze" the reminder just as you would an alarm clock so that it reminds you again later. You can also dismiss it or view the item. If you choose to dismiss it, you will never see that reminder again, so be careful. This dialog is identical to the Reminder dialog used by Microsoft Outlook, incidentally.

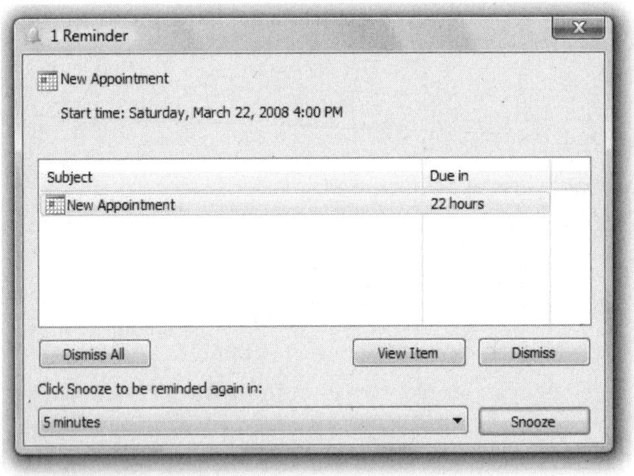

Figure 22-14: Outlook users will find the Reminder dialog to be familiar.

◆ **Participants:** This feature integrates with the Contacts database in Windows Vista, enabling you to add people from your address book to the appointment. See Chapter 20 for more information about Windows Contacts.

◆ **Notes:** This large text entry area enables you to write or paste in large blocks of text that may be pertinent to the appointment.

After you've created a new appointment, you might notice small icon-like symbols in the colored blocks that represent the appointment in the calendar view. For example, if you specify a reminder, a small alarm clock icon will appear. You can also get a bit more information about a particular appointment by moving the mouse cursor over it. When you do so, a small balloon help window will appear and display the title, location, and time of the appointment. This is especially useful in Month view, where you can't see starting and ending times for individual appointments.

The display of appointments varies according to their type. Appointments with starting and ending times appear as colored rectangles in the calendar view, but all-day and multi-day events appear in the upper well of the Day, Work Week, and Week views, as shown in Figure 22-15.

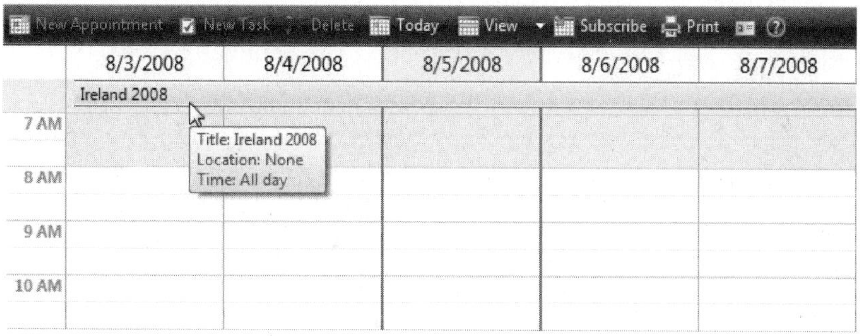

Figure 22-15: All-day events appear in the well at the top of Windows Calendar when in Day, Week, and Work Week views.

In Month view, multi-day events visually expand across all of the applicable days, as shown in Figure 22-16.

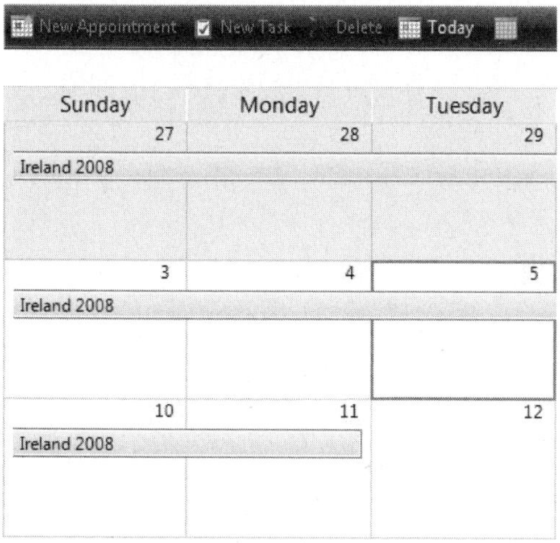

Figure 22-16: Multi-day events visually expand to include all of the days you specify.

If you want to view or edit an appointment later, select it in the calendar view. The appointment details appear in the Details pane.

If you just need to edit the title of an appointment, simply double-click it in the calendar view. The appointment title will be highlighted, enabling you to type a new title.

Configuring Appointments

You can access exactly two appointment-related options in the Windows Calendar Options dialog, which, again, is confusingly available via the File menu. In this dialog, you can specify the starting length of new appointments (the default is one hour) and the default reminder time (the default is none). It can be handy to change these defaults if your new appointments typically share common characteristics. If you almost always want to be reminded about an appointment one day early, for example, you could change the default reminder value to one day. This won't prevent you from changing the reminder on an appointment-by-appointment basis, of course.

Taking Calendar to Task...with Tasks

In addition to scheduling appointment events, Windows Calendar also enables you to create and configure various tasks. As its name suggests, a task is a to-do item that you want to ensure is completed. As with appointments, you can set reminders for tasks, and you can configure individual tasks to repeat at regular intervals. When you complete a task, you can mark it as completed from within Windows Calendar.

Like appointments, tasks are associated with calendars. This makes sense if you think about it. If you do choose to organize Windows Calendar with various calendars, it's likely you'll want to associate certain tasks with home, work, or whatever other categories you may choose to use for other scheduling needs. That said, tasks are relegated to the Tasks section of the Navigation pane and are not added to the main calendar view. This is actually pretty confusing, as many calendars add a task pane at the bottom of certain calendar views.

Creating Tasks

To create a new task, first select a calendar in the Calendars section of the Navigation pane. Then, click the New Task button in the Windows Calendar toolbar. (There are other ways to initiate a new task. You can right-click an empty spot in the Tasks section and choose New Task; or simply select File ➪ New Task from the Windows Calendar menu. You can also select Ctrl+T. You want options, I've got options.)

However you do it, a new task will appear in the Tasks section with its name highlighted for editing, as shown in Figure 22-17. Additionally, information about the task appears in the Details pane so you can configure it as needed.

Figure 22-17: Creating a new task in Windows Calendar.

In the Details pane, you'll see a number of options for your newly created task:

- ◆ **Title:** This is how you identify the task. You can use any title you'd like.
- ◆ **Calendar:** This specifies the calendar to which the task is attached.
- ◆ **URL:** If a Web address is associated with the task, you can enter it here.
- ◆ **Task Information:** In this section, you specify whether the task is completed, a priority rating (Low, Medium, High, or None), and optional starting and ending dates (but not times). When a task is marked as completed, that task includes a check mark in the Tasks section of the Navigational pane, as well as in the Task Information section of the task's Details pane. If you want to be reminded of an upcoming task you need to complete, it often makes sense to set up at least a starting date for the task. That way, when you enter a reminder time in the next section, it has something to work from.
- ◆ **Reminder:** As with appointments, you can configure Windows Calendar to remind you when tasks are due. These reminders behave identically to appointment reminders.
- ◆ **Notes:** This large text entry area enables you to write or paste in large blocks of text that may be pertinent to the task.

tip   What's the difference between a task and an appointment? Appointments typically
        come and go at specific times, but tasks are often more open-ended and have a com-
        pletion requirement. In addition, appointments can involve other people. With a task,
        you're on your own. Then again, when a task is completed, you don't have to share the
        glory. Live by the sword, die by the sword.

Configuring Tasks

You can configure a number of task-related features from the Options dialog for Windows
Calendar. These options include whether and when to hide completed tasks (which might
otherwise clutter up the Tasks section if you're highly productive), the default reminder
time, and the default color to use to mark a task that's overdue. (No surprise, the default
color is red.) That's right—Windows Calendar can get nasty if you don't keep on top of
your tasks.

tip   There's another option in the Options dialog that's pertinent to tasks. In the Calendar
        section of this dialog is an option titled *Reminders should show when Windows
        Calendar is not running*. For the most part, you will want to ensure that this option is
        enabled. Otherwise, you'd have to remember to run Windows Calendar in order for
        task (and appointment) reminders to pop up, which kind of defeats the purpose of a
        reminder. Maybe you could set a reminder that would remind you to run Windows
        Calendar. Never mind.

tip   You can also change how tasks appear in the Tasks section of the Navigation pane. If
        you right-click in this area and choose Sort By, you can sort by due date, priority, title,
        and calendar name.

Sharing Calendars

So far, everything covered in this chapter will be familiar to you if you've used an
application such as Microsoft Outlook or even the calendar functionality of a Web mail
solution such as Hotmail or Yahoo! Mail. (Microsoft itself has created a newer Web calendar called Windows Live Calendar, covered later in the chapter.) But what really sets
Windows Calendar apart from those products is that Windows Calendar adheres to the
iCal Internet-based calendaring standard. This means that it's extremely easy to share
calendars with people from all over the world, as long as they too use Windows Calendar
or another application (such as Apple iCal or Mozilla Sunbird) that also respects this
standard.

Importing and Exporting Calendars

Previous to Windows Calendar, Microsoft supported only static calendar data interoperability in its various calendar products. That is, you could *import* or *export* calendar data in specific formats so that you could copy or move information from one calendar to another. This functionality has been added to Windows Calendar as well; and although it's not as exciting as the sharing technologies described later in the chapter, it's still useful.

Windows Calendar can only import (and export) to industry-standard ICS format, which is sometimes referred to as iCalendar format. This format is supported by applications such as Apple iCal and Mozilla Sunbird, but not by Microsoft Outlook (though Outlook 2007 does allow you to open files in ICS format).

Follow these steps to export a calendar to ICS from Windows Calendar:

1. Select the calendar you wish to export and then select File ⇨ Export.
2. Select a location to which to save the file using the Export dialog, and then give it a description name.
3. You can now import this file into another compatible calendar application.

To import an ICS calendar into Windows Calendar, you follow a similar set of steps, although this time you obviously need an ICS file to import. There are a few ways to get such a file. If you have a calendar application that supports exporting into ICS, then you could obviously use that; but a better method is to download one of the many ICS files out there on the Web. We'll look at this scenario in the next section.

Publishing and Subscribing to Calendars

Importing and exporting is nice, but both of these operations are like slices in time because they can't help you if future changes are made to any of the calendars you've exchanged. What's needed, of course, is a way to automatically *synchronize* data between calendars so that you can ensure that your calendar is always up-to-date. This, of course, is where the iCal standard comes in. Using the publish and subscribe functionality that's built into Windows Calendar, it's possible to subscribe to any number of online calendars and even publish your own calendars online.

Subscribing to Calendars

Before you can subscribe to an online calendar, you need to find one. There are several online calendar resources that you can peruse. One of the best is Apple's iCal Library (**www.apple.com/downloads/macosx/calendars/**) because Apple was one of the first major software companies to embrace the iCal standard. Apple's site includes professional sports schedules, worldwide holidays, movie openings, and much more. Another excellent resource is iCalShare (**www.icalshare.com/**), which lists even more calendars to which you can subscribe, in a bewildering list of categories.

Using either site, or a similar resource, you can browse different calendars until you find one to which you'd like to subscribe. Say you're a Boston Red Sox fan. (I know, who isn't?) If you search for "Red Sox" on iCalShare, you'll see a number of calendars devoted to the schedule of Boston's major league baseball team.

Secret

You might think that you could subscribe to one of these calendars simply by downloading it. Unfortunately, it's not that simple. Instead, you must right-click the link to an online calendar and copy its Web address, or URL, to the clipboard. To do this with Internet Explorer, right-click and choose Copy Shortcut. (In Firefox, it's Copy Link Location.) Then, switch to Windows Calendar and click the Subscribe button in the toolbar. This displays the Subscribe wizard, shown in Figure 22-18.

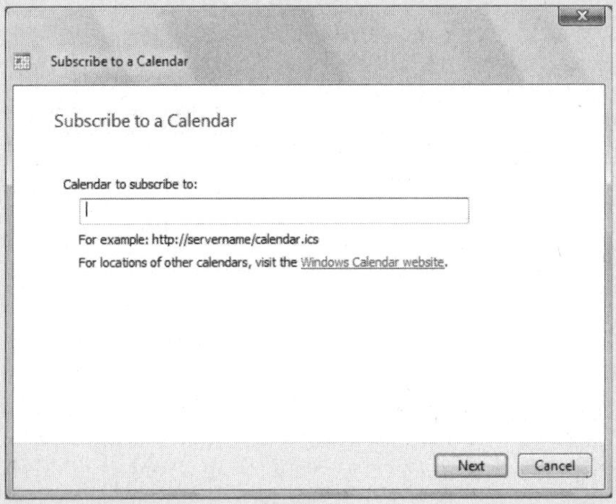

Subscribe to a Calendar

Subscribe to a Calendar

Calendar to subscribe to:

For example: http://servername/calendar.ics
For locations of other calendars, visit the Windows Calendar website.

Next   Cancel

Figure 22-18: It's nice that you can subscribe to online calendars, but it's not very automated.

Paste the URL for the calendar into the text box and click Next. Windows Calendar will connect to the Web and discover details about the calendar. In the next phase of the Subscribe wizard, you'll see the name of the calendar (which you can and likely will want to change), along with options for how often it should refresh (or synchronize with) the remote calendar. If reminders or tasks are included with the calendar, you can optionally enable them as well, as shown in Figure 22-19.

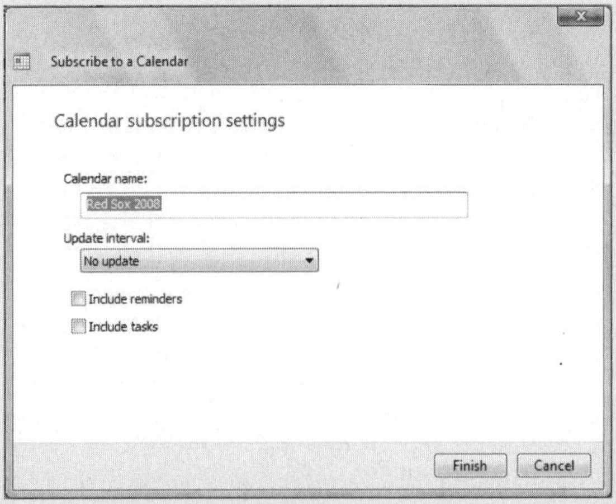

Subscribe to a Calendar

Calendar subscription settings

Calendar name:

Red Sox 2008

Update interval:

No update

☐ Include reminders
☐ Include tasks

Finish   Cancel

Figure 22-19: It's unlikely that you'll want to be issued reminders from a remote calendar, but it's nice to have the option.

continues

continued

Click Finish and you'll complete the subscription. This process is similar to creating your own calendars. For example, you'll see a new calendar appear in the Calendars list, along with its associated appointments, all displayed in a custom color, as shown in Figure 22-20. You can edit the name of the calendar, delete it, or change its display color if you'd like. (Might I recommend a light red color for that Red Sox schedule you just configured?)

Figure 22-20: Subscribed calendars appear alongside local calendars in Windows Calendar.

There are key differences between subscribed and local calendars as well. Subscribed calendars are read-only, which means you cannot add or change appointments with them. (As such, the New Appointment, New Task, and Delete toolbar icons are disabled when you select such a calendar.) You can only view them (or, as noted above, change their name and color within Windows Calendar). The people who publish the calendars to which you are subscribing are free to change them, of course. If they do change a calendar you're subscribing to, you can get the latest changes by setting up a refresh schedule when you subscribe, or by synchronizing, described shortly.

Publishing Your Calendars

If you have access to a Web server to which you can copy an ICS file, you can publish your own calendars. Because this isn't as common as subscribing, Windows Calendar doesn't include a Publish toolbar button, but it does include a full-featured Publish Calendar wizard that steps you through the process. To find it, select a calendar and then navigate to

Share ⇨ Publish from the Windows Calendar menu. This displays the Publish Calendar wizard, shown in Figure 22-21.

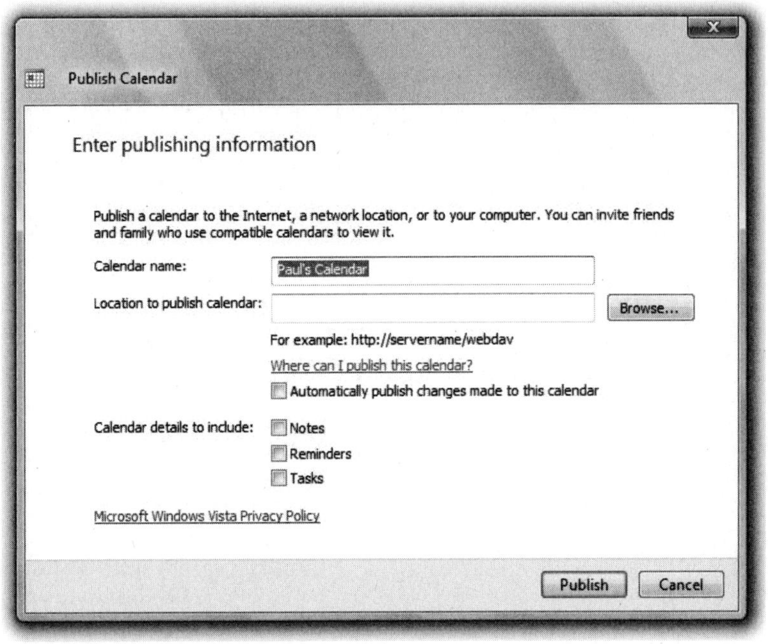

Figure 22-21: With this simple wizard, you can publish your own calendars online.

To publish a calendar directly to a Web server, that server must be compatible with the Web-based Distributed Authoring and Versioning (WebDAV) standard, a set of technologies aimed at making it easier to manage files on remote Web servers. If you don't have access to such a server, then you can always export your calendar to a local ICS file and then upload it to a Web server using FTP or whatever uploading tool you choose. However, when you do this, you lose the best feature of publishing, which is the capability to keep the remote (or published) version of your calendar up-to-date as you make changes to it from within Windows Calendar.

In the Publish Calendar wizard, you first provide a name for your calendar (Windows Calendar uses the calendar name by default). Then, enter a URL where you'd like to publish the calendar. This URL is formatted just like any Web address, using the HTTP prefix. If your Web server is named **winsupersite.com** and you have dedicated a remote folder for calendar sharing called **ical**, you might type in the address **www.winsupersite.com/ical**. Then, determine whether you want the published calendar to be automatically updated when changes are made and decide whether to include Notes, Reminders, and Tasks. When you're ready, press the Publish button.

Now, Windows Calendar will publish your calendar to the Web site you specified. At this point, you can continue making changes to the calendar; stop publishing it, if you're not happy with the results; or announce the calendar, giving friends and family an opportunity to discover it and, it is hoped, subscribe. The latter two options are available in the Share menu.

Synchronizing Your Calendars

With the proliferation of local and shared calendars on your system, you're going to want some way to ensure that everything is up-to-date. Fortunately, Microsoft has included a synchronize function in Windows Calendar that performs two key functions. If you have a remote calendar to which you've subscribed, then synchronizing will ensure that you have the very latest version; and if you are publishing a calendar, Synch will ensure that the remote copy is up-to-date with the changes you've made locally. You can choose to synchronize only the currently selected calendar or Synch All, which will sync all of your calendars, in both directions. Both options are available from Windows Calendar's Share menu.

Searching Calendars

In keeping with the Windows Vista instant search-centric user interface, Windows Calendar provides a handy Search box in the upper-right corner of the application window, from which you search for both appointments and tasks. If you type a term into the Search box, then by default Windows Calendar will search all appointment and task events and display the results in a Search Results pane that appears at the top of the Windows Calendar window, shown in Figure 22-22.

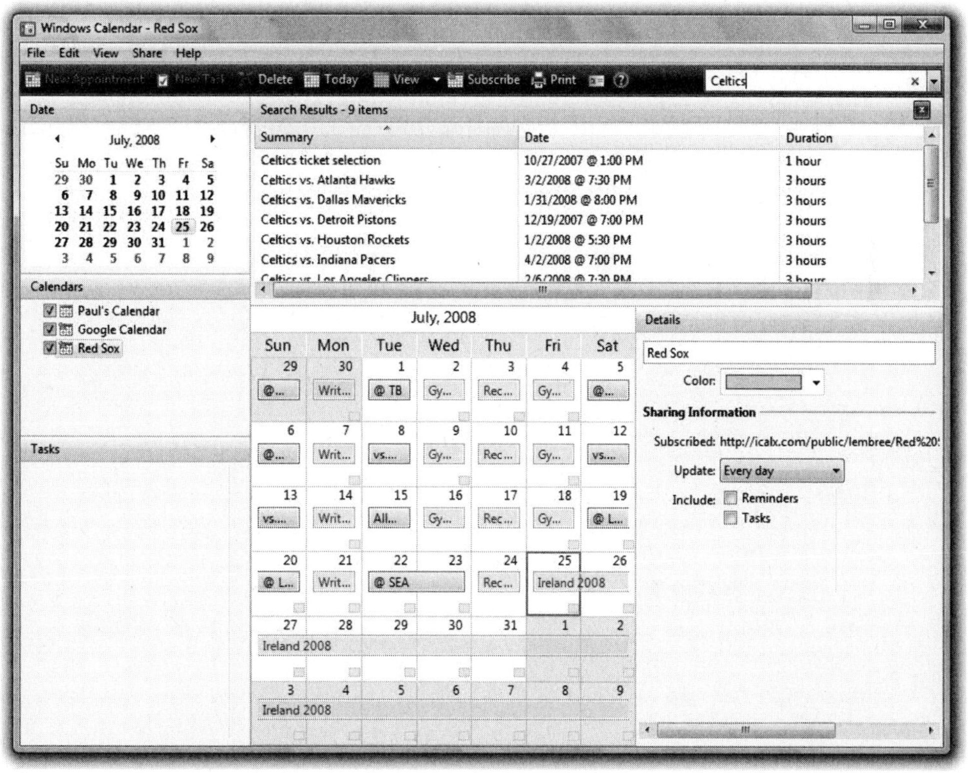

Figure 22-22: The Search feature in Windows Calendar works with both appointments and tasks.

You can also limit searches with certain criteria. If you look to the right of the Search box, you'll see a drop-down menu. This menu enables you to limit the search to today's events, the next 7 days, the next 14 days, the next 31 days, this calendar month, all future events, or the currently selected day.

Secret It's not obvious, but the search feature in Windows Calendar is limited in two key ways. First, it will search only selected calendar(s), so make sure you've selected the calendar(s) you want in the Navigation pane before performing a search. Second, search will search only the title field. You can't search for items in Location, Notes, or other Details pane fields.

Printing Calendars

This may seem a bit antiquated in this day of digital tools, but Windows Calendar includes a nice printing component, which enables you to print your calendars in various attractive ways. This is handy for people who need a quick printout or haven't otherwise embraced the notion of personal digital assistants (PDAs) or smartphones. Sometimes, a piece of paper just works.

Before you print, you need to decide which calendars to include in your printout. Any calendars that are selected, or checked, in the Calendars list in the Navigational pane will print, so deselect any calendars you'd like to exclude first.

Next, click the Print button in the Windows Calendar toolbar. This launches the Print window, shown in Figure 22-23. Here, you can configure various print options.

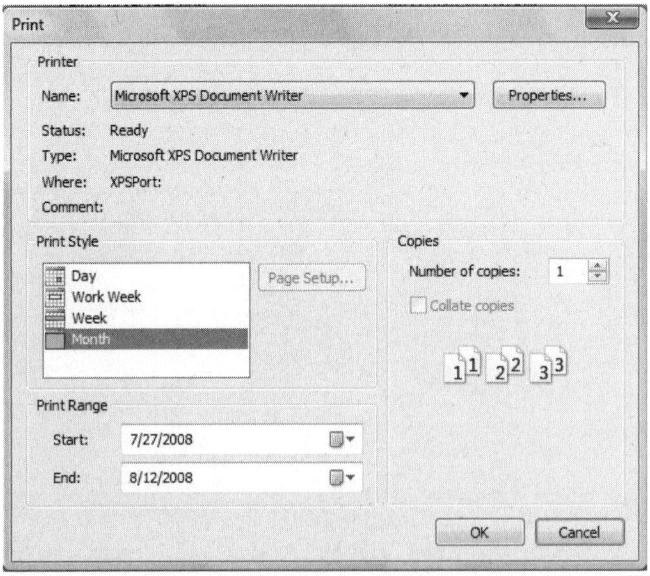

Figure 22-23: When printing calendars, you can choose between various view styles.

Key among these options is Print Style. Here, you can pick between Day, Work Week, Week, and Month views. You can also specify a date range and other options. The actual printouts are surprisingly nice. They provide an attractive calendar display but none of the Details information found with each appointment.

Secret The printing functionality in Windows Calendar prints only appointments, not tasks.

Integrating with Other Windows Vista Applications

Finally, no discussion about Windows Calendar would be complete without a short look at how this application integrates with other Windows Vista applications. Actually, Windows Calendar integrates with only a handful of Windows Vista applications, and only one of them, Windows Contacts, is particularly meaningful. While Microsoft tends to boast about how its applications "talk" to each other, this communication is fairly minimal in the real world.

In the case of Windows Calendar and Windows Contacts, I already mentioned how you can add a list of participants to appointments. What I glossed over is that you can also *invite* these people to meetings and other appointments you create.

Here's how it works: Suppose you create an appointment for a meeting between you and several co-workers. In the Participants section of the details for this appointment you select contacts from a pop-up window that appears when you click the Attendees button. The contacts you see in this list are populated from the database of contacts found in Windows Contacts. (And in a nod toward the integration mentioned earlier, you can actually add a new contact to Windows Contacts from this window if you're so inclined.)

Once you've added attendees to the appointment, you can also optionally choose to invite them. This invitation is sent via e-mail, using Windows Mail (another integrated part of Windows Vista) or whatever mail client you've configured as the default. (See Chapter 20 for information about Windows Mail and configuring the default mail client.) The e-mail invitation uses the e-mail address that's configured for each contact you've invited. The subject is the title of the appointment, and attached to the e-mail is an ICS file for the appointment, as shown in Figure 22-24. If your recipients execute this attachment, the appointment will be added to their own calendars. Neat! (Assuming they're cool with running attachments, of course.).

Windows Calendar also features a small, unnamed icon in its toolbar that, for some reason, launches Windows Contacts. It's the second to last icon on the toolbar, the one that looks sort of like a contact card. There's also a Contacts entry in the View menu that, yes, launches Windows Contacts as well. Ah, "integration."

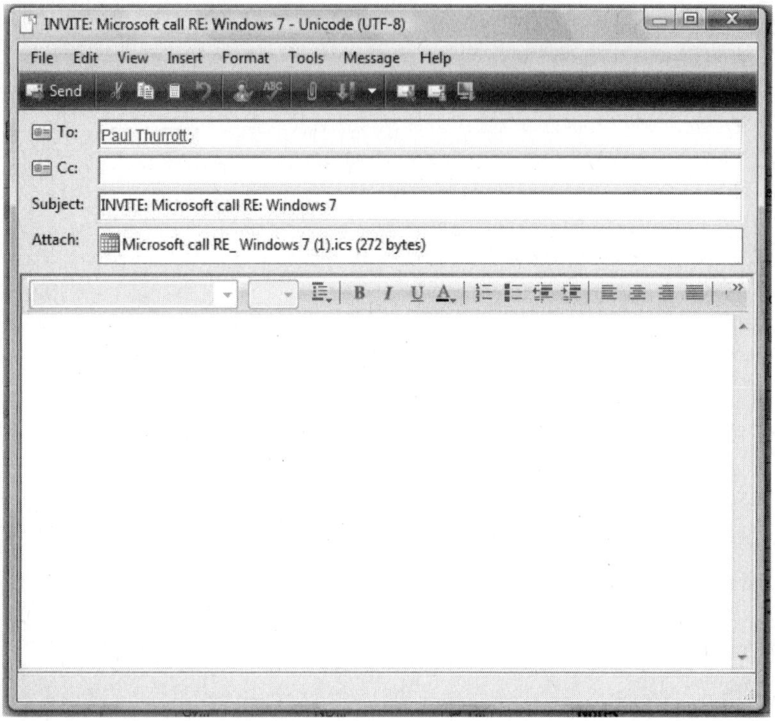

Figure 22-24: You can invite people to meetings and other appointments using e-mail-based invitations with ICS attachments.

A Quick Look at Windows Live Calendar

In addition to its desktop-based Windows Calendar tool, Microsoft has created a calendaring standards-based Web calendar called Windows Live Calendar, which is part of its Windows Live suite of online services. Windows Live Calendar replaces the company's previous stab at an online calendar, the horrid calendar component of Hotmail. Like Windows Calendar, Windows Live Calendar can import ICS files, and it supports multiple calendars. However, as of this writing, you cannot publish Windows Live Calendars and subscribe to them from other ICS-compatible clients such as Windows Calendar. That may change by the time you read this, however. Stay tuned to the SuperSite for Windows for updates (**www.winsupersite.com**).

Windows Live Calendar does have a few unique features, however. In addition to being available from any PC thanks to it being a Web-based service, Windows Live Calendar also integrates with other Windows Live services, such as Windows Live Events, Microsoft's Evite-like service, enabling you to create events that you can easily share with others in pretty impressive ways.

You can get a closer look at Windows Live Calendar in Chapter 21, but my hope is that this service eventually becomes the ideal online companion for Windows Calendar, especially for those who have invested heavily in Microsoft's various online services. Windows Live Calendar is shown in Figure 22-25.

Figure 22-25: Windows Live Calendar is a bit immature as I write this book, but it will likely be far more usable by the time you read this.

Summary

Windows Calendar is a decent standards-based calendar, and given the fact that no such functionality existed in Windows XP or previous Windows versions, it's a welcome addition to the growing collection of Windows Vista applications. With Windows Calendar, you can maintain one of more calendars, subscribe to Web-based calendars, and publish your own calendars so that others can keep up with your activities. It is hoped that this chapter has inspired you to discover this application's many and varied features. Unless you require Exchange compatibility or Windows Mobile device integration, this application should meet all of your scheduling needs.

Keeping Your Data Safe

♦ ♦

In This Chapter

Backing up and restoring data

Utilizing the Backup and Restore Center

Creating and restoring data backups

Managing automatic backups with Windows Backup

Backing up an entire PC using system images

Restoring an entire PC using the Windows Recovery Environment

Using Shadow Copies to recover old versions of data files

Repairing Windows with System Restore

♦ ♦

With Windows Vista, Microsoft has finally given users pervasive and reliable backup and restore solutions for both data files and the entire computer. You can use the File and Folder Backup Wizard to copy your important files and folders to a safe location, the Complete PC Backup tool to create a system image that can be used later to restore a broken PC, and the Backup Status and Configuration tool to enable automatic data backups or restore data backups or system images. There's even a cool new feature borrowed from Windows Server that helps you recover old versions of data files if you save the wrong version, and an updated version of System Restore that can help your PC "go back in time" and remove bad drivers or applications. You may never need to turn to a third-party backup and restore utility again.

Secret   That's right: Years before Apple shipped a feature called Time Machine in Mac OS X 10.5 that it promoted with a "go back in time" marketing mantra, Microsoft had this feature in Windows Server and then later in Vista first—and you thought only Microsoft copied features from other operating systems.

Different Backups, Different Goals

Now that you've moved to digital storage for your most valuable data, it's time to start thinking about creating backups, copies of your original data that are ideally kept elsewhere for safekeeping. Many people don't even consider backing up until the unthinkable happens: a hard drive breaks down, literally taking all the data with it, or fire or theft occurs. Whatever the situation, you should be prepared for the worst before it happens. This is all the more important because many people now manage both their professional and private lives on their PCs. It's one thing to lose this week's meeting agenda, but quite another when a hard-drive crash takes away the only copies you had of five years' worth of digital photos. Those are *memories*, for crying out loud.

Given the almost complete lack of decent backup solutions in previous Windows versions, you may be surprised to discover that Windows Vista offers an almost mind-boggling array of backup and restore solutions, each aimed at a different need. Best of all, Vista also includes a friendly front end to all these capabilities, so that even the most nontechnical user can get up to speed quickly. Before getting into that, however, consider the various types of data safety facilities that Windows Vista supports.

Data Backup

If you think of your Documents folder as the center of your data universe, and keep an elaborate series of folders and files there, then you'll understand the necessity of backing up these crucial files on a regular basis. To this end, Windows Vista supports both automatic and manual data backup options, enabling you to choose which files to back up and when. You can then restore your backups at any time to recover previous versions of documents, or to replace a file you may have accidentally deleted.

Complete PC Backup

There's nothing worse than discovering that you need to reinstall Windows for some reason. Not only do you have to take the time and make the effort to reinstall the operating system again, you also have to ensure that you have drivers for all your hardware, find and reinstall all the applications you use regularly, reload all your personal data, and reconfigure all of the system's options so that it's exactly the way you used to have it. Rather than go through this rigmarole, you can use a new Windows Vista feature called Complete PC Backup to create what is called a *system image* or *snapshot*. This image—which is essentially a huge backup file—contains the entire contents of your PC as it existed the day you created the image. If you need to recover your entire PC, you can simply restore the system image and get right back to work.

File Recovery

Windows Vista offers the following two excellent ways to recover lost files:

- ♦ **Shadow Copies:** If you want to recover an older version of a document, perhaps because you made an editing error and then saved it, you can use this feature to access previous versions of the file.
- ♦ **System Restore:** If you make a change to your system that renders the PC unstable, such as installing a bad driver, you can use this feature to return to a previous state in time, or *restore point*. When you reboot, none of your data has been changed, but the rest of your system configuration returns to that of the day and time the restore point was first made.

Add all that up, and what you have is the makings of a full-featured data recovery software suite. Amazingly, Microsoft provides all of that functionality in Windows Vista, free.

Available Tools in Various Vista Versions

Now the bad news. As explained in Chapter 1, different product editions of Windows Vista include support for different features. These differences can be dramatic in some cases—digital media feature support is an obvious example—and this is true of Vista's backup and recovery functionality as well, unfortunately. Put simply, lower-end versions of Windows Vista do not include some of the platform's best data and PC reliability features.

As a reminder, Table 23-1 outlines the Vista technologies highlighted in this chapter and explains which are available in each mainstream Windows Vista product edition.

Table 23-1: Reliability Features

	Home Basic	Home Premium	Business	Enterprise	Ultimate
Manual file backup and recovery	Yes	Yes	Yes	Yes	Yes
Automatic file backup	Yes	Yes	Yes	Yes	Yes
Shadow Copies	—	—	Yes	Yes	Yes
System image backup and recovery	—	—	Yes	Yes	Yes

Throughout this chapter, I also highlight when certain features are unavailable in certain Windows Vista product editions so there's no confusion.

One Tool to Rule Them All: Using the Backup and Restore Center

Although various data recovery tools are available scattered through the Windows Vista user interface, a single application—the Backup and Restore Center—provides a handy front end to most of them. Shown in Figure 23-1, this application helps you back up and restore files on your PC, and create and restore complete PC backups as well. (Backup and Restore Center also has links to System Restore.)

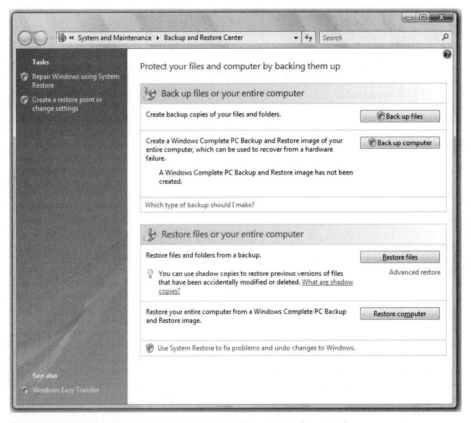

Figure 23-1: It's a one-stop shop for all your data protection needs.

Actually, the version of the Backup and Restore Center shown in Figure 23-1 is available only in Windows Vista Business, Enterprise, and Ultimate editions. If you have Windows Vista Home Basic or Home Premium, you see the Backup and Restore Center shown in Figure 23-2. This version lacks links to the Complete PC Backup functionality, which is not present in those versions of Vista.

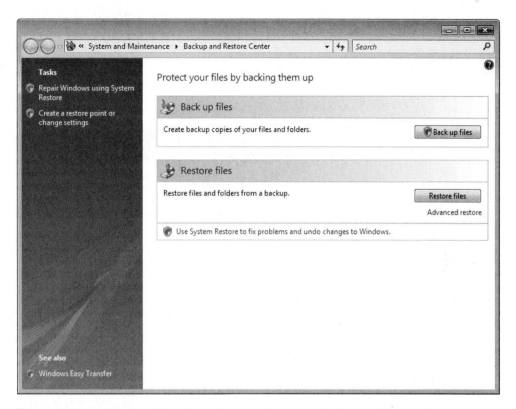

Figure 23-2: In Windows Vista Home Basic and Premium, Backup and Restore Center is somewhat scaled back.

Because the Backup and Restore Center basically sits in front of most of the other data recovery functions included in Windows Vista, I use this as the obvious starting point for most of the data, file, and system backup and restore features discussed.

tip The Backup and Restore Center can be found in the Start Menu under All Programs ➪ Maintenance, but the easiest way to find this application, as always, is Start Menu Search: Type **backup and restore** and press Enter.

Backing Up Documents, Pictures, and Other Data

If you want to create a data backup, you can use the Back Up Files Wizard, which is available from the Backup and Restore Center. To do so, launch the Backup and Restore Center and click the Back Up Files button. This launches the wizard shown in Figure 23-3.

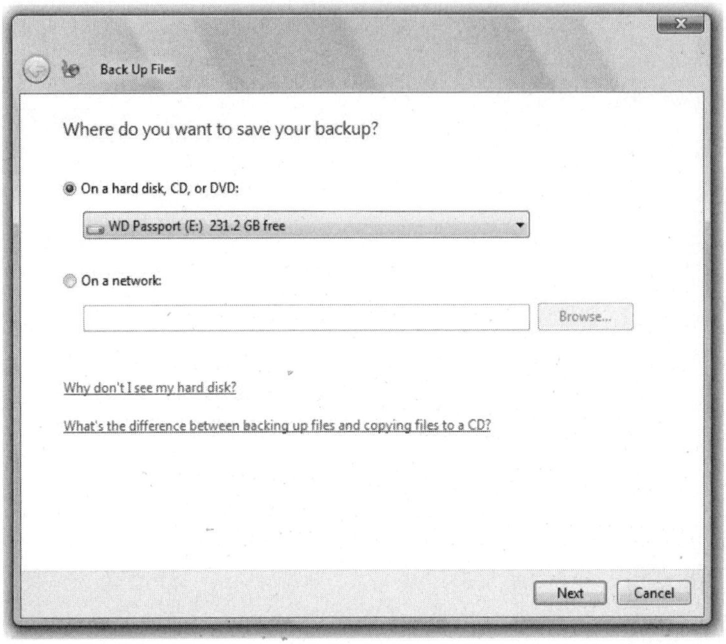

Figure 23-3: The Back Up Files wizard helps you manually create a backup of your important data files.

In the first step of the wizard, you must choose a location to store the backup. You can save a backup to an internal or external hard disk or other storage device, a recordable optical disk (typically a writeable CD or DVD), or a network share. The amount of space you need, of course, depends on the amount of data you are backing up. The wizard autoselects the local storage offering the most free space, but you can change this selection, of course.

> **tip**   Microsoft does not allow you to back up to the disk or partition you are backing up. That is, if you are backing up data from the C: drive, you cannot save the backup to the C: drive.

In the second step, shown in Figure 23-4, you select which disks (or partitions) to include in the backup. If you have only a single disk, then this is simple, but many people are using multiple disks and partitions, so the wizard gives you the option to include those as well.

> **Secret**   You don't see step two? This second step appears only if you are trying to back up on a system that has two or more hard disk partitions. On a typical single-drive system, such as a portable computer, you proceed directly to the third step.

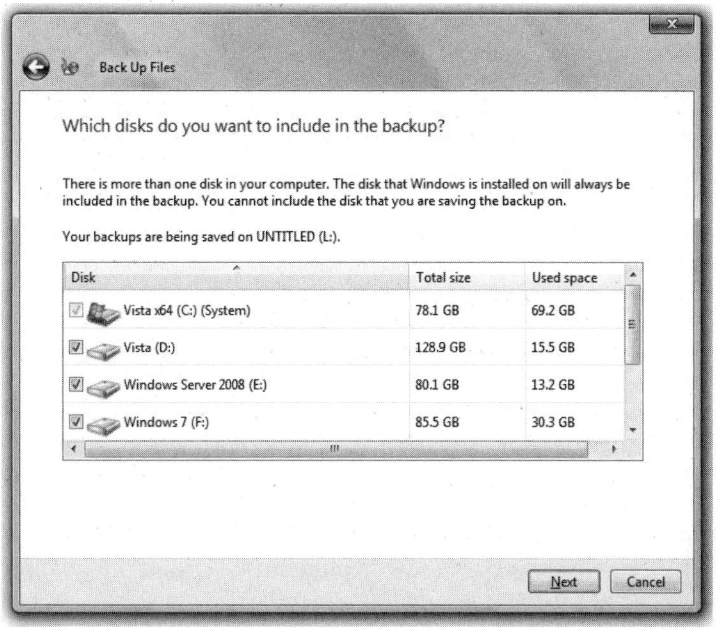

Figure 23-4: This step in the backup wizard appears only on multipartition systems.

In the next step, select which types of data files you'd like to back up, as shown in Figure 23-5.

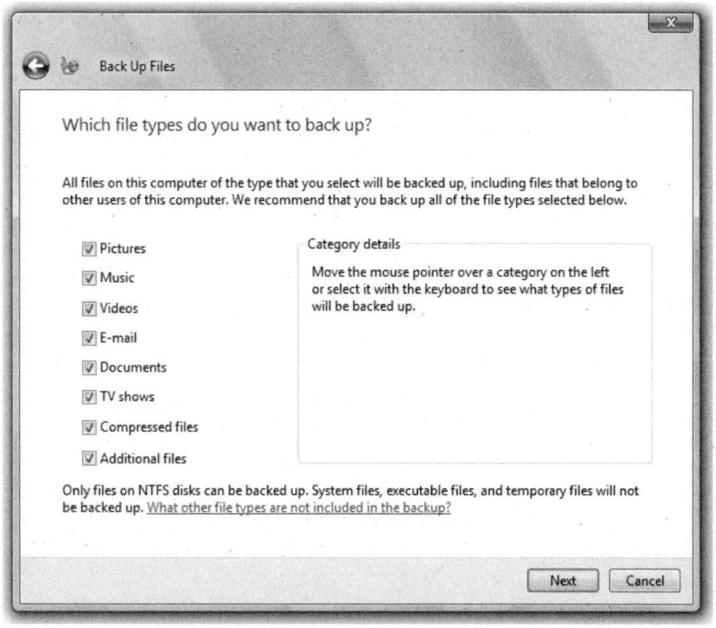

Figure 23-5: Rather than make you step through a series of document locations, the wizard intelligently finds the data files you specify, regardless of their location.

You can choose between a variety of general file types, including the following:

◆ **Pictures**, such as digital photos, drawings, scanned pictures, faxes, clip art, and other image files

◆ **Music**, or, more accurately, all audio files, including songs, playlists, and other audio files

◆ **Videos**, which includes any digital movie files in common formats such as WMV, MPEG, and AVI

◆ **E-mail**, which consists of files created by Microsoft e-mail applications such as Windows Mail, Windows Live Mail, and Microsoft Outlook. Note that only local files are backed up. If you leave e-mail messages on the server, these e-mails are not backed up.

◆ **Documents**, such as Word documents and other word processing files, Excel spreadsheets and other spreadsheets, PowerPoint presentations, PDF and XPS files, text files, and the like

◆ **TV shows,** such as those recorded with Windows Media Center

◆ **Compressed files**, including those that are stored in common compressed file formats, e.g., ZIP, CAB, ISO, WIM, and VHD. (If you use Vista's Compressed Folders feature, those folders are considered compressed files as well.)

◆ **Additional files,** which can be a number of other file types that don't neatly fall into the preceding categories.

Secret
Although the wizard doesn't offer any way to fine-tune exactly which data file types to back up, you won't have to worry about it missing anything. As long as you leave every data file type checked in this step of the wizard, Windows Backup will be overly thorough and back up all known data types plus virtually anything it can't recognize.

Secret
As always, there are exceptions. Prior to Windows Vista Service Pack 1 (SP1), Backup couldn't back up files stored in Encrypted File System (EFS) protected locations. However, this capability was added in SP1, yet another reason to upgrade. Regardless of which version of Vista you use, Backup cannot back up program files, files in the Recycle Bin, temporary files, files stored on FAT-formatted hard disk partitions, and some other file types.

In the next step of the wizard, Microsoft subtly guides you toward a regular, automatic backup strategy by noting that new and changed files can be added to subsequent backups according to the schedule you configure here. As shown in Figure 23-6, it's suggested that you automatically back up at least weekly.

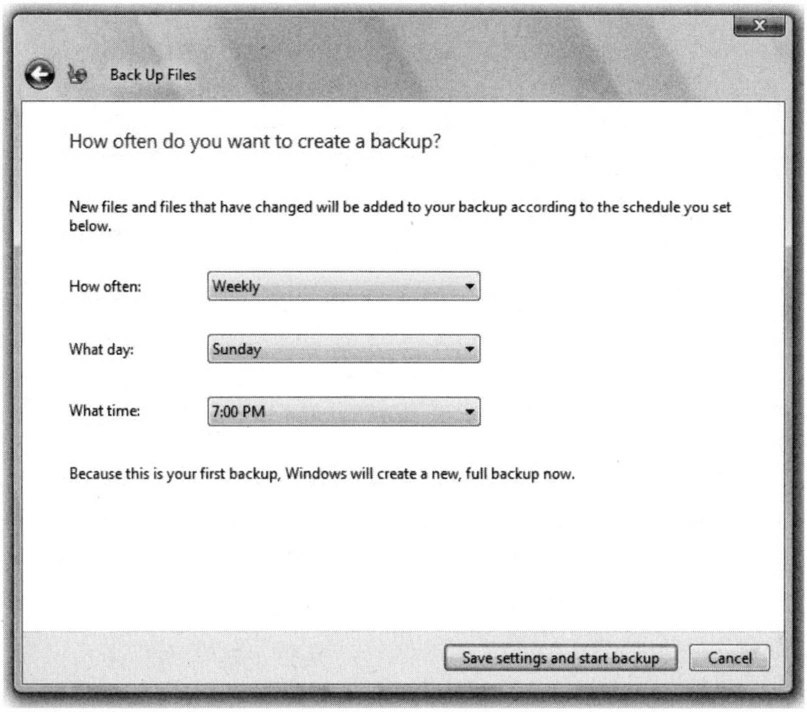

Back Up Files

How often do you want to create a backup?

New files and files that have changed will be added to your backup according to the schedule you set below.

How often: Weekly

What day: Sunday

What time: 7:00 PM

Because this is your first backup, Windows will create a new, full backup now.

Save settings and start backup   Cancel

Figure 23-6: The wizard enables you to access the Backup Status and Configuration automatic backup functionality as well.

Secret

What the wizard doesn't tell you is that by configuring this schedule here, you are actually configuring another Windows Vista tool, Backup Status and Configuration, to make regular partial backups that include files that have changed since the first full backup. You can in fact run Backup Status and Configuration separately, as shown in Figure 23-7, if you want. This is the tool that handles scheduling all forms of automatic backups. (The Vista Home Basic and Premium version of Backup Status and Configuration is slightly different, as shown in Figure 23-8.)

continues

continued

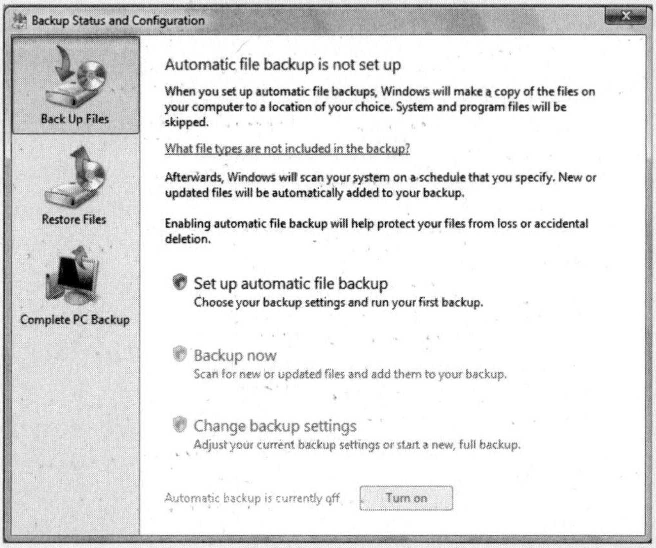

Figure 23-7: Backup Status and Configuration enables users with Windows Vista Business, Enterprise, and Ultimate to schedule regular, automatic backups.

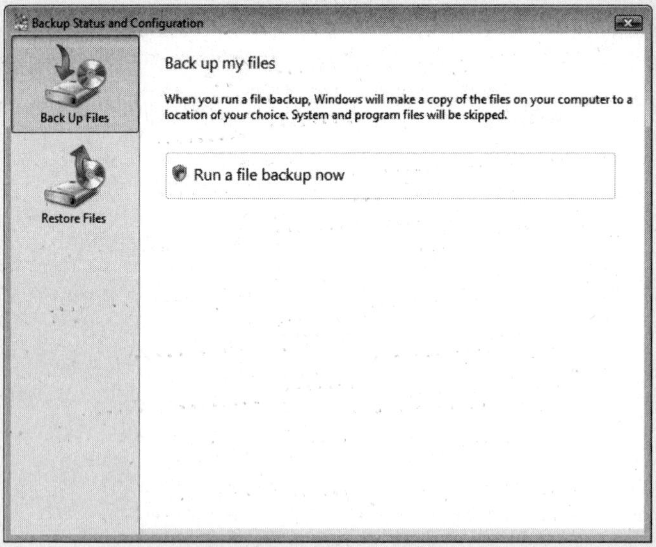

Figure 23-8: In Windows Vista Home Basic or Home Premium, the Backup Status and Configuration utility lacks features related to Complete PC Backup.

tip

> **tip**
>
> If you set up an automatic backup schedule now, Windows Vista will monitor your PC usage and prompt you to perform occasional full backups over time as well.

Now you're prompted to start the backup, which typically runs in the background, though the first manual backup will display a Back Up Files progress window, shown in Figure 23-9. As the backup runs, a small Windows Backup icon sits in the system tray, so you can view the status of the backup's progress if desired.

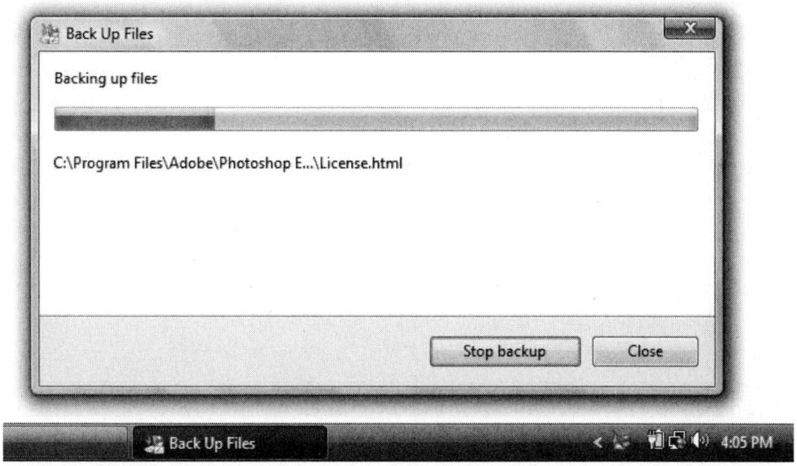

Back Up Files

Backing up files

C:\Program Files\Adobe\Photoshop E...\License.html

Stop backup   Close

Back Up Files   4:05 PM

Figure 23-9: You can always check the backup's status by clicking the File Backup Is Running tray icon.

Secret

The Backup utility in Windows Vista uses standard ZIP files to store its backups, so if you need to recover the files from a non–Windows Vista–based PC, you won't have any problems. Backups are saved to a folder on the backup device, named in the form of *Backup Set–date–unique identifier;* and if you drill into those folders, you'll find a Backup Files folder full of ZIP files. These files contain all of your data backups. Note that each time you dive deeper into this folder structure, you will have to deal with User Account Control (UAC) prompts: Microsoft wants to ensure that you're not mucking around in there and deleting things by mistake.

> **tip**
>
> You can create multiple automatic data backup schedules this way if you want. For example, you may want to back up different drives or data file types at different times or with different regularity.

Managing Backups

Once you have created your first data backup, a few things change. First, the Backup and Restore Center indicates that you've completed a backup, as shown in Figure 23-10. This is the one-stop locale for almost all your backup needs, after all.

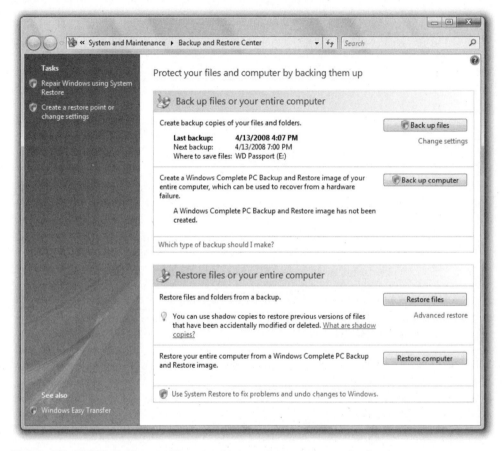

Figure 23-10: The Backup and Restore Center reflects the recent backup.

Second, the Backup Status and Configuration tool mentioned earlier has also changed. Now, instead of the big grayed-out options shown earlier in Figure 23-7, this utility has also been updated now that automatic backups have been configured, as shown in Figure 23-11.

Backup Status and Configuration is used to manage the automatic backup of your data, to restore data that has already been backed up, and to provide access to Vista's Complete PC Backup functionality. You can find the Backup Status and Configuration shortcut in the Start Menu by selecting All Programs ⇨ Accessories ⇨ System Tools—or with Start Menu Search by typing **backup**.

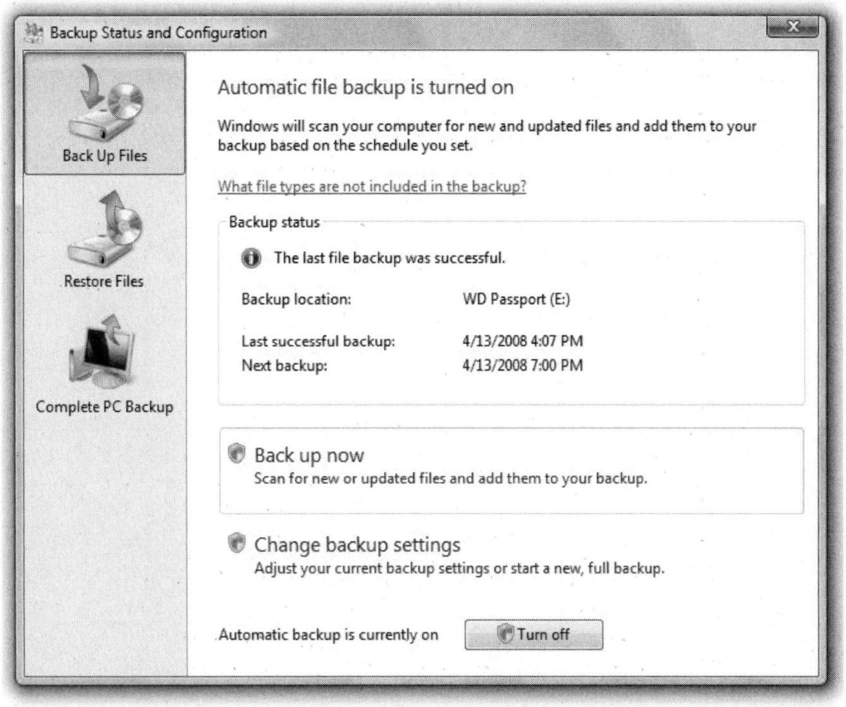

Figure 23-11: Now that Backup Status and Configuration has been given something to do, it springs to life.

If you click Change Backup Settings, you'll return to the Backup Files wizard, where you can change any of the settings you previously configured. The Back Up Now link enables you to manually trigger a backup, using your previously configured settings. You may occasionally need to do this if you make a lot of changes to data files well in advance of your next backup. You can turn off automatic backups by clicking the Turn Off button at the bottom of the window.

Restoring Files

You can restore files you have previously backed up using either Backup Status and Configuration (click the Restore Files button) or with the Backup and Restore Center. Both offer access to the following two types of data restore operations:

 ◆ **Wizard-Based Restore:** Restore files and folders you backed up previously using a simple wizard.

 ◆ **Advanced Restore:** With this type of restore, you can perform more advanced restoration tasks, such as restoring files from a different PC.

Follow these steps to trigger a data restore:

 1. Open the Backup and Restore Center and click the Restore Files button.

 2. The Restore Files wizard, shown in Figure 23-12, appears, enabling you to choose between files from the latest (most recent) backup or files from an earlier backup.

If you choose the second option, you can select the backup you want from a list of the backups that have been performed.

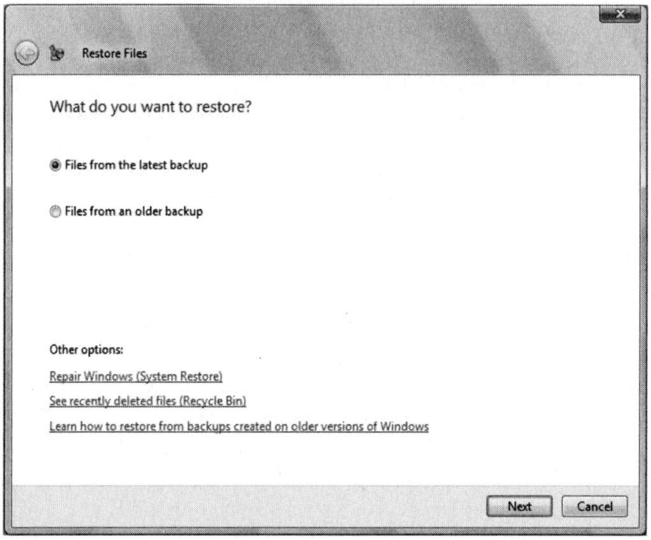

Figure 23-12: Wizard-based data restoration is the simplest option.

3. In the next phase of the Restore Files wizard, shown in Figure 23-13, you select which files to restore. This is more complicated than it seems. You must click the Add Files or Add Folders button to navigate to backed up locations in the file system and then choose those files and/or folders you wish to restore. Note that you can do this multiple times and create a list of files and/or folders to restore. You can also click the Search button to search for files and folders to restore.

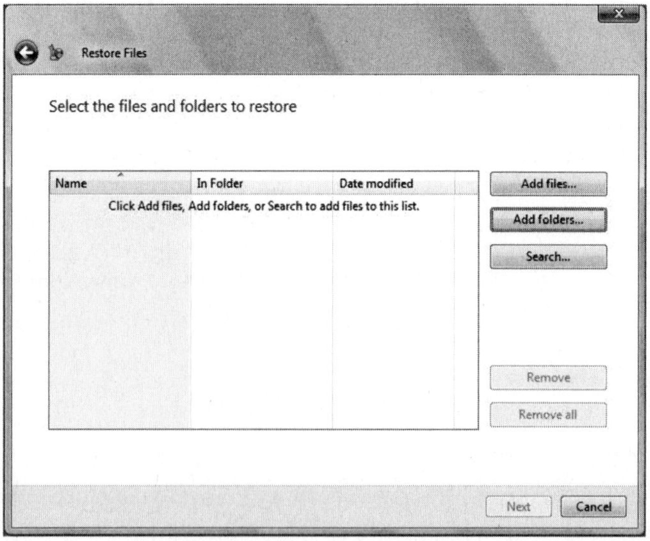

Figure 23-13: Here, you have to find the file(s) you wish to restore.

4. After you select all the files and folders you wish to restore, click the Next button. In this phase of the wizard, shown in Figure 23-14, you indicate where you want to save the restored files. You can restore in the original location, which is the default, or select a different location. If you select a different location, you also have the opportunity to create a unique directory structure that emulates the directory structure of the original backup.

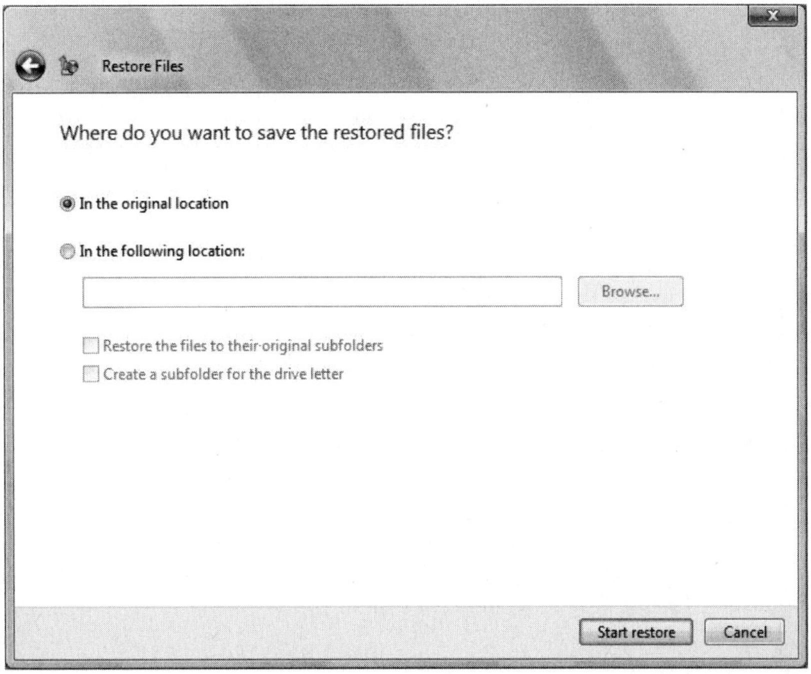

Figure 23-14: The Restore Files wizard is pretty generous about where restored files can be copied.

5. Click the Start Restore button to begin restoring files.

If file restoration will cause files to be overwritten, as it will if you choose to restore the files to their original location, you will see a standard Windows Copy File dialog (see Figure 23-15). This dialog enables you to overwrite the existing file, keep the existing file, or keep the existing file and rename the restored version.

That's all there is to it: After the copy phase, the wizard completes. Click Finish to close the wizard.

Copy File

There is already a file with the same name in this location.
Click the file you want to keep

➜ Copy and Replace
Replace the file in the destination folder with the file you are copying:

080311.docx
Backup Device (WD Passport (E:))
Size: 30.8 KB
Date modified: 3/10/2008 11:20 AM

➜ Don't copy
No files will be changed. Leave this file in the destination folder:

080311.docx
080311 (C:\Users\Paul Thurrott\Documents)
Size: 30.8 KB
Date modified: 3/11/2008 12:33 AM

➜ Copy, but keep both files
The file you are copying will be renamed "080311 (2).docx"

☐ Do this for all conflicts   Cancel   Cancel

Figure 23-15: This dialog ensures that you understand you will be overwriting an existing file if you're not careful.

Backing Up the Entire PC

Backing up and restoring data files is important and should occur on a regular basis; but over the past few years, a new type of backup utility that backs up entire PC systems using *system images* has become quite popular. These types of backups protect against a hardware disaster: If your hard drive completely fails, for example, you can purchase a new drive and use the system image to restore the PC to its previous state.

System imaging utilities aren't actually all that new; corporations have been using them for years. But now that consumer-oriented system-imaging utilities have gained in popularity, Microsoft has created its own version and bundled with Windows Vista.

Secret

You can only back up your entire PC if you are running the correct version of Windows Vista. Vista's system image creation utility is called Windows Complete PC Backup, and it's available only in the following editions: Windows Vista Business, Enterprise, and Ultimate. Vista Home Basic and Home Premium users do not have Complete PC Backup. If you're running Windows Vista Home Basic, you have two options: One, you can upgrade to Windows Vista Ultimate via Windows Anytime Upgrade (at a cost of $199 or $159 U.S., depending on which version you already own). This process is discussed in Chapter 2. Alternately, you can purchase a third-party system image utility such as Symantec Norton Ghost for considerably less (www.symantec.com/norton/).

Secret

System imaging utilities typically compress the data on your hard drives so that the image file takes up a lot less space than the original installation. Various solutions use different compression schemes, but you may be interested to know that Windows Vista uses the tried-and-true Virtual Hard Disk (VHD) format that Microsoft also uses in its Virtual PC and Virtual Server products. That means system images created with Windows Vista will be supported for a long time to come.

caution

System images contain complete PC environments. You can't arbitrarily restore only parts of a system image, as you can with data backups. Instead, when you restore a system image, it restores the entire PC and overwrites any existing operating system you may already have on there. That means you should be careful before restoring a system image: Any data you have on the disk will be overwritten. Of course, you're using automatic backups, too, right?

To create a system image, launch the Backup and Restore Center and click the Back Up Computer button. This launches the Windows Complete PC Backup wizard, shown in Figure 23-16, which walks you through the steps needed to completely back up your PC system. You can save system images to hard disks or optical storage (such as recordable CDs or DVDs).

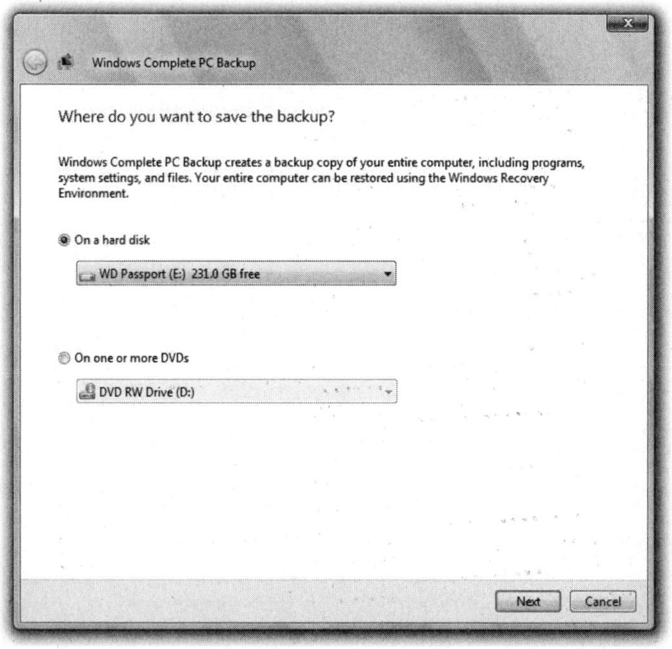

Figure 23-16: Complete PC Backup is one of the best features in Windows Vista, but it requires Vista Business, Enterprise, or Ultimate.

Secret

You can only write a system image to a hard disk that is formatted with the NTFS file system. That's because system images often exceed the 4GB file size limit imposed by the older and less reliable FAT32 file system.

Secret

Unlike the Backup Files wizard, Complete PC Backup cannot write a system image to a network share. Only locally attached storage will work.

If you have more than one hard disk (or hard disk partition), you'll see the dialog shown in Figure 23-17 next. From here, you can choose which disks (really, which partitions) you want included in the backup.

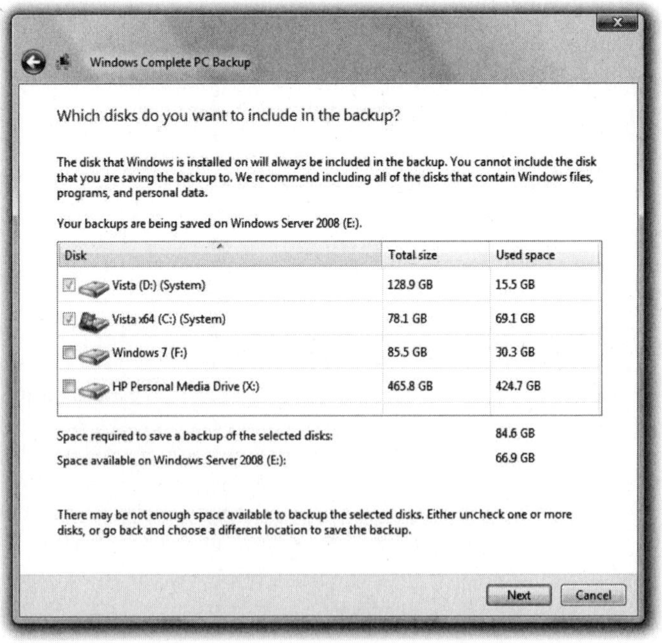

Which disks do you want to include in the backup?

The disk that Windows is installed on will always be included in the backup. You cannot include the disk that you are saving the backup to. We recommend including all of the disks that contain Windows files, programs, and personal data.

Your backups are being saved on Windows Server 2008 (E:).

Disk	Total size	Used space
☑ Vista (D:) (System)	128.9 GB	15.5 GB
☑ Vista x64 (C:) (System)	78.1 GB	69.1 GB
☐ Windows 7 (F:)	85.5 GB	30.3 GB
☐ HP Personal Media Drive (X:)	465.8 GB	424.7 GB

Space required to save a backup of the selected disks: 84.6 GB
Space available on Windows Server 2008 (E:): 66.9 GB

There may be not enough space available to backup the selected disks. Either uncheck one or more disks, or go back and choose a different location to save the backup.

Next   Cancel

Figure 23-17: Multipartition households will have to do some planning.

Secret

Two file system locations must be included in the system image—what Microsoft refers to as the *boot partition* and the *system partition*. The boot partition is always C:\, whereas the system partition is the drive with the Windows Vista Windows directory. This is typically C:, but if you installed Vista in a dual-boot setup with a previous Windows version, the system partition might be in a different location. If you have other drives or partitions, you can optionally choose to include them in the system image as well.

Windows Complete PC Backup will provide an estimate of the amount of space needed to create a system image, as shown in Figure 23-18. The required storage space varies according to the size and usage of the hard disk on your PC.

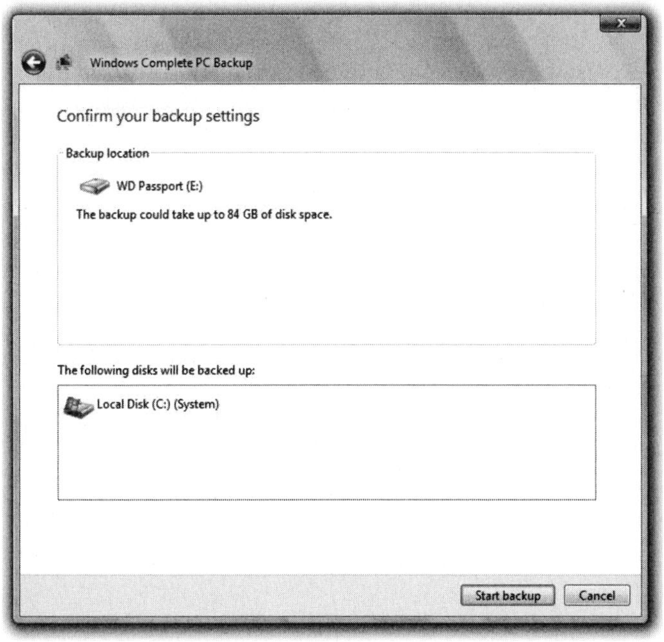

Figure 23-18: Though complete PC backups are huge, they are compressed and therefore much smaller than the actual disk to which you are backing.

Click Start Backup to back up the PC. Creating a system image is typically a lengthy process, so you should ensure that your system is exactly the way you want it before you start imaging the PC.

Restoring the Entire PC

Although a Restore Computer option appears in the Backup and Restore Center, you can't actually trigger an entire PC restoration from within Windows. Instead, you need to reboot your system and utilize the Windows Recovery Environment, which should be installed on your system, or the Windows Vista installation DVD. This is because the recovery process literally overwrites all of the data on your hard drives. Obviously, you want to be sure you have backed up any crucial data before attempting this process.

Follow these steps to restore your entire PC using a system image:

1. Reboot the computer.
2. After your PC has finished its BIOS sequence, hold down the F8 key. If you don't see an option for the Windows Recovery Environment, just boot up your computer with the Windows Vista DVD instead.
3. After Windows Vista setup begins, you'll be brought to the Install Now dialog. Instead of installing Vista, however, choose the System Recovery Options link.
4. You'll be guided through a series of steps. Choose your keyboard layout (U.S. for U.S. residents) when requested to do so.
5. Setup searches for Windows installations to repair. When you are asked what type of repair task you'd like to accomplish, select Windows Complete PC Restore.
6. The Windows Disaster Recovery Wizard launches. If you haven't already attached a hard drive or DVD containing the system image, do so now. The wizard will step you through the process of recovering the system image, rebooting, and loading your newly recovered system. As with creating a system image, this can be a very lengthy process, so budget an hour or more to complete this recovery.

Recovering Old Versions of Data Files

One of the most useful new features for information workers in Windows Server 2003 was *Volume Shadow Copy*, which silently and automatically created tiny backups, called *snapshots*, of data files stored on the server every time a user made any changes. In a managed environment like those based on Windows Server, Volume Shadow Copy is a wonderful feature, because users who save documents on the server can easily recover older document versions without having to summon an administrator to restore an old backup from a tape or a hard drive.

With Windows Vista, Microsoft has added Volume Shadow Copy to its client operating system as well and renamed it slightly, to Shadow Copies. This means that any Windows user can take advantage of this amazing bit of functionality and recover seemingly lost versions of files they have mistakenly edited. No server operating system is required.

The trade-off, of course, is disk space. Because Windows must store multiple copies of your data files, Shadow Copies does eat up a bit of disk space; but because Shadow Copies saves only the parts of files that have changed, or what Microsoft calls the *delta changes*, the disk space loss is not as bad as it would be otherwise. In fact, you probably won't even notice it's happening.

Unlike with Windows Server, you can't really manage how much disk space Volume Shadow Copy uses, or even the drives on which it is enabled. Instead, Microsoft enables the service across all drives, folders, and data files on a Windows Vista PC.

Secret   Shadow Copies is yet another Windows Vista reliability feature that requires certain Vista product editions. Shadow Copies is available on Windows Vista Business, Enterprise, and Ultimate editions only; users with Vista Home Basic and Home Premium need not apply.

To access this feature, find a document that you have changed a lot recently, right-click it, and choose Properties. Then, navigate to the Previous Versions tab. As shown in Figure 23-19, Windows maintains a number of previous versions, each of which you can restore if needed.

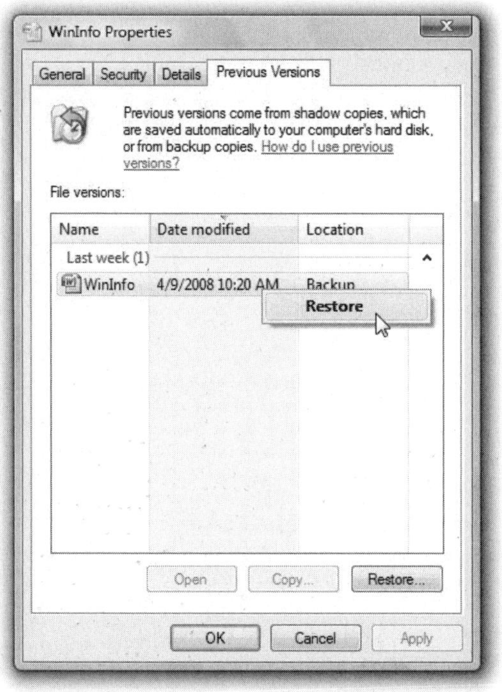

WinInfo Properties

General | Security | Details | Previous Versions

Previous versions come from shadow copies, which are saved automatically to your computer's hard disk, or from backup copies. How do I use previous versions?

File versions:

Name	Date modified	Location
Last week (1)		
WinInfo	4/9/2008 10:20 AM	Backup
	Restore	

Open | Copy... | Restore...

OK | Cancel | Apply

Figure 23-19: Shadow Copies makes it possible to resurrect old versions of data files.

To restore an older version of a file, select the file version you want and click the Restore button. As with any other file copy operation, you are prompted to either replace the existing file, keep the existing file, or keep the existing file and rename the newly recovered version.

Secret   The number of previous versions shown in this dialog depends on a number of factors, including how long your system has been up and running and how many times the document has been edited. In some cases, you may see no previous versions. If so, make sure that the System Restore service is running. I show you how in the very next section.

Using System Restore to Repair Windows

One of the best features in Windows Millennium Edition (Me) and Windows XP was System Restore, which has proven itself to be a life saver in my own experience. This feature carries forward in slightly improved form in Windows Vista. System Restore automatically backs up key system files at opportune times, such as when you're installing a new hardware driver. (Otherwise, an automatic restore occurs once every 24 hours.) That way, if a driver or application wreaks havoc with your PC, you can use System Restore to reload older system file versions and get back up and running again.

Secret   System Restore is the underlying technology that makes Shadow Copies, discussed in the previous section, possible. Shadow Copies work only on hard disks (or partitions) that are protected with System Restore.

System Restore has the following two main interface points:

♦ **System Protection:** This is located in the System Properties dialog and is annoyingly much harder to find in Windows Vista than it was in previous Windows versions. The quickest way to access it is to open the Start Menu and type **System** in Start Menu Search, locate the System link, and press Enter. Then, click the System Protection tab in the System Properties window.

As shown in Figure 23-20, this interface enables you to configure which disks or partitions you will automatically protect (typically only the system volume, which is usually drive C:). You can also manually create a system restore point by clicking the Create button. You need to supply a name for the restore point.

♦ **System Restore wizard:** This wizard restores your PC's key system files to a previous point in time. To launch this wizard, open the Start Menu and navigate to All Programs ➪ Accessories ➪ System Tools ➪ System Restore. (Or just type **system restore** in Start Menu Search.)

In the introductory page of the wizard, shown in Figure 23-21, you can choose the recommended restore point (typically the most recent one) or choose a different restore point.

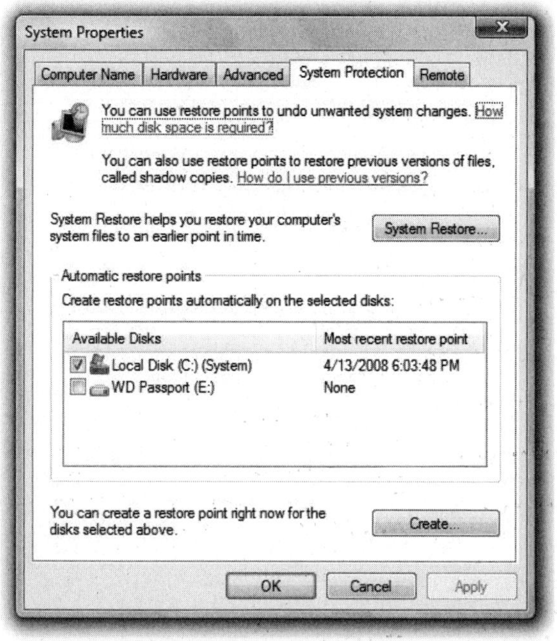

Figure 23-20: From System Protection, you can configure System Restore.

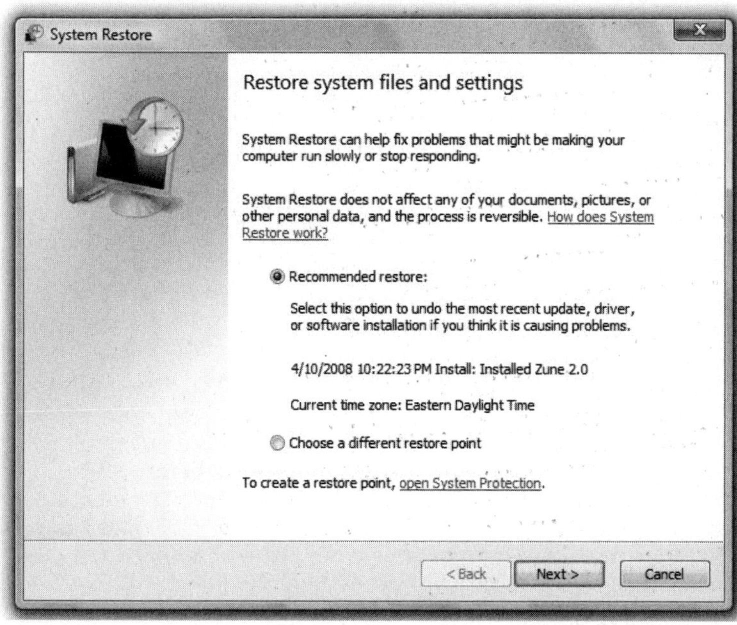

Figure 23-21: Automatic or manual? With System Restore, the choice is yours.

As shown in Figure 23-22, when you select the latter option, you get a list of restore points. Most of these will have been automatically created by the system and will include a description of what was going on when each restore point was created. If you manually created your own restore points from System Protection, those restore points will have "Manual:" appended to the front of the restore point name.

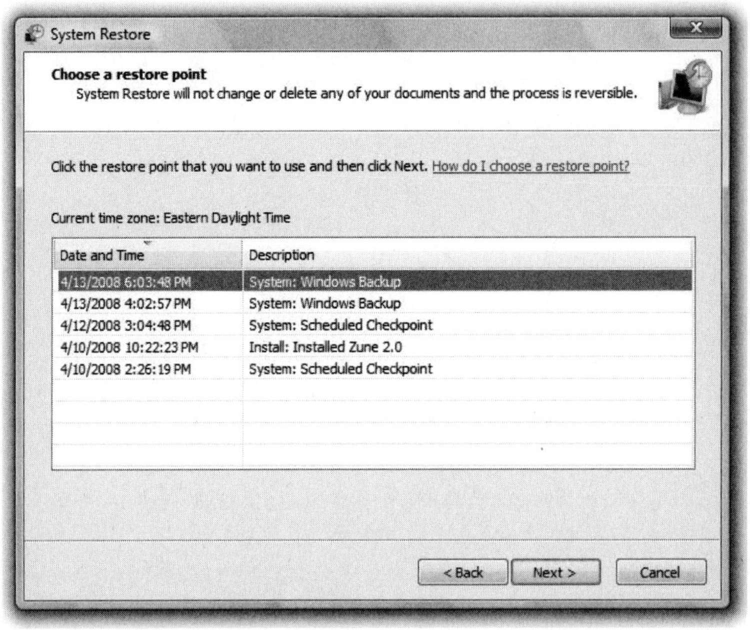

Figure 23-22: Here, you can choose the restore point you'd like to use.

When you select a restore point, Windows will move into the secure desktop and begin restoring your system to its previous state. This requires the PC to reboot. Note that any applications you have installed since that restore point will almost certainly need to be reinstalled.

Summary

Windows Vista includes a surprisingly rich set of features for backing up and restoring documents and other data files, as well as the entire PC. This is one instance where Vista really distances itself from Windows XP. With Windows Vista, you get handy file backup and restore wizards, a system-imaging utility that enables you to recover completely from almost any PC calamity, and a nice front end from which to manage all of this functionality. It will be interesting to see how the third-party utility market responds to these changes, though Microsoft has certainly left one big opening by not supporting some of these technologies in the Home Basic and Home Premium editions of Vista.

Automating Windows Vista with Windows PowerShell

Chapter
24

◆ ◆

In This Chapter

Understanding the new Windows command line and scripting environment

Downloading, installing, and running Windows PowerShell for the first time

*Working with the new **.ps1** scripts*

Constructing Windows PowerShell commands

Finding all available Windows PowerShell commands

Drilling down to the specific parameters supported by each command

Exploring why Microsoft developed a new language for Windows

Providing a PowerShell Quick Reference

Finding out more about PowerShell

◆ ◆

Microsoft Windows PowerShell is a new command-line and scripting environment with capabilities far beyond the older command interpreters that were included with previous versions of Windows (and, still are, in Windows Vista). Based on Microsoft's .NET technologies, Windows PowerShell was created because Microsoft wanted to better support the ever-evolving needs of system administrators. For this audience, Windows PowerShell provides an unprecedented level of control, along with a consistent and logical interactive shell that is self-documenting and discoverable. Put more simply, Windows PowerShell makes it easier than ever to automate repetitive tasks; and for power users of all kinds, this new environment points the way to the future.

Today, Microsoft uses PowerShell as the underpinnings of its Exchange Server messaging product, for example, providing a UNIX-like command-line environment on which all of the familiar GUI management tools are actually based. In addition, PowerShell is an integrated part of Windows Server and will be included in future desktop versions of Windows after Vista.

Getting PowerShell

Windows PowerShell isn't installed by default on Windows Vista, so you need to take the following steps to obtain and run this new command-line and scripting environment:

1. Visit **www.microsoft.com/powershell**, Microsoft's Web site for Windows PowerShell.
2. Find the Download link for the latest version of Windows PowerShell. At the time of this writing, PowerShell 1.0 is the current version, but Microsoft will likely release Windows PowerShell 2.0 by the time you read this.
3. Download and run the installer. Note that there are different installers for the 32-bit (x86) and 64-bit (x64) versions of Windows Vista.
4. Click Start and type **powershell** in Start Menu Search to open this new environment.

You can also start Windows PowerShell from the Windows command line: Run the command prompt (**cmd.exe**), type **powershell,** and press Enter to start PowerShell.

To exit Windows PowerShell, type **exit** from within this environment and then press Enter. This closes the PowerShell character mode window, or, if you started **cmd.exe** before starting PowerShell, returns you to **cmd.exe**. You can exit **cmd.exe** in the same way.

The Windows PowerShell is shown in Figure 24-1.

When either PowerShell or **cmd.exe** is running, you can also simply click the X button in the upper-right corner of the window to close the shell. There's no need to type **exit.** You can, however, put the **exit** command to good use within a script to close any window your script may have opened.

Figure 24-1: Not too imposing, is it? Windows PowerShell is the future of Windows command-line environments.

Understanding PowerShell

Released around the same time as Windows Vista, Windows PowerShell is an extensive scripting environment that is far richer than the batch language included with the command-line environment in previous versions of Windows. (For backward compatibility, Windows Vista still includes this older command-line environment.) PowerShell can also be downloaded and run on Windows XP and Windows 2000. This means PowerShell scripts you write can also run on most other Windows PCs in operation today.

As noted previously, PowerShell represents so much capability that Microsoft's Exchange 2007 e-mail application is written in it. You probably won't need to write anything that complex; but regardless of the size of your project, Microsoft has built PowerShell so it has few limitations. It's worlds away from Windows' old batch language, which is run by the **cmd.exe** command interpreter, and is even more powerful—and certainly more consistent—than any UNIX command-line environment.

As just one of the features PowerShell brings to Windows that Microsoft's older command-line environments did not, you can use PowerShell commands to read from and write to hives in the Windows Registry as though they were ordinary drives. For example, you access **HKEY_LOCAL_MACHINE** through a drive named **HKLM**, and **HKEY_CUURENT_USER** via **HKCU**.

PowerShell scripts normally bear a file extension of **.ps1,** for PowerShell version 1. This contrasts with Windows' built-in c**md.exe,** which runs batch files ending in **.bat**. Presumably, if a future PowerShell version 2 is released, scripts that require the more advanced language will bear the extension **.ps2,** and so on.

Microsoft wisely avoided making **.ps1** files execute automatically if you happen to open one. Under a new Microsoft policy announced before Vista was released, a potentially harmful feature is not turned on by default unless at least 90 percent of Windows users would regularly use it.

For example, almost everyone sends files to a printer, which isn't particularly dangerous, so printing capabilities are automatically enabled in Vista.

Running scripts, however, can silently install worms or Trojan horses if you inadvertently open one. Hacker Web sites and untrustworthy e-mails will undoubtedly try to use PS scripts to slip rogue programs onto users' PCs.

To give you an idea of the problem, the **.ps1** extension sounds like it might have something to do with PostScript. You can imagine virus writers sending out mass e-mails after Vista becomes widely installed, saying things like "See the naughty pictures in the attached PostScript file." Noticing the unfamiliar **.ps1** extension, many users might assume the attachment were a harmless image file. In reality, although a racy picture might be displayed, a powerful script could also be silently launched, infecting a user's PC.

Keeping PowerShell disabled, except for those users who need such scripts and turn them on, is Microsoft's way of minimizing the risk. If you know what you're doing, enabling PowerShell isn't particularly dangerous. If you don't need PowerShell, however, you don't need it. Viruses can't run rampant via PowerShell scripts if most Windows users have PowerShell turned off.

Secret

Running PowerShell Scripts Safely

By default, Microsoft disables the operating system's ability to run PowerShell scripts merely by clicking or opening them; but if you use PowerShell scripts, you should take the following three steps to protect yourself against hacked Web sites or e-mails that might find ways to run them without your knowledge:

1. Obtain a digital certificate and digitally sign any scripts you develop in house. Require that scripts you obtain from other parties be signed by them.

2. Configure PowerShell so it will run only those scripts that are signed by parties you know and trust.

3. Secure your list of trusted certificates. It doesn't do any good to restrict scripts to a list of trusted parties if a virus or Trojan horse is able to quietly add other signatures to your list.

If you don't know how to take the preceding steps, get a professional to set up your system in this way—or don't configure your system to run any scripts that happen to be opened.

Constructing a PowerShell Command

It's impossible to adequately document the Windows PowerShell language in a single chapter—entire books deal with this subject, and I recommend that you study one if you want to become proficient. See the recommendations at the end of the chapter for some suggestions. Instead, this section provides an introduction and a quick reference that will get you started.

The Windows PowerShell language draws from several older programming languages. Its grammar is based on POSIX, a character-based command language that's also called a *shell* (because it sits over the operating system *kernel*). POSIX is a subset of the Korn Shell, which is widely used in UNIX environments.

Windows PowerShell, however, is not a copy of POSIX. Instead, it adopts many of the features of the object-oriented Microsoft .NET programming model. In a nutshell, .NET objects have properties and methods, both of which are defined in well-understood ways. For example, a file object has properties such as size (in bytes), a date and time when the file was last modified, a read-only flag (which may be on or off), and so forth.

In creating the commands that would be available in Windows PowerShell, Microsoft's developers used a *verb-noun* naming convention. Some common Windows PowerShell commands are as follows:

```
Get-ChildItem
Get-Content
Remove-Item
```

In each case, the first word is a verb, followed by a hyphen and then a noun on which the verb operates. (Speaking of case, all Windows PowerShell commands are case insensitive. That is, **GET-childITEM** does the same thing as **get-childitem**. I'm documenting commands here with initial capital letters for the same reason Microsoft does—to improve readability—but you're free to write them in whatever mixed case you wish.)

These commands seem awfully long—and you haven't seen anything yet. Fortunately, shorter versions of Windows PowerShell commands, called *aliases,* are also built in to the system for most commands. Additionally, you can define your own aliases. The three Windows PowerShell commands previously shown are equivalent to the following **cmd.exe** commands that you probably know:

```
dir
type
del
```

That's right—Microsoft has defined long, hard-to-remember commands to replace **dir** (which shows a directory listing of filenames), **type** (which displays a file's contents), and **del** (which erases a file).

Microsoft explains the length of its new PS commands by saying it helps developers remember and understand them. It also makes it possible to get a synopsis of a group of commands by using the command **get-help**, though to be fair, many people will use the command's short, memorable alias instead: **help**.

For example, you can see a listing of all the Windows PowerShell commands that retrieve, or *get*, some kind of information using the following syntax:

```
help get-*
```

When you enter this at the PowerShell command line and press Enter, the following output is provided:

```
PS C:\Users\Paul> help get-*
Name                            Category       Synopsis
Get-Command                     Cmdlet         Gets basic information about...
Get-Help                        Cmdlet         Displays information about Windows P...
Get-History                     Cmdlet         Gets a list of the commands entered ...
Get-PSSnapin                    Cmdlet         Gets the Windows PowerShell snap-ins...
Get-EventLog                    Cmdlet         Gets information about local event l...
Get-ChildItem                   Cmdlet         Gets the items and child items in on...
Get-Content                     Cmdlet         Gets the content of the item at the ...
Get-ItemProperty                Cmdlet         Retrieves the properties of a specif...
Get-WmiObject                   Cmdlet         Gets instances of WMI classes or inf...
Get-Location                    Cmdlet         Gets information about the current w...
Get-PSDrive                     Cmdlet         Gets information about Windows Power...
Get-Item                        Cmdlet         Gets the item at the specified locat...
Get-PSProvider                  Cmdlet         Gets information about the specified...
Get-Process                     Cmdlet         Gets the processes that are running ...
Get-Service                     Cmdlet         Gets the services on the local compu...
Get-Acl                         Cmdlet         Gets the security descriptor for a r...
Get-PfxCertificate              Cmdlet         Gets information about .pfx certific...
Get-Credential                  Cmdlet         Gets a credential object based on a ...
Get-ExecutionPolicy             Cmdlet         Gets the current execution policy fo...
Get-AuthenticodeSignature       Cmdlet         Gets information about the Authentic...
Get-Alias                       Cmdlet         Gets the aliases for the current ses...
Get-Culture                     Cmdlet         Gets information about the regional ...
Get-Date                        Cmdlet         Gets the current date and time.
Get-Host                        Cmdlet         Gets a reference to the current cons...
Get-Member                      Cmdlet         Gets information about objects or co...
Get-UICulture                   Cmdlet         gets information about the current u...
Get-Unique                      Cmdlet         Returns the unique items from a sort...
Get-Variable                    Cmdlet         Gets the variables in the current co...
Get-TraceSource                 Cmdlet         Gets the Windows PowerShell componen...
```

You can also see those commands that operate on objects:

```
PS C:\Users\Paul> help *-object

Name             Category     Synopsis
ForEach-Object   Cmdlet       Performs an operation against each o...
Where-Object     Cmdlet       Creates a filter that controls which...
Compare-Object   Cmdlet       Compares two sets of objects.
Measure-Object   Cmdlet       Measures characteristics of objects ...
Tee-Object       Cmdlet       Pipes object input to a file or vari...
New-Object       Cmdlet       Creates an instance of a .Net or COM...
Select-Object    Cmdlet       Selects specified properties of an o...
Group-Object     Cmdlet       Groups objects that contain the same...
Sort-Object      Cmdlet       Sorts objects by property values.
```

Seeing All the Commands

PowerShell provides a command, known as **Get-Command**, that displays all the built-in commands available. Unlike the old **cmd.exe**, which relies on external, on-disk files for most of its features, PowerShell has a wealth of internal commands. These are known as *cmdlets*, pronounced *commandlets*.

The alias for **Get-Command** is **gcm**. Both the cmdlet and its alias require the addition of a pipe (|) and the **more** command to keep the output from scrolling off the top of the screen. The following lines show how to use the **more** command:

```
PS C:\Users\Paul> gcm | more

CommandType     Name              Definition
Cmdlet          Add-Content       Add-Content [-Path] <String[]> [-Value] ...
Cmdlet          Add-History       Add-History [[-InputObject] <PSObject[]>]...
Cmdlet          Add-Member        Add-Member [-MemberType] <PSMemberTypes>...
...
Cmdlet          Get-PSProvider    Get-PSProvider [[-PSProvider] <String[]>]...
<SPACE> next page; <CR> next line; Q quit
```

> **note** If you often use batch commands or PowerShell scripts, you'll probably want to expand the character-based window in which the commands appear. The Layout tab of the Command Prompt Properties dialog enables you to do just that, similar to how you would make such changes to the cmd.exe Command Prompt window (see Figure 24-2).

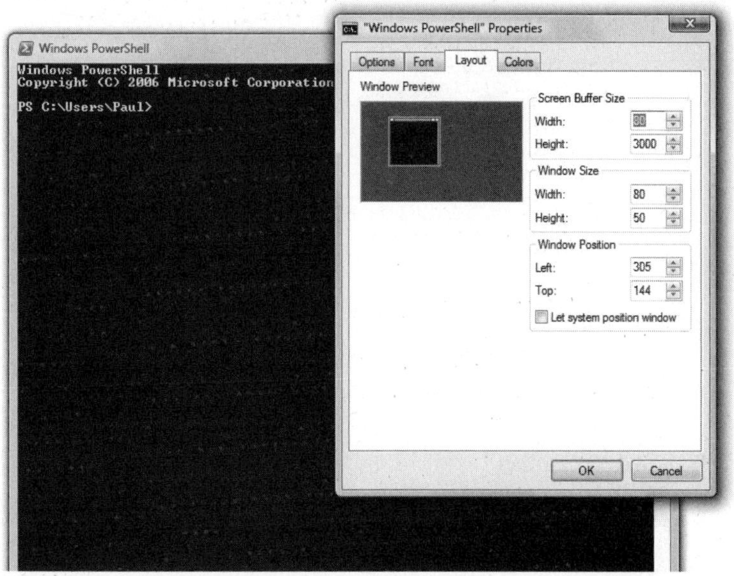

Figure 24-2: You can change the width and height of the Windows PowerShell command-line environment to meet your expanding needs.

Getting Help with Commands

To find the syntax and all the parameters of a command, type **help** and the name of the command or its alias. This command automatically pages the output, so no more than one screenful appears at a time:

```
PS C:\Users\Paul> help foreach


NAME
     ForEach-Object


SYNOPSIS
     Performs an operation against each of a set of input objects.


SYNTAX
     ForEach-Object [-process] <ScriptBlock[]> [-inputObject <psobject>] [-begin
<scriptblock>] [-end <scriptblock>] [<C
     ommonParameters>]


DETAILED DESCRIPTION
     Performs an operation against each of a set of input objects. The input objects can
be piped to the cmdlet or specified by using the InputObject parameter. The operation
to perform is described within a script block which is provided to the cmdlet as the
value of the Process parameter. The script block can contain any Windows PowerShell
script. Within the script block, the current input object is represented by the $_
variable. In addition to the script block that describes the operations to be carried
out on each input object, you can provide two additional script blocks. One, specified
as the value of the Begin parameter, runs before the first input object is processed.
The other, specified as the value of the End parameter, runs after the last input
object is processed. The results of the evaluation of all the script blocks, included
the ones specified with Begin and End, are passed down the pipeline.


RELATED LINKS
     Where-Object
     Compare-Object
     Group-Object
     Select-Object
     Sort-Object


REMARKS
     For more information, type: "get-help ForEach-Object -detailed". For technical
information, type: "get-help ForEach-Object -full".
```

Why a New Language?

Windows PowerShell has far more capabilities than the old Windows command prompt, **cmd.exe**. Take a look at a very simple example to see what you can do with Windows PowerShell.

The **dir** command, as you probably know, displays a directory listing of the files in the current directory or any specified directory. The output of **dir** looks the same in both **cmd .exe** and Windows PowerShell, but PowerShell enables you to do a lot more.

In **cmd.exe**, the **dir** command simply outputs the name, size, and other attributes of the files it lists. If you wanted to see whether a particular set of files would fit onto a single CD-R, for example, you might look at the output of a **dir** command:

```
dir
Mode        LastWriteTime        Length    Name
--------    -------------------  --------  --------
-a---       12/31/2007 10:00 AM  20123456  File1.doc
-a---       12/31/2007 10:30 AM  21234567  File2.doc
-a---       12/31/2007 11:00 AM  22345678  File3.doc
```

You could then add up the length of the files in your head or on a calculator; or you could try to write a batch file that would accept the output of **dir**, extract the byte sizes, and then somehow add them up and display a total.

With Windows PowerShell, determining the size of a directory in bytes can be accomplished with just three lines of code. First, you define a variable, **$bytesize**, and set its initial value to zero. Next, you pipe the output of the Windows PowerShell cmdlet alias **dir** into the **foreach** alias and add up the bytes. Finally, you display the total. The whole thing looks like this:

```
$bytesize = 0
dir | foreach {$bytesize += $_.length}
$bytesize
```

In response to the third line of code, Windows PowerShell displays the value of **$bytesize**:

```
63703701
```

Instead of using the third line of this script, which simply outputs the total onscreen, you could feed the number into another process, write the total into a file for later analysis, or any other number of alternatives. For example, if the selected files were too large for a single CD-R, a script you wrote could show you the message "Whoa, boy! You'll need two CDs for those files," or three, or four, or whatever number was calculated.

Notice that I've used the aliases **dir** and **foreach** to make the second line of the script concise. If I had used the non-alias name of each cmdlet, the script might look as follows:

```
$bytesize = 0
get-childitem | foreach-object {$bytesize += $_.length}
$bytesize
```

Because a percent sign (%) is also an alias for the **for-eachobject** cmdlet—as shown in the next section—you could also make the original script even shorter, at the expense of being less readable:

```
$bytesize = 0
dir | % {$bytesize += $_.length}
$bytesize
```

The percent sign in this case doesn't have anything to do with calculating a percentage. It's just an alias for the command **foreach-object**. This use of symbols may be confusing, but it does reduce the amount of typing developers have to do, which is always a good thing.

Windows PowerShell Quick Reference

Most programming reference guides provide long lists of commands presented alphabetically in a single block. Instead of doing that, this quick reference breaks the commands into groups sorted by verb. (Remember that all Windows PowerShell cmdlets have a long name in the form *verb-noun*.) Understanding PowerShell's verbs makes it easier to drill down and learn the details of any nouns you'll actually need to use.

Many, but by no means all, cmdlets also have shorter, built-in aliases. Where these exist, they're shown in the left column.

Secret

No alias? No problem, as it appears that the makers of Windows PowerShell have thought of nearly everything: When no alias exists for a cmdlet, you can easily make one up using **Set-Alias**.

Add

The **Add** command inserts contents or entries into an object, into the console, or into the session history (see Table 24-1).

Table 24-1: Add Cmdlets

Alias	Cmdlet
ac	Add-Content
	Add-History
	Add-Member
asnp	Add-PSSnapin

Clear

The **Clear** command removes contents or properties of an object without deleting the object (see Table 24-2).

Table 24-2: Clear Cmdlets

Alias	Cmdlet
clc	Clear-Content

continues

Table 24-2: (continued)

Alias	Cmdlet
clear	Clear-Host
cls	Clear-Host
cli	Clear-Item
clp	Clear-ItemProperty
clv	Clear-Variable

Compare

The **Compare** command finds differences in the properties of objects (see Table 24-3).

Table 24-3: Compare Cmdlet

Alias	Cmdlet
diff	Compare-Object

Convert

The **Convert** command changes the form of an input to a particular output format (see Table 24-4).

Table 24-4: Convert Cmdlets

Alias	Cmdlet
cvpa	Convert-Path
	ConvertFrom-SecureString
	ConvertTo-Html
	ConvertTo-SecureString

Copy

The **Copy** command makes a duplicate of an object or its properties in another location (see Table 24-5). (**Copy-Item** has three aliases that do the same thing, copying—so to speak—the syntax of older languages.)

Table 24-5: Copy Cmdlets

Alias	Cmdlet
copy	Copy-Item
cp	Copy-Item
cpi	Copy-Item
cpp	Copy-ItemProperty

Export

The **Export** command writes content to a file, the console, CLiXML (Constraint Language in XML), CSV (comma-separated values), and so on (see Table 24-6).

Table 24-6: Export Cmdlets

Alias	Cmdlet
epal	Export-Alias
	Export-Clixml
	Export-Console
epcsv	Export-Csv

ForEach

The **ForEach** command performs actions on a series of objects (see Table 24-7).

Table 24-7: ForEach Cmdlets

Alias	Cmdlet
%	ForEach-Object
foreach	ForEach-Object

Format

The **Format** command creates output with specific tabular or columnar arrangements (see Table 24-8).

Table 24-8: Format Cmdlets

Alias	Cmdlet
fc	Format-Custom
fl	Format-List
ft	Format-Table
fw	Format-Wide

Get

The **Get** command fetches various objects, properties, processes, and other information (see Table 24-9). Notice that **Get-ChildItem** is the same as **dir** and two other aliases.

Table 24-9: Get Cmdlets

Alias	Cmdlet
	Get-Acl
gal	Get-Alias
	Get-AuthenticodeSignature
dir	Get-ChildItem
gci	Get-ChildItem
ls	Get-ChildItem
gcm	Get-Command
cat	Get-Content
gc	Get-Content
type	Get-Content
	Get-Credential
	Get-Culture
	Get-Date
	Get-EventLog
	Get-ExecutionPolicy
help	Get-Help
ghy	Get-History
h	Get-History

continues

Table 24-9: *(continued)*

Alias	Cmdlet
history	Get-History
	Get-Host
gi	Get-Item
gp	Get-ItemProperty
gl	Get-Location
pwd	Get-Location
gm	Get-Member
	Get-PfxCertificate
gps	Get-Process
ps	Get-Process
gdr	Get-PSDrive
	Get-PSProvider
gsnp	Get-PSSnapin
gsv	Get-Service
	Get-TraceSource
	Get-UICulture
gu	Get-Unique
gv	Get-Variable
gwmi	Get-WmiObject

Import

The **Import** command extracts values from an alias list or an XML or CSV file (see Table 24-10).

Table 24-10: Import Cmdlets

Alias	Cmdlet
ipal	Import-Alias
	Import-Clixml
ipcsv	Import-Csv

Invoke

The **Invoke** command executes a string as an expression, executes a previously run command, or opens a file (see Table 24-11).

Table 24-11: Invoke Cmdlets

Alias	Cmdlet
iex	Invoke-Expression
ihy	Invoke-History
r	Invoke-History
ii	Invoke-Item

Join

The **Join** command merges path elements into a single path (see Table 24-12).

Table 24-12: Join Cmdlet

Alias	Cmdlet
	Join-Path

Measure

The **Measure** command calculates the execute time for code or computes the properties of objects (see Table 24-13).

Table 24-13: Measure Cmdlets

Alias	Cmdlet
	Measure-Command
	Measure-Object

Move

The **Move** command changes the location of objects or the properties of objects (see Table 24-14).

Table 24-14: Move Cmdlets

Alias	Cmdlet
mi	Move-Item
move	Move-Item
mv	Move-Item
mp	Move-ItemProperty

New

The **New** command sets a new property of an object or creates new objects, services, drives, and so on (see Table 24-15).

Table 24-15: New Cmdlets

Alias	Cmdlet
nal	New-Alias
ni	New-Item
	New-ItemProperty
	New-Object
mount	New-PSDrive
ndr	New-PSDrive
	New-Service
	New-TimeSpan
nv	New-Variable

Out

The **Out** command determines the destination of output, such as to a file, a printer, or a pipeline (see Table 24-16).

Table 24-16: Out Cmdlets

Alias	Cmdlet
	Out-Default

continues

Table 24–16: *(continued)*

Alias	Cmdlet
	Out-File
oh	Out-Host
	Out-Null
lp	Out-Printer
	Out-String

Pop

When you use the **Pop** command, the location determined by the latest stack entry becomes the current location (see Table 24-17).

Table 24-17: Pop Cmdlets

Alias	Cmdlet
popd	Pop-Location

Push

The **Push** command places a location on the stack (see Table 24-18).

Table 24-18: Push Cmdlet

Alias	Cmdlet
pushd	Push-Location

Read

The **Read** command gets a line of data from the host console (see Table 24-19).

Table 24-19: Read Cmdlet

Alias	Cmdlet
	Read-Host

Remove

The **Remove** command deletes an item, object, or property; removes a drive from its location, and so on (see Table 24-20). Notice that **Remove-Item** is the same as **del**, **erase**, and four other aliases.

Table 24-20: Remove Cmdlets

Alias	Cmdlet
del	Remove-Item
erase	Remove-Item
rd	Remove-Item
ri	Remove-Item
rm	Remove-Item
rmdir	Remove-Item
rp	Remove-ItemProperty
rdr	Remove-PSDrive
rsnp	Remove-PSSnapin
rv	Remove-Variable

Rename

The **Rename** command changes the name of an item or property (see Table 24-21).

Table 24-21: Rename Cmdlets

Alias	Cmdlet
ren	Rename-Item
rni	Rename-Item
rnp	Rename-ItemProperty

Resolve

The **Resolve** command determines the meaning of wildcards in a path (see Table 24-22).

Table 24-22: Resolve Cmdlet

Alias	Cmdlet
rvpa	Resolve-Path

Restart

The **Restart** command starts a service that was stopped (see Table 24-23).

Table 24-23: Restart Cmdlet

Alias	Cmdlet
	Restart-Service

Resume

The **Resume** command starts a service that was suspended (see Table 24-24).

Table 24-24: Resume Cmdlet

Alias	Cmdlet
	Resume-Service

Select

The **Select** command matches objects, files, or strings that have specified parameters or patterns (see Table 24-25).

Table 24-25: Select Cmdlets

Alias	Cmdlet
select	Select-Object
	Select-String

Set

The **Set** command establishes a value, property, and so on, for an object, service, or the host computer (see Table 24-26).

Table 24-26: Set Cmdlets

Alias	Cmdlet
	Set-Acl
sal	Set-Alias
	Set-AuthenticodeSignature

continues

Table 24-26: *(continued)*

Alias	Cmdlet
sc	Set-Content
	Set-Date
	Set-ExecutionPolicy
si	Set-Item
sp	Set-ItemProperty
cd	Set-Location
chdir	Set-Location
sl	Set-Location
	Set-PSDebug
	Set-Service
	Set-TraceSource
set	Set-Variable
sv	Set-Variable

Sort

The **Sort** command sorts objects into ascending or descending order (see Table 24-27).

Table 24-27: Sort Cmdlet

Alias	Cmdlet
sort	Sort-Object

Split

The **Split** command divides a PowerShell path into individual components, such as parent path or leaf item (see Table 24-28).

Table 24-28: Split Cmdlet

Alias	Cmdlet
	Split-Path

Start

The **Start** command runs a service that was stopped, begins a period in which activities are suspended, or starts a transcript of a session (see Table 24-29).

Table 24-29: Start Cmdlets

Alias	Cmdlet
sasv	Start-Service
sleep	Start-Sleep
	Start-Transcript

Stop

The **Stop** command halts processes or services, or ends a transcript that had been started in a session (see Table 24-30).

Table 24-30: Stop Cmdlets

Alias	Cmdlet
kill	Stop-Process
spps	Stop-Process
spsv	Stop-Service
	Stop-Transcript

Suspend

The **Suspend** command pauses a service that had been running (see Table 24-31).

Table 24-31: Suspend Cmdlet

Alias	Cmdlet
	Suspend-Service

Tee

The **Tee** command routes selected objects to two different places (see Table 24-32).

Table 24-32: Tee Cmdlet

Alias	Cmdlet
tee	Tee-Object

Test

If a specified path exists, the **Test** command returns **true**; otherwise, it returns **false** (see Table 24-33).

Table 24-33: Test Cmdlet

Alias	Cmdlet
	Test-Path

Trace

This turns on tracing for a command line, multiple command lines, a pipeline, and so on (see Table 24-34).

Table 24-34: Trace Cmdlet

Alias	Cmdlet
	Trace-Command

Update

The **Update** command changes information in format data files or PowerShell's **types .psxml** file (see Table 24-35).

Table 24-35: Update Cmdlets

Alias	Cmdlet
	Update-FormatData
	Update-TypeData

Where

The **Where** command allows operations to be conducted only on objects in a pipeline that meet certain criteria (see Table 24-36).

Table 24-36: Where Cmdlets

Alias	Cmdlet
?	Where-Object
where	Where-Object

Write

The **Write** command outputs a string, an object, or a message to the display, pipeline, and so on (see Table 24-37).

Table 24-37: Write Cmdlets

Alias	Cmdlet
	Write-Debug
	Write-Error
	Write-Host
echo	Write-Output
write	Write-Output
	Write-Progress
	Write-Verbose
	Write-Warning

Taking It to the Next Level

Because it is impossible to provide a thorough overview of something as sophisticated as Windows PowerShell in just a single chapter, this section highlights some PowerShell resources that I've found to be very useful.

Useful Windows PowerShell Web Sites

♦ **Windows PowerShell Web Site:** Microsoft's Windows PowerShell Web site is the obvious starting point for any investigation of this innovative new scripting environment.

   www.microsoft.com/powershell

♦ **Sample Windows PowerShell Script Repository:** This valuable collection of administrative scripts demonstrates how powerful Windows PowerScript can be in the real world.

   www.microsoft.com/technet/scriptcenter/scripts/msh/default.mspx?mfr=true

♦ **PowerShell Script Center:** An excellent collection of Windows PowerScript resources, including betas of the next version, free books and courseware, and much documentation.

   www.microsoft.com/technet/scriptcenter/hubs/msh.mspx

♦ **Windows PowerShell Blog:** The developers behind Windows PowerShell discuss the inner workings of this environment in a regularly updated blog.

   http://blogs.msdn.com/PowerShell/

◆ **Windows PowerShell Scriptomatic:** This amazing utility writes Windows PowerScript scripts for system administration and management. www.microsoft.com/downloads/details.aspx?FamilyID=d87daf50-e487-4b0b-995c-f36a2855016e&DisplayLang=en

Recommended Windows PowerShell Books

◆ *Windows PowerShell in Action* by Bruce Payette (Manning Publications, 2007)

This book, by Windows PowerShell co-creator Bruce Payette, is how I cut my teeth on Microsoft's latest scripting environment. It's full of examples and well written.

◆ *Pro Windows PowerShell* by Hristo Deshev (Apress, 2008)

A professional-level reference that focuses on real-world PowerShell, *Pro Windows PowerShell* is an excellent guide for those seeking information on using this environment to control Windows, applications, and the network.

◆ *Professional Windows PowerShell Programming: Snapins, Cmdlets, Hosts, and Providers* by Arul Kumaravel et al. (Wiley, 2008).

◆ *Professional Windows PowerShell* by Andrew Watt (Wiley, 2007).

Summary

In this chapter, you've only scratched the surface of what Windows PowerShell, the new scripting language, can do. It's a complete development language, and to take full advantage of it, you'll need to study one or more books dedicated to this topic. But I've tried to give you in this chapter a quick overview and a few tricks to get you started.

Now that you've read this chapter, you'll be able to access the properties of objects in ways impossible in **cmd.exe**, understand how PowerShell commands work and how to use aliases, and use the Quick Reference to find particular commands to study further.

Beyond Vista: Managing Multiple PCs

Windows Vista is Microsoft's most impressive desktop operating system to date, but in today's world, few users actually access a single PC. In addition, you use online services, have portable devices such as smartphones and portable media players, and manage home networks with two or more PCs, some of which are laptops and other mobile computers. Throughout this book, I've tried to maintain this sense of perspective, because Windows Vista doesn't exist in a vacuum. Instead, it's part of a complex and growing electronic ecosystem. That's why I've also covered Zune and Microsoft's Live services, as well as many non-Microsoft solutions.

However, there's a final topic to cover before heading off toward the distant future of Windows 7, Vista's successor. Today, Microsoft sells two Windows Vista companion products that, among other things, provide multi-PC management capabilities. Better still, these products, Windows Live OneCare and Windows Home Server, also perform other useful functions. Both products are uniquely beneficial to Windows Vista users, in particular, and extend the capabilities of this desktop platform. This chapter takes a close look at them.

Windows Live OneCare

Windows Live OneCare is an all-in-one, self-updating PC care service. Shown in Figure 25-1, this software combines antivirus, antispyware, and firewall security features with PC tune-up functionality and a first-class PC backup and restore service. Newer versions of the product add centralized multiple-PC management, monthly progress reports, online photo backup, and other new features, which is why Windows Live OneCare is covered in this chapter. For the first time, this innovative PC protection suite adds functionality that enables you to oversee all of the PCs on your home network from a single location.

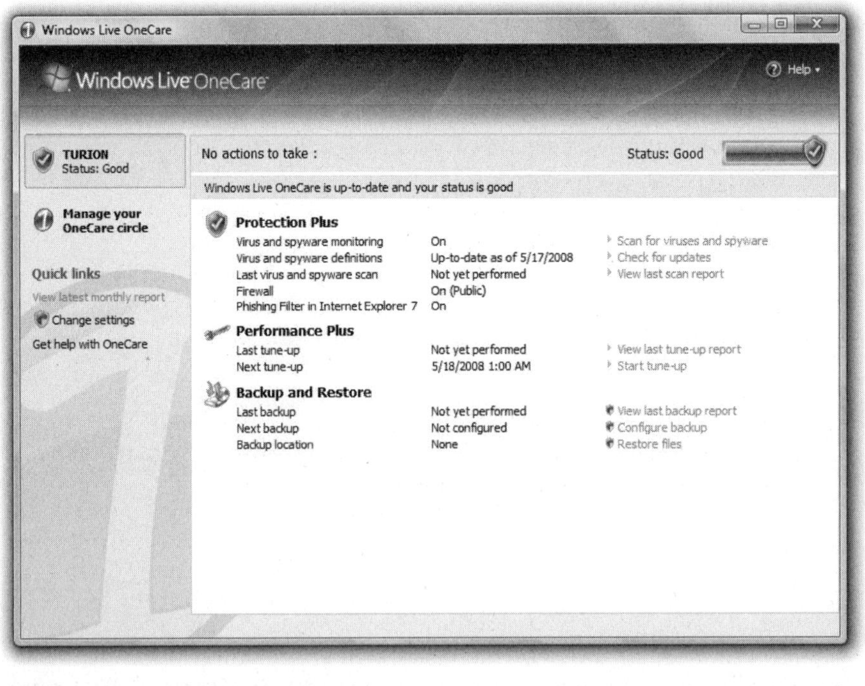

Figure 25-1: Windows Live OneCare really completes the picture for Windows Vista on your home network.

That OneCare does this for an extremely low cost—about $50 a year retail, but often found for much less online—is nothing short of amazing. In fact, it has turned the PC security industry on its head. McAfee, Symantec, and other major players are now offering OneCare-like products, too. I guess imitation really is the sincerest form of flattery.

The first version of OneCare shipped for Windows XP in early 2006 and was generally excellent, though Microsoft mucked things up a bit with the release of Vista, which duplicated some of the core functionality of OneCare. By the time the Vista-specific OneCare 1.6 version shipped in early 2007, I was ready to give up the all-in-one security service for good, thanks largely to its annoying and near-constant pop-up messages. OneCare 1.6 was just too intrusive and many of its other features seemed unnecessary in Vista.

With Windows Live OneCare 2, launched in late 2007, Microsoft turned things around. Now, OneCare has been fleshed out with many new features, as noted previously, and has largely lost the annoyances. Just as important, OneCare isn't a heavy abuser of system resources. You won't notice its presence as you do with, say, those heavyweight Symantec suites. OneCare 2 is all about getting out of your way for the most part. It is an important change and an excellent addition to your home network.

> **tip** You can purchase Windows Live OneCare in a number of ways, the easiest of which is to visit the product's Web site (http://onecare.live.com) and download it directly: Microsoft allows you to try OneCare for 90 days before purchasing, although this isn't usually the least expensive way to purchase OneCare. Instead, search online retailers such as Amazon.com and shopping aggregation sites such as CNET Shopper.com for the best deals. You can usually find OneCare for much less than its retail price, which is the price you pay if you buy directly from Microsoft.

Windows Live OneCare Management Concepts

Windows Live OneCare features multiple-PC management functionality that has two goals. The first is beneficial only to Microsoft: The company wants to ensure that customers don't install OneCare on more than three PCs. In earlier versions of the software, OneCare could actually be installed on a virtually unlimited number of machines; but starting with OneCare 2, you are limited to three installs per product key. That's fine, of course, but anyone who was happily installing a single copy of OneCare on more PCs will have some thinking to do.

Secret   If you do have more than three PCs at home and you'd like to use OneCare to manage them all, you can do so, but you have to purchase a second version of OneCare, with its own product key, for each set of three PCs.

The second aim of this system, of course, is to provide customers with a way to manage up to three PCs from a single location, and this system works surprisingly well.

OneCare uses a management entity called a *circle*, which is a group of PCs on the same home network, all running OneCare. In this circle of up to three PCs, one or more PCs can be denoted as *hub* PCs, which are capable of monitoring all of the PCs in the circle and, in very limited circumstances, triggering remote PC health fixes. Non-hub PCs simply operate like OneCare-enabled PCs before version 2: They're unaware of other OneCare-running PCs on the network and operate as if in a standalone install.

Under this system, a hub PC's OneCare console has two health shield icons, one for the local system and one for the circle, as shown in Figure 25-2.

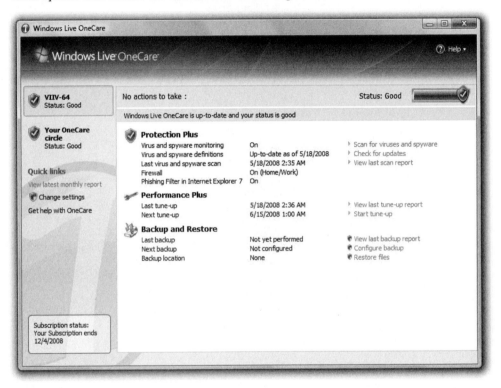

Figure 25-2: The OneCare management console on a hub PC monitors the health of both the PC and the entire OneCare circle.

On a non-hub PC, you'll only see a single health shield icon, as shown in Figure 25-3.

Regardless of whether the PC is configured as a hub or not, the goal is for these shield icons to remain green, which indicates good health. A yellow icon indicates fair health, such as when a tune-up, backup, or automatic update is overdue. A red icon is more serious: In this case, a PC is at risk and requires immediate attention.

Hub PCs monitor not only their own health but the health of the other PCs on the network too, so if your PC's health is fine but another PC in the circle requires a tune-up, for example, the local PC's status will be good (green), while the OneCare circle's status will be fair (yellow). This is reflected both in the aforementioned console and in the OneCare tray icon, which also uses the same three-color system.

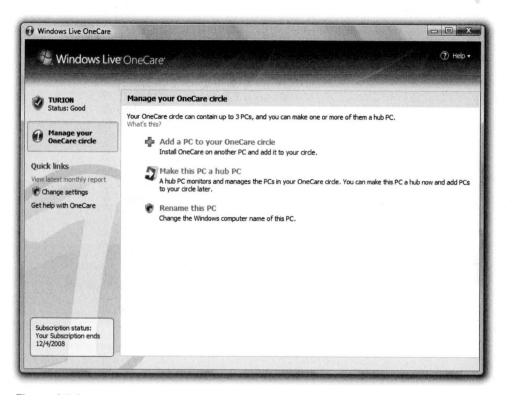

Figure 25-3: Non-hub PCs monitor only their own health and essentially operate in a standalone mode.

I mentioned earlier that you could use this system to fix other PCs in very limited circumstances. What you can't do is arbitrarily run remote tasks, such as backups and tune-ups, on remote PCs. But if another PC in your circle requires attention, you can in fact address that need from a hub PC's OneCare console. My advice is to make your own PC the hub PC in your circle and then configure the other PCs in the house as non-hub PCs. That way, when you sit down at the PC each day, you can respond to any issues that crop up without having to physically visit the other PCs. This is a wonderful bit of functionality and it works quite well.

Installing and Configuring Windows Live OneCare

Installing Windows Live OneCare is quite simple. First, navigate to the Windows Live OneCare Web site (**http://onecare.live.com**) and download the free 90-day trial. Run the Setup application on your first PC and link it to your Windows Live ID (described in Chapter 21). Then, as shown in Figure 25-4, specify whether you want to make the PC a hub PC. You should do so for any machines on which you think you'll want to perform maintenance tasks.

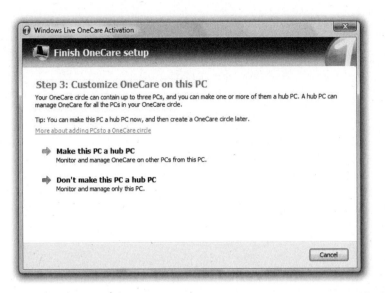

Figure 25-4: In the most crucial stage of OneCare setup, you must decide whether to make the PC a hub PC.

Once setup is complete, you'll need to reboot the computer. After that's done, your desktop will reappear with Windows Live OneCare. You will also probably see your first Windows Live OneCare Firewall notification window, shown in Figure 25-5. These windows appear whenever an application that is unknown to OneCare—and is thus potentially dangerous—tries to run.

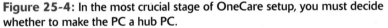

Figure 25-5: When you first run OneCare, you'll probably see a number of these notification windows.

Windows Live OneCare Features

Windows Live OneCare provides a comprehensive set of functionality. While most security suites also bundle antivirus, antispyware, and firewalling functionality in a single, easy-to-digest package, Windows Live OneCare goes the extra mile by adding other useful features designed to keep your PC running smoothly. This more holistic approach to PC health—which goes beyond simple malware protection—as well the product's multi-PC management, sets this service apart from the competition. The following sections examine each of the features OneCare provides.

Anti-malware

In the Protection Plus section of the Windows Live OneCare application window, you'll see links to the product's various PC security features, including the antivirus, antispyware, and firewall features, and its front end to Internet Explorer's phishing filter (the latter of which is described in Chapter 19).

The antivirus and antispyware functionality work in tandem and provide two services: A feature called viruses and spyware monitoring ensures that your system is constantly being monitored for any suspicious malware activities. There's also a malware scanning function. This works automatically on a schedule, but you can also run the scan manually. Either way, OneCare checks the files on your hard drive for infections. (This latter functionality is exposed through a tune-up feature that's also available in Performance Plus.)

When files are found to include a known virus or other malware, they are quarantined by OneCare. You can view quarantined files by clicking the Change settings task in the Quick Links section of the main application window and then choosing the Viruses and Spyware tab; then, click the Quarantine button. In the resulting dialog, you can attempt to clean infected files (which doesn't always work), delete them, or restore them (which is obviously not recommended).

Secret

> The spyware scanning functionality in Windows Live OneCare is based on the same code as that used by the Windows Defender feature that's included with Windows Vista. When you install OneCare, however, Windows Defender is disabled automatically and OneCare becomes the default antispyware tool.

OneCare includes a firewall that is dramatically better than the firewall built into Windows Vista. Unlike the Vista firewall, the OneCare version is bi-directional—that is, it scans electronic communication both heading out of your system and attempting to enter your system.

Secret

> As with the antispyware functionality, OneCare's firewall replaces the firewall that ships with Windows Vista.

You configure the OneCare firewall from the Firewall tab of the Settings dialog. The default protection setting is On, of course, where only known good programs are allowed to access the Internet. You can add or remove programs from the OneCare firewall's known programs list by accessing Advanced Settings. As shown in Figure 25-6, the resulting dialog provides a fine-grained list of applications, ports and protocols, and network connections you can manually configure. You will typically simply leave these settings as is.

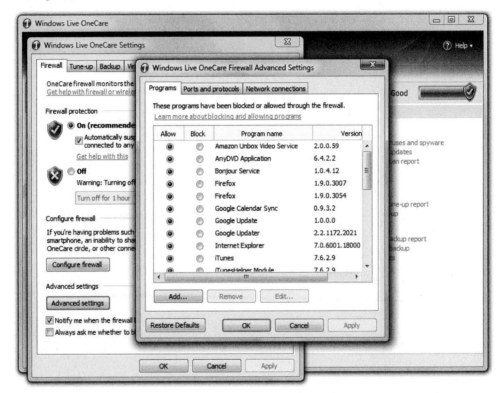

Figure 25-6: Looking for fine-grained control of the OneCare Firewall? Here it is.

There's an option on the Firewall tab of the Windows Live OneCare Settings window that specifies whether the application will display a notification when the firewall blocks an application. I usually leave this checked because I want to know when OneCare blocks a program from running. A second option, *Always ask me whether to block or allow programs*, can be enabled if you are suspicious about what's happening on your PC. This option essentially enables you to bypass OneCare's built-in logic about known good applications.

PC Performance

In the Performance Plus section of the main application window, OneCare provides a link for running what it calls a tune-up. This tune-up, shown in Figure 25-7, involves several tasks that help to keep your system secure and performing at a high level.

Figure 25-7: The OneCare tune-up keeps your PCs in top-notch shape.

---

tip

Does this tune-up look familiar? To me, it seems like a direct descendant of the Windows 98 Maintenance Wizard, which inexplicably disappeared when Microsoft migrated its OS to the NT codebase with Windows XP in 2001.

OneCare tune-up tasks include the following:

♦ **Remove unnecessary files:** This optional task, which is disabled by default, will delete or compress files that are on your hard drive but not needed. Fear not, OneCare won't delete the latest version of your next novel, but it will delete files such as unnecessary program installation routines, Windows temporary files, temporary Internet files, and the like. The idea here is to save hard drive space, not overthink which files you are and aren't using. You enable this functionality via the Tune-up tab in Windows Live OneCare Settings.

♦ **Hard disk defragmentation:** This task triggers the Disk Defragmenter that's built-into Windows Vista, enhancing the overall performance of your system. This is handy, but somewhat unnecessary in Windows Vista, as the built-in Defragmenter runs automatically anyway.

♦ **Virus and spyware scan:** Not to be confused with OneCare's live anti-malware monitoring, this feature actually runs a virus and spyware scan against the files on your PC, ensuring that none are infected. You should run a full scan when you first install OneCare, but if you don't, it will eventually prompt you to do so.

♦ **Backup:** This feature checks the backup plan you've created for the PCs you have configured with OneCare and then backs up any files that have changed since the last backup. You'll look at Windows Live OneCare's Backup functionality later in this section.

♦ **Automatic Updates:** OneCare manually runs Automatic Updates to see whether there are any new updates to download from Microsoft Update. These updates can be for Windows or for other supported Microsoft applications, including OneCare itself.

When you run the Tune-up manually, the Windows Live Tune-up dialog shown earlier appears and runs through the list of tasks you've configured. Unfortunately, there's no way to skip parts of the tune-up, so if you just ran a manual malware scan and then launch Tune-up, you have to sit through another full scan, sorry. By default, the tune-up runs automatically once every 4 weeks at 1:00 a.m. on Saturday morning, but I've set mine up to run weekly. It's a bit resource intensive, so you should try to schedule it to run when you know you won't be sitting in front of the computer.

To configure the few tune-up features you can configure, take a look at the Tune-up tab of the Windows Live OneCare Settings dialog. Here, you can configure the tune-up schedule and whether OneCare should remove unnecessary files each time the tune-up is run. There's also a button dedicated to the new start-time optimizer, where you can control what applications run when Windows boots.

The reason this tool is here, I believe, is that it replaces similar functionality in Windows Defender, which, as you know, is disabled when OneCare is installed. As shown in Figure 25-8, the Windows Live OneCare start-time optimizer presents a list of the applications that are configured to automatically run each time your system boots. By minimizing this list, you can speed boot time (and rid yourself of unnecessary and unwanted utilities).

Figure 25-8: OneCare provides a hidden but useful tool for limiting the number of applications that run each time your system boots.

What makes this feature special is that you actually get some information about each application, which is accessed by clicking the little carat character that's found between the icon and name of each entry. This, along with recommendations found next to most but not all entries, should help nontechnical users make better decisions about which applications to disable at boot-time. After all, it's not always clear which things are safe to disable.

Backup and Restore

In the Backup and Restore section of the main application window, OneCare provides a front end to its full-featured backup and restore functionality, which goes beyond what's available in Windows Vista by providing multi-PC backup and restore features, as you will see shortly.

Secret Though the Backup and Restore functionality is a superset of what's available in Windows Vista, that's only true of file backup. You still need to use Vista's image-based Complete PC Backup and Restore functionality for full system backups. This and other Vista backup features are covered in Chapter 23.

Before you can use OneCare's backup and restore functionality, you need to configure a backup plan. This is done via the Backup tab of the Windows Live OneCare Settings window. Click the Configure Backup button and you'll see the Backup Configuration dialog, shown in Figure 25-9.

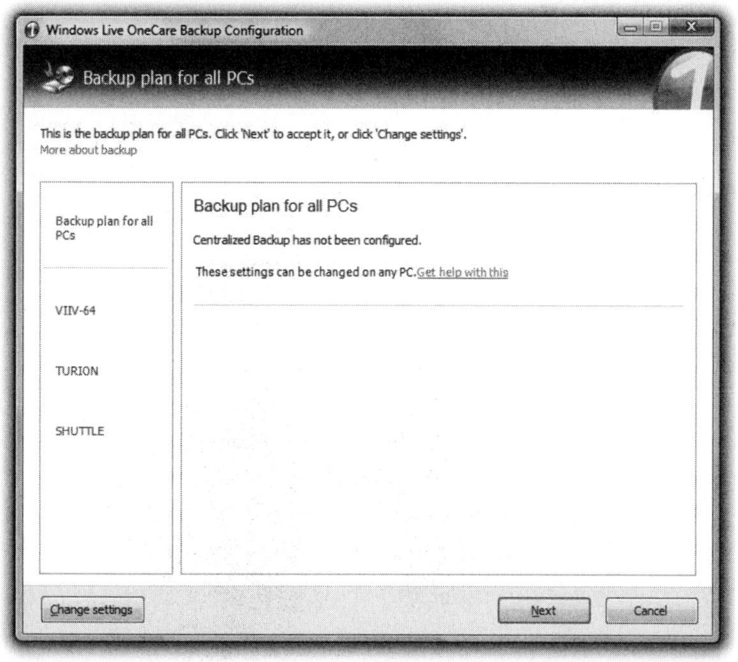

![Screenshot of Windows Live OneCare Backup Configuration dialog. Title bar reads "Windows Live OneCare Backup Configuration". Header: "Backup plan for all PCs". Text: "This is the backup plan for all PCs. Click 'Next' to accept it, or click 'Change settings'. More about backup". Left panel lists: "Backup plan for all PCs", "VIIV-64", "TURION", "SHUTTLE". Main panel: "Backup plan for all PCs — Centralized Backup has not been configured. These settings can be changed on any PC. Get help with this". Buttons: "Change settings", "Next", "Cancel".]

Figure 25-9: On hub PCs, you can configure a backup plan for all the machines in your circle.

If you access this feature from OneCare's hub PC, you will see links for each PC in your OneCare circle, plus a way to configure a common backup plan for all PCs simultaneously. Otherwise, you'll only be able to configure the backup plan for the PC you're currently using.

To configure a backup plan, select a PC from the list or choose *Backup plan for all PCs*. OneCare presents three very simple options: Where, When, and What. In this case, "Where" represents the device you'll use to store PC backups. Acceptable backup devices include an external hard disk (typically USB based), a writable disk burner (CD-R, CD-RW, DVD-R, DVD-RW, DVD+R, DVD+RW, or DVD+R DL)—obviously, the bigger the capacity the better; a network share; or a portable device such as an SD memory card or portable media player.

"When" refers to the schedule: By default, OneCare will back up your PC(s) automatically each week, on Friday at 7:00 a.m. You can change this to occur during the OneCare tune-up, daily, every 2 weeks, or every 4 weeks.

"What," of course, reflects which files will be backed up. By default, OneCare will back up all document and data types, but you can click the Change Settings link to fine-tune the file types, as shown in Figure 25-10. This list isn't particularly fine-grained—you can't, for example, tell it to back up all files in certain locations—but it's designed to be idiot-proof. No offense.

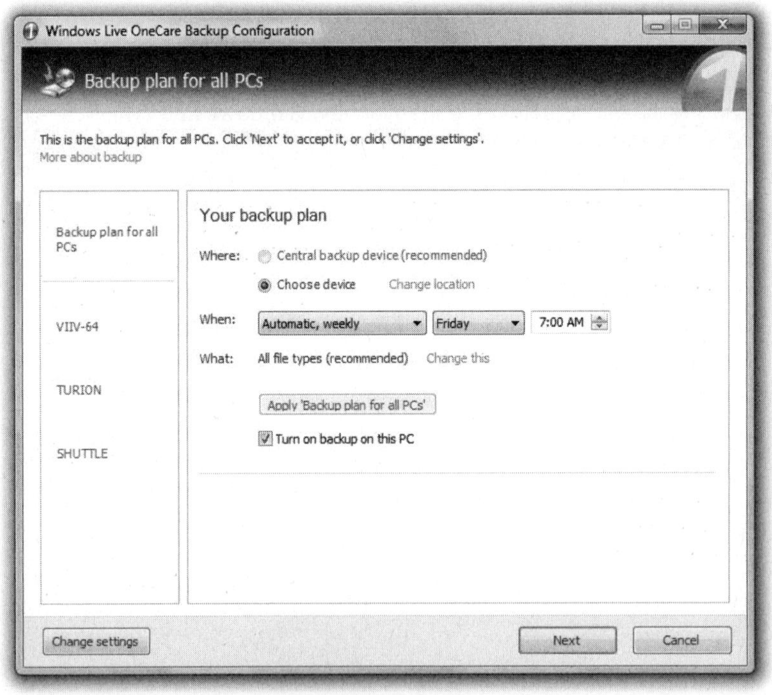

Figure 25-10: Plain English makes for simple configuration anyone can understand.

Once you have OneCare Backup configured correctly, click Next to commit to the backup plan. After that, OneCare Backup will run regularly according to the schedule you made.

When you are restoring backups, a similar wizard is employed. You can choose from a list of backup collections and then specify whether to restore all missing files, select files to restore by type, or even search for specific files to restore, which can be very convenient. The wizard also enables you to choose how to handle restored files with the same name as files on your PC: You can copy the restored files to a temporary folder or choose not to restore duplicates.

OneCare also offers a related online photo backup feature, Microsoft's first move toward true offsite backup (the current feature cannot be used to back up documents or other file types, only photos). However, online photo backup is considered a premium feature and thus costs an additional $50 per year for a paltry 50GB of storage. That's not a good deal at all: Google charges just $20 for 10GB of storage as I write this, and that storage can be used across its Gmail, Picasa Web, and other services. Furthermore, keep in mind that this feature is intended only for offsite backup. It cannot be used to share photos online, as is the case with most other online photo storage solutions.

tip	Put simply, I think you should skip this service. If you're looking for a way to back up photos online, consider Google Picasa Web or Yahoo!'s excellent Flickr service instead. They're not as automated as OneCare Online Photo Backup, but they're not nearly as expensive.

Monthly Reports

In keeping with its multi-PC management philosophy, Windows Live OneCare also generates comprehensive monthly reports that appear onscreen on the hub PCs in your circle. These reports provide an excellent overview of the health of your circle and spell out what steps OneCare may have made during that period. The reports are interactive where required as well, so you can address problems. If you're not using a particular OneCare feature, for example, the report provides a way for you to enable it without having to dive into the OneCare console or Settings dialog. In Figure 25-11, you can see a typical monthly report.

Automatic Printer Sharing

While Windows Vista enables users to manually share printers with each other on a home network, many people are simply unaware of this functionality. For this reason, OneCare includes the capability to automatically share printers between all of the PCs in a OneCare circle.

Secret	There's only one problem with automatic printer sharing, from what I can tell: If one of your PCs is running an x64 version of Windows, OneCare won't share printers from the 32-bit PCs and vice versa.

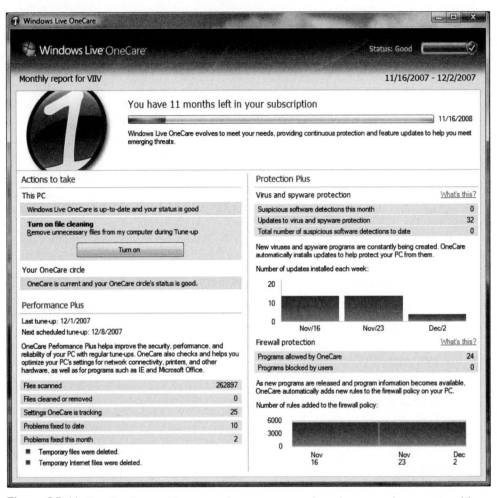

Figure 25-11: OneCare's monthly reports keep you up-to-date about your home network's health.

Windows Home Server

In late 2007, Microsoft's PC maker and hardware partners began shipping specially designed home server products based around a new operating system called Windows Home Server. Code-named "Q" (and previously code-named "Quattro"), Windows Home Server is just what its name suggests, a home server product. It provides a central place to store and share documents, along with other useful services for the connected home.

Windows Home Server is designed to be almost diabolically simple, and after 2½ years of active development, Microsoft decided that it had achieved an interface that was both simple enough for the most inexperienced user and powerful enough for even the most demanding power user.

Okay, maybe that's a bit of a stretch; but given what it does—bring the power of Microsoft's server operating system software into the home—Windows Home Server is pretty darned impressive. And if you're in the Windows Home Server target market—that is, you have broadband Internet access and a home network with two or more PCs—this might just be the product for you. In many ways, it's the ultimate add-on for Windows Vista.

From a mile-high view, Windows Home Server provides four basic services: centralized PC backup and restore, centralized PC and server health monitoring, document and media sharing, and remote access. I'll examine all of these features in just a bit.

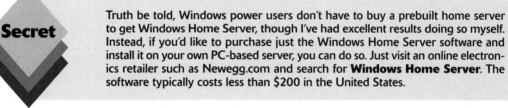

Secret

Truth be told, Windows power users don't have to buy a prebuilt home server to get Windows Home Server, though I've had excellent results doing so myself. Instead, if you'd like to purchase just the Windows Home Server software and install it on your own PC-based server, you can do so. Just visit an online electronics retailer such as Newegg.com and search for **Windows Home Server**. The software typically costs less than $200 in the United States.

Windows Home Server Installation and Configuration

Depending on how you acquire Windows Home Server, your one-time install and initial configuration experience will either be long and reasonably difficult or long and reasonably easy. Those who purchase new home server hardware will have the simpler and, in my mind, superior experience, but configuring the server is a time-consuming proposition in either case. That said, it's a one-time deal. For the most part, you'll install the server just once and then access it remotely occasionally after that.

Secret

Some PC makers, notably HP, have gone to great lengths to make the Windows Home Server initial setup experience much easier than the Microsoft default. See my review of HP's MediaSmart Server on the SuperSite for Windows (www. winsupersite.com/reviews/whs_hp.asp) to see what I mean.

Once you've purchased a Windows Home Server machine, you simply plug it into your home network, turn it on, and then access it remotely from other PCs on your network. (Check the server documentation for the exact setup procedure, which varies from PC maker to PC maker.)

You won't normally sit down in front of your home server with a keyboard, mouse, and screen, and access it as you would a normal PC. Indeed, many commercial home server machines don't even come with a display port of any kind, so you couldn't plug in a monitor even if you wanted to. Instead, Microsoft expects you to interact with Windows Home Server solely through a special software console.

Secret

You may not be surprised to discover that you can bypass the Windows Home Server administrative console and access the bare-bones operating system if you know the trick. Here's how it works: On a Windows Vista–based PC, launch the Remote Desktop Connection utility (type **remote** in Start Menu Search), type the network name of your home server into the Computer field (typically something like HOME-SERVER), and supply the name *administrator* as the user name and the password for the master account that you configured during home server setup. Ta-da! You can now access the Windows Home Server Desktop, shown in Figure 25-12, just as you would any other computer. Note, however, that Windows Home Server is designed to be used remotely via the console, and not interactively, so be careful about installing software or making other changes via this remote desktop interface.

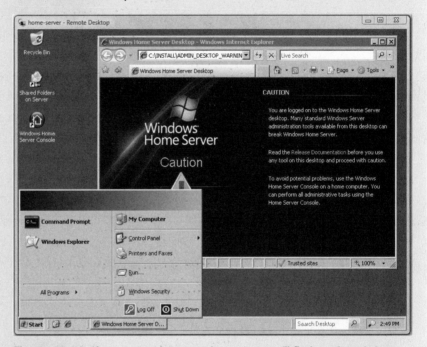

Figure 25-12: If you remotely access the server, you'll find a stripped-down version of Microsoft's enterprise-oriented Windows Server products.

The initial configuration of Windows Home Server involves first installing the Windows Home Server Connector software, which comes on its own CD, on a client PC running Windows XP with Service Pack 2 or 3 or any version of Windows Vista. (You can also access the Connector software via your home network; it can be found at \\HOME-SERVER\ Software\Home Server Connector Software\ by default.) The installer will "join," or connect, your PC to the server (see Figure 25-13) for later backup purposes and then complete the setup process.

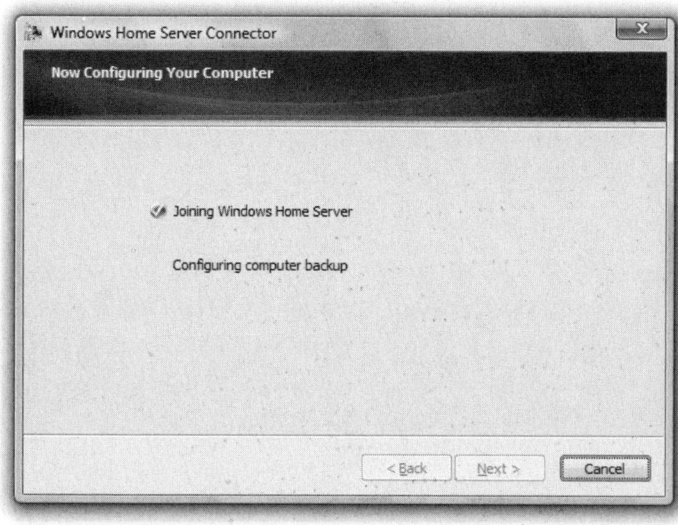

Figure 25-13: Windows Home Server connects to your PC, establishing a backup and management relationship.

Secret

As is the case with any other PC-like network resource, you must log on to the Windows Home Server in order to access it remotely, and that's true regardless of how you plan to access the server (via shared folders, the administrative console, or the Connector tray software). While it's possible to maintain different logons on your PC and the server, it's simpler to make them identical. That way, you will automatically and silently log on to the server every time you need to access it. In fact, Windows Home Server will prompt you to do this, as shown in Figure 25-14, if the passwords don't match. Note, too, that if you configure Windows Home Server for remote access (detailed later in this chapter), the passwords you use need to meet minimum length and complexity guidelines, for your security.

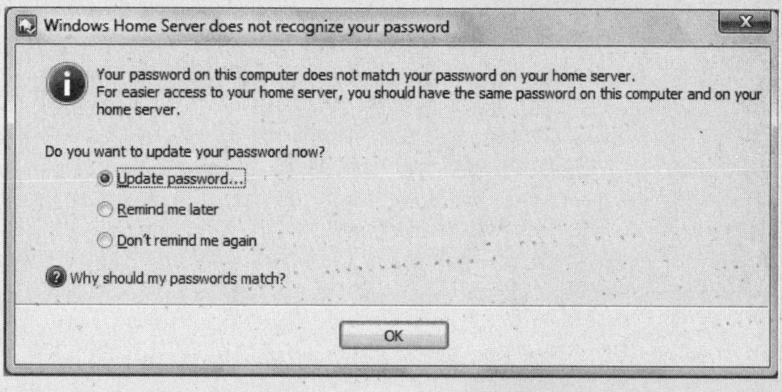

Figure 25-14: It's not required, but your life will be easier if you sync passwords between your PC and your Windows Home Server user account.

Admin Console Drive-By

You can launch the Windows Home Server management console from the new Windows Home Server Connector icon in the tray notification area. This icon is a colored square with a white home on it, as shown in Figure 25-15. The color of the icon relates to the overall health of your home network and home server: Green is healthy, yellow indicates a warning, and red means something is very wrong.

The Windows Home Server Console is a unique application running remotely on the server. It's an odd little application.

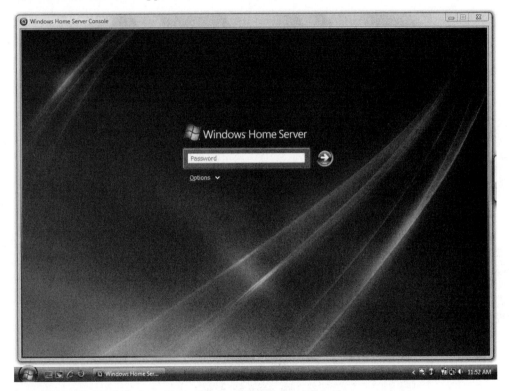

Figure 25-15: The Windows Home Server Console logon interface.

You log on to the console with the Windows Home Server password you configured during initial setup. Once the (overly lengthy) logon process completes, you'll be presented with the UI shown in Figure 25-16. From here, you can manage and configure the various features of the Windows Home Server.

On a standard Windows Home Server install, you'll see a very simple interface with tabs at the top titled Computers & Backups, User Accounts, Shared Folders, and Server Storage. There's also a Network health shield icon and links for settings and help. Most PC makers add other tabs, however. Figure 25-17 shows two additional tabs: MediaSmart Server (which was put there by HP, the PC maker) and Jungle Disk Online Backup, a Windows Home Server add-on I installed for remote backup services. (For more information about Windows Home Server add-ons, keep reading.)

Figure 25-16: The Windows Home Server Console presents a simple, multi-tabbed user interface.

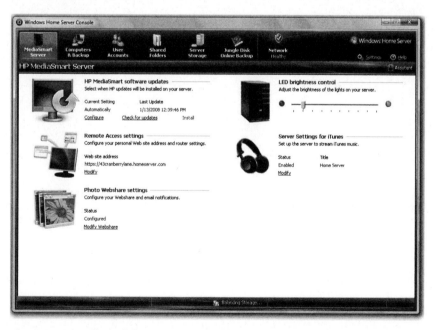

Figure 25-17: Some PC makers add additional functionality—and UI elements—to Windows Home Server.

The following sections describe what's available in the Windows Home Server management console user interface, regardless of how you obtained the server.

Computers & Backup

From this tab, you manage the computers that are connected to Windows Home Server (that is, the systems on which you've installed the Windows Home Server Connector software). A connected PC is one that will be completely backed up to the server by default, but you can configure this at the drive level. For example, you might want to back up only one hard drive on the system regularly, but not the other. By default, Windows Home Server will back up individual PCs overnight.

To configure backups on a PC-by-PC basis, navigate to the Computers & Backups interface in the Windows Home Server Console, right-click the PC you'd like to manage, and choose Configure Backup. The Backup Configuration Wizard will appear, as shown in Figure 25-18, enabling you to choose which disks to back up and other details related to the process.

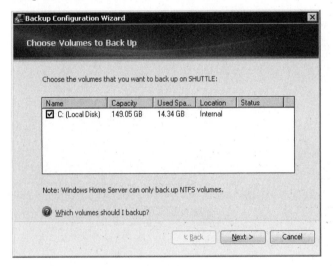

Figure 25-18: The Backup Configuration Wizard.

You can manually trigger a backup from the Connector tray icon on the client PC or from within this interface. You can even trigger backups from other PCs if you'd like. Remember: Windows Home Server is all about central management of your PCs, so you're free to trigger backups and other activities from any PC that has access to the Windows Home Server Console.

User Accounts

In the User Accounts tab, you can create user accounts that allow individuals to access various features of the server. By default, there is a guest account, but you will typically create accounts that map to accounts on the PCs you use and thus to people in your home. For example, I created a *paul* account, assigned it a complex password (required in Windows Home Server by default), and gave it Full access to all shared folders (see Figure 25-19).

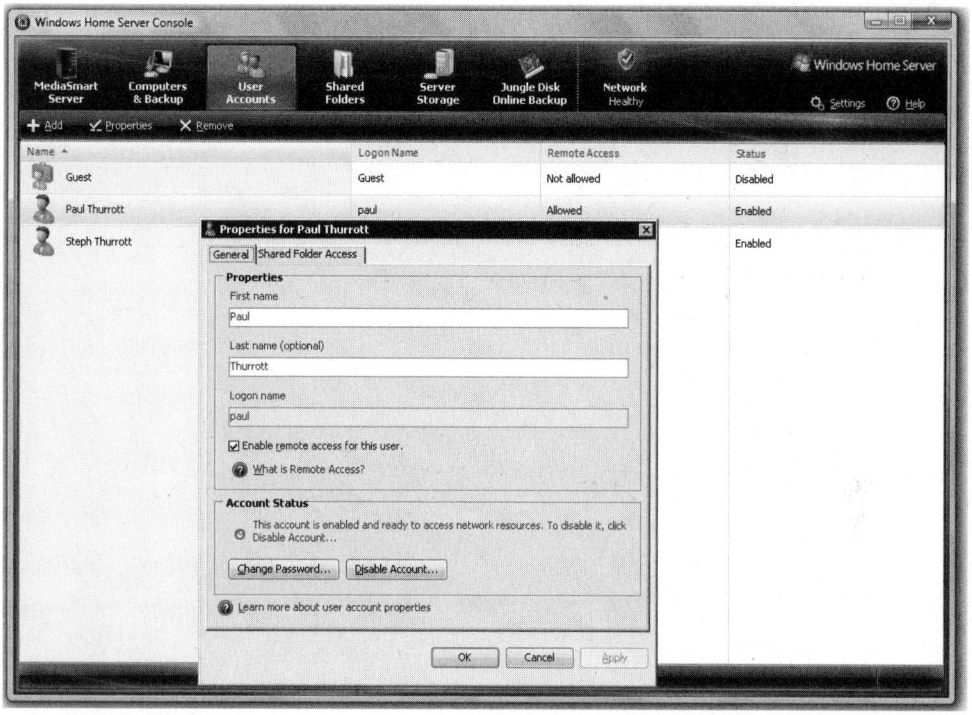

Figure 25-19: Individual user accounts are configured via a simple dialog.

If you want to provide remote access, you need an even more complex password; and you can, of course, specify which users can access which shared folders (described in the next section). That way, your children, for example, could have access to certain shared folders but not others that you want to keep private.

Shared Folders

Here you'll see all of the shared folders that are configured on the server, along with a simple Duplication option for each. The feature determines whether data in that folder is copied to two hard disks for reliability purposes. (Note that you must have at least two physical hard disk drives in the server to access this feature.) You can add and configure shares from here and determine access rights on a user-by-user basis. The Shared Folders tab is shown in Figure 25-20.

Server Storage

This section of the Windows Home Server user interface lists all of the hard drives currently attached to your server, whether or not they're configured for use by the server, and other related information, as shown in Figure 25-21. You can add new storage to the server here or repair a hard drive that's encountering errors. (When this happens, you'll see a health alert in the Windows Home Server Connector tray icon on each connected PC.) You can also remove a hard drive using this interface if necessary.

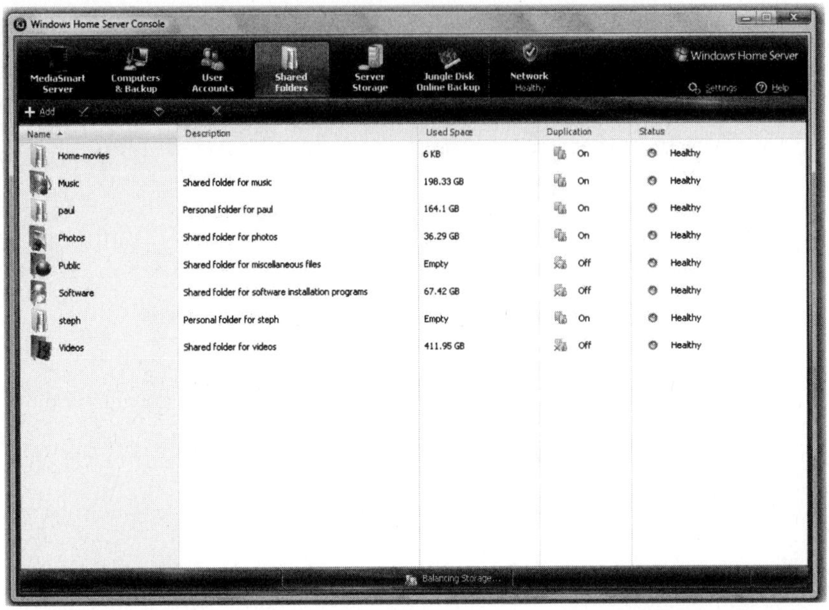

Figure 25-20: This interface is a front end to all of the shared folders on the server.

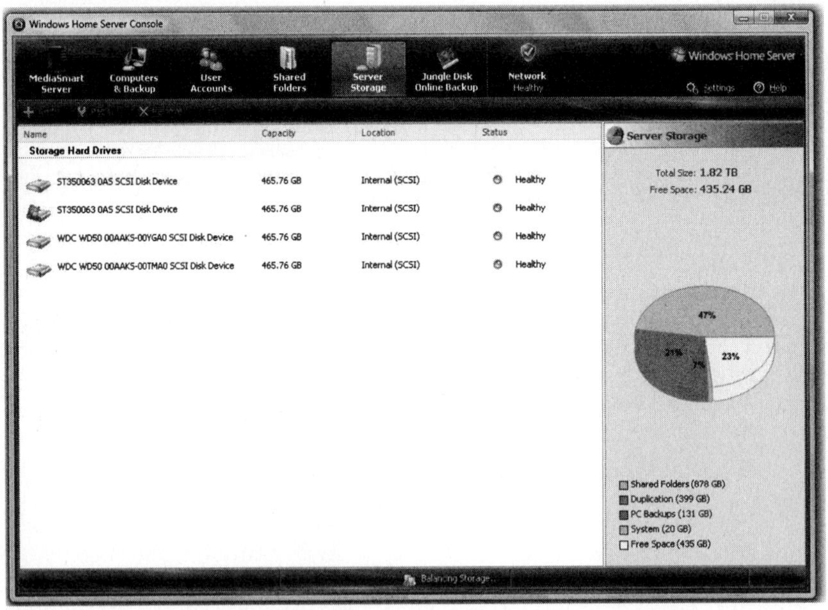

Figure 25-21: Server Storage shows which drives are configured for use with the server and how storage is allocated.

What you can't do in Windows Home Server is specify where files will be stored. This is handled automatically by Windows Home Server. All you do is create shares, determine whether they're duplicated across disks, and then copy files to that location. In the Server Storage tab, the only thing you can do with a healthy disk is choose to remove it. Simple, right?

Settings

The inauspicious little Settings link in the upper-left corner of the Windows Home Server Console opens the most complex UI you'll see here, as shown in Figure 25-22—a Settings dialog with seven sections by default, though preinstalled versions of the server have more.

Figure 25-22: The most complex UI in Windows Home Server is accessed via an almost hidden link.

Default sections in the Settings dialog include the following:

- ◆ **General:** Configure date and time, region, Windows Update, and other basic settings.
- ◆ **Backup:** Configure various default settings related to PC backups, including the backup time window (12:00 a.m. to 6:00 a.m. by default); how much time to retain monthly, weekly, and daily backups; and so on.
- ◆ **Passwords:** Windows Home Server requires very strong passwords by default, because malicious hackers accessing the server over the Web could gain control over the system, and thus all of your valuable files and, potentially, other PCs

on your network if they were able to brute-force attack their way past a weak password. That said, you can change the password policy here if desired. I don't recommend it.

◆ **Media Sharing:** Windows Home Server can share digital media files via default Music, Photos, and Videos shared folders. The server uses standard Windows Media Connect technology to do so, so if you enable this sharing, PCs and compatible devices on your network (e.g., an Xbox 360 or other Windows-compatible digital media receivers) will "see" the Home Server shares and be able to access that content over the network.

◆ **Remote Access:** In this important and sometimes confusing section, shown in Figure 25-23, you can turn on the Home Server's Web server, configure your home router for remote access and Web serving, and configure your custom domain name (**something.homeserver.com**).

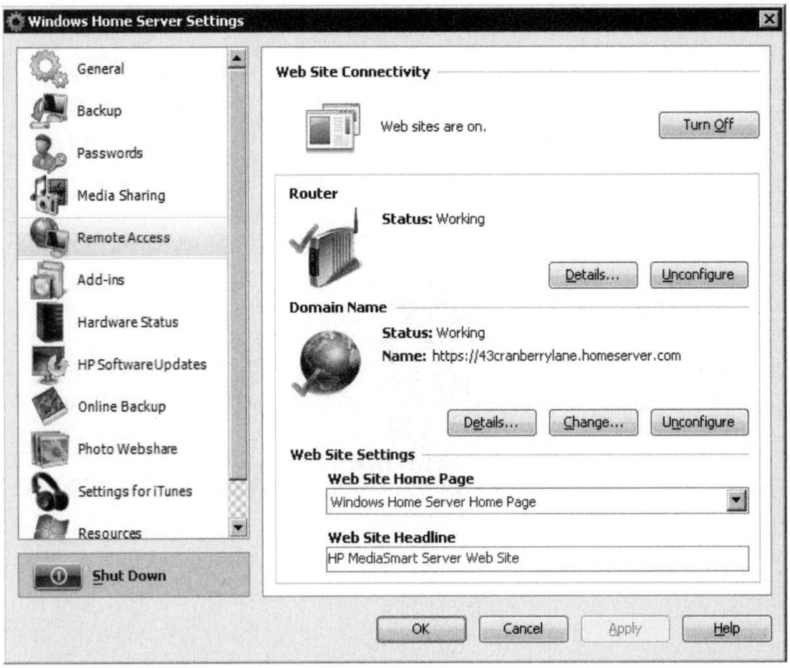

Figure 25-23: Remote Access is a bit of a black art, but Windows Home Server will try to automatically configure your router.

◆ **Add-ins:** Here, you can install or uninstall any Windows Home Server add-ins. (The Jungle Disk Online Backup mentioned earlier in the chapter is one such add-in.)

Secret

Microsoft maintains a list of Windows Home Server add-ins on its Web site: www.microsoft.com/windows/products/winfamily/windowshomeserver/add-ins.mspx

◆ **Resources:** This seventh section acts as an About box for Windows Home Server.

◆ **Other settings:** Depending on how you acquired your Windows Home Server, you may see other settings listed in this dialog. For example, the HP MediaSmart Server I use has additional settings that are unique to HP's hardware; and the aforementioned Jungle Disk Online Backup add-in adds its own link here, as do other add-ins.

Deep Dive: Windows Home Server Features

Mousing around the Windows Home Server Console UI is a nice way to see what's available, but it's time to take a closer look at each of the core features of Windows Home Server, with an emphasis on the benefits that each feature brings.

PC Backup and Restore

With the advent of Windows Home Server, Microsoft now offers three levels of backup protection to Windows Vista users. Windows Vista introduces the Backup and Restore Center, for image-based backup of the entire PC as well as more typical file backup. Vista also includes Previous Versions, a way to retrieve older versions of documents and other files directly from the file system, as well as tools such as System Restore. (These tools are all described in Chapter 23.)

As discussed earlier in this chapter, Windows Live OneCare offers an even better backup experience, with a centralized backup tool for up to three OneCare-enabled PCs on your home network. (OneCare also offers a semi-related online photo backup feature.)

Windows Home Server offers a third level of backup protection. As with similar functionality in OneCare, this Windows Home Server feature provides a centralized backup solution that applies to the PCs on your home network (and unlike OneCare, it is not limited to three PCs). However, Windows Home Server is a better solution than what OneCare offers because the backups are stored in a more logical place—the headless "back room" Home Server, and because it reduces the required hard drive space by not creating duplicate copies of files that haven't changed.

Windows Home Server Backup provides two basic services: It backs up the entire PC and then performs incremental backups on a daily basis going forward, enabling you to restore your computer to a previous state using a Computer Restore CD that's included with the server. It also provides a way to access and restore individual files and folders, similar to the way Previous Versions works on the local system.

This interface is a bit hard to find. Open the Windows Home Server Console and navigate to the Computers & Backup tab. Then, right-click the computer whose backups you'd like to access and choose View Backups. The dialog shown in Figure 25-24 will appear.

To access backed up files from a specific date, choose the date from the list at the top and then click Open. If the backup contains files backed up from two or more drives or partitions, you'll be prompted to pick one. Then, Windows Home Server will open the backup—a process that can take a few minutes depending on the size of the backup—and provide a standard Explorer window, like that shown in Figure 25-25.

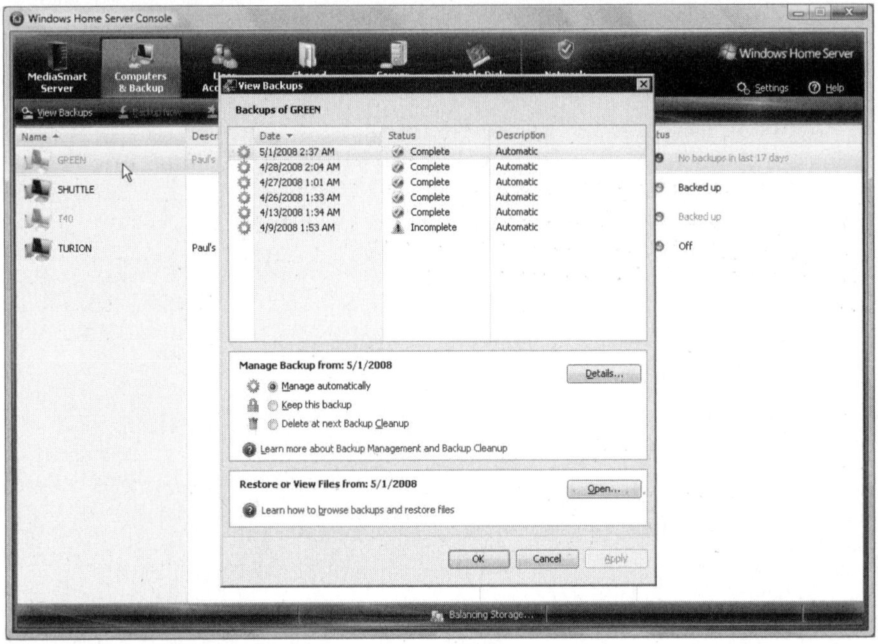

Figure 25-24: You can view all of the backups associated with a particular PC.

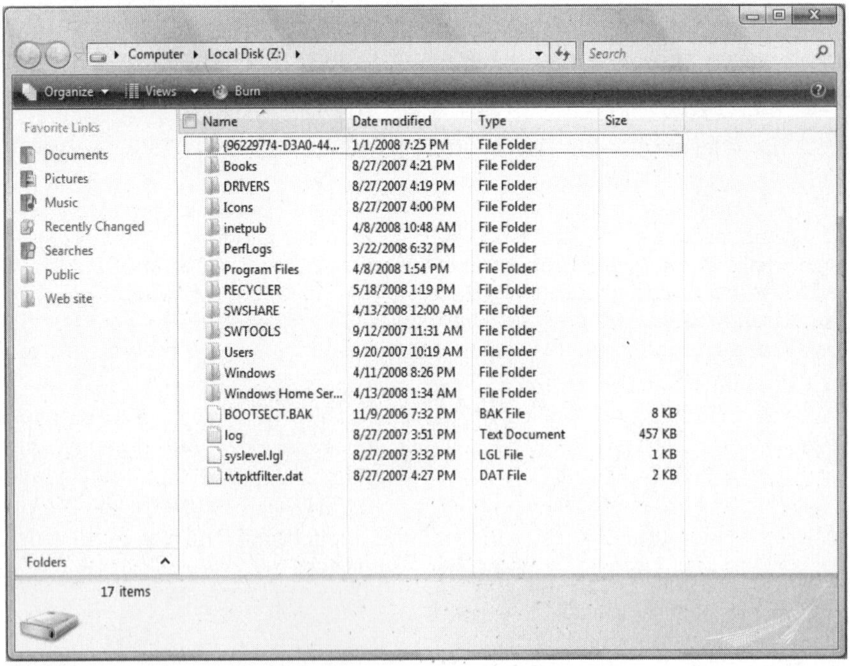

Figure 25-25: Backup sets can be navigated using a standard Windows Explorer window.

From here, you can navigate around the virtual file system of the backup, find the files you need, and drag and drop them onto your PC as you would any other files. When you close this special Explorer window, the connection with the backup is lost.

PC and Server Health Monitoring

Windows Home Server includes health monitoring, both for the server itself and all of the connected PCs. In this way, it's again a bit like Windows Live OneCare, which offers similar functionality. The overall health of the entire system—the server and all the clients—is optionally communicated via the Windows Home Server Connector icon that appears in the system tray of any connected PCs. If it's green, all is well; yellow indicates a risk; red is a critical problem; and blue means that the PC is being backed up.

Windows Home Server monitors several things to determine overall health. On the server, it monitors the integrity and free space of the attached hard drives (both internal and external). On the PC clients, it monitors backups to ensure they're proceeding without problems, and, on Vista systems in particular, it integrates with Windows Security Center to ensure that each PC is up-to-date with anti-virus and other security controls. That way, you know when a PC elsewhere in the house is behind on updating its security features and can take proactive steps to correct the situation.

Notifications, which appear when there are issues, can be annoying, as anyone who's used Windows OneCare or similar notification-based security software will know, but individual users can elect to just turn off tray-based health notifications, which isn't a bad idea for all the non-administrators in the house (that is, everyone else in your family).

Document and Media Sharing

While it's relatively simple to create a shared folder on a Windows Vista PC, Windows Home Server builds on this basic functionality in a number of ways. From a general standpoint, a server is an ideal place to store file archives of any kind, though this may be a foreign concept to many consumers currently. Though I had been using Windows Server–based servers for years at home, I switched over entirely to Windows Home Server in late 2007. It's a product I use and recommend.

From a file-sharing perspective, Windows Home Server works like any Windows-based machine. It includes a number of prebuilt shares, such as Music, Photos, Public, Software, and Videos, and it creates a default share for each user you create (at **\\home-server\users** **user name** by default). These shares have standard rights associated with them, so whereas even a guest has read access to the Public folder, only a user who was explicitly given the correct credentials can access any share with Full rights. The UI for configuring this is far simpler than what's available in Windows Vista, and you can, of course, add other shared folders if you wish. To do so, just navigate to the Shared Folders tab in the Windows Home Server Console and click the Add toolbar button.

Windows Home Server isn't just about simplicity. In addition to making it very easy to access and control access to whatever is available on the server, Windows Home Server also includes a unique and innovative approach to disk storage. Instead of using the arcane drive letter layout that still hobbles Windows Vista today, any hard drive you connect to Windows Home Server is added to the pool of available storage, and you don't need to deal with any disk management arcana. Just plug in the drive, external or internal, navigate to Server Storage, right-click it, and choose Add.

In a nice nod to future expansion, Windows Home Server will work with as much storage as you can throw at it, and it's basically limited only by the USB 2.0, Firewire, ATA, and

S-ATA connections on your server. My Home Server setup currently utilizes a whopping 2TB of storage, although much of that is used for file duplication.

Indeed, this file duplication functionality is another innovative Windows Home Server feature. Rather than burden users with complicated existing technologies like RAID, Windows Home Server instead supplies a very simple interface that ensures that important files are duplicated across at least two physical drives, ensuring that if one drive fails, you won't lose anything critical. I've configured Windows Home Server so that all of my digital photos and documents are duplicated in this fashion, for example, while videos are not. File duplication is configured on a per-share basis and is automatic if you have two or more drives connected. You can, however, configure this feature as you will.

Finally, Windows Home Server also makes it easy to remove storage. This way, if you want to disable older, less voluminous storage devices and plug in newer, bigger drives, you can do so without interruption. Windows Home Server first copies whatever data is on the older drives to other drivers, and then it removes that drive from the storage pool so you can disconnect it. (Obviously, this requires enough free space on other drives.) It's a brilliant scheme and works as advertised.

Remote Access

I used to subscribe to Logmein.com's Log Me In Pro service at a cost of about $100 a year. This service enabled me to connect to my home-based Windows Server machine, which until late 2007 was my main data archive, from anywhere in the world I could find an Internet connection. For someone who travels as much as I do, this kind of service is crucial: I can't tell you how often I've been out on the road and realized I forgot to copy an important file to my laptop. With Log Me In, I was able to download those files and even remotely access the server UI over the Internet to perform other tasks. It was incredibly valuable.

Windows Home Server includes a superset of this functionality, and it does so at no additional or annual cost. Thanks to the Windows Home Server remote access features, you can access the home server as well as most connected PCs in your home network using a simple and effective Web interface, shown in Figure 25-26.

Note the word *most* there: Due to limitations of Microsoft's home-oriented Windows versions, you can only remotely control PCs on your home network running Windows XP Pro or XP Tablet PC with Service Pack 2 or higher, or Windows Vista Business, Enterprise, or Ultimate.

Secret

Fortunately, you can bypass this built-in remote desktop limitation with Microsoft's Live Mesh software, a free solution described in Chapter 21.

Figure 25-26: The Windows Home Server Web interface enables you to use all of the server's remote access features.

Remote access consists of three related features:

♦ **Windows Home Server shared folders:** The contents of any folders that are shared from Windows Home Server, such as Music, Photos, Public, Software, and Videos, as well as any other folders you've shared, are accessible via the Web interface, shown in Figure 25-27. There's even a Windows Live Search box to help you find exactly what you need.

♦ **Connected PCs:** PCs that are connected to Windows Home Server can be remotely controlled, similar to the way you can control a Windows client or server using Remote Desktop. Obviously, the experience can be fair to middling depending on your connection speed, but it's still great to be able to do this with desktop machines when you're on the road.

♦ **Windows Home Server Console:** You can also access the Windows Home Server management console when you're online but off the home network. The management experience is identical to when you're connected locally, aside from potential speed issues and the fact that the console appears within the browser and not via the traditional console window.

![Screenshot of Windows Internet Explorer window showing "Now browsing: HOME-SERVER\Photos\". The browser address bar reads https://43cranberrylane.homeserver.com/Remote/files.aspx?share=08f3b543-13c8-482a-81d2-f9fc0cab3d... The Windows Home Server page displays "HP MediaSmart Server Web Site Remote Access, Welcome, Paul!" with tabs for Home, Computers, and Shared Folders. It lists folders in Photos.]

	Name	Size	Type	Date Modified
	2000		File Folder	3/29/2008 9:21:51 PM
	2001		File Folder	3/29/2008 9:23:37 PM
	2002		File Folder	3/29/2008 9:26:44 PM
	2003		File Folder	3/29/2008 9:41:49 PM
	2004		File Folder	3/29/2008 9:50:44 PM
	2005		File Folder	3/29/2008 10:11:07 PM
	2006		File Folder	3/29/2008 10:37:58 PM
	2007		File Folder	5/2/2008 3:40:10 PM
	2008		File Folder	5/12/2008 10:58:15 AM
	Favorites		File Folder	5/17/2008 8:17:51 PM
	Jon and Jamie		File Folder	3/29/2008 11:36:56 PM
	Old pictures		File Folder	3/29/2008 11:53:05 PM
	Wallpapers		File Folder	3/29/2008 9:14:38 PM
	_Scans and other photos to sort		File Folder	3/29/2008 9:17:31 PM
	ehthumbs_vista.db	799.5 KB	Data Base File	5/17/2008 12:59:21 PM
	SyncToy_1eff06bd-3a77-4ec3-95ce-51cad818f5...	24.08 MB	DAT File	5/17/2008 8:17:53 PM

Figure 25-27: Server-based shared folders via the Web interface.

In addition to all this great functionality, Microsoft has made it really easy to configure and use. By default, remote access is disabled, so you need to utilize the Remote Access link in the Settings dialog to first turn it on and then configure it. Enabling remote access can be either dead simple or utterly painful, depending on what kind of router you're using on your home network. The trick is to use a modern, Universal Plug and Play (UPnP) router: Windows Home Server will automatically configure it for remote access, and all will be well. If you don't have such a device, you need to manually configure your router using fairly technical instructions in the Windows Home Server help files.

Secret

To enable remote access to specific PCs, you need to do a little work on each PC, as there's no way to make it work using just the Windows Home Server console. In a Windows Vista–based PC, open the Start Menu, right-click Computer, and then select Properties. Then, click Advanced System Settings and navigate to the Remote tab in the System Properties dialog that appears. Under Remote Desktop, select *Allow connections from computers running any version of Remote Desktop (less secure).* If you choose the *more secure* version, it won't work.

Once remote access is up and running, Microsoft (or the PC maker from whom you purchased the server) will give you a free custom URL like ***something.homeserver.com*** where *something* is replaced by whatever name you prefer. Then you can access your home server resources from the Web using a standard Web address.

Windows Live OneCare/Windows Home Server Integration

You may have noticed that Windows Live OneCare and Windows Home Server have a bit of functional overlap: Both products offer a number of common features, including centralized backup and restore, and centralized PC health monitoring. That said, each is also unique in certain ways. Best of all, they can even work together: Microsoft has designed each product to be aware of the other so that overlapping features won't get in the way if you're using both, as I do. It's time to see how this works.

First, Windows Home Server is the more comprehensive of the two and, of course, the most expensive, especially if you acquire the software with new server hardware. In cases where features overlap, the Windows Home Server version is generally superior to that offered by Windows Live OneCare. What Windows Home Server lacks, however, is any form of PC security software: The product can ensure that your PCs' security solutions are up-to-date, but it does nothing to actually protect them against electronic attacks. For this reason, those using Windows Vista with Windows Home Server will still need, at a minimum, a decent antivirus solution. This is described in Chapter 8.

Both Windows Live OneCare and Windows Home Server include centralized PC backup and restore functionality. The difference between the two solutions is that the Windows Home Server backup and restore functionality backs up data to the server, whereas OneCare typically relies on USB-based storage that is attached to one of the PCs in the circle. Conceptually, the solutions are similar, though the Windows Home Server solution is more sophisticated and provides a way to easily access backed up files. If you have both Windows Live OneCare and Windows Home Server, obviously you don't want or need two similar and competing backup solutions running simultaneously.

If you install Windows Live OneCare on a system that is already protected by Windows Home Server, the OneCare Backup feature is automatically disabled, with no user intervention required on your part. Of course, you're free to go into the UI for either or both solutions and configure things differently, but it's nice that Microsoft thought this one through.

Regarding PC security monitoring, because redundant monitoring won't harm your PCs or institute a performance hit, both services can run concurrently.

Summary

While Windows Vista is an excellent solution for standalone PCs, you must look to additional tools if you want to manage multiple PCs on your home network from a central location. Microsoft offers two tools that offer this kind of functionality. One is Windows Live OneCare, an all-in-one suite that provides security and PC care features. The other,

Windows Home Server, is typically obtained with new home server hardware but can also be purchased separately. Windows Home Server provides four basic services: centralized PC backup and restore, centralized PC and server health monitoring, document and media sharing, and remote access. While each of these products is interesting in its own right, the combination of Windows Vista, Windows Live OneCare, and Windows Home Server provides a comprehensive management suite suitable for any home network.

Index

H